I0031682

Gen. Samuel B. Webb.

Hon. Silas Deane.

Chief Justice Thomas S. Williams.

Chief Justice Stephen Mix Mitchell.

Hon. Martin Welles.

Hon. David Lowry Seymour.

SOME OF WETHERSFIELD'S DISTINGUISHED SONS.

Families of Ancient Wethersfield, Connecticut

Consisting of Volume II of
The History of Ancient Wethersfield

Comprising the Present Towns of
Wethersfield, Rocky Hill, and Newington; and of
Glastonbury Prior to Its Incorporation in 1693

From Date of Earliest Settlement
Until the Present Time

With Extensive Genealogies and
Genealogical Notes on Their Families

Part 1

Henry R. Stiles

HERITAGE BOOKS
2019

HERITAGE BOOKS

AN IMPRINT OF HERITAGE BOOKS, INC.

Books, CDs, and more—Worldwide

For our listing of thousands of titles see our website
at
www.HeritageBooks.com

A Facsimile Reprint
Published 2019 by
HERITAGE BOOKS, INC.
Publishing Division
5810 Ruatan Street
Berwyn Heights, Md. 20740

— Publisher's Notice —
In reprints such as this, it is often not possible to remove blemishes from
the original. We feel the contents of this book warrant its reissue despite
these blemishes and hope you will agree and read it with pleasure.

International Standard Book Number
Paperbound: 978-0-7884-5892-7

Henry R. Stiles. A.M. M.D.

PREFACE.

While, in the *historical* part (Vol. I) of this work, I builded largely upon the labors of my deceased predecessor, W. S. ADAMS, Esq., yet, for this volume (*Genealogies*), I alone am responsible. The favorable reception which was accorded to my *Windsor* History has fully confirmed my belief that no history of a town can be fully and satisfactorily written, unless it contain, in a greater or lesser degree the genealogies of the families and the biographies of the individuals, whose lives and acts have been, in fact, the vital essence of its corporate existence.

My main idea in preparing these genealogies, has been, *firstly*, to gather up and preserve *all* the genealogical data to be found on Town, or other original, Records; and *secondly*, to supplement, enlarge and reinforce these with such additional data as I could gather from printed works, or from family records and correspondence. *Absolute completeness* may not thus, in all cases be obtained; but it affords the reader or user of these pages a pretty full *resume'* of what has, *thus far*, been ascertained concerning any family in which he may be interested; and suggests clues which—with more time at his disposal—he may follow out to a still higher degree of perfection.

The form of arrangement, or notation, given these genealogies, though not so elaborate as might be deemed necessary in the genealogy of a special family, will, I trust, be found to be sufficiently clear to answer the needs of those who have occasion to consult these pages. Simplicity has been studied in this respect.

The sources of these genealogical statements have, for the most part, been indicated in the Preface to Volume I, as well as in connection with the genealogies themselves. I have been especially careful in this respect, both on account of wishing to satisfy the demands of those who may naturally wish to know my *authorities*, and from a desire to give due credit to each and every one of the kind friends who have so cheerfully communicated to me of the fruits of their own knowledge and labors. The names of many of these are given in the Preface to Volume I.

In this, as in my *Windsor* genealogies, I have been careful to note all baptisms, whose records are attainable. This I have done from the same motive as given in my Windsor book, and which I venture here to quote: "*Baptismal* records, generally only used by genealogists to *approximate dates of birth* where the latter are wanting, seem to me to have a deeper significance than is usually accorded to them. To the Christian they signify the date of the individual's birth into the Family of God. Thus, their sacramental import gives them a value co-ordinate with that of the record of the natural birth. I have, therefore, carefully preserved and recorded all baptismal data which I could find—knowing that, to some, it would be a matter of sincere interest to know that they and their ancestry were, and are of the 'baptized children of God'—and such knowledge in these days is not always obtainable."

Several articles prepared as Appendices for this work have been unavoidably omitted, for want of room. Among these were (1) The *Mix Baptismal Records, 1697-1735*, and also (2) *Rev. Mr. Lockwood's Records of Births, Marriages and Deaths*, of First Congregational Church of Wethersfield, *1739-1745*, as well as a careful copy of the *Records* of the Third Church (or Stepney Parish) from *1765 to 1756*, made for me by *Mr. Edwin Stanley Welles*. These records, however, have practically been embodied in the genealogies of this work (the former, indeed, having been printed lately in the *Connecticut Magazine*) ; and as these MSS. will be deposited in the archives of the Connecticut Historical Society, their absence from our printed pages, is less to be deplored.

The same may be said of a voluminous *List of Civil and Military Officers*, of and from Wethersfield, compiled by the late Judge Adams, and added to by Mr. E. Sweetzer Tillotson; also a *List of Ship-Yards, Landing Places and Warehouse Grants by the Town,* by Judge Adams; *List of Subscribers to the Building of the Brick Church, 1761,* by Judge Adams; and *Extracts from Old Wethersfield Tax-Books 1730-1789,* compiled by Mr. E. Sweetzer Tillotson; as also several of lesser interest.

Mistakes and inconsistencies may be found in these family records, but the reader may be assured that they do not arise from carelessness on the part of the compiler. Working genealogists will, from their own experiences, know the difficulties of such work, and will make kindly allowance for all errors found.

Condensation, both as to form of expression and arrangement of matter, has been forced upon me by the large amount of material placed at my disposal, and in these genealogies especially, this has taken the form of *abbreviations,* of which a list follows this Preface.

The adverse conditions of health, referred to in the Preface to the first volume, have continued with me during the completion of these genealogies; and at the most critical part of my work (*i. e.,* the proof reading) my eyes became so overstrained as to threaten not only its entire stoppage, but the permanent loss of my eyesight. From both these dilemmas, however, I have been saved by the assistance volunteered by my sister, Miss CHARLOTTE E. STILES, and my daughter, Mrs. FREDERICK E. TRUESDALE, by whose patient labor this work has been brought to its present happy issue.

The reader, will, perhaps, understand and sympathize with me, when I say that, in view of all the hindrances which I have had in the carrying on of this undertaking, I feel very much as quaint old COTTON MATHER felt, when he first looked upon the printed and bound copy of his great *Magnalia Christi Americana,* of which event he makes this mention, in his diary, under date of August 30, 1702: "Yesterday, I first saw my Church History since ye publication of it. A gentleman arrived here from New Castle, in England, that had bought it there. *Wherefore I sett apart this Day, for a solemn Thanksgiving unto God, for His watchful & gracious providence over the work,* & for ye Harvest of so many prayers, & cares, & Tears & Resignation, as I had Employed upon it."

Henry R. Stiles. A.M. M.D.

HILL-VIEW.
October 1, 1904.

CONTENTS OF VOLUME II.

ILLUSTRATIONS.

FAC SIMILE AUTOGRAPHS.

LIST OF ABBREVIATIONS.

abt.—about
acc.—according to
ae.—aged
auth.—on the authority of
app.—appointed
A. C. N. H.—Mrs. A. C. N. Hawley
b.—born
bp.—baptized
batt.—battalion
bro.—brother
btwn.—between
bo't—bought
bu.—buried
ch.—church; *chh.*—churches
ch.—children
Col.—Colony, or Colonial
comm.—commission
connect.—connected
Conn.—Connecticut
Cont.—Continental
Co.—County
Ct.—Court
d.—died
dau.—daughter
dec.—deceased
dth.—death
des.—deserted
disch.—discharged
emig.—emigrated
Eng.—England
exc.—exchanged
est.—estate
enl.—enlisted
exam.—examined
fam.—family
ftr. or *fth.*—father
fm.—from
Far.—Farmington
gen. or *geneal.*—generation, or genealogy
gd-f.—grandfather
gd-s.—grandson
gd-dau.—granddaughter
grad.—graduated
Htfd.—Hartford
ho.—home
ho-lot.—home-lot
Ind.—Indian
inf.—infant, or infancy
inhab.—inhabitant
invent.—inventory
k.—killed
Ld. Rec.—Land record
ld.—land; *lds.*—lands

ldd.—landed property
m.—married
marr.—marriage
ment.—mentioned
Mix MSS.—the Mix Ch. Rec.
mcht.—merchant
mdze.—merchandize
mthr.—mother's right—as applied to a baptism, signifies that the inf. rec'd the rite, through the right of his mother (father, or grand-parents, as the case might be), as a member of the church—under the old "Half-Way Covenant" system.
mort.—mortuary
Midd.—Middletown, Ct.
N. Y.—New York
New.—Newington, Ct.
neph.—nephew
N. C. R.—Newington Ch. Rec.
nr.—near
occup.—occupied
ord.—ordained
per.—perhaps
poss.—possibly
possess.—possessed, or possessions
ppy.—property
prob.—probably
pub.—public or published
Q-M.—quarter-master
Rec. or *Recs.*—record, records
rep.—represented, or representative
res.—residence, or resided
resig.—resigned
Revol.—Revolution, the American
rem.—removed
ret.—returned
Ry-H.—Rocky Hill, Ct.
s. p.—*sine prole,* i. e., without issue
shp.—ship
slp.—sloop
schr.—schooner
S. C. R.—Stepney Ch. Recs.
schl.—school
sett.—settled, or settler
Step.—Stepney
val.—value, or valued
Weth.—Wethersfield
W. T. V.—Weth. Town Votes
W. Ld. Rec.—Weth. Land Rec.
wk.—week
y. or *yr.*—year
yg.—young

OLD AND NEW STYLE.

At the time of the first settlement of New England, the English people began the year on the 25th of March, Annunciation, or Lady Day. Any dates between January 1st and March 25th, appearing on the records of those times, should have one year added. Later, a new form of designating the year was adopted; the first time of its being used by the General Court, being "this 20th day of March, 1649-50," or 1650, by our present reckoning. This style prevailed for about one hundred years; and the dates of all the months of the year should be carried forward—thus, between 1600 and 1700, *ten* days; between 1700 and 1752, when the English Government changed their dates from Old to New Style, there should be *eleven* days added. In 1752, the British Parliament made September the 3rd, the 14th.

ERRATA.

The errors, thus far discovered in this volume, are mostly of a typographical character, and largely due to the trouble with my eyesight which overtook me while this portion of the work was passing through the press.—H. R. S.

Those which *need* correction are the following:

Page 34, line 29 from bottom of page—for "Polemus," read *Polhemus.*

Page 55, line 11 (Note) from bottom of page, for "Weston," read *Webster;* and on last line but one of same note, for "Stow," read *Starr.*

Page 61. The names of the children of Sally Drusilla Beckley, should be *Hamlin,* not "Hamblin."

Page 119, line 23, for "Vedderw," read *Vedder.*

Page 120, Last line, for "FAM. 14¾," read FAM. *42*

Page 129, line 5, for "Boltin," read *Bolton;* line 3 from bottom, for "Guadeloupe" read *Guadaloupe.*

Page 147, *Bucker,* line 26, read Chapt. VII.

Page 152, line 5, for "rigorous," read *vigorous;* and line 13, for "elder," read *holder.*

Pages 159, 6th line; 163, 23rd line, and 175, 3rd line, for "Tanitor," read *Taintor.*

Page 161, line 2 for "*rts,*" read *res;* and for "Buckinham," read *Buckingham.*

Page 171, first line of Note, for "Manmarning," read *Manwaring.*

Page 184, line 3, for "Morrison," read *Munson.*

Page 229, line 3, for "Hubbartam," read *Hubbardtown,* Vt.

Page 233, line 16, for "liviest," read *liveliest.*

Page 271, line 19, for "Fern," read *Fenn.*

Page 279, line 23, the ancestral line of FAM. 35, should read thus, *Ebenezer,[2] Ebenezer,[2] John.[3]*

Page 334, line 27, for "Tyral," read *Tryal.*

Page 345, line 19, the year-date "1685," should read *1885.*

Page 386, line 27, from bottom of page, for "spacious," read *spurious;* and eleven lines below, for "Boot," read *Booth.*

Page 455, the ancestral line of *Enos*, FAM. 2, should read *Gideon*,[4] *Samuel*,[3] *Nathaniel*,[2] *George*.[1]

Page 550, line 22, for "Page 567," read Page *570*.

Page 607, lines 6 and 7 from bottom of page, for "Samuel m. Jedidiah Lord," etc, read Samuel, m. *wid. of Jedidiah Lord, Mrs. Jedidiah Lord m. (2) Abiel Hancock.*

Page 735. FAMILY OF DANIEL, 19. *Somehow*, poss. by virtue of the "total depravity of inanimate things," (especially noticeable in *types*) much confusion has crept into the printed page, in the 3rd to 5th lines of this family history. The reader is simply requested to *supply the year of death* of Daniel's wife. viz: *15Apl., 1808*, and to *omit all of the 4th and 5th lines and the date 1808, at* beginning of 6th line.

Page 738, line 4.   Strike out all relating to marr. of Abigail.

Page 743, line 33, in Family 44, Samuel should read *Samuel L.*

Page 763, line 2nd, (above the Note), "Silver Bills and Plate," should read "*Silver, Bills and Plate.*"

Page 767, line 27, should read, "m. his own cousin, *Abigail* (dau. Rev. William & Hannah *Wolcott*) **Burnham.**"

Page 785, line 35. "prob. the P. who b. Horace Hough" should read "who *m.*" etc.

Page 791, line 2nd from bottom of page, "Ebenezer Moreley," should prob. read "*Moseley.*"

Marsh Family Additions and Corrections, Vol. I.

The statement, page 337, that there were *four* emigrant bros. of the name is *not proven.*

Page 338. For "Aenesiphorus," read *Onesiphorus*. Same page, line 9, from bottom, for "very duly," read *was duly, etc.*

Page 339, line 11, for "61 years," read *over 62 yrs.* Same page, line 29, for "the Williams'," read the *Williamses.*

Page 341, line 22, for "Bremmer," read *Brimmer*. Same page, line 4 from bottom, for "1808," read 1806, and add, *he had rec'd his A. M. degree from Y. C. in 1774.*

Vol. II, page 497, *footnote.* The name "Wilson" should be spelled *Willson*. Jared Willson's death (lines 2 and 3 of note) should be 1880. Mary Bolton Watson (Chapin) d. 2 Apl., 1848. Sarah Dana Watson was b. 4 Aug., 1855, and her husband's name should be spelled in the Danish form of Andersen. The name of Ellsworth Daggett's wife was *June* (not Jane) Spencer. Their children ment. in the text are both dead. The eldest, Oliver E. (Daggett), d. 1875, *not* 1815.

Richard Henry Dana, Jr., and Sarah Watson, his wife are credited only with 2 children. They had 4 others, one of whom is (3) *Elizabeth Ellery Dana*, b. 3 Apl., 1846, of Cambridge, Mass., who has been very helpful to this history; (4) *Mary Rosamond (Dana)*, b. 1 Sept., 1848; m. 26 Aug., 1878, Henry Fearing **Weld**; (5) *Richard Henry (Dana)*, Jr., b. 3 Jan., 1851; m. 10 Jan., 1878, Edith (dau. of the poet H. W.) **Longfellow**; (6) *Angela Henrietta (Dana)*, b. 22 Feb., 1857 m. 25 June, 1892, Henry Whepple **Skinner**, their son Richard Dana (Skinner), was b. 21 Apl., 1893.

RICHARD H., Jr., & Edith Longfellow (Dana), had (1) Richard Henry (Dana), b. 1 Sept., 1879; (2) Henry Wadsworth Longfellow (Dana), b. 26 Jan., 1881; (3) Frances Appleton (Dana), b. 25 May, 1883; (4) Allston (Dana), b. 29 Sept., 1884; (5) Edmund Trowbridge (Dana), b. 25 Oct., 1886; (6) Delia Farley (Dana), b. 2 Oct., 1889.

FRANCIS O. LYMAN & Ruth Charlotte, his wife, had, besides the 2 ch. ment.

in note, (3) *Charlotte Dana (Lyman)*, b. 9 Aug., 1885; (4) *Richard Dana (Lyman)*, b. 5 Feb., 1888.

Footnote. "Onesephorus" is a misprint for *Onesiphorus*. Rev. Dr. Marsh's age at death was 78, *not* 79 yrs. His son Ebenezer Grant Marsh's age at dth. was 26 *not* 27 (line 8, p. 497).

Page 497, line 29, Rev. O. E. Daggett d. 31 Aug., 1880. Line 35, the "d. at Rome, Italy, &c.," refers to *Mr.* Richard Henry Dana, Jr., Mrs. Sarah Watson Dana, his wid. is still living—1904.

Line 4 from bottom of page, "Walter F." should be Walter Scott. His wife Sarah Watson (Swayne), d. 4 May, 1902.

Page 498, line 31. Insert *d.* before the word Chicago.

Same page, line 37. The surname of Ebenezer Grant Marsh's 1st wife was *Western*, not Webster: and that of his second, Elizabeth *De Voe* (not De Noe) *Palen* (not Palem). Their son Charles Van Rensselaer was m. Feb. 1903. Their 4th daughter's name was Bessie *Kate* (not Bessie *Reitor*).

GENEALOGIES AND BIOGRAPHIES.

ABBOTT, ROBERT, from Watertown, Mass., where he was adm. freeman, 3 Sept., 1634, name then spelled *Abbitt* in *Col. Rec.;* adm. freeman at Hartford, 1640; thence to Weth., where he had ld. rec. 1641.—See Chapt. VII., Vol. I; juror same yr.; rem. to New Haven, there adm. freeman, 6 Aug., 1642, and where his s. John ("b. many mos. before"—*Savage*), was bp., 7 Oct., 1649. By his request his ld. was set out to him at Branford, but res. in N. H. till 6 May, 1645 (*A. Gen.,* tho' *Savage*—prob. more correctly, says 1649) ; he seems to have d. 1658; a shoemaker, and had a hard struggle to get along, as the court records at New Haven show. (*Htfd. Times,* Jan. 7-28, 1901) : his est. distrib. 1660, to 6 ch. all prob. b. at B., or N. H., concerning whom see *Savage* (I, 5), and *A. Gen.* (174), accepting, perhaps, the former's deductions concerning them as more reliable than those of the latter. The *Gen.* says his wid. Mary m. 4 Nov., 1659, John **Robbins;** the former says "name of wife unknown," and that the Mary, or Maria, who m. this Robbins (a clergyman and leader of a colony of early settlers of Branford, which rem. to R. I."), was not the wid. of Robert A., but his dau. which could hardly be, if, as rec., she was b. 13 May, 1657.

JOHN—*Hinman* says (2d edit.)—had lds. at Weth., 1641.

ABBY (*Abbe*), GEORGE, of Chatham, m. Mary **Brooks,** 5 Feb., 1784; their ch. ae. 11 mos. bu. 28 Apl., 1810.—*W. C. R.*

LUCY, m. Chauncey **Shepard,** of Chatham, 7 Nov., 1832.—*W. C. R.*

MARY STOCKING, (adult) bp. July, 1832.—*W. C. R.*

REUBEN, of Glast., m. wid. Mary **Tryon,** of Chatham, 9 July, 1812, "in 1st Soc'y."

RICHARD, called in *Co. Ct. Rec.,* Nov., 1719, an attorney.

ABRO, TENOR, d. 5 Apl., 1705, in his 25th yr.—*Weth. Ins.*

ACKERLY, (*Acerly, Accorly*), HENRY, *Hinman* says was poss. from Weth. and rem. with 3d Company to Stamford, where he sett. early; house carpenter; d. at S. 1650, *Savage* says 1658, 17 June, wh. is date of his will; name, however, does not appear on *Weth. Rec.;* nor does *Savage* ment. him at all in connection with Weth.

ACKLEY, MICHAEL, m. Anne **Hunt,** 13 Nov., 1853.—*W. C. R.*

MIRIAM (wid.), d. 9 May, 1850, ae. 87.—*S. C. R.*

WILLIAM, m. Harriet **Price,** 26 Jan., 1825.

ADAMS, (*this genealogy furnished by* Mr. BENJAMIN ADAMS, A. M., *formerly of Weth., now of Brooklyn, N. Y.*)

FAM. 1. BENJAMIN. On the 20th Jan., 1676, this person, presumably then a res. of Htfd., and Samuel Williams, testified under oath that they had served under Capt. John Edwards, of Weth., in the recent (1675) war against the Indians (*Htfd. Co. Rec.*, III, 156). There is every reason to believe that he was a son of *William* Adams, of Farmington, Conn., who d. 18 July, 1655, leaving a wid. Elizabeth, and two ch. a son Benjamin, ae. 6 yrs., and a dau. Elizabeth, ae. 3 yrs.* Benjamin was "bp. and adm. to full communion," Mch. 31, 1678, in the Second (South) Church at Htfd. (*Parker's Hist.*, *2d Ch.*, 292); abt. 1690, he m. Elizabeth (dau. of Thomas & Hannah *Crow*) **Dickinson,** of Weth., and gd-dau. of the Settler Nathaniel D. of that town, and of Hadley, Mass. For the next few yrs., he was apparently a res. of Htfd., tho' it does not appear that he owned ld. there. Before 28 Dec., 1696, he had rem. to Weth., as appears from a mention of his home-lot on Weth. *Town Rec.* I, 124; see also, Chapt. VII, Vol. I; in 1700, he was chosen as "lister" (assessor), and in 1712, a grand-juror;[1] in 1702-3, was made appraisor of stray cattle; in 1711, was plff. in suit *vs.* James Poisson, a French Huguenot physician of Weth. for the value of 71 bu. of onions sold by him to the latter, and which suit was decided in his favor. Though he may have farmed to some little extent, his est. inventory shows no farming implements; while the mention of saws, hammers, chisels, etc.,, would indicate his trade to have been that of a carpenter, or builder; for *land rec.*, see Vol. I, Chapter VII. He d. 28 Jan., 1712-13, "between break of day and sunrise." Letters of adminst. granted to his dau. Abigail, 7 Sept., 1725, twelve yrs. after his death; invent. taken 3 Dec., same yr. *Htfd. Prob. Rec.* XII, 203.) Mrs. Elizabeth (Dickinson) Adams, is ment. (in connection with her father's est.) as living in 1720; and also, in *Weth. Town Rec.* II, 18, in Dec., 1722; she prob. d. abt. 1725, in which yr. her husband's est. was adm. upon and his son Amasa required to choose a guardian.

Children:

1. John, bp. (*Cat.*, *1st Ch. Htfd.*, 170) 27 Nov., 1692; d. unm'd before 3 Jan., 1721.
3. A son, bp. (*Hist. 2d Ch. Htfd.*, 306) 28 Oct., 1694; prob. d. inf.
4. Elizabeth, b. abt. 1696; unm'd in 1722.
5. Abigail, b. abt. 1700; m. 26 June, 1755, Capt. Samuel **Butler,** of Weth., as his sec-

ond wife. He d. 21 June, 1774; his wid. Abigail was living as late as 1779.
6. Amasa, bp. (*Weth. Ch. Rec.*) 24 Oct., 1708. FAM. 2.
7. Zeruiah, bp. (*Weth. Ch. Rec.*) 15 Apl., 1711.—*Mix Mss.*

FAM. 2. AMASA[2] (*Benjamin[1]*), b. 1708; bp. 3 Aug., 1708; chose as his guardian his uncle Eben[er] Dickinson, of Weth., 3 Aug., 1725; m. 16 Mch., 1731-2, Hannah **Camp,** (bp. Htfd., Sept. 28, 1712), dau. of Joseph Camp of Htfd., and gd-dau. of John & Mary (*Sanford*) Camp; in 1735, he bo't ld. of Isaac Riley, in Weth.; was a farmer, tho' not a large ld-owner, and was also a ship-builder, as in July, 1743 he is credited on the books of the great Weth. shipping firm of Elisha Williams & Co., "for work for Sloop *Lark*," and in 1754, was employed in the bldg. of sloops built in Stepney Parish (Ry-Hill), for the West Ind. trade, two of which, the *Dove* and the *Dolphin*, were mostly built by him. For over 20 yrs., he was a pt-owner of the old "Chester Mill," estab. in 1637, of which he bo't a ¼ interest in 1760, and another quarter in 1769. One of these parts he conveyed to his son John, in 1772, and the other to son Joshua, in 1782, from which latter date the mill became known as the "Adams Mill,"

---

* This William Adams, who was prob. the father of Benjamin, came to Htfd., from Mass., in 1640; rem. to Farmington, where he was an early settler; m. Elizabeth, wid. of William Heacock, of F.; by her had ch. Benjamin, bp. abt 1649, and Elizabeth, b. abt. 1652. Mrs. A.'s death, 3 Aug., 1655, as well as her husband's death are rec. *Far. Town Rec.* II, 320. Inventory of his est. 6 Sept., 1635, am't £36.03.00. The ch. (both Heacock and Adams) were ordered by the Court to be "placed out" by Mr. Steele and Thos. Judd" as well as they can."
Careful research by the late Judge Sherman W. Adams and others failed to connect this William with any of the somewhat numerous branches of the A. family in America, or with any of those who located in Htfd. or neighboring towns. Nor is there any record of the son Benjamin, after the death of his parents in 1655, unless he is the person whose deposition (as given above) was made at Htfd. some 20 yrs. later.
[1] The first time such appt. was made in Weth. as far as records show.

and the business was carried on by successive generations of the Adams family for almost a century; tho' Amasa Adams held few, if any, town offices and appears not to have been prominent in public affairs, he yet was not lacking in public spirit. He contributed his share (£24, 14, 01) to the erection of the present Cong. Ch. edifice in 1761; and later, he assisted in bldg. the dwelling-house presented to Rev. James Lockwood by his parishioners. His loyalty to the patriot cause is evidenced by his contribution to the fund raised in Weth. (1775), for the relief of the sufferers by the Boston Port Bill. He joined the First Cong. Ch., 5 Feb., 1737-8, during the pastorate of Rev. Stephen Mix, by whom his 13 ch. were bap.; he lived to see 11 of these ch. married and 12 survived him. He d. 6 July, 1790, ae. 82, "leaving 12 ch. and 2 dec'd; 54 gd-ch. and 16 dec'd; and 19 gt-gd-ch. and 1 dec'd; in all 103."— *Conn. Courant.—W. C. R.;* his wid. Hannah d. 28 Sept., 1798, ae. 86; at the time of her death, the gd-ch. had increased to 78 and the gt-gd-ch. to 66.—*Conn. Courant.—W. C. R.*

Children (bp. from *Weth. Ch. Rec.*) :

1. Lydia, b. 8 (bp. 14, *Mix*) Jan., 1732-33 ; m. 3 Dec., 1800, Capt. John **Bulkeley**, of Weth., who was for many yrs. eng. in W. I. trade, and in 1780, commanded the Schr. *Experiment* in Rev. war ; he d. 27 Mch., 1807, ae. 81 ; his wid. Lydia d. 15 July, 1814.
2. Abigail, b. 5 [*Mix MSS.* say bp. 3] Mch., 1734 ; m. 12 Jan., 1758, William **Loveland**, of Weth. ; she d. 3 Sept., 1795, and Mr. L. m. (2) Mary ————— ; he d. Weth., 1804 ; wid. Mary rem. to Winchester, Ct. *Issue:*
   i. Abigail (Loveland), b. 16 Mch., 1763 : m. 21 July, 1785, Capt. Moses **Hatch**, she d. 3 Nov., 1850.
   ii. Anna (Loveland), bp. Apl., 1764 ; m. 11 Jan., 1784, Simon **Frasier**, res. Aurelius, N. Y. ; d. before Nov., 1839
   iii. Hannah (Loveland), b. 1767 ; m. Elisha **Coleman**, of Weth. ; d. 3 May, 1819.
   iv. Eunice (Loveland), d. unm'd 5 Apl., 1839, ae. abt. 70.
   v. Thomas (Loveland).
   vi. Lydia (Loveland), m. 7 Jan., 1790, James **Grimes.**
   vii. Prudence, bp. 24 Apl., 1774 ; m. Roger **Deming.**
   viii. Sarah, bp. 4 June, 1775 ; m. Christopher **Stillwell**; d. before Nov., 1839.
   Note.—Prob. Recs. (1805) mentions these 8 ch. of Wm. Loveland ; but several others are known to have d. before that time.
3. Benjamin, b. 1 Dec., 1735. FAM. 3.
4. Susannah, b. 17 Nov., 1737 ; m. 27 Apl., 1772, Nath'l **Hurlburt, Jr.**, of Weth. ; she d. 4 Feb., 1800, and he m. (2) wid. Sarah **Clark**, by whom he had 4 *ch.*; the wid. d. 5 Jan.,1811. He d. 16 Aug., 1817, ae. 75. *Issue (by first wife)* :
   i. Amasa (Hurlburt), bp. 8 May, 1774 ; m. Rhoda **Kilby.**
   ii. David (Hurlburt), bp. 15 July, 1775 ; d. Sept., 1800, in W. I.
   iii. Elizur (Hurlburt), b. 29 July, 1777 ;. m. 3 Jan.,1798, Mary **Deming**; d. Weth., 22 Apl., 1834.
   iv. Lucy Camp (Hurlburt), bp. 18 June, 1786 : m. 4 Jan., 1802, James **Pearl**; d. Weth., 29 Aug., 1849, ae. 69.
5. Camp. b. 9 Oct., 1739. FAM. 4.
6. Lucretia, b. 21, bp. 26, July, 1741 ; m. 5 Aug., 1779, David **Dunham**, of Sheffield, Mass. (*W. C. R.*) ; res. until abt. 1793, on Harris Hill, Weth. ; she d. 20 July, 1796.
7. Hannah, b. 5, bp. 9 Oct., 1743 ; m. 14 Jan., 1768, Daniel **Warner**, of Weth. (b. 29 June, 1748, son of Wm. & Elizabeth *Mitchel*) Warner ; she d. 7 Sept., 1801 ; the bapt. of

9 ch. of a Daniel W. (prob. this above) are given in *Weth. Ch. Rec.*, as follows :
Elizabeth (Warner), Hannah (Warner), Sarah (Warner), bp. 16 Nov., 1777 ; Mary (Warner), Daniel (Warner), Billy (Warner, bp. 16 Nov., 1783 ; Levi (Warner), bp. 1 Feb., 1784 ; Horace (Warner), bp. 30 Apl., 1786 ; Hiram G. (Warner), bp. 21 Feb., 1790.
8. John, b. 9 Aug., 1745 ; bp. sometime betw. Aug. and Sept. 1, 1745. FAM. 5.
9. Elizabeth, b., bp. 9 Aug., 1747 ; m. 28 Oct., 1770, Christopher **Warner**, (b. 16 Aug., 1742, son of William & Elizabeth *Mitchell*), who d. before 17 July, 1794, since his 2 ch. were bp. in Weth., as ch. "of the wid. Elizabeth W." She res. with her mother Hannah Adams, from whom she had, in 1796, the gift of an int. in the old A. homestead on South Hill. She d. 29 Aug., 1825, leaving ppy. to dau. Abigail **Larkin** and the latter's ch. *Issue:*
   i. Abigail (Warner), bp. 17 July, 1774 ; m. Isaac Larkin, who d. 29 Dec., 1821 ; she d. Weth., 14 Nov., 1844, ae. 74.
   ii. Moses, bp. 17 July, 1774 ; rem. to Sandisfield, Mass. (?).
10. Joseph, b. 7, bp. 10 Sept., 1749 ; d. 19 May, 1753.
11. Amasa, b. 15, bp. 18 March, 1753. FAM. 6.
12. Joseph, b. 1755. FAM. 7.
13. Mary, bp. 16 Oct., 1757 ; m. 27 Aug., 1778, Joseph **Waterbury**, of Stamford, Ct., res. in the Belden House, Harris Hill, Weth. ; he was a Rev. soldier and pensioner ; he d. 6 Oct., 1834, ae. 78 ; she d. 17 Dec., 1827, ae. 70. *Issue (Weth. Ch. Rec.)* :
   i. Huldah Steward (Waterbury), bp. 9 Nov., 1783 ; d. unm., 19 Sept., 1848.
   ii. William (Waterbury), bp. 10 Oct., 1784 ; d. 30 Jan., 1805, ae. 24, at Guadaloupe, W. I. ; sailor.
   iii. Simeon (Waterbury), bp. 15 Apl., 1787 ; d. 28 Oct., 1808, ae. 24, in Jamaica, W. I. ; sailor.
   iv. Samuel (Waterbury), bp. 16 Feb., 1790. bu., 17 Feb., 1790, ae. 6 wks.
   v. John (Waterbury), bp. 31 Mch., 1791 ; bu. Apl., 1791.
   vi. Mary (Waterbury), bp. 15 July, 1792 ; m. 9 Jan., 1817, Wm. A. **Havens**; d. Weth., 6 Sept., 1865.
   vii. Joseph, bp. 20 Sept., 1795 ; d. at sea, 17 Nov., 1825, ae. 30.
   viii. John, bp. 21 Apl., 1799 ; d. 25 Sept., 1803, ae. 4.
   ix. Sally, bp. 8 Oct., 1803 ; d. 9 Oct., 1803.

FAM. 3. BENJAMIN,[3] (Amasa,[2] Benjamin,[1]), m. 5 Feb., 1761, Patience (dau. William & Thankful Nott) **Blinn**, of Weth.; for his ld-rec., see Vol. I, Chapt. VII; was a carpenter and bldr.; subs. £1-10-00 toward the erection of the Lockwood parsonage, 1767, "to be paid in joiner work"; farmed and owned considerable ld.; had an int. in the Chester Mill and during his later life was actively eng. in milling business; in 1774, was a grand juror; 1779, chosen surveyor of highways; in 1780, tythingman; was rec'd to full communion in First Cong. Ch. Weth., in 1761; d. in his ho. on South Lane, Weth., where he had res. for half a century, 27 Nov., 1816, in his 81st yr.—*W. C. R.* His wid. d. 26 Oct., 1818.—*W. C. R.* His invent. taken Dec., 1816, amt'd to $3,803.18.

Children (bp. *Weth. Ch. Rec.*) :

1. Persis, b. 8, bp. 15, Nov., 1761 ; m. 18 Feb., 1795, John **Montague**, of Weth. ; res. in old M. ho. on So. Hill ; he d. 9 Nov., 1811 ; she d. 7 Jan., 1826. *Issue:*
   i. Martha (Montague), b. 1797 ; d. unm. 12 Sept., 1822.
   ii. Mary (Montague), b. 10 Nov., 1799 ; m. 20 Aug., 1823, Geo. L. **Adams**; she d. 10 Sept., 1828.
   iii. John (Montague), b. 22 Nov., 1801 ; m. 20 Nov., 1833, Lucy **Wright**; he d. 16 Jan., 1880.
   iv. Huldah, b. 6 July, 1789 ; m. 1804 ; d. unm. 7 Aug., 1828.
   v. Harriet (Montague), b. 6 Oct., 1806 ; d. unm. 3 Aug., 1888.

2. Lucinda, b. 3, bp. 10 Sept., 1763 ; m. 30 Jan., 1783, Thomas **Havens**, of Weth. ; he had been an apprentice to his father-in-law, Benj. Adams, and was a carpenter and builder of vessels, as well as houses. He res. in South Lane and d. 14 Sept., 1825, ae. 61 ; his wid. d. 7 Sept., 1828. *Issue:*
   i. Sarah (Havens), b. 9 Aug., 1783 ; d. 16 March, 1805.
   ii. Sylvester (Havens), b. 19 Sept., 1785 ; m. Caroline M. **Hills**; d. 9 Oct., 1852.
   iii. Thomas (Havens), b. 19 Sept., 1787 ; m. Patty **Blinn**, who d. 21 May, 1864 ; he d. 10 May, 1857.
   iv. Uzziel (Havens), b. 24 Nov., 1789 ; m. 1813, Rachel **Jagger**; d. in Cuba, 11 Feb., 1825.
   v. Nancy (Havens), b. 6 Mch., 1792 ; d. 16 Aug., 1792.
   vi. William Adams (Havens), b. 27 Oct., 1793 ; m. Mary **Waterbury**; d. 28 Aug., 1865.
   vii. Henry (Havens), b. 14 May, 1796 ; m. Chloe W. **Keen**; d. June, 1868.
   viii. Nancy (Havens), b. 6 July, 1798 ; d. unm. 4 Aug., 1887.
   ix. Hiram (Havens), b. 17 May, 1803 ; m. 13 Feb., 1833, Mary W. **Adams**; d. 30 Oct., 1886.

   x. Sarah (Havens), b. 29 Jan., 1807 ; d. unm. 31 Aug., 1868.
3. Sinalda, b. 5 Sept., 1765 ; d. unm. 12 May, 1796.—*W. C. R.*
4. Uzziel, b. 3, bp. 10 Jan., 1768. FAM. 8.
5. Thankful, b. 2, bp. — Feb., 1770 ; m. Mch., 1791, Samuel **Hayford**, of Far., who d. soon after, and she m. (2) Silas **Goffe**, of Far., 12 May, 1814 ; she d. Weth., Apl. 10, 1849. *Child (by first husband)* :
   i. Samuel, bp. 12 Nov., 1797 ; m. Hannah **Blinn**, who d. 15 Aug., 1878 ; he d. 10 Jan., 1816, ae. 25 yr.
6. Huldah, b. 20 Apl., 1772 ; d. unm. 26 Dec., 1853.
7. Charlotte, b. 1, bp. 2 Oct., 1774 ; m. 14 Jan., 1798, Josiah **Griswold**, of Stepney Parish (Ry-H.), son of Solomon & Sarah *Deming* Griswold, and b. 21 Nov., 1775 ; he d. at Stp., 19 Dec., 1832 ; she d. 3 Sept., 1847. *Issue:*
   i. Charlotte (Griswold), b. 9 July, 1799 ; m. 2 June, 1824, Horace **Blinn**.
   ii. Sarah Deming (Griswold), b. 11 Feb., 1801 ; m. 3 Sept., 1823, Chester **Wilcox**; she d. 15 Jan., 1852.
   iii. Josiah (Griswold), b. 3 Dec., 1802 ; m. Eliza **Cummings**; d. 3 Dec., 1841.
   iv. Solomon (Griswold), b. 2 Jan., 1805 ; m. 11 Nov., 1827, Elizabeth W. **Arnold**; he d. 23 Aug., 1853.
   v. Melissa (Griswold), b. 9 Jan., 1807 ; m. 10 Mch., 1831, Walter **Warner**; d. 1898.
   vi. Mercy Miller (Griswold), b. 2 Mch., 1809 ; m. 26 Nov., 1829, Russel **Adams**; she d. 30 Aug., 1865.
   vii. William (Griswold), b. 12 Apl., 1811 ; m. Julia A. **Gibbs**; d. 14 Aug., 1880.
   viii. Martha (Griswold), b. 2 Apl., 1813 ; d. 25 Jan., 1833.
   ix. Lester (Griswold), b. 15 July, 1815 ; d. 3 Feb., 1816.
   x. Mary (Griswold), b. 19 Mch., 1817 ; m. James **Reiley**, 24 Oct., 1847.
8. William, b. 18 Feb., bp. 7 Mch., 1779. FAM. 9.

FAM. 4. CAMP,[3] (Amasa,[2] Benjamin,[1]), at age of 18 was a soldier in Fr. and Ind. Wars, under Capt. Eliphalet Whittlesey, from Apl. 10 to 15 Nov., 1758; m. at Weth. (*Weth. Ch. Rec.*), 13 Dec., 1759—(*W. C. R.*), Mehitabel (dau. of Timothy & Sarah *Kilbourne*) **Baxter**; b. 25 May, 1740; res. So. Lane, Weth., in an ancient ho. erected *circa* 1735, and near by was a workshop in which he worked as a cabinet-maker and in which bldg. it is said, he made with his own hands complete sets of furniture (except the chairs) for each of his seven daus. as they were successively married. In 1788, he became pt. owner of the old Chester grist mill; and was prominent and useful in all town and Ch. affairs; held the offices of grand juror, tythingman and surveyor of highways in 1772, 1778 and 1786, respectively; was elected as listor (assessor) from 1787-1794, inclusive; d. Weth., 20 Mch., 1823, ae. 84; his wid. d. 15 Aug., 1825, ae. 85.—*W. C. R.*

Children (bp. from *Weth. Ch. Rec.; corroborated by his Fam. Bible, in possess. of Mrs. Frances H. Corbin, of New Haven*):

1. Mehitable, b. 27 Dec., 1759 ; bp. 16 Mch., 1760 ; m. 16 Mch., 1780, James **Hatch**, b. 26 Oct., 1757, who was lost at sea, 23 Oct., 1791 ; she d. 20 Dec., 1831. *Issue:*
   i. Jerusha (Hatch), b. 23 May, 1781 ; m. Abijah **Savage, Jr.**, of Cromwell ; d. 21 Feb., 1814.
   ii. Mehitable (Hatch), b. 3 Aug., 1783 ; m. 8 Mch., 1804, Daniel **Harris** of Midd.
   iii. George (Hatch), b. 15 July, 1785.
   iv. Sarah Kilburne (Hatch), b. 21 June, 1788 ; m. Amasa **Savage**, of Cromwell ; she d. 15 July, 1865.
   v. John (Hatch), b. 21 Sept., 1791 ; d. in Providence, R. I., Aug., 1829.
2. **Sarah**, b. 1?, bp. 20 Sept., 1761 ; m. 16 June, 1799, Capt. Chas. **Francis**, of Weth., who d. at W. May, 1850, ae. 87 ; she d. 5 Jan., 1852. *Issue:*
   i. Sarah (Francis), b. July, 1801 ; m. Hosea **Harris**, 7 Aug., 1821.
   ii. Charles (Francis), b. 3 Jan., 1803 ; m. 5 Oct., 1825, Emily **Blinn**; he d. 9 Apl., 1885.
3. Martha, b. 20 Apl., 1764 ; m. 4 Jan., 1787, Joseph **Treat**, who d. E. Htfd., 12 Nov., 1827 ; she d. 2 Jan., 1849. *Issue:*
   i. Martha (Treat), b. 27 Jan., 1788 ; m. Ozias **Roberts**; d. 3 Jan., 1809.
   ii. Harriet (Treat), b. 15 Dec.., 1789 ; m. Ozias **Roberts**; d. 19 July, 1822.
   iii. Sally (Treat), b. 13 Jan., 1792 ; m. 16 Jan., 1812, Eli **Olmsted**; d. 28 Sept., 1875.
   iv. Ashbel (Treat), b. 17 Sept., 1793 ; d. 29 Sept., 1793.
   v. Ira (Treat), b. 13 Mch., 1795 ; d. 28 Nov., 1817.
   vi. Adna Adams (Treat), b. 8 Apl., 1797 ; m. 15 Feb., 1826, Jane **Relley**; res. Denver, Col.
   vii. Mary (Treat), b. 20 Aug., 1799 ; m. 11 Sept., 1822, Ralph **Pitkin**; d. 9 Sept., 1848.
   viii. Joseph Camp (Treat), b. 11 Oct., 1802 ; m. 3 Nov., 1825, Jane A. **Roberts**; d. 2 Mch., 1880.
   ix. Royal (Treat), b. 25 Feb., 1806 ; m. (1) Nancy **Crane**, 6 Mch., 1828 ; m. (2) Hepzibah **Porter**, 23 Apl., 1834 ; d. 28 Aug., 1859.
4. James Camp, b. 13, bp. 16 Feb., 1766 ; m. 23 Dec., 1790, Sarah **Barrett** (b. 8 Aug., 1771), dau. of James & Anna *Carrington* Barrett ; res. So. Lane, Weth., in father's old ho. where he d. 11 Aug., 1820 ; wid. d. 13 Aug., 1845. *No issue.*
5. Hannah, b. 18, bp. 24 Jan., 1768 m. 27 Nov., 1788, Oliver **Corey**, of Stepney ; d. R. I., 11 Jan., 1835, ae. 67 ; had large family of ch.
6. Rebecca, b. 14 Aug., 1770 ; m. in Stepney, 1 Jan., 1795, Capt. Humphrey **Woodhouse**, of Weth. (son of Sam'l & Thankful *Blinn* Woodhouse) ; he d. 27 May, 1827 ; wid. d. 29 Aug., 1845. *Issue:*
   i. Humphrey (Woodhouse), b. 11 Aug.,

1795 ; m. 10 Mch., 1818, Clarissa **Harris**; d. 19 Aug., 1872 ; res. Weth.
   ii. James (Woodhouse), b. 23 June, 1797 ; d. 14 Nov., 1798.
   iii. James (Woodhouse), b. 6 May, 1800 ; d. 27 May, 1819.
   iv. Rebecca (Woodhouse), b. 5 July, 1802 ; m. 16 Sept., 1822, Oliver **Robbins.**
   v. Julia (Woodhouse), b. 19 May, 1806 ; m. (1) Wm. **French**, of Oxford, O. ; m. (2) Hon. Royal R. **Hinman**, of Htfd. ; d. 10 June, 1888.
   vi. George Washington (Woodhouse), b. 17 Mch., 1809 ; d. 31 Aug., 1825.
   vii. Charles (Woodhouse), b. 11 Nov., 1812 ; m. 19 Dec., 1834, Lepha L. **Guernsey**; d. 15 Oct., 1894, in Rutland, Vt.
7. Mary Ann, b. 22 Feb., 1773 ; m. 26 May, 1793, Dea. Simeon **Francis**; res. on Wolcott Hill, Weth., in present John Hanmer ho. ; he d. 7 Sept., 1823 ; she d. 18 Sept., 1822 ; fam. res. Weth., but rem. West. *Issue:*
   i. Charles (Francis), b. 19 Mch., 1794.
   ii. Simeon (Francis), b. 8 May, 1796.
   iii. Mary Ann (Francis), b. 9 Aug., 1798.
   iv. Calvin (Francis), b. 12 June, 1802 ; m. 21 Oct., 1823, Abigail D. **Francis**; d. 27 June, 1886, at Athens, Ill.
   v. Josiah (Francis), b. 14 Jan., 1805 ; not ment. in father's will.
   vi. Edwin (Francis), b. 9 Oct., 1808.
   vii. Huldah (Francis), b. 10 May, 1810.
   viii. Allen (Francis), b. 1814 ; d. 4 Aug., 1887, in Ontario.
   ix. Newton (Francis), b. —
8. Ashbel, b. 12 Apl., bp. 16, 1775 ; d. 3 May, 1775.—*W. C. R.*
9. Honor, b. 13, bp. 30, June, 1776 ; m. 20 May, 1798, Elijah **Crane, Jr.**, wheelwright, who res. at Weth., Sandisfield, Mass., and Sheffield, Mass., in which last named place he d. Mch., 1863 ; she d. in Sheffield, 20 Apl., 1836. *Issue:*
   i. Sarah (Crane), b. 16 Nov., 1798 ; d. 16 July, 1806.
   ii. Rebecca (Crane), b. 1 May, 1800 ; m. (1) Rossiter **Robbins**; m. (2) T. W. **Stillman**, of Sheffield ; d. 7 Sept., 1877.
   iii. Harriet (Crane), b. 6 Aug., 1802 ; m. 11 Feb., 1825, Josiah **Robbins**, of Weth. ; d. 16 May, 1886.
   iv. Calvin Camp (Crane), b. 28 Oct., 1805 ; m. Lucretia **Mott**, of Marlborough, Mass. ; d. 20 Apl., 1881.
   v. Sarah Adams (Crane), b. 30 June, 1807 ; m. 15 June, 1824, William **Adams**; d. 3 Oct., 1858.
   vi. George (Crane), b. 26 Feb., 1810 ; d. unm. 18 Apl., 1855.
   vii. Royal (Crane), b. 23 May, 1812 ; m. Mary **Beach.**
   viii. Elizabeth (Crane), b. 14 Dec., 1815 ; m. (1) John **Keep**; m. (2) Wm. **Carley, Jr.**, of Chatham, N. Y. ; d. Dec., 1894.
   ix. Martha (Crane), b. 23 Nov., 1820 ; d. unm. 18 Aug., 1850.

FAM. 5. JOHN,[3] (*Amasa,*[2] *Benjamin,*[1]), b. 1745; m. 6 Dec., 1774—(*W. C. R.*), Mary (dau. Abraham & Rebecca *Hurlburt*) **Crane**—(*W. C. R.*); res. on So. Hill, Weth., in present Frank H. Belden ho.—the "new ho." referred to in his father's will; was a farmer and with his bros. operated the Adams' mill; his wife d. 20 May, 1794, ae. 41—(*W. C. R.*); he d. 7 Aug., 1795.—(*W. C. R.*) Est. valued at £574-2s-2d. A John A., *prob.* the same, m. 7 Aug., 1795, Martha **Curtis**—(*W. C. R.*); the wid. Martha A., m. (2) John **Goodrich**, who d. 23 Dec., 1830; she d. 30 Apl., 1830, ae. 78.

Children—(*W. C. R.*) :

1. Lucy, b. 25 Nov., 1777 ; m. Stepney, 28 Aug., 1800, Curtis **Crane, Jr.** (b. 24 June, 1777), mariner, lost at sea, 16 Sept., 1810, on schr. *Sally*, wrecked off Barnegat Shoals ; she d. in Angelica, N. Y., 5 May, 1867. *Child :*
    i. Mary, b. 25 July, 1801 ; m. 22 Jan., 1822, in Eaton, N. Y., Lyman **Gardner;** she d. 29 Apl., 1844.
2. Mary, b. 25 Feb., 1779 ; bp. 1 Feb., 1795 ; m. 11 Apl., 1799, Roger **Wolcott,** who d. Trenton, Oneida Co., N. Y., 20 Oct., 1829 ; she d. at T., 24 Feb., 1859. *Issue (all except first, b. at T.*) :
    i. John Adams (Wolcott), b. 25 June, 1800 ; d. unm. 1 Apl., 1847.
    ii. Mary (Wolcott), b. 9 Oct., 1802 ; m. 3 July, 1834, C. C. **Cunningham,** of Russia. N. Y. ; d. 22 Jan., 1892.
    iii. Harriet (Wolcott), b. 10 Mch., 1805 ; m. Henry S. **Deming,** of Trenton, N. Y. ; d. 4 July, 1864.
    iv. Horace (Wolcott), b. 25 Dec., 1807 ; d. 22 Aug., 1840.
    v. Alfred (Wolcott), b. 15 Feb., 1810 ; d.

21 Apl., 1829.
    vi. Sarah Camp (Wolcott), b. 15 May, 1812 ; m. 12 Jan., 1860, Henry **Jones;** res. Amesville, N. Y.
    vii. Eliza Blinn (Wolcott), b. 7 Sept., 1814 ; m. Gideon **Hinman,** 2 Oct., 1834 ; res. Trenton, N. Y.
    viii. Gardner (Wolcott), b. 20 Mch., 1817 ; m. Sept., 1849, Abby **Bronson;** res. Eldorado, Wis.
    ix. Austin Roger (Wolcott), b. 7 May, 1822 ; m. 14 Jan., 1882, Mrs. Sarah H. **Dodge;** res. Gould Farm, Mo.
3. Hannah, b. 1786 ; bp. 1 Feb., 1795 ; m. before 1813, Hosea **Tarbox;** res. in Trenton and Ellicottville, N. Y. *Issue :*
    i. John (Tarbox).
    ii. Martha (Tarbox).
    iii. Elvira (Tarbox).
    iv. Mary (Tarbox).
Four other ch. d. in inf.—*Weth. Ch. Rec.,* viz. : Two (twins) bu. 19 Nov., 1781, and one bu. 11 Jan., 1777, perhaps also the ch. ae. 5 mos. and the ch. ae. 9 mos., who d. 25 Aug., 1786.—*W. C. R.*

FAM. 6. AMASA, Jr.[3] (*Amasa,*[2] *Benjamin,*[1]), b. 1753 ; in Apl., 1775, was one of Capt. Chester's Lex. Alarm Co. ; served during the following yr. in Capt. Hez. Welles' Co., in Col. Elisha Wolcott's Reg. ; in 1778, enl. in Capt. Elijah Wright's Co., of Col. Enos' reg. ; prob. served until close of war, Jan. 15, 1783 ; he m. in Stepney, Sarah *Deming* **Griswold,** wid. of Solomon G. ; she d. 12 June, 1794, in 42d yr. ; he m. (2) 24 Jan., 1796—(*W. C. R.*), Caroline **Dalebe,** wid. of Jonathan(?) Dalebe, of Weth. ; she d. 13 Aug., 1798. In Nov., same yr., he rem. with his 3 ch. to Bristol, Ct., and within next 2 yr., he m. (3) Mrs. Lydia **Belden,** he was a farmer ; d. at B., 16 Jan., 1819 ; his wid. Lydia d. 9 Sept., 1836, ae. 76.

Children :

1. Sylvester, b. 29 Oct., 1783 ; bp. 7 Mch., 1784 ; m. Betsy ———— ; was a shipbuilder. res. at Stepney, and later at Midd., where he d. *No issue.*
2. Horace, b. 8, bp. 28, Jan., 1787. FAM. 10.
3. Roxana, b. 25 Apl., 1790 ; m. at Bristol Ct., 25 Sept., 1812, Chauncey **Boardman,** of B., but b. in Stepney, Weth., 16 Nov., 1790 ; he d. at B., 11 Aug., 1867 ; wid. d. 29 July, 1862. *Issue :*
    i. Sarah Caroline (Boardman), b. 23 Jan. 1813 ; m. 23 Nov., 1832, Joseph A. **Wells,** of Plymouth, Ct. ; d. 17

Jan., 1839.
    ii. Martha A. (Boardman), b. 16 Jan., 1816 ; m. 11 Sept., 1838, Theron **Ives,** of Htfd. ; d. 5 Aug., 1888.
    iii. Lydia E. (Boardman). b. 15 Feb., 1823 ; m. 8 Dec., 1847, Charles **Toote,** of Canton, Ct.
    iv. Jane R. (Boardman), b. 3 July, 1826 ; m. 19 Nov., 1851, Wm. L. **Rogers,** of Htfd.
    v. Ellen A. (Boardman), b. 28 Aug., 1836 ; d. 24 Jan., 1839.

FAM. 7. JOSEPH,[3] (*Amasa,*[2] *Benjamin,*[1]), b. 1755 ; m. 7 Dec., 1780, Mehitable **Barrett,** both of Step.—(*W. C. R.*), who d. Weth., 4 Dec., 1798, ae. 39. He m. (2) Mary (wid. of Leonard) **Dix,** 9 Jan., 1800—(*W. C. R.*) ; res. Harris Hill, Weth., oppo. ho. of late Chauncey Harris ; farmer and miller ; after his mar. to Mrs. Dix, he rem. to her home in West Hill, where he d. 10 Sept., 1801 ; wid. d. 8 Aug., 1830, ae. 68.—(*W. C. R.*)

Children (by *first marriage*) from *Family Bible :*

1. Sally, b. 7 June (17th *Town Rec.*), 1781 ; bp. 10 Apl., 1785 ; m. Htfd., 3 June, 1801, Luther **Burt,** who. d. 26 May, 1824 ; she d. Htfd., abt. 1830. *Issue* (auth. *MS. Julia Coleman,* of New Britain, Ct.) :
    i. George (*Burt*).
    ii. Mary Ann (Burt) ; d. unm. 1834.
    iii. Alfred (Burt) ; m. Adaline **Allen.**
    iv. Henry (Burt) ; m. ————.
    v. Charles (Burt), m. Eveline **Allen.**
2. Joseph, b. 6 Aug., 1783 ; bp., 10 Apl., 1785. FAM. 11.

3. William Barrett, b. 22 Nov., 1785 ; d. 26 Aug., 1786.
4. Persis, b. 26 Sept., bp. 11 Nov., 1787 ; m. Htfd., 22 May, 1808, Samuel **Skinner,** of Bolton, Ct., who d. abt. 1820 ; she m. (2) ———— **Rogers,** of Baltimore, Md., wh'ther she rem. ; by her first mar. she had at least two ch., Mehitable, b. abt. 1810, and Lucy.
5. William, b. 7 Oct., 1790 ; bp. 16 Jan., 1791 ; d. 20 Jan., 1808, in Kingston, Jamaica.
6. James, b. 1 July, bp. 1 Dec., 1793. FAM. 12.

7. Emily, b. 21 Feb., bp. 23 Oct., 1796 ; d. unm., 9 Sept., 1824.
8. Henry, b. 4 Dec., 1798 ; rem. to Philadelphia, before 1825, where it is supposed he m. Louise ————, who d. a few yrs. after; and he m. (2) in Phila., 10 Nov., 1829, Ann Miller; he d. 23 Feb., 1832, and had several ch. of whom nothing is known ; he had estab. a successful bus. as a bookbinder, in Phila.
9. Lura, b. 10 Aug., 1800 ; bp. 6 Oct., 1805 ; m. 30 Jan., 1821, Solomon Woodhouse (b. 30 Aug., 1798), son of Capt. Samuel & Abigail *Goodrich* Woodhouse ; cabinetmaker ; res. on the Common, in Weth. ; he d. 19 May, 1853 ; wid. d. 25 Feb., 1888. *Issue:*
  i. Mary Hatch (Woodhouse), b. 17 Dec., 1821 ; m. 15 Sept., 1845, Wm. B. Clarke; m. (2) Ephraim Pickering; she d. 28 Aug., 1887.
  ii. Abigail Goodrich (Woodhouse), b. 10 Oct., 1823 ; m. 2 Apl., 1846, Benj. Bliss;

res. Htfd.
iii. Lura Ann (Woodhouse), b. 12 Dec., 1825 ; m. 5 Jan., 1853, John C. Hatch.
iv. George Butler (Woodhouse), b. 12 Mch., 1828 ; went to Cal., Nov., 1847.
v. William Henry (Woodhouse), b. 22 June, 1830 ; d. 15 May, 1832.
vi. Elizabeth Butler (Woodhouse), b. 2 Apl., 1833 ; m. 8 Dec., 1881, Fred. T. Chapman, of Weth., d. 9 Dec., 1886.
vii. Elvira Maria (Woodhouse), b. 18 Apl., 1835 ; m. 18 Dec., 1861, Geo. L. We'les, of Weth, who d. 3 Nov., 1890.
viii. Henry William (Woodhouse), b. 27 Mch., 1838 ; drowned 26 June, 1847.
iv. Edward Gardner (Woodhouse), b. 24 Feb., 1841 ; m. 30 Nov., 1864, Louisa Rogers, who d. 21 Dec., 1896 ; res. Weth.
x. Herbert Hayden (Woodhouse), b. 24 June, 1843 ; m. Frances Ellen Wolcott, 10 July, 1867 ; res. N. Y. City.

FAM. 8. UZZIEL.[4] (*Benj.,*[3] *Amasa,*[2] *Benj.,*[1]). b. 1768; m. at Weth., 14 Sept., 1794— (W. C. R.). Clarissa Lucas; was a carpenter; res. on E. side So. Lane in ho. owned by late E. G. Adams; he d. 16 Aug., 1825, ae. 57; wid. d. 18 Apl., 1854, ae. 78.

Children (bp.—W. C. R.) :

1. Fanny, b. 28 July (Feb.—*Town Rec.*), 1795 ; d. 18 Dec., 1796.—W. C. R.
2. George Lucas, b. 20 Apl., bp., 12 Nov., 1797. FAM. 13.
3. Fanny, b. 9 Mch., bp. 30 June, 1799 ; d. unm. 25 Sept., 1877.
4. Miles, b. 19 Feb., bp. 28 June, 1801. FAM. 14.
5. James Benjamin, b. 16 Mch., 1803 ; bp. 6 Apl., 1806. FAM. 15.
6. Horace, b. 23 Feb., 1805 ; bp. same time

with James B. (Feb. 21.—*Town Rec.*) FAM. 16.
7. Clarissa, b. 2 Dec., 1806 ; d. unm. 7 Dec., 1887.
8. Walter, b. 3 May, 1810. FAM. 17.
9. Watson, b. 3 (5—*Town Rec.*), Jan., 1812. FAM. 18.
10. Orson S., b. 4 June, 1814. FAM. 19.
11. Thomas, b. 27 Feb., 1816. FAM. 20.

FAM. 9. WILLIAM,[4] (*Benj.,*[3] *Amasa,*[2] *Benj.,*[1]). b. 1779; m. 25 Nov., 1801, Mary (dau. Elijah & Sarah *Balch*) Welles, of Weth.—(W. C. R.) ; res. So. Lane in ho. now owned by R. T. Hewitt; was a prominent farmer and miller; d. 28 Nov., 1852; wid. d. 23 Aug., 1854.

Children:

1. William, b. 12 Mch., 1803. FAM. 21.
2. Welles, b. 6 Dec., 1804. FAM. 22.
3. Russel, b. 8 Jan., 1807 ; bp. 11 May, 1813. FAM. 23.
4. Chauncey, b. 6 Nov., 1808. FAM. 24.
5. Mary Welles, b. 25 Oct., 1811 ; m. 13 Feb., 1833, Hiram Havens, of Weth. (son of Thos. & Lucinda *Adams* Havens) ; she d. 19 Nov., 1876 ; he d. 30 Oct., 1886. *Issue:*
  i. Katherine Adelia (Havens), b. 27 Sept., 1834 ; m. Judge Thomas McManus; res. Htfd.
  ii. Emma Eliza (Havens), b. 7 Oct., 1836.
  iii. Edward Newton (Havens), b. 12 Oct., 1838.
  iv. Francis Wayland (Havens), b. 2 Dec., 1845.
  v. Charles Hiram (Havens), b. 15 July, 1849 ; d. 17 Sept., 1850.
6. Sarah Balch, b. 28 Oct., 1814 ; prob. the Sarah Balch A., who was bp. 6 Apl., 1834—W. C. R.; m. 20 Jan., 1836, Simeon Blinn, of Weth., b. 24 June, 1804 ; she d. 4 Oct., 1877 ; he d. 3 Dec., 1880. *Issue:*
  i. Adelaide Amelia (Blinn), b. 18 Jan., 1837 ; m. 10 Sept., 1856, Levi Goodwin, who d. 7 June, 1880 ; she res. So. Weth.
  ii. Alfred Alonzo (Blinn), b. 13 Nov., 1838 ; d. 16 Dec., 1843.
  iii. Ellen Theresa (Blinn), b. 1 Feb., 1842 ; m. 12 Feb., 1862, S. Broadbent Morgan, who d. Denver, Col., 11 Dec., 1897.

iv. Alice Gertrude (Blinn), b. 25 Sept., 1844 ; res. So. Weth.
v. Frank Stuart (Blinn), b. 2 May, 1850 ; res. So. Weth.
7. Emily, b. 30 Oct., 1816 ; m. 19 Sept., 1837, Franklin W. Griswold, b. 28 Mch., 1815, d. at Weth. 21 Dec., 1886. *Issue:*
  i. Franklin Clinton (Griswold), b. 10 Sept., 1838 ; m. 1865, Sarah E. Putnam; m. (2) 1882, Ella Hall. They have (a) Edwin F., b. 17 Apl., 1866 ; (b) Chas. C., b. 16 Apl., 1871 ; (c) William P., b. 23 Dec., 1875 ; (d) Harry A., b. 21 April, 1884 ; (e) Ella May, b. 19 Oct., 1885 ; (f) Emily A., b. 23 Jan., 1887 ; (g) Mary E., b. 29 Oct., 1888 ; (h) Stanley E., b. 10 Mch., 1890 ; (i) Ruth H., b. 24 Sept., 1891 ; (j) Mildred W., b. 31 July, 1893 ; (k) Franklin W., b. 17 Nov., 1895 ; (l) Leslie W., b. 28 Mch., 1898 ; res. Minn.
  ii. Emily Augusta (Griswold), b. 9 Mch., 1843 ; m. 31 Dec., 1863, John M. Morris; had (a) Arthur F., b. 29 July, 1865, d. 2 Aug., 1866 ; (b) Emily, b. 11 Jan., 1872, d. 15 Sept., 1873 ; (c) John M., b. 7 Nov., 1873, d. same day. Mrs. Morris m. (2) 29 June, 1881, Jedidiah Deming, of Newington.
  iii. Henry Adams (Griswold), b. 21 July, 1847 ; m. 15 Feb., 1887, Maude Holley,

of Highblow, Md., res. in Washington, D. C.
iv. Mary Helen (Griswold), b. 20 Aug., 1849; m. 28 Dec., 1870, John Leslie **Welles,** of Weth.; had (a) Harry L., b. 19 May, 1874; (b) Franklin G., b. 9 July, 1876; (c) Clifford Y., b. 29 Oct., 1877; (d) Joseph F., b. 8 Mch., 1880; (e) Clayton W., b. 22 Apl., 1883; (f) Ruth Morris, b. 31 July, 1884; (g) Emily Adams, b. 26 Aug., 1886; (h) Eleanor M., b. 6 Oct., 1887; res. Weth.
v. Ella Francis (Griswold), b. 13 Sept., 1856; m. 30 Oct., 1879, Edward **Deming;** had (a) Edward A., b. 12 Nov., 1880; (b) Mabel, b. 20 Sept., 1882; (c) Clinton D., b. 21 Aug., 1884; (d)

Winifred G., b. 25 Sept., 1887; (e) Dorothea, b. 14 May, 1892; (f) Ella C., b. 22 Oct., 1896; res. Htfd.
8. Eliza, b. 2 Nov., 1818; m. 6 Oct., 1846, Henry Prudden **Allen,** of Htfd., who d. Brownsville. Tex., 25 June, 1865; she d. Weth. *Issue:*
i. Ella Frances (Allen), b. 25 July, 1847; d. 23 Nov., 1862.
ii. William Henry (Allen), b. 18 June, 1854; died.
iii. Mary Eliza Adams (Allen), b. 18 Jan., 1858; m. P. A. **Lester,** 28 Feb., 1894; res. Niantic, Ct.; died.
iv. Frederick James (Allen), b. 12 July, 1861; d. 6 Aug., 1861.
9. Martha, b. 20 Aug., 1821; d. unm., 2 Sept., 1892.

FAM. 10. HORACE,[4] (*Amasa,*[3] *Amasa,*[2] *Benj.,*[1]), b. 1787; m. at Bristol, Ct., Oct. 29, 1812, Lois **Wilcox,** b. 15 Dec., 1792, (dau. of Benjamin & Philena *Rowe*) Wilcox; he was a soldier in War of 1812, serving at New London, Ct.; rec'd a pension and bounty grant of 160 acres of Western ld.; was for a time in the clock selling business in employ of his bro-in-law Chauncey Boardman; in Nov., 1825; rem. to Triangle Broome Co., N. Y., where he had previously bo't a farm and where he d. 27 May, 1878; wife d. 2 Aug., 1817. Of his 10 ch., 7 at one time or another taught school.

Children:

1. Celona Jenette, b. 24 July, 1813; m. 25 Aug., 1844, John **Leach,** of Triangle, N. Y.; she d. 21 Nov., 1845. *No issue.*
2. Andrew Jackson, b. 29 July, 1815. FAM. 25.
3. Franklin, b. 14 July, 1818. FAM. 26.
4. Maryette, b. 4 Oct., 1820; m. 24 May, 1840, Lewis **Ticknor,** who d. at Triangle, N. Y., 24 Feb., 1872; she d. 5 Dec., 1892. *Issue:*
   i. Jane (Ticknor), b. 14 Mch., 1841; m. Chas. **Rogers,** 15 Apl., 1862.
   ii. Nancy (Ticknor), b. 1 Dec., 1842; m. E. B. **Smith,** of Marathon, N. Y.; res. Nebraska.
   iii. Verranus, b. 17 Oct., 1844; d. 9 May, 1863.
5. Chester Wilcox, b. 31 Dec., 1822; d. 1 Jan., 1825.
6. Helen, b. 31 Mch., 1825; m. 14 Nov., 1847, in Southville, N. Y., Homer **Hurlburt,** of Barker, N. Y.; she d. at Ithaca, N. Y., 19 Jan., 1893. *Issue:*
   i. Eugene B. (Hurlburt), m. Ruth **Rolfe,** 2 Sept., 1869.
   ii. James R. (Hurlburt), m. Mary **Foster,** 1 Sept., 1869.
   iii. Horatio (Hurlburt).
   iv. Adelia (Hurlburt).
   v. Caroline (Hurlburt).
   vi. Alice (Hurlburt), m. Searls **Casterlaine,** 14 Nov., 1887.
7. Horace Perry. FAM. 27.
8. Emily Jane, b. Triangle, N. Y., 11 Jan., 1830; m. 10 Jan., 1852, William **Ball (b. in** Winchesdon, Mass.); res. Barker, N. Y., where he d. 4 Jan., 1855; she m. (2) 28 Feb., 1872, Leverett **Jeffers,** who d. 30 Sept., 1895, ae. 76. *Issue:*
   i. Lewis (Ball), b. 12 Dec., 1852; m. 22 May, 1883, Fannie E. **Amsbry,** b. 1858; had (a) Jennie b. 25 Nov., 1884; (b) Bessie, b. 23 July, 1887; (c) Anna, b.

13 July, 1890; (d) b. 4 Oct., 1895.
   ii. Celona Jane (Ball), b. 30 Aug., 1859; m. 13 May, 1883, Augustus **Lewis,** b. 1852; had (a) Frank A. (Lewis), b. 16 Aug., 1884; (b) Ray (Lewis), b. 1 Dec., 1885.
9. Charlotte, b. 13 Dec., 1832, at Triangle, N. Y.; m. at Binghamton, N. Y., 7 Nov., 1855, Wm. D. **Wilcox,** b. 1821; res. at Triangle, N. Y.
   To Mrs. Wilcox we are indebted for the very full account of the descendants of her ancestor, Amasa Adams, Jr.
10. Angeline, b. in Triangle, N. Y., 27 Apl., 1835; m. 26 Oct., 1856, Orlando R. **Fuller,** b. 9 Sept., 1828; res. Nanticoke, N. Y. *Issue:*
   i. William D. (Fuller), b. 21 Dec., 1857; m. 18 Nov., 1880, Jennie **Morgan,** b. 1861; had (a) Bessie, b. 14 Sept., 1881; (b) Orlando, b. 1 Dec., 1882; (c) Jessie, b. 15 Jan., 1884; (d) Angeline, b. 8 Aug., 1885; (e) Mary, b. 21 Mch., 1890; (f) Horace, b. 14 Apl., 1893.
   ii. George (Fuller), b. 23 Mch., 1860; he d. 5 Mch., 1890; m. 25 Aug., 1883, Sarah **Padget;** had (a) Merl D., b. 2 June, 1885; (b) George, b. 23 Mch. 1889; d. 21 July, 1890.
   iii. Frederick B. (Fuller), b. 4 Sept., 1863; m. 24 Feb., 1886, Julia **Pollard,** b. 1867; had (a) Guy, b. 3 Apl., 1887; (b) Grace, b. 5 Apl., 1891.
   iv. Andrew (Fuller), b. 27 May, 1866; m. 2 Feb., 1890, Nellie **Edwards,** who d. 14 Dec., 1892; had (a) Ray, b. 7 Aug., 1891 ;Mr. And. Fuller m. (2) 13 Sept., 1896, Ann **Beebe.**
   v. Lottie (Fuller), b. 23 July, 1875; m. 23 Apl., 1893, Wm. F. **Barden;** had (a) Ellen, b. 10 Dec., 1894.

FAM. 11. JOSEPH,[4] (*Joseph,*[3] *Amasa,*[2] *Benj.,*[1]), b. 6 Aug., 1783; m. 3 Mch., 1802, at Htfd., Sally (dau. of Dr. Matthew) **Bronson,** and b. 12 Sept., 1783; res. a few yrs. in Htfd.; then occup. his father's homestead on Harris Hill, Weth.; kept a general store on Main St.; also was in commis. business; d. 6 Oct., 1834; wid. d. 29 Sept., 1860.

Children:

1. Emeline, b. 3 Feb., 1803; m. Htfd., 11 Aug., 1839, Daniel **Avery** (b. Monson, Mass., 1806), a hatter; res. Weth.; he d. 6 Feb., 1854; wid. d. New Britain, Ct., 24 Jan., 1891. *Issue:*
   i. Sarah Jane (Avery), b. 15 Sept., 1840; m. 26 July, 1864, Philo W. **Hart**, who d. N. B., 16 Feb., 1892.
   ii. William (Avery), b. 24 Dec., 1842; d. Apl., 1844.
2. Julia, b. 28 Apl., 1810; m. 18 Dec., 1836, Curtis **Coleman** (b. 22 Feb., 1807), of

Weth., who d. 22 Nov., 1868; she resides in New Br., with her dau. Mrs. Henry O. Nash. *Issue:*
   i. William Adams (Coleman), b. 13 Oct., 1837; killed at battle of Chancelorsville, 3 May, 1863.
   ii. Franklin Curtis (Coleman), b. 22 July, 1839; m. 23 Jan., 1867, Anna M. **Smith.**
   iii. Isabel Julia (Coleman), b. 11 Dec., 1841; m. 18 Nov., 1862; Henry O. **Nash**, of New Britain, Ct.

FAM. 12.   JAMES,[4] (*Joseph,*[3] *Amasa,*[2] *Benjamin,*[1]), b. 1793; m. 17 Apl., 1817, Mary (dau. George & Betsy) **Tinker**—(*W. C. R.*); was a contractor and builder; and did much business in the South; res. Weth., on Harris Hill; d. 11 Aug., 1844; wid. d. 22 Mch., 1858, ae. 60.

Children:

1. George, b. 10 Mch., 1818; d. 12 Dec., 1824.—*W. C. R.*
2. Mary Tinker, b. 25 Oct., 1819; m. 18 May, 1850, Augustus **Parish**, of Pomfret, Ct.; she d. Weth., 11 Sept., 1855. *Issue:*
   i. Walton Augustus (Parish), b. 21 May, 1852.
   ii. William Adams (Parish), b. 4 June, 1854.
3. James, b. 25 Apl., 1821. FAM. 28.
4. Levi Hatch, b. 4 Mch., 1823. FAM. 29.
5. Lucy Howard, b. 3 Apl., 1825; m. 20 July, 1845, Harvey **Goodrich**; res. Weth.; d. 6 Nov., 1861; Mr. G. res. Falls Village, Mass. *Issue:*
   i. Inez, b. 14 Mch., 1847; m. Chas. **Fletcher**; res. Manchester, N. H.
6. Sarah Buck, b. 22 Oct., 1828; m. 9 Jan., 1848, James W. **Roberts**, of Htfd.; she d. 7 June, 1862; Mr. R. was a bookbinder; res. in Weth., and Htfd., and d. 7 Aug., 1895. *Issue:*
   i. Fanny Weeks (Roberts), b. 20 Dec., 1849; m. Jas. L. **Adams.**
   ii. Lizzie (Roberts), b. 6 June, 1852; d. 1 June, 1858.
7. Elizabeth Prudence, b. 19 Oct., 1830; m. 26 May, 1852, Joseph H. B. **Butler**; res. So. Hanson, Mass. *Issue:*
   i. Mary Elizabeth (Butler), b. 18 Jan., 1855; d. 22 Feb., 1862.
   ii. Arthur Deney Blakely (Butler), b. 23 Apl., 1859; m. 14 June, 1885, Mabel **Howe.**
   iii. Lucius Franklin Robinson (Butler), b. 9 Aug., 1863; m. 8 Jan., 1887, Imogene W. **Beals**, who d. 3 Feb., 1890.
8. William Henry, b. 10 Jan., 1834; m. wid. Martha **Bulkeley**, 17 Dec., 1860; res. Rocky Hill, Ct.
9. Jenette Fortune, b. 29 Apl., 1837; m. 11 Jan., 1858, Schuyler **Penfield**; res. Htfd., Ct. *Issue:*
   i. George Schuyler (Penfield), b. 19 July, 1859; m. 22 Apl., 1887, Fanny M. **Perry.**
   ii. Jennie Louise (Penfield), b. 11 Nov., 1860; m. 22 June, 1887, Chas. F. **Doebler.**
   iii. Mary Elizabeth (Penfield), b. 9 Jan., 1862; d. 10 May, 1862.
   iv. William Adams (Penfield), b. 28 Sept., 1864.
   v. Raymond Whiting (Penfield), b. 1 Oct., 1867; m. 11 Oct., 1893, Elizabeth **Oakes.**
   vi. Mary Lizzie (Penfield), b. 2 May., 1873.
10. Louise Augusta, b. 17 Mch., 1839; m. 11 Feb., 1861, Darius A. **Russell**, of Wallingford, Ct., who d. Dec., 1867; she m. (2) 24 July, 1873, Walter C. **Griswold**, of Rocky Hill; res. Bridgeport, Ct. *Issue*
    (*by first marriage*):
    i. Benjamin Franklin (Russell), b. 24 Mch., 1863.
    Issue (by second marriage):
    ii. Alfred Wyllys (Griswold), b. 14 May, 1874; d. 28 Sept., 1876.
    iii. Bessie Louise (Griswold), b. 12 Oct., 1876.
    iv. Alfred Wyllys (Griswold), b. 7 Feb., 1879.
    v. Walter Garfield (Griswold), b. 29 Nov., 1881.

FAM. 13.   GEORGE LUCAS,[5] (*Uzziel,*[4] *Benj.,*[3] *Amasa,*[2] *Benj.,*[1]), b. 1797; m. 20 Aug., 1823, Mary (dau. John & Persis *Adams*) **Montague**—(*W. C. R.*), b. 10 Nov., 1799; a sailor, in the W. I. trade; was lost in storm off Cape Hatteras, Aug., 1827; wid. d. 10 Sept., 1828.—(*W. C. R.*)

Children:

1. Martha Montague, b. 6 Aug., 1824; d. unm. 27 Dec., 1873.
2. George Wilson, b. 24 Dec., 1826; bp. 13 Oct., 1828. FAM. 30.

FAM. 14.   MILES,[5] (*Uzziel,*[4] *Benj.,*[3] *Amasa,*[2] *Benj.,*[1]), b. 1801; m. 29 Oct., 1830, Mary Ann S. (dau. Samuel & Hannah *Blinn*), **Hayford**—(*W. C. R.*), b. 1 Nov., 1809; was a carpenter; res. So. Lane, Weth.; d. 14 Feb., 1874; she d. 12 Apl., 1863, ae. 56.

Children:

1. Samuel Hayford, b. 24 Feb., 1832. FAM. 31.
2. Cornelius Franklin, b. 8 Jan., 1834.
3. Jemima Blinn, b. 6 Nov., 1835 ; d. 5 May, 1855.
4. Miles Stoddard, b. 26 Feb., 1838. FAM. 32.
5. Stoddard Miles, b. twin to Miles Stoddard ; d. 27 Feb., 1838.
6. Edward Payson, b. 27 Mch., 1843 ; m. Louisa F. Hays; res. Ashfield, Ct.

7. Walter, b. 25 Oct., 1845. FAM. 33.
8. Mary Ann, b. 11 Dec., 1847.
9. Callie Dix, b. 27 July, 1849 ; m. 4 Dec., 1889, Edwin M. Havens, of Weth., where they reside.
10. Albert Harvey, b. 24 Mch., 1851 ; m. 24 Mch., 1891, Laura Bulkeley, of Ry-H. ; res. at Weth.; an officer in the State Prison.

FAM. 15.   JAMES BENJAMIN,[5] (*Uzziel*,[4] *Benj.*,[3] *Amasa*,[2] *Benj.*,[1]), b. 1803 ; rem. to New Marlboro, Mass., where he m. Rachel (dau. Orson & Nancy Blinn) Smith; about 1837, he rem. to Sheffield, Mass.; his wife d. 3 Feb., 1838, and he m. (2) Julia A. Peck; in 1851, he located in East Windsor, Ct., and d. in Broad Brook, Ct., 3 Aug., 1854 ; wid. d. 23 Mch., 1875; was a stonecutter and for some yrs. owned a marble quarry in Canaan, Ct.

Children:

1. Alfred J., b. New Marlboro, Mass., 25 Aug., 1827 ; m. 24 Apl., 1854, Emma Louise (dau. of Dennis & Rhoda *Elton*) Rood, b. 1831 ; who d. 12 Aug., 1862 ; had Emma Louise, b. 31 July, 1862.
2. Sophia M., b. 24 Jan., 1830 ; m. in E. Windsor, Ct., 7 June, 1854, Edwin Barber, who d. 2 Nov., 1860 ; she m. (2) 27 Sept., 1865, Nelson Osborn, who d. 7 Aug., 1894. *Issue (by first marriage)* :
   i. Irving A. (Barber), b. 6 Apl., 1855 ; d. 27 Aug., 1861.
   ii. Eveline Martha (Barber), b. 17 May, 1857.
3. Horatio N., b. 22 Mch., 1832. FAM. 33.
4. Emily Jane, b. 8 Dec., 1834 ; in Sheffield ; m. 2 June, 1858, Joseph W. Smith, of Ellington, Ct. ; who d. 17 Oct., 1885 ; res. Melrose, Ct. *Issue:*
   i. Frederick E. (Smith), b. 4 Mch., 1861 ; d. 25 Jan., 1862.

   ii. Florence A. (Smith), b. 23 Dec., 1862.
   iii. Inez (Smith), b. 6 June, 1865 ; m. 3 Dec., 1885, Clarence E. Sexton.
   iv. Burton W. (Smith), b. 6 Sept., 1868 ; m. 26 Oct., 1892, Luella J. Bancroft; res. Jewett City, Ct.
   v. Edith J. (Smith), b. 1 Feb., 1878.
5. Georgietta, b. 12 Feb., 1839 ; m. 21 Jan., 1879, Geo. Kress, lawyer ; res. Westfield, Mass. *Issue:*
   i. Eva Julia, b. 5 Apl., 1881.
6. Henry Martin, b. 18 Aug., 1840 ; m. 7 Dec., 1871, Abaline Howe Allen; is Supt. of Temp. Home for Children, Warehouse Point, Ct.
7. Miriam Rachel, b. 5 May, 1842 ; m. Alonzo K. Reed. *Issue:*
   i. Mamie, b. 3 Mch., 1873.
8. Stanley Burdette, b. 23 Jan., 1844. FAM. 34.

FAM. 16.   HORACE,[5] (*Uzziel*,[4] *Benj.*,[3] *Amasa*,[2] *Benj.*,[1]), b. 1805 ; m. 24 Nov., 1829, Emeline (dau. Ebenezer, Jr., & Sally *Chappel*) Goodale; res. Weth., and d. 30 Mch., 1882; wid. d. 14 Dec., 1883. She was bp. 7 Sept., 1834.—(*W. C. R.*)

Children:

1. Celia Ann, b. 30 Aug., 1830 ; m. 13 May, 1856, Minor D. Briggs, of Broadalbin, N. Y. *Issue:*
   i. Florence Adeline (Briggs), b. 13 Nov., 1857 ; m. 21 Oct., 1881, Geo. H. Lincoln.
   ii. Merton B. (Briggs), b. 20 May, 1860 ; d. 1 Jan., 1891, in San Antonio, Tex.
2. Ebenezer Goodale, b. 2 Apl., 1832. FAM. 35.
3. Newell Hurd, b. 18 June, 1835 ; m. Celista Kibbie, of Somers, Ct. ; he d. 5 Feb., 1871.
4. Adaline, b. 14 Feb., 1840 ; d. 25 Sept., 1856.

5. Albert, b. twin to Adaline ; d. 9 Dec., 1843.
6. Adelia Maria, b. 21 Jan., 1842 ; m. 17 Mch., 1888, John Havens, of Weth., b. 19 Oct., 1819 ; he d. ————.
7. Margaret, b. 23 Mch., 1844 ; m. W. W. Adams.
8. Alice Rosetta, b. 23 May, 1846 ; d. unm. 30 May, 1874.
9. Albert Raymond, b. twin to Alice R. ; d. 6 Dec., 1846.
10. Wilson Raymond, b. 22 Nov., 1848 ; d. unm. 22 Apl., 1886.

FAM. 17.   WALTER,[5] (*Uzziel*,[4] *Benj.*,[3] *Amasa*,[2] *Benj.*,[1]), b. 1810 ; m. 24 Apl., 1838, Nancy A. (dau. Levi & Nancy *Woodruff*) Blinn, of Weth.; res. Weth., Bristol and Southington, Ct.: clock case maker; d. 22 June, 1880; wid. d. 28 Jan., 1891, ae. 79.

Children:

1. Nancy A., b. ————— ; d. Nov., 1848. | 2. Walter, b. 30 July, 1850 ; d. 8 Sept., 1850.

FAM. 18.   WATSON,[5] (*Uzziel*,[4] *Benj.*,[3] *Amasa*,[2] *Benj.*,[1]), b. 1812 ; m. in New Haven, Grace (dau. David) Ritter, of N. H.; was in marble bus. at Weth., New Haven and Rockville, Ct.; d. Rockville, 27 Oct., 1885 ; wid. d. Melrose, Mass., 28 May, 1893.

Children:

1. David Ritter, b. 12 Aug., 1834. FAM. 36.
2. Angela Dwight, b. 19 Dec., 1836.
3. George Watson, b. 26 Jan., 1840. FAM. 37.
4. Elizabeth Williams, b. 19 Jan., 1842 ; d. 7 Jan., 1843.
5. Julia Elizabeth, b. 20 Aug., 1844 ; m. 21 Mch., 1865, Geo. E. **Nettleton**; res. New Haven ; he is in Ins. bus. *Issue;*
   i. Charles E. (Nettleton), b. 21 Feb., 1868 ; m. Bessie **Francis.**
   ii. Frederick Lester (Nettleton), b. 26 Dec., 1875.
6. Adelia A., b. 27 Nov., 1848 ; m. 31 May,

1872, Thos. R. **Rhodes**; res. in Melrose, Mass. *Issue:*
   i. Grace Adelia (Rhodes), b. 23 Feb., 1873.
   ii. Martha Alice (Rhodes), b. 16 Apl., 1876.
   iii. Walter Adams (Rhodes), b. 6 July, 1880 ; d. 4 Sept., 1883.
   iv. Thomas Harold (Rhodes), b. 19 July, 1886.
7. Thomas Ritter, b. 24 Sept., 1850 ; m. 28 Apl., 1875, Josephine W. **Eldridge ;** res. Rockville ; ch. Howard E., b. 4 Oct., 1881.

FAM. 19. ORSON S.,[5] (*Uzziel*,[4] *Benj*.,[3] *Amasa*,[2] *Benj*.,[1]), b. 1814; m. 25 Apl., 1838, Eunice (dau. Thos.?) **Robbins,** of Weth.; res. at Unionville and Southington, Ct.; he d. 16 Oct., 1852; wid. m. (2) 1860, Lemuel **Clark,** who d. 7 Sept., 1862, and she m. (3) James Griswold, of Weth., where she now res.

Children (by first mar.) :

1. Thomas Edgar, b. 13 Feb., 1841 ; d. unm. 28 Mch., 1895.
2. Dewey F., b. 11 Aug., 1842. FAM. 38.
3. Olive S., b. 23 Aug., 1852 ; m. 27 June, 1876, Sherman **Blakeslee.** *Issue:*
   i. Lulu Carrie (Blakeslee), b. 28 Mch., 1877 ; d. 18 Apl., 1878.
   ii. Dewey Sherman (Blakeslee), b. 19 Nov., 1882.

FAM. 20. THOMAS,[5] (*Uzziel*,[4] *Benj*.,[3] *Amasa*,[2] *Benj*.,[1]) b. 27 Feb., 1816; m. 8 Dec., 1841, in E. Windsor, Ct., Huldah (dau. Joshua & Eunice *Crane*) **Wells,** of E. W.; she d. 1 Apl., 1857, in Htfd., and he m. (2) 17 Nov., 1858, Jeanette (dau. Henry C. & Statira *Hurd*) **Bulkeley,** of Middle Haddam, Ct.; he was in the marble and granite bus. in Htfd., and d. there 16 Jan., 1886.

Children (by first marriage) :

1. Arthur Thomas, b. 17 July, 1843 ; m. 10 May, 1876, Caroline L. **Parker,** who d. 18 June, 1894 ; he d. 21 Dec., 1892.
2. Julia Maria, b. 25 Feb., 1846.
3. Fanny Louise, b. 2 Feb., 1850 ; m. 23 Oct.,

1878, Edward H. **Judd,** of Htfd.
4. Charles Henry, b. 22 Feb., 1852 ; m. 1 Mch., 1890, Belle F. (dau. Wm.) **Scoville;** res. Htfd.
5. Ella Clarissa, b. 16 Jan., 1854 ; d. ———.

Children (by second marriage) :

6. Jennie Hurd, b. 31 Mch., 1860 ; d. 2 July, 1860.
7. Nettie Roberts, b. 27 Sept., 1862.

FAM. 21. WILLIAM, Jr.,[5] (*William*,[4] *Benj*.,[3] *Amasa*,[2] *Benj*.,[1]), b. 1803; m. 15 June, 1824, Sarah (dau. Elijah & Honor *Adams*) **Crane,** b. 30 June, 1801; res. in Weth.; woodworker; d. 4 Dec., 1839; wid. d. 3 Oct., 1858, at LaCrosse, Wis.

Children:

1. William Chauncey, b. 13 Oct., 1825 ; d. unm. 21 Feb., 1854.
2. Cordelia, b. 5 Jan., 1828 ; m. 24 Mch., 1852, Harvey S. **Dickinson,** of Wis.; res. West Salem, Wis. *Issue:*
   i. Arthur (Dickinson), b. Dec., 1852 ; d. 1 Feb., 1865.
3. Frances Honor, b. 10 May, 1830 ; m. 31 Mch., 1852, Walter William **Webb,** of Meriden, Ct.; rem. West, abt. 1860 ; res. La Crosse, Wis. *Issue:*
   i. Minnie Olive (Webb), b. 29 Mch., 1858 ; m. 23 Nov., 1880, Elric C. **Cole,** of Kenosha, Wis.; res. in Kans.,

where he is Judge of Appellate Court.
   ii. Frances Anna (Webb), b. 22 Dec., 1861.
   iii. Walter Butler (Webb), b. 23 May, 1863 ; d. 30 Dec., 1890.
4. Ellen M., b. 10 July, 1832 ; m. 10 Dec., 1857, John D. **Johnson,** of Htfd., who d. Tenn., 1892.
5. Frank N., b. 5 Oct., 1834 ; m. 14 Dec., 1859, Hannah **Peterson;** railroad man at Spokane Falls, Wash. *No issue.*
6. George Crane, b. 25 Oct., 1836. FAM. 39.
7. Sarah, b. 10 Feb., 1838 ; m. 6 Feb., 1859, Fred W. **White,** of Htfd.

FAM. 22. WELLES.[5] (*Wm*.,[4] *Benj*.,[3] *Amasa*,[2] *Benj*.,[1]), b. 1804; m. 25 Nov., 1828, Mary W. (dau. Thos. & Mary *Wolcott*) **Griswold,** b. 11 Aug., 1806; she d. 27 Apl., 1865; he m. (2) 18 Sept., 1866, Elizabeth R. (dau. Thos. & Patty *Blinn*) **Havens;** he d. 18 Feb., 1876; wid. d. 1 Mch., 1895. He was an influential citizen of Weth., serving the town in several official capacities; rep. to State Leg., 1837, 1853 and 1864; was many yrs. in the commis. bus.

Children:

1. Augustus Franklin, b. 9 Oct., 1829; bp. 1 June, 1830.—*W. C. R.* FAM. 39a.
2. Thomas Griswold, b. 21 June, 1832; bp. 6 Jan., 1833. FAM. 40.
3. William Welles, b. 31 Oct., 1833. FAM. 41.
4. Sherman Wolcott, Esq., b. 5 May, 1836; d. 19 Oct., 1898; *the historian of Weth.*— See *Biog.*, Vol. I, of this history.
5. Mary Eliza, b. 22 Jan., 1839; m. 17 Oct., 1866, Clarence E. Bailey, of Weth.; res. Mass. *Issue:*
   i. Sherman Adams (Bailey), b. 8 Mch.,

1870; d. New Lond., 28 May, 1893.
   ii. Mabel Elizabeth (Bailey), b. 24 Au.., 1873; m. 24 Aug., 1898, Webster W. Bolton, Mass.; res. Mass.
   iii. Freddie Welles (Bailey), b. 11 Apl., 1875; d. 4 May, 1876.
   iv. Nellie May (Bailey), b. 20 Oct., 1879.
6. Luther Walton, b. 20 Dec., 1841. FAM. 42.
7. Henry Mortimer, b. 18 Sept., 1844; d. 30 July, 1845.
8. Martha Antoinette, b. 3 Apl., 1847; d. 21 Sept., 1849.

FAM. 23. RUSSEL,[5] (*Wm.*,[4] *Benj.*,[3] *Amasa*,[2] *Benj.*,[1]), b. 1807; m. 26 Nov., 1829, Mercy Miller (dau. Josiah & Charlotte *Adams*) Griswold, b. 2 Mch., 1809, of Stepney; she d. 31 Aug., 1865, and he m. (2) Charlotte A. (dau. of Horace & Charlotte *Griswold*) Blinn; he d. 28 June, 1885; wid. res. in Weth.; he was prominent in Weth. town affairs; rep. in State Leg., 1852 and '58.

Children:

1. Maria Louise, b. 5 Feb., 1832; d. 21 Nov., 1832.
2. Albert Russell, b. 7 Oct., 1833; d. 4 Apl., 1834.
3. Alfred Russell, 6 Apl., 1835. FAM. 43.
4. Josiah Griswold, b. 19 Dec., 1839. FAM. 44.
5. Leslie Emerson, b. 25 Feb., 1847; m. 5 June, 1895, Jennie W. (dau. Fred. A. &

Jemima *Dunham*) Havens, of Weth., b. 3 Feb., 1855; res. in Weth.; he rep. town in State Leg., and prominent in public school matters.
6. Frances Adelaide, b. 8 June, 1850; m. 4 Mch., 1888, Clayton E. Webster, who d. in Dec., 1903.

FAM. 24. CHAUNCEY,[5] (*Wm.*,[4] *Benj.*,[3] *Amasa*,[2] *Benj.*,[1]), b. 1808; m. 10 Oct., 1843, Julia Ann Willard; he rep. in State Leg., 1856.

Children:

1. Clarence Eugene, b. 15 Aug., 1844. FAM. 45. | 2. Ellis Dwight, b. 1 Aug., 1846. FAM. 46.

FAM. 25. ANDREW JACKSON,[5] (*Horace*,[4] *Amasa*,[3] *Amasa*,[2] *Benj.*,[1]), b. 1815; m. 1 Nov., 1846, at Athens, Pa., Harriet M. (dau. Myron & Lois *Fuller*) Cole, b. 9. Feb., 1825; was in lumber bus.; rem. to Triangle, N. Y., abt. time of mar.; after he set. at Greene, Chenango Co., N. Y., where he d. 19 Dec., 1854.; wid. m. (2) ———— Palmer, and m. (3) Wendover; she d. 21 Dec., Auburn. N. Y., 1894.

Children:

1. Charles Eugene, b. Pine Creek, Pa., 24 Feb., 1849; m. 3 May, 1888, at Triangle, N. Y., Caroline (dau. Wm. & Clarissa *Kelsey*) Benson.
2. George DeWitt, b. Barker, N. Y., 17 July, 1851; m. 29 Apl., 1879, Lottie L. (dau. Romantus & Hester *Quade*) Cody.
3. Theodore Ozellas, b. 16 May, 1853.

FAM. 26. FRANKLIN,[5] (*Horace*,[4] *Amasa*,[3] *Amasa*,[2] *Benj.*,[1]), b. 1818; m. in Triangle, N. Y., 18 Oct., 1847, Delilah (dau. Eliakim & Lydia *Phillips*) Shippey, b. 14 Apl., 1828; lumber and sawmill bus. at T.; d. 13 May, 1896. No *issue.*

FAM. 27. HORACE PERRY,[5] (*Horace*,[4] *Amasa*,[3] *Amasa*,[2] *Benj.*,[1]), b. 1827; m. N. Y. Mills, N. Y., 24 Oct., 1854, Diana (dau. of Edward & Eleanor *Houghtaling*) Manning; he res. Whitney's Pt., Triangle, N. Y., cooper.

Children:

1. Martin Perry, b. 25 Aug., 1856; m. at Nayaug, Pa., 16 Oct., 1895, May (dau. Wm. Peter & Emma *Dixon*) Latimer.
2. Lizzie, b. 10 June, 1859; m. 5 Jan., 1881, Elbert J., Moore, 26 Aug., 1860. *Issue:*

   i. Bertha Lois (Moore), b. 24 Oct., 1881; d. 14 June, 1882.
   ii. Clive Adams (Moore), b. 22 Nov., 1886.
3. Frank Manning, b. 15 Apl., 1866.

FAM. 28. JAMES,[5] (*James,*[4] *Joseph.*[3] *Amasa,*[2] *Benj.,*[1]), b. 1821; m. 4 Feb., 1852, Margaret **Clark,** of N. Y.; was a carpenter; res, N. Y. City and Weth.; d. at W. 3 Feb., 1858

Children:

1. Mary, b. ————.
2. James, b. 6 Dec., 1854; d. ————.

3. Charlotte, b. 8 Mch., 1856; d. 23 Apl., 1856.

FAM. 29. LEVI HATCH,[5] (*Jas.,*[4] *Jos.,*[3] *Amasa,*[2] *Benj.,*[1]), b. 4 Mch., 1823; m. 5 Apl., 1846, Nancy Amelia (dau. Loren) **Whitford,** of Weth.; she d. 18 Sept., 1858, ae. 33; he m. (2) 4 Mch., 1859, Mrs. Harriet (Morgan) **Boyington;** he was a carpenter; res. Newington, Ct.; d. 26 Apl., 1860; wid. d. 11 Feb., 1873.

Children:

1. Julia Elizabeth, b. 4 Mch., 1847; m. 17 Apl., 1867, Perkins Robbins **Livermore;** res. Marshfield Hills, Mass. *Issue:*
   i. Ella Frances (Livermore), b., 16 Apl., 1868.
   ii. Grace Margaret (Livermore), b. 13 Dec., 1869.
   iii. Maud Eunice, b. 29 July, 1873; m. July, 1894, Leonard G. **Ewell.**
   iv. Annie Elizabeth, b. 7 Jan., 1882; d. 28 May, 1883.

2. James Levi, b. 10 Feb., 1849; m. 13 Aug., 1895, Fannie Weeks (dau. James W. & Sarah Adams) **Roberts;** res. in Windsor, Ct.
3. William Stoddard, b. 3 Mch., 1852; d. unm. 27 Jan., 1873.
4. Charles Alfred, m. 31 May, 1884, Elizabeth P. **Holmes;** res. in Ridge Hill, Mass.; one ch. Mabel Elizabeth **Adams,** b. 6 Aug., 1889.
5. George, b. 4 Sept., 1858; d. 16 Sept., 1858.

FAM. 30. GEORGE WILSON,[6] (*Geo. Lucas,*[5] *Uzziel,*[4] *Benj.,*[3] *Amasa,*[2] *Benj.,*[1]), b. 1826; m. 31 Dec., 1863, Caroline E. (dau. Wm. J.) **Stoddard,** b. 30 Sept., 1833; he was Sgt. in Co. B, 22d Conn. Reg., in War of Civil Rebellion; res. in Weth.

Children:

1. Charles Stoddard, b. 22 June, 1866.
2. Bertha May, b. 18 July, 1870; m. 30 Dec., 1893, Chas. P. **Backus,** of Danielson, Ct.,

where they res. 1 ch.
3. May Montague, b. 21 June, 1873.

FAM. 31. SAMUEL HAYFORD,[6] (*Miles,*[5] *Uzziel,*[4] *Benj.,*[3] *Amasa,*[2] *Benj.,*[1]), b. 1832; m. 8 Feb., 1857, in Rome, Ga., Susan E. (dau. of Robinson C.) **Bennett,** of Utica, N. Y.; hotel keeper, Hunter, No. Dak.

Children:

1. Charles Robinson, b. 12 Oct., 1858. FAM. 47.
2. Mary Jemima, b. 19 Nov., 1860; m. 1 May, 1864, in Cincinnati, O., Lawrence **Cook;** carpenter; res. Hunter, No. Dak. *Issue:*
   i. Dudley Lawrence (Cooke), b. 27 Nov., 1885.
   ii. Stanley Adams (Cooke), b. 18 June, 1887.
3. Edward Oscar, b. 13 Nov., 1862; m. 23

Oct., 1889, Mrs. Olive Crosby **Watson;** res. Cincinnati, O.
4. Ernest Miles, b. 30 July, 1867; m. 14 Jan. 1892, Fannie (dau. Dennis) **Ward,** of Cincinnati; farmer; res. Page, No. Dak. *No issue.*
5. Frank Hayford, b. 25 June, 1872; m. Maggie **Miller.**
6. Howard Raymond, b. 10 Jan., 1880.

FAM. 32. MILES STODDARD,[6] (*Miles,*[5] *Uzziel,*[4] *Benj.,*[3] *Amasa,*[2] *Benj.,*[1]), b. 1838; m. 14 Dec., 1881, Martha C. (dau. Hez. & Harriet *Welles*) **Butler,** of Weth.; served in Co. B, 22d Reg., Conn., in Civil War.

Children:

1. Mabel Butler, b. 3 Aug., 1884.

2. Martha Hayford, b. 8 May, 1887.

FAM. 33. HORATIO N.,[6] (*Jas. Benj.,*[5] *Uzziel,*[4] *Benj.,*[3] *Amasa,*[2] *Benj.,*[1]), b. 1832; m. Broad Brook, Ct., 17 Jan., 1860, Elizabeth (dau. Henry & Alice *Wolstenholme*) **Dawson.**

Children:

1. James Benjamin, b. 15 Apl., 1861; m. 24
   June, 1886, in Almoral, Iowa, Sarah P.
   Stevens; res. Blair, Neb., where he is
   treas. of Crowell Lumber & Grain Co.
   Issue.
      i. Beulah Stevens (Adams), b. 7 June,
        1887.
      ii. Robert Wolstenholme (Adams), b. 9
         Aug., 1889.

       iii. Lloyd Hadley (Adams), b. 24 June,
         1892.
       iv. Alfred Lester (Adams), b. 21 Jan.,
         1896.
2. Herbert Madison, b. 26 June, 1863.
3. Elsie Marie, b. 29 Aug., 1864.
4. Mary Elizabeth, b. 27 Jan., 1866.
5. Lester Horatio, b. 20 Jan., 1867.

FAM. 34. STANLEY BURDETTE,[6] (*Jas. Benj.,*[5] *Uzziel,*[4] *Benj.,*[3] *Amasa*[2] *Benj.,*[1]),
b. 1844; m. Broad Brook, Ct., 18 Oct., 1817, Eliza (dau. Benj. L. & Abigail
Irene *Hastings*) **Bissell**, who d. 2 Oct., 1887; he res. Bd. Bk.

Children:

1. Carleton Benjamin, b. 30 Oct., 1878.
2. Grace Edith, b. 28 Feb., 1884.

3. Stanley Burdette, b. 9 Sept., 1887.

FAM. 35. EBENEZER GOODALE,[6] (*Horace,*[5] *Uzziel,*[4] *Benj.,*[3] *Amasa,*[2] *Benj.,*[1]),
b. 1832; m. 19 Oct., 1859, Frances **Firman**, of Somers, Ct.; he d. 6 Jan., 1898.

Children:

1. Elmer E., b. 24 June, 1861; m. 23 May, 1893,
   Lizzie Howard **Kingsbury.**
2. Ernest Clinton, b. 2 Oct., 1864.
3. Mertin Louise, b. 14 July, 1870; m. 18 Sept.,

    1889, Geo. **Sanford.** *Issue:*
      i. Harold (Sanford), b. 4 Dec., 1891.
4. Dora M., b. 15 Aug., 1875.

FAM. 36. DAVID RITTER,[6] (*Watson,*[5] *Uzziel,*[4] *Benj.,*[3] *Amasa,*[2] *Benj.,*[1]) b. 1834;
m. 14 Apl., 1859, Mary E. (dau. Wm. H. & Matilda) **Carey**; is carriage maker
in New Haven, Ct.

Child:

1. Hattie, b. 12 Sept., 1860.

FAM. 37. GEORGE WATSON,[6] (*Watson,*[5] *Uzziel,*[4] *Benj.,*[3] *Amasa,*[2] *Benj.,*[1]), b.
1840; m. 30 July, 1859, Catherine E. (dau. of Wm. & Ella *Kelsey*) **Burns**;
railroad man; res. New Haven, Ct.

Children:

1. John Quincy, b. 16 Apl., 1860; m. 12 June,
   1889, Etta C. **Battersby.**
2. George W., b. 13 Jan., 1866.

3. Thomas David, b. 6 July, 1867.
4. Frederick Dibble, b. 6 June, 1870.

FAM. 38. DEWEY FREDERICK,[6] (*Orson S.,*[5] *Uzziel,*[4] *Benjamin,*[3] *Amasa,*[2] *Benjamin,*[1]), b. 1842; m. 8 May, 1813, Julia M. (dau. Horace P. & Harriet N.)
Winsor, of Syracuse, N. Y.; res. Providence, R. I.

Children:

1. Frederick Howard, b. 24 Aug., 1874.
2. Charles Fowler, b. 23 Sept., 1876.

3. Harriet Louise, b. 6 Oct., 1879.
4. Dewey Frederick, b. 5 July, 1882.

FAM. 39. GEORGE CRANE,[6] (*Wm.,*[5] *Wm.,*[4] *Benj.,*[3] *Amasa,*[2] *Benj.,*[1]), b. 1836; m.
6 Jan., 1856, Hannah M. (dau. Wm. Henry & Mary Ann *Dutton*) **Snow**;
in Aug., 1862, enl. in 1st Conn. Cavalry and served till close of war; set.
in Baltimore where he res.

Children:

1. Lillian Emma, b. 9 Aug., 1859; m. 10 Aug.,
   1879, James Franklin **Ward**; res. Baltimore.
   Issue:
      i. Arthur (Ward), b. 9 Jan., 1882.
2. George Clinton, b. 25 Nov., 1861; m. 6 Feb.,
   1883, Ella **Armitage.** *Issue:*
      i. Joseph Clinton (Adams), b. 30 Oct.,
        1887.
      ii. Frank (Adams), b. 26 Apl., 1884.

3. Otelia, b. 6 Sept., 1866; d. 12 Mch., 1867.
4. Flora May, b. 30 May, 1870; m. 13 June,
    1895, Isadore V. **Hart.**
5. Nettie, b. 26 Nov., 1872; m. Dr. Herbert J.
    Standish, of Weth.; res. Htfd.
6. Frank Chauncey, b. 16 Nov., 1873.
7. Rosa Estelle, b. 26 Apl., 1878.
8. Earl, b. 24 July, 1879; d. 17 Aug., 1879.

WELLES ADAMS.

THOMAS GRISWOLD ADAMS.

FAM. 39a. AUGUSTUS FRANKLIN,[6] (Welles,[5] William,[4] Benjamin,[3] Amasa,[2] Benjamin,[1]), b. 1829; m. Martha **Griswold**, of Ry-H.; res. at Weth.; served in the War of the Civil Rebellion; d. at Weth. 5 Sept., 1881.

Children:

1. Ida Mabel, b. 14 Sept., 1856; m. 28 Oct., 1879, Elisha (s. of Hon. S. W.) Johnson **Robbins**, who d. 26 Nov., 1894; wid. res. Weth. *Issue:*
   i. Jane Johnson (Robbins), b. 19 June, 1882.
2. Charlotte, m. Thomas **Elliott**; res. Htfd. *Issue:*
   i. Howard (Elliott).

FAM. 40. THOMAS GRISWOLD,[6] (Welles,[5] Wm.,[4] Benj.,[3] Amasa,[2] Benj.,[1]), b. 1832; m. 21 Nov., 1855, Lucy Stillman (dau. Ransom & Lucy *Smith*) **Dickinson**, of Weth.; commis. mcht.; res. Weth.; d. 22 Apl., 1902. She b. 25 Jan., 1835; d. 29 Dec., 1901. After completing his education at Williston Seminary, East-hampton, Mass., Thomas Griswold Adams began his bus. career in New York with the Alexandre Line of steamships, long since merged into the Ward Line. Not long after marriage he retd. to Weth. to succeed his father in business. For many years, principally as the head of the firm of Adams & Hanmer, he was one of the most prominent commission mchts. in Hartford Co. Although tobacco was his specialty he did a large trade in onions and garlic. He was the founder of the Village Improvement society, and a memb. of the Eccles. soc. He was for years sec. and treas. of the First School soc., and for fifteen years its chairman, and it was largely through his influence that the addition to the ancient cemetery was provided. He was selectman in 1880-81; a memb. of the High School comm., and chairman of the bldg. comm. for the new high school, until he was succeeded by George W. Harris in 1893. Until 1901 he was at the head of the Weth. Wharf Co. In politics he was a Demo-crat, although never taking an active part in political affairs. Eminently one of the most public-spirited citizens whom Weth. has ever produced, and pos-sessing an uncommonly broad and liberal mind, he was active in all that made for the good of his native town.

Children:

1. Emma Dickinson, b. 5 Nov., 1856; d. 15 June, 1858.
2. Mary Annette, b. 2 Feb., 1858.
3. Laura Stillman, b. 2 Mch., 1861; d. 5 Oct., 1862.
4. Henry Sherman, b. 1 Aug., 1864; journalist, Brooklyn, N. Y.
5. Thomas Welles, b. 14 Dec., 1867.
6. Bertha Louise, b. 15 Apl., 1870; d. 9 July, 1873.
7. Jalon Dickinson, b. 25 Dec., 1871.
8. Benjamin, b. 20 Sept., 1873; grad. Y. C.; Sup't Dept. of Traveling Libraries, Brook-lyn (N. Y.), Pub. Library; in 1904, prom. to Asst. Sup't of Circulating Dep't of New York Pub. Library.

FAM. 41. WILLIAM WELLES,[6] (Welles,[5] Wm.,[4] Benj.,[3] Amasa,[2] Benj.,[1]), b. 1833; m. 26 Apl., 1856, Sarah Newson **Robbins**, who d. 6 Feb., 1862; he m. (2) 7 Jan., 1864, Margaret (dau. Horace & Emeline *Goodale*) Adams; he d. 1896; wid. res. Weth.

Children (by first marriage):

1. Lella Florence, b. 26 July, 1857; m. 6 Oct., 1886, Clayton Thos. **Willard**; res. Griswoldville, Weth. *Issue:*
   i. Warren Adams (Willard), b. 7 Oct., 1887.
2. Minnie Grace, b. 23 Feb., 1859; m. 29 Oct., 1879, William Goodrich **Griswold**; res. So. Weth. *Issue:*
   i. Margaret (Griswold), b. 15 Sept., 1880.
   ii. Fred. Albert (Griswold), b. 21 May, 1882.
   iii. Wm. Goodrich (Griswold), b. 2 Feb., 1886.
   iv. Samuel Adams (Griswold), b. 3 Sept., 1888.
   v. Robbins Newson (Griswold), b. 11 Oct., 1892.
   vi. Donald Williams (Griswold), b. 19 Aug., 1895.
   vii. Rich. Whitmore (Griswold), b. 11 Feb., 1898.
3. Nellie Robbins, b. 23 Jan., 1861; d. 20 Sept., 1861.
   (*By second marriage*):
4. Nellie Edith, b. 20 Oct., 1865; d. 5 Jan., 1896.
5. Emma Gertrude, b. 7 Apl., 1867; d. 22 Feb., 1886.
6. William Welles, b. 6 May, 1869.
7. Alice May, b. 25 Aug., 1871.

s. Newell Burton, b. 1 Nov., 1873.
9. Margaret Elizabeth, b. 13 Sept., 1875; d. 30 June, 1879.
10. Frederick Orson, b. 13 Jan., 1878; d. 1 June, 1886.
11. George Lucas, b. 12 Dec., 1879.
12. Horace Howard, b. 6 Dec., 1881.
13. Robert Stanley, b. 3 July, 1885; d. 17 Mch., 1886.
14. Stanley Goodale, b. 9 Jan., 1888.

FAM. 42.   LUTHER WALTON,[6] (*Welles,[5] Wm.,[4] Benj.,[3] Amasa,[2] Benj.,[1]*), b. 1841; m. 20 Dec., 1864, Martha B. (dau. Wm. & Lucy *Barrett*) **Dix**, of Weth.; b. 1 Dec., 1843; she d. 28 Jan., 1879; he m. (2) Mrs. Nellie A., **Miner;** res. So. Weth.

Children (by first marriage):

1. Lucy E., b. 27 Sept., 1866.
2. Luther Franklin, b. 6 Nov., 1868.
3. Harry M., b. 24 Oct., 1870.
4. Grace F., b. 17 Oct., 1872 ; d. 31 Aug., 1885.
5. Stephen Dix, b. 28 Feb., 1875.
6. Mattie B., b. 22 May, 1877 ; d. 1 Sept. 1885.
(By second marriage):
7. Walton, b. 28 Mch., 1881.
8. Lyman Wayne, b. 6 Mch., 1883.
9. Lulu May, b. 5 May, 1884 ; d. 17 Aug., 1885.
10. Herbert Maxwell, b. 19 Feb., 1886 ; d. 22 June, 1892.
11. Viola G., b. 20 July, 1887.
12. Claude M., b. 14 Dec., 1891.

FAM. 43.   ALFRED RUSSEL,[6] (*Russel,[5] Wm.,[4] Benj.,[3] Amasa,[2] Benj.,[1]*), b. 1835; m. 25 Dec., 1865, Margaretta Jane (dau. John & Martha *Hayford*) **Tiebourt,** of N. Y.; res. So. Weth.

Children:

1. Frank Tiebout, b. 8 Mch., 1861; d. 8 Sept., 1862.
2. Alfred Leslie, b. 7 May, 1864 ; m. 19 Nov., 1891, Alethea H. (dau. Henry) **Zoble,** of
Brooklyn, N. Y., where they res.
3. Cornelia Tiebout, b. 23 Apl., 1870 ; m. 10 Nov., 1898, J. Fred. (son of David) **Hunter,** of Brooklyn, N. Y.

FAM. 44.   JOSIAH GRISWOLD,[6] (*Russel,[5] Wm.,[4] Benj.,[3] Amasa,[2] Benj.,[1]*), b. 1839; m. 30 Dec., 1863, Ellen M. (dau. Horace & Abigail *Hills*) **Warner,** of Weth.; res. in Weth.; as a Repub. he is prominent in local and county politics; serving as first Selectman for 14 consecutive years, and rep. town in State Leg., 1876; is eng. in wholesale farm produce commis. bus. and for many yrs. a member of the firm of Adams & Hanmer; is now (1904) at head of the First School soc. and the custodian of the ancient cemetery of Weth.

Children:

1. Carrie Rosalie, b. 6 Apl., 1866 ; m. 11 Dec., 1889, Chas. C. (son of Chancey & Emeline *Wells*) **Harris,** of Weth.; res. So. Weth.
   Issue:
   i. Burton Adams (Harris), b. 2 July, 1891.
2. Fred. Russell, b. 7 June, 1869 ; d. 3 Jan.,
1871.
3. Arthur Burton, b. 23 May, 1872 ; d. 13 May, 1873.
4. Ada Frances, b. 23 Aug., 1874 ; m. 27 Oct., 1897, Gideon (s. of Dudley & Felecia *Hanmer*) **Wells,** of Weth., where they res.
5. Mabel Hills, b. 1 May, 1879.

FAM. 45.   CLARENCE EUGENE,[6] (*Chauncey,[5] Wm.,[4] Benj.,[3] Amasa,[2] Benj.,[1]*), b. 1844; edu. at the W. Acad. and Williston Sem., Easthampton, L. I.; freq. town collector of taxes, constable; and in 1891, rep. W. in Gen. Assembly. One of the orginators of the Grange in Weth., and for two yrs. Deputy Master of the State Grange—also thrice master and lecturer of Central Pomona. He is Dea. in W. Cong. ch.; m. 22 Dec., 1869, Alice S. **Bailey;** res. Weth.

Children:

1. Lena Maud, b. 24 Sept., 1870.
2. Etta May, b. 16 Mch., 1872.
3. Harriet Julia, b. 22 Mch., 1874.
4. Clarence Willard, b. 24 Nov., 1877 ; d. 27
Nov., 1877.
5. Alice Lockwood, b. 25 May, 1879.
6. Willard Carleton, b. 28 Feb., 1884.
7. Jessie Eugenia, b. 17 Apl., 1885.

FAM. 46.   ELLIS DWIGHT,[6] (*Chauncey,[5] William,[4] Benj.,[3] Amasa,[2] Benj.,[1]*), b. 1846; m. 22 May, 1873; Harriet Sargent (dau. Rev. Aaron C. & Harriet *Johnson*) Adams, b. 18 Sept., 1847, at Montclair, N. J.; res. Weth.; he is an officer of the Comstock, Ferre Seed Co.

Children:

1. Kate Ellis, b. 16 Aug., 1876.
2. Arthur Chester, b. 19 Apl., 1884.

FAM. 47. CHARLES ROBINSON,[7] (*Samuel H.*,[6] *Miles[5] Uzziel*,[4] *Benj.*,[3] *Amasa*,[2] *Benj.*,[1]), b. 1858; m. 23 Oct., 1879, Carrie (dau. Henry) **Brown**, of Delaware, Ind.; res. Hunter, No. Dak.

Children:

1. Alice Edith, b. 28 June, 1880.
2. Elsie May, b. 30 Mch., 1882.
3. Susie Emmaletta, b. 27 May, 1890.

4. Edward Hayford, b. 29 Oct,. 1892.
5. Eugene Charles, b. 31 Aug., 1894.

Miscellaneous:—Concerning others of the Adams surname found in *Weth. Records;* but, as far as can be ascertained, not connected with the foregoing line.

ADAMS, REV. AARON C., b. at Bangor, Me., 7 April, 1815; grad. Bowdoin College, 1836; studied theol. at Lane Theol. Sem., Cincinnati, O., and grad. Bangor Theol. Sem., 1839; pastor at Gardiner, Me., Walden, Mass., Auburn, Me.; settled at Weth., 18 Mch., 1868, and remained till 30 June, 1879. His published works were:

Historic Sketch of the First Church of Christ in Weth., given from the pulpit, July 9, 1876. Hartford, 1877, 8vo. pp. 24.

Fifty Years among the Churches and Ministers. A Sermon preached in the First Church of Christ in Weth., Conn., July 21, 1889. Hartford, 1889, pp. 24.

H. S. A., 1813-1892. [A Memorial of Harriet Sargent Adams, by Rev. A. C. Adams, 1893.] pp. 26.

DANIEL, adm. freeman at Htfd., 13 May, 1686.—*Conn. Col. Rec.*, III, 199; "adm. an inhab." of Weth., 19 Aug., 1695.—*Weth. Town Notes*, 1, 120.

JAMES, apparently a native of Killingly, Ct., was a leading mcht. in Weth., in 1790, and prob. for some yrs. previous; owned a warehouse at Stepney and largely interested in shipping; m. at Stepney, abt. 1788, Martha **Wright**, who d. 18 May, 1791, in her 38th yr. (*tombstone*); Jas. A., d. 19 Aug., 1892, in 30th yr. (*tombstone*).

THOMAS, land owner in Weth., 1640; see Vol. 1, Chap. VII.

Marriages:

EUNICE, m. William **Smith**, 2 Sept., 1832.—*Weth. Ch. Rec.*

MARY, m. Lewis **Bettlehauser(?)**, 18 Nov., 1778; both "of Weth."—*Weth. Ch. Rec.*

NELLIE M., m. Chester P. **Bliss**, 16 Dec., 1862.—*Weth. Town Rec.*

ADKINS, SAMUEL, "from Milford, but earlier from Weth., the s. of Josiah Adkins, of that place, sett. in New Milford, about 1717. * * * sold out and rem. from town abt. 1755; no ch. rec. to him there." Orcutt's *Hist. of New Milford, Ct.*, p. 67, 69, *et alios.* Fam. of Midd. origin.—See *Savage*, i, 19.

AIKEN, Rev. WILLIAM POPE, pastor at Newington, (for *biog.* see Vol. I p. 819), b. Fairhaven, Mass., 9 July, 1825, son of Lemuel Smith & Sarah (Coffin) Aiken; grad. Y. C., 1853; tutor at Y. C. 1855-57; sett. at New., 15 Jan., 1857; m. 15 Aug., 1857, Susan C. (dau. of Edwin, Esq.) **Edgerton**, of Rutland, Vt.

Children (*b. at New.*):

1. Edward Edgerton (Rev.), b. 1 Mch., 1859; grad. Y. C., 1881; m. Maud (dau. Geo. H.) **Lockwood**, of Brooklyn, N. Y., who d. 1889; he is a missionary in China.
2. Susan Curtis, b. 14 Apl., 1861; m. 6 Oct., 1881, Chas. Wm. **Ferry**, of Rutland, Vt.;

had Alice L., who m. 1 June, 1887, Dr. Chas. Allen **Gale**, of Rutland.
3. Alice Louise, b. 19 Oct., 1863.
4. William Pope, b. 1 Feb., 1865; grad. Y. C., 1889; lawyer.

AKINS, BENJAMIN, d. ae. 87, 7 Jan., 1806.—*W. T. R.;* JOSEPH had Reuben, bp. 17 Nov., 1765.—*S. C. R.*

REUBEN, s. of Joseph, bp. Nov. or Dec., 1765.—*W. Rec.*

ALCOCK, "Mr." PHILIP. *Savage*, I, p. 22, credits him to New Haven; as perhaps
s. of Thos.; and as having m. 5 Dec., 1672, Elizabeth, dau. of wid. of Thomas
Mitchell; also as having 4 ch., b. betw. 14 July, '75 and 19 Nov., '81, "and perhaps more," wh. as they are not rec. at Weth. were prob. b. at N. H.; also says,
"had come to N. H., from Weth.; was said to have been a prop'r, 1685," (query—
at Weth. or N. H.?), "and m. (2) 4 Apl., 1699, Sarah, wid. of Nath'l **Butler,"**
(might have been wid. of the Nath'l Butler who d. at Weth., 9 Feb., 1797, ae.
abt. 56.) Alcock's first and only appearance on *Weth. Rec.* is as a "lister."
18 Aug., 1701. *Savage* says he d. 1715. We incline to believe that his res.
in Weth. began abt. 1681.—*H. R. S.*) *Hinman* (2d Edit.) notes that Philip
and wife Sarah, of Weth., were app. as adm'rs on est. of Nath'l Butler, dec'd,
of Weth., on a judg't rendered in favor of Mr. Wm. Gibbons of Boston, before
Nathan Stanley, Assist., June 10, 1700.—See, also, Chapt. VII, Vol. I.

ALDEN, JOHN B., of Htfd., m. Huldah **Clapp,** 17 June, 1827.—*W. C. R.*

Children:

1. Jane Olivet, b. 12 Mch., 1828.
2. Eunice Brown, b. 19 June, 1829.
3. John B., b. 1 June, 1831.

4. Clarissa Ann, b. 26 Aug., 1833 ; d. 30 Sept., 1833.

ALEXANDER, EBENEZER, m. Mehitable (dau Henry) **Buck,** 10 Oct., 1709.

Child (b. *Weth.*):

1. Elias, b. 25 (bp. 30, *Mix MSS.*) July, 1710.

Miscellanea:

THOMAS, of Wrentham, Mass., m ¹emima **Cole,** 26 Apl., 1779.

Children (*W. C. R.*):

1. Anne, bp. 6 Aug., 1780.—*W. C. R.*
2. James, bp. 21 Sept., 1783.—*W. C. R.*

ALLEN, (from *Weth. Town Rec.* and *Weth. Ch. Rec.*) AUSTIN, m. Abby Ann
Goodrich, both of Ry-H., 29 Oct., 1840.

ISAAC, of E. Windsor, m. Mary S. **Prudden,** 5 July, 1818.

MARY, m. Simeon **Drake,** of E. Windsor, 26 Nov., 1837.

ELISHA, the wife of, ae. 47, bu. Nov., 1813.—*W. C. R.*

HANNAH, dau. of Susannah, bp. 9 Feb., 1706-7.—*Mix MSS.*

ALLIS, (synon. with *Ellis*) WILLIAM,[3] (acc. to *Allis Gen.*, p. 4) (s. of *John*,[2]
s. of *Wm.*,') freeman at Braintree, Mass., 1640; who rem. abt. 1661, to Hatfield
—(Judd's *Hadley*, p. 447; *Savage*, i, 42)'; was b. 16 May, 1684; res. in Weth.,
where he was m. by Rev. Mr. Mix, 15 Dec., 1709, to Mary .(dau. Jacob) **Griswold;** appears in Weth. as collector in 1712; as lister, also as packer, 1713.
Hinman (2d Edit.) says he was an aged man in 1756, made his will, in wh.
he appt'd Isaac North, exc.; Est. £151-12-8; res. in Kensington (Berlin).

Children (*Weth. Rec.*[6]; *Allis Gen. for marriages*):

1. Mary, b. 22 bp. 25 (*Mix Rec.*) Nov., 1711 ;* m. Ebenezer **Sanford.**
2. Lydia, b. 14 Sept., bp. 11 Oct., (*Mix Rec.*), 1713 ;* m. John **Collins,** 1739.—See **Collins.**
3. Sarah, b. 6 Oct., 1715 ;* m. Ezekiel **Kelsey,** 1743.—See *Kelsey.*
4. Ann, b. 1720 ; m. Samuel **Pike.**

5. John, b. 11 Sept., 1726 ; d. 18 May, 1756, in 29th yr., by wh. the family name became extinct in Weth. The wid. of John, Sen. (acc. to *Hinman*, 2d Edit.), m. (2) David **Webster,** by whom she had a son John (Webster), who d. ae. 6 yrs.

Miscellanea :

ABIGAIL, of Weth., d. 1672.—*Hinman*, 2d Edit.

WILLIAM E., d. 22 Sept., 1892; his wife Harriet A. **Kimball,** d. 10 Dec., 1882.— *Weth. Inscr.*

ALLYN, Capt. otherwise "Mr." JOSEPH, came to Weth. from Plymouth, Mass., sometime betw. 1702 and '03—See Chap. VII, Vol. I; his wife was Mary **Doty;** administration on his est. granted to his son-in-law, Nath'l Stillman, 6 Apl., 1742; an agreement for settlement of the estate was exhib. in Ct., 25 Jan., 1743-4; accepted and ordered to be kept on file.

Children (b. in Plymouth, Mass.) : [*]

1. Elizabeth, b. 1700; m. Hezekiah **Kilborn.**
2. Mary, b. 1702; m. Col. James **Otis,** and was the mother of James Otis, "the patriot" of Boston.
   (*Born in Weth.*) *Rec. I. 76.*
3. Hannah, b. 17 May, 1705; m. Rev. Eben'r **Wright.**

4. Samuel, b. 24 Feb., 1706-7.
5. Sarah, b. 17 Aug., 1708; m. Nath'l **Stillman.**
6. Martha, b. 22 Oct., 1710.
7. Abigail.
   (The *Mix. Mss.* records all these ch. as being bp. 11 Sept., 1715; the mother owning the Covenant at the same time.)

THOMAS. *Savage* says (1, 44) of "Weth., 1636, not migrat. from Watertown, for Bond has not named him, was bro. of Matthew [of Windsor] with whom he had extraordinary controversies in the law, as is fairly infer. from Trumbull's *Col. Rec.,* I, 211: was made freeman, 1652; rep. 1656; and soon after d. as might be concluded from not seeing his name as rep. in any year subseq., nor in the list of freemen for that town, 1669; yet he may have rem. to Midd., as no list of that sort is found from that place in Trumbull, and one of the name there was deacon, who d. 16 Oct., 1688, having had no ch., but leaving wid. Martha, perhaps, who had been wid of Roger Jepson, and d. 1690. She calls in her will, Obediah Allen, of Midd., "cousin." Y is not seen in the last syllable of his name, tho' in his bp. rec. Apl. 1664 (if he were s. of Samuel. of Chelmsford Co.. Essex, Eng.), the spell. is the other way." This statement agrees perfectly with that given in Stiles' *Hist. of Ancient Windsor,* Rev. Edit. II, 27; but Dea. Thomas Allyn's name does not occur upon Weth. Rec., as in anywise showing him to have been resident or interested in Weth.; and we have no excuse for placing him here, except upon Savage's authority.

HENRY, (s. of Capt. John & Ruth) d. 27 June, 1774, ae. 2 yrs., 4 mo.—*C. L. C.*

ALVERT (Alvord?) SAUL, m. Eleanor **Kellogg,** 14 Apl., 1779.—*N. C. R.*

AMES, (orig. a Mass. family, tracing back to Briton Co., Somerset, Eng.), JOHN, of Rocky Hill (Weth.), b. Nov., 1733; d. 16 July, 1790.

JOHN, m. Abigail **Butler,** who was b. 30 June, 1737, and d. 23 Feb., 1800, in 63d yr. *P. F. R.'s* notes says he was one of the two sons of Richard Ames, who set. at New London. 1696, and d. there 1 Jan., 1735; and that Richard had a bro. Nathaniel, who for many yrs. in the Colonial period was celebrated for his almanacs, and whose son was Fisher H. Ames, the celebrated Boston orator, who was the first rep. to the Federal Congress, 1774-1789.

Children (Hinman, 1st Edit.; bp. from Step. Rec.) :

1. David, b. 1 Feb., 1751; d. 19 Nov.,1822; lost an arm by a pistol shot; res. Southington, Ct., and after this injury, taught school for many years.
2. Philemon, b. 8 Oct., 1758; d. 9 June, 1797;

m. Ruth (dau. David) **Hurlburt,** of M. Haddam, who was b. Oct., 1760; was a ship carpenter, or builder (draftsman) and master of the Ship-yard at Ry-H.; possessed affable manners and much firmness

---

[*] Davis'*Ancient Landmarker of Plymouth,* p. 6, Part II; p. 170, Part I; Freeman's *Hist. Cape Cod,* I 274, note : Tudor's *Life of James Otis,* p. 497.

and integrity of character; d. ae. 39; left but one ch. *Eunice*, bp. 26 Aug., 1787.—*S. C. R.*, who m. Fred. **Robbins**, Jr., of Weth.
3.   John, b. 31 Aug., 1760; d. smallpox, 12 July, 1776, ae. 16.
4. Benjamin, b. 29 Oct., 1762; d. 19 Nov., 1795 (1794, acc. to *Step. Rec.*), ae. 33. FAM. 2.
5. Mehitable, b. 21 Mch. (bp. 7, Apl.), 1765; d. ae. 10.
6. William, b. 31 July, bp. 2 Aug., 1767; d.

2 July, 1811. FAM. 3.
7. Eunice, b. 4, bp. 10 Sept., 1769; d. 1775.
8. Robert, b. 20, bp. 26 Apl., 1772; d. 1775.
9. Abigail, b. 3, bp. 12 June, 1774; m. Russell McKee; in 1840, was res. at Midd.; family.
10. John, b. 1 May, 1777; d. 1778.
11. Mary, b. 1 June, 1780; d. 1821. Pos. the Polly A., who m. 19 Nov., 1807, Rev. Salmon King, of E. Htfd.—*S. C. R.*

FAM. 2.   BENJAMIN,[2] (*John*,[1]), b. 1762; m. 8 Sept., 1785, Lois **Warner**, she prob. the "wid. Lois," who d. 23 Mar., 1841, ae. 78, Glast. He d. 19 Nov., 1794, ae. 32.

Children (Step. Rec.) :

1. Rhoda, bp. 8 July, 1787.
2. Robert Butler, bp. 1 Mar., 1789.
3. Roger Warner, bp. 31 Mar., 1791.

4. Inf.; d. 19 Nov., 1792.
5. Benjamin, bp. 17 Aug., 1794; "Benj. Ames, 2d, d. 22 Oct., 1795."

FAM. 3.   WILLIAM[2] (*John*,[1]), b. 1767; m. 14 Apl., 1796, Lydia **Callender**; who d. 3 Dec., 1828, ae. 62, in P. Ho. He d. 3 July, 1811, ae. 44.—*S. C. R.*

Miscellanea:

WILLIAM, m. Jerusha **Goodrich**, 4 Nov., 1790; she d. 15 Dec., 1793.—*S. C. R.*

IRA, s. of William 3d, bp 16 Jan., 1793; d. 26 Sept., 1795, in 3d yr.—*S. C. R.*

DANIEL had John, who d. 30 Aug., 1784, in 4th yr.—*S. C. R.*

ROBERT, (prob. from Mass., and also prob. bro. of John, above), was prob. the R. of Stepney, who m. Sarah **Moreton**, "both of S.," 20 Feb., 1765—*W. Ch. Rec.*, and d. 10 Nov., 1770. Accor. to *Hinman*, his est. distrib. 1772, amt'd to £373-13-7; wid. Sarah had dower; he owned ld. at Barkhamstead, Ct., left his s. William, £199, 4s.; to dau. Sarah, £49, 12s., besides life int. in est. to wid.

Children (Weth. Rec.) :

1. William, inf. bp. 27; d. 29 Jan., 1767.
2. Wiliam, b. 7, bp. 14 Aug., 1768.
3. Sarah, b. 24, bp. 28 (*Step. Rec.*) Apl., 1771.

4. John.
5. Perhaps others.

From *Stepney Ch. Rec.:*

WILLIAM, inf. s. of Robert Ames, bp. 27 Jan., d. 29 Jan., 1767.

RICHARD, d. 12 Nov., 1770.

JERUSHA, wife of William, d. 15 Dec., 1793, ae. 27.

ABIGAIL, (*wid.*) d. 23 Feb., 1800, ae. 63.

AMIDON, JOHN, native of Ashford, Ct., came with a family, to Htfd. 20 yrs. ago, and later to Weth., where he d. ae. 74. At breaking out of the Civil War, he rem. to N. Y. City and eng. in mfre. of umbrellas, in which he acquired a competence. He built the country store on Htfd. Ave. cor. of High St. and Sandy Lane, Weth., later occup. by Walkely & Damery—and still later by T. E. Damery.

ANDRUS, (*Andrews*, but almost uniformly spelled *Andrus*—sometimes *Andross*, in *Weth. Rec.*). The genealogy of this Conn. fam. has already been well compiled,[*] as also has that of the Mass., Maryland and other families of the name; and we simply present here such A. records as are found in the *Town, Church and Graveyard Records of Weth.*

---

* *Geneal. Hist. of John and Mary Andrews*, who set. in Farmington, Conn., 1640, embracing their descendants to 1872, etc., etc. By Alfred Andrews Andrews, Hartford, Ct., 1872, 8 vo., 672 pp.

JOHN ANDRUS, the progenitor of the Conn. fam., was, 1672, one of the 84 orig.
pprs. of Tunxis or Farmington, which town bounds Weth. on the west; and he
res. very near the Weth. line. He had nine ch.—three of whom were daus.,
one of whom, Rachel, m. 1675, Ezekiel **Buck**, of Weth. His fourth son

JOSEPH, b. 26 May, 1651, who res. abt. the centre of New. parish, became a large
ld. owner; had ld., 1684, near Pipe-Stave Swamp, on the "West lots," or "West
Division," by purchase from John and Joseph Riley, who held by right of the
first gen. division of lds. in New., Feb., 1670-1; and, in 1702, he bo't the sawmill
which had been erected there by auth. of the Town; and, among the 165 inhab.
who shared in the second div. of New. lds., we find his name as owner of lot
145. He is prob. the J. A., adm. inhab. 1703, and is also, by trade, named as
one of the three earliest set. of New., and his house, which the annalist of
New. says (in 1876) "still stands," was abt. 20 or 30 rods from the old meeting
house, and was at one time fortified as a house of refuge and defence from
Ind. attack. He d. 27 Apl., 1706—*N. Rec.*, and invent. of his est. taken 23 May,
1706, by Nath'l Stoddard and John Curtis, Jr., amt'd to £413-07-04; his will
devises to his wife Rebecca ————, and sons, and his "dau's portions, as the
Ct. shall think meet;" none of his lds. to be sold "except to one [or] another of
my sons." His will was duly exhib. to the Ct., June 5, 1706, by wid. and eld. s.,
and the Ct. app. Daniel Andrus, of Far.; Ephriam Whaples and Samuel Hum,
of Weth., to div. and distrib. the estate, which was done 18 Feb., 1709-10—the
personal est. going to daus. Rebecca and Anne.—*Htfd. Prob. Ct. Rec.*

Children:

1. Joseph (Dr.), b. abt. 1686. FAM. 2.
2. Benjamin. FAM. 3.
3. Ephraim, b. abt. 1685.
4. Caleb, ae. 15, b. Mch. 1694; m. 15 Feb., 1722, Mary **Gillett**, of Htfd. FAM. 4.
5. Rebecca, ae. 17; m. a **Gillett**, of Htfd.
6. Anne, b. abt. 1696, ae. 13; m. John **Camp**. (Caleb, ae. 15; Rebecca, ae. 17; Anne, ae. 13, all, in 1700, chose their mother as guardian.)

FAM. 2. Dr. JOSEPH,[3] (*Joseph*,[2] *John*,[1]), b. abt. 1686; "of Htfd," was m. to Sarah
Curtis, of L. I., 18 Nov., 1706, "by Joshua Hobart, Minister in Southold"—
Weth. Rec.; res. New.; is named in Rev. Mr. Belden's List of New Ch. memb.
at time of his ord. 1747; he d. 18 Jan., 1756, ae. 78; his wid. d. 23 May, 1760.

Children (Weth. Rec.):

1. Joshua, b. 11 Dec., 1707; bp. 22 Feb., 1707-8.
2. William, b. 24 May, 1710; bp. 2 July, 1710; prob. FAM. 5; prob. the one referred to in following doc. from *Htfd. Co. Prob. Rec.:* "William Andrews, invent. £112-00-00 taken 4th Aug., 1722, by Samuel Hunn, John Deming, John Camp, *Ct. Rec.*, 3 July, 1722, *whereas*, William Andrews, late of Weth., being gone to sea and having
been absent abt. 14 yrs., and not heard of that he is alive, and a motion being made that adm. should be granted on s⁴ estate—adm. gr. to Joseph Andrews, a bro. of s⁴ William Andrews."
4. Joseph, bp. 29 Nov., 1713; d. yg.
5. Benajah, b. 26 Mch., 1717. FAM. 6.
6. Elijah, b. 1719, m. Feb., 21, 1745, Phœbe **Hurlbut.**

FAM. 3. BENJAMIN,[3] (*Joseph*,[2] *Joseph*,[1]), m. 19 Dec., 1704, Elizabeth ————.
See Chap. VII., Vol. I.

Children (Weth. Rec.):

1. Jemima, b. 2 Oct., 1706.
2. Joseph, b. 5 May (bp. 22 June—*Mix*), 1707.
3. Rebecca, b. 3 Feb., bp. 27 Mch, 1708-9.
4. Phinehas, b. 22 July, 1711.
5. Phinehas, b. 26 May, 1712.
6. Timothy, b. 2, bp. 11 July, 1714.

FAM. 4. CALEB,[3] (*Joseph*,[2] *John*,[1]), b. abt. 1696; m. Mary (dau. Joseph) **Gillett**,
of Htfd., 15 Feb., 1721-2; res. New., d. 1775, ae. 79.

Children (Weth. Rec.):

1. Mary, b. 15 Feb., 1723-24.
2. Hannah, b. 7 May, 1725; prob. the H. who d. 15 Sept., 1748.—*W. C. R.*
3. Amos, b. 14 Nov., 1726; prob. d. 5 Sept., 1748.—*N. C. R.*
4. Rhoda, b. 6 May, 1728.
5. Lydia, b. 20 July, 1730.
6. Abel, b. 6 May, 1735. FAM. 7.
7. Eli, b. 8 Jan., 1736-7; d. P. H., 16 Apl., 1811, ae. 75.—*N. C. R.*
8. Clemont, b. 31 Oct., 1739.
9. Esther (acc. to *A. Genealogy*).

FAM. 5. WILLIAM,[3] (Joseph,[2] John,[1]), b.————; Poss. the Wm. who m. Irene **Griswold**,, who d. 10 Sept., 1758—N. C. R.; he m. (2) 4 Jan., 1759, wid. Lois **Stephens**.—N. C. R.

Children (Weth. Rec.; bp. N. C. R.) :

1. Miles, b. 22 May, 1735. FAM. 8.
2. Elisha, b. 1 Mch., 1738. FAM. 9.
3. William, b. 28 Oct., 1740 ; prob. the Wm., Jr., who m. Silence **Wright**, 22 Mch., 1762, and had (N. C. R.) Lemuel bp. 28 June, 1772 ; Naomi bp. 22 Sept., 1782.
4. Joseph, b. 13 Apl., 1743. FAM. 10.
5. Chloe, b. 3 (bp. 6—N. C. R.), 1747-8.
6. A "Sarah of William,' d. 14 Dec., 1751.— N. C. R.
    (By second marriage) :
7. Sarah, bp. 25 Nov., 1759 ; prob. the S., "inf. dau.," who d. 20 Feb., 1761.—N. C. R.
8. Sylvia, b. 17, bp. 18, Apl., 1762.
9. Cynthia, b. 15 bp. 20 Oct., 1765.
10. Rhoda, b. 14 Oct., 1768 ; bp. 19 Feb., 1769.

FAM. 6. BENAJAH,[4] (Joseph,[3] Joseph,[2] John,[1]), b. 1717; m. Anne **Clark**, 25 Jan., 1745.

Children (Weth. Rec.; bp. N. C. R.) :

1. Elizur, b. 13, bp. 27 Dec., 1747 ; d. 4 Dec., 1829 ; ae. 82.—N. C. R. Anna, his wife, d. 16 Feb., 1836, ae. 81.—N. C. R.
2. Silas, b. 23 Apl., bp. 20 May, 1750 ; prob. the S. who d. (N. C. R.) 16 Apl., 1821, ae. 75.

FAM. 7. ABEL,[4] (Caleb,[3] Joseph,[2] John,[1]), b. 1735; m. 2 Dec., 1764, Eunice **Stod-dard**, of W. Htfd.; she is said to have been a model of patience and pleasant-ness. Abel was adm. to N. Ch. 4 Sept., 1785, and his 2d wife Rhoda adm. 3 Sept., 1787, on letter fm. W. Htfd. Ch. She died Jan. 23, 1785, and he m. (2) April 16, 1787, Rhoda **Sedgwick**, wid. of Elisha **Seymour**, He d. 15 May, 1811, ae. 76.—N. C. R. He is believed by some to be the hero and his second wife the heroine of the following story told in Barger's *Conn. Hist. Coll.* p. 116.

"Mr. A———— of this place, (Newington) who was a very religious and con-scientious man, married for a wife one of the most ill-natured and troublesome women which could be found in the vicinity. This occasioned universal sur-prise wherever he was known, and one of his neighbors ventured to ask him the reasons which governed his choice. Mr. A———— replied, that having had but little or no trouble in the world, he was fearful of becoming too much attached to things of time and sense. And he thought by experiencing some afflictions, he should become more weaned from the world, and that he married such a woman as he thought would accomplish the object. The best part of the story is, that the wife, hearing of the reasons why he married her, was much offended, and *out of revenge*, became one of the most pleasant and dutiful wives in the town, declaring that she was not a going to be made a *pack horse* to carry her husband to heaven."

It is but fair to say that Dea. Joshua Andrus and Asher Atwood are thought, by some, to be the hero of the above story.

Children (Weth. Rec.; bp. N. C. R.) : *all by first marr.*

1. Amos, b. 17 Mch., bp. 12 May, 1765 ; d. 21 Feb., 1826, ae. 63—N. C. R.; m. 10 Mch., 1813, "Milly" **Welles**; she, Amelia (wid. of A.), d. 3 May, 1842, ae. 75.— N. C. R Amos Andrus was a thrifty farmer. It was said of him that the "sun never shone upon his milk pail." He milked his cows before sunrise in the morning, and after sunset at night. The fact that he was treasurer of the Ecclest.
Socy. from 1812, until his death (21 Feb., 1826) caused him to feel an interest in the prosperity of the Society, and as he left no children, he willed his ppy. to the said Socy.—See Chapt. XVIII.
2. Ruth, b. 9 Oct., 1766.
3. Jared, b. 16 Apl., 1769.
4. Allen, b. 25, bp. 28 July, 1771.
5. Hannah, b. 1, bp. 6, Feb., 1774.
6. Lydia, bp. 20 May, 1781.

FAM. 8. MILES,[4] (Wm.,[2] Joseph,[2] John,[1]), b. 1735; m. Phebe **Hurlbut**, of Goshen, 1 May, 1759.

Children (Weth. Rec.; bp. N. C. R.) :

1. Miles, b. 7 July, bp. 24 Oct., 1759.
2. Irene, b. 17, bp. 25, Jan., 1761.
3. Mehitable, b. 25 Apl., and bp. 23 May, 1762.
4. Clorinde, b. 15 June, 1753 ; bp. 1 July, 1764.
5. Phebe, b. 10, bp. 17 Aug., 1766.
6. Jason, b. 17 Feb., bp. 8 May, 1768-9.
7. Benajah, b. 13 Nov., 1769 ; bp. 15 Apl., 1770.

FAM. 9. ELISHA,[4] (*Wm.*,[3] *Joseph*,[2] *John*,[1]), b. 1738; m. Phebe **Hurlbut**, 21 Feb., 1745—*Weth. Rec.;* he d. 3 Nov., 1750; she d. 13 Nov., 1772.—*N. C. R.*

Children (Weth. Rec.):

1. Asa, b. 10 Apl., 1746.
2. Josiah, b. 16 May, 1749.

3. Elijah, b. 16 Oct., 1752.
4. Rose, b. 20 Sept., 1755.

FAM. 10. JOSEPH,[4] "2nd," (*William*,[3] *Joseph*,[2] *John*,[1]), b. 1743; m. Asenath

Children (Weth. Rec.; bp. *N. C. R.):*

1. Ruth, b. 27, bp. 30 Jan., 1763.
2. Pamela, b. 5, bp. 9 or 17 (?) Sept., 1764.
3. Joseph, b. 9 Aug., bp. 7 Dec., 1766.
4. Polly, b. 8 June, 1770.
5. Roxalena, b. 14 Dec., 1771.

6. Elisha, b. 11 Oct., 1773.
7. William, b. 16 Nov., 1775.
8. Sarah, b. 11 Sept., 1777.
9. Asenath, b. 22 May, 1779.

Unconnected Families:

BENJAMIN, m. Anne **Churchill**, 30 Oct., 1760.

Children (Weth. Rec.; bp. *N. C. R.):*

1. Anne, b. 14, bp. 19 Sept., 1762.
2. Lorana, b. 1 Dec., 1764; bp. 27 Jan., 1766;

d. 3 May, 1768.
3. Thankful, bp. 29 Mch., 1767.

DANIEL, (s. of *Joseph*, s. of *John*, of Far.?), m. 30 Oct., 1707, Mabel (dau. Jacob) **Goff;** he d. 21 Aug., 1748, ae. 75; *A. Gen.* says he d. 16 June, 1740; res. Weth., but belonged to Kens. parish; bu. Chr. Lane Cemetery.

Children (Weth. Rec.):

1. Abigail, b. 22 July, 1713.
2. Mabel, b. 6 June, 1715.
3. Eunice, b. 18 Sept., 1717.
4. Daniel, b. 12 May, 1720. FAM. 2.

5. Hannah, b. 8 Sept., 1723.
6. Jacob, b. 24 Jan., 1728. FAM. 3.
7. Hezekiah, b. 14 Aug., 1731.

FAM. 2. DANIEL, Jr., (Daniel), b. 1720; m. 6 Feb., 1746, wid. Eunice **Kelsey,** who d. 23 Feb., 1763; he m. (2) Mary **Mitchell,** 2 Aug., 1764.

Children (Weth. Rec.):

1. Daniel, b. 24 Aug., 1748.
2. Eunice, b. 29 Apl., 1750.
3. Mabel, b. 17 June, 1754.
4. Sybil, b. 20 or 30 May, 1756.

5. Abigail, b. 4 May, 1759.
6. Martin, b. 30 May, 1761.
   (*By second marriage*):
7. Justus, b. 9 Mch., 1765.

FAM. 3. JACOB,[2] (*Daniel, Sr.*,[1]), b. 1729; m. Eunice ———— —.

Children (Weth. Rec.):

1. Jacob, b. 20 Jan., 1760.
2. Caroline, b. 20 Oct., 1762.

3. Sarah, b. 7 Jan., 1765.

DAVID, m. Margaret ————————; prob. the D. who d. 24 Aug., 1748.

Child (Weth. Rec.):

1. Mary, b. 1 Apl., 1748.

ELIAS, m. Tabitha **Bissell,** of E. Windsor, 20 Nov., 1780.

Child (Weth. Rec.):

1. Clarissa, b. 4, bp. 20—N., 1781.

ELIJAH, m. Phebe (dau. Joseph & Sybil) **Hurlbut,** 21 Feb., 1745; she d. 13 Nov., 1772, (*Weth. Rec.*); he d. ae. 73, bu. 3 Sept., 1792.—*W. C. R.*

Children (Weth. Rec.):

1. Asa, b. 10 Apl., 1746; m. Chloe **Andrus**, 16 Mch., 1768; had (*N. C. R.*):
   i. Inf. bp. 5, d. 15 Dec., 1770.
   ii. Frederic, bp. 25 Mch., 1770.
   iii. Chloe, bp. 16 Apl., 1775 (or 3 ?).
2. Josiah, b. 16, bp. 21 May, 1749.

3. Elijah, b. 16 Oct., 1752; prob. the E. who m. Sarah **Hurlbut,** both of Weth., 22 Nov., 1774—*W. C. R.;* had *Clarissa* bp. 30 Mch., 1783, and a dau., ae. 2 yrs., bu. 30 Mch., 1783.—*W. C. R.*
4. Rose, b. 20, bp. 26 Sept., 1755.

EPHRAIM, see Chap. VII, Vol. I.

JOHN, b. at Far., 10 June, 1680; m. Mary (dau. Jacob) **Goff**, 26 June, 1712; he d. 16 June, 1740; adm. gr. wid. and s. David, 20 Jan., 1740-1; he is prob. the J. adm. inhab. 1703, and called an attorney in *Co. Ct. Rec.*, 1709.

Children (Weth. Rec.):

1. David, b. 28 Jan., 1718-9; a D. d. 21 Aug., 1748; poss. the same.

2. Moses, b. 12 May, 1722.

JOSEPH, m. Sarah **Wells**, 3 Apl., 1746.

Children (Weth. Rec.):

1. Levi, b. 23 Feb., 1747; m. Chloe **Welles**, 20 Dec., 1770.—*N. C. R.*
2. Elias, b. 16, bp. 18)*N. C. R.*) Feb., 1752-3; d. 15 Apl., 1827, ae. 74.—*N. C. R.*
3. Sarah, b. 12, bp. 25 (*N. C. R.*) Jan., 1756.

4. A "Ruth, of Joseph," was bp. 31 Mch., 1751; d. 5 Apl., 1751.—*N. C. R.*
5. A "Joseph, of Joseph, Jr.," was bp. 7 Dec., 1765.—*N. C. R.*

JOSHUA, (——————————), m. Sibel ——————.

Children (Weth. Rec.):

1. Jeremiah, b. 16 Jan., 1732.
2. Epaphras, b. 16 Apl., 1735.
3. Fitch, b. 12 Oct., 1739; m. Mary **Wells**, 26 July, 1764.—*N. C. R.* (*N. C. R.* gives d. of Lois, "wife of F.," 30 May, 1805, ae. 43.)
   i. Three ch. at a birth, 8 Jan., 1742;

all d. same day.
ii. Three ch. (one named Sybil), b. 3 Mch., 1743; all d. same day.
iii. Two ch. (one named Sybil), b. 1 June, 1744, of which one d. same day; the other was named *Curtis*, who d. 31 Jan., 1756.—*S. C. R.*

Miscellanea:

PHINEHAS, (——————————); m. Lois **Williams**, 16 Oct., 1751; in 1778, he manumitted his slave "Prince Nauque" prob. for service in Continental Army. The "wid. Lois" d. P. H., betw. 1 July and 1st Oct., 1825, ae. 96.

Children (Weth. Rec.):

1. Keturah, b. 14 Nov., 1752; bp. 12 Nov.— *N. C. R.*
2. Appleton, bp. 14 Aug., 1757.—*N. C. R.*

3. Phinehas, b. 19, bp. 24 July, 1763—*N. C. R.;* m. 23 Jan., 1783, Seely **Stoddard**.

Miscellanea: ARTHUR, s. of Elizur, m. Mary **Ingraham**, 20 Jan., 1805, both of Weth.—*N. C. R.* FITCH & Lois, had Joshua bp. 28 Apl., 1805, she d. 30 May, 1805, ae 43.—*N. C. R.* HANNAH, d. 15 Sept., 1748.—*N. C. R.* ELISHA, ae. 50, d. 4 Mch., 1810.—*N. C. R.* EPAPHRAS, m. 6 Jan., 1808, Abigail **Wells**. —*N. C. R.* HEZEKIAH, of Far., m. 1757, Anne **Stedman**.—*W. C. R.* JOSEPH, of Chatham, m. Elizabeth **Weaver**, 16 Feb., 1778.—*W. C. R.* JOSHUA, of Weth., m. Prudence **Camp**, of Hafd., 18 Sept., 1814.—*W. T. R.* MOSES, (s. of Moses & Lydia), d. 30 Nov., 1753, ae. 1 yr. *Chr. Lane Cemetery.* LOIS, ae. 96, d. 19 Sept., 1825.—*N C. R.* OBED, of Glast., m. Abigail A. **Russell**, 10 Mch., 1830. OBED, m. Loretta **Caswell**, both of Glast., 1 May, 1832. OLEDINE, d. at Long Meadow, ae. 34, 24 June, 1808.—*N. C. R.* RHODA M., m. Wm. F. **Wallis**, of Manchester, Ct., 29 Sept., 1835.—*W. T. R.* RUTH (wid.), from Berlin, d. P. H., 25 Dec., 1825, ae. 97.—*S. C. R.* SARAH (wid.), d. 23 May, 1760. SAMUEL, m. ——————; had (*N. C. R.*) Samuel Johnson bp. 3 June, 1763; Whiteley Horn bp. 11 Sept., 1768; Theode bp. 29 Mch., 1771; Jemima bp. 25 July, 1773; Samuel (Andross) of Wintonbury (poss. the S. above), m. Rebecca **Tryon**, of Weth., 7 Apl., 1763.— *W. C. R.* SAMUEL, Jr., m. Chloe Ann **Francis**, 26 Sept., 1832; had (*W. T. R.*) Ann Elizabeth, b. 19 Jan., 1826, and Mary Francis, b. 9 May, 1838.—*W. T. R.* HENRIETTA (adult), bp. 22 Nov., 1795.—*W. C. R.*

ANDREWS, CHARLES McCLEAN, Prof. of History in Bryn Mawr College, since 1889; b. Weth., 23 Feb., 1863, (s. of Rev. William Watson Andrews, by his 2nd wife, E. B. **Williams**); grad. Trinity Coll., Htfd., Ct., 1884; A. M. 1890; Ph. D. Johns Hopkins 1889; m. 1895, Evangeline Holcombe **Walker**, and has two ch.; he is author of *The River Towns of Connecticut; The Old English Manor; The Historical Development of Modern Europe, etc.*, also occasional articles in reviews and historical journals.

Rev. WILLIAM WATSON, although not a native, was long a resident of Weth.; and allied by marr. with one of its oldest and most distinguished families; his personality, Christian character, social relations and literary ability conferred an honor upon the town and community in which he lived, which justifies us in giving him a niche in this Weth. history. Mr. Andrews was b. in Windham, Conn., 26 Feb., 1810, and was the eldest son of William and Sarah (*Parkhill*) Andrews. His father was successively, pastor of Congregational churches in Windham, Danbury and South Cornwall, and had six sons, of whom five became ministers. The American ancestor of the family was William Andrews, of New Haven, one of twelve men chosen to do the "foundation work" of the church, in 1639.

Watson Andrews (as he was generally called) graduated at Yale in 1831. President Porter of Yale and Professor Atwater of Princeton were his classmates and lifelong friends, and these three, with a few others, were nearly the earliest disciples of Coleridge in America, forming a group of which Dr. Gilman, the retiring president of John Hopkins University, made honorable mention at the recent bi-centennial anniversary at New Haven. Much was expected of Mr. Andrews; he was a good scholar, and greatly excelled as a writer and speaker. In 1833, he married Mary Anne, the second daughter of James and Susan (*VanWyck*) **Given**, of Fishkill, N. Y. Her father was Scotch-Irish, and was for many years an elder in the Reformed Dutch church; her mother was of Dutch descent, one of her ancestors being the first minister of Brooklyn, John Theodore Polemus. In 1834, Mr. Andrews was ordained pastor of the Congregational church in Kent, in his native State. The picturesque scenery of Kent was a source of endless delight to its young minister, but his chief interest was in his work. He had rare power in the pulpit, though the accomplished orator was soon forgotten in the man of God with his message. And this, with his pastoral fidelity and wisdom, his ready sympathy and the pleasure which he took in their society, fast won the affections of his people. He keenly enjoyed wit and humor: bursts of laughter from the study used to announce to his wife the arrival of the *Charleston Mercury*, edited by one of his wittiest classmates, John Milton Clapp. His domestic life contributed much to his influence, both by its light and its shadows. Around his wife the shadows lay thickest, through her early loss of health and the burden of unaccustomed tasks, but from her proceeded the light that shone brightest for others. The blending of refinement and high intelligence with a simplicity which was almost bareness, was a profitable lesson for rich and poor. Far more so was the religious atmosphere in which Puritanism had something of its strictness, but none of its gloom, and Sunday was perhaps as pleasant as Saturday, an atmosphere which was so sweet and pure because of the heavenly love flowing into it through the unbroken fellowship of the human parents with the Father and the Son. The strong attachment between Mr. Andrews and his first congregation seemed to become an inheritance in its various families, and hardly to have grown weaker when he died. To him the relation was very sacred, and he would not have dissolved it for the sake of outward advancement. But the death of his wife in 1848, and the subsequent scattering of his children (the youngest an infant) were followed by an important change, the way for which had long been preparing.

He had scarcely left college when his attention was drawn to the supposed revival in Scotland of the primitive gifts of healing and prophecy. The movement took form by degrees in the restoration, as was believed, of the primitive ministries of apostle and prophet, and the gathering of congregations, not as a new sect, but as a portion of the Catholic church accepting and seeking to use a grace offered to the whole. The adhesion of the wonderful Scotch preacher, Edward Irving, then a Presbyterian pastor in London, led careless observers to call all adherents Irvingites. They would themselves use no name except Catholic Apostolic, but they freely acknowledged the equal right of all bodies of baptised persons to use it, and did not wish it applied to them as a distinctive, or a sectarian, name. And undoubtedly the offensive and inaccurate nickname, Irvingite, was often employed by others who had no desire to offend, and simply because nothing properly distinctive had been provided. In 1843, a visit to Great Britain, made desirable by impaired health, brought Mr. Andrews, already convinced, into contact with the chief representatives of the movement. He was struck by their freedom from the usual marks of *a fanatical spirit, their sober, reasonable attitude towards the present order of things, and their hearty acceptance of their duties as subjects and members of society, and as members, for the most part, of the church of England. And, somewhat to his surprise, he found himself bidden to remain in his Congregational parish, as being there a lawful minister of Christ, and to seek to maintain and strengthen its spiritual life. And when, in May, 1849, he sought and obtained an orderly dismissal at the hands of the North Consociation of Litchfield, in order, as he believed, to serve directly under Apostles, he did not regard himself as withdrawing from the Congregational ministry, and he remained a member of the Association (consisting of ministers only) for several years longer. He was at once placed in charge of a small congregation in Potsdam, in northern New York, and there, still a pastor, he remained until the close of 1856. Now, for the first and only time in his life, he seemed almost entirely cut off from sympathy and friendly companionship. This isolation, due to the failure of his new neighbors to understand his position, disappeared as they learned at least to understand him. In 1853, he was called on to define his relations to his Association in Connecticut, and after a full statement on his part, the name was removed from its lists. He was afterwards, however, chosen an honorary member of the Hartford Central Association, and regularly took part in its discussions. On leaving Potsdam he entered the order of evangelists, with the duty of carrying the Gospel not to unbelievers but to believers presumed to have missed its full significance. His message embraced the evangelist's call to repentance and faith, but to repentance chiefly, for the common sins of Christendom, its worldliness and its divisions, and to faith in Christ as renewing the gift of Pentecost.

In July, 1858, Mr. Andrews married, at Wethersfield, Elizabeth Byrne, youngest daughter of John and Mary (*Dyer*) **Williams,** and descended from a line of ministers. To a man of his temperament the return to life in a true home was the greatest of earthly blessings. The house at Wethersfield became, as far as was necessary, the home also of his three older children, two of them now grown. Here his eldest daughter and his second son (the latter during a short visit), died in 1874 and 1880, respectively, after having received the tenderest care. Here three younger children were born and reared, and here, to the end of his long life, he enjoyed in a rare degree the domestic happiness which had been so sadly broken off in Kent. He often preached in the old parish church, and was often called on, particularly in times of sorrow, for the exercise of his pastoral gifts. He was the friend, sometimes the intimate friend, of the successive parish ministers. Habitually using with delight a rich liturgy, having its centre in the Eucharist, as the earthly counterpart of Christ's Heavenly intercession, he would attend by preference the Congregational service when compelled to choose between that and any other save his own. And he probably took part in public worship for the last time at a Congregational prayer meeting in Wethersfield. It would have been a grievous wrong had Congregationalism wholly disowned so affectionate a son.

The evangelistic work of Mr. Andrews (ultimately including the oversight of other evangelists in America, and involving frequent journeys) were performed in the pulpits of friendly ministers, in public halls through the secular and sometimes the religious newspapers, through the publication in other ways of various writings, and through an extensive correspondence. He never expected large results; he and those with and under whom he served were to be used, as they believed, merely in gathering the first fruits of an immeasurably vaster harvest, which should be reaped at Christ's second advent. But he had hoped for more than he ever saw, and frankly confessed his disappointment, though without the smallest weakening of his faith. And the magnitude of the result was after all a matter of detail; a substantial result was visible. He had drawn to his side men, his peers in intellectual and spiritual strength, who sometimes suffered more than he from the heavy hand of sectarianism, and he had brought to the apostolic "sealing" not a few devout and thoughtful Christians, who were often instructed to remain in the bodies in which they had been baptized, because they had not joined a sect. And most who knew him felt the silent, ceaseless influence of his sanctity, of that dwelling in love which is dwelling in God, which so often made men think of the beloved disciple. To many he also imparted convictions which made them stronger and happier, convictions about our Lord's second coming, the unity of the church, the dignity of worship, and the incarnation, as the central truth of Christianity. And since he would call no man a heretic who accepts the ancient creeds, he in effect defended that freedom of Christian thought which is our birthright, frankly to be recognized, if brethren would dwell together in unity. He had, indeed, thrown all his strength into a movement forming no insignificant part of the great Catholic movement of the nineteenth century, which has sought in so many ways to develope the brotherhood of Christians, and of men.

The last years of Mr. Andrews were happy ones, for he worked until the night came, and beautiful with the ripened fruit of holiness. In October, 1897, he was attacked by influenza, and though the attack did not seem very severe, old age, like a mild but universal disease, had prepared the organs in general to give way. He had long hoped to escape death through his Lord's return to the earth, and it may be that he never knew of this crowning disappointment, while he always knew how to make God's will his. On the evening of the 17th of October, he devoutly and thankfully received the Holy Communion. At ten, when all but his nurse had left him, thinking him to be in no immediate danger, he asked her the hour. Then he said "good night" to all. as if all were with him, and as if he expected in a little while to say "good morning," and so "fell on sleep" until the morning of the resurrection from the dead. The funeral was held in the Congregational church at Wethersfield, and, besides the reading of the burial office by two ministers with whom he had served, two others, a Congregationalist and an Episcopalian, paid affectionate tributes, as to a father in God. Thus the last rites were in harmony with that love for all saints which had made his life a benediction, and with his belief in the real if obscured unity of the Church Universal.

A life of Mr. Andrews was prepared by his brother the Rev. Dr. S. J. Andrews of Hartford, and published by the Putnams in 1900.—*Rev. J. G. A.*

Rev. Mr. Andrus, by his first wife, had children, of whom mention will be found in the *Williams Geneal.* in this volume.

ARCHER, BENJAMIN, d. 10 July, 1853, ae. 76; m. 18 July, 1822, Chloe (**Williams**), who d. 7 Jan., 1821, ae. 44 —*W. Rec.*; also, wife of B. prob. 2d. wife), d. 21 Nov., 1856, ae. 73; had by 1st mar. Israel Williams, bp. 5 May, 1826, who d. 15 Feb., 1849, ae. 24.—*S. C. R.*

ARNOLD, AARON C., of Midd., m. Eliza Ann **Smith,** 17 Nov., 1830.—*Weth. Rec.* HARRIET, d. 12 Aug., 1843, at Northampton, in 21st yr.—*Weth. Rec.* JULIUS (from Hartford, d. 25 Apl., 1847, in 43d (or 63d) yr.—*S. C. R.* LAURA, d. 2 Sept., 1839, in 10th yr.—*S. C. R.* SOPHIA, d. 3 Sept., 1834, in 15th yr.— *S. C. R.* TALCOTT A., m. Caroline **Holmes,** both of Ry-H., 5 (*Ch. Rec.,* 9; *Town Rec.*) Mch., 1834; their dau. d. 2 July, 1843, in 2d yr.

ASPINWALL, ELEAZUR, m. Elizabeth **Steel,** 28 June, 1775.—*N. C. R.*

ARTHUR, BARBARA, dau. of Gen. & Barbara, d. 28 Sept., 1861, ae. 6 mos.— *Chr. Lane Cemetery.*

ATWELL, JOHN, s. of John, of Saybrook. who m. [Quartermaster] **Crowfoot's** dau., of Saybrook, bp. 22 May, 1709.—*Mix MSS.* JOSEPH, s. of John, of Saybrook, bp. 21 Oct., 1711.—*Mix MSS.*

ATWOOD, assistance acknowledged from Rev. E. F. ATWOOD, of Hartford, Ct., who credits much of his information to the material gathered by Mr. Francis Atwood, gt-gd-son of Josiah, s. of Dr. Thomas, the Weth. pioneer.

This has been a family of some consequence in Great Britain, no less than sixteen families of the name having their arms entered in the Herald's College. On each side of the Atlantic, it has been a prolific family; and ten of the name had grad. at American colleges prior to 1853.

The name appeared earlier in Mass., than in Conn., JOHN, "Gent.," from London, was made a freeman 1636, and was an assistant in the Plymouth Colony, 1638; he bro't over the value of a large est. with him, and d. in 1644. PHILIP, of Malden, Mass., 1653, came over, ae. 13, in the *Francis,* 1635; HARMON, of Boston, was a memb. of the Anc. and Hon. Artillery Co., 1644, and freeman, 1645; and STEPHEN was founder of the Cape Cod family of the name, 1643.

The *Weth.* Atwoods are descendants of THOMAS, said to have been a captain of a company raised by himself, in Cromwell's "Ironsides" reg't, and that at the battle of Marston Moor, a spent bullet knocked out two front teeth and lodged in his mouth—tho' Savage discredits the tale, and says that he was no captain, but only a physician. He is supposed to have descended from Thomas, "Gent," of Bromfield Co., Essex, Eng., and came to Plymouth, Mass., about 1640, and m. in 1667, Abigail ————————, she being then 17, and he 57 yrs. of age. Trad., also, says that their log cabin was erected on the spot now, at beginning of 20th century, occup. by the Cong. Ch. at P.; and that later he built on the same site, a brick mansion, destroyed by fire within the memory of some recently living. He was joined by a nephew, Edward, from Eng., who engaged with him in the W. I. trade; and it is said that they built the first sea-going vessel at Rocky Hill, and that later, they built vessels, but the nephew d. at sea, and their ppy. was lost.

He came to Weth., not as *Savage* says, in 1688-9, but as *Weth. Rec.* show, as early as 1663; and was a householder there in 1670—see Chapter VII, Vol. I; m. Abigail ————; d. prob. early part of 1682, as the invent. of his est. (£148-06-09) was taken by John Kilborn, Sen., and Thos. Wright, on 24 Oct., of that yr.—see *Ct. Rec.*; 13 Dec., 1682.—*Htfd. Co. Prob.* As a physician, Thomas Atwood had an extensive "ride," extending (as we learn from certain bills and notes found in *Htfd. Prob. Rec.*,) from Saybrook on the South, to Woodbury on the West; and he owned ld. in Rocky Hill, and also West of the Mountain, in Newington, where his ygst. son sett. and this is still occup. by his descendants.

Children (Weth. Rec.):

1. Abigail, b. last day of Sept., 1668.
2. Andrew, b. first day Sept., 1671; drew ld. in the allotment of 1694.—*Weth. Rec.;* d. s. p.
3. Jonathan, b. 8 June, 1675; settled in Wood-bury, Ct.—(See Cothren's *Hist. Woodbury,* I, 490; II, 1471.)
4. Josiah, b. 4 Oct., 1678. FAM. 2.
5. Mary, b. 29 May, 1681.

FAM. 2. JOSIAH,[2] (*Thomas,*[1]), m. to Bathsheba (dau. Bezaleel, dec'd) **Lattimer,** 16 Feb., 1709-10, by John Chester, Ass't. Settled in Newington parish.

Children (Weth. Rec.):

1. Abigail, b. 6 Dec., (bp. 10—*Mix MS.*), 1710; d. 22 Aug., 1747, in 36th yr.—*Weth.* (*N.*) *Insc.*
2. Oliver, b. 1 Mch., 1715-6. FAM. 3.
3. Jedidiah, b. 28 June, 1719. FAM. 4.
4. Josiah, } FAM. 5.
   } twins, b. 13 Apl., 1727.
5. Hezekiah, } FAM. 6.
6. Asher, b. 27 Dec., 1729. FAM. 7.

FAM. 3. OLIVER,[3] (*Josiah,*[2] *Thos.,*[1]), b. 1715-16; m. to Dorothy **Curtis,** 23 Nov., 1746, by Rev. Jas. Lockwood.—*W. C. R.* He was a chairmaker.

Children (Weth. Rec.):

1. Abigail, b. 28 Aug., 1747.
2. Elijah, bp. 26 Oct., 1750.—*N. C. R.*
3. Elijah, b. 28 Aug., 1751, prob. the E. who d. 4 June, 1770.—*N.*
4. Levi, b. and bp. (*N. C. R.*), 10 May, 1752.
5. John, b. 16, bp. 20 Apl., 1755—*N. C. R.;* was a Revol. soldier and d. soon after his disch. from confinement in the Sugar House Prison in N. Y. City.

FAM. 4. JEDIDIAH,[3] (*Josiah,*[2] *Thos.,*[1]), b. 1719; m. (1) Susannah **Deming,** 29 Nov., 1747; she d. 16 Sept., 1758, (*N.*); he m. (2) 22 Nov., 1759, Sarah **Loomis,** res. New.; he was fined Nov., 1745, for criticising the doctrines of Rev. Mr. Wadsworth, of Htfd. 1st Ch.—*Co. Ct. Rec.,* Case 43, Vol. R. *Hinman* says he rem. to N. Y. State.

Children (Weth. Rec.):

1. Timothy, b. 9 Sept., 1749.
2. Bathsheba, (dau. of Jed.), d. 20 Feb., 1761.—*N. C. R.*
3. Josiah, (s. of Jed.), d. 17 Jan., 1758.—*N. C. R.*

FAM. 5. JOSIAH,[3] (*Josiah,*[2] *Thos.,*[1]), m. 13 Apl., 1751, Caroline **Mygatt;** res. New.

Children (Weth. Rec.; bp. N. C. R.):

1. Huldah, b. 28 Jan., d. 22 Oct., 1752.
2. Huldah, b. 13, bp. 24 Mch., 1754.
3. Josiah, d. 3 Feb., 1754.
4. George, bp., 9 Jan., 1756; d. 26th.—*N.*
5. Rhoda, bp. 9 Oct., 1757.
6. Inft. unbp. d. 17 June, 1759.
7. Rhoda, bp. 11 May, 1760.
8. Solomon (Salmon ?).
9. Hosea.
10. Elijah, who res. in Berlin.

FAM. 6. HEZEKIAH,[3] (*Josiah,*[2] *Capt. Thos.,*[1]), m. acc. to the Hinman copy from *Weth. Rec.,* pub. in *N. Eng. Hist. Gen. Register,* XV, 242, wid. Abigail **Hunn;** but D. Williams Patterson, the eminent genealogist, lately dec'd, makes the following note (*N. Eng. Reg.*, XVII, 358) concerning this, viz.: "In examining the *original* record, in Apl., 1862, its position directly after that of Zebulon Stoddard, who m. wid. Abigail Hunn, 21 Mch., 1745, and d. 19 Apl., 1761, led me to suspect an error, which suspicion was confirmed by the *N. Ch. Rec.*, which gives the marr. of Hez. Attwood and wid. Abigail **Stoddard**, 28 Apl., 1763, wh. is confirmed also by *N. Ch. Rec.* He with his wife and two sons, rem. to Gt. Barrington, Mass.

Children (Weth. Rec.):

1. Hezekiah, b. 29 Sept., 1764; Hez. bp. 7 | 2. Phinehas, b. 11, bp. 28 Sept., 1766.—*N. C.* Oct., 1763 (?).—*N. C. R.* | *R.*

FAM. 7.   ASHUR,[3] (*Josiah*,[2] *Thomas*,[1]), b. 1729; he was, in Nov., 1754, a tanner in Weth.—*Co. Ct. Rec.;* m. by Rev. Joshua Belding, Apl., 1757, to Mary **Mitchelson**, of Simsbury; res. Newington parish; he d. 2 Apl., 1808, ae. 77; wid. d. 27 Mch., 1816, ae. 88.—*Weth.* (*N.*) *Inscr.*

Children (Weth. Rec.):

1. Elizabeth, b. 6 Feb., 1759; d. single (*Hin-* | d. (*N. C. R.*) 7 May, 1838, ae. 75.
man)—*N. C. R.* says 11 Oct., 1842, ae. 84. | 3. Ezekiel, b. 19 Aug., 1764. FAM. 8.
2. Mary, b. 12 Dec., 1762; prob. the M. who |

FAM. 8.   EZEKIEL,[4] (*Ashur*,[3] *Josiah*,[2] *Thomas*,[1]), b. 1764; m. 21 Jan., 1793, by Ashbel Gillette (Bapt. Elder) to Hannah **Francis**, sister of the mother of Hon. Francis Gillette. He d. 29 Oct., 1853, ae. 89; she d. 23 Nov., 1833, ae. 64.—*Weth.* (*N.*) *Inscr.*

Children (Weth. Rec.):

1. Josiah, b. 26 Apl., 1794. FAM. 9. | i. Sarah M. (Stanwood), m. ————
2. Sarah, b. 11 Mch., 1796; m. Rev. Henry | **Thomas**, and res. Kalamazoo, Mich.
Stanwood, who d. Missouri, 1860, ae. 64. | 3. Francis, b. 29 Aug., 1803. FAM. 10.
Issue: |

FAM. 9.   JOSIAH,[5] (*Ezekiel*,[4] *Ashur*,[3] *Josiah*,[2] *Thomas*,[1]), b. 1794; m. (*N. C. R.*) 18 Oct., 1819, Prudence (dau. Capt. Martin) **Kellogg**, of New.

Children (Weth. Rec.):

1. Charles Kellogg, b. 24 Dec., 1820; bp. 5 | i. Francis (Kirkham).
Aug., 1821—*N.;* killed on railroad, unm. | ii. Henry K. (Kirkham).
6 Aug., 1898. | iii. Thomas A. (Kirkham), of Bridge-
2. Josiah Elbert, b. 20 Feb., bp. 6 July (*N.*), | port, Ct.
1823; m. Jerusha **Ellis**, 1854; had a s. | iv. John H. (Kirkham), lawyer, New
Elbert, who m. and had a s. | Britain, Ct.
3. Thomas Robbins, b. 20 Jan., bp. 24 Oct. | v. Mary H. (Kirkham).
(*N*), 1824; unm. | 5. Mary Kellogg, b. and bo. 26 Feb., 1830
4. John Mitchelson, b. 11 Feb., 1826, bp. 4 June | (*N.*); m. 17 Jan., 1885, the widower of her
(*N.*), 1826, unm.; lawyer and judge at | sister Hannah P., viz.: J. S. Kirkham.
Witchita, Kan.; now a farmer. | *No issue.*
5. Hannah Prudence, b. 17 May, bp. 19 Aug. | 6. Julia Norton, b. 5 Sept., 1831; bp. 10 June,
(*N.*), 1827; m. 1 Dec., 1859, J. S. **Kirkham**; | 1832—*N.;* unm.; res. Newington, Ct.
she d. 1 Dec., 1882, ae. 55. *Issue:* |

FAM. 10.   FRANCIS,[6] (*Ezekiel*,[5] *Josiah*,[4] *Ashur*,[3] *Josiah*,[2] *Thomas*,[1]), b. 1803; m. Eunice **White**, 14 July, 1840; she d. 23 Dec., 1895; he d. 9 Oct., 1881, ae. 78. —*Weth.* (*N.*) *Inscr.*

Children:

1. Herman, b. 22 Nov., 1841. FAM. 11. | 3. Henry Stanwood, b. 18 June, 1847. FAM. 12.
2. Oliver, b. Sept., 1843; d. unm. 11 Feb., 1888. |

FAM. 11.   HERMAN,[7] (*Francis*,[6] *Ezekiel*,[5] *Josiah*,[4] *Arthur*,[3] *Josiah*,[2] *Thomas*,[1]), b. 1841; m. Josephine **Chamberlain**. He was a prominent druggist and Vice Pres. of the College of Pharmacy in N. Y. City.

Children:

1. Carrie L. | 2. Mable J.

FAM. 12. HENRY STANWOOD,[7] (*Francis,[6] Ezekiel,[5] Josiah,[4] Arthur,[3] Josiah,[2] Thomas,[1]*), b. 1847; m. 31 Mch., 1886, Hattie M. **Brewer**, of New Britain, Ct.

Children:

1. Louise, b. 27 July, 1887. | 2. Florence, b. July, 1892 ; d. 1895. | 3. Shirley, b. 31 Mch., 1896.

Descendants of Doctor JONATHAN ATWOOD, second son of Dr. (or Capt.) Thomas, who removed to Woodbury, Ct.

In 1854, Cothren (*Hist. Woodbury, Ct.*) records 278 descendants of this Dr. Jonathan, in that town; and, in 1868, 54 voters of the name were registered in the town of Woodbury and in Watertown, adjoining.

Dr. JONATHAN,[2] (*Thomas,[1]*), m. Sarah **Terrell**, 5 Nov., 1701.

Children:

1. Nathan, b. Sept., 1702 ; m. and d. 1726. *Issue ;*
  i. Elijah, b. 11 Apl., 1704 ; d. 1804. 1804.
  ii. Sarah, b. 29 June, 1726.
2. Mary, b. Oct., 1703 ; d. Dec., following.

3. Mary, b. 20 Apl., 1705 ; mother of Dr. Seth Atwood **Bird**.
4. Jonathan (Lieut.), b. 9 Sept., 1710 ; d. 1783.
5. Oliver, b. 11 Mch., 1717 ; d. 30 Jan., 1810. FAM. 2.

FAM. 2. OLIVER,[3] (*Dr. Jonathan,[2] Dr. Thomas,[1]*), b. 1710; m. (1) 12 Nov., 1740, Lois **Wheeler;** m. (2) Nancy **Wells;** m. (3) Naomi **Fairchild.**

Children:

1. Nathan (Dea).
2. Gideon.
3. Elisha.
4. Ann.

  (*By second marriage*) :
5. John, b. 19 Mch., 1749. FAM. 3.
6. Wells.
7. Nancy.

FAM. 3. JOHN,[4] (*Oliver,[3] Dr. Jonathan,[2] Dr. Thomas,[1]*), b. 1749; m. (1) Concurrence **Hurd;** m. (2) Martha **Brooks;** m. (3) Phebe **Northup.**

Children (by first marriage) :

1. Lucy. | 2. Truman. | 3. Ann. | 4. James, b. 1775 ; d. 1862. FAM. 4

FAM. 4. JAMES,[5] (*John,[4] Dr. Jonathan,[3] Oliver,[2] Thomas,[1]*), b. 1775; m. (1) Prudence **Stoddard**, 24 Aug., 1798; m. (2) Abigail **Lewis;** m. (3) Rosetta **Cheveroy.** His 1st wife, b. 11 Aug., 1775, was gt-gd-dau. of Rev. Anthony Stoddard, who for 61 yrs. was pastor of the 1st Ch. of Woodbury, Ct., and her mother was Esther Warham, dau. Rev. John, the 1st pastor at Windsor, Ct. James Atwood was an active founder of the first Meth. Epis. church in Woodbury, Ct., and for 36 yrs. a class-leader.

Children (all by first wife) :

1. Olive. m. Elmore **Judson.**
2. Frederick Stoddard, b. 1800. FAM. 5.
3. Sylvia, m. Hiram **Warner** (?).

4. John Bird, m. Maria **Lewis;** had three daus. and a s. who d. in Civil War.

FAM. 5. FREDERICK STODDARD,[6] (*James,[5] John,[4] Dr. Jonathan,[3] Oliver,[2] Thomas,[1]*), b. 1800; m. (1) Maria **Tuttle;** m. (2) wid. Awelia **Scott;** m. (3) wid. Sarah **Hurd.**

Children (by first marriage) :

1. Abiram Stoddard, b. 9 Apl., 1824 ; d. 2 May, 1872. FAM. 6.
2. Chauncey H., m. Abby **Hamlin**, of Bristol, Ct. ; had a s.
3. Jannet, m. Nathan **Warner, Jr.;** had a dau.

4. George, m. Huldah **Carrington**, of Bristol, Ct., 1858 ; had a s., Chauncey, and dau. Jennie, who m. Camillus **Johnson;** res. in Newington, Ct. ; has 10 ch.

FAM. 6. ABIRAM STODDARD,[7] (*Fred. S.,[6] James,[5] John,[4] Dr. Jonathan,[3] Oliver,[2] Thomas,[1]*), b. 1824 ; m. wid. Cornelia **North**, Jan., 1846 ; res. Bristol, Ct.

Children:

1. Eugene (Rev.), b. 14 Mch., 1847; served 3 yrs. as private in War of the Civil Rebellion before he was 18; prepared for college at a private acad. in Woodbury, and at the Colgate Academy, Hamilton, N. Y.; ent. Oberlin College, Ohio, 1870; grad. June, 1875, from Oberlin Theol. Sem.; ordained at Arcade, N. Y., Dec., 1875; spent 3 yrs. in home missionary work at Deadwood, Dak.; ret. to Conn., has held several pastorates: chaplain of Weth. Prison for 2 yrs.; retired 1895; res. Hartford, Ct.
2. Ernest, m., res. Oakland, Cal.; has 4 ch.
3. Mary, m. John **Tanner**; res. Terryville, Ct.; one son, Leverett.
4. Nellie G., m. Egbert **Healy**; res. Plainville, Ct.; one son.
5. J. Hubert, m. Addie **Norten**; res. Bristol, Ct.; two sons.

MARY, ae. 88, d. 27 Mch., 1816.—*N. C. R.*

AUSTIN, BENJAMIN, had Anne Goodrich bp. 25 Nov., 1798.—*W. C. R.* CALEB inf. bu. 22 Feb., 1831. ae. 1 yr.: MOSES, bp. 16 Dec., 1830.—*W. C. R.* ABIGAIL, dau. of *Caleb & Laura*, b. 10 Aug., 1833.—*W. T. Rec.* ANNE

AVERY, ELISHA P., of Breckesville, O., m. Betsy **Goodrich**, 27 May, 1841.— *S. C. R.*

AYRAULT, (Arolt). This name said to be Belgian; always referred to on *Weth. Rec.* as French. Assistance in this sketch acknowledged, esp. in later descendants, from Mrs. MARIA H. BURDITT, of Weth.

NICHOLAS and PIERRE,* brothers and both physicians, came to this country, 1687, shortly after the revocation of the Edict of Nantes, as members (some say leaders) of a party of Huguenots. PIERRE† set. and d. in Rhode Island. NICHOLAS m. there, Marian **Bretoun**, also a Huguenot, whose acquaintance he had made on the voyage hither. He sett. in Weth., was apparently a man of means and good social standing. "Dr. Nicholas Ayrault, a French Huguenot, Died May 6, 1706-7, aged 37."—*Weth. Ins. Weth. Rec.* says he "d. 4 Mch., 1705-6, ae. abt. 50 yrs., his age not clearly known." His will, made 2 Mch., 1706-7, in presence of Moses Crafts. Steph. Hurlbutt and P. Alcock, witnesses, and proven on the 8th of Mch., devising "the Worldly Goods & Estate the Lord hath Lent me," gives to his "dear and loving wife Marian Ayrault," whom he constitutes his sole executrix, "all the rest and residue of my estate, goods & chattels whatsoever, in France, not herein before bequeathed, after my debts and funeral expenses are discharged" to be at her disposal, "so long as she continues a wid.;" but, in default thereof, two-thirds of his est. to be div'd among his ch. To his son Peter, he gave his "gold buttons." Dr. Ayrault's wid. d. 27 Aug., 1741, ae., 60.—*Weth. Ins.*

Children (Weth. Rec.):

1. Mary (prob. Marian), who d. 13 Aug., 1778, in 85th yr., which would make her b. 1693 (?).—*W. C. R.*
2. Easter (Esther), b. 5 Mch., 1698-9.
3. Peter, b. 4, bp. (6 Dec.—*Mix MSS.*), 1702-3. FAM. ?.
4. Nicholas, b. 2 Oct., 1705. FAM. 3.

PETER,² (*Dr. Nicholas,¹*), bp. 1702-3; m. 12 Nov., 1744, Mary **Francis**—*Weth. Rec.*;* prob. the Peter who d. (*W. C. R.*) 28 Oct., 1779, ae. 77; wid. m. (2) John Francis,† by whom she had three children.

---

* *Hinman* (p. 90) speaks of two Ayraults, but calls him Samuel, instead of Pierre; and thinks Dr. Nicholas was prob. a bro. or son of Dr. Samuel. *Savage* (I, 85), referring to this supp. of Hinman's, says: "It would not surprise me to have it ascertained that Hinman's Samuel was the same as *Stephen*, Newport, 1685, one of the blessed army of French Protestant exiles. His s. ·Daniel m. 9 May, 1703, Mary Robinson of N. Y."
Another account says that he m. Mary Dodd, of Htfd., and that they had also, *Elizabeth*, b. 1752, who m. James Hosmer; *Stephen*, b. 1749; *Lydia*, b. 1754; *Peter*, b. 1760. But we accredit only what the *Weth. Rec.* and *Ins.* give, as above.
† Prob. the wife of Peter A., who was bp. 17 Aug., 1771.—*W. Ch. Rec.*

Children (*Weth. Town and Ch. Rec.*):

1. Stephen, b. and bp. 8 Aug., 1743; d. 9 Aug., 1745.
2. Marianna, b. 26, bp. 29, Sept., 1745; bp. 16 Nov., 1746; m. Simeon **Griswold**, 4 May, 1769.—See *Griswold*.
3. Stephen, b. 22, bp. 27 Sept., 1747.
4. Peter, bp. 13 Oct., 1754.
5. Elizabeth, bp. 3 Sept., 1749.
6. Lydia, bp. 5 July, 1752.

FAM. 3. Capt. NICHOLAS,[2] (*Dr. Nicholas,*[1]), b. 1705; m. Jane (dau. Daniel) **Stocking,** of Midd., 17 Apl., 1730.—*Weth. Rec.;* he d. 29 Apl., bu. 2 May, 1775—*W. C. R.;* ae. 70; she d. 26 or 31—*W. C. R.,* Oct., 1783, ae. 70.—*Weth. Ins.* A *Co. Ct. Rec* of Apl., 1732, shows him to have been a tanner.

Children (*Weth. Rec.*):

1. James, b. 17 Sept., 1730.
2. Marian, b. (and bp.—*Mix MSS.*) 6 May, 1733; d. 26 Jan., 1737-8.—*Weth. Ins.*
3. Daniel, b. 8 Dec., 1735. FAM. 5.
4. Marian, b. 25 Feb., 1737; d. 5 Sept., 1741; *Hinman* erroneously says d. 1749.
5. Nicholas, b. and d. 1 May, 1740.
6. Jane, b. 6, bp. 24 Mch., 1741-2; m. Ashbel **Riley.**
7. Nicholas, b. 11 (18—*Hinman*), bp. 21 (*Weth. Ch. Rec.*) Oct., 1744; d. 29 Mch., 1749-50.
8. Marian, b. 5 Nov., 1746; d. 26 (25—*Weth. Ins.*) Feb., 1747-8.

FAM. 4. JAMES,[3] (*Capt. Nicholas,*[2] *Dr. Nicholas,*[1]), b. 1730; m. Abigail **Kilborn,** 2 Jan., 1755.—*W. Ch. Rec. Ch. Rec.* ment. James & wife as having joined the church in 1754.

Children (*Weth. Ch. Rec.*):

1. Ebenezer, bp. 11 Dec., 1748.
2. Mary Ann, bp. 6 Feb., 1757.
3. Jane, bp. betw. 10 Apl. and May 1, 1757.
4. Dau. bp. 14 Jan., 1759.
5. Nicholas, bp. 14 June, 1761.

FAM. 5. DANIEL,[3] (*Capt. Nicholas,*[2] *Dr. Nicholas,*[1]), b. 1735; m. (1) 26 July, 1759; —*Weth. Ch. Rec.* says betw. June 19 and 20; (*Hinman* says, erroneously, 20 Mch. 1750), Lucy **Williams;** he d. 8 Mch., 1807, ae. 71—*W. C. R.;* she d. Sept., 5, 1852, ae. 100.—*Weth. Ins.;* she prob. the wife who d. ae. 44, 2 Oct., 1781 —*W. C. R.;* he m. (2) Mary (dau. Ebenezer) **Balch.** 1784, who d. 16 Sept., 1852, ae. 100.

Children (*Weth. Ins.*):

1. Lucy (in rec. *Lousy,* prob. for Louise, the Fr. name), b. 12 May, bp. betw. 20 Apl. and Sept. 18 (*Weth. Cr. Rec.*), 1760; prob. the L. who m. Abner **Wilcox,** of Killingworth, 22 July, 1782.—*Weth. Ch. Rec.*

Children (*by second marriage*):

2. Daniel, b. Oct., bp. 12 Nov., 1786. FAM. 6.
3. Mary, b. May, bp. 11 June, 1785—*W. C. R.;* d. Feb., 1854; who m. Edward **Shepherd;** had *issue:*
   i. Charles (Shepherd).
   ii. Edward (Shepherd).
   iii. Elizabeth (Shepherd).
   iv. Mary Ann (Shepherd).
   v. Daniel Ayrault (Shepherd), res. Cleveland, O., 1884. *et alios.*

FAM. 6. DANIEL,[4] (*Daniel,*[3] *Capt. Nicholas,*[2] *Dr. Nicholas,*[1]), m. Hepzibah **Kentfield:** he d. 11 Nov., 1862 or 8, ae. 82; she d. 23 Aug., 1871, ae. 74.—*Weth. Ins.*

Children:

1. Mary M., b. 1826; d. 29 Apl., 1895, ae. 69.—*Weth. Ins.; unm.*
2. Jane, m. Rev. Joseph **Bailey,** of Midd. *Issue:*
   i. Joseph, Rev. (Bailey), of Edgartown, Mass.; no ch.
   ii. Marian Bretoun (Bailey), m. ——— **Langzethel.** *No children.*
   iii. Jennie Bretoun (Bailey), m. ——— res. in Middlefield; four ch.
   iv. Vincent (Bailey), res. Htfd., unm.
3. Antoinette, m. Geo. **Story,** of Htfd. *Issue:*
   i. Arthur N. (Story), m. Charlotte **Carroll,** of Htfd.; six ch.
   ii. Louis (Story), res. N. Y.; four ch.
4. Louise, m. Ed. D. Redfield, of Essex, Ct. *Issue:*
   i. Mary (Redfield), m. Geo. **Dickinson;** is now a wid., Essex, Ct.
   ii. Hosmer P. (Redfield), m. Mary **Welles,** of Weth.; res. Htfd.; had a son Dudley.
   iii. Edward D. (Redfield), m. Marietta **Griswold,** of Fulton, Ill.; res. Htfd.; two ch.
   iv. Lily (Redfield), m. Walter H. **Wright;** res. Centerbrook, Ct.; four ch.

Miscellanea:

DANIEL, d. 5 Sept., 1846, ae 7.—*Weth. Ins.* DANIEL, m. Mary **Balch**, of Weth.,
1 July, 1784.—*N. C. R.* DANIEL, wife of, ae. 44, bu. 2 Oct., 1781.—*W. C. R.*
MARY, dau. of Daniel, ae. 2, bu. 31 Dec., 1824; DANIEL, s. of Daniel, bp.
5 Nov., 1786; MARY, dau. of Daniel, bp. 5 June, 1785.—*W. C. R.* STEPHEN,
bu. 26 Dec., 1759.—*W. C. R.* PETER, the wife of, d. 17 Aug., 1776.

BACKUS, Rev. SIMON, s. of Joseph, of Norwich, Ct., and b. 11 Feb., 1701; became
pator of ch. at New.—see Chapter XVIII, Vol. I; m. 1 Oct., 1729—(*Weth.
Rec.*), Eunice (dau. Rev. Timothy) **Edwards**, of (E.) Windsor, Ct.; he d.
Louisburg, Isld. of Cape Breton, "having gone there as Chaplain of the Army
of the New Eng. Colonies," 2 Feb., 1746. His wid. d. E. Windsor, 1 June,
1788, ae. 83.

Children (Weth. Rec.):

1. Clorinda, b. 31 Oct., 1730; m. Zebadiah
   Lathrop, of Norwich, Ct., abt. 1750, and
   d. 25 Oct., 1803, ae. 73; six ch.—See Goodwin's *Geneal. Notes,* 303.
2. Eunice, b. 15 Jan., 1732-3; d. E. Windsor,
   1808; unm.
3. Elizabeth, b. 19 May, 1734; m. David **Bissell**, prob. of E. W., 25 Feb., 1761; he d.
   16 Dec., 1799; 6 ch.—See *Goodwin's Gen.
   Notes* 303. See, also, *Stiles' Ancient
   Windsor, II,* 87, where an erroneous parentage is given to Elizabeth (*Backus*)
   Bissell.
4. Simon (Rev.), b. 13 Feb., 1738; pastor (1)

   of ch. at Granby, Mass., and (2) of ch.
   in Guilford, Ct.; see for desc'ts *Goodwin's
   Gen. Notes, 304.*
5. Esther, b. 19 Nov. 1739; m. 1 June, 1758,
   Benj. **Ely**, of West Springfield (Holyoke),
   Mass.; she d. 19 Sept., ae. near 81.—See
   Goodwin's Geneal. Notes, 304-5.
6. Joseph, b. 30 May, 1741; d. abt. 1 Jan., 1742.
7. Jerusha, b. 13 Jan., 1743; m. abt. 1765,
   Smith **Bailey**, of E. W.; 4 ch.—See *Goodwin's Geneal. Notes, 305.*
8. Mary, b. 24 Mch., 1745; d. E. W., 27 Dec.,
   1751.

ELIZUR, of Albany, m. Elizabeth **Chester**, 8 June, 1809.—*W. T. R.* See Goodwin's
Geneal. Notes, 17.

BACON, RICHARD had (*W. C. R.*):

1. Richard, } bp. 20 June, 1791.
2. Henry, }
3. Allyn, bp. 20 June, 1791.
4. George, bp. 11 Mch., 1792.

BATHSHEBA—Wid. of Joel, d. 22 Dec., 1849, ae. 80.—*Weth. Ins. (B. Q.)*

BADGER.—This name, in Weth., dates from 1812, when ELEAZER,[6] (s.
of *Moses*[5] & Jerusha Janes; s. of *Daniel*,[4] b. 1698, & Mary Weld, of No. Coventry;
s. of *Nathaniel*,[3] b. 1676, & Mary Sweet; s. of *John*,[2] mcht. of Newbury, Mass.,
by his 2d wife, Hannah *Weave;* s. of *Giles*,[1] the emigrant to America, 1635,
& Elizabeth Greenleaf), rem. here from No. Coventry: and m. 1812, Harriet
(dau. Michael & Catherine *Perrin*) **Bridgen**, who was b. 28 Jan., 1780. They
both rem. to and d. at Sanquoit, N. Y.

Children:

1. Charles Whiting, b. 1 Apl., 1814. FAM. 2.
2. Alfred Goodrich.
3. Cornelia.
4. Harriet.

FAM. 2. CHARLES WHITING,[7] (*Eleazor*,[6] *Moses*,[5] *Daniel*,[4] *Nath'l*,[3] *John*,[2] *Giles*,[1]),
rem. to Newark, N. J., 1836; invested largely in real estate while N. was yet a
town; m. 12 Oct., 1842, in Weth., Rhoda **Stillman**.

Children (b. Newark, N. J.):

1. Harriet E., b. 9 Oct., 1843; m. Robert S.
   Grummon, of N., 22 Jan., 1864. *Issue:*
   i. Charles Alfred (Grummon), b. 31 Oct.,
   1864.
2. Kate B., b. 3 Jan., 1846.
3. Alfred S., b. 11 Nov., 1848; d. Jan., 1863.

BAILEY.—(*From Step. Ch. Rec.*)—ALFRED, had dau. Rosella **Clark**, bp. 1 Jan., 1830; he d. 20 Aug., 1862, ae. 69. JAMES, of Hadd., m. Nancy **Belden**, 15 Apl., 1848. JOHN A., of N. Y., m. Sarah **Kelsey**, 15 Oct., 1854; ROMANZO N., of St. Louis, Mo., m. Adeline **Pulsifer**, 15 Aug., 1848.

ASA STANTON, m. Amelia **Stillman**, 28 Nov., 15——*W. C. R.;* he d. 21 Mch., 1821, in 34th yr.—*Weth. Ins.;* she d. 2 Mch., 1874, ae. 81—*W. Ins.;* had (*Weth. Ins. and W. C. R.*) : 1. Henry Stillman, b. 16 Aug., bp. 13 Oct., 1816; d. 13 Nov., 1838. 2, Jane Amelia, b. 26 Apl.; bp. 11 Oct., 1818; d. 13 May, 1838. 3. Caroline Maria, b. 25 Aug., bp. 25 Nov., —*W. C. R.*, 1821; d. 1 Nov., *W. C. R.*, 1821; d. 1 Nov., 1838, ae. 17 yrs.—(*Weth. Ch. Rec.*) :

From Weth. Ins.:—FREDERICK W., d. 3 May, 1876. SARAH, wife of *Timothy*, d. 14 Mch., 1823, ae. 49 yrs. EVERETT L., b. 15 Aug., 1852; d. 30 July, 1854. THERESA. B., b. 31 Aug., 1849; d. 5 Oct., 1873. ARNOLD, b. 17 Dec., 1814, d. 18 Mch., 1865. WILLIAM, d. 16 May, 1846, ae. 64; Polly **Goodrich**, his wife, d. 22 Nov., 1871, ae. 79. ————, s. of Mrs. J., ————., d. 31 Oct., 1852.—*S. C. R.*

BAKER, SAMUEL.—*Hinman*, p. 110, says he m. (1) Sarah **Cook**, 1670, and (2) Mary ————, 19 May, 1687.—*Weth. Rec. Children* (*Weth. Rec.*) : 1. William, b. 14 June, 1689. 2. Ann, b. 15 Nov., 1691.

TIMOTHY, of Weth., d. 1709; ment. by *Hinman: Htfd. Co. Prob. Rec.* shows that the invent. of his est. was taken 15 Dec., 1709, by Moses Craft and Hez. Deming; value £21·08·08; adm. gr. to Jonathan Deming, Jr., and that Wm. Brown of N. J., appeared before the Ct. with proof that he was the "only brother" to the dec'd, and the est. was paid over to him.

EBENEZER, of Boston, m. Prudence **Bulkley**, 9 Aug., 1812.—*S. C. R.*

JOHN, ae. 16, d. 13 Nov., 1815.—*W. C. R.*

MARTYN, of New Lond., m. Mabel **Weaver**, of E. Htfd., 4 Oct., 1792.—*W. C. R.*

BALCH.—(Name derived from the "baldechin," or canopy carried over princes, or over the Host in public processions, etc.—old form *Balchin.*)

EBENEZER,[5] (*Joseph*,[4] a sea-captain, dr. at Antigua, 1732, & Mary Osgood: *Samuel*,[3] b. 1659; *Benjamin*,[2] said to be the first white male b. in the Bay Colony, 1628 ; *John*,[1] who came from Co. Somerset, Eng., to Salem, Mass., 1623) ; b. at Boston, 1723, goldsmith and clock-maker; rem. to Htfd. early as 1744, and 12 Apl., 1756, rem to Weth.; m. (1) 28 June, 1750, Sarah (dau. Capt. Jonathan) **Belding**, of Weth. (*W. C. R.*), who d. 3 Apl., 1756, in 29 yr.; m. (2) Lois (dau. Ezra) **Belding**, and cousin of his first wife, 29 Nov., 1756; she d. 22 May, 1793, ae. 56,—*W. C. R.* He d. at W. Htfd. 28 Apl., 1807, ae. 84.

Children (*Weth. Rec.; mar. from Balch Geneal.*[*]) :

1. Sarah, b. Htfd., 1 Apl., 1751 ; m. 12 Nov., 1772, Elijah (s. Joseph) **Welles**, of W. ; b. 27 Feb., 1751 ; she d. W., 4 Mch., 1823.
2. Mary, b. Htfd., 17 Nov., 1752 ; m. 1784, Daniel (s. Capt. Nicholas) **Ayrault**; d. W., 16 Sept., 1852, ae. 100 yrs.
3. Jonathan Belding, b. Htfd., 14 Nov., 1754 ; m. W., 8 Dec., 1766, Hopeful (dau. Sam'l) **Hulburt**; *W. C. R.;* res. Htfd. ; Revol. soldier, see Vol. I, XI ; m. 18 Jan., 1819,

Elenor **Whitman**; he d. 16 Feb., 1825. 6 ch.
4. Levi, b. 27 Feb., 1758 ; d. 15 Aug., 1760.
5. Joseph, b. 16 or 20 Dec., 1760 ; bp. 17 Feb., 1760-1; d. Johnstown, N. Y.; was drummer boy in Revol. ; clockmaker and silversmith ; rem. to J. 1810, and m. Mary **Watson**; 7 ch.
6. Lois, b. 16 or 20 Dec., 1760 ; bp. 17 Feb., 1760-1; m. Oliver (s. Joseph & Sarah) **Talcott**, of Glast. ; res. Southwick, Mass.;

[*] *Geneal. of the Balch Families in America.* By Galusha B. Balch, Salem, Mass., 1897, 8 vo., 553 pp.

rem. 1819 to Cleveland, O., where she d. 1852.
7. Lucy, b. 21 Dec., 1763 ; m. Wait **Goodrich** (sea capt.), of Weth. ; d. 17 July, 1854 ; bu. Weth.
8. Ebenezer, b. Weth., 30 Aug., 1766 ; m. abt. 1790, Sarah (dau. James & Abigail *King*) **Burchard**; was a goldsmith and clockmaker, but did not follow the trade ; in 1800 rem. to Plattsburg, N. Y., built a ho. and engaged in shipping timber to Quebec

by rafts ; built the first Pres. ch. at P.; was in the battle of P. in War of 1812 ; he d. 31 Dec., 1843.
9. Timothy, b. Weth. 26 Oct., 1768 ; m.Ann **Whitman**; rem. to Plattsburg, N. Y., and res nr. his bro. Ebenezer ; he d. 22 Nov., 1844 ; had 9 ch.
10. William, b. 17 May, bp. 19 July, 1778 ; carpenter ; m. Ann **Smith**; d. W. Htfd. 31 Mch., 1857 ; 6 ch.

NATHANIEL, of Stonington, Ct., m. Esther **Deming**, 23 Dec., 1777.—*W. C. R.*

BALDWIN, HIRAM'S ch. d. 8 Oct., 1844, in third year.—*S. C. R.* JUNIUS E., of Winchester, Ct., m. Mehitable S. **Belden**, 30 Mch., 1845. MERRITT, of New Htfd., m. Rhoda **Wells**, of Weth., 1 Nov., 1807.—*W. T. R.* NATHAN, m. Mary **Deming**, 7 Dec., 1783, both of Weth.; she bu. 30 Nov., 1787, ae. 29. —*W. C. R.* THEODORE W., d. abt. 7 Apl., 1855, ae. 16.—*S. C. R.*

BAMBOREA, (*Bemborea*), HENRY, d. 26 Dec., 1805, in 61st yr.—*S. C. R.; had inf. which d. 10 May, 1792.—*W. C. R.*

BANCROFT, THOMAS, of West Hampton, d. 2 Aug., 1800, ae. 20.—*W. C. R.*

BARBER, GRANDISON, of Windsor, m. Laura [dau. of Maj. Justus] Francis, of Weth., 20 Nov., 1816.—*N. C. R.*

BARBOUR, GEORGE H., (desc'd from *Thomas*, the Settler at Windsor, Ct.) ; m. 23 June, 1869, Kathren (dau. Wm. H. and Susan *Robertson*) **Hawley**; sett. at Detroit, Mich.

Children

1. Edwin S., b. 11 May, 1870.
2. Grace L., b. 5 Aug., 1874 ; m. Joshua **Rhodes**, of Pittsburg, Pa., 26 Oct., 1898.

They have two daus.
3. Estelle, b. 30 June, 1878.
4. George, b. 25 Nov., 1880.

BARNARD, JOHN, from Htfd.; owned lds. in Weth. Great Meadow, 1660. Is this the J. of Hadley, formerly of Htfd., whose will ment. the ch. of his kinsman Henry Hayward of Weth.?

JAMES, of Htfd., m. Elizabeth **Goodrich**, 8 Sept., 1805.

Dr. ——————, inf. of, bp. 1 Aug., 1788.—*W. C. R.*

EBENEZER, m. Thankful Neckels, (**Nicolls**) of Htfd., 17 July, 1747.—*W. Ch. Rec.*

SAMUEL, m. Mehitable **Wells**, 6 July, 1786; had (*W. C. R.*) :

Children :

1. Nancy Clarke, bp. 25 Mch., 1787.
2. Sylvester, bp. 3 Jan., 1790.
3. John, bp. Oct., 1791.

4. Mary Wells, bp. 29 Sept., 1793.
5. Catharine, bp. 28 Aug., 1796.

BARNES, JOHN,[1] (furnished by Mrs. R. M. TUTTLE, Hornellsville, N. Y.), b. Eng., 1708; immigrated to America, 1730; m. a **Hesselton**, of Boston; served as a soldier at Quebec, under Gen. Wolfe; d. at Quebec, of "hepatic consumption," after its surrender to the Br., in 1762.

Children :

1. Joseph.
2. Josiah.

3. John. FAM. 2.
4. Amos.

5-6-7. And 3 daus.

Fam. 2. JOHN, Jr.,[2] (*John*,[1]), b. Concord, Mass., 19 Sept., 1740; was a soldier, with his father, under Wolfe at Quebec; and while there made and figured a powder-horn, dated Quebec, Dec. 20, 1762. After his return home, 1763, he went to Htfd., to visit a sister (wife of Nicholas Brown) and there he prob. met with Esther **Blin,** of Weth., whom he m. 23 Feb., 1764, and of whom her son Aziel has left this description, written in his 85th yr.:

"Our mother was a woman rare,
Of French extract, uncommon fair,
Her stature short, she seemed the height
Of God's own angels robed in light.
A form genteel, a sprightly mind,
Discreet, chaste, modest and refined
And in the kingdom of her home
She was Cornelia of Old Rome.

"Our mother, lovely Esther Barnes,
Was worthy of her thousand charms,
Her blooming cheeks, a mouth most
  sweet,
Her swelling bust, her little feet,
Her forehead broad, her auburn hair,
Her piercing eyes made her most fair
And handsome to her seven boys!
She was their queen—they were her
  joys."

John Barnes early entered the army, upon the opening of the War of the Revol., and, as sergeant, served for 5 yrs.; after its close, he rem. 1787, to Benson, Vt., and d. there, 16 May, 1790, "from the fatigues of the war." His account book, from 1764 to '87, is still in possession of his desc'ts, containing the names of many of the Weth., residents during that period, and with the signatures of both parties, where settlements were effected. He was a "general" mechanic, and his entries are for all kinds of work, from making a coffin to mending a chaise, from articles of furniture to squares of window sashes. In July and August, 1776, there are many charges for mending gunstocks. An astonishing thing to us, of this day, is the number of entries, both credit and contra-credit, of "a qt. Rum." It was in 1764, and as the eye goes along the columns, it is also noticeable that for years there is no mention of coffee, and only occasionally of a pound of tea. Cider was plenty and probably was used in the same manner as the common wine of the old country. The bookkeeping is scrupulously exact, although "a days' work, and a piece of a day," would convey to the mind of a person now a different idea from the time it was written. The charges are in pounds, shillings and pence. It is a book of deal with fellowcraftsmen and not strictly a family expense book, albeit there are items in the contra-credit column of articles for family use, as, shoes for "Edmund" and "Melvin" and "a pair of shoes for my wife." Sugar is bought in small quantities. There were maple sugar and honey and molasses for common sweets. Tobacco was used, and was smoked, as there are entries for pipes. Snuff is also a commodity used, beef and mutton were bought by the quantity, in the fall, and not by the pound as is customary at present.

The spelling and penmanship are excellent, though the spelling is sometimes phonetic, giving the pronunciation of 1764. Chair is "chear," and chest is always "chist." Flax and wool were used, and wheels and spools were of the things made and mended. Onions were sold by "ropes," not bushels. "To onions fifty ropes" is one charge. Hannah Dickinson, who is charged with a "case of draws made" and one "skeel" must have been a dressmaker for there is contra-credit "a gown altered" and a "boy's gown" made. Widow Sarah Riley had a "chist" a "pair of fliers," and two spools made. Abraham Blinn, a "set chist," 3 dozen button-molds, a bread bowl and candle-stand mended, Square tables and round tables and candle-stands were made and gun stocks and teapot-handles made as good as new; coffins were made and cradles mended in the workshop of Grandfather John; and the story is an interesting one of work done.—*E. G. T.*'

Children (*Weth. Rec.**; *Fam. Rec.†*; *bp. S. C. R.*) :

1. John, b. Monday,† 10 June, bp. 20 Oct., 1765 ; d. in Old Jersey Prison Ship July or Aug., 1782.†
2. Aziel, b. Friday,† 21 Aug., 1767 ; bp. 27 Sept., 1767.—*S. C. R.* FAM. 3.
3. Edmund, b. Wednesday, 17 Jan., 1770 ; bp. 1 Apl., 1770 ; d. 1779 ;† "Edmund Barnes, son of Mr. John Barnes & Mrs. Esther Barnes, who passed the painful operation of cutting for the stone in the bladder,

March 3d, 1779 & died on the 23d in the 10th yr. of his age. FAM. 3.—*Weth. Inscrip.*
4. Melvin, b. Friday,† 8 May, bp. 26 July, 1772.*
5. Anson, b. Saturday,† 4, bp. 7 Mch., 1775 ;* d. 1793.†
6. Edmund, b. Thursday,† 2 Dec., 1779.*
7. John Hesselton, (Hazeltine, *S. C. R.*), b. Wednesday, 7 Aug., bp. 3 Nov., (*S. C. R.*), 1782 ;* d. 1828.†

FAM. 3. AZIEL,[3] (*John,*[2] *John,*[1]), b. 1767; rem. to Benson, Vt., 1787; m. 14 June, 1792, Eleanor, (dau. Ebenezer & Lydia) **Cooley;** he died at Hornellsville, N. Y., 19 Sept., 1857; was a builder, and the birthplaces of his ch. indicate some of the places where he took contracts.

Children (*Fam. Rec.*) :

1. Esther, b. Williamstown, Mass., 26 June, 1794 ; m. 17 Jan., 1816, at Boston, Vt., Levi Smith **Goodrich,** M. D.; she d. at Howard, N. Y., 24 June, 1825. *Issue:*
   i. Eleanor Charlotte (Goodrich), b. at Benson, Vt., 1 Jan., 1818 ; m. 25 June, 1835, at Howard, N. Y., Edward **O'Brien,** a lawyer, b. at Gt. Barrington, Mass., who d. at Big Creek, N. Y., 20 Dec., 1872 ; she d. Humboldt, Iowa, 21 May, 1886 ; they had (a) Esther (O'Brien), b. Newark Valley, N. Y., 4 Dec., 1831 ; m. at Big Creek, N. Y., 28 Oct., 1857, Gilbert **Bogart, Jr.,** M. D., of Castile, N. Y.; Dr. B. b. at Union Cors., Liv. Co., N. Y.; practiced in Castile, N. Y., and Humboldt and La Porte, Iowa; was Assist. Surg. 23 Mich. Vols. in the Civil War; d. at St. Paul, Minn., 20 Dec., 1888 ; (b) Edward (O'Brien), b. Dansville, N.Y., 8 Sept., 1840 ; d. at Big Creek, N. Y., 30 Oct., 1860 ; unm.
2. Sophia, b. Norwich, Mass., 2 Nov., 1797 ; m. at Benson, Vt., 23 Dec., 1816, Seymour **Howard,** of B., rem. to Howard, N. Y., where she d. 18 Sept., 1865. Mr. H. d. at Avoca, N. Y., 21 Aug., 1884, ae. nr. 90 yrs. *Issue:*
   i. Harriet (Howard), b. Benson, Vt., 12 Mch., 1818 ; m. at Howard, N. Y., 31 Jan., 1847, Wm. R. **Van Campen,** of Almond, N. Y.; they had (a) Aziel Barnes (Van Campen), b. at A., 24 Aug., 1848 ; m. ae. 48 yrs., Ella **Hosser,** of Ohio; res. Raymond, Cal.; (b) Azelia B. (Van Campen), b. Almond, N. Y., 19 Oct., 1850 ; m. A. O. **Bruce;** 7 ch.; res. Wawona, Cal.; (c) Howard N. (Van Campen), b. A., 19 Apl., 1853, d. Cal., 8 Dec., 1874, unm. Mr. Wm. R. Van Campen d. Nov., 1892 ; Mrs. V. C. d. 9 Sept., 1884, at Merced, Cal.
   ii. Jane (Howard), b. Benson, Vt., 25 Dec., 1819 ; m. at Howard, N. Y., 8 July, 1852, Robert **Mackie,** b. at Glasgow, Scotland, 11 June, 1816. Both d. at Avoca, N. Y., she 1st Feb., and he 21 Oct., 1897. They had (b. at *Avoca, N. Y.*) (a) Frank (Mackie), b. 15 July, 1855 ; m. 20 June, 1877, Hannah **Eells,** of A.; (b) Sophia (Mackie), b. 24 May, 1857 ; m. 8 July, 1877, Frank **Evans,** of A.; d. at Wallace, N. Y., 10 Feb., 1893.
   iii. Cooley Blinn (Howard), b. Benson, Vt., 2 May, 1825 ; m. at Avoca, N. Y., 14 Oct., 1858, Hannah **Paine,** she d. 14 Apl., 1865 ; m. (2) 17 Oct., 1865, Samantha (Paine) **Hoogland,** who d. at Hornellsville, N. Y., 7 Feb., 1887. They had (b. *Howard, N. Y.*) (a) Cooley Ward (Howard), b. 11 Aug., 1861 ;

m. 15 Sept., 1891, Sarah Ann **Darling,** of North East, Pa.; (b) Nellie Sophia (Howard), b. 27 July, 1862 ; m. 11 Oct., 1881, John **Miller** (one ch. d. inf.) ; m. (2) 20 Nov., 1889, Geo. Philip **Wettlin,** d. 23 June, 1894 ; (c) Ida Hannah, b. 14 Apl., 1865, d. inf.
   iv. Sidney Seymour (Howard), b. Benson, Vt., 21 Aug., 1830 ; m. at Milton, Wis., 16 Aug., 1856, Lovisa W. **Reynolds,** of M.; res. Dana, Kas., where she d. 29 Jan., 1891; had (a) Frank and (b) Melvin (Howard).
   v. Frank Seymour (Howard), b. Milton, Wis., 29 Nov., 1858 ; m. Uniontown, Kas., 23 Sept., 1884, Laura B. **Anderson;** had (a) Floyd Merton (Howard), b. U. Kans., 8 July, 1885 ; (b) Warren Anderson (Howard), b. Dana, Kans., 16 Nov., 1890 ; (c) Lella Grace, b. 1889.
   vi. Melvin (Howard), b. Howard, N. Y., 10 May, 1863 ; unm.
3. Lydia, b. Montgomery, Mass., 14 Feb.,1800 ; m. at Benson, Vt., 22 Aug., 1822, Augustus Asher **Olmsted,** b. 1806. *Issue:*
   i. Angeline Augusta (Olmsted), b. Benson, Vt., 31 Mch., 1824 ; m. Howard, N. Y., 21 Jan., 1841, Otis Allen **Bullard,** artist, of Howard, N. Y., who, apprenticed, ae. 14, to trade of wagon making and sign painting, early developed a taste for art, became a self-taught portrait painter and finally sought and found competent instruction and became a successful artist. His crowning work was his Panorama of New York City, which cost him over four yrs labor, and more than $15,000 in its production. He d. N. Y. City, 13 Oct., 1853. *Issue:* (a) George Washington (Bullard), b. 27 Mch., 1852 ; m. at Howard, N. Y., 24 June, 1874, Emma **House;** he d. Hornellsville, N. Y., 18 Nov., 1891.
   ii. Laura Esther (Olmsted), b. Benson, Vt., 10 June, 1828 ; m. at Howard, N. Y., 22 June, 1845, Henry **Zeilly;** their only ch. Eleanor (Zeilly), d. ae. 12 yrs.
   iii. Ten Eyck Gansevoort (Olmsted), b. Howard, N. Y., 23 Feb., 1833 ; m. at Chicago, Ill., 1860, Eliza **Cole,** who d. at Manitowoc, Wis., 1877 ; she d. 1865. Mr. Ten E. G. Olmstead served in War of Civil Rebellion as Lt.-Col. 27th Wis. Vols.
   iv. Mary Fanny Briscoe (Olmsted), b. Howard, N. Y., 10 Apl., 1835 ; m. at Manitowoc, Wis., 1862, T. C. **Barnes;** had one dau. Elsie Olmstead (Barnes), b. 27 Mch., 1864 ; m. (1) 2 June, 1888, I. F. **Ingersoll,** who d. 12 Mch., 1898 ; she m. (2) 27 Sept., 1900, Dr. S. Mical **Hagar,** of Chicago.

4. Aziel Anson, b. Burlington, Vt., 19 July, 1802 ; d. 1 Aug., 1809.
5. Laura Eleanor, b. Benson, Vt., 19 July, 1806 ; m. at B., 11 Sept., 1826, Levi Smith **Goodrich, M. D.** She was ten yrs. old when the doctor m. her sister Esther, and she sat on his knee at the time of the home wedding. Dr. G. b. in Benson, Vt., 22 May, 1793 ; grad. at Fairfield Med. College, 1815 ; m. at B., 17 Jan., 1816, Esther Blinn Barnes ; practiced med. at Moravia, Howard and Almond, N. Y., d. at A., 16 Sept., 1846—see *Goodrich Geneal.*, by L. W. Case, 1889. Mrs. Laura E. G. d. Hornellsville, N. Y., 13 Jan., 1892, ae. 85 yrs. and 6 mos., after 45 yrs. of widowhood. Their children were :
  i. Ellen Goodrich, b. Howard, N. Y., 25 Feb., 1829 ; grad. at Ontario Female Sem., Canandaigua, N. Y., 1851 ; m. 13 July, 1852, at Hornellsville, N. Y.,

Rev. Darius R. **Ford**, D. D., of Alfred, (N.Y.) Acad., of which she became preceptress 1856-7 ; she d. H. 30 Sept., 1857. Prof. Ford was a grad. of Brown Univ. ; prof. of Greek and Chemistry at A. Acad. and Alfred Univ., 1851-62 ; prof. of Nat. Sciences, Elmira (N. Y.) Coll., 1863-99.
  ii. Ervilla Goodrich, b. Howard, N. Y., 23 July, 1840 ; grad. 1861, at the Emma Willard School, Troy, N. Y. ; m. 7 Nov., 1867, at Hornellsville, N. Y., Russell M. **Tuttle.**—(See *Tuttle Gen.*, by Geo. F. Tuttle.) For further notice of Mrs. R. M. T. see Mrs. Russell Sage's *Emma Willard and her Pupils*, p. 494.
6. Aziel Cullen, b. Benson, Vt., 26 Mch., 1809 ; d. Howard, N. Y., 22 Nov., 1833.
7. Cooley Blinn, b. Benson, Vt., 3 Oct., 1812 ; d. 19 Jan., 1813.

Miscellanea :—HARTWELL, of Far., m. Hannah **Clark**, 27 May, 1783.—*S. C. R.* MARY, dau. of James, bp. 14 Feb., 1768.—*W. C. R.* MARTIN & Ruth had Ruth bp. 5 Sept., 1819.—*S. C. R.* REUBEN, of Midd., m. Nancy **Webb**, 15 May, 1814.—*S. C. R.* WILLIAM, m. Sarah **Holmes**, 8 Oct., 1821.—*W. T. R.*

BARNS, MATTHEW,[1] supp. by *Hinman* to have been an older bro. of Thomas, of Midd. ; m. (1) Experience ————, 12 Jan., 1678 ; m. (2) Abigail ————, Jan. 12, 1692. For ld. holdings see Chapter VII, VOL. I.

Child (Weth. Rec.) :

1. Matthew, b. Aug., 1694.

BARNABY, JAMES, d. ae. 76, Nov. 25, 1831.—*N. C. R.*

BARNISH, JOHN, of Htfd., m. Louisa **Nott**, of Step., 11 Nov., 1779.—*N. C. R.*

BARNSTABLE, WILLIAM, m. Hannah **Pelton**, of Weth., 3 Oct., 1779.—*W. C. R.*

BARNUM, JOHN, of Danbury, m. Catharine **Kilbey**, 27 Aug., 1782—*W. C. R. ;* she d. (wid.) 7 Jan., 1821, ae. 76.—*W. C. R.*

BARREL, JOSEPH, of Boston, m. Sarah **Simpson**, 18 Nov., 1778.—*W. C. R.*

BARRETT, JAMES, m. Ann **Carrington**, 3 Dec., 1761.

Children (Weth. Rec.) :

1. Selah, b. 24 Dec., 1762 ; m. 2 or 8 Oct., 1783, Lucy **Dickinson**.—*W. C. R. ;* he d. 26 Sept., 1825 ; she d. 9 Aug., 1857 in 95 yr. *Issue :* (1) Thomas, d. at Niagara, Nov., 1913, ae. 27 [in the war?] ; (2) Sophia, d. 18 Aug., ae. 32 ; (3) Inf. d. ae. 4 mos., 22 Oct., 1806 ; (4) Chauncey, d. at sea, ae. 24, 9 Aug., 1823.—*W. C. R.*
2. Anne, b. 4, bp. 9 Sept., 1764.
3. Martha, b. 27 June, 1766.
4. Mary, b. 9 Feb., 1768 ; d. 5 Aug., 1769, ae. 1 yr. 5 mo., 27 d.—*W. Ins.*
5. Mary, b. 7 Sept., 1769 ; poss. the Mary who d. 27 Mch., 1857 ae. 64.—*W. Ins.*
6. Sarah, b. 8 Aug., 1771.
7. Ruth, b. 17, bp. 23 Apl., 1775.
8. James, b. 7, bp. 9 Mch., 1777 ; m. Anne **Warner**, 3 July, 1804.—*W. C. R.*

Miscellanea :—GEORGE, of Htfd., m. Rebecca **Dix**, 2 Apl., 1794. HULDAH, d. 9 Dec., 1811, ae. 21.—*W. C. R.* MARTHA, d. 26 Jan., 1844, ae. 55.— *W. Ins.* SAMUEL, of Weth., ord. by Particular Ct., 5 Dec., 1645, to serve Arthur Smith for one yr. for £8.—*Hinman.* THOMAS, d. 15 July, 1813, ae. 29.— *W. Ins.* WILLIAM, d. 17 July, 1777, ae. 40.—*W. C. R.* WILLIAM, d. 7 Apl., 1858, ae. 62 yr., 9 mo.—*W. Ins.* ELIZABETH, wife of Wm., d. 30 July, 1845, ae. 53.—*W. Ins.* LUCY, dau. of Wm. & Elizabeth, d. 22 Sept., 1850, ae. 24— *W. Ins.*

BARROWS, ASHBEL, had (*S. C. R.*) Samuel Ward bp. 14 Sept., 1844; Andrew Otis bp. 5 Nov., 1847.

BARTHOLOMEW, LATHROP, of Harwinton, m. Martha **Deming**, 13 Mch., 1804.

BARTLETT, SAMUEL, m. Dency Smith, of Glast., 11 Feb., 1800.

BARTON, WILLIAM, of Far., m. Elizabeth **Hopkins**, 19 Aug., 1781.—*W. C. R.* WILLIAM had (*Mix MSS.*) Sarah bp. 22 Feb., 1729-30; Mabel, bp. 18 June, 1732.

BASCUM, (*Bascombe, Boscum, Bassum, Bossum*), WILLIAM, of Weth., 1636; prob at Guilford, Ct., 1665.—*Hinman.* Savage (I, 136) suggests that he may have been a bro. of the Thomas, early sett. at Windsor and Northampton; also, that the name, as given to Wm. of Watertown, may be an abbreviation of "Bassumthwaite," who d. early and his wid. had. share of lds. with other Wat. settlers, at Sudbury, 1639.—See Chapt. VII, Vol. I; also *Conn. Col. Rec.*, 1, 4.

BASSETT, JONATHAN, m. Mary ————.

Children (Weth. Rec.):

1. Abigail, b. 6 Sept., 1739.
2. Jonathan, b. 14, bp. 20—*L. Mss.*, Nov., 1743.
3. Mary, b. 20 May, bp. betw. that date and Sept. 1, 1745.
4. Hannah, b. 13 Feb., 1747.
5. William, b. 28, bp. 30 Apl., 1749.
6. Nathan, b. 11 Dec., 1751.
7. Elisha, b. 6, bp., 13 May, 1753.

BATES, see *Betts.*

BAXTER,[*] Capt. THOMAS, the founder of the Cape Cod, or Barnstable (Mass.) family of Baxters came into notice in the Conn. Colony in Sept., 1653, when under a so-called commission from Rhode Island, "to offend the Dutch," and with a purpose to prevent a carrying trade with the colony at New Amsterdam, he seized the vessel of one Mayo, a Barnstable man, within the jurisdiction of the Plymouth Colony. The matter stirred up quite an official excitement; and when it got into the courts for adjudication, the case went against Baxter. In 1653, a special warrant was issued against him by the Conn. Gen. Ct. for committing several misdemeanors within the jurisdiction of that colony, and was given to Jonathan Gilbert to arrest him, with power to raise forces to execute the warrant, if needed. Evidently, the Capt. was not in good odor with the Conn. authorities. In 1654, he is ment. as of Weth.; in May, 1662, (see *Hazard*, II, 285), the Gen. Ct. granted divorce (for desertion) to Bridget Baxter, from Thomas, who at the time, was in England. In this matter, the parties are described as being of Long Island; *Savage* says Newfield. Disgusted with Conn., Capt. B. next settled at Yarmouth, Mass., the town adjoining Barnstable. He had two sons:

1. THOMAS, who m. Temperance (wid. of Edward) **Sturgis**, 1679; he d. 1713, leaving three sons, the second of whom was

[*] *Mary Baxter* got divorce from husband, Thomas, March, 1729; on ground of desertion. —*Co. Ct. Rec.*

2. THOMAS, b. in Yarmouth, Mass., who m. (1) Mary (dau. Sgt. John) **Lattimer,** of Weth., 3d May, 1705;* m. (2) Hannah **Crowell.**

Children * (*Weth. Rec.*) :

1. Timothy,* b. 26 Feb., 1706. FAM. 2.
2. Elizabeth,* b. 23 Mch., 1708, bp. 9 Oct., 1709.
3. Thomas, b. 17 Dec., 1710. FAM. 3.
4. Cornelius, b. 30 Nov., 1712; m. (1) Dorcas **Gage,** 11 Feb., 1737; m. (2) Joanna **Merchant,** 1749 ('47 *Baxter Geneal.*) ; had

10 ch.
5. Leah, b. 17 Dec., 1715; had a son Simeon (Berry), b. 1739.
6. Malachi, b. 30 Apl., 1718; m. Thankful **Kelly,** 18 Mch., 1738; res. at Yarmouth; had 7 ch.

FAM. 2. TIMOTHY,[2] (*Thos.,*[1]), m. Sarah **Kilborn,** 14 July, 1726; was called (in *Co. Ct. Rec.*) a tanner, in 1733; d. 18 Apl., 1777, ae. 73.—*W. C. R.;* wid. d. ae. 86, 23 Dec., 1785.—*W. C. R.*

Children (*Weth. Rec.*) :

1. John, b. 28 Dec., 1726; was a Revol. soldier and pensioner; enl. Nov., 1775 under Lieut. Noah Allen, in Capt. Soule's Co., Col. Insley's Reg., which subsequently joined the Co. was merged into a Co. Whitcomb's Reg. of Sandisfield, Mass., in which town Mr. B. was then a res.; he was at Roxbury after the Br. left Boston; at B. until Aug., '76; at Ticonderoga until Jan. 1, '77, where his Co. was disch'd Apl., '77; he enl. again in Capt. Elizur Deming's Co. and served for 1½ mos.; again enl. June, '77, in Capt. Insley's Reg., which subsequently joined Gen. St. Clair's army and formed a part of the Northern Army under Gen. Gates, until 1 June, 1778, when Mr. B. became a gunner on board the privateer *Gen. Putnam,* Capt. Thos. Allen, and cruised for 3½ mos. during which time they captured several Br. vesels. In July, 1780, he enl. in Capt. Noah Allen's Co. and joined the select infantry Co. under Gen. Lafayette under whom he served in N. J. and was disch'd 15 Dec., 1780. He m. Candace Emerson, July, 1806, and he d. 17 Apl., 1847, ae. 89 yrs., 8 mos. His reputed age at dth. would better agree with the John who was b. at Weth. 19 Aug., 1757. In 1788 he rem. to Herkimer Co., N. Y., and abt. 1822 to Brownsville, Jeff. Co., N. Y.—*Memoir of Baxter Family, by Joseph Nickerson Baxter, Boston, 1879.*
2. Honour, b. 2 Mch., 1729; prob. the H. who m. 7 Dec., 1752, John **White,** of Htfd.
3. Martha, b. Dec., 1730. (The 3 foregoing ch. bp. 26 Mch., 1732, the parents at the same time owning the Covenant.—*Mix MSS.*)
4. Elisha, b. 29 Oct., bp. 3 Dec., 1732. FAM. 4.
5. Sarah, b. 28 Dec., 1735.
6. Mehitable, b. 25 May, bp. 5 June, 1740, by Mr. Lockwood

FAM. 3. THOMAS,[3] (*Thos.,*[2] *Thos.,*[1]), b. 1710; m. Zilpha **Nickerson,** of Chatham, 8 Nov., 1740.

Children:

1. Benjamin, b. 20 Sept., 1741; m. Elizabeth **Ryder.**
2. Reuben, b. 2 May, 1745; m. Elizabeth **Crowell,** 31 Oct., 1765.
3. Stephen, b. 1 July, 1748; injured in head and insane.
4. Ruth, b. 5 June, 1751; m. Reuben **Snow,** 1768.
5. Thomas, b. 3 Sept., 1755; m. Prudence **Baker,** 6 Dec., 1790.
6. Zilpha, b. 1 Oct., 1758.

FAM. 4. ELISHA,[3] (*Timo.,*[2] *Thos.,*[1]), b. 1732; m. 13 or 14 Dec., 1756, Honor **Wolcott;** he d. 2 Aug., 1804, ae. 74; she d. 31 July, 1809, ae. 73.—*W. C. R.*

Children (*Weth. Rec.*) :

1. Honor, b. 8 Sept., bp. 22d, 1757, privately, being ill; d. 3 Oct., 1757.
2. Rhoda, b. 24, bp. 10 Sept., 1758.
3. Elisha, b. 8, bp. 17 Feb., 1762.
4. Honor, b. 17, bp. 24 Feb., 1765.
5. Lucy, b. 20, bp. 21 Mch., 1768.
6. Leonard, b. 28 Oct., 1771.
7. Prudence, b. 8, bp. 19 Feb., 1775.
8. Anne, b. 20, bp. 28 June, 1778.
9. Polly Wolcott, b. 1 Oct., 1781, bp. 4 Dec. 1785.

Miscellanea:—*Baptisms* (*W. C. R.*) JOHN, s. of John, bp. 21 Aug., 1757.—See John, No. 1 of FAM. 2, above. LOIS, dau. of John, bp. betw. 19 June and 16 Sept. 1759. MARY (Baxter), dau. Sarah Kilby, b. 28 Oct., 1791.

Marriages:—(*W. C. R.*) MARTHA, m. Chas. **Dix,** 25 Jan., 1753, poss. the M. No. 3 of FAM. 2. MARY, m. James Cook **Dodge,** of New Boston, N. H., 22 Dec., 1813.—*W. C. R.*

Deaths:—(*W. C. R.*) ABIGAIL (wid.), d. 8 Sept., 1782, ae. abt. 55. An inf. of JONATHAN'S, d. 29 Oct., 1798. PRUDENCE, of Elihu, ae. 12, d. 8 Nov., 1787. SAMUEL, d. 29 Jan., 1729, ae. 6 yr., 7 mo.—*Weth. Ins.*

BEACHGOOD, EDWARD, s. of Hannah, bp. 15 Apl., 1781.—*S. C. R.*

BEADLE, (*Beedle*), ROBERT, of Weth., an early sett.; stole gunpowder from Mr. Blackman, of Stratford, two sacks from wid. Foote, 2 sacks from Thos. Welles, a blanket from Rich. Mills and a sack from Thos. Tracy; the Ct. ord. that he should restore double for each theft, be severely whipped and branded in his hand, on the Wednesday, Dec. 12, 1644; and, for his loathsome demeanor on the 5th day of Mch., 1644, he was ord, to be severely scourged and kept in the house of correction two weeks longer, and then again whipped and be then bound to appear at every Quarter Ct., and be whipped until the Ct. see some reformation in his conduct. In Mch., 1645, William Latham was charged, by the desire of Mr. Robins, in his inventory of debts, £1, 14s., for having delivered Robt. Beadle at Fisher's Island, by oruer of the Ct. On the 17th of May, 1649, he and Cary Latham were named to appear at Ct., for suffering an Ind. to escape, who had been committed to them for safe-keeping.—*Hinman,* 2d Edit., 165. *Savage* (i, 152) places this entirely disreputable person as of New London, 1648, and says "had, perhaps, been at Weth., where *Hinman* (164) ranks him among first sett. there; had Robert, b. 1642, and he rem. 1650, to Newbury, Mass., a good riddance for the Conn. Colony!

DAVID, m. Abigail —————, d. 28 Apl., 1782, ae. 67.

Children (Weth. Rec.):

1. Benjamin, b. 18 Dec., 1741.
2. Jonathan, b. 20 June, bp. 2 July, 1744.
3. Ruth, b. 30 June, bp. 17 July, 1748; per. the R. who m. 19 Aug., 1779, Aaron **Draper,** of Roxbury.—*W. C. R.*
4. David, b. 12 Sept., bp. betw. Aug., and Oct., 1750; m. 24 Apl., 1776, Jerusha **Hatch,** both of Weth. (*W. C. R.*); she prob. the "wife of David 2d," who d. 23 Dec., 1777, ae. 22.
5. Sarah, bp. 17 Feb., 1754.

JONATHAN, (prob. the second s. of David above), m. Elizabeth —————, who d. 23 Jan., 1793, ae. 39—*W. Ins.;* had (*W. C. R.*) Jonathan, ae. 20 mos., bp. 6 Oct., 1779; Polly, William, Betsy, Jerusha, bp. 28 Nov., 1779; Salome bp. 2 Jan., 1780; John bp. 16 Nov., 1783; Abigail bp. 14 Aug., 1785, prob. the A. who m. 2 Oct., 1805, Alex. **White,** of Midd.—*W. C. R..;* inf. bu. 13 Oct., 1789; Manning, bp. 11 Feb., 1787; Jonathan's wife d. 23 Jan., 1793, ae. 38.—*W. C. R.*

MANNING, (or *Manna?* prob. s. of *Jona,* above), m. Emily **Abby,** both of Weth., 4 Sept., 1810—*W. C. R.;* had (*W. C. R.*) Abbe, b. 4 Sept., 1810; John Palmer, Jerusha and Henry, bp. 12 Aug., 1821; Elizabeth Palmer, bp. 13 Oct., 1822; Manna, bp. 17 Jan., 1830, "of the late Manna, who d. 9 Dec., 1829, ae. 42;" but another acc. says, he d. 4 Dec., 1831, ae. 42. His wife Emily A., d. 10 Aug., 1879, ae. 89.

JERUSHA, m. Wm. **Lockwood,** of Gilead, Ct., 16 Jan., 1841.

WILLIAM, murderer and suicide. This man's history and tragic ending may be found in Vol. I, Chapt. XVII. The only items of his family on *Weth. Recs.* are *Lydia,* b. 1 Nov., 1774; *Mary,* b. 6 Oct., 1776, both with their mother, killed by father, Dec., 1782.   ,

Miscellanea:—ABIGAIL, m. Roger **Robbins,** 19 June, 1759; RUTH, m. Nathaniel **Colman,** 19, Jan., 1744; ELIZABETH, m. Edw'd **Hopkins,** 17 Aug., 1768. —*W. C. R.*

BEADSLEY, HEZEKIAH, of Stratford, Ct., m. Mary **Roach,** Weth., 6 Sept., 1789.—*W. T. R.*

BEAUMONT, (*Bemont*), LUCIUS W., m. Martha G. **Bulkley**, 27 Nov., 1845— *S. C. R.;* had *Laura Mabel*, bp. 6 June, 1847, and *William Lucius*, bp. 9 May,. 1852.—*S. C. R.*

(*Bemont*), IRA, of E. Htfd., m. Mabel Bulkley, 10 Oct., 1811.—*S. C. R.*

BEAVIE, GIDEON N., m. wid. Lydia G. **Shaylor**, 12 July, 1837.—*S. C. R.*

BEBE, (*Beebe?*), WILLIAM, m. Elizabeth **Dunston**, 7 Apl., 1780; CHRISTOPHER, m. Mary **Taylor**, 30 June, 1791.

BECKET, JONAS, of Bristol, m. Hannah **Deming**, 1789.

BECKLEY. (Furnished by Mrs. C. B. SHEPPARD, New York City.) Sergeant RICHARD, the first settler of Beckley Quarter, Weth., b. acc. to trad. in Hampshire, Eng., 1618, is first heard of on Am. soil, in New Haven, Ct., 5 Feb., 1639, where he was app. on a comm.; and his name appears freq. on the *N. H. Town* and *Ch. Recs.* up to 1659, and on the *Ld. Recs.* still later. July 1, 1644, he was on a list of men to be governed by Theophelus Aaton; he joined with others, at different dates, in trying to secure a neck of ld. now in E. Haven, the ld. being finally gr. 3 Dec., 1651; and his share he sold to Thos. Harrison, 1662; in 1646, and again 11 Feb., 1655-6, he sat in the men's second seat at ch., and his wife ("Sister" or "Goodwife") Beckley was in the women's second seat; but was not on the ch. seating list of 20 Feb., 1661-2; in 1648, he was chosen for the yr. as a Sargeant of the Artillery Co.; in 1659, on two occasions, he was a witness in N. Haven, Ct.; his coming to Weth. is marked by the Town's voting him "inhabitance," 22 Feb., 1660; he is said to have voted in Weth., 1662; was on jury from Weth., Mch. 2 and June 15, 1664, June 16 and Sept. 7, 1665, 6 Sept., 1666, 2 Mch., 1670-1; and on list of Weth. freemen, nominated May 13, and elected Oct., 1669; in ————, bo't from Tarramuggas, Indian chief, 300 acres of ld. lying on both sides of the Mattabesett River, "whereon were his house and barnes;" when (8 Oct., 1668) the Gen. Ct. confirmed his possession.—(See Vol. I, Chapter VII, also Chapter I.) In 1669 (Dec. 24), he complained to the Particular Ct., at Hartford that, during his absence, one Sunday, two Inds. had ent. his house and pilfered; for which loss he received an order for £3-13-6. Sgt. Beckley may have m. twice; m. (2) wid. Frances. He d. 5 Aug., 1690; his will, drawn 15 May, 1689, exhib. to and approved by Prob. Ct., 4 Sept., 1690, provided handsomely for wid. and six ch.—*Htfd. Co. Prob. Rec.*, V, 72. Invent. of est. £383-05-00. Est not fully distrib. until 13 Nov., 1701 after dth. of his s. Nath'l.

Children (*b. New Haven*) :

1. Sarah, m. John (s. of Rich. & Anne), **Church**, at Htfd., 21 Oct., 1657 ; he b. 1637 ; d. 1691, prob. at Htfd. ; she d. after 1689. *Issue :*
   i. Richard (Church), b. abt. 1663, at Htfd. ; d. at Colchester, 1 Apl., 1730 ; m. 3 Mch., 1692, Elizabeth (dau. Thos. & Hannah *Warner* or *Warriner*) **Noble**; b. at Westfield, Mass., 9 Feb., 1673 ; d. at Colchester, Conn., 10 Aug., 1757.—*Noble Gen.* and *R. R. Hinnman.*
   ii. Sarah (Church) m. (1) Geo. **Knight**; m. (2) Samuel **Hubbard.**
   iii. John (Church), d. 1735 ; m. Apl., 1695 or '99, Abigail (dau. Thos. & Elizabeth

   Stebbins) **Cadwell**; b. Htfd., 26 Nov., 1670.
   iv. Mary (Church), m. 20 Mch., 1690, Thomas (s. Thos. & Susanna *Church*) **Standish**; she d. 20 Jan., 1705.
   v. Ruth (Church).
   vi. Samuel (Church), b. abt. 1670 ; d. 1719 ; m. twice, his 2d wife was Mrs. Elizabeth **Clark**, whom he m. abt 1710.
   vii. Anne (Church), b. 1673 ; m. Jonathan **Clarke**. Some *recs.* indicate that she m. before Feb., 1724, Benj. Cleveland, of Canterbury, Ct. b. 1701 ; if so, she was 28 yrs. older than her husband. "Feb. 13, 1724, Elizabeth Church and Benjamin Cleveland and his wife Ann"

deeded lds. In Htfd.—*S. R. J. Hoyt.*
It is, however, very possible that
Jonathan Clark was the husband of
Elizabeth (No. viii of this Church
family).—*MSS. C. B. S.*
ix. Joseph (Church), b. 1676.
x. Deliverence (Church), b. 1679 ; d.

Westfield, Mass.?
2. John, b. 6 Mch., 1642. FAM. 2.
3. Mary, bp. 12 Sept., 1647.
4. Benjamin, b. 27 Jan., 1650. FAM. 3.
5. Nathaniel, b. 13 Oct., 1652. FAM. 4.
6. Hannah, b. 14 Oct., 1656.

FAM. 2. JOHN,[2] (*Sgt. Richard,*[1]), b. 1642; was nomin. freeman in Weth., 13 May, 1669; inherited 100 acres, with the ho. already built thereon for him—see Chapter VII, Vol. I; m. (prob. before 1670) a dau. of John and Honor *Treat* **Deming,**[*] who was living 1701, when final set. of his est. was made. He d. before 8 Apl., 1696.

Children:

1. Hannah,[3] m. Robert (s. Rob't & Susannah *Treat*) **Webster,** at Htfd. 10 Sept., 1689 ; he b. 1662 ; d. Feb., 1744 ; she d. 1715. *Issue b. Htfd.:*[†]
   i. Robert (Webster), b. Oct., 1689.
   ii. Abraham (Webster), b. 1 Sept., 1693.
   iii. Hannah (Webster, b. 7 Nov., 1695 ; m. 1719, Ebenezer (s. John & Sarah *Mygatt*) Webster ; b. 1689 ; d. 12 Feb., 1776 ; she d. Nov., 11, 1775.
   iv. Matthew (Webster), b. 17 Apl., 1698 ; d. 2 Feb., 1707.
   v. Joseph (Webster), b. 7 Mch., 1700.
   vi. Caleb (Webster), b. 22 Feb., 1702-3.
   vii. Mary (Webster), b. 5 Dec., 1704 ; d. yg.
   viii. Abigail (Webster), b. 22 Jan., 1710-1.
2. Richard,[3] b. FAM. 5.
3. Deborah,[3] b.   ; m. before 1696, Samuel (s. Obediah & Mary *Desbrough*) Spencer, b. Htfd ; d. Haddam (?) betw. 20 Apl. & July 5, 1756 ; she d. after 14 Dec., 1740. *Issue, b. Htfd.:*
   i. John (Spencer), b. 10 Oct., 1696 ; d. 12 Mch., 1757 ; m. 4 Nov., 1741, Elizabeth Taylor, who b. 1717 ; d. 31 Jan., 1807, ae. 89.
   ii. Mehitable (Spencer), bp. 5 Mch., 1698 ; m. 10 Aug., 1726, Sam'l (s. of Sam'l & Abigail *Whitmore,* or Wetmore) Bishop; b. at Guilford, 14 Mch., 1699.
   iii. William (Spencer), bp. 12 Feb., 1699 ; prob. d. yg.
   iv. Deborah (Spencer), b. 28 Apl., 1700 ; m. 25 Jan. 1717, Wm. Roberts, of Htfd., Ct.
   v. Hannah (Spencer), b. 27 Mch., 1703 ; d. yg.
   vi. Nathaniel (Spencer) ,b 5 Dec., 1704 ; m. (1) 1 Mch., 1733, Abigail Hurlburt; m. (2) 29 Sept., 1757, Ruth Purple.
   vii. Abigail (Spencer), bp. 23 Nov., 1707 ; living unm. 1770.
   viii. William (Spencer), bp. 15 Aug., 1708 ; prob. d. yg.
   ix. Lucy (Spencer), b. 7 Sept., 1710 ; m. Nov., 1731, Joseph (s. Joseph & Mary *Hoyt*) Crittenden, of Guilford ; she d. 13 July, 1796.
   x. Hannah (Spencer), bp., 10 Jan., 1714. (Not mentioned in father's will.)
   xi. Samuel, b. 7 May, 1717. (Not mentioned in father's will.

4. Abigail,[3] b. 1675 (?) ; m. 25 Mch., 1695, Matthew (s. of Thos. & Elizabeth *Stebbins* Wilson) Cadwell; b. Htfd., 5 Oct., 1668 ; d. 22 Apl., 1719 ; Abigail Beckley, wid. Matthew Cadwell ; d. Nov., 10, 1755 ; prob. Guilford, Ct., having m. (2) May 10, 1721, as his sec. wife, Caleb (s. Elizabeth Jordan & Andrew) Leete, of Guilford, Ct., ; b. Dec., 10, 1673 , d. Dec. 3, 1760. No ch. by sec. m.—*Leete Fam. Gen. Prob. and Town Rec. Issue (all b. Htfd.) :*
   (*Printed Ch. Rec.*) Matthew, Abigail, Daniel, Daniel, Abigail, Elias ; and (from *Dwight's Fam. Gen.*) Matthew, Abigail, Anne, John, Abel.
   i. Matthew (Cadwell), bp. June, 1697 ; b. 11 June, 1696?) d. Htfd. 27 Dec., 1723 ; m.
   ii. Abigail (Cadwell), bp. 30 Apl., 1699 ; (b. 28 Apl., 1698?) d. Htfd., Ct., bef. 1712.
   iii. Ann (Cadwell), bp. 18 May, 1701 ; (b. 6 May, 1700?)
   iv. John (Cadwell), bp. 6 Dec., 1702 ; (b. 30 Nov., 1702) d. 2 Apl., 1746 ; m. Dorothy (dau. Thos.) Kilbourne.
   v. Abel (Cadwell), bp. 3 Dec., 1704 ; (b. 27 Nov., 1703?) d. 1780 ; m. 1731, Anne dau. Nath'l & Mehitable Partridge) Dwight; b. 2 July, 1710.
   vi. Daniel (Cadwell), bp. 20 Oct., 1706 ; d. yg.
   vii. Daniel (Cadwell), bp. 21 May, 1710. (b. 18 May, 1710?)
   viii. Abigail (Cadwell), bp. 8 June, 1712 ; m. 1728 (?), Jonathan Starr, b. 10 Feb., 1702 ; d. E. Guilford, Ct., 4 Sept., 1765.
   ix. Elias (Cadwell), bp. 1-7 Mch., 1711 ; d. Aug., 1760 ; m. 1 Apl., 1735, Hannah Davis, who d. 18 Jan., 1752.
5. Catharine,[3] b. abt. 1684-5 ; m. (1) 27 Sept., 1706, Daniel (s. Jeddiah & Sarah *Orton*) Dewey; b. Westfield, Mass., 9 Mch., 1679? d. Far. abt. 1 Jan., 1717 ; m. (2) 12 Aug., 1731, Dea. John (s. Ebenezer & Sarah) Deming; b. N. 25-26 July, 1679 ; d. N. 1 May, 1761. *Issue:*
   i. Daniel (Dewey), b. 24 Aug., 1707 ; m. 27 Jan., 1731, Rebecca (dau. Thos. & Mary *Goodrich*) Curtis; he d. 28 Oct., 1786. 5 ch.
   ii. Sarah (Dewey), b. 2 Aug., 1712 ; m. 8 Mch., 1744.

---

* In connection with this *see Note* to JOHN BECKLEY'S (FAM. 2) dau. Hannah, whose "misbehavior," Sept., 1689, only a month before her marr. to Robert Welston, had been concealed from John Deming until revealed by the action of the Court, two years and a half later, and whose displeasure was shown by the codicil in his will of ————. His will, also, shows no other Beckley gd-ch. and though a Hannah appears both in the family of Richard and that of John Beckley, yet, as Richard Beckley's will made no provision for the support of *his* dau. Hannah and left her only a small money gift, it is but reasonable to suppose that she was married before 1689; nor do the *Court recds.* show any misbehavior of a Hannah, or Ann. Beckley. So, we are left to the conclusion that John's wife was John Deming's daughter.
† From the well known genealogist FRANK FARNSWORTH STOW, of Middletown, Ct., we have the following : The *Genealogical Notes* of Nathaniel Goodwin, printed 1856, p. 235, states

FAM. 3. BENJAMIN,[2] (*Sgt. Richard,*[1]), b. New Haven, 27 Jan., 1650; inherited 100 acr. of ld. with house already built thereon, and his father's will directs his bro. Nathaniel to help him build a barn; he m. (1) at Weth., 7 (or 17) Oct., 1685, Rebecca ————, see, also, Chapter VII, Vol. I; m. (2) in New Lond., 12 Nov., 1702, Miriam **Stevens**, who d. before 13 Sept., 1742. He d. 27 Apl., 1736, ae. abt. 86. His will was made 28 June, 1728.—*Weth. Rec.*

Children (Weth. Rec.):

1. Martha, b. 15 Oct., 1692; m. 1710, Hezekiah (s. Capt. Thos. & Ruth Hawkins) **Hart.**
   Issue:
   i. Rebecca (Hart), b. 27 Aug., 1711; m. Nath'l **Sage**, of Midd.
   ii. Hezekiah (Hart), b. 11 Dec., 1714; d. 29 Mch., 1730.
   iii. Martha (Hart), b. 5 Aug., 1717; m.
   16 Dec., 1736, Joseph (s. Jacob & Dinah Churchill) **Deming**, b. 13 Dec., 1713; she d. 26 Nov., 1748, at Berlin.
   iv. Lucy (Hart), b. 5 Sept., 1720; m. her sister's husband's bro., Jacob **Deming.**
   v. David (Hart), b. 11 Aug., 1724; d. 1786; m. Lucy **Peck.**
   vi. Ruth (Hart), b. Kens. 1 Nov., 1726; d.

that a daughter of John Deming married "a Beckley," his Christian name not being given. In 1860, Hon. James Savage issued the first vol. of *Genealogical Settlers of New England.* On p. 151, he states that the second wife of Richard Beckley "was a d(aughter) of John Deming." Other writers have evidently taken Savage as authority and this statement seems to have been accepted without question. In my studies of some Goodwin matters, I have been puzzleing over this problem and am obliged to differ from Savage in my conclusions.

RICHARD BECKLEY made his will in May, 1689, in which he provided for his wife Frances. Thus far I have not been able to find any record of their marr., nor of her death, neither can I find any record of the marr. of his son John, through whom came the lines of descent. JOHN DEMING, Sen., of Weth., made his will June 26, 1690, in which he gave £5 to his "daughter Beckley" also "to my grandchild Ann Beckley, five pounds to be paid her by my Executor at her day of marriage." I have been unable to find any Ann Beckley. The nearest to that name is Hannah, of which there were two. One, the daughter of Richard, born October 14 or 15, 1656, and living in May, 1689, the other a daughter of Richard's son John, her date of birth being unknown. The latter m. in Sept., 1689, Robert **Webster.** The fact that she was marr. at the date of this will is probably the reason that persons have supposed that it was RICHARD BECKLEY, who married Deming's daughter. At the date of this will the Beckley families were living in what is still known as "Beckley Quarter" and John Deming was presumably living in Weth. village, at least six miles distant in a straight line, and evidently an old man for those days. The clue to a solution of the problem lies in the codicil to Deming's will made February 3, 1692, which reads "and whereas in my Will I give my grand child Ann Beckley five pounds, She haveing miscarryed I withdraw my guift from her." I have spent considerable time looking for a rec. of the bad behavior of an Ann or Hannah Beckley, but without success. The *Hartford Town recs.* have the marriage of Robert Webster and Hannah Beckley, daughter of John, as taking place September 10, 1689, and the birth of their first child in the following month, the day not being given in the record. I have made an examination of the *Htfd. Co. Ct. R.,* and find this entry under date of May 26, 1692 " Robt. Webster & his wife for Incontenensy before Marriage confest by them are fined forty shillings." This seems to me to be the solution of the problem. Deming and the Beckleys living so far apart it was perhaps possible to conceal from Deming the fact of the marriage of Hannah Beckley to Robert Webster, which was necessitated by the birth of their child to occur in the next month. If Deming did not know of these matters, the wording of his will is perfectly natural. When the actions of Webster and his wife became a subject for the County Court to pass judgment upon, it made the matter too public to be kept from Mr. Deming any longer. Consequently in the following February, he makes a codicil in which he revokes the legacy made in his will to Ann Beckley. The evidence seems to me conclusive that John Beckley, not Richard, married a daughter of John Deming of Wethersfield and that his daughter Hannah, was the grandchild referred to in Deming's will and codicil.

Since writing the above, I have discovered the fact that in Dec., 1699, John Deming, Sr., was appointed one of the distributors on the estate of John Beckley. If my inference is correct as to Beckley's marriage, Deming was appointed to distribute the estate of his son-in-law.

9 July, 1773 ; m. (1) Daniel (s. Daniel)
Beckley; m. (2) Abraham Harris.
vii. Zerviah (Hart), b. 16 Dec., 1728 ; m.
(1) John (s. Wm.) Allis; b. 11 Sept.,
1726 ; d. 18 May, 1756 ; m. (2) as sec.
wife, 19 Dec., 1761, David (s. John &
Esther Judd) **Webster;** b. Glast., 29
Jan., 1721 ; d. 12 May, 1806 ; she d.
17 Jan., 1786 ; had 4 ch.
viii. Hezekiah (Hart), b. 7 Jan., 1730 ; m.
10 Jan., 1757, Abigail **Adkins;** he d.
14 Apl., 1804.
ix. Hepzibah (Hart), b. 16 Apl., 1732 ; d.
1792 ; m. 18 Jan., 1753, Isaac (s. Isaac
& Mary *Woodford*) **North;** b. 1729.
x. Zachariah (Hart), b. 5 Jan., 1734 ; d.
26 Dec., 1811 ; m. 23 Mch., 1758, Abigail
dau. Joseph & Mary Judd) **Beckley;**

b. 22 Dec., 1737; and d. 12 July, 1765.
2. John, b. 16 Oct., 1695. FAM. 6.
3. Benjamin, b. 16 Dec., 1698 ; bp. 26 Mch.
FAM. 7.
4. Miriam, b. 4 May, bp. 15 June,—*Mix.* 1707 ;
m. 5 Dec., 1745, Thomas (s. of John &
Sarah *Stanley*) **Wadsworth,** b. Far., 1680 d.
1771, ae. 92, s. p. ; she d. 1759.
5. Hannah, b. 24 Mch., bp. 2 July, 1710 ; m.
6 May, 1742, Jonathan (s. Samuel & Mary
Bradford) **Benton.** *Issue:*
i. Lydia (Benton), b. Weth., 1 Feb.,
1743.
ii. Samuel (Benton), b. Weth., 4 Sept.,
1745.
iii. Jonathan (Benton), b. Weth., 18 Mch.,
1748.

FAM. 4.   NATHANIEL,[2] (*Sgt. Richard*,[1]), b. New Haven, 1652, though unmarried
when his father d. was made sole executor, and rec'd the homestead and 100
acr. of ld.—the farm, with prob. a third ho. thereon, which is still occupied
(1900) by descts. of the Beckley name.—See Chapter VII, VOL I. He m. at
Weth., 18 May, 1693, Comfort (dau. Jona., Sr., & Sarah) **Deming,** b. 5 June,
1668. He d. 30 Oct., 1697; his estate, invent. taken 13 Apl., 1698, val. at
£200-09-00 ; est. set. by wid. and ch. by agreement.—*Htfd. Co. Prob.* His wid.
m. (2) Thomas **Morton,** 2 Feb., 1710.—*Talcott.*

Children (Weth. Rec.) :

1. Daniel, b. 8 May, 1694. FAM. 8.
2. Joseph,[3] b 19 Sept., 1695. FAM. 9.
3. Mary,[3] b. 1 Mch., 1697 ; m. 1 Mch. 1717,
Thos. (s. Hannah & John, or Stephen &
Sarah *Judd*) **Hopkins;** she d. 7 Mch., 1759,
at Htfd. *Issue* (b. *Htfd.*) :
i. Abigail (Hopkins), b. 11 Mch., 1718 ;
d. yg.
ii. Sarah (Hopkins), b. 28 Oct., 1719.
iii. Stephen (Hopkins), b. 8 May, 1722 ;
d. 1804.
iv. Thomas (Hopkins), bp. 10 Aug., 1724 ;
m. (1) Anne ————, who d. 30
Mch., 1759 ; m. (2) Alice (dau. Samuel
& Alice *Hooker*) **Howard,** who b.
1740 (?), d. 23 Apl., 1778.

v. Moses (Hopkins), m. 7 Apl., 1763,
Elizabeth **Deming,** who d. 7 July,
1767 ; m. (2) Mary (dau. Bevil &
Lydia *Dodd*) **Seymour,** b. New., 4
Dec. 1735 ; d. 6 Nov., 1795.
vi. Aaron (Hopkins), b. 14 July, 1729 ;
d. 16 (?) Dec., 1755.
vii. Elisha (Hopkins), bp. 17 Oct., 1731 ;
d. Htfd., 9 Apl., 1777.
viii. Benjamin (Hopkins), b. 11 May, 1734 ;
d. Mch. (6 ?), 1764 ; m. Rachel (dau.
Eliphalet & Katherine *Marshfield*)
Steele, bn. 4 Sept., 1737 ; d. 12 (?)
June, 1763.
ix. Abigail (Hopkins), b. 28 Aug., 1737.

FAM. 5.   RICHARD,[3] (*John*,[2] *Sgt. Rich'd*,[1]), b. ————————— ; m. Weth., 23 Nov.,
1699, Elizabeth (dau. Jonathan, Sr., & Elizabeth *Gilbert*) **Deming,** b. 15
June, 1674 (or 12 June, 1677), at W., d. 23 Nov., 1765.—See Chapter ————,
Vol. I.

Children (Weth. Rec.) :

1. Nathaniel, b. 27 Aug., (bp. 3 Nov.—*Mix*),
1700 ; d. Weth., 14 Mch., 1760, unm. ; willed
his ppy. to bro. and sister.
2. Abraham, b. 12 Jan. (bp. 26 Apl.—*Mix*),
1702. FAM. 10.
3. Elizabeth, b. 27 June (bp. 29 Aug.—

Mix), 1703 ; m. 10 or 20 Mch., 1743, Jonathan (s. Jona. & Mercy) **Boardman,** of
Weth., b. 1697 ; she d. 30 Aug., 1776. *Issue:*
i. Elizabeth (Boardman), m. 4 Dec.,
1773, James **Price.**

FAM. 6.   JOHN,[3] (*Benj.*,[2] *Sgt. Richard*,[1]), b. Oct. 16, 1695; d. Mch. 24, 1765, Weth.;
m. 16 Mch., 1727, Mary (dau. Jno. & Elizabeth *Thompson*) **Woodruff,** b.
Jan. 30, 1699 or 1700 ; d. Apl. 19, 1761.

Children (Weth. Rec.) :

1. Sarah, b. 27 June, 1728 ; m. 28 Apl., 1748,
Dea. Richard (s. Geo. & Mercy *Seymour*)
Hubbard, of Midd., b. 1713, d. at Berlin,
1795 ; she d. 24 Mch., 1778.
2. Mary, b. 16 July, 1730 ; d. before 14 Mch.,
1765.
3. John (Lieut.), b. 22 Dec., 1732. FAM. 11.
4. Elias (Capt.), b. 27 Feb., 1735. FAM. 12.
5. Achsah, b. 25 Jan., 1743 ; m. Weth., Ct.,

20 Dec., 1764, Abijah (s. Samuel & Joanna
Judd) **Hubbard,** b. Far., Ct., 4 Oct., 1741 ;
d. Berlin, Ct., 9 Feb., 1811 or 1814. *Issue:*
i. Abijah (Hubbard), b. 1764 ; d. 2 Aug.,
1789.
ii. John (Hubbard), b. 1768 ; d. Berlin,
Ct., 25 Apl., 1845 ; m. Catharine **King,**
b. 1774 ; d. 26 Nov., 1824.
iii. James (Hubbard), b. 1769.

iv. Sarah (Hubbard), b. 2 Feb., 1780 ; d. 13 June, 1867 ; m. (1) 29 Oct., 1798, Agathus (s. Raphael & Sarah) **Hurlburt**, b. 28 June, 1776 ; d. ————— ; m. (2) 28 Aug., 1833, Abijah **Hubbard**.

v. Harvey (Hubbard), b. Mch., 1782 ; d. 7 Aug., 1863 ; m. (1) Jennie Doane **Galpin**, 26 Nov., 1807 ; m. (2) 10 Apl., 1825, Huldah **Galpin**.

vi. Polly, b. 1785 ; d. 2 Nov., 1808, unm.

FAM. 7. BENJAMIN,[3] (*Benj.,[2] Richard,[1]*), b. 1698; m. Mary (dau. Stephen & Elizabeth *Royce*) **Lee**, of Far., 4 Mch., 1730; he d. 12 Nov., 1777; she d. 26 Sept., 1782 or 89.

Children (Weth. Rec.) :

1. Rebecca, b. 22 Apl., 1732 ; m. Dec., 1752, Caleb (s. of Caleb & Elizabeth *Baldwin*) **Galpin**, of Midd. ; she d. prob. at M., before 1765. *Issue :*
   i. Mary (Galpin), b. 21 Oct., 1753.
   ii. Abel (Galpin).

   iii. Perhaps others.
2. Benjamin (Lieut.), b. 30 Apl., 1738. FAM. 13.
3. Theodore, b. 12 Sept., 1740 ; d. same month.
4. Mary, b. 9 Feb., 1742 ; prob. d. before 1765.
5. Theodore, b. 1744 ; m. Lucy **Kirby**. FAM. 14.

FAM. 8. DANIEL,[3] (*Nathaniel,[2] Sgt. Richard,[1]*), b. 1694; m. 6 Aug., 1719, Martha (dau. Thos.) **North**, of Far.

Children (Weth. Rec.) :

1. Martha, b. 27 Oct., 1720 ; m. 4 Aug., 1742, John (s. Sgt. Thos. & Mary *Goodwin*) **Savage;** she res. E. Berlin Ct. *Issue (all b. Midd.)* :
   i. Ruth (Savage), b. 12 Apl., 1743.
   ii. Nathaniel (Savage), b. 22 Oct., 1745.
   iii. Lemuel (Savage), b. 28 Mch., 1749.
   iv. Huldah (Savage), b. 25 Mch., 1752 ; m. 1779, Josiah (s. of Daniel & Sarah *White*) **Wilcox.**
   v. Martha (Savage), b. 5 Aug., 1754 ; d. unm. 3 May, 1833.
   vi. Mary (Savage), b. 4 Jan., 1757.
2. Daniel, b. 29 Nov., 1724. FAM. 15.
3. Lois, b. 17 Nov., 1730 ; m. 15 Nov., 1753, Peat (s. Caleb & Elizabeth *Baldwin*) **Gal-**

pin. *Issue (all b. in Midd.)* :
1. David (Galpin), b. 19 Sept., 1754.
ii. Jehiel (Galpin), b. 22 Dec., 1756 ; d. Nov., 1793.
iii. Lois (Galpin), b. 10 Dec., 1758 ; m. Zenas **Goodrich**, b. Nov., 1763 ; rem. to New Dunham, N. Y.
iv. Goodrich (Galpin), b. 6 Nov., 1763 ; d. 1818.
v. Caleb (Galpin), b. 23 July, 1761 ; d. 20 Mch., 1764.
vi. Caroline (Galpin), b. 2 Apl., 1765.
vii. Orrel (Galpin), b. 5 July, 1767.
viii. Son (Galpin), b. 5, d. 8 June, 1769.
ix. Caleb (Galpin), b. 29 Nov., 1771.

FAM. 9. Lieut. JOSEPH,[3] (*Nathaniel,[2] Richard,[1]*), b. 1695; m. (1) Mary (dau. Benj. & Susannah *North*) **Judd**, of Far., 23 Oct., 1823, who d. 16 Apl., 1750, ae. 48; he m. (2) Sybil **Porter**, 29 Mar., 1753; he d. 30 Jan., 1772; she d. at W., 6 July, 1783. He was prob. the Joseph B. licensed as a taverner, by the Co. Ct., 1733, '34 and '42.

Children (Weth. Rec.; marr. and dths.—C. B. S.) :

1. Mary, b. 6 Apl., 1725 ; d. inf.
2. Josiah, b. 28 Apl., 1726 ; m. Ann ————, who after his dth. m. (2) Ephraim **Hollister**, of Far., Ct. *Issue (by wife Ann)* :
   i. Mary (Beckley), b. Weth., 1754-5 ; prob. m. Calvin **Hulbert**, of Weth., 29 July, 1773.
   ii. Chloe (Beckley). b. 15 Oct., 1756 ; m. 25 Sept., 1777, Gideon **Cole**, of Far. *Issue :*
     i. Anna (Cole), b. 25 Sept., 1778 ; d. Chili, N. Y., 30 Oct., 1830 ; m. Benj. **Wood.**
     ii. Henderson (Cole), b. 8 Apl., 1780 ; d. Elkhart, Ind., 9 Sept., 1851 ; m. Betsey **Parmalee.**
     iii. Nancy (Cole), b. 19 Oct., 1781 ; d. Prattsburgh, N. Y., Oct., 1851 ; m. George (or Israel) **Gardner.**
     iv. Betsey (Cole), b. 30 Jan., 1783 ; d. Jerusalem. N. Y., 1807 ; m. 12 Sept., 1800, Timothy **Barnes**, b. 30 Jan., 1780.
     v. Amanda (Cole). b. 26 Sept., 1785 ; d. Pultney, N. Y., 11 Jan., 1807 ; m. Joel **Stanton.**
     vi. Emily (Cole), b. 27 Jan., 1788 ; d. Vernon, N. Y., 1807 ; m. (1) David **Parmalee**; m. (2) Anson **Bull.**
     vii. Almira (Cole), b. 17 Jan., 1791 ; d. Prattsburg, N. Y., 26 Aug., 1820 ;

m. 7 Nov., 1808, Timothy **Barnes**, as second wife.
     viii. Horace (Cole), b. 1 July, 1792 ; d. Roscoe, Ill., 1862 ; m. Abby **Frisbie.**
     ix. Rhoda (Cole), b. Apl., 29 1795 ; m. John **Bramble.**
     x. Hiram (Cole), b. 4 Mch., 1797 ; d. Prattsburgh, N. Y., 26 Feb., 1847 ; m. Fanny **Frisbie..**
     xi. Chloe (Cole), b. 24 Mch., 1799 or 1800 ; d. Milford, Mich., 1873-5 ; m. Theron **Lindsley.**
     xii. Harmon (Cole), b. 29 June, 1802 ; d. Apl., 1825.
3. Joseph, b. 23 Aug., 1727. FAM. 16.
4. Thankful, b. 11 Nov., 1728 ; m. Lieut. Nathaniel **Dickinson.**—See *Dickinson.*
5. Ruth, b. 11 Oct., d. 3 Nov., 1730.
6. Eunice, b. 11 Nov., 1731 ; m. 20 Mch., 1755—*N. C. R.*, Job (s. Isaac & Elizabeth *Whaples*) **Hart**, b. Far., 3 Jan., 1732 ; res. Stockbridge, Mass., where they d. *Issue :*
   i. Jabish (Hart), bp. 2 Jan., 1757 ; m. Jemima **Brace.**
   ii. Candace (Hart), bp. 8 Feb., 1758 ; m. Roswell **Barnes**, of Oneida, N. Y.
   iii. Job (Hart), bp. 11 Mch., 1759 ; m. Rachel **Ball.**
   iv. Harvey (Hart), bp. 28 Dec., 1760 ; d. 3 Dec., 1780, unm.
   v. Leverett (Hart), bp. 27 June, 1762 ;

d. unm.
vi. Eunice (Hart), bp. 30 Oct., 1763 ; d.
Victor, N. Y., 29 June, 1822 ; m. at
Stockbridge, Mass., 30 Oct., 1783,
Abijah (s. of Joshua & ———
Clark) Williams, bp. 1756 ; who d.
28 Feb., 1840.
vii. Joseph (Hart), bp. 17 Mch., 1765 ; m.
Beulah Warner.
viii. Simeon (Hart), bp. 21 July, 1766 ;
m. Betsy Treat.
ix. Reuben (Hart), bp. 17 Jan., 1768 ; m.
wid. Boughton.
x. Comfort (Hart), bp. 25 Aug., 1771 ;
m. Sibel Churchill, Pompey, N. Y.
xi. Hepzibah (Hart), bp. ; m. Solomon
Williams, Chenango, N. Y.
xii. Betsy (Hart), bp. 4 June, 1775 ; d. yg.
7. Mary, b. 12 Jan., 1733 ; m. 21 July, 1755,
Isaac (s. John & Hannah Norton) Pratt,
b. Htfd., 1734 ; she d. Goshen, Ct., 11 Dec.,
1807 ; he d. G., 3 Sept., 1814. Issue :
i. Mary (Pratt), b. 26 Oct., 1758 ; m.
John Taylor.
ii. Sarah (Pratt), b. 19 Apl., 1760.
iii. Honor (Pratt), b. 1 Sept., 1762.
iv. Caroline (Pratt), b. 21 Apl., 1766.
v. Candace (Pratt), b. 10 Aug., 1767.
vi. John (Pratt), b. 21 Sept., 1770.
vii. Isaac (Pratt), b. 22 Dec., 1771.
8. Zebedee, b. 8 Mch., 1734. Fam. 17.
9. Hepzibah, b. 16 Apl., 1735 ; m. 18 Jan.,
1753, John (s. Elixodon & ———) Woods;
she d. Bristol, Ct., 1793. Issue :
i. Eli (Woods), b. 23 Oct., 1753.
ii. Huldah (Woods), b. 13 Oct., 1754 ; m.
June, 1773, Daniel(s. Rufus & Mary)
Clark.
iii. Hepzibah (Woods), b. 8 Jan., 1756 ;
m. Judah Barnes, 3 Nov., 1774.
iv. Ruth (Woods), b. 13 Mch., 1757.
v. Silas (Woods), b. 7 Feb., 1759.
vi. Charlotte (Woods), b. 21 Apl., 1763.
vii. Silence (Woods), b. 10 Oct., 1764.
viii. Abigail (Woods), b. 10 Oct., 1766 ;
m. Benoni Johnson.
ix. John (Woods), b. 1 Apl., 1768.

x. Thankful (Woods), b. Oct., 1770.
xi. Zadoc (Woods), b. Apl., 1772 ; m.
Huldah (Winchell) Mildrum.
10. Silas, b. 5 Nov., 1736 ; d. 11 Nov., 1757.
11. Abigail, b. 22 Dec., 1737 ; m. 23 Mch.,
1758, Zachariah (s. Hez. & Martha Beckley)
Hart, of Far., b. 5 Jan., 1734 ; she d.
Weth., 12 July, 1765 ; he m. (2) Sarah
(of John) Parsons. Issue :
i. Olive (Hart), b. 24 June, 1759 ; d.
2 Oct., 1833 ; m. (1) Solomon (s.
Abijah & Sarah Clark) Flagg, b.
Bristol, Ct., 1758 ; m. (2) Ithamar
Morgan.
ii. Joseph (Hart), b. 14 Oct., d. Nov.,
1760.
iii. Zachariah (Hart), b. 1 Sept., 1761 ;
d. Jan., 3, 1762.
iv. Caroline, b. 21 Oct., 1762 ; d. 26 Oct.,
1841 ; m. Abel (s. Ephm. & Ann
Beckley) Hollister, b. Far., 10 Feb.,
1761, and d. 25 May, 1809.
v. Zachariah, b. 26 May, d. 17 Nov., 1764.
12. Ruth, b. 7 Apl., 1739 ; d. 16 Apl., 1740.
13. Comfort, b. 4 Sept., 1740 ; d. 28 Apl., 1741.
14. David, b. 17 Feb., 1742. Fam. 18.
15. Jonathan, b. 12 Feb., d. 28 Mch., 1743.
16. Dorcas, b. 6 Mch., 1744 ; m. David (s.
Joseph & Martha Hart) Deming, at Weth.,
12 Dec., 1765.
17. Honor, b. 3 July, 1745 ; m. at W., 29
Nov., 1764, Elisha (s. of Gen. Isaac &
Susannah Pratt) Marsh, b. Litchfield, Ct.,
15 Nov., 1742, who d. 20 Jan., 1804 ; she d.
Sept., 1809. Issue :
i. Honor (Marsh), b. 23 July, 1766 ;
m. 25 Dec., 1788, Obed. Buell.
ii. Abigail (Marsh), b. 15 Nov., 1769 ;
m. 31 May, 1794-5, Ellada Osborn, of
Litchfield, Ct.
iii. Elisha (Marsh), b. 27 Aug., 1772 ; d.
16 Dec., 1841 ; m. 1802, Rhoda Kilbourne.
iv. Mary (Marsh), b. 4 Nov., 1781 ; m.
2 Oct., 1803, Dr. Isaac (s. Isaac &
Martha Lyman) Marsh, who, b. 18
Feb., 1777, d. 1 Sept., 1829.

Fam. 10. ABRAHAM,[4] (Rich.,[3] John,[2] Rich.,[1]), b. 12 Jan., 1702; m. (1) Martha
Heart, who was b. 1700 (?); m. (2) Deborah ———. She d. Jan., 1792.

Children (C. B. S.) :

1. Richard.
2. Mehitable, m. 28 Nov., 1782, as his 2d
wife, Timothy (s. of Timothy & Betsy
Leonard) Hubbard; they had a dau.
Letitia, b. 1783.
3. Jason, b. 4 Sept., 1767 ; this man, or his
ch. left Weth. ; he had 8 ch., of whom
Horace (the third), b. 1812; m. 9 May,

1838, Minerva (dau. Peter & Mattie Lattin)
Augur, of Hartwick, N. Y., who d. at H.
7 Oct., 1882.
4. Elijah, b. 1768 (?) : m. and prob. left
Weth. ; d. 14 Apl., 1830.
5. Isaac, prob. left Weth.
6. Ch. d. 7 Feb., 1765 ; bu. at Beckley Quarter.
7. Elizabeth, b. d. (prob. unm.) 8 Oct., 1775.

Fam. 11. JOHN,[4] (John,[3] Benj.,[2] Rich.,[1]), b. 1732; m. at Kens., Jan. or June,
1758, Ruth Hubbard; res. Weth., where he d. 14 Feb., 1776; was a Lieut. in
battle of Lexington, 1775.

Children (b. Weth.) :

1. Lydia, b. 1759 (?) ; m. 6 Apl., 1780, Ashbel
Belden (?).
2. Sarah, b. 1761 (?) ; m. Levi Butler (?).
3. Ruth, b. 1762-3 ; m. Chas. Priestley, or
4 Mch., 1783, Silas Belden (?), prob.
the first ; her mother Ruth, wid. of John,
prob. m. the second.
4. Ch. d. 26 Aug., 1765.
5. Mary, b. 1766-7 (?) ; m. 11 Feb., 1787,
Luman Deming, of Weth., b. 1766, who
d. W., 30 May, 1821 ; she d. 29 Sept., 1836,
at W. Issue (all b. Rocky Hill) :
i. Lucy (Deming), b. abt. 1788-9 ; bp.
19 July, 1801.
ii. John Beckley (Deming), b. 1791 ; bp.
19 July, 1801 ; d. Weth., 26 Feb., 1842.

iii. Achsah (Deming), bp. 19 July, 1801.
iv. Hannah (Deming), b. 1797; d. 29 Oct.,
1800.
v. Erastus (Deming), b. 1800, bp. 19
July, 1801 ; d. 8 Feb., 1853, Suffield,
Ct. (?) ; m. Charlotte ———.
vi. Linus (Deming), b. 1805 ; d. Weth.,
11 Jan., 1891.
(Perhaps others.)
6. John, b. 1768-9 ; m. Mary Blinn (wid.
of Luman) Beckley. Fam. 19.
7. Asahel, b. 1770; d. 7 Oct., 1830; blind for
many yrs. ; unm.
8. Achsah, b. 1772-3 (?).
9. Child, d. 11 Mch., 1775.

FAM. 12. ELIAS,[4] (*John*,[3] *Benj*.,[2] *Sgt. Richard*,[1]), b. Weth., 1735; m. at Kensington, 4 Aug., 1757, Lois (dau. John) **Parsons,** b. 1740; d. Weth., 3 May, 1815. He d. W., 14 Feb., 1816.

Children (Weth. Rec.) :

1. Lois, b. 28 July, 1758; d. 26 Dec., 1773, in 16th yr.
2. Elias, b. 13 Feb., 1760. FAM. 20.
3. Rowena, b 2 Apl., 1763; m. Weth., Samuel **Porter,** b. 1762, who d. at Berlin (?), 21 Jan., 1818; she d. 23 Jan., 1830; willed her ppy. to her nephew James E. Smith; had no ch.
4. Olive, b. 17 June, 1765; m. at Weth., Joseph **Porter,** who d. after 12 July, 1835; she d. at Kennebunk, Me., in Dec., 1834.
5. Selah, b. 31 Mch., 1767. FAM. 21.
6. Sylvester, b. 1 Apl., 1771. FAM. 22.
7. Lois, b. 16 Nov., 1773; m. (1) Elnathan (s.

Elnathan & Chloe *Lee*) **Smith,** who d. Berlin, 22 Feb., 1801; m. (2) John **Dunham,** who d. Berlin, 13 Apl., 1826; she d. before 1833. *Issue (by first marriage)* :
  i. Maria (Smith), b. 1797 (?); d. 27 June, 1815.
  ii. James E. (Smith), m. before 1838. *Issue (by second marriage)* :
  iii. Laura Ann (Dunham), b. 1811; m. a **Grannis.**
  iv. Maria Smith (Dunham), b. 1815; m. a **Gilbert.**
  v. Mary Jane (Dunham), b. 1823.

FAM. 13. BENJAMIN,[4] (*Benj*.,[3] *Benj*.,[2] *Sgt. Richard*,[1]), b. Weth., 1738; m. at W., 23 Apl., 1761, Eunice **Williams,** b. 1736; he d. at W. 3 Mch., 1794; she d. at W., 22 Sept., 1789.

Children (b. Weth.) :

1. Oliver, b. 16 Sept., 1762. FAM. 23.
2. Hannah, b. 8, d. 28 Dec., 1764.
3. Luman, b. 27 May, 1766. FAM. 24. 27 May, d. 15 Aug., 1798. FAM. 24.
4. Hannah, b. 13 July, 1768; m. Joseph **Crowfoot.** *Issue:*

  i. Eunice (Crowfoot).
  ii. Sally (Crowfoot).
  iii. Hannah (Crowfoot).
  iv. Joseph (Crowfoot).
  v. Betsy (Crowfoot).

FAM. 14. THEODORE,[4] (*Benj*.,[3] *Benj*.,[2] *Sgt. Richard*,[1]), b. Weth., 1744; m. at Kens., 25 Dec., 1771, Lucy **Kirby,** b. W., 1748, d. 14 July, 1780. He d. W., 26 Jan., 1806.

Children (Weth. Rec.) :

1. Lucy, b. 17 Sept., 1772; m. at Guilford, Ct., 28 Nov., 1792, Jesse (s. Samuel & Rebecca *Norton*) **Hart,** b. Far., 3 Jan., 1768; d. Berlin, 15 Mch., 1827. *Issue:*
  i. Lucy (Hart), b. 23 Oct., 1793; d. 21 Oct., 1846; m. 25 Apl., 1819, Edward **Norton.**
  ii. George (Hart), b. 15 Aug., 1795; d. Berlin, 16 Nov., 1825; m. Weth., 1818, Caroline (dau. David & Eunice *Williams*) **Beckley,** b. Weth., 10 Oct., 1796; d. B., 15 Nov., 1881.
  iii. Harriet (Hart), b. 22 Sept., 1798; d. 12 June, 1863; m. 3 Mch., 1822,

Norris **Wilcox.**
  iv. Rebecca (Hart), b. 7 Feb., 1802; d. 9 Feb., 1807.
  v. Elizabeth (Hart), b. 17 Dec., 1806; m. 17 Aug., 1828, Fred **Weston,** of Sandy Hill.
  vi. Emma (Hart), b. 12 Sept., 1809; m. 19 Sept., 1826, Howard **White,** of Danbury, Ct.
2. Seth (Capt.), b. 7 Jan., 1775; m. Huldah **Richardson;** he d. Cape Francois, Island of Hispaniola, 1802, "seafaring man, active and useful in his profession," ae. 27 at dth.

FAM. 15. DANIEL,[4] (*Dan'l*,[3] *Nath'l*,[2] *Sgt. Rich*.,[1]), b. 1724; m. Ruth (dau. Hez. & Martha *Beckley*) **Hart,** of Far., b. 1 Mch., 1726; he d. W. 4 Mch., 1760; she m. (2) Abraham **Harris,** and d. July, 1773.

Children (C. B. S.) :

1. Seth, b. 28 July, 1753—(*Weth. Rec.*); d. 27 Feb., 1769.
2. Jonathan, b. 1755. FAM. 25.
3. Daniel (Dr.), b. 11 June, 1758. FAM. 26.

FAM. 16. JOSEPH,[4] (*Joseph*,[3] *Nath'l*,[2] *Sgt. Rich*.,[1]), b. at Canaan, Ct., 1727; m. (1) Pede (dau. Daniel & Rachel) **Hancock,** who d. at C., 28 June, 1776; m. (2) at Newington, Ct., 19 Nov., 1778—*N. C. R.*, Elizabeth (dau. Nath'l & Ruth *Parker*) **Boardman,** He, then "of Weth.," got a deed, 15 May, 1749, from Jeremiah Lawrence, of Canaan, Ct., which prob, marks abt. the date of his rem. to C., where some of his descts. still live in his old homestead.

Children (b. Canaan—C. B. S.) :

1. Joseph, b. 3 May, 1749. FAM. 27.
2. Samuel, b. 25 or 27 July, 1751. FAM. 28.
3. Chloe, b. 25 Mch., 1755; m. Elijah **Whitney.** *Issue:*
  i. Elijah (Whitney).

  ii. Elisha (Whitney).
  iii. Joseph (Whitney).
  iv. Flecta (Whitney).
  v. William (Whitney).

FAM. 17. ZEBEDEE,[4] (Joseph,[3] Nath'l,[2] Sgt. Rich.,[1]), b. 1734; m. Hannah ————;
he d. 4 Dec., 1776; she d.(?) 25 Aug., 1810, ae. 79.

Children (b. Wcth.):

1. Solomon, b. 12 Sept., 1756. FAM. 29.
2. Hannah, m. Charles (s. Charles & Hannah *Aspenicall*) **Nott**, 28 July, 1775; he was b. W., 11 June, 1754; d. at Berlin, Ct., before 7 Feb., 1816; she d. after 1781. *Issue (b. Weth.):*
  i. Sylvester (Nott), b. 22 Aug., 1776.
  ii. Zebedee (Nott) b. 20 Mch., 1778; d. 1 Apl., 1827.
  iii. Hannah (Nott), b. 17 June, 1779; prob. d. unm. 12 Jan., 1849.
  iv. Jonathan (Nott), b. 4 Feb., 1781; prob. d. 17 Nov., 1858; prob. m. Prudence **Belden**, who d. 9 Feb., 1882, ae. 88.
3. Rhoda, b. ————; d. after 1779; m. 17 Dec., 1776, Isaac **Bidwell**, of Glast.
4. Ann, b. Aug., 1762; m. 28 Mch., 1782, Benj. **Dix**, who was b. 26 Mch., 1757, and d. 19 June, 1827; she d. 9 July, 1827; they prob. rem. to Barre, Vt., with her bro. Zebedee Beckley. *Issue:*
  i. John (Dix), b. 12 June, 1784.
  ii. Lucy (Dix), b. 10 Sept., 1785; d. 18 June, 1812.
  iii. Dorcas (Dix), b. 28 Aug., 1787; d. 11 July, 1802.

  iv. Jemima (Dix), b. 12 Aug., 1789; d. 27 June, 1795.
  v. Jerusha (Dix), b. 8 Oct., 1791; d. Mch., 30, 1869; m. 7 Apl., 1811, Thos. M. (s. of Enos) **Towne**; d. So. Barre, Vt., 7 May, 1867.
  vi. Leonard (Dix), b. 18 Apl., 1793; d. 14 Aug., 1827; m. Betsy Sanborn.
  vii. Relief (Dix), b. 8 Apl., 1795; d. Mch., 1872.
  viii. Betsy (Dix), b. 1 Aug., 1798; d. 10 Jan., 1855; unm.
  ix. Benjamin (Dix), b. 3 July, 1800; d. 23 June, 1817; unm.
  x. Lavinia (Dix), b. 12 Dec., 1802; d. 23 Oct., 1854.
  xi. Reuben (Dix), b. 9 Aug., 1805; d. 12 June, 1852; unm.
  xii. Ozias (Dix), b. 18 Nov., 1807; d. 10 May, 1861; m. 1837 (?), Grace **Holmes**.
5. Zebedee, b. 31 Dec., 1763. FAM. 30.
6. Abigail, d. May, 1798; m. Isaac **Judd**.
7. Josiah, b. 1 May, 1768; m. Mary **Norton**. FAM. 31.
8. Theodosia, b. 10 July, 1772; m. after 1804, Simeon **Stedman**.

FAM. 18. DAVID,[4] (Lt. Joseph,[3] Nath'l,[2] Sgt. Richard,[1]), b. 1742; m. 23 Sept., 1763, Hepzibah (dau. Daniel & Sarah *White*) **Wilcox**, b. Midd., 31 Jan., 1745; d. Weth., 19 Feb., 1821; he d. Weth., 10 Nov., 1798.

Children (Weth. Rec.):

1. David, b. 31 Mch., 1765. FAM. 32.
2. Silas, b. 28 Sept., 1766. FAM. 33.
3. Caroline, b. 8 Sept., 1768; m. Selah **Beckley**; d. 8 Oct., 1820.
4. Joseph, b. 2 Feb., 1771; d. 12 Apl., 1772.

5. Hepzibah, b. 9 Mch., 1773; d. 23 Aug., 1775.
6. Luther, b. 11 Oct., 1778.
7. Joseph, b. 12 Nov., 1775; d. 25 Jan., 1777. FAM. 34.

FAM. 19. JOHN,[5] (John,[4] John,[3] Benj.,[2] Rich.,[1]), b. Weth., 1768-9; d. Weth., 22 May, 1839, m. abt. 1799, Mary **Blinn** (wid. of Luman) Beckley, b. 1771-2; who d. 4 Feb., 1835.

Children (b. Weth.):

1. Lydia, b. 6 Sept., 1800; m. at Berlin, abt. 1816, Edmund **Sanford**. *Issue (prob. all b. E. Berlin, Ct.):*
  i. Lucy Ellen (Sanford), b. 6 Oct., 1817; m. 21 Oct., 1839, Harvey **Penfield**.
  ii. Urban (Sanford), b. 1819; m. Jane **Harlow**.
  iii. Daniel (Sanford), b. 1820, or 21; d. unm. in Beckley Qr.
  iv. Angeline (Sanford), b. 1822, or 23; d. ae. 1 yr., 9 mos.
  v. Edmund (Sanford), b. 15 Dec., 1824; m. (1) Weth., 7 May, 1845, Emily (dau. Aaron & Miriam *Beckley*) Por-

ter, who d. abt. 1855 (?); m. (2) Julia **Stocking**.
  vi. Harriet (Sanford), m. (1) 7 Jan., 1856, Tertius H. (s. of Jonathan) **Belden**; m. (2) 1881, Alfred **Hemingway**.
  vii. Lotan (Sanford), d. New Britian, ae. 21 yrs.
2. Eliza, m. at Rocky Hill, 16 Nov., 1845, Hiram **Hubbard**. *Issue:*
  i. Elizabeth (Hubbard), m. Geo. **Smith**.
  ii. Harriet (Hubbard).
  iii. Henry (Hubbard).
  iv. Walter (Hubbard).

FAM. 20. ELIAS,[5] (Elias,[4] John,[3] Benj.[2] Sgt. Rich.,[1]), b. Weth., 1760; m. (1) at E. Berlin, Rachel (dau. Elisha & Thankful *Johnson*) **Savage**, 23 Jan., 1783; she b. Midd., 10 Apl., 1761, d. at B. 26 Aug., 1826; he m. (2) at B., 14 Apl., 1828, Abigail Norton Smith Stanley (dau. Zacheus & Sarah *Parsons*) **Hart**, of Far., b. 1768, d. B., 4 July, 1845. He d. B., 4 Oct., 1828.

Children (C. B. S.) :

1. Orrin, b. 17 Jan., 1784. FAM. 35.
2. Lyman, b. 1 Jan., 1786. FAM. 36.
3. Allen, b. 7 Mch., 1788. FAM. 37.
4. Ch. d. 13 May, 1792.
5. Milicent, b. 3 Sept., 1793 ; m. 8 May, 1821,
   Nathaniel **Parmalee**, of Berlin, Ct. *Issue:*
   i. Cornelia (Parmalee), b. 1822-3 ; m.
      1843, Norris **Bailey**, of New Britain,
      Ct. ; 1 ch.
   ii. Orrin (Parmalee), res. Santa Anna,
       Cal., m. 1 ch.
   iii. Leverett Allen (Parmalee), b. 1824 ;
        d. 1827.
   iv. William L. (Parmalee), b. 1826 ; d.
       1892-3.
   v. Walter A. (Parmalee), b. abt. 1830 ;
      d. unm., in Cal.
   vi. Frances Clarissa, b. abt. 1833 ; d. unm.,
       in Cal.
6. Clarissa, b. 9 Dec., 1799 ; d. Berlin, Ct.,
   26 June, 1880 ; m. 28 Oct., 1822, at Berlin,
   Lotan (s. Moses & Rhoda *Smith*) **Porter**,
   b. 1799 ; who d. 30 Oct., 1858. *Issue* (b. in

Beckley Qr.) :
   i. Frederick Lyman (Porter), b. 23 Aug.,
      1823 ; d. 28 July, 1833.
   ii. Linus Alanson (Porter), b. 17 July,
       1825 ; d. 15 Sept., 1826.
   iii. Edwin Alanson (Porter), b. 22 Sept.,
        1827 ; d. 29 Mch., 1867.
   iv. Linus Augustus (Porter), b. 9 Apl.,
       1830 ; d. 29 Nov., 1862.
   v. Emily Fidelia (Porter), b. 18 May,
      1832 ; d. 29 Oct., 1871.
   vi. Caroline Elizabeth (Porter), b. 26
       July, 1834 ; m. (1) 8 July, 1861, Chas.
       E. **Steele**, who d. 13 Apl., 1863 ; m.
       (2) 4 Dec., 1885, Franklin Dwight
       Jones.
   vii. Frederick Allen (Porter), b. 16 June,
        1836, d. unm. 24 Feb., 1885.
   viii. Henry Lyman (Porter), b. 4 Jan.,
         1840 ; m. (1) Mary L. **Wilson**; m. (2)
         Ruda Carter (dau. Fred B. & Char-
         lotte *Wilson*) **Loomis.**

FAM. 21. SELAH,[3] *(Elias,[4] John,[3] Benj.,[2] Rich.,[1])*, b. Weth., 31 Mch., 1767 ; m.
at W., 10 Nov., 1787, Caroline (dau. David & Hepzibah *Wilcox)* **Beckley,**
b. Weth., 8 Sept., 1768, and d. Stow, O., 8 Oct., 1820.

Children (all except Hepzibah, rem. to Little Britain, O.) :

1. Dan, b. 10, d. 18 Oct., 1788.
2. Hepzibah, b. 7 Dec., 1789 ; d. 17 Oct., 1794.
3. Noel, b. 19 July, 1791. FAM. 37a.
4. Lotan, b. 3 Nov., 1793. FAM. 38.
5. Hepzibah, b. 11 Aug., 1795 ; m. Berlin,
   18 Aug., 1817, Russell (s. Wait & Abigail
   Russell) **Dickinson**, b. Weth., 25 Oct., 1794 ;
   d. B., 26 May, 1881. *Issue (all prob. b.
   Rocky Hill)* :
   i. Caroline Beckley (Dickinson), b. 22
      Dec., 1818 ; d. Meriden, Ct., 17 Feb.,
      1863-4 ; m. (1) Wm. Sylvester **Beckley**,
      and m. (2) Alfred Luther **Beckley.**
   ii. Jerusha (Dickinson), b. 26 Oct., 1820 ;
       d. at Sterling, Neb., 16 Oct., 1873 ; m.
       at Berlin, Ct., 7 June, 1847, Andrew
       F. (s. Gideon & Dorothy *Hays*) **Mills**,
       b. Hudson, O., 29 May, 1820 ; d.
       Sterling, Neb., 1 Mch., 1887.
   iii. Celestia (Dickinson), b. 16 May, 1822 ;
        m. at Ry-H., 5 Dec., 1839, Seabury
        (s. Simeon & Emily *Beckley*) **Belden**,
        b. Ry-H., 17 May, 1817.

   iv. Hepzibah (Dickinson), b. 23 Mch.,
       1824 ; d. 3 Jan., 1827.
   v. Child, b. and d. 24 June, 1826.
6. Rowena Porter, b. 17 Oct., 1799 ; m. a
   Bowen; had, at least, two ch.
7. Elnathan Smith, b. 2 Apl., 1801. FAM. 39.
£. Lois, b. 13 Jan., 1803 ; d. 24 Sept., 1823,
   at Stow, O., m. 25 Mch., 1821, William
   Whitmore. *Issue:*
   i. Lotan (Whitmore), d. 12 Sept., 1823,
      ae. 1 yr., 8 mos.
9. Edwin, b. 3 Feb., 1806. FAM. 40.
10. Sally Drusilla, b. 10 Aug., 1807 ; m. 30
    Aug., 1827, Charles **Hamlin.** *Issue:*
    i. Caroline (Hamblin).
    ii. Mary (Hamblin).
    iii. Harriet (Hamblin).
    iv. Evelyn (Hamblin).
    v. Charles (Hamblin).
    Prob. two others.
11. Ahira, b. 17 Dec., 1809. FAM. 41.

FAM. 22. SYLVESTER,[5] *(Elias,[4] John,[3] Benj.,[2] Rich.,[1])*, b. Weth., 1 Apl., 1771 ;
d. Berlin, Ct., 17 Dec., 1821 ; m. at Kennebunk, Me., Hannah (dau. Samuel)
Moody, b. K., 1770 ; d. B., 18 Mch., 1838.

Children:

1. Adelia, b. Weth., 7 Feb., 1802 ; d. Stafford,
   Ct. ; m. Apl., 1825, at B., Lysis **Lamb,**
   b. 1801 ; d. 9 Mch., 1862. *No issue.*
2. Louise, b. Weth., 1803-4 (?) ; d. Brattleboro, Vt. (?) ; m. (1) Berlin, Ct., 9
   Nov., 1823, Linus (s. Moses & Rhoda
   Smith) **Porter,** b. 1803 ; d. B., 14 July,
   1825 ; m. (2) Brattleboro, Vt., 24 Dec.,
   1837, as his 2d wife Ashbel (of Thos.)
   Dickinson. *Issue (by first marriage)* :
   i. Fidelia (Porter), b. Berlin, Aug.,
      1824 ; m. Jas. **Burt**, of Bkln., N. Y.

Issue (by sec. mar.; b. Brattleboro) :
   ii. Clarence (Dickinson), b. ———.
   iii. Lucy (Dickinson), b. 1842 ; m. Fred.
        Field.
3. William Augustus, b. Weth., abt. Dec.,
   1805 ; d. 30 July, 1811.
4. William Sylvester, b. 1812 ; FAM. 42.
5. Sylvester Augustus, b. Berlin, Ct., abt.
   1817 ; d. 17 Apl., 1828.
6. Emilius Lysander, b. 29 Sept., 1819.
   FAM. 43.

FAM. 23. OLIVER,[5] *(Benj.,[4] Benj.,[3] Benj.,[2] Sgt. Rich.,[1])*, b. 1762 ; m. Lucinda
(dau. Richard) **Belden**, of Weth., 19 Jan., 1785, who was b. 1764 (?) ;
d. 22 Mch., 1857. He d. Sept., 1819 (?), or 28 Jan., 1820.

Children (b. Weth.):

1. Polly, b. 21 Nov., 1785 ; m. Lyman **Sanford;** she d. at E. Berlin, Ct. *Issue:*
    i. Caroline (Sanford).
    ii. Henry (Sanford), m. Polly (dau. Samuel & Sophronia Adaline) **Beckley.**
    iii. Lyman (Sanford).
    iv. James (Sanford).
    v. Jane (Sanford).
2. James, b. 13 Nov., 1787 ; d. Weth., 19 Aug., 1817 ; unm.
3. Rodney, Blendall, b, 28 Dec., 1789. FAM. 44.
4. Samuel, b. 25 Feb., 1791. FAM. 45.
5. Theodore, b. 10 Feb., 1794. FAM. 46.
6. Sydney, b. 28 Sept., 1797 ; m. bef. 1814, at W. Reuben (of Richard & Susanna *Wilcox*) **Beckley,** who b. 31 Dec., 1789 ; d. E. Berlin, Ct., 6 Sept., 1871 ; she d. Meriden, Ct., 17 Mch., 1880. *Issue:*
    i. Eliza (Beckley), b. 31 Dec., 1814 ; d. yg.
    ii. Clarissa (Beckley), b. 5 Apl., 1818 ; d. yg.
    iii. Juliette (Beckley), b. 10 June, 1820 ; m. at Meriden, Ct., 11 May, 1842, Warren P. **Beach,** d. E. Berlin, Ct. (?), 27 July, 1843.
    iv. Nancy O. (Beckley), b. 28 Dec., 1822 ; m. Wm. **Morgan,** of E. Berlin, Ct.
    v. Reuben (Beckley), b. 12 Jan., 1825 ; d. Lime Rock, Ct., 24 Apl., 1897 ; m. (1) at Weth., 8 Apl., 1847, Elizabeth (dau. Sophronia Blinn) **Tucker;** m. (2) ————
    vi. Clarissa (Beckley), b. 25 Nov., 1828 ; d. ————.

vii. Laura A. (Beckley), b. 28 Nov., 1830 ; d. Yalesville, Ct. (?), 18 Apl., 1897 ; m. Meriden, Ct., 12 Dec., 1852, as his sec. wife, Jonathan **Morley.**
viii. Fidelia Jane (Beckley), b. 3 Feb., 1835 ; d. E. Berlin, Ct. (?), 26 Sept., 1856 ; m. 8 Mch., 1856, Geo. D. (s. Leonard & Miranda *Beckley*) **Pattison.**
ix. William H., b. 1 Jan., 1839 ; d. 4 July, 1856, at E. Berlin, Ct.
7. Betsy Williams, b. 18 Apl., 1801 ; d. Midd., 5 Mch., 1883 ; m. Norman **Crittendon,** b. at Cromwell, Ct.
8. Nancy, b. 28 Oct., 1803 ; m. (1) at E. Berlin, Ct., 24 Nov., 1825, Chester (s. Israel & Martha *Stocking*) **Kelsey,** b. W. Cromwell, 7 July, 1804 ; who d. New Haven, 4 Oct., 1829 ; she m. (2) at Midd., 12 Sept., 1833, David (of Nich. & Abigail *Stocking*) **Ames,** who b. and d. Portland, Ct., 21 June, 1841 ; she m. (3) at Midd., 17 Apl., 1850, John (of Wm. & Sally *Cotton*) **Cornwell,** b. Westfield, Ct., 1800, who d. 21 Jan., 1873. She was living in Midd. 1899. *Issue:*
    i. Lucinda Elizabeth (Kelsey), b. 23 Jan., 1827 ; d. 21 July, 1887, prob. at Midd. ; m. Thos. C. **Canfield,** of Midd.
    ii. Nancy Maria (Kelsey), b. 13 Dec., 1828 ; m. Seth **Savage.**
        Issue (by second marriage) :
    iii. David (Ames), b. Cornwall, Ct., 25 July, 1833 ; d. unm., on Paraguay Expedition.

FAM. 24. LUMAN,[5] (*Benj.,[4] Benj.,[3] Benj.,[2] Sgt. Rich.,[1]*), b. 1766 ; m. Polly **Blinn,** and d. Berlin, Ct., 15 Aug., 1798 ; she m. (2) John **Beckley,** and d. Feb., 1833.

Children (b. Berlin, Ct.):

1. Lucy, b. 3 Feb., 1793 ; m. 22 May, 1812 at Weth., Urbane (s. Asahel & Content *Parsons*) **Kelsey,** of Berlin ; b. 1787 ; she d.in Ohio, 8 Oct., 1874. *Issue:*
    i. Angeline (Kelsey), b. 15 Dec., 1812 ; d.

10 Sept., 1822.
    ii. Sarah Ann (Kelsey), b. 4 Oct., 1826 ; unm.
    iii. Benjamin (Kelsey), b. 6 May, 1829 ; m.
2. Benjamin, b. 1794-5. FAM. 47.

FAM. 25. JONATHAN,[5] (*Daniel,[4] Daniel,[3] Nath'l,[2] Sgt. Richard,[1]*), b. 1755 ; m. 11 May, 1774, at Weth., Mary (dau. David & Lydia *Andrus*) **Webster,** of Newington, who, b. 28 Feb., 1754, d. at Berlin, Ct., 25 Dec., 1831 ; he d. W., 30 June, 1804.

Children (b. Weth.):

1. Amos, d. 17 Oct., or Nov. 1776, in 1st yr. of age.
2. Ruth, b. 12 Aug., 1777 ; m. 1 Jan., 1798, John (s. John & Hannah *Dewey*) **Goodrich;** b. Berlin, Ct., 19 May, 1776, and who d. at B. 4 May, 1886 ; she d. B. 16 Jan., 1849. *Issue:*
    i. Darius Newton (Goodrich), b. 14 Mch., 1799 ; d. 29 Aug., 1867 ; m. in N. Y. City 15 June, 1829, Maria **Forsyth.**
    ii. Nathan Fenn (Goodrich), b. 22 June, 1801 ; d. 1 Mch., 1883 ; m. Eveline **Todd.**
    iii. Lydia Gilbert (Goodrich), b. 9

Sept., 1805 ; m. Henry **Stowe,** of New Haven, Ct. ; d. 7 Aug., 1846.
    iv. Mary Webster (Goodrich), b. 12 June, 1807 ; m. Horace **Haskell;** d. 2 Jan., 1834.
    v. Hannah Dewey (Goodrich), b. 7 Sept., 1814 ; m. Aaron **Dutton,** of Claremont, N. H. ; d. 30 Oct., 1893.
    vi. Martha H. (Goodrich), b. 25 Oct., 1817 ; d. 7 Sept., 1823.
3. Hosea, b. 18 Dec., 1779. FAM. 48.
4. Roxy, b. 1783 ; d. unm, 18 Dec., 1865.
5. Norman, b. 1794 ; m. Mary **Evans.** FAM. 49.

FAM. 26. DANIEL,[5] (*Dan'l,[4] Dan'l,[3] Nath'l,[2] Sgt. Rich.,[1]*), b. Weth. 1758 ; m. Waterbury, Ct. (?), 23 Mch., 1787, Levia (dau. John & Sarah *Gordon*) **Lewis,** b. July, 1770, and who d. Waterbury, Ct., 16 Feb., 1797. He d. Utica, N. Y., 9 Nov., 1843 ; descendants now mostly in the West.

Children:

1. Gordon Lewis, b. Waterbury, Ct., 17 Oct., 1788 ; m. Phoebe **Barnes.**
2. Flora, b. Waterbury, Ct., 27 Apl., 1791 ; m.

Clark **Scott.**
3. Levia, b. Naugatuck, Ct., 28 Feb., 1795 ; m. Ely **Platt.**

FAM. 27. JOSEPH,⁴ (*Joseph*,³ *Nath'l*,² *Sgt. Richard*,¹), b. 1749, m. (1) 5 Jan., 1769, Jane **Bosworth**—*Canaan Ch. Rec.;* m. (2) Peddey. **Hancox,** of Canaan, May, 1747.—*C. T. R.*

Children (C. B. S.):

1. David, b. 29 Feb., 1772; m. Polly **Reed.**
2. Jonathan, b. 29 May, 1775; d. Ohio.
3. Pedee, b. 29 June, 1777; m. Sam'l **Bushnell.**
4. Chloe, b. 6 Sept., 1780; m. John Ashley **Dutcher.**
5. Joseph, b. 3 May, 1785; m. Clarissa **Jeffries.**—*Canaan T. Rec.*
6. Amelia,b. 4 July, 1786; m. Chas. **Burrill.**
7. Daniel, b. 5 Aug., 1790; m. Sally **Camp.**
8. Solomon, b. 12 Aug., 1792; m. Laura **Scovel.**

FAM. 28. SAMUEL,⁵ (*Joseph*,⁴ *Joseph*,³ *Nath'l*,² *Rich.*,¹), b. Canaan, Ct., July 25-27, 1751; d. Caanan, Ct., Jan. 13, 1840; m. (1) Southington (?), Ct., May 28, 1771, Sarah (dau. Samuel & Sarah *Webster*) **Root,** b. Southington, Ct., Dec. 15, 1750; d. Canaan, Ct., Oct. 2, 1809; m. (2) Canaan, Ct., Nov. 22, 1810, Mrs. Naomi (*Gaylord*) **Kellogg** (dau. Nehemiah & Lucy *Loomis*) **Gaylord,** b. Canaan, Ct. (?), Feb. 8, 1757; d. Canaan, Ct. (?), Mch. 12, 1830.

Children (all b. Canaan, Ct.):

1. Billa, b. Canaan, Ct., Aug., 29, 1773; m. Weltha **Hosmer.**
2. Samuel, b. June 15, 1776; m. Sarah **Adams.**
3. Luther, b. Dec. 31, 1779; m. Jette **Beebe.**
4. Silas, b. Jan. 11, 1786; m. Lydia **Tanner.** FAM. 49.ⁿ
5. Oliver, b. Oct. 11, 1793; d. Mch. 5, 1798, prob. Canaan, Ct.

FAM. 29. SOLOMON,⁵ (*Zebedee*,⁴ *Joseph*,³ *Nath'l*,² *Sgt. Rich.*,¹), b. 1756; m. at Weth., 11 July, 1776, Chloe (dau. Nath'l & Rosetta *Blinn*) **Kirkham,** b. Weth., 1757, who d. W., 9 Nov., 1818. He d. W., 4 Feb., 1836.

Children (b. Weth.):

1. Solomon, b. 14 Aug., 1778. FAM. 50.
2. Chester, b. 12 May, 1780. FAM. 51.
3. Chloe, b. Nov. 3, 1782; m. N. Y. City, June, 1813, James **Lamb,** who was b. Midd, 6 Apl., 1777, and d. Berlin, Ct., 9 Feb., 1833; she d. B. 1 Sept., 1862. *Issue:*
   i. Huldah (Lamb), b. N. Y. City 30 June, 1814; d. B. 11 Dec., 1836; m. 1835, Jas. B. **Carpenter,** of B.
   ii. Loomis (Lamb), b. N. Y. City 22 Nov., 1815; d. Midd., Mch., 1870; m. Midd., Ct., 6 Aug., 1839, Mary E. **Curtis,** of Meriden.
   iii. Leverett (Lamb), b. N. Y. City 8 Oct., 1816; d. yg.
   iv. James Lockwood (Lamb), b. Berlin, Ct., 23 Oct., 1818; d. Winthrop, Ct., Apl., 1890; m. at W. (?) Minerva **Jones.**
   v. Louisa (Lamb), b. B. 12 Nov., 1822; m. B. 22 July, 1844, James B. **Carpenter,** above.
   vi. Lorenzo (Lamb), b. B. 30 May, 1826; m. Berlin, Ct., Lucy (dau. Horace & Elizabeth *Goodwin*) **Steele,** of Berlin.
4. Orrin, b. 9 Feb., 1785. FAM. 52.
5. Justus, b. 20 Apl., 1787. FAM. 53.
6. Miriam, b. 16 Apl., 1789; m. Berlin, Ct., 1816, Aaron (s. Aaron & Lois *Kelsey*) **Porter;** b. 1786, who d. at B. (?) 4 Dec., 1849. Ile b. 1786; d. B. 9 Mch., 1852. *Issue:*
   i. Orrin Beckley (Porter), b. 4 July, 1817; d. B. 1 Jan., 1876; m. Jane M. **Smith.**
   ii. William Henry (Porter), b. 10 Sept., 1819; d. 18 Sept., 1849; m. Martha **Belding.**
   iii. James Robinson (Porter), b. 8 Oct., 1821; m. (1) Lucy **Culver;** m. (2) Mrs. Lucy (Andrus) **Blake.**
   iv. Andrew (Porter), b. 9 Jan., 1824; d. bef. 1895.
   v. Emily (Porter), b. 5 Nov., 1825; d. 1855 or '56; m. 7 May, 1845, Edmund (s. Edmund & Lydia *Beckly*) **Sanford.**
   vi. Fidelia (Porter), b. 18 Apl., 1828; d. bef. 1895; m. Osborne **Roberts.**
   vii. Maria (Porter), b. 5 May, 1831; m. John **Miller,** of New Haven, Ct.
7. Nathaniel, b. 25 May, 1791. FAM. 54.
8. Emily, b. 27 May, 1794; d. 15 Nov., 1877; m. at Berlin, Ct., 10 May, 1816, Simeon (s. Rich. & Mercy *Collins*) **Belden,** b. Ry-H., 15 July, 1793; he d. Midd., Ct., 18 May, 1835; she d. 15 Nov., 1877, at B. *Issue:*
   i. Seabury (Belden), b. Ry-H. 17 May, 1817; m. (1) 5 Dec., 1839, Celestia (dau. Russell & Hepzibah *Beckley*) **Dickinson,** who d. 1 May, 1881; he m. (2) 15 Apl., 1885, Mrs. Sarah A. (Porter) **Barnes,** dau. of Marvin & Rebecca Porter.
   ii. Susan Melvina (Belden), b. 13 May, 1819; d. Midd. 1874; m. Wm. (s. Chauncey & Emily *Dudley*.
   iii. James Perry (Belden), b. 3 Aug., 1821; d. 30 Sept., 1822.
   iv. Perry (Belden), b. 8 Feb., 1823; d. E. Berlin, 5 Jan., 1892; m. Margaret **Hills.**
   v. Alonzo (Belden), b. 12 Oct., 1824; d. 25 Sept., 1825.
   vi. Alonzo (Belden), b. 26 Mch., 1826; d. abt. 1882; m. Ann Eliza **Meldrum.**
   vii. Nelson (Belden), b. 16 Aug., 1827; d. Ore., 3 Nov., 1874.
   viii. Emily (Belden), b. 14 Sept., 1829; d. 1 May, 1834.
   ix. Charlotte (Belden), b. 30 May, 1831; m. Midd. 29 Dec., 1882, James (s. Matt. & Ann) **Houston.**
   x. Sarah (Belden), b. 17 Nov., 1832; d. 11 Nov., 1833.
9. Nancy, b. 6 Nov., 1796; d. Berlin, Ct., (?) 3 Feb., 1884; m. Weth. 8 Dec., 1814, Samuel **Goodrich;** b. 1793, who d. Ry-H. 14 Apl., 1863. *Issue:*
   i. Adelia (Goodrich); m. John **Smith,** of Cromwell.
   ii. Norris (Goodrich); m. ——— **Culver.** (?)
   iii. Nathaniel (Goodrich); m. ——— **Belden.** (?)
   iv. Walter (D.?) (Goodrich), m. at Ry-H. 7 May, 1862, Mary B. **Goodrich.**
   v. Alonzo, m. Electa ——— (?).
   vi. Sarah, m. Osborne **Belden.**
   vii. Elizabeth, unm. "Out West."
   viii. Cornetia, m. Theo. **Burr,** of Hadd., Ct.

FAM. 30. ZEBEDEE,[5] (*Zeb.*,[4] *Joseph*,[2] *Nath'l*,[2] *Sgt. Rich.*,[1]), b. 1763, rem. to Barre, Vt., where a large number of his descts. are now resident; none left in Weth. He m. 8 Feb., 1789, Elizabeth **Belding**, of Far., b. 1769, and d. in Barre, Vt., 25 Aug., 1856; he d. B., 5 Feb., 1851.

Children:

1. Horace, b. Weth. 13 Feb., 1792 ; m. (1) Abigail **Wellington**; m. (2) Mrs. **White**; m. (3) Hannah **Blanchard.**
2. Oramel, b. Weth. 15 July, 1793 ; m. Betsy **Thompson.**
3. Samuel, b. 10 Feb., 1796 ; m. Roxana **Colby.**
4. Ch. ; d. Bristol, Ct., 1796. (?)
5. Oran, b. 30 June, 1802 ; m. Phebe **Sawyer.**
6. Luther, b. 12 Jan., 1809 ; m. Lovila D. **Goodale.**

FAM. 31. JOSIAH,[5] (*Zebedee*,[4] *Joseph*,[3] *Nath'l*,[2] *Sgt. Rich.*,[1]), b. 1768; rem. to Wethersfield, Vt., where he d. 12 Oct., 1861, and his numerous descts. are mostly in the West; none in Weth. He m. 1787, Mary (Molly) **Norton**, b. at Whitehall, N. Y., 29 Dec., 1767, who d. Weth., Vt., 29 Nov., 1838.

Children (b. Weth., Vt.):

1. Chester, b. 24 Mch., 1788 ; m. Eunice **Field.**
2. Josiah, b. 19 Oct., 1789 (or 15 Oct., 1790), m. (1) Lucretia **Nichols**; m. (2) Lydia ————; m. (3) Minerva **Bird.**
3. Lovina, b. 6 Sept., 1791 ; d. 30 Sept., 1799.
4. Sarah, b. 22 Mch., 1794 ; m. Cleveland **Redfield.**
5. Cyrus, b. 7 Mch., 1796 ; m. (1) Lucinda (**Fifield?**) m. (2) Lucretia **Davis.**
6. Asel, b. 7 Oct., 1797 ; d. 15 Aug., 1814.
7. Olive, b. 11 Nov., 1799 ; m. Summer **Hicks.**
8. Martha, b. 24 Nov., 1802 ; m. Emery **Gale.**
9. Dorcas, b. 26 Oct., 1803 ; m. John D. **Abbott.**
10. Guy (Rev.), b. 25 Dec., 1805 ; m. (1) Caroline **Walker**; m. (2) Phylia **Baker.**
11. Luke, b. 18 Apl., 1808 ; m. Mrs. Emma **Taylor.**
12. Dau., b. 4 Dec., 1810 ; d. 1 Mch., 1811.
13. Son, b. 7 Mch., 1812 ; d. 4 July, 1812.
14. Nancy, b. 18 June, 1814 ; m. Sabin **Felch.**

FAM. 32. DAVID,[5] (*David*,[4] *Joseph*,[3] *Nath'l*,[2] *Rich.*,[1]), b. 1765; d. Berlin, Ct., 16 Oct., 1822; m. Weth., 31 Mch., 1785, Eunice (dau. Moses & Martha *Robbins*) **Williams**, b. 1759; she d. B., 10 Mch., 1838.

Children:

1. Julia, b. 20 Nov., 1785 ; m. Orrin **Beckley.**
2. Son b. and d. 11 Jan., 1788.
3. Honor, b. 11 Oct., 1789 ; d Berlin, bef. 8 June, 1853 ; m. prob. bef. Feb., 1812, Abigail **Flagg.** *Issue:*
   i. Henry William (Flagg), d. bef. June, 1857 ; m. Cornelia **Cook.**
   ii. Norris Robbins (Flagg), d. yg.
4. Moses Williams, b. 7 Oct., 1791. FAM. 55.
5. Eunice, b. 18 Mch., 1795 ; m. 1816, Freedom (s. of Asabel & Abigail *Cowles*) **Hart**; b. 1796 ; she d. 31 Aug., 1823. *Issue,* (prob. *all b. in Berlin*) :
   i. Julia Beckley (Hart), b. 26 June, 1816 ; m. Harlow W. **Heath.**
   ii. William Cook (Hart), b. 13 Mch., 1818 ; m.
   iii. Sarah Ann (Hart), b. 5 Feb., 1820 ; m. Orin **Savage.**
   iv. James (Hart), b. 1 Apl., d. Dec. 7, 1822.
   v. Child, b. and d. 21 Aug., 1824.
6. Caroline, b. 10 Oct., 1796 ; d. Berlin, 15 Nov., 1881 ; m. (1) at B. 19 Mch., 1818, Geo. (s. Jesse & Lucy *Beckley*) **Hart**, who d. B. 16 Nov., 1825 ; m. (2) at B. 12 Sept., 1827, William (s. of Justus & Mabel *Boardman*) **Bulkeley**, who b.Weth. 7 Dec., 1797 ; d. Berlin, 10 Nov., 1878. *Issue,* (by first *marr.*) :
   i. Harriet (Hart), b. 27 Oct., 1819 ; m.

at B. 11 June, 1844, Nath'l (s. of Nath'l) **Dickinson.**
(*By second marr. at Berlin, Ct.*) :
   ii. William (Bulkeley), b. 6 July, 1829 ; unm.
   iii. George (Bulkeley), b. 27 Apl., 1837 ; d. ae. 2 yrs.
   iv. Julia (Bulkeley), b. 9 Sept., 1839 ; d. unm.
7. Dau., b. and . 6 Oct., 1798.
8. Inf., d. 1 Oct., 1798.
9. Miranda, b. 25 May, 1800 ; d. Berlin, 7 May, 1872 ; m. at B. 17 Sept., 1826, Leonard (s. Luther & Abigail *Miller*) **Pattison**, of Berlin, who d. B. 11 Jan., 1872. *Issue:*
   i. George (Pattison), b 1827 ; m. (1) Mch. 8, 1856, Fidelia Jane (dau. Reuben & Sydney) **Beckley**, who d. 28 Sept., 1856 ; be m. (2) Hannah **Downs.**
   ii. Frank (Pattison), b. 1829 ; d. unm.
   iii. Jane (Pattison), b. 1831 ; d. unm.
   iv. Miranda (Pattison), b. 1833, and d. yg.
   v. Harriet (Pattison), b. 1835 ; d. yg.
   vi. Sarah (Pattison), b. 1837 ; m. Henry **Jones.**
   vii. Norris (Pattison), m. Lucinda **Whaples.**
   viii. William Le Roy (Pattison), b. 1845 ; d. unm.

FAM. 33. SILAS,[5] (*David*,[4] *Joseph*,[3] *Nath'l*,[2] *Sgt. Rich.*,[1]), b. 1766, d. 1 Oct., 1823; m. 4 Nov., 1798, Patience (dau. of Jedediah & Sarah *Wilcox*) **North**, of Far., b. 1775, who d. Windsor, Ct., 29 Feb., 1836.

Children (b. Weth.):

1. Emma, b. July, 1799 ; m. 7 May, 1821, Horace **Potter**; had 12 ch.
2. Silas, b. 21 Apl., 1802. FAM. 55.

FAM. 34. LUTHER,⁵ (David,⁴ Joseph,³ Nath'l,² Rich.,¹), b. Weth., 11 Oct., 1778; d. Berlin, Ct., 11 Jan., 1841; m. 18 Sept., 1803, Sarah (dau. Solomon & Olive Hart) **Flagg**, who was b. 10 Aug., 1785, and d. Midd., 21 Feb., 1861.

Children (all b. in Beckley Qr.) :

1. Horace, b. 30 Aug., 1804. FAM. 56.
2. Ralph Henry, b. 15 Aug., 1806. ҐAM. 57.
3. Walter, b. 22 June, 1808. FAM. 58.
4. Alfred Wyllis, { twins b. 18 Dec., 1809;
5. Albert Wells, { d. 10 Apl., 1811; d. 16 Apl., 1811.
6. Albert Wyllys, b. 12 Sept., 1812. FAM. 59.
7. Olive Amelia, b. 20 Apl., 1814; m. Berlin, 14 May, 1835, Horace C. (s. Samuel & Sarah Stanley) **Sheldon**; b. B. 16 Feb., 1805; d. Htfd., 31 Aug., 1884. *Issue:*
   i. Frances Amelia (Sheldon), b. 3 Mch., 1836; m. Wm. **Goodrich**; d.
   ii. Fidelia Angeline (Sheldon),
   iii. Fred., Augustus (Sheldon), twins, b. 1 Mch., 1840; d. yg.
   iv. Sarah Beckley (Sheldon), b. 8 Dec., 1843; d. yg.
   v. Julia (Sheldon), b. 31 July, 1845; m. Frank N. **White**, of Boston.
8. Luther, b. 16 Aug., 1815; d. 15 Dec., 1816.
9. Alfred Luther, b. 28 Oct., 1817. FAM. 60.
10. Sarah, b. 30 Mch., 1820; m. at New Haven, Ct., 1841, John (s. of John & Nancy *Miller*) **Collins**, of Midd., b. 1818; who d. New Orleans 22 Jan., 1855; she d. Ravenna, O., 21 Apl., 1880. *Issue:*
    i. Emma (Collins), b. 15 Dec., 1846; d. 11 Oct., 1854.
    ii. Sarah Beckley (Collins), b. 13 Jan., 1852; unm.
11. George, b. 3 Oct., 1821. FAM. 61.
12. Joseph, b. 1 Apl., 1823; d. 3 Apl., 1824.
13. William, b. 2 Oct., 1826. FAM. 62.

FAM. 35. ORIN,⁶ (Elias,⁵ Elias,⁴ John,³ Benj.,² Sgt. Rich.,¹), b. 1784; d. at Berlin, Ct., 9 Mch., 1836; m. (1) at B., 20 Oct., 1805, Julia (dau. David & Eunice *Williams*) **Beckley**, b. Weth., 20 Nov., 1785; d. B., 16 Oct., 1808; m. (2) at B., 26 Apl., 1812, Harriet (dau. Shubael & Sarah *Hart*) **Pattison**, b. B., 3 Oct., 1788; d. B., 11 Sept., 1847.

Child (by first marriage) :

1. Son ; d. 16 June, 1808 ;ae. 31 hrs.
(By second marriage) :
2. Julia Maria, b. 16 Jan., 1813; m. B. 8 Sept., 1836, Sidney Smith (s. Amos & Mehitable *Simons*) **Allcott**; b. Ballston Spa, N. Y., 20 Dec., 1803, and d. Boston, Mass, 1 May, 1867 ; she d. Newton, Mass., 30 Oct., 1860. *Issue:*
   i. William Seymour (Alcott), b. 23 Nov., 1838 ; d. 5 May, 1844.
   ii. Julius Lee (Alcott), b. 20 Aug., 1839 ; d. 17 Jan., 1840.
   iii. Julia Maria (Alcott), b. 15 Dec., (1842?) d. 11 Apl., (1842?)
   iv. Charles H. (Alcott), b. 11 Jan., 1844 ; d. 4 Sept., 1862.
   v. Frank (Alcott), b. 15 Sept., 1845 ; d. Meriden, Ct., 29 Dec., 1891 ; m. at New Haven, Ct., 15 Sept., 1875, Elvira Minerva **Thompson** (dau. Leverett), b. Branford, Ct., 25 Nov., 1852.
3. Lyman, b. 10 July, 1815. FAM. 63.
4. Emily, b. 11 May, 1817 ; m. 29 Nov., 1840, Horace Gardiner **Smith**; b. Bath, N. H. *Issue:*
   i. Murray Winchester (Smith), b. 1 Nov., 1842 ; m. Emmogene **Nellis**, 1867 ; d. Denver, Col.
   ii. Charles Lowell (Smith), b. 30 Aug., 1848 ; d. Ill., 1864.
   iii. Mary Glenwood (Smith), b. 5 May, 1852 ; d. Denver, 1874.
   iv. Jessie Frances (Smith), b. 27 Mch., 1854 ; unm. 1900.
5. Jane, b. 28 Dec., 1819 ; d. 21 June, 1823.
6. Jane Eliza, b. 16 Sept., 1823 ; d. 21 Sept., 1826.
7. Harriet Pattison, b. 22 Nov., 1825 ; m. 15 Apl., 1846, Augustus Pattison (s. Augustus B. & Lydia *Bishop*) **Collins**; d. 19 Mch., 1890, at New Britain, Ct. *Issue:*
   i. Auguta (Collins), b. 16 d. 18 Sept., 1847.
   ii. Charles Orin (Collins), b. 12 Oct., 1849 ; m. at Mt. Vernon, N. Y., 7 Jan., 1874, Elizabeth A. (dau. Thos. & Margaret *Hallock*) **Stubbings**.
8. Caroleen, b. 27 July, 1829 ; m. at N. Britain, Ct., 7 Apl., 1858, John Woodruff (s. of John & Prudence *Woodruff*) **Clark**, of N. B. ; b. 3 July, 1822 ; she d. N. Y. City, 13 Apl., 1891. *Issue:*
   i. Mary Eleanor (Clark), b. Brooklyn, N. Y., 18 Jan., 1859 ; m. 8 Oct., 1879, Mancius Holmes (s. Mancius Smedes & Gertrude *Holmes*) **Hutton**, D. D. b. N. Y. City, 13 Oct., 1837.
   ii. Edward Herbert (Clark), b. New Britain, Ct., 18 Nov., 1860 ; m. at New Britain, Ct., 31 Oct., 1883, Emma Louise (dau. Thos. Abiram & Martha *Fitch*) **Conklin**, b. N. B., 8 Jan., 1861.
   iii. Caroleen Beckley, b. Kensington, Ct., 12 June, 1862 ; m. at New Brunswick, N. J., 15 Oct., 1890, Geo. Beekman (s. Wm. Phil'ips & Elizabeth Martha *Rowan*) **Sheppard**, b. Bklyn., N. Y., 7 Sept., 1858. Mrs. Sheppard is the main author of this Beckley Geneal.
   iv. John Hilliard (Clark), b. 30 Nov., 1863, and d. 28 Oct., 1864, Kensington, Ct.

FAM. 36. LYMAN,⁶ (Elias,⁵ Elias,⁴ John,³ Benj.,² Rich.,¹), b. Weth., 1786; d. at Sault Ste. Marie, Mich., 17 Sept., 1863; m. in Ohio, 1832-3, Sarah (dau. Abijah & Polly *Penfield*) **Sturdevant**, b. Harford, Pa., 8 Apl., 1805; d. Caledonia, Mich., on 23 July, 1892

Children:

1. Everett Allen, b. Stow Corners, O., 9 Sept., 1835 ; living, unm. in 1901.
2. Clara Augusta, b. 28 Aug., 1842 ; m. Albert Wolcott **Stow**.
3. Wilson S., b. Starr Corners, O., 26 Oct., 1845 ; d. 8 May, 1866, at Cascade, Mich.

FAM. 37. ALLEN,[6] (*Elias,*[5] *Elias,*[4] *John,*[3] *Benj.,*[2] *Sgt. Rich.,*[1]), b. Weth., 7 Mch., 1788; d. Berlin, Ct., 3 Oct., 1832; m. (1) at B., 27 Sept., 1809, Marcia **Carter,** who, b. 1790, d. B., 3 Sept., 1815; he m. (2) at B., 6 June 1817, Miriam (dau. Elijah & Miriam) **Clapp,** b. Berlin, 1795; d. B., 24 Sept., 1879.

Children (*b. Berlin*):

1. Evelyn, b. Feb., 1811. FAM. 64.
2. Almira, b. 13 Aug., 1815; d. 27 Jan., 1816.
(*By second marriage*):
3. Henry Clapp, b. 21 May, 1818. FAM. 65.
4. Aurelia Wells, b. 6 Mch., 1825; m. 18 Nov., 1845, Jas. H. **Goodrich.** *Issue:*
   i. Emma Clarissa (Goodrich), b. 1847; d. 1847.
   ii. Ella Josephine (Goodrich), b. 1849; d. 1868.

   iii. Chas. Allen (Goodrich), b. 26 Sept., 1852; m. 1878, Julia **Hays.**
   iv. Emma Aurelia (Goodrich), b. 1855; m. 1880, Arthur C. **Bliss.**
   v. Frank Henry (Goodrich), b. 1857; m. 1889, Ella **Mackay.**
   vi. Edward Wells (Goodrich), b. 1861; m. 1890, Hattie J. **Allen.**
   vii. George Edward (Goodrich), b. 31 Oct., 1865.

FAM. 37a. NOEL,[5] (*Selah,*[4] *Elias,*[3] *Benj.,*[2] *Sgt. Rich.,*[1]), b. 1791; d. Stow, O., 10 Mch., 1858; m. S., 21 Oct., 1827, Margaret (dau. James & Losina *Wright*) **Lindsley,** b. Burlington, Vt., 7 Apl., 1709; she d. S., 26 Oct., 1880.

Children:

1. Caroline, b. 31 Oct., 1828; m. Madison **Andrews.**
2. Edwin, b. 18 or 19 July, 1830; m. Maria **Cowly.**
3. Laura, b. 19 Sept., 1832; m. Josiah **Gay-**
lord.
4. Noel, b. 8 July, 1834; m. Martha **Randall.**
5. Lois Rowena, b. 12 Dec., 1839; d. unm. S., 12 July, 1876.

FAM. 38. LOTAN,[6] (*Selah,*[5] *Elias,*[4] *John,*[3] *Benj.,*[2] *Sgt. Rich.,*[1]), b. Berlin, 3 Nov., 1793; d. at Huntington, O., 25 Sept., 1847-8; m. Berlin, 16 Oct., 1829, Lucy Kirby (dau. Seth & Huldah *Richardson*) Beckley, b. Weth., 28 Aug., 1800; d. H., 1875 or '76.

Children:

1. Lois Deming, b. Berlin, Ct., 13 May, 1822; d. 25 Sept., 1822.
2. Seth, b. B., 5 Oct., 1823; d. 9 Sept., 1825.
3. Ammi Deming, b. B., 26 June, 1826. FAM. 66.
4. Huldah Richardson, b. B., 11 June, 1827; d. 13 Aug., 1830.
5. Harriet Richardson, b. Stow, O., 24 Sept., 1834; d. Huntington, O., 15 Feb., 1856.
6. Caroline, b. H., 10 Mch., 1841; m. 3 Jan., 1860, George (s. of Eleazer & Polly *Davis*) **Fisher;** she d. Cleveland, O., 8 Mch., 1904. *Issue* (*b. Wellington, O.*):

   i. Erwin Lotan (Fisher), b. 13 Mch., 1861; m. in Ohio, 25 June, 1890, Fanny **Madison.**
   ii. Everett George (Fisher), b. 15 Mch., 1863.
   iii. Ada (Fisher), b. 3 July, 1866; d. 12 Jan., 1867.
   iv. Leona (Lucy) (Fisher), b. 22 Jan., 1868; m. 1885, Ruloff **Schenck.**
   v. Nellie Harriet (Fisher), b. 28 Jan., 1870; m. 1892, Robt. Armour **Edmeston.**

FAM. 39. ELNATHAN SMITH,[6] (*Selah,*[5] *Elias,*[4] *John,*[3] *Benj.,*[2] *Rich.,*[1]), b. Berlin, Ct., 1801; d. Huntington, O., 11 Dec., 1872; m. bef. 1827, Polly Fidelia (dau. Isaac & Lucy *North*) **Wilcox,** b. 1805; prob. d. H., 7 May, 1891.

Children:

1. Lyman, b. 5 Apl., 1827. FAM. 67.
2. Elouisa Lucy, b. 27 Apl., 1832; m. At Huntington, O., as 2d wife, 1871, Madison (s. Theo. R. & Axie *Richardson*) **Andrews;** b. 1826. *Issue:*

   i. Estella Madeline (Andrews), b. 1872; m. Orville B. **McClellan.**
   ii. Lucy Beckley (Andrews), b. 17 Feb., 1879.

FAM. 40. EDWIN,[6] (*Selah,*[5] *Elias,*[4] *John,*[3] *Benj.,*[2] *Rich.,*[1]), b. 1806; d. Morley, Mich., 23 Dec., 1872; m. at Stow, O., 7 Feb., 1835, Polly (dau. Recompense & Polly *Moore*) **Tiffany,** b. Gd. Isld., N. Y., 6 Feb., 1813; who d. Ind., 22 May, 1851.

Children:

1. George, b. Perry, Ind., 6 Sept., 1840; m. Martha Jane **Hart.**
2. Henry C., b. 30 Apl., 1846; m. Mar-
guerite E. **Main.**
3. Edwin, b. 12 May, 1851; m. Belle **Chapin.**

FAM. 41. AHIRA,[6] (*Selah*,[5] *Elias*,[4] *John*,[3] *Benj*.,[2] *Rich*.,[1]), b. 1809; d. Stur., O., 1 Nov., 1856; m. S., 21 Dec., 1834, Lucy (dau. Orin A. & Sarah *Wilcox*) **Stevens**, b. S., 3 May, 1818; d. Cleveland, O., 12 June, 1888.

Children:

1. Luther, b. Stow, O., 23 Apl., 1836; d. 10 May, 1836.
2. Charles Selah, b. Stow, O., 17 Jan., 1839; d. Morley, Mich., 20 July, 1880.
3. Sarah Hepzibah, b. Stow, O., 11 July, 1840; d. Cuyahoga Falls, O., 19 Apl., 1882; m. 21 Feb., 1878, at Akron, O., Julian **Marshall**. *No issue.*
4. Julia Amelia, b. Stow, O., 6 Aug., 1843;

m. James **Turner**.
5. Andrew Olin, b. Cuyahoga Falls, O., 10 July, 1846; m. Fanny **Ray**.
6. Eunice Marian, b. Monroe Falls, O., 25 June, 1849; m. (1) Albert Squires; m. (2) Henry **Strong**.
7. Lucy Augusta, b. Stow, O., 1 Oct., 1855; m. Harry **Pritchard**.

FAM. 42. WILLIAM SYLVESTER,[6] (*Sylvester*,[5] *Elias*,[4] *John*,[3] *Benj*.,[2] *Rich*.,[1]), b. Weth., 1812; d. Berlin, Ct., 3 Sept., 1844; m. at B., 9 May, 1839, Caroline (dau. Russell & Hepzibah *Beckley*) **Dickinson**, b. Weth. (Ry-H.), 22 Dec., 1818; d. Meriden, Ct., 17 Feb., 1863-4.

Child (*b. Berlin, Ct.*):

1. Frances Hannah, b. 1839; d. Midd., 25 Apl., 1861; m. Midd., 12 Oct., 1858, Edgar **Beckley**.

FAM. 43. EMILIUS LYSANDER,[6] (*Sylvester*,[5] *Elias*,[4] *John*,[3] *Benj*.,[2] *Rich*.,[1]), b. Berlin, Ct., 20 Sept., 1810; d. Stafford, Ct., 24 June, 1874; m. at B., 8 Apl., 1845, Sarah Jane (dau. Horace & Elizabeth *Goodwin*) **Steele**, b. Berlin, 5 June, 1825.

Child:

1. Ella Elizabeth, b. No. White Creek, N. Y., 14 Aug., 1848; m. at Stafford, Ct., 4 Apl., 1886, Eugene Sylvester (s. of Dydemus Freeman & Emeline Almira *Cady*) **Howlett**, b. 1858. *No issue.*

FAM. 44. RODNEY BLENDALL,[6] (*Oliver*,[5] *Benj*.,[4] *Benj*.,[3] *Benj*.,[2] *Rich*.,[1]), b. Weth. 1789; d. Boston, Mass. (?), 21 Nov., 1822; m. at B. Clarissa (*Bartlett*) **Nash**.

Children:

1. James Rodney, b. B., 12 Jan., 1815; m. (1) Nancy **Pray**; m. (2) Hope S. **Keene**.
2. William Bartlett, b. and d. at Weymouth, Mass.
3. Clarissa, b. Weymouth, 1819; m. Washington **Merritt**.

FAM. 45. SAMUEL,[6] (*Oliver*,[5] *Benj*.,[4] *Benj*.,[3] *Benj*.,[2] *Rich*.,[1]), b. Weth., 25 Feb., 1791; d. Rockport, O., 18 Mch., 1876; m. Midd., Ct., 5 May, 1815, Sophrania Adaline (dau. Ephm. & Nancy *Rogers*) **Coe**, b. Granville, Mass., 24 Mch., 1796; d. 31 Mch., 1869.

Children:

1. Polly, b. Middletown, Ct., 15 Sept., 1816; m. Henry **Sanford**.
2. Susan, b. Berlin, 3 Dec., 1818; m. Paul **Knowlton**.
3. Samuel, b. Granville, Mass., 22 July, 1821; d. Dover, O., 10 Oct., 1840.
4. Harriet, b. Ridgeville, O., 22 Oct., 1823; m. Harry **Bratton**.
5. James Rodney, b. Dover, O., 12 Jan., 1825; m. Angeline **Steadman**.
6. Caroline Sophronia, b. Dover, O., 15 Nov., 1827; m. Osborne **Cook**.
7. Ephraim Loren, b. Dover, O., 9 Oct., 1832; m. Sarah Ann **Kelly**.
8. Nancy Lucinda, b. Dover, O., 29 Sept., 1836; m. Jos. Henry **Wood**.

FAM. 46. THEODORE,[6] (*Oliver*,[5] *Benj*.,[4] *Benj*.,[3] *Benj*.,[2] *Rich*.,[1]), b. Weth., 1794; d. Glast., 17 Sept., 1829; m. Midd., 20 Oct., 1823, Eliza (dau. Asher) **Belden**; she m. (2) Elijah **Stanley**.

Children:

1. Oliver, b. 'Glast., 1824 (?); d. Guilford, Ct., 6 Oct., 1864; unm.
2. Chester, b. Glast., 1 July, 1825; m. Mary Elizabeth **Belden**.
3. Lyman, b. Glast., 23 Nov., 1826; m. Mary **Page**.
4. John, b. Berlin, 27 Feb., 1829; m. Mary Hall **Curtis**. FAM. 68.

FAM. 47. BENJAMIN,[6] (Luman,[5] Benj.,[4] Benj.,[3] Benj.,[2] Rich.,[1]), b. Berlin, 1794-5; d. Huntington, O., 5 Dec., 1843; m. B. Lucette **Porter,** who d. B., 29 Sept., 1837.

Children (b. Berlin):

1. Harriet.
2. Marrietta, d. Berlin, 3 Aug., 1836, ae. 16 yrs. 6 mos.
3. Margaret, m. ————.
4. Luman Horace, d. 10 Mch., 1826, ae. 6 mos.

FAM. 48. HOSEA,[6] (Jona.,[5] Daniel,[4] Daniel,[3] Nath'l,[2] Rich.,[1]) b. 1779, at Weth.; d. Chesterfield, N. H., 15 Oct., 1843; m. Killingworth, Ct., 21 Sept., 1808. Lydia (dau. Abraham & Lydia Redfield) **Pierson,** b. K., 8 June, 1785.

Children:

1. Lydia Sophia, b. 17 Aug., 1809 ; d. 24 Mch., 1856 ; unm.
2. Fanny Emily, b. 11 Oct., 1811 ; d. 11 Sept., 1826.
3. Jane Louisa, b. July, 1815 ; m. (1) Nelson W. **Herrick**; m. (2) Alonzo Church **Wood.**
4. Abraham Pierson, b. 29 May, 1820 ; d. 25 Oct., 1843 ; unm.
5. David Webster, d. 25 Oct., 1822 ; m. Mary Hough **Chase.**

FAM. 49. NORMAN,[6] (Jona.,[5] Daniel,[4] Daniel,[3] Nath'l.,[2] Rich.,[1]), b. Weth., 1794; d. Berlin, 7 June, 1836; m. Weth. (N. C. R.), 13 June, 1819, Mary **Evans,** b. 1796; who d. B., 27 Jan., 1861.

Children:

1. Levi, b. 1820 ; d. 17 May, 1852 ;unm.
2. Lewis, b. 23 Nov., 1823. FAM. 69.
3. Linus, b. 1824 (?). FAM. 70.
4. Mary Anna, b. 1828 (?) ; m. Geo. S. **Johnson,** b. Midd., 1827 (?). Issue:
   i. Charles (Johnson).
   ii. Mary (Johnson).
   iii. Child (Johnson), d. yg.
   Perhaps others.
5. Emiline Jane, b. Apl., 1830 ; d. 30 Aug., 1832.
6. Emily J., b. 16 June, 1833 ; m. Berlin, 18 Sept., 1854, Philip H. (s. Philip & Sally Andrus) **Deming,** b. B. 1836, who d. B. 1862. Issue:
   i. Wilbur (Deming), b. 29 June, 1855.
   ii. Clarence (Deming), b. B., 6 Mch., 1857 ; m. ————.
   iii. Mary (Deming).
7. Emeline L., b. twin to Emily J., m. 18 Sept., 1854, Abraham **Warner,** b. 1829, at Berne, N. Y. Issue:
   i. Levi (Warner).
8. Norman, b. 3 and d. 6 Aug., 1836.

FAM. 49a. SILAS,[6] (Samuel,[5] Joseph,[4] Joseph,[3] Nath.,[2] Rich.,[1]), b. Canaan, Ct., Jan., 11, 1786; d. New York, N. Y., Oct., 5, 1869; m. Warren, Ct., Mch. 11, 1808, Lydia (dau. Ephriam & Huldah Monson) **Tanner,** b. Warren, Ct., Mch. 2, 1788; d. Canaan, Ct., Nov. 20, 1864.

Children:

1. Laura Talmadge, b. Warren, Ct., 7 Aug., 1809 ; d. Canaan, Ct., 21 Sept., 1810.
2. Samuel Marvin, b. Warren, Ct., 22 Nov., 1811. FAM. 70a.
3. Van Antwerp.
4. Maria Eveline, b. Canaan, Ct., 4 Oct., 1818 ; d. Canaan, Ct., 28 June, 1841.
5. James Falconer, b. and d. Canaan, Ct., 5 Dec., 1830, 22 Oct., 1834.

FAM. 50. SOLOMON,[6] (Solomon,[5] Zebedee,[4] Joseph,[3] Nath'l,[2] Rich.,[1]), b. Weth., 1778; d. Berlin, 5 Feb., 1858; m. (1) at Wilmington, Del., 4 Apl., 1802, Ann **French,** b. Wilm., 1 Aug, 1786; d. B., 29 Apl. 1816; he m. (2) at Wilm., 3 July, 1817, Lucretia (dau. Howell) **Evans,** b. Wilm., 27 Oct. 1793; d. B., 4 Feb., 1854.

Children (all b. Beckly, Qr.)

1. William, b. 22 Apl., 1803. FAM. 71.
2. Justus, b. 27 Feb., 1805 ; d. 3 July, 1806.
3. Sally, b. 14 Nov., 1807 ; m. 2 Nov., 1831—N. C. R., Andrew **Abernathy,** of New Htfd. ; had a s. Henry.
4. Elizabeth, b. 1 Feb., 1810 ; m. Chas. **Clark.**
5. Emily, b. 29 Mch., 1812 ; m. at B., 10 Oct., 1831, Walter (s. Ebenezer & Polly Goodrich) **Andrews,** b. New Britain, Ct., 14 June, 1811 ; she d. Watertown, Wis., 21 Jan., 1885. Issue (b. Watertown, Wis. ?) :
   i. Ellen M. (Andrews), b. 18 July, 1833 ; m. Wat., Wis., 1 Oct., 1861, Elnathan **Breckenridge.**
   ii. George (Andrews), b. 7 May, 1835 ; d. 16 Mch., 1840.
   iii. George (Andrews), b. 6 Feb., 1842 ; d. 14 Oct., 1843.
   iv. Sarah Augusta (Andrews), b. 5 May, 1845 ; d. 13 July, 1847.

v. Charles (Andrews), b. 8 July, 1847;
  m. at Milwaukee, Wis., 14 Dec., 1869,
  Mary **Cubitt**.
6. Rebecca, b. 3 Oct., 1814; m. Aaron **Mor-**
  ley, at B., 17 Feb., 1833; d. Brooklyn,
  N. Y., 8 Jan., 1891. *Issue:*
  i. Albert William (Morley), b. 27 Mch.,
    1834 ; m. (1) 1865, Sarah **Wiggins;** m.
    (2) ————.
  ii. Caroline E. (Morley), b. 26 Nov.,
    1835 ; d. 9 June, 1894 ; m. Apl., 1855,
    Wm. **Lewis.**
  iii. Sarah A. (Morley), b. 6 Feb., 1838 ;
    d. 4 Mch., 1891 ; m. (1) ————
    Needham; m. (2) 25 June, 1864, Geo.
    Strong.
  iv. Charles A. (Morley), b. 28 Oct., 1840 ;
    d. 27 Aug., 1841.
  v. Mary E. (Morley), b. 22 Mch., 1844 ;
    d. 30 Sept., 1844.
  vi. Emma R. (Morley), b. 3 Nov., 1845 ;
    d. 4 Aug., 1847.
  vii. Alice Q. (Morley), b. 23 Oct., 1848 ;
    m. 17 Apl., 1872, James **Wiggins,** of
    Brooklyn, N. Y.
  viii. Edward A. (Morley), b. 16 July,
    1851 ; d. 27 July, 1867.
  ix. Franklin E. (Morley), b. 6 Dec.,
    1853 ; d. 24 Oct., 1854.
  x. Frederick A. (Morley), b. twin to
    Franklin A., b. 6 Dec., 1853; m. 1
    Mch., 1879, at Bkln., N. Y., Mary
    Strong.
  xi. George H. (Morley), b. 2 Nov., 1856 ;
    d. 13 Jan., 1884 ; m. 8 Aug., 1881.
  (*By second marriage*) :
7. Mary Jane, b. 25 May, 1818 ; m. at B.,
  27 Apl., 1840, Reuben (s. of Job & Polly
  Gladden) **Root,** b. Kens., 4 Sept., 1815 ; d.
  Berlin, 19 May, 1879 ; she d. Meriden, 8
  Jan., 1901. *Issue* (*b. Berlin, Ct.*) :
  i. Almira (Root), b. 11 Nov., 1843 ;
    unm.
  ii. Julia (Root), b. 15 Mch., 1847 ; m.
    Henry **Snow.**

iii. Edward (Root), b. 14 Nov., 1849 ;
  m. Carrie **Norton.**
8. James Henry, b, 23 Sept., 1819. FAM. 72.
9. Franklin Wiles, b. 8 May, 1821. FAM. 73.
10. Cornelia Sloops, b. 14 Oct., 1822 ; m. at
  Ry-H. 5 July, 1840, Davis D. **Stevens;** b.
  New Haven, Feb., 1815 (?) ; d. B. 9-11,
  Oct., 1891. She d. Ry-H. 12 Feb., 1883.
  Issue:
  i. Henry Davis (Stevens), b. 19 Dec.,
    1841 ; unm. 1899.
  ii. Lovira Jane (Stevens), b. 26 Sept.,
    1846 ; m. (1) Geo. **Gilbert;** m. (2)
    ————.
  iii. Corean A. (Stevens), b. 5 Nov., 1848 ;
    m. ———— **Sanford.**
  iv. Frank H. (Stevens), b. 14 Dec., 1850 ;
    m. 5 Sept., 1875, Eliza **Semker.**
  v. Clifford B. (Stevens), b. 30 Apl., 1853 ;
    d. yg.
  vi. Charles I. (Stevens), b. 23 June, 1855 ;
    d. yg.
  vii. Edgar D., b. 9 Sept., 1857.
  viii. Elmer E. (Stevens), b. 3 May, 1862 ;
    m. ———— **Goodrich.**
  ix. Birdsey S. (Stevens), b. 5 Feb., 1867 ;
    unm. 1898.
11. Almira Evans, b. 3 Jan., 1824 ; m. B. 5
  May, 1847, Horace (s. of James & Olive
  Wilcox) **Booth;** b. New Britain, 6 Nov.,
  1821.
  Children (*all b. New Britain, Ct.*) :
  i. Horace Wilcox (Booth), b. 18 Oct.,
    1849 ; m.
  ii. Olive Almira (Booth), b. 24 July,
    1856 ; d. 1885 ; m. J. R. **Andrews.**
  iii. Mattie Lucetta (Booth), b. 25 Oct.,
    1863 ; m. 1886, Albert N. **Abbe.**
  iv. Lyman (Booth).
12. Ch. D. b. 9 d. 10 June, 1832.
13. Caroline Elizabeth, b. 25 June, 1834 ; m.
  Berlin, 3 Jan., 1859, Myron S. (s. of
  Nathan'l & Eliza *Peck*) **White;** b. Norfolk, Ct., 14 Aug., 1824. *No issue:*
14. Ch. b. and d. 18 July, 1840.

FAM. 51. CHESTER,[6] (*Solomon*,[5] *Zebedee*,[4] *Joseph*,[3] *Nath'l*,[2] *Rich.*,[1]) b. Weth.,
12 May, 1780; d. Wilmington, Del., bef. July 31, 1822; m. (1) ————;
m. (2) Sally (dau. James & Eleanor) **Lyle,** b. 1792; both wives from Wilmington, prob.

Children :

1. Sydney Ann, m. Midd., Ct., 13 June, 1843,
  William **Warner;** d. bef. 1895. *No issue.*
2. Elizabeth, m. Walter (s. Rich. & Mercy
  Collins) **Belden;** b. Ry-H. 25 Jan., 1807.
  Issue:
  i. Helen (Belden), m. ———— **White.**
  ii. Henry (Belden), d. Htfd. prob. abt.

  1895 ; m. Sophronia ————.
  iii. Orlando (Belden), d. in Andersonville
    Prison during Civil War, 1864.
  iv. Frances (Belden), m. Hiram **Belden;**
    d.
3. Henry Vining, b. near Wilmington, Del.,
  11 Feb., 1815 ; m. Sarah **Ducker.**

FAM. 52. ORRIN,[6] (*Solomon*,[5] *Zebedee*,[4] *Joseph*,[3] *Nath'l*[2] *Rich.*,[1]), b. Weth.,
9 Feb., 1785; d. at sea betw. Wilmington and Savannah, Nov., 1815; m. Prudence **Jeffers,** b. Wilm., 8 June, 1791, and d. there 8 Mch., 1818.

Children (*b. Wilmington, Del.*) :

1. Caroline, b. 30 July, 1813 ; m. ————
  Martin.
2. Anna Maria, b. 26 Aug., 1814 ; m. Jacob

  Hampton.
3. Orin Lewis, b. 18 Dec., 1815 ; m. Nancy
  Maria **Zimmerman.**

FAM. 53. JUSTUS,[6] (*Solomon*,[5] *Zebedee*,[4] *Joseph*,[3] *Nath'l*,[2] *Richard*,[1]), b. Weth.,
1787, d. Wilm., Del., m. at Wilm., Sally (Robinson) **Hustice,** (dau. John &
Marg't *Robinson*.)

Children (*b. Wilmington, Del.*) :

1. Robinson, who seems to have had a dau.
  Margaret and a son George.
2. Wm. Henry.

3. Sally Ann.
4. 'Louisa, who m. James **Mantenay.**

FAM. 54. NATHANIEL,⁶ (Solomon,⁵ Zebedee,⁴ Joseph,³ Nath'l,² Richard,¹), b. Weti..,
1791; d. Balt., May, 1850; m. 1808, Elizabeth (dau. James & Eleano) Lyie, b.
31 Dec., 1787; d. Camden, N. J., 26 July, 1870.

Children:

1. Sally Ann, b. Balt., 25 Dec., 1813; m.
   Joseph J. Shipman.
2. William Henry, b. Balt., 21 June, 1816;
   m. Ann Rebecca Van Meeter.

3. Susan Amanda, b. Wilmington, Del., 17
   Oct., 1818; m. John Davis Tustin.
4. Elizabeth Emily, b. Balt., 9 Nov., 1828;
   m. Perry Tulley Carroll.

FAM. 55.ᴬ MOSES WILLIAMS,⁶ (David,⁵ David,⁴ Joseph,³ Nath'l,² Richard,¹),
Weth., 1791; d. Southington, Ct., 27 Sept., 1868; m. at Kans., 4 Apl., 1816;
Mary (dau. Rob't & Sarah Hart) Cornwall, b. 12 July, 1798; d. at ˈS.,
7 Sept. 1885.

Children (all b. New Britain, Ct.):

1. Sarah Cornwall, b. 14 Jan., 1818; m.
   Southington, Ct., 7 Dec., 1840, Francis
   Woodruff (s. Chauncey & Lois Woodruff)
   Lewis, b. S., 21 Jan., 1816; d. S., 14 Sept.,
   1888. Issue:
   i. Vernelia E. (Lewis), b. 11 Apl., 1845;
      m. at Suffield, Ct., 1 Jan., 1894, Fay-
      ette C. Slate.
   ii. Hattie A. (Lewis), b. 9 Oct., 1846; d.
       at Wallingford, Ct., 16 Dec., 1889; m.
       at S., 17 May, 1876, Fayette C. Slate.
2. William Redfield, b. 24 June, 1820. FAM. 74c.
3. Eunice Robbins, b. 17 July, 1822; m. 17
   July, 1822; d. Southington, 13 Oct., 1884;
   m. at S., 9 July, 1844, John (s. Noah &
   Luanna Andrews) Gridley, b. S. 4 Aug.,
   1815; he d. S., 5 Apl., 1878. Issue:
   i. John William (Gridley), b. 9 Apl.,
      1846; m. 24 Apl., 1866, Julia (dau.
      David) Pratt; m. (2) Mary Ida (dau.

   Geo. W.) Robbins.
   ii. Eunice E. (Gridley), b. 12 Nov., 1852;
       d. 7 Nov., 1853.
   iii. Mary E. (Gridley), b. 5 Oct., 1855;
        m. 7 Sept., 1887, Rev. Fred. L.
        Stevens.
   iv. Julia E., b. 1 Mch., 1857; d. 27 July,
       1895; m. 30 Nov., 1880, Clinton San-
       ford Haviland.
4. Caroline Matilda, b. 6 June, 1824; m. at
   Southington, Ct., 16 May, 1847, Edwin (s.
   Josiah & Lydia Hubbard) Stannard, b.
   Haddam, Ct., 9 Nov., 1820, who d. Golds-
   boro, N. C., 29 Mch., 1865; she d. S.,
   9 July, 1850. Issue:
   i. Alida Caroline (Stannard), b. 3 Oct.,
      1849.
5. George, b. 1826; d. 5 July, 1830.
6. Moses Williams, b. 8 June, 1828. FAM. 75.

FAM. 55. SILAS,⁶ (Silas,⁵ David,⁴ Joseph,³ Nath'l,² Richard,¹), b. Weth., 1802;
d. New Haven, Ct., 22 Feb., 1882; m. 30 Nov., 1825, Amelia (dau. Jared &
Eunice Dickerman) Atwater, b. Hamden, Ct., 30 Sept., 1801; and d. N. H.,
8 Apl., 1885.

Children (prob. b. Hamden, Ct.):

1. William Augustus, b. 16 Oct., 1827; d. 11
   May, 1892; m. Cordelia (dau. James &
   Eunice Dickerman) Wheeler; had no ch.;
   adopted a boy and girl.
2. Cornelia Eunice, b. 10 Oct., 1830; d. 1
   Dec., 1859; m. Robert Dayton. No issue.
3. George Washington, b. 3 May, 1833; m.
   Margaret T. Peok.

4. Elizabeth Maria, b. 10 Mch., 1835; d. 11
   Nov., 1835.
5. Elias Cornelius, b. 10 Feb., 1837; d. 29
   Apl., 1837.
6. Ellen Maria, b. 5 Aug., 1838; m. Chas.
   Foster Beckley. No issue.
7. Elihu Atwater, b. 20 May, 1840; m. Elizabeth J. Bartlett.

FAM. 56. HORACE,⁶ (Luther,⁵ David,⁴ Joseph,³ Nath'l,² Rich.,¹), b. Weth., 1804;
d. Berlin, 21 July, 1843; m. Berlin, 16 Apl., 1826, Mary (dau. Ebenezer M. (?)
& Polly Pierce) Roberts, of Midd., who d. 25 Dec., —— (?).

Children:

1. Edgar, b. 24 July, 1827. FAM. 76.
2. Harriet Maria, b. 10 Oct., 1829; m. at
   Berlin, July, 1850, James F. (s. Isaac &
   Ursula Francis) Lewis; b. New Britain,
   Ct., 11 Mch., 1813, and who d. N-B. 1 Jan.,
   1880. Issue:
   i. Lillian L., m. Chauncey Fuller.
3. Mary Amelia, b. 6 June, 1833; m. at Berlin, 28 Oct., 1851, Frank Cordin; b. Wil-

   mington, Ct., 26 July, 1828. Issue:
   i. Clara, m. Fred. C. Wilson.
   ii. Howard Curtis, d. 1893; m. Helen
       Plerson.
4. Josephine Alice, b. 26 Oct., 1838; m. 14
   Sept., 1854, Alva W. (s. Alvah & Emma
   Cooke) Spaulding. No issue.
5. Birdsey Judson, b. 27 Feb., 1841; d. battle
   of Fredericksburg, Va.

FAM. 57. RALPH HENRY,⁶ (Luther,⁵ David,⁴ Joseph,³ Nath'l,² Rich.,¹), b. Weth.,
1804; d. Meriden, Ct., 13 Mch., 1883; m. (1) at B., 24 June, 1832, Lucinda
(dau. John) Miles, b. Cheshire, Ct.; who d. 14 Sept., 1834; m. (2) at Meriden,
Ct., 1 May, 1836, Abigail (dau. of Collins & Rebecca Guy) Hall, b. M., 25
Nov., 1796, and who d. New Haven, 15 Apl., 1890.

Children (b. Meriden):

1. John Miles, b. 28 Sept., 1833 ; d. Cheshire, Ct., 10 Aug., 1853.
2. Charles Foster, b. 24 Dec., 1836 ; m. New Haven, Ct., 30 Jan., 1866, Ellen Maiha (dau. Silas & Amelia Atwater) **Beckley**;
   b. Hamden, Ct., Aug. 5, 1838.
3. Harriet Abigail, b. 29 Oct., 1841 ; m. 10 June, 1891, Chas. Hooker **Risley, of Berlin,** Ct., s. p.

FAM. 58. WALTER,[6] (*Luther*,[5] *David*,[4] *Joseph*,[3] *Nath'l*,[2] *Rich.*,[1]), b. Weth., 1808; d. Ravenna, O., 3 Jan., 1893; m. at Berlin, Ct., 12 Jan., 1832, Maria (dau. Joseph & Roxana *Caldwell*) **Butler,** b. B., 7 Feb., 1804; d. Mt. Pleasant, Tex., 12 July, 1860.

Children:

1. Frances Laura. b. B. 15 Oct., 1832 ; m. Alex. H. **Mallory.** *Issue:*
   i. Herbert W. (Mallory), b. 1 May, 1853.
   ii. Clarence B. (Mallory), b. 29 June, 1855 ; d. 29 Dec., 1855.
   iii. Richmond E. (Mallory), b. 2 Apl., 1857.
   iv. Walter L (Mallory), b. 8 May, 1859.
   v. Laura M. (Mallory), b. 24 Sept., 1863.
   vi. Florence D. (Mallory), b. 29 Nov., 1865 ; d. 12 Feb., 1894.
2. Henry Augustus, b. 10 Mch., 1834 ; d. 22 Oct., 1844.
3. Jane Maria, b. 23 July, 1836 ; d. 29 Sept., 1849.
4. Joseph Walter, b. 10 Nov., 1837 ; d. Texas, 14 Aug., 1866.
5. George Alfred, b. Randolph, Vt., 13 May,
   1839 ; m. Phœbe Caroline **Lowe.** *Issue:*
   i. Walter, b. 9 May, 1881.
   ii. George, b. 7 July, 1882.
6. Rosina Maria, b. Stow, O., 13 Sept., 1847 ; m. (1) Richmond S. **Horn;** m. (2) Henry **Johnson.** *Issue:*
   i. Elbert (Horn), b. Texas, 17 July, 1862.
   ii. Bernand (Horn), b. Ft. Smith, Ark., 24 Jan., 1866.
   iii. Clara Evelyn (Horn), b. Ravenna, O., 10 Mch., 1868 ; d. 18 Feb., 1872.
   iv. George Francis (Horn), b. Medina, O., 26 May., 1875.
   v. Raymond Leon (Horn), b. Medina, O., 5 Feb., 1878.
7. Frank Ludovici, b. 4 Sept., 1845 ; d. unm. Texas, 22 June, 1864.

FAM. 59. ALBERT WYLLIS,[6] (*Luther*,[5] *David*,[4] *Joseph*,[3] *Nath'l*,[2] *Rich.*,[1]), b. Weth., 12 Sept., 1812 ; d. Ravenna, O., 1 Oct., 1889; m. at Rootstown, O., 18 Nov., 1840, Sarah (dau. David & Clarissa *Buell*) **Root,** b. at R., 1813; she d. Ravenna, O., 5 July, 1846.

Children:

1. Albert Luther. b. 20 Sept., 1841 ; d. 23 Aug., 1876 ; unm.
2. Alfred Wyllis, b. 16 Sept., 1842 ; d. 22
   July, 1843.
3. Charles Alfred, b. 10 Aug., 1844 ; m. Henrietta Eliz'h **Brigham.**

FAM. 60. ALFRED LUTHER,[6] (*Luther*,[5] *David*,[4] *Joseph*,[3] *Nath'l*,[2] *Rich.*,[1]), b. Berlin, Ct., 1817 ; d. Rockville (?), Ct., 13 Mch., 1900; m. (1) at Clinton, Ct., 30 Nov., 1843, Clarissa (dau. Josiah & Sue *Field*) **Kelsey,** b. C., 6 Aug., 1823; d. 1846; m. (2) at B., Clarissa Beckley (Dickinson) **Beckley,** (dau. Russell & Hepzibah *Beckley*) **Dickinson,** b. Ry-H., 22 Dec., 1818; who d. Meriden, Ct., 17 Feb., 1863 or '64; he m. (3) at Tolland, Ct., 22 July, 1864, Emma (dau. James & Elizabeth *Flexney*) **Gamage,** b. Eng., 20 May, 1839.

Children:

1. Walter Henry, b. 30 Sept., 1846.
2. Sarah Louise, b. 29 Sept., 1851 ; d. 6 Oct., 1861.
3. Alfred Russell, b. 28 Feb., d. 27 Sept., 1855.
4. Carrie Emma, b .19 Oct., 1856 ; m. Linneus Fremont **Turner.**
5. George Alfred, b. 18 Apl., d. 13 Sept., 1865.
6. Alfred Gamage, b. 2 Apl., 1867 ; m. Margaret **Laws.**
7. Harry, b. 18 July, 1869 ; d. 11 Oct., 1870.
8. Alfred Horace, b. 16 Apl., 1875 ; not m. 1900.

FAM. 61. GEORGE,[6] (*Luther*,[5] *David*,[4] *Joseph*,[3] *Nath'l*,[2] *Rich.*,[1]), b. 1821, in Berlin; d. Meriden, 9 Sept., 1894; m. at M., 30 Nov., 1842, Maria (dau. Patrick Munn & Maria *Hull*) **Lewis,** b. M., 10 Dec., 1824; who d. M., 6 Feb., 1892.

Children:

1. Henry Foster, b. M. 11 Jan., 1844; m. Elizabeth **Wright.**
2. Lucy Eudora, b. M. 10 May, 1846; m. Edwin Hamlin **Wright.**
3. Georgietta Maria, b. M. 4 Aug., 1848; m. Wesley Grant **Kelsey.**
4. Frank Lewis, b. M. 26 Sept., 1850; m. Ida **Northrop.**
5. Ralph William, b. Stamford, N. Y., 2 Oct., 1852; m. at Clinton, Ct., 4 July, 1880,

     Mary Etta (dau. Horace Edgar & Flora *Woodstock*) **Griswold**; b. C. 13 Feb., 1858; who d. M. 26 Mch., 1895.
6. George Albert, b. 11, d. 19 May, 1855.
7. Edgar Miles, b. Northford, Ct., 4 July, 1856.
8. Harriet Melissa, b. N. 12 May, 1859; m. Willis Norman **Barber.**
9. Lillian Ethleen, b. Clinton, Ct., 14 Dec., 1856.
10. Geo. Hallam (M. D.), b. Clinton, Ct., 28

FAM. 62. WILLIAM,[6] (*Luther*,[5] *David*,[4] *Joseph*,[3] *Nath'l*,[2] *Rich*.,[1]), b. Berlin, Ct., 2 Oct., 1826; was living in 1901; m. (1) at New Haven, Ct., 10 Occt., 1853, Sarah (dau. Russell & Sally *Moulton*) **Dickinson**, b. Enfield, Ct., 6 Dec., 1832; d. Meriden, Ct., 10 Nov., 1866; m. (2) Lucinda Fuller (dau. Lucius & Lydia Eleanor *Fuller*) **Munson**, b. Litchfield, Ct., 28 Dec., 1736.

Children:

1. Pauline Celestia, b. Midd., 10 Mch., 1855; d. 6 July, 1855.
2. Clarence William, b. Midd., 11 Dec., 1856; m. Minnie E. **Blake.**
3. Minnie Sarah, b. Htfd. 11 Dec., 1861; d.

     Meriden, Ct., 31 May, 1863.
     (*By second marriage*):
4. Harriet Lewis, b. 5 Dec., 1870; d. 1 Mch., 1871.

FAM. 63. LYMAN,[7] (*Orin*,[6] *Elias*,[5] *Elias*,[4] *John*,[3] *Benj*.,[2] *Rich*.,[1]), b. Berlin, Ct., 10 July, 1815; d. B., 13 Sept., 1860; m. B., 13 Mch., 1850, Cornelia (Hall) **Andrus**, (dau. Archibald Hall, M. D., & Harriet *Deming*) **Hall**, b. Weth., 28 Dec., 1821; d. at Woodbridge, N. J., 3 Sept., 1890.

Children:

1. Harriet Pattison, b. New Britain, Ct., 2 Dec., 1851; m. John Blanchard **Edgar**. of Woodbridge, N. J.
2. Caroleen, b. Berlin, Ct., 13 Jan., 1855; d. Woodbridge, N. J., 8 Feb., 1871.

FAM. 64. EVELYN,[7] (*Allen*,[6] *Elias*,[5] *Elias*,[4] *John*,[3] *Benj*.,[2] *Rich*.,[1]), b. Berlin, Ct., Feb., 1811; d. Hampden, Ct., 21 Nov., 1840; m. at Meriden, 8 July, 1832, Elizabeth Ann (dau. Joseph & Triphena) **Farrington**, b. M., 1812.

Children:

1. Henry Allen, b. M. 22 Feb., 1834; d. unm. Galveston, Tex., April, 1863.
2. Elizabeth Ann, b. M. 19 Mch., 1836; m. Joseph Marshall **Ward.** *Issue:*
   i. Frank Weston (Ward), b. 6 July, 1860; m. Jan. 1881, Maude (dau. P. Y. & Ann) **Cooney**, of Detroit, Mich.; have s. Joseph Marshall.
   ii. George Henry (Ward), b. 16 Oct., 1862; m. June, 1884, Minnie A. (dau. Ed. & Mary) **Coffae**, of Detroit, Mich.; have s. Geo. H.
   iii. William Beckley (Ward), b. 16 Oct., 1863; m. Mch., 1893, Mary Alice (dau. Orville & Jane) **Harris**, of Battle Creek, Mich.

   iv. Joseph Farrington (Ward), b. 26 July, 1868; d. Oct., 1868.
3. Jane Caroline, b. M. 12 Aug., 1838 · d. N. Y. City May, 1862; m. 11 June, 1860, Moses W. **Ward**; b. 1830 (?).
4. Eveleen Jeanette, b. Hanover, Mich., 22 Mch., 1841; m. Silas **Stiles.** *Issue:*
   i. Mabel C. (Stiles), b. 1 May, 1862.
   ii. Jennie B. (Stiles), b. 11 Nov., 1865; d. 24 July, 1888.
   iii. Henry C. (Stiles), b. 18 Feb., 1870.
   iv. Ethelyn S. (Stiles), b. 18 Apl., 1872; d. 10 May, 1873.
   v. Clare A. (Stiles), b. 26 Sept., 1877.
   vi. Ethel C. (Stiles), b. 27 Aug., 1881.

FAM. 65. HENRY CLAPP,[7] (*Allen*,[6] *Elias*,[5] *Elias*,[4] *John*,[3] *Benj*.,[2] *Rich*.,[1]), b. Berlin, Ct., 21 May, 1818; d. Forestville, Ct., 14 Nov., 1865; m. 9 June, 1846, Emily P. **Botsford**, of Bristol, Ct.

Children:

1. Miriam Clapp, b. 12 Mch., 1847; unm.
2. Henry Evelyn, b. 22 Feb., 1849; d. unm. 14 Jan., 1887.
3. Rosalie Althea, b. Forestville, Ct., 31 Oct., 1851; m. Moses W. **Ward.** *Issue:*
   i. Ethel Beckley (Ward), b. 27 Jan., 1882; d. 7 Oct., 1882.
   ii. Allen Beckley (Ward), b. 30 July,

     1884.
   iii. William Parmalee b. Nov., 28, 1888.
4. Frank Allen, b. F. 6 Jan., 1853; d. Htfd. 24 July, 1885, unm.
5. Carrie Hall, b. 20 Mch., 1856; d. unm. Bristol, Ct. (?), 22 June, 1892.
6. Jannie Cornelia, b. 27 Apl., 1858; d. unm. 5 Oct., 1876.

FAM. 66. AMMI DEMING,[7] (*Lotan*,[6] *Selah*,[5] *Elias*,[4] *John*,[3] *Benj.*,[2] *Rich.*,[1]), b. Berlin, Ct., 26 June, 1826; m. Huntington, O., 10 Feb., 1853, Eliza (dau. Anner & Mary *Harris*) **Kelsey;** b. H. 28 Aug., 1832; d. 13 Apl., 1896.

Children:

1. Harriet Louisa, b. 1 Jan., 1856; d. 17 Feb., 1864, at H.
2. Walter A., b. 21 Apl., 1858; d. 9 Dec., 1880, at Htfd, unm.
3. Rowena L., b. 12 Feb., 1862; m. Robert Dell **Boice.**
4. Ella Elizabeth, b. 15 June, 1865; d. 16 Mch., 1883, at H.

FAM. 67. LYMAN,[7] (*Elnathan Smith*,[6] *Selah*,[5] *Elias*,[4] *John*,[3] *Benj.*,[2] *Rich.*,[1],), b. 1827; d. 5 Jan., 1896; m. at Huntington, O., 19 Oct., 1848, Mary Jane (dau. Rev. Harlow P. & Susan *Mallory*) **Sage;** b. Rochester, O., (?) 1831.

Children:

1. Harley O., b. 6 June, 1851; m. Mary **Peet.**
2. Delmar Irving, b. 26 May, 1861; m. Rose

May **Adams.**
3-4. 2 Ch. d. yg.

FAM. 68. JOHN,[7] (*Theo.*,[6] *Oliver*,[5] *Benj.*,[4] *Benj.*,[3] *Benj.*,[2] *Richard*,[1]), b. Berlin, Ct., 27 Feb., 1829; d. Meriden, Ct., 11 Dec., 1877; m. Meriden, Ct., 17 Nov., 1850, Mary Hall (dau. Eli E. & Julia A.) **Curtis;** b. Meriden, Ct., 18 Jan., 1834; d. Htfd. 7 Apl., 1881.

Children:

1. Ida Amelia, b. M. 7 June, 1853; m. Henry Edward **Chapman.**
2. Elroy Arthur, b. M. 1 Mch., 1857; d. 4 Feb., 1878.

FAM. 69. LEWIS,[7] (*Norman*,[6] *Jona*,[5] *Daniel*,[4] *Daniel*,[3] *Nath'l*,[2] *Richard*,[1]), b. Berlin, Ct., 1823 (?); d. Berlin, 18 Nov., 1891; m. Midd. 30 Apl., 1849, Roxanna (dau. Elijah & Harriet *Lucas*) **Tryon;** b. Midd. 1831 (?); d. B. 23 Nov., 1891.

Child. b. Midd.:

1. Norman Lewis, b. 7 Aug., 1856; m. 27 Dec., 1888, Flora E. (dau. Isaiah W. &

Maria *Nettleton*) **Hurlburt.** FAM. 77.

FAM. 70. LINUS,[7] (*Norman*,[6] *Jona*,[5] *Daniel*,[4] *Daniel*,[3] *Nath'l*,[2] *Rich.*,[1]), b. B. 1824; d. 2 Dec., 1864; m. Clinton, Ct., Louise E. (dau. Russell) **Wright.**

Children:

1. Etta, b. B. Aug., 1861; d. 20 Sept., 1864.
2. Edward Linus, b. B. 12 July, 1864; m.

Nellie **Hutchings.** FAM. 78.

FAM. 70a. SAMUEL MARVIN,[7] (*Silas*,[6] *Samuel*,[5] *Joseph*,[4] *Joseph*,[3] *Nath'l*,[2] *Rich.*,[1]), b. at Warren, Ct.; d. at N. Y. City 5 Apl., 1885; m. at N. Y. 29 July 1834, Margaret De Milt (dau. John & Sarah *Leggett*) **Van Antwerp;** b. N. Y. City 20 Sept., 1815. and who d. at N. Y. 21 Apl., 1887. Mr. Beckley was brought up and educated at Canaan, Ct., and completed his educ. at Litchfield (Ct.), High School. In 1828 he ent. the dry gds. ho. of Don Alonzo Cushman, in N. Y. City and, while yet a young man, was taken into partnership by that firm. In course of time he set up in bus. for himself, on Broadway, nr. Cedar St., and still later estab. the firm of Clapp, Kent & Beckley, dry gds. jobbers, and was very successful in bus. until his retirement in 1860. He possessed excellent judgment as a buyer of gds., and his wide acquaintance in the trade, together with his high probity and enterprising commercial spirit rendered him a prominent figure among the N. Y. mchts. of that day. He was a member of Rev. Dr.Cox's Ch. but, after his marr., joined the Dutch Ref. Ch. in Lafayette Place; and later with the Fourth Ave. Pres. Ch. In politics he was a Rep., and before that an active Henry Clay campaigner. He was one of the Grand Jury which investigated the frauds of the "Tweed Ring."

Children (all b. N. Y. City) :

1. Samuel Falconer, b. 10 Aug., 1835 ; d at Canaan, Ct., 18 Aug., 1836.
2. Margaret Van Antwerp, b. 23 Dec., 1836 ; m. Seth Hastings **Grant,** of Newburgh, N. Y., at one time Comptroller of N. Y. City. *Issue:*
   i. Edith (Grant), b. 1 Jan., 1860 ; unm. 1899.
   ii. Arthur Hastings (Grant) Rev., b. 16 Nov., 1865 ; m. at Sioux Falls, S. D., 3 Mch., 1892, Amy Deborah (dau.

   Samuel Viel & Dorcas Emma *Hill*) **Allison;** b. Farrington, Wis., 22 Dec., 1870.
3. Silas Webster, b. ——, d. yg.
4. Maria Eveline, b. and d. 1841.
5. Sara Louisa, b. 13 Nov., 1843 ; m. John **Brower.**
6. Samuel Leslie, b. 15 June, 1851 ; d. Stirling, N. J., 4 Sept., 1874, unm.
7. Ernest Grant, b. 4 Dec., 1867 ; d. Chatham, N. Y., 2 Nov., 1872.

FAM. 71. WILLIAM,[7] (*Sol.*,[6] *Sol.*,[5] *Zebedee*,[4] *Joseph*,[3] *Nath'l*,[2] *Richard*,[1]), b. Weth. 22 Apl., 1803; d. Wilmington, Del., Oct., 1832; m. Berlin, 18 Apl., 1822, Roxana (dau. John & Roxy *Galpin*) **Deming,** b. B. 19 June, 1796. (*Had two children*) :

FAM. 72. JAMES HENRY,[7] (*Sol.*,[6] *Sol.*,[5] *Zeb.*,[4] *Joseph*,[3] *Nath'l*,[2] *Richard*,[1]), b. Berlin, Ct., 23 Sept., 1819; d. Southington, Ct., 29 Aug., 1884; m. at Bristol, Ct., 30 Mch., 1846, Emeline A. **Blake;** b. Midd., 4 Mch., 1826.

Children:

1. Lafayette Rollin, b. Bristol, Ct., 23 May, 1847 ; m. (1) at Troy, N. Y., 12 Feb., 1874, Annie V. **Baldwin,** who d. T. 23 Nov., 1890 ; m. (2) at Bkly., N. Y., 10 Feb., 1897, Rachel A. **Tilton.** *No issue.*
2. Albert James, b. Bristol, Ct., 19 Aug., 1851 ; m. (1) Elizabeth Amelia **Tuttle;**
   m. (2) Eva Calista **Tuttle.**
3. Eugene Franklin, b. Ry-H., 27 Aug., 1853 ; d. Ry-H., 20 Sept., 1854.
4. Arthur E., b. Ry-H., 16 May, 1856 ; unm. 1896.
5. Caroline Elizabeth, b. Ry-H., 22 Sept., 1860-2 ; m. Adolphus David **Washburn.**

FAM. 73. FRANKLIN WILES,[7] (*Sol.*,[6] *Sol.*,[5] *Zeb.*,[4] *Joseph*,[3] *Nath'l*,[2] *Richard*,[1]), b. Berlin. Ct., 8 May, 1821; d. at New Britain, 26 July, 1877; m. (1) at B. 1 Jan., 1849, Eliza Maria (dau. James & Anna Maria *Morgan*) **Belden;** b. B. 1830 (?); d. B. 6 Sept., 1852; no issue; m. (2 at Meriden, 20 Sept., 1853, Catharine Jane **Parsons.**

Children (by second marriage) :

1. Ella Jane, b. B., 11 Sept., 1855 ; unm. 1894.
2. Franklin Sumner, b. B., 25 Oct., 1859 ; m. Frances **Kraemer.**
3. Carlton, b. B., 24 Sept., 1865 ; d. 14 Mch., 1868.
4. Archer Edward, b. B., 9 July, 1869 ; d. 24 Feb., 1871.

FAM. 74. WILLIAM REDFIELD,[7] (*Moses Williams*,[6] *David*,[5] *David*,[4] *Joseph*,[3] *Nath'l*,[2] *Richard*,[1]), b. New Britain, Ct., 24 June, 1820; d. Stamford, N. Y., 28 Dec., 1896; m. at S. 1 Sept., 1846, Hannah Rebecca (dau. of Samuel Brooks & Mary *Judson*) **Maynard;** b. S. 1 Aug., 1827; d. N. Y. City 10 Mch., 1900.

Children (b. Stamford, N. Y.) :

1. Harry Fremont, b. 26 Sept., 1848 ; d. Wattsburgh, Pa., 3 Sept., 1852.
2. Mary Frances, b. 19 Aug., 1853 ; m. Wm.
   Riseley.
3. William Maynard, b. 2 Oct., 1867 ; m. Cornelia Laraway **Preston.**

FAM. 75. MOSES WILLIAMS,[7] (*Moses W.*,[6] *David*,[5] *David*,[4] *Joseph*,[3] *Nath'l*,[2] *Richard*,[1]), b. New Britain, Ct., 8 June, 1828; d. Southington, Ct., 10 Feb., 1875; m. Middlebury, Ct., 2 June, 1865, Elizabeth (dau. Joseph Perkins & Mehitable Ann *Thompson*) **Platt;** b. Midd. 13 Nov., 1837.

Children (b. Southington, Ct.) :

1. Grace Elizabeth, b. 14 Feb., 1867 ; unm. 1900.
2. Charles Williams, b. 15 Mch., 1869 ; m. Helen **Frost.**
3. Alice Louise, b. 16 Feb., 1871 ; m. Paul Clifford **Woodruff.**
4. Bertha Thompson, b. 17 Oct., 1874 ; unm. 1900.

FAM. 76. EDGAR,[7] (*Horace*,[6] *Luther*,[6] *David*,[4] *Joseph*, *Nathn'l*,[2] *Richard*,[1]), b. Berlin, Ct., 24 July, 1827; d. 3 Oct., 1895; m. (1) at B. 11 July, 1849, Jane E. (dau. Edmund) **Warner;** divorced and m. (2) Midd., Ct., 12 Oct., 1858,

Frances Hannah (dau. Wm. Sylvester & Caroline Beckley *Dickinson*) **Beckley;** b. 1839; who d. Midd. 25 Apl., 1861; m. (3) Htfd. 24 Sept., 1862, Elizabeth Goodwin (dau. Chauncey Henry & Eliza Ann *Butler*) **Winship;** b. Htfd., 3 Feb., 1841.

Children:

1. Mary Amelia, b. and d. 23 Dec., 1850.
2. Eugene Forrest, b. Meriden or Htfd., Ct., 3 Mch., 1851; m. Harriet A. **Whitmore;** m. (2) Imogene L. (*Colton*) **Twiss;** m. (3) Emma Lewis **Woodruff.**

   (*By second marriage*):
3. Clinton Edgar, b. Midd., 13 Dec., 1859; unm. 1900.

   (*By third marriage*):
4. Alice Josephine, b. Milford, Ct., 26 Aug., 1863; m. Irville Leslie **Dow.**
5. Birdsey Judson, b. M., Mch., 4 1869; d. 17 Sept., 1878.
6. Harriet Eliza, b. M., 8 Jan., 1875; unm. 1899.
7. Henry Chauncey, b. Htfd., 13 Feb., 1879; unm. 1898.

FAM. 77. NORMAN L.,[8] (*Lewis*,[7] *Norman*,[6] *Jona*,[5] *Daniel*,[4] *Daniel*,[3] *Nath'l*,[2] *Rich*.,[1]), b. Berlin, Ct., 1862 (?); m. at Cromwell, Ct., abt. 1893, Flora E. **Hurlburt;** b. C. 1863 (?).

Children (b. Berlin, Ct.):

1. Lewis Raymond, b. 28 July, 1894.
2. Doris Hurlburt, b. 22 Sept., 1901.

FAM. 78. EDWARD LINUS,[8] (*Linus*,[7] *Norman*,[6] *Jona*,[5] *Daniel*,[4] *Daniel*,[2] *Nath'l*,[2] *Richard*,[1]), b. Berlin, Ct., 12 July, 1864; m. Midd., 26 Nov., 1890, Nellie (dau. John & Maria *Fountain*) **Hutchins;** b. Midd., 1868.

Children:

1. Etta Maria, b. Midd., 16 Sept., 1891.
2. Leah Alice, b. Midd., 23 Oct., 1893.

BECKWITH, THOMAS, of Lyme; m. Betsy **Brown,** 14 Dec., 1796.

NATHAN, of Htfd.; m. Betsy **Rich,** 25 Nov., 1783.—*W. T. R.*

MARY, ae. 28; d. 8 Nov., 1807.—*N. C. R.*

LOT. & *Mary Ann* had ch. d. 17 Sept., 1828, ae. 1; inf. d. 2 May, 1829.—*N. C. R.*

BELDEN (*Baylden*), The author of a recent Belden genealogy* traces the Eng. hist. of this family for over 800 yrs. from before the battle of Hastings, 1066, and gives the arms as follows: *Baylden of Baylden.* Arg. a fesse betw. 3 fluer-de-lis *sable;* or, another with the fluer-de-lis *gules;* another Arg. a chevron betw. 3 fluer-de-lis *sable,* from the chief, a pile descending to the top of chevron. The arms in possess. of the descendants of Richard of Wethersfield, have an added motto, "God my Leader." The name was first spelled *Baylden* until 1641; then on the *Weth. Recs. Beldon* from 1641-43: *Belding* from 1643-1736; *Beldon* from 1736-1753; *Belding* from 1753—1825; *Belden* from 1825 to the present time. *Hinman* (*N. Eng. Gen. Reg. XV. 297*) says that the spelling of the name was changed and restored to the orig. orthography through the exertions of Rev. Joshua Belden, minister at Newington, Ct., abt. 1772, by Col. Elisha Williams, at that time Town Clerk of Weth., who showed to him, on the early records, three several and distinct autographs of the elder John Belden, signed clearly John *Belden* and thus convinced him of the corruption of form which the name had undergone. The Rev. Joshua, thereupon, instituted a correspondence with different members of the family, with a view to their general adoption of a uniform spelling of the name. A tradition, in some branches of the fam. that the family is of Welch origin, that the name was orig. *Bellenden,* and that there was some connection with the British earldom of that name, need not be seriously credited.

---

* Concerning Some of the Ancestors and Descendants of Royal Denison and Olive Cadwell Belden, by Jessie Perry Van Zile Belden [Mrs. James M. Belden], Printed for Private Circulation, by J. B. Lippincott & Co., Philadelphia, MDCCCXCVIII, 200 copies, pp. 245.

RICHARD, the Weth. settler, is supposed to have been (by the Geneal. above referred to) a son of Sir Frances Baylden, of Kippax, Co. Yorkshire, Eng., and to have been bp. 26 May, 1591. If he is the same Rich. Baylden whose bold, well written signature was affixed to a document (26 Mch., 1613) stating that he was aged "19 yrs. of age, born at Kippax, in Com. Ebor,"* and "intending to pass over for Bredaugh, to be a soldier under Cap [t] en [afterwards Sir George] Blundell," and "hath taken the oath of allegiance," it is prob. that our Richard of Weth. had seen some military service in the Low Countries, before emigrating hither. The identification of the Weth. Richard with the Kippax Richard, seems to have hinged largely, in the mind of a member of the English family (quoted, by the *Belden Geneal.*, referred to, as a high authority in its history) on his belief that the latter "was the only Richard, so far as I know, who would have had money to spend in the purchase of land, as Richard of Weth., did."

It is true that the lds. belonging to Richard Baylden in Weth., comprising eight pieces in all, are located and described in *Land Recs., Sec'y States' Office*, Book I, p. 19, and referred to in *W. T. Recs.*, under date of "2d month & 7th daie, 1641, as those given him by the Towne and those he bo't of Jonas Woode," but it does not follow that he paid out much hard cash for them; for a portion were undoubtedly his *by grant* from the Town.—See Chapter I, Vol. I. We need not, then, infer that he was a man of much superior means to his neighbors in the new settlement, more especially as the inventory of his estate, taken at his death in 1655, by John Talcott and John Nott, foots up only to £111-19-00.—*Htfd. Co. Prob. Rec.*, II, 58.

He must have been 48 or 50 yrs. of age when he came to Weth., 1641, and he d. 1655; but during his brief American life he accumulated considerable real estate, which he left to his children; and the family which he founded has certainly exhibited a marked financial ability, as well as a high degree of moral and intellectual force. His home lot was on the cor. of Broad Street, and "the waye leading into the Great playne," and was sold in 1742, by his gt-gd-son Silas, to Josiah Smith, whose desc't James Smith, in 1885, occupied it and had the orig. deed, and whose ho. is on nearly the same site as the orig. Rich. Belden ho.†

Richard Belden was appointed, in 1646, one of the Town's cow-keepers or "herders" to look after the settlers' cattle, during their daily pasturing in the meadows belonging to the Town—an office which in nowise affects our estimate of his character or social standing—since in those old days, men seem to have been willing to serve the community in any duty which was assigned to them.—See, also, Chapter VII, Vol. I. He bro't with him, to America, three sons, men grown.

Children (Weth. Rec.; b. in Eng.):

1. William, b. abt. 1622. He has been supp. to have been a *brother* of Richard, the Settler.† FAM. 2.	2. Samuel, b. abt. 1629. FAM. 3.
	3. John, b. abt. 1631.; FAM. 4.

---

* Comitate Ebor—*i. e.*, County of York. Yet, the bp. rec. of 26 May, 1591, would make him 22 instead of 19 yrs. old at the time of signing this doc., whereas the acceptance of his own statement as to his being 19 yrs. old, would make him to have been born in 1594, not 1591.

† If the identification of Richard Belden, of Weth., with Richard, b. 1591, son of Sir Francis B., of Kippax, is accepted, even presumptively, William of Weth., could not have been his bro. By a second wife, Sir Francis had sons William, Richard and others younger ; William dying before 1615. Richard *might* name a son after his deceased elder bro., but could hardly have produced him at Weth. Richard, the Settler, in the only one named in *Weth. Rec.*, as having a ho or lds. in the town, until the children of William and John (presumably his son) begin to be recorded, but as for Samuel, we have recorded evidence that he was Richard's son, and that he was at Branford as early as 1644, on his own account.

‡ "John Belding, of Weth.," testified, 16 Feb., 1661, that he was "abt. 27 yrs. old."—*New Haven Col. Rec.*

FAM. 2. WILLIAM,[4] (*Richard*,[1]), b. abt. 1622, in Eng.; was, like his father, app. one of the Town's "herders," 1648; his wife's Christian name was Tomasin [Tamasine (?)]. He d. 27 Mch., 1655. Invent. taken 1 June, same yr. Value, £142-06-08.—*Htfd. Co. Prob.*, II, 69. *Savage* says he rem. to Norwalk, which can hardly be, as his invent. is drawn by John Deming, Samuel Smith and Nath'l Dickinson, who subscribed themselves as being "his townsmen." In his will he requests the two latter friends to act "as supervisors," and pathetically asks them "to do what they can to advise and counsel my wife, and do the best they can to take care of my little ones, and to see my body honorably buried." His name is here spelled *Beldin*.

Children (b. Weth.) :

1. Samuel, b. 20 July, 1647.
2. Daniel, b. 20 Nov., 1648; m. 10 Nov., 1670, Elizabeth (dau. Nath'l, Jr.) **Foote**, of Weth.; rem. to Deerfield, Mass., where in the massacre of 1696 by the Inds. his wife and 3 ch. were slain and 2 other ch. taken captive; he d. at D., 14 Aug., 1732, in 86th yr. See *Foote Geneal.*, xxviii, xxix, 49; Judd's *Hadley Geneal's*, 432; Sheldon's *Deerfield*, 80-81.
3. John, b. 9 Jan., 1649-50—*S. W. A.* queries

if this was the J. who drew ld. in 1694 allot. at Weth., and was a lister, 1715, and says this appears to be the J. who rem. to Norwalk,—See Sheldon's *Narrative of Stephen Williams*. (Sheldon's *Deerfield* credits William Belden also with the following children) :
4. Susanna, b. 5 Nov., 1651 or '52.
5. Mary, b. 2 (or 20) Feb., 1652-3.
6. Nathaniel, b. 13 (or 14) Nov., 1654.

FAM. 3. SAMUEL.[2] (*Richard*,[1]), b. abt. 1625, in Eng., betw. 1644 and '46, was at Branford, Ct.; in 1661, was at Hatfield, Mass., and served valiantly in the King Philip's War. His wife Mary being killed by the Inds., 19 Sept., 1677, at Hatfield, Mass.; he m. (2) 25 June, 1678, Mary (wid. of Thos.) **Wells**, and dau. of Thos. **Meakim;** she d. 20 Sept., 1691; he m. (3) Mary (wid. of John) **Allis**, and (4) 10 Apl., 1705, the wid. of John Wells. He rec'd a gift of ld. from his father, Oct., 1654; was made freeman in Conn., 21 May, 1657, before going to Mass. He d. at Hatfield, Mass., 3 Jan., 1713. By his first wife he had 7 ch.

Children (b. Weth.) :

1. Mary, b. 10 July, 1655; m. Daniel **Weld**, of Deerfield, Mass.—*C. G. H.*
2. Samuel, b. 6 Apl., 1657. FAM. 4a.
3. Stephen, b. 28 Dec., 1658; m. 16 Aug., 1682, Mary (dau. of Thomas) **Wells**, of Hadley. He d. 6 Oct., 1720, in 62d yr.; his wid. m. (2) 2 Jan., 1723, Capt. Joseph **Field**, of Sunderland, Mass., and d. 5 Mch., 1751. *Ch.:* Stephen, *Jr.* (eld.), *Samuel, Jonathan, Joshua, Elizabeth* (Scott), *Mary* (Waite), *Esther.* It is the line of this Stephen, Jr., b. 22 Feb.,

1689, at Northfield, which is traced in the *Belden Geneal.* referred to. The descendants of his bro. *Joshua* will be found in Temple's *Hist. of Whately, Mass.*; see, also, Judd's *Hadley*, pp. 452, 453.
4. Sarah, b. 30 Sept., 1661.
5. Anna, b. 27 Jan., 1665.
6. Ebenezer, b. 16 Nov., 1667; m. Abigail ————, and d. 21 Nov., 1739; had dau. *Martha*, b. 1693.
7. John, b. 13 Nov., 1669.
(These last four from Notes of *C. G. H.*)

FAM. 4. JOHN,[2] (*Richard*,[1]), b. abt. 1631, (see Note to p. —), m. Lydia (dau. Thomas & Susanna) **Standish**—*C. B. H.*, (24 Aug., Apl. ?) 1657; was made a freeman, 1657; was enl. trooper under Capt. John Mason 1657-8; active in Town affairs; for ld-holdings, see Chapter VII, Vol. I. He d. 27 June, 1677, ae 46; est., £911. He was prob. a mcht. as in Dec. 1662, one Samuel Edsall of New Amsterdam [New York], gave him a due bill for £14, payable in "trading cloth" at 9s. per yard, and "Osenbridge,, [Osnaburg] at 20d. per yard, to be paid by the last of the following April, if Benfield [prob. the master of some trading vessel] come to the Manattans" [Manhattan]. *S. W. A.* supposes this John Belden to have been the one who was licensed to be a tavern-keeper, in Weth., in 1673, as the only two other Johns of the same name were aged respectively, only 15 and 25. He also thinks this was not the John who rem. to Norwalk, Ct. *Weth Ld. Recs.*, pp. 225 and 258, bear his autograph signature, "John belden."

Children (Weth. Rec.):

1. John, b. 12 June, 1658. FAM. 5.
2. Jonathan (Lieut.), b. 21 June, 1660. FAM. 6.
3. Joseph, b. 23 Apl., 1663. FAM. 7.
4. Samuel, b. 3 Jan., 1665. FAM. 8.
5. Sarah, b. 31 Mch., 1668.
6. Daniel, b. 12 Oct., 1670; *Hinman* says supposed to have gone to Norwalk, to his gd-uncle William, and to have been the progenitor of the Norwalk Beldens. But if, as we have reason to believe, said uncle never rem. to N., or, if Daniel did go there, it must have been "on his own hook."
7. Ebenezer, b. 8 Jan. (or June), 1672. FAM. 9.
8. Margaret, b. 29 Mch., 1677.

9. Lydia (acc. to *C. G. H.*), b. Mch., 1675; m. 8 May, 1694, Stephen (s. Joseph) **Kellogg**, b. 1668; d. 1772; had:
   i. Stephen, b. 1695.
   ii. Lydia, b. 1697.
   iii. Moses, b. 1700.
   iv. Abigail, b. 1702.
   v. Daniel, b. 1704.
   vi. Ephraim, b. 1707.
   vii. Mercy, b. 1709.
   viii. Noah, b. 1711.
   ix. Silas, b. 1714.
   x. Amos, b. 1717.
   xi. Aaron.

FAM. 4.[a]   SAMUEL,[3] (*Samuel,*[2] *Richard,*[1]), b. 1657; m. (1) Sarah (wid. Samuel,) **Billings;** m. (2) Mary (wid. Thos.) **Hastings.**

Children:

1. Samuel, b. 25 July, 1689. FAM. 9a.
2. Daniel, b. 14 Feb., 1691.
3. Gideon, b. 24 Mch., 1693.
4. Prudence, b. 12 Feb., 1694.

5. Richard, b. 18 Apl., 1699.
6. Matthew, b. 3 June, 1701.
7. Hannah, b. 25 Sept., 1704.

FAM. 5.   JOHN,[3] (*John,*[2] *Rich.,*[1]), b. 1658; m. Dorothy (dau. Josiah) **Willard,** 15 June, 1682; who d. 28 Feb., 1754, ae. abt. 91. He d. 10 Jan., 1713-4, ae. abt. 56. Invent. of est. taken 17 Feb., 1713-14, by Jona. Belding, Jacob Griswold and David Wright; amt. £891-00-03; admin. gr. to wid. and eld. s. Josiah, whom the two younger boys chose as their guardian.—*Htfd. Co. Prob.*

Children (Weth. Rec.):

1. Josiah, b. 14 Feb., 1682-3. FAM. 10.
2. John, b. 3 Dec., 1685. FAM. 11.
3. Benjamin, b. 13 Jan., 1687. FAM. 12.
4. Lidia, b. 9 Apl., 1690; d. 6 Apl., 1693.
5. Hannah, b. 12 Sept., 1692.
6. Lidia, b. 30 Nov., 1694.

7. Stephen, b. 21 May, 1697.
8. Ezra, b. 27 Nov. (bp. 3 Dec.—*Mix MS.*), 1699. FAM. 13.
9. Dorothy, b. 11 (bp. 17—*Mix MSS.*) May, 1702; d. 2 July, 1704.

FAM. 6.   Dea. JONATHAN,[3] (*John,*[2] *Rich.,*[1]), b. 1660; selectman 1695; see also Chap. VII, Vol. I; m. Mary (dau. Thos. & Eliz, *C. G. H.*) **Wright,** 10 Dec., 1685; he d. 6 July, 1734, ae. 74, *Weth. Ins.;* she d. 8 Sept., 1741 in 76 yr. *Weth. Ins.;* her will dated 10 Mch., 1735-6, proven 2 Jan., 1741-2,devised her est. to her two daus.—*Htfd. Co. Prob. Rec.*

Children (Weth. Rec.):

1. Jonathan, b. 11 Nov., 1686.
2. Mary, b. 11 Sept., 1687; m. 8 June, 1710, David **Wright**. (Ment. in mother's will.)
3. Silas, b. 29 July, 1691. FAM. 14.
4. Jonathan (Capt.), b. 30 Mch., 1695. FAM. 15.

5. Elizabeth, b. (and bp.—*Mix MS.*) 1 Oct., 1698; m. Ezra **Belding**. (Ment. in mother's will.)
6. Mabel, "of Jona.," bp. 1 Oct., 1704.— *Mix MS.*

FAM. 7.   JOSEPH,[3] (*John,*[2] *Rich.,*[1]), b. 1633; m. 27 Oct., 1693, Mary or Mercy **Willard** (*C. G. H.*), who d. 17 Mch., 1739-40; collector, 1690; he is called "clerk" in 1705, was appraiser of cattle, 1708. See, also *Chap. VII, Vol. I.* D. 7 Dec., 1724, ae. 62.—*Weth. Ins.*

Children (Weth. Rec.; bp. Mix MSS.):

1. Sarah, b. 1 June, 1695; m. (acc. to mother's will) a **Burnham.**
2. Joseph (Capt.), b. 28 Dec., 1697; d. 26 Apl., 1754, in 57th yr.—*Weth. Ins.;* m. Elizabeth ————, who d. 5 June, 1740, in 37th yr.—*Weth. Ins.*
3. Thomas (Capt.), b. 9 (bp. 15), Sept., 1700. FAM. 16.

4. Mary, b. 23 (bp. 25), Apl., 1704; m. (acc. to her mother's will) a **Boardman.**
5. Amos, b. 15, bp. 17 Aug., 1707.
6. Easter (Esther), b. 26 June, bp. 2 July, 1710; m. (acc. to mother's will) a **Wolcott.**
7. Eunice, b. 16 June, 1714.

FAM. 8. SAMUEL,[3] (*John*,[2] *Rich.*,[1]), b. 1665; m. Hannah (acc. to James N. Belden, of Bridgeport, Ct.,—*Handy;* dau. of Richard H.; and gd-dau. John **Elderkin,** a first sett. of Norwich), 14 Jan., 1685; he d. 27 Dec., 1738. *Weth. Rec.* give death of a Samuel as 27 Dec., 1733, but date of his will seems to fix it at 1738. Invent. est val. £381-16-01—taken 25 Jan., 1739.—*Htfd. Co. Prob.* Wid. d. 20 Jan., 1741-2. *Hinman* supposes him to have rem. to New Lond., and to have been the progenitor of the New Lond. Beldens. *S. W. A.* queries in his MSS. notes, "Was he prob. the Samuel. whose house was one of the six to be "fortified," in 1703? If so, it was the orig. Nathaniel Dickinson's ho. S. W. side of Broad St."

Children (*Weth. Rec.; bp. Mix MSS.*) :

1. Dau. b. Nov., 1687 ; d. Apl., 1688.
2. Samuel, b. 25 July, 1689. FAM. 17.
3. Daniel, b. 14 Feb., 1690-1. FAM. 18.
4. Gideon, b. 24 Mch., 1692-3. FAM. 19.
5. Prudence, b. 12 Feb., 1694.
6. Eunice, b. 14 Apl., 169 ; d. 26 Dec., 1797.
7. Richard, b. 18, bp. 23 Apl., 1699.
8. Matthew, b. and bp. 13 June, 1701 ; m. Elizabeth (dau. Sam'l) **Williams,** 1 (or 16) Apl., 1729. *Issue:*
   i. Mercy, b. 10 Feb., 1729-30.
9. Hannah, b. and bp. 25 Sept., 1704.

FAM. 9. Sgt. EBENEZER,[3] (*John*,[2] *Rich.*,[1]), b. 1672; m. Abigail (dau. Nath'l & Martha) **Graves;** during his active life, held nearly every town office, from hayward and constable to that of Selectman. For ld. holdings see Chapt. VII, VOL. 1. He d. 2 Nov., 1739 ae. abt. 72.—*Weth. Ins.*

Children (*Weth. Rec.; bp. Mix MSS.*) :

1. Ebenezer (Lieut.), b. 7 Sept., 1697. FAM. 20.
2. Thankful, b. 16, bp. 22 Nov., 1700, or 1702 ; m. 5 Dec., 1723, Samuel (bro. of her

bro. Ebenezer's wife) **Talcott;** he d. 6 May, 1739, at Weth.

FAM. 10. Mr. JOSIAH,[4] (*John*,[3] *John*,[2] *Rich.*,[1]), b. 1683; m. Mabel (dau. Sgt. Samuel) **Wright,** 1 May, 1707, who d. 11 Oct., 1767, *Weth. Ins.;* he d. 5 Sept., 1746; was lister, 1713; tythingman, 1715; he res. and d. at Rocky Hill, 5 Sept., 1746, in 64 yr.—*Weth. Ins.*

Children (*Weth. Ins.; bp Mix MSS.*) :

1. Mabel Wright, b. 9 Feb., 1707-8.
2. Dorothy, b. 4, bp. 6 ———, 1708-9.
3. Rebecca, b. 12, bp. 14 Jan., 1710-11; d. 19 of same mo.—*Mix MS.*
4. Rebecca, bp. 20 July, 1712.
5. Josiah, b. 11, bp. 14 June, 1713. FAM. 21.
6. Ozias, b. and bp. 18 Nov., 1714 ; d. 29 Nov., 1731, ae. 17 yr. 11 d.
7. Rebecca, b. 19, bp. 24 June, 1716 ; d. 18 Aug., 1736.—*Weth. Ins.*
8. Abigail, b. 17 Nov., 1719.
9. Return, b. 28 Jan., 1721; d. 24 Jan., 1764.
in 48d yr.—*Weth. Ins.*
10. Solomon, b. 22 May, 1722 ; prob. the Sol. who m. 27 June, 1768, Elizabeth **Rockwell;** he was bu. 6 Jan., 1776. *Issue* (*Weth. and W. C. R. Rec.*) :
    i. Hannah, b. 23 May, bp. 4 June, 1769.
    ii. Solomon, b. 9 Sept., 1772 ; idiot, bu. 8 Nov., 1829, ae. 57.
    iii. Stephen, b. 15, bp. 21 Aug., 1774.
11. Lidia, b. 6 Sept., 1725.
12. Hannah, b. 20, bp. 22 Mch., 1730.

FAM. 11. JOHN,[4] (*John*,[3] *John*,[2] *Rich.*,[1]), b. 1685; m. (1) Keziah (dau. Sgt. Benj.) **Gilbert,** 1 May, 1712, who d. 2 Dec., 1712, ae. abt. 21; m. (2) Patience (dau. Esq. Josiah) **Rosseter,** 22 Mch., 1714-15, who d. 9 Mch., 1715-16, ae. 24; m. (3) Sarah (dau. Jacob) **Griswold,** 16 Dec., 1718. There was a John B. whose invent. (val. at £851-13-09) was taken 24 June, 1725, and acc. to *Court Rec.* 6. July, 1725; adm. gr. to wid. *Mary,* and his will mentions John, Ebenezer and Timothy as "sarviving." If, as acc. to this doc. his wid's name was Mary, he must have m. a *fourth* time.

Children (*Weth. Rec.; by 1st wife*) :

1. Dau., b. and d. 29 Nov., 1712.
(*By second marriage*) :
2. John, b. 1, bp. 11 Mch., 1715-16. FAM. 21a.
(*By third marriage*) :
3. Ebenezer, b. 6 Dec., 1719.
4. Keziah, b. 21 Aug., 1722.
5. Timothy, b. 26 Dec., 1723 ; m. 4 Mch., 1746, Abigail (dau. William & Susanna *Bonen*) **Hurlbut;** she d. 1786, Sheffield, Mass.— *W. C. R.*

FAM. 12. BENJAMIN,[4] (*John*,[3] *John*,[2] *Rich.*,[1]), b. 1687; m. Anne (dau. Lt. Benj.) **Churchill,** 29 Jan., 1713-14; licensed as a tavernkeeper same yr.; collector, 1712; in a deed of gift 1711, is called "feltmaker."

Children (*Weth. Rec.; bp. Mix MSS.*) :

1. Mary, b. 9, bp. 18, Dec., 1715. (In *Mix MSS.* this name is *Martha.*)
2. Benjamin, b. 9, bp., 16 Feb., 1717-18.
3. Charles, b. 13 Mch., 1719-20.

FAM. 13. EZRA,[4] (*John*,[3] *John*,[2] *Rich.*,[1]), b. 1699; m. 13 or 15 Feb., 1721-22, Elizabeth (dau. Dea. Jonathan,[3] *John*,[2] *Rich.*,[1]) **Belding.**

Children (*Weth. Rec.; bp. Mix MSS.*) :

1. Ezra, b. 29 Nov., 1722; prob. the Ezra who had a s. Jonathan bp. 20 Jan., 1751.
2. Aaron, b. 9 Sept., 1725.
3. Elizabeth, b. 28 Oct., 1728.—*Mix MS.*
4. Aaron, b. 1 Oct., 1731. FAM. 22.
5. Eunice, b. 20, bp. 25 ———, 1733; d. 7 Aug., 1754.—*Mix MS.*
6. Elizabeth (acc. to *C. G. H.*).
7. Lois, b. 24 Apl., 1737.

FAM. 14. Mr. SILAS,[4] (*Dea. Jona.*,[3] *John*,[2] *Rich.*,[1]), b. 1691; m. Abigail (dau. Capt. Joshua & Elizabeth *Butler*) **Robbins,** 30 Nov., 1716. (*Hinman* p. 181,) says of him, that, "while he remained in Weth. he was highly respected and employed in public business, was chosen hayward, 1712; sold his ppy. in W. intending to rem. to Canaan, Ct., where he had bo't a large tract of ld. as also in Dutchess Co., N. Y., and in Berkshire, Mass., on which to sett. In autumn of 1741, he ret. to W. to close up his affairs there, was suddenly taken ill, and d. there. Mrs. Abigail d. 16 Feb., 1783, in 86 yr.—*W. Ins. Canaan Ct. Recs.* show him to have had a ppro's share in the first division of that town, 1718; also a deed to Isaac Lawrence of C. 22 Aug., 1739, and one from Cornelius Brown, of Windsor, 20 Feb., 1739-40; his wid. Abigail was adm. memb of 1st. Ch. of C. (now S. Canaan) from Ch. in Weth. 1 July, 1753. In all these recs. he is ment. as "of Weth."

Children (*Weth. Rec.*) :

1. Silas, b. 13 Nov., 1717; sett. at Canaan, C:.—*Hinman.*
2. Abigail, b. 4 Nov., 1720; m. 12 Dec., 1744, Thos.[4] (*Thos.*,[3] *Stephen*,[2] *Thos.*,[1]) **Hurlburt,** of Weth.
3. Joshua (Rev.), b. 19 July, 1724. FAM. 23.
4. Charles, b. 4 May, 1728; sett. at Dover, N. Y.—*Hinman.* FAM. 23a.
5. Lydia, b. 1, bp. 3 May, (*Mix*). 1730.
6. Oliver, b. and bp. (*Mix*) 19 Nov., 1732. FAM. 23b.
7. Jonathan (Dea.), b. 16 Nov., 1737; m. 22 Mch., 1759, Sarah *Belding.*—*N. C. R.* (From this family sprang the Beldens, of Litchfield, Ct.; Hampshire Co., Mass., and Dutchess Co., N. Y.)

FAM. 15. Capt. and Esq. JONATHAN,[4] (*Dea. Jonathan*,[3] *John*,[2] *Rich.*,[1]), b. 1695; m. Martha (dau. John) **James,** 29 Dec., 1715; he d. 20 Aug., 1768, from injuries rec'd by the falling of his cellar stairs (*Conn. Courant*) ; was J. P. and Town Treas. of Weth. for many yrs. and much in public affairs.

Children (*Weth. Rec.*) :

1. David, b. 4 Oct., bp. 5 Aug., acc. to *Mix Rec.*), 1716; bu. 18 Dec., 1785, ae. 70. —*W. C. R.* FAM. 24.
2. Jonathan (Lieut.), b. 18 Mch., 1718-19; d. 10 July, 1736.—*Weth. Ins.*
3. Moses, b. 29 Dec., 1720; d. 6 Sept., 1741, in 21st yr.—*Weth. Ins.*
4. Mary, b. 9 Nov., 1723.
5. Sarah, b. 11 June, 1727.

FAM. 16. Capt. THOMAS,[4] (*Joseph*,[3] *John*,[2] *Rich.*,[1]), b. 1700; m. Mary (dau. Rev. Stephen) **Mix,** who d. 14 Apl., 1742, in 42d yr. *Weth. Ins.;* he d. 13 Apl., 1761, in 61st yr.

Children (*Weth. Rec.; bp. Mix. MSS.*) :

1. Mary, bp. 12 Oct., 1729.
2. Mary, b. 18 Aug., 1730; m. Capt. Edward **Howard;** d. 2 Mch., 1761.—*Weth. Ins.*
3. Thomas, bp. 15 Aug., 1731.
4. Thomas (Col.), b. 9 Aug., 1732. FAM. 25.
5. Joseph, b. 4 (or 14) Nov., 1732; bp. 3 Dec., 1733; grad. Y. C.; rem. from Weth. in early life. *Hinman* says he had a s. Thomas who d. in Htfd. *No issue.*
6. Rebecca, b. Oct., 1735.
7. Simeon, b. 24 Feb., 1736-7. FAM. 26.
8. Lucy, b. 17 Apl., 1741.
9. Elizabeth, ¦ twins, b. 11 Nov., 1744.—
10. Eunice, ¦ *W. C. R.*
11. James, bp. 20 Apl., 1760.—*W. C. R.*
12. Rebecca, bp. 1746. Possibly these last four may belong to Fam.—.)

FAM. 17. Mr. SAMUEL,[4] (Sam'l,[3] John,[2] Rich.,[1]), b. 1689; m. 10 Apl., 1712, Mary **Spencer**, of Haddam, Ct., who d. 28 Oct., 1751—in 60 yr.—*W. Ins.* He d. 31 July, 1771. The "wife of Sam'l," who d. 23 Feb., 1775, may have been a second wife.

Children (Weth. Rec.; bp. Mix. MSS.):

1. Samuel, b. 26 Apl., bp. 3 May, 1713; d. 10 Jan., 1782, ae. 69.—*S. C. R.* FAM. 27.
2. Jared, b. 19, bp. 30 Jan., 1714-15.
3. Nathaniel, b. and bp. 24 June, 1716; prob. the N. who m. Lois **Deming**, 28 Mch., 1751.—*W. Ins.*
4. Lydia, b. 24 May, 1718.
5. Asa, b. 1 Apl., 1720; d. 16 Feb., 1800, ae. 80.—*S. C. R. and W. Ins.*
6. Mary, b. 11 Dec., 1721; d. 9 Oct., 1751.
7. Ann b. 7 Nov., 1723.
8. Seth, b. 18 Sept., 1725; d. 8 Oct., 1751, in 25th yr.—*W. Ins.*
9. Daniel, b. 19 May, 1727; acc. to *Hinman* he m. 8 May, 1750, Mary **Miller**;

he d. 6 Aug., 1752.* *Issue:*
    i. James (Belden), b. 16 Mch., 1750-5, from whom (per. s. Martin and gr. s. Austin) descended James N. Belden of Bridgeport, Ct., James, who in youth, accompanied his mother to Sandisfield, Mass., where he became the ancestor of a large B. family.
10. Richard, b. 30 Dec., 1728. FAM. 28.
11. Phinehas, b. 14 Sept., 1730. FAM. 29.
12. Dorothy, b. 6 Sept., 1732.
13. Esther, b. 22 June, 1734.
14. Martha, "dau of Samuel," b. 6 June, 1736; d. 9 Oct., 1751, in 16th yr.—*W. Ins.*

FAM. 18. DANIEL,[4] (Sam'l,[3] John,[2] Rich.,[1]), b. 1691; m. wid. Margaret **Clark** dau. of Peter *Blinn*), 28 Nov., 1714. He prob. the D. who d. 31 Mch., 1774. Dr. *C. G. H.* gives this Daniel as s. of *Samuel* b. 1657, s. of *Samuel* b. 1625, s. of *Richard* the Settler, in the Hatfield line. But we believe him to have been s. of *Samuel, John* and *Richard*—the Weth. line.—*H. R. S.*

Children (Weth. Rec.):

1. Margaret, b. 10 (bp. 11—*Mix*) Sept., 1715.
2. Lois, b. 14 June, 1717.
3. Prudence, b. 28 Jan., 1719.
4. Eunice, b. 17 Mch., 1722.
5. Thankful, b. 10 Nov., 1724.

FAM. 19. GIDEON,[4] (Sam'l,[3] John,[2] Rich.,[1]), b. Weth. 1693; m. Elizabeth (dau. Zech.) **Seimer** [Seymour], 7 Feb., 1711-12. Her father, Zachary S. (s. of Rich., of Htfd., Far. and Norwalk, who d. 25 Nov., 1655), m. at Weth., 9 Feb., 1688, the wid. Mary **Gritt** [Garrett]; he d. Weth., Aug., 1702 ae. 60. Gideon Belden d. 1733; invent. est. £79-18-00; taken 28 Dec., 1733; adm. gr. 1 Jan., 1733-34 to his wid., Elizabeth. †

Children (Weth. Rec.):

(The same remark as made regarding his bro. Daniel, FAM. 19, applies also to this Gideon.)
1. Ebenezer, b. 10 Mch., d. 12, 1713.
2. Eunice, b. 12 July, 1714.
3. Elisha, b. 22 July, 1715. FAM. 30.
4. Ruth, b. 23 Sept., 1717; m. David[4] (David,[3] John,[2] Thos.,[1]) **Hurlbut, Jr.**——See *Hurlbut Geneal.*
5. Elizabeth, b. 10 Oct., 1719. Dr. C. G. Hubbard says she m. Elijah **Hurlbut**, b. 1719, of Weth., and had ch. as follows: (1) Elijah; (2) Simeon; (3) Levi, b. 1748; m. 1777, Sarah **Cook**; (4) Thomas, m. Eunice **Gant**; (5) Robert; (6) Stephen, m. 1782, Phebe **Pelton**; (7) Rebecca; (8) Hetty; (9) Elis; (10) Eunice. But, Mr. Homer W. Brainard, of Htfd., gives her rec. as follows: "A careful study of *Weth. Recs.* leads me to think that E. D., who m. Jonathan Burr, 29 Oct., 1740, was the dau. of Gideon, and gd-dau. of Samuel & Hannah Belden. There is but one other Eliz. and her age is not so suitable. Jonathan[4] Burr was b. Midd., 21 Mch., 1712-13, (s. Jona.,[3] & Abigail) Burr, and gd-s. of Samuel[2] of Htfd., eld. s. of Benjamin,[1] first of the name in Conn. Jonathan[4] and his bros. Ebenezer and Nathaniel, early sett. in

Middle Haddam, south of Hog Hill, and in 1738-40, were petitioners for a new eccl. soc., which was formed in 1740, and named Middle Haddam. The issue of Elizabeth Belden & Jonathan Burr, were:
    i. Jonathan (Burr), b. 3 Aug., 1741; m. Priscilla **Freeman**, 17 Mch., 1763; rem. to Ludlow, Mass.; had a large fam.—See *Burr Geneal.*, and Noon's *Hist. Ludlow.*
    ii. Elizabeth (Burr), b. 1742 or '43; m. 16 Sept., 1761, Lieut. Abner **Brainard**, as his 2d wife; res. Chatham, nr. East Haddam.
    iii. Mary (Burr).
    iv. Abigail (Burr).
    v. Ebenezer (Burr).
    vi. Experience (Burr), b. 1752.
    vii. Jeremiah (Burr), bp. 1756.
6. Abigail, b. 10 Sept., 1721.
7. Hannah, b. 4 Sept., 1723.
8. Hezekiah, b. 20 Oct., 1725; d. 20 Oct., 1793, in 69th yr.—*S. C. R.*
9. Sarah, b. 4 Apl., 1727.
10. Experience, b. 6 Jan., 1729; d. Nov., 26, ——.
11. Gideon, ae. 5 mos., at father's dth.
12. Three others that d. before 1734.

---

* But *Weth. Ins.* gives tombstone rec of a Daniel B., son of Mr. Samuel and Mrs. Mary, who d. 28 July, 1752, in 26th yr.—So *Hinman* may have got hold of the wrong Daniel.
† The *Ct. Rec.* (Htfd. Co. Prob.) names *Esther* as Gideon's wid.; the est. as insolvent, and ch. put under guardianship, as follows, viz.: *Elisha*, ae. 19, to Josiah Churchill; *Ruth*,

FAM. 20. Lieut. EBENEZER,[4] (*Sgt. Ebenezer,[3] John,[2] Rich.,[1]*), b. 1697; m. Mary (dau. Cornet Samuel) **Talcott**, 7 Dec., 1720; she bp. 30 June, 1697; d. 23 Jan., 1784; Lieut. Ebenz'r d. 26 Dec., 1783. Like his father he filled many offices of town trust.

Children (Weth. Rec.):

1. Martha, b. 24 Sept., 1721.
2. John, bp. 9 Aug., 1730.—*Mix MS.* FAM. 31.
3. Anne, m. Rev., Joshua **Belding.**

4. Eunice (?), d. 7 Aug., 1754, in 21st yr.— *Weth. Ins.*

FAM. 21. JOSIAH,[5] (*Josiah,[4] John,[3] John,[2] Rich.,[1]*), b. 1713; m. (1) 13 Feb.,1745-6 Thankful **Nott** (*W. C. R.*) who d. 27 Jan., 1751 (*Weth. Ins.*); he m. (2) 31 Jan., 1759 (*W. C. R.*), Mehitable **Robbins**, who d. 28 Apl., 1784, ae. 57; he was bur. 18 Oct., 1787, ae. 70 yr.—*Weth. Ins.*

Children (Weth. Rec.):

1. Ozias, b. 5, bp. 12 Apl., 1747; bu. 8 Nov., 1810.—*Weth. Ins.*
2. Rebecca, bp. 25 Sept., 1748.
3. Josiah,   } twins, b. 21 Jan., 1751.—
4. Thankful, }   *Weth. Ins.*

(By second marriage):
5. Josiah, b. 16 May, 1761; bu. 26 Sept., 1775, ae. 14.—*W. C. R.*

FAM. 21a. JOHN,[5] (*John,[4] John,[3] John,[2] Richard,[1]*), b. 1716; m. Sarah **Kellogg.**

Children (C. G. H.):

1. John Kellogg, b. 19 May, 1740. FAM. 31a.

FAM. 22. AARON,[5] (*Ezra,[4] John,[3] John,[2] Rich.,[1]*), b. 1731; m. Mercy (dau. Matthew) **Belden**, 5 Feb., 1756.—*W. C. R.* Prob. the "wife of Mr. Aaron," who d. 27 Dec., 1807, ae. 78.—*Weth. Ins.* He d. 9 Dec., 1816.—*C. G. H.*

Children (Weth. Rec.; bp. W. C. R.):

1. Moses, b. 14 Aug., 1756. FAM. 32.
2. Benjamin, b. 25, bp. 30 Oct., 1757.
3. Asahel, b. 18, bp. 23 Sept., 1759. This may *poss.* be the *Ashbel* who m. Lydia **Beckley,** 6 Apl., 1780, both of Weth.— *N. C. R.*
4. Silas, b. 28 Dec., 1761; d. 5 Mch., 1824, in 63d yr.—*S. C. R.*; m. 4 Mch., 1783, Ruth **Beckley**, prob. the "wid. of Silas,"

who d. 20 Mch., 1830, ae. 70.—*S. C. R.*
5. Roswell, b. 21 Jan., bp. 13 Nov., 1763; d. 16 Dec., 1817; wid. "of late," *R.* d. 31 Jan., 1835, in 58th yr.—*S. C. R.*
6. Justus, b. 23 Jan., 1767. FAM. 33.
7. Aaron, b. 14 Sept., 1769. FAM. 34.
8. Elizabeth, b. 14 Sept., 1771; bp. and d. 27 Oct., 1772.—*S. C. R.*

FAM. 23. Rev. JOSHUA,[5] (*Silas,[4] Dea. Jona.,[3] John,[2] Rich.,[1]*), b. 1724; grad. Y. C.

1743; while at Col!, was one of the converts at that instit. of the "Great Revival;" studied theology and on 1st Oct., 1745, being then of Canaan, Ct., where his father had rem. some time before his dth.) he was licensed by the Htfd. No. Consociation to preach the gospel. He was ord. at Newington, 11 Nov., 1747. His full biog. will be found in Chapt. VIII, Vol. I, in connection with the history of Newington parish. It was he who became convinced in middle life (1772), of the propriety of changing the spelling of the fam. name from Belding to Belden, and who was instrumental in obtaining a large degree of uniformity, in this respect, among the different B. families. He m. (1) 30 Nov., 1749, Anne (dau. Lieut. Ebenezer) **Belding**, who d. 29 Oct., 1773, in 47 yr. (*Weth. N. Ins.*); he m. (2) 14 Nov., 1774, Honor (wid. of Charles) **Whiting**, of Norwich, and dau. of Esq. Hezebiah Goodrich of Weth., who d. 21 Aug., 1801 in 70th yr. (*Conn. Courant*). He d. 23 July, 1813, ae. 89 yrs. and in 66th year of his ministry.*

---

ae. 16, to her uncle, Daniel Belding; as, also, *Ebenezer*, ae. 3 yrs. The mother retained the guardianship of *Elizabeth*, ae. 14 yrs.; *Hannah*, 11 yrs.; *Hezekiah*, ae. 8; *Sarah*, ae. 7 yrs., and *Gideon*, ae. 5 mos. The invent. of est., however, was exhib., 1 Jan., 1733-4, by and adm. gr. to *Elizabeth* Belding.
* None of Mr. Belden's writings were published, except the Charge prepared to be

Children (Weth. Rec.; bps. N. C. R. and dths. from Weth. N. Ins.) :

1. Martha, b. 14, bp. 20 Jan., 1750-1; d. 27 July, 1761.
2. Anne, b. 23, bp. 26 Jan., 1762 ; d. 23 Sept., 1758.
3. Abigail, b. 10, bp. 12 Aug., 1754 ; m. James **Lusk**, of New., later of Enfield—*Hinman;* she d. 11 Oct., 1777.
4. Mary, b. 9 Dec., 1755 ; m. Justus **Francis**, of New., and d. 5 Mch., 1735.
5. Sarah, b. 29 Sept., 1757 ; d. 28 Jan., 1779.
6. Anne, b. 7, bp. 8 July, 1759 ; d. — 1773, ae. 29.

7. Martha, b. 24, bp. 26 July, 1761 ; m. Joseph **Lynde**, druggist, of Htfd.
8. Octavia, b. 27, bp. 30 Oct., 1763 ; m. Rev. Nathaniel **Gaylord**, of Hartland, Ct.
9. Rhoda, b. 29 May, bp. 1 June, 1766 ; m. Rev. Silas **Churchill**, of New Lebanon, N. Y.; she d. 28 May, 1823.
10. Joshua (Dr.), b. 29 Mch., bp. 3 Apl., 1768. FAM. 35.
11. Mary, bp. 14 Dec., 1775.
12. Hezekiah, b. 17, bp. 22 Feb., 1778. FAM. 36.

FAM. 23a.   CHARLES,[5] (*Silas,*[4] *Jona.*[3] *John,*[2] *Rich.,*[1]), b. 1728; sett. at Canaan, Ct.; m. Hannah **Hockaboom**; (Hoogeboom? Hocaboom?).

Children (b. So. Canaan, Ct.) :

1. Abigail, bp. 13 Nov., 1753 ; m. 2 Oct., 1773, Roswell **Dean**, of So. Canaan.
2. Charles, bp. 28 Aug., 1754. FAM. 36a.
3. Jettie, b. 20 Apl., 1756 ; m. 3 Mch., 1774, Isaac **Beebe**.
4. Hannah, b. 9 Sept., 1757 ; m. 19 Feb., 1778, John **Whiting**.
5. Bartholomew, b. 30 Dec., 1759.

6. Joshua, b. 17 Dec., 1761.
7. Mary, b. 3 Dec., 1763.
8. Elizabeth, b. 23 Feb., 1766.
9. Rachel, b. 28 Nov., 1767.
10. Daniel, b. 6 June, 1772.
11. Jeremiah, b. 15 Apl., 1774 ; m. Elizabeth **Kellogg**.
12. David, bp. 22 Sept., 1773.—*sic* on rec.

FAM. 23b.   Capt. **OLIVER**,[5] (*Mr. Silas,*[4] *Dea. Jona.,*[3] *John,*[2] *Rich.,*[1]), b. 1732, in Weth., rem. to Lenox, Mass., where he d. Sept. 16, 1811; he was Capt. Co. 7 2d Berkshire Reg. in Rev. War; he m. (1) Abigail ———, who d. Nov. 6, 1767; m. (2) June 16, 1768, Anna (supp. dau. of Jona. & Sarah *Langdon*) **Woodruff**, b. Jan. 26, 1736, d. in L. 19 Feb., 1828.

Children (by first marr.) :

1. Abigail, b. Canaan, Ct., 14 Feb., 1756 ; d. Chenango Falls, N. Y., 11 Oct., 1839 ; m. Simon **Willard**.
2. Lydia, b. 30 June, 1757 ; d. July, 1789 ; m. Josiah **Pond**, of Shoreham, Vt.
3. Theodosia, b. 9 May, 1759 ; d. 14 Feb., 1818 ; m. Eliakim **Culver**, of Shorham.
4. Oliver, Jr., b. 13 Mch., 1762 ; d. 15 ———, 1821 ; m. Anna **Steele**, of Lenox.
5. Anna, b. 15 May, 1765 ; d. May, 1808 ; m. Isaac **Flagg**, of Shoreham.
   (*By second marriage*) :
6. Chauncey, b. 27 Mch., 1769 ; d. 13 Oct., 1817 ; m. Ruth **Martindale**.
7. Levi, b. 22 Aug., 1770 ; d. 22 Sept., 1854, at Lenox ; m. Esther **Collins**.
8. Samuel, b. 10 Sept., 1772 ; d. Charlton, N. Y., 23 Oct., 1865 ; m. Betsy **Curtis**.
9. Ezekiel, b. 6 Jan., 1775 ; d. 21 June, 1862 ; m. Susan **Choate**.
10. Alma, b. 7 Jan., 1777, at Lenox; d. 4 Jan., 1828, at Chenango Forks, N. Y.; m. (1) 4 Jan., 1801, Nathan **Hubbard**, b. at Pittsfield, Mass., Feb., 1775 ; d. Middlebury, Vt., Mar., 1813 ; she m. (2) 1817, David **Seymour**, Jr., of Chenango Forks, N. Y.
    Issue:
    i. Franklin B. (Hubbard), b. 1801; d. 1865 ; m. Mariah **Seymour**.
    ii. Chauncey P. (Hubbard), b. Pittsfield, 17 Nov., 1803 ; d. Fredonia, N. Y., 10 Apl., 1894; m. 3 Aug., 1831, his cousin Mary (dau. of Stephen) **Wells**, b. 25 Jan., 1807, in Lenox; d. in Fredonia, N. Y., 8 Sept., 1898; had (a) Emily

Hubbard), b. 1832 ; m. Daniel S. **Hubbard**, of Syracuse, N. Y.; (b) Ann M. (Hubbard), b. 27 Apr., 1834 ; m. Amasa **Cooke**, of Austerlitz, N. Y.; (c) Adelaide (Hubbard), b. 11 Feb., 1837 ; (d) Mary A. (Hubbard), b. 1839 ; d. 1841 ; (e) Albert W., Rev. (Hubbard), b. Cameron, N. Y., 18 Oct., 1841 ; grad. Amherst Coll. 1867 ; d. Sivas, Turkey, Asia, 13 Apl., 1899 ; a Miss. of the Am. Bd. ; m. 1871, Emma R. **Spencer**, of Corning, N. Y. ; (f) Theodore S. (Hubbard), b. 6 July, 1843, at Geneva, N. Y. ; m. 1871, Carrie M. **Gilbert**, of Fredonia, N. Y. ; (g) Chauncey G., M. D. (Hubbard), of Hornellsville, N. Y., b. 16 Oct., 1845 : m. 1880, Florence N. **Prentice**, of Jasper, N. Y. ; (h) Alma Rose (Hubbard), b. 22 Feb., 1850 ; (i) Mary A. (Hubbard), b. 1851 ; d. 1853.
    iii. Fanny B. (Hubbard), b. Dec., 1805 ; d. 1857 ; m. Dr. Ezra **Gleason**, of Boston, Mass.
    iv. Nathan Pomeroy, Capt. (Hubbard), b. 1813 ; d. 1882, unm., at Battle Creek, Mich.
    (*By second marriage*) :
    v. Sarah B. (Seymour), b. 21 Dec., 1818 ; d. 2 July, 1821.
    [Dr. HUBBARD has compiled a list of 1,450 names of descendants of this Oliver Belden, which was expected to be inserted here ; but at the last moment it was crowded out for want of space.—H. R. S.]

delivered at the ordination of his successor, Rev. Joab Brace, and which may be found in the *Appendix* to Dr. Brace's *Half Century Discourse,* 1855.
An Elegy written and published soon after the death of Mr. Belden's wife, bears this title.
An *Elegy on the Death of Mrs. Anne Belding,* late wife of the Reverend Mr. Joshua Belding, of Newington, who died October 29, 1773. Humbly inscribed to him, by a Youth of his Parish, Hartford, 1774, pp. 9.
For a sketch of Mr. Belden's life, see *Conn. Evangelical Magazine,* 2d Series, Vol. VI, pp. 429-437.

FAM. 24. DAVID,[5] (*Capt. Jona.*,[4] *Dea. Jona.*,[3] *John*,[2] *Richard*,[1]), b. 1716 Stepney parish; m. 3 Aug., 1769, Hepzibah **Goodrich.**. He d. ae. 70, 18 Dec., 1785.—
W. C. R.

Children (bp. from S. Ch. Rec.):

1. Martha, b. 29 June, 1772.—*Weth. Rec.*
2. Daniel, ⎰ bp. 29 Apl., 1781.
3. Selah, ⎱
4. Burrage, bp. 2 Feb., 1783.
5. Milly, bp. 12 Nov., 1786.
6. Asa, ⎰ twins, bp. 8 Feb., 1789.
7. Asahel, ⎱
8. Harvey, bp. 13 Nov., 1791.
9. Rosanna, bp. 14 Nov., 1793.
10. Calvin, b. 30 Oct., 1796.

11. Lois, b. 18 Feb., 1798.
12. David, b. 31 Oct., 1802.
13. Josiah Wolcott, bp. 3 May, 1801.
(*Note*, these last two named may have been ch. of another David—as *N. Rec.* state that a David m. Lois **Wolcott**, of Stepney, 18 Feb., 1779.
14. Jona. "of David," bp. 1 Oct., 1775.—*W. Ch. Rec.*

FAM. 25. Esq. and Col. THOMAS,[5] (*Thos.*,[4] *Joseph*,[3] *John*,[2] *Rich.*,[1]), b. 1732; m. 1 Aug., 1753, Abigail, (dau. Dr. Ezekiel) **Porter**, who d. 17 Mch., 1798, ae. 61; Col. Thomas d. 22 May, 1782, ae. 50; wid. m. (2) Oct., 1796, Rev. James **Dana**, D. D., of New Haven. Col. Thos. grad. Y. C. 1751; was highly esteemed, active in public affairs and held many town offices.

Children (Weth. Rec., W. C. Rec. and Weth. Ins.):

1. Ezekiel Porter (Col.), b. 12 Feb., 1756. FAM. 37.
2. James, b. 19, bp. 20 Apl., 1760; d. 27 Nov., 1779, ae. 20; bu. Litchfield.—*W. C. R.*
3. Mary, b. 22, bp. 27 May, 1770; m. Fred **Butler**, of Htfd., b. 23 July, 1776; d. 5 Apl., 1843; she d. 17 June, 1811, ae. 40. *Issue:*
   i. Abigail Porter (Butler), b. 26 Feb., 1798; m. 27 Mch., 1824, James **Bidwell**, of Utica, N. Y.; she d. 6 Feb., 1832; had (a) Esther E. (Bidwell), b. 21 July, 1826; res. in old Porter-Belden ho., Main St., Weth.; (b) Abigail Butler (Bidwell), b. 21 Jan.,

1832; m. Chas. S. **Cozzens**, 9 Nov., 1850; d. 7 June, 1892; had an only ch.: Frederick Butler Cozzens, b. 15 May, 1860, and d. 2 Aug., 1861.
   ii. Thomas Belden (Butler), late Chief Justice of the State of Conn., b. 22 Aug., 1806; d. at Norwalk, Ct., 8 June, 1873; "a profound and enthusiastic scientist, a high minded and judicious legislator, both in the State and Nation; an able and distinguished lawyer, and a conscientious, upright, learned, impartial and incorruptible judge."
4. Abigail, d. Mch., 1772, ae. 2 mos.

FAM. 26. Esq. SIMEON,[5] (*Thos.*,[4] *Joseph*,[3] *John*,[2] *Rich.*,[1]), b. 1737; grad Y. C. 1762; m. Martha (dau. Rev. James) **Lockwood**, of Weth., 3 Nov., 1765, who was bur. 5 Dec., 1830, ae. 88; he d. 29 Oct., 1820; was a mcht. and held many town offices; was, also, for many yrs. Dep. Sheriff of Htfd. Co.

Children (Weth. Rec.):

1. Simeon, b. 3 or 4 Oct., 1767; d. 3 Feb., 1768.
2. Simeon, b. 27, bp. 30 Apl., 1769; sett. at Fayetteville, N. C.—*Hinman.* A Simeon m. Emily **Beckley**, 13 Feb., 1787.
3. Charlotte, b. 24 Dec., 1770; m. Hon. Lewis B. **Sturgis**, of Fairfield, Ct.—*Hinman.*
4. Martha, b. 1 Dec., 1772; m. ———— **De Witt**, Esq., of Milford, Ct.—*Hinman.*
5. James Lockwood, b. 15, bp. 23 Oct., 1774.

FAM. 38.
6. Joseph, b. and bp. 29 Dec., 1776; grad. Y. C., 1795; commenced bus. as a druggist; later was a general book agent and made the bus. profitable to himself and employees; m. Hannah (dau. John) **Reynolds**, of Enfield, Ct., 13 Nov., 1813; d. 7 Aug., 1826. *No issue.*
7. Mary Mix, b. 15, bp. 17 Aug., 1783; m. Barzillai Buck **Deane**, of Weth.
8. Mehitable, bp. 17 Aug., 1783.—*W. C. R.*

FAM. 27. SAMUEL,[5] (*Sam'l*,[4] *Sam'l*,[3] *John*,[2] *Rich.*,[1]), b. 1713; d. 10 Jan., 1789, ae. 69; m. Elizabeth ————————; res. Step. Sam'l B.'s wife d. 23 Feb., 1775.—
S. C. R.

Children (Weth. Rec.):

1. Prudence, b. 12 July, 1742.
2. Abner, b. 12 Jan., 1744; m. 24 Oct., 1771, Mary **Standish.**—*S. C. R.*
3. Bildad, b. 9 Sept., 1745. FAM. 39.
4. Seth, b. 7 Aug., 1747. FAM. 40.

5. Moses, b. 18 June, 1749; d. 16 Aug., 1750.
6. Rebecca, b. 27 Mch., 1751; poss. the R. who m. Daniel **Woodruff**, of Far., 28 Feb., 1775.—*W. C. R.*
7. Mary, b. 3 Jan., 1753.

FAM. 28. RICHARD,[5] (*Samuel*,[4] *Samuel*,[3] *John*,[2] *Rich.*,[1]), b. 1728; m. 30 Oct., 1749, Elizabeth (dau. Wm. & Susannah) **Hurlbut**, *W. C. R.*, and d. at Step., 28 July, 1797, in 69 yr.—*Weth. Ins.*

Children (S. C. Rec.) :

1. Amos, b 26 Oct., 1750; m. Comfort **Blinn,** Oct., 1773.
2. Jeremiah, b. 26 Mch., 1753. Fam. 40.
3. Othniel, b. 27 Mch., 1755. Fam. 41.
4. Caleb, b. 10 Feb., 1757, (idiot) d. 17 Aug., 1794.—*S. C. R.*
5. Richard. (prob.), who d. 31 Jan., 1848, ae. 87, P. H.; b. therefore, 1758; m. 28 Sept., 1785, Mary **Cole** [man ?] ; his wife d. 22 Feb., 1844. He was a Revol. pensioner, res. S. side road opp., but E. of Dea. *T. P.*

William's place.—Dr. R. W. G. He had issue (*S. C. R.*) :
  i. Inf. who d. 5 Mch., 1792.
  ii. Son (Belden), who d. 29 Apl., 1799, in first year.
  iii. Richard (Belden), who d. P. H., 1 Apl., 1848, ae. 45.
6. Samuel (Spencer, prob.)—a "Samuel Spencer, s. of Rich." was bp. 11 Aug., 1771. Fam. 43.

Fam. 29. PHINEHAS,[5] (*Sam'l,[4] Sam'l,[3] John,[2] Rich.,[1]*), b. 1730; m .Hannah **Deming,** 22 Mch., 1750-1.

Children (b. Weth.) :

1. Charles, b. 3 Apl., 1752.—*Pittsfield* (Mass.) *Rec.,* give pub. of intent of marr. between Charles B. and Wid. Elizabeth **Chandler;** she adm. to P. Ch., 1776; had issue (*P. Ch. Rec.*) :
   i. Chandler (Belden), bp. 1 Dec., 1776.
   ii. Charles (Belden), bp. 8 May, 1779.
2. Mary, b. 8 Aug., 1753.
3. Lucy, b. 1 Apl., 1773.
4. Ch. bu. 28 Nov., 1775.—*W. C. R.*
5. Ebenezer, b. 7 July, 1776; prob. the E.

who m. Anne **Fosdick,** 29 July, 1804, and who was bu. 19 Jan., 1806, ae. 29. *W. C. R.*
6. Sarah, b. 11 Oct., 1778; bp. 7 Mch., 1779.
7. Nancy, b. 5, bp. 10 Dec., 1780.
8. Harriet Mann, b. 4 Feb., bp. 7 Sept., 1783—prob. the *"Marcia,* of John, bp. 6 Sept., 1801."—W. C. R.
  (Poss. the "Sarah, dau. of John," bp. 19 June, 1774, may have belonged to this family.)

Fam. 30. ELISHA,[5] (*prob. s. of Gideon,[4] Sam'l,[3] John,[2] Rich.,[1]*), b. 1715; prob. the E. who d. 29 Sept. 1813, ae. 77; the "wid. of Elisha," who d. at Berlin (*S. C. R.*) 11 July, 1817 in 87 yr.

Children (S. C. R.) :

1. Joshua, bp. 30 Sept., 1764; it may have been his wife who d. 18 Apl., 1825 in 38th yr.—*S. C. R.*
2. John, bp. 2 Feb., 1766.
3. Honor, bp. 29 Nov., 1767.
4. Aziel, b. *Fam. Bible Rec.* says, 28 Mch., bp. 6 (?) Apl., 1770. Fam. 44.
5. Elisha, bp. 8 Dec., 1771. Fam. 45.

6. Prudence, bp. 29 May, 1774.
7. Lydia, bp. 6 Aug., 1775.
8. Isaac, bp. 10 Oct., 1779; pos. the I. who m. Marietta **Holmes,** 16 July, 1829.—*S. C. R.*
9. Joel, bp. 26 May, 1782.
10 (?), Eunice, bp. 7 Oct., 1792.

Fam. 31. JOHN,[5] (*Ebenezer,[4] Ebenezer,[3] John,[2] Rich.,[1]*), b. ————; m. Rebecca **Reynolds,** 12 June, 1766, filled his round of town offices, as did his father and grandfather. Is prob. the Capt. John who, ae. 55, was bu. 16 Aug., 1790.

Children (b. Weth.) :

1. Elizur, b. 7, bp. 10 Sept., 1763; ent. Y. C. A lugubrious *"Funeral Oration on the Death of Mr. Elizur Belden, of Weth., a Senior Sophister in Yale College,* who d. 8 Apl., 1786, at ae. 23, by Reuben Hitchcock, 1786," preserves his memory in printed form.*

2. Rebecca, b. 28 May, bp. 9 June, 1765.
3. Mary, b. 27 Dec., 1767.—*W. C. R.* says bp. 8 Nov., 1767.
4. John, b. 26, bp. 30 July, 1769.
5. Ebenezer (Capt.), b. 7 July, bp. 1 Dec., 1771.
6. Sarah, } bp. 27 May, 1781.
7. Esther, }

Fam. 31a. JOHN KELLOGG,[6] (*John,[5] John,[4] John,[3] John,[2] Rich.,[1]*), b. 1740; m. 8 Nov., 1769, Mercy (sister of Noah) **Webster,** b. 8 Nov., 1749, and d. 12 Aug., 1820. He d. 22 Nov., 1815.

Children (C. G. H.) :

1. Mercy, b. 26 Mch., 1771; d. 1777.
2. Lucinda, b. 15 Feb., 1772; d. 31 Jan., 1831.
3. John, b. 14 Jan., 1774. Fam. 45a.
4. Rachel, b. 5 Aug., 1776; d. 1777.
5. Ebenezer, b. 9 Sept., 1778; d. 1826. Fam. 45b.

6. Mercy, b. 2 May, 1782; m. ——— **Dennison.**
7. Betsy, b. 18 Mch., 1786; m. Rev. Elihu **Mason,** Castleton, Vt.

---

* Pres. Ezra Stiles' *Literary Diary,* iii, 213, records "Last Saturday, d. at Weth., Elizur Belden, a Senior Soph. in this College   I directed the Senior Class & they elected Hitchcock to make a Funeral Oration upon his classmate Belden."—(p. 214).   The whole Senior Class in mourning for Belden, their Classmate.   A black Ribbon round the left arm.—(p. 222-5, June, 1786.)   A Funeral Oration delivered this day in Chapel by Hitchcock.   His father and mother present."   The Pres. improved the opportunity to secure from the mother,

FAM. 32. Mr. MOSES,[6] (Aaron,[5] Ezra,[4] John,[3] John,[2] Rich.,[1]), b. 1750 (5?); m. Ruth ————, "Ruth wid. of Moses," d. 17 Sept., 1846, ae. 88.—Weth. Ins. He d. 14 June, 1824, in 69th yr.

Children (S. C. R.):

1. Lois, ⎰ bp. 6 May, 1781.
2. Sarah, ⎱
3. Oliver, bp. 26 Jan., 1783; d. 11 Dec., 1797

in 14 yr.—Weth. Ins.
4. Cynthia, bp. 18 Jan., 1789.
5. Mary, bp. 4 Jan., 1795.

FAM. 33. JUSTUS,[6] (Aaron,[3] Ezra,[4] John,[3] John,[2] Rich.,[1]) b. 1767; d. 19 Oct., 1846, ae. 80—Weth. Ins.; m. (1) Mary **Riley**, 17 Apl., 1792—S. C. R.; she prob. the wife of J., who d. 25 Nov., 1792—S. C. R.; m. (2) 3 Dec., 1797, Hannah **Morton**, who d. 17 Oct., 1854, ae. 77—Weth. Ins.

Children (bp. S. C. R.):

1. Son, ae. 5, d. 22 July, 1797.—S. C. R.
   (By second marr.):
2. Mary, bp. 29 Nov., 1799.
3. Solomon, bp. 6 Dec., 1801.
4. Thomas Morton, bp. 5 Aug., 1804; prob. the T. who d. 1 Nov., 1829, in 25th yr.

5. Lucy, bp. 4 May, 1806; poss. the ch. who d. 23 Oct., 1806, in 1st yr.
6. Mercy, bp. 18 Sept., 1808.
7. Betsy, bp. 18 Nov., 1809.
8. Aaron, bp. 14 Aug., 1814.

FAM. 34. AARON, Jr.,[6] (Aaron,[5] Ezra,[4] John,[3] John,[2] Rich.,[1]), b. 1769; m. 30 July, 1797, Rhoda **Wright**; he d. 18 July, 1814, ae. 44; she d. 8 Feb., 1866, ae. 87.

Children (S. C. Rec.):

1. Ashbel, bp. 14 Oct., 1798; m. Philia **Blinn**, 27 Feb., 1823.
2. Leonard, bp. 2 Oct., 1800; d. 16 Nov., 1853, ae. 53; m. Lucretia **Holmes**, 6 Aug., 1826; she d. 15 Feb., 1853, ae. 45.

3. Emily, bp. 5 Oct., 1806; d. 12 Dec., 1840, ae. 35.—Weth. Ins.
4. Juliana, bp. 29 Jan., 1809.
5. Elliott (of "the late Aaron, Jr."), bp. 14 Aug., 1814.

FAM. 35. Dr. JOSHUA,[6] (Rev. Joshua,[5] Silas,[4] Dea. Jona.,[3] John,[2] Rich.,[1]), b. 1768; grad. Y. C., 1778, or 1781; became a physician, and set. in New., where he built the ho. now occup. by Mr. Olin Wetherell, but after a few yrs. abandoned his profession for farming in New.; m. Dorothy (·dau. Lieut. Lemuel) **Whittlesey**, 9 Jan., 1797—N. C. R.; he d. 6 June, 1808—Weth. Ins.; esteemed and greatly lamented. His wid. (b. 8 Mch., 1770) d. 10 Sept., 1846.—Weth. (N.)·Ins.

Children (Hinman):

1. Lemuel Whittlesey (Dr.), b. 6 Jan., bp. 1 Mch., 1801. FAM. 46.
2. Joshua, b. 3 Aug., 1802. FAM. 47.
3. Chauncy, b. 15, bp. 25 (N. C. R.) Oct.,

1804. FAM. 48.
4. John Mason, b. and bp. (N. C. R.) 26 Aug., 1806. FAM. 49.

FAM. 36. HEZEKIAH,[6] (Rev. Joshua,[5] Silas,[4] Dea. Jona.,[3] John,[2] Rich.,[1]), grad. Y. C., 1796; was for sometime a mcht. in New Haven, where he m. 28 Dec., 1818, Harriet Halsted (dau. Esq. Underhill) **Lyon**, of Rye., N. Y.; losing his wife, he rem. to Richmond, Va., and, in connection with others, became a contractor for transportation of the U. S. mails, 1823-42; then ret. to Weth. of which he became the Town Clerk.—Hinman. He d. at W., 22 Mch., 1849, ae. 71.—W. T. R.

Children (Hinman):

1. George Hubertus, b. in N. Haven, 12 Oct., 1819; engineer on N. Y. & Erie R. R.
2. Mary Honoria, b. in N. H., 20 Sept., 1821.

---

a long and curious account of her late son's illness and infirmities in childhood, especially the hip disease and a total loss of sight at age of 3-7 yrs., the latter having been entirely and suddenly cured by a German quack doctor, in a manner which greatly excited the President's curiosity, as evidenced by the fulness of details entered in his diary.

FAM. 36a. CHARLES, Jr.,[5] (*Chas.*,[5] *Silas*,[4] *Jona.*,[3] *John*,[2] *Rich.*,[1]), b. So. Canaan, Ct., 7 Sept., 1754; m. 17 Dec., 1782, Lois **Bosworth.**

Children (b. So. Canaan):

1. Hannah, b. 30 June, 1785; d. 1811, unm.
2. Charles 3d, b. 19 Mch., 1789; d. 1846 in Ohio; m.
3. Clarissa, b. 2 Nov., 1789; m. 15 Dec., 1810, m. Gaylord **Kellogg**, of Canaan; d. 1817; 3 ch.

4. Henry, b. 23 Jan., 1793. FAM. 49a.
5. Miles, b. 18 Apl., 1795; d. 1880. *No issue.*
6. Polly, b. 27 June, 1797.
7. Betsy, b. 1800; m. Asabel **Benedict; d.** 1839, at Spencertown, N. Y.; 5 ch.

FAM. 37. Col. EZEKIEL PORTER,[6] (*Col. Thos.*,[5] *Thos.*,[4] *Joseph*,[3] *John*,[2] *Rich.*,[1]), grad. Y. C. 1775; served creditably in Revol. War (see Vol. I, pp. 507-8), retiring from the army with title and rank of Capt. and brevet of Major, subsequently was active in militia; m. (1) 26 Sept., 1781, Elizabeth (dau. Esq. and Capt. Elisha) **Williams,** who was b. 28 Oct., 1756, and d. 30 Oct., 1789, ae. 33— *W. C. R.;* he m. (2) Mary **Parsons,** of Amherst Mass., 1 Nov., 1790, who d. 21 Mch., 1845, ae. 88. Col. Belden d. 9 Oct., 1824, in 69th yr.—*W. C. R.;* he was repeatedly chosen Selectman; was elected J. P. in 1812, and held the office uninterruptedly until his death; was a member of almost all the town committees; rep. the town in Gen. Assemb., in 49 sessions, and was elected to two more, which he declined to serve; was a man of kindly and social feeling, gentlemanly and amiable manners, and active in public affairs.

Children (Weth. Rec. and W. C. R.):

1. Abigail, b. 26, bp. 30 June, 1782; m. 1 Men., 1809 (*W. C. R.*), Justin **Ely**, Jr., Esq., of West Springfield, Mass., where she d. 7 Apl., 1864.
2. Elizabeth, b. 10, bp. 26 Jan., 1784; m. 30 Jan, 1812, Daniel (s. of Daniel & Sarah *Saltonstall*) **Buck**, of Weth.; res. in Htfd. and Poquonock; after his death she rem. to Weth., where she d. 3 Mch., 1887, ae. 103, "highly esteemed and blessed by all who knew her." Had 6 cb.
3. Thomas, b. 29 July, bp. 7 Aug., 1785; d. unm., 24 Feb., 1831.
4. Inf. b. and d. 29 June, 1787.

(*By second marriage*):
5. Inf. b. and d. 21 Feb., 1789.
6. James, b. 1 Oct., bp. 20 Nov., 1791; d. 13 (14 *W. C. R.*) Sept. 1800.
7. Ezekiel Porter, Jr., b. 18, bp., 29 Mch., 1794; d. 2 Apl., 1818.—*W. C. R.*
8. Mary Foote, b. 1 June, bp. 19 July, 1795; m. 22 May, 1821, Erastus F. **Cooke,** of Oppenheim, N. Y.
9. Cella, b. 5 Oct., bp. 27 Nov., 1796; m. Heman **Ely**, of Elyria, N. Y.
10. Julia, b. 27 Aug., bp. 16 Dec., 1798; m. James L. **Belden**, of Weth.
11. Hannah, b. 19 Mch., bp. 29 June, 1800; m. 29 Oct., 1828, George **Pryor**, Jr., of Canaan.

FAM. 38. JAMES LOCKWOOD,[6] (*Simeon*,[5] *Thos.*,[4] *Joseph*,[3] *John*,[2] *Rich.*,[1]), b. Weth., 1774. *Hinman* says he was a successful mcht., but had reverses; lost his ppy. and turned his attention to horticulture; estab. the Weth. Seed Garden, by which he retrieved his fortunes, and accumulated a handsome ppy.; he m. Julia (dau. Esq. Ezekiel Porter) **Belden,** 28 Sept., 1819; while res. in Weth., was highly esteemed; was for a number of yrs. P. M.; resigned to enter into civil affairs of the state; was several times elected rep. of W. to the Gen. Assemb.; J. P. from yr. to yr.; in 1840, rem. to New Haven, for purpose of educating his sons; d. in N. Y., 1 Feb., 1847.—*Weth. Ins.*

Children:

1. Ezekiel Porter, bp. 18 Nov., 1821; bu. 8 Nov., 1822, ae. 14 mos. *Weth. Ins.*
2. Ezekiel Porter, b. 24 Apl., bp. 3 Aug., 1823; grad. Y. C. 1844; was a modeler in wood in N. Y. and N. Haven.

3. Celia Mix, b. 14 June, bp. 20 Aug., 1820; d. 9 Oct., 1824 in 4½ yr.—*Weth. Ins.*
4. James Lockwood, b. 23 Mch., bp. 7 Aug., 1825—sailor.

FAM. 39. BILDAD,[6] (*Samuel*,[5] *Samuel*,[4] *Samuel*,[3] *John*,[2] *Rich.*,[1]), b. 1745; m. Mary **Riley,** 14 Feb., 1770—*S. C. R.;* she d. 6 July, 1871, in 62d yr.

Children (S. C. R.):

1. Rosanna, inf. bp and d. 16 Sept., 1770.
2. Susannah, bp. 5 Jan., 1772; d. 26 Mch., 1782.

3. Rosanna, bp. 8 Sept., 1782.
4. Bildad Butler, bp. 13 Nov., 1785.
5. Clifford, bp. 5 Apl., 1789.

FAM. 40. SETH,[6] (Samuel,[5] Samuel,[4] Samuel,[3] John,[2] Rich.,[1]), b. 1747. Abt. this man there is uncertainty, and absence of record. As near as we can make out he m. (1) Sally ————, who d. 16 Mch., 1799, in 21st yr.—Weth. Ins.; and m. (2) 16 Apl., 1772, at Weth., Christian **Dickinson**, who was bp. 1755. Is said (by writer in Geneal. Dept. Htfd. Times) to have been a private in Col. Huntington's reg. and killed at Battle of L. I., Aug., 1776, and to have had, in add. to the ch. given below, a son Seth, who lived in Cornwall, Ct.

Children (bp. S. C. R.; by second marriage):

1. Sally, bp. 10 May, 1801.
2. Inf., d. 28 Dec., 1802.

3, Lucy, ⎰ twins, bp. 15 Jan., 1804.
4. Lucius, ⎱
5. Harriet Sage, bp. 23 Nov., 1806.

FAM. 41. JEREMIAH,[6] (Rich.,[5] Sam'l,[4] Sam'l,[3] John,[2] Rich.,[1]), b. 1753; m. ————.

Children (S. C. R.):

1. Polly, bp. 13 Nov., 1785.
2. Ezekiel, bp. 17 Sept., 1786.
3. Lotta, bp. 21 June, 1789.
4. Philanda, bp. 6 Nov., 1791; d. 28 June, 1794.
5. Jerusha, bp. 22 Dec., 1793.

6. Andrew, bp. 19 June, 1796.
7. Alfred, bp. 28 July, 1799.
8. Henry, bp. 18 Oct., 1801.
9. Philomela, bp. 15 Apl., 1804.
10. Nancy, bp. 13 Apl., 1806.

FAM. 42. OTHNIEL,[6] (Rich.,[5] Sam'l,[4] Sam'l,[3] John,[2] Rich.,[1]), b. 1755; m. 4 Dec., 1778, Sarah **Lindsey** (both of Stepney)—W. C. R.; rem. to Chester, Mass., where he d. Oct., 1834; she 1837; he was a Revol. pensioner.

Children (S. C. R.):

1. Amos, bp. 29 Apl., 1781.
2. Ruth, bp. 14 Apl., 1782.
3. Sylvester, bp. 26 June, 1785; prob. the S. who m. Abigail Wright, 29 July, 1804.
4. Hannah, bp. 14 Aug., 1790 (S. C. R.); d. 23 Aug., 1796.
5. Sarah, bp. 3 Oct., 1790 (?).
6. Salmon, bp. 19 Feb., 1792. (And a geneal. enquirer in Htfd. Times, 12 Aug., 1901, gives the following—prob. b. at Chester,

Mass.)
7. Abby, who m. a **Waite.**
8. Lavinia, who m. a **Cannon.**
9. Asenath, who m. a **Foote.**
10. Sarah, who m. a **Moore.**
11. Mercy, who m. 1 Mch., 1826, Walter S. **Hatch**, of Brandford, Mass., at New Lebanon, N. Y.—She tho't to be the ygst. of Othniel's ch.
12. Othniel.

FAM. 43. SAMUEL SPENCER,[6] (Rich.,[5] Sam'l,[4] Sam'l,[3] John,[2] Rich.,[1]), b. 1771; d. 24 Sept., 1849, in 78 yr.—S. C. R.; m. Margaret ————, who d. 8 Oct., 1862, in 90th yr.

Children (S. C. R.):

1. Olive, bp. 14 Sept., 1800; prob. the O. who m. John Scovell, of Stockton, N. Y., 12 Nov., 1834.
2. Philip, bp. 11 Apl., 1802; Weth. Ins. gives dth. of Philip C. 30 Apl., 1840, ae. 40.
3. Asa, bp. 28 Apl., 1805; d. 19 Sept., 1865, ae. 61. "A kind Husband, Father and

Friend."—Weth. Ins.
4. Mary, bp. 31 Jan., 1808; prob. the ch. who d. 19 Dec., 1808 in 1st yr.
5. Edward, bp. and d. 19 Dec., 1808.—Weth. Ins.: tombstone gives this as date of dth. of Edmund.

FAM. 44. AZIEL,[6] (Elisha,[5] Gid.,[4] Sam'l,[3] John,[2] Rich.,[1]), b. 1770; m. Azubah **Goodrich**, 2 Mch., 1794—N.; who was b. 25 Mch., 1774; and who d. 4 Mch., 1809, at 6:30 p. m., in her 35th yr.—Weth. Ins.; he m. 29 Oct., same yr., wid. Abigail **Miller**—S. C. R., and d. 1 Dec., 1830, ae. 60. Both bu. in "Ch. St." cemetery at Newington. He res. Berlin.

Children (Family Bible Rec.):

1. Ira, b. 19 June, 1794.
2. Alven, b. 25 Jan., 1796.
3. Oren, b. 12 May, 1799.
4. Mary, ⎰ twins, b. 4 Nov., 1802.
5. Maria, ⎱
6. Jerusha, b. 11 July, 1805.
7. Walter, b. 4 May, 1811; m. Elizabeth

Beckley, 6 May, 1830; had inf. d. 26 Feb., 1835; had ch. d. 15 Oct., 1839.
8. Azubah, b..26 July, 1812.
9. Orpha, b. 13 Sept., 1814.
10. Honor, b. 28 Nov., 1816.
11. Edwin, b. 13 Oct., 1818.

FAM. 45. ELISHA,[6] (*Elisha*,[5] *Gid.*,[4] *Sam'l*,[3] *John*,[2] *Rich.*,[1]), b. Weth., 1771; m. ——————, prob. the "wid. of Elisha," who d. 26 Mch., 1848, in 81st yr. He prob. the E. who d. 25 Feb., 1848, in 77th yr.—*S. Ch. Rec.*

Children (Step. Ch. Rec.) :

1. George, bp. 3 Dec., 1797.
2. Barzillai, bp. 13 Oct., 1799.
3. Nancy, bp. 24 May, 1801.
4. Isaac, bp. 22 May, 1803; d. 18 Mch., 1882, ae. 79.—*Weth. Ins.*
5. A ch. of Elisha B., Jr., d. 25 Sept., 1805, in 2d yr.—*S. C. R.*
6. Sophia, bp. 25 Sept., 1805.

7 .Otis, bp. 11 Oct., 1801; "disappeared" 20 Sept., 1840, in 33d yr. *S. Ch. Rec.* ; m. Mary W. **Butler**, 10 Sept., 1837. *W. Rec.* Charlotte Ann, who d. 31 Mch., 1842, ae. 3 yr, 3 mos., and Alice Maria, who d. 19 Apl., 1842, were daus. of Otis & Mary W. Belden.—*Weth. Inscrip.*

FAM. 45a. JOHN,[7] (*John Kellogg*,[6] *John*,[5] *John*,[4] *John*,[3] *John*,[2] *Rich.*,[1]), b. 1774; m. 19 Apl., 1795, Asenath **Darrow**, of Philadelphia, Pa.; he d. at Far., Ct., 14 Oct., 1851; she b. 30 Nov., 1774, d. 6 Oct., 1840.

Children (C. G. H.) :

1. John, b. 15 Jan., 1796; d. same yr. FAM. 51.
2. Benjamin, b. 15 Aug., 1797.
3. Mary A., b. 3 Mch., 1800; m. a **Griswold**, 11 May, 1862.
4. Mercy W., b. 14 Feb., 1802; d. 1804.

5. Lucy Benjamin, b. 13 Dec., 1803; d. 1804.
6. Edwin Webster, b. 19 Sept., 1805. FAM. 52.
7. Henry J., b. 1 Mch., 1813; d. same yr.
8. Eliza Jane, b. 21 Aug., 1814; m. Dr. E. E. **Crofoot**; d. 7 Mch., 1901, Syracuse, N. Y.

FAM. 45b. EBENEZER,[7] (*John Kellogg*,[6] *John*,[5] *John*,[4] *John*,[3] *John*,[2] *Rich.*,[1]), b. 1778; m. 27 ——————, Jane **Whitehall**, who was b. in Philadelphia, Pa., 1780; he d. at Batavia, N. Y., 27 May, 1826.

Children (C. G. H.) :

1. John, d. in Calif.
2. James G. (M. D.), b. 22 Apl., 1821; d. at N. Orleans, 5 July, 1896; m. Arabella E. **Treat**, of Buffalo, N. Y.

3. Joseph, d. in Calif.
4. William W. (Rev.), b. 25 June, 1820. FAM. 49a.
5. Ann.

FAM. 46. Dr. LEMUEL WHITTLESEY,[6] (*Dr. Joshua*,[5] *Rev. Joshua*,[4] *Silas*,[3] *John*,[2] *Rich.*,[1]), b. 1801; grad. Y. C., 1821; sett. as phys. in Springfield. Mass.; m. Catharine (dau. Esq. Stephen) **Chester**, 7 May. 1829; who d. Jan., 1887—*C. G. H.*; he d. 26 Oct., 1839, "a man of great purity of mind, of amiable manners and some attainments, and was rapidly rising into eminence."

Child :

1. Donald Chester, b. 21 Jan., 1831; d. 1 June, 1837.—*W. C. R.*

FAM. 47. JOSHUA,[7] (*Dr. Joshua*,[6] *Rev. Joshua*,[5] *Silas*,[4] *Dea. Jona.*,[3] *John*,[2] *Rich.*[1]), b. 1802; grad. Y. C., 1825; rem. to and became a mcht. at St. Louis, Mo.; being unsuccessful, rem. to Glasglow, Mo., and retrieved his losses; m. 1834. Agnes Morton Graves **Lewis**, of G., whose father (Henry Lewis) was a large ld. ppr. and of the ancient Lewis fam. of Va. Mr. Joshua Belden became a prosperous resident of G., where he was known as "the honest man." He d. 2 Mch., 1870.

Children :

1. Agnes Whittlesey, b. 23 Feb., 1835, bp. 14 Aug., 1836.—*N. C. R.*
2. Dorothy, b. 6 Jan., 1836.
3. Elizabeth Merton, b. 25 Feb., bp. Apl., 1838; m. Oct., 1859, Dr. Stephen **Bowles**.

Issue (C. G. H.) :
i. Elizabeth (Bowles).
ii. Wallace (Bowles).
iii. John (Bowles).
iv. Henry (Bowles).

FAM. 48. Dr. CHAUNCEY.[7] (*Dr. Joshua*,[6] *Rev. Joshua*,[5] *Silas*,[4] *Dea. Jona.*,[3] *John*,[2] *Rich.*,[1]), b. 1804; grad. Y. C., Med. Dept., 1829; set at W. Springfield. Mass.; m. Lucy B. (?) (dau. Justin) **Ely**, of W. S. Nov., 1834; was highly respected as a man and in his profess.; d. 22 Nov., 1845, ae. 41.—*Weth. Ins.*

Children:

1. Theodore. b. 8 (or 18) June, 1836.
2. Elizabeth, b. May, 1838.
3. Chauncey Herbert. b. 6 Feb., 1844 ; m. 1878, Nellie **Miller.** *Issue (C. G. H.):*

i. Chancy M., b. Dec., 1879.
ii. Charles, b. 1880.
iii. Herbert.

FAM. 49. JOHN MASON,[7] (*Dr. Joshua,[6] Rev. Joshua,[5] Silas,[4] Dea. Jona.,[3] John,[2] Rich.,[1]*), b. 1806; m. Mary E. (dau. of Nathan) **Hale,** of Glast., 14 June, 1838; sett. as a farmer in New. on the ancestral Belden homestead. He d. 7 Sept., 1876; she b. 16 Mch., 1812, d. 3 Feb., 1888.—*Weth. Ins.*

Children (N. C. R.):

1. Mary Elizabeth, b. 8 Sept., 1839 ; bp. 9 Feb., 1840.
2. Agnes Whittlesey, b. 10 , bp. 16 July, 1843 ; d. 15 Oct., 1845.—*N. C. R.*
3. Cornelia Hale, b. 11 Apl., bp. 20 July, 1845 ; d. 19 Apl., 1881.

4. Agnes Whittlesey, b. 18 Jan., 1845 ; bp. 4 July, 1847.
5. Joshua, b. 18 Nov., 1848, bp. 1 Apl., 1849.— *W. T. R.*
6. Julia M., b. 17 Dec., 1852.

FAM. 49a. HENRY,[7] (*Charles, Jr.,[6] Chas.,[5] Silas,[4] Jona.,[3] John,[2] Rich.,[1]*), b. 1793; m. Sally **Beebe;** d, 1864.

Children (C. G. H.):

1. Clarissa, d. yg.
2. Henry, b. and d. St. Lou's, Mo., 1853, unm.
3. Louise, b. 1835 ; d. 1859, unm., in N. Carolina.

4. Kate, m. 9 Mch., 1863, M. J. **Thompson.** *No issue.*
5. Augustus, b. 1837. FAM. 50.
6. Charles, d. 1868, unm., in San Francisco, Cal.

FAM. 49b. Rev. WILLIAM W.,[8] (*Ebenezer,[7] John K.,[6] John,[5] John,[4] John,[3] John,[2] Rich.,[1]*), b. in Moscow, N. Y., 1820; grad. Y. C.; Presb. clergyman; d. New Haven, Ct., Dec., 1901; m. (1) Sarah **Treat,** of Orange, Ct.; m. (2) Ellis **Passmore,** of Smithfield, R. I.

Child:

1. William P., grad. Y. C. 1878 ; editor of the *Amsterdam Democrat* (N. Y.) ; d. 1903.

FAM. 50. AUGUST,[8] (*Henry,[7] Chas.,[6] Chas.,[5] Silas,[4] Jone.,[3] John,[2] Rich.,[1]*), b. 1837; m. 25 June, 1874, at Bunker Hill, Ill.; Susan **Adams.**

Children (C. G. H.):

1. Pearl L., b. 15 May, 1875 ; m. a **Chadwick.**
2. Harry O., b. 20 Jan., 1878.
3. Katharine, b. 12 Dec., 1879 ; res., unm., E.

Northfield, Mass.
4. Miles B., b. 13 Mch., 1884, Cove, Ore.

FAM. 51. BENJAMIN,[8] (*John,[7] John K.,[6] John,[5] John,[4] John,[3] John.,[2] Rich.,[1]*), b. 1797; m. 3 May, 1820, Ann **Francis.**

Child (C. G. H.):

1. Sarah, b. 15 Mch., 1821 ; m. 15 May, 1844, Lyman **Hotchkiss,** of Boston, Mass. *Issue:*
   i. Elizabeth B. (Hotchkiss), b. 21 July, 1853 ; d. 23 June, 1897, unm.

ii. Ella (Hotchkiss), b. 19 June, 1847 ; m. 14 Sept., 1870, Edmund B. **Cowles,** of Boston, Mass. *No issue.*

FAM. 52. EDWIN WEBSTER,[8] (*John,[7] John K.,[6] John,[5] John,[4] John,[3] John,[2] Rich.,[1]*), b. 1806; m. 17 Feb., 1830, Sophia **Brace,** who d. 23 Aug., 1882; he d. 22 Jan., 1893.

Children (C. G. H.):

1. Henry John, b. 8, d. 23 Feb., 1831.
2. Edgar Andrews, b. 11 Aug., 1833. FAM. 53.
3. Annette S., b. 9 Oct., 1835 ; m. 27 Oct., 1859, Joseph E. **Brace;** she d. 4 Oct., 1874.

Issue:
i. William S. (Brace), b. 1869, June 20.
4. William, b. 1840 ; d. 1841.

FAM. 53.   EDWIN A.,[9] (*Edwin W.*,[8] *John*,[7] *John K.*,[6] *John*,[5] *John*,[4] *John*,[3] *John*,[2] *Rich.*,[1]), b. 1833; m. 4 Dec., 1866, Alice K. **Flagg; res.** Htfd, Ct.

Child (*C. G. H.*) :

1. Ettie S., b. 6 June, 1870.

THE NORWALK (CONN.) LINE.—Descended from WILLIAM, b. 1671; son of *Daniel*, b. 1648, of Weth.; son of *William*, b. abt. 1622, in England; son of *Richard Belden, the Settler, of Weth.* (Furnished by C. G. HUBBARD, M. D., of Hornellsville, N. Y.)

FAM. 1.   WILLIAM,[4] (eld. s. of *Daniel*,[3] *William*,[2] *Rich.*,[1]), b. 1671; m. 2 May, 1700, Margaret (dau. Wm. & Johanna *Hawkes*) **Arms,** who was b. 6 Oct., 1683; res. at Norwalk, Ct.

Children:

1. Margaret, b. 10 Feb., 1701 ; m. Nath'l **Slosson;** she d. 14 Apl., 1780 ; 12 ch.
2. Daniel, b. 14 Sept., 1702 ; m. 1727, Esther **Smith.**
3. Elizabeth, b. 10 Nov., 1704 ; m. Daniel **Cole.**
4. Thankful, b. 9 Feb., 1706 ; d. 1717.
5. Mary, b. 25 June, 1709 ; ш. Nathan **Betts.**
6. Abigail, b. 4 Jan., 1710 ; m. John **Rockwell.**
7. Ruth, b. 18 Jan., 1712 ; m. John[4] (*John*,[3] *Thos.*,[2] *Rich.*,[1]) **Seymour,** b. 1710. *Issue:*
   i. John (Seymour).
   ii. William (Seymour), m. 6 Jan., 1757, Lydia **St. John.**
   iii. Seth (Seymour), m. Anna **Benedict.**
   iv. Sarah (Seymour).
   v. Matthew (Seymour).
   vi. David (Seymour), b. 1744 ; m. Lucy **Alvord.**
   vii. Jonathan (Seymour).
   viii. Ira (Seymour), m. Jerusha **Parsons.**
   ix. James, m. 13 Feb., 1774, Rebecca **Keeler.**
8. Miriam, b. 11 Nov., 1714 ; m. Samuel **Higgins.**
9. Esther, b. 11 Oct., 1716 ; m. Daniel **Hurlbut.**
10. Thankful, b. 5 Oct., 1718 ; m. Alex. **Resique.**
11. Sarah, b. 20 Aug., 1720 ; m. Zebulon **Crane.**
12. Azor, b. 10 Dec., 1723. FAM. 2.

FAM. 2.   AZOR,[5] (*Wm.*,[4] *Dan'l*,[3] *Wm.*,[2] *Rich.*,[1]), b. Deerfield, Mass., 1723; m. Mary ————————; res. Norwalk, Ct.

Children (*C. G. H.*) :

1. Azor (Capt.), b. 1749. FAM. 3.
2. Abigail, b. 1754 ; d. 1806 ; unm.
3. Eunice, m. Zalmon **Hull.**
4. Mary, b. 14 Jan., 1759 ; m. Justus **Cray.**
5. David (Rev.), b. 16 July, 1764. FAM. 4.
6. Esther, b. 16 Dec., 1768 ; m. Lewis **Taylor.**

FAM. 3.   Capt. AZOR,[6] (*Azor*,[5] *Wm.*,[4] *Dan'l*,[3] *Wm.*,[2] *Rich.*,[1]), b. in Norwalk, Ct., 1749 ; m. 22 Apl., 1775, Hannah (dau. Steph.) **Smith;** he m. (2) Hannah **Fitch,** b. 1766.

Children (*C. G. H.*) :

1. William (Rev.), b. 16 July, 1781. FAM. 5.
2. Charles (Dr.), b. 1783.
3. Anne, b. 1784 ; m. Stephen **Olmstead.**
4. Lewis, b. 1787. FAM. 6.
5. Joseph, b. 23 Dec., 1790.
6. Daniel, b. 4 Nov., 1793. FAM. 7.
7. Benjamin (Dr.), b. 23 Sept., 1797 ; d. single.
   (*By second marriage*) :
8. George Fitch, b. 21 ——, 1802. FAM. 8.
9. Platt, b. 19 Feb., 1804. FAM. 9.

FAM. 4.   Rev. DAVID,[6] (*Azor*,[5] *Wm.*,[4] *Dan'l*,[3] *Wm.*,[2] *Rich.*,[1]), b. 1764; m. 3 Dec., 1794, Martha **Hull,** who was b. 1774.

Children:

1. David Hull, b. 21 Dec., 1797. FAM. 10.
2. Jane, b. 27 May, 1799 ; m. Reuben **Boothe.**
3. John Arms, b. 24 Sept., 1802. FAM. 11.
4. Elizabeth, b. 31 July, 1814 ; m. Edgar S. **Tweedy.**

FAM. 5.   Rev. WILLIAM.[7] (*Capt. Azor*,[6] *Azor*,[5] *Wm.*,[4] *Dan'l*,[3] *Wm.*,[2] *Rich.*,[1]), b. 1781; m. 5 Feb., 1807, Abigail F. (dau. Nath'l & Mary) **Hatch,** who was b. 9 Nov., 1785; he grad. Y. C., 1803, and was for 40 yrs. Principal of Schools in New York City.

Children:

1. Nathaniel H., b. 23 Jan., 1809.
2. William, b. 20 Aug., 1811.
3. Henry, b. 9 Apl., 1813.

4. Abigail, b. 19 June, 1817.
5. Mary, b. 30 May, 1819.
6. Lucy, b. 21 (or 25) Mch., 1822.

FAM. 6.   LEWIS,[7] (*Capt. Azor,*[6] *Azor,*[5] *Wm.,*[4] *Dan'l,*[3] *Wm.,*[2] *Rich.,*[1]), b. 1787; m. Rachel **Banks;** m. (2) Anne M. **Frelinghuysen.**

Children:

1. Maria, b. 1818; d. unm.
2. Ebenezer, b. 1820.
3. Eunice, b. 12 Feb., 1826.

(*By second marriage*) :
4. Anna Jackson, b. 31 Jan., 1831; m. 1856, James Wells **Randall.**

FAM. 7.   DANIEL,[7] (*Capt. Azor,*[6] *Azor,*[5] *Wm.,*[4] *Dan'l,*[3] *Wm.,*[2] *Rich.,*[1]), b. 1793; m. Sarah (dau. Frederick) **Curtis.**

Children:

1. Charles A., b. 15 Jan., 1828.
2. Frederick C., b. 1831.
3. Joseph, b. 1 Apl., 1833.

4. Sarah F., b. Sept., 1835.
5. Louisa A., b. 27 Oct., 1840.

FAM. 8.   GEORGE FITCH,[7] (*Capt. Azor,*[6] *Azor,*[5] *Wm.,*[4] *Dan'l,*[3] *Wm.,*[2] *Rich.,*[1]), b. 1802; m. 28 Oct., 1823, Nancy **Hanford,** of Wilton, Ct.

Children:

1. Henry H., b. 19 Nov., 1825.
2. Charlotte, b. 24 Aug., 1827.

3 George Fitch.

FAM. 9.   PLATT,[7] (*Capt. Azor,*[6] *Azor,*[5] *Wm.,*[4] *Dan'l,*[3] *Wm.,*[2] *Rich.,*[1]), b. 1804; m. 1 Sept., 1829, Mary (sister of Rev. Horace) **Bushnell.**

Children:

1. Charlotte, b. 12 Feb., 1832.
2. Frederick, b. 1834.

3. William, b. 1 Apl., 1837.
4. Horace, b. 4 Oct., 1840.

FAM. 10.   DAVID HULL,[7] (*Rev. David,*[6] *Azor,*[5] *Wm.,*[4] *Daniel,*[3] *Wm.,*[2] *Rich.,*[1]), b. 1797; m. (1) 1824, Cornelia **Johnston,** of Newton; he m. (2) Susan **Johnson;** he m. Anne **Clark,**

Children:

1. Jane, b. 21 Dec., 1825; m. Joshua D. **Berry.**
(*By second marriage*) :
2. Cornelia, b. 29 Dec., 1829.
3. Clarissa, b. 1830; unm.
4. David, b. 14 Aug., 1832.

5. John, b. 1834.
(*By third marriage*) :
6. Mary F., b. 1845.
7. Frederick.
8. Howard.
9. Reuben B., b. 28 Sept., 1849.

FAM. 11.   JOHN ARMS,[7] (*Rev. David,*[6] *Azor,*[5] *Wm.,*[4] *Dan'l,*[3] *Wm.,*[2] *Rich.,*[1]), b. 1802; m. 11 Nov., 1825, Betsy C. **Marvin.**

Children:

1. Nathan, b 17 Aug., 1826; d. 28 July, 1855, at Wilton, Ct.
2. Samuel B., b. 3 Apl., 1828.
3. John A., b. 25 June, 1830.

4. Charles, b. 16 June, 1833.
5. Frances, b. 12 Nov., 1835; m. Benj. F. **Bulkley.**
6. Martha, b. 31 Dec., 1839.

BELKNAP, SAMUEL, m. Elizabeth ————.

Child (*Weth. Rec.*) :

1. Elisha, b. 1 Dec., 1718.

BELL, FRANCIS. *Hinman* says "an important man in the Col., a firm Puritan in form and principles," favorably noticed (in connection with Slosson) by Cotton Mather. Francis and *Abraham* were at Weth., 1637-38; their relationship not known; tho' *S. W. A.* entertained the opinion that A. was father to Francis. Abraham afterwards sett. at New Haven, as also did *James*, presumably a bro. of A. and who (*Geneal. Guide to Early Sett. of America*) is said to have taken the oath of fidelity, 1644, and to have rem. to Taunton, Mass.

ABRAHAM, acc. to *Charlestown (Mass.) Rec.*, appears in that town "from New Haven," in 1647, and m. Kate **Waffe**, and d. 1662-3; she d. 1692, which dates agree with that of *Savage*, who says that "adm. of his est., £154·01·01, was given to his wid. Cath., who d. 29 Aug., 1692, ae. 68;" and that he (*Savage*) recs. no ch., but Isaac, bp. at C., 12 Oct., 1662; but *C. Rec.* give him Hannah, Mary, Abraham, Dorothea, all apparently older than the Isaac, ment. since he is named last. Gillespie's *Picturesque Stamford* gives (p. 33) a photograph *facsimile* of a page of the *Bell Fam.* Bible, now preserved in that town, containing the following autographic geneal. rec., viz: *Jonathan Bell,* [s. of Francis, and the first ch. b. in S.], b. in Sept., 1641. *Elizabeth Bell,* b. Aug., 1643. *Mary Bell,* b. in the last of May,, 1646.

This Bible was used by Abraham Bell, who added to it, on same page as above, the following record of his own children, viz: My dau., *Mary,* b. 7 Dec., 7 day, 1714. My son, *Samuel,* b. 25 Sept., 25 day, 1718. My son, *Abraham,* was b. April, 17 day, 1721.

FRANCIS, of whom *Savage* says, he "had been early at Weth.; was a Lieut., 1660, but not a freeman of Conn. Col., before 1676, tho' he was adm. inhab. of New Haven, 1641. He became a set. of Stamford, Ct., 1640. Huntington *Hist. Stamford* thinks it doubtful if he came thither from Weth., and, if he did, that he must have been young, but recs. prove him to have been first at Weth. His wife Rebecca, d. 1684, and he d. 8 Jan., 1690; invent. est. val. at £317·12·00— *Fairfield Prob. Rec.*, p. 116; from his will of 24 May, preceding, we gain something as to his family," etc.—See Huntington's *Hist. Stamford*. The genealogist of the family is Mr. Jared W. Bell, 248 Lexington Ave., New York City. And a *Bell Geneal.* has been prepared by John V. Acker, of Newtown, Ct.

LUCY ANN, m. Hiram **Smith**, of E. W., 17 Jan., 1833.

ISAAC BELL, b. 20 Mch., 1783; d. in Rocky Hill, 2 Oct., 1835. His father was of Glastonbury (prob. Eastbury) ; he was a soldier in the Revolution.—*Conn. Mag.*, Vol. III, p. 240.

BEAUMONT, LUCIUS, M., had (*S. C. R.*) :

1. Laura Mabel, bp. 6 June, 1847. | 2. William Lucius, bp. 9 May, 1852.

BEMENT, WILLIAM, m. Phebe ————.

Children (*Weth. Rec.*) :

1. Phebe, b. 22 Jan., 1733-4.
2. Penelope, b. 11 Oct., 1735.
3. William, b. 21 Aug., 1737.
4. Asa, b. 4 Feb., 1738-9 ; m. Ruth Neal, 15 Jan., 1761 ; had (*Weth. Rec.*) *Rebecca,* b. 10 Mch., 1762.
5. Ebenezer, b. 3 Jan., 1740-1.
6. Samuel, b. 25 Dec., 1742.
7. Hannah, b. 25, bp. 28 Oct., 1744 ; d. 21 Oct., 1746.
8. Edith, b. 14, bp. 21 Sept., 1746.
9. Edith, b. 26 Apl., bp. betw. that date and 17 July, 1748.
10. Sarah, b. 10 June, bp. 15 July, 1750.
11. Chloe, b. 7, bp. 17 May, 1752.
12. Freelove, b. 26 Mch., 1754.
13. Rebecca, b. 18, bp. 23 Nov., 1755 · d. 11 July, 1767.
14. Rebecca, b. 11, bp. 18 Sept., 1757 ; d. 4 Nov., 1760.

BENFIELD, ————, divorced from wife Elizabeth, 6 Dec., 1662.

BENJAMIN, CALEB, acc. to Chapin's *Glast. Cent.*, 186, was never a resident of the town, tho' *Hinman* calls him "of Weth." *Savage* speaks of him as "of Weth. or Hartford," and certain it is acc. to *Weth. Rec.*, that he was fence-viewer for Naubuc and Nayaug, 1678, and was gr. ld. 1672—see Chapter VII, Vol. I; his wife Mary was (acc. to *Savage*) the dau. of Samuel **Hale,** of Weth(Glast.) ; *Hinman* says he was adm. freeman 1669, but *where* he does not say; and that, in 1682, he with others petit. the Gen. Ct. for leave to sett. and form a plantation in the Wabaquasset country, prob. N. of the Pequot country (poss. in present Windham county), and that tho' he res. in Htfd., he d. in Weth., 8 May, 1684.—*Weth. Rec. Savage* (I, 165) thinks him a bro. of Abel, of Charlestown, Mass., and a son of John, the Settler, at Watertown, Mass., 1632. See, also, Chapter I, Vol. I, this Hist. *Hinman* (1st Edit., pp. 114, 115) credits him with the following ch. to which *Savage* adds the dates of birth, acc. to *Glast. Centennial,* p. 186.

Children:

1. Mary, b. 15 Sept., 1671; m. Benj. **Dibble.**
2. Abigail, b. 27 Apl., 1673; m. Ebenezer **Hills.**
3. Sarah, b. 17 Feb., 1675-6.
4. John, b. 5 Nov., 1677.
5. Samuel, b. 14 Feb., 1679-80.
6. Martha, b. 19 Jan., 1680-1.
7. Caleb, (acc. to *Savage and Chapin*), b. 1683; and the latter says he d. 1700, before wh. time his bros. John and Samuel seem to have d. also, his estate being set to his sisters.

FAM. 2. JOHN, (prob. s. *John*, s. of *John*, the Settler, and b. 1679), m. Ann **Latimer,** 26 July, 1699.

Children (Weth. Rec.) :

1. John, b. and bp.—*Mix,* 12 May, 1700.
2. Ann, b. 1 Jan., 1703-4; bp. same mo.—*Mix.*

SAMUEL, d. 1669-70.—See Chapter VII, Vol. I. Bro. of Caleb?; was he of Weth. or Htfd.? His wid. res. in Weth., 1670.

BENSON, EDWARD, of New Bedford; m. Rhoda C. **Gladding,** 13 Aug., 1818— *W. T. R.;* LEVI, Co. B, 25 Conn. Reg. Inf., d. 22 June, 1872.—*W. Ins.*

BENTON. (Assistance acknowledged from FRED M. STEELE, Esq., of Chicago, Ill.) Two of this name came to Weth. early, ANDREW and EDWARD. Trad. says they were bros. and that Edward was the eldest, which, however, does not seem probable; nor were they from Co. Kent, as hitherto claimed, but (as recent investigations indicate) from Co. Essex, Eng.[*]

ANDREW, b. 1620, came prob. first to Watertown, Mass.; is next found at Weth. among the earliest there; in Nov., 1639, was one of the "free planters" at Milford, Ct., whither he prob. came with Rev. Mr. Prudden's party of Weth. and New Haven men. He, with his wife (who was adm. 13 Oct., 1649) were both memb. of Ch. at Milford, Ct., and in 1666, took letters of dismission to the Ch. at Hartford, where they had evidently rem. some time before, as we

---

[*] A letter from JOHN H. BENTON, of N. Y., to FRED. M. STEELE, of Chicago, Ill., Nov., 1902, states that from personal examination, by HORACE BENTON, of Cleveland, of the parish records (Vol. XII) of Epping, Co., Essex, Eng.—18 miles N. E. of London, it was found that a *John* Benton & Mary Southmayd were m. 24 (or 25) May, 1618, and that their s. *Andrew* was bp. 15 Oct., 1620; which agrees with his age at death, as given on his tombstone, 1683; and would account for the persistency with which he endeavored to perpetuate his father's name (John) in his own family—it having been given to no less than three of his children. He, also, gave his mother's name (Mary) to his 2d dau., and his s. Ebenezer had a s. named John.

find him serving as a juror at H., 4 Feb., 1664, and res. that yr. in Weth. Lane; was freeman at H., 1665; later a fence viewer and land owner. He and wife Hannah were, 22 Feb., 1670, among orig. memb. of the Second ch. at H., in full communion. He m. (1) Hannah (dau. Geo. & Anna) **Stocking**— See *N. E. Gen. and H. Register*, Apl., 1896; he m. (2) Ann, "the witch," (dau. of John **Cole**, who d. 19th Apl., 1686. He d. at Htfd., 31 July, 1683, ae. 63; gravestone still štdg. in Old Centre Bu-gd., near rear of ch. His est., £364, 15s., 4d., adm. by his youngest son Joseph, who filed invent., 18 Dec., 1683, and which names "children, Andrew, Samuel and Joseph; daus. Mary and Dorothy (by first wife), and (by second wife) Ebenezer, ae. 10, Lidia, ae. abt. 7; Hannah, ae. 5.

Children (by first wife; m. abt. 1648):

1. Hannah, d. yg.
2. John, b. 9 Apl., 1650; d. 24 May, 1650.
3. John, b. 7 Oct., 1653; d. yg.
4. Andrew, b. 12 Aug., 1655, (acc. to *Milford Rec.*); m. Martha, b. 19 May, 1657, (dau. Sgt. Thos.) **Spencer**; he d. 1704, prob. the Benton killed by Ind., spoken of *N. E. Gen. & Hist. Register*, XI. FAM. 2.
5. Mary, b. 16 Aug., 1656; m. Nathaniel (s. Jno.) **Cole**, 23 Oct., 1684.
6. Samuel, b. 15 Aug., 1658: m. Sarah **Pomeroy**. FAM. 3.
7. Dorothy, b. 1660.
8. Joseph, b. 1661; m. Sarah (dau. Bevil) **Waters**, of Htfd., 10 Feb., 1698; res. Milford, Ct., 10 Feb., 1697; he d. 12 Aug., 1753; res. Newington, 1726.
   (By second marriage):
9. Ebenezer, bp. 4 Jan., 1673; unfortunate and feeble minded.
10. Lydia, bp. 13 Feb., 1675; adm. to 2d. ch. Htfd., 25 Apl., 1697.
11. Hannah, bp. 26 Jan., 1678.
12. John, bp. 30 May, 1680; d. yg.

FAM. 2. ANDREW,[2] (*Andrew*,[1]), b. 1655; m. Martha (dau. Sgt. Thomas) **Spencer;** b. at Htfd. 19 May, 1657. *Hinman* says Martha Spencer m. a Benton; and, by exclusion, Andrew, Jr., is the only Benton who could have wed her, all others being m. and wives living; the fact of the second dau. being named Martha also helps to confirm this conclusion (by the same process of exclusion, we are led to conclude that the Benton killed by the Inds. 1704, was Andrew, the father). He owned covenant in Second ch. Htfd. 6 Jan., 1677, and he, with wife, were adm. to its membership 10 Dec., 1694. He d. 5 Feb., 1704.

Children (all b. Htfd. and bp. in 2d ch.):

1. Hannah, bp. 6 Jan., 1677; m. Edw'd **Scoville**, 20 Feb., 1700.
2. Martha, bp. 1 Aug., 1679.
3. Andrew, bp. 31 July, 1681.
4. Mercy, bp. 9 Oct., 1683.
5. John, bp. 22 Feb., 1685.
6. Dorothy, bp. 22 Apl., 1688; m. Jno. **Gridley**,
2 May, 1716.
7. Mary, bp. 2 Nov., 1690.
8. Ebenezer, bp. 18 Oct., 1696; m. Eliz. **White**,[4] (*Jno*,[3] Capt. *Nath'l*,[2] Elder *Jno*,[1]). FAM. 4.
9. Elizabeth, bp. 12 Feb., 1698.

FAM. 3. SAMUEL,[2] (*Andrew*,[1]), b. 1658, in Milford, Ct., adm. to 2d Ch., Htfd., 23 Sept., 1716; surveyor of highways in Htfd., 1713; name appears (with that of his s. Samuel, Jr.,) on the orig. deed of Tolland, as among its grantees: on 20 Feb., 1719, deeds ld. to his s. Daniel and describes himself as of Htfd.; will dated 4 Apl., 1744; prob. at Htfd., 3 June, 1746, mentions wife Sarah and all ch. given below; he m. Sarah **Pomeroy**.

Children:

1. Samuel, bp 28 Jan., 1680; m. 2 Jan., 1704, Mary, b. 15 Feb., 1684, (dau. Dea. (Medad) **Pomeroy**. The "ch. of Sam'l" bp. 2 July, 1710—*Mix MS.*, may have been a son of this Samuel, as also, may have been Nathaniel, bp. 11 Mch., 1713-14.
2. Sarah, bp. 28 Sept., 1685; m. 1 Jan., 1702, Moses **Blatchley**. *No issue.*
3. Hannah, b. 14 Mch., 1688; m. 11 May,
1711, Samuel **Kellogg.**
4. Abigail, b. 9 Dec., 1691.
5. Caleb. b. 1 Mch., 1695; m. Hannah ————, in 1719, perhaps parents of Prudence, bp. 12 Feb., 1748-9—as "of Caleb."
6. Daniel, bp. 26 June, 1696; m. Mary **Skinner**, 3 Jan., 1722.
7. Jacob, bp. 21 Sept., 1698: m. (1) Abigail **Carter**; m. (2) Elizabeth **Hinsdale**. FAM. 5.

FAM. 4. EBENEZER,[3] (*And*,[2] *And*,[1]), b. Htfd.; bp. 2d Ch. 18 Oct., 1696; res. and d. Htfd.; bu. 1 Dec., 1770; m. Elizabeth (dau. *John* Capt., *Nath'l*,[2] Elder

Jno.,[1]), **White,** of Midd., she bp. 11 June, 1698; *bu. rec.* reads "mother Jno. Benton, wid'. Ebenezer bu. 9 Mch., 1791"; gravestone reads (So. Bury. Gd. Htfd.) d. 8 Mch., 1791, ae. 96; also states that she was m. in 1720.

Children (bp. 2d Ch. Htfd.) :

1. Anne, bp. 16 Dec., 1722; m. 12 July, 1741, Elijah,[4] (*s. Thos.*,[3] *Capt. Preserved, Capt. Roger*,[1]) **Clapp.** The *Clapp Geneal.* says that Elijah Clapp m. *Mary* **Benton** in 1735; but no authority has been found confirmatory of this statemnt; and, in searching for a mar. rec. to confirm *Hinman's* statement that Elijah Clapp, in 1741, m. *Anne* Benton, Mr. E. Stanley Welles found in an orig. rec. of marriages performed by Jno. Marsh, Esq., of Htfd. (now in possess. of *Conn. Hist. Soc.*) the statement that Elijah Clapp m. in the evening July 12, 1741, Ann Benton; and as Anne (dau. of Ebenezer) was bp. 16 Dec., 1722, and was the first and only one of the B. family bearing that name, in 1741, we are forced to the conclusion that she must be *the* one and there are no other claimants for her hand. Further, Elijah Clapp d. 13 May, 1777; and *Htfd. Co. Prob. Rec.* shows that his wid. *Ann* was app. adm'x, and she is so spoken of as late as 17 Oct., 1785. *Issue (all res. and d. Htfd., except Norman)* :

  i. Elijah (Clapp), b. 1753; m. Miriam **Jones;** he d. 17 Feb., 1800, ae. 47.
  ii. Norman (Clapp), b. 1761; sett. Weth., and d. there; m. 1782, Huldah **Wright,** who d Weth., Apl., 1801, ae. 40; he m. (2) Mary Frances **Wright.** He d. Weth., May, 1830, ae. 69.—See *Clapp.*
  iii. Oliver (Clapp), b. 1760; m. Lucy G.[5] (dau. Ozias) **Goodwin;**[4] who d. 26 Jan., 1842; he d. 19 Aug., 1840, ae. 80.
  iv. Capt. John (Clapp), m. Mabel **Cotton,** who d. 14 Apl., 1817, ae. 39.
  v. Elizabeth (Clapp), m. Wm. **Bunce.**
  vi. Eunice (Clapp), m. Thos. (s. Daniel) **Steele;** had 7 ch.
  vii. Mary (Clapp), b. 1747; m. Lemuel (s. Daniel) **Steele.**
  viii. Anne, m. Neal **McNeal.**
  ix. Sarah, m. Jno. **Roberts.**
2. John, bp. 15 Nov., 1724.
3. Mary, bp. 26 Feb., 1727.
4. Asa, bp. 28 Feb., 1731.
5. Ebenezer, jr., m. Ruth ————; he bu. 10 Feb., 1764; wid. living 1764.

FAM. 5. JACOB,[3] (*Samuel*,[2] *Andrew*,[1]), b. 1698; bp. 2d Ch. Htfd. 26 Sept., 1698; rec'd into that ch. 20 June, 1723; rem. to Tolland and the first Town meeting was held at his ho. in 1737; was active in bldg. the Cong Ch. there; and was elected its first deacon, 1738; took the first deed in Harwinton, Ct., 1732; went there to live, 1735; the earliest book of town records are in his handwriting, and he its first town clk., 1737-1741; rep. the town in Gen. Asemb. three sessions, 1756-8, and often Selectman. He m. (1) in 1st Ch. Htfd. 6 July, 1724, Abigail **Carter;** b. 26 Apl., 1697 (dau. *Joshua*,[3] *Joshua*,[2] *Joshua*,[1] & *Mary Skinner*) Carter; who d. 22 Sept., 1725; he m. (2) 4 Apl., 1728, Elizabeth, b. 9 Jan., 1702, (dau. *Barnabas*) **Hinsdale.** His will, dated 11 June, 1761; prob. 30 Nov., 1761; he d. 2 Nov., 1761.

Children (by first marriage) :

1. Abigail, bp. 19 Sept., 1725; m. Timothy[3] (*Edw'd*,[2] *Jno.*,[1]) **Dodd.**
  (*By second marriage b. Htfd.*) :
2. Jacob, b. 8 Jan., 1729.
3. Phineas, b. 10 Jan., 1731; d. 16 Aug., 1744.
4. Amos, b. 10 Nov., 1732; m. (1) Eliz.

White, of Htfd., 13 May, 1756; (2) Jerusha **Buck,** 18 Jan., 1759.
5. Barnabas, b. 3 Jan., 1735; m. Martha **Griswold,** 15 Oct., 1758, at Harwinton.
6. Elizabeth, b. 17 June, 1738.

EDWARD Benton, who appears upon *Weth. Rec.* abt. 1660, and who has been supp. to be s. of Edward of Guilford, Ct., *may* have been the bro. of Andrew, the Sett. at Weth., but could hardly have been his elder bro., for (1) in June, 1684, he testified in the Naubuck Case (Hollister *vs.* Bulkeley, *Private Controversies,* Vol. VII, Sec. of State's, Office Htfd.) that he was then "ae. 46 yrs. or thereabouts;" (2) he d. 20 Feb., 1698, ae abt. 60; both of which dates would make him to have been b. 1638; and (3) instead of coming to Weth. with Andrew, he does not appear on record here until 1660, some 21 yrs after Andrew's coming here. So that the alleged identity of their parentage does not appear to be confirmed. His wid. Mary ————, d. 8 Aug., 1702, ae. 59 yrs. 8 mos. *Weth. Rec.* He had charge of the Town House at Weth. 1665; was hayward, 1692; for his ld. holdings see Chapt. VII, Vol. I. *Htfd. Co. Prob. Recs.* show that the invent. of his est. amt'd to £342-10-00.

Children, (Htfd. Co. Prob. Rec. ment. in his will and all, except Edward, of age) :

1. Samuel. FAM. 2.
2. Edward.
3. Rebecca, m. 7 Dec., 1699, Isaac **Borman.**
4. Mary, m. 23 Oct., 1684, Nath'l **Cole.**
5. Ellen (or Eleanor), b. 1670; m. Daniel (s. of James & Dorcas *Weed*) **Wright,** 20 Aug., 1705; she d. 27 Sept., 1749. *Issue:*

i. Ruth (Wright), b. 5 June, 1711; m. Elizur **Talcott,** 1730; d. 12 Sept., 1791.
6. Dorothy.
7. Edward. FAM. 3.
8. Daniel, b. "last of Mch.," d. "beginning of" July, 1682.

FAM. 2. SAMUEL,² (prob. s. *Edward,*¹) ; m. 5 Feb., 1704, Mary (dau. Sam'l) **Bradfield.** He d. 24 July, 1752, *Weth. Rec.;* she d. 6 Dec., 1747; he was surveyor, 1703; cattle appraiser, 1724; for ld. holdings see Chapt. VII, Vol. I.

Children (Weth. Rec.) :

1. Mary, b. 19 Mch., 1704-5.
2. Sarah, b. 19, bp. 23 (*Mix*) Mch., 1706-7.
3. Hannah, b. 1 July, 1710.
4. Nathaniel, b. 8 Mch., 1714; d. 9 days old; may have the N. ment. in *Mix MSS.* as

being bp. 1713-14.
5. Jonathan, b. 23 Oct., 1715. FAM. 4.
6. Nathaniel, b. 9 Apl., 1718. FAM. 5.
7. Abigail, b. 4 Nov., 1720.

FAM. 3. EDWARD,² (*Edward,*¹) ; m. Mary **Hale,** 16 Oct., 1702, who d. 3 May, 1756, ae. 73 yrs.

Children:

1. Josiah, b. 16 June, 1705. FAM. 6.
2. Ephraim, b. 19 Aug., 1707.

3. Mary, b. 27 ——, 1710.

FAM. 4. JONATHAN,³ (*Sam'l,*² *Edward,*¹), b. 1715; m. (1) Hannah **Beckley,** 6 May, 1742, who d. 18 Jan., 1750 in 40 yr; m. (2) 24 Aug., 1750, Deborah (dau. Sam'l & Mary) **Williams,** who d. 12 Nov., 1786.—*Weth. Rec.*

Children (Weth. Rec.) :

1. Lydia, b. 1 Feb., 1742-3.
2. Samuel, b. 4 Sept., 1745.

3. Jonathan, b. 18 Mch., 1747-8.
4. Hannah, b. 13 Jan., 1749.

FAM. 5. NATHANIEL,³ (*Samuel,*² *Edward,*¹) b. 1718; m. 13 Oct., 1745, Dorothy **Cook.** He d. 3 Dec., 1753.—*Weth. Rec.*

Children (Weth. Rec.) :

1. John, b. 13 Mch., bp. 19 Apl., 1746. FAM. 7. | 2. Mary, b. 30 Mch., 1751.

FAM. 6. JOSIAH,³ (*Edward,*² *Edward,*¹), b. 1705; m. Hannah **House,** 5 Feb., 1736.

Children:

1. Josiah, m. Dorothy **Smith.**
2. Edward, m. Sarah **Talcott,** 8 Feb., 1770; d. 26 June, 1815.

3. Mary, m. Samuel **Wright.**
4. Prudence, m. David **Goodrich,** 7 Nov., 1754.

FAM. 7. JOHN,⁴ (*Nath'l,*³ *Samuel,*² *Edward,*¹), b. 1746; m. Mary **Blinn,** 3 May, 1764; was a Revol. soldier; d. 6 Feb., 1808, ae. 62.—*W. C. R.* "John B.'s wife" d. 6 June, 1787.—*W. C. R.*

Children (Weth. Rec.) :

1. Nathaniel, b. 29 June, 1765.
2. George, b. 1 July, 1768—tho' one rec. says 1 July, 1765.
3. Mary, b. 30 Jan., 1771.
4. Rebecca, b. 21 Feb., 1773.
5. Hannah, bp. and d. (?) 14 May, 1775.— *W. C. R.*
6. Dorothy, b. 22 Aug., 1776; bp. 4 May, 1777; m. Sam'l **Crane,** 9 Apl., 1799; for ch. see *Crane Geneal.*
7. John, b. 16 Feb., bp. 3 Oct., 1779.
8. Simeon, b. 15 Apl., bp. 2 Dec., 1781; poss.

the S. who m. Anne **Hubbard,** of Chatham, Ct., 11 July, 1799, and had a ch. who d. P. H., ae. 3 yrs., Mch., 1811.—*W. C. R.*
9. Nancy, b. 14 (19 ?) Mch., 1784; m. Nathan **Harris,** rem. to N. Y. State, 1819. There was a rec. of a Mary, who m. *Nath'l* Harris of Coventry, Ct., 28 Jan., 1802. Can these be the same parties?
10. Harriet, b. 22 Mch., 1786.
(From this point, the record of this family are to be traced to Htfd., Glast., Tolland and other places than Weth.)

BERRY, MANDERS; m. Sally **Wright,** 2 Oct., 1814; his inf. ch. d. 17 Feb., 1815.—
S. C. R. Inf. ch. d. 28 Jan., 1816.—*S. C. R.*

PETER, m. Mabel **Deming,** 9 Oct., 1788. Peter, ae. 23, bu. 12 Jan., 1790. Inf. d.
1 Feb., 1789.—*W. C. R.*

BESWICK, GEORGE, named by *Savage* (I, 172) as "of Weth."; d. 1672.—See
Chapt. VII, Vol. I.

BETTLEHEISER, LEWIS m. Mary **Adams,** 18 Nov., 1778.

BETTS (*Bates, Bet, Bett, Betes, Beete, Beetes,*), Sgt. JOHN, b. Claydon, Eng.; bp.
5 May, 1627 (*Boardman Gen.*), was, with
his mother, among the first sett. at
Htfd.—his father being then dead; poss,
and prob. d. on the voyage hither. She
had a gt. of ld. for his home lot, among the first sett. of Htfd. and seems to have
supported herself by keeping a school for young ch.; Rev. Mr. Stone of Htfd.,
writing, July 19, 1647, to Rev. Thos. Shepard of Cambridge, ment. the dth. of
"Goody Bets, the school dame" in a then prevailing epidemic. After her dth.
it is prob. that the ch., John and Martha (ae. 11), found a home in Weth. with
their sister Mary, who had been for 4 or 5 yrs. the wife of Samuel Boreman
(*Boardman*) of that town.

Sgt. John Betts m. Abigail (dau. John) **Elderkin;** b. Dedham, Mass., 13 Sept.,
1641; prob. m. at New London, where the E. fam. were at that time res'g. Betts
was an esteemed citizen of Weth. see Chapt. VII, Vol. I; is ment. in *W. T. V.*
as surveyor; was chosen constable Mch., 1665-6; juror in Ct. of Magistrates,
May, 1652, '53, '54, '55, '59, '60, '61; comm. Sgt. by Gen. Ct. May, 1657; rec'd the
3d lot (30½ r. wide and containing 182 acr.) in the division of Naubuc Farms on
E. side Gt. River. After 1651 his domestic life was embittered by conduct of his
wife, then ae. 21. For blasphemy (not the only or least of her offences) the
Ct. in Mch., 1662-3, ord. her to be led to the place of execution, with a rope
around her neck and there to ascend the gallows and stand for a time in the
public view; and further, that she should be remanded to the "tuition and government of her father, until further notice from the Court" with "the advice of
Rev. Mr. Fitch and Rev. Gersham Buckley. Though Sgt. Betts attempted again
to live with her as his wife, she proved incorrigible (see *Ct. Rec.*) from which
it appears that, for "lascivious conduct"—she was with 4 (named) partners, of
Weth., she was "*whipped upon the naked body,*" and, finally, 14 Oct., 1672,
he was gr. a divorce from her. Mch. 13, 1672-3 he m. (2) Mrs. Abigail (wid.
of John,[2] s. Jeremy,[1]) **Adams,** whose husband had d. 1870, leaving 7 yg.
ch. The following item from *Court Rec.* 1 Apl., 1673, p. 131, seems to
refer to this marr. "John Betts produced a writing in this Court, subscribed by Rebekah Boreman, Mary Wright, Martha Smith and Sarah
Butler, which signifieth that the 13 March, 1672-3, John Betts was married to
Abigail Betts & that the said John Betts took her in clothes of his own providing to her shift and staveless being stript as aforesaid by the aforesaid
women; and the sd. John Betts in Court renounced all claym & Interest to the
est., both Debts and Credits." His whole conduct towards this second wife and
her seven yg. ch. (as shown by records at Huntington) seems to have been
most liberal and fatherly. In Jan., 1680-1, Betts sold his ho. and lot on E.
side Broad St. in Weth. and, prob. abt. that time, rem. to Huntington, L. I.,
where within the same mo. he bght. lds. and prospered—becoming, by 1683, the
7th in the list of those who had valuable est. in that town, and where he d. a

little before May 6, 1690. *Htfd. Prob. Rec.* contains an invent. of est. of John Betts "formerly of Weth., late of Huntington, L. I., dec'd in the Col. of Conn. in lds., taken by John Chester, Sen., and Nathan'l Foote, on a bond of £200 for faithful adm. of sd. est." Val. of Invent. £188-00-00—no date, but abt. 1697. See, also, Chapt. VII, Vol. I, this Hist.

Child (by first marr.) :	(By second marriage) :
1. Abigail.	2. John, as *Savage* says b. "before 1648, who d. at Huntington, 1691.

BATES, BENJAMIN ROBINSON ; m. Laura Ann **Peters**, of Glast., 2 Jan., 1852.

JACOB, Jr., m. Mary **Robbins**, 13 May, 1808.—*N. C. R.*

ROBERT, poss. from Watertown, Mass., (*Savage* says "Watertown, 1636," but *Bond* can tell no more), early at Weth., (considered by Chapin *Glast. Centennial*) as the ancestor of the fam. of the name in Glast; was a lot owner of 182 acres here in 1640 (see Vol. I, p. 248) which he sold, on or before May 4, 1641, being abt. to remove, to Wm. Gibbons; rem. to Stamford, Ct., among the first settlers and d. there 11 June, 1675; his will, prob. 1 Nov., same yr., bequeathes to a son *John;* a dau. Mary, wife of Adam Ambler, also to daus. of his s. John; to a gd-son, John, and a son-in-law John Cress. He m. as 2d wife, Susanna (dau. of Simon) **Hoyt;** also provides for the freeing (when they should reach the age of 40) of several Negro slaves. (*See Huntington's Hist. Stamford.*)

BEVIN (*Bevan, Bevans or Bevens*), ARTHUR, of Glast., came to Weth., before Glast. was set off as a separate town; d. at Glast., 15 Dec., 1697; but was not a ld. or ho-holder until subsequently; est £269; had wife Mary, and following children.

Children (according to *Hinman* and *Chapin*):

1. John, b. 1676.	7. Arthur, b. 1686.
2. Mary, b. 1678.	8. Joanna, b. 1687.
3. Grace, b. 1679.	9. Elizabeth, b. 1690.
4. Mercy, b. 1681.	10. Abigail, b. 1692.
5. Thomas, b. 1682 ; was a tax-payer in Glast 1713.	11. Sarah, b. 1694.
6. Desire, b. 1684.	12. Anna, b. 1696.

BIBBARD (?), MABEL; m. Samuel **Colton**, betw. June 19 and 16 of Sept., 1759.—*L.*

BIDWELL,[*] (*Bydewell, Biddle*, orig. *Saxon*,—Biddulph "War Wolf," seems to be orig. of Cos. Norfolk and Devon, Eng.) Assistance rec'd from *Mrs. Anna C. N. Hawley*, of Htfd.; also Chapin's *Glast. Centennial;* Stiles' *Anc. Windsor, Ct., Goodwin's Geneal. Notes.*

JOHN, a prop'r of Htfd. "by courtesie of the Towne," 1640, had a home lot in the town and a tan-yard on an island in Little River; was an orig. and early memb. of 1st Ch. 1687, (*Hist. 1st Ch. Htfd.*, p. 13), m. Sarah (dau. of John & Sarah *Bidell)* **Wilcocks**, of Htfd.;[†] was chosen chimney-viewer, 1655-61; 9 Nov., 1670 was freed from watching, warding and training, *Htfd. Co. Mem. Hist.*, I, 230; he and wife memb. (1685) of 1st, afterwards (1687) of Second, or So. Ch. Htfd., Feb., 1670; he d. 1687. Invent. est. 4 June, that yr. £419-10-06, *Htfd. Co. Prob. Rec.*, IV, 253; will dated 23 Aug., 1683, ment. wife and all ch. given below; wid. d. 15 June, 1690.

---

[*] A Geneal. of this family has been pub. by EDWIN M. BIDWELL, Albany, N. Y., 1884, 12 mo., pp. 123.

[†] John Bidwell receives a legacy from his father-in-law John Wilcox's will, July 24, 1651, dated (after the death of his wife) of £10, also £40 to be devided among his &, daughter Sarah Boddell's living children. Also made "Sole executor" of widow Mary Wilcox's (John' will, Oct. 4, 1666.—*MSS. A. C. N. H.*

Children (Htfd. Co. Mem. Hist., II, 230):

1. John, b. 1641; m. 7 Nov., 1678, Sarah (dau.
   Thomas & Hannah *Tuttle*) **Welles,** of
   Htfd.; adm. memb. Co. Ch., 21 Feb., 1685;
   d. 3 July, 1692; she d. 1708; invent.
   £1,081. For desc'ts see *Goodwin's Geneal.
   Notes*, 256, and for those in line of his s.
   Jonathan see *Stiles' Anc. Windsor, Ct.*,
   II, 72-74.
2. Joseph, b. Weth., E. side River; m. 18
   May, 1675, Mary (dau. Wm.) **Colefax;**
   adm. So. Ch. Htfd., Feb., 1672; fence-
   viewer E. side River, 1687-8; d. 1692.
   Fam. 2.
3. Samuel, b. 1650, Midd.; m. 14 Nov., 1672,
   Elizabeth (dau. Thomas) Stow, of Midd.;
   m. (2) Sarah (dau. Capt. Daniel) **Harris;** m. (3) Abigail ————; he d. 5
   Apl., 1715.
4. Sarah, m. William **House,** of Htfd.; adm.

So. Ch. Htfd., 31 Mch., 1678.
5. Hannah, m. John [1] **Waddams,** of Weth.
6. Mary, m. Lieut. John **Meekims,** Sen. of
   E. Htfd. *Issue:*
   i. John (Meekims).
   ii. Joseph (Meekims).
   iii. Samuel (Meekims).
   iv. Mary (Meekims), m. ———— **Belding.**
   v. Sarah (Meekims), m. Thos. S. **Spencer,** Htfd.
   vi. Rebecca (Meekims), m. Thos. **Hurlbut,** Htfd.
   vii. Hannah (Meekims), m. John **Arnold,**
   of Htfd.,
7. Daniel, b. 1655, m. (1) Elizabeth ————;
   m. (2) Dorothy ————; res. E. Htfd.,
   where he was first constable, 1699; held
   other town offices; d. 29 Nov., 1719.

Fam. 2. JOSEPH; m. Mary **Colefax,** 8 May, 1675; sett in that part of Weth.
afterwards known as Glast.; was an orig. member 2d Ch. Htfd., 1672; in 1669
had a gr. of timber ld. for a sawmill in Eastbury; his will exhib. 2 July, 1692;
he d. at Weth.—*Bidwell Geneal.*, 38, 34.

JOSEPH Bidwell; Invent. £254-04-00 taken 17 June, 1692 by Samuel Hall, Jr.,
Joseph Hill, Thomas Fitch. Will dated 2 June, 1692: My will is that my wife
have my entire estate for her maintenance and the bringing up of my children;
if she marry then make an equal distribution to all my children of all my estate
which is left, excepting her thirds; my wife to be sole executrix. I desire
Deac. Samuel Butler and my brother Jonathan Cole to be Overseers. Joseph
Bidwell.   The children: Amy, 14 years of age; Joseph, 12; Benjamin, 9,
Ephriam, 6; Lydia, 3, & Mary, 4 months.   Witnesses to will: Sarah House, wife
of William; Elizabeth Arnold, wife of Henry.

Children (Weth. Rec.):

1. Mary, b. 12 Mch., 1675-6; d. bef. father.
2. Anne, b. 1 Oct., bp. 17 Nov., 1678; m.
   Jonathan **Sage,** 1 Nov., 1705; res. Midd.
3. Joseph, b. 20 or 24, Jan., 1680; bp. 10 Apl.,
   1681; res. Glast.; d. abt. 1753.
4. Benjamin, b. 15 or 26 Sept., 1683 or '84;
   res. Glast.

5. Ephraim, b. 16 Aug., 1686; d. 1753; res.
   Glast.; m. 3 Nov., 1713, at Wallingford,
   Ct., Elizabeth **Lewis.**
6. Lideah, b. 13 May, 1689; m. 24 May, 1717,
   Eleazur (s. Samuel) **Foote,** of Hatfield;
   two children.
7. Mary, b. 18 Mch., 1692.

Miscellanea:

Mrs. BIDWELL, (dau. Hez. Welles), d. 18 Aug., 1778, ae. 28,—*W. C. R.;* she
(adult) bp. 27 Dec., 1795.—*W. C. R.*

SAMUEL, "a person under infirmity of understanding, but of capacity," chose Noah
Waddams to be his guardian on 5 Mch., 1727-8.

JAMES, Esq., of Htfd., m. Sarah **Welles,** of Weth., 12 June, 1777.—*N. Ch. Rec.*

ISAAC, of Glast., m. Rhoda **Beckley,** of Worthington, Ct., 7 Dec., 1776.

SALMON & Cath., had ch. d. 13 Aug., 1803.—*W. C. R.*

From Weth. Ins.:

ABBY BUTLER, wife Chas. L. **Cozzens,** b. 21 Jan., 1832; d. 7 June, 1892; their
s. *Frederick Butler,* (Cozzens), b. 18 May, 1860, d. 2 Aug., 1861.

JAMES, of Utica, N. Y., s-in-law of Fred'k Butler, d. 21 July, 1875, ae. 86.

CARRIE M., wife of Edgar E. **Spencer,** d. 31 Jan., 1879, ae. 22.—(*Ry-H.*)

SAMUEL, m. Charlotte *Kirkham* **Price,** 5 Nov., 1833.

SAMUEL, bu. 13 Aug., 1803.

BENJ., of E. Htfd., m. Rhoda **Deming,** 5 Mch., 1811.—*W. C. R.*

FABIUS, of G., m. Laura **Riley,** of Weth., 16 Nov., 1819.—*W. C. R.*

———, m. Betsy **Strong,** both of Glast., 2 Oct., 1799.

PRUDENCE, of Samuel, bp. 20 Sept., 1818.

SALMON & Kath. Bidwell, had *Edmund,* bp. 13 Aug., 1803.

BIGELOW (*Baguley, Bigullah, Bigullaough, Bigalow, Bigelow, Bigeloe, Bigelo, Biglow*), JONATHAN,[4] (*Jona.,[3] Jona.,[2] Jno.,[1]*) ; bp. 27 Jun. 1714; betw. 1735 and '36, m. Tabitha **Coleman** (Lieut. Jno.,[3] Jno.,[2] Thos.,[1]. He d. 23 Jan., 1779; she d. 17 Sept., 1785, ae. 70. See, also, *Goodwin's Geneal. Notes,* p. 52 for this family.

Children:

1. Jonathan, m. and had 3 sons bp. 7 May, 1797.
2. Thomas, d. 5 Oct., 1767, ae. 31.
3. Dau. b. 19 Sept., 1755—a ch. bu. that day. Of 5 daus. ment in his will (dated 5 June, 1778) were
4. Hannah, b. 14 Aug., 1738, who m. 2 Dec., 1759, Capt. Jno. (s. John) **Barnard,** of Htfd. He was b. 25 Dec., 1732, and served during nearly the whole of Revol. War and was an orig. memb. of Soc. of Cincinnati. She d. 13 Mch., 1800, ae. 62 ; he d. 28 Dec.,

1813, ae. 81 ; they were the gd-parents of Hon. Henry Barnard, LL. D., Sup't of Pub. Schools of Ct., and Pres. Conn. Hist. Soc. After her dth., Capt. B. m. (2) Martha (wid. Frederic) **Stanly,** of Htfd., and sister of his first wife.
5. Martha, b. 1752 ; m. (1) Frederic **Stanly,** of Htfd., b. 1752, who d. 7 Jan., 1795 ; she m. (2) as second wife, Capt. John **Barnard,** widower of her sister Hannah. She d. 11 Nov., 1823.—(*Communicated by Fred. M. Steele, Esq.*)

Miscellanea: JOHN, ld.-holder in Glast., 1709, and a taxpayer in 1713; no rec. of fam. nor of any of name until 1762, when DAVID J. m. Patience (dau. Nathaniel Jr.) **Foote.** *Glast. Centenn.* p. 195.

BIGGS, WILLIAM, of Midd.; acc. to *Savage,* owned lds. in Weth. near the So. line of township; in 1681, the yr. of his decease. Invent. of est. £139; left a wid. and 6 ch., as follows: *Wiliam,* ae. 15; *Mary,* ae. 14; *Thomas,* ae. 9; *Elizabeth,* ae. 8; *Sarah,* ae. 6; *John,* ae. 4. He had been, in Oct., 1676, excused, on acc. of age, from watching, warding and training. See, also, Chapt. VII. Vol. I.

SARAH, adult, perhaps the dau. of William above; bp. and owned Cov't 3 Feb., 1711-12.—*Mix. MSS.*

JOHN, of Htfd.; m. Elizabeth **Curtis,** 22 Jan., 1778.—*W. C. R.*

THOMAS,—See Chapt. VII, Vol. I.

BINGHAM, EBENEZER; m. Huldah **Blinn,** 7 Jan., 1892 (*W. C. R.*) ; he d. 15 July, 1817 or 19 (?) ae. 43; she bu. 5 Jan., 1829, ae. 50; they had (*W. C. R.*) ; *William,* bp. 13 d. 14 Aug., 1806; *Eliza,* bp. 2 Nov., 1806; *William,* bp. 11 Sept., 1808; *Henry,* bp. 18 Nov., 1810; *Jane,* bp. 7 July, 1816.—*W. C. R.*

JESSE, of E. Hadd.; m. Roxy **Robbins,** 12 Oct., 1817.—*W. C. R.*

JOSEPH, of Htfd.; m. Mary **Wells,** of Weth., 12 Mch., 1744-5.—*W. C. R.*

BIRDSEY, KATHERINE, of Weth.; early rem. to Weth. from New Haven; m. Joseph **Hawley,** of Stratford, Ct., who came there abt. 1639 from Roxbury, Mass., and who d. at S. 1690. The first ch. of Joseph Hawley & Kath. Birdsey, was Samuel; b. 1647.—Note by *F. F. Starr.*

The Geneal. Guide to Early Settlers of America, says (p. 41) : that Dea. *John* Birdsey is said to have come from Reading, Berkshire, Eng., to Am. 1636, and sett. first in Weth., Ct., where he m. Phillipe, dau. of Rev. Henry Smith. [If this marr. be correctly given, it must have been to one of Rev. Smith's two daus.

by his first wife—who both m. and had ch. berore their father's death—their
names being unknown.—See *Goodwin's Gen. Notes.—H. R. S.*   Trad. says his
bro. [who may have been the father of the Kate above ment.] came to Weth.
with him and remarried and that his ch. were all daus., and one of them m.
Joseph Hawley, first of the name in Stratford, Ct., where he came in 1649, from
Milford.—*See Savage's Geneal.* Dict., I, 183; *Orcutt's Stratford, Ct., Hinman's
Conn. Settlers,* and note in *N. Y. Mail & Express,* of 25 Apl., 1903.

BISHOP, JOHN; m. Sarah ————, Jan., 1675; see Chapt. VII, Vol. I. *Hinman* says he was in the Colony 1648. For lds. see Chapt. VII, Vol. I.
From a letter of R. M. Chipman, Bethlehem, Ct., to *S. W. A.*, dated in 1887, we
gather that this John *Bishop* was son of Thomas, of Ipswich, Mass., and grand-
son of Dr. John B., of Bradford and Medford, Mass., and he had a bro.
Thomas.   Sarah, wife of this John—in deed given in 1683-4—called herself
"of Weth. wid. and adm'x of John B., late of Weth.," and conveys his interest
in same est. that had been bequeathed to the bros. John and Thos. by the will
of their father, (Thos. of Ipswich) in 1670-1.—See, also, *Col. Rec. Conn.*, I, 177;
and Chapt. VII, of Vol. I of this History.

Child (Weth. Rec.) :

1. Sarah, b. 3 July, 1676.

BLACK, JEREMY (?) ; d. 16 Feb., 1818, ae. abt. 50.

BLACKLEACH, JOHN. *Savage* says (1. 189), that he was of Salem, Mass., 1634;
freeman 6 May, 1635, an active mcht.; rep. 1636. He rem. to Boston, acc. to
Savage, thence rem. to Htfd.; went home [i. e. to Eng.] prob. in 1678 (unless
that it was his s. John that went), but next yr. came again, where he remained
until his dth. See Chapt. VII, Vol. I. *Hinman* calls him a "gent. of estate;"
tho' he left only £373, among such of his ch. as were living at the time of his
death, 23 Aug., 1683 (*Weth. Rec.*) ; his wife having d. on 20th of preceding
month. (*Weth. Rec.*)   His Invent. amtg. to £373-16-06, was taken 3 Sept.,
1683, by Samuel Talcott, James Treat and Samuel Butler, Selectmen (*Ct. Rec.*) ;
6 Sept., 1683—adm. gr. to Samuel Butler and Mrs. Exercise Hodges; ord. for
distrib. to John Blackleach, Mrs. Exercise Hodges, Mary Jefferies and Benoni
Blackleach. Htfd. Prob. Rec. He is found in the pub. rec. as having once been
fined £30 for slandering the Court.   The Ct. was of the opinion that the fine
should have been £100, but owing to a weakness incident to the culprit, it was
reduced to the above amt.
Vol. 111, p. 211, of *Private Controversies,* Sec'y of State's Office, Htfd.; contains
rec. of an appeal of Mrs. Elizabeth Blackleach, to the *Ct. of Assistants,* relative
to the will of one Christian **Harbor** (or **Harbert ?**), wife of Benjamin Harbert,
who seems to have been her father. And, p. 201, of same Vol. contains a bond
(1687) given by John Blackleach, for the support of his father[-in-law]
Benj. Harbord, and his mother[-in-law] Jane Harbord, in consideration of their
making over their est. to him. It appears from this bond that the will of
Christian Harbord, who d. some time before her husband, was made with his
consent, and gave ppy. to her bros. in Eng.; and, when it came abt. that support was given by John Blackleach to his wife's parent, or parents, Mrs.
Elizabeth Blackleach (smart woman that she was) made her appeal as to the
illegality of said will.   But what concerns us most in the matter, is to know
who were her parents. Presumably *Christian* was her own mother, and *Jane*
a step-mother. For ld. holdings see Chapter VII, Vol. I.

Children (of John & Elizabeth Blackleach, as given by Savage, 1, 189):

1. John, Jr., of whom *Savage* says he had a s. John, b. 1660; that next yr., he rem. to Htfd., and there bo't of his father the est. that the latter had bo't of Elder Goodwin ; that he went to Eng., 1678; but the next yr. set sail for Boston in the *Mayflower*, with a ch. who may have been sent over to Eng., for educat., and after a long res. d. in Weth., 9 Sept., 1703, æe. abt. 77, and, in *Savage's* opinion "the rec. is prob. aggravated by 10 yrs." Also that his wid. d. 12 June, 1708, in 74th yr.—*Weth. Rec.*

John, 3d, s. of John, Jr., and ment. above as b. in 1660, sett. in Farmington. His wife's name is not known, but the following doc. from *Htfd. Co. Prob.* would seem to prove that she d. during his absence, prob. on a voyage to Eng.

Elizabeth Blackleach, wid. of John, Jr., invent., £272-02-06, taken August, 1708, by Joseph Wadsworth and Capt. Aaron Cooke. She died 12 June, 1708—Will—Nuncupative—Evidence of John Stedman cousin 8 June 1708 s. of Thomas Wickham and Sarah Benjamin that Mrs. Elizabeth Blackleach, ordered her will from the custody of Thomas Wickham saying for I will have none out for my daughter Mary shall have it and do what she will with it for Mary shall have all that I have for I see what has become of what Betty had and I see how it is with Mrs. Jesse now, for Mary hath not carried herself so—To Mary Olcott saying take the will and keep it, and do what you will with it for I give you all I have to dispose of as you see cause Record by Caleb Stanly Clerk Court Record 2 August 1708 will annuled John Olcet & Mary Olcott his wife one of the dau. of Mrs. Elizabeth Blackleach evidences accepted by the Court Adm* to John & Mary Olcot'.

John Blackleach Sen. Invent. £1076-19-00 Taken by Benjamin Churchill Thomas Wickham Sen—Debts yet due at Antigua and Inventory cannot be put in the Will. He died 7 September 1703—Whereas my wife Elizabeth Blackleach hath been for divers years past left in the management of my concerns in Hartford and Wethersfield and hath taken much pains and care and thereby hath found difficulty and she knowing how my children have behaved towards her and also out of that care and respect that I bear toward her Comfortable Maintenance I do in this my Last Will and Testament give and bequeath all my estate both real & personal unto my beloved wife Elizabeth Blackleach Leaving the Settlement thereof to her * * * hereby giving her full power to will and bequeath the said estate as she shall see meet and I do—appt. my wife Elizabeth Blackleach to be sole Executrix desiring Mr. John Chester and Joshua Robbins to be

Overseers—In case my wife die Intestate I say it to be remembered that I have given my dau. Elizabeth Harris in Boston and considerable est. not short of £500 Signed John Blackleach, 3 Sept., 1703. Witnesses John Chester, Thomas Wickham Senr., Ct. Rec. 15 Sept., 1704—approved. "John Blackleach, Jr., Invent. £145-00-00, taken 8 Apl., 1700, by Thomas Chester and Benjamin Churchill, Court Record. Whereas, Mr. John Blackleach, Jr., being gone to sea, and his wife taken away by death in his absence, and no person appearing to preserve his estate, until his return, or further order, Mrs. Elizabeth Blackleach [his mother ?] moving this Court that Ciprian Nicols, and Mr. John Olcott, should take the estate into their hands for its preservation, this Court join in Mr. Samuel Hooker with them. Mrs. Elizabeth Blackleach requests this Court to appoint Mr. John Olcott, guardian to the child of Mr. John Blackleach dec'd, whose name is John, abt. 2½ yrs. old, 17 Jan., 1698-9. Court Rec. Adm. gr. to Mr. John Olcott, est. of Mr. John Blackleach, Jr., of Farmington, dec'd.— *(Note, by Mr. E. A. R. Manwaring.)* These dates conflict a little. The *First Ct. Rec.* should have an earlier date. As the inventories are on one side of the book, and Ct. Recs. on the other, or in another volume, they come out of order in some cases ; and dates are not always given in the originals.) In addit. to the s. John, b. 1660, acc. to *Savage*, John, Jr., had two daughters, viz. : 1. *Elizabeth*, who m. a **Harris**, of Boston, and rec'd £500 in distrib. of her father's est. 2. *Mary.* who m. John **Olcott**, having previously been the wife of Thomas **Welles**; and who, after Olcott's dth., m. Joseph **Wadsworth**, "the intrepid preserver of the Col. Charter in the famous Charter Oak of Htfd."

2. Exercise, bp. 24 Jan., 1637 ; m. a **Hodges** —as see her father's will. *Savage* says she m. in Boston, 24 Aug., 1660, Richard **Rasor**. If both his statements and that of her father's will are correct, it must be that she was twice married.
3. Joshua, bp. 23 Feb., 1639.
4. Elizabeth, bp. 12 Dec., 1641 ; d. soon.
5. Benoni, bp. May, 1643.—See Chapter VII, Vol. I.
6. Elizabeth, bp. 4 Aug., 1644.
7. Solomon.
8. Mary, (acc. to *Savage*) who m. a **Jeffries.** —as see her father's will.
Orcutt's *Hist. of Stratford, Ct.,* gives record of a Blackleach family in that town, originating abt. 1678, with Richard, a mcht. and (as also his s. Rich.) a man of considerable prominence in the community. No proven relationship to the Weth. Blackleaches, tho' in point of time, ages, etc., John of W. and Richard of S. may have been bros.

BLAKELY, JOSEPH, of Willink, N. Y., m. Sally **Williams,** 7 Feb., 1816.

JOSEPH, the wife of, d. 8 Aug., 1842, at Aurora, N. Y.

JOHN, m. Jane E. (dau. Ackley & Harriet) **Williams,** b. 23 Sept., 1816; d. 17 Dec., 1858, bu. at Sardinia, N. Y.

BLAKEMAN, JOHN, of Weth., acc. to Savage (I, 195), bro. of James of Stratford and Deliverance of Stonington, and all sons of Rev. Adam, first minister of Stratford, Ct. John m. abt. 1653, Dorothy (dau. Rev. Henry) **Smith,** of Weth., and rem. to Stratford; had *John, Ebenezer* and *Joseph;* and d. 1662;

104 GENEALOGIES AND BIOGRAPHIES OF ANCIENT WETHERSFIELD.

will prov., 26 Nov., following; wid. m. (2) 31 Oct., 1665, Francis **Hull**, of S., who d. 1687; she m. (3) Mark **Sension**, of Norwalk, who d. 1693, and she m. (4) Dea. Isaac **Moore**, of Far.; she d. 1706. A considerable rec. of John's desct's, through his sons John, Ebenezer and Joseph, will be found in Orcutt's *Hist. Stratford, Ct.*

BLANNOT, HENRY, m. Harriet **Blinn**, 2 May 1816 (?).—*N. C. R.*

Children:

1. Harriet,		6. Henry, prob. the H. who d. ae. 10 yr., 22 June, 1822.—*W. Ins.*
2. Fanny,		
3. Edwin Washington,	bp. 18 June, 1820.	7. Franklin Blinn, bp. 21 Oct., 1821.
4. Mary,		8. Henry James, bp. 20 July, 1823.
5. Nancy,		9. Martha Edwards, bp. 25 Sept., 1825.

BLINN, (*Blin, Blen, Blynn*), of French (prob. Huguenot) origin; largely a Stepney parish family.

PETER, first of the name in Weth., m. Johanna ————; he is said to have been a joiner. See Chapter VII, Vol. I, this Hist. His will (*Htfd. Co. Prob. Rec.*) here given, gives his wid. name as Mary, prob. a second wife, and that he had (prob. by her) four other sons, whose names are not given in *Weth. Rec.*, viz.: Peter, James, Jonathan and Deliverance. PETER BLYNN. Invt. £79-00-01, taken 18 Mch., 1724-5, by David William Warner, Richard Montague. Will dated 2 March, 1724-5, "age 84 years being in health of Body," I give to my wife (Mary Blynn) to my son Peter Blynn, to James, to Williams, to my daughter Mary Hurlbut, to my gr. son Daniel son on my son Daniel Blynn, to my son Jonathan to Deliverance Blynn, to my dau. Margaret Belding. I give my silver headed cane to my gr. son George Blynn, son of my son Deliverence Blynn. My son Deliverence to be Executor.

PETER BLYNN, O

Witness: David Goodrich David Williams Christopher Graham.

Proven 4 May, 1725.

Children (Weth. Rec.):

1. William, b. 1 July, 1675. FAM. 2.	(*By second marriage*):
2. Mary, b. 2 Dec., 1677; m. ——— **Hurlbut.**	5. Peter.
3. Daniel, b. 2 Mch., 1679.	6. James.
4. Margaret, b. 10 Mch., 1681; m. ——— **Belden.**	7. Jonathan. FAM. 3.
	8. Deliverance. FAM. 4.

FAM. 2. WILLIAM,[2] (*Peter*,[1]), b. 1675—see Chapter VII, Vol. I, this Hist.; m. Anna (dau. John) **Coltman** (dec'd), 13 Nov., 1701, she d. 17 Oct., 1724, in 45th yr.—*Weth. Rec.;* he m. (2) Thankful (dau. John) **Nott, 22** Dec., 1725.

Children (Weth. Rec.; bp Mix MS.):

1. Daniel, b. 27 Dec., 1703; bp. Jan., 1703-4. FAM. 5.	*Conn. Mag.*, Vol. II, p. 289.
2. Mary, b. 18 Mch., 1705-6.	7. Thankful, b. 9 Aug., 1720; d. 25 Oct., 1724. *Weth. Ins.*
3. William, b. 29, bp. 31 July, 1709. FAM. 6.	8. Gershom, b. 18 Sept., 1726. FAM. 8.
4. Anna, b. 4 Feb., 1712-3.	9. Thankful, b. 24, bp. 30 Nov., 1729.
5. Peter, b. 4 Feb., 1712-3. FAM. 7.	10. Patience, b. 16, bp. 20 May, 1732.
(Twins bp. 8 Feb., 1712-3.)	11. Samuel, b. 12 Apl., 1735. FAM. 9.
6. Ephriam, b. 21, bp. 29 Jan., 1715-16. *Enhriam Blinn*, of Farmington, May 13, 1768, and Lenox, Sept. 23, 1781; also records lands in Berkshire Co. records.—	12. Abraham, b. 2 Feb., 1738; d. 28 Mch., 1739.
	13. Elizabeth, b. 7 Apl., 1741.

FAM. 3. JONATHAN,[2] (*Peter*,[1]), b. ————; m. 9 Dec., 1708, Hannah (dau. Wm.) **Clark;** she d. 11 Sept., 1713; he m. (2) Abigail **Nott,** 26 June, 1740.—See, also, Chapter VII, Vol. I.

Children (Weth. Rec.) :

1. Jonathan, b. 1 (bp. 7, *Mix.*) Oct., 1711. | 2. Lucy, b. 2 (bp. 6, *Mix.*) Sept., 1713.
FAM. 10.

FAM. 4. Mr. DELIVERANCE,[2] (*Peter,*[1]), b. ————; m. 5 Feb., 1713, Mary **Stillman**, who d. 30 June, 1735, ae. 46— *Weth. Insr.;* he d. 3 Nov., 1736, in 48th yr. Est. £600; invent. taken 1 Dec., 1736; *Ct. Rec.* 4 Jan., 1736-7; adm. gr. to Benj. Stillman. Rec. £800, with John Stillman.—*Htfd. Co. Prob. Rec.* He was licensed as a taverner, Nov., 1725; Feb., 1727; and in Nov., 1722, sold liquor; also, again in Feb., 1734.—*Co. Ct. Rec.*

Children:

1. Martha, b. 17 (bp. 19, *Mix.*) Feb., 1715-16; poss. the M., wife of Philip **Mortimer**, rope maker, of Boston, 1743.—*S. W. A.*
2. Mary, b. 23 Sept., 1718.
3. Rebecca, b. 10 Sept., 1721.
4. George, b. 9 Nov., 1724; in Apl., 1739, he chose his uncle, Nathan'l Stillman, as his guardian. See, also, his father's will.

FAM. 5. DANIEL,[3] (*Wm.,*[2] *Peter,*[1]), b. 1703; m. Martha (dau. Thos.) **Stillman**, 15 June, 1736.

Children (Weth. Rec.) :

1. Martha, b. 21 Nov., 1736.
2. Daniel, b. 18 May, 1738.
3. Hezekiah, b. 5 July, 1741.
4. Esther, b. 20 Mch., 1742-43. FAM. 11.
5. Justus, b. 29 Nov., 1748.

FAM. 6. WILLIAM,[3] (*Wm.,*[2] *Peter,*[1]), b. 1709; m. Sarah ————.

Children (Weth. Rec.) :

1. Solomon, b. 26 Mch., (bp. Apl. 7, *Mix.*) 1731. FAM. 12.
2. Deliverance, b. 13 Jan., 1739.
3. Mary, bp. 1740.
4. Elizabeth, bp. 12 Apl., 1741.—*S. C. R.*
5. William, b. 14 Sept., 1742. FAM. 13.
6. Hosea, b. 1 (bp. 2, *S. C. R.*) Dec., 1744. (*L.*) FAM. 14.
7. Sarah, b. 28 Sept., (bp. 5 Oct., 1746. *S. C. R.*)

FAM. 7. PETER,[3] (*Wm.,*[2] *Peter,*[1]), b. 1713; m. Martha **Collins**, 10 Mch., 1734; he d. 7 Mch., 1793, in 85th yr.—*Weth. Insc.*

Children (Weth. Rec.) :

1. David, b. 10 Oct., 1735.
2. Christian, b. 17 Aug., 1737; d. 27 May, 1755.
3. Anne, b. 17 Aug., 1739.
4. Abraham, b. 14 Jan., 1742.
5. Lois, b. 13 May, 1745.
6. Comfort, b. 15 Oct., 1749.
7. Peter, b. 7 Dec., 1752.

FAM. 8. GERSHOM,[3] (*Wm.,*[2] *Peter,*[1]), b. 1726; m. Chloe **Butler**, 29 (28—*Fam. Bible*) Dec., 1756—*Weth. Rec.;* she b. 31 Jan., 1739; d. 10 June (one acc. says 23 Apl.), 1821, ae. 82; he d. 1 or 2 Nov., 1810, ae. 84.—*Weth. Rec., and data furnished from Fam. Bible*[6] *by* Mrs. ADELAIDE A. GOODWIN.)

Children (Weth. Rec.) :

1. Mehitable, b. 6, bp. 12 June, 1757; m. 20 Feb., 1781, Joshua Cone; she d. 8 Apl., 1839.
2. Gershom, b. 15 Nov., 1759. (*Fam. Bible.*)
3. Son, b. 14 Nov., 1760. (*Fam. Bible.*)
4. Gershom, b. 2 Dec., 1761; d. 25 Oct., 1768.
5. Simeon, b. 26 Mch., bp. 5 (or 1) Apl., 1764. FAM. 15.
6. Mary, b. 23 June, 1766.
7. Gershom, b. 13, bp. 21 Oct., 1770; d. 1 Nov., same yr.
8. Thankful, b. 21 Oct., 1771.
9. Levi, b. 7 May (*Fam. Bible*), bp. 19 June, 1774.
10. A son, b. 28 Mch., 1777. (*Fam. Bible.*)
11. Huldah, b. 27 July, 1778 (*Fam. Bible*); m. Ebenezer **Bingham**, Jan., 18, 1802. (*Fam. Bible.*)
12. Levi, bp. 5 Aug., 1781; d. 9 Sept., same yr.
13. Lucy, b. 21 Nov., 1782; bp. 6 Apl., 1783; m. 19 Mch., 1810, Ashbel **Hurlburt**; she d. Pawlet, Vt., 1811.—*Weth. Ins.*
A ch. of Gershom d. 2 May, 1776, ae. 3 yr.—*W. C. R.*

FAM. 9. SAMUEL,[3] (*Wm.,*[2] *Peter,*[1]), b. 1735; m. Elizabeth **Welles**, 30 Mch., 1755, who d. 13 Nov., 1784, ae. 47.—*Weth. Insc.*

Children (Weth. Rec.) :

1. Elizabeth, b. 10 Nov., bp. 10 Dec., 1758; d. 18 of 19 Feb., 1807, ae. 49.—*Weth. Inscr.*
2. George (Capt.), b. 1, bp. 9 Sept., 1764; d. 20 May, 1796, "in Cape St. Nichola Mole,
W. I."
3. Huldah, d. 2 Oct., 1773, ae. 5 yr.—*Weth. Instrp.*

FAM. 10. Mr. JONATHAN,⁴ (Daniel,³ Wm.,² Peter,¹), b. 1711; d. 17 July, 1789, in 78th yr.—Weth. Insc. He m. Sarah ————, who d. 18 Aug., 1805, in 79th yr.—Weth. (N.) Insc.   Res. Newington.

Children (Weth. Rec.):

1. Sarah, b. 1, bp. 10 Feb., 1759.
2. Jonathan, b. 28 Sept., bp. 3 Oct., 1762; d. 8 June, 1803, in 40 yr.—Weth. (N.) Inscr.
3. Lucy, b. 8, bp. 19 Jan., 1766.
4. A James, s. of Jonathan Blinn, was bp. 20 Dec., 1730, by Mr. Mix.

FAM. 11. JUSTUS,⁴ (Daniel,³ Wm.,² Peter,¹), b. 1748; m. Margaret **Crofoot,** Sept., 1772, who d. 2 July, 1798, in 48th yr.—S. C. R.; he m. (2) wid. Mary **Stoddard,** 27th June, 1800; res. Stepney; he d. 19 Apl., 1833 in 86th yr.—S. C. R.

Children (Weth. Rec.):

1. Justus, b. 17 Jan., 1775.
2. William, b. 29 Oct., 1777.
3. Elizabeth, b. 1 Feb., 1781.
4. Joseph, b. 23 Oct., 1784.
5. Esther, b. 12 May, 1787; d. 7 Mch., 1789.—
(S. Ch. Rec.)
6. Ch. b. and d. 21 Mch., 1789.—(S. Ch. Rec.)
7-8. 2 ch. (twins) d. 29 June, 1790.—(S. Ch. Rec.)
9. Charles, b. 11 June, 1798.

FAM. 12. SOLOMON,⁴ (Wm.,³ Wm.,² Peter,¹), b. 1732; m. 30 Sept., 1784, Desire **Andrus**—S. Ch. Rec.; he d. ae. 74, bu. 19 Jan., 1808.—W. C. R.

Children (Weth. Rec.):

1. Polly, b. 20 Sept., 1785.
2. Levi, b. 6 Jan., 1787; d. 4 Dec., 1834, ae. 48; had (W. C. R.) Henry D., Cornelia and Harriet bp. 31 July, 1822; Lucy Ann bp. 28 Sept., 1823; Levi bp. 2 Mch., 1833; inf.
d. 4 Mch., 1833, ae. 10 wks.
3. Hannah, b. 8 Sept., 1788.
4. Hervey, b. 4 Feb., 1791.
5. Barzillai, b. 31 Jan., 1793.
6. George, b. 27 Feb., 1796.

FAM. 13. WILLIAM,⁴ (Wm.,³ Wm.,² Peter,¹), b. 1742; m. 7 Nov., 1782, Nancy **Lucas.**—W. C. R.   He d. at Gt. Barrington, Mass., 1 Aug., 1822, ae. 80.— Stockbridge Star, item from R. H. C.

Children (Weth. Rec.):

1. Nancy, b. 4 Oct., bp. 30 Nov., 1783.
2. Hepzibah, b. 16, bp. 25 Sept., 1785.
3. Patty, b. 14, bp. 22 June, 1788.
4. William, b. 14, bp. 18 July, 1790.
5. Emily, b. 3, bp. 17 June, 1792.
6. Joseph, b. 1795.

FAM. 14. HOSEA,⁴ (Wm.,³ Wm.,² Peter,¹), b. 1744; m. 8 Nov., 1773, Ruth **Smith** —S. Ch. Rec.; he d. 6 Aug., 1815, in 71 yr.—W. Insc.; she prob. the Ruth who d. 28 July, 1826, ae. 87.—Weth. Ins.

Children (Weth. Rec.):

1. Sarah, bp. 10 Dec., 1775.
2. Hannah, b. 4 July, 1776.
3. Hosea (Capt.) b.   , bp. 7 July, 1776; bu. 15 June, 1819, ae 43; "lived beloved and d. lamented." (Weth. Ins.) m. Mehitable **Wolcott,** 15 Apl., 1798.
4. William, bp. 25 Apl., 1779.
5. Roger, bp. 10 Feb., 1782.
6. James, bp. 6 Mch., 1785; d. 8 Feb., 1848, ae. 63.—Weth. Ins.
7. John, bp. 30 May, 1790.

FAM. 15. SIMEON,⁴ (Gershom,³ Wm.,² Peter,¹), b. 1764; m. 19 Feb., 1801, Damaris **Crane,** who d. 12 Apl., 1834; he d. 12 Apl., 1837, ae. 73.—Weth. Insc.

Children (Fam. Bible):

1. Emily, b. 27 July, 1802, bp. 3 July, 1803; d. 20 Dec., 1883; m. Charles **Francis;** 4 ch.
2. Simeon, b. 24 June, bp. 4 Nov., 1804.
FAM. 16.
3. Lucy, b. 25 Oct., 1811, bp. 7 June, 1812; d. 20 Dec., 1889; m. Horace **Wells;** their s. was (1901) res. Weth.

FAM. 16. SIMEON,⁵ (Simeon,⁴ Gershom,³ Wm.,² Peter,¹), b. 1804; m. Sarah Balch **Adams,** 13 June, 1836—W. T. R.; she b. 28 Oct., 1814; d. 4 Oct., 1877; he d. 3 Dec., 1880.—Weth. Insc.

Children (Fam. Bible) :

1. Adelaide Amelia, b. 18 Jan., 1837 ; m. 11 Sept., 1856, Levi **Goodwin**, b. 28 Feb., 1819, and who d. 7 June, 1880. *Issue :*
    i. Albert Ward (Goodwin), b. 30 June, 1857 ; m. 1 Oct., 1884, Amelia Dora **Zimmerman**; have
    (a) Margaret /Adelaide (Goodwin), b. 14 Feb., 1890.
    ii. Stephen Buckland (Goodwin), b. 18

May, 1860 ; unm.
2. Alfred Alonzo, b. 13 Nov., 1838 ; d. 16 Dec., 1843.
3. Ellen Theresa, b. 1 Feb., 1842 ; m. 12 Feb., 1862, Samuel Broadbent **Morgan**, who d. 11 Dec., 1897.
4. Alice Gertrude, b. 25 Sept., 1844 ; unm.
5. Frank Stuart, b. 2 May, 1850 ; unm.

Families Unattached :

ABRAHAM,[4] (*prob. of Peter,*[3]—FAM. 7—, *Wm.,*[2] *Peter,*[1]), bu. 14 Mch., 1790, in 49th yr.—*S. C. R.;* wife's name Polly ————; had *Levi* and *Shingleton* (*Singleton?*) bp. 22 May, 1785, the latter d. 21 Mch., 1808, in 36th yr.— *S. C. R.*

DAVID,[4] (*prob. eld. bro. of Abraham above and s. of Peter,*[3] *Wm.,*[2] *Peter,*[1]), b. 1735; m. Prudence **Goodrich**, 14 Dec., 1790.

Children (S. C. R.) :

1. Emily, bp. 28 June, 1795.
2. Sophia, bp. 19 June, 1796.
3. David, bp. 22 Apl., 1798.
4. Pamela, bp. 4 May, 1800.
5. Julia, bp. 13 June, 1802.
6. Lucretia, bp. 29 Apl., 1804.

7. Prudence, bp. 22 Dec., 1805.
A *Prudence* Blinn (prob the wife of *David* above) had
1. Roxy, bp. 29 May, 1791.
2. James, bp. 28 Apl., 1793.

BELA, m. Hannah (dau. Joseph & Hannah) **Hurlbut**, 16 Dec., 1756; she b. Weth., 7 Nov., 1736.

Children (N. C. R.) :

1. Asa, bp. 6 Feb., 1757.
2. Wiliam, bp. 8 Oct., 1759.
3. Jonathan, bp. 1 Mch., 1761.
4. Seth, bp. 8 Apl., 1764.

5. Hannah, bp. 18 May, 1766.
6. Samuel, bp. 9 Feb., 1772.
7. Hannah ("of Bela Blin of Canaan") bp. 23 Oct., 1774.—*N. Ch. Rec.*

ELISHA, of New., m. Esther W. **Griswold**, 23 Nov., 1831; prob. the E. who d. 20 Oct., 1878.—*N. C. R.*

Children :

1. Elisha Burritt, bp. 15 June, 1834.
2. Franklin, bp. 2 Aug., 1835.
3. Esther, bp. 27 Aug., 1837.
4. Elisha, bp. 1 July, 1838.
5. Mary Jane, bp. 24 July, 1842.

6. Levi Welles, bp. 10 Nov., 1844 ; d. 5 Oct., 1851, ae. 7 yr., 5 mos.—*W. C. R.*
7. Harriet Lavinia, bp., 10 Oct., 1847.
8. Alice A., d. 17 July, 1857, ae. 2 yr.— *W. C. R.*

EPHRAIM.

Children (N. C. R.) :

1. Hannah, bp. 3 Feb., 1751 ; d. 23 Apl., 1752.
2. Hannah, bp. 29 Oct., 1752.

3. Rosel (Rosewell), bp. 10 Nov., 1754.
4. Silas, bp. 23 Jan., 1757.

JAMES, m. Lois **Wolcott**, who d. wid. 12 Mch., 1820—*W. T. R.;* he d. 25 Aug., 1808, ae. 78.—*N. C. R.*

Children (Weth. Rec.; bp. New. Ch. Rec.) :

1. Lois, b. 17 Mch., 1757.
2. James, b. 14. bp. 18 May, 1760.
3. Elisha, b. 24, bp. 27 M·h., 1763 ; d. 20 Oct., 1818, by cart wheel passing over his head, in 56th yr.—*Weth. (N.) Inscr.*
4. Unni, b. 25, bp. 31 Mch., 1765 ; m. Holly

Hunter, 17 Feb., 1789. (*N. Ch. Rec.*) ; prob. the U. who d. (*N. C. R.*) 18 Feb., 1840, ae. 75.
5. Abigail, b. 23 Mch., bp. 7 Sept., 1777.
6. Nancy, b. 13 Oct., 1778, bp. 6 June, 1779.

JAMES, Jr., (prob. s. of *James*, ment. above), m. Irene **Andrus** (she on a sick bed) ; he is prob. the James, "of New.," who m. Anna **Butler**, 14 Oct., 1826— *W. C. R.;* was a mariner and d. at ae. of 63; prob. the Capt. James, who d. at South, 21 May, 1833.—*W. C. R.*

Children (N. C. R.) :

1. James Butler, bp. 22 June, 1828.
2. Delia Ann, bp. 13 May, 1832.
3. Chauncey Wright, bp. 2 Aug., 1835.—

N. C. R.
4. Lucy Francis, bp. 31 May, 1842 ; d. 2 June, 1842.—*N. C. R.*

JONATHAN, the *Mix Rec.* gives date of bp. of ch. *James* and *Mary*, 20 Oct., 1728.

JONATHAN.

Children (N. C. R.) :

1. Sally.
2. Lucy.
3. Erastus.

4. Polly—these 4 bp. 30 July, 1797.
5. Jonathan, bp. 29 Nov., 1798.
6. Sabra, bp. 8 Aug., 1802.

JOHN, b. 31 Jan., 1813; d. 2 May, 1853; his wife Martha **Harris,** b. 19 Apl., 1811; d. 1 Feb., 1876.

Children:

1. Cordelia Harris, b. 8 Oct., 1815 ; d. 11 May, 1893.
2. Hosea Harris, b. 22 July, 1799 ; d. 16 Oct., 1874 ; his wife, Sarah **Francis,** b. 30 July,

1801, d. 27 Dec., 1854.
3. Timothy R. Harris, b. 15 Mch., 1802 ; d. 20 Feb., 1853.

JOHN, the *Mix Rec.* gives date of bp. of his s. *Charles*, 2 Sept., 1733.

HANNAH, the wid. who d. 27 Feb., 1812, in 70 yr.; had (*N. C. R.*) *Asabel, Daniel, Mary, Hannah, Levi*, bp. 9 Sept., 1785.

BOARDMAN, (diff. forms of spelling *Borman, Boreman, Bordman, Boardman).*

~Bozeman~

The exhaustive and admirable *Boardman Genealogy* says that the American family descends from the *Boreman's*, and that the name *Bordman* or Boardman was "from the first entirely distinct from Boreman, and has an altogether different derivation * * * * Curiously and unaccountably, the descendants both of Thomas Boreman of Ipswich, Mass., and of Samuel Boreman of Weth., having at first generally employed the spelling BORMAN, by inserting, after a few generations, the *d*, and sometime later the *a*, gradually changed their name to its present form, and so made it not only different from the one by which their ancestors were called, but identical with that of an entirely distinct family." "This change from Boreman or Borman to Boardman, first appears in the Weth. line in the record of Richard of Newington, 1707, nearly 70 yrs. after the first appearance of Samuel B. in New England. The new form was adopted by most of the family in Weth., till 1780, when the *a* is first added in the record of Elijah, son of Israel of Newington." The plan adopted by the author of the Genealogy referred to, is to give to the first two generations, the name *Boreman*, to the third and fourth *Bordman*, and *Boardman* to the remainder.

The Eng. ancestry of Samuel, the Weth. sett., is traced as follows— from (1) *William* Boreman, of Banbury, Oxfordshire, 1525; (2) *Thomas,* "the elder," of Claydon, 1546, d. 1579; (3) *Thomas,* "the younger," of Claydon, m. Dorothy **Gregory,** 1580; (4) *Christopher,* of Claydon b. 1581, d. 1640, m. Julian (dau.

---

* BOARDMAN GENEALOGY, 1525-1895.—The English Home and Ancestry of Samuel Boreman, of Wethersfield, Conn., and Thomas Boreman, of Ipswich, Mass., With Some Account of their Descendants (now called *Boardman*) in America. Illustrated with Views, Autographs and an English Pedigree. Compiled by Charlotte Goldthwaite, Published by Mr. F. J. Boardman, Hartford, Conn., 1895 ; 8vo. xiii, 778 pp., 350 copies printed—in every respect a superb work.

HOMESTEAD OF SAMUEL BOREMAN, SEN., ON BROAD STREET, WETHERSFIELD, AS IT APPEARED WHEN KEPT AS A TAVERN, 1816-1827, BY HEZEKIAH AND DOSHA CRANE. Built about 1660.

From a painting in possession of William F. J. Boardman.

From Boardman Genealogy.

Felix) **Carter;** (5) *Samuel,* bp. Banbury, Oxfordshire, Eng., 20 Aug., 1615, came early to Weth. (from Ipswich, Mass., where his name first appears on rec. 1639.) But the B. genealogy makes it quite clear that his removal to Weth. was in 1641 and intimates a possibility that his wife Mary **Betts,** whose mother was "the Widoe" Betts, of Htfd., "school dame" in that town, may have been a *second* wife m. at Hartford, his first having d. at Ispwich. His wife was Mary (dau. of John & Mary) **Betts,** of Claydon, Oxfordshire, Eng., from which place they undoubtedly emig. tó America—as William Boardman (6th in gen. from the Settler) had in his possession a letter written from that place, in 1641, to Samuel Bordman, from his mother; of which the following is a copy from the original in possession of Mr. Wm. F. J. Boardman, of Hartford, Conn.:

"Good Sonne. I have received yoʳ letter, whereby I understand that you are in good health, for wch. I give God thankes, as we are all, praysed be God for the same; whereas yoʳ desire is to see yoʳ brother Christopher with you he is not provided for so great a Journey, neither doe I think that he dare take uppon him so dangerouse a voyage. Yoʳ Five sisters are all alive & in good health & remember their love to you. Yoʳ Father hath been dead allmost this two yeares & thus troubling you noe further at this time, I rest, praying God to blesse you and yoʳ wife unto whome we all kindly remember oʳ loves

Yoʳ everloving
Mother

[Cley] don the
5th of February   JULIAN BORMAN
1641

[Superscription]
To her very loving Sonne
Samuel Boreman at
Ipswich in New-England
give this with
Trust."

Mrs. Samuel Borman d. Aug., 1684, ae. prob. 61; her est. inventoried at £277-01-02.

Mr. Borman received large grants of ld. at Weth. both from the Town and also from the Indians, by each of whom he seems to have been greatly trusted and respected. (See Chapt. VII. Vol. I.) A portion of the land (30 acres) which he had from the Town, Jan., 2, 1649-50, was at the S. end of the present Rocky ' Hill, being the first piece of ld. at that end of the Town granted to a private individual. It furnished great quantities of saplings, suitable for the making of pipe staves—then a very important industry in the infant colonies, and as Mr. B. was a cooper by trade, it may have been one of the inducements which led him to leave Mass., where the supply was rapidly being exhausted. The earliest reference in the *Weth. Rec.* to Mr. B. is the entry (*T. V.* I p. 4) of description of his "earmark" for cattle.

He rep. Weth. as dep. to Gen. Ct., (commencing Oct., 1657) for 18 terms, being present at 34 sessions; was app. by Gen. Ct., 1649, as Town Sealer of Weights and Measures; also, 1659, Customs Collector for Weth., being the first incumbent in that office; juror for 15 yrs., betw. 1646 and '62; Grand Juror in 1660 and '62, and frequently placed on Committees to settle church disputes, estates, town bds., and differences with the Indians. He d. intestate in Apl., 1673; est. valued £742·15.

Children (Weth. Rec.):

1. Isaac, b. 3 Feb., 1642-3. FAM. 2.
2. Mary, b. 14 Feb., 1644-5 ; m. (1) John Robbins; m. (2) ——— Denison; she d. 19 May, 1721.
3. Samuel, b. 28 Oct., 1648. FAM. 3.
4. Joseph, b. 12 Mch., 1650 ; rec'd 16 ac. ld. at Rocky Hill, 1674, by distrib. of father's est ; he d. unm. 1676.
5. John, b. 12 June, 1653, rec'd 7 ac. ld. in N. cor. (now Hewitt's) So. Weth., 1674, by distrib. of father's est.
[Presumptive evidence tends to show that

those two bros. d. in the service, in King Philip's War.] Invent. taken 27 Feb., 1676.
6. Sarah, b. 4 Mch., 1655 ; m. Thomas Fitch, of Weth., who d. 18 Oct., 1704.
7. Daniel, b. 4 Aug., 1858. [yr. wanting in *W. Rec.* prob. 1656.—*S. W. A.*] FAM. 4.
8. Jonathan (Lieut.), b. 4 Feb., 1660. FAM. 5.
9. Nathaniel b. 12 Apl., 1663. FAM. 6.
10. Martha, b. 12 Aug., 1666 ; m. (1) Benj. Crane; m. (2) Samuel Terry, of Enfield, Ct. ; d. 29 May, 1743.

FAM. 2.   ISAAC,[2] (*Samuel,*[1]), b. 1642; m. Abiah (dau. of Thos. & Alice) Kimberly, of New Haven, and sister of Eleazer Kimberly, school-teacher at Weth., and later Sec'y of the Colony. He was chosen surveyor, drew 52-ac. lot in 1685; his father gave him the homestead W. side Rose Lane (now Main St.) next S. of James Wright's, 1674 ; he drew lots in allotment of 1694; chosen fence-viewer, 1684; surveyor of highways, 1689; sealer of weights and measures, Selectman, Constable, etc.; cooper by trade. He d. 12 May, 1719 in 77th yr.; Invent. est. £14-18-19; wid. d. 6 Jan., 1722-3.

Children (Weth. Rec.):

1. Isaac, b. 21 July, 1666. FAM. 7.
2. Samuel, b. 7 July, 1668. FAM. 8.
3. Thomas, b. 14 Nov., 1671. FAM. 9.
4. Sarah, b. 1673 ; m. Sam'l Frary; d. 1 Mch., 1733-4.
5. Abiah, d. unm., 8 Feb., 1740-1 ; "found dead in her bed being in her usual state of health the night preceding."—*Weth. Rec.*

6. Eunice, b. 29 June, 1682 ; m. (1) 24 Dec., 1702, Ab'm Williams; m. (2) Obadiah Dickinson. Issue (*by first marriage*) :
   i. Eunice (Williams), b. 20 July, 1704.
   ii. Rebecca (Williams), b. 25 Apl., 1706.
   iii. Abigail (Williams), b. 22 Feb., 1707-8.
   iv. Abia (Williams), b. 26 Jan., 1709-10.
   v. Silence (Williams), b. 20 Feb., 1711-12.

FAM. 3.   SAMUEL,[2] (*Samuel,*[1])—called in *Weth. Rec.* "Clerke," also, "Sgt.," and, after his father's dth. "Samuel, Sen.," to distinguish him from his bro. Isaac's s. Samuel—; m. Sarah (dau. Lieut Samuel & Mary *Boosey*) Steele, of Far., 8 Feb., 1682 ; he d. Dec. 23 (will dated 20th), 1720, ae. 72. For lds. see Chapt. VII, Vol. I; owned ld. in Rocky Hill, gr. to his father, but exch. with his bro. Jonathan for the homestead, in Weth. proper, where he res.; was a cooper by trade; chosen surveyor of highways, 1679; collector, 1683; on Comm. to lay out road in Fearful Swamp, 1687; lister, 1693, etc. His est. invent. £1,085-18-10. His wid. d. 23 Jan., 1732-3. Her est. invent. 2 Mch., 1732-3, at £103-00-06; in in will, dated 25 Mch., 1727-8, says: "I, Sarah Boardman, of Weth., wid. reliet of

AN INVENTORY OF THE ESTATE OF MR. SAMUEL BOREMAN OF WETHERSFIELD, DECEASED, TAKEN AND APPRAISED BY THE SELECTMEN THE 2D OF MAY, 1673.

The original in possession of William F. J. Boardman.

Mr. Samuel Boardman, dec'd—being very aged." His will ment. "Cousin Jemima Graves" and states that ½ of his Weth. Division lot was given to him from the town of Weth. *Children (Weth. Rec.):*

1. Mary, b. 13 Nov., 1683; m. Daniel **Warner,** 3 Oct., 1706. *Issue:*
  i. Sarah (Warner), b. 2 Feb., 1707-8.
  ii. William (Warner), ⎫ b. 1 Oct., 1715.
  iii. Hannah (Warner), ⎭
2. Sarah, b. 13 Mch., 1686; d. 17 d. old.
3. Hannah, b. 27 June, 1687; d. 16 May, 1688.
4. David, b. 1 June, 1692; m. Abigail (dau.

James, Jr., & Prudence *Chester*) **Treat,** 6 Dec., 1717; res. in the old home of his father and gd-father, Broad St., cor. Fletcher Lane, which, as he had no issue, he left to his nephew, Samuel (the merchant), s. of his bro. Joseph.
5. Joseph, b. 6 Apl., 1695. FAM. 10.
6. Josiah, bp. 19 Mch., 1698-9.—*Mix MSS.*

FAM. 4. DANIEL,[2] (*Samuel,*[1]), b. 1658; m. Hannah (dau. Samuel) **Wright,** 8 June, 1683; appears on rec. as fence-viewer, 1684; sheep master, 1694; town school comm., 1715; d. 20 Feb., 1724, ae. 67; he was a glazier by trade; held lds. in Litchfield and New Milford, Ct.; his wid. who m. (2) James **Treat,** of Weth., d. 25 Feb., 1746, ae. 82. Invent. est. taken at Litchfield 8 Apl., 1725 and also at Weth. Will, dated 13 Feb., 1725; gives s. Timothy ½ of his Newington lds; and Joshua & Benj. were to share his Litchfield & New Milford lds.; his s. Charles' (d. same day as his father) share was to go to his bros. and sisters. *Children (Weth. Rec.):*

1. Richard, b. 1 Sept., 1684-5. FAM. 11.
2. Daniel (Rev.), b. 12 July, 1687. FAM. 12.
3. Mabel, b. 30 May, 1689; m. (1) John **Griswold,** 1711; m. (2) Josiah **Nichols.**
4. John, b. 18 Nov., 1691; d. 31 Dec., 1712.
5. Hannah, b. 18 Dec., 1693; m. John **Abbe.**
6. Martha, b. 19 Dec., 1695; m. Ens. Sam'l **Churchill,** 26 June, 1717.
7. Israel, b. 6 Oct., 1697. FAM. 13.
8. Timothy, b. 5 July, 1699, d. 19 July, 1699.
9. Timothy, b. 20 July, 1700. FAM. 14.
10. Joshua, b. 18 Nov., 1702; m. at Litchfield, 14 Feb., 1724-5, Sarah (dau. Quinten) **Stockwell,** of Hatfield, Mass., b. 1704; he m. (2) Amy (dau. Capt. Rich. & Amy *Reed*) **Case,** of Simsbury, Ct., who d. abt,

1792, ae. abt 89. They seem to have res. in Litchfield, Ct., Housatonick and Sheffield, Mass.; he d. 1761; had 8 ch.
11. Benjamin, b. 10 Mch., 1705; shared with his bro. Joshua, their father's ldd. ppy. in New Milford and Litchfield; res. in latter place until 1736, when he bo't lds. in and rem. to Sheffield, whither Joshua had already gone. Two yrs. later he rem. to Sharon, Ct., where he d. He m. abt. 1735, Deborah (dau. Am.) **Goodrich,** of Weth.; had 5 ch., descendants of some of which res. in Otsego Co., N. Y.
12. Charles, b. 13 June, 1707; d. same day as his father, 20 Feb., 1724; both prob. of an epidemic then prevailing in Weth.

FAM. 5. Lieut. JONATHAN,[2] (*Samuel,*[1]), b. 1660; m. Mercy (dau. John) **Hubbard,** of Hatfield, Mass., 22 Oct., 1685; fence viewer, 1692 and '97; drew lots in 1694 allotment; bridge comm'r, 1698; surveyor, 1700-1; seating the meeting-house, 1707; selectman, 1702; appraiser of cattle, 1703; had in 1677, 13½ ac. in Rocky Hill, coming from his bro. Joseph's est., and he also bo't 19½ ac. on W. side of the Rocky Hill. This became his home and contin. in family for many yrs., some of it as late as end of last century. He was commis. by Gen. Ct. May, 1698, as Ens. of the Trainband in So. end of Weth. and Lieut., May, 1703; he was also one of the three in charge of the fortified Deming house, known as "Fort Deming." He d. 21 Sept., 1712, in 52d yr. *Weth. Rec.* Invent. of est. £693-19-05, taken by Jonathan Smith, Joseph Grimes. Will (nuncupative—not signed): He gave ½ his estate to his wife during her natural life; the other ½ to his son Jonathan; "he paying Legacies to his younger sisters, an amount to each to be made equal to what his sister Mary Wright had received—the two Negros to his wife during her life." She with son John Wright to be executors—Proven 3d Nov., 1712. Witnesses, Stephen Mix, Joseph Grimes.

Children:

1. Mercy, b. 4 July, 1687; m. John **Wright**, 4 July, 1706, who d. 8 Mch., 1714, ae. abt. 35.
   i. Mercy (Wright), b. 29 June, 1707.
   ii. John (Wright), b. 31 May, 1709.
2. Joseph, b. 18 Apl., 1690; d. 15 Feb., 1692-3.

3. Jonathan, b. 16 May, 1697. FAM. 15.
4. Abigail, b. 20 May, 1700; d. 1718, unm.
5. Hepzibah, b. 16 Feb., 1702-3; m. Dea. David **Goodrich, Jr.**, 21 Dec., 1721; had 10 ch.— See *Goodrich*.

FAM. 6. NATHANIEL,[2] (*Samuel*,[1]), b. 1663; m. Elizabeth (dau. Lieut. Return & Sarah, dau. Rev. John *Warham*) **Strong**, of Windsor, 30 Apl., 1707; he being then in his 44th and she in her 37th yr. *Dr. R. W. Griswold* says: "He sett.

Nathaniel Boreman [signature]

at So. end of Rocky Hill ab't same time as his bro. Lieut. Jonathan; his ld. and ho. being on a road (now closed) that led directly W. from where (for so many yrs. later) the Burying Ground was located; the ho. being a few rods W. of the Boardman-Holmes place. See, also, Chapt. VII, Vol. I. He d. 29 Nov., 1712, in same yr. as his bro. Jonathan, a yr. of much mortality in Weth. There were 6 dths. in the B. family this yr., viz: Jonathan, Sen., ae. 53; Nathaniel, Sen., ae. 49; John, a gd-son, ae. 28; a son of John & Mary (Boardman) Robbins, ae. 22; a s. of Daniel Boardman; Mr. Williams, husband of Isaac Boardman's dau. Eunice; and Isaac, s. of Martha Boardman, who m. Benj. Crane—this evidences the great severity of the epidemic, which became known as "the yr. of y⁰ greate sicknesse." Invent. est. £433-15-00. His wid. m. (2) William (s. of Dea. Wm.) **Warner**, of Weth. as his second wife, 6 Jan., 1714. He was "Capt." of the Train Band in South part of Weth. and from this marr. sprang William Warner, Jr., and the large Warner tribe of Stepney Parish.

Children (Weth. Rec.):

1. Nathaniel, b. 19 Feb., 1711-12. FAM. 17.

FAM. 7. ISAAC,[3] (*Isaac*,[2] *Samuel*,[1]), b. 1666; m. Rebecca (dau. Wid.) **Benton**, 7 Dec., 1699. He d. 9 May, 1719 in 53d yr., three days before his father, having been an invalid for several yrs.; his four sons were amply provided for by their gd-father, Isaac, Sen.

Children (Weth. Rec.):

1. Isaac, b. 11 Sept., 1700. FAM. 17.
2. Edward, b. 6 Nov., 1702. FAM. 18.
3. Josiah, b. 30 June, 1705; m. 5 Aug., 1734, Rachel **Cole**; sett. Midd.; d. 1781; 10 ch.

4. Ephraim, b. 15 Feb., 1711; m. Mehitable **Cole**, 1734, who d. 1769; res. of Midd. 1731-2, later at Far. (Southington), where he d. 2 Jan., 1761.

FAM. 8. SAMUEL,[3] (*Isaac*,[2] *Samuel*,[1]), b. 1668; m. Mehitable (dau. Thos. & Elizabeth *Stebbins*) **Cadwell**, of Htfd., 5 Nov., 1696; res. in Midd., where he had much ldd. ppy. He d. 6 Sept., 1732.

Children (Weth. Rec.):

1. Stephen, b. 5 Aug., 1698; rem. with father to Midd. abt. 1719; m. Abigail **Savage**, of Midd., 21 Mch., 1726; rem. to Bolton, Ct., where he d. 20 Apl., 1776; she d. 1753; had 8 ch.
2. Moses, b. 8 May, 1701; rem. with father to Midd.; m. 20 Nov., 1724, Silence **Cornwell**; he d. 16 Dec., 1737, leaving 3 ch.; wid. m. (2) Ebenezer **Fox**.
3. Mehitable, b. 20 June, 1703; m. 23 Apl., 1721, Richard **Goodrich**, as 2d wife.
4. Abia, b. 19 Nov., 1704; m. Samuel **Stocking**, 20 July, 1726.
5. Rachel, b. 16 Nov., 1706; m. Janna **Wilcox**, 29 Apl., 1725.

6. Sarah, b. 7 Sept., 1708; d. unm., 2 Aug., 1741; bu Portland, Ct.
7. Anna, b. 16 July, 1710; m. John **Savage**, 1 May, 1735.
8. Deborah, b. 13 Mch., 1712; m. John **House**.
9. Elizabeth, b. 22 Dec., 1713; m. 21 Oct., 1736, John **White**.
10. Abigail, b. 3 Sept., 1717; m. Josiah **Wright**.
11. Thankful, b. 19 Nov., 1719; m. 1 Mch., 1738-9, James **Pennock**.
12. Jonathan, b. 28 Feb., 1724; d. prob. 1790; had 9 ch.

GRAVESTONE OF SAMUEL BORDMAN. 1720.

Fam. 9. THOMAS,³ (*Isaac,*² *Samuel,*¹), b. 1671; m. Mary (dau. Nath'l) **Chillinton,** (*Chittenden?*), of Guilford, "toward latter part of May, 1699;" m. (2) Sarah (wid. Ab'm) **Kilborn,** 15 Oct., 1718, who d. 17 Oct., 1719; m. (3) Hannah (wid. Wm.) **Butler,** 24 Dec., 1729; he was hayward, 1693; gr. an earmark for cattle, 1701; appraiser of strange cattle, 1717.

Children (*Weth. Rec.*) :

1. Prudence, b. 15 Aug., 1700; m. a **Miller;** her heirs, 1758, supp. to be in No. or So. Carolina.
2. Thomas, b. 19 Oct., 1707; m. Martha —— ;

d. 1757; no issue. wid. m. (2) Thos. **Brigden,** of Weth.
3. Mary, b. 6 Nov., 1709; m. Thos. **Fox,** 6 Nov., 1729. (See *Fox.*)

Fam. 10. Cornet JOSEPH,³ (*Samuel,*² *Samuel,*¹), b. 1695; m. Mary (dau. Joseph) **Belding,** 17 Feb., 1726; d. 19 Jan., 1771; she d. 30 Apl., 1769, ae. 66; he was a man of substance and prominent in Weth. affairs; selectman 1755, when the Fr. prisoners were quartered in the town, under his care and that of Nich. Ayrault and Sam'l Curtis; was comiss. Qr. Ms. of the Troop of Horse, 6th Mil. Reg. 11 May, 1749; and Cornet in same reg. by Gen. Ct., 1751; dep. to Gen. Ct. Oct., 1754, Jan. & Mch., 1755, Oct., 1759, May, 1760.

Children (*Weth. Rec.*) :

1. Mary, b. 4 Mch., 1727; m. Hez. **Welles,** 17 Dec., 1747; d. 23 May, 1786.
2. Sarah, b. 4 Feb., 1730-1; m. 24 Nov., 1748, Capt. Crafts **Wright;** m. (2) 10 Jan., 1770, Esq., John **Robbins;** she d. 10 Feb., 1784. *Ch. Rec.* Did she d. 1768?—a Sarah Wright was app. adm'x, with Appleton Robbins, 8 Apl., 1768.
3. Eunice, b. 11 Nov., 1733; m. (1) 22 Aug., 1754, David **King;** m. (2) Hosea **Harris;**

d. 2 Apl., 1813.
4. Hannah, b. 20 Apl., 1736; m. 1 May, 1755, David **Goodrich.**
5. Levi, b. 6 May, 1739. **Fam. 19.**
6. Rhoda, b. 29 Apl., 1742; m. 13 Sept., 1762, Francis **Hanmer, Jr.** (*W. Ch. Rec.*) ; d. 20 Nov., 1801.
7. Samuel, b. 4, bp. 9 (L) Dec., 1744. **Fam. 20.**
8. Abigail, b. 7 May, 1748; m. 27 Oct., 1767, Joseph **Butler;** descts. in Pittsfield, Mass.

Fam. 11. Lieut. RICHARD,³ (*Daniel,*² *Samuel,*¹), b. 1684; m. Sarah (dau. Edward & Mehitable *Smith*) **Camp,** of Milford, Ct., 11 Mch., 1707—this rec. in Weth. Town Bks. is the first instance where the name is spelled with a "*d.*" Res. in Newington parish; for the estab. of which he was, 1712 one of the petitioners. He d. 7 Aug., 1756, ae. 71; *N. C. R.* She (b. 1683) d. 28 Dec., 1768. *N. Ch. Rec.* He was prominent in all N. affairs; served as ensign in the New. militia Co. org. 1726.

Children (*Weth. Rec.*) :

1. Sarah, b. 13 June (Jan. in rec.), 1708; m. 24 Nov., 1730, John **Parmalee.**
2. Gamaliel, b. 2 Oct., 1711; m. Sarah **Sherman;** d. 17 Sept., 1754, ae. 43; two yrs.

before his father. **Fam. 21.**
3. Mary, b. 19 Sept., 1719; m. Martin **Kellogg, Jr.,** 1 July, 1742. *Issue* (See *Kellogg*) :

Fam. 12. Rev. DANIEL,³ (*Daniel,*² *Samuel,*¹), b. 1687; grad. Y. C. 1709, immediately took charge of the Hopkins Grammar School at Hadley, Mass., for 8 mos., when he was called to preach (May 17, 1712) at New Milford, Ct., where a ch. had just been estab.; was ord. 21 Nov., 1716; "gave tone and character to the new sett. by his devotion and active service;" was the first sett. minister there and d. there 25 Aug., 1744; was largely interested in the conversion and civilization of the Indians in Litchfield Co., with whom he had great influence; he m. (1) 26 Feb., 1716-17, Hannah **Wheeler,** of Milford, Ct., who d. 20 June, 1719; m. (2) (1 Nov., 1720) Mrs. Jerusha (wid. Ebenezer) **Selly,** of Poquonock Parish Stratford; she was one of the 9 daus. of Dea. David *Sherman,* of Poq. Parish, Stratford; b. 1693; d. 30 Aug., 1777.

Children (by first marriage):

1. Hannah, b. 12 Jan., 1717-18; m. Josiah
   Dayton; d. 25 May, 1758.
   (By second marriage):
2. Penelope, b. 26 Dec., 1721; m. Dr. Riverius
   Carrington; d. 13 Oct., 1799.
3. Tamar, b. 26 Mch., 1723; m. Rev., Nath'l
   Taylor, D. D.; her father's successor in
   the N. M. pastorate; she d. 27 June, 1795;
   he m. again.
4. Mercy, b. 9 Feb., 1725; m. Gilead Sperry;
   she d. 17 Oct., 1795-6.
5. Sherman, b. 12 Aug., 1728; m. 1755, Sarah
   Bostwick; became the most prominent

man in N. Milford; dea. in ch.; Capt. in
Mil.; 21 times rep. the town in Gen.
Assem.; d. 1801.
6. Jerusha, b. 4 May, 1731; m. 20 Oct., 1765,
   Rev. Daniel Farrand, of So. Canaan, Ct.,
   where she d. 16 Aug., 1806.
   [Ebenezer Seelye, only ch. of Mrs. Jerusha
   Seelye, was b. 5 Nov., 1717 and bro't up
   and educated by Rev. Mr. Boardman.]
   This *New Milford* line of Boardmans will
   be found in *Orcutt's History of New Mil-
   ford, Ct.*

FAM. 13.   ISRAEL,[3] *(Daniel.[2] Samuel,[1])*, b. 1697; m. Elizabeth (prob. dau. Jacob)
    Gibbs, Windsor, Ct.; and sett. in Newington, Ct., but, 1722, rem. to Stamford,
    Ct.; in 1725 sold out at S. and ret. to Weth. where he d. 24 Apl. of that yr.;
    was a glazier. Invent. £561.

Children (Weth. Rec.):

1. Olive, b. 10 Aug., 1718.
2. Elisha, b. 20 Feb., 1720. FAM. 22.
3. Israel, (Capt.), b. 19 Mch., 1725; b. in
   Stamford; but his father's fam. rem. to
   Weth. very soon after his birth and his
   father d. very soon after the rem. to
   Weth; his mother m. (2) abt. 1729, Thos.
   Waterbury, of S., and d. 1730, leaving her
   3 ch. orphans. Israel, then ae. 5, was
   left in charge of an aunt in S., and on
   arriving of age (1746) sold to his bro.
   Elisha all his right to mother's Weth.
   ppy.; his subsequent life was mostly identified with S., and with Pensacola, Fla.,

where, in 1763, he unfortunately invested
in a plantation, and where he d. He was
a sailor, owning and commanding his
own vessel; a staunch Episcopalian, a
man of Christian principle and Puritan
ideas, with the courage to defend them—
and he possessed energy, decision and a
spirit of enterprise; he m. (1) 1745-6, Mary
(dau. Josiah) Blackman, of T.; m. (2)
at Weth., Sybil (dau. Jonathan & Mary
Burnham) Warrinor, of Springfield; had
2 ch. by 1st, and 5 by 2d wife, who ret.
to Weth. and Htfd.

FAM. 14.   TIMOTHY,[3] *(Daniel,[2] Samuel,[1])*, b. 1700; m. Hannah (dau. Israel &
    Lydia *Wright*) Crane, 21 Dec., 1721; res. Newington, and d. 27 Dec., 1753, ae.
    54; impounder of cattle, 1731; wid. d. Dalton, Mass., 20 Feb., 1780, ae. 80. See
    Chapt. VII, Vol. I.

Children (Weth. Rec.):

1. Damaris, b. 11 Nov., 1722; m. (1) Alex.
   Frazier; m. (2) Simeon Judd.
2. Charles, b. 4 Sept., 1725. FAM. 23.
3. Timothy (Dea.), b. 2 Dec., 1727; carpenter, shipbuilder, cabinet-maker; m. Jemima Johnson, and sett. in Middletown;
   10 ch. Dea. Timothy's 5th son, *Elisha*, b.
   11 July, 1760; m. 29 May, 1783, Mary
   Wright; rem. to and was mcht. and for
   many yrs. postmaster at Weth. Before
   1816 he rem. to New Haven, where he d.
   28 Dec., 1838. and his wife d. 31 Jan.,
   1817. *Issue (bp. W. C. R.)*
   i. Horace, b. 13 June, 1784; d. 16 Feb.,
      1792.
   ii. Laura, b. 31 Oct., 1787, bp. 9 Dec.;
       unm.
   iii. Mary Wright, b. 26 Jan., bp. 27 Apl.,
        1794; d. 10 Aug., 1813, ae. 18, at Far.
   iv. Eliza, b. 13 Aug., 1797; bp. 24 Sept.;
       m. Aug., 1819, Dr. John H. Kain; d.
       2 Jan., 1846.
   v. Emeline Frances, b. 12 June, bp. 15
      Sept., 1799; m. (as 2d wife) Capt.
      Chas. Goodrich Boardman, of Rut-
      land, Vt. *No issue.*
4. Hannah, b. 12 Dec., 1729; m. Jonathan
   Dickinson, Jr., 8 May, 1754. *Issue (see
   Dickinson):*
5. Elizabeth, b. 14 Oct., 1731; d. 6 Nov.,
   1731.

6. Daniel, b. 29 Sept., 1732; m. (1) Sarah
   Foote, of Weth.; sett. in Pittsfield (now
   Dalton), Mass.; m. twice again; had 7
   ch. most of whom m. and rem. to N. Y.
   State. [Poss. the D. who m. Eunice
   Belden, 29 Jan., 1756.—*Weth. Rec.*,] and
   who had *Anne*, bp. 27 Mch., 1757; *Sarah*,
   bp. 26 May, 1765, and *Mary*, bp. 29 Mch.,
   1767.
7. John, b. 6 Aug., 1735; m. and rem. to
   N. Y. State.
8. Elizabeth, b. 5 Oct., 1737; m. 2 Mch.,
   1761, Jona. Brigden.
9. Seth, b. 21 Apl., 1742; m. N. 6 Feb.,
   1772, Abigail (prob. dau. Ezekiel & Abigail *Wright*) Fordick—*N. Ch. Rec.*; was
   a Rev. soldier in Capt. Chester's Co.,
   at siege of Boston, 1775; at Bunker Hill;
   under Gen. Gates in the North, 1777,
   lost his right thumb at Stillwater, N. Y.,
   1777; pensioner 1818, on invalid pens.
   list, 1833-4; cordwainer; res. at Spencertown, Waterford. Attica. Canandaigua,
   N. Y., Lenox, Mass., and went West;
   at Newington, 25 Feb., 1831, ae. 89; had 5
   ch. who survived; m. and went West;
   one dau's dth. rec. in *W. C. R.*, 1777, ae.
   13 mos.
10. Olive, b. and bp. 3 Nov., 1745; m. 10
    Nov., 1768, Theo. Lee.

FAM. 15.   Lieut. and Dea. JONATHAN, Jr.,[3] *(Jonathan,[2] Samuel,[1])*, b. 1697; m.
    Mabel (dau. Jonas & Sarah) Holmes, 30 June, 1725; she d. 15 Nov., 1741; he
    m. (2) 10 Mch., 1743, Elizabeth Beckley; he was for many yrs. (from 1716)

THE OLD JONATHAN BOARDMAN HOMESTEAD, ROCKY HILL.

View taken shortly before it was pulled down about 1892.

From Boardman Genealogy.

the school master of Rocky Hill. He d. 25 Dec., 1775. *S. Ch. Rec.* The ld. rec'd from his father had two houses on it, which were afterward moved together, forming the curious old double Boardman house, under one roof, pulled down in 1893. His father, who d. when he (Jonathan, Jr.) was abt. 15 yrs. old, left him one-half of his personal estate to be improved for his learning and bringing up " and the benefit of certain lds." for the same use; and his education was undoubtedly superior to that of most young men of his day. He was, for many yrs. the schoolmaster at the North end of Weth. township. The first Rocky Hill school house, erected 1712, was nearly opp. to his house.

Children (by first marriage; b. Weth. Rec.) :

1. Jonathan, b. 27 Mch., 1726. FAM. 24.
2. Elnathan, b. 17 Oct., 1727. FAM. 25.
3. John (Capt.), b. 5 Dec., 1729. FAM. 26.
4. Mercy, b. 12 Apl., 1733 ; m. Sam'l **Churchill**, 16 July, 1770. *Issue:*
   i. Dau. (Churchill), d. unm.

ii. Mary Anna (Churchill), b. 25 Apl., 1782.
(*By second marriage*) :
5. Elizabeth, b. 7 July, 1744 ; m. James **Price**; had Elizabeth Price, b. 19 June, 1776.

FAM. 16. Sgt. NATHANIEL,[3] (*Nath'l*,[3] *Samuel*,[1]), b. 1711-12; of Rocky Hill; m. 28 Feb., 1733, Ruth (dau. Joseph & Ruth *Williams*) **Parker;** inherited the place where his father res.—the Boardman-Holmes farm; he d. 12 May, 1776. S. Ch. Rec.; wid d. 7 May, 1790, ae. 84.

Children (Weth. Rec.) :

1. Nathaniel, b. 25 Jan., 1734. FAM. 27.
2. Elizabeth, b. 22 Sept., 1736 ; m. 19 Nov., 1778, Joseph **Beckley**, of Canaan.
3. Sarah, b. 20 Oct., 1739 ; m. (1) Nich. **Cady**; m. (2) 29 Nov., 1769, Dea. Jesse **Churchill.**
4. Return, b. 14 Sept., 1744—(*Jan. T. Rec.*) ; d. unm. 6 Sept., 1831—*S. Ch. Rec.;* was

of Weth. Lex. Alarm Co., 1775 ; named after his gt-gd-fth. Return Strong of Windsor, res. in old Boardman ho. Ry-H.; gave his farm to his sister Eunice's s. Allen Boardman Holmes, from whom the old Samuel Boardman farm takes its present name, the Boardman-Holmes Farm.

FAM. 17. ISAAC,[4] (*Isaac*,[3] *Isaac*,[2] *Samuel*,[1]), b. 1700; m. Elizabeth ————; rem. to Bolton, Ct., and had hardly got sett. when his house was struck by lightning and burned, leaving him in such destitute circumstances that he was officially commended by the Governor and Council, May, 1727-8, to the charity of the churches of Bolton and Weth. for relief; he d. Bolton, 20 Apl., 1766.

Children:

1. Ichabod, b. Weth., 25 Oct., 1725 ; m. Mary **Fenn**, and rem. 1761, to Nova Scotia.
2. Elizabeth, b. Bolton, (prob.) 26 Dec., 1727 ; m. Mr. **Riley.**
   (From *Co. Ct. Recs.*, we learn of the following add. ch., viz.:)

3. Eunice, who m. Amos **Williams**, of Newark N. J.
4. Sarah, who m. Samuel **Frary**, of Midd.
5. Samuel, who res. Midd.
6. Obediah, who res. Midd.

FAM. 18. EDWARD,[4] (*Isaac*,[3] *Isaac*,[2] *Sam'l*,[1]), b. 1702; m. 30 Jan., 1726-27, Dorothy (dau. Benj. & Hannah) **Smith**, of Glast., where they sett. and he taught school in Eastbury parish. Abt. 1740 he rem. to Midd. (Westfield Soc.) ; where he d. 28 Apl., 1772 ae. 70; wid. d. at Sandisfield, Mass., 21 Dec., 1777, ae. 74.

Children (b. Glast.) :

1. Hannah, b. 18 Oct., 1729 ; m. 22 Jan., 1752, David **Higby**; d. 2 July, 1800.
2. Benjamin (Rev.), b. 3 Aug., 1731 ; grad. Y. C., 1758, and was tutor there 2 yrs. ; ord. at Midd. Haddam, where he remained in ministry until 1783 ; from 1784 to 1791, was pastor of So. Ch., Htfd.; served as chaplain in Revol. army, being known among the soldiers, as "Big Gun of the

Gospel" on account of his sonorous voice ; m. 11 Feb., 1762, wid. Ann **Bowers**, who had been first the wid. of Steph. **Hosmer**, of E. H.; had no issue ; adopted a nephew Jeduthan, s. of his bro. Elizur ; d. 12 Feb., 1802.
3. Elizur, b. 31 May, 1738 ; m. Rebecca **Sage**; res. Cromwell ; later, rem. to Sandisfield, Mass., where he d. 1790.

FAM. 19. LEVI,[4] (*Joseph,*[1] *Samuel,*[2] *Samuel,*[1]), b. 1739; m. 23 Apl., 1761, Esther* (dau. Gamaliel & Sarah *Sherman*) **Boardman**, of Newington; was prominent in Weth. public affairs; selectman, 1773, '74, '75; res. in Broad St.; d. 22 Mch., 1782; wid. m. (2) 11 Nov., 1784, Wm. **Warner**, and d. 1 Sept., 1797, ae. 54. Invent. of est., £1023·15·3, included a number of books, some in Greek and Latin; seems to have taken youths into his family for purposes of education; prob. for a time he kept tavern cor. Broad St. and Fletcher's Lane.

Children (Weth.) :

1. Joseph, b. 5, bp. 6 Mch., 1763 ; d. 6 Oct., 1775.
2. Levi, b. 30 Jan., bp. 10 Feb., 1765. FAM. 28.
3. Sarah, b. 21 Dec., 1766 ; d. 7 Feb., 1768.*

4. Simeon, b. 9 Nov., 1770 ; d. 25 July, 1775.
5. Joseph Simeon, b. 3 May, bp. 25 May, 1780. FAM. 29.

FAM. 20. SAMUEL,[4] (*Joseph,*[3] *Sam'l,*[2] *Sam'l,*[1]), "the Merchant", b. 4 Dec., 1744; m. (1) 14 Dec., 1769, Ann (prob. dau. Elizur & Sarah *Goodwin*) **Wright**, who d. 27 May, 1774; m. (2) Naomi (dau. Capt. Sam'l & Naomi) **Butler**; was one of the Weth. Lexington Alarm Co. Apl., 1775 (See Vol. I, pp. 440, 509) ; with Daniel Hinsdale (Samuel Boardman & Co.), in 1775, he built saltpetre works at Weth., at foot of Broad St., abt. opp. the old Simon Hale house, where large quantities were mfd. for the use of the government. He was "one of the most enterprising mchts. in Weth."; was large ship-owner and did a large W. I. trade, etc. See Chapter on *Maritime Hist.* His first res. was cor. Broad St. and Fletcher's Lane, the home of three gen. before him; becoming involved in business debts the ppy. passed from his hands in 1774—was later known as Crane's Tavern, and destroyed by fire in 1827. His later res. was on E., end High St. in the part called "the Common"; where he d. 8 Aug., 1822, ae. 78; wid. d. 26 Jan., 1826, ae. 73.

Children (by first marriage) :

1. Belden, b. 31 Dec., 1771 ; d. at sea, 1799, ae. 28.
2. Son, ae. 2. d. 26 Sept., 1775.—W. C. R.
3. Samuel, b. 14 Sept., 1773 ; d. 6 Sept., 1776.
(*By second marriage*) :
4. Samuel, b. 20 Sept., 1776 ; d. at sea, ae. 18.
5. Anne, b. 19 June, 1778 ; m. 28 Sept., 1803, Joseph **Talcott**; d. 5 Nov., 1863, ae. 85.
6. Butler, b. 19 Apl., 1780 ; d. at sea, Aug., 1806, ae. 26 yr.

7. Abigail, b. 1 Oct., 1785 ; m. 13 Dec., 1808, Rich. **Deming**; d. 22 Apl., 1860, ae. 75.
8. Julia, b. 31 July, 1787 ; d. unm., 4 Apl., 1876, ae. 89.
9. Eunice, b. 30 May, 1790 ; m. 13 Sept., 1821, Chauncey W. **Deming**; d. 20 Jan., 1844, ae. 54.
10. Sally, b. 29 June, 1793 ; m. 28 Dec., 1824, David **Warren**; of E. Htfd.—W. C. R.; d. 8 Mch., 1863, ae. 71.

FAM. 21. GAMALIEL,[4] (orig. called Richard), (*Rich.,*[3] *Daniel,*[2] *Samuel,*[1]), b. 1711; m. Sarah **Sherman**, and d. 17 Sept., 1754—N. Ch. Rec., two yrs. before his father; wid. m. (2), 1759, Samuel (s. "Worshipful" Sam'l & Abigail *Collins*) **Wolcott**, of Midd., who d. 6 Mch., 1794, ae. 78.

Children (Weth. Rec.) :

1. John, b. 9 Feb., 1740 ; d. 7 Jan., 1759.
2. Sherman, b. 17 July, 1741 ; m. 16 Apl., 1761, Sarah **Deming**; res. Newington ; last appears on Weth. Rec. in 1771, on a deed of ld. sold by him, prob. rem. abt. that time. Issue :
   i. John, b. 11 May, 1764 ; d. 25 Nov., 1770 ; N. Ch. Rec. gives bp. of a John

Sherman, who was bp. 20 May, 1763.
   ii. Gamaliel, (twins b. 6, bp. 17, d. 18
   iii. Sarab, (Mch., 1768.—N. Ch. Rec.
   iv. Rhoda, bp. 28 Oct., 1770.
3. Esther, b. 22 Dec., 1743 ; m. (1) Levi **Boardman**, 23 Apl., 1761 ; m. (2) 11 Nov., 1784, Wm. **Warner**; d. 1 Sept., 1797, ae. 54.

---

* A Levi B., had dau. Sarah bp. privately, being ill, 13 Mch.. 1769.

THE BOARDMAN HOMESTEAD, 1719-1866, AT THE SOUTHWEST END OF BROAD STREET, WETHERSFIELD.

Built by Samuel Boreman, Jr., for his son Cornet Joseph.

From a painting by D. F. Wentworth in possession of William F. J. Boardman.   From Boardman Genealogy.

FAM. 22. ELISHA,[4] (*Israel*,[3] *Daniel*,[2] *Samuel*,[1]), b. 1720; m. his cousin, Hannah (dau. Leonard & Abigail *Gibbs*) **Dix**, 2 Aug., 1739; res. on Wolcott Hill road; d. abt. 1754, intestate; wid. m. (2), Elizur **Wright.**

Children (Weth. Rec.):

1. Lucy, b. 12 Apl., 1740; m. John **Rose**; was of New Canaan, N. Y., 1768.
2. Olive, b. 9 Feb., 1743, at Canaan, N. Y., 1768.
3. Leonard, b. 1, bp. 9 Feb., 1746; m. 14 Dec., 1769, Exeprience **Pelton**; d. 9 Nov., 1807; *no issue;* was a Revol. soldier.
4. Ozias, b. 16, bp. 23 Apl., 1749; m. 23 Apl., 1772, Lydia **Hinsdale**, in Canaan, Litchfield County, Ct., where he sett.; d. 11 Apl., 1785; she at Morristown, Vt., where her s. Ozias sett.
5. William, d. yg. and unm., 1758-65.

F M. 23. Capt. CHARLES,[4] (*Timo.*,[3] *Daniel*,[2] *Sam'l*,[1]), b. 1725; m. (*Weth. Ch. Rec.*) 7 Aug., 1753, Abigail (dau. Dea. John & Mary *Wolcott*) **Stillman**, she prob. the wid. of Chas., who d. ae. 86, Aug., 1818—*W. C. R.;* rem. to Midd., soon after m., but later ret. to Weth. where his children's births are rec; was a mariner and master (prob. owner also) of vessels in the W. I. trade. He d. W. 12 Aug., 1793, ae. 68.—*W. C. R.*

Children (Weth. Rec.):

1. William, b. 3 Feb., 1756; lost at sea, Sept., 1775, ae. 19.
2. Rhoda, b. 29 July, 1757; m. 17 Dec., 1781, Joseph **Stillman, Jr.**, of Weth., d. 10 Oct., 1841.
3. Abigail, b. 20 Mch., 1759; m. 4 Sept., 1781, John **May.**
4. Charles, b. 4, bp. 15 Feb., 1761; was a marine on the Conn. Man of War *Oliver Cromwell*, in Jan., 1776; was lost at sea, Oct., 1780, ae. 19.
5. George (Capt.), b. 22, bp. 28 Nov., 1762; m. 27 Nov., 1788, Mary (dau. Francis &
Rhoda *Boardman*) **Hanmer**; d. 11 July, 1857. FAM. 30.
6. Hannah, b. 24 July, bp. 4 Aug., 1766; m. 22 Nov., 1786, Rev. Jesse **Churchill**; d. 10 Dec., 1804.
7. Sarah, b. 13 Apl., bp. 29 May, 1768; m. 6 Feb., 1797, Josiah **Francis**; d. 11 Nov., 1856.
8. John, b. 17 Nov., 1770; m. 29 Jan., 1794, Abigail **Goodrich**; d. 19 Aug., 1853. FAM 31.
9. Mary, b. 31 Oct., 1772; m. 23 Nov., 1795, Norman **Smith**; d. 3 Aug., 1820.

FAM. 24. JONATHAN,[4] (*Jona.*,[3] *Jona.*,[2] *Samuel*,[1]), of Rocky Hill, b. 1726; m. 13 June, 1754, wid. Martha **Cole**, of Newington, whose first hubd. had been Phinehas Cole, of N.; he occup. the same ho. as did his father and gd-father; was Sgt. in Capt. Josiah Buckingham's Co.; Col. Elihu Chauncey reg. 8 Sept. to 28 Oct., 1755, in Fr. War; he d. 1798; wife of Jno. d. 13 Sept., 1776,—*S. C. R.*

Children (Weth. Rec.):

1. Abigail, b. 22 Oct., 1755; m. 24 Aug., 1780, Capt. Rich. **Price**, of Ry-H., sea capt. in foreign trade.
2. Mercy, b. 2 Aug., 1757; m. 16 July, 1778, Sam. **Churchill**; d. 24 Jan., 1834.
3. Mabel, b. ————; m. 22 Mch., 1781, Justus **Bulkley**; d. 11 Sept., 1804.
4. Jonathan, b. 1763; m. Zerviah **Hosford**, Apl., 1803; rem. 1797, to Bristol, Ct., where he d. 7 Apl., 1804, and wife d. Oct., 1824; had 6 ch., of which the 3 eldest were b. in Ry-H., viz.:
   i. Juliana, bp. 20 Nov., 1781; d. at
Bristol, Ct., 1857, in 67th yr.—*R. W. G.*
   ii. Chauncey, b. Weth., 16 Nov., 1790, bp.; m. 25 Sept., 1812, Roxana **Adams**; he d. 11 Aug., 1857; became a famous clock-maker.
   iii. Martha, b. 21 Feb., bp. 2 Sept., 1792; m. 9 Aug., 1818, Levi **Marsh.**
   iv. Jonathan, b. Weth., 23 Jan., bp. 25 Oct., 1795; m. and rem. to Danby, Tompkins County, N. Y., where he d. 1874.

FAM. 25. ELNATHAN,[4] (*Jona.*,[3] *Jona.*,[2] *Samuel*,[1]), b. 1727; res. Rocky Hill; m. abt. 1752, Jerusha (prob. dau. David & Lydia) **Goffe**; res. a little N. of his bro. Jona.; d. 9 May, 1811—*S. Ch. Rec.;* wife d. 26 Sept., 1805, in 73d yr. *Dr R. W. Griswold's MSS. Notes* says of him—that he res. in a ho. a little N. of his son, Elnathan, Jr.—*S. Ch. Rec.*

Children:

1. William, b. abt. 1753; bp. and d. 5 Sept., 1765; run over by cart.
2. Elijah, bp. 17 Nov., 1756; m. 16 Sept., 1781, Mary **Nott**; d. 4 Sept., 1808. FAM. 32.
3. Elnathan, bp. 3 Sept., 1765; served in Rev. War in Capt. Nath'l Pomeroy's Co., Col. Chapman's Reg., at Newport, Aug. and Sept., 1778; was of Kent, Ct., 1777.— (See our *Revol. List.*)
4. Sarah, bp. 3 Sept., 1765; m. Samuel **Steb-**
bins, of Sherburne, N. Y., 1831.
5. Candace, d. 24 Sept., 1767.—*S. Ch. Rec.*
6. Candace, bp. 5 Feb., 1769; m. 23 May, 1798, Thos. **Steel, Jr.**, of Lenox, Mass.
7. Lucy, bp. 16 Feb., 1772; m. 9 Aug., 1812, (as 3d wife) Dea. Seth **Hart**, of Ry-H.; m. ———— **Warner.**
8. Hannah, bp. 21 Aug., 1774; m. 14 May, 1800, Elias **Robbins**; d. 12 Sept., 1859.

FAM. 26. Capt. JOHN,[4] (*Jona.*,[3] *Jona.*,[2] *Samuel*,[1]), of Ry-H., b. 1729; first of fam. to become, from abt. 1755, exclusively a sailor; was engaged in W. 1. trade; shipwrecked and rescued in 1772. From the *Conn. Courant*, 3 Nov., 1772 we gain the following item: "Capt. Cornelius White, arrived here [Boston] from Cape Nichola Mole, came across a wreck, which proved to be Capt. John Boardman, of Weth., in Conn., who, together with his crew, Capt. W. took off and brought in." Finally lost at sea in 1780; res. in N. pt. of old double Boardman ho. (which he or his father built) while his son, Capt. Jason, occupied the S. part; he m. (1), Grace (dau. Stephen & Abigail *Holmes*) **Riley**, of Ry-H., who d. 17 Dec., 1754; m. (2), 29 Jan., 1756—*Weth. Rec.*, Elizabeth (dau. Capt. Jona.) **Warner**, who d. 17 Mch., 1825, ae. 87.

Children by first marriage:

1. John, b. Jan., 1754; m. abt. 1773, it is supp. Martha **Curtis**; d. early and wid. m. (2) John **Adams**; m. (3) John **Goodrich**. *Issue (by first marriage)*:
   i. Allyn,[6] (*John*,[5] *John*,[4] *Jona.*,[3] *Jona.*,[2] *Sam'l*,[1]), b. Weth., 1774, m. 1 Jan., 1797, at Gt. Barrington, Mass., Phebe (dau. Stephen & Eunice *Lathrop*) **Woodworth**; was a tanner and currier; in Mch., 1799, rem. fam. and gds. on ox-sleds to Covert, N. Y., where he res. until dth., 12 Feb., 1837; wid. d. 28 Sept., 1856, in 80 yr.; 12 ch. (*By second marriage*):
2. Rebecca, b. 27 July, 1760; m. 27 Dec., 1780, Constant **Griswold**, a soldier of the Revol.; d. 20 Mch., 1825.
3. Jason (Capt.), b. 16 Jan., 1762; m. 7 July, 1784, Hepzibah **Curtiss**. FAM. 33.
4. Mehitable, b. 21 Aug., 1763; m. 29 May, 1791, Capt. Pownall **Deming**, of Lyme, Ct., mch. Htfd.; m. (2) 2 Apl., 1799, Maj. Luther **Colton**.
5. Frederic, b. 16, bp. 23 June, 1765; m. 28 July, 1790, Chloe (dau. Gershom) **Bulkley**; d. 24 Oct., 1821; followed the sea; mate of one of his father's vessels. FAM. 34.
6. Ashbel, b. 13, bp. 20 Sept., 1767; lost at sea with his father, 1780.
7. Daniel, b. 30 Apl., bp. 5 May, 1771; m. Elizabeth **Bell**, of Glast.; d. 29 Jan., 1834. *No issue.*
8. Elizabeth, bp. 11 Dec., 1774; m. 15 May, 1791, Chas. **Morgan**, of Htfd.; d. ae. 27.

FAM. 27. NATHANIEL,[4] (*Nath'l*,[3] *Nath'l*,[2] *Sam'l*,[1]), of Ry-H., b. 1734; m. Mabel (prob. dau. Wm. & Hannah *Hale*) **Holmes**, and d. 4 May, 1776—*S. C. R.*, eight days before his father's dth.; wid. d. in Nov., 1777, leaving a family of s. orphan ch., the elder s. Levi (ae. 18), and the eld. dau. Mehitabel, took charge and bro' up the y-gr. ch.

Children:

1. Levi, b. 21 Sept., 1759; m. 4 Jan., 1789, Rachel **Riley**; d. 16 Jan., 1818. FAM. 35.
2. Mehitable, b. 3 Nov., 1761; m. 4 Jan., 1781, Levi **Collins**, of Ry-H.
3. Eunice, b. 13 May, 1763; m. 17 Oct., 1787, Daniel **Holmes**; d. 30 Nov., 1849.
4. Sineon, b. 26 Aug., 1765; bp. 31 Aug., 1766; d. unm. 23 Nov., 1815.—*S. Ch. Rec.*
5. Ruth, b. 17, bp. 18 Dec., 1768.
6. William, b. 27 Jan., 1770; bp. 24 Feb., 1771; m. 12 Nov., 1797, Elizabeth **Holcomb**; res. Canaan, Ct.; had 9 ch.
7. Sarah, b. 7 Jan., 1773; bp. 17 Apl., 1774.
8. Rhoda, b. 9, bp. 21 Mch., 1776.

FAM. 28. LEVI,[5] (*Levi*,[4] *Joseph*,[3] *Sam'l*,[2] *Sam'l*,[1]), of Weth., b. 1765; m. 2 Sept., 1790, Elizabeth **Warner**, of Weth.; res. old homestead on Broad St., where he d. 20 May, 1808, ae. 43. In 1816 wid. sold old place and rem. with sons *Henry* and *Levi* to Sheffield, Mass. until her dth., 5 Jan., 1858, ae. 84.

Children (b. Weth., all bp. 5 Nov., 1795):

1. Henry, b. 2 Jan., 1791; d. 26 Nov., 1822, unm.
2. William, b. 15 Aug., 1792; m. 4 July, 1815, Abigail **North**; was a cabinet maker; res. Htfd. and Berlin; rem. 1824 to Sheffield, Mass., and became a farmer; d. 21 Apl., 1869; wid. d. 25 Feb., 1870, ae. 79; had 7 ch.
3. Levi, b. 28 July, 1795; m. 5 Dec., 1817, Sally **Callender**; d. 1 Sept., 1875.

FAM. 29. JOSEPH SIMEON,[5] (*Levi*,[4] *Joseph*,[3] *Sam'l*,[2] *Sam'l*,[1]), of Weth., b. 3 May, 1780; m. 31 July, 1803, Lucinda (dau. Joseph & Hannah *Harrison*) **Canfield**; cordwainer; rem. to Lenox, Mass., in 1804, and engaged largely in the tanning bus. In 1805 ret. to Weth., where he res. till his

HOMESTEAD OF RETURN BOARDMAN, ROCKY HILL.

FROM PHOTOGRAPH TAKEN IN 1894. STILL STANDING IN 1903.

From the Boardman Genealogy.

dth., 13 Nov., 1827, when as super-cargo of the sloop Eliza, bd. fm. Weth. to N. Y., he and all on board were shipwrecked and lost; his wid. m. 19 Sept., 1832. Ezra **L'Hommedieu**, of Chester, Ct., where she d. 6 Mch., 1850, ae. 64. Mr. B. was a man of remarkably earnest christian character and experience, and very careful and accurate in bus. matter.

Children (Weth. Rec. and W. C. R.):

1. William, b. 25 Feb., 1805; m. 3 Jan., 1828, Mary **Francis**; d. 3 Nov., 1887. FAM. 36.
2. Hannah, b. 2 Apl., 1807; bp. 29 Sept., 1816; m. 23 Jan., 1828, Mason **Holmes**; m. (2) 1843, John A. **Clark**; d. 1 Sept., 1891.
3. Joseph, b. 8 Aug., 1810; d. 21 Sept., 1810.

4. Joseph Canfield, b. 4 May, 1813; bp. 29 Sept., 1816; physician at Trenton, N. J.; d. 26 July, 1896, unm.
5. Maria Lucinda, b. 3 Jan.; bp. 4 June, 1820; m. 17 Oct., 1836, John **Daniels**; d. 21 Aug., 1864.

FAM. 30. Capt. GEORGE,[5] (*Chas.,*[4] *Timo.,*[3] *Daniel,*[2] *Sam'l,*[1]), of Weth., b. 1762; m. 27 Nov., 1788, Mary (dau. Francis & Rhoda *Boardman*) **Hanmer;** was a mariner, commanding several vessels in the foreign trade; rem. to Schenectady, N. Y., and d. 14 July, 1857, ae. 75; wife d. 6 Feb., 1829, in 65th yr.

Children (Weth. R. and W. C. R.):

1. William, b. 1789; bp. 11 Jan., 1795; d. 6 Dec., 1797, ae. 8.
2. Child, b. and d. 2 Mch., 1790.
3. Betsy, b. 23 June, bp. 5 July, 1792; d. 9 July, 1792.
4. Clarissa, twin to Betsy; m. 22 Dec., 1811, John R. **Vedderw**; d. ae. abt. 93.
5. Mary, bp. 30 Dec., 1794; d. 18 June, 1796.
6. Mary Hanmer, b. 22 Mch., bp. 11 June, 1797; m. Rev. Henry **Hotchkiss**; d. 1892.
7. William, b. 16 July, bp. 13 Oct., 1799;

m. 28 Apl., 1828, Alida **Pruyn**; d. 13 Feb., 1885.
8. Frances M., b. 6 Mch., bp. 29 June, 1805; m. 17 June, 1835, Dr. James S. **Duglass**; d. July, 1892.
9. Inf. [Harriet ?] bp. 5 [or 20 ?], d. 21 Sept., 1803.
10. Elizabeth Hanmer, b. 2 Apl., bp. 16 Aug., 1807; m. 15 Sept., 1830, Rev. Geo. W. **Eaton**, D. D.; d. 18 Jan., 1893.

FAM. 31. JOHN,[5] (*Chas.,*[4] *Timo.,*[3] *Daniel,*[2] *Sam'l,*[1]), of Weth., b. 1770; m. there, 29 Jan., 1794, Abigail **Goodrich**, of Weth.; app. to a trade; in 1792 (ae. 18), went to Georgia. In 1792, he settled in Albany, N. Y., where he spent the rest of his life as a prominent builder. He was a ruling elder of the First Presbyterian church at Albany, 1805-1815; and from 1815 to the time of his death, Aug. 19, 1853, ruling elder of the Second Presbyterian church of that city.

The sermon preached at his funeral bears this title: *A Sermon preached on Sabbath Afternoon, August 21, 1853, in connection with the Funeral Solemnities of John Boardman, Ruling Elder of the Second Presbyterian church, Albany.* By Wm. B. Sprague, D. D., Albany, 1853—8 vo. p. 33.

Children:

1. Charles, b. 12 Dec., 1794; d. unm. at Elmira, N. Y., 22 July, 1849.
2. George Smith, b. 29 Dec., 1796; m. 19 May, 1823, Alida M. **Lane**; m. (2) Feb., 28, 1832, Sarah **Brayton**; m. (3) 16 June, 1856, Sophia Ledyard **Childs**; d. 7 Feb., 1877.
3. William Goodrich, b. 23 Oct., 1800; m. 10 July, 1826, Amanda **Parker**; d. 25 Jan., 1882.
4. John S., b. 3 Jan., 1802; d. 26 Mch., 1805.

5. Mary Ann, b. 29 Mch., 1805; d. unm. 15 Nov., 1862.
6. John, b. 13 July, 1809; d. unm. 14 Mch., 1864.
7. James Stillman, b. 12 Jan., 1812; unm.; res. N. Y. City.
8. Ann Eliza, twin to James S., d. 25 Oct., 1813.
9. Ann Eliza, b. 8 Mch., 1816; d. 5 Sept., 1816.

FAM. 32. ELIJAH,[5] (*Elnathan,*[4] *Jona.,*[3] *Jono,*[2] *Sam'l,*[1]), b. Ry-H. 1756; m. 16 Sept., 1781, Mary **Nott**—*S. Ch. Rec.;* rem. to Htfd.; where he became keeper of the jail, from 1800 till his dth; landlord of the City Hall tavern, combining both offices (in same bldg.) with success; was a member of Christ ch. (Epis.) and much respected citizen; served, also, honorably in the Revol. Army; he d. 4 Sept., 1808, at Htfd.; wid. d. Wallingford, 23 Feb., 1838, ae, 85; both bu. Ry-H.

Children:

1. William Elnathan, bp. 15 Dec., 1784; d. 26 (16—*S. Ch. Rec.*) Dec., 1784.
2. William Henry, bp. 17 July, 1785; d. 6 Mch., 1786.
3. Henry, bp. 10 Nov., d. 24, 1786.—*S. Ch. Rec.*
4. Elijah (Maj. U. S. A.), b. Ry-H., bp. 30 Dec., 1787; m. Htfd., 27 Apl., 1809, Frances (dau. Robert) **Seymour.** In 1815 (being

then Capt. 6th U. S. Inf.), he was on recruiting service in Htfd; was stationed at Plattsburgh, N. Y., 1818-19, and last at Niagara, where he d. 22 Mch., 1832; wife d. 29 Sept., 1829, ae. 41.
5. James (Capt.), bp. 26 Sept., 1790. FAM. 37.
6. Inf., d. 13 Oct., 1793.—*S. Ch. Rec.*

FAM. 33. Capt. JASON,[5] (*John,*[4] *Jona.,*[3] *Jona.,*[2] *Sam'l,*[1]), b. Ry-H., 1762; m., 7 July, 1784, Hepzibah (dau. Dea. Thomas & Dorothy *Bulkely*) **Curtis,** of Ry-H.; at dth. of father he (then 18 yrs. old), succeeded him on the old homestead, and as sailor and sea captain, and later (from abt. 1785 and for 50 yrs. on) was a prominent shipbuilder and owner; owned a line of packets sailing fm. Conn. River to Richmond, Va., of which his sons Capt. Ashbel and Capt. John were masters; and was also in W. I. trade. His wife d. 4 Jan., 1807 and he m. (2), 3 Jan., 1808, Lydia **Deming,** who d. 11 Feb., 1842, ae. 65.—*S. Ch. Rec.* Capt. Jason, a man of fine appearance and dignified and courteous manners, d. 6 Feb., 1844, ae. 83.—*S. Ch. Rec.*

Children (bp. S. Ch. Rec.):

1. Rhoda, b. 11 May, bp. 14 Oct., 1787; m. 2 Jan., 1811, Sabin **Colton,** of Long Meadow Mass.; d. 10 Dec., 1852; their s. Sabin Woolworth Colton, m. Susannah **Beaumont;** had 7 ch., of whom was *Julia* (Colton), who m. Harrison **Allen,** M. D., of Phila., Pa. *Issue:*
   i. Harrison (Allen), b. 1875; d. 1899.
   ii. Dorothea W. Harrison (Allen), b. 1880.
2. John, b. 28 Feb., bp. 29 Mch., 1789; d. 25 Nov., 1792.
3. Ashbel (Capt.), b. 2 Jan., bp. 19 Sept., 1790. FAM. 38.
4. Julia (Juliana on bp. rec., bp. 20 Nov.), b. 2 Aug., 1791; m. 17 Mch., 1835, Rich. **Gillet,** of Far., d. at Rome, s. p.
5. John, b. 20 Aug., bp. 3 Sept., 1793. FAM. 39.
6. Hannah, b. and bp. and d. 17 Dec., 1795.
7. Thomas Curtis, b. 29 Mch., 1797; bp. 22 July, 1798; so named from his gd-father Dea. Thos. Curtis; went to Haddam when a yg-man as clk. became cashier of E. Hadd. Bk. till his dth, 1865; killed on steamboat dock, by a piece of wood breaking off from strain of boat's cables; he

m. Sophrania (dau. Hon. Wm.) **Palmer,** of E. H.—*R. W. G.*
   (*By second marriage*):
8. Jason, b. 1, bp. 11 Jan., 1809. FAM. 39a.
9. Norman, b. 16 Apl., bp. 18 Aug., 1811; was assoc. with Chester B. Goodrich in mercantile bus. at Little Rock, Ark.; later a mcht. in N. Y. City; d. 1873; m. (1) Caroline A. (dau. Truman) **Sweet,** of Htfd.; m. (2) 1846, Annie T. (dau. Thos.) **Williams,** of N. Y.—*R. W. G.*
10. Luther, b. 26 Dec., 1812; bp. 6 Feb., 1813; began (ae. 16) in trade of brittannia and hollow ware at Meriden, Ct., then at Chester, later at E. Hadd., in 1842, began mfgr. of silver-plated ware and built up a large bus.; was vice pres. of Conn. Valley R. R.; a director of Nat. Bk. of New Eng.; pres. of Htfd. & L. I. Steamboat Co.; d. 29 Mch., 1887.—*R. W. G.*
11. Mary Jane, b. 20 Mch., bp. 2 July, 1820; m. 6 Apl., 1842, Dea. Thos. Danforth **Williams,** of Ry-H., where she d. 7 Aug., 1888, ae. 68; the last of a fam. prominent in old Step. parish for full 200 yr.

FAM. 34. FREDERIC,[5] (*John,*[4] *Jona.,*[3] *Jona.,*[2] *Samuel,*[1]), of Ry-H.; b. 1765; m. 28 July, 1790, (*S. C. R.*) Chloe (dau. Gershom & Thankful *Belden*) **Bulkley;** sailor, mate of one of his father's vessels; he d. 24 Oct., 1821, ae. 57,—*S. C. R.;* wid. d. 28 Jan., 1825.

Children by first marriage:

1. William Bulkeley, b. 15 Sept., 1791, bp. 5 June, 1791 (*sic., S. C. R.*); d. 24 July, 1793.
2. William Bulkely, b. 4 May, bp. 29 June, 1794; m. Sarah (dau. Col) **Buell,** of Marlborough, Ct., where and at E. Hadd. and

Htfd., he was a mcht., d. 17 Feb., 1834.
3. Rebecca, b. 2 June, 1798, bp. 4 Aug., 1799; m. 16 Apl., 1823, Levi **Boardman;** she d. 20 Mch., 1864.
4. Roland, bp. 18, d. 19 Apl., 1804.—*S. Ch. R.*

FAM. 35. LEVI,[5] (*Nath.,*[4] *Nath.,*[3] *Nath.,*[2] *Nath.,*[1]), of Ry-H.; b. 1759; m. 4 Jan., 1789, Rachel (dau. David & Rachel *Curtis*) **Riley;** he d. 16 Jan., 1818;—*S. Ch. Rec.;* wid d. 1847.

Children:

1. William, b. 22 Oct., 1789; res. unm. Canaan, Ct.
2. Sylvester, b. 22 Oct., 1791; res. Evansville, Ind.
3. Eleazer, b. 24 Mch., 1794; res. LeRoy,

N. Y.
4. Levi, b. 1 July, 1799; m. 16 Apl., 1823, Rebecca (dau. Frederic) **Boardman;** d. 20 Aug., 1876. FAM. 41⅗.

Mary Francis Boardman

1803 - 1884.

William Boardman

1805-1887

Fam. 36. WILLIAM,[7] (*Joseph*,[6] *Simeon*,[5] *Levi*,[4] *Joseph*,[3] *Samuel*,[2] *Samuel*,[1]), b. Lenox, Mass., 25 Feb., 1805; m. 3 Jan., 1828, Mary (dau. Capt. Daniel & Mehitable *Goodrich*) **Francis**; was educated at Weth.; learned printer's trade in office of *Hartford Times*, then owned by Samuel Bowles and John Francis; in summer of 1824, accompanied Mr. Bowles to Sp'f'ld (on a flat boat loaded with press and all the equipment of a printing office), where Mr. Bowles started the *Springfield Republican*, of which Mr. Boardman set up and printed a part of the first issue; in 1828 in co. with Wm. Faulkner (Boardman & Faulkner) he edited and started the *Norwich* (*Ct.*) *Republican*, the second paper in Conn., to support the election of Andrew Jackson for the Presidency; in 1830, pub. the *Tolland Advocate* for an association; in 1832, with Alfred Francis, he pub. B. L. Rayner's *Life, Writings and Opinions of Thomas Jefferson*, the printing, binding, etc., being all done in Weth., in bldg. yet standing cor. opp. May's tavern, on the N.—a subscription book of which a large edition was favorably rec'd by the public; in 1834, he became foreman of the *Hartford Times* office; in 1837-9, was largely engaged in raising silkworms and making sewing silk; also cigar-making from tobacco of his own raising; in 1841, he (and John Fox) established in Weth. a large grocery bus., the first in New Eng. outside of Boston, to roast, grind and pack coffee and spices for the wholesale trade. The partnership being dissolved in 1844, he took up the business, 1 Jan., 1845, in his own name, and in 1850 rem. to Htfd., where with his son, Wm. F. J. B. he estab. the firm of Wm. Boardman & Son; introduced steam-power and modern machinery, and with gradually increasing facilities conducted the most complete factory of the kind in New Eng. until his death, 3 Nov., 1887, since which it has been continued by the younger of his sons, and a grandson. Mr. B. was largely interested, also, in many mfg. and financial institutions, and in the formation of many industries, whose success has redounded to that of the City of Hartford. He also held several public offices in earlier life, rep. Weth. in Leg. in 1852, and was app. State Prison Director, 1834 and '52. He was an earnest liberal Christian in the fellowship of the M. E. church; the Boardman Chapel in Weth., to the bldg. of which he contributed liberally, was named after him, and the Boardman Memorial Chapel ded. in 1886, was erected by him in remembrance of his wife, who d. 14 Dec., 1884, ae. 81,—a woman of liberal spirit and kindly heart, interested in all good works, both pub. and private.

Children (*b. Weth.*):

1. William Francis Joseph, b. 12 Dec., 1828; Fam. 40.
2. Thomas Jefferson, b. 27 May, 1832; Fam. 41.
3. Arethusa Maria, b. 15 Dec., 1836; d. 20 July, 1837.
4. Alpheus Francis, b. 26 June, 1838; d. 26 May, 1839.
5. Mary Lucinda, b. 1 June, 1841; m. 28 Dec., 1870, Geo. W. **Atwood**.
6. Emma Jennette, b. 25 June, 1846; d. 18 Apl., 1860.

Fam. 37. Capt. JAMES,[6] *U. S. A.*, (*Elijah*,[5] *Elnathan*,[4] *Jona.*,[3] *Jona.*,[2] *Sam'l*,[1]), b. Ry-H. abt. 1790; m., abt. 1810, Lydia (dau. Maj. Isaac) **Foote**, of Branford Ct.; commiss. 1st Lt. in 26 Reg. Inf. U. S. A., 21 Apl., 1814, and remained in service until June, 1815, when they rem. fm. Wallingford to N. Y. City, where he was inspector of customs, 1835, until dth., which was before 1842; wid. d. 30 Apl., 1857.

Children:

1. James Rockwell, M. D., b. 3 Mch., 1811; m. 9 June, 1836, Sarah W. **Mudge**; d. 11 Apl., 1865.
2. Martha Foote, b. 31 Aug., 1812; m. (1) Wm. **Ackerman**; m. (2) Wm. **Knickerbocker**; d. 17 Aug., 1889.
3. Winfield Scott, d. yg.

FAM. 38. Capt. ASHBEL,⁶ (*Jason*,⁵ *John*,⁴ *Jona.*,³ *Jona.*,² *Sam'l*,¹), b. Ry-H. 1790; m. 11 Mch., 1822, Eveline (dau. Hon. Wm.) **Palmer,** of E. Hadd.; was master of the *Richmond*, one of a line of packets owned by his fthr. and plying to Richmond, Va., and to W. I.; was lost at sea (with three other yg. men fm. Ry-H.) Nov., 1823, on a voyage to Martinico; wid. m. (2) Rich. W. **Miller,** of E. Hadd.

Child:

1. Ashbel, b. 16 Nov., 1823; m. 4 Apl., 1854,   Aug., 1874; she d. 11 Feb., 1885.
   Cath. **Stevens;** res. E. Haddam; d. 19

FAM. 39. Capt. JOHN,⁶ (*Jason*,⁵ *John*,⁴ *Jona.*,³ *Jona.*,² *Sam'l*,¹), b. Ry-H. 1793; m. 27 Apl., 1828, Sally (dau. Oliver & Hannah *Adams*) **Corey;** was a seaman and mstr. of one or more vessels; d. 18 Oct., 1837; wid. m. (2) as 2d wife, Charles **Hurlburt,** and d. 6 June, 1859.

Children:

1. Emily Curtis, b. 13 Mch., 1829; m. 12 Dec., 1847, Jas. A. **Smith,** New Britain, Ct.
2. Hannah Elizabeth, b. 21 Mch., 1831; unm.
3. Martha Jane, b. 13 Feb., 1834; m. 31 Oct., 1855, Francis N. **Penfield,** New Britian, Ct.
4. John Henry, b. 22 Sept., 1836; m. 18 Apl., 1867, Sarah Hanmer (dau. Roswell & Nancy *Robbins*) **Dix,** of Newington. *Issue:*
   i. Carrie Elizabeth, b. 4 Sept., 1870.
   ii. Minnie Dix, b. 14 Sept., 1873.

FAM. 39a. JASON,⁶ (*Capt. Jason*,⁵ *John*,⁴ *Jona.*,³ *Jona.*,² *Sam'l*,¹), of Ry-H., b. 1809; m. 12 Jan., 1831, Maria **Bradley;** d. Aug., 1867.

Children (all b. in old Jona. B. house, Ry.H.):

1. Eliza Jane, b. 29 Aug., 1833; m. 8 Oct., 1854, Truman **Griswold.**
2. Andrew Jackson, b. 4 Jan., 1836; enl. 1862, in 27th Conn. Vols.; Corp'l Co. G.; wd. at Fredericksburg, Va., 1862; disch. Mch., 1863; d. 9 Oct., 1867; bu. Ry-H.
3. Lemuel Henry, b. 18 Sept., 1837; m. 9 Jan., 1882, Anzonetta E. **Stevens;** enl. 1861, for 3 mos., Co. I, 2d Conn. Reg.; enrolled again 1862, as 1st Lieut. Co. I, 22d Conn. Reg.; honorably disch., 1863. *Issue:*
   i. Clyde Coe, b. 8 Oct., 1887.
4. James William, b. 24 Aug., 1839; m. 14 Oct., 1865, Harriet E. **Tippett;** was 1st Sgt. Co. E., 1st Heavy Artill., 1861; disch. 1864.
5. Julia Maria, b. 10 Aug., 1841; m. 29 Mch., 1867, Fred J. **Wassum.**
6. Frederic, b. 31 Oct., 1843; m. 8 June, 1867, Abbie **Chapman;** 4 ch.
7. Lydia Ann, b. 28 Jan., 1847; unm.
8. John Bradley, b. 6 Jan., 1850; m. 15 Nov., 1870, Lillie **Ranney;** 2 ch.
9. Anna Williams, b. 30 Aug., 1854; m. 13 Sept., 1882, Walter **Gamwell;** 2 ch.
10. Susan Amelia, b. 25 Aug., 1857; m. Herbert **Church.** *No issue.*

FAM. 40. WILLIAM FRANCIS JOSEPH,⁸ (*Wm.*,⁷ *Joseph*,⁶ *Simeon*,⁵ *Levi*,⁴ *Joseph*,³ *Sam'l*,² *Sam'l*,¹) b. Weth. 1828, m. 7 Jan., 1852, Jane Maria (dau. Dr. Chas. & Electa *Toocker*) **Greenleaf,** of Htfd.; was edu. at Weth. Academy; in 1846 ent. in bus. with his father; became partner 1850, and retired, on acct. of ill health, fm. the firm in 1888, after 42 yrs. connection with it; was an orig. member of the Putnam Phalanx; in 1863 was elected a memb. of Htfd. Common Council; in 1862 became a director of State Bk. of Htfd. and was actively engaged in many business and mfg. enterprises. To his liberality and love of ancestry the family is indebted for the admirable *Boardman Genealogy,* to which reference has already been made, and also for much both of material and help to this history, of his native town. Mrs. Boardman d. 20 Aug., 1899.

Child:

1. William Greenleaf, b. 29 June, 1853; m. 29 Oct., 1874, Eliza Fowler **Root.** *Issue:*
   i. Francis Whittier, b. 6 Apl., 1876;

   d. 5 Apl., 1885.
   ii. Cedric Root, b. 23 Jan., 1886.
   iii. Dorothy Root, b. 26 Apl., 1889.

FAM. 41. THOMAS JEFFERSON,⁸ (*Wm.*,⁷ *Joseph*,⁶ *Simeon*,⁵ *Levi*,⁴ *Joseph*,³ *Sam'l*,² *Sam'l*,¹),b. 1832; m. 14 Oct., 1858, Julia Amanda **Ellis,** who. d. 24 Nov., 1858; he m. (2) 24 Oct., 1861, Mary Charlena **Ellis,** (sister of his first wife), who d. 16 Jan., 1890; he m. (3) 29 Apl., 1893, Mary Adah (dau. Fred. H.)

William F. J. Boardman

Jane M. Greenleaf Boardman

1835-1899.

Simpson; he was educ. at Weth. and at Wilbraham, Mass.; clerked it for a time in a country store, then accepted a position with his father and bro.; in 1853, was adm. as partner in firm of Wm. Boardman & Sons, and now is head of the concern. Is an active Sunday School and church worker in the Universalist denomination.

Children (by second marriage):

1. Howard Francis, b. 22 Sept., 1862; m. 12 Jan., 1886, Catherine Augusta **Belchor.** *Issue:*
   i. Harold Ellis, b. and d. 16 Nov., 1890.
   ii. Mariel Wildes, b. 31 May, 1893.
2. Emma Julia, b. 13 Oct., 1865; m. 11 Apl., 1888, Geo. Robley **Howe.** *Issue:*
   i. Majorie May (Howe), b. 16 May, 1890.
3. Minnie Gertrude, b. 2 May, d. 4 Aug., 1868.
4. William Ellis, b. 1 June, 1869.
5. Helen May, b. 13 Mch., 1879; d. 29 June, 1888.
(By third marriage):
6. Thomas Bradford, b. 9 Mch., 1895.
7. George Frances, b. 31 May, 1896.

FAM. 42. LEVI,[6] (*Levi*,[5] *Nath'l*,[4] *Nath'l*,[3] *Nath'l*,[2] *Sam'l*,[1]), b. Ry-H. 1799; m. 16 Apl., 1823, Rebecca (dau. Fred. & Chloe *Bulkley*) **Boardman;** farmer; democrat; dea. of Bap. ch. in Cornwall; wife d. 20 Mch., 1864; he m. (2) Mercy (Belden) wid. James **Goodrich;** he d. 20 Aug., 1876.

Children:

1. Sarah Buell, b. 26 Feb., 1824; m. 27 Apl., 1848, Samuel C. **Cowles.**
2. Chloe Bulkley, b. 28 Jan., 1826; m. 7 Nov., 1843, Wm. S. **Whitford;** d. 30 Nov., 1872.
3. Mary, b. 31 Aug., 1829; m. 7 Jan., 1855, Wm. Leroy **Webb.**
4. Ann Eliza, b. 17 Feb., 1835; m. 12 Oct., 1856, Chas. S. **Robinson.**
5. William Bulkley, b. 25 Jan., 1837; unm.; res. Ry-H.
6. Henry, b. 9 Dec., 1840; d. 28 May, 1842.

ISRAEL BOARDMAN, of Newington, Conn. There is no evidence connecting him with the Samuel Boardman family; b. 1721; m. 4 Aug., 1740,—(*W. C. R.*) Rebecca (dau. Joseph & Mary) **Meekins,** of (E.) Htfd. b. 1723. He was a clothier, sett. and owned ch. cov't in Newington, 13 Dec., 1747; births of ch. rec. in Weth.; bps (of all but Elijah's) in Newington Ch. Rec.; had mill ppy. in Simsbury; he d. 2 Nov., 1796, ae. 75; wid. d. 9 Dec., 1814, ae. 91.—(*Ch. Rec.*)

Children (Weth. Rec. and New. Ch. Rec.):

1. Theodore, b. 22 Dec., 1746, bp. 31 Jan., 1746-7; m. Eunice **Lusk,** 24 Aug., 1794.—*W. C. R.*
2. Benejah, b. 14, bp. 21 May, 1749; m. (1) Lucy Price; m. (2) 22 Dec., 1794, Martha **Churchill.** *N. C. R. Issue:*
   i. *Samuel,* bp. 27 Feb., 1780.—*N. C. R.*
3. Elijah, b. 31 Mch., 1752; m. Nancy **Deming,** 6 Apl., 1780.—*W. C. R.*
4. Samuel, b. 24, bp. 26 Jan., 1755; d. in Prison Ship in Revol. War.
5. Rebecca, wife of ———; d. Mch., 1779, ae. 50 yr.—*S. W. A.*
6. Rebecca, b. and bp. 3 June, 1759; m. 11 May, 1789, Sion (s. Ezekiel & Mary *Gibbons*) **Wentworth,** of Newington, as his 2d wife; his 1st wife having been Anna Stoddard, b. 11 Jan., 1769; d. 2 Aug., 1780 in Weth.; he was a Revol. soldier, and d. Apl., 1823; *no issue.* Mrs. Rebecca (Boardman) Wentworth, d. 21 Mch., 1814, ae. 55.—*Ch. Rec.*
The genealogy of 5 generations of this family will be found in the *Boardman Genealogy,* pp. 669-684.

LEVI,—one of this name, from Weth., sett. in Suffield, May, 1816; was farmer mcht.; m. a Mrs. **Callender,** of S.; had 8 ch. A dau. *Sarah,* m. Ralph **Little,** mcht. and prominent man of S.

Miscellanea: ELIZABETH, adm. to Sheffield (Mass.) ch. from Weth. ch. 7 July, 1816—*R. H. C.*

BOOSEY, Lieut. JAMES, an early sett. at Weth., of which he was a prominent citizen; and active also in Colon. affairs; rep. to Gen. Ct. fm. 1639 until his dth.; also, in 1644, he was app. by the Gen. Ct. on a comm. with the Gov. Edw'd Hopkins, the Dep. Gov., John Haynes, Capt. John Mason and Mr. John Steele, to treat with Mr. Geo. Fenwick abt. the purchase of the fort, etc., at Saybrook; his earmark for cattle rec. *W. T. V.,* I, p. 3; and fence-tax, 1647,

Ibid. I, 29; was rep. to Gen. Ct. from 1639 until dth. 22 June, 1649; a man of considerable ppy.—See Chapt. VII, Vol. I. Savage (*Gen. Dict. N. E. I*, 211) says his wife Alice ————, m. (2) James **Wakeley** and d. 1683. Lieut. Boosey's will is on rec. in *Htfd. Co. Prob. Off.*, invent. £983-08-00 ment.; his 5 ch. makes his wife sole exec'x, and app. Mr. Welles, brother Nath'l Dickinson and brother Smith, Jr., overseers; Samuel Smith, Sen. and Nath'l Dickinson, witnesses. His will dated 21 June, 1649—he d. 22 June, 1649; gives to his s. Joseph £200 to be pd. to him on coming of age of 20, in lds.; home-lot with barn standing wh. were bo't of Mr. Olcott, wh. was Thomas Sherwood, the younger, all the upland bo't of Robt. Coe; to his s. Joseph £100 in lds.; to his dau. Mary (Steele); to dau. Hannah; to dau. Sarah. He willed all his lds. to his sons Joseph and James, after their mother's dth—Joseph to have all the purchased lds., except 4 acres in the Great Meadow wh. was John Simmons' and Jeremy Jagger; refers to this 4 ac. as in Beaver Meadow; to his s. James he willed his dwelling ho., ho-lot, barns, and houses thereon, with all the ld. wh. was given him by the Town, and then in possession, viz.—12 acs. in Great Meadow, 56 acs. upland and swamp, with 4 acs. in Beaver mead. before named. The excess of value of these lds. above the £300 thus given to the sons, was to be divided proportionately betw. his 5 ch. Its valuation by the appraiser was £400, and the extra £100 was so divided, as per will.—*Ibid.* Vol. 2, 178, 179, 189. The name became extinct in Weth. in the second generation.

Children (*Weth. Rec.*) :

1. Joseph, b. perhaps bef. his father sett. at Weth.; m. Esther ————; res. at Fairfield, 1655; d.* West Chester; his wid. m. Jehu **Burr.**
2. Mary, b. 10 Sept., 1635; m. Lieut. Samuel (s. Mr. John) **Steele** (b. 1626-7), of Far.; dep. from Far. to Gen. Ct. from May, 1669 to May, 1677; afterwards rem. to Weth.,

which town he rep. in Gen. Ct. 1681; d. Weth. 15 Aug., 1685. See *Steele.*
3. Hannah, b. 10 Feb., 1641-2; m. (supp.) John **Pratt.**
4. Sarah, b. 12 Nov., 1643; m. 2 June, 1659, Nath'l **Stanley**; she d. 18 Aug., 1716.
5. James, b. 1 Feb., 1645-6; d. yg.

BOOTH, EUNICE, of Weth. m. Benjamin Mallery, of Stratford, 22 Dec., 1715.— Cotton's *Woodbury.*

SALMON, of Berlin, m. Lois **Wright,** 19 Apl., 1797.

ELISHA, m. Esther Hollister, 5 Dec., 1751.—*N. C. R.*

LYMAN, m. Keziah Andrews, of Burlin, 5 May, 1825.—*N. C. R.*

ROBERT, d. 17 Dec., 1750, ae. 60.—*C. L. C.*

BORELL, HARRY, the ch. of, inf. d. Jan., 1819, in 2d yr.—*S. C. R.*

BURRELL, ABRAHAM, and wife Mary; he b. in 1729, and she in 1730. It is a trad. of the family that they came from Weth., Conn., and afterwards moved

---

* His nuncupative will, "that which was spoken by of Joseph Boosey as his last will before his wife Esther and Josias Gilbert, being in his perfect senses. He gave to his wife Esther, and the s^d Ester to pay out of the est. two oxen to James Wakeling, of Weth., being his free gift to the said Wakeling; they are to be the same oxen that was bo't of James Wakeling by Joseph Boosey upon condition that the said James W., must acquit all accounts between them; and the remainder of the est., in care he left his wife with child, the said Esther is to give his est. to the ch., when the child is of age, provided that all debts that doth appear upon just accounts due be satisfied in the first place. Invent. of lds. and gds. of Joseph Boosey, lately dec'd in Westchester, 24 July, 1655. £504-10-00, taken by Thos. Wheeler. (*Private Controversies,* Vo.l II, 178, Sec'y State's Office.) *Savage* (I, 211), says he had no ch.; res. at Fairfield, 1655, but d. at Westchester, N. Y., and that his wid. m. John **Burr.**

to Sheffield, Mass. Children: *Mary, Jonathan, David, Lois, Arnold, Arnold, Jabez, Rebecca, Samuel, James, Abraham, Sary, Isaac.* Abraham moved to Washington Co., N. Y. and Jonathan rem. to near Little Falls, N. Y.

There is now at Little Falls, N. Y., the firm of D. H. Burrell & Co. said to be the largest house in the cheese manufacture in the world. Stiles' *Anc. Windsor* furnishes two items (pp. 652, 744 Vol. 2) viz.: That Mary (dau. of Col. Charles) **Burrell**, of Canaan, Ct., m. 1793, Timothy Rockwell, and d. 7 Aug., 1794, in 33d yr.; also that Return Strong of Windsor, m. (2) Elizabeth **Burrell**, of Htfd., 19 June, 1700. As Canaan is near Sheffield, Mass., these items may possibly bear some reference to the family of this Abram who rem. from Weth. to Sheffield.

BOSWELL, JAMES, *Savage* credits him to Weth., 1658; d. 24 Dec., 1660, prob. without family.—See Chapt. VII, Vol. I.

BOSTWICK, ELIJAH, of New Canaan, m. Sarah **Bulkeley,** 11 Oct., 1793.—*W. T. R.* This is the Capt. Elijah at whose house in Lebanon, N. Y., Miss Elizabeth Mygatt, a nat. of Weth., d. in 1835, ae. 84.—See *Mygatt.*

BOSWORTH, ISAAC, of Buffalo, N. Y., m. Martha A. **Clark,** of Weth., 20 Apl., 1832.—*N. C. R.*

BOTELL, (*Boutelle*) ELLERLAR, of Meriden, m. Amanda Aurelia **Beckley,** 9 Feb., 1834.

BOWEN (*Bowin*), JOSIAH, m. Susannah (dau. Wm.) **Clarke,** 9 Nov., 1694; was "cast away in a storm as is conjectured," latter end of Oct., or first of Nov., 1703—*Weth. Rec.;* wid. m. Samuel **Curtis.** His invent. taken 3 Dec., 1717, by Moses Crafts and John Howard, amt'd to £40—est. consisted of a piece of ld. in Weth. 6 rods, 3 ft. in length, by 3 rods, lacking 3 ft., in breadth, abutting on a highway E. and ld. of Wm. Clarke, W.; on ld. of Benj. Adams N., and Wm. Clarke, S., * * with a dwelling ho. thereon, also, the following items, an old poor bed and bedstead 8s.; 5 small pewter dishes, old cup, an old porriger, 14s. 6d.; old warming pan and old skillet, 6s.; small iron pot, little iron kettle, 10s.; two small earthen dishes, one broken, 10d; old green rugg, 18s.; 2 old Turkey work cussions [cushions], 7s.; large good chest, 7s.; one small trammel (?); an old frying pan, 6s., 6d, which equals £3-17-10. A sorry list of household goods, indeed! By *Ct. Rec.* of 1 Oct., 1717, upon motion of Joseph King that adm'n be granted on the est. Susannah Curtis "sometime wife of y* s^d Bowen" was cited to appear and show cause why adm^n should not be gr. and Samuel Curtis, "the present husband of s^d Susannah" appeared and took adm^n, 5 Nov., 1717.—*Htfd. Co. Prob. Rec.*

CHARLES, ae. 13, bu. 14 June, 1794.—*W. C. R.*

DANIEL, m. Esther (dau. Rev. Stephen) **Mix.**—*S. W. A.* See Chapt. VII, Vol. I.

BOWERS, a Stepney family. BENAJAH, m. wid. Esther **Benton,** 27 Nov., 1791;—*S. C. R.;* he d. after Sept., 1823, ae. 81. *Children* (*S. C. R.*) : *Lotta* and *Lucinda,* bp. 21 Apl., 1793.

EPHRAIM, (adult) bp. 20 June, 1802; his wife d. 17 Dec., 1834—*S. C. R.;* he d. 1 Apl., 1840, in 63d yr.

Children (*bp. S. C. R.*) :

1. Eunice, bp. 18 Sept., 1803; d. 28 Sept., 1826, in 18th yr.
2. Mary, bp. 2 Aug., 1818.
3. Mercy.
4. Henry, d. at Hebron, Ct., 10 Jan., 1824, in 15th yr.
5. Jason Burrell, bp. 2 Aug., 1818.
6. Esther Maria, bp. 2 Aug., 1818.
7. Ephriam, bp. 2 Aug., 1818; d. 1826, in 12 yr.
8. Otis, bp. 20 Apl., 1806; d. at New Lond., 3 Apl., 1821, in 17th yr.
9. Eunice, bp. 17 Nov., 1822.
10. Rachel, bp. 1 Aug., 1829.
11. Sarah, bp. 2 Aug., 1818.

EPHRAIM, (whether the above is not certain), of Ry-H, m. wid. Hannah **Stevens,** of Glast. 22 Nov., 1835.—*S. C. R.*

EPHRAIM, of Chatham, m. Esther **Benton?** 5 Mch., 1801.—*S. C. R.*

JOHN, of Chatham, m. Hannah **White,** 6 Feb., 1803.

JOHN, (adult, poss. the above), bp. 3 Nov., 1805; had: *Walter* and *Jerusha,* bp. 10 Nov., 1805.—*S. C. R.*

JOHN, bp. 12 JUNE, 1808.—*S. C. R.*

JAMES, bp. 12 June, 1808.—*S. C. R.*

RACHEL, bp. 1 Aug., 1819.—*S. C. R.*

SARAH, m. Joel **Hart,** of Burlington, Ct., 7 Sept., 1820.—*W. T. R.*

WILLIAM, d. N. Y. City, 26 Dec., 1825, in 24th yr.—*S. C. R.;* prob. the Wm. Tyler, s. Ephm., b. 15 Aug., 1802.

BOWMAN, NATHANIEL, d. 1707; will dated 14 Jan., 1706-7, gives all his est. to Samuel Buck, of Weth., "he paying all my debts and funeral exp." Invent. of est. taken by Wm. Goodrich and Philip Alcock, £13-08-06, Sam'l Buck granted admⁿ.—*Htfd. Prob. Rec.*

Of this Nathaniel, the author of the *Boardman Geneal.* says (p. 207, note): "The name of Nathaniel *Bowman* occurs often about this time in Weth. Rec's, and is easily confounded with that of Nathaniel Boreman. The former was considerably the older of the two, and is supposed to have come from Water-town, Mass. He m. Rebecca, dau. of Rev. Henry Smith, of Weth. A Nathaniel Bowman, who d. in Weth. 1707, leaving his small est. to Samuel Buck is con-jectured to have been their son." The fact that Mabel Buck is also one of the witnesses to this will, may possibly hint at some relationship between the Bucks and this Nathaniel Bowman. See, also, Chapter VII, Vol. I, of this Hist. *Savage* (I, 225) says, "Nathaniel, Weth. 1668, prob. s. of Nath'l of Watertown, Mass., important man; in 1669, m. Rebecca (dau. Rev. Henry) **Smith,** who had been divorced from her husband, Lieut. Samuel Smith, of New London, on acc. of his desertion of her.—(See *Smith*). He d. Jan., 1707; *no issue.*

NATHANIEL, m. Ann (dau. John) **Barnard,** of Watertown.—See Chapt. VII, Vol. I, *S. W. A.*

BRACEY, (*Bracie, Brassey, Brasy, Brase*), "Mr." JOHN, d. Weth. 19 Jan., 1708-9, "ae. abt. 70, as thought"—*Weth. Rec.;* was at Weth. early as 26 Apl., 1661, when he sold to Samuel and Pheobe Martin (she being his—Bracies' mother), his interest in the homestead occup. by the said Martins. His mother, the aforesaid Pheobe Martin, was the dau. of William Bisby, or Bigsby, of London, and her father had bo't for her and her ch., by a former marr., this ppy. in Weth. *Savage* says (I, 227), that John Bracie came first from N. Haven, abt. 1647, "where he first, with respect of prefix, sat down" in 164·.

Children:

1. Susannah, bp. 5 Sept., 1647.
2. John, bp. 5 Sept., 1647.

THOMAS, bro. of John above ment., rem. to Hatfield, Mass., before 1678—See Chapt. VII, Vol. I, this hist.; also, Judd's *Hadley*, p. 458, which gives his ch.; he d. 1704.

BRACE, Rev. JOAB, D. D., (s. Zenas & Mary *Skinner*), of W. Htfd.; b. 13 June, 1781; grad. Y. C. 1804; licensed to preach 24 Sept., same yr.; ord. 7 Oct., 1804, over ch. at New.; m. 21 Jan., 1805, Lucy **Collins;** she adm. to New. ch. 1805; and d. 16 Nov., 1854, ae. 72. Rev. Joab Brace resigned his pastorship 16 Jan., 1855, and d. 20 Apl., 1861, at Pittsfield, Mass. For *biog.* see Chapter XVIII, Vol. I.*

Children (New. T. & Ch. Rec.) :

1. Mary Skinner, b. 6 May, bp. 8 June, 1806; m. 11 Mch., 1827, Rev. John **Todd,** of Groton, Mass.—W, T. R. 9 ch.
2. Martha, b. 2 Nov., 1808, bp. 26 Mch., 1809; m. 28 Aug., 1832, Rev. Samuel N. **Sheperd,** of Madison, Ct.; 5 ch.
3. Seth Collins (Rev.), b. 3, bp. 11 Aug., 1811; grad. Y. C. 1832; d. 26 Jan., 1897.
4. Joab (Rev.), b. 16 June, bp. 7 Aug., 1814; grad. Y. C. 1837; sett. at Lanesboro, Mass.,
   where he d. 1 Sept., 1845, ae. 31; m. Elizabeth J. **Watson,** of Pittsfield.
5. Samuel (Rev.), b. 24 Feb., bp. 25 May, 1817; grad. Y. C. 1841, and was tutor there m. (N. C. R.) Sarah R. **North,** of New Britain. Ct., 19 Aug., 1847 (dau. of Alvin North).
6. John Whitman, b. 9 Feb., bp. 29 Aug., 1824; d. 2 Jan., 1846, ae. 21½ yrs.

JOAB, Rev. E., bro. of Rev. Dr. Joab, d. 22 Sept., 1846, ae. 31; bu. at Lanesboro, Mass.

BRADDOCK, JOHN, m. Emily Wells, Jr., 22 Apl., 1819.

BRADFORD, WILLIAM, d. 21 Sept., 1824, ae. 65 (tombstone says 64); his wid. Elizabeth, d. 13 Oct., 1828, in 71st yr.—(S. Ch. Rec.)

Children (Weth. S Juror & S. Ch. Rec.)

1. William, bp. 26 Sept., 1784.
2. George, bp. 28 Mch., 1790; d. Fayetteville, N. C., 30 Sept., 1846.—Weth. (S.) Inscr. says, ae. 58.
3. Horace, bp. 27 Oct., 1793; d. Fayetteville,
   N. C., 27 Jan., 1827, ae. 36.
4. Fanny, bp. 8 Nov., 1795.
5. Charlotte, bp. 30 July, 1797.
6. Sophia, bp. 18 Oct., 1801; m. Chas. H. **Hill;** d. N. Y., 24 Feb., 1841.

NANCY, wife of Sylvester **Bulkley,** d. 21 Oct., 1872, ae. 86.—(Weth. (S) Inscr.)

JAMES, b. at Sheffield, Mass., 2 July, 1817; he a lawyer; m. Mary A. **Hale,** of Weth. He was a desc'dt of Gov. Wm. Bradford—and had 3 ch.—R. H. C.

BRADLEY, CHARLES, of Plymouth, Ct., m. Caroline **Smith,** of Htfd., 4 May, 1829.—S. C. R.

DANIEL, m. Sarah **Judd,** 20 Nov., 1751.—N.

NATH'L, m. Dorothy **Ashley,** of Worthington, 1 June,1775.—N.

WM., of Htfd., m. Julia **Montague,** 23 Dec., 1813.—W. C. R.

---

* Mr. Brace's published works were:
1. *War Inconsistent with the Gospel of Christ,* and destructive of human happiness. Address delivered before the Peace Society, at their semi-annual meeting in West Hartford, Sept. 12, 1820, Hartford, 1829, 8 vo., pp. 20.
2. *Half-Century Discourse.* History of the Church in Newington, Its Ministers, Its Doctrines, Its Experience; presented in the Discourse delivered on Tuesday, the 16th of January, 1855, on his relinquishment of active service at the close of half-century from his ordination in that place. Hartford, 1855, 8 vo., pp. 75.
3. *Account of a Revival of Religion in Newington.*—See *Christian Spectator,* May, 1822.
Mr. Brace's ordination Sermon was preached by Rev. Nathan Perkins, of West Hartford, and was published with the title, "*The Character of a faithful minister of the Gospel delineated,*" in a Discourse delivered January 16, 1805, at the ordination of the Rev. Joab Brace to the work of the Christian ministry over the church and congregation in Newington, a parish in Weth. By Nathan Perkins, D. D., Hartford, 1807, 8 vo., pp. 23.
The sermon preached by Rev. John Todd, at Dr. Brace's funeral, was published in the *National Preacher,* October, 1861.

ISAAC, m. Mary **Larkin**, 26 Aug., 1832.—*W. T. R.*

IRA, of Northampton, m. Emily **Woodhouse**, 31 Dec., 1810.—*W. C. R.*

JOHN, a son, ae. 10 yr., d. 3 Oct., 1789.—*W. C. R.*

BRAINARD, Mary A., of Ry-H., m. Ethel **Sanger**, of New Br., 17 Apr., 1836.—
W. T. R.

EDWARD, d. ae. 5, 3 Dec., 1846.—*N. C. R.*

EZRA, of E. Htfd., m. Lovisa **Robbins**, 14 May, 1809.—*W. C. R.*

BRAMAN Henry I., of Newport, m. Melinde M. **Curtis**, of Weth. 13 Apl., 1829.—
N. C. R.

BRANDEGEE, (*Brundig, Brandig, Brandish, Brandiger, Brondiger, Brandigat, Brandisley, Brondish, Boundikee,*), are various spellings of a name found in old records, and all of which seem to connect with and apply to one JOHN BRUNDISH, who was at Weth. prob. as early as 1635-7, and of whom only one record exists, and that incidentally, in *Weth. Land Recs.* as being the owner of a home-lot which bounded another man's ppy.—See Chapt. VII, Vol. I. These various spellings of the name, as given above, together with the fact that some of the earlier generations resided in the neighborhood of New York City, (Westchester and Duchess Cos.), has given rise to the very natural opinion that the family was of Dutch origin. But this opinion is controverted by Mr. Marius Brandegee, of Elizabeth, N. J., who considers it to be of English stock, in which view we also concur. It will also be noted that the terminal of the name is spelled variously—dage, digge, dyge, by members of the same stock; and that all the spellings contain the same consonants, B. R. N. D., with the first vowel O. U. or A. rather broad, and the terminal S. H. or G. E., indicating that the G. should be pronounced *soft* and not hard, as the G. in geese.

As to the John Brundish, the acknowledged ancestor of this race, he had died before the 27 Oct., 1639, which is the date of the inventory of his estate, leaving a widow (Rachel) and five children. Judge ADAMS, in endeavoring to identify the Wethersfield men who were killed by the Indians in the Massacre of 1637, suggests, with some degree of probability that Brundish may have been one of the number; but owing to the loss of the Weth. records for those first early years, one may never know whether this conjuncture is correct. Savage, in his *Geneal. Dict. of New Eng.*, mentions (p. 284) John *Brundish*, and (p. 218) John *Brandisley*, with an evident suspicion that the two were identical, as he gives exactly the same information concerning each of them. viz., that he prob. came to Weth. from Watertown, Mass., where he was made freeman in 1639, and that his widow, Rachel, m. (2) Anthony **Wilson**, of Fairfield, [or Stamford?] Ct.; also, that by B. she had 5 children, 4 daus. and a son. *Weth. Rec.* also shows that she sold the ho-std. to Elder Clement Chaplin, before 1 May, 1641, and, with that, the name disappears from the town for awhile.

We seem to pick up the interrupted trail of the family again, in John, (one of eleven settlers from Greenwich, Ct., 1660, of the town of Rye, in Winchester Co., N. Y.,), who signs his name, July 26, 1662, to a declaration of loyalty to Charles II, as *Brondish*, being one of three of the eleven who did not sign their names with a mark. In Jan., 1663, he signed his name *Brondig*. He was elected first Town Clerk of Rye, was deputy to the Gen. Ct. in 1677 and 1681, and d. 1697, and in the accounts of those days was called "Stout Old

John Brondig." He was one in 1662 of the original pprs. of Manusing Island and Poringoe Neck in Westchester Co., and left four sons, *John, Joseph, David and Joshua*, of whom Joseph and *David* are held (by family trad.) to be the ancestors of the families since bearing the name in that county. One account says that a *Jonathan* was one of these bros.—See Boltin's *His. of Westchester, N. Y.*, II. 713, and Meade's *Hist. of Greenwich, Ct.*, 306.

Of the descendants of DAVID, the above mentioned son of John, of Rye, we learn this much from a letter of the Rev. Abner Brandagee, of Brookfield, Ct., written in 1842. In this he says, "The name of my great-gd. father was *David* He had 2 bros. of whom I have heard my father speak, *Jacob and Joseph;* but where the desc'ts of Jacob were or whether he had any, I know not. *Joseph's* desc'ts are somewhat numerous and dispersed throughout Duchess and Westchester Co's , N. Y. Some are in the city of N. Y., of good standing as brokers and merchants.

"The desc't's of my gt-gd-father *David* are also numerous, tho' I believe my gd-father *James*, was the only son, b. 3 May, 1734. On setting out in life he rem. from Nine Partners, Duchess Co., N. Y., to Bedford, Westchester Co., N. Y., where my father, *Israel*, was born; a few years after, he and his wife Phebe **Seamons,** moved back again to Nine Partners, where the rest of the family were born, viz., Zebulon, James, Reuben, (who was a physician and afterwards a clergy-man), Sarah, Elizabeth, Stephen, Phebe, Abraham, Nancy. Of these were liv-ing in 1842, only Abraham, res. in Western N. Y.; Phebe, res. nr. Catskill, N. Y.; and Nancy, res. Caldwell, N. J. The younger generations were dispersed in New York, Penn., New Jersey. 'Unexpectedly to myself,' says the narrator, I was providentially called back to Duchess and Westchester Counties, the vicinity of my ancestors, where I spent 5 yrs. of my ministry, and thence, 20 yrs. ago this mo. I came to this place." *Israel*, his father, as also his uncles James and Stephen, lived and d. in Essex Co., N. J.

The re-instatement, in the town of original settlement (viz. Wethersfield), of the family of Brondish, (under the changed form of the name—*Brandegee*), seems to have been through the coming hither, abt. the middle of the 18th Century, of one Jacob *Brandigot*. Whether he was a son of the John, or of Jonathan,* both sons of "Stout Old John," of Rye, N. Y., and both of whom sold out their rights at Rye, abt. 1726 and rem. prob. to Nine Partners, as many other Rye families did, is as yet an undetermined matter. We lean how-ever to the idea that he was a son of John—consequently John 3rd. But, a Jacob it was who, according to a firm family trad., *ran away* from his father's family, and curiously enough found his life-work in Stepney, a parish of the same old Conn. town where his first American ancestor was buried a hundred yrs. before. According to Andrews, (*Hist. New Britain, Ct.*, 130), he came to New Britian from Nine Partners, (Dutchess Co), N. Y., when 13 yrs. old. He is said to have been b. 1729; and his mother's name was Brock. [If it was *Buck*, which is an old Weth. name, it may in some way account for his heading this way, in leaving his N. Y. home]; he was by trade, a weaver, and, at one time kept a store in Great Swamp Village, now Kensington. He m. at Newington, Ct., 11 Oct., 1753, Abigail Dunnum (Dunham)—*Annals of Newington*, 106, and from the same authority we learn that he owned the Covenant, at Kensington, 27 July, 1755, being then called *Brandigee*. He was in later life, engaged in the W. I. trade, sailing his vessels from Rocky Hill, and d. at sea on a return voyage from Guadeloupe, Mch., 26, 1763. His wid. m. (2) Rev. Edward Eells, of Upper Midd., (*Cromwell, Ct.*,) she d. 25 Jan., 1825.

---

* And both of whom sold out their rights at Rye, abt. 1726, and rem. prob. inland to Nine Partners, as many other Rye families did.

JACOB,⁴ (John,³(?) John,² John,¹), m. Abigail **Dunham**, and d. 1763, as above stated.

Children (Kensington Recs.):

1. Elishama, b. 17 Apl., 1754. FAM. 2.
2. Rhoda, b. 5 Oct., 1756, bp. 2 Jan., 1757.
3. Persis, b. 31 Aug., 1758; d. 3 Aug., 1845, at Silver Creek, Chatauqua Co., N. Y.; m. 20 Aug., 1782, Rev. Charles (s. of Capt. Azel & Kezia *Woodruff*) **Brace** (incorrectly given as Beard in *Early Conn. Marriages*), of Hartland, Ct., who was b. 4 May, 1764, and d. 3 Apl., 1832, and is bu. at So. Winfield, Herkimer Co., N. Y., to which place they rem. 1793. *Issue:*
   i. Nancy (Brace), m. Asa **Gage**, of Winfield, N. Y. and had 7 ch., of whom the 3d Persis Brandegee (Gage) m. Wm. D. **Talcott**, and had 8 ch.; and the 4th Nancy (Gage) m. a **Roll**, and whose dau. Ellen (Roll) m. a Brace—and their ch. is Charles Talcott of Richmond Hill, L. I.
   ii. Persis (Brace), m. Fred. (?) **Avery**.
   iii. Polly (Brace), m. Abraham **Woodruff**; s. p.

   iv. Lavinia (Brace), m. John **Hewett**; had:
     (a) Candace; (b) Harriet, and (c) Jane.
   v. Sally (Brace), m. 1815, Loring **Chapin**, of Silver Creek, Chat. Co., N. Y., had *issue:*
     (a) Woodruff (Chapin); (b) Dr. Marvin (Chapin); whose dau. Ellen Persis, m. Edw'd **Browne**; res. Chicago, Ill.; (c) Charles (Chapin); (d) Persis Brandegee (Chapin), d. ae. 18; (e) Alice (Chapin).
   vi. Candace (Brace), m. Samuel **Angell**; had dau. Jennie (Angell); res. Coopertown, N. Y.
4. Abigail, b. 31 Aug., 1760; d. 26 Sept., 1823; m. Timothy **Hart**, 13 Nov., 1781.— (*Early Conn. Marriages.*)
5. Mary, b. 18 Dec., 1763; d. Dec., 1764.
6. Jacob, b. 4 Jan., 1765.

FAM. 2. ELISHAMA,⁵ (Jacob,⁴ John,³ John,² John,¹), b. 1754; m. Mrs. Lucy (dau. of Samuel & Patience Ward *Plumb*, and wid of Jeremiah) **Weston**, 10 Mch., 1778. She d. 1 Feb., 1827; he d. 26 Feb., 1832.

Children (b. at Berlin Ct.):

1. Jacob, b. 11 Nov., 1779. FAM. 3.
2. Lucy, b. 15 July, 1781; m. Sept., 1824, Giles **Curtis**, of Meriden, Ct., who d. Jan. 10, 1842; *S. P.*; she d. 9 Aug., 1855.
3. Elishama, b. 5 Nov., 1784. FAM. 4.
4. John, b. 19 Nov., 1786. FAM. 5.
5. Sally Milnor, b. 2 Aug., 1793; d. 14 Nov., 1809, unm.

FAM. 3. JACOB,⁶ (Elishama,⁵ Jacob,⁴ John,³ John,² John,¹), b. 1779; m. April, 1824, Jeanette Caroline **Chastant**; d. in New Orleans, 14 Aug., 1808, and she d. 19 July, 1882. He d. 20 Feb. 1849.

Children:

1. Henriette Marie, b. N. O., 4 Apl., 1825; m. 30 June, 1851, Wynant **Van Zandt**, of N. Y. City; she d. 27 July, 1886, Wichita, Kans. *Issue:*
   i. Camillus Wynant (Van Zandt), b. Belleville, N. J., 13 June, 1852; d. Bath Beach, N. J., 16 July, 1892, bu. Avondale, N. J., unm.
   ii. Elodie Odile (Van Zandt), b. N. Y. City, 18 June, ——; m. 25 Dec., 1885, Monroe **Wheeler**, of Avondale, N. J., who d. 2 July, 1897; their s. Stephen (Van Zandt), b. 1886, res. Wichita, Kans.; Mrs. Henrietta M. Van Zandt d. at W. 27 July, 1886.
2. Clothilde Caroline Angeline, b. 3 May, 1827, in N. Y. City; m. Harry **Lloyd**, of Lloyd's Manor, Lloyd's Neck, L. I., 8 May, 1848; she d. 12 Mch., 1886, N. Y. City. *Issue:*
   i. John Henry (Lloyd), b. 31 Jan., 1849, in N. Y. City, d. N. Y. City, 10 Nov., 1886.
   ii. John Nelson (Lloyd), b. 2 Nov., 1855 at Lloyd's Manor, d. 10 Aug., 1856.
3. Adelaide Madeleine Odile, b. 13 Mch., 1830, at Norwalk, Ct.; m. Andrew Stelle **Hamersby**, of N. Y. City, 24 Jan., 1853; she d. 1 Feb., 1871, Norwalk, Ct. *Issue:*
   i. Andrew Stelle (Hamersby), b. 20

Nov., d. Dec., 1853.
   ii. Odile (Hamersby), b. 27 June, 1860; m. 7 Dec., 1881, Herbert Melville **Southwick**, of New Baltimore, Md. *Issue:*
     i. Andrew Worthington (Southwick), b. 26 Dec., 1882, at Bayonne, N. J.
     ii. John Hamersby (Southwick), b. N. Y. City, 21 July, 1885.
     iii. Wm. Livingston (Southwick), b. 28 Jan., ——, d. 15 Jan., 1894, in N. Y. City.
4. Elodie Celeste Agnes, b. 8 May., 1833, and d. N. Y. City, 3 Nov., 1843.
5. John Camillus, b. 31 July, 1836; d. 14 Dec., 1886. FAM. 6.
6. Marie Stephanie Aloysia, b. 21 Aug., 1839, in N. Y. City; m. 20 Dec., 1856, Harvey **Sparks**, of San Francisco, Cal., b. 30 Oct., 1830; d. May, 1889. *Issue:*
   i. Eugenie Stephanie Caroline (Sparks), b. Paris, France, 13 Feb., 1857.*
   ii. Elodie Floyd (Sparks), b. N. Y. City, 2 Nov., 1858.
   iii. Harvey Brandegee (Sparks), b. 15 July, 1860, at West Point, N. Y.; m. 1889, Henrietta W. **Pinkney** (dau. of William); she d. 26 Dec., 1891; had Harvey Pinkney, b. 10 Dec., 1891; d. 6 Mch., 1893.

---

* Eugenie Stephanie Caroline Sparks, m. N. Y. City, 30 Oct., 1885, John Henry Dorrity, who d. 31 Dec., 1899. *Issue:* i. Elodie Floyd (Sparks), m. Edward L. Deslonde, N. Y. City, 16 Oct., 1889; has (a) Stephanie Brandegee (Deslonde), b. 12 July, 1890; d. 28 Oct., 1892; (b) Edward Darrington (Deslonde), b. 4 July, 1892; (c) Orville Chastant (Deslonde), b. 20 Mch., 1894; (d) Camillus Brandegee (Deslonde), b. 22 Jan., 1897; (e) Eugenie Celeste (Deslonde), b. 3 Apl., 1900.

FAM. 4. ELISHAMA,[6] (*Elishama,*[5] *Jacob,*[4] *John,*[3] *John,*[2] *John,*[1]), b. 1784; m. 14 Oct., 1811, Emily **Stocking,** who was b. 1793, and d. 7 June, 1833; he m. (2) 28 Nov., 1833, Anna Booth **Mygatt,** b. 8. Mch., 1798, and d. 3 Aug., 1836.

Children:

1. Jacob Sheldon, b. 9 Sept., 1812; m. Sarah M. **Hinsdale,** of Berlin, Ct., 15 May, 1839; he d. 4 Aug., 1851; his wid. m. ——— **Sample,** and d. in Keokuk, Ill.
2. Elishama, b. 14 Jan., 1814. FAM. 7.
3. John, b. 25 Aug., 1816. FAM. 8.
4. Camillus Marius, b. 26 Apl., 1820; d. 5 May, 1821.
5. Marius, b. 8 Mch., 1823. FAM. 9.
6. Henry Justus, b. 29 July, 1831; m. 11 Mch., 1858, Sarah Kipp **Miller;** d. 7 Oct., 1861; *s. p.;* wid. res. Brooklyn, N. Y.
7. Sarah Elizabeth, b. 24 May, 1833; res. Farmington, Ct.; m. 10 Apl., 1858, Danford Newton **Barney,** of N. Y. City. *Issue:*
   i. Danford Newton (Barney), b. 10 Jan., 1859; res. Far., Ct.; m. 22 May, 1890

Laura B. (dau. Austin C. & Lucy *Root*) **Dunham,** of Htfd. *Issue:*
   (*a*) Mary Elizabeth (Dunham), b. 12 June, 1891.
   (*b*) Danford Newton (Dunham), b. 21 July, 1892.
   (*c*) Laura Jennette (Dunham), b. 17 Mch., 1895, d. 21 Apl., 1900.
   (*d*) Austin Cornelius (Dunham), b. 7 Nov., 1896.
   (*e*) Sarah Brandegee (Dunham), b. 11 Apl., 1901.
   (*By second marriage*):
8. Julia Maria, b. 28 Oct., 1836; res. Farmington, Ct.
9. Anna, b. ———, d. 3 Aug., 1838.

FAM. 5. JOHN,[6] (*Elishama,*[5] *Jacob,*[4] *John,*[3] *John,*[2] *John,*[1]), b. 1786; m. (1) Mary Ann (dau. Daniel & his wife Sarah *Packwood*) **Deshon,** of New London, Ct., b. 3., 1800, and d. 31 July, 1853; m. (2) Sarah (dau. Dr.) **De Camp,** of Saratoga Spgs., N. Y.

Children:

1. ———, b. 12, and d. 14 ———, 1822.
2. John Jacob, b. 15 July, 1823, at N. Lond. FAM. 10.
3. Frank Deshon, b. 12 Oct., 1826, at N. Lond., d. 4 Sept., 1853, unm.
4. Mary Jane, b. 27 Feb., 1825, at N. Lond.; m. 5 Oct., 1843, Theo. T. (s. James & Eliza Halstead *Meeker*) **Wood,** of Morristown, N. J. *Issue:*
   i. John Brandegee (Wood), b. 25 June, 1844; res. at Riverside, Cal.; m. 20 Aug., 1874, Sarah (dau. of Rutger B. & Mary *Seymour*) **Miller,** of Utica, N. Y., who d. 3 Mch., 1896. *Issue:*
      i. Mary Brandegee, who d. 3 Mch., 1896, at Utica, N. Y.
   ii. Clement (Wood), b. 3 Mch., 1846; d. same yr.
   iii. Theodore Talbot (Wood), b. 20 Feb., 1847; m. 1874, Helen **Bryant,** c. Mendham, N. J.; he d. 9 Jan., 1886; *s. p.;* wid. res. Dresden, Ger.
   iv. Mary Deshon (Wood), b. 3 May, 1851; m. 23 June, 1876, Fred'k Getman **Fincke,** of Utica, N. Y.; she d.

19 Nov., 1901, Buffalo, N. Y. *Issue:*
   i. Frances Amelia (Fincke), b. 12 June, 187—; m. B. Leonard **Hand,** of Albany, N. Y., 1902.
   ii. Reginald (Fincke), b. 26 Nov., 1878.
   v. Frank Deshon Brandegee (Fincke), b. 10 Apl., 1853; d. 17 Nov., 1857.
   vi. Augustus Brandegee (Fincke), b. 4 July, 1854; d. 31 Aug., 1900; unm.
   vii. Walter Brandegee (Fincke), b. 7 Jan., 1857; res. Pasadena, Cal.; unm.
   viii. William Meeker (Fincke), b. 3 Aug., 1858; m. 8 Nov., 1893, Grace **Mosher,** of N. Y. City; he d. Paris, France, 29 May, 1900.
   ix. Sarah DeCamp (Fincke) b. 27 Jan., d. 30 July, 1861.
   x. Clarence Brandegee (Fincke), b. 9 July, 1863; m. 20 Apl., 1900, Mary Alston **Channing;** no ch.
5. Augustus, b. 12 July, 1826, at N. Lond. FAM. 11.
6. William Edward, b. 23 Dec., 1829; d. 27 Feb., 1830.
7. Helen, b. 7 Dec., 1832; d. 4 Oct., 1834.

FAM. 6. JOHN CAMILLUS,[7] (*Jacob,*[6] *Elishama,*[5] *Jacob,*[4] *John,*[3] *John,*[2] *John,*[1]), b. 1836; m. Harriet Hanks **Coffee,** of Astoria, L. I., 25 Apl., 1872; she d. 12 July, 1894, at Lloyd's Neck, L. I. He d. Brooklyn, N. Y., 14 Dec., 1886.

Children (b. Astoria, L. I.):

1. William Camillus, b. 30 Mch., 1873; d. 24 May, 1902, unm.
2. Coralie Chastant, b. 29 Dec., 1874; m. Nov., 1896, Clarence Barclay **Ward,** of

Huntington, L. I.
3. Adele Rosine, b. 19 Feb., 1881, in Huntington, L. I.

FAM. 7. ELISHAMA,[7] (*Elishama,*[6] *Elishama,*[5] *Jacob,*[4] *John,*[3] *John,*[2] *John,*[1]), b. 1814; m. 26 Apl., 1841, Florence (dau. Maj. Townsend & Katherine *Potter*) **Stith,** of Petersburg, Va., she was b. at Florence, Italy, 8 Nov., 1822, and d. at Berlin, Ct., 26 Dec., 1901.

Children:

1. Dau. b. and d. 14 Feb., 1842.
2. Townshend Stith, b. 26 Feb., 1843 ; m. Mary K. **Curran** (*nee Layne*), 30 May, 1889 ; res. at San Diego, S. Cal.
3. Charles, b. 12 Dec., 1845 ; m. Mabel (dau. John G. & Augusta L. *Warner*) **Daggett,** of Summerville, Mass. ; have a dau. Hilda, b. 12 Apl., 1887.
4. Florence Stith, b. 1 Jan., 1845 ; res. Berlin, Ct., unm.
5. Robert Bolling, b. 4 Apl., 1849. **Fam.** 12.
6. Emily Stocking, b. 6 Apl., 1851 ; res.

Berlin, Ct., unm.
7. Katharine, b. 3 June, 1853 ; res. Berlin, Ct., unm.
8. Henry Melville, b. 31 May, 1855 , d. 28 June, 1893, in Helena, Montana, unm.
9. Edith Victorina, b. 4 Sept., 1857 ; d. 22 Nov., 1863.
10. Horace Stocking, b. 13 Sept., 1859 ; d. 29 Mch., 1864.
11. Arthur Latimer, b. 23 Aug., 1862 ; res. Berlin, Ct., unm.
12. Edward Newton, b. 28 Mch., 1865. **Fam.** 13.

Fam. 9. MARIUS,[7] (*Elishama,*[6] *Elishama,*[5] *Jacob,*[4] *John,*[3] *John,*[2] *John,*[1]), b. 1823 ; m. Mary Ann **Bulkeley,** of Berlin, Ct., (dau. of Sylvester & wife Mary *Johnson*), 13 Nov., 1845. He d. 6 June, 1881.

Children:

1. Mary Emily, b. 15 Sept., 1846 ; d. 23 June, 1863.
2. William Sylvester, b. 16 Dec., 1858 ; m. 16 July, 1884, Elizabeth (dau. James & Eliza) **Reed,** of Newington, Ct. *Issue:*

i. Mary Elizabeth (Brandegee), b. 23 July, 1887.
ii. Marjorie (Brandegee), b. 1 June, 1889.
iii. Frank Augustus (Brandegee), b. 16 Aug., 1890.

Fam. 9. MARIUS,[7] (*Elishama,*[6] *Elishama,*[5] *Jacob,*[4] *John,*[3] *John,*[2] *John,*[1]), b. 1823 ; m. 22 Nov., 1847, Catharine Amelia **Fountain,** of N. Y. City.

Children:

1. Emily Stocking, b. 7 Sept., 1848 ; d. 12 July, 1849.
2. Elizabeth Gaulladette, b. 17 Apl., 1850.
3. William Partridge, b. 16 Apl., 1864 ; m. Caroline **Morris,** of N. J., 27 Dec., 1888. Res. N. Y. City. *Issue:*

i. Ruth Morris (Brandegee), b. 16 Oct., 1889.
ii. Morris Marius (Brandegee), b. 3 Sept., 1892.
iii. Wm. Partridge (Brandegee), b. 11 June, 1894.

Fam. 10. JOHN JACOB,[7] (*John,*[6] *Elishama,*[5] *Jacob,*[4] *John,*[3] *John,*[2] *John,*[1]), b. 1823 ; m. Martina Louisa (dau. of Lewis & Martina *Elmendorf*) **Condit,** on Morristown, N. J., b. 8 Feb., 1826, who is living 1903.

Children:

1. John Elmendorf, b. 9 July, 1853, in Litchfield, Ct. ; lawyer (Miller, Fincke & Brandegee), Utica, N. Y.
2. Lewis Condit, b. 25 Nov., 1855, at Utica, N. Y. ; d. 29 Nov., 1873, at Htfd., Ct., unm.
3. Edward Deshon, b. 10 Oct., 1857 ; res. Utica, N. Y. ; unm.
4. Martina Elmendorf, b. 18 Oct., 1861 ; res. Utica, N. Y. ; unm.

Fam. 11. AUGUSTUS,[7] (*John,*[6] *Elishama,*[5] *Jacob,*[4] *John,*[3] *John,*[2] *John,*[9]), b. 1826 ; m. 5 Sept., 1854, Nancy Christine (dau. Wm. Chapman & Mary Eliza *Platner*) **Bosworth,** of Lee, Mass., who d. 27 Mch., 1881.

Children (b. at New London, Ct.) :

1. Augustus, b. 17 July, 1855 ; m. wid. of Ferris **Duglass,** of New Lond., Ct.
2. Helen, b. 9 May, 1858 ; m. 24 Sept., 1890, Moses Gray **Zabriski,** U. S. A. ; have i. Augustus Brandegee (Zabriski), b. 13 Aug., 1896 ; d. 4 June, 1897 ; she
res. New Lond.
3. Frank Bosworth, b. 8 July, 1864 ; res. New London, unm.
4. Marian Christina, b. 18 Aug., 1866, at New Lond., d. 11 Oct., 1884 ; unm.

Fam 12. ROBERT BOLLING,[8] (*Elishama,*[7] *Elishama,*[6] *Elishama,*[5] *Jacob,*[4] *John,*[3] *John,*[2] *John,*[1]) b. 1849 ; m. 17 Mch., 1898, Susan (dau. Joseph & Lucy *Meech*) **Lord,** of Northampton, Mass.

Child:

1. Robert Lord, b. 31 Dec., 1898.

Fam. 13. EDWARD NEWTON,[8] (*Elishama,*[7] *Elishama,*[6] *Elishama,*[5] *Jacob,*[4] *John,* *John,*[2] *John,*[1]), m. 26 Oct., 1899, in Helena, Mon., Harriet R. (dau. Francis & Hannah) **Pope,** of Helena.

Child :

1. Florence Pope, b. 30 Oct., 1902.

BRANDISLY, *Savage* (I, 238) ment. a JOHN of this name, who was of Watertown, perhaps; a freeman 4 Mch., 1635; rem. early to Weth.; d. 1639, leaving wid. Rachel, who. m. Anthony **Wilson,** of Fairfield, Ct., and 1 son and 4 daus. —See *Brandegee* and *Brundish.*

BRATTLE, WILLIAM, m. (*Weth. Rec.*), Mary **Wright,** 21 Sept., 1743, who d. in Pittsfield, Mass., May, 1802, ae. 90; she was adm. to P. ch. 1764. This William is ment. by the author of *Descendants of Capt. Thomas Brattle,* as being one of the three only distinct B. families in New Eng., (the other two being of Boston), but adds nothing to our knowledge of him, beyond what is here given. The fam. prob. rem. fm. Weth. to P. between 1755 and '64; he is found on the P. town-list of 1772.

Children (Weth. Rec.) ; items starred * furnished from *Pittsfield Record.*

1. Sarah, b. 11 July, 1744 ; m. 1780, Jacob **Ward; was** adm. to P. ch., 1766.
2. William, b. 29 Aug., bp. 1 Sept., 1745. FAM.
3. Elizabeth, b. 13 Jan., 1746-7 ; m. 1787, Uriah **Judd.***
4. Mary, b. 25, bp. 31 July, 1748 ; m. Oswald **Williams.***
5. John,* b. 11, bp. 10 Aug., 1779, gravestone at P. says d. 15 Dec., 1832, ae. 82.
6. James (Dea.), b. 23 Nov., 1751 ; d. 8. May,

1803 in 53d yr. (gravestone at Pittsfield, Mass.), *Town Rec.* says May 10, and 51 yr. ; his wid. Edith, poss. a 2d wife, d. 6 Oct., 1803, in 44th yr. ; she adm. to P. ch. 1786 ; he in 1778.*
7. Martha, b. 22 Feb., 1753 ; m. Stoddard **Williams.***
8. Anne, o. 15 Aug., 1755 ; m. 1777, Sol. **Butler;*** she, then a res'd of Benson, Vt. ; m. (2) 15 June, 1822, Jacob **Ward,** of Pittsfield, Mass.—*R-H. C.*

FAM. 2. WILLIAM,[2] (*William,*[1]), b. 1745 at Weth.; m. (1) Abigail (dau. Nath'l & Judith) **Fairfield,**—marr. pub. 8 Oct., 1774; she bp. at P. 17 Aug., 1766; she d. 1778; he m. (2) Lucy **Leffingwell,** of Lenox, Mass., b. 1765; mar. pub. 17 Aug., 1787; she d. 26 Feb., 1791; he m. (3) at Weth., 5 Feb., 1793,— *W. T. R.,* Hannah **Welles,** of Killingworth—who was adm. to ch. at P. 1832.

Children (by third wife):

1. ————, b. 18, d. 20 Oct., 1793.
2. Welles, b. 16 June, 1795 ; rem. West abt. 1850.
3. Julia, b. 22 Sept., 1797 ; m. A. **Burbank,** of Htfd., Ct. ; adm. to Ch. 1821.
4. Maria, b. 22 Feb., 1800 ; m. Benedict **Clark;** res. Saratoga, N. Y.

5. Charles, b. 30 Jan., 1805 ; d. unm., Pittsfield.
6. Ch., d. 25 July, 1788, ae. 3 wks.
7. Ch., d. 1790.
We are indebted to ROLLIN H. COOK, Esq., of Pittsfield, Mass., for the Pittsfield data concerning this family.)

BREWER, THOMAS, came from Midd. (acc. to *Glast. Centenn.*) to Glast. parish, and was rejected as an inhab. by the Town's Vote of Dec. 25, 1682, but said vote was cancelled (apparently the same day and session), and in Mch., 1676, was chosen fence-viewer, also, in 1697; and 13 Feb., 1690-1, was one of petitioners for a new church on E. side the Gt. River. He m. Sarah ————, of Glast., 13 Jan., 1682.

Children:

1. Mary, b. 28 Jan., 1685.
2. Thomas, b. 17 Feb., 1687 ; m. Martha **Goodale,** of Midd., 4 May, 1710.
3. Hezekiah, b. 23 Feb., 1690 ; m. Eunice ————, 1757.
4. Sarah, b. 9 Dec., 1692 ; m. Ebenezer **Goodale,** Midd., 15 Mch., 1717.
5. Joseph, b. 20 Mch., 1695 ; m. Dinah

Smith, 29 May, 1727.
6. Benjamin, b. 13 Aug., 1697.
7. Daniel, b. 25 Mch., 1699 ; m. Eleanor **Goodrich,** Midd., 1719.
8. Lydia, b. 27 July, 1701.
9. Nome (*sic.*), b. 28 Sept., 1703.
10. Elexsander (*sic.*), b. 5 Oct., 1706.

JOHN, of E. Htfd., m. Hannah **Curtis,** 22 Oct., 1799.

An "aged Mrs. BREWER," d. 21 May, 1787.—*S. C. R.*

BREWSTER, ELIJAH, Jr., of Midd., m. Margaret **Curtis,** 16 Apl., 1777.

BRIGDEN, THOMAS, yeoman, fm. Faversham, Co. Kent, Eng., embarked fm. Sandwich, in slp. *Hercules,* for New Eng., in 1634, with wife Thomasin and two ch., viz.: *Sarah* and *Thomas,* Jr., (Fam. 2), and his wife Mildred. They sett. at Charlestown, Mass., where he d. 20 June, 1668, and his wife Thomasin d. 12 Mch., 1669. A third ch. (Rev.) Zachariah, was b. to them 2 Aug., 1639.

FAM. 2. THOMAS,[2] (*Thomas,*[1]), m. Mildred (only dau. of Michael) **Cartrick** (?), of Ispwich. He d. at C. 24 July, 1683; wife Mildred d. July, 1726, ae. 96 yrs., at Charlestown, Mass.

Children:

1. Sarah, b. 3 Jan., 1656.
2. Zachariah, b. 1658.
3. Thomas, b. 1660. FAM. 3.
4. John, b. 1661.

5. Michael, b. 2 June, 1664. FAM. 4.
6. Nathaniel, b. 1666.
7. Timothy, b. 1670.
8. Elias, b. 1672.

FAM. 3. THOMAS,[3] (*Thos.,*[2] *Thos.,*[1]), b. 16 Sept., 1703; m. (1) 16 Feb., 1726, Grace **Livermore;** who d. 26 Jan., 1767, in 62d yr.—*Weth. Ins;* m. (2) Martha, (supp. to have been wid. of Thos.) **Boardman,** of Weth., 24 Mch., 1768. He d. 4 Feb., 1781, ae. 78.—*W. C. R. and Weth. Ins.* The *Boardman Geneal.* says, he left her all the est. she had at time of marr. and the No. half of his ho. on E. side of High St. formerly that of Mr. Chas. Bulkley. She d. 21 Oct., 1789, ae. 83 or 86.—*W. C. R.*

Children (by first marriage b. in Charlestown, Mass.):

1. Johanna.
2. Grace (*Weth. Ins.*), d. 19 Aug., 1819, ae. 90—*W. C. R.,* hence b. 1729.
3. Rebecca (*Weth. Ins.*), d. 12 Mch., 1829, ae. 97, hence b. 1732.—*W. C. R.*
4. Thomas.

5. Jonathan. FAM. 5.
   (*By second marriage*):
6. William, b. 3 Aug., 1740; d. 14 July, 1750.
7. Michael, b. 16, bp. 20 Nov., 1743. FAM. 6.
8. Sarah, b. and bp. 9 Aug., 1747.
9. Timothy, b. 7, bp. 26 Mch., 1749.

FAM. 4. MICHAEL,[3] (*Thomas,*[2] *Thos.,*[1]), b. 1664, m. 1687, Johanna (dau. Edward & Mary *Hale*) **Wilson.**

Children (by second marriage—Weth. Rec.):

1. Timothy.
2. Johanna.

3. Michael.
4. Michael.

5. Mary.
6. Sarah.

FAM. 5. JONATHAN,[4] (*Thos.,*[3] *Thos.,*[2] *Thos.,*[1]), b. ————; m. 2 Mch., 1761, —*W. C. R.,* Elizabeth (dau. Timothy & Hannah *Crane*) **Boardman;** b. 5 Oct., 1737, res. at Midd.

Children (Midd. Rec.):

1. William, b. 25 Mch., 1762.

2. Jonathan, b. 29 Oct., 1763.

FAM. 6. MICHAEL,[3] (*Thomas,*[2] *Thomas,*[1]), b. 1743; m. Catharine (dau. Dr. Thos.) **Perrin,** 2 Nov., 1773; he was one of the volunteers in the Weth. Lex. Alarm Co. Apl., 1775; and also one of the vol. co. who went to N. Y. in sloop *Ann,* Aug. 23, '76, and prob. took part in battle of L. I. on the 27th that mo. He d. 21 Jan., 1828, ae. 84; his wife d. 1 Oct., 1820, ae. 75.—*Weth. Ins.*

Children (Weth. Rec.):

1. Michael, b. 2 Nov., 1774; bp. 7 May, 1775. FAM. 7.
2. Katharine, bp. 5 Oct., 1776; prob. the inf. bu. 15 Oct., 1776.
3. Hezekiah, b. 24 Oct., 1777.
4. Harriet, b. 24, bp. 28 Jan., 1780; m. Eleazer **Badger,** 1812.—See *Badger.*

5. Thomas, bp. 4 July, 1783; may have been the inf. bp. 5th same mo.—*W. C. R.*
6. Catherine, b. 25 Nov., 1784; bp. 30 Apl., 1786; d. 1 June, 1872.—*Weth. Ins.*
7. William, b. 24 Jan., 1788; bp. 2 Mch., 1800, ae. 12.
8. Hezekiah Whiting, bp. 10 May, 1798 (?).

FAM. 7. MICHAEL,[3] (*Michael*,[2] *Thos.*,[1]), m. 3 Jan., 1809,—*W. C. R.*, Asenath **Woodhouse**, who was bp. (adult) 1 Nov., 1818 and d. 12 Aug., 1866, ae. 83; he d. 16 (14—W. C. R.), June, 1815. He carried on chair-making in a shop formerly standing in rear of Dr. Cooke's store.—*Weth. Ins.*

Child:

1. Martha, b. 30 Nov., 1810—*W. T. R.*; d. 1 Oct., 1854, ae. 44.—*Weth. Ins.*

BRIDGMAN, ISAAC, (may have been the ISAAC ment. by *Savage* (i. 250) as one of the ch. of *John* of Northampton, only surviving son of James, of Htfd. and Springfield), m. Dorothy (dau. Sgt. John) **Curtis**, 11 Apl., 1700.

Children (*Weth. Rec.*) :

1. Lidia, b. 9 Feb., 1707.
2. Gideon, b. 2 Oct., 1708.

3. Dorothy, b. 10, bp. 15—*Mix*, Oct., 1710.

BRIGGS, WILLIAM, a tanner, adm. inhab. from Lyme, Ct., Dec. 1681, he desiring to carry on his trade; orig. from Boston, 1673.

BRISTOL, JOSIAH WARNER, m. Mary **Goodrich**, 16 Jan., 1816.—*W. C. R.*

Children (*W. C. R.*) :

1. Frances, b. 19 Dec., 1816; bp. 16 Mch., 1817.
2. Thomas Warner, b. 3 Mch., bp. 4 June, 1820.

3. Hannah (or Harriet) Treat, b. 24 Apl., bp. 13 July, 1823.
4. Martha Barnes, bp. 28 Aug., 1825.

BROADBENT, (*Weth., Ins.*), Dr. SAMUEL, b. 29 Mch., 1759; d. 2 Apl., 1828, ae. 69,—*W. C. R.*, m. Abigail ————, who was b. 6 June, 1773, and d. 27 (or 29) Jan., 1874.

ROWENA, b. 13 Nov., 1813.

SAMUEL & Catherine had s. b. 15 Apl., 1849.

BROADFIELD, (*Bradfield*), LESLY (or Leslie), see Chapt. VII, Vol. I.

BROCKWAY, PEREZ & Rebecca S., had *Lucy S.*, b. 5 Aug., 1837, d. 25 Sept., 1852. Mrs. Rebecca S. Brockway d. 25 May, 1880 ae. 70.

BROMSON, (*Brownson Bronson, Brunson,*) JOHN, prob. a son of John, of Htfd., 1639, who rem. to Far. and was one of the founders of the Far. Ch.,(*Savage*, I. 280) ; m. Hannah ————, 25 Oct., 1664.

Children (*Weth. Rec.*) :

1. John, b. 25 Aug., 1665; prob. the J. ment. by *S. W. A.* as having m. Mary **Deming.**— See Chapt. VII, Vol. I.
2. Mary, b. 15 Sept., 1668.

3. Sarah, b. 22 Aug., 1671.
4. Abraham, b. 26 Nov., 1673.
5. Joseph, b. 19 May, 1677.
6. Grace, b. 7 Sept., 1679.

ISAAC, (*Savage* thinks him prob. s. of John, of Htfd.), m. Thankful (dau. Samuel) **Dibble,** of Windsor, 30 Jan., 1706-7.

Child (*Weth. Rec.*) :

1. Samuel, b. 30 Dec., 1707.

LUKE, Capt., m. wid. Martha **Griswold**, 4 Dec., 1816.

SAMUEL, d. 23 Jan., 1741-2, ae. 76; his wife Sarah, d. 25 Oct., 1741, ae. 75.— *C. L. C.*

TIMOTHY, Dorcas, wife of, d. 30 Apl., 1747, ae. 42.—*C.L.C.*

BROOKS, SAMUEL, rec'd gt. of common ld. from the town of Glast., 1692; m. Sarah ————,—*Glast. Centennial.*

Children (b. Glast.):

1. Sarah, b. 8 Jan., 1693.
2. John, b. 8 Mch., 1695.
3. Samuel, b. 27 May, 1697; m. Mary ————; had 10 ch.
4. Mary, b. 6 Feb., 1699.
5. Timothy, b. 28 Oct., 1701.
6. "Ledda" [Lydia], b. 23 May, 1704.
7. Hannah, b. 29 Sept., 1706.
8. Abigail, b. 4 May, 1708.
9. Elizabeth, b. 24 Jan., 1711.

SUSANNAH Brooks, (who seemes to have belonged to this family,) nuncupative will, 10 September, 1721, testimony of Abigail Robbins and Lucy Robbins. "She would give to Thomas Robbins her chest in the chamber; to Lydia Brooks, dau. of Samuel Brooks, of Glast., £6. money, now in the hands of Samuel Robbins; she gave to his children each £20., the remainder she gave to Joshua Robbins & Richard Robbins,"—Abigail Robbins. *Court Record,* will accepted, proven.— Lucy Robbins except the disposing 50s. to Joshua Robbins. Samuel Brooks adms. exhibit account. Order to Dist. gr. to Samuel Brooks & Elizabeth Smith to Mercy Brooks and Lydia Cook, brother & sisters of the dec., to each £5-19-8½.

JONATHAN, m. Hannah **Clarke**, 12 Sept., 1749.

Children (W. C. R.):

1. Joseph.
2. Mary, bp. 3 Mch., 1765.
3. Dau. of, bp. 16 Oct., 1757, on mother's account.
4. Joseph, "son of Hannah," his parents being dead, bp. 9 Oct., 1768, on the right of his grandmother; he was dr. ae. 21; bu. 1 Feb., 1786.

JONATHAN, ae. 86, bu. 13 May, 1807.—*W. C. R.*

JOSEPH, (poss. the s. of Jona. & Hannah above ment.), m. 17 Jan., 1786, Lucy **Smith**, of Glast.—*S. C. R.*

MARTHA, ae 23, d. 22-23 Sept., 1775.—*W. C. R.*

THOMAS, the wife of, d. ae. 71; bu. 22 May, 1793.—*W. C. R.*

BROOME, Col. JOHN, had (*W. C. R.*)

1. Catherine Hutchinson, bp. 28 Jan., 1780-1. | 2. Caroline, bp. 7 Sept., 1783.

BROWN, EDWARD, m. Elizabeth **Graham,** (*alias* Dillings) 17 Jan., 1771, (*N. C. R.*); bu. 18 Apl., 1800, ae. 77; had

1. John, bp. 9 July, 1775. | 2. James, bp. 13 Mch., 1774. | 3. Betsy, bp. 11 July, 1779.

ELMER E. & Lottie L., had *Sadie G.;* d. 10 July, 1887, ae. 6 mos. 14 d.— *Weth. Ins.*

HERBERT W., d. 30 May, 1896, ae. 19 yr.—*Weth. Ins.*

HENRY, ae. 64, d. 20 May, 1823.—*N. C. R.*

ISAAC had, (*W. C. R.*):

Children:

1. Isaac, bp. 30 Aug., 1795; bu. 13 Sept., 1795, ae. 9 wks.
2. Isaac, bp. 14 June, 1801; bu. 1 Apl., 1804, ae. 6.

JOHN, m. Sarah **McDoonan;** 20 Jan. 1778.—*W. C. R.*

LYMAN, d. 9 Oct., 1821, ae. 37; his wife Sarah d. 15 Sept., 1855, ae. 71.

Children (Weth. N. Ins.) :

1. Joseph, d. 7 Mch., 1847, ae. 40 yr.
2. Julia, d. 12 Feb., 1856, ae. 42.

3. Rhoda, d. 17 May, 1808.

MARTIN, m. Elizabeth C. **Kirkham**, 9 Apl., 1846,—*N. C. R.*

MARY, m. EDWARD **Rose**, of Granville Mass., 20 Jan., 1811.—*W. C. R.*

RICHARD had *Sally;* bp. 5 Nov., 1795.

ROGER, of Stamford, m. Mehitable **Nott**, 22 Apl., 1781.

SAMUEL (Browne) had *Martha Washington;* bp. 18 Jan., 1778.—*W. C. R.*

THOMAS, m. Rebecca **Bar**, [?], both of 1st. Soc'y.

THOMAS, ae. 25, d. Nov. or Dec., 1812.—*W. C. R.*

THOMAS, ch. of, bu. 20 Sept., 1812; wid. of, ae. 26, bu. 8 July, 1813.—*W. C. R.*

ZACCHEUS, of Killingly, m . Sarah **Hale**, 8 Oct., 1808, who d. 3 Nov., 1872, ae. 92; he d. 20 Dec., 1861 ae. 80.

Children (Weth. N. Ins.) :

1. Deborah, d. 14 Oct., 1866, ae. 86.
2. Sarah A., d. 14 July, 1881, ae. 64.
3. Abigail K., d. 21 Aug., 1881, ae. 68.

4. Walter F., b. 5 Mch., 1820, d. 26 Nov., 1885 ; his wife, Elizabeth, b. 13 Feb., 1818, d. 24 May, 1893.

BRUNDISH, JOHN, of Weth.—See *Brandegee.* For 1d-ppy. see Chapt. VII, Vol. I, p. 253.

BUCK, *(Bouk, Book).* There were three families of this name among the early settlers of Weth., prob. related to each other, though in what degree we know not. Of these, the oldest of record, and most distinctively of Weth., by length and permanence of residence was that of EMANUEL. The others were those of HENRY and JOHN. If, as *S. W. A.* states (Chapt. VII, Vol. I.) *Enoch* Buck rec'd a grant of land from the Town in 1649, then there were *four* B. families, but we incline to the thought that this Enoch was a son of Ezekiel, and gr-son of Emanuel. There are two genealogies of the Emanuel Buck family,* in print, of which we have availed ourselves in the preparation of this sketch—our excerpts therefrom being indicated by being placed in brackets, thus [   ] followed by the initials of the author quoted. Our own sketch has rec'd valuable corrections and additions from a MSS. note-book compiled by ROSWELL R. BUCK, in 1863, and kept up to date by members of the Weth. family, and furnished to us by Mr. HENRY ROBINSON BUCK, of Weth.

The Emanuel Buck Family.

EMANUEL BUCK was in Weth. before 1640. In most printed accounts his name is followed by "or Enoch," why this apparent incertitude, we are unable to discover. *Savage* (1. 283) aptly says, "a strange confusion of names, yet the *Weth. Recs.* mention the man by both prefixes, in different places." A writer in the Geneal. dep't of *Htfd. Times* (Nov. 17, 1902) offers the following suggestion as to the possible explanation of this: "A court record is headed 'Emanuel Buck,' but followed two or three times by 'Emanuel, alias Enoch

---

* 1. *Origin, history and genealogy of the Buck family,* * * * and a complete tracing of every lineal descendant of James Buck and Elizabeth Sherman, his wife [Descendants of Emanuel and Henry Buck of Weth., Conn., 1647]. By Cornelius B. Harvey, Jersey City, N. J.. J. J. Griffiths, printer, 1889, 8 vo., 273 pp.
2. *Genealogy of the* SAMUEL BUCK [b. abt. 1730] *family of Portland, Conn.,* to the year 1894 [and their prob. descent from Emanuel Buck, early of Weth.], by Horace B. Buck, Worcester, Mass. ; press of Oliver B. Wood, 1894, 12 mo., 54 pp.
3. The *Saltonstall Genealogy.* From this splendid genealogy we have greatly enriched the line of Daniel & Sarah Saltonstall's descendants.

Buck.' I could find no reason for this except possibly in some earlier record Enoch, son of Ezekiel, appeared to act for Emanuel, his probable uncle, because of his age and feebleness. From such a source may have come the idea of these names referring to the same person." He m. (2) 17 Apl., 1658, Mary (dau. John) **Kirby**, of Htfd., b. 1637, who d. 12 Jan., 1711-12. For ld-est. see Chapt. VII, Vol. I. [He died intestate, abt. 1700, prob. b. 1623.—*Harvey.*]

Children (Weth. Rec.) by first wife:

1. Ezekiel, b. 15 Jan., 1650. FAM. 2.
2. John, b. the later end of Nov. [30—*Harvey*], 1652.
3. Jonathan, b. 8 Aug., 1655. [An old deed indicates that he m. and res. on ld. adjoining his bro. Ezekiel—not known if he had ch.—*Harvey.*] See, also, Chapt. VII, Vol. I.

(By second marriage) :
4. Mary, b. 1 Jan., 1758-9.
5. David, b. 3 Apl., 1667; d. 20 Sept., 1738. FAM. 3.
6. Sarah, b. 1 Apl., 1669.
7. Hannah, b. 12 Apl., 1671.
8. Elizabeth, b. 4 June, 1676.
9. Thomas, b. 10 June, 1678.
10. Abigail, b. 5 Aug., 1682.

FAM. 2. EZEKIEL,[2] (*Emanuel*,[1]), b. 1650; m. Rachel (dau. John) **Andrews**, of Far., 18 Mch., 1675. By purchase or otherwise he obtained the greater part of his father's lds. and in 1652 had planned (with others) to leave Weth. and settle in the Wabaquasset country, but was denied by the Gen. Ct.,* in 1698, he was one of the orig. purchasers and pprs. of the Durham grant. See also Chapt. VII, Vol. I. In 1712 he and his sons, with others, petit. the Gen. Ct. for a new parish—which being granted took the name of Newington, where he afterwards res.; he was a farmer and an officer in the militia; d. 1 or 31 Mch., 1713, leaving a large pers, and landed est.; wid. survived him, date of her death unknown. Invent. est. £308-15-09, taken 17 Mch., 1712-3, by James Patterson and Joshua Robbins; will dated 2 Mch., 1712-13, gives ho. and ½ of his lds. to wid. during her life, with reversal on dth. to his gd-s., Ezekiel (s. of his eldest s. Ezekiel), the rest to his other ch., his 2 marr. daus. had rec'd their portions before. Son Enoch, exec. *Htfd Co. Prob. Rec.*

Children:

1. Ezekiel, b. 8 Jan., 1676. FAM. 4.
2. Rachel, b. 23 July, 1678. [m. 1697, John (eld. s. of John) Bronson, of Far., b. 25 Aug., 1665; she d. and he m. (2) Mary **Chatterton**, of New Haven, and shortly after, rem. from Weth. to So. Carolina.] *Issue:*
   i. John (Bronson).
   ii. Mary (Bronson), m. ———— Ford.
   iii. Sarah (Bronson), m. ———— Mc-Gregor.—*Harvey.*]
3. Jonathan, b. 23 July, 1679; m. Mary **Andrus'** 4 Mch., 1700-01. *Children (Weth. Rec.; Mix MS.)* :
   i. Mary, bp. Jan., 1701.
   ii. Ruth, b. 23 Jan., bp. 21 Feb., 1702-3.
   iii. Joseph, b. 20 June, 1706.
   iv. Mary, bp. 28 Sept., 1707.
   v. Jonathan, b. 10 Oct., 1708.
   vi. Moses, b. 12, bp. 16 Sept., 1711.
   vii. Mary, b. 3, bp. 8 Aug., 1714.
   [Jonathan, called *Jr.*, in the *Mix Rec.* (except in last rec. of bap.) rem. to New Milford, Ct. (acc. to *Harvey & Orcutt*), in 1715 ; the latter author, *Hist. New Milford*, pp. 670-1, gives names and births of four ch. b. at New M. and a short geneal. of his descendants.]
4. Stephen, b. 2 Feb., 1680. FAM. 5.

5. [Mary, b. 1682; m. 23 Nov., 1704, John **Kelsey**, farmer of Weth.—See *Kelsy.*]
6. Enoch,† b. 5 Apl., 1683; [m. 2 May, 1717, Mary (dau. of Samuel) **Beebe**, of Old Milford, Ct., b. 26 Sept., 1699, and d. abt. 1745.—*Harvey.* The geneal. of this line will be found in Orcutt's *New Milford, Ct.*, pp. 671-2.]
7. Sarah, b. "abt. the" 8 Apl., 1685, "as is remembered," [m. 13 Mch., 1703, John **Welton**, or Wilton, of Waterbury, Ct.; had ch.—*Weth. Ch. Rec.*; give rec. of John (Welton), bp. 22 June, 1707; *Ezekiel*, "of Ezekiel Buck, Sr., his s. Wilton, of Waterbury, I think."
8. Mary, b. 31 Jan., 1687-8.
9. Hannah, b. 1 Jan., 1688-9; [was living at time of father's dth., as his will provides for her.—*Harvey.*]
10. Abigail, b. Jan., 1690-1; [rem. to New Milford with her bros. and there m. John **Noble**; had ch.—*Harvey.*]
11. Comfort, b. 7 Dec., 1692; [res. at Weth., where she prob. m.—*Harvey.*‡]
12. Ebenezer, b. 2 Sept., 1697; d. 10 Dec., 1712.

* Orcutt (*Hist. New Milford*, p. 670) says he "set. at New Lond., abt. 1667, and afterwards rem. to Weth."

† There seems to have been another *Enoch* (at least he is the only other E. ment. on *Weth. Rec.*, who m. Mercy (dau. Sam'l) Taylor, and had *William*, b. 13 Oct., 1708—tho' this may be a 1st marriage of this Enoch, s., of Ezekiel.

‡ CHARLES H. WOODRUFF, Esq., of N. Y. City, suggests, with much probability of correctness, that she m. Capt. Jacob **Griswold**, of Weth., New Milford and Litchfield, of which

FAM. 3. DAVID,[2] (*Emanuel*,[1]), b. 1667, m. 14 June, 1690, Elizabeth (dau. Daniel) **Hubbard,** of Guilford, Ct., b. 1669 or 70, who d. 25 Mch., 1734-35, ae. 66. He d. Weth. 20 Sept., 1738, ae. 71.—*W. Ins.* See also, Chapt. VII, Vol. 1.

Children (Weth. Rec.; bp. Mix. MSS.) :

1. Elizabeth, b. 16 Feb., 1690-1; [supp. to m. William **Perkins**; had dau. Elizabeth Perkins, who m. Samuel **Jacobs**; had *issue :*
   i. William (Jacobs).
   ii. Philip (Jacobs).
   iii. Daniel Buck (Jacobs).—*Harvey.*]
2. Ann, b. 25 Apl., 1693; [d. inf.—*Harvey.*]
3. Daniel (Rev.), b. 13 Sept., 1695; [grad. Y. C., 1718, studied for ministry, was never ord. rem. to Southington, Ct.; m. Elizabeth **Perkins**, of Norwich, Ct., 11 June, 1722; had dau. Elizabeth, b. 11 May, 1723 --*Harvey*], and poss. the dau. Hannah (dau. D. & E.), b. 4 Feb., 1724-5.—*Weth. Rec.* Invent. taken 11 Apl., 1726—*Ct. Rec.;* 5 May, 1726, adm. gr. to wid. & John Sage, of Midd.—*Htfd. Ct. Prob.*
4. David, Jr., b. 13 Mch., bp. Mch., 1698. FAM. 6.
5. Mary, b. 9, bp. 15 Sept., 1700; [d. 19 Mch., 1726, unm.—*Harvey.*]

6. Josiah, b. 16, bp. 17 Jan., 1702-3. FAM. 7.
7. Joseph, b. 5, bp. 8 Apl., 1705; [d. inf., 14 Sept., 1712.—*Harvey.*]
8. John, b. 18, bp. 20 July, 1707; d. 4 Feb., 1726—*Weth. Ins.;* unm.
9. Eunice, b. 19, bp. 25 Dec., 1709.
10. Mabel, (*Weth. Ins.* gives this name as *Mary*), b. 5 June, 1712; [m. 3 Mch., 1732, James **Mitchell**, of Weth., as his first wife and d. 5 Aug., 1739; he m. (2) Rebecca (dau. of Rev. Stephen) **Mix**; *Weth. Ins.* says he was b. Scotland, near Glasgow, and d. in 71 yr., 11 Feb., 1776; his third wife was Arminal (wid. of Mr. Donald **Grant**, mcht.), who d. 14 Mch., 1814, ae. 94; bu. at Weth. *Issue by Mitchell:*
    i. James, b. 2 Mch., 1733.
    ii. Mabel, b. 26 Jan., 1736.
    iii. David, b. 28 Dec., 1738.—*Harvey.*]

FAM. 4. EZEKIEL,[3] (*Ezekiel*,[2] *Emanuel*,[1]), b. 1676; m. Sarah (dau. Jno.) **Bronson,** of Far., 13 Jan., 1697-98; she bp. 13 Aug., 1699,—*Mix. MSS.* He was unfortunate and the *Weth. Town Rec.* contains rec. of a town-vote, or order, 1715, relative to giving him assistance "because of his physical infirmities." He d. soon after this entry.

Children (Weth. Rec. and Mix. Miss.) :

1. Ezekiel, b. 5 (or 25), bp. 7 May, 1699; rem. from Weth. to Litchfield, thence to New Milford, where he m. and his dec'ts are given by Orcutt.—*Hist. New Milford,*

Ct., p. 1673.
2. Sarah, b. 8 Feb., bp. 20 Apl., 1700-1; m. and res. Weth.
3. Rachel, bp. 3 (13 ?) May, 1711.

FAM. 5. STEPHEN,[3] (*Ezekiel*,[2] *Emanuel*,[1]), b. 1680; m. Anne (dau. Jacob) **Johnson,** 11 Apl., 1703; she owned cov't & was bp. 23 July, 1710.—*Mix MS.*

Children (Weth. Rec. and Mix MS.) :

1. Benjamin, b. 15 May, bp. 4 June, 1704.
2. Anna, b. 4 Feb., 1705-6.
3. Esther, bp. 26 Jan., 1708-9.
4. Hester, b. 18 Dec., 1710.
5. Deborah, bp. 18 Mch., 1710-11.

6. Deborah, b. 25 Mch., 1713.
7. Stephen, b. 15 June, 1714.
8. Ebenezer, b. 25 Jan., 1717. FAM. 8.
9. Jacob, b. 13 Mch., 1719.
10. Elizabeth, b. 17 May, 1723.

FAM. 6. DAVID,[3] (*David*,[2] *Emanuel*,[1]) b. 1698, m. 19 Dec., 1723, Eunice (dau. James) **Treat,** who d. 5 Mch., 1725-26. It may be that she m. soon after as there is in *Htfd. Prob. Ct. Rec.*, a Ct. Rec., 2 Apl., 1728, gr. adm. & ord. of distrib. to Eunice Buck. wid., and David, only son, age 3 yrs., and Jonathan Riley and Eunice Riley were made the child's guardians.

Child (Weth. Rec.) :

1. David, b. 14 Nov., 1724.

latter place he was an original settler, and one of its most distinguished citizens. He bases his theory on the following strong circumstantial evidence, seemingly proving that she was the dau. of Ezekiel Buck, of Weth. :
1. Ezekiel Buck had a daughter *Comfort.*
2. There is no record of her marriage to any other.
3. She was of suitable age, b. Dec. 7, 1692. J. G. was born Mch. 26, 1690.
4. There is no record of his marriage.
5. Their families were neighbors and intimate.
6. Their respective grandfathers bought land together.
7. On the settlement of New Milford, J. G. removed there in 1712-13, secured a "home lot" and built him a house, and was therefore (probably) then married.
8. Comfort Buck was then 20 years old.
9. Two years later, 1715, her brothers Jonathan & Enoch followed to and settled in New Milford.
10. In 1720, J. G., with his wife Comfort, removed to Litchfield.
11. Jonathan Buck accompanied him from New Milford to the new settlement.
12. Ezekiel, another brother of Comfort, with his son Ezekiel, joined them from Wethersfield.

FAM. 7.   JOSIAH,[3] (David,[2] Emanuel,[1]), b. 1703, m. 28 May, 1731, Ann (dau. Chas.) **Deming**, of Boston, b. 1711. He d. 8 Feb., 1793, ae. 90, (Weth. Ins.), she d. 9 Mch., 1772, in 61 yr.—Weth. Rec. He may be called the founder of the "Bucktown" settlement in Weth.*

Children (Weth. Rec.):

1. Ann, b. 26 Feb., 1732; m. Joshua **Hemp-stead**, of Htfd., and d. 7 July, 1799.
2. Mary, b. 31 Oct., bp. 4 Nov., 1733.
3. Elizabeth, b. 7 Apl., 1735; m. Gideon **Wright**, of Sandisfield, Mass., and d. 25 May, 1770.
4. Prudence, b. 15 Dec., 1737; m. 18 Jan., 1776, Luke **Fortune**, of Norwich, Ct., d. 17 Feb., 1825. *Issue:*

    i. James (Fortune), b. 8 Oct., 1777.
5. Josiah, b. 23 Apl., 1742; d. 16 Oct., 1807.— Weth. Ins. FAM. 8.
6. Daniel, b. 13, bp. 21 June, 1774; d. 6 Jan., 1808. FAM. 9.
7. Mabel b. 22, bp. 27 Mch., 1748; m. 10 Nov., 1774, Justus **Riley**, and d. 28 May, 1843, ae. 95.

FAM. 8   Capt. JOSIAH,[4] (Josiah,[3] David,[2] Emanuel,[1]), b. 1742; m. 26 Jan., 1775, Hannah (sister Silas) **Deane**, of Groton, Ct. She, wid., d. ae. 70, bu. 3 Sept., 1824.—Weth. Ins. He d. ae. 66; bu. 16 Oct., 1807.

Children:

1. Josiah, b. 29 Dec., 1775; bp. 7 Apl., 1776; d. unm. 1812.
2. Elizabeth, b. Feb., bp. 12 Apl., 1778; d. unm. 13 May, 1801.
3. Barzillai Deane, b. 16 Mch., bp. 1 Apl., 1781; d. Sept., 1842. FAM. 10.

4. Hannah, b. 23 June, bp. 7 Aug., 1785; m. Chester **Bulkeley**, of Albany, N. Y.; had 7 ch.; all d. yg. A Josiah Buck, m. Sarah **Riley**, 30 Dec., 1776.

FAM. 9.   DANIEL,[4] (Josiah,[3] David,[2] Emanuel,[1]), b. 1744; m. 3 Dec., 1775, Sarah (dau. Gurdon) **Saltonstall**, of New Lond., Ct., who d. 19 Nov., 1828, ae. 74.— Weth. Ins.

Children (Weth. Rec.):

1. Anna, b. 24 Nov., d. 12 Dec., 1776, ae. 3 wks.—Weth. Ins.
2. Gurdon, b. 30 Dec., 1777; bp. 3 May, 1778. FAM. 11.
3. Daniel, b. 27 Oct., bp. 14 Nov., 1779; d. Jan., 1860. FAM. 12.
4. Charles, b. 21, bp. 31 Mch., 1782; m.

Cath. **Bradford**, of N. Y.; he d. 5 June, 1858.
5. Winthrop, b. 9, bp. 26 Dec., 1784. FAM. 13.
6. Ann, b. 12, bp. 15 Oct., 1786; d. 6 Feb., 1788.—Weth. Ins.
7. Dudley, b. 25 June, bp. 6 Sept., 1789; d. 8 May, 1867. FAM. 14.

FAM. 10. BARZILLAI DEANE,[5] (Joseph,[4] Josiah,[3] David,[2] Emanuel,[1]), b. 16 Mch., 1781; m. Mary Mix (dau. Simeon) **Belden**, of Weth., 31 Mch., 1812; she b. 9 Aug., 1781, d. 26 Feb., 1866—Weth. Ins; he d. ae. 61.—Weth. Ins.

Children:

1. Hannah, b. 28 Jan., bp. 12 June, 1812; d. unm.
2. Josiah, b. Nov., 1814, bp. 9 Apl., 1815; d. 24 Sept., 1873. FAM. 15.
3. Mary Mix, b. Jan., 1816, bp. 8 June, 1817; m. 8 Oct., 1845, Chauncey E. **Wetmore**, of Midd., Ct.; rem. to Baltiomre, Md.,

and to Cal.
4. Barzillai Deane, b. Nov., 1819, bp. 23 May, 1819—W. C. R.; d. 19 May, 1831.— Weth. Ins.
5. Lucy, b. 1821, bp. 2 June, 1822; m. J. D. **Pratt**, of Baltimore, Md.

FAM. 11.   GURDON,[5] (Daniel,[4] Josiah,[3] David,[2] Emanuel,[1]), m. 20 Apl., 1805, Susannah (dau. David) **Manwaring**, of N. Lond., they res. N. Y. City, who d. 19 Nov., 1828; he d. 4 Aug., 1852.

---

* An undisputed trad. in the B. family is that Josiah[3] (FAM. 7) and possibly his father David[2] (FAM. 3) orig. res. in a small ho. where that of Henry[6] (FAM. 22) now stands; and that he (Josiah[3]) erected the present houses for his sons, that on the E. side of the road, for Josiah[4], in 1774; and that on the W. side, on the site of the old ho., for Daniel[4], in 1775. Josiah[3] made his home with Daniel in the latter house until his dth. in 1793. The foundation walls of the old ho. were uncovered abt. 1890, while excavating for a new furnace in this house.

Children:

1. David, b. 29 Jan., 1806. FAM. 16.
2. Gurdon (M. D.), b. 4 May, 1807. FAM. 17.
3. Charles Dudley, b. 29 Nov., 1808. FAM. 18.
4. Daniel Winthrop, b. 27 Nov., 1810; d. unm. at St. Croix, W. I., 4 Mch., 1832.
5. Sarah, b. 28 Dec., 1812; m. Jona. D. Steele, as his 2d wife; d. Dec., 1855; he d. Aug., 1872. *Issue:*
   i. William Dayton (Steele), b. 1851.
   ii. James Alexander (Steele), b. 16 July, 1853.
6. Elizabeth, b. 16 Nov., 1816; m. John Auchincloss, of N. Y., 3 June, 1835. *Issue:*
   i. Henry Buck (Auchincloss), b. 7 June, 1836; m. Mary Cabell, of Charlotte, Va.; 7 ch.
   ii. Sarah Ann (Auchincloss), b. 3 July, 1838; m. 1859, James Coates, of Paisley, Scotland; she d. 12 ——, 1887, at Providence, R. I.
   iii. John Stuart (Auchincloss), b. Mch., 1840.

   iv. William Stuart (Auchincloss), b. 19 Mch., 1842; m. Martha Tuttle (dau. W. C.) Kent, of Phila.; 3 ch.
   v. Elizabeth Ellen (Auchincloss); b. 3 July, 1844.
   vi. Edgar Sterling (Auchincloss); m. 21 May, 1872, Maria LaGrange (dau. Samuel & Maria E.) Sloan; 7 ch.
   vii. Fred. H. Lauton (Auchincloss), d. Yokohama, Japan; m. Joanna Howe.
   viii. John Winthrop (Auchincloss), m. Caroline Howe (dau. C. H. & Caroline H.) Russell; 4 ch.
   ix. Hugh Dudley (Auchincloss), b. 1858.
7. Rebecca Coit, b. 6 Nov., 1818; d. unm. 18 July, 1870, at Rye Beach, N. Y.
8. George, b. 14 Aug., 1821; d. N. Y. City; unm., 1824.
9. Edward, b. 6 Oct., 1814. FAM. 19.
10. Henry, b. 6 Nov., 1824; d. 3 Sept., 1891, in N. Y. City.

FAM. 12. DANIEL,[5] (*Daniel,[4] Josiah,[3] David,[2] Emanuel,[1]*), b. 1779; m. 14 (Sept. or) Oct., 1805, Julia (dau. Hon. Stephen *Mix*) Mitchell, of Weth., who d. 9 Oct., 1807, ae. 26, *Weth. Ins.*, without issue; he m. (2) Elizabeth (dau of Ezekiel Porter) Belden, of Weth., 30 Jan., 1812, who was b. 10 Jan., 1783-4; d. 3 Mch., 1887, ae. 103 yrs. 1 mo. & 24 days. He d. Jan., 1860, at Poquonnock, Ct. *Children*: [*births from Harvey's Buck Gen.*]

1. Daniel, b. 26 Feb., 1814. FAM. 20.
2. Ezekiel, b. 31 Jan., 1816; d. 21 Mch., 1844, unm.
3. Charles, b. 26 Dec., 1817; d. 28 Aug., 1845, unm.
4. Julia, b. 16 July, 1820; d. unm. 7 June, 1897.
5. John, b. 16 Dec., 1822; d. 21 Mch., 1847, unm.
6. Susan, b. 3 Mch., 1825; res. Weth.

FAM. 13. WINTHROP,[5] (*Daniel,[4] Josiah,[3] David,[2] Emanuel,[1]*), b. 1784; m. 29 Jan., 1812, at Weth., Eunice H. (*Weth. Ins.* says *W.*), (dau. Gideon) Parsons, of Amherst, Mass. She d. 5 Aug., 1812, ae. 24, without issue; he m. (2) 28 Dec., 1814, Eunice (dau. Dr. Abner) Moseley, of Weth., who d. 24 Aug., 1862.— *Weth. Ins.* He d. 19 Aug., 1862.—*Weth. Ins.*

Children (all but 2 last bp., 1 Apl., 1827):

1. Martha Ann, b. 26 Nov., 1815; d. unm., 12 Aug., 1900.
2. Winthrop, b. 16 Dec., 1816. FAM. 21.
3. Eunice, b. 31 Dec., 1819; d. unm., 12 Mch., 1897.—*Weth. Ins.*
4. Maria, b. 30 Jan., 1821; m. 5 Feb., 1856, Edmund G. Howe, of Htfd., who d. 23 Apl., 1872; she d. 8 Dec., 1895, without issue.
5. Robert, b. 8 Mch., 1823; d. 16 Aug., 1881 —*Weth. Ins.;* m. (1) at Hastings, Minn., Lucinda M. (dau. Jona.) Emerson, of Lebanon. N. H.; she d. 7 June, 1859; he m. (2) 5 Aug., 1860, Helen Frances (dau. Elisha L.) Jones, of St. Albans, Vt.; d. 16 Aug., 1881. *Issue:*
   i. Robert Moseley, b. 5 Sept., 1865; m. Mary (dau. Richard) Marcy, of Watertown, N. Y.
6. Roswell Riley, b. 21 Oct., 1826. FAM. 22.
7. Kate Moseley, b. 1 Feb., bp. 3 Nov., 1833; m. 6 Nov., 1866, John Buckingham, of Chicago, who d. 21 Aug., 1881. *Issue:*
   i. Henry Winthrop (Buckingham). b. 28 Nov., 1868.
   ii. Arthur Hale (Buckingham), b. 27 Oct., d. 3 Aug., 1871.
   iii. Clifford Hale (Buckingham), b. 1 Jan., 1876.
8. Henry, b. 6 Dec., 1834; bp. 3 June, 1835. FAM. 23.

FAM. 14. DUDLEY,[5] (*Daniel,[4] Josiah,[3] David,[2] Emanuel,[1]*), b. 1789; m. 25 Sept., 1827, Hetty G. (dau. John) Hempstead, of Htfd., who d. 12 June, 1834; he m. (2) 12 Sept., 1837, Martha C. (dau. Nath'l) Adams, of Portsmouth, N. H., who d. 20 Feb., 1864. He d. 8 May, 1867, ae. 65. *Children:*

1. George, b. 16 Sept., 1830. FAM. 24.
2. Mary, b. 8 Sept., 1832; d. 3 Aug., 1833.
3. Dudley, b. 5 June, 1834;d. 20 Nov., 1836.

(*By second marriage*):
4. Dudley, b. 10 Mch., 1839.—(*MS.*) FAM. 25.
5. James, b. 17 Nov., 1840; d. 20 July, 1842 (*MS.*)

FAM. 15. JOSIAH,[6] (*Barzillai,[5] Josiah,[4] Josiah,[3] David,[2] Emanuel,[1]*), m. 4 Mch., 1855, Juliette (dau. Sylvester) Goodrich, of Pawlet, Vt. She res. New London, Ct. *Child*:

1. Barzillai D., b. 4 May, 1858; res. Htfd. d. 1883.

FAM. 16. DAVID,[6] (*Gurdon,[5] Daniel,[4] Josiah,[3] David,[2] Emanuel,[1]*), b. 1806; m. 8 May, 1837, Matilda Stewart **Hall**, of Boston, Mass.; he d. 15 Aug., 1875, at Marblehead, Mass.

Children:

1. Florence, b. 15 July, 1839; d. 18 Aug., 1864.
2. Stewart Manwaring, b. 24 Oct., 1842. FAM. 26.
3. Eleanor, b. 24 May, 1850.
4. Henry Hall, b. 11 Mch., 1854; lawyer in Boston.
5. Howard Mendenhall, b. 16 May, 1856; physician in Boston.

FAM. 17. GURDON,[6] (*Gurdon,[5] Daniel,[4] Josiah,[3] David,[2] Emanuel,[1]*), b. 1807; m. 27 July, 1836, Henrietta (dau. Albert Henry) **Wolf**, of Geneva, Switzerland, d. 6 Mch., 1877, in N. Y. He was a distinguished surgeon.

Children:

1. Amelia Henrietta, b. 11 Feb., 1838; m. 24 Sept., 1863, Alfred **North**, M. D., of Waterbury, Ct.
2. Susan Manwaring, b. 1 Nov., 1839.
3. Louisa Munsell, b. 9 Sept., d. 4 Dec., 1841.
4. Albert Henry, b. 20 Oct., 1842; ni. Laura (dau. Rev. J. S. C.) **Abbott**, of N. Haven;
   i. Winifred.
   ii. Harold Winthrop.
5. Alfred Linsley, b. 8 Nov., 1844; d. 10 Feb., 1848.
6. Gurdon Saltonstall, b. 23 Oct., 1848; m. (1) Clara **Tillon**; m. (2) Anna **Tillon**.
7. Francis Dudley, b. 11 Oct., 1850.

FAM. 18. CHARLES DUDLEY,[6] (*Gurdon,[5] Daniel,[4] Josiah,[3] David,[2] Emanuel,[1]*), b. 1808; m. at Ellington, 18 Sept., 1844, Sophronia **Smith**, of Wilbraham, Mass.

Children:

1. Charles Gurdon, b. 13 Apl., 1847; res. San Rafael, Cal., 1904.
2. Grace Winthrop, b. 20 July, 1851.
3. Margaret Smith, b. 29 Apl., 1857; res. San Francisco, Cal., 1904.
4. William, d. 30 Sept., 1870, at Orange, N. J.

FAM. 19. EDWARD,[6] (*Gurdon,[5] Daniel,[4] Josiah,[3] David,[2] Emanuel,[1]*), b. 1814; fitted for coll. at Mt. Pleasant School, Amherst, Mass., ent. Y. C. 1831, grad. 1835, studied law and commenced practice in N. Y. City, 1838 rem. to Boston, 1843, where the practiced, and res. from 1855 until his dth., 16 July, 1876; m. 8 June, 1841, Elizabeth Greene (dau. Hon. Samuel, L. L. D.,) **Hubbard**, of Boston, a justice of the Mass. Supreme Ct. A good lawy., a modest but distinguished scholar, of a somewhat quaint and humorous character and a faithful, cheerful christian.

Children:

1. Helen Alice; res. Andover, Mass.
2. Walter, b. 29 Sept., 1847; grad. Y. C. 1870.
3. An inf. d.

FAM. 20. DANIEL,[6] (*Dan.,[5] Dan.,[4] Josiah,[3] David,[2] Emanuel,[1]*), m. 4 June, 1839, Mary E. (dau. W. H.) **Imlay**, who d. 17 Nov., 1862; acc. to Harvey's *Buck Gen.* rem. to 'San Francisco, Cal.; d. I Jan., 1892.

Children:

1. Daniel Winthrop.
2. William Imlay.
3. Frederic Clarence.
4. Charles Ezekiel.
5. Mary Elizabeth.

FAM. 21. WINTHROP,[6] (*Winthrop,[5] Dan'l,[4] Josiah,[3] David,[2] Emanuel,[1]*), b. 1816; m. 24 Dec., 1845, Charlotte (dau. Sylvester) **Woodhouse**, of Weth., who was b. 19 Oct., 1819, d. 15 Jan., 1896.

Children:

1. Edward Winthrop, b. 28 Feb., 1847; m. 12 Sept., 1876, Abigal B. (dau. Reuben C.) **Osborn**, of New. *Issue:*
   i. Winthrop, b. 18 Sept., 1878.
   ii. Edward Osborn, b. 25 June, 1883.
   iii. Helen Dudley, b. 2 July, 1888.
2. Louis Dudley, b. 13 Aug., 1850; m. 10 Feb., 1881, Laura (dau. Sam'l O.) **Church**, of Htfd., d. 19 Mch., 1887. *Issue:*
   i. Charlotte, b. 21 Aug., 1882.
   ii. Mary Church, b. 17 May, 1885.
   iii. Louise Dudley, b. 26 Mch., d. 16 Aug., 1887, ae. 5 mos.—*Weth. Ins.*

FAM. 22. ROSSWELL RILEY,[6] (*Winthrop*,[5] *Daniel*,[4] *Josiah*,[3] *David*,[2] *Emanuel*,[1]),
b. 1826; m. 8 Nov., 1866, Maria C. (dau. Dr. Josiah) **Barnes,** of Buffalo, N. Y.

Children:

1. Harriet Moseley, b. 16 Aug., 1867.
2. Winthrop Seymour, b. 13 May, 1870; d.
    24 May, 1878.
3. George Sturges, b. 10 Feb., 1875.

FAM. 23. HENRY,[6] (*Winthrop*,[5] same as above), b. 1834; m. 30 Nov., 1875, Theresa
(dau. Geo.) **Robinson,** of Htfd.

Children (births from Harvey's Buck Gen.):

1. Henry Robinson, b. 14 Sept., 1876; m. 3
    Dec., 1901, Mary Ladoyett (dau. Charles)
    Wolcott, of Weth. *Issue:*
    i. Henry Wolcott, b. 15 May, 1903.
2. John Saltonstall, b. 7 May, 1879.
3. Charles Howe, b. 2 Aug., 1881.

FAM. 24. GEORGE, (*Dudley,* same as above), b. 1830; m. Lucy Farrer (dau. Rev.
Rich.) **Hall,** of New Ipswich, N. H., who d. 16 July, 1870; he m. (2) 5 Apl.,
1877, Josephine Louise **Hitchcock,** of Southington, Ct.

Children:

1. Horace Hall, b. 28 June, 1855.
2. Mary Eliza, b. 12 Oct., 1857; d. 14 Apl.,
    1860.
3. Lucy Farrer, b. 5 July, 1859; d. 10 Sept.,
    1881.
4. Mary Eliza, b. 30 Apl., 1861; d. 5 Aug.,
    1886.
5. George Dudley, b. 16 Aug., 1863; d. Nov.,
    1882.
6. William Winthrop, b. 22 Mch., 1866.
7. Hetty Saltonstall, b. 10 July, 1868.
    (*By second marriage*):
8. Grace Hamilton, b. 2 Feb., 1880.

FAM. 25. DUDLEY, (*Dudley,* same as above), b. 1834; m. 3 Oct., 1865, Lizzie
Van Wagner, of Burlington, N. J.

Children:

1. Edward Terry, b. 23 Sept., 1866.
2. Dudley Saltonstall, b. 5 Apl., 1868.
3. Madeline, b. 15 May, 1871; m. 27 Feb.,
    1900, Francis **Blossom.**

FAM. 26. STEWART MANWARING, (*David, Gurdon,* same as above), b. 1842;
m. 30 Oct., 1872, Grace **Ross,** of Bangor, Me.

Children:

1. Clifford Ross, b. 12 Feb., 1874.
2. Katharine, b. 12 Oct., 1877.
3. Theda, b. 31 July, 1879.

THE HENRY BUCK FAMILY.

HENRY, m. 31 Oct., 1660, Elizabeth (dau. Josias) **Churchell,** freeman;
constable (Mch., 1670-1); blacksmith—(*Weth. Ld. Rec.* 1718); farmer. See
Chapter VII, Vol. I; d. July, 1712, ae. 86, which shows him to have been
b. 1626.

Children (Weth. Rec.):

1. Henry, said to have been b. 1662.* FAM. 2.
2. Samuel, b. 2 Feb., 1664. FAM. 3.
3. Martha, b. 15 Oct., 1667; m. 27 Oct., 1687,
    Jonathan **Deming.**—See *Deming.*
4. Elizabeth, b. 6 June, 1670; prob. d. yg.
5. Mary, b. 12 Mch., 1672-3; m. 14 Mch.,
    1700, Benj. **Smith,** b. 1673; d. 1761. *Issue:*
    i. Josiah (Smith), b. 1707; m. 1740,
6. Sarah, b. 25 July, 1678; prob. d. yg.; but
    one acc. says m. Sgt. John (s. Daniel,
    Sen.) **Rose,** 8 July, 1697.
7. Ruth, b. 4 Dec., 1681, prob. d. yg.
8. Mehitable, b. 4 Jan., 1684; m. 10 Oct.,
    1709, Ebenezer **Alexander.** *Issue:*
    i. Elias (Alexander), b. 25 July, 1710.

    Mary **Treat;** d. 17 Oct., 1793.

FAM. 2. HENRY,[2] (*Henry*,[1]), b. abt. 1662; m. ————; rem. to Cohanzey, N. J.

Child (see note below):

1. Henry,[3] ————. FAM. 4.

* The fact of the existence of this son (who appears not on *Weth. Rec.*) seems to be
estab. by *Weth. Land Recs.* (IV, opp. p. 6), contains a deed from Henry, Sen., to this son,
"now inhab. of Cohanzey, Salem Co., N. J.," dated 17 Aug., 1709.
    It is further confirmed by the following entry in Rev. Mr. Mix's *bp. rec.:* "Henry, of
Henry Buck, of Cohansey, bp. 14 Nov., 1708, a pretty big boy."
    Harvey says that "*one* of the sons of Henry & Elizabeth (Churchill) Buck, had a son
Ephraim, who m. (1) Judeth Nixon. who d. 6 Mch., 1769, ae. 33, and that he m. (2) Abigail

Fam. 3. SAMUEL,[2] (*Henry,*[1]), b. 1664; m. 23 Jan., 1690, Sarah (dau. Dea. Samuel) **Butler;** he d. 23 (acc. to *Prob. Rec.* 26) Apl., 1709, ae. 44 yrs., 2 mo. (*Weth. Rec.*) ; d. before his father, who 17 Aug., 1709, deeds a 50 acr. lot to Samuel's 3 sons, *Isaac, Peletiah* and *Samuel.—Weth. Ld. Rec.,* IV, 6. His invent. taken 26 Jan., 1709-10 amt. £350-12-06; *Ct. Rec.* of adm. gr. 6 Feb., 1709-10 to wid. Sarah.—See, also, Chapt. VII, Vol.I.

Children (*Weth. Rec.*) :

1. Isaac, b. 12 Apl., 1693. **Fam. 5.**
2. Dorothy, b. 29 July, 1695; d. yg.
3. Peletiah, b. 2, bp. 11 Sept., 1698. **Fam. 6.**
4. Sarah, b. 25, bp. 30 Mch., 1701; d. yg.
5. Elizabeth, b. 13, bp. 15 Aug., 1703 ; d. yg.
6. Samuel, b. 12 July, 1705. **Fam. 7.**
7. Martha, b. 21, and bp. Oct., 1707 ; d. yg.

Fam. 4.   HENRY,[3] (*Henry,*[2] *Henry,*[1]), bp. 1708?

Children:

1. Joseph, b. 1 May, 1753. **Fam. 8.**
2. Ephraim. **Fam. 9.**
3. Judith, m. Jeremiah **Barnett.**
4. Ruth, m. William **Stratton.**
5. Reuben. **Fam. 10.**
6. Jeremiah (Josiah ?), b. 3 July, 1764. **Fam. 11.**

Fam. 5.   ISAAC,[3] (*Samuel*[2] *Henry,*[1]), b. 1693 (?) ; m. 25 Nov., 1712, Elizabeth (dau. James) **Wright.**

Children (*Weth. Rec.*) :

1. Elizabeth, b. 4 Nov., 1719-20.
2. Samuel, b. 20 June, 1722 ; m. 10 Feb., 1751, (acc. to *Harvey*) Sarah **Hurlbut.**
3. Abigail, b. 11 Mch., 1724.
4. Justus, b. 11 Mch., 1725-6.
5. Mehitable, b. 19 Oct., 1728.
6. Hannah, b. 29 Nov., 1730.
7. Mariamne, b. 20, or 24 Feb., 1734.

Fam. 6.   PELETIAH,[3] (*Samuel,*[2] *Henry,*[1]), m.* 25 Mch., 1724, Lydia (dau. John) **Stoddard,** who d. 29 July, 1726; m. (2) 18 Jan., 1745, ——————— (*Weth. Rec.*) ; "the first burial in the New yd."—*Weth. Ins.*

Children (*Weth. Rec.*) :

1. Lydia, b. 22 Apl., 1725.
2. Peletiah, b. 25 July, 1726. **Fam. 12.**

Fam. 7.   Sgt. SAMUEL,[3] (*Samuel,*[2] *Henry,*[1]), m. 28 Dec., 1727, Sarah (dau. John) **House,** of Glast.—*Weth. Ins.;* she d. 11 Oct., 1751; he m. (2) Elizabeth M. **Lead.**—(*Weth. Rec.*) ; he d. 17 Oct., 1758.

Children (*Weth. Rec. and Mix Rec.*) :

1. Sarah, b. 3, bp. 8 June, 1729.
2. John, b. 11 July. 1731 ; m. Sarah **Hurlbut,** 10 Feb., 1757.—*Weth. Rec.* **Fam. 13.**
3. George, b. 11, bp. 14 Oct., 1733 ; (*Mix MSS* says a George, s. of Samuel, was bp. 18 July, 1731.
4. Titus, b. 27 Jan., 1736; m. Caroline **Seaward.** **Fam. 14.**
5. Samuel, b. 10 June, 1738. **Fam. 15.**
6. Daniel, b. 23 Apl., 1742.
7. Betty, b. 30 Nov., bp. 2 Dec., 1744.
8. Isaac, b. 20 Feb., bp. 22 Nov., 1747.
9. Jesse, b. 20 Feb., 1749 ; bp. 4 Mch., 1750. **Fam. 16.**
   (*By second marriage*) :
10. William, b. 21, bp. 26 Nov., 1752 ; d. 22 Dec., 1753.

Fam. 8.   JOSEPH,[4] (*Henry,*[3] *Henry,*[2] *Henry,*[1]), m. Ruth **Seeley.**

Children:

1. John, b. 1 Apl., 1784. **Fam. 17.**
2. Maria, b. 25 Sept., 1785 ; d. 26 Sept., 1798.
3. Sarah, b. 11 Aug., 1787 ; m. (1) ——————— **Ogden;** m. (2) Henry **Shepard.**
4. Jane, b. 4 Oct., 1789 ; m. Daniel P. **Stratton.**
5. Hannah, b. 1791 ; m. Nathan L. **Stratton.**
6. Naomi Seeley, b. 13 Sept., 1793 ; d. 26 Sept., 1798.
7. Ephraim, b. 23 Feb., 1795.
8. Joseph, b. 23 Dec., 1796 ; m. Emily **Fithian.** **Fam. 18.**
9. Jeremiah, b. 8 Sept., 1803 ; d. abt. 1860.

——————— (whose fam. name seems, from other sources, to have been **Russell**), and that he d. 1777."

There is evident confusion in the recs. which have been handed down to us—involving the loss of one generation. Henry[2] said to have been b. 1662, is said to have m. Judith Nixon and is credited with a fam., the eldest of whom was b. 1753; which, considering date of his birth, is improbable. Furthermore, his s. Ephraim is cred. with having m. Judith Nixon (?). Our own idea is that Henry[2] (s. Henry,[1] the Settler) was the Henry who rem. to Cohansey, N. J., and had a son Henry,[3] the "pretty big boy" bp. by Rev. Mix, and who was the father of Ephraim,[4] who m. Judith Nixon, —- Aug., 1709.

FAM. 9. EPHRIAM,⁵ (*Ephriam,⁴ Henry,³ Henry,² Henry,¹*), m. Elizabeth **Hendry.**

Children:

1. Anna M., m. Thos. B. **Black.**
2. Sarah H., m. Robt. H. **Reeves.**
3. Mary H.
4. Bowman H., m. Caroline **Ayers.**
5. Hannah S., m. Horace **Saunders.**

6. Elizabeth H.
7. Joseph.
8. Ephraim, m. Mary J. **Westcott.**
9. Emily H., m. Robert J. **Brown.**
10. Charles H.

FAM. 10. REUBEN,⁴ (*Henry³ Henry,² Henry,¹*), m. Sarah **Strattes,** pos. the wid. S. who. d. 7 June, 1800, ae. 89.—*S. C. R.*

Children:

1. Violetta F., b. 24 Mch., 1793; d. 22 May, 1838.
2. Reuben, b. 17 Nov., 1794.
3. Sarah S., b. 7 Oct., 1796; m. Levi **Stratton.**

(*By second marriage*):
4. Mary.
5. Abigail.
6. Ruth.

FAM. 11. JEREMIAH,⁴ (or Josias?) (*Henry,³ Henry² Henry,¹*), m. Sarah **Holmes,** who d. 10 Oct., 1832.

Children:

1. Rachel Holmes, b. 24 Sept., 1792; d. 28 Apl., 1794.
2. William Ramsay, b. 21 Jan., 1799; d. 12 May, 1822.
3. Mary Holmes, b. 5 Oct., 1800; d. 18 Aug., 1817.
4. Robert Shute, b. 17 Sept., 1802. FAM. 19.

5. Frank Nixon, b. 26 July, 1804. FAM. 20.
6. Sarah Holmes, b. 8 Jan., 1808; d. Mch., 1880.
7. Jeremiah, b. 13 Sept., 1809; d. 1 Sept., 1810.
8. Jeremiah More, b. 20 July, 1814. FAM. 21.

FAM. 12. PELETIAH,⁴ (*Peletiah,³ Samuel,² Henry,¹*), m. 9 Nov., 1754, Hannah **Hills.**—*Weth. Rec.*

Child (Weth. Rec.):

1. Lydia, b. 15 Sept., 1753.

FAM. 13. JOHN,⁴ (*Samuel,³ Samuel,² Henry,¹*), m. Martha **Hawthorne.**

Children:

1. Martha Hawthorne, m. Dr. W. S. **Bowen.**
2. Jane, m. Chas. C. **Morgan.**
3. John, m. Rebecca **More.**
4. Maria Therese, d.
5. Smith Bowen, d.
6. Williiam Bowen, m. Sallie **Bispham.** No

issue.
7. Mary Holmes, d.
8. Caroline P.
9. Louisa, m. Chas. **Reeve.**
10. Jeremiah.
11. Theodore, m. Mary **Clarke.**

FAM. 14. TITUS,⁴ (*Samuel,³ Samuel,² Henry,¹*), m. Caroline **Seaward,** 1 Oct., 1760; who d. 5 Oct., 1778, in 40th yr.—*Weth Ins.;* he d. 25 Aug., 1776— (*Weth. Rec.*)

Child (Weth. Rec.):

1. Sarah, b. 2 bp. 9 Aug., 1761.

FAM. 15. SAMUEL,⁴ (*Samuel,³ Samuel,² Henry,¹*), m. 22 Apl., 1762, Elizabeth (**Blin**—*Weth. Rec.*), who d. 8 Feb., 1787, ae. 46, and who may have been "wid. of S." d. ae. 57, bu. 17 Apl., 1830. He d. ae. 83, 15 Jan., 1821.—*Weth. Ins.*

Children (Weth. Rec.):

1. John, b. 7 May, bp. 7 Nov., 1762.
2. Betty, b. 31 Dec., 1763; bp. 8 Jan., 1764; d. 25 May, 1792.
3. Mehitable, b. 4 June, 1766; bu. ae. 13, 1 Sept. 1779.
4. Samuel, b. 12 Nov., bp. 4 Dec., 1768; d. 12 Aug., 1828; his wife Lucy **Goodrich,** d. 16 Apl., 1830, ae. 56.—*Weth. Ins.*

5. George, b. 2 Apl., 1771.
6. Titus, b. 4, bp. 10 Apl., 1774.
7. Bille, bp. 31 July, 1774.
8. Gershom, b. 16 May, 1778; bp. 31 Jan., and d. 7 Feb., 1779.
9. Sally, b. 25 Oct., 1781; bp. 21 Dec., 1804.— *W., C. R.*

FAM. 16. JESSE,[4] (*Samuel,*[3] *Samuel,*[2] *Henry,*[1]), m. Ann **Goodrich**, of Chatham; who bu. 2 July, 1785; he m. (2) Esther **Seaward**, of Durham, Ct.; he d. 19 Apl., 1789—*Weth. Rec.;* d. at sea—news rec'd May, 1789.—*W. C. R.*

Children (*Weth., Rec.*) :

1. Prudence, b. 4 Dec., 1775; bp. 23 Sept., 1787.
2. Caroline, b. 4 Dec., 1777; d. 24 Nov., 1782.
3. Jesse, b. 24 Mch., 1780; bp. 23 Sept., 1787.—*W. C. R.;* may be the J. of Litchfield, who m. Sally **Coleman**, of Weth., 17 Sept., 1803.
4. Richard, b. 13 Dec., 1782; bp. 23 Sept., 1787.—*W. C. R.*

5. Anne, b. 28 June, 1785; bp. 23 Sept., 1787. —*W. C. R.*

(*By second marriage*) :

6. Henry, b. 12 Feb., 1787.
7. Caroline, b. 12, bp. 24 Mch., 1789 ; poss. the dau. of "*wid.* of Jesse," ae. 3 ; bu. 10 Jan., 1792.

A Prudence of Jesse, bp. 23 Sept., 1787.
A Hy., ae. 30, d. W. I., 11 June, 1815.

FAM. 17. JOHN,[5] (*Joseph,*[4] *Henry,*[3] *Henry,*[2] *Henry,*[1]), m. Rebecca **Moore.**

Children:

1. Jane B., m. Wm. C. **Bowen.**
2. Emma G.

FAM. 18. JOSEPH,[5] (*Joseph,*[4] *Henry,*[3] *Henry,*[2] *Henry,*[1]), m. Emily **Frithrian.**

Children:

1. Harriet.
2. Ephraim.
3. Charles.
4. Margaretta.
5. Martha.
6. Joseph Fithian.

FAM. 19. ROBERT SHUTE,[5] (*Jeremiah,*[4] *Henry,*[3] *Henry,*[2] *Henry,*[1]), m. Caroline **James.**

Children:

1. Sarah Holmes, b. 2 Dec., 1838.
2. Robert Shute, b. 16 Mch., 184--; d. 1842.
3. Clara M. R., b. 4 Mch., 1843 ; m. Frank L. **DuBois,** U. S. N.
4. Robert James, b. 27 Apl., 1845 ; m. 29

June, 1871, Sidney E. **Reeves.** FAM. 22.
5. Chester Jones, b. 31 May, 1847 ; m. Eliz'th R. **DuBois.**
6. Caroline James, b. 23 Aug., 1849 ; m. Leslie **Lupton.**

FAM. 20. FRANCIS NIXON,[5] (*Jeremiah,*[4] *Henry*[3] *Henry,*[2] *Henry,*[1]), m. Jane E. **Coe.**

Children:

1. William Ramsay, b. 20 July, 1828 ; d. 6 Aug., 1828.
2. Louise Stitcher, b. 5 Dec., 1829 ; d. 1 Mch., 1830.
3. Richard Coe, b. 4 Dec., 1830 ; d. 19 July, 1832.
4. Charles Elton, b. 13 May, 1833. FAM. 23.

5. Mary Coe, b. 11 June, 1835 ; d. 21 Feb., 1860.
6. Robert Shute, b. 22 July, 1846 ; d. 21 May, 1847.
7. Albert Henry, b. 15 June, 1848 ; d. 22 May, 1859.

FAM. 21. JEREMIAH MORE,[5] (*Jeremiah,*[4] *Henry,*[3] *Henry,*[2] *Henry,*[1]), m. Mary **Bush.**

Children:

1. Francis Nixon, m. 18 Jan., 1814, Margaret C. **Douglass;** had Ellen Sinclair, b. 9 Dec., 1884.
2. Mary Kane, m. Dr. David W. **Maull** (?).

3. Laura Matilda, m. Chas. **Easman.**
4. Lewis Poller Bush, m. Martha ————.
5. James, bp. 27 Mch., 1774.

FAM. 22. ROBERT JAMES,[6] (*Rob't Shute,*[5] *Jeremiah,*[4] *Henry,*[3] *Henry,*[2] *Henry,*[1]), b. 1845; m. Sidney E. **Reeves.**

Children:

1. Robert Sidney, b. 28 Nov., 1872.
2. Ellis Reeves, b. 8 Aug., 1875.
3. Elizabeth Steinman, b. 17 July, 1817 : d.

12 Aug., 1818.
4. Laura Maxwell, b. 17 July, 1877.
5. George Franklin, b. 21 Feb., 1881.

FAM. 23. CHARLES ELTON,[6] (*F. Nixon,*[5] *Jeremiah,*[4] *Henry,*[3] *Henry,*[2] *Henry,*[1]), b. 1833; m. Sophia N. **Stratton.**

Children:

1. Charles Elton, b. 12 Mch., 1858 ; d. 31 July, 1859.
2. Eleanor Stratton, b. 31 Dec., 1861 ; d. May, 1884.

3. Agnes Elton, b. 7 Jan., 1868 ; d. 16 July, 1868.
4. Albert Henry, b. 9 Mch., 1873.
5. Charles Elton, b. 19 June, 1875.

A JOHN BUCK FAMILY.

BUCK, JOHN, Hinman (*Puritan Settlers of Conn.* edit., p. 367) mentions a JOHN BUCK, sett. at Weth. who m. Deborah **Hewes**, of Guilford, Ct. (prob.) 10 Oct., 1665. He may have been a bro. or cousin of Emanuel and Henry Buck, Their son *Thomas*, b. abt. 1666,* m. Sarah **Judd**, of Farmington or Htfd. [12 May, 1709.—*Harvey*.]

Children:

1. Sarah, b. 19 Jan., 1710 [June 10—*Harvey*].
2. Thomas, b. 6 Sept., 1712 [6 Feb.—*Harvey*].
3. Mary, b. 5 [11—*Harvey*] Nov., 1715.
4. Ebenezer, b. 11 Nov., 1717.
5. John, b. 24 Mch., 1722 [1721—*Harvey*] ; d. same yr.

The younger Thomas is said to have had lds. at Midd., as early as 1671,—*N. Eng. Gen. & Hist. Reg.*, XIV, 64 ; he d. soon after and his wid. Hannah m. (2) Joseph **Baker**, b. 16 June, 1665, by whom she had *Joseph* (Baker), b. 13 Apl., 1678 ; and *Lydia* (Baker), b. 5 July, 1681 ; who are put down (*N. Eng. & Hist. Reg.*, V, 65) as being at Windsor.

SAMUEL, m. Hannah **Wright**, 22 Mch., 1758; she b. 1737?

Children:

1. Peletiah, bp. 3 Apl., 1763 ; m. 2 Nov., 1786, Hannah **Sage**, of Cromwell.
2. Jeremiah, bp. 20 Mch., 1764 ; m. 1786, Mary **Butler**; rem. to Stockbridge.
3. Hannah, bp. 30 Aug., 1767 ; m. David **Brewer**; rem. to Vt.
4. Isaac, bp. 3 Mch., 1772 ; rem. to Tunbridge, Vt.
5. James, bp. 27 Mch., 1774.
6. Polly, bp. 17 Mch., 1778 ; m. Joel **Rannsey**; rem. to Vt.
7. Samuel, d. yg.

8. Samuel, bp. 3 May, 1779 ; m. Ruth **Goodrich**; res. Portland, Ct.
9. Justus, } twins, b. 3 Sept., 1789.
10. Esther, } Esther, m. Ezekiel **Goodrich**. If m. 1790, acc. to Portland rec., would make her birth in 1789 impossible, even if her mother at 52 would be likely to give birth to twins then.
11. Betsy, m. Reuben **Loveland**.
12. Rose, } twins (?).
13. Sally, }

BUCKER, The widow. See Chapt. Vol. I.

BUCKINGHAM, Rev. ———————— supplied the Weth. pulpit, 1663-4.

ARTHUR H., b. 27 Oct., 1870; d. 3 Aug., 1871.

ISAAC, m. Lucy **Belden,** of Weth., 11 May, 1794.—*N. C. R.*

BUCKLAND, LEONARD, ae. 28; bu. 20 Feb., 1811.—*W. C. R.*

BULKELEY,† (*Bulkley, Buckley*). The name, orig. spelled (temp. King John, 1199-1216) Buclough, and (temp. Henry IV and Edward IV) Bulclough, signifies "a large mountain."‡

The Weth. fam. of Bulkeley can clearly trace its descent, acc. to Collins' and Sir H. Nicholas' *Peerages* and other equally reliable works, from Robert Bulkeley, Esq., Lord of the Manor of Bulkeley, in the Co. Palatine of Chester, Eng. (temp. King John) through twelve generations, to Rev. Edward Bulkeley, D. D. (9th

---

* Glast. graveyard has the tombstone of a *Thomas Buck*, who d. 30 Aug., 1732, ae. 70, which would mean that he was b. 1662. May this not be the date of birth of this Thomas, instead of 1666, which is evidently an approximate date?

† THE BULKELEY FAMILY, *or the Descendants of Rev. Peter Bulkeley, who set. at Concord, Mass., in 1636.* Compiled for Joseph E. Bulkeley, of Rocky Hill, by Rev. F. W. Chapman, Htfd., 1875, 8 vo., 289 pp.

‡ The *name* is only correctly spelled *Bulkeley*. That branch of the family which went to New York is the only one which ever altered the spelling ; although it is *usually* pronounced Buckley in Conn. It is not misused in Mass.—*C. K. B.*

In this sketch, the Concord (Mass.) and Fairfield (Conn.) families of Bulkeley have not been followed out.

gen.)* who was b. at Ware(?) Shropshire, Eng.; m. Almark Irlby or Islby)
of Lincolnshire (Harvey's *Hist. Hundred of Willey*, p. 364-6); was. adm. to
St. John's Coll., Cambridge, 6 Apl., 1560—(Baker's *Hist.* of that Coll., I. 287
and 333); is ment. in same work as curate of St. Mary's, Shrewsbury, 1550;
prebend of Chester; prebend of Litchfield, abt. 1580—(*Geneal. Bulfordiensis*—
Bladys); rector of All Saints, Odell, in the Hundred of Willey, Bedfordshire.
where he d. and was succeeded by his eld. son.

PETER, B. D., (10th gen.), b. 31 Jan., 1582-3, at Odell, Bedfordshire, Eng., ent. St.
John's Coll., Cam. (ae. 16) 22 Mch., 1604-5—(Baker's *Hist.* that Coll., I,
292); fellow, 1608, M. A. degree; and "said, but on doubtful auth. to have
proceeded Bach. of Divinity," *Hinman;* succeeded his father, Rev. Edward,
as rector of Odell (Woodhill, *Wahull*) in the Hundred of Willey, Co. Bedf.
He was known to be a non-conformist, but "the Lord Keeper Williams, formerly
his Diocesan, and his personal friend, desired to deal gently with his non-
conformity"—Hotten (I, p. 368 *Palfrey*), and connived at it, as he had at his
father's for twenty years—but when Laud became Primate of Eng. 1633, and
trouble came to good Bishop Williams, Mr. Bulkeley was silenced and with no
hope of reinstatement, sold a goodly est. sailed for New Eng. in 1635, at the age
of 52.

His first wife, to whom he was m. abt. 1613, was Jane (dau. of Mr. Thomas)
Allen, of Goldington—(Blady's *Geneal. Bulfordiensis*), and by whom he had
10 sons and 2 daus., (of whom a few only reached maturity) had d. at Odell,
1626; and he m. (2d) after 8 yrs. of widowerhood, Grace (dau. of Sir Richard,
Knt. & Dorothy *Needham*) **Chetwoode;** who was b. (?) in the Manor of Odell,
1602.—See Nicholas' *Historic Peerages of Eng.;* various *Harleian MSS.*, etc.).

Here we follow *Savage* I. 291: "He came in the *Susan* and *Ellen*, emb. 9 Mch.,
1635], his age at the custom house called 50, and (for more perfect deception
of the government spies) his wife *Grace*, ae. 33, appears to be embarked in another ship [the *Elizabeth and Ann*]; and son *John* 15, some weeks earlier, beside *Benjamin* 11, and *Daniel* 9, (which two, though not names of his sons,
yet may stand for them, all three in the same ship with himself, but set down
at intervals in the record, both of time and space;† and, of course, his clerical
character did not appear, or he would have been stopped." The family evi-

---

* The line of descent is elsewhere thus set forth more particularly, viz:
1. Baron Robert de Bulkeley, A. D. 1199-1216.
2. Baron William de Bulkeley, m. a dau. of Thomas Butler.
3. Baron Robert de Bulkeley, m. Jane (dau. Sir William) Butler.
4. Baron William de Bulkeley, m. 1302, Maud (dau. Sir John) Davenport.
5. Baron Robert de Bulkeley, m. Agnes ————.
6. Baron Peter de Bulkeley, m. Nicola (dau. Thos.) Bird.
7. Baron John de Bulkeley, of Houghton, m. Arderne Fitley.
8. Baron Hugh de Bulkeley, m. Helen (dau. Thos.) Wilbraham.
9. Baron Humphrey de Bulkeley, m. Grisel Molton.
10. Baron William de Bulkeley, of Oakley, m. Beatrice (dau. William) Hill.
11. Baron Thomas de Bulkeley, m. Elizabeth (dau. of Randelle) Grosvenor.
12. Rev Edward de Bulkeley, Rector of Odell (s. of Thos. & Elizabeth Grosvenor) Bulkeley,
    m. Olive Ilsly, of Lincolnshire.
13 Rev. Peter de Bulkeley, the Emigrant to America.
† There are discrepancies in the several lists of passengers to New Eng. given by *Hotton,
Drake* and others, which are a little puzzling as to the manner of exodus of this family
from Eng. *Hotton's* list of passengers on the *Susan and Ellen* gives Peter, Daniel, ae.
9, and *Benjamin* Bulkeley—but in list of Rev. Peter's fam. there appeareth no *Benjamin*,
tho' poss. the name may have been assumed temp. by one of the other ch.
    Another list of pass. by same vessel gives names of *Grace Bewlie*, ae. 20, and *Jo. Backley*,
ae. 15, which seems to dispose of *Savage's* statement that Grace, wife of Rev. Peter, embarked
on another ship, *i. e.*, if we assume (as is quite poss.) that she did not give her married
name to the Customs officers. It, also, allows of our accepting the curious tradition current,
apparently, in all branches of the family (and not otherwise explainable, unless she was
on board the same vessel with her husband) as to the *trance* into which she fell, while on
the voyage.
    It is evident enough, however, from a careful comparison of passenger lists of the
Simon and *Ann* (as well of other somewhat similarly named vessels, sailing for New Eng.
at abt. this date) and also of family rec. of births in Rev. Peter's fam., that its members
were distributed, and left Eng., in different vessels, at about the same time.

dently came over in different vessels, leaving Eng. on (?) the day or so after the other.

A curious and very live tradition in the family, is connected with the mother's, Mrs. Grace Bulkeley's voyage across the Atlantic, viz., to the effect that while on the way hither, "she apparently died, and that her husband, supposing land to be near and unwilling to consign the beloved form to a watery grave, urgently entreated the Captain that the body might be kept one day more and yet another day, to which, as no signs of decay appeared, he consented. On the third day, symptoms of vitality were observed, and before land was reached, animation so long suspended, was restored, and though carried from the ship an invalid, she recovered and lived to old age."—Caulkins' *New London*, 132.

Some antiquarians have treated this as a fairy-tale; but, after, all, fm. a physicians' standpoint, it may be quite true. The strongest argument against the validity of the trad. is the fact that *Savage* says that Rev. Peter and his *bride* came over to N. Eng. in separate ships. *Hotten* confirms this, but he also mentions a Grace Bewlie, ae. 30, as on the same ship *with* ·Peter and Jo. *Backlie* and the other ch., so that Hotten can be used to prove either theory. And it is quite improbable that Rev. Peter would, if he could have managed it otherwise, have allowed his new and young wife to be separated from him in this long and tedious voyage to their new home. It being assumed, then, (Savage to the contrary) that husband and wife were on the same ship—we have only to remember, as to the *trance*, that such swoons, or trances, are apt to occur with pregnant women (especially in first pregnancies), at about the time of their "quickening"—and it would be nothing strange or impossible that Mistress Grace, a young and impressible woman, passing through all the anxieties and excitement of such a leaving of home and such a rough voyage, should have, at the time of her "quickening" (which must, fm. the dates, have occurred while on the ocean) experienced a nervous disturbance of the nature of a trance. Gershom, her first-born, was. b. abt. 4 months after his parents arrived in New Eng.; and the name (Gershom) which was given him, meaning, as it does, "an exile" ("I have been a stranger in a strange land."—*Exodus* II, 22) affords us a glimpse, perhaps, of the thoughts, anxieties and forebodings which filled the young mother's heart.

Rev. Peter, upon his arrival in N. Eng., first sett. at Cambridge, but the next yr. with 12 others, he began the sett. of Concord, and with them endured the miseries of their first winter there, which he was fortunately able somewhat to mitigate out of the abundance of his own estate, and which was recompensed 3 yrs. later, by a grant fm. the Gen. Ct. of 300 acr. of ld. at Cambridge.* His position at Concord was that of *Teacher* to the ch. of which Rev. John Jones was pastor; but the latter being soon called away to Fairfield, Mr. B. was install. 6 Apl., 1637, and always spoken of as "the first minister of C." He seems to have been much esteemed by his fellow ministers for learning, purity of life and good judgment. In 1637, he was, with Hooker, app. Moderator of a Synod, convened to discuss the Antinomian, or Perfectionist question then troubling the good people of the colony. His name also heads the list of the clerical members of the Standing Council app. by the Colony, in 1638, to take charge of the preparation of a "Body of Liberties," or Constitution, first undertaken in 1635. One, at least, of the laws in this doc. bears the impress of his views, since it was his life-long conviction and practice—"As to Servants, when they had rendered diligent service seven yrs., they were not to be sent away empty."—

---

* Another account says that "while he buried a considerable estate in the Wilderness, he raised one for almost every one he employed in the affairs of his husbandry. Mr. B. had brought with him from Eng., £6,000, a large fortune for those days; nearly all of it was consumed in helping forward the enterprise of the settlement.

Palfrey, *Hist. N. Eng.*, II, 30). Cotton Mather, in his Magnalia, III, 96-98, gives a sketch of his life, and quotes some Latin poems as speciments of his classical attainments. Mr. B. also pub. a volume (Lond. 1646) entitled The *Gospel Covenant*, made up of sermons preached at Concord; and an Elegy on his friend Rev. Hooker. It is also worthy of note that he was among the first (with Flint and Willard), prior to the Apostle Eliot, "to instruct the Indians in the knowledge of the Gospel," and the singular immunity from Ind. attacks, which Concord enjoyed, was largely credited, by trad., to his sanctity and influence. He d. at C. 9 Mch., 1658-9, in his 76th yr. His will, (given in *N. Eng. Gen. Reg.*, X, 167-70) dated 14 Apl., 1658, with codicils of 13 Jan. and 26 Feb., following was prob. 20 June next.—(*N. Eng. Gen. and Hist. Reg.*, X, 167). It names 7 ch.; notes that Thomas was dead, yet remembered his wid.; calls Mr. Samuel Haugh "cousin"; and gives his folio Bible to Oliver St. John, Lord Chief Justice of the Common Pleas, his nephew and makes his wife exex[x]. The wid. of his son Thomas got the "value of one Kow"; two of his sons were to halve a set of books--or, if each wished to possess the whole set let them buy a second set and divide the two so that each might have half the books which had been his father's! His wid. Grace d. 21 Apl., 1669, at New Lond., Ct., where she had rem. 1663, with her eld. son and had bo't a house there; she was called "a woman of great piety and wisdom."

Children (by first marr. born in Eng.) :

1. Edward, b. 17 June, 1614, at Odell, Eng., came to N. Eng., before his father; adm. memb. Ch. at Boston, as a single man, 22 Mch., 1635; adm. freeman, 6 May, same yr.; adm. inhab. Plym., Col., 5 June, 1644; ord. as minister at Marshfield, 1642, (succeeding Mr. Blinman, who had preceded his bro. Gershom at New London), served till 1658, and next yr. succeeded his father in ministry at Concord; d. at Chelmsford, Mass., 2 Jan., 1696.
2. Mary, b. 1615; bp. 24 Aug., d. few hrs.
3. Thomas, b. 11 Apl., 1617; came to Am. in the *Plaine Joanne*, May, 1635, ae. 32— *Hotten's Lists;* freeman, Mch., 1638-9; m. Sarah (dau. of Rev. John) *Jones*, of Concord; and with him rem. to and sett. in Fairfield, Ct., d. abt. 1658, and was the father of the F. branch of the B. family.
4. Nathaniel, b. 29 Nov., 1618; d. 1627, ae. 9.
5. John (Rev.), b. 11 Feb., 1620; came to N. Eng., in same ship with his fthr.; made freeman 18 May, 1642; ret. to Eng., instituted into a living at Fordham by a Parliamentary Committee, but, being ejected 1662, rem. to Wapping (Lond.), where he duly qualified and practiced medicine with success, and d. abt. 1689.— *Calamy's Acc. of Ejected Ministers*, II, 311-12. Savage says he was of the first class grad. at H. C., 1642, and ranks on the catal. next after Sir Geo. Downing. He gave to H. C. an acre of ld. in Cambridge, afterwards known as "The Fellows' Orchard," and yet in possess. of the Coll. The deed is curious, as being in Latin, and as for the affection it indicates for Pres. Dunster. He is said to have left a wife and 3 ch.
6. Mary, b. 1 Nov., 1621; d. 1624, ae. 3.
7. George, b. 17 May, 1623, not known to have marr.
8. Daniel, b. 28 Aug., 1625.
9. Jabez, b. 20 Dec., 1626; d. under 3 yrs.

10. Joseph, (prob.) b. 1619.—*Hotten.*
11. William, of Ipswich, 1648, came to N. Eng., in the *Expedition*, 20 Nov., 1635.
12. Richard.—See *Hotten.*
A *Humphrey* Buckley, ae. 18, came on the *Globe*, 7 Aug., 1635. *Humphrey* is a family name with the B.'s, and may have been an *alias* for another of the sons.
(By second marriage, b. New Eng.) :
13. Gershom, b. 6 Dec., 1636, (or 2 Jan., as fam. memorial has it.—*Savage*). F[A]M. 7.
14. Eleazer, b. prob. 1638; of whom *Savage* says he was "living in 1659, when his father's will provides well for him; d. prob. in no long time after, as he is never ment. as freeman', or otherwise."
15. Dorothy, b. 2 Aug., 1640, at Concord, Mass.[*]
16. Peter, b. 12 Aug., 1643,[*] at Concord; res. Fairfield, Ct.; his wife d. prob. before date of his will (25 Mch., 1691), wherein she is not ment. He rem. to F. prob. abt. the same time that his mother and his eld. bro. rem. to New Lond. (1663); he was a physician; his will names his two eld. daus. *Grace* and *Margaret* and a son *Peter*. For the remainder of his ch., we are obliged to refer to the will of his bro. Rev. and Dr. Gershom, to whose care he had left them and in whose bequests they shared, viz.: *Gershom*, b. or bp. 1675, (or '79, as given in *Year Book of Soc. of Colonial Wars*) : *Dorothy* and *Peter*, b. 25 Dec., 1683; who m. Hannah *Ward*, and known from his occup. as "Peter, Weaver," to distinguish him from his cousin "Peter, Cooper."— *W. H. Perry*. This Ger[s]hom, b. 1675 or 9, is prob. the G., of Fairfield, Ct., who figures so largely as *Capt.* Gershom, in *Conn. Col. Rec.*, VI, 72, 340; VII, 7, 350, 356, 523; VIII. IX, 424, 555; X. 77, 554-592, 598; XI, 2. Undoubtedly, this gives the rec. of *two* men—that of the sec-

[*] A Register of the Births and Burials in Concord "from the yeare 1639 and until the first month 1644, according to our account."
"Dorothie, the daughter of Mr. Peter Bulkeley, was born the — (6), 1640."
"Peter, the sonne of Mr. Peter Bulkeley, was born the 12, (6) 1643."
"Peter, the sonne of Mr. Peter Bulkeley, was born the 3 (11) 1640."
"Sarah, the daughter of Mr. Thomas Buckley, was born the 12 (11) 1640."—*Register*, Vol. 3 p. 271.

ond man beginning prob. in 1734, with the formation of the Coldchester Train-band.—*C. K. B.* These are the initials of Mrs. Caroline Kemper Bulkeley, whose husband, Louis Carleton Bulkeley, is of the Fairfield line of Bulkeleys, and who res. at Avalon, Alden's Bridge, La. To this lady we are under deep obligations for much useful material concerning the B. family, into whose history she has made strenuous investigation. Mr. B.'s descent from this Gershom is as follows: *Gershom,* m. Rachel (dau of Lt. Col. John) **Talcott.** Their s. *Peter,* m.

Ann (dau. of William) **Hill,** of Fairfield. Their s. Gershom, m. (1) Elizabeth **Chapman;** m. (2) Wid. Hannah **Raymond;** m. (3) Mary Burr **Bartram,** wid. of Daniel Osborn, Jr. By his first wife (Elizabeth), he had *William,* who m. Mary Bartram **Osborn** (dau. Gershom's 3d wife) ; their s. *Philemon Carpenter,* m. Mary Jane **Moody** of New Rochelle, N. Y., b. Eng.; their son, *Louis Carleton,* m. *Caroline* (dau. Andrew Carr & Louisa Anderson) **Kemper,** of Cincinnati, O. Their *ch.* are *Louise* (Bulkeley), b. 1895; *Grace Chetwood* (Bulkeley), b. 1897.

FAM. 2. *Rev.* and *Dr.* GERSHOM,[2] (*Rev. Peter,*[1]), b. 6 Dec., 1636, at Concord; grad. H. C. 1655, being then not quite 19 yrs. old; given by *Oldmixon,* as a Fellow of the Coll., only one since 1653, "next to Hon. Peter Bulkeley (son. of Dr. Edward, s. of Peter[1]) with only one name between"; m. 26 Oct., 1659, Sarah (dau. of Rev. Charles) **Chauncey,** Pres. of Harvard Coll. She was b. at Ware, Eng., 13 June, 1631. In 1661, he became minister of the 2d ch. at New Lond., Ct., but, after a few yrs. some difficulty arising with his people, he rem. to Weth. and in 1666-7 was installed as pastor, succeeding four or five clergymen, who had served the ch. as supplies since the departure of Rev. John Russell, who had rem. to Hadley, in 1659. After 10 yrs. ministry here, Mr. Bulkeley, in 1676, asked for a dismission from pastoral office on account of impaired health (Miss Caulkins says "a weak voice") ; and he thereafter devoted himself to the practice of medicine and surgery, in which he attained much success and reputation. He was also an ardent student in Chemistry and Philosophy; and was master of several languages, including Latin, Greek and Dutch; and was also an expert surveyor.

During his pastorate, 1675, he was appointed, by the Gen. Ct., as surgeon to the Conn. troops in King Philip's War, and was also placed on the Council of War; and the Ct. also gave orders to have him taken especial care of. Trumbull speaks of him as a great surgeon of his day in the colony. While on this expedition the party to which he was attached, was attacked by a number of Indians, near Wachusett Hill, Mass., and in the fight he rec'd a wound in the thigh.

Dr. Bulkeley was a man of very positive character and very pronounced opinions— his courage being always equal to the backing up—by word or deed—of his convictions. He was well versed in law, and as a Magistrate, much respected. He insisted upon unqualified obedience to authority; naturally, an ardent Royalist, it is not strange that in the days of political excitement which arose in consequence of Sir Edmund Andros' attempt to interfere with the government of the colonies, he could not espouse the popular side; but raged in person, and with all the power of his forceful pen, against the assumptions of the colonial government. But, it must be conceded, that his keener insight into the political field foresaw that the course which the colonists were then pursuing would ultimately lead to the triumph of democratic principles which they disavowed, and which eventually culminated in the Revolution. His personal connection with the events of that troublous time, and with the authorship of the famous tract *Will and Doom,* will be found more fully discussed in Chapt. of our 1st Vol. His only other pub. work, besides *Will and Doom* was an Election Sermon, delivered 1680, (Romans XIII, 7) printed at Boston. He has come down to us in history as "always a troublesome and discontented person," a "bigoted partisan," "a man of strong prejudices," etc.—but his ability and honesty of purpose no one has ever questioned; and it is not at all unlikely that, like many another man, stout in heart and strong in the courage of his own convictions, he may have had a softer side to his nature, known only to his family and friends. The closing sentence of the epitaph graven upon his tomb, concedes that he was "of a most exemplary and Christian life." That being so, his other and less pleasing characteristics may easily be condoned as mere foibles, not seriously dimning the lustre of the most rigorous and useful personality which has ever graced the annals of Weth. Chapin's *Glast. Centennial* (pp. 181-2) gives a brief view of the memorable case at law between him and Mr. John Hollister, which largely occup. the attention of the Gen. Ct. for two sessions, and resulted in an order by that body for a resurvey (by Eleazur Kimberly and Hugh Welles) of all the lots on the East side of the river from East Hartford line to the South line of the Nayaug section.

Rev. and Dr. Gershom Bulkeley, after he ent. upon the practice of med. and surgery, became a land elder in Glastonbury; but, though he died there, 2d Dec., 1713, at the home of his dau. Dorothy (wid. of Mr. Thomas) **Treat**, we have no reason to believe that he was ever other than a resident of Weth. proper. For ld. ppy, see Chapt. VII, Vol. I. His wife Sarah, had d. 3 June, 1699.

His monument in Weth. Cemetery, says of him: "He was honorable in his descent, of rare abilities, excellent in learning, master of many languages, exquisite in his skill, in divinity, physic and law, and of a most exemplary and Christian life. *In certam spem beatae resurrectiones repositus.*

His will, dated 28 May, 1712 (see *Bulkeley Geneal.* 81-86) is a long, curious and characteristic doc. of which the following (*Htfd. Co. Prob. Ct.*) is an abstract. GERSHOM BULKELEY, Wethersfield, (*alias* Glastonbury,) Invent. not shown. Will dated 26 May, 1712. I give to my son *Charles;* dau. *Hannah* (Goodrich); to my dau.-in-law Hannah *Avery*, and Hannah *Wolcott;* to my son Edward's present wife Dorothy; to my brother Peter's children Gershom, Peter, Grace, Margaret, Dorothy, I give to my son *Edward* the clock now standing in his house, my Seal Ring, the Great Gilt Spoon, a Silver Porringer and all the Books and Manuscripts there touching Law. Except some notes I have written. I give to my son *John* all my books and Manuscripts as concern only Divinity and other Learning except Law; also, such as concern Medicine and Chymistry. To my grand son *Richard Treat*, (son of Thomas and Dorothy Treat) all my books which concern Medicine and Chymistry. I give to him if he hold and pursue his present inclination to study. Otherwise, I give them to his mother, my dau. *Dorothy*, to dispose of; to my dau. *Catharine* (Treat) Decd., I have given yet to her only child Catharine Treat I give my Silver Tankard, Silver cucumbit, the Silver Salt-Seller and the small Silver Dram Cups; or, if she die, to her Father Richard Treat. The rest of my estate to my dau. Dorothy Treat, Richard Treat to be Executor.

Witness. John Hollister, Samuel Brooks, } Daniel Andrews.   } GERSHOM BULKELEY,   (   )

Addition 4 November, 1714, as my son Richard Treat has Deceased I ordain my daughter Dorothy, now widow, Sole Executrix. He gives Her his Negro Maid Hannah.

                          GERSHOM BULKELEY,   (   )

Witness, Samuel Brooks, Joseph Easton, Sarah Brooks.

7 March 1714, Rev. John Bulkeley of Colchester, accused the Executrix of embezlement from the estate.

Will approved 7 December, 1713. 7 June, 1715, the Executrix moved the Court to Compel Rev. John to take an invt. of estate in his hands, he having neglected to do so.

TOP OF TABLE MONUMENT OF REV. GERSHOM BULKELEY,
showing a rude sculpture of the Bulkeley Arms.

Children:

1. Catharine, b. abt. 1660-1; m. Richard (s. Rich'd) **Treat**, 20 Aug., 1704; d. soon after. See ref. to her in her father's will.
2. Dorothy, b. abt. 1662; m. 5 July, 1693, Lieut. Thomas **Treat**, (bro. of her sister Cath's husband) "of Nayaug;" he was one of the petitioners for incorporation of Glast., and by Dr. Gershom B.'s will was made his exec'r, but, dying 17 Jan., 1713, ae. 44, before the Dr.'s dth., the executorship was transferred to his wid., Mrs. Dorothy T., who d. 1757; 8 ch. See *Treat.*
3. Charles (Dr.), b. abt. 1663; stud. med., prob. with his father; was licensed to practice, 1687, as appears by Ct. Rec.; settled New Lond.; m. and d. before his father. *Issue:* Hannah, m. 18 May, 1709, Richard **Goodrich**, of Weth.; also res. in Glast., later in Midd.
4. Peter, b. abt. 1664; m. Rachel **Talcott**, 21 Mch., 1700; was lost at sea in a storm, abt. 22 Nov., 1701, ae. 37. (*Weth. Rec.*)* Invt. 67-03-00, taken by Robert Welles, Samuel Wright, David Goodrich, 30 Mch., 1702; Invt. not complete—money due at Deleware and parts of a broken sloop at Block Island. *Court Record*—Peter Bulkeley, Mariner—Rachell the Relict appointed Adms. Bond with Ebenezer Kilbourne

£100. Invt. Present account 12 March 1701-2 there being no issue the surviving children of Rev. Gershom Bulkeley, having an Interest in the estate quit claim to the sd. estate desiring that the entire estate might be distributed to the Widow Reserving to the heir of Mr. Charles Bulkeley late of New London Dec. her part if she should ever demand it for this Security was given by Mrs. Rachel Bulkeley widow. We are informed by that very careful geneal. Rev. M. E. DWIGHT, M. D., of Plainfield, N. J., that the final fig. 1, in the date of yr. 1701, is written suspiciously like a 2; also, what is of more importance (and which has been discovered by Dr. D.) that Peter's wid., Rachel (dau. Capt. Samuel) Talcott, of Weth., m. (2) Mr. Henry[2] **Wolcott** (s. of Simon,[1]), of Windsor, Ct., as his second wife; which finds corroboration in the Rev. Gershom's will, wherein he ment. "my dau.-in-law, Rachel Wolcott;" Mrs. Rachel (Talcott) Bulkeley-Wolcott, d. 8 Jan., 1726, having had, by her Wolcott husband, three ch., viz: *Peter, Rachel* and *Gideon*—the latter the ancestor of Mrs. M. E. Dwight.

5. Edward, b. 1672. FAM. 3.
6. John (Rev.), b. 1679. FAM. 4.

FAM. 3. Capt. & Esq. EDWARD,[3] (*Rev. & Dr. Gershom,[2] Rev. Peter,[1]*), b. 1672; m. Dorothy (dau. Jonathan) **Prescott**, 14 July, 1702, of Concord, Mass., he d. Weth., 27 Aug., 1748, in 75 yr. The Bulkeley arms given herewith, are copied fm. those sculptured on his tombstone in Ry-H. bu-gd. He was collector 1703, selectman 1708, was adm. an attorney, *Co. Ct. Rec.* June, 1711. In Apl., 1712, he prosecuted Massecup and Peter Sachme, Indians for stealing some cloth from his fulling mill---the cloth being owned by John Edwards, John Gills and Edward Wigley—value @ 6s to 7s per yd. *Co. Ct. Rec.* From same *Rec.* we learn that in Apl., 1716, Mr. B. tho' then one of the Justices of the Peace, was prosecuted and fined 6s. 8d. for forging land recs. (he being Register) the forging being upon a conveyance from Josiah Churchill to said Bulkeley, in which doc.

BULKELEY ARMS.

the word *January* had been erased, and the word *May* substituted therefor. But, on appeal, the jury found him not guilty. Mr. B's wid. d. 30 Nov., 1760, in 81 yr. —*W. Ins.*

---

* There has been much confusion as to the parentage of the two Rachel Talcotts who m. into the Bulkeley family; and *Savage* argues the question at great length (considering the limitations of space of his immense *Geneal. Dict.*); but fails to determine the point.
Our version is this—Lt.-Col. *John* Talcott, of Weth., had a dau. Rachel, b. 23 Feb., 1681, who m. Gershom Bulkeley, of Fairfield, son of Dr. Peter B., of F. His cousin Peter Bulkeley (son of Rev. Gershom) m. 1700, Rachel (dau. of Capt. *Samuel*) Talcott, also of Weth., and d. next yr. leaving no issue; his wid. m. (2) Henry Wolcott.

Children (Weth. Rec.); the last three from *B. Geneal.*

1. Charles, b. 25 (bp. 28 *Mix*) Mch., 1702-3. FAM. 5.
2. Elizabeth, b. 24 (bp. *Mix*) Jan., 1704-5, m. Joseph **Smith**, res. Midd.
3. Sarah, b. 8 (bp. 9 *Mix*) Feb., 1706-7; m. Joseph **Stowe**; d. at Midd.
4. Rebecca, b. 2 (bp. 7 *Mix*) Feb., 1708-9; m. her first counsin, Isaac **Treat.**
5. Peter, b. 19 (bp. 25 *Mix*)   , 1710-11; d. inf.
6. Peter, b. 11 (bp. 16 *Mix*) Mch., 1711-12. FAM. 6.
7. Gershom, b. 29 July, (bp. 1 Aug., *Mix*) 1714. FAM. 7.
8. Dorothy, b. 11 Sept., 1716; m. Thomas **Curtis.**
9. Jonathan, b. 11 Sept., 1718. FAM. 8.
10. Abigail, b. 1720; m. John **Marsh.**
11. Lucy, b. 1723; m. Charles **Butler.**

FAM. 4. Rev. JOHN,[3] (*Rev. Gershom,*[2] *Rev. Peter,*[1]   ) b. 1679, grad.
H. C. 1699; m. 1701, Patience (dau. John & Sarah) **Prentice,** of New Lond.,
stud. theol., became pastor at Colchester, Ct., 20 Dec., 1703, where he ministered
until his dth. in June, 1731; held high rank among the clergy of his day.
Pres. Chauncey, of H. C., certainly a competent critic, after a full estimate of
the character and abilities of Rev. John's father (Dr. Gershom) and his gd-
father, (Rev. Dr. Peter), hesitates not to say, "but, by all that I have been
able to collect, the Colchester Bulkeley surpassed his predecessors in the strength
of his intellectual powers;" and he classes him among the three most eminent
for strength of genius and powers of mind, that New Eng. had then produced—
the others being the Rev. Jeremiah Dummer, and Mr. Thomas Walter. He was
"a famous casuist and sage counsellor."[*]

Children:

1. Sarah, b. 8 Apl., 1702; m. (1) Jonathan **Trumbull**; m. (2) John **Welles.**
2. Dau. b. 6 May, 1704; lived 3 hrs.
3. John, b. 19 Apl., 1705; m. (1) Mary **Gardiner**; m. (2) Abigail **Hastings.**
4. Dorothea, b. 28 Feb., 1706.
5. Gershom, b. 14 Feb., 1709. FAM. 9.
6. Charles, b. 26 Dec., 1710.
7. Peter, b. 21 Nov., 1712.
8. Catherine, b. 21 May, 1715.
9. Oliver, b. 29 July, 1717; d. 1 Jan., 1719.
10. Lucy, b. 29 June, 1720.
11. Irene, ⎰ twins, b. 10 Feb., 1722; d. 20
12. Joseph, ⎱   Feb., 1722; d. 25 Feb., 1722

FAM. 5. Mr. CHARLES,[4] (*Edward,*[3] *Rev. & Dr. Gershom,*[2] *Rev. Peter,*[1]) b. 1703;
m. 28 May, 1724, Mary (dau. John) **Sage,** of Midd., where they res.; he d.
21 Feb., 1758 in 55 yr., she d. 5 Oct., 1756, ae. 57 yr.—*Weth. Ins.*

Children (Weth. Rec., Mix. MSS.):

1. Mary, b. 9 June, 1725; m. David **Webb,** 20 May, 1750.
2. John (Capt.), b. 9 July, 1726. FAM. 10.
3. Catharine, b. 7 Sept., 1728; m. ————. **Cadwell.**
4. Giles, bp. 14 Dec., 1729. FAM. 11.
5. Benjamin, bp. 1 Aug., 1731. FAM. 12.
6. Sarah, b. 20 Apl., 1733; m. Cephas **Smith,** 5 Aug., 1756.
7. Charles (Capt.), bp. 10 Nov., 1734. FAM. 13.
8. Olive, b. 5 Apl., 1736; m. James **Deming.**
9. Thomas, b. 28 Sept., 1739.
10. Edward, b. 8 Nov., 1741; bp. 15 Nov., ————? FAM. 14.
11. Prescott (Capt.), bp. 5 Aug., 1744. FAM. 15.

FAM. 6. PETER,[4] (*Edward,*[3] *Rev. & Dr. Gershom,*[2] *Rev. Peter,*[1]) b. 1712; m.
(1) 2 Apl., 1741 Abigail **Curtis,** who d. 27 Nov., 1762 in 55th yr.; m. (2)
Christian **Smith,** 26 Jan. 1769—*S. Rec.;* prob. the wid. Christian who d. 22

---

* Rev. John Bulkeley's published works were:
1. *The Necessity of Religion in Societies;* and its Serviceableness to Promote the Due and Successful Exercise of Government In Them; Asserted and Shown.   A Sermon Preach'd before the General Assembly of the Colony of Connecticut, at Hartford, May 14, 1713, [N. D.] 1713, pp. 70.
2. *An Impartial Account of a late Debate at Lyme* in the Colony of Connecticut, on the Three following Heads, viz.: I.   The Subjects of Baptism.   II.   The Mode of Baptism. III.   The Maintenance of the Ministers of the Gospel.   Giving a Summary of what was there delivered on both sides. * * *   New London, MDCCXXIX, 16 mo. pp. 200.
3. *The Usefulness of Revealed Religion to Preserve and Improve that which is Natural;* as it was Represented in a Sermon Preached at Colchester, on the Occasion of the Ordination of the Rev. Mr. Judah Lewis, December 17th, 1729, N. London, MDCCXXX, pp. 48.
4. He also wrote the Preface (60 pp.) to Roger Wolcott's *"Political Meditations,"* New London, 1725.
The following sermon, occasioned by Mr. Bulkeley's death, was published:
A Discourse Delivered at Colchester, June 13, 1731, the Day after the Funeral of the Rev. Mr. John Bulkeley, Pastor of the Church of Christ in that Place.   By Eliphalet Adams, M. A., New London, MDCCXXIV, pp. 46.

Dec., 1802,—*S. C. R.;* was app J. P. for Htfd. Co., May 1775; d. 4 Apl., 1776.—
S. C. R.; res. Weth. (Stepney).

Children (Weth. Rec.):

1. Joseph, b. 28 Jan., 1742. FAM. 16.
2. Abigail, b. 13 Apl., 1743; m. Nath'l **Miller,**
   of Ry-H.; rem. to Brookville, N. Y.; d.
   14 Apl., 1834.
3. Oliver, b. 5 Dec., 1744; m. and d. at sea,

Apl., 1776.—*S. R.*
4. Solomon, b. 21 Mch., 1747. FAM. 17.
5. Dorothy, b. 17, d. 28 July, 1749.
6. Justus, b. 24 Dec., 1752. FAM. 18.

FAM. 7. Mr. GERSHOM,[4] (*Edward*,[3] *Rev. & Dr. Gershom*,[2] *Rev. Peter*,[1]) b. 1714;
m. Thankful (ygst. dau. of Daniel & Marg't *Blinn*) **Belding,** 17 Feb., 1743, a
wife of Gershom d. 17 or 18 Dec., 1794 in 71 yr.; a wife of Ger. d. 23 Dec., 1798
in 57 yr.—both rec.—*S. C. R.*, which belongs to G. I do not know; he d. 21
Aug., 1800 in 87 yr.—*S. C. R.*

Children (Weth. Rec.):

1. Thankful, b. 20 May, 1744.
2. Jehiel, b. 23 Oct., 1745. FAM. 19.
3. Gershom (Rev.), b. 3 Dec., 1747. FAM. 20.
4. Mabel, b. 2 May, 1750.
5. Ruth, b. 17 May, 1752.
6. William, b. 2 Sept., 1754; m. Olive (dau.
   Capt. Elias & Prudence) **Williams,** 31
   Jan., 1776 (*S. R.*), who d. in childbirth
   26 Nov., 1777.—*Weth. Ins.* He was
   drowned at sea, 23 July, 1788. *Issue:*

i. William, d. ae. 10 yr.; prob. the
   "Wm., s. of Wm." bp. 25 Mch., 1781—
   S. R.
7. Hosea (Capt.), b. 1756. FAM. 21.
8. Thankful, b. abt. 1760; m. Samuel **Dimock;**
   d. 14 Oct., 1798, or was she the one who
   d. 20 June, 1765 (*S. C. R.*), ae. 38.—
   Weth. Ins.
9. Chloe, bp. 24 Sept., 1765 (*S. C. R.*); m.
   Fred. **Boardman,** 28 July, 1790.

FAM. 8. JONATHAN,[4] (*Edward*,[3] *Rev. & Dr. Gershom*,[2] *Rev. Peter*,[1]), b. 1718; m.
Abigail **Williams,** 13 Nov., 1746. He d. 16 June, 1777 in 59th yr.—*Weth. Ins.*

Children (B. Geneal.):

1. Eleanor, b. 11 Nov., 1747.
2. Stephen, b. 19 Dec. (*Nov. in Fam. Bible
   Rec.*), 1749. FAM. 22.
3. Edmund, (Edward in *S. C. R.* of dth.) b.
   17 Dec., 1751; d. 20 Jan., 1806 in 54th yr.
   (*S. C. R.*)
4. Jonathan, b. 5 Nov., 1753; d. 11 July, 1756,
   ae. 2 yr. 8 mos. 6 d.—*Weth. Ins.*
5. Frederick Treat (*Fam. Bible Rec.*), b.
   27 Aug., 1755; d. 20 Jan., 1777.
6. Son, b. 25 Jan., 1758; d. nxt. eve'g.
7. Jonathan, b. 10 May, 1759. FAM. 23.
8. Lydia, b. 9. May, 1761.
9. Dau., (stillborn) 11 May, 1762.

10. Moses, b. 7 Feb., 1764.
11. Dorothy, b. 8 Apl.; prob. bp. 11 May; d.
    18 Aug., 1766.
12. Burrage, b. and bp. (*S. C. R.*) 9 Nov.,
    1767—*Fam. Bible Rec.* gives 8 Aug., and
    S. C. R. gives bp. as 9th Aug., so the
    B. Geneal. date must be an error. He was
    one of 22 men, taken prisoner by a Br.
    War vessel, and who d. in one of the New
    York prisons in 1782. (*Step. Ch. Rec.*)
    See Revol. Chapt. Vol. 1.
13. Dorothy, b. (acc. to *Fam. Bible Rec.*)
    19 May, 1770; bp. 8 July. (*Step. Rec.*)

FAM 9. GERSHOM,[4] (*Rev. John*,[3] *Rev. & Dr. Gershom*,[2] *Rev. Peter*,[1]) b. 1709; m.
Abigail (dau. Joshua & Abigail *Warner*) **Robbins.**

Children:

1. Sarah, b. 10 June, 1735; m. Joseph **Isham,**
   17 June, 1765.
2. John, b. 23 May., 1737. FAM. 24.
3. Joshua, b. 24 Feb., 1741; m. Lois **Day,**
   9 Nov., 1761.
4. Daniel, b. 13 May., 1744; m. Dorothy
   Olmstead, 16 May, 1764.

5. Eunice, b. 14 May, 1747; m. Elihu **Lord,**
   25 May, 1769.
6. David, b. 18 July, 1749; m. Hannah
   Brenith, 18 Dec., 1781.
7. Roger, b. 14 Sept., 1751; m. (1) Jerusha
   Root; m. (2) Rhoda **Loomis;** m. (3) Polly
   Champion.
8. Ann, b. 11 May, 1758.

FAM. 10. Capt. JOHN,[5] (*Chas.*,[4] *Edwd.*,[3] *Rev. & Dr. Gershom*,[2] *Rev. Peter*,[1]), b.
1726; m. Honor **Francis,** 17 July, 1750. *Weth. Rec.*, who d. 6 May, 1903 in
66 yr.—*Weth. Ins.* He d. ae. 81, bu. 27 Mch. 1807.—*W. C. R.*

Children (Weth T. & Ch. Rec.):

1. John, b. 10, bp. 18 Nov., 1750. FAM. 25.
2. Honor, b. 14 Mch., bp. 14 Apl., 1753; m.
   Sylvanus **Bronson;** 6 ch.
3. William, b. , 1754; lost at sea, Sept.
   or Oct. 1802 (?).
4. Elizabeth, bp. 16 Feb., 1755; m. John
   Mygatt; 1 ch.

5. Frances (Capt.), bp. 31 July, 1757. FAM.
   26.
6. Benjamin, b. 1761; d. yg.
7. Sarah, bp. 16 June, 1765; d. yg.
8. Edward, b. 1767. FAM. 26a.
9. Sarah, bp. 1 July, 1770; m. ———
   Beskirk.

FAM. 11. GILES,⁵ (*Chas.*,⁴ *Edwd.*,³ *Rev. & Dr. Gershom,*² *Rev. Peter,*¹) b. abt. 1728; m. ———; he d. 4 Aug., 1785 in 57 yr.—*S. C. R.*

Children (bp. S. C. R.):

1. Levi, bp. 30 Sept., 1764; prob the L. who d. at sea, 3 Nov., 1789, ae. 26.
2. David, bp. 3 Aug., 1766. FAM. 27.
3. Abigail, bp. 22 Oct., 1769.
4. Daniel, bp. 28 June, 1772.
5. Hetty, bp. 15 Apl., 1781.

FAM. 12. BENJAMIN,⁵ (*Chas.*,⁴ *Edw'd.*,³ *Rev. & Dr. Gershom,*² *Rev. Peter,*¹), b. 1731; m. (1) 3 Nov., 1757, Susannah **Kirby**, who d. 27 May, 1776, ae. 42,— *Weth. Ins.;* m. (2) Elizabeth **Brownell**, 6 Feb., 1777—*W. C. R.;* he d. ae. 91, bu. 16 or 17 Aug., 1822.—*Weth. Ins.*

Children (Weth. Rec.):

1. Thomas, b. 2, bp. 8 Oct., 1758. FAM. 28.
2. Lucy, b. 18 Sept., 1760; m. Joseph **White**.
3. George, b. and bp. 28 Nov., 1762; m. Martha **Webster**, of Compton, R. I.
4. Huldah, b. 1, bp. 7 Oct., 1764; m. John **Francis**, Jr., 7 Nov., 1792; she d. 14 Apl., 1833.—*Weth. Ins.*
5. James, b. 11 Sept., 1766; m. Caroline **Hallam**, of Charleston, S. C.; *no issue.*
6. Stephen, b. 18 Nov., 1768. FAM. 29.
7. Abigail, b. 30 Dec., 1770; m. Jasper **Lacy**; rem. to Ohio.
8. Martha, b. 26 Apl., 1773, bp. 27 Feb., 1774;
   m. George **Webster**, of Whitestone, N. Y.
9. Hannah, b. 25 June, bp. 9 July, 1775; m. Amos **Woodruff**, of Stockbridge, Mass.
   (*By second marriage*):
10. Benjamin, bp. 5 Mch., 1780.
11. Benjamin, b. 16 Feb., 1782, bp. 13 May, 1782. FAM. 30.
12. Samuel, b. twin to Benjamin, bp. 24 Sept., 1784.
13. Brownell. FAM. 31.
14. Betsy, m. Philo **Yale**, and d. without issue, July, 1864.

FAM. 13. Capt. CHARLES,⁵ (*Chas.*,⁴ *Edw'd.*,³ *Rev. & Dr. Gershom,*² *Rev. Peter,*¹) b. abt. 1739; m. (1) 10 Mch., 1760, Mary **Griswold**, who d. 24 Jan., 1771, who d. 24 Jan., 1772, ae. 31.—*Weth. Ins.;* m. (2) Eunice **Welles**, 7 Oct., 1773, who d. "wid." 10 Sept., 1827 ae. 81.—*Weth Ins.* He prob. the C. who d. ae. 78, 10 Nov., 1812.—*Weth. Ins.*

Children (Weth. Rec. & *S. C. R.):*

1. Charles,* b. 19 May, (9 Mch. *tombstone*) and bp. before 18 Sept., 1760; he d. in W. I., 15 Dec., 1787 ('99 *tombstone*).— *S. C. R.* FAM. 32.
2. Justus,* b. 15 Mch., 1762.
3. Mary,* b. 13, bp. 15 June, 1764 (*S. R.*); m. Elisha **Wetherell**.
4. Elizabeth, b. and bp. 25 Jan., 1766.
5. Daniel, bp. 14 Aug., 1769.
6. Eunice, bp. 11 Dec., 1774.
7. Nancy, bp. 27 Apl., 1777; prob. d. 6 May, 1779; m. Joshua **Goodrich** (?).
8. Inf., bu. May, 1779; prob. the Nancy bp. 2 May, 1779.
9. Chester, bp. 25 Feb., 1781 ('82 on *tombstone*) of Albany, N. Y.; m. (1) 5 Oct., 1806, Hannah **Buck** (*Conn. Comut.*); m. (2) 20 Nov., 1833, Martha **Riley**, of Weth. He d. 4 Dec., 1848, ae. 68. (*W. T. R.*) *Weth. Ins.* notes tombstone inscription of *Maria*, his wife, who b. 8 Mch., 1798, d. 17 Sept., 1872.
10. Polly, b. 30 Oct., 1785. (*S. C. R.*)
11. Mary Griswold, bp. 26 Oct., 1783.— *W. C. R.*
12. (?) Horace Welles, bp. 16 July, 1786.— *W. C. R.*
   (Had ch. d. 4 Oct., 1784.—*W. C. R.*)

FAM. 14. Major EDWARD,⁵ (*Chas.*,⁴ *Edw'd.*,³ *Rev. & Dr. Greshom,*² *Rev. Peter,*¹) b. abt. 1741; m. (1) 27 Oct., 1771, Rachel (only ch. of Lieut. Oliver & Mary) **Pomeroy**, (*S. C. R.*), who d. 14 Aug., 1774 in 20 yr., (*S. C. R.*) m. (2) 24 Mch., 1782, Prudence **Welles**; he d. 30 May, 1787 in 46 yr.—*S. C. R.*, she d. 26 Jan., 1825 ae. 72.—*Weth. Ins.* He res. at Ry-H. in what was known as the Long house (built by Pomeroy) near The Landing. His title of Major was obtained in the Revol. war.—*Dr. R. W. G.*

Children (Weth. *Rec. & S. C. R.):*

1. Roxa, bp. 25 Oct., 1772; m. Selah **Francis**, of Weth., 25 Feb., 1793.
2. William, bp. 2 Nov., 1773; drowned at sea, 23 July, 1788; he m. Mabel ———; their only ch. *William*, d. 14 Feb., 1790, in 10th yr.—*Weth. Ins.*
   (*By second marriage*):
3. Rhoda, bp. 11 Aug., 1776; m. Josiah **Edwards**.
4. Fanny, bp. 29 Apl., 1781; m. Elihu **Frisbie**, of Albany, N. Y., 29 Oct., 1813; 2 ch.
5. Rachel,* b. 13 Dec., 1782; bp. 16 Feb., 1783; prob. the R. who m. 11 Aug., 1805, Serenus **Swift**, of Manchester, Vt.—
   W. C. R.
6. Pamela,* b. and bp. 6 June, 1784; d. 16 Sept., 1814, in 31st yr.—*S. C. R.*
7. Rodney, bp. 13 June, 1784; d. 22 Sept., 1786.—*S. C. R.*
8. Prudence, bp. 1 Apl., 1787; m. Ebenezer **Parker**, of Boston, 9 Aug., 1812.
9. Oliver Pomeroy,* b. 31 Jan., bp. 8 Apl., 1787; d. 14 Nov., 1852.—*Weth. Ins.*
10. Edward Rodney, bp. 5 July, 1789.— *S. C. R.*
11. Charlotte, bp. 23 Jan., 1799; m. Orrin **Lewis**.—*S. C. R.*
12. Inf., d. 13 Feb., 1792.

FAM 15. Capt. PRESCOTT,[5] (Chas.,[4] Edwd.,[3] Rev. & Dr. Gershom,[2] Rev. Peter,[1])
b.————————; m. 1774, Lois **Williams.** He d. 10 Sept., 1791, ae. 47.—S. C. R.

Children (bp. S. C. R.) :

1. Simeon, bp. 21 Aug., 1774 ; d. Oct., 1793, in W. I., ae. 18 ; unm.
2. Horace, bp. 10 Oct., 1779 ; d. Leyden, N. Y., 1813.
3. Nancy, b. 1 Oct., bp. 11 Nov., 1781 ; m. Nathan **North,** of Exeter, N. H., 1805.
4. Laura, bp. 21 Mch., 1784 ; d. insane, 23

Mch., 1841 at Leyden, Wis.
5. Louisa, b. 30 Jan., bp. 9 Apl., 1786 ; m. John G. **Post.**
6. Lydia, b. and bp. 24 Feb., 1788 (S. C. R.) ; m. P. **Irwin.**
7. Belinda, b. 5 June, bp. 29 Aug., 1790 (S. C. R.) ; m. Dr. Sam'l **Bass.**

FAM. 16. Capt. JOSEPH, Esq.,[5] (Peter,[4] Edw'd,[3] Rev. & Dr. Gershom,[2] Rev. Peter,[1])
b. 1742 ; m. Mary (dau. Moses & Martha) **Williams,** 3 May, 1776.—S. C. R.
She b. 3 Jan., 1756, d. 23 Dec., 1848, ae. 92 (tombstone 1845, ae. 89, 11mo.).
He was a mcht. at Ry-H.; and rep. to State Leg. He d. 31 Mch., 1821, ae.
80.—S. C. R.; was one of the old mchts. at The Landing, Rocky Hill; many
yrs. J. P. and rep. the Town in Assembly of Oct., 1798, May and Oct., 1800,
May, 1801, Oct., 1803; both sess. of 1804, 1805, '6, '7, '8, '9, and May, 1810,
both of 1813, Oct., 1814. He occup. the ho. now (1902), res. of Justus L.
Bulkeley.

Children:

1. Mary, b. 18 Dec., 1778, bp. 10 June, 1781 ; m. Joseph **Butler,** 23 May, 1803.
2. Rhoda, b. 21 Jan., bp. 10 June, 1781 ; m. Wyllis **Williams,** 19 June, 1799.
3. Ralph, b. 14 Sept., bp. 26 Oct., 1783 ; he d. N. Y., 4 Feb., 1860, ae. 77 yrs. 4 mos.; m. Eliz'th **Bradford,** 21 Jan., 1808 (S. C. R.) ; she b. 28 Aug., 1782 ; d. Ry-H. 26 Nov., 1876, ae. 94 yrs. 3 mos.—Weth. Ins.
4. John, b. 28 Oct., bp. 11 Dec., 1785 ; d. 2 June, 1806.—Weth. Ins.
5. Edmund, b. 6 Dec., 1787, bp. 3 Feb., 1788.— S. C. R. FAM. 33.

6. Joseph, b. 28 Oct., 1789, bp. 21 Feb., 1790 (S. C. R.) ; grad. Y. C. 1810 ; from 1815 practiced law in N. Y. City with success for many yrs.; but from losses incurred thro' his bro. Ralph, became discouraged and did not do so well in later life ; d. at Ry-H. 21 Mch., 1851.—Weth. Ins.; unm.
7. Henry, b. 10 (11 tombstone) June, bp. 1 Aug., 1793 (S. C. R.) ; m. Martha **Tucker.** FAM. 34.
8. Walter Williams, b. 15 Sept., 1797, bp. 28 Jan., 1798. FAM. 35.

FAM. 17. SOLOMON,[5] (Peter,[4] Edw'd,[3] Rev. & Dr. Gershom,[2] Rev. Peter,[1]), b.————
————————; m. Martha (dau. Moses) **Williams,** 6 June, 1776—(S. C. R.) ; he
d. 4 Mch., 1790, ae. 43—S. C. R.; his wid. m. (2) Elizur **Goodrich,** 6 Mch.,
1796.

Children :

1. Sally.
2. James ; poss. the Jas. who d. 11 Jan., 1860, ae. 82.—Weth. Ins.

3. Oliver.
4. George.

6. Nancy.
5. Martha.

FAM. 18. JUSTUS,[5] (Peter,[4] Edw'd,[3] Rev. & Dr. Gershom,[2] Rev. Peter,[1]), b. ————
————————; m. (1) Mabel **Boardman,** 22 Mch., 1781, who d. 11 Sept., 1804, ae.
44—Weth. Ins.; m. (2) Lucretia Churchill(?), wid. of Ackley **Riley,** of
Stepney, 19 June, 1805, who. d. 12 Sept., (Oct., tombstone) 1826, ae. 75 ; m. (3)
wid. Mehitable **Curtis,** 12 Nov., 1826, who d. 13 Mch., 1851, in 82d yr.; he
d. (9 or 22) Mch., 1829, in 77th yr.—Weth. Ins.; res. Rocky Hill.

Children (bp. S. C. R.) :

1. Ch., d. 11 June, 1781.
2. Sophia, bp. 6 Oct., 1782.
3. Chesterfield, bp. 7 Nov., 1784 ; d. Nov., 1845, in 62d yr.—S. C. R.
4. Inf., [Justus?] d. 19 Oct., 1786.—S. C. R.
5. Lora, b. 4, bp. 7 Nov., 1790.

6. Clarissa, bp. 1 May, 1791.
7. Betsy, bp. 1 Aug., 1793.
8. Justus, bp. 25 Sept., 1795 ; d. yg.
9. William, bp. 14 Apl., 1799.
10. Harriet, bp. 11 Oct., 1801.
11. Julius, bp. 13 Nov., 1803 ; m.; had 5 ch.

FAM. 19. JEHIEL,[5] (Gershom,[4] Edw'd,[3] Rev. & Dr. Gershom,[2] Rev. Peter,[1]), b.
1747 ; m. Mary **Robbins,** 2 Mch., 1775—S. C. R.

Children (S. C. R.):

1. Inf., d. 29 Apl., 1781.
2. Chauncey, bp. 8 Sept., 1782 ; prob the Ch.

who m. Nancy **Hart**, 27 Aug., 1805.—
S. C. R.

FAM. 20. Rev. GERSHOM,[5] (*Gershom,[4] Edw'd,[3] Rev. & Dr. Gershom,[2] Rev. Peter,[1]*),
b. 1747; m. Mabel **Huntington**; grad. Y. C. 1770; studied theol.; licensed by
Htfd. So. Assoc., 1772; sett. at 2d or North parish of Midd. Upper Houses
(Cromwell), Ct., June 1778; dismissed fm. there 1808, after 30 yrs. service;
and remained at C. until his dth., 7 Apl., 1832, ae. 86. He m. (2)—(*Weth.
Rec.*) Hope **Warner**, of Step., 30 Sept., 1778; who d. 1 Oct., 1813, ae. 63.

Children:

1. Dau. | 2. Dau. | 3. Leonard ; m. Polly **Williams.**

FAM. 21. Capt. HOSEA,[5] (*Gershom,[4] Edw'd,[3] Rev. & Dr. Gershom,[2] Rev. Peter,[1]*), b.
————; m. Abigail **Griswold**, of Weth., 1 May, 1781—S. C. R., who d.
28 Aug., 1823, ae. 63.—S. C. R. He d. 4 Nov., 1838, in 82d yr.—S. C. R. Their
home was the old Butler tavern in the So. Dist. of Ry-H., on ppy. descending to
him fm. his gt-gd-fthr., Rev. Dr. Gershom B.

Children (bp. S. C. R.):

1. Amelia, b. 24 Apl., bp. 5 May, 1782 ; m.
   Allen **Robbins**, 17 Oct., 1804.
2. Ursula, b. 8 June, bp., 27 July, 1783 ; d.
   27 Mch., 1873.—*Weth. Ins.*
3. John Griswold, b. 3 Jan., bp. 17 Apl.,
   1785. FAM. 36.
4. Sylvester (Dr.), b. 1 June, bp. 22 July,
   1787. FAM. 37.
5. Gershom, b. 11 Feb., bp. 19 Apl., 1789 ;
   prob the G. who m. Esther **Neff**, 30 May,
   1816 (S. C. R.) ; altho. *Weth. Ins.* seems
   to give him a wife *Laura*, b. 4 Feb., 1795,
   who d. 8 July, 1864. He d. 19 Jan., 1867.—
   Weth. Ins.
6. Inf., d. 13 Nov., 1790.
7. Mabel, b. 13 Nov., 1791, bp. 26 Feb., 1792 ;
   m. Ira **Beaumont**, of E. Htfd., 10 Oct., 1811 ;
   9 ch. ; she d. 22 Mch., 1884.

8. Olive, b. 1 Sept., bp. 2 Nov., 1794 ; m.
   Revilo **Chapman**. of Hadd., 29 Apl., 1823.—
   W. T. R.
9. Abigail, b. 17 Sept., bp..29 Nov., 1795 ;
   prob. the ch. d. 8 June, 1798, in 3d yr. ;
   Weth. Ins. says d. 6th June, ae. 2 yr. 8
   mo. 11 dys.
10. Abigail Stanley, bp. 28 Apl., 1799 ; m.
    Davis **Smith**, Mch., 1819, inkeeper at
    Haddam, but later rem. to Ry-H. They
    had a family of ten children ; four of these
    died in infancy ; Mary I. was the second
    wife of Ambrose Wolcott, now deceased,
    and Margaret W., the first wife of William
    C. Williams, formerly of Rocky Hill. Mrs.
    Smith was a most estimable woman and
    truly one of the "mothers in Israel."

FAM. 22. Capt. STEPHEN,[5] (*Jonathan,[4] Edw'd,[3] Rev. & Dr. Gershom,[2] Rev. Peter,[1]*), b.
1749; m. (1) Martha (dau. Mr. John & Abigail) **Marsh**, who d. 26 (6th *tombstone*) Apl., 1804, in 53rd yr.; m. (2) Susan **Riley**, 16 Sept., 1805; he d. 6 May,
1813.

Children (bp. S. C. R.):

. Honor, b. 5 May, bp. 25 Sept., 1774 ; m.
  David **Edwards, Jr.,** of Midd.
2. Stephen, b. 18, bp. 28 Apl., 1776 ; d. 29
   Sept., 1779.—*Weth. Ins.*
3. Catharine, b. 15 Oct., 1778 ; d. 11 Oct.,
   1799.
4. Kate, b. 2 Sept., 1780, bp. 4 Mch., 1781 ;
   m. Zenas **Edwards**, 7 Dec., 1803.
5. Stephen, b. 30 Mch., bp. 1 June, 1783 ; m.
   Eliza **Riley.**
6. Allen, b. 19 July, bp. 27 Aug., 1786 ; d. 17
   Aug., 1855, ae. 69 (*Weth. Ins.*) ; he m. 26
   June, 1823, (*W. T. R.*) Eliza Ann Riley,
   who d. 4 Oct., 1857, ae. 51 (*Weth. Ins.*).

They had *Harriet Abbot*, d. 6 Oct., 1829, ae.
1 yr. 13 d ; *John Marsh*, d. 29 Apl., 1836,
ae. 23 ; *Joseph*, d. in Calif. 14 Dec., 1849,
ae. 23.
7. Polly (Patty on *tombstone*), bp. 2, d. 4
   May, 1790.—*Weth. Ins.*
8. Frederic, b. 1 bp. 3 June, 1792 ; m. Nancy
   Riley. FAM. 38.
9. Dau., b. 18 Dec., 1796 ; poss. the inf. who
   died this yr., one hr. old.
   (*By second marriage*) :
10. Burrage, b. 22 Dec., 1805. FAM. 39.
11. Stephen, b. 4 Mch., 1807. FAM. 40.
12. Inf. d. 11 Oct., 1810.

FAM. 23. JONATHAN,[5] (*Jona.,[4] Edw'd,[3] Rev. & Dr. Gershom,[2] Rev. Peter,[1]*), b.
1759; m. Mary **Edwards**, 16 Jan., 1787—S. C. R.; he d. 30 Mch., 1836, in 77th
yr.—S. C. R.; she d. 14 Feb., 1823, in 62d yr.—S. C. R.

Children (S. C. R.):

1. Sally, bp. 2 Dec., 1787 ; m. Elisha **Goodrich**, of Glast., 30 July, 1821 ; 2 ch.
2. Nably (Abigail), bp. 19 Feb., 1792 ; m.
   Isaac **Stevens**, of Portland, Ct., 20 Apl.,
   1819 ; 4 ch.

3. Prescott, b. 8 Feb., bp. 11 June, 1797. FAM.
   41.
   Jona B.'s inf., who d. 29 Oct., 1798—prob.
   of this family.

Fam. 24. JOHN,⁵ (Gershom,⁴ Rev. John,³ Rev. & Dr. Gershom,² Rev. Peter,¹), b. 1737; m. 11 Jan., 1757, Judith (dau. Elijah & Mary *Welles*) **Worthington.** (*This fam. communicated by B. W. Pierson, Esq., of N. Y. City.*)

Children:

1. John, b. 7 Oct., 1759; m. Theo. **Foote.**
2. William, b. 30 Aug., 1761; m. Mary **Champion.**
3. Gershom, b. 3 Oct., 1763.
4. Elijah, b. 29 Jan., 1766; m. Pamela **Loomis.**
5. Nabby, b. 30 Dec., 1769; m. Roger **Tanitor.**
6. Joshua Robbins, b. 2 Nov., 1771. Fam. 42.
7. Mary, b. 2 Feb., 1774; m. Aaron **Buckland.**
8. Judith, b. Jan., 30, 1775; m. Solomon **Tanitor.**
9. Gurdon, b. 15 Mch., 1777; m. (1) Fanny **Wright**; m. (2) Nancy **Porter.**
10. Gad, b. 20 Feb., 1779; m. Orra **Barstow.**
11. Lydia, b. 25 Apl., 1781; m. (1) John **Worthington**; m. (2) Dr. Wm. **Mason.**
12. Dan, b. 20 Mch., 1784; m. Phebe **Burnet.**
13. Harriet, b. 22 Jan., 1787; m. Samuel **Moseley.**

Fam. 25. JOHN,⁶ (John,⁵ Chas.,⁴ Edw'd,³ Rev. & Dr. Gershom,² Rev. Peter,¹), b. 1750; m. Sarah **Wright.**

Children:

1. John, bp. 30 Nov., 1783; m. ———— **Daggett.**
2. Elizabeth (Patty), bp. 30 Nov., 1783; m. James Goodrich.

Fam. 26. Capt. FRANCIS,⁶ (John,⁵ Chas.,⁴ Edw'd,³ Rev. & Dr. Gershom,² Rev. Peter,¹), b. ————————; m. (1) Rhoda (dau. Capt. Elisha & Abigail) **Griswold,** 18 Jan., 1781—*W. C. R.;* who d. 6 Mch., 1795, ae. 38—*Weth. Ins.;* m. (2) Elizabeth **Fosdick,** 5 Jan., 1796 or 7—*Weth. Ins.;* he d. on board of the brig. *Ontario,* Timothy Stillman, mstr., 26 Apl., 1813.

Children (b. Weth., W. C. R.):

1. William, b. 11 Nov., 1781; bp. 30 Nov., 1783.
2. Clarissa, b. 20, bp. 28 Mch., 1784; m. Charles **Noyes,** of Canaan, N. Y., 30 Dec., 1807.—*W. C. R.*
3. Harriet, b. 13, bp. 23 Apl., 1786; d. 7 Oct., 1786.—*Weth. Ins.*
4. Francis, b. 6 Nov., bp. 9 Mch. (?), 1788; m. Content **Mix,** of N. Haven, 9 Nov., 1811; was lost at sea (1817) in brig *Regent,* off Cape Trafalgar, ae. 29.
5. Chauncey, b. 12 June, bp. 18 July, 1790; d. ae. 2, bu. 14 May, 1792.
6. Harriet, b. and bp. 4; d. 13 Feb., 1795.

(*By second marriage*):
7. Chauncey, b. 16, bp. 18 June, 1798; **grad.** at Coll.; taught school in Phila.; studied law; adm. to bar in 1822, in P.; alderman in that city, 1845-50, much esteemed; d. 23 May, 1860, ae. 62.
8. James Henry, b. 23 July, 1799; bp. 3 Aug., 1800; rem. to Phila. 1814; m. Adaline **Alexander,** 26 June, 1828; had 11 ch. all b. in P.; of whom James Henry, Jr., b. 1834; d. 1875, served in U. S. N. during the Civil War, and later in China and Japanese waters.
9. Charles, b. 27 Apl., bp. 28 June, 1801; rem. to Phila. 1814; m. Eliza **Hunt.**

Fam. 26a. EDWARD,⁵ (Chas.,⁴ Edw'd,³ Rev. & Dr. Gershom,² Rev. Peter,¹), b. 1767; m. Diana (Dinah, on tombstone) **Bunce,** 9 July, 1795; he d. 5 Feb., 1805; she d. Dec., 1804, ae. 35.—(*Weth. Rec.*)

Children (Weth. Rec.):

1. Honor Francis, b. 22 Aug., 1795; bp. 3 July, 1796; m. Joel **Chapin, Jr.,** of Oxford, N. Y., 6 Oct., 1823.—*S. C. R.*
2. John Bunce, b. 2 May, bp. 2 July, 1797; d. at Port au Prince, W. I.
3. Eliza, b. 20 May, 1799; bp. 8 Nov., 1801; m. Rich. **Green.**
4. Edward, b. 7 Aug., bp. 8 Nov., 1801; joined 1st Cong. Ch., Weth., 1822; rem.
to New Haven, Ct., in 1828; m. 1832, Lucy **Mansfield;** was one of the founders of Chapel St. Church (Ch. of the Redeemer in that city).
5. Mary, bu. 20 Mch., 1803; b. 16, bp. 19, d. 20 Mch., 1803.
6. Wealthy, b. 28 May, 1804; m. Jesse St. **John.**

Fam. 27. DAVID,⁶ (Giles,⁵ Chas.,⁴ Edward,³ Rev. & Dr. Gershom,² Rev. Peter,¹), b. 1766; m. Elizabeth **Flint,** 6 May, 1789.

Children:

1. Inf., bu. 13 Feb., 1790.
2. Harriet, bp. 9 Nov., 1794.
3. Ch., bp. 24 May, 1795.
4. Levi, ae. 16 mos., bu. 31 July, 1796.—See *Weth. Ins.*
5. William, bp. 10 Sept., 1797.
6. S. ae. 15 mos., bu. 17 Aug., 1798.
7. Levi, bp. 5 May, 1799.
8. Charlotte, bp. 28 June, 1801.
9. David Collins, bp. 5 May, 1805.
10. John Lathrop, bp. 22 Oct., 1809.

FAM. 28. THOMAS,[6] (*Benj.,*[5] *Chas.,*[4] *Edw'd,*[3] *Rev. & Dr. Gershom,*[2] *Rev. Peter,*[1]), b. 1758, m. Bathsheba **Sage**.

Children:

1. George, poss. the G. who d. W. I., 1 July, 1805, in 19th yr.—*S. C. R.*
2. Laura.
3. Fanny.
4. Henry.
5. Sophia.

FAM. 29. STEPHEN,[5] (*Benj.,*[4] *Edw'd,*[3] *Rev. & Dr. Gershom,*[2] *Rev. Peter,*[1]), b. 1768; m. —————————; purchased the Wadsworth (Charter Oak) pl. at Htfd.; he d. 17 Oct., 1841, ae. 73.—*Weth. Ins.*

Children:

1. George, ae. 1 yr., bu. 7 Oct., 1829.—*W. C. R.*
2. Caroline, m. Hon. I. W. **Stuart** ("*Scoeva*") of Htfd.

FAM. 30. BENJAMIN,[5] (*Benj.,*[4] *Edw'd,*[3] *Rev. & Dr. Gershom,*[2] *Rev. Peter,*[1]), b. 1764; m. Sarepta (dau. Solomon) **Woodruff**, of Far.

Children:

1. Martha.
2. Lucy.
3. Samuel.
4. Julia.

FAM. 31. BROWNELL,[5] (*Benj.,*[4] *Edw'd,*[3] *Rev. & Dr. Gershom,*[2] *Rev. Peter,*[1]), b. 1782; m. Dolly **North**, of Far.; rem. to Coventry, N. Y.

Children:

1. George, b. 20 Nov., 1814; m. Esther **Pendleton**.
2. Francis, b. 10 Apl., 1819; m. Grace **Adams** (?).

FAM. 32. CHARLES,[5] (*Chas.,*[4] *Edw'd,*[3] *Rev. & Dr. Gershom,*[2] *Rev. Peter,*[1]), b. 1760; m. Eunice **Robbins**, 15 (24—*S. C. R.*) Oct., 1782; she d. 29 Mch., 1835—*Weth. Ins.*; res. Weth. He d. in W. I., 15 Jan., 1799.—*Weth. Ins.*

Children:

1. Mary, b. 8 Apl., bp. 30 Oct., 1785; m. Thomas **Seldon**, of E. Hadd.
2. Augusta, b. 26 (28—tombstone) Jan., bp. 8 Apl., 1787—*S. C. R.;* d. N. Y. City, 18 Apl., 1859, unm.
3. Henry, b. 7 Mch., bp. 31 May, 1789; m. Betsy **Dodd**, 15 Apl., 1812.
4. Archibald, } twins, b. 6 Apl., 1792.
5. Ashbel, }
   Arch.bald, m. Wealthy Ann **Burr**, Sept., 1815.
   Ashbel, m. Ann Eliza **Fanning**, 25 May, 1816.

(*Note.—Step. Ch. Rec.* gives bp. of *Asher* and *Ashbel*, twins of Chas. B. 3 June, 1792; prob. the same.)
6. Erastus, } twins, b. 6 Nov., 1798; bp. 21
7. Mehitable, } May, 1797.—(*Sic., S. C. R.*)
   Erastus, d. Brooklyn, N. Y., 10 Jan., 1880; Mary **Walbridge**, his wife, b. 26 Sept., 1796; d. B., 23 Mch., 1872.—*Weth. Ins.*
   Mehitable, m. S. H. R. **Hall**, 14 May, 1826. (*Note.—Step. Ch. Rec.* gives *Emiline*, instead of Mehitable, as name of one of these twins.)

FAM. 33. EDMUND,[6] (*Joseph,*[5] *Peter,*[4] *Edw'd,*[3] *Rev. & Dr. Gershom,*[2] *Rev. Peter,*[1]), b. 1787; m. 18 Apl., 1811, Nancy **Robbins**,—(*S. C. R.*); he d. (6 or) 26 Feb., 1853; she b. 29 Aug., 1791; d. N. Y. City, 14 Sept., 1862.

Children (bp. S. C. R.):

1. Joseph Edmund, b. 9 Feb., 1812; bp. 23 May, 1819; m. Mary Lawrence **Bicknell**. FAM. 43.
2. Justus Robbins, b. 15 June, 1813; bp. 28 May, 1819; m. Mary K. **Adams**, 1 May, 1851; mcht. at Augusta, Geo., 1834-52, when he rem. to N. Y. City. After what were known as the Schuyler frauds in connection with N. Y. & New Haven R. R. his good reputation led to his appt. as

Pres. of that corporation, an office which he held from 1855, until his dth. in 1862.
3. Julius Huntington, b. 9 Mch., 1815—*Weth. Ins.;* bp. 23 May, 1819; d. Washington, N. C., 30 July, 1833.—*Weth. Ins.*
4. Susan Mansfield, b. 20 (30—tombstone) Apl., bp. 10 Sept. (*S. C. R.*), 1825; d. 30 Sept., 1832.—(*Tombstone.*)
5. Susan Mansfield, b. ——————; m. Hiram H. **Webb**, of Rockingham, N. C., 1855.

FAM. 34. HENRY,[6] (*Joseph,*[5] *Peter,*[4] *Edw'd,*[3] *Rev. & Dr. Gershom,*[2] *Rev. Peter,*[1]), b. 1793; a mcht. at the Landing, Ry-H.; was the first Town Clerk at Rocky Hill.

Ct.; rep. the Town in Leg. and held the office until spring of 1860, during all which time, also, he was J. P.; rts. in old B. homestead just S. of the Centre Corner; held many other offices of trust; m. 16 May, 1847, Martha **Tucker**, of Weth.; he d. 10 June, 1860.—*Weth. Ins.* which also calls his wife Martha **Adams**, and date of her dth. 24 Dec., 1893.

Children:

1. Henry William, b. 30 June, 1847; *Weth. Ins.* says b. 16 June, 1848; d. 19 Apl. 1891.
2. Martha Robbins, b. 31 Dec., 1848.
3. Mary, b. 23 Feb., 1850.
4. Joseph, b. 16 Oct., 1851.

5. Walter, b. 1 June, 1853.
6. John, b. 6 Feb., 1855.
7. Laura, b. 22 Nov., 1856.
8. Julia, b. 13 Nov., 1857.
9. Elizabeth, b. 7 July, d. 18 Aug., 1860.—*Weth. Ins.*

FAM. 35. WALTER WILLIAMS,[6] (*Joseph*,[5] *Peter*,[4] *Edw'd*,[3] *Rev. & Dr. Gershom*,[2] *Rev. Peter*,[1]), b. 1797; m. 17 June, 1830, Lucy (dau. Levi) **Robbins**; was merchant at Ry-H.; lost his life from exhaustion from burning of steamboat *Pennsylvania*, on the Delaware River, 5 Mch., 1834; she d. 5 Mch., 1887.—*Weth. Ins.*

Children:

1. Amelia, m. Rev. Horace **William**.
2. Susan M., m. Hiram H. **Webb**, of Rock-

Ingham, N. C., 8 Oct., 1855.—*S. C. R.*

FAM. 36. JOHN G.,[6] (*Hosea*,[5] *Gershom*,[4] *Edw'd*,[3] *Rev. & Dr. Gershom*,[2] *Rev. Peter*,[1]), b. 1785; m. (1) Abigail **Hart**, 25 Nov., 1804—(*S. C. R.*); m. (2) wid. Mary **Hubbard**, 12 Jan., 1830, who. d. 24 Nov., 1855, ae. 68—*Weth. Ins.*, (*S. C. R.*), prob. the M. wife of J. who d. 28 May, 1850, ae. 43—*Weth. Ins.;* he d. 14 (4 *tombstone*) Nov., 1829, in 46th yr.—(*S. C. R.*)

Children (all bp. 26 July, 1818,—S. C. R.):

1. William, d. unm. poss. the Wm. who d. 13 Mch., 1840 ae. 35.—*Weth. Ins.*
2. Amelia Ann, m. Norman **Butler.**
3. Ursula Bull, m. Josiah **Butler.**
4. John, d. unm. 22 Sept., 1832.
5. Hosea, m. Susan **Patch**, of Midd.; had dau. May, b. 12 June, 1842, who m. Edw'd S. **Thompson**, of Glast.

6. Caroline Hart, m. Philip **Butler**, of Midd., 28 Nov., 1833—*W. T. R.;* res. Cromwell.
7. Benjamin Griswold, m. Emily Abigail **Clark**, of Meriden, 1839; res. M.; 4 ch.
8. Frances Amelia, m. Wm. **Clark**; res. Meriden.
9. Mary Sophia, bp. 2 Sept., 1838.—*S. C. R.*

FAM. 37. SYLVESTER, M. D.,[6] (*Hosea*,[5] *Gershom*,[4] *Edw'd*,[3] *Rev. & Dr. Gershom*,[2] *Rev. Peter*,[1]), b. 1787, at Ry-H.; prepared for college under Rev. Calvin Chapin; grad. Y. C. 1810; taught school in Weth.; studied med. with Dr. Daniel Fuller, of Ry-H.; attended lectures at Dart. Coll. Med. School; rec'd his M. D. degree 1812; commenced practice at Haddam; after 8 yrs rem. to Chester; ret. to Higganum (Hadd.) in partnership with Dr. Munger; then located at Cromwell for 12 yrs.; then, after taking a post-grad. course in N. Y. City, ret. to Ry-H. in 1848, where he succeeded Dr. Barrows, who had gone to Htfd. He d. 1 Feb., 1857. Of him it was justly said: "He performed his duties as a man and a physician carefully, faithfully and honestly, and was gathered to his fathers like a shock of wheat fully ripe to the harvest." He, then "of Mdd." m. Nancy **Bradford**, May 1, 1825—*S. C. R.*; she d. 21 Oct., 1872, ae 86.—*R. W. G.*

Children:

1. Sylvester, d. yg. at Cromwell, Ct.
2. William, m. Lurania **Belden**.

3. Mary Ann, m. John **Brundage**.

FAM. 38. FREDERICK,[6] (*Stephen*,[5] *Jona.*,[4] *Edw'd*,[3] *Rev. & Dr. Gershom*,[2] *Rev. Peter*,[1]), b. 1792; m. Nancy **Riley**, 6 Oct., 1814—*S. Rec.;* he d. 28 Sept., 1850; she d. 23 Dec., 1857, ae. 65.—*Weth. Ins.* .

Children:

1. Martha, (M. on *tombstone*) March ; b. 15 Oct., 1815 ; bp. 1 Sept., 1821 ; d. 1 Apl., 1870, unm.
2. Julia, twin Jane, b. 2 Jan., 1819 : bp. 1 Sept., 1821 ; d. 21 Feb., 1890 ; unm.
3. Jane, twin Julia, bp. 1 Sept., 1821 ; m. Walter **Edwards**, 15 Nov., 1843 ; he d. 31 May, 1874, ae. 50 ; she d. 27 May, 1888. *Issue :*
   i. Elizabeth (Edwards), b. 29 Oct., 1844 ; m. Edward T. **Francis**, 24 Mch., 1870 ; had (*a*) Everett H. (Francis), b. 26 Sept., 1872 ; (*b*) Bernice (Francis), b. 14 Jan., 1874.
   ii. Fanny Maria (Edwards), b. 28 Aug., . 1846 ; d. 3 Sept., 1849.
   iii. Frederick Bulkeley (Edwards), b. 14

Oct., 1850.
   iv. Frank Daniel (Edwards), b. 12 Feb., 1853 ; d. 25 June, 1889.
4. Nancy R., b. 30 Dec., 1822 ; bp. 13 July, 1823 ; m. Benj. H. **Tower**, 3 Jan., 1865.
5. Stephen, b. 6 May, bp. 28 Aug., 1825. FAM. 48a.
6. Kate E., b. 23 Apl., 1834 ; ("Fr. Cath. of Med." bp. Jan., 1835.) m. 20 Nov., 1872, John **Warner**. *Issue :*
   i. Kate Bulkeley (Warner), b. 11 Oct., 1873 ; d. 26 Aug., 1893.
   ii. Gertrude Edwards (Warner), twin iii, b. 7 Dec., 1875.
   iii. Grace Chetwood, (Warner), d. 19 Oct., 1896.

FAM. 39. BURRAGE,[6] (*Steph.*,[5] *Jona.*,[4] *Edw'd*,[3] *Rev. & Dr. Gershom*,[2] *Rev. Peter*,[1]), b. 1805 ; m. Caroline **Miller**; res. at Dividend, Ry-H. ; he d. 26 (20, tombstone) Feb., 1874, ae. 68 ; she d. 14 Mch., 1887, ae. 75.

Children:

1. Henry W., b. 25 Sept., 1833.
2. Burrage, b. 15 Jan., 1836 ; lived 3 days.
3. Albert, b. 26 Jan., 1838 ; prob. the s. of B. who d. 16 Aug., 1845, in 7th yr.
4. Mary D., b. 19 Sept., 1840 ; unm.
5. Joseph A., b. 3 Nov., 1843 ; m. Emma Jane **Whitman**.
6. Carrie M., b. 4 Mch., 1846 ; m. Franklin E. **Davenport**.

FAM. 40. WAIT C.,[6] (*Steph.*,[5] *Jona.*,[4] *Edw'd*,[3] *Rev. & Dr. Gershom*,[2] *Rev. Peter*,[1]), b. 1807 ; m. (1) —————— ; m. (2) Charlotte **Whitmore**, both of Ry-H., 10 May, 1838—*S. Rec.*; he d. 2 Feb., 1849, in 42d yr.—*S. C. R.*

Children:

1. Charles.
2. Edward, poss. the one who d. 8 Oct., 1856, ae. 16.—*S. C. R.*
3. Mary.
4. Lucy.
5. Inf., d. 14 Nov., 1840.—*S. C. R.*

FAM. 41. PRESCOTT,[6] (*Jona.*,[5] *Jona.*,[4] *Edw'd*,[3] *Rev. & Dr. Gershom*,[2] *Rev. Peter*,[1]), b. 1797 ; m. Penelope **Tryon**, 15 Sept., 1822 ; he d. 1874 ; she d. 30 Sept., 1864, ae. 59 yrs., 8 mos.—*Weth. Ins.*

Children (bp. 29 June, 1838—S. C. R.) :

1. Lucy,* b. 17 June, 1823 ; m. Hamilton **Horton**, 1 Aug., 1844.
2. Laura,* b. 8 Feb., 1825 ; m. George **Smith**.
3. Martha Edwards,* b. 8 Jan., 1827 ; m. William **Fyler** (?), 1850.
4. Mary, } perhaps one of these was the
5. Mary,* { "ch. of P.," who d. 3 Oct., 1842, in 8 yr., and the other the "Inf. of P.," who d. 26 or 28 Jan., 1831.—*S. C. R.*
6. Horace,* b. 1830 ; d. 11 June, 1848, in 18

yr., at So. Glast.
7. Walter,* m. Electa **Hunt**, 1852.
8. Ellen Louise,* m. Samuel **Abbey**, 1866.
9. Harriet Griswold, bp. 1 May, 1840— *S. C. R.*; m. Lyman **Kellum**, 1865.
10. Abby Jaue, bp. 3 July, 1846—*S. C. R.*; m. Harry **Hutchinson**.
11. Noah Edwards, b. 3 Mch., 1843 ; bp. 3 July, 1846—*S. C. R.*; unm.
12. Imogene Lawrence, b. 7 Nov., 1851.

FAM. 41a. STEPHEN,[7] (*Frederick*,[6] *Stephen*,[5] *Jona.*,[4] *Edward*,[3] *Rev. & Dr. Gershom*,[2] *Rev. Peter*,[1]), b. 1825 ; was an excellent farmer, and of the pioneer tobacco growers of Weth., as also a large buyer of the plant for a New York firm. He was a capable and successful business man, and highly esteemed for his business sagacity and integrity. Prior to the Civil War, he was a Democrat, but after that became a Republican in politics ; and in his religious faith, he was Episcopalian. His fellow townsmen repeatedly testified their esteem for him by electing him to town offices. In 1861, he served as selectman, and a member of the Board of Relief, as also in 1882-3. In 1883, he rep. the Town in the Conn. Legislature. He was one of the founders, and an esteemed member of the Conn. society of the patriotic order *The Sons of the American Revolution.*

Stephen Buckley

As a public spirited citizen, he was ever a staunch supporter of the Town's educational interests. He m. 23 Jan., 1850, Prudence Mary (dau. of John) **Warner,** of Weth. He d. 21 June, 1891; she (b. 5 Feb., 1827) d. 29 Nov., 1887.

Children:

1. Fanny R., b. 2 Nov., 1850; m. John **Han-mer,** 28 Jan., 1874; res. Weth. *Issue:*
   i. Alice Elizabeth (Hanmer), b. 6 Nov., 1874.
   ii. Mary Goodrich (Hanmer), b. 6 Oct., 1878.
   iii. Fanny Bulkeley (Hanmer), b. 6 Oct., 1878.
2. Alice May, b. 9 Apl., 1852; res. (1902) Weth.
3. Prudence Warner, b. 24 Jan., 1854; res. (1902) Weth.
4. Frederick, b. 8 Feb., 1856; d. 2 Apl., 1860.
5. Edward J., b. 23 Apl., 1858; m. Jennie Sage, 28 Apl., 1886. *Issue:*
   i. Rachel Eugenia (Bulkeley), b. 7 Sept.,

1887.
6. Stephen, b. 4 Jan., 1861; edu. at Weth. and Htfd.; grad. Htfd. High School, 1880; and in same yr. rem. to Brooklyn, N. Y., where he ent. employ of the late Henry H. Dickinson (a native and res. of Weth.), druggist, and on Mr. D's retirement from bus. 1885, Mr. Bulkeley succeeded to the bus. which he still carries on. He is a memb. of the Church Club and of the Crescent Athletic Club of Brooklyn.
7. Charles, ⎱ res. Weth.
8. Chester, ⎰ twins, b. 25 Apl., 1864.
   d. 27 Oct., 1867.
9. Robert, b. 9 Sept., 1866; res. (1902) Weth.

FAM. 42. JOSHUA ROBBINS,[6] (*John,*[5] *Gershom,*[4] *Rev. John,*[3] *Rev. & Dr. Gershom,*[2] *Rev. Peter,*[1]), b. 1771; m. 17 Sept., 1793, Sarah Bulkeley (dau. John & Sarah *Bulkeley*) **Tanitor.** Her mother's parents were Gershom & Abigail **Bulkeley.** (*This fam. communicated by Mr. B. W. Pierson, of N. Y. City.*)

Children:

1. Clarissa Tanitor, b. 21 Nov., 1794; m. 24 Sept., 1815, Job **Pierson;** she d. 19 Dec., 1865.
2. Mary Augusta, b. 29 May, 1797; m. Parker Learned **Hall;** she d. 30 Aug., 1857.
3. John Robbins, b. 29 Apl., 1800; d. 8 May, 1800.
4. Caroline Emily, b. 25 Apl., 1803; m. Charles Seymour **Benjamin;** she d. 1 July,

1844.
5. John Robbins, b. 17 Apl., 1805; d. 17 Oct., 1887, unm.
6. Charles Taintor, b. 28 Aug., 1808; d. 23 Nov., 1872; m. Oct., 1840, Mary Henrietta
7. Sarah Abigail, b. 22 May, 1812; d. 27 Sept., 1871, unm.

FAM. 43. JOSEPH EDMUND,[7] (*Edmund,*[6] *Joseph,*[5] *Peter,*[4] *Edw'd,*[3] *Rev. & Dr. Gershom,*[2] *Rev. Peter,*[1]), b. 1812, at Rocky Hill; at ae. of 13 became clerk in N. Y. City; early engaged in wholesale leather trade, amassed a competence; m. Mrs. Mary (dau. John Laurence) **Bicknell,** of Newtown, L. I., 23 Oct., 1837. The summers of the later yrs. of his life were spent at Weth.; he. d. abt. 1884.

Children:

1. Elizabeth L. (adopted), m. Geo. A. **Welles.**
2. Edmund Wm., b. 2 Oct., 1838; m. Caroline J. **Turner.**
3. Justus Lawrence, b. 4 July, 1840; m. Laura E. **Caldwell.**
4. Josephine, b. 13 Dec., 1841; m. Theo. M. **Barnes.**
5. Mary L., b. 24 Aug., 1843; m. Fred. S. **Entz.**
6. Marguerite, b. 13 June, 1847.

BULL, AMOS, m. Mary ————; he d. 8 Jan., 1775, ae. 50; she may have been the wid. Mary, who had *Beriah* bp. 21 Mch., 1775, and who d. 5 Sept., 1834, ae. 83.—*W. C. R.*

Child (Weth. Rec.):

1. James, b. 10 Aug., 1772.

2. Inf. "of Wid. Bull," bu. 21 Mch., 1775.— *W. C. R.*

SAMUEL, m. Fanny ————.

Children (Weth. Rec.):

1. Eleazer Huntington, b. 14 Feb., 1800.
2. Seth Pitkin, b. 31 Dec., 1801.
3. Fanny White, b. 2 Aug., 1803; m. 4 Jan., 1820, Lyman **Burke,** of E. Hadd.
4. Samuel Griswold, b. 6 Apl., 1805; d. 9 Apl., 1806.
5. Samuel Griswold, b. 17 Apl., 1807; d. 13

Oct., 1810.
6. Melissa Amelia, b. 9 Feb., 1809; d. 7 Dec., 1811.
7. Edward Leonard, b. 5 Feb., 1811.
8. Lorenzo Solon, b. 8 Mch., 1813.
9. Melissa Amelia, b. 9 Jan., 1815.

From *Steph. Ch. Rec.* verified by *Weth. Ins.*:

AARON had *Mary* and *George Horsford*, bp. 5 May, 1796.

AARON d. 17 Apl., 1797, in 43d yr.—*Weth. Ins.*

EUNICE, m. Isaac **Bell**, of Glast. 24 Oct., 1803.

JONATHAN, of Far., m. Mary **Smith**, 10 Aug., 1794; a *Mary*, wife of Jona., d. 5 Sept., 1834, ae. 83.—*Weth Ins.*

ROGER, m. Ruth **Russell**, 19 Nov., 1767.—*S. C. R.*

ROGER, Mr., d. 23 May, 1783, in 41st yr.; had *Russell* bp. 1 Mch., 1772; *Ursula* bp. 9. June, 1782, d. 9 Dec., 1782.

RUSSELL (or Roswell?), m. 17 Dec., 1795, Lucy (dau. Daniel & Sarah *Warner*); she d. 14 Dec., 1808, ae. 34—*S. C. R.; Weth Ins.* say 33.

SAMUEL, had ch. d. 17 Apl., 1806, in 2d yr.; had ch. d. 13 Oct., 1810, in 4th yr.; had dau. d. 8 Dec., 1811, in 3d yr.

BUNCE. The first two generations of this family were residents of Hartford, to which town THOMAS, their orig. ancestor came, in 1637, from Mass.; he served as an ensign in the Htfd. contingent of vols. in the Pequot War, and "for his good services therein," was gr. 60 acr. of ld. by the Gen. Ct., of 11 Mch., 1671, to which, in 1672, was added 50 acr. more.—*Col Rec.* II, 154. In 1673 he was a memb. of a Comm. of Safety app. by the Ct.—*Col. Rec.* II, 375. *Savage* thinks his wife was a dau. of Capt. Thos. **Bull,** of Htfd. Ensign Bunce d. 1683.

Children (Savage, I, 298):

1. Thomas. FAM. 2.
2. John.
3. Sarah, m. (1) John **White**, of Htfd.; m. (2) Nicholas **Worthington**.
4. Mary, b. 17 Sept., 1645; m. (1) Thos. **Meakins'** of Htfd.; m. (2) John **Downing**.
5. Elizabeth, m. Jacob **White** of Htfd., bro. of her sister Sarah's husband.

FAM. 2. THOMAS,[2] Jr., (*Ens. Thomas,*[1]); will said to have been dated 25 Apl., 1759.

Children:

1. Thomas.
2. Joseph.
3. Jonathan (prob. FAM. 3).
4. Susanna.
5. Sarah.
6. Abigail.

FAM. 3. JONATHAN,[3] (*Thos., Jr.,*[2] *Ens. Thos,*[1]), to whose wife Sarah ————, and to Robert Sanford, prob. of Htfd., adm. on his est. was gr. in Dec., 1717. *Weth. Rec. Rev. Mix's Bapt. Recs.* credits him with the following

Children:

1. Zachariah (Zaccheus?), bp. 13 Nov., 1702. FAM. 4.
2. Susannah, bp. 19 Nov., 1704.
3. Abigail, bp. 6 June, 1708; poss. the A. who m. Caleb **Griswold**, 30 July, 1730.— *S. C. R.*

FAM. 4. ZECHARIAH,[4] (*Jonathan,*[3] *Thos., Jr.,*[2] *Ens. Thomas,*[1]), b. 1702; m. Elizabeth (dau. Ens. Michael) **Griswold**; he d. Apl., 1781, ae. 78; his wid. d. 16 May, 1782, ae. 79.—*W. C. R.*

Children (Weth. Rec.):

1. Elizabeth, b. 29 May, 1726.
2. Zechariah (Capt.), b. 5 Oct., 1728, bp. 12 Oct., 1729.—*Mix Rec.* FAM. 5.
3. Ann, b. 8 Aug., 1731; bp. 13 Aug., 1732.—*Min.*
4. Prob., also, Abigail, who was bp. during Rev. Mr. Lockwood's ministry, betw. 22 Jan. and 1 June, 1744.

FAM. 5. Capt. ZECHARIAH,[5] (*Zechariah*,[4] *Jonathan*,[3] *Thomas*,[2]*Jr.*, Ens. *Thomas*,[1]),
b. 1728; m. 13 June, 1753, Sarah **Bowen**. He d. 19 Sept., 1784, in the W. I.,
in his 56th yr.—*W. Ins.*

Children (Weth. Rec.) :

1. Sarah, b. 8 Mch., 1755 ; m. Moses **Lockwood**, 9 Sept., 1773.—*S. C. R.*
2. William, b. 28 Nov., 1757 ; m. Elizabeth **Lloyd**, both of Weth., 4 July, 1779.— *W. C. R.*
3. James, b. 16 Feb., 1760.
4. **Richard** (Capt.), b. 2 May, 1766, bp. (adult) 5 Nov., 1795. FAM. 6.
5. Simeon, b. 25 Mch., 1768.

FAM. 6. Capt. RICHARD,[6] (*Capt. Zachariah*,[5] *Zachariah*,[4] *Jonathan*,[3] *Thomas Jr.*,[2]
Thomas,[1]), b. 1766; m. 12 Sept., 1790, Olive **Montague**, "both of Weth."; she
d. ae. 40, 12 July, 1808, and he m. (2) Fanny ————, who d. (wid.) 9
Sept., 1832, ae. 48; he d. in the W. I., 9 Jan., 1823, ae. 58.—*W. Ins.*

Children (S. C. R. and W. Ins.) :

1. Sally, bp. 5 Nov., 1795.

(*By second marriage*) :
2. Caroline, b. 13 Nov., 1817 ; d. 17 Feb., 1840.

Capt. JARED, was a somewhat prominent memb. of this family; a well-known and
highly respected sea-captain, and commanded, at least during the latter
part of his life, a packet (passenger) vessel plying betw. Philadelphia, Pa.,
and Charleston, S. C., in which latter city he died. A finely executed minia-
ture of him is in possession of a descendant, Mr. Lanneau, of C. Aside fm.
the data concerning Capt. Jared furnished by the *Weth. Recs.*, we are indebted
to the late well-known and careful genealogist ALLYN S. KELLOGG, of Vernon,
Ct., for such facts as here have his initials appended to them.

Capt. Bunce m. (1) Mary (dau. of Timothy & Mary *Mygatt*) **Stanley**,
b. 2 June, 1737; they were prob. m. in Harwinton, Ct., whence they rem. to
Htfd., where they owned the Cov't in the First Church, 25 June 1756; she d.
at Htfd. 16 May, 1763; he m. (2) Lydia ————, who was b. at Weth.,
and d. 23 Mch., 1799, ae. 43; he m. (3) Mary Ann ————, of
Charleston, S. C., fm. the Cong'l ch. of which city she presented a letter to
the ch. of Weth., 5 Sept., 1802, prob. shortly after her marr.—*A. S. K.*

Children (by first marriage, Htfd. First Ch. Rec.) :

1. Huldah, bp. 29 Feb., 1756.
2. Jared, bp. 7 July, 1757 ; d. 8 Oct., 1758.
3. Jared, bp. 20 May, 1759.
   (*By second marriage, Weth. Ch. Rec.*) :
4. Mary Stanley, bp. 5 Dec., 1784 ; m. 1807, Rev. Dr. Benjamin M. **Palmer**, of Charles-town, S. C., and both d. 1847. She went to school in Weth.; was a poetess and author of the hymn, "I'm a Pilgram, I'm a Stranger."—*E. E. D.*
5. William, bp. 25 June, 1786.
6. Sarah, bp. 16 Dec., 1787.
7. Jared, bp. 19 July, 1789.
8. Elizabeth, bp. 1 May, 1791.
9. Lydia, bp. 31 Mch., 1793.
10. Harriet, bp. 30 July, 1797 ; m. Rev. Alfred **Wright**, missionary to the Choctaws, 1825.
11. Anne, bp. 31 Mch., 1799. The mother d. of childbed fever 8 days before, ae. 43. (An inf. d. 19 Mch., 1785.—*W. C. R.*)

JONATHAN. There was one of this name, who m. 21 Nov., 1765 (*W. C. R.*)
Elizabeth **Ranney**, (tho' the name *may* be Rannals, or Reynolds), who was
prob. the "wife of Jonathan" who d. ae. 62, 8 Jan., 1809.

Children (Weth. Rec.) :

1. Jonathan, b. 8 Mch., 1766 ; prob. the Jona-than, Jr., who m. Merrelus **Baldwin**, 13 Apl., 1788.—(*W. C. R.*).
2. Elizabeth, b. 24 Mch., 1768.
3. Dinah, b. 4 Mch., 1770 ; m. Edward **Bulke-ley**, 9 July, 1795 (*W. C. R.*) ; she d. 6 Dec., 1804
4. John, b. 20 Apl., 1774 ; father (prob.) of "John, s. of John" who d. at Hispaniola,
   W. I., July, 1795.
5. Charles, b. 5 Sept., 1779 ; m. Roxana **Lati-mer**, 5 Aug., 1804 ; he d. 15 Apl., 1813, ae. 34 ; she (wid.) d. 7 Aug., 1814.—*W. C. R.*
6. William, b. 26 June, 1782.
7. Zachariah, b. 20 July, 1784.
8. Abigail, b. 25 Aug., 1788 ; m. Wm. **Thrasher**, both of Weth., 8 Feb., 1809.

BURBRIDGE,WILLIAMS, inf. d. 4 Dec., 1793.—*S. C. R.*

————, ch. d. 10 Dec., 1812, in 2d yr.—*S. C. R.*

BURGEE, (Burge?) JOHN, m. Hannah **Flowers,** 17 Oct., 1769.—*W. C. R.*

BURKIT, JOHN, of Midd., m. Polly **Marsh,** 7 Nov., 1816—*S. C. R.*

JOHN, d. 9 May, 1841, in 51st yr.—*S. C. R.; Mary,* wife of, d. 30 Oct., 1867, ae. 72.— *S. C. R.*

JOHN, d. 9 Apl., 1890, ae. 69.

From *Weth. Ins.,* JULIA (dau. John & Mary) and wife of James H. **Lathrop,** d. 28 Nov., 1836, ae. 18.

JANE M. (dau. of John & Mary), and wife of Albert H. **Warner,** d. 6 Dec., 1848, ae. 25.

(Burkett) SUSAN, m. Hiram **Dewing,** of Charleston, S. C., 29 Aug., 1850.—*S. C. R.*

BURNHAM, The Weth. Burnhams are descts. of Thomas (b. 1617, of Herefordshire descent, Eng.), who came to Htfd. abt. 1647-8, an educated man and lawyer—who bo't large tracts of land at Podunk in prest. So. Windsor, and also lds. in E. Htfd.; had 9 ch.—See Stiles' *Anc. Windsor, Ct.,* II, 128.

The first of the name who appears in *Weth. Rec.* is

FAM. 2. WILLIAM,[2] (7th of the 9 ch. of above *Thomas,*[1] of Htfd and Podunk,), prob. the constable of 1692, and who drew lds. in 1694; m. acc. to *Weth. Rec.,* Elizabeth (dau. of Nath'l) **Loomis,** June 28, 1681, who d. Nov. 19, 1717. He d. 12 Dec., 1730.

Children:

1. Elizabeth, b. 20 May, 1682; m. 12 May, 1699, Michael **Griswold**; d. 9 Sept., 1741.
2. William, b. 17 July, 1684. FAM. 3.
3. Joseph, b. 7 Aug., 1687, probably unm.; d. 20 Apl., 1760 (?).
4. Nathaniel, b. 3 Jan., 1690. FAM. 4.
   From *Weth. Rec.*:
5. Jonathan, b. 21 Mch., 1692; d. 24 Jan., 1752. FAM. 4.
6. Mary, b. 2 Sept., 1694, unm.; d. 17 Apl., 1715.
7. Abigail, b. 16 Dec., 1696; m. 1 Jan., 1716, Nathaniel **Phelps**; d. 2 Jan., 1724.
8. David, b. 12 Oct., 1698, probably unm.; d. 10 Sept., 1741 (?).

FAM. 3. Rev. WILLIAM,[3] (s. of *William,*[2] *Thomas,*[1]), b. 17 July,. 1684; grad. H. C. 1702; in 1709 res. on ld. in Great Swamp, Far., (later Kensington parish—now Berlin township), where he had fm. the Town, 50 acs., with a special view of having him as pastor of a new parish there; m. 18 May, 1704, Hannah (dau. Capt. Samuel) **Wolcott,** by his wife Judith *Appleton;* and 10 of Dec., 1712, the long contemplated new ch. in Great Swamp (Kensington, since May, 1722) was org. with 10 memb. and Mr. B. formally installed as its pastor, and served until his death, 23 Sept., 1750, in 38th yr. of his ministry. *C. L.* His wife Hannah, d. 16 Mch., 1747-8, ae. 63.—*C. L. C.* He m. (2) wid. **Buckinham,** of Htfd. He had 9 ch. His will, says Rev. Mr. Robbins' *Hist. Sketch of Kensington, Berlin, Ct.,* 1886 dated 15 July, 1748, was accepted by prob. first Tuesday, Apl., 1759, but never recorded. It contained, among other provisions, the following:—"excepting concerning my Spanish Indian woman, Maria, my will is that after my decease she shall have liberty to dwell with any of my ch. where she likes best; and, concerning my molatto boy James, is that, acc. to my deceased wife's desire, my dau. Abigail, may have liberty to take him at what price he shall be valued at." For- ld. rec. See Chapt. VII, Vol. I. The only published work of Mr. Burnham is an Election Sermon entitled *"God's Prudence in placing men in their Respective Stations & Conditions.* Asserted and shewed. A sermon preached before the General Assembly of the Colony of Connecticut, at Hartford, May 10, 1722. The day of Electing the Honorable the Governour, the Deputy Governour, the Worshipful Assistants there. Published by order of Authority, 1722."

Children (Weth. Rec.) :

1. William, b. 5 Apl., 1705 ; bp. ent. in Rev.
   Mr. *Mix's Rec.*, as "William, of William,
   Jr., Baccalour*, 8, 2d., 1705."
2. Samuel, b. 28 May, 1707 ; privately bp.
   by Mr. Mix.
3. Hannah, bp. 2 Jan., 1708-9.—*Mix*.
4. Lucy, bp. 22 July, 1711.—*Mix*.
5. Sarah ("dau. of Rev. Wm."), d. 23 Nov.,
   1726, ae. 7.—*C. L. C.*

FAM. 4. NATHANIEL,[3] (*William,*[2] *Thomas,*[1]) surveyor, the Town bo't his instruments in 1713, chosen Town Clerk, 1716; m. 1 or 5 May, 1714, Mehitable (dau. Maj. John) **Chester**; he d. 16 Dec., 1754; she d. 18 Mch., 1773, ae. 84.— *Weth. C. R.*

FAM. 5. JONATHAN,[3] (*William,*[2] *Thomas,*[1]), m. Mary (dau. Maj. John dec'd) **Chester**, 1 Jan., 1718; she d. 19 Apl., 1766; he d. 24 Jan., 1761-2; chosen hayward, 1713.

Children (Weth. Rec.) : *

1. Jonathan, b. 7 Nov., 1718 ; d. 15 Mch.,
   1739-40.
2. Elizur, b. 21 Mch., 1721-2 ; d. 25 Dec., 1724,
   ae. 2 yr., 9 mos., 4 d.—*Weth. Ins.*
3. Abigail, b. 17 Aug., 1727.
4. Prudence, b. 1, bp. 7 Dec., 1729—*Mix
   MS.*; d. 27 June, 1730.
5. Elizur, b. 24 June, bp. 1 July—*Mix*, 1733 ;
   m. Chloe **Rose**, of Bramford, 19 Aug., 1762.
6. Mary, b. 9 Aug., 1735 ; d. 25 Aug., 1735.

Families unattached:

JONATHAN, m. Mary **Bassett.** *

Children (Weth. Rec.) :

1. John, b. and bp. 1 Oct., 1716.—*Mix* (?).
   Weth. Rec. says b. 21 Oct.
2. Nathaniel b. 16 Jan., 1718-9 ; d. 3 June,
   1776.
3. Mehetable, b. 15 Dec., 1720.
4. Peter, b. 22 Mch., 1722-3. FAM. 6.
5. Jeremiah, b. 24 July, 1725 ; d. 1 Sept.,
   1741, ae. 16 yrs., 1 mo., 8 d.—*Weth. Ins.*
6. Julia, m. John **Dimmick**, of E. Htfd., 18
   Mch., 1727.—*W. T. R.*

FAM. 6. Capt. PETER,[2] (*Nathaniel,*[1]), m. (1) 16 or 17 Nov., 1757, Hannah **Deming,** who d. 26 June, 1776; m. (2) 13 Mch., 1777, Elizabeth **Ward;** he d. 11 Jan., 1790, ae. 67.

Children (Weth. Rec. & W. C. R.) :

1. John, b. 15 Oct., 1758.
2. Hannah, b. 6, bp. 16 Dec., 1761.
3. Jeremiah, b. 22 June, 1763 ; d. Feb., 1827,
   ae. 64.—*Weth. Ins.*
4. Abigail, b. 19, bp. 21 June, 1767.
   (*By second marriage*) :
5. Simeon, bp. 4 Jan., 1778.—*W. C. R.*
6. George Ward, b. 2, bp. 4 Jan., d. 11 Apl.,
   1778.—*Weth. Ins.*
7. Elizabeth, b. 17, bp. 23 May, 1779 ; d. 22
   Mch., 1780, ae. 10 mos., 6 d.
8. Samuel, b. 29 Sept., bp. 1 Oct., 1780 ; d.
   14 Sept., 1781.
9. Samuel Ward. b. 13, bp. 21 Sept., 1783.
   (Peter had ch. d. 14 July, 1781 ; inf. d.
   12 Apl., 1778 ; inf. dau. d. 23 Mch., 1780.—
   W. C. R.)

---

* JONATHAN, m. Mary Bassett. *Children* (*Weth. Rec.*) :
  Abigail, b. 6 Sept., 1739. | May. b. 20 May, 1745.
  Jonathan, b. 14 Nov., 1743. | Hannah, b. 13 Feb., 1746-7.
If it were not for record of dth. of this Jonathon's wife Mary, as 1766, we might think these children here given, a second lot, by a *second marriage* (?), which is also suggested by the interval of time between birth of Mary, No. 6, of the family, and the birth date of Abigail, the first of the lot given in this note. Is it not possible that the death dates of the first wife Mary and her youngest dau. Mary should be *exchanged?* This would make a second marriage possible to Jonathan.

---

* Will and Inventory of a MARTHA BURNHAM—*Htfd. Prob. Recs.*
Will dated, 7 August, 1733. Invt. taken. I bequeath five Sixths (5-6) of all my Estate unto my Children now living, viz : my Son Eleazer Gaylord, Marth Wilcocks Elizabeth Gaylord Sarah Bissell and Hannah Orvis, and the other Sixth part I give to my grand Children the Children of my Son Samuel Gaylord Dec^d, to Samuel 1-3 part of s^d Sixth part—to Eleazer his brother one third part and to Millicent one third of s^d Sixth part—Nathaniel Gaylord my soninlaw to be Sole Executor
Witness Daniel Williams   MARTHA BURNHAM Q
Daniel Harris Benjamin Woodbridge
Court Record 4 September 1733. Will now exhibit

Court Record 12 January 1730-1 Cept. Joseph Southmayd to be guardian to Millicent Gaylord age 10 *years* and Samuel Gaylord age 7 years and Eleazer Gaylord of Middletown to be guardian to Eleazer Gaylord age 4 years all children of Samuel Gaylord Deed.

BURR, SAMUEL, of Htfd., m. Rebecca **Stillman,** 7 July, 1773,.—*W. C. R*

BURROWS, (*Burrough*), communicated by Miss M. F. SMITH. Mr. ROBERT, was
one of the company who came in the ship *Arbella*, which sailed from Cowes,
Isle of Wight, 29 Mch., and reached N. Eng., 12 June, 1630.—*Winthrop's
Journal*, Addenda 2 p. 340. Trad. gives Manchester as his Eng. home,
and also that two brothers (John and William) came with him, that they were
Bapt. and "driven out of Eng. by relig. persecution," and that they sett. finally
one in N. Y. and the other in Penn.—see small pamplet of a branch of the B.
family, by Rev. F. Denison, who however, is unable to give orig. of the trad.
A part of the *Arbella's* Co. went to Salem, another part to Weth. where Mr.
Burrows owned a ho-lot, on the Htfd. road, before 1640; his fence tax is rec.
W. T. V. I, 29. See Chapt. VII, Vol. I. Abt. 1643 he rem. from Weth. to
Gov. Winthrop's new plant, at Pequot (New Lond.) and there rec'd a special
gt. of ld. from that town, 2 June, 1650. In July, 1651, his name occurs
among those who "wrought at the Mill-dam" (*Caulkins' Hist. New Lond.*) of
the old (or *Winthrop*) mill, on the div. of the lds. vacated by the Pequots,
in Groton. Burrows, John Packer and Robert Park sett., on the W. side of
Mystic River, his gt. dated 3 Apl., 1657, being "a parcel of ld. betw. the W.
side of the River and a high mountain of rocks." "Goodman Robt. Burrows"
was also chosen the first ferryman across Mystic River, for a groat (four-
pence) and he is supp. to have been the first actual sett. of Mystic. With
his ho-lot in New Lond. and his estate at Pequanoc, (betw. New Lond. and
Mystic) and on the Mystic; he was by 1664, the third gentleman in the New
Lond. sett. in the amt. of his taxable ppy. viz. £246.

From his being a fellow passenger in the *Arbella*, with Mr. (Sir?) Robert Park
and Gov. Winthrop, it is not improbable that the three were friends in Old
Eng. and that Park and the Burrows bros. were both from the Co. Lancaster.
He was evidently on intimate terms with Gov. Winthrop, who often visited
him during his res. at Mystic. *Thomas Miner's Diary*, 1653-1684, p. 35, rec.
that "1659, June, Sabbath day the 12, Mr. Tomson taught [preached] at Mr.
Burrowe's. Mr. Winthrop was there."

Robert Burrows ho-std at Mystic, occup. the same site as that since occup. by
that of the late John Burrows (of 7th gen.) and was held in the fam. until
within a few yrs. Among the lds. gr. to R. B. was Fort Hill, in Groton,
4 miles E. of New Lond., it was the site of the original fortress of Sassacus,
the Pequot Chieftian. This remained in the B. family for 215 yrs. and was
the ho-std. of Rev. Roswell, 5th in desc't from the settler.

Mr. Burrows m. (1) 1645, Mary, (wid. of Samuel) **Ireland,** who had d. 1639, (see
Ireland). "Goodwife Burrows" d. at M. Dec., (but acc. to the *Miner Diary*,
(p. 113, 3 Oct.), 1672; he seems to have marr. again acc. to the following item,
p. 117 of the same *Miner Rec.* above referred to)—"1673, Thursday, the 17 of
June Robert Burrows was married." This is our only auth. for his second marr.
—the dates are those of Old Style. Mr. Burrows d. Aug., 1682. He had two
sons, *John*, (FAM 2), and *Samuel*, both of whom were presented for free-
manship in the Colony, in Oct., 1669; of the later we have no certain information. This estate reverted to Bro. John's[2] family. Samuel had d. prior to
1712.—*Groton P. Rec.*

FAM. 2. JOHN,[2] (*Mr. Robert,*[1]), b. Weth. 1642; m. 14 Dec., 1670, Hannah (dau.
Edward & Ann *Ellice*) **Culver,** who was b. at Roxbury, Mass., 11 Apl., 1651,
R. Recs.; he res. in Groton, and his grave (in the Wightman Burying Ground)
is marked by a large granite slab, inscribed "J. B. 74, dyed 1716." He and

his wife were memb. of the first Cong. Ch. at Stonington, where also his ch. were all bp.; his burial place adjoins the site of the 1st Bp. Ch. in Groton (and in Conn.), of which he was also a liberal supporter; his wife survived him, the invent. of her estate, being dated, May 24, 1733, (*N. Lond. Prob. Rec.*) had 5 sons and 2 daus., whose bap. are given in record of First Cong. Ch., of Stonington, Ct.—See Wheeler's *Hist. Stonington.* His son

JOHN,[3] (*John,*[2] *Robert,*[1]), b. Groton, 2 Sept., 1671; m. 14 Oct., 1700, Lydia **Hubbard,** (dau. Hugh & Jane *Latham*), b. 7 Feb., 1675, at N. Lond., by whom he had 5 sons and 3 daus.; by his will, dated 5 Dec., 1748, he gave the homestead which descended to him from his gd-fthr. Robert, to his son John, and the ppy. called Fort Hill to his son Amos, besides making provisions for his other child, his gd-ch., and a liberal provision for his wid. He d. 26 May, 1752. his son

JOHN,[4] (*John,*[3] *John,*[2] *Rob't,*[1]), familiarly known as "Sergt." Burrows, from his having been orderly sergeant in some campaign of the Fr. and Ind. War, was present at the capture of Quebec in 1759, under Gen. Wolfe, and his pocket order-book and journal were in the possession of his gd-son, John,[7] of Mystic, Conn., containing minute and interesting details of operations at Crown Point and Ticonderoga. His brother

NATHAN,[6] 1746-1808, also saw service in the Revol. War, making two trips with ox-teams from Groton to Boston, conveying supplies to the patriot army. He d. at Chenango, N. Y., and his descendants are numerous in Conn. and R. I.

HUBBARD,[5] 1739-1781, (*Hubbard,*[4] *John,*[3] *John,*[2] *Robt,*[1]) served in the Revol., 1776 and again in 1781; was one of the gallant defenders of Fort Griswold, at the battle and massacre of Groton Heights, where he was killed.—*Battle of Groton Heights,* by Chas. Allyn, 1882, pp. 93, 135, 204-36, 250-54.

AMOS,[4] (another s. of *John,*[3] *John,*[2] *Robert,*[1]), b. Groton, 1714, d. 1773; res. at Fort Hill, Ct.; m. 1736-7, Elizabeth **Rathbone,** of Colchester, Ct., a direct descendant of John R., of Block Island; was an unordained preacher of the (New Ligt) Separate Cong. Ch., at Pequanoc, Groton, Ct. His two sons, *Elisha, Nathan* and son-in-law Solomon Tift were all in the battle of Groton Heights, and suffered imprisonment on the Br. prison ship, *Old Jersey.*

The Rev. SILAS,[5] (*Amos,*[4] *John,*[3] *John,*[2] *Robert,*[1]) 1741-1818, was the.founder and pastor of the Second Bap. Ch. at Fort Hill, Groton, Ct. was ord. abt. 1765 and served that ch. as pastor for 53 yrs. being succeeded by his s. Rev. Roswell, 1768-1837; ord. in 1806—See Sprague's *Annals of Am. Pulpit.* "Elder" Silas m. 7 Apl., 1764, Mary (dau. of Isaac & Esther *Denison*) **Smith,**[5] (*Isaac,*[4] *Nehemiah,*[3] *Nehem.*,[2] *Nehem.*,[1]), they had 6 sons and a dau., who lived to maturity. Of these sons three have been already mentioned, viz.: Daniel, Roswell, Enoch and a fourth Jabez, b. 1772; settled at Mayville, N. Y., and had three sons, who lived to maturity; their dau. Mary[6] (Burrows) m. Jedidiah Randall, and their dau. Frances E.,[7] (Randall) m. William Parsons Smith, parents of Mary F. Smith,[8] of New York.

Rev. DANIEL,[6] (*Rev. Silas,*[5] *Amos,*[4] *John,*[3] *John,*[2] *Robert,*[1]), 1766-1858, was a Meth. minister, ord. by Rev. Bishop Seabury; res. at Hebron and Midd., at the latter place his descendts. now res., also in Penn. and the West. He was also Rep. from Conn., in 17th U. S. Cong., 1821- 23; app. Surveyor and Inspector of Customs at Midd., which office he held through all changes of admin. for 24 yrs., when he resigned.

Rev. ROSWELL,[6] (*Silas,*[5] *Amos,*[4] *John,*[3] *John,*[2] *Robert,*[1]) had 3 sons, all prominent in the pioneer history of Western New York, viz.

1. LATHAM A., 1792-1855; grad. of Brown Univ., stud. law with Richard Riker, of N. Y. City; was an officer, in service on the frontier, in War of 1812; practiced law at Owego, Tioga Co., N. Y., and was for many yrs. the first Judge of that Co. His last years were spent in Buffalo, N. Y.

2. ROSWELL S., 1798-1879, took a partial course at Y. C., from which, in 1867, he rec'd the hon. degree of A. M.; went to Albion, N. Y., in 1824, and was a mcht. there for several yrs., later he estab. a bank of which he was pres. at time of his dth.; refused all public office, except the Collectorship of the Canal Revenue, in 1825, which office he held for six yrs. He was an honored citizen, interested in all public matters, especially of an educational and religious nature.

3. LORENZO, 1803-1885, res. of Albion, N. Y., and partner with his bro. Roswell S.; rep. to U. S. Congress, 1849-53; Comptroller of State of N. Y., 1855, held the office for 2 yrs. In 1858 was chosen Second Regent. of State of N. Y., and held office until dth.; was in all the relations of life esteemed for his perfect integrity and ability.

ENOCH,[6] (s. Rev. Silas,[5] Amos,[4] John,[3] John,[2] Rob't,[1]), 1770-1852, was a mcht. and hon. citizen of Stonington, Ct., rep. to Gen. Assemb., 1810, '11, '15, '16 and '17; elected an Assist. under the old Charter, and State Senator under the Constitution of 1818, for 1819-20-21. In his later yrs. res. in Troy, N. Y. His son,

SILAS E.,[7] (Enoch,[6] Silas,[5] Amos,[4] John,[3] John,[2] Rob't,[1]) 1794-1870; was vol. in defense of Stonington, War of 1812; a mcht., lived much abroad and traveled extensively, his descts. are in Eng. and N. Y.

The late Judge ROSWELL L.[8] Burrows, 1821-1897, was an able lawyer and an esteemed citizen of Buffalo, N. Y.

GEO. L.[8] Burrows, a Banker, of Saginaw, Mich.

Geo.[9] L. Burrows, Jr., Latham[9] A. BURROWS, both of Saginaw.

LORENZO[8] Burrows, of Albion, N. Y.,

Dr. CHAS.[9] M. Burrows, of Albion.

Hon. A. C.[9] Burrows, a lawyer of Albion, N. Y.

Dr. LORENZO[9] Burrows., Jr., of Buffalo, N. Y.

All these are direct descendants of the old Pilgrim settler Robert Burrows.

BUSHNELL, ————, m. Prudence **Welles,** 25 Oct., 1748.—*W. C. R.*

BUTLER, (*Boteler*). A most ancient and numerous family, said to be of Irish origin, although there are in Chesire and Yorkshire, many ancient families of the name, from which the Irish lines may have descended. In the peerage of Ireland the name is one of the oldest, the surname being derived from the Chief Butlership of that Kingdom. Theobald Fritz Walter, who derived his pedigree from the Duke of Normandy, was created the Chief Butler of Ireland, in 1177, by Henry II, and was possessed of the baronies of Upper and Lower Ormande, as well as of numerous other places. His son and heir, Theobald, was the first to assume the name of Butler, 1221.

Butler genealogies of the American families are understood to be in preparation by Mr. W. P. Butler, of Minneapolis, Minn., and by Ex-Mayor Butler, of Cincinnati, Ohio.

The authorities referred to in the following sketch, are: *Weth. Town and Church Recs.; Weth. Inscriptions; Stepney Parish (Weth.) Recs.; MSS.* of the late EDWIN STEARNS, and correspondence of Mrs. F. B. WIGHTMAN, of N. Y. City;

MRS. GEORGE H. BUTLER, of Cromwell, Ct.; (Joseph Butler line) Mrs.
EDWARD DEMOREST, (Comfort Butler line) and Mrs. A. A. HAXTUN, in the *N. Y. Mail & Express*, editress of the Geneal. Dep't of that paper.

Dea. RICHARD BUTLER, the American ancestor of the Butlers of Weth., came
to this country in 1633,—(Paige's *Hist. Cambridge, Mass., p.* 32,) from
Braintree, Co., Essex, Eng., became a freeman at C., 14 May, 1634, and a
member of Rev. Thos. Hooker's Ch., at Hartford, Ct., (1642), where he was,
with his bro. William, among the first settlers,—*Mem. Hist. Htfd.* Co., I, 233),
rec'd 16 acr. land in first division; was a deacon in First Ch. there; juror,
1643, '44, '47, '48; grand juror, 1660-2; selectman, 1649, '54, '58; dep. to Gen.
Ct., 1656-60; app. clerk of Gen. Ct. 20 May, 1658, (*Conn. Col. Rec.* I 313, 314,
315, 346); res. in Htfd. on So. side of Little River, "on the cor. where the
road fm. Geo. Steele's intersects the road fm. the Mills to the country," and
owned ho-lot and other lds. in Weth. He was twice marr.—name of first wife
unknown—one acc. says he came hither, "mourning the loss of wife and inf."
He m. (2), acc. to *Hinman*, and before coming to Htfd., Elizabeth **Bigelow**;
but by some she is thought to have been of Htfd. He d. at H. in a ripe old
age, 6 Aug., 1684. The inventory of his est. amt. to £654-15-00, and was taken
12 Sept., same yr., by Paul Peck and Geo. Graves.* Mrs. Elizabeth (Biglow)
Butler d. 26 Feb., 1656-7.

Will of Richard Butler.

April 2 1677

Know all men whom it may concerne that I Richard Butler of Hartford upon
Connecticut river being in bodily health and of sound and perfect memory doe
make and ordayne this my last will and testiment in forme and manner as
followeth
Impimis—
I doe give to my sonne Thomas Butler my uper lot in the longe meddow.
I doe give to my sonne Samuel all my meadow land in Wethersfield meadow
I doe give to Nathaniel my sonne my meddow lot neare the long meddow gate
I doe give to Joseph Butler my sonne all my land in the south meddow
I doe give to my sonne Daniel Butler my now delling house with all apurtenances
of building and grounds about it and also I do give to my sonne Daniel my lot
commonly caled ten-acres I doe give my 3 daughters Mary Wright, Elizabeth
Olmsted and hanah Greene twentie shillings apece (to be payd out of my
moveable estate by my present wife Elizabeth whom I appoint my executrix to
this my last will) *** Also it is my will that none of these children aforesaid
doe possess or enjoy any of these lands or aught else mentioned, but with the
consent of death or change of the mother's condition, that is by marrying againe.
But if my wife Elizabeth Butler should change her condition and marry againe
then my will is that all aforesaid sonnes and daufters do posses every one his
legacy and my wife only the thirds and for the rest of chattels and household
goods I give them all to my wife provided as aforesayd she continues in widowhood but if she marry againe then to take the thirds of all as of the house and
lands so of chattels and household stuff and the rest equally to be divided
amonge all my children afore mentioned and that this may by divers willes
extant that I have written with my owne hand yet this my last and shall
stand Written with my owne hand—Richard Butler

* Mr. C. W. MANMARNING, to whom we are indebted for our excerpts from the *Htfd. Co.
Prob. Office*, remarks in regard to records of inventories:
I have come to the conclusion that the Invent. of an Estate is not of great consequence,
because in so many cases, it means only personal estate or what may be left after. A
Esther has made over lands by Deeds, of gift, or provided Marriage Portions, to the married
daughters—the Estate of Richard Butler appears to be completed.

April 2-1677 ***(I also appoint my two sonnes Thomas & Samuel Butler to
be my overseers of this my last will ***(my will also is that my daughter
Mary Wright shal have one feather bed after her mother's decease)
Witnesses
   Samuel Wright
   Samuel Butler
              Richard Butler
***Sworn in Court & accepted with 5 above written interlinings
                J. Talcott C. C.
William Butler a Brother left a will 1648.

Dea. Richard's elder, and unmarried bro. WILLIAM, sett. also at Htfd., at abt.
the same time, but d. 1648, giving his ppy. to Richard, and requesting him to
pay certain legacies to their two sisters, a Mrs. West and a Mrs. Winters, in
Old Eng., and to certain friends in Htfd.; also, £60 to the Htfd. ch. It is
prob that the four were all of the family.—(Copy of an old MSS. mem. found
in an old chest in a Northampton (Mass.) garret, and communicated to the
N. Y. Mail & Express by Mr. *W. G. Duyckinck*, of Morristown, N. J.

Children (b. at Hartford, Ct.):

1. Thomas, b. abt. 1637; inher. the upper lot
   lot on Long Meadow, Htfd.; m. Sarah
   (dau. Rev. Samuel) **Stone**, of H., where he
   sett. on Main St.; but rem. further W.
   of the Town; he d. 1688. *Issue:*
    i. Thomas.
    ii. Samuel.
    iii. John.
    iv. Dau., m. Edward **Cadwell**.
    v. Dau. m. John **Day**.
    vi. Hannah, m. Thos. **Cadwell**.
    vii. Mary, m. John **Porter**.
    viii. Dau. m. Cornelius **Halibut** (Hurl-
     but ?).
    ix. Margaret.
    x. Hope.
    xi. Susanna.

2. Samuel,* (Dea.), b. abt. 1639. FAM. 2.
3. Nathaniel,* b. abt. 1641. FAM. 3.
4. Joseph,* b. abt. 1648. FAM. 4.
5. Daniel (Sgt.), b. at Weth. FAM. 5.
6. Mary,* b. abt. 1635; m. 29 Sept., 1659,
   Samuel **Wright**, of Weth.; she d. Feb.,
   1690.
7. Elizabeth,* b. abt. 1643; m. (1) Nehemiab
   (or John ?) **Olmstead**, of Htfd.; m. (2)
   Obediah **Gilbert**. *Issue (by first marr.):*
    i. Sarah (Olmstead).
    (*By second marr.*):
    ii. Obadiah (Gilbert).
    iii. Benjamin (Gilbert).
    iv. Josiah (Gilbert).
8. Hannah, m. ———— **Greene**.

In regard to the Weth. Butlers, the notes of the late Dr. R. W. GRISWOLD, say
that "they were, fm. an early period, mostly residents of that portion of the
town known as Stepney parish, now Rocky Hill. In the first quarter of the
19th century, there were *eight* Butler families within the limits of Stepney
parish—only two of which were nearly related. These two were those of
SAMUEL BUTLER and SAMUEL, Jr., whose home was on the site of the present
Charles C. Butler's residence. ELNATHAN BUTLER lived "by the gate" at the
South end. WILLIAM SAGE BUTLER, (lost at sea in 1823), lived where his son
afterwards did. SIMEON BUTLER, the grist-mill man, lived on the corner West
of the mill; Capt. JOSIAH BUTLER, opposite the meeting-house; Capt. JOSEPH
BUTLER, on the S. E. corner of "the Centre"; and another JOSIAH had his
home under the big elm where, for many years, Alfred Daily lived, and H. C.
Holmes now resides. This last named Josiah was a brother of the Ebenezor
Butler, who kept the tavern in Cromwell, just below the Rocky Hill South town-
line." It will be seen, therefore, how naturally some of the Butlers, living
close to the Middletown (Upper Houses) line, strayed into the towns of
Cromwell and Middletown.

FAM. 2. Dea. and Ens. SAMUEL,² (Dea. Richard,¹), b. 1639, sett. in Weth. where
in 1668, he was chosen Town School Master; a res. householder in 1670—
(*Weth. Ld. Rec., Vol. I*), see also Chapt. Vol. I; selectman, 1689. "Ensign
Samuel Butler, deacon at Weth." d. 31 Dec., 1692, "ye last day of the week,
ye last day of the month, ye last day of the year; and, as he had sayd, soe it

proved, ye last day of his life."—(*Weth. Rec.*) He inher. all his father's meadow-ld. in Weth. meadows.—See Chapt. VII, Vol. I. His invent. amt'd to £529-07-00, taken 25 Feb., 1692-3, by John Wiard and Joseph Churchill. His will, dated 30 Nov., 1692 gives dwelling ho-lot, etc., with other lds. to his s. Samuel, he to pay his sister Mary (**Hopkins**) £5, and his sister Dorothy (prob. then unm'd) £10; remainder to sons James, Jonathan and George and dau. Elizabeth (**Emmons**); son Samuel to be exec'r.—*Htfd. Co. Prob.* He m. Elizabeth —————, who d. 17 Oct., 1681. The preface of his will shows the character of the man.

"In the name of God Amen this 30th Day of December in ye fourth year [1692] of ye Reigne of our Sovereinge lord & lady William & Mary by ye grace of God of England Scotland France & Ireland King & Queen Defender of ye faith etc in ye year of our lord God one Thousand Six hundred ninety two I Samuel Butler of Wethersfield in ye County of Hartford in their magesties Territory and Dominion of new England in America being sick & weake of body but of good & perfect memory thanks be to Almighty God And calling to remembrance ye uncertain estate of this present, life & that all flesh must yield unto Death when it shall please Almighty God to call Doe make constitute ordain & Declare this my last will & testament Revoking and Ad nulling by these presents all and every testament & testaments will & wills heretofore by me made either in word or writing and this onely to be taken for my last will & testament & no other. And first being penitent & sorry for my sins past humbly Desiring forgiveness for the same I give and comitt my soule to Almighty God my Savior & redeemer in whom & by ye meritts of Jesus Christs Death & passion I trust & believe Assuredly to be Saved & to have full remission and forgiveness of all my Sins & yt my Soule with my body at the generall Day of resurection Shall rise again with Joye & through ye merits of Jesus Christ possess & inheritt ye kingdom of heaven prepared for his elect & chosen and my body to ye earth from whence it was taken to be buried in such decent & Christian like maner as ye my executors here after named shall be thought meet & convenient.

& for ye Settling my temporall estate & such goods & chattels as it hath pleased God far above my Deserts to bestow upon me I give & bequeath ye same as followeth & first I will yt all those debts & duties yt in right or conscience I ow to any maner of person or persons be well & truly payd by my executor hereafter named," etc.

Children (Weth. Rec.) :

1. Samuel. FAM. 6.
2. James. FAM. 7.
3. Jonathan. FAM. 8.
4. George, —————; d. unm., 5 May, 1698; invent. £49-11-08, taken 15 Aug., 1698; est. div. by agreement among his bros. and sisters.—*Htfd. Co. Prob.*
5. Mary, —————; m. Eben. **Hopkins**, of Htfd., 21 Jan., 1691-2.
6. Dorothy, —————; m. ————— **Kilbourn.**
7. Elizabeth, b. 20 Aug., 1667; m. Samuel **Emmons.**
8. Sarah, —————; m. Samuel **Buck.**

FAM. 3. NATHANIEL,[2] (*Dea. Richard,*[1]), b. abt. 1641; res. ld. owner in Weth. 1694— (See Chapt. VII, Vol. I); sett. Weth.; was a res. householder, 1670. He d. 9 Feb., 1697-8, "ae. 56 yrs. or thereabouts." Invent. amtd. to £299; adm. given to wid.—*Htfd. Co. Prob.* He m. (1. prob.) Sarah —————. He inher. mead.-lot near the Long Meadow gate; Mary, wife of Nathaniel, d. 9 Apl., 1725, ae. abt. 26 yrs.

Children (*Weth. Rec.*) :

1. Samuel, rem. to Southampton, L. I. (Mass. ?).
2. William, m. ————. FAM. 9.
3. Hannah, m. ———— **Case.**
4. Ann, m. ———— **Riley.**

5. Abigail, m. John **Cram** (Crane?), who d. 23 Oct., 1694, ae. 30; she m. (2) ———— **Walker.**
6. Ruth.

FAM. 4. JOSEPH,[2] (*Dea. Richard,*[1]), b. abt. 1648, at Htfd.; sett. in Weth. where he inher. fm. his father, lds. in the South Meadow—(See Chapt. VII, Vol. I) ; was made a freeman 1668; rem. to and became a ho-hldr. in Rocky Hill dist. Mch., 1670-1; m. (1), before 30 Jan., 1667, Mary (dau. Ens. William) **Goodrich;** he m. (2) Margaret ————.* His will, dated 8 July, 1725, and prob. 6 Mch., 1732-3; invent, 28 Feb., 1732-3, amt. to £1,000—*Htfd. Co. Prob. Rec.* and *Weth. Ld. Rec.*, II, 176. He d. at Stepney 10 Dec., 1732, ae. 84†; his wid. 1 June, 1735.—*Weth.* (*S.*) *Ins.*

Children:

1. Richard, b. abt. 1668. FAM. 10.
2. Benjamin, b. 1673. FAM. 11.
3. Joseph, *Cromwell Ch. Rec.* says, "7 Dec., 1740, we had the news of Joseph Butler being drowned at sea"—prob. unm. and without issue.‡
4. Gershom, b. 1685. FAM. 12.
5. Charles, b. 1685. FAM. 13. Said to have been twins.
6. Mary, d. Jan., 1795, ae. 88, therefore, b. abt. 1703; m. David (s. of Josiah & Mary *Churchill*) **Edwards.**§ He b. in Southampton, L. I., 6 Apl., 1707; d. 7 Jan., 1795; she d. 10 July, 1786. *Issue:*
   i. Mary (Edwards), b. 1735; m. Moses **Hall,** 29 July, 1752.
   ii. Ann (Edwards), b. 1738; m. Jehiel **Williams,** 10 Jan., 1757.
   iii. Mercy (Edwards), b. 1739; m. Eben **Backus,** 26 Nov., 1760.
   iv. Sarah (Edwards), b. 18 May, 1741; m. Rev. Edward **Élls,** 27 Jan., 1763.
   v. Churchill (Edwards), b. 28 Feb., 1742.
   vi. Joseph (Edwards), b. 7 Mch., 1744.
   vii. Martha (Edwards), b. 18 Mch., 1746; m. a **Ranney.**
   viii. Hepzibah (Edwards), b. 9 Feb., 1747.
   ix. David (Edwards), b. 24 Dec., 1749.
7. Charles (2d), b. 1715. FAM. 13a.

---

* We may infer that he had two wives, from the following entry in *Co. Ct. Recs.* (18 Apl., 1677) from which it appears that in a suit against his (Joseph's) "now wife," damages being held at £40, Joseph being prest to go forth in the country's service, trial was deferred until the (next) Sept. Court."

This supposition is supported by the following letter rec'd from the veteran genealogist, FRANK FARNSWORTH STARR, of Midd., Ct., who says: "A singular fact exists as to Joseph Butler. In his will [1725], he states that he has given by deed to his sons *Richard* and *Gershom,* who were both then living, and to his son *Charles,* who was then dead, all the ppy. that his small estate would admit and they nor their heirs were not to have anything more. To his wife Mary he gave 1-3 of the personal estate in fee and the life use of 1-3 of the real estate and appointed her executor. To his daughter *Mary* he gave 2-3 of his personal estate and £25 to be paid to her by his other sons. The rest of the estate was given to "my three sons now living with me" *Benjamin, Joseph* and *Charles.* The *Htfd. Co. Ct. Recs.* show that before Jan. 30, 1677, Joseph Butler had married a daughter of Ensign William Goodrich, but does not give her name. The *Midd. Ld. Recs.* show that in July, 1694, he had a wife named *Mary* and Mary is the name of the wife mentioned in his will of 1725. His son *Gershom* was eighty years old at his death in 1765, therefore born about 1685. The son *Charles,* who is mentioned in the will as being dead, must have been the husband of Susanna Williams, and the Wethersfield records give his death as Sept. 25, 1711, age not stated. The daughter Mary married David Edwards & died in Jan., 1795, aged 88, therefore born about 1707. As to Benjamin's age I am uncertain. The Charles who was living when the will was made was evidently the husband of Jerusha Goodrich and died in 1785, aged 70, therefore born about 1715. The dates of birth of these various children would indicate that Joseph Butler must have had two wives at least. Mary, Joseph & Charles belonging to the second set of children and also Benjamin, unless the latter was far past middle life when he married in 1734. *Midd. Land Records* show that in 1740-41, Richard, Gershom, Benjamin and Charles Butler and Mary wife of David Edwards convey their interest in the real estate of their *brother* Joseph Butler dec[d]. Mary and Bathsheba daughters of Charles & Susanna Butler of Wethersfield convey their interest in the lands of their *uncle* Joseph Butler dec[d]. These facts prove that Joseph Butler, son of Joseph, died before 1741, without issue and probably unmarried.

† There seem to have been two *Joseph Butlers,* often ment. in the *Hartford Recs.,* one generally named as "of Weth.," and the other as "of Htfd."

‡ Goodwin was in error (*Geneal. Notes,* p. 82) in giving this Joseph in marr. to Patience Horton, since the *Midd. Ld. Recs.* incontestibly prove that the husband of said Patience was the son of a Samuel Butler, who came to Midd. from Wallingford.

§ Mr. David Edwards d. 7 Jan., 1787, ae. 87; his wife (Mary Butler) d. 10 July, 1786, ae. 80 (Jan., 1795, ae. 88). In 1741, Benjamin and Gershom Butler (Nos. 2 and 4 of above family) David Edwards and wife Mary, and Charles Butler (No. 5 above) sold to Richard Edwards 24 acres of land on the Russell Plain, Upper Middletown, which belonged to their bros. Joseph Butler dec'd. In 1741, Elijah Miller and wife Bathsheba sold to Benj. Miller 37 acres land in Upper Houses, which belonged to their uncle Joseph Miller.—*Town Recs. Midd.*

FAM. 5. DANIEL,[2] (Dea. Richard,[1]), b. in Weth.; sett. at Htfd., where he inher. his father's home-lot, dw-ho, and barns, also 10 acres ld.; he m. Mabel ————; he d. 28 Mch., 1692; wid. m. (2) ———— **Taintor.**

Children:

1. Sarah, b. 28 Sept., 1680.
2. Mabel, b. 12 Aug., 1684.
3. Hannah, b. 22 Nov., 1686.

4. Elizabeth, b. 7 Nov., 1689.
5. Mary, b. 17 Nov., 1691.

FAM. 6. SAMUEL,[3] (Dea. Samuel,[2] Dea. Richard,[1]), m. 26 Nov., 1696 (or 2 Mch., 1704), Mary (dau. Sgt. John) **Kilborn;** he d. 10 Dec., 1711; she d. 27 Aug., 1752.—*Weth. Rec.* His invent. of est., taken 27 Feb., 1711-2, amt. £233-06-00. Will (nuncupative)proven 24 Dec., 1711.—(*Htfd. Co. Prob.*)

Children (Weth. Rec.):

1. Elizabeth, b. 20 Apl., 1698.
2. Samuel, b. 29 June, bp. 5 July,—*Mix*, 1702; poss. the S. who m. 4 Apl., 1751, Naomi **Kilburn**, who d. 13 Aug., 1752: he m. (2) Abigail **Adams**, 26 June, 1755.— *W. C. R. Issue:*
　i. Naomi, b. 10 May, 1752.—*Weth. Rec.*
3. George, b. 6 Oct., 1704; d. 26 Feb., 1725.—
4. Daniel, b. 8, bp. 9 Feb., 1706-7. FAM. 14.

5. Abraham, b. 19 Mch., 1708-9; the following entry in Rev. Mr. *Mix's Bp. Rec.*, prob. refers to this birth: *"Abr'ah. of* Samuel Butler (I think it was) bp. Mch. 1 (?), 1708-9; this I say Mch. 27, 1709." This is prob. the *Abraham*, who d. 5 Feb., 1777, ae. 68; and whose wid. Abigail d. 10 Jan., 1803, ae. 97.—*W. C. R.*

FAM. 7. *Mr.* JAMES,[3] (Dea. Samuel,[2] Dea. Richard,[1]), b. ——, ————; m. 6 May, 1703, Hannah (dau. Joseph) **Edwards;** he was hayward, 1699; highway surveyor, 1715; he d. 7 Nov., 1765, in 89th yr.; she d. 10 Jan., 1741-2.—*Weth. Rec. & Ins.*

Children (Weth. Rec.);

1. Hannah, b. 26 Sept., 1705; (bp. 30 Sept., 1705.—*Mix.*)
2. Hezekiah, b. 29 Apl., bp. 2 May, 1708. FAM. 15.

3. James, b. 4 (bp. 3—*Sic. Mix*) Feb., 1712; d. 13 Jan., 1736, in 25th yr.—*W. Ins.*
4. William, b. 8 Feb., 1714-15. FAM. 16.

FAM. 8. JONATHAN,[3] (Ens. Samuel,[2] Dea. Richard,[1]), b. 1678; m. (1) 18 Sept., 1709, Mary (dau. John & Elizabeth) **Easton,** who d. abt. 1728; he m. (2) prior to 2 Jan., 1729, Elizabeth (dau. Edward & Elizabeth Cadwell, and wid. of Jonathan) **Easton,** who was b. 5 Dec., 1687.—*Htfd. Co. Prob. Rec.* and *Easton Geneal.* He d. in 1756; dist. of est. ordered 26th July, and reported as effected: "We also find the ye sd. Jonathon Butler deas. by way of settlement gave and advanced to the sd. Jonathan Butler, Jr., near two hundred acres of land in the town of Harwinton, which is more than a double part and share of sd. estate. We also find that Elizabeth (Mygatt), Mary (Edwards), Sarah (Merrell), Rebecca (Barrett) and Dorthy Butler, and each of them, (who are the daughters of sd. deas.) have already received their full part and share of sd, estate. We therefor Distribute the Real estate of sd. deas. as follows—to Daniel and to Moses and to George Butler to each L.1153 12—11. Old Tenor. Thomas Seymour, Isaac Sheldon, Jonathan Seymour."

Children (by first marriage):

1. Jonathan, bp. 26 June, 1708.
2. Elizabeth, bp. 21 June, 1710; m. Nov., 1730, Joseph **Mygatt.**
3. Daniel, bp. 8 Mch., 1713.
4. Moses, bp. 30 Aug., 1716.
5. Mary, bp. 20 Apl., 1718; m. 21 Feb., 1750, Richard **Edwards**, and d. 20 Sept., 1795; he d. 5 Mch., 1770.
6. Sarah, bp. 14 Aug., 1720; m. 28 Apl.,

1746, Hezekiah **Merrells.**
7. John, bp. 27 Sept., 1721.
8. Rebecca, bp. 23 June, 1723; m. ———— **Barrett.**
　(*By second marriage*):
9. George (Capt.), b. 17 Nov., 1728; bp. 27 July, 1729. FAM. 17.
10. Dorothy, b. 13 June, 1731.

FAM. 9. WILLIAM,[3] (Nath'l,[2] Dea. Richard,[1]), b. ——, ————; m. Hannah (dau. Wm.) **Hill,** 23 May, 1695; for ld. holdings see Chapt. VII, Vol. I; he d. 20

May, 1714—(*W. C. R.*), and it is his est. prob. which was inventoried 17 Nov. of that yr., at £67-08-10; she prob. the H. who d. 17 Apl., 1743, in 71st yr.— *W. Ins.*

Children (*Weth. Rec. & Mix Rec.*) :

1. Eunice, b. 12 Jan., 1696.
2. Sarah, b. 11 Jan., 1698.
3. Peter, twins, b. 9 Apl., 1700; bp. 4
4. Sarah, June, 1704.—*Mix Rec.*
5. Ruth, b. 29 Apl., 1702; bp. 4 June, 1704.—

Mix Rec.
6. Abigail, bp. 6 Aug., 1704.
7. John, bp. 13 Apl., 1707.
8. Mary, bp. 9 Oct., 1709.
9. Esther, bp. 6 Apl., 1712.

Fam. 10.   RICHARD,[3] (*Joseph,*[2] *Dea. Richard,*[1]), b. 1667-8; sett. in Step. parish; m. his cousin Sarah (dau. of Ephraim) **Goodrich,** of Weth. 15 Dec., 1725. From the evident disparity of their ages, (he being 58 and she 27 yrs., at time of marr., a difference not so common in the olden time as now), there has been some doubts expressed as to whether *this* Richard was the son, or grandson of Richard the emigrant ancestor; but much special research has been spent upon the question without shaking the correctness of the recorded facts. He was a tything-man in 1694; for his ld-holdings see Chapt. VII, Vol. I; he d. 27 Oct., 1737; she d. 6 May, 1795, ae. 98.—*W. Ins.*

Children (*Weth. Rec.*) :

1. Sarah, b. 20 Feb., 1727; m. ————
   Grimes, of Simsbury, Ct.
2. Joseph, b. 20 Dec., 1729; d. 3 Aug., 1736.—

W. (S.) Ins.
3. Charles (Lieut.), b. 19 July, 1732. Fam. 18.

Fam. 11.   BENJAMIN,[3] (*Joseph,*[2] *Dea. Richard,*[1]), b. 1673; sett. at Upper Houses (Midd.) now Cromwell, where he res. in 1741, when he and his bro. Joseph sold ld. in Rocky Hill, to their bro. Charles, of Weth.; he m. 5 Dec., 1734, Thankful (dau. John & Hannah) **Sage,** who was b. 9 Feb., 1711; he was largely engaged in exporting cattle to the W. I.; he d. 1750; wid. m. (2) as his second wife Elisha **Stocking.**

Children:

1. Mary, b. 7 Sept., 1735; m. 30 Nov., 1752, Willett **Ranney;** she d. 1823. *Issue:*
   i. Chloe (Ranney).
   ii. Mary (Ranney).
   iii. James (Ranney).
   iv. Lucretia (Ranney).
   v. Seth (Ranney).
   vi. Sarah (Ranney).
   vii. Sybil (Ranney).
2. Lucia, b. 31 Sept., 1736; m. 16 Mch., 1758, Joseph **Ward,** of Midd. *Issue:*
   i. Olive (Ward).
   ii. Joseph (Ward).
   iii. Eber (Ward).
   iv. Lucia (Ward).
   v. Bela (Ward).
   vi. Olive (Ward).
   vii. Phebe (Ward).
3. Comfort, b. 23 Jan., 1738. Fam. 20.
4. Eli, b. 26 May, 1740. Fam. 21.
5. Joseph, b. 26 Aug., 1742; m. 27 Oct., 1767.

Abigail (dau. Cornet Joseph & Mary Belding) **Boardman.**—*W. C. R.* The *B. Geneal.* says, p. 221, that their desc'ts are said to have res. in Pittsfield, Mass.
6. Martha, b. 21 Aug., 1744; m. Thos. **Wright,** of Ry-H.
7. Hannah, b. 26 June, 1746; m. Rev. Samuel **Ells,** of Midd., 7 Nov., 1770—as of Edward & Martha Ells; grad. Y. C., 1766; sett. at No. Branford, Ct.; a patriotic clergyman of the Rev. period, moved by the earnest appeals from Gen. Washington, to rally for the country's defense, he preached on the subject to his people; and at the close of service, one Sunday morning, took command of a Co. of 60, with whom he joined the army at N. Y.
8. Chloe, b. 2 Oct., 1747.
9. Grace, b. 30 Jan., 1749; m. Ebenezer **Wright.**

Fam. 12.   GERSHOM,[3] (*Joseph,*[2] *Dea. Richard,*[1]), b. 1685, at Midd. (Cromwell); m. 1719, May (dau. Jonathan & Sarah) **Deming,** of Weth., b. 24 Oct., 1692, who d. 2 Apl., 1771; he d. 1 May, 1765, ae. 81.

Children:

1. David, b. 14 May, 1720. Fam. 21.
2. Ann, b. 7 Feb., 1722; m. Joseph **Wilcox,** of Midd., 6 (or 10) May, 1742. *No issue.*
3. Millie, b. 3 Mch., 1724; m. Asa **Belden,**

12 Oct., 1749.
4. Gideon, b. 29 May, 1727; d. 7 Feb., 1740.
5. George, b. 19 June, 1730. Fam. 22.
6. Gershom, b. 14 Feb., 1737. Fam. 23.

FAM. 13. CHARLES,² (*Joseph*,² *Dea. Richard*,¹), b. 1685?; m. 17 May, 1704, Susanna (dau. Amos, dec'd) **Williams**, and sett. in Weth.—See Chapt. VII, Vol. 1. *Weth. Recs.* say, "Mr. Charles Butler being in the Queen's service, d. at Milford, 25 Sept., 1711, as he was coming home." He was ment. in the will of his father Joseph, as being at that date (1725) dead.

Children (Weth. Rec. & Mix Rec.) :

1. Mary, b. 25 Feb., 1706; m. Jona. **Smith**, 14 Jan., 1731; *issue*, 6 ch., see *Smith*.
2. Bathsheba, b. 21 Sept., bp. 18 Dec., 1709;

m. Elijah **Miller.** See Note to FAM. 4.
3. Charles (posthumous), b. 11 Mch., bp. 13 Apl., 1712;* d. 1 May, 1713.

FAM. 13a. CHARLES,³ (*Joseph*,² *Dea. Richard*,¹), b. 1715; m. Jerusha **Goodrich**, 19 Nov., 1740; she d. at Step. 12 Dec., 1761, in 40th yr.; he m. (2) Lucy **Bulkeley**, who d. at Ry-H. 17 Jan., 1781, in 57th yr. He d. 26 June, 1785, in 71st yr.—*W. (S) Ins.*, which would make him b. 1714. The discrepancy between age as given on tombstone and that given in res. is prob due to mistake by family.

Children :

1. Jerusha, b. 21 Jan., 1742 ; m. Hezekiah **Goodrich.** *Issue :*
   i. Eli.
   ii. Jerusha (Goodrich).
   iii. Hezekiah (Goodrich).
   iv. Joseph Butler (Goodrich).
   v. Joshua (Goodrich).
2. Ruth, b. 15 Feb., 1744 ; m. Ephraim **Williams**, of Ry-H. *Issue :*
   i. Levi.
   ii. Lucretia (Williams).
   iii. Elias (Williams).
   iv. William (Williams).
   v. Chester (Williams).
   vi. Allen (Williams).
   vii. George (Williams).
   viii. Sylvanus (Williams).
3. Joseph, b. 4 Nov., 1745. FAM. 23a.
4. Moses, b. 20 Mch., 1747 ; m. Azubah ——— ; both d. New Britain, Ct. *Issue :*
   i. Joseph (Butler).
   ii. Solomon (Butler).
   iii. Horace (Butler).
5. Benjamin, b. 5 Jan., 1750-1. FAM. 23b.
6. Mercy, b. 20 Dec., 1753 ; m. Gurdon (s. of Ephraim) **Griswold**; he d. Ry-H.; she d. at Sheffield, Mass. *Issue :*
   i. Barnabas (Griswold), } twins.
   ii. Elizur (Griswold), }
   iii. Abigail (Griswold).
   iv. Silas (Griswold).
   v. Jerusha (Griswold).

vi. Eleazur (Griswold).
vii. Mercy (Griswold).
viii. John (Griswold).
7. David (acc. to one acct.) ; he m. Patience **Conley**; both d. Westfield, Mass. *Issue : S. C. R.* give bp. rec. of ch. of a David, whom we suppose must be the same D., viz :
   i. Frederick, }
   ii. Leonard, } bp. 28 Dec., 1790.
   iii. Lena, }
   iv. Charles, }
   v. Alvin,
   vi. Levi, bp. 17 Apl., 1791.
   vii. David, bp. 16 June, 1793.
   viii. Sylvanus, bp. 23 Aug., 1795. Inf. d. 22 July, 1801.
   (By second marriage) :
8. Stephen ; prob. the "S. s. of Charles," who was bp. 21 Oct., 1764 (*W. C. R.*), and who d. at sea Dec., 1803 in 41st yr. ; m. 1788 Ruth **Russell**, who d. in N. Y. State, and who was poss. wid. Ruth who d. N. Y. City abt. 7 Apl., 1855, in 79th yr.— *S. C. R.* Had :
   i. Rixa (?) (or Rhoda), bp. 1 Sept., 1796.—*S. C. R.*
   ii. Cyrus, bp 1 Sept., 1799.—*S. C. R.*
   iii. Erastus.
   iv. Lucy.
   v. Harriet.

FAM. 14. DANIEL,⁴ (*Sam'l*,³ *Dea. Samuel*,² *Dea. Richard*,¹), b. 1707; m. Arminel (dau. Josiah) **Churchill**, of Weth., 14 May, 1730; she d. 27 Aug., 1752.— *Weth. Rec.*

Children (Weth. Rec.) :

1. Elizabeth, b. 11, bp. 21 Mch., 1730-1.— *Mix.*
2. Mary, b. 18 Oct., 1732 ; d. 20 July, 1748.
3. Sarah, b. 11 Sept., 1734.
4. Abigail, b. 10 Feb., 1737.
5. Eunice, b. 26 July, 1739.
6. Prudence, b. 21 Oct., 1741.
7. George, b. 26 Dec., 1743 ; d. 1747.
8. Samuel, b. 19 Feb., 1746 ; prob. the S. who d. 27 Aug., 1810, in 65th yr.—*Weth. Ry-H. Ins.*
9. Lydia, } twins, b. 12 Apl., 1748.
10. Hannah, }

11. George, b. 22 Feb., 1749-50 ; m. Oct., 1776, Chloe **Bidwell**, of Glast., who was b. 1752 and d. 21 Sept., 1836, ae. 84 ; rem from Ry-H. to Pittsfield, Mass., in 1777 ; was a Revol. soldier ; d. 19 Aug., 1837, ae. 88½ yrs. ; had 11 Ch., of whom the eldest was b. in Glast., the other 10 in P. Their 4th ch. was Samuel, b. 25 Sept., 1784, bp. May, 1795 ; adopted by his uncle Samuel B.; d. in Ry-H.—*Ry-H. Cem.* acc. to *J. W. B.*, of Meriden, Ct., in *Htfd. Times Geneal. Dept.*

* Specially ment. in the *Mix Rec.* as being "the son of Charles, dec'd ; and there was, at that time, no other C. B. who could have been referred to as his father.

FAM. 15. HEZEKIAH,[4] (*James*,[3] Dea. *Samuel*,[2] Dea. *Richard*,[1]), b. ——, ————;
m. 19 Jan., 1732, Rebecca **Standish**, who d. 12 Mch., 1776, in 67th yr—
W. Ins.; he d. 17 Dec., 1786, in 79th yr.—*Weth. Rec. & Ins.*

Children (*Weth. Rec.*) :

1. Lois. b. 9, bp., 19 Nov., (*Mix.*) 1732; d. 26 Apl., 1741.—*Weth. Ins.*
2. Rebecca, b. 12 May., 1735.
3. James, b. 9 Dec., 1736; poss. the J. who m. 8 Apl., 1769, Hannah **Wright**, and had (1) *Lucy*, b. 3 May, 1769, and (2) *Roger*, b. 20 Apl., 1771.—*Weth. Rec.*
4. Hezekiah, b. 6 Apl., 1740; d. 9 May, 1814, in 74th yr.—*Weth. Ins.;* had a s. *Hezekiah*.[6]—See FAM. 23c.
5. Lois, b. 3 Nov., 1742; d. 14 Sept., 1746.— *Weth. Inscr.*
6. Josiah, b. 8 July, 1745. FAM. 24.
7. John, b. 24 Apl., 1753. FAM. 25.

FAM. 16. WILLIAM,[4] (*James*,[3] Dea. *Samuel*,[2] Dea. *Richard*,[1]), b. ——, ————;
m. Lucy **Goodrich**, 8 Nov., 1739—*Weth. Rec.;* she prob the Mrs. Lucy, who d.
17 Jan., 1781, in 57th yr.—*Weth.* (*S.*) *Ins.*

Children (*Weth. Rec.*) :

1. William, b. 16 Apl., 1741.
2. Marianne, b. 22 Dec., 1742; d. 30 Sept., 1750 in 8th yr.
3. Theodore, b. 26, bp. 30 Sept., 1744. FAM. 25a.
4. A William of William was bp. 1745, betw. 24 Mch., and 31 May; prob. the Wm. who
   m. Sarah **Baldwin**, of Saybrook, 12 Dec., 1774; "William the son of William" who d. 22 May, 1776, may have been their son.— *W. C. R.*
5. Roger, b. 20 Sept., 1746. FAM. 25b.
6. Chloe, b. 7 Nov., 1750.

FAM. 17. Capt. GEORGE,[4] (*Jonathan*,[3] Ens. *Samuel*,[2] Dea. *Richard*,[1]), b. 1728;
res. Htfd; m. abt. 1753, Mary ————; he d. before 1789. She b. 18 May,
1728, d. after 1790. Capt. George d. insolvent—*Htfd. Co. Prob. Rec.*, XXIV, p.
140, 60-3; invent. £61-02-03.—*Ct. Rec.*, pp. 49, 63, 72, 100.

Children (*Fam. Recs.*) :

1. Polly, b. 15 May, 1754.
2. Richard, b. 30 June, 1756. FAM. 26.
3. George, b. 11 Mch., 1758; d. soon.
4. George, b. 21 May, 1760.
5. Anne, b. 11 July, 1762.
6. Welthea, b.
7. Charles, b. 19 Oct., 1767.

FAM 18. Lieut. CHARLES,[5] (*Charles*,[4] *Richard*,[3] *Joseph*,[2] Dea. *Richard*,[1]), b. 1732;
m. 24 Oct., 1754, Azubah **Ranney**; he d. 18 Jan., 1783, in 51st yr.; was a
Revol. soldier, enl. Apl., 1775, and served as sgt. in the Lexington Alarm, for 8
days; is said to have been at Bunker Hill, and in Arnold's Quebec expedition;
in May, same yr., was comm. Ens. in the 2d Cont. Reg., Col. Joseph Spencer,
and in 9th (Capt. John Chester's) Co.; disch. 10 Dec., 1775; in 1776, comm.
2d Lieut. in 22 Cont. Reg., Col. Samuel Wylly's; 10 Apl., 1777, was comm. 1st
Lieut. in Col. Thos. Belden's Reg., Capt. Chester Wells' Co.; disch. 22 May,
1777; fm. 1777-1778, is said to have served as surgeon, with rank of Capt., in
Militia reg. under Gen. Spencer(?). Is said to have died fm. effects of exposure in the service.

Children (*Weth. Rec.*) :

1. Simeon (Dea.), b. 13 Aug., 1755. FAM. 27.

FAM. 19. Capt. ELI,[4] (*Benjamin*,[3] *Joseph*,[2] Dea. *Richard*,[1]), b. Midd., Ct. 26 May,
1740; m. 20 Feb., 1765, Rachel **Stocking**, of Midd., b. Jan., 1744. In Spring of
1789, he visited his old neighbor and kinsman, Hugh White, who had sett. at
Whitestown, N. Y., in '84, and before ret. to Ct., he purchased lds. in (present
town of) Paris, Oneida Co. to which his two sons Sylvester and John rem. in
the fall of that yr. In 1793, visiting these sons in Oneida Co., he was so
pleased with the county that he bo't a farm just S. of New Htfd., 17 Apl.
1793, on to which he rem. in winter of 1795. His title of Capt. was gained by
service in the War of Revol. as Capt. of cavalry—in Col. Seymour's Reg. of
Light Horse, at N. Y. City, Aug., 1776, and in Sheldon's Light Dragoons.—
(*Conn. Men in Rev.*)

THE BUTLER FAMILY. 179

Children:

1. Ashbel, b. 28 Nov., 1765. FAM. 28.
2. Sylvester, b. 18 Apl., 1767. FAM. 29.
3. John, b. 28 Mch., 1769. FAM. 30.
4. Lucy, b. 1771; m. Benjamin **Morris,** wid'r with 3 ch.; he killed by falling of a tree. *Issue:*
   i. George W. (Morris), d. 1884, s. p.
   ii. Harriet (Morris), m. Wm. **Stone.**
   iii. Caroline (Morris), d. unm.
   iv. Benj. Butler (Morris), b. 21 Sept., 1804; m. 16 Aug., 1836, Mary **Cox;** m. (2) 16 Oct., 1855, Wid. Abby **Kirkland,** of Utica, N. Y.
5. Rachel, b. 10 Apl., 1773; d. 2 Mch., 1854; m. 31 Dec., 1797, Richard **Sawyer,** of New Htfd., N. Y.; b. 26 Dec., 1769 and d. 8 Aug., 1843. *Issue:*
   i. Gerry Elbridge (Sawyer), b. 11 Nov., 1798.
   ii. Henry Kirkland (Sawyer), b. 11 Nov., 1799; m. Caroline **Prentise;** res. N. Y.; d. 4 June, 1864.
   iii. Eliza (Sawyer), b. 28 May, 1802; d. Sept., 1853; m. Freedom **Tibbitts.**
   iv. Jedidiah (Sawyer), b. 13 Aug., 1805; m. Frances **Hall;** d. Oct., 1876.
   v. Richard (Sawyer), b. 10 Sept., 1810; d. 8 Nov., 1842.
6. Martha, b. 14 May, 1775; m. her cousin Joseph (s. Joseph & Abigail *Boardman*) **Butler,** 1 Feb., 1804; he b. New Htfd., N. Y., 22 July, 1770; d. 28 Jan., 1857; she d. 22 Apl., 1841. *Issue:*
   i. Juliette Adams (Butler), b. 27 May, 1805.
   ii. Cornelia Eliza (Butler), b. 20 Sept., 1806.
   iii. Charles Joseph (Butler), b. 3 July, 1809; d. unm., Galveston, Tex., 25 July, 1838.
   iv. Emily Louise (Butler), b. 29 July, 1812.
   v. Frederic Julius (Butler), b. 23 , 1819.
7. Chloe, b. 28 Mch., 1777; m. Moses (s. of Lemuel) **Maynard,** 1810 or 11*; she d. 19 Dec., 1821, Madison, N. Y., ae. 45; he d. 27 May, 1853, ae. 77. *Issue:*
   * His second wife; his first was a Lincoln, by whom he had 4 ch.; his 3rd wife was Mrs. Curtis; he res. Madison, Mad. Co., N. Y.; was sheriff of that Co. for many yrs.
   i. Butler (Maynard), b. 1 Jan., 1812.
   ii. Edward (Maynard), b. 1813.
   iii. iv. Twins, b. and d.
   v. Jane M. (Maynard); m. W. R. **Griswold,** farmer, Mad. Co., N. Y., abt. 1845; she d. Aug., 1856.
   vi. Mary Anne (Maynard), m. ――― **Cook;** res. nr. Ann Arbor, Mch.; 2 s. 1 dau.

vii. DeWitt Clinton (Maynard), d. yg. 1821.
8. Eli, b. 28 Mch., 1779. FAM. 31.
9. Sarah, b. 4 Mch., 1781; m. 17 May, 1805, Asa (s. John & Ruth *Stone*) **Eames,** who was b. 17 May, 1780, at N. Htfd, N. Y., and d. Sept., 1832, at Vernon, N. Y.; she d. 23 Mch., 1864. *Issue:*
   i. Harriet (Eames), b. 7 Mch., 1806.
   ii. Charles Butler (Eames), b. 22 Feb., 1811; m. 1833, Helen **Stevens;** d. s. p.
   iii. Cornelia (Eames), b. 11 Jan., 1813; m. 1841, Anthony Rhoades **Kinney;** 4 ch.
   iv. Charlotte (Eames), b. 17 Jan., 1817; m. 1845, Stephen **Dinsmore;** d. 1892 at DeWitt, Iowa.
   v. Sarah Frances (Eames), b. 16 Mch., 1821; m. 1873, Horace **Duryea.**
10. Perces, b. 1783; m. 17 May, 1805, Hez. (s. John & Ruth *Stone*) **Eames,** who was b. 17 May, 1780; d. 23 Sept., 1826; she d. Milwaukee, 14 June, 1843. *Issue:*
   i. Clarissa, ⎱ b. 24 Feb., 1806, d. at
   ii. Son, ⎰ birth.
   iii. Edward Franklin (Eames), b. 16 Feb., m. 1832, Maria (dau. of Asa & Phebe) **Broadwell;** d. 30 Jan., 1871; she d. 2 Jan., 1883, ae. 75; 5 ch.
   iv. Caroline (Eames), b. 4 Dec., 1811, at New Htfd., d. Milwaukee, 14 Sept., 1858; m. 1840, Joseph (s. of Wm. & Lydia *Trask*) **Carey;** 5 ch.
   v. Henry F., b. 27 Jan., 1815; m. Emily (dau. Jacob & Jerusha Huntington) **Sherrell,** 3 Sept., 1839; was many yrs. Pres. Continental Nat. Bk., Chicago, Ill.; 7 ch.
   vi. Lester H. (Eames), b. 18 May, 1817; d. Chicago 10 Sept., 1895, unm.
11. Clarissa, b. 3 Apl., 1785; m. 9 Jan., 1814, Col. James (s. Abram & Hannah *Washburn*) **Berthrong,** who was b. 13 Nov., 1780; d. 23 Oct., 1850. Abram B. and a bro. came from France and he sett. Middlebury, Vt., but never heard of his bro. after they landed. Col. James B. (the son) and Hez. Sage were both Cols. and contractors; built the Albany Basin and part of the Erie Canal. *Issue:*
   i. Lucius Washburn (Berthrong), b. 26 Oct., 1814; m. 25 Apl., 1844, Maryette **Farr;** m. (2) Sarah (dau. Edward & Hannah *Turner*) **Root,** 8 Oct., 1861; she b. 16 Nov., 1822; 1 ch.
   ii. Jane Eliza (Berthrong), b. 9 May, 1816; m. 4 Jan., 1843, Martin (s. Oramel & Elizabeth *Webber*) **Shapley;** b. 25 June, 1817; she d. Binghampton, N. Y., Feb., 1897; 3 ch.

FAM. 20. COMFORT,[4] (*Benj.*,[3] *Joseph,*[2] *Dea. Richard,*[1]), b. 1738; m. Sibel (dau. Daniel & Esther *Stor*) **Ranney,** 6 May, 1762, who was b. 29 Aug., 1744 and d. 16 Aug., 1781, ae. 37 yrs.; he m. (2) Elinor (wid. Stephen) **Bush,** of Chatham, 1st Feb., 1790.

Children (b. Midd. Upper Houses):

1. Mary, bp. 13 Nov., 1763; m. Capt. Reuben **Kirby,** of Up. Midd., Capt. K. d. 29 June, 1833, ae. 65; Wid. Mary d. Htfd., 31 May, 1853, ae. 80. *Issue:*
   i. Abel (Kirby), d. 28 Nov., 1889, ae 90 yrs.
   ii. Maria (Kirby), d. unm.
   iii. Horace (Kirby).
   iv. Nicholas (Kirby).

v. Thomas (Kirby).
vi. Lucia (Kirby). Htfd., d. 20 June, 1846, ae. 41.
2. Benjamin, b. 25 May, 1765. FAM. 32.
3. James (Capt.) b. 4 June, 1767. FAM. 33.
4. Daniel. FAM. 34.
   (*By second marriage*):
5. Comfort, b. 29 Apr., 1791. FAM. 35.

FAM. 21. DAVID,[4] (*Gershom,*[3] *Joseph,*[2] *Dea. Richard,*[1]), b. 1720; m. Hannah **Cook.**

Children:

1. David. | 2. Samuel. | 3. John. | 4. George. | 5. Hannah.

FAM. 22. GEORGE,[4] (*Gershom*,[3] *Joseph*,[2] *Richard*,[1]), b. 1727; m. (1) Anna **Plum,** 10 Apl., 1755, who d. 2 June, 1766; he m. (2) Desire **Dimock.** He rec'd by deed of gift, 1751, ld. in No. Soc. Midd., which he sold to John Alsop of N. Y. City in 1777; he subsequently owned his father's ld. at Ry-H., which he prob. got by exch. with some of his father's other heirs.

Children (by first marriage):

1. Mary, b. 1756.
(*By second marriage*):
2. David; poss. the D. who d. 17 Mch., 1765-6. W. C. R.

3. Selah, b. 1768; d. 1853. FAM. 36.
4. Silas, b. 1776.
5. Josiah.

FAM. 23. GERSHOM,[4] (*Gershom*,[3] *Joseph*,[2] *Dea. Richard*,[1]), b. 1737; m. Prudence ————; he d. 12 Apl., 1812, ae. 76.—*Cromwell Bu-gd. Insc.*

Children:

1. Anne.
2. Gideon.
3. Ebenezer, d. 16 Feb. 1825.
4. Josiah.
5. Rosetta.

6. Gershom; one rec. says he d. at W. I. Oct., 1793, ae. 24, and that his wid. m. Stephen **Webster.**
7. Oliver, d. 2 June, 1798, ae. 18.

FAM. 23a. JOSEPH,[4] (*Chas.*,[3] *Joseph*,[2] *Dea. Richard*,[1]), b. 4 Nov., 1745; m. 30 Nov. 1774, Elizabeth **Brooks.**

Children:

1. Simeon, b. 1775.
2. Simeon, b. 1778.
3. John, b. 1780.
4. Daphne, b. 1782.
5. Joseph, b. 1784.
6. Theodosia, b. 1786.
7. Sophronia, b. 1788.
8. Dorcas, b. 1790.

9. Abijah, b. 1792
10. Marcus, b. 1794; m. ———— **Allyn;** had a s. *Clark,* b. 1827; who was father of Jesse B. Butler, of Farmersville, Ind.
11. Sylvia, } twins, b. 1796.
12. ————, }
13. Elizabeth, b. 1797.
14. Washington, b. 1800.

FAM. 23b. BENJAMIN,[4] (*Charles*,[3] *Joseph*,[2] *Dea. Richard*,[1]), b. 1750; m. 13 Dec., 1775, Eunice (dau. Nath'l & Mary) **Robbins;** he was dr. 21 Aug., 1813, in 64th yr.—*W. (S.) Ins.;* she (wid.) d. at Upper Midd., 1 Oct., 1847, ae. 92.—*W. (S.) Ins.* This Benj. prob. the one who enl. 11 July, 1775 in 1st Cont. Reg., Col. Webb— and in 2d Co.—disch. 20 Dec., 1775; in Dec. 1776, was in Wadsworth's Brigade; enl. 10 Apl., 1777, in 3d. Cont. Capt. Abby's Co., Col. Sam. Wylly's Reg., for 3 yrs.; was of those detached, Nov., 1781, to serve in Ormond's Cavalry and with it (as Corp'l) July, 1782.

Children (S. C. R. and Fam. Rec.):

1. Joseph, b. 3 June, bp. 28 July, 1776. FAM. 35a.
2. Demas, b. 25 Feb., 1778; d. at sea, 14 Nov., 1800.
3. Jerusha, b. 13 June, 1780, bp. 15 Apl., 1781; d. 3 Oct., 1851.
4. Allen, b. 3 Sept., bp. 2 Nov., 1783. FAM. 36a.
5. Sylvester, b. 23 Aug., bp. 20 Nov., 1785; d. 14 Nov., 1861; his wid. Anne, d. 4 Apl., 1864. FAM. 36b.
6. Mary, b. 12 Sept., 1788, bp. 7 June, 1789; d. 24 May, 1790, ae. 1 yr. 8 mos.—*S. C. R.*
7. Mary, b. 30 Sept., 1790, bp. 17 Apl., 1791; became 29 Apl., 1822, the 2d wife of Comfort (s. of David) **Starr,** of Midd.; b. 12 July, 1786; joiner and farmer, who d. 28 Mch., 1829. *Issue: (by first marr.)* : *Mary Elizabeth,* b. 1811; (*by second marr.*) *Sophia Butler* (Starr), b. 1826, and *Harriet Lucy* (Starr), b. 1824; the latter m. John Roberts **Williams;** no issue; Mrs. Mary Butler Starr d. 5 Sept., 1863.

8. Eunice, b. 19 Feb., bp. 31 Mch., 1793; m. 14 May, 1815, Ichabod (s. of) **Chapman,** who was b. 14 Nov., 1777; he d. 1855; Mrs. Chapman d. 13 Jan., 1877. *Issue:*
   i. Daniel (Chapman), b. 1 Nov., 1818; m. 15 Sept., 1841, Juliette **Childs,** of Pittsfield, Mass.; 3 ch.
   ii. James Ichabod (Chapman), b. 3 Sept., 1821; d. 1837.
   iii. Eunice Jennette (Chapman), b. 16 May, 1829; m. (1) Nathn'l **Messor;** m. (2) Prof. **Ford.**
9. Benjamin, b. 25 bp. 28 Feb., 1795; d. 27 Mch., 1795.
10. Jerome (or Jamin?), b. 8 Mch., bp. 21 Aug., 1796; dr. 13 (or 30) May, 1813, in 18 yr.—*W. (S.) Ins.*
11. George, b. 10 Mch., bp. 4 Nov., 1798. FAM. 36c.
12. Sophronia (or Sophia), b. 9 Aug., 1800, bp. 17 Jan., 1802; d. at Marietta, O., 1 June, 1888.

FAM. 23c. HEZEKIAH,[6] (*Hez.,[5] Hez.,[4] James,[3] Dea. Samuel,[2] Dea. Richard,[1]*), b. 1789, prob. 25 Sept.; m. 7 Oct., 1824, Harriet **Wells**, of Pittsfield, Mass.; he d. 26 Aug., 1863, ae. 74; she d. 11 Dec., 1876, ae. 76.

Children (*W. C. R.*) :

1. Harriet, b. 22 Oct., 1825, bp. 27 Aug., 1826.
2. Sarah, b. 3 Dec., 1827.
3. John, b. 16 Apl., bp. 17 Oct., 1830.
4. Inf. bp. 10 Aug., 1828.
5. Hezekiah, b. 4 Apl., bp. 3 Nov., 1833.
6. Love Smith, b. 14 Nov., 1835.
7. Lucy Wells, b. 24 Nov., 1838.
8. Levi Wells, b. 2 May, 1841.
9. Martha Ann, b. 15 Apl., 1843.

FAM. 24. JOSIAH,[5]* (*Hez.,[4] James,[3] Dea. Sam'l,[2] Dea. Richard,[1]*), b. 1745; m. Elizabeth **Russell**, 11 Nov., 1790; res. Midd. He prob. the "J. of Upper Midd.," who d. 4 Mch., 1845, in 78th yr.; "E., wid. of Josiah," d. 14 Sept., 1847, ae. 87.—*S. C. R.*

Children:

1. Julia, m. her cousin, Horace **Butler**, of N. Y.
2. Maria, m.   **Cook**; both d. yg., leaving 2 ch., viz:
    i. Russell (Cook), who d. Calif.
    ii. Maria E. (Cook) ; was for many yrs. the matron of the Wadsworth Orphanage for boys, at Htfd.; still living 1903 ; res. N. Y. City.
3. Sophia, m. Dea. Jared **Dimock**, of Ry-H. *Issue* see *Dimock*.
4. Russell, d. at sea, unm ; Calif. ; prob. the R. who d. at sea 19 July, 1821, in 29th yr. *W. C. R.*
5. Gershom, d. at sea, unm.
6. Philip Russell, b. 16 Sept., 1810 ; m. Caroline H. ——, who was b. 8 Aug., 1813 :

d. 1 June, 1858; he d. 13 Feb., 1898. *Issue:*
    i. Richard N. (Butler), b. 9 Nov., 1838 ; d. 19 July, 1841.
    ii. Susie L (Butler), b. 23 Jan., 1842 ; d. 27 Oct., 1867 ; m. Benj. H **Ranney**, of Cromwell.
    iii. Henry Richard (Butler) (twin), b. 12 Apl., 1845 ; d. 15 Jan., 1872.
    iv. Horace Russell (Butler) (twin), b. 12 Apl., 1845 ; m. a cousin (dau. of Joseph **Wilcox**, of Cromwell.
    v. Carrie Alberta (Butler), b. 7 Apl., 1852 ; m. Arthur E. (s. Isaac L.) **Coe**, of Midd. ; their only dau. Claudine Alberta (Coe), m. Dr. D. Lewis **Maitland**, of Midd.

FAM. 25. JOHN,[5] (*Hez.,[4] James,[3] Dea. Samuel,[2] Dea. Richard,[1]*), b. 1753; m. Love **Smith**, 9 Feb., 1777—*Weth. Rec.;* he d. 12 Dec., 1831, ae. 79—*W. Ins.;* she d. 14 Sept., 1830, ae. 75—*W. Ins.*

Children (*Weth. Rec.*) :

1. Sarah, b. 26 Apl., bp. 21 June, 1778.
2. Betsy, b. 8, bp. 15 Oct., 1780 ; poss. the B. who m. Josiah **Curtis**, of Lenox, Mass., 17 Feb., 1805.—*W. T. R.*
3. Hope, b. 22 Feb., bp. 6 Apl., 1783.
4. Polly, b. 19 June, bp. 7 Aug., 1785.
5. Clarissa, b. 8 Jan., bp. 2 Mch., 1788 ; d. 30 Mch., 1858, ae. 70.—*W. Ins.*
6. Hezekiah, b. 18 Jan., 1790.
7. Emily, b. 30 Mch., 1793.

FAM. 25a. THEODORE,[5] (*William,[4] James,[3] Dea. Samuel,[2] Dea. Richard,[1]*), b. 1746; m. Nancy **Baldwin**, of Saybrook, 3 Dec., 1786; he d. 11 Jan., 1818, ae. 73; she d. 27 May, 1813, ae. 44.

Children (*W. C. R.*) :

1. Nancy, bp. 6 and d. 8 July, 1796.
2. George,
3. Abigail,   } bp. 28 Aug., 1796.
4. William, bp. 16 Sept., 1798.
5. Henry, bp. 23, bu. 24 Sept., 1806, ae. 7 mos.
6. Nancy, bp. 6 Sept., 1808.
7. Son, } twins (Leonard?), d. 27 July,
8. Son. } 1808.

* We find on record another JOSIAH[?] (*Hezekiah,[2] James,[1]*), who *may be* the rightful claimant to this place. This Josiah, b. 1745, m. 16 Oct., 1769, **Ranney** (*Weth. Rec.*) though another acc. gives her name as Martha **Riley**. *Weth. Recs.* give the following *children:*
1. Simeon, b. 25 Mch., 1770.
2. Lois, b. 3 Mch., 1773.
While the *W. C. R.* also give as children of Josiah (& Martha *Riley*) Butler, these following, poss. by a 2d marr.:
3. Martha, } bp. 24 Apl., 1774.
4. William, }
5. Rhoda, bp. 7 Aug., 1776.
6. Allen, bp. 12 Mch., 1780.
7. Sylvester, bp. 7 Aug., 1785 ; m. Huldah (dau. Eli. & Mary *Wells*) **Stoddard**; who d. 10 May, 1872, ae. 87, at Pittsfield, Mass., where they had 8 ch. rec. His age at dth. agrees with yr. of his birth.—*R. H. C.*
8. Prudence, bp. 13 Apl., 1788.

FAM. 25b. ROGER,⁵ (William,⁴ James,³ Dea. Samuel,² Dea. Richard,¹), b. 1746; m. Hannah **Hanmer,** 22 Feb., 1769; she d. 23 Feb., 1780, in 30th yr.; he m. (2) Lucretia ————, who d. "wid. of the late" Roger, 10 Mch., 1837, ae. 82—W. C. R.; he. d. 28 July, 1799, ae. 53.

Children (W. C. R. & W. R.) :

1. Lucy, b. 3 May, 1769.
2. Roger, b. 30 Apl., 1771 ; bu. 4 Oct., 1792.
3. Roger, bp. 3 Apl., 1774.
4. William, bp. 6 Nov., 1774
5. Martha, bp. 10 July, 1774.
6. Hannah, bp. 3 Oct., 1779.

(By second marriage) :
7. Henry Goodrich, bp. 2 Oct., 1785.
8. Eli, bp. 26 June, 1789 ; prob. the ch. bu. 14 Apl., 1790.
9. Charlotte, bp. 26 Feb., 1792.

FAM. 26. RICHARD,⁵ (Geo.,⁴ Jona.,³ Ens. Samuel,² Dea. Richard,¹), b. 1756; sett. Windsor, Ct.; m. 12 May, 1786, Lucy **Ranney,** b. 1762 (dau. of Stephen & Patience *Ward*) Ranney, of Midd.—*Midd. Recs.*

Children (Fam. Recs.) :

1. Nancy, b. 19 May, 1787.
2. Richard, b. 12 Dec., 1788.
3. Walter, b. 19 Feb., 1791.
4. George Stephen, b. 18 Oct., 1793 ; d. inf.
5. George Stephen, b. 8 July, 1795. FAM. 37.
6. Daniel Ranney, b. 31 Aug., 1797.
7. Lucy, b. 12 Apl., 1800 ; poss. the L. who m. 2 Nov., 1834, William **Camp,** of Htfd.
8. Charles Frederick, b. 25 June, 1803.
9. Mary Ann, b. 16 Apl., 1805.

FAM. 27. Dea. SIMEON,⁶ (Lieut. Chas., Jr.,⁵ Charles,⁴ Richard,³ Joseph,² Dea. Richard,¹), b. ——, ——— ; m. 18 Sept., 1783, Anna Moses **Marsh**; they res. abt. one mile above Cromwell line—the present Gardiner place. He was a farmer and miller, and d. 29 Dec., 1831, in 77th yr.; his wid. d. 13 Aug., 1849, in 88th yr.

Children (W. C. R.) :

1. Abigail, bp. 2 Oct., 1785 ; d. 13 Aug., 1849.—*S. C. R.*
2. Nancy, bp. 27 May, 1788.
3. William (Capt.), bp. 21 Aug., 1790 ; res. with his sister Nancy, in his father's old place ; was a farmer and miller.
4. Eunice (Ermina or Emera?), bp. 29 Mch., 1792 ; d. ae. 1 yr.—*S. C. R.*
5. Ulysses, bp. 7 June, 1795 ; m. Orpha **Robbins,** 29 Mch., 1820 ; d. at Chatham, 21 Sept., 1823, ae. 28; had

i. Fred Robbins (Butler), bp. 25 Mch., 1823.
6. Norman, bp. 15 Dec., 1798 ; m. ——— **Bulkely**; res. in West; d. at Chatham, 1 Sept., 1823.—*S. C. R* .
7. Anselma, bp. 11 Apl., 1802 ; d. 15 Nov., 1825, ae. 24.—*S. C. R.*
   An Abigail (of Simeon & Anne), d. 13 Aug., 1821, ae. 39.—*W: (S.) Ins.*—prob a second Abigail.

FAM. 28. ASHBEL,⁵ (Capt. Eli,⁴ Benj.,³ Joseph,² Dea. Rich.,¹), b. 1765; m. 5 Apl., 1791, before leaving Midd., Sarah (dau. Jehiel & Anne *Edwards*) **Williams,** who was b. 12 Mch., 1770 and d. 22 Feb., 1862; he d. 8 Mch., 1828.

Children:

1. Horace (or Harris), b. 9 July, 1792, bp. 27 Jan., 1793. FAM. 38.
2. Chester, b. 30 Jan., 1795. FAM. 39.
3. Lyman, b. 16 Sept., 1796, bp. 8 Jan., 1797 ; m. Mary **Dutton**; d. 2 Apl., 1859 ; *no issue*.
4. Hiram, b. 16 Oct., 1799 ; m. Harriet **Talmadge**; he d. at Phelps, N. Y., leaving a son C. Worden Butler, of Buffalo, N. Y.
5. Charles, b. New Htfd., N. Y. ; m. Laura **Harrington**; res. Jamestown, Catt. Co., N. Y. ; had a son *Oscar*.
6. Laura, m. Curtis **Ryder,** of Warsaw, N. Y. ; had 2 ch., *Butler* and *Frances* (Ryder).
7. Sarah, b. 8 Oct., 1802 ; d. 1862 ; m. Thos. L. **Morgan.**

FAM. 29. SYLVESTER,⁵ (Capt. Eli,⁴ Benj.,³ Joseph,² Dea. Richard,¹), b. 1767; m., in Midd., 26 Jan., 1792, Lydia **Wetmore,** b. 19 Jan., 1773, and d. 22 July, 1855; he d. 20 July, 1805. They res. Midd.

Children:

1. Lucy, b. 11 Aug., 1794 ; d. 15 Sept., 1807.
2. Sylvester Eli, b. 25 Nov., 1796. FAM. 40.
3. Lucy, Beatta, b. 8 Jan., 1797 ; m. 14 May, 1818, at Paris, N. Y., Joseph (s. Joseph &

Submit *Luce*) **Howard, Jr.,** who d. at Aurora, N. Y., 16 Sept., 1836 ; she d. 13 Jan., 1871 ; 7 ch.
4. Joseph Wetmore, b. 9 June, 1801.

FAM. 30. JOHN,[5] (*Capt. Eli,[4] Benj.,[3] Joseph,[2] Dea. Richard,[1]*), b. 1769; m. 12 Mch., 1797, Hannah (dau. Capt. Asa Todd of Wallingford, Ct., & Sarah) **Potter,** of Branford, Ct.; she was b. 20 Oct., 1775, d. 23 Apl., 1856; they rem. to Sanquoit, N. Y., and he d. 16 May, 1851.

Children:

1. Eliza, b. 17 Jan., 1798; d. 8 (9) Oct., 1869; m. 1 Oct., 1823, Wm. W. (s. James & Martha *Parmalee*) **Hickox,** of Durham, Ct.; he d. Winfield, N. Y., 21 Aug., 1871; 4 ch.
2. John Milton, b. 18 Mch., 1799; d. 6 May, 1824, unm
3. Son, b. 1801.
4. Chauncey Sage, b. 27 Dec., 1802. FAM. 41.
5. Son, b. 1804.
6. Amni Todd, b. 26 Aug., 1805. FAM. 42.
7. Asa Alanson, b. 16 Feb., 1808. FAM. 43.
8. Lucy Maria, b. 6 Feb., 1810; m. Sterling **Ackley,** 3. Nov., 1840; d. 18 Feb., 1887; *no* issue.
9. Julia, b. 11 Oct., 1812; d. 20 July, 1838, unm.
10. Henrietta, b. 12 June, 1815; d. 7 Jan., 1842, unm.
11. George Hamilton, b. 2 Jan., 1823. FAM. 44.

FAM. 31. ELI,[5] (*Capt. Eli,[4] Benj.,[3] Joseph,[2] Dea Richard,[1]*), b. 1779; m. 1 Sept., 1806, Rachel **Kellogg,** of New Htfd., N. Y.; was a farmer on "Butler Farm"; wife was dau. of Truman & Hannah *Merrill* Kellogg and was b. 11 June, 1788, and d. 18 Apl., 1871. He d. 3 Sept., 1832; farmer and prominent citizen.

Children:

1. Morgan L., b. 7 June, 1807; m. 10 Feb., 1841, Marianne (dau. Rufus & Nancy *Hungerford*) **Howard;** b. 6 July, 1815; he d. 3 Aug., 1892; *no issue;* a farmer (stock-farm); blt. and pres. to New Htfd, its *Memorial* (Butler) *Town Hall.*
2. Francis, b. 23 Dec., 1808; m. 12 May, 1853, Harriet (dau. Jacob & Jerusha *Huntington*) **Sherrill;** b. 28 Sept., 1817; d. 25 Dec., 1887; he d. 21 Nov., 1889. *Issue:*
   Morgan Sherrill, b. and d. 1856; and *Emily Huntington,* b. '58; m. Rev. Israel N. **Terry;** had inf. s. who d. 1882.
3. Truman Kellogg, b. 31 Oct., 1810; d. 11 Nov., 1888, unm.; donated lds. and bldgs.
for St. Luke's Hospital and Home, and ld. for St. Luke's ch., Utica; a benevolent man.
4. Harriet, b. 23 Oct., 1814; m. Chas. P. (s. Amos & Lucy *Olmsted*) **Wetmore,** of Detroit, Mich., 10 Oct., 1844; *no issue.*
5. Mary, b. 1 Feb., 1817; m. 1 June, 1853, George (s. Robert & Mary Spaulding) **Burch;** she d. 15 Apl., 1892; 1 ch. d.
6. Hannah, b. 14 Feb., 1820; m. Dr. J. B. **Brown,** 3 Aug., 1858, at Little Falls, N. Y.; she d. 13 Apl., 1870; *no issue.*
7. Sophia D.. b. 14 Oct., 1823; d. 30 Sept., 1893, unm.
8. Henry, b. 2 June, 1826. FAM. 45.

FAM. 32. BENJAMIN,[5] (*Comfort,[4] Benj.,[3] Joseph,[2] Dea. Richard,[1]*), b. 1765; m. Mary **Treadway,** 22 June, 1787, who d. 15 Jan., 1843, ae. 73 yrs. We judge that he was the B. of Step., who, with Isaac Boardman, owned the brigantine *Hiram,* in 1795; also, the slp. *Two Brothers,* and the schooner *Betsy and Nancy,* in 1797; also, in 1803, the sloop *Allen* and schr. *Kitty.* A Benj. of Ry-H. d. 1813, ae. 64, whether at sea or not, is not known.

Children:

1. Mary, b. 1790, bp. 17 Apl., 1791; m. Hiland **Hill,** of Catskill, N. Y.
2. Harriet, b. 1792; d. yg.
3. Clarissa, b. 1794; m. Stephen **Taylor,** of Midd.
4. James Harvey, b. 1796; d. at Havana, Cuba, 1822; a ship-master.
5. Harriet, b. 1798; m. John **Pratt,** of Milford, Ct.
6. Edwin, b. 1800; ship-master; d. at Havana. Cuba, 1832.
   A Benjamin had Benjamin bp. 28 Jan., 1795, who d. inf., 27 Feb., same yr.— S. C. R.

FAM. 33. Capt. JAMES,[5] (*Comfort,[4] Benjamin,[3] Joseph,[2] Dea. Richard,[1]*), b. 1767, at Cromwell, Ct.; m. 25 or 28 Sept., 1800, Clarissa **Sage,** who was b. 27 May, 1776. He d. at sea 2 Jan., 1807, ae. 39; his wid. d. 11 Oct., 1836, in ho. of Stillman K. Wightman, her s-in-law.

Children:

1. James, b. 7 Aug., 1803. FAM. 46.
2. Clarissa, b. 27 Oct., 1805; m. 18 Oct., 1827, Hon. Stillman K. (only s. of Rev. Fred'k & Polly *King*) **Wightman,** of R. I.; he grad. Y. C. 1825; was at one time memb.
of Leg. of Conn.; sett. and resided in Midd. until 1843, when he rem. to N. Y. City and practiced law until his dth, 27 May, 1899, ae. 96; she d. 28 Jan., 1897, ae. 92. *Issue:*

i. Frederick Butler (Wightman), b. 2 May, 1829; m. Abby (dau. Robert M. & Ellen *Morrison*) **Hartley.***

ii. Clarissa King (Wightman), b. 19 Feb., 1831, d. 26 June, 1833.

iii. James Stillman (Wightman), b. 20 Mch., 1833; m. (1) Lilly **Hunter,** 1863; m. (2) 1885, Mrs. Sarah H. Davis **Whitlock.**

iv. Edward King (Wightman), b. 27 Apl., 1835; grad. Coll., City N. Y.;

a man of letters; killed at Fort Fisher, 15 Jan., 1865.

v. Charles Stephens (Wightman) Rev., m. Mary **Earle,** 20 Dec., 1882.

vi. Mary Clarissa (Wightman), b. 24 Sept., 1839; d. 19 July, 1890.

vii. Ellen Augusta (Wightman), b. 21 Nov., 1841; m. John **Hunter;** she d. 9 Dec., 1899; their dau. Clarissa Augusta (Hunter), m. Vincent S. **Cronk.**

FAM. 34. Capt. DANIEL,[5] (*Comfort,*[4] *Benj.,*[3] *Joseph,*[2] *Dea. Richard,*[1]), m. Mary **Keith,** who d. 11 Apl., 1812, ae. 35; Capt., Daniel d. at New Orleans, 1813; res. in ho. S. of the old Butler mansion (lately torn down) at Cromwell, Ct.

Children:

1. Janette.
2. Mary, d. Midd., 21 Sept., 1822, ae. 18.
3. David, d. St. Pierre, Martinique, 1826,

ae. 21.
4. Alexander, d. Cincinnati, O.
5. Benjamin, b. 6 Aug., 1810.

FAM. 35. COMFORT,[5] (*Comfort,*[4] *Benj.,*[3] *Joseph,*[2] *Dea. Richard,*[1]), b. 1791; m. 30 Sept., 1815, at Broadalbin, N. Y., Martha **Brown,** of B. b. 2 May, 1797, who d. 14 Sept., 1882; he d. 14 Apl., 1864; rem. to Blyn.; bu. Greenwood Cemetery, Bklyn., N. Y.; saddle and harness mkr.; in old age entirely blind.

Children (all b. Utica, N. Y.):

1. William Comfort, b. 9 Sept., 1816.
2. Jane Maria, b. ————; m. (1) Nelson **Roth.** *Issue:*
   i. Charles Volkert (Roth), m. Letitia A. **Carey.**
   ii. John (Roth), d. 27 Feb., 1866.
   iii. Henry Albert (Roth), d. yg.
   iv. Arthur Franklin (Roth), m. Addine A. **Williams;** had (*a*) Nelson John (Roth); (*b*) Harold Butler (Roth).
   v. Cornelia Maria (Roth), m. John C. **Balis;** had (*a*) Florence Cornelia (Balis); (*b*) Grace Louisa (Balis).
   iv. Mary Ann, d. yg.
3. Mary Ann, b. 10 Sept., 1820; m. Frank B. **Austin;** had a son, who d. inf.
4. Catherine Eliza, b. Aug., 21, 1822; m. Alvin M. **Bennett.** *Issue:*
   i. Emma Louise (Bennett), m. Eslor J. **Boddy;** had (*a*) Ralph Tower (Boddy); (*b*) Arthur Dearing (Boddy).
   ii. Fannie Butler (Bennett), m. A. J.

Newbury, had (*a*) Irving Covel (Newbery).
   iii. Clarissa Austin (Bennett), m. L. J. **Amsden;** had (*a*) Edith Bennett.
5. Harriet Ells, b. 26 Apl., 1824; m. E. F. **Nelson.** *Issue:*
   i. Mary Evelyn (Nelson), m. Wm. J. **Ladd.**
   ii. Isabella Louise (Nelson), m. C. F. **DeGolyer;** had (*a*) Ella Louise (DeGolyer); (*b*) Charles Frederic (DeGolyer), d. yg.; (*c*) Reginald Butler (DeGolyer; (*d*) George Nexsan (DeGolyer).
6. Amelia Wright, b. 26 June, 1826; d. 14 Sept., 1854.
7. Charles Carroll, b. 12 Mch., 1828; m. Emma **Gates.** FAM. 47.
8. James Henry, b. 7 Feb., 1830.
9. George Frederic, b. 28 Aug., 1834. FAM. 48.
10. Edward Demorest, b. 16 Aug., 1836. FAM. 49.

FAM 35a. *Capt.* JOSEPH,[5] (*Benjamin,*[4] *Charles,*[3] *Joseph,*[2] *Dea. Richard,*[1]) b. 1776; m. 23 May, 1803, Mary (dau. Joseph & Mary) **Bulkeley,** who d. Ry-H., 22 Mch., 1854, in 75 yr.—*S. C. R.* He d. Ry-H., 9 Feb., 1826.—*S. C. R.*

---

* FREDERICK B. WIGHTMAN, Esq., lawyer, of N. Y. City, & Abby his wife have the following children:
1. *Clara Belle* (Wightman), b. and d. 16 Jan., 1860.
2. *Frederick Hartley* (Wightman), b. 26 Oct., 1864; m. 23 June, 1891, Cecilia G. **Proud;** d. at Lake Placid, Adirondacks, N. Y., 7 Aug., 1894.
3. Rev. *Percy Butler* (Wightman), b. N. Y. City, 13 Feb., 1871; grad. N. Y. Univ., 1893; at Auburn Theol. Sem., 1895; Ass't Pastor Westminster Presb. Ch., Buffalo, N. Y., 1896-8; Post-Grad. Study at New College, Edinburg, Scotland, and Auburn Theol. Sem., 1898-99; pastor of Pres. Ch. at Fayetteville, N. Y., 1899, to date; m. 9 Oct., 1900, Edith **Lewis,** dau. of Rev. Henry M. Booth, D. D., LL. D., and late Pres. Auburn Theol. Sem. *Issue:* Henry Booth Wightman, b. 8 Aug., 1901.
4. *Orrin Sage* (Wightman), M. D., b. 6 May, 1873; grad. A. B., N. Y. Univ., 1895; grad. in Med. N. Y. Univ., 1898; Alumnus of Gouverneur Hospital, N. Y. City. Is engaged in private practice, N. Y. C., since 1900.
5. *Robert Stillman* (Wightman), b. 9 Sept., N. Y. City, 1876; grad. A. B., N. Y. Univ., 1897; at Auburn Theol. Sem., 1900; traveled abroad, 1899; missionary in Presb. Ch., in the Adirondacks, 1900, at De Grasse, St. Law. Co., N. Y.; contributor to *Auburn Review* and *Christian Work and Evangelist,* on Adirondack Mission Work.

Children, (Fam. Recs.) :

1. Mary Williams, b. 8 Jan., 1805 ; bp. 4 May, 1806 ; m. 13 Sept., 1827, Thomas **Danforth, Jr.**, b. 6 July, 1792 ; she d. 27 May, 1858. *Issue :*
   i. Henry Tallman (Danforth), b. 1 June, 1828.
   ii. Mary Bulkeley (Danforth), b. 13 May, 1830.
   iii. Ellen Cornelia (Danforth), b. 5 Apl., 1833 ; d. 1 Apl., 1834.
   iv. Walter Williams (Danforth), b. 4 Apl., 1835.—See *Danforth.*
2. Julia Ann (Julianna), b. 31 Mch., bp. 21 May, 1809 ; d. at Suffield, Ct., Sept., 1864 ; she m. 12 Nov., 1840, Jonathan T. **Fairfield.** *Issue :*
   i. Joseph Butler (Fairfield), b. 11 July, 1846.
   ii. Mary Elizabeth (Fairfield), b. 2 Oct., 1852.
3. Cornelia, b. 17 (or 19) Sept., bp. 15 Nov., 1812 ; d. Ry-H., 30 Dec., 1875 ; m. 17 May, 1837, Benjamin (s. Eliakim) **Smith;** she d. Ry-H., 30 Dec., 1875. *Issue :*
   i. Adelaide Williams (Smith), b. 12 Feb., 1838 ; m. Charles **Wright**; had 1 ch., s. Chas. Stewart W.
   ii. Ellen Cornelia (Smith), b. 3 Sept., 1840.
   iii. Mary Bulkeley (Smith), b. 29 Feb., 1844.
   iv. Charles Edmond, (Smith), b. 2 Dec., 1849.
4. Eunice Robbins, b. 17 May, bp. 11 Sept .

1814 ; d. Pittsfield, Mas., 13 Jan., 1879 ; m. George W. **Fairfield,** 2 June, 1847.
5. Joseph Henry Bulkeley, b. 26 Oct., 1817 ; bp. 2 Aug., 1818 ; m. 26 May, 1852, Elizabeth P. **Adams;** 3 ch. He d. 7 Feb., 1892.
6. Nancy, b. 6 Oct., 1815 ; bp. 18 June, 1820 ; d. Ry-H., 6 Jan., 1869 ; m. 15 May, 1843, as his 2d wife, Albert Gallatin **Parker**, of Bridgehampton, L. I., who d. Ry-H., 26 Nov., 1871. *Issue* (b. *Ry-H.*) :
   i. Gertrude Amelia (Parker), b. 26 Feb., 1844 ; res. (1903) Whitman, Mass. ; m. Robert E. **Wilcox**, of Ry-H., 26 Oct., 1864 ; had 2 ch.
   ii. Mary Matilda (Parker), b. 10 Feb., 1846 ; d. 24 June, 1847.
   iii. Mary Elizabeth (Parker), b. 11 Dec., 1847 ; m. Nathan P. **Sykes**, of Htfd. ; res. H.
   iv. Cornelia Albertina (Parker), b. 16 Aug., 1849 ; d. Htfd., 23 Oct., 1872.
   v. Emily Josephine (Parker), b. 21 July, 1851 ; m. 13 Oct., 1869, Dr. Joseph M. **Pettengill** of Kenosha, Wis. ; res. Hudson, Mass. ; has son, Dr. Clarence A. Pettengill, of Hudson, Mass.
   vi. Ellen Bulkeley (Parker), b. 25 June, 1854 ; m. 4 Mch., 1878, Harvey B. **Domar**, of New Haven, who d. 6 Nov., 1902 ; 2 ch.
   vii. Fannie Florence (Parker), b. 1 Feb., 1859 ; m. 1 May, 1877, Dr. James F. **Brogan**, of N. H. ; she d. 13 May, 1884 ; 2 daus.

FAM. 36. SELAH,[5] (*Gideon*,[4] *Gershom*,[3] *Joseph*,[2] *Dea. Richard*,[1]) b. 29 Sept., 1768, at Midd.; prob. accompanied his father's fam. to Blandford, Mass., 1777, where he remained until abt. 1820, when he rem. to Andover, Ohio; m. Lucy **Hall**, abt. 1788.

Children:

1. George, b. 1789. FAM. 49.
2. Lucy, b. 1792, m. Jonathan **Shepard**, of Tolland, Mass. *Issue :*
   i. Jonathan (Shepard), b. 1812 ; d. 1879.
   ii. Lucius B. (Shepard), b. 1813 ; d. 1893.
   iii. Joseph H. (Shepard), b. 1819 ; d. 1894.
   iv. Norman W. (Shepard), b. 1829 ; d. 1872.
   v. Philander T. (Shepard), b. ———.
   vi. Henry B. (Shepard).
   vii. George E. (Shepard).
   viii. Elmira R. (Shepard), b. 1816 ; d. 1892.
   ix. Cynthia M. (Shepard), b. 1821.
   x. Fidelia A. (Shepard), b. 1827 ; d. 1896.
   xi. Caroline (Shepard).
3. Orpha, b. 1797.
4. Norman, twin Cynthia, b. 1799. FAM. 50.
5. Cynthia, twin Norman ; m. Pierrepont **Potter**, a lawyer, of Jamaica, L. I. ; had several ch.
6. Selah, b. 1803. FAM. 51.

FAM. 36a. ALLEN,[5] (*Benjamin*,[4] *Chas.*,[3] *Joseph*,[2] *Dea. Richard*,[1]) b. 1783 ; m. Sarah (dau. Epaphras & Elizabeth *Wells*) **Sage**, of Upper Midd., Ct., 5 Feb., 1817, she d. 15 Sept., 1864 ; he d. 5 Oct., 1825, at U. Midd.

Children:

1. Catharine Maria, b. 24 Apl., 1818 ; d. 14 Oct., 1821.
2. Sarah, b. 28 Oct., 1822 ; d. 11 Jan., 1832.
3. Catharine Louise, b. 21 Oct., 1824 ; m. 12 Sept., 1844, in Sumpter Co., Ala., Philip **May**, who d. 16 Nov., 1880 ; she d. 29 Oct., 1862. *Issue (all b. in Ala.) :*
   i. Frank (May), b. 30 June, 1845 ; d. 20 Oct., 1856.
   ii. Annie (May), b. 30 Sept., 1846 ; d. 22 Oct., 1858.
   iii. C. Louise (May), b. 30 July, 1848 ; m. 20 Jan., 1868, C. B. **Jones;** d. at Coffeeville, Tex., 2 Feb., 1893 ; 7 ch.
   iv. George Butler (May), b. 15 Sept., 1855 ; d. 15 Sept., 1883 ; was one of the Texas Rangers—in service on frontier.
   v. Mary W. (May), b. 12 Nov., 1850 ; m. 21 Dec., 1874, John B. **Lacy**, who d. in Texas, 9 Nov., 1890 ; now a wid. with 4 ch., 2 of whom are married. *Issue :*
   i. Walter Philip (Lacy), b. 6 Nov., 1876.
   ii. Elizabeth May (Lacy), b. 11 Aug., 1882 ; m. John G. **Lloyd**, 1 May, 1902.
   iii. Herbert Ross (Lacy), b. 15 Oct., 1878 ; d. 1778.
   iv. Mary Ross (Lacy), b. 2 Oct., 1886 ; d. 1887.
   v. Ora Lee (Lacy), b. 31 Dec., 1887.
   vi. John (May), b. 12 Nov., 1852 ; res. at Laurel, Miss. ; m. Susy **McNoble**, of Livingston, Ala., May, 1893. *No issue.*
   vii. Annie, b. 13 Mch., 1858 ; res. Belmont, Ala. ; she m. (1) Capt. Viceroy **Tull**; m. (2) ——— **McCormick**. *Issue (by Tull) :*
   i. John Lacy, b. 16 Mch., 1880.
   ii. Ora May, b. 31 Jan., 1889.
   iii. Katherine Byrd, b. 11 Aug., 1890 ; d. 1896.
   iv. B. Viceroy, b. 26 Oct., 1892.

FAM. 36b. SYLVESTER,[5] (*Benj.*,[4] *Charles*,[3] *Joseph*,[2] *Dea. Richard*,[1]), b. 23 Aug., 1785; bp. 20 Nov., (*S. C. R.*) m. 28 Dec., 1814, Anna **Butler**, b. at Harperfield, N. Y., 19 Feb., 1796. She was a des'c'd of a Jona. Butler, who came from 'Scotland to Ct. abt. 1698, and settled at Saybrook.

Children:

1. Amelia, b. 7 Dec., 1815.
2. Benjamin, b. 22 Dec., 1817; d. 26 Aug., 1822.
3. George Henry, b. 26 Oct., 1820. FAM. 51a.
4. Anne Maria, b. 7 June, 1831.
5. Mary Ellen, b. 8 Feb., 1836.

FAM. 36c. GEORGE,[3] (*Benjamin*,[2] *Charles*,[1]), b. 1798; m. Mary Fisk (dau. James & Mary) **Greene,** of Saratoga, or Ballston Spa., N. Y.; mcht. in N. Y. City, wholesale for dealer and mfr.; ill health caused his removal to Texas, where he d. at Bastrop, 5 Mch., 1841; wid. ret. to Saratoga, N. Y.

Children, (Fam. Recs.) :

1. George, b. 20 June, 1826.
2. William Sylvester, b. 9 Oct., 1837; d. at Bastrop, Tex., 5 Oct., 1846.

FAM. 37.   GEORGE STEPHEN,[5] (*Richard*,[4] *Jonathan*,[3] *Ens. Samuel*,[2] *Dea. Richard*,[1]) b. 1795; m. 21 Nov., 1822, Cornelia (dau. J. Whiting & Elizabeth *Ostrander*) **Warner,** of Htfd., rem. soon after to Louisville, Ky.; he was for many yrs. a Warden in Christ P. Epis. Ch., at L., and d. there 5 Aug., 1831, of yellow fever; wid. and fam. rem. to Oswego, N. Y., where her sisters lived.

Children, (Fam. Recs.) :

1. Mary Elizabeth, b. 19 Feb., 1827; m. 7 Oct., 1847, Walter Mann, who b. 16 Sept., 1827; d. 16 Aug., 1892; Mrs. Smith has furnished her line of descent from Dea. Richard, the Emigrant. *Issue:*
   i. Cornelia (Mann), b. 1849; d. unm.
   ii. Walter Butler (Mann), b. 1851; d. 1864.
   iii. Eliza Stewart (Mann), b. 1855; m. 5 Aug., 1880, Dr. Chas. Eastwick **Smith;** res. St. Paul, Minn. *Issue:*
      i. Mary Guest (Smith), b. 7 Oct., 1881.
      ii. Charles Eastwick (Smith), b. 14 Jan., 1883.
   iv. Catharine Phelps (Mann), b. 1859;

   m. James **Burnes,** 1878; d. 1897.
   v. Frederick Clarke (Mann), b. 1860; m. 1896, Caroline **Hill.**
   vi. Charles Edward (Mann), b. 1870; m. 1895, Anna H. **Comstock;** had (a) Charles Edward, b. 1898; d. 1901.
2. Cornelia Ann, b. 1 (?) Apl., 1828; d. unm.
3. Charles Henry, b. 19 Oct., 1829; m. Cath. **Slocum,** 9 Oct., 1860. *Issue:*
   i. Georgiana (Butler), b. 1862.
   ii. Charles Warner (Butler), b. 1863.
4. Georgiana, b. 21 Feb., 1831; m. Dr. Chas. **Bowman;** d. 1881. *Issue:*
   i. Mary Cornelia, b. 1856.

FAM. 38.   HORACE,[5] (*Ashbel*,[5] *Capt. Eli*,[4] *Benj.*,[3] *Joseph*,[2] *Dea. Richard*,[1]) b. 1792; m. Hannah, (dau. Borden & Lydia *Grey*) **Wilbur,** who d. at Orange. N. J., 6 Nov., 1897, ae. 99. The largest tax payer in the town, a "man of affairs", promoter of mfrs., raised fine horses on his farm,etc., was over 6 ft. 2 in. in height, a silent man.

Children:

1. James Lawrence, b. 3 Feb., 1818. FAM. 49.
2. Samson Wilbur, b. Apl., 1820, d. yg.
3. Deborah Wilbur, b. 15 Sept., 1823; d. yg.
4. Horace, b. 13 Nov., 1824; res. Calif., unm.
5. Mary Eliza, b. 25 Dec., 1834; m. Jas. W.

   Frisbie; d. Detroit, Mich.; 3 ch.
6. Charles (Chester ?), b. 30 (10 ?) July, 1836; m. 30 Nov., 1864, Elinor J. **Smith;** res. N. Y. City, have s. *Charles Bell.*

FAM. 39.   CHESTER,[6] (*Ashbel*,[5] *Capt. Eli*,[4] *Benj.*,[3] *Joseph*,[2] *Dea. Richard*,[1]), b. 1795; m. Nancy (dau. Tertius) **Ellenwood,** who was b. 12 July, 1794, d. 19 July 1863; farmer res. New Htfd., N. Y., he d. 4 July, 1854.

Children:

1. William, b. 2 Nov., 1816; m. Frances **Walker,** of Chicago; he d. 16 Aug., 1879; of 3 sons—one *Walter L.,* of Chicago, is living.
2. Mary E., b. 22 Jan., 1820; m. Jas **Littlewood,** 1 Sept., 1846; res. Beloit, Wis., farmer—one son *George.*
3. Jane E., d. 11 Aug., 1843, ae. 19.
4. Charles, b. 20 July, 1826; m. Cornelia

   (dau. Amma & Hester *Kellogg*) **Nichols;** he d. Elgin, Ill., 12 Nov., 1861; one s. *William Kellogg.*
5. Henry Ashbel, 14 Sept., 1829; m. Christiana E. **Allen,** 20 Mch., 1854; mcht. at Ottawa, Ill.; 3 ch.
6. Sarah, d. 2 July, 1845; ae. 9 yr., 4 mo., 17 d.

FAM. 40. SYLVESTER ELI,⁶ (*Sylvester,*⁵ *Capt. Eli,*⁴ *Benj.,*³ *Joseph,*² *Dea. Richard,*¹) b. 1796; m. 18 Mch., 1819, Martha (dau. Rufus & Lavinia *Benton*) **Luce,** b. 27 Jan., 1799 and d. 31 May, 1878, in Utica, N. Y.

Children:

1. Lucy, b. 17 Sept., 1820; m. 28 Apl., 1841, Erastus B. (s. Isaac & Laura *Buck*) **Mason,** of New Htfd.; she d. 1898; 2 ch.
2. Abigail, b. 11 June, 1822; m. 10 May, 1843, Lewis (s. Oliver G. & Deborah *Lewis*) **Rogers;** 2 ch.
3. Emily, b. 9 Oct., 1824; d. 28 Sept., 1841.
4. Beatta, b. 10 Jan., 1829; d. 22 Feb., 1836.

5. Henry S., b. 27 Aug., 1831; d. 28 Aug., 1864; m. Mary Anne **Beebe,** Dec., 1859. *No issue.*
6. Charles H., b. 10 Dec., 1839; d. 1840.
7. Mary, b. 26 July, 1841; m. 1864, Wm. M. (s. of Peter & Betsy) **Price,** b. 14 Nov., 1819; he d. Utica, N. Y., 18 Aug., 1883; 2 ch.

FAM. 41. CHAUNCEY SAGE,⁶ (*John,*⁵ *Capt. Eli,*⁴ *Benj.,*³ *Joseph,*² *Dea. Richard,*¹) b. 1802; m. (1) Elizabeth (dau. Abel. & Sarah *Warren*) **Mosher,**—or Mosier—Hugenot descent, of Pepperell, Mass., May 9, 1826, she d. Sanquoit, N. Y., 29 Mch., 1836; m. (2) Julia (dau. Jacob & Jerusha *Huntington*) **Sherrell,** of Windham, Ct., 3 Oct., 1844, she d. at S., 22 Aug., 1878. He d. at S., 28 Mch., 1893. A true country gentleman, occupying various positions of trust, with one other he founded the Oneida Co. Bk., of Utica N. Y., 1853; in his younger days active in mil. affairs, Col, of 6th N. Y. Reg. Cavalry, the last survivor of the Body Guard which escorted Gen. Lafayette on his visit to U. 1825, a liberal and benevolent man.

Children:

1. John Milton, b. 9 July, 1827; grad. Ham. Coll., 1848; pres. of Oneida Co. Bk., Utica, N. Y.; d. Jan., 27, 1899, unm.
2. Charles Addison, b. 10 Aug., 1829; grad. Ham. Coll., 1851; m. 23 Aug., 1871, Martha (dau. Samuel C. & Elizabeth *Davis*) **Gilbert,** of Gilbertsville, Otsego Co., N. Y.; she d. 4 Feb., 1898, at U.; had 3 ch.
3. Elizabeth Jenette, b. Sanquoit, 21 Aug., 1834; m. 11 Sept., 1861, P. V. (s. Dr. Ralph & Sarah *Corse*) **Rogers,** of Watertown, N. Y., who was b. 30 Dec., 1824; and d. Utica, 2 July, 1895. He was a grad.

of Ham. Coll.; pres. of First Nat. Bk., of Utica. *Issue:*
  i. Charles Butler (Rogers), b. U., 23 Jan., 1865; m. 31 Jan., 1894, Susan (dau. Edw'n Salisbury & Catharine *Curtenius*) **Brayton,** b. 9 Nov., 1865; she d. 3 Apl., 1898; Mr. C. B. Rogers is a grad. of H. C. and of Univ. of Berlin (Germany), and succeeded his father in pres. of the First Nat. Bk. of Utica, N. Y.; he m. (2) 3 May, 1900, Eugenia Dumaux **Forgery,** of Dayton, O.

FAM. 42. AMMI TODD,⁶ (*John,*⁵ *Capt. Eli,*⁴ *Benj.,*³ *Joseph,*² *Dea. Richard,*¹) b. 1806; mcht. in Utica, and later, for many yrs., a banker in Syracuse, N. Y., m. 13 Sept., 1832, Susan Jennette (dau. Joseph & Susan *Germond*) **Mott,** (Quakers); he d. Sanquoit, 4 Feb., 1888; she d. Utica, 25 Oct., 1889.

Children:

1. John Germond, b. 16 Mch., 1834; m. (1) 8 Aug., 1861, Annie Eliza (dau. Judge Enoch Huntington & Caroline J. *Beach*) **Rosekrans,** of Glens Falls, N. Y.; raised a Co. at beg. of Civil War; was Capt. 3d N. Y. Inf., and Col. of 147 N. Y. Vols. He m. (2) Mabel Helen **Gilman,** of Baltimore, Md., June, 1890. *Issue:*
  i. Rose Huntington, b. 30 Sept., 1865; m. (1) Henry B. **Rich;** m. (2) Lloyd **Taylor,** who d. 23 Dec., 1896.
  (*By second marriage.*)
  ii. John Germond, Jr., b. Baltimore, 26

July, 1894.
2. Mary Smith, b. 8 July, 1835; m. 24 Oct., 1854. Edward Salisbury (s. Gaius B.) **Rich.** of Buffalo, N. Y. *Issue:*
  i. Jeanette Butler (Rich), b. 2 Feb., 1856; m. 12 Feb., 1874, Rev. Chas. Hall (s. Parshal) **Strong,** of N. Orleans; rector of St. John's ch., Savannah, Ga.; 3 ch.
  ii. Harriet Salisbury (Rich), b. 11 Oct., 1858; d. 30 Sept., 1860.
  iii. Washington Irving (Rich), b. 4 May, 1861; d. 9 Feb., 1897.

FAM. 43. ASA ALANSON,⁶ (*John,*⁵ *Capt. Eli,*⁴ *Benj.,*³ *Joseph,*² *Dea. Richard,*¹), b. 1808; m. (1) 3 Sept., 1835, Mary Anne (dau. Abel & Sarah *Warren*) **Mosier,** b. N. Htfd., 10 Oct., 1810, d. Sanquoit, 11 Apl., 1838; he m. (2) 25 Mch., 1841, Sally (dau. John & Betsy *Snow*) **Chadwick,** she b. 1810, d. 11 Apl., 1893. He d. 21 Sept., 1851.

Children:

1. Julia Adelaide, b. 7 July, 1836; m. 26 May, 1868, Erastus Z. (s. Zenas & Melinda *Beach*) **Wright**, b. Utica, N. Y., 10 Mch., 1829. *Issue:*
   i. Mabel (Wright), b. 6 Nov., 1869.
   ii. Elizabeth Butler (Wright), b. 3 Aug., 1871; m. Willis N. **Mills**, Menominee, Mich., 13 Sept., 1896; had dau. Eliz.

beth, b. 4 Jan., 1899.
iii. Benjamin Hager (Wright), b. 27 June, 1873.
iv. Julia Henrietta (Wright), b. 17 June, 1877; m. 20 June, 1899, James De-Peyster (s. James & Sarah *Johnson*) **Lynch.**

FAM 44. GEORGE HAMILTON,[6] (*John*,[5] *Capt. Eli*,[4] *Benj.*,[3] *Joseph*,[2] *Dea. Richard*,[1]) b. 1823; m. 13 Apl., 1865, Mary J. (dau. Wm. P. & Harriet *Bailey*) **Johnson,** b. 26 May, 1837. He d. 17 Aug. 1887.

Children:

1. Harriet Eliza, b. 4 June, 1866; d. 16 Dec., 1869.
2. William Johnson, b. 1 Oct., 1868.
3. Charles Milton, b. 29 Apl., 1870.

FAM. 45. HENRY,[3] (*Eli*,[2] *Capt. Eli*,[1]) b. 1826; m. 12 June, 1855, Ella P. (dau. Uriah & Jerusha *Chaffee*) **Farmer,** who was b. 14 Sept., 1833, and d. 25 Feb., 1897, at Brooklyn, N. Y. He d. 3 Dec., 1863.

Children:

1. Nellie Rachel, b. 12 June, 1857; d. 1 Feb., 1858.
2. Truman Francis, b. 2 Oct., 1860; d. 22 Dec., 1861.
3. Frances Sophia, b. 2 Oct., 1860; m. 11 Sept., 1888, Erastus Wright **Gillespie,** d. Auburn, N. Y., 2 Apl., 1889.
4. Mary Burch, b. 7 July, 1862; m. Frank A.

(s. Wm. B. & Mary *Boardman*) **Parker,** 15 Aug., 1883. *Issue:*
i. Henry Butler (Parker), b. 28 Jan., 1885.
ii. Florence Sophia (Parker), b. 30 Jan., 1889.
iii. Grace Louise (Parker), b. 25 May, 1891.

FAM. 46. Capt. JAMES,[6] (*Capt. Jas.*,[5] *Comfort*,[4] *Benj.*,[3] *Joseph*,[2] *Dea. Richard*,[1]) b. 1803; m. (1) 3 June, 1824, Mary **Streeter,** of Ashford, Ct., b. 11 Apl., 1805, who was the adopted dau. of Elder (Rev.) Frederick Wightman, of Cromwell, Ct., she d. 11 Sept., 1825, bu. in Cromwell; he m. (2) Mary King **Topliff,** of Ashford, Ct., and also an adopted dau. of Rev. Fred'k Wightman, 12 July, 1829. He was a shipmaster & d. at Matamorey, Mex., 5 June, 1881.

Children (by 1st Marr.):

1. James Frederick, b. 13 Jan., 1825. FAM. 38.
(*By second marriage*):
2. Mary Augusta, b. 9 Apl., 1830; m. 6 Aug., 1850, John **Hastings;** he d. 23 June, 1876; she d. Muscatine, Iowa, 11 Mch., 1893. *Issue:*
   i. Frances Augusta (Hastings), b. Weth. 12 May, d. 6 Sept., 1851.
3. Agnes Martha, b. 19 Aug., 1831; m. (1) 3 Nov., 1852, Roswell **Bronson,** M. D., at Oxford, Ct., who d. 8 Dec., 1855. *Issue:*
   i. John (Bronson), b. 19 Sept., 1855; d. 20 Aug., 1856.
The wid. Bronson m. (2) at Cromwell,

Ct., 11 Dec., 1861, Israel Louis **Graham,** M. D., who d. 3 Dec., 1886, at Muscatine, Iowa. *Issue:*
ii. James Butler (Graham), b. 25 Aug., 1863; d. 10 Oct., 1863.
iii. Ida (Graham), b. 4 June, 1865; d. 28 Apl., 1866.
iv. Mary (Graham), b. 5 Aug., 1866; m. John A. **Robbins,** D. D., 18 Sept., 1894, and d. 20 Dec., 1897. *Issue:*
(*a*) Agnes (Robbins), b. 3 May, 1896;
(*b*) Mary Graham (Robbins), b. 5 Dec., 1897.

FAM. 47. CHARLES CARROLL,[6] (*Comfort*,[5] *Comfort*,[4] *Benj.*,[3] *Joseph*,[2] *Dea. Richard*,[1]), b. 1828; m. Eunice **Gates.**

Children:

1. Leila, m. Ellis W. **Hedge.** *Issue:*
   i. Beatrice (Hedge).

ii. Leila (Hedge).
2. Emma.

FAM. 48. EDWARD DEMAREST,[6] (*Comfort*,[5] *Comfort*,[4] *Benj.*,[3] *Joseph*,[2] *Dea. Richard*,[1]) b. 1836; m. Adelaide **Taylor.**

Children:

1. Estella Tracy, m. John H. **Shipnay.** *Issue:*
   i. Geo. Edward (Shipnay).
   ii. Walter Butler (Shipnay).

iii. Margaret Estella (Shipnay).
iv. Warren (Shipnay).
2. Blanche Carroll.

FAM. 49. GEORGE,[6] (*Selah*,[5] *Geo.*,[4] *Gershom*,[3] *Joseph*,[2] *Dea. Richard*,[1]), b. 1789; m. Eliza **Cochran,** 1825; farmer, Andover, Ohio.

Children:

1. George E., b. 1826.
2. Eliza, b. 1831.
3. Eliza J., b. 1833.
4. John R., b. 1835.

5. Cecilia M., b. 1838.
6. Martha C., b. 1840.
7. Lucius C., b. 1842; d. 1862.
8. Augusta, b. 1844; d. 1846.

FAM. 50. NORMAN,[6] (*Selah*,[5] *Geo.*,[4] *Gershom*,[3] *Joseph*,[2] *Dea. Richard*,[1]) b. 1799; m. 1831, Mary A. (dau. Josiah & Mary *Cannon*,) **Starr,** of Stowe, O., res. at at Andover, O.

Children:

1. Cyntha E., b. 1833.
2. Norman S., b. 1834.
3. Charles W., b. 1836, d, ——.
4. Francis A., b. 1838; d. 1879
5. Mary Ellen, b. 1842; d. 1845.
6. Cyrennus J., b. 1844; d. ——.

7. Julia A., b. 1846.
8. Bradner W., b. 1848; d. ——.
9. Mary Ella, b. 1854; d. ——.
The dth. of a Norman B.'s ch., ae. 5, is rec. (S. C. R.), 7 Dec., 1833, and of another in 1st yr., 25 Mch., 1835.

FAM. 50a. JAMES LAURENCE,[7] (*Horace*,[6] *Ashbel*,[5] *Capt. Eli*,[4] *Benj.*,[3] *Joseph*,[2] *Dea. Richard*,[1]), b. 3 Feb., 1818; m. (1) 22 July, 1841, Lydia Pauline (dau. Joseph & Susan *Gernard*) **Mott,** b. 4 Oct., 1818, d. Syracuse, N. Y., 22 Feb., 1851; he m. (2) Martha (dau. Jesse) **Patrick,** of Troy, N. Y., 10 May, 1853, who d. 12 Nov., 1883; he d. Mch., 1894.

Children:

1. Emma Mott, b. 10 Feb., 1847; m. Bradford S. **Seymour;** res. Dakota; 8 ch.

2. Lydia Pauline, b. 13 Feb., 1851.
3. Florence Nina, b. Troy, N. Y., 12 Oct., 1862.

FAM. 51. SELAH,[4] (*Selah*[5], *Geo.*,[4] *Gershom*,[3] *Joseph*,[2] *Dea. Richard*,[1]) b. 1803; m. Mary **Crowell,** res. Andover, O., until late in life he rem. to Mich., where he died.

Children:

1. Edwin.
2. Arminia.

3. Harriet.
4. Cynthia.

5. Jane.
6. Almena.

7. Emerson.
8. Exenia.

FAM. 51a. GEORGE HENRY,[6] (*Sylvester*,[5] *Benj.*,[4] *Charles*,[3] *Joseph*,[2] *Dea. Richard*,[1]), b. 1820, m. Lucinthia (dau. Dr. Ira & Lucintha *Cone*) **Hutchinson,** 9 Nov., 1854. He a farmer; for more than 25 yrs. deacon in the Cong'l Church at Cromwell, Ct. and Sup't of its Sabbath School.

Children:

1. Ernest Preston, b. 2 Oct., 1855. FAM. 52.
2. Kate Hutchinson, b. 27 Nov., 1858; m. 21 Jan., 1880, Chauncey M. **Warner,** of Cromwell, Ct. *Issue:*
   i. George Marvin (Warner), b. 10 Nov., 1880, at La Crosse, Wis.; grad. Wesleyan Univ., 1903.

ii. Willis Chauncey (Warner), b. at Weth., Ct., 21 Feb., 1883; grad. from Midd. High School; employed in Electrical Vehicle Co., Htfd.
3. Anna Lucintha, b. 2 Apl., 1864; d. 31 Aug., 1867.
4. George Sylvester, b. 20 Mch., 1866. FAM. 53.

FAM. 52. ERNEST PRESTON,[7] (*George H.*,[6] *Sylvester*,[5] *Benjamin*,[4] *Charles*,[3] *Joseph*,[2] *Dea. Richard*,[1]), b. 1855, m. 4 Aug., 1881, Julia Gertrude **Hatch,** of So. Windham, Ct.; res. Cromwell, Ct. She d. 24 Oct., 1885.

Child:

1. Frederick Tabor, b. at Windham, Ct., 21 Feb., d. 26 July, 1882.

FAM. 53. GEORGE SYLVESTER,[7] (*George H.*,[6] *Sylvester*,[5] *Benjamin*,[4] *Charles*,[3] *Joseph*,[2] *Dea. Richard*,[1]), b. 1866; grad. Midd. High School 1895; and in same year established the business of cultivation of small fruit, from which has grown the large plant of the Butler & Jewell Co.'s Nursery at Cromwell, Ct., of which he is Pres. and Manager. He m. 25 June, 1891, Carrie Augusta (dau. of Dea: Ralph Bulkeley & Sarah A.) **Savage,** of Cromwell, Ct.

Children (*b. Cromwell, Ct.*):

1. Sylvester Benjamin, b. 26 July, 1892.
2. Ralph Savage, b. 10 Apl., 1894.

3. Lucinthia, b. 14 May, 1896.

Families unattached.

FREDERICK, (s. of Jonathan & Ruth, of Htfd.,) b. Weth., 23 July, 1766; grad. Y. C. 1785, res. through life in Weth., where he d. 5 Apl., 1843, ae. 78.— *W. T. R.* He m. Mary (dau. Col. Thomas & Abigail) **Belden,** 11 Jan., 1787, she b. 22 May, 1770, d. 17 Jan., 1811.—*Weth. Rec.* Mr. Butler led a literary life and published quite a number of historical and geographical works.

These were:

1. *A Catechetical Composed of General History,* Sacred and Profane, from the Creation of the World to year 1817 of the Christian Era. 3rd Ed. Hartford, 1818, 12 mo., pp. 216, First Edition, 1817 (?).

2. *Sketches of Universal History, Sacred and Profane,* from the Creation of the World to the year 1818 of the Christian Era. In three parts, with an Appendix. Hartford, 1818 (?), 12 mo.

3. The same, Third Edition, corrected by the Author, Htfd., 1821, 12 mo., pp. 407.

4. *The Farmer's Manual,* being a plain, practical Treatise on the Art of Husbandry, designed to promote an acquaintance with the modern improvements in Agriculture, together with remarks on Gardening, and a Treatise on the Management of Bees. Hartford, 1819, 12 mo., pp. 224.

5. *The same.* Weth., 1821, 12 mo., pp. 224.

6. *A Complete History of the United States of America,* embracing the whole period from the Discovery of North America, down to the year 1820. 3 Vols., Hartford, 1821, 8 vo.

7. *The Elements of Geography and History,* combined in a catechetical form: Accompanied with an Atlas. Weth., Published by Deming and Francis, 1825, 12 mo., pp. 360.

8. The same. Second Edition. Weth., Pub. by D. & F., 1825, 12 mo., pp. 408.

9. *Memoirs of the Marquis de la Fayette,* Major-General in the Revolutionary Army of the U. S. Together with his Tour through the U. S. Weth., 1825, 12 mo., pp. 418.

10. *A History of the U. S. States of America.* Weth., 1827, 12 mo.

11. *The Same,* Third Revised and Improved Edition. Weth., Pub. by D. & F., 1828, 12 mo., pp. 452.

12. *Life of Washington* (?).

Children (*Weth. Rec. & Inscr.*):

1. Mary Porter, b. 18 Apl., bp. 8 June, 1788; d. 15 Nov., 1832.
2. Charlotte, b. 16 Feb., bp., 28 Mch., 1790; d. 16 Nov., 1858.
3. Frederick Augustus, b. 17 July, bp. 2 Sept., 1792; drowned in the Mississippi, near the mouth of the Ohio, 20 Sept., 1815.
4. Roswell, b. 24 Apl., bp. 2 Aug., 1795; d. 5 Mch.,1884.

5. Abigail Porter, b. 26 Feb., bp. 22 Apl., 1798; d. 6 Feb., 1832, at Utica, N. Y.
6. Elizabeth, b. 7 Aug., bp. 10 Oct., 1802; d. 12 Mch., 1833.
7. Julia Ann, b. 30 July, bp. 14 Oct., 1804; d. 6 Oct., 1889.
8. Thomas Belden (Chief Justice), b. 22 Aug., bp. 19 Oct., 1806. "A profound and enthusiastic scientist | a high minded and judicious legislator | both in the State |

and Nation, | An able and distinguished | lawyer, and a conscientious | upright, learned, impartial | and incorruptible Judge."—*Monument in Weth. Cemetery.*
Judge THOMAS BELDEN BUTLER rec'd a classical education, ent. the Med. School of Yale College, 1826, rec'd the degree of M. D., in 1828; practiced med. for 8 yrs., in Norwalk, Ct.; then began the study of Law; was adm. to the Bar in 1837; was a memb. of Conn. Ho. of Rep., 1832-46, and of the State Senate, 1848-53; rep. dist. in U. S. Congress in 1849. In May, 1855, he was app. a Judge of the Superior Ct., of Conn., and in 1861, of the Supreme Ct., of which he was

made the Chief Justice in 1870. He d. at Norwalk, Ct., 8 June, 1873. He was profoundly versed in scientific matters, especially in atmospheric problems. His pub. works on these subjects were:
1. *Philosophy of the Weather*, New York, 1856.
2. *Concise, Analytical and Logical Development of the Atmospheric System*, and Prognostication of the Weather, Norwalk, 1871.
3. *The Atmospheric System as God made It*, and of the Elements of Prognostication of the Weather. Numerous engravings, pp. 403; Hartford. Printed for tne Author, 1870.

FREDERICK had *Martha, Marsh, Julia* and *Jane* bp. 2 Sept., 1821.—*W. C. R.* Fred'k's wife, ae. 29, d. 26 Nov., 1850.

FREDERICK A., Sgt. Co. G. 24 Conn. Vols., d. 15 Mch., 1893; his wife Harriet Louisa, d. 14 Nov., 1851, ae. 28.—*Weth. (S.) Ins.*

FREDERICK R., m. Elizabeth **Goodrich**, 6 May, 1853; Fred R's infant d. 19 Feb., 1844,—prob. by a 1st marr. He res. in Ry-H. until after the Civil War, then rem. to Chester, Ct., where he d. They are both bu. in Cromwell, Ct.; *issue*:

i. Lily (Butler), who m. and rem. to | Lyme, Ct.
ii. Fluvia (Butler), d. in Htfd. Hospital.

SAMUEL, Capt.,[4] (*Sam'l*,[2] *Dea. Sam'l*,[3] *Dea. Rich.*,[1]?), b. 1712; m. 4 Apl., 1751, Naomi **Kilborne**, who d. 13 Aug., 1752, ae. 31; he m. (2) 26 June, 1755, Abigail **Adams**, (*Weth. Ch. Rcc.*) had Naomi b. 10 May, 1752, (*Weth. Rec. & Ins.*) who m. Mr. Samuel **Boadman**, who d. 7 Aug., 1822, ae. 78; she d. 26 Jan., 1826, ae. 73; *issue*:

1. Samuel, d. at sea, 1794, ae. 18.
2. Butler, d. at sea, Aug., 1806, ae. 26.— *Weth. Ins.*

SAMUEL, of Ry-H., b. 25 Sept., 1784; m. 28 Oct., 1808, Prudence (dau. of Elisha & Sarah) **Hurlbut**, b. Chatam, Ct., 19 Mch., 1787. He d. 19 May, 1848, ae. 63.—*W. C. R.;* she m. (2) Manly, bro. of her first husband.

Children:

1. Elisha Hurlburt, b. 12 Sept., 1809.
2. Samuel Bidwell, b. 27 Sept., 1812; m. Charlotte Kirkham **Price**, 5 Nov., 1833.— *W. T. R.*
3. Prudence, b. 2 Apl., 1816.
4. George Augustus, b. 28 Feb., bp. 18 July, 1819.
5. Charles Churchill, b. 1 Jan., bp. 21 June, 1821.—*Hurlburt Geneal.*

THOMAS, (poss. s. of *Thomas*, s. of *Thomas*, eld. son of Dea. *Richard*, of Htfd.), m. Sarah **Churchill**, 22 Nov., 1737.

Children:

1. Chloe, b. 31 Jan., 1739.
2. Huldah, b. 15 Feb., 1741.
3. Rhoda, b. 7 Jan., 1743.
4. Josiah, b. 12 Nov., 1745.
5. Sarah, b. 1 Feb., 1747.
6. Elisha, b. 2 Dec., 1748.
7. Elizabeth, b. 19 Aug., 1753.—*Weth. Rec.*

JOSEPH, m. Asenath **Andrus**.

1. Ruth, b. 27 Jan., 1763.
2. Pamela, b. 5 Sept., 1764.
3. Joseph, b. 9 Aug., 1766.
4. Polly, b. 8 June, 1770.
5. Roxalina, b. 4 Dec., 1771.
6. Elisha, b. 11 Oct., 1773.
7. William, b. 16 Nov., 1775.
8. Sarah, b. 11 Sept., 1777.
9. Asenath, b. 22 May, 1779.

BUTTOLOPH. Name derived from St. Botolphs or Buttolph, (perhaps orig. "Boat-help") the Saint of sea-faring men, who is said to have died 680 A. D. The Saxon Chronicles state that he, with his brother Adolph, was educated in Germany; that he returned to Eng., and, through the favor of Ethelmund, King of the South Angles, estab. a monastry near the present site of the Cathedral of St. Bottolph, at Boston. Lincolnchire, Eng., which place derives (as well as Boston, Mass.,) its name from St. Bottolph's town. This saint is commemorated on the 17th of June, which is also the date of the battle of Bunker Hill.

BUTTOLPH (or *Buttles* as spelled by a part of the American family.) Valuable assistance acknowledged from HARRY T. BUTTOLPH, of Buffalo, N. Y., and LUCIUS A. BARBOUR, of Hartford, Ct.

THOMAS, ae. 32, and Ann, his wife, ae. 24, sailed from London, 1635, in the ship *Abigail*, Capt. Hackwell, master. [Mr. Chas. H. Townsend of New Haven, states (*N. Eng. Hist. & Gen. Register* 1898, p. 318,) that he finds in the recs. of the tenantry of the Townshend estates at Raynham Co., Norfolk, Eng., the names of Buttolph, Cooper, Armitage and others prominently associated with Boston and vicinity.] He became a freeman, 2 June, 1641; constable, 1647, in Boston, Mass., where he was a glover and leather dresser. He became a memb. of the 1st. Ch., of Boston, Sept., 1639, where his ch. were bp.; and was present at the whipping of Obadiah Holmes, for heresy, informing on John Spor, for "giving aid" to Holmes, thus causing the imprisonment of Spor, who was liberated on his fine being paid by friends. Buttolph's "eight acres" pasture was in the vicinity of the State House, Boston, and Buttolph's St., (changed in 1855, to Irving Place) was laid out on its eastern border. In early times, the deeds of this ld. ran to the colored citizens Scipio, Pompey and others. He d. 1667; will of 25 May, prob. 18 June, that yr. is given in *N. Eng. Gen. Reg.* XVI. 159. His wid. d. 1680.

Children (b. Boston, printed Commissioners' Records):

1. Thomas, b. 12 Aug., 1637; bp. 29 Sept., 1639. FAM. 2.	Thomas **Bingley.**
2. John, b. 28 Dec., 1639, bp. 29 Feb., 1639-40. FAM. 3.	4. Samuel, b. 18 May, 1646; d. yg.
	5. Samuel, b. 12 Sept., 1647; d. yg.
3. Abigail, b. 18 Dec., 1642; bp. 19 Feb., 1643; m. (1) David **Saywell;** m. (2)	6. Samuel, b. 1648; d. yg.
	7. Mehitable, b. 26 Oct. (or Aug.), 1651.

FAM. 2. THOMAS,[2] (*Thos.*,[1]) b. 1637; m. to Mary (dau. of Nicholas) **Baxter,** 5 Sept., 1660, by Deputy-Gov.? Richard Bellingham; he d. Jan., 1669; wid. m. Joseph **Swett.**

Children:

1. Thomas, b. 5 d. 10 Oct., 1661.	1 Apl., 1690, Joseph (s. Joseph & Ruth) **Belknap.** *Issue:*
2. Thomas, b. 15 Feb., 1662-3; m. 3 Dec., 1689, Abiel (thus in printed rec. but prob. should be Abiah) **Sanders;** he d. 30 Nov., 1690; she m. (2) George **Beard,** 17 Dec., 1691. Thomas Buttolph d. 30 Nov., 1690.	i. Hannah (Belknap).
	ii. Abigail (Belknap), b. 1692.
	iii. Mary (Belknap), b. 1694.
	iv. Nicholas (Belknap), b. 1695.
3. Mary, b. 21 Jan., 1664-5; m. (1) Joseph **Thaxter,** who d. 1687; m. (2) Robert **Guttridge** (Goodrich), who d. 1717, by whom she had *issue:*	v. Buttolph (Belknap), b. 1697.
i. John (Goodrich).	vi. Nathaniel (Belknap), b. 1699.
ii. Buttolph (Goodrich).	vii. Ruth (Belknap), b. 1704.
iii. Mary Ann (Goodrich), b. 1711.	viii. Elizabeth (Belknap), b. 1708.
i. Abigail, b. Jan., 7, 1666; m. as 2d wife,	ix. Lydia (Belknap), b. 1710.
	x. Abraham (Belknap), b. 1711.
	5. Nicholas, b. 3 Mch., 1668. FAM. 4.

FAM. 3. Lieut. JOHN,[2] (*Thomas,*[1]) b. 1639, a glover by trade, rem. to Salem, Mass.; where he m. (1) 16 Oct., 1663, Hannah (dau. George) **Gardner,** of S. who was b. 5 Dec., 1644; by 1669 he had ret. to Boston, and later, (prob. after 1674), rem. to Weth. prob. induced to do so by the fact that his father-in-

law, George Gardner, had rem. from Salem to Htfd., Conn., where he died. He was chosen constable at W. 1679, was townsman (selectman) 1686, bo't ld. in W. from John Coleman, who had rem. to Hatfield.—See Chapt. VII, Vol. I., his wife, Hannah, d. 6 June, (Jan. 26 ?) 1681, and he m. (2) 27 June, 1682. Abigail ————, who d. 5 June, 1687, ae. abt. 27,—(*Weth. Rec.*) He m. (3) Susannah (wid. of Nathaniel) **Sanford**, "sometime of Htfd. (see deed *Htfd. Ld. Rec.* I pp. 155-6, dated 20 Mch., 1692). He was Lieut. in Train-band, memb. of Gen. Ct., and had a large est. in Weth. and Boston. He d. 14 (or 18) Jan., 1692-3, ae. abt. 53.—(*Weth Rec.*) *Htfd. Co. Prob.* gives his will, etc., thus John Buttolph died 14 January, 1692-3. Invt. £1042-03-02. Taken by Robert Wells, John Chester, Jr., Joshua Robbins, Benjamin Gilbert, it included ("Land at Norich, (new villeg.), 3000 or 4000 acres") Will dated 13 January, 1692. His eldest son *John* Buttolph to have a double portion; his dau. *Abigail* to have the best feather bed with all the furniture to it, the rest of her portion to be in pewter, brass or Irons and if that is not enough it shall be made out of the land at Norwiche that I had with her mother; I declare that the worshipful Capt. Mason and my eldest son Buttolph shall be Executors. I desire these two men shall take care of my youngest children, *Jonathan, Abigail, James;* my son *George*, his wife Elizabeth Buttolph shall have £10. in such goods as she shall choose for her own proper estate . . . for her loving careful pains in attending me in my sickness. Proven 6th. March, 1692-3.

Children:

1. John, b. 11 July, 1664, at Salem. FAM. 5.
2. Jonathan, b. 9 day, 2d mo., 1665, at Salem, Mass.
3. George, b. 15 Oct., 1667, at Salem, Mass. For geneal. of desc'dts see separate sketch at end of this genealogy. See, also, Chapt. VII, Vol. I.
4. David, b. 7 May, 1669, at Boston. FAM. 6.
5. Hannah, b. 15 Jan., 1670, at Boston.

6. Samuel, b. 18 May, 1673, at Boston.
7. Mercy, b. 2 Mch., 1674, at Boston.
8. Jonathan, b. 8 Jan., 1677, at Weth.
9. Joseph, b. 12 Dec., 1680, at Weth.; d. 14 Oct., 1683. (*Weth. Rec.*) (*By second marriage*):
10. Abigail, b. 3 Apl., 1683, at Weth.
11. James, b. 22 Dec., 1684, at Weth.; lds. were confirmed to this James in New Lebanon, Ct.

FAM. 4. NICHOLAS,[5] (*Thos.*,[2] *Thos.*,[1]) b. 1668; m. 21 June, 1699, Mary **Guttridge**, (Goodrich) ; he was a bookseller, 1705 to 1727 in the Cornhill (now a part of Washington St.) Boston; a memb. of the Ancient & Honorable Artillery Co., of Boston; he d. 29 Jan., 1727, and was bu. in the Granary Burying-ground, Boston.

Children:

1. Thomas, b. 12 Aug., 1700.
2. Mary, b. 8 May, 1703; m. John **Phillips**; had a son *William*, b. 29 Aug., 1727; who m. Margaret **Wendall**, and their son *John* (Phillips), b. 26 Nov., 1770 was Boston's first Mayor; he m. Sally **Walley** and had *Issue*:
   i. Thomas W. (Phillips).
   ii. Sarah (Phillips), m. *Savage* I, 323, says "2 Nov., 1665 or by another version of the numerals in the rec. 9 Apl., 1666" (1) Thomas **Jenks**; m. (2) Alonzo **Gray**.
   iii. Margaret (Phillips) m. Edward G. **Reynolds**.
   iv. Marian (Phillips), m. Rev. Geo. H.

   Blagden, pastor of Old South Ch., Boston.
   v. John (Phillips), Rev.
   vi. George W. (Phillips).
   vii. Wendell (Phillips), the eminent orator and philanthropist.
   viii. Granville T. (Phillips).
3. Abigail, b. 23 Nov., 1704; m. 1 Feb., 1725, Knight **Leverett**, s. of Thos. Hudson Leverett; she d. 26 Jan. 1774. *Issue:*
   i. John (Leverett), b. 28 Jan., 1726-7.
   ii. Rebecca (Leverett), b. 5 Dec., 1728.
   iii. Thomas (Leverett), b. 3 Apl., 1730.
   iv. Abigail (Leverett), b. 25 Feb., 1731.
4. Nicholas, b. 13 May, 1706.

FAM. 5. JOHN,[3] (*John*,[2] *Thos.*,[1]) b. 1664; m. (1) Hannah—one acc. says *Sarah* (dau. John & Alice *Flint*) **Pickering**; m. (2) Priscilla ————; was a lieut. in Capt. John Higginson's Co., of Salem, so called 2 July, 1695; from a deed of 24 Nov., 1696, we learn that he was a baker, and eld. s. of John of Weth., trader, dec'd; was exect[r] of his father's will, as appears from *Htfd. Ld. Rec.*

See also Chapt. VII, Vol. I. He d. 10 May, 1713, acc. to tombstone in Charter St. Burying-gd., Salem, Mass.; his wid. Priscilla, m. (2) 25 July, 1722, Dea. Simeon **Willard**, and d. 21 July, 1731. John B. passed some yrs. of his youth in Weth.

Children:

1. John, b. 1 July, 1688. FAM. 7.
2. Hannah, b. 9 Oct., 1689; m. 29 Mch., 1710, ,Nathaniel (s. John & Hannah *Abbott*) **Osgood.**
(*By second marriage*):

3. Priscilla, b. 31 July, 1692; m. 6 Dec., 1711, John **Lansford.**
4. Sarah, b. 30 Jan., 1693-4; m. 18 Nov., 1713, John **Allen.**
5. William, b. 7 Sept., 1695; d. 23 Sept., 1721.

FAM. 6. Sgt. DAVID,[3] (*John,*[2] *Thos.,*[1]) b. 1669; m. Mary ————; res. in Weth., See Chapt. VII, Vol. I, and later sett. in Wintonbury parish, Windsor; in 1700 rem. to Simsbury, Ct., where he d. 15 Apl., 1717; was a cordwainer and shoe-maker; his wid. prob. the Wid. B. who m. (pub. 7 Oct.,.1725), Benjamin **Smith**, of Springfield.

Children:

1. Jonathan (Dr.), b. abt. 1692-3. FAM. 8.
2. Martha, b. 2 Apl., 1694; m. 25 Dec., 1712, Thomas (s. of Sgt. Daniel & Mary *Pinney*) **Adams.** *Issue:*
   i. Martha (Adams), b. 30 Sept., 1713.
   ii. Mary (Adams), b. 20 Jan., 1715.
   iii. David (Adams), b. 28 Aug., 1718; d. 1801; m. Mindwell (dau. Daniel & Penelope *Buttolph*) **Case,** who was b. 24 Oct., 1721; d. 16 Feb., 1813.
   iv. Hezekiah (Adams), b. 13 Aug., 1724; d. 1784; m. (1) 1749, Lydia (dau. Thos. & Hannah *Phelps*) **Phelps;** b. 1725; d. 10 Nov., 1760; m. (2) Sarah (dau. Thomas & Mary *Watson*) **Phelps.**
   v. Mercy (Adams), b. 25 June, 1728.
   vi. Thomas (Adams), b. 20 Dec., 1731; m. Rosanna ————.
   vii. Hosea (Adams), b. 22 Mch., 1736.
3. Penelope, b. 1 Oct., 1699; m. 7 May, 1719, Daniel (s. John & Sarah *Holcomb*) **Case,** who d. 27 June, 1746. *Issue:*
   i. Daniel (Case), b. 31 Jan., 1720; d. 24 May, 1801; m. 22 Feb., 1750, Mary (dau. Cyprian & Abigail) **Watson,** who d. 25 May, 1807.
   ii. Mindwell (Case), b. 24 Oct., 1721; m. David **Adams.**
   iii. Dudley (Case), b. 23 Nov., 1723; d. 1792; m. 14 Apl., 1742, Dorcas (dau. Charles & Hepzibah *Pettibone*) **Humphrey.**
   iv. Susannah (Case), b. 20 Sept., 1726; m. Joseph (s. of Joseph & Hannah *Adams*) **Mills,** 1795.
   v. Zacheus (Case), b. 1728; d. 1812; m. Abigail (dau. Thomas & Mercy *Case*) **Barber;** b. Feb., 1730-1; d. 1798.
   vi. Ezekiel (Case), b. 30 Sept., 1731; m. (1) 2 Aug., 1753, Lucy (dau. James & Amy *Butler*) **Cornish;** m. (2) Wid. Mary (Allyn) **Hoskins.**
4. Silence, b. 21 Feb., 1701; m. 7 Nov., 1721, William (s. of Atherton & Rebecca *Stoughton*) **Mather,** of Suffield, Ct. *Issue:*
   i. Timothy (Mather), b. 4 Aug., 1722; d. 28 Oct., 1802; m. (1) 25 Oct., 1748, Hannah **Fuller,** who d. 7 Apl., 1757; m. (2) 6 Mch., 1760, Lucy **Kellogg.**
   ii. Increase (Mather), b. 12 Aug., 1725; d. 7 May, 1799; m. 5 Sept., 1768, Apphia **Norton,** who d. 10 June, 1837.
   iii. Rebecca (Mather), b. 8 Sept., 1727; d. 29 Sept., 1794; m. ———— **Rising.**
   iv. Apphia (Mather), b. 5 Aug., 1730; d. 12 June, 1811; m. 15 June, 1753, Chas

Hathaway, who d. 27 June, 1808.
   v. Eusebius (Mather), b. 10 Dec., 1732.
   vi. William (Mather), b. 25 Apl., 1735; d. 22 May, 1810; m. (1) 10 Apl., 1760, Helena (Allyn) **Talcott,** who d. 6 Dec., 1770 (dau. of Paletiah); m. (2) Martha **Dickinson,** who d. 29 May, 1809.
   vii. Benoni (Mather).
5. Mehitable, b. 25 Aug., 1704; m. Lieut. David **Holcomb,** of Simsbury (s. of Nathan'l & Martha *Buell*) **Holcomb;** Lieut. H. m. (2) Wid. Elizabeth **Hoskins,** who d. 20 July, 1779. *Issue:*
   i. Mehitable (Holcomb), b. 1722.
   ii. David (Holcomb), b. 1724.
   iii. Deborah (Holcomb), b. 1726; d. 1772; m. 15 Oct., 1740, Joseph (s. Joseph & Rebecca *North*) **Phelps,** who was b. 18 Oct., 1716; d. 14 May, 1775.
   iv. Son (Holcomb), b. 28 Sept., 1726.
   v. Martha (Holcomb), b. 1727; m. Asahel (s. of Samuel & Elizabeth *Wilcoxson*) **Hayes;** b. 3 June, 1732.
   vi. Reuben (Holcomb), b. 1728-9; m. Susannah (dau. Samuel & Elizabeth *Wilcoxson*) **Hayes.**
   vii. Susannah (Holcomb), b. 1734; m. 15 Nov., 1756, Dr. Josiah **Topping.**
   viii. Simeon (Holcomb), b. 1734; m. 8 May, 1760, Huldah (of Nathan'l & Thankful *Hays*) **Holcomb.**
   ix. Ezra (Holcomb), b. 1735; m. Phebe **Gillett.**
   x. Lydia (Holcomb), d. Feb., 27, 1822; m. 1749, Solomon (s. Nathan'l & Abigail *Filer*) **Higley.**
   xi. Ezekiel (Holcomb), b. 1738.
   xii. Jedidiah (Holcomb), b. 1740; d. 1779; m. Mercy ————.
   xiii. Eli (Holcomb), b. 1741.
6. Mary, b. Feb., 1707; m. 23 July, 1729, Joseph **Wilcox;** prob. m. (2) Capt. Nathn'l (s. Nathan & Martha *Buell*) **Holcomb,** as his 2d wife, 14 Dec., 1771. *Issue:*
   i. Hosea (Wilcox), b. 10 May, 1730
   ii. Elizabeth (Wilcox), b. 20 Jan., 1731.
   iii. Mary (Wilcox), b. 3 Nov., 1733.
   iv. Mindwell (Wilcox), d. 2 Feb., 1736-7.
   v. Susanna (Wilcox), b. 21 Feb., 1735-6.
   vi. Joseph (Wilcox), b. 6 June, 1738; d. 15 Jan., 1759.
   vii. David (Wilcox), b. 30 Apl., 1740.
   viii. Mindwell (Wilcox), b. 24 Oct., 1742.
7. David, b. 24 May, bp. 5 June, 1709.* FAM. 9.
8. Hannah, b. 20 Feb., 1711-12; m. 11 Mch.,

* DAVID.—In Rev. Dudley Woodbridge's *Ch. Rec.*, Simsbury, it is rec. that David Buttolph had a son b. 24 May, bp. 5 June, 1709, but the name has been torn off from the orig. and appears in brackets.—L. A. B. He is said to have m. Mary **Holcomb,** 3 Sept., 1731.

1765, Judah (s. Nathan'l & Martha *Buell*) **Holcomb**; she d. 11 Mch., 1765; he d. 5 Jan., 1802. *Issue:*
  i. Rosanne (Holcomb), b. 24 June, 1732; d. 8 Nov., 1814; m. 1750, Samuel (s. Samuel & Elizabeth *Wilcoxson*) **Hayes.**
  ii. Silas (Holcomb), b. 17 Nov., 1734.
  iii. Ozias (Holcomb), b. 3 Mch., 1736-7.
  iv. Hannah (Holcomb), b. 28 Aug., 1740;

m. 1757, Silas (s. of Samuel & Eliz'th *Wilcoxson*) **Hayes;** she d. 23 June, 1823.
  v. Benajah (Holcomb), b. 12 Nov., 1741.
  iv. Rhoda (Holcomb), b. 7 Feb., 1743-4.
  vii. Judah (Holcomb), b. 27 Aug., 1746.
  viii. Dan (Holcomb), b. 21 Oct., 1748.
  ix. Penelope (Holcomb), b. 29 Feb., 1752.
9. Temperance, b. 12 July, 1713 or '15.

FAM. 7. JOHN,[4] (*John,[3] John,[2] Thos.,[1]*), b. 1688; m. 19 June, 1710, Mehitable **Lord**; was a wine mcht., rented the basement of the Town Hall, of Boston, until 1740; held lds. in Rutland, Mass.

Children:

1. Mary, b. 25 May, 1711.
2. John, b. 23 Sept., 1712.
3. Mehitable, b. 4 Dec., 1714; d. yg.
4. Sarah, b. 23 Sept., 1716; m. 20 Nov., 1735, John **Parker.**
5. William, b. 17 Feb., 1718; d. yg.
6. Thomas, b. 29 Nov., 1719.
7. Mehitable, b. 24 Jan., 1722; m. Ebenezer **Ward,** 10 July, 1758.
8. William, b. 7 May, 1725.

FAM. 8. Dr. JONATHAN,[4] (*David,[3] John,[2] Thos.,[1]*), b. 1692-3; m. (1) 21 Feb., (or July), 1723, Martha (dau. Nath'l & Martha *Buell*) **Holcomb,** who d. 24 Jan. 1725; m. (2) 29 (or 24) Apl., 1729, Elizabeth **Cornish;** m. (3) 15 Feb., 1758, Martha **Loomis** Phelps, (dau. William & Martha *Morley*) Loomis, wid. of Jona. Phelps.

Children:

1. Jonathan, b. 8 Mch. (May ?), 1724. FAM. 10.
2. Benoni, b. 29 Jan., 1725.
  (*By second marriage*):
3. Daniel, b. 7 Apl., 1730.
4. Elizabeth, b. 3 Apl., 1731; m. 6 Mch., 1751, Noah (s. Noah & Hannah *Case*) **Humphrey,** who b. 15 Jan., 1726-7; d. 1790. She d. 6 June (or 8 Jan.), 1762.
5. Isaac, b. 15 Jan., 1732-3; m. (1) Sarah ————, who d. 12 Jan., 1753, ae. 54; m. (2) 15 July, 1754, Elizabeth (dau. Joseph & Dorothy *Alfred*) **Segor;** he may have been the Isaac ment. in the N. Y. State's men in Revol. as a private in Capt. Vosburg's Co., Col. Whiting's Reg., at Albany, N. Y., King's Dist.

FAM. 9. DAVID,[4] (*David,[3] John,[2] Thos.,[1]*), b. 1709; m. Mary **Holcomb**, 3 Sept., 1731. The identity of this family has been proven by Elam J. and Jonathan Buttolph, of Iowa Falls, Iowa; see also Smith's *Hist. of Dutchess Co., N. Y.,* p. 246.

Children:

1. David, b. 2 Aug., 1732; res. at North East, N. Y.; he adopted his nephew Milton; but d. intestate, before he reached his majority.
2. Roger, b. 4 Oct., 1734; was in the battle of Bunker Hill, from Hartland, Ct., in a Mass. Reg't; res. at Great Barrington, Mass.
3. Elijah, bp. 1742. FAM. 11.
4. John, b. Simsbury, Ct., 18 July, 1749. FAM. 12.

FAM. 10. JONATHAN,[5] (*Jona.,[4] David,[3] John,[2] Thos.,[1]*), b. 1724; m. Jerusha **Dibble,** of Simsbury, 3 July, 1746; she d. and he m. (2) 15 Feb., 1758, wid. Martha **Phelps.** This family has adopted the form of *Buttles,* as their name.

Children (acc. to Mrs. Enoch Buttles, of Granby, Ct.):

1. Jonathan, b. 10 Nov., 1747; his numerous descendants will be found in the *Whitney Genealogy.*
2. Joel, b. 27 Nov., 1750; d. at Granby, Ct., ae. 37; was a Revol. soldier; m. Hannah **Hayden,** of Windsor, Ct., who d. 1880. *Issue:*
  i. Benoni (Buttles).
  ii. Enoch, (Buttles), m. Phileta **Rice.**
  iii. Hannah (Buttles).
  iv. Levi (Buttles).
3. Jerusha, b. 10 Jan., 1753.
4. Levi, m. Sarah **Phelps;** rem. 1803, to Worthington, Ohio, where he d. 1805, ae. 42.
5. Abijah, b. 4 Dec., 1741; m. Olive **Waters;** res. on State line, at Granville, Mass. FAM. 13.
6. Daniel, b. 17 June, 1748; served in Revol. war in Capt. Colton's Co., Col. Brewer's reg't; sett. at Lucerne, N. Y.; had s. *Orin,* who had *issue:*
  i. J. Doane, res. Rome, N. Y.
  ii. Myron, res. Tahawus, N. Y.
  iii. Emory, res. Glens Falls, N. Y.
7. Asa, b. 14 Nov., 1756.
8. Patty, b. 27 Feb., 1758.
9. Temperance.
10. Polly.

FAM. 11. ELIJAH,[5] (David,[4] David,[3] John,[2] Thos.,[1]), b. 1742; res. Salisbury, Ct.; m. Feb., 1780, Deborah (wid. of Joseph) **Plumly**, and res. at Middlebury, Vt., where she d. 5 Mch., 1796, ae. 41. They were both charter members of the ch. at Midd'y, which was orig. in a barn, 5 Sept., 1789. History of this family furnished by Mr. Jonathan Buttolph, of Iowa Falls, Iowa, and Mrs. Isadore E. Brown, Bloomington, Ill.

Children:

1. Ezekiel, b. 27 Nov., 1784. FAM. 14.
2. Elijah, d. 14 Apl., 1814, ae. 26; hence b. 1788.
3. Sally, d. 15 Apl. (one acc. says 25 Mch.), 1814.
4. David, d. at Middlebury, Vt., 30 June, 1869, ae. 79, hence b. 1790; m. Almira **Little**, of Shoreham, Vt.
5. Joanna, d. 1 May, 1818, ae. 37, hence b. 1781.
6. Joseph, b. 1786; d. ae. 86. FAM. 15.
7. Jonathan, b. 1 Aug., 1797; m. and rem. to Potsdam, N. Y., where he was a millwright and kept the first hotel in that town. *Issue:*
   i. Myron (Buttolph), m. and has sons, Oscar and Orman.
   ii. Seymour (Buttolph), b. 1819.

FAM. 12. JOHN,[5] (David,[4] David,[3] John,[2] Thos.,[1]), b. 1749; m. Sylphia **Holmes**, who was b. 20 Jan., 1757, and d. 29 June, 1815; he d. 20 July, 1823; res. in North East, Dutchess Co., N. Y.

Children:

1. Lavinia, b. 29 Dec., 1777; m. ——— **Simmons**, and d. 10 Apl., 1843.
2. David, b. 28 Oct., 1779. FAM. 16.
3. Asa, b. Oct., 1781. FAM. 17.
4. Philomela, b. 29 Aug., 1783; m. ——— **Mead**; d. Pine Plains, N. Y., 28 Feb., 1826.
5. Morris, b. 16 Apl., 1786; m. Mary **Pattison**, of N. J.; had a son *Eugene* (Pattison) killed in a R. R. accident in West.
6. Sylvia, b. 18 Apl., 1788; d. 12 Dec., 1842.
7. John (Rev.), b. 4 Apl., 1790. FAM. 18.
8. Clarissa, b. 1 Nov., 1794; d. 9 June. 1816.
9. Horace. b. 1800.
10. Milton (Rev.), b. 29 May, 1792. FAM. 19.
11. Warren, m. ——— **McAllister**; d. 3 Sept., 1843, at Canaan, Ct. *Issue:*
   i. Horace.
   ii. Chas. W.
   iii. John W.
   iv. Fanny.

FAM. 13. ABIJAH,[4] (Jona.,[5] Jona.,[4] David,[3] John,[2] Thos.,[1]), b. 1741; m. Olive **Waters**; res. on State Line, Granville, Mass.

Children:

1. Olive.
2. Patty.
3. Silence.
4. Cephas, b. 11 Apl., 1791. FAM. 20.
5. Laura.
6. Marian.
7. Florinda.
8. Rensselaer, m. and had a son.
9. Levi, b. 2 Apl., 1806; m. had a dau.
10. Caroline H., b. 27 Oct., 1805.

FAM. 14. EZEKIEL,[6] (Elijah,[5] David,[4] David,[3] John,[2] Thos.,[1]), b. 1764; m. 6 Jan., 1791, Desire (dau. John & Desire *Holt*) **Phelps**, of Canaan, Ct. In February following they packed everything they had on a pung, bed clothes, kettles, skillet, pans, plates, spoons, and forks and with a three year old colt went to Rutland, Vt., and by marked trees through Brandon and Salisbury to Middleburg to his father Elijah; when the snow was off in the spring, he made a "pitch" of 200 acres in New Haven, Vt.; he d. 4 Feb., 1805.

Children (b. New Haven, Vt.):

1. Isaac, b. 2 Dec., 1792. FAM. 21.
2. Joanna, b. 1 Oct., 1794; d. 25 Feb., 1796.
3. Annis, b. 9 July, 1796; m. Alvin **Walker**; res. Essex, Vt.
4. Calvin, b. 25 May, 1797; m. 25 Dec., 1821, Jerusha **Sprague**; rem. to Essex, Vt., in 1828; where he d. 1876. *Issue:*
   i. Melissa, m. Wm. **Brew**; had large family; rem. from Essex to Burlington, Vt.
   ii. Electa, d. Essex, 1839.
5. Abiram, b. ———; m. Betty **Sprague**, and rem. to Potsdam, N. Y., was a farmer and fork mfr. *Issue:*
   i. Sewall, res. Potsdam, N. Y.; served in Civil War.
   ii. Seymour.
   iii. Maria (Mrs. Bacon), d.
6. John Phelps, b. 2 June, 1801. FAM. 22.

FAM. 15. JOSEPH,[6] (Elijah,[5] David,[4] David,[3] John,[2] Thos.,[1]), b. 1786; m. Harriet **Treadway**, who d. 28 Dec., 1822, ae. 32; he m. (2) Rosetta **Branch**; res. at Orwell, Vt., after 1850.

Children (by first marriage):

1. Joseph S., d. at Hague, N. Y., 1882.
2. Jonathan, b. 10 Dec., 1826.
3. Harriet E., d. 24 Aug., 1844, ae. 24.

(By second marriage):
4. Dau., wife of E. R. **Hustls,** Ft. **Edward,** N. Y., and ae. (1896) 60.

FAM. 16. DAVID,[6] (*John,[5] David,[4] David,[3] John,[2] Thos.,[1]*), b. 1779; m. 27 May, 1818, Urania **Lyman,** b. 1 Jan., 1792, of Middlefield, Ct., a cousin of Rev. Dr. Lyman Beecher. Mr. David B. grad. Wms. Coll.; practiced law at Norwich, N. Y.

Children:

1. Urania, b. 12 Apl., 1819; d. 20 July, 1834.
2. Ably Cornelia, b. 24 Feb., 1821; d. 24 June, 1830.

3. Jane Adaline, b. 20 Dec., 1826; d. 19 Aug., 1875.
4. David Lyman, b. 24 Dec., 1822; d. 28 Aug., 1830. FAM. 23.

FAM. 17. ASA,[6] (*John,[5] David,[4] David,[3] John,[2] Thos.,[1]*), b. 1781; res at North East, N. Y.

Children:

1. Caroline, m. Joseph **Flood,** of Marilla, N. Y., d. 1896.
2. Hiram, m. Loretta **Colly;** res. Darien, N. Y.
3. Lucius, m. Eliza **Carter.**
4. Ransom.

5. Morris.
6. Eliza Ann, m. Henry **Freed;** res. 1896, Buffalo, N. Y.
7. Harriet, m. Jos. P. **Bidlack.**
8. Mary, m. Lorenzo **Burr,** Darien, N. Y.

FAM. 18. Rev. JOHN,[6] (*John,[5] David,[4] David,[3] John,[2] Thos.,[1]*), b. 1790; was a Baptist; sett. (1823) in Detroit, Mich., being the first minister of that denomination to sett. in that State; in 1826, he sett. at Pontiac, Mich., where he d. 1 Oct. same year; he m. Mary **Douglas,** 1816.

Children:

1. Sylvia, b. 1817; d. 1836.
2. Henry D., b. 1818; d. 1847.
3. John G., b. 1822. FAM. 24.

4. James W., b. 1823. FAM. 25.
5. Judson A., b. 1825. FAM. 26.
6. Sarah M., b. 1827; m. ———— **Gerls.**

FAM. 19. Rev. MILTON,[6] (*John,[5] David,[4] David,[3] John,[2] Thos.,[1]*), b. 1792; m. ———— **Christy,** of Cornwell, Ct.; he was a Pres. clergyman.

Children:

1. Edward A., d. unm., ae. 37; was a lawyer at Poughkeepsie, N. Y.
2. Annie E., m. ———— **White,** of Castile.

N. Y.
3. Sarah.
4. John Henry, d. 1887; an electrician.

FAM. 20. CEPHAS,[7] (*Abijah,[6] Jona.,[5] Jona.,[4] David,[3] John,[2] Thos.,[1]*), b. 1791; m. 25 May, 1820, Nancy **Stoughton,** b. at Windsor, Ct., 23 Feb., 1794; they rem. to Milton, Pa.; she d. 27 Dec., 1869; he d. 17 May, 1878.

Children (b. Milton, Pa.):

1. Anson W., b. 22 June, 1821. FAM. 27.
2. Olive, b. 29 Nov., 1822; m. Paul **Juneau,** Jr., of Milwaukee, Wis., 28 Feb., 1848.
3. Oscar Babbitt, b. 25 Dec., 1824; d. 9 Mch., 1884; a dentist in Boston; m. 3 Aug., 1854, Camilla **Mygatt.**

4. Cephas Augustus, b. 6 May, 1829; d. 6 May, 1881.
5. Laura Ann, b. 26 May, 1826; d. 30 Apl., 1830.
6. Frederick Stoughton, b. 1 Jan., 1831.
7. Orrin Mortimer, b. 23 May, 1833.

FAM. 21. ISAAC,[7] (*Ezek.,[6] Elijah,[5] David,[4] David,[3] John,[2] Thos.,[1]*), b. 1792; m. Electa **Towsley,** who was b. 15 June, 1795; res. New Haven, Vt.

Children:

1. Lydia Ann, b. 4 Aug., 1817; m. ———
   Hoyt; d. 17 May, 1852.
2. Royal C., b. 9 May, 1819; res. Iowa.
3. Desire, b. 7 Sept., 1821; m. (1) Rich
   Tucker; m. (2) Newman Hill. *Issue (by
   first marriage)* :
   i. Henry (Tucker), b. 7 Mch., 1851.
      (*By second marriage.*)
   ii. Burton (Hill), b. 22 Mch., 1857; d.
      13 Apl. 1863.
   iii. Arthur (Hill), b. 30 May, 1859.
4. Henry A., b. 6 Oct., 1823; m. ———
   Smith; res. So. Burlington, Vt.; d. 1
   Sept., 1876; 3 ch., all d. of diphtheria,
   1862.
5. Hannah, b. 13 Jan., 1825; m. Albert Bliss;

6. Albert, b. 4 May, 1828; d. 28 July, 1852, at
   Westville, N. Y.
7. Anne J., b. Aug., 1830; m. Wesley Warner, Essex, Vt.; she d. 30 Mch., 1892, in
   Ill. *Issue:*
   i. Herman (Warner), res. Chicago.
   ii. Electa (Warner).
8. Emily, b. 4 May, 1834; m.. 25 Feb., 1858,
   at N. Haven, Vt., Curtis A. Rathburn,
   who was b. 13 Mch., 1828. *Issue:*
   i. Edson M. (Rathburn), b. 31 Mch.,
      1859.
   ii. Orson R. (Rathburn), b. 28 Feb.,
      1861; d. 20 Feb., 1862.
   iii. Reed H. (Rathburn), b. 16 Jan., 1863.
   iv. Ruble D. (Rathburn), b. 4 Aug., 1870.

FAM. 22. JOHN PHELPS,[7] (*Ezek.,[6] Elijah,[5] David,[4] David,[3] John,[2] Thos.,[1]*), b. 1801;
m. 24 May, 1825, Abigail N. Jewett, res. Essex, Vt.

Children:

1. Othniel Jewett, b. 3 Aug., 1826; d. Buffalo,
   N. Y.

2. Elam Jewett, b. 8 Aug., 1828. FAM. 28.

FAM. 23. DAVID LYMAN,[7] (*David,[6] John,[5] David,[4] David,[3] John,[2] Thos.,[1]*), b.
1832; m. 10 June, 1850, at Colonel's Isld. Geo., Laura E. Maxwell.

Children:

1. Charles E. Maxwell, d. yg., 21 Mch., 1857.
2. James David, b. ——————; res. 53 E.
   86th St., N. Y. City.

3. William, m. and has 3 sons: 1 dau.
4. Susan Mary.
5. Wallace, d. 11 Aug., 1899.

FAM. 24. JOHN G.,[7] (*Rev. John,[6] John,[5] David,[4] David,[3] John,[2] Thos.,[1]*), b. 1822; m.
1847, Melissa Phillips; res. Pontiac, Mich., where Melissa d. 1857, and he m. (2)
Julia Carnfield ,1857, who d. 1896.

Children (by first marriage) :

1. Mary, b. 1847; d. 1862.
2. Dwight, b. 1850; d. 1887.
3. Valina, b. 1854.
(*By second marriage*) :
4. Lucy, b. 1858.
5. Julia, b. 1860.
6. Charles, b. 1863; m. ———.

7. Jennie, b. 1864.
8. Anna, b. 1866; m. ———.
9. Edward, b. 1868.
10. Willis H., b. 1870; dentist at Kenton, O.
11. Louis, b. 1876.
12. Henry, b. 1878.

FAM. 25. JAMES W.,[7] (*Rev. John,[6] John,[5] David,[4] David,[3] John,[2] Thos.,[1]*), b. 1823;
m. Mary Friece, 1846.

Children:

1. Frank W., b., 1848; d. 1892.
2. John N., b. 1852.

3. Viola, b. 1854.

FAM. 26. JUDSON A.,[7] (*Rev. John,[6] John,[5] David,[4] David,[3] John,[2] Thos.,[1]*), b. 1825;
m. Lydia Alger, 1848.

Children:

1. Sarah A., b. 1852.
2. Jennie E., b. 1857.

3. James M., b. 1861.
4. Henry J., b. 1872.

FAM. 27. ANSON W.,[8] (*Cephas,[7] Abijah,[6] Jona.,[5] Jona.,[4] David,[3] John,[2] Thos.[1],*), b.
1821; m. 15 June, 1850, Cornelia H. Mullins; res. at Milwaukee, Wis.

Children:

1. Kate S., b. 15 Mch., 1851; m. 27 Dec.,
   1876, Geo. B. Porson; has 2 sons.
2. Olive Louisa, b. 10 June, 1853; m. 15
   Oct., 1878, Chas. B. Patton; has 2 daus.
3. Iola Jenette, b. 15 Apl., 1855.
4. Cephas, b. 27 July, 1857; m. May, 1889,

   Grace E. Roberts; 1 son.
5. Anson M., b. 7 Feb., 1859.
6. Cornelia Cora, b. 5 May, 1861; m. 24
   June, 1884, Daniel M. Kneeland; 2 sons,
   1 dau.
7. Augusta Henry, b. 20 Apl., 1863.

FAM. 28. ELAM JEWETT,[8] (*John Phelps*,[7] *Ezek*,[6] *Elijah*,[5] *David*,[4] *David*,[3] *John*,[2] *Thos.*,[1]), b. 1828; m. 14 Sept., 1853, Mary Elizabeth **Tracey;** rem. to Buffalo, N. Y., in 1869.

Children:

1. Harry Tracey, b. 6 May, 1855; engineer in the Municipal service of the City of Buffalo, N. Y. He is the one to whom the family of Buttolph are most indebted for this history of their name in America, and has printed a blue-print Pedigree Chart of the family, which is of great

interest.
2. John Phelps, b. 16 Jan., 1857.
3. Charles Jewett, b. 22 Dec., 1859; d. 9 Aug., 1865.
4. Abbie Huldah, b. 1 June, 1864; d. 24 July, 1865.
5. Benjamin Gilbert, b. 3 Aug., 1866.

BUTTOLPH, GEORGE, 3rd. ch. and s. of Lieut. John, of Salem, Mass., and Weth., Ct., was b. 15 Oct., 1667, at Salem; came to Weth. with his father abt. 1676— *Savage* (I, 323); drew ld. in 1694, as a res. landowner; rec'd, in 1693, fm. his father's estate, a half of the homestead ppy. which his father had occupied on the N. W. cor. of Broad and Short Sts., Weth.; and d. 1696, leaving the following *children:*

1. George, then ae. 6 yrs. FAM. 2.
2. Elizabeth, ae. 3; Peter Lattimore, on 11 Nov., 1746, was app. adm'r for her; described as "late of New London, Conn."
3. Joseph, ae. 2 yr.; blacksmith, see Po-

quonnoc *Rec. of Deeds*, I, p. 496. His wid. exhib. the invent. of his estate, 3 May, 1696.—See *Prob. Rec.* The family appears to have drifted away to the New London region.

FAM. 2. GEORGE, *Jr.*,[4] (*George*,[3] Lieut. *John*,[2] *Thos.*,[1]), m. Lydia ——————, who appeared before Prob. Ct., as his wid., 6 Feb., 1738-9, and was app. guardian of the two younger of their children.

Children:

1. Lydia, m. Titus Hurlbut, 19 Aug., 1734.
2. Jonathan, m. Elizabeth (dau. Thos. & Elizabeth) **Edgecombe,** of Groton, Ct.; their dau. *Elizabeth (Buttolph); m. abt. 1770, Rich. **Starr;** rem. to Hinsdale, Mass.,

1781; d. at Dalton, Mass., 11 Sept., 1828, ae. 81.
3. George, b. New London, 1726. FAM. 3.
4. Mary.
5. Ann, ment. in Jonathan's will.

FAM. 3. GEORGE,[5] (*Geo.*,[4] *Geo.*,[3] Lieut. *John*,[2] *Thos.*,[1]), b. 1726; m. (1) —————— **Collins,** who d. leaving an inf. son, George. He m. (2) Anna **Baker,** at Stonington, Conn., 29 Oct., 1756; and rem. to Chester, Mass.

Child (by first marriage):

1. George. FAM. 4.
(*By second marriage*):
2. Starr. FAM. 5.
3. Moon; d. inf.

4. Rachel.
5. Joseph. FAM. 6.
6. Three daus.

FAM. 4. GEORGE,[6] (*Geo.*,[5] *Geo.*,[4] *Geo.*,[3] Lieut. *John*,[2] *Thos.*,[1]), while yet a minor, enl. and served 4 yrs. in the War of the Revol.; was at the battle of Monmouth, N. J.; and for several weeks a prisoner in one of the old prison buldgs. at N. Y.; m. —————— **Dye,** of Stonington, Ct.

Children (by first marriage):

1. Dau., m. —————— **Brown;** fam.
2. Dau., m. —————— **Dewey;** fam.
(*By second marriage*):
3. George, b. 1817; drowned at Htfd., Ct., ae.

26.
4. Charles, b. 14 Apl., 1819; d. 1895, at Preston, Ill.

FAM. 5. STARR,[6] (*Geo.*,[5] *Geo.*,[5] *Geo.*,[4] *Geo.*,[3] Lt. *John*,[2] *Thos.*,[1]), rem. to Penn., and 1829, to Ohio, and d. in Lorraine Co., in 1840.

Children:

1. William.
2. Thomas.
3. George.
4. Ashbel, b. 1808, at Norwich, Mass.; m.

and had:
i. Charles, res. Chicago, Ill.
ii. William A., m. 19 Oct., 1892, Marian Lydia **Buck,** Alliance, O.

FAM. 6. JOSEPH,[6] (*Geo.*,[5] *Geo.*,[4] *Geo.*,[3] *Lieut. John*,[2] *Thos.*,[1]), rem. to and d. at Schoharie, N. Y., 4 Sept., 1854, ae. 75.

Children:

1. Joseph, m. ——— Wood; has a s. George, living (1901).
2. Elisha, m., has a s. Alonzo; res. at Syracuse, N. Y.
3. Sarah, m. ——— Cloes; res. at Chadwicks, N. Y.; was ae. 84 in 1896.
4. Melissa.

BYSBIE,—See *Bisbee.*

BUTTON, JOSIAH, of E. Hadd., m. Ursula B. **Bulkeley,** ———.

MANLEY, of Ephratah, N. Y., m. Prudence **Butler,** 31 July, 1851.—*S. C. R.*

BUTTRICKS, EDWARD, m. Nabby **Kilborn,** 16 Jan., 1788.—*N. C. R.*

CABLES, MARTYN, of Htfd., m. Rebecca **Flint,** 23 Feb., 1806—*W. C. R.*, had (*W. C. R.*) Rebecca, bp. betw. 27th and 31st Aug., 1817—the mother being dead.

REBECCA, m. Perez **Brockway,** of Spgfld., 24 Nov., 1831—had Lucy (Smith) b. 5 Aug., 1837.—*W. T. R.*

CADY, NICHOLAS, m. Sarah **Wright,** 12 Oct., 1749—(*Weth. Rec.*), who. d. 14 Jan., 1757, in 31st yr.; res. Ry-H.—*Weth. Ins.*

Child (Weth. Rec.):

1. Butler, b. 27 Aug., 1750; d. 25 Nov., 1754.

WALTER GOODALE, of Htfd., m. Julia Ann **Stoddard,** 7 Mch., 1838.

CADLEY, (Cadwell?) TIMOTHY, of Westfield, m. Cath. **Bulkeley,** 10 May, 1756.

CADWELL, ELISHA C., of Torrington, m. Sophia **Holmes,** 30 Apl., 1833?—*W. T. R.*

ESTHER, d. 30 Aug., 1847, ae. 7 mos.

HENRY, d. 29 Aug., 1848, ae. 1 mo.

ROXANA, wife of *Benjamin,* d. 6 Mch., 1849, ae. 53 yrs.—*Weth. Ins.*

THEODOTIA, d. 22 Sept., 1844, ae. 7 mo.—*Weth. Ins.*

WILLIAM MARTIN, (s. of *Amasa* & *Mary*) d. 22 Mch., 1842, ae. 6 yrs.—*Weth. Ins.*

CHESTER, of Springfield, m. Mary **Hurlbut,** 19 Sept., 1809.

CALDER, JOHN, m. Hannah ———; had—(*Weth. Rec.*), Thomas, b. 5 June, 1738.

Child:

1. Thomas, b. 5 June, 1738.

CALKINS, MARIA A., m. Dunham E— ———, 18 Jan., 1846.—*N. C. R.*

ASAHEL, d. ae. 49, 1 Nov., 1825—*W. T. R.;* Abigail his wife, ae. 40, d. 4 Sept., 1823.—*Ibid.*

CASE, ASA, m. Abigail **Blinn,** 12 Apl., 1794.

HULDAH, m. Wm. **McClintock,** of Palmer, Mass., 13 Sept., 1821—*W. T. R.*

CALLENDER, ELI, d. 19 Nov., 1816, in 80 yr.—*S. C. R.;* ELISHA, m. Sarah **Crane,** 25 Sept., 1766—*S. C. R.;* ELISHA, Sally, wife of, d. 7 Feb., 1820, in 41st yr.— *S. C. R.;* ELISHA, Experience, wife of, d. 9 Feb., 1853, ae. 76—*W. Ins.;* FANNY, (adult) bp. 19 Oct., 1794—*S. C. R.;* FRANCIS, of Bristol, m. Prudence **Butler,** 5 June, 1836—*S. C. R.;* HORACE, m. Betsy **Robbins,** 23 Oct., 1817; he d. 2 Mch., 1846, in 57th yr. in Weth.—*S. C. R.;* JOHN, of Glast., m. Sally **Dickinson,** 12 Oct., 1803; LAURA, m. 15 Dec., 1845, Francis **Colvin**—*W. T. R.;* MARY, (adult) bp. 22 Nov., 1796—*S. C. R.;* NANCY, d. 30 Jan., 1797, ae. 25 yrs.; she was bp. 22 Nov., 1796—*S. C. R.;* NANCY, (wife of Sylvester **Clark**), d. 28 Jan., 1881, ae. 70;POLLY (adult) bp. 19 Mch., 1797—*S. C. R.;* SARAH (wid.), d. 5 Feb., 1823, ae. 80, in P. H.—*S. C. R.;* SARAH, of Ry-H., m. Albert N. **Fitch,** of Htfd., 1 May, 1843—*S. C. R.;* WILLIAM, an inf. of, d. 21 —— 1819— *S. C. R.;* WILLIAM, 2d, m. Charlotte **Kelsey,** 14 July, 1825—*S. C. R.;* he d. 21 Mch., 1826, in 22d yr.—*S. C. R.;* WILLIAM, m. Lucy **Dickinson,** 29 Oct., 1807—*S. C. R.;* their dau. Eliza, d. 20 Apl., 1819, ae. 9 mos.—*W. Ins.;* Mrs. Lucy Callendar was bp. 17 May, 1823; WILLIAM, the wife of, d. 22 May, 1823, in 39th yr.—*S. C. R.;* WINTHROP, m. Julia **Roberts,** 15 May, 1843.—*W. T. R.*

CAMP. This Weth. fam. prob. desc. fm. Edward of New Haven, who m. Mary ————, and d. Mch., 1721—will in *N. H. Rec.* V. 5, 56-57. Invent. est. 29 Mch., 1721—*Ibid.* p. 65; had s. *Edward,* d. 1650.

Capt. JOHN, m. (1) Mary ————; he d. 4 Feb., 1747, in 72d yr.— *Weth. Ins.;* "wid. of Capt. John" *Rebecca,* d. 26 Feb., 1769—*Weth. Ins.;* res. in New.; was prob. the *John,* s. of John (See *Savage,* I, 331) freeman of Htfd., who was b. 13 Feb., 1675, which would agree with age (72) as above given.

Child:

1. Mary, b. 25 Oct., 1713—*Weth. Rec.;* poss. the dau. of John & Rebecca, who acc. to note in *Htfd. Times,* Feb. 28, 1901, m. 1735, Thos. **Stoddard,** of Weth.

FAM. 2. Dea. JOHN, Jr., m. Penelope **Deming,** 1 Nov., 1739, who d. 15 Apl., 1784, in 67th yr. Dea. John d. 27 July, 1782, in 81st yr.—*Weth. Ins.*

Children (Weth. Rec.):

1. Mary, b. 10 Dec., 1740.
2. Anne, b. 1 Dec., 1742.
3. Joseph, b. 27 July, 1744. FAM. 3.
4. James, b. 30 Nov., 1746. FAM. 4.
5. Lucy, b. 27 Mch., bp. 2 Apl., 1749; prob. the L., who m. Timothy **Lee,** 23 Apl., 1772. —*N. C. R.*

FAM. 3. JOSEPH,[3] (*Dea. John,*[2] *Capt. John,*[1]), b. 1744; m. Anna **Kellogg,** 5 Dec. 1768—(*N. C. R.*); she d. 2 Aug., 1804, in 56th yr.; he d. 15 Apl., 1812, ae. 68.— *Weth. Ins.*

Children (Weth. Rec. & N. C. R.):

1. Anna, bp. 29 Apl., 1770; d. 26 May, 1772.
2. Anna, b. 15, bp. 9 May, 1773; d. 11 May, 1853, ae. 80.—*Weth. Ins.*
3. Eleanor, b. 17, bp. 30 July, 1775.
4. Sarah, b. 6 June, bp. 2 Aug., 1778; d. 1 Mch., 1836, ae. 58.—*N. C. R.*
5. Joseph, b. 26 Mch., bp. 8 July, 1781.
6. James, b. 15 Mch., bp. 20 June, 1784. FAM. 5.
7. Alma, b. 31 Jan., bp. 20 May, 1787; d. 3 Apl., 1845, ae. 58.—*N. C. R.*
8. Lucy, b. 12 May, bp. 1 Aug., 1790.

FAM. 4.   JAMES,[3] (John, Jr.,[2] Capt. John,[1]), b. 1746; m. Elizabeth **Kilborn,** 4 Dec., 1769; he d. 22 June, 1782, ae. 35.—*Weth. Ins.*

Children (Weth. & N. Ch. Recs.):

1. John, b. 6 Apl., 1770, bp. 26 May, 1771 (?), N.
2. Samuel, b. 25 Aug., bp. 6 Sept., 1772.
3. Abigail, b. 30 Oct., 1773; bp. 6 Nov., 1774.
4. Moses, b. 15 Apl., bp. 14 Sept., 1777; prob. the M. who m. Chloe **Stoddard,** in Nov., 1802.
5. Mary, b. 14 Oct., 1778; bp. 26 Sept., 1779; prob. the M. who m. Thos. **Stoddard,** 18 Dec.—*Weth. Rec.*
6. Elizabeth, b. 24 Mch., bp. 4 July, 1782.

FAM. 5.   JAMES KELLOGG,[4] (Joseph,[3] John, Jr.,[2] Capt. John,[1]), b. 1784; m. Caroline (dau. John & Susannah *Cowles*) **Deming,** of Far., who was b. Far., 27 May, 1789; was a mcht. at Far.; he d. 6 Apl., 1845, ae. 61, at Far.; she d. at F., 2 Sept., 1843, in 55th yr. (*This fam. rec. furnished by Capt. Edw'd Hooker, U. S. N.*)

Children (b. Far.):

1. John Deming, } bp. 17 June, 1821; moth-
2. Fanny Cowles, } er bp. at same time.
3. Samuel Kellogg, } Samuel of Far., m. Mary (dau. Gen. Martin) **Kellogg,** 20 Apl., 1847.—*N. C. R.*
4. Joseph Walker, bp. 6 July, 1823; m. a **Hale;** was connected with the *N. Y. Jour. of Commerce.*
5. Susan Ann, b. 4 Sept., 1825; d. 10 Sept., 1826.
6. Susan Ann, b. 3 June, 1827; m. Rev. Mr. **Whittlsey,** of Newington; rem. to Peoria, Ill.
7. Ch., unnamed, b. and d. 1813.
8. Ch., unnamed, b. and d. 1819.

Miscellanea:

CAROLINE, b. 29 Jan., 1835; d. 21 May, 1874; *Dan,* a ch. of, ae. 8, d. 1 Jan., 1808.—*N. C. R.*

ELIZA W., b. 3 Feb., 1861; d. 20 Sept., 1892.

ERASTUS & Salome, had *Mary Araline,* bp. 6 May, 1827.

JOSEPH, m. Lydia **Francis,** 23 Jan., 1833—*N. C. R.;* she d. 25 Apl., 1836, ae. 36—*N. C. R.;* had *Lydia* and *Joseph,* bp. 8 June 1845.

JOSEPH, (s. of John, by wife Mary (dau. of Robert) **Sanford,** of Htfd.) b. 30 Jan., 1679, was a ld-holder at Htfd. and also in Weth., where he res.; he m. Abigail ————. From *So. Ch. Rec.,* of Htfd., p. 320, we find that their dau. *Hannah* was bp. 28 Sept., 1712, and fm. *Htfd. Co. Prob. Rec.,* VIII, 228, we learn that she was their only ch.; she m. Amasa **Adams,** of Weth. 16 Mch., 1731-2.—See *Adams.* Her father Joseph' invent. of est. was taken 23 Dec., 1712, by Thos. Richard and Wm. Webster—amt. £226·10·05—*Ct. Rec.;* 15 Dec., 1712, gr. adm. to Abigail Camp, wid., and Samuel Benton, Senr., of Htfd., 6 Dec., 1714. Distributors of J. C.'s est. William Webster of Htfd. & Hez. Deming of Weth. Prob. Ct. 6 Dec., 1714. The *Htfd. Daily Times* of Apr. 6, 1904, gives an opinion regarding Abigail ———— the wife of Joseph Camp. From combined evidence given, he is inclined to believe she was dau. of Samuel Benton, b. 9 Dec., 1691—(*Benton Genealogy*). Saml. Benton had a dau Abigail, b. at above date, who was ment. in her father's will as Abigail in 1744—and as he was an adm. on Joseph Camp's will with Abigail, is one reason for believing so. The same writer (H. W. B.) also suggests that Abigail Camp was prob. dau. of Saml. Benton, for reasons given, and that she may have m. (2) Rich'd Montague, of Weth.—reason—"Mrs. Abigail Mantague's known age at death agrees perfectly with Abigail Benton's birth-date."

HOMER, of Washington, Ct., b. 17 Oct., 1797, m. Delia **Whittlesey;** he d. 9 Oct., 1891; she b. 1 Aug., 1808, d. 21 Oct., 1894—*Weth. Ins.;* had (*Weth. Ins.*) *Laura*

Kellogg bp. 10 June, 1832, prob. the *Laura A.*, who m. Nelson **Peters,** of Wilbraham, Mass., 25 Mch., 1849—*S. C. R.; Lemuel Whittlesey,* bp. 20 June, 1830; *Caroline Anne,* bp. 11 Oct., 1835; an *inf.* of, d. 20 Mch., 1845 ae. 2 d.— *W. C. R.*

LOUISA JANE A., of New., m. Nelson **Peters,** of Wilbraham, Mass., 25 Mch., 1849.—*W. C. R.*

LEMUEL WHITTLESEY, (s. of Homer & Delia, above), m. Eliza E. **Webster,** who was b. 13 Oct., 1831, d. 14 May, 1872; had—(*Weth. Ins.*) *Mary,* d. 12 Sept., 1868, ae. 17 mos.; *Grace,* d. 26 Mch., 1873, ae. 11 mos.; *Alice M.,* d. 17 June, 1873, ae. 3 yrs. 10 mos. *Lemuel W.,* prob. m. (2) Mary **Robbins,** who d. 27 Mch., 1892, ae. 57.

PHILIP, m. Mary **Green,** 29 Nov., 1827.—*W. T. R.*

SAMUEL K., m. Mary **Kellogg;** he d. 26 Mch., 1884, ae. 64; she d. 14 May, 1852, ae. 33—*Weth. Ins.;* had (*Weth. Ins.*) *Mary K.,* d. 14 Oct., 1859, ae. 9; had by wife *S. K*————, *Laura H.,* d. 6 Apl., 1864, ae. 8; *Anna K.,* d. 15 Feb., 1862, ae. 1 yr.; and *Sarah K.,* d. 24 Dec., 1872, ae. 7 yrs.

SHEM, m. Data **Webster,** 17 Nov., 1811.—*W. T. R.*

WILLIAM, of Htfd., m. Lucy **Butler,** 2 Nov., 1834.—*W. T. R.*

CANDEE, JUSTUS, of Oxford, m. Delia **Merriam,** 15 Oct., 1833; he d. 30 Aug., 1877, ae. 74; she d. 27 July, 1878, ae. 79.—*Weth. Ins.*

CANFIELD, DAVID, of Sandisfield, Mass., m. Betsy **Wolcott,** 4 Feb., 1800.

PRESTON & Mary A., had—(*Weth. Ins.*) *Lucia H.,* d. 30 Apl., 1892; *Bertha,* d. 25 Feb., 1897, ae. 5 yrs.

CARPENTER, JOHN,—See Chapt. VII, Vol. I.

CARRINGTON, RICE, m. Abigail **Fox,** 20 Jan., 1811.—*N. C. R.*

JOHN, in Weth., 1647.—See Chapt. VII, also, Chapt. XVII, Vol. I.

CARTER, DAVID, m. Susannah ————, [prob. Tryon,] and prob. a 2d marr. as we find a rec. of dth. of *Joanne,* wife of David Carter, 14 Sept., 1751, in 17th yr.—also, of a s. David, abt. 1 mo. old.

Children (*Weth. Rec.*) :

1. Joanna, b. 23 Jan., 1759.
2. David, b. 18 Sept., 1761.
3. George, b. 26 Jan., 1763; bp. and d. 28 Nov., 1767.
4. Elisha, b. 26 July, bp. 1764 (prob. in Aug.).
5. Jason, b. 8 Jan., 1767.
6. George, b. 25 Sept., 1768.
7. Susannah, b. 18 Jan., 1771.
   A. ———— "late," had Susannah Tryon bp. 2 Nov., 1783.—*W. C. R.*

Miscellaneous: ALFRED H., m. Cynthia C. **Chapman,** both of E. Hadd., 3 Sept., 1829—*S. C. R.;* ABIGAIL, dau. of David, bp. 20 Mch., 1763; DAVID, s. of Joshua, bp. 21 Feb., 1730-1; ELIJAH H., s. of Dea. Elijah, of Keene, N. H., a beneficiary of 3d Cong. Ch. of Beverly, Mass., d. at Weth., 10 Aug., 1822 ae. 21—memb. Soph. class of Y. C.; HENRY, m. Belinda **Steel,** of New Britain, (Berlin), 21 Sept., 1836—*W. T. R.;* HOPLEY, (wid.), a s. of, d. 6 bu. 7 Sept., 1828—*W. C. R.;* JOHN, of Htfd., m. Sarah **Miner,** of Weth., 28 Nov., 1779— *W. C. R.;* JOHN, of Htfd., (prob. same as above) m. Hopey **Butler,** 8 Dec.,

1805; JONATHAN, ae. (supp.) 92, bu. 9 Mch., 1790—*W. C. R.;* JONATHAN (prob. above) m. Elizabeth **Latimer**, 19 Mch., 1727-28, had *David*, b. ? Feb., 1730-1—*W. T. R.;* LAURA W., d. 22 Nov., 1895 ae. 76; LYMAN & Laura, had *William S.*, bp. 2 Aug., 1847, and a *son* bu. 30 Apl., 1849; MR. & MRS. ———, had *Nancy* and *Sarah Porter*, bp. 2 Oct., 1828—*W. C. R.;* NANCY, prob. dau. of the "Mrs" above, m. Lewis **Whitman**, of Ry- H., 19 Apl., 1843; ROSEWELL & Hannah, had *George*, bp. 6 Oct., 1811 and *Hannah*, bp. 29 Sept., 1816— *W. C. R.;* SARAH P., m. Geo. W. **Tuttle**, of Bristol, 21 Oct., 1846; W. L. & Augusta had *L. Leroy*, who d. ae. 2 yr. 6 mos.—*W. Ins.*

CASTLE, HANNAH, wife of Silas, b. Weth., 11 Nov., 1769.—Cothren's *Woodbury, Ct.*

CASWELL, JARED, of Glast., m. (*W. C. R.*) Marinda **Rhodes**, 17 Oct., 1832.

PRUDENCE, wife of Francis, d. 21 Apl., 1837, ae. 21.—*Weth. Ins & S. C. H.*

CATLIN, (Cattelin, Cattling, Cattell,) THOMAS, of Htfd., abt. 1640; was b. Eng., 1612; was a considerable ld. owner and an active citizen of Htfd., of which he was constable fm. 1662-1674.—See Chapt. VII, Vol. I. His wife d. before 1675, and he m. (2) Mary (wid. of Edward) **Elmore**, of Windsor, Ct., who had been killed by Inds. in King Philip's War. Mr. Thomas C. d. 1690, ae. 78.

By his first wife Mary (b. in Eng., as supp.) he had:

1. Mary.
2. Mary, b. 6 May, 1649, who is supp. to have m. a **Burnham**, as his will contained a bequest to a gd-dau. Mary Burnham.
3. John, b. in Eng. prob., and therefore the eldest. FAM. 2.

FAM. 2. JOHN,[2] (*Thos.,*[1]), b. Eng.; owned with his father, a large amt. of ld. in Htfd.; and rec'd by deed of gift, dated 29 Jan., 1689-90, other ppy. fm. his father. He m. (*acc. to Weth. Rec.*) Mary ———, 23 Sept, 1662, by whom he had—(*Weth. Rec.*) :

Child:

1. John, b. 26 July, 1663, and may be the John (who acc. to a writer in *N. Y. Mail & Express*, 18 June, 1898), m. Isabella **Ward** (?), and whose *son* went to Deerfield, Mass.

The *Boardman Gen.* (p. 342) says, John, Sen., m. Mary **Marshall**, 27 July, 1665, and that she d. 20 Oct., 1716; he dying not long after. If this is so—it must have been a *second* marr. and would account for the family of 6 ch. there given him—which, however, do not appear on the Weth. Rec. In the *Candee Gen.* it is surmised that he rem. to Newark, N. J.; but there is, altogether, considerable uncertainty, fm. all the accounts given (by *Savage*, Chipman's *Harwinton*, the *Candee Gen., and Boardman Gen.*), concerning John, and his relationship to Thomas, of Htfd. *Savage*, (I, 349), ment. a JOHN, of Deerfield, who came fm. Newark, N. J., before 1663, with his mother Isabel, "but they had some yrs. before gone fm. Conn., of course. The bap. name of her first husband is unknown, for she m. James **Northam**, of Weth., who d. 1662 and she rem. and had third husband, Joseph **Baldwin**, of Hadley."

BENJAMIN, a pretty lively soldier and seaman of the Revolutionary War, (See Chapt. XI, Vol. I) was undoubtedly a descendant of the foregoing. He was bu. 9 Feb., 1782; his wife was bu. 26 Apl., 1781. *Weth. Ch. Rec.* cr. them with an inf. bu. 3 May, 1781; a son bu. 25 July, 1777, ae. 4.

(The *Boardman Gen.* contains much interesting Catlin matter.)

The late excellent genealogist, Miss Charlotte Goldthwaite, furnished (1889,) theh following note to Judge S. W. Adams concerning Benjamin Catlin's family. "BENJAMIN of Weth. was a desc't of Thomas, of Htfd., in the following line, viz. *Thomas*,[1] of Htfd., *John*,[2] *Benjamin*,[3] b. Htfd., 1681; rem. 1738 to Harwinton; *Benjamin*,[4] b. 1723, in Htfd., rem. to Harrington; *Benjamin*,[5] Rev. soldier and writer of the Bunker Hill letter [see Vol. I. p. 450.] This last Benj. m. Anna (dau. of Elisha) **Deming**, of Weth., and *Weth. Ch. Rec.* show that his wife d. 26 Mch., 1781, and Benjamin Catlin d. Feb., 9, 1782,—*W. C. R.*, and besides the two ch. they lost in infancy [see line 10, above], they left a son *George*, b. 1778 and a dau. *Honor*, as I find from *Prob. Rec.*, but what became of these ch. I do not know."

CENTOR, JONATHAN, ae. (supp.) 92, bu. 9 Mch., 1790.

CHADWICK, WILLIAM, m. Mehitable **Smith**, 25, Mch., 1790.

Children (*Weth. Ch. Rec.*) ;

1. Nancy, bp. 22 May, 1792.
2. William, bp. 26 Dec., 1793 ; prob. the "inf.   s." who d. 27th same month.

CHALKER, RUSSELL, of Saybrook, m. Cynthia **Wolcctt**, (wid. of Wm. Nott Wolcott,) 22 Mch., 1809, she ae. 38 bu. 11 Oct., 1824.—*W. C. R.;* a dau. ae. 18, bu. 15 July, 1827.—(*W. Ch. Rec.*)

CHAMBERLAIN, ELISHA, of Pittsfield, m. Ruth **Hurlbut**, 12 Nov., 1797. (*W. C. R.*) ; *Rebecca*, d. Sept., 1807.—*W. C. R.*

JOSEPH, of Weth., Hadley and Colchester, m. 8 June, 1688, Mercy, (dau. John) **Dickinson**, who came from Woburn, Mass.—*Htfd. Times*, 2 Feb., 1903.

CHAMBERS, (*Step. R.*) GEORGE ORLANDO, of Midd., m. Martha (dau. Elijah) **Robbins**, 14 Dec., 1825.—*S. C. R.;* he b. 15 Sept., 1801, d. 18 Dec., 1884; she b. 29 Aug., 1796, d. 12 June, 1849—*Weth. Ins.*; they had *Francis*, bp. 31 Oct., 1828—*S. C. R.; Henry Richard*, bp. 2 Nov., 1832; and *Martha Augusta*, bp. 6 Apl., 1827—*S. C. R.*

JOHN,   ⎫
DEBORAH,   ⎬ ch. of Phebe., bp. 17 Nov., 1768.—*S. C. R.*
POLLY,   ⎭

Wid. RUTH, d. 13 Oct., 1833, in 56 yr.

CHAMPLIN, OLIVER, d. 4 Mch., 1821.—*W. C. R.*

CHAPIN, (*Step. Ch. Rec. & Weth. (S.) Ins.*,) Rev. CALVIN, D. D., (for whose biog. see Vol. 1., pp. 854-864) m. 2 Feb., 1795, Jerusha (dau. of Rev. Jonathan) **Edwards,** Pres. of Union College, N. Y., she was b. 30 Jan., 1776 and d. 5 Dec., 1847, in 72d yr., at Ry-H.

Children (*S. C. R. & Goodwin's Geneal. Notes*) :

1. Jerusha, b. 12 Feb., bp. and d. 1 Mch., 1796; d. at age of 18 days.
2. Eliza, b. 4 Apl., bp. 14 May, 1797; m. Ashor **Robbins**, of Weth.
3. Edward. b. and bp. 19 Feb., 1799; m. Sarah McGrath, of York, Pa.; is a lawyer.
4. Jerusha, b. 2 Apl., bp. 20 June, 1802; d. 26 Nov., 1826, ae. 54.

D^r. Chapin also entered upon his Ch. book of Baptisms, the following entries of the deaths of his parents, brothers and others of his father's family: Dea. EDWARD, of and at Springfield, Mass., d. Jan., 1800 in 76th yr.; EUNICE, wid. of Dea. Edward of and at Springfield, d. 8 Apl., 1806 in 78 yr. EDWARD, Jr., d. at Springfield, 22 June, 1795 ae. 40; ALPHEUS, of and at Springfield, d. 18 Feb., 1826 in 61st yr.; AMZI, of Northfield, Ohio, d. 19   , 1835 ae. 67; AARON, d. of and in Htfd., 25 Dec., 1838, ae. 86; JOEL, (Rev.), d. at Bainbridge, N. Y., 8 Aug., 1845 ae. 84; EUNICE, wife of Rev. Joel, d. at B., 16 Apl., 1837, ae. 66; JOEL W., of Oxford, N. Y., m. Honor Francis **Bulkeley**, 6 Oct., 1823; LAERTES, d. 30 Oct., 1847 in N. Y. City, bu. at Htfd.; LUCIUS, d. 24 Dec., 1842, at Hamilton, Ohio, in 33d yr.

CHAPLIN, CLEMENT, Cambridge, of whom *Savage* says (I. 360),"came in the *Elizabeth and Ann*, from London, 1635, was a chandler of Bury St., Edmunds Co., Suffolk, Eng., ae. 48, and tho' the Custom House rec. tells no more, he bro't prob. the wife who was Sarah **Hinds**, dau. of a goldsmith in that borough, but no ch. is ever ment. Freeman (Cam.) 3 Mch., 1636; soon after removed to Htfd., with Hooker and his friends, was one of the purchasers of that beautiful city; but finally sett. down at Weth., the next year was treas. of the Colony; dep. 1639, and drew ld. in the ld. div. of that yr., rep. 1643 and '44, was living 1646; gave all his est. to his wife who went home, but date of his dth. or of her rem. is equal. unknown.—See 3 *Mass. Hist. Soc. Coll.*, X 168. He was the Ruling Elder of the Weth. Ch. In 1643, was fined £15 for signing a paper defamatory to Rev. Henry Smith, of Weth.; by order of the Ct., an official doc. was drawn up and publicly read in each town of the Col. exculpating Mr. Smith, with a warning that if hereafter, any one repeated or divulged any charges against Mr. S. he should be fined 40s." See, also Chapt. VII, Vol. I. Altogether, not a lovable character in Weth.'s early history.

CHAPPELL, GEORGE, then ae. 20, came to Windsor, Ct., in 1635, in the ship *Christian*, from London, as one of a party of workmen sent out by Sir R. Saltonstall to prepare him a place at Windsor, where he intended ultimately to settle. This party were in charge of Mr. Francis Stiles, a citizen and master builder of Lond., whom Saltursall had chosen as the agent and manager of his proposed plantation, and Geo. Chappel and some others of the passengers were indentured as apprentices to Stiles, as appears from order of Ct. at Htfd., 28 Mch., 1637, "ord. that Mr. Francis Stiles shall teach *George Chapple*, Thomas Cooper, and Thomas Barber, his servants, in the trade of a carpenter, according to his promise, for their service of their term, behind 4 days in a week only to saw and slitte their own work." He seems not long to have remained at W. for before April, 1641, (See Chapt. VII, Vol. I) he had a house and lot in Weth. nor is his further connection with Weth. known after rec. of birth of his 3d ch. in Oct., 1649. He m. Christian ————, and prob. rem. soon after that date—perhaps New Haven way.

Children (Weth. Rec.):

1. Abigail, b. 1 Sept., 1644.
2. Sarah, b. 21 (26—*S. W. A.*) Sept., 1647.
3. Rachel, b. 10 Oct., 1649.
   S. W. A. (Chapt. VII, Vol. I) ment. a GEORGE, Jr., s. of George (?) and *Margaret*, called in the *Rec.* the "R." George, and b. 17 Mch., 1653; from which we might infer a second marr. of George, Senr.; and

he also speaks of another George, "a cooper's apprentice, 1637, or thereabouts, apparently not related to either of the foregoing Georges—a dissolute man, of little account; but as to this, we imagine he has confused him with George, the orig. emigrant, of Windsor.

Miscellaneo: ROSWELL (*or Russell*) m. Jerusha **Hurlbut**, 16 June, 1825—W. C. R.; SOLOMON, d. 23 Dec., 1829, in 70 yr.—*S. C. R.*

CHAPMAN, (a Stepney parish family), all from *Weth. Ins. & S. C. R.* AMY, wife of David, d. 6 June, 1829 ae. 80, *Weth. Ins.*

DANIEL, (or David? see *Weth. Ins.* where the same rec. is given once under head of *Daniel*, and once under *David*, d. 19 Nov., 1820, ae. 73; his s. *Jacob*, d. *W. I.* 26 Oct., 1817, ae. 38; dau. *Susan* d. N. Haven, 29 June, 1819, ae. 36.

GILBERT m. Sabra **Winchel,** 24 May, 1806, (*N. C. R.*) 23 May, 1806; their s. *Russel G.* d. 5 Nov., 1823, ae. 1 yr. 5 mo. *John* d. 31 Mch., 1869, ae. 66.

REVILO m. Olive **Bulkeley,** res. at Rocky Hill, he b. 28 Apl., 1793, d. 15 Mch., 1866; she b. 1 Sept., 1793, d. 7 Jan., 1866; their s. *Harry B.,* b. 25 Jan., 1825, d. at Sippican, (Rochester) Mass., 4 Aug., 1842; *Sarah Jane,* b. 4 Dec., 1828, (*W. C. R.* say bp. 3 July, 1829), d. 3 June, 1874; *Amelia Maria,* bp. 29 July, 1827.

SARAH ANN, b. 6 May, 1836.

IRA, of Glast, m. Sally **Glossenger,** 31 Dec., 1811.

HENRY B., d. Aug., 1842, Rochester, N. Y., in 19th yr.

JULIUS, of E. Hadd., m. Fanny **Robbins,** 9 Dec., 1807.

PELEG, of Chatam, m. Lucy **Benjamin,** of E. Htfd., 2 Feb., 1797.

ORRIN, s. Sarah, had Whiting,? ae. 2, d. 10 Dec., 1828.—*N. C. R.* Orrin d. 16 June, 1842, ae. 45.—*N. C. R.*

CHAUNCEY, KATHARINE (dau. Rev. Nath'l, of Dunham, and wife of Mr. Benjamin) **Stillman,** d. 12 June, 1736, in 22d yr.—*Weth. Ins.*

CHARLES, of Phila., m. Hannah **Chester,** 26 Sept., 1808; she d. 6 Feb., 1821.— *W. Ch. Rec.*

EUNICE, d. 1 May, 1814, in 46 yr.—*S. C. R.*

EUNICE, d. betw. July and Oct., in P. H., ae. 28, 1825.—*S. C. R.*

EUNICE, dau. of Oliver, bp. 26 May, 1765.—*S. C. R.*

JOHN, 2d ch. of, d. 6 Jan., 1836.—*S. C. R.*

HULDAH, wid., d. 27 Feb., 1798, ae. abt 70.—*S. C. R.*

LUCY, (dau. of John & Amelia B.,) d. 7 Jan., 1836, ae. 1 yr. 5 m. 16 days.

CHERRY, JOHN, for lds. see Chapt. VII, Vol. I, m. Sarah ————, 26 June, 1669.

Children (Weth. Rec.):

1. John, b. 1 July, 1672. | 2. Henry, 14 Feb., 1673.

CHITTENTON, "The aged Mrs.," d. 29 Apl., 1767.—*N. C. R.*

CHILSON, DANIEL, m. Sybil ————.

Child (Weth. Rec.):

1. Daniel, b. 9 Feb., 1745-6.

CHESTER.   In the Ancient Burying Ground of Wethersfield, there yet standeth a

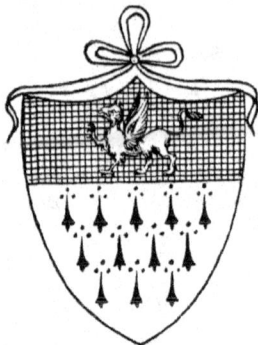

THE CHESTER ARMS.

table monument, upon which is rudely cut a coat of arms, and the following inscription, "Here lyes the body of Leon | ard Chester, Armiger, late | of the Town of Blaby and | severall other Lordships | in Leicestershire deceased | in · Wethersfield Anno | Domini 1648 oetatis 39." This monument, conspicious amid its humbler (headstone) neighbors, by reason of its early date, size, form, armorial device and inscription, and betokening a degree of inherited wealth and social standing not common in the earlier settlements, has always possessed for Wethersfieldians a certain romantic charm, which has been further heightened by the tradition of his perilous adventure amid the forests of Mt. Lamentation, (See Chapt. XVII Vol. I), to this day,
a "household tale" in every Weth. family. The interest thus centering on the Chester family has been also greatly accentuated by the personal character, services and influence of its members in the three earlier generations—so that we find the names *Chester* and *Leonard* incorporated—either in token of intermarriage, or of respect, into nearly all the older families of this ancient town. On the Weth. Rec. of Births, Marriages & Deaths, the Chesters number but 8 families; and the name (except as represented by marriage into other families) has long since been extinct in the old town. In Nath'l Goodwin's *Genealogical Notes, or Contributing to the Family History of some of the First Settlers of Conn. and Mass.*, is a genealogical sketch of this honorable family of which, in connection with *Weth. Rec.*, and other sources of information at our disposal, we have made free use of the record herewith presented.

Concerning the *pedigree* and *arms* of the family, the late Hon. J. Hammond Trumbull, the well known Conn., historical student thus speaks in a communication addressed to Judge Sherman W. Adams:

"The pedigree of the Chesters of Blaby is given in Nichols's *History of Leicestershire*, Vol. IV. pt. 2, p. 52, and in the *Visitation of the County of Leicestershire, in* 1619. (by Wm. Camden, Clarencieux), published by the Harleian Society, 1870, p. 138. Leonard Chester, "etat. 10, 1619," was son and heir of John, of Blaby, who married "Dorothia, filia Tho. Hooker de Com. Leie," and who was the son of Leonard of Blabỳ, by his second wife, Bridget, dau. of John Sharpe of Frisbie. The arms were blazoned (1619) "Ermine, on a chief sable a griffin passant with wings endorsed argent." A copy of the armorial seal of Col. John Chester (eldest son of John, eldest son of John, eldest son of Leonard) from an impression made in 1799, was engraved for *The Heraldic Journal*, Vol. II, p. 44.

Mr. Savage, in his *Genealogical Dictionary, of New Eng.*, alludes to "some diversity of opinion" as to the maiden name and parentage of Mary, the wife of Leonard Chester, himself "guessing, it may be she was the widow of Nicholas Sharpe and daughter of Wade." Dr. Bond, *Hist. of Watertown*, p. 736 calls her Mary *Nevill*, and that he was right as to the surname, the seal used by Judge James Russell, son of her second husband, Hon. Richard Russell, supplies strong proof. This seal was engraved, from a document dated 1700, in *The*

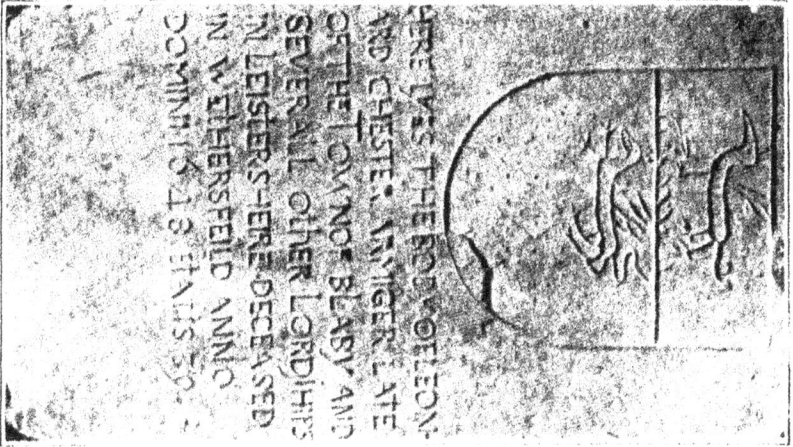

THE LID, OR TOP STONE, OF THE LEONARD CHESTER TABLE-MONUMENT, showing a rude attempt at sculpture of the Chester Arms. *(Photo by A. Morgan.)*

TABLE-MONUMENT OF LEONARD CHESTER.

Heraldic Journal, Vol. IV, p. 32. It bears the name of Russell, impalling the saltire (argent?) of the Nevills, with a mark of difference (a martlet·) The saltire, anciently the arms of Raby, became the arms of the Nevills, when their surname was assumed by the Lords of Raby, after the marriage of Robert of Raby with the heiress of Galfred Nevill.

The will of Leonard Chester of Wethersfield mentions a bequest to him and his heirs by Nicholas Sharpe. The Chesters of Blaby and the Sharpes of Frisbie Super Wreke in the same county were nearly related by marriage. The grandmother of our Leonard was the daughter and co-heiress of John Sharpe; and two of her daughters married Sharpes of Frisbie,—Anna, was in 1619, the wife of Robert Sharpe, and Alicia the wife of Richard Sharpe.

Of Leonard Chester's "father Wade," to whom he had sent a letter of attorney, before Aug. 2, 1648, I find no trace. Was Mary Nevill a *second* wife? And is the note quoted by Mr. Goodwin (*Geneal. Notes*, p. 8) to be relied on,— that Leonard Chester first "married Mary Wade, widow (?), daughter of Mr. Nicholas Sharpe?"

The Widow of Leonard Chester, Esq., who, it will be remembered, was a wid. at the time of her marr. to him was married a third time (1655) to the Hon. Richard **Russell**, of Charlestown, Mass., being his second wife. Mr. Russell, whom Frothingham calls the ancestor of a distinguished family in this country, was of a family no less celebrated in Eng. He was b. in Hertford, Hertfordshire, Eng., in 1611. *Savage* says his father was Paul Russell, and that this son Richard was an apprentice in the City of Bristol, 4 Dec., 1628 and came to New Eng. with his newly marr. wife Maude ————, in the ship *St. John*, in 1639-40. It appears of record that the "City Council of London, gave permission to the ship *St. John*, Richard Russell and partners, Masters, Stephen Goodyear, Mcht. New Haven, Owner, Jan. 26, 1639-40, to transport 250 passengers to New Eng." Mr. R. was adm. inhab. of Charleston, Mass., 1640; and with his wife, was adm. to Ch., 22 May, 1641; and made freeman 2 June, same year; chosen a selectman of C., 1642, and his name stands at the head of the Board of Selectmen for 17 yrs., and as a member 26 yrs. In 1644 was chosen a rep. to Gen. Ct., for 2 successive yrs., and Speaker of the House five years; was an Assistant 16 yrs. and for 20 yrs. Treasurer of the Colony. He was also largely engaged in commerce and merchandizing; and in navigation as early as 1645. With his son, James, he built wharves and storehouses in the Charleston River near where the C. bridge now crosses to Boston and was one of the largest real-estate owners in the country, including by purchase from Dea. Edward Collins, 1600 acres of ld. which composes the greater part of the present town of Medford, Mass., he also owned ¼ of the Pemaquid Patent (now Saco, Me.) and d. possessed of a large fortune. His wife Maude, d. 1652; and in 1655 he m. Mary, wid. of Leonard Chester, of Weth.

Hon. Richard Russell d. at C. 14 May, 1676, in his 65th yr.; will dated 29 Mch., 1674; prob. 18 May, 1676; mentions his wife Mary (Chester) Russell, her eld. dau., wife of Samuel Whiting and 7 ch.; her second dau. then living, wife of Thomas Russell and 2 ch.; her third dau. Eunice; and her son Stephen Chester; his own son James R., wife and 3 ch.; his dau. Katherine, wife of Wm. Rosewell and her son Wm.; his dau. Elizabeth, wife of Nath'l Graves; his sister Elizabeth (Corbett); his sister Sarah (wid.) of Bristol, Eng.; sister Mary (Newell,) wid. and her sons John and Joseph, Mary (Golden) and Eleazer Allen. He gave the £100 to the Ch., £50 towards a home for the ministry; £200 to the Town of C. for a poor fund; £100 to Harvard Coll. as "a continuous revenue to educate two poor students."

It is said on auth. of H. G. Somerby, the eminent genealogist, that the Hon. Richard Russell has now no male descendants in America.

His wid. Mary (Chester) Russell d. 30 Nov., 1688, ae. abt. 80 yrs. Her will, dated 20 Nov., 1688, proved 1 Oct., 1689, mentions eld. son John Chester, to whom she bep. £30; dau. Dorcas **Whiting**, £30; & to her husband Rev. Samuel Whiting, £10; certain chattels to their dau. Elizabeth Whiting; to son Stephen Chester, mcht. £40; to her dau. Prudence Russell's orphans, viz: Thos. R. "my gd-son" the brick ho. and part of wharf bo't of my step-son Daniel Russell; to Mary and Prudence Russell "my gd-ch.," house furniture and plate with "the Chester arms;" sons in law, James Russell and Richard Sprague, £5 each, etc.

FAM. 1. LEONARD, Esq., the English ancestry of Chester has been traced back for

many generations, but it will suffice for our purpose to say that the Weth. settler was the *son* of John Chester, of Blaby, (m. Dorothy,* dau. of Thos. **Hooker**, of Leicester, and sister of the celebrated Rev. Thos. Hooker, of Htfd.) ; and *gd-son* of Leonard Chester, of Blaby, who m. (1) the dau. of Nicholas **Saville;** and (2) m. Bridget, dau. of John **Sharpe**, of Frisby, Super Wreke, Eng., and *gt-gd-son* of William Chester, Bart., of London, and of Barnet Co., Hertford, Eng.

He was b. 1610; m. Mary Wade, came to Watertown, Mass., 1633, was prop'r there, and "Chester's Meadow" and "Chester Brook" in Waltham still perpetuate his memory in Mass., was one of the first settlers of Weth., 1635; was a grand juror, his name occurring 13 times in Vol. I, of *Cam. Col. Rec.*, built, (VII) the first corn-mill in Weth.; for his land rec. see Vol. I, Chapt. VII. Was evidently an active, influential and highly respected citizen; d. in Weth. 11 December, 1648, ae. 39; will dated 2 Aug., 1648; app. his wife sole executrix, and refers incidentally to ppy. "remaining still in Old England," and to his "father Wade" and "Uncle Newton" (first minister of Farmington, Conn., and later second minister at Milford, Ct.). This will is given in full in Goodwin's *Geneal. Notes*, p. 8. There was, however, a previous will dated 22 Nov., 1637, on file in *Htfd. Co. Prob. Office.*

His wid. m. (2) abt. 1655, (as his 2d wife) the Hon. Richard Russell, of Charlestown, Mass., a prominent merchant and citizen of that place, whose first wife, Maud, had d. some 3 yrs. before. He d. in 1676, and she survived him, dying at C., 30 Nov., (*Savage* says Dec.,) 1688, ae. abt. 80.—*Charleston Recs.*

Her will dated 20 Nov., 1688, at C., app. her son Stephen and her son-in-law Rev. Sam'l Whiting, exec's, and devises considerable ppy. to ch. and gd-ch.; among personal effects she mentions "brass andirons," "silver tankards," "to servant John Coultman, of Weth., a silver wine cup, marked M. I. D.," and a "silver plate with the Chester arms on it," and "a painted carpet," See Goodwin's *Notes* p. 9.

Leonard Chester's Will—22 November, 1637—Beaqueaths to his wife Mary, to his Mother Dorothy Chester, to d. Mary, to the Children of My Uncle Thomas

---

* *Savage* (I, 375) speaking of the diversity of opinion as to this lady's maiden name, says: "Bond calls her *Neville*, but Chester's will, that had not been seen by him, speaks of his 'father Wade;' and yet Goodwin, in his geneal. of the fam. (*Notes*, 8) quotes an authority that calls her 'Wid. Wade, dau. of Nich. Sharpe;' and, in my guess, it may be that she was wid. of Sharpe and dau. of Wade."

† The name of Mrs. Dorothy Chester appears on the records as grantees of three lots of land in Hartford, among the 1st settlers in 1639 ; probably the mother of Leonard.

Hooker now Pastor of the Church in Hartford—appoints his wife Executrix. Mr. John Plume and Henry Smith, Overseers, 2 August, 1648. Codicil making Provisions for children born Since the Original Will was written . Proven 21 July, 1651. Invt. £1062-01-08.

Children (Weth. Rec.) :

1. John (Capt.), b. 3 Aug., 1635, at Watertown, Mass.* Fam. 2.
2. Dorcas, b. 5 Nov., 1637; m. 12 Nov., 1656, Rev. Samuel **Whiting**; grad. H. C. 1653; 1st min. at Billerica, Mass. (s. of Rev. Samuel W., 1st min. of Lynn, Mass., by his 2d wife, dau. of Rt. Hon. Oliver St. John, of Eng.) ; she d. 16 Feb., and he 28 Feb., 1713, ae. respectively 76 and 80. *Issue:*
    i. Elizabeth (Whiting), b. 6 Oct., 1660; m. Rev. Thos. **Clark**, 2d min. Chelmsford, Mass., as 2d wife.
    ii. Samuel (Whiting), b. 19 Dec., 1662; cornet in the Troop; d. 1714.
    iii. John (Whiting), Rev., b. 1 July, 1664 ; H. C. 1685 ; 2d min. at Lancaster, Mass. ; was shot and scalped by Inds. 11 Sept., 1697; left wid. and ch.
    iv. Oliver (Whiting), b. 8 Oct., 1665 ; many years a "mag." ; left wid. and 6 ch. ; he d. 1736.
    v. Mary (Whiting), b. 28 Apl., 1667.
    vi. Dorothy (Whiting), b. 23 Aug., 1668.
    vii. Joseph (Whiting), b. 7 Jan., 1670; d. 6 Aug., 1701.
    viii. James (Whiting), b. 20 July, 1671 ; d. 1 Aug., 1671.
    ix. Eunice (Whiting), b. 6 Aug., 1672; d. 20 Aug., 1672.
    x. Benjamin (Whiting), b. 26 Aug., 1675 ; d. 18 Sept., 1675.
    xi. Benjamin (Whiting), b. 5, d. 20 Oct., 1682.
3. Stephen, b. 3 Mch., 1639 ; d. Htfd., 23 Apl., 1705, unm. ; for 1d. holdings see Chapt. VII, Vol. I. His est. (invent. taken 7 May, 1705) by Thos. Wickham, Sen., and Samuel Butler, amt'd to £200-15-06 ; the *Prob. Ct.* made his nephew, Maj. John

Chester, his adm'r, and ordered the est. distrib. 1-3 part to the ch. of Capt. John Chester (bro. of the dec'd) ; 1-3 part to Rev. Samuel Whiting, of Billerica, Mass., who had marr. the dec'd's sister Dorcas ; and 1-3 part to the surviving ch. of Capt. Thomas Russell, "late of Charlestown, dec'd," who marr'd the dec'd's sister Prudence.
4. Mary, b. 15 Jan., 1641, at Charlestown, Mass., d. 15 Sept., 1669, unm.
5. Prudence, b. 16 Feb., "or thereabouts," 1643 ; m. 30 Dec., 1669, Capt. Thomas **Russell**, of Charlestown, a son, or nephew of Hon. Richard, of C., who d. 21 Oct., 1676, ae. 35 ; Mrs. Prudence Russell d. 2 Oct., 1678, ae. 35. *Issue:*
    i. Mary (Russell), b. 27 Sept., 1670 ; m. John **Watkins**.
    ii. Thomas (Russell), b. 30 Mch., 1672.
    iii. Prudence (Russell), b. ; m. —— **Dole**, of C.
6. Eunice, b. 15 Jan., "or thereabouts," 1645 ; m. 25 Feb., 1672-3, Capt. Richard **Sprague**, of Charlestown, Mass.; she d. 27 May, 1676, ae. 31; he m. (2) Wid. Catherine **Anderson**; he d. 7 Oct., 1703, ae. 78 ; no issue by either marr.
7. Mercy, b. "the middle of" Feb., 1647 ; d. Charlestown, Mass., 15 Sept., 1669, leaving a will of that date, by which she gave her est. to her sisters, Dorcas (Whiting), Prudence Chester, and Eunice Chester, then both of C., and to her bro., Stephen, also of C., "in such proportion as the testator's dear mother, Mrs. Mercy Russell shall prescribe,"—but making no mention of her sister Mary, who from the rec. must have d. on same day as herself.

Fam. 2. Capt. JOHN,[2] (*Leonard,*[1]) "Worshipful Capt. John Esq.," b. 1635; m. Feb., 1653-4, Sarah (dau. of Hon. Thomas) **Welles**; successively Treas'r, Sec'y, Lt-Gov., and (4th) Gov. of Conn.; he was adm. freeman, May, 1658; was dep. May, 1676, and was a very prominent and useful citizen of the Colony; res. Weth.; d. 23 Feb., 1697-8, ae. 62 yr. 6 mo. 20d.—*W. Ins.;* his wid. d. 12 Dec., 1698, "ae. abt. 67."—*W. Ins.*

Will of *Capt. John Chester.* Died 23 February, 1697-8. Invt. £1133-00-00 taken 25 March, 1697-8 by William Warner and Thomas Welles. Will dated 21 February, 1697-8. I give to my son John Chester my dwelling house with my house lott and Land adjoining to him and to his Male heirs forever. In default of Male heirs—I give—bequeath said house Homelott-Lands to my son Thomas Chester and to his Male heirs forever and this is all the estate which I give conditionally; all the remainder I give positively. I give to my eldest son John Chester—my grist-mill also Land lying at the landing near my brother's [Stephen's] warehouse; also half my farme which the General Court gave me wch was laid out by Doct. John Brockett & Capt. Thomas Yale. I give to my son Thomas

—I ratify to the heirs of my son Stephen Chester, Dec'd. All those Lands which I gave him, I give to my wife, so much of my lands houseing and pastureing as I am now in possession of as she shall see meet to improve during her life. I give to her my plate, viz. Tankard Porringe [r]s, Wine Cups, Silver Spoons, to her and to be at her dispose to give hereafter to such of her children as she shall please. I give to my three dau. Sarah, Prudence, & Eunice, their sums of £100. to be paid to them in Current Country pay, viz. what is yet behind I give to the dau⁸ of my dau, Mary the former wife of Mr. John Wolcott. In lieu of their mothers £25. to Sarah £25 to Prudence £25. to Eunice £25. to be paid in current country pay either before or after their mother's decease— as my wife shall be willing to part with the movables—I give to my brother Stephen Chester £5. I give to the Towne of Wethersfield the Land at the burying yard which I bought of Samuel Willis, Esq., reserving a benefit and privilege therein for my own family & successors. I app't my sons John & Thomas Chester Executors.

JOHN CHESTER, SEN. O.

Witness Stephen Chester ⎫   Court Record 13 April, 1698—Will—Invt—Exhibit
Peter Bulkeley.   ⎭   Sarah Chester the widow.

Children (*Weth. Rec.*) :

1. Mary, b. 23 Dec., 1654 ; m. 14 Feb., 1776-7, John **Wolcott**, of E. Windsor, s. of Henry W., Sen.ʳ; she d. 10 July, 1689, ae. 34 ; he m. (2) 1692, Hannah **Nichols**, of Stamford, Ct. ; he d. 3 Jan., 1712, ae. 68. *Issue* (*by first marr., 6 ch.*) See *Stiles' Hist. & Geneal. of Ancient Windsor*, Vol. II.
2. John (Maj.), b. 10 June, 1656. FAM. 3.
3. Sarah, b. Nov., 1657 ; m. 5 Dec., 1689, Simon **Wolcott**, of Windsor, Ct., s. of Simon and gd-s. of Henry Wolcott, Sen. ; he d. 3 Aug., 1732, in 66th yr. ; she d. 3 Aug., 1723, in 66th yr. *Issue* (6 ch.) See *Stiles' Ancient Windsor*, Vol. II.
4. Stephen, b. 26 May., 1660. FAM. 4.
5. Thomas, b. 23 Mch., 1662. FAM. 5.
6. Samuel, b. 23 May, 1664 ; d. unm., 12 May, 1689.

7. Prudence, b. 10 Dec., 1666 ; m. 17 Dec., 1691, James **Treat**, of Weth. ; she d. 25 May, 1727 ; he m. (2) Hannah (wid. of Daniel) **Boardman**, of Weth. ; he d. 18 Feb., 1742 ; she d. 25 Feb., 1746, ae 82. *Issue,* see *Treat.*
8. Eunice, b. 7 May, 1668 ; m. 17 May, 1694, Rev. Timothy **Stevens**, minister of Ch. at Glast. ; she d. 16 June, 1698, ae. 30 ; he m. (2) Alice (wid. Rev. John) **Whiting**, of Lancaster, Mass. Rev. Mr. Stevens d. 14 Apl., 1726, ae. 61. *Issue:*
   i. Timothy (Stevens), b. 23 Mch., 1695 ; d. 1 Apl., 1695.
   ii. Sarah (Stevens), b. 19 Mch., 1696 ; d. 25 Sept., 1717.
   iii. John (Stevens), b. 4, d. 27 June., 1698.

FAM. 3.   Major JOHN,³ (*Capt. John,*² *Leonard,*¹), Esq., Judge, Speaker of Assembly;

b. 1656; m. 25 Nov., 1686, Hannah (dau. Hon. Samuel) **Talcott**, of Weth., adm. to communion, "Mr. Jno. Chester, Jr., 7. 12 '96, as I remember."—*Mix. Dairy;* for ld. ppy. see Chapt. VII, Vol. I. Major John d. 14 Dec., 1711, ae. 55. Invt. of est. £4277-07-11, taken 26 Jan., 1711-12, by Jona. Belding, Joshua Robbins, 2d, and Samuel Wolcott; will dated 5 Dec., 1711, gives to his two sons, the sum of £200 each; makes his wife Hannah and sons John and Thomas, exec'rs, and by a codicil (10 Dec., 1711) divides equally betw. his sons the ld. given him by he Town. "The goods lying in bottom [ship[which came from Eng., for me, to be distrib. among the family," and the "estate in Eng. and the income thereof, that my executrix and my son* when capable should improve. [employ] Mr. Noah Neal, Esq., of Stamford in the County of Lincoln and his son and heir after him". Will witnessed by Rev. Stephen Mix and Rob't Welles, proven 4 Feb., 1711-12.—*Htfd. Co. Prob. Rec.* His wid.. d. 23 July, 1741, in 77 yr.—*W. Ins.*

---

* His son John was then abt. 9 yrs. old ; and son Thomas d. in May following the father's dth.

Children (Weth. Rec.) :

1. Penelope, b. 21 Oct., 1687; d. 1 Apl., 1688.
2. Mehitable, b. 29 Jan., 1688-9; m. 1 May, 1714, Nathan'l **Burnham**, of Weth., who d. 16 Dec., 1754; she d. 18 Mch., 1773, ae. 84. *Issue:*
   i. Nathaniel (Burnham), b. 16 Jan., 1719.
   ii. Mehitable (Burnham), b. 15 Dec., 1720.
   iii. Peter (Burnham), b. 22 Mch., 1723.
   iv. Jeremiah (Burnham), b. 24 July, 1725.
3. Mary, b. 8 Mch., 1690-1; m. 1 Jan., 1718, Jonathan **Burnham**, of Weth., who d. 24 Jan., 1752, ae. 60; she d. 19 Apl., 1766, ae. 75. *Issue:*
   i. Jonathan (Burnham), b. 7 Nov., 1718; d. 15 Mch., 1740.
   ii. Elizur (Burnham), b. 21 Mch., 1722; d. 26 Dec., 1724.
   iii. Abigail (Burnham), b. 17 Aug., 1727.
   iv. Prudence (Burnham), b. 1 Dec., 1729; d. 27 June, 1730.
   v. Elizur (Burham), b. 24 June, 1733.
   vi. Mary (Burnham), b. 9 Aug., 1736.
4. Penelope, b. 18 Nov., 1693; m. May 24, 1716, Rev. Eleazer **Williams**, 1st min. of Pomfret, Ct., ordd. Oct., 1715; s. of Dea. Samuel, and gd-s. of Robert Williams, one of the first sett. of Roxbury, Mass.; he d. 28 Mch., 1753 in 63d yr.; she d. 27 June, 1764 in 77th yr. *Issue:*
   i. Samuel (Williams), b. 27 May, 1717; d. 17 July, 1717.
   ii. Chester (Williams), b. 29 June, 1718; min. of Hadley, Mass.; m. Sarah (dau. Hon. Eleazur) **Porter**, of H., 1744; he d. 13 Oct., 1752, ae. 36; she d. 5 Feb., 1774, ae. 48; 5 ch.
   iii. Ebenezer (Williams), b. 26 May; d. 11 June, 1720.
   iv. Nehemiah (Williams), b. 15 Sept., 1721; d. 17 Mch., 1739.
   v. Ebenezer (Williams), b. 22 Nov., 1725; Col. Wms. d. 22 Aug., 1780, ae. 57, a distinguished man. His wid. (Jerusha, dau. Hon. Eleazer **Porter**, of Hadley) d. 23 Sept., 1805, ae. 71; had 13 ch.—of whom Elisha (the 12th), b. 1773, became a very distinguished jurist at Hudson, N. Y.
   vi. Hannah, b. 3 July, 1732; m. Jabez **Huntington**, Esq., of Norwich, Ct., 10 July, 1740, as his 2d wife.
5. Hannah, b. 15 May, 1696; m. 30 Nov., 1716, Gideon **Welles**, Esq., of Weth., who d. 28 Mch., 1740, ae. 48; she d. 29 May, 1749, ae. 53. *Issue*, see *Welles*.
6. Prudence, b. 4, (bp. 5 *Mix*) Mch., 1698-99;

m. 13 Dec., 1713, Col. John (grad. H. C. 1701, son of Rev. Solomon) **Stoddard**, of Northampton, Mass., who d. 19 June, 1748; she d. 11 Sept., 1780. *Issue:*
   i. Mary (Stoddard), b. 27 Nov., 1732; m. John **Worthington**, Esq., of Springfield, Mass., 7 Dec., 1768, as 2d wife; he d. 25 Apl., 1800, in 81st yr.; she d. 12 July, 1812. *Issue by sec. marr:*
      i. John (Worthington), b. 22 Apl., d. 11 Aug., 1770.
   ii. Prudence (Stoddard), b. 28 May, 1734; Ezekiel **Williams**, Esq., of Weth., 6 Nov., 1760; he d. 1818, ae. 86. *Issue*, see *Williams' Gen.*
   iii. Solomon (Stoddard), b. 29 May, 1736; sett. Northampton, Mass.; m. (1) Martha **Partridge**, of Hatfield, 21 Nov., 1765; m. (2) Eunice **Parsons**, of Amherst, Mass.; he d. 19 Dec., 1787, ae. 51; 3 ch. by each marr.
   iv. Israel (Stoddard), b. 28 Apl., 1741; sett. in Pittsfield, Mass.; m. Eunice **Williams**, of Hatfield; he d. 27 June, 1782, ae. 41.
   v. Hannah (Stoddard), b. 13 Oct., 1742; d. 5 Aug., 1743.
7. Eunice, b. 11 May, ("bp. the Sabbath following."—*Mix Rec.*), 1701; m. as 2d wife, Col. Joseph **Pitkin**, of E. Htfd.; (his 1st wife was Mary (dau. Rich.) **Lord**, of Htfd.; his third was Eunice (wid. of Gen. Jona.) **Law**, of Milford, Ct. Col. Pitkin d. 3 Nov., 1762, ae. 67; Mrs. Eunice his 2d wife, d. 25 June, 1756, ae. 55; no issue by her.
8. John, b. 30 June (bp. 4 July—*Mix*), 1703. Fam. 6.
9. Sarah, b. 1 July (bp. 13 July—*Mix*), 1707; m. abt. 1731, Col. Israel **Williams**, of Hatfield; grad. H. C. 1729; she d. 18 (8 *gravestone*) 1770, ae. 63; he d. 10 June, (Jan. on *gravestone*) 1788 in 79th yr. *Issue:*
   i. John (Williams), b. 26 May, 1732; grad. H. C. 1751; d. same yr.
   ii. William (Williams), b. 1734; in pub. bus. until Revol.
   iii. Israel (Williams); d. unm.
   iv. Sarah (Williams); m. Dr. Perez **Marsh**, of Dalton, Mass.
   v. Eunice (Williams), m. Maj. Israel **Stoddard**; prob. of Northampton, Mass.
   vi. Jerusha (Williams), m. Elisha **Billings**, Esq., of Conway, Mass.
   vii. Lucretia (Williams), m. John Chandler **Williams**, Esq., of Pittsfield, Mass.
10. Thomas, b. 31 Aug. (bp. 2 Sept. *Mix*), 1711; d. 29 May, 1712, ae. 8 mos. 29 d.

Fam. 4. STEPHEN,[3] (*Capt. John*,[2] *Leonard*,[1]) b. 1660, for ldd. ppy. see Chapt. VII, Vol. I; m. Jemina (dau. Lieut. Jas. & Jemina) **Treat**, of Weth., 17 Dec., 1691; she was b. 15 Mch., 1668; he d. 9 Feb., 1697-8; ae. 37¾ yr.; she d. 5 Oct., 1755.—*W.* (*N.*) Ins. Invent. of est. valued at £1140-00-00.

Children (Weth. Rec.) :

1. Dorothy, b. 5 Sept., 1692; m. Martin **Kellogg**, of Weth., 13 Jan., 1716; res. Newington parish; he d. 13 Nov., 1753 in 68th yr.; wid. d. 26 Sept., 1754, ae. 62.—*W. Ins. Issue* (6 cb), see *Kellogg*.
2. Sarah, b. 5 Mch., 1693-4; m. Joseph **Lamb**, of Southold, L. I.*
3. Mary, b. 26 Oct., 1696.
4. Stephen John, b. (posth.) 14 Feb., 1697-8;

d. 8 June, 1725.—*Weth. Ins.*; being b. five days after his father's dth. (Feb. 9), and his gd-father dying on 23d of same mo. he rec'd the names of both of these progenitors, being thus the first of the fam. to bear more than one Christian name. He grad. Y. C. 1721; d. in 28th yr. unm.—*Yale Biog.* 245.

---

* On authority of the following doc. in *Htfd. Co. Prob. Office:* "An agreement made 27 June, 1738, by Martin Kellogg and Dorothy his wife, of Weth., and by *Joseph Lamb* and *Sarah his wife*, of Southold, L. I., Co. of Suffolk, in the Province of New York, and Mercy Chester, of Weth., the only surviving heirs and co-heirs of Stephen John Chester, do for ourselves and heirs, mutually agree for a division of the estate. Signed and Sealed, Test. Jos. Talcott, Jr., Clerk."

FAM. 5.   THOMAS,⁴ (*Capt. John,³ John² Leonard,¹*), b. 1662; m. Mary (dau. Rich.,
Esq.) **Treat,** of Weth., 10 Dec., 1684—for ldd. ppy. see Chapt. VII, Vol. I; he d.
4 Dec., 1712, in 53d yr.—*W. I.;* wid. d. 1 Jan., 1748, ae. 81.—*W. Ins.* Invent.of
est. taken 23 Jan., 1712-13—amt. £1648-09-01, wid. made adm'r; est. distrib.
to wid.; to dau. Eunice (Williams) : to dau. Mary.—*Htfd. Co. Prob.*

Children (*Weth. Rec.*) :

1. Eunice, b. 22 Nov., 1685 ; m. 23 Feb., 1714, Rev. Elisha **Williams,** 1st pastor of Newington parish, Weth. ; Rector of Yale Coll. ; Colonel and Judge of Superior Ct. of Conn. ; she d. 31 May, 1750 ; he m. (2) Elizabeth (dau. Rev. Thos. **Scott,** of Norwich, Eng., who after his death (1755) m. (2) Hon. Wm. **Smith,** of N. Y. City, 1761, and after his death she resided at Mr. Sheriff Williams, Weth., until her death,

13 June, 1776, at ae. of 68.   *Issue* (*by first marr.*), see *Williams.*
2. Samuel, b. 29 (or 30) 1696 ; d. 17 Mch., 1710-11.—*W. Ins.*
3. John, b. 17 Dec., 1699 ; d. 14 Dec., 1700.
4. Mary, bp. 5 Apl., 1702.
5. Mary, b. 6 Jan., 1705-6 ; m. Thomas **Welles,** Jr., of Weth., 14 June, 1738. *Issue,* see *Welles.*

FAM. 6.   Col. JOHN,⁴ (*Major John,³ Capt. John,² Leonard,¹*), Col. Judge, b. 1703;
grad. H. C. 1722; m. 19 Nov., 1747, Sarah (dau. Rev. James) **Noyes,** her
father being pastor of the First ch. in New Haven, Ct. Mr. Chester frequently
served as a memb. of the Gen. Assembly, and as an Assistant; was Judge of
the Co. Court and an important man in Town and Colony. He d. suddenly,
while superintending work in the hay-field, 11 Sept., 1771. In 1748 he was
said to be the only male, in his line, of the Chester name. The bell in the
belfry of the First ch. of Weth., was his gift, imported fm. Eng. and inscribed
"John Chester, 1761."

His dth. was thus noticed in the *Conn. Courant:* "Wethersfield, 20th Sept.,
1771. On Wednesday the 11th inst., suddenly departed this life, the Hon.
John Chester, Esq., of this Town. He appeared in the morning quite well,
and in high health. About 9 o'clock he rode near three miles into the meadow,
with *Capt. Fisk,* of *Farmington,* where he found some of his hay that needed
opening. After having opened a few cocks, as he was walking from one of
them to another, conversing with a young man who was there concerned in and
about the hay, he suddenly set his fork into the ground, laid his hand on his
breast, and cried out, O dear! and instantly sank down. Capt. Fisk and the
young man ran to his assistance; but no symptoms of life appeared. The
doctors, as soon as possible, were with him, let him blood, and used other
means to recover him, but all to no purpose. His death appears to have been
as sudden as can well be conceived of.

He was a Gentleman, in many views, highly distinguished—was descended from a
train of honorable ancestors—liberally educated at Cambridge, and excellently
furnished by the God of Life, with a genius and superior accomplishments, for
public usefulness and service. In the earlier part of his life he was constantly
a member of the General Assembly; for many years was Colonel of the Sixth
Regiment of Militia; and one of the Assistants of the Colony, and employed in
various other stations of trust and importance in the government; in which
he acquitted himself to his own honor, and the acceptation of the public. He
was a gentleman of great penetration and a settled judgment; of inflexible uprightness, truth and fidelity in his administration; sagacious to discern what was
just and right to be done; steady and firm in pursuing the dictates of his own
mind, and the welfare of the community. As a member of the General Assembly,
and as one of the Hon. Council, he was ever distinguished for his upright and
independent conduct. His inclination and genius, equally with his affluent circumstances in life conspiring to render him, in the departments he sustained
unbaised, either by popular applause or disapprobation, to act contrary to his
sentiments; which, though uncommonly modest in delivering, yet he gave them

when called on, with a freedom and firmness, which demonstrated to his honor, that he had first weighed them, and convinced himself of their justness. He was a friend to, and promoter of order and peace; a steady and exemplary attendant on the worship of God's House and the ordinances of the Gospel, and a friend to its ministers. He was highly esteemed and valued by the people in this place, whose peace and prosperity he wisely and steadily pursued. In a broad wisdom and a sound mind, steadiness, impartiality and integrity; an uncommon spirit of government, and skill and ability to promote the common good; virtue and a solemn profession of the religion of the Son of God; the virtues and duties of the social life; and in the smaller circle of his own family, prudence and fidelity, kindness and economy, with a veil of humility and modesty cast on the whole, marked and distinguished his character.

A strong pillar fell, when Chester died. The execution of his great abilities, for a course of years for the welfare of the Colony, and the peace and happiness of this place, justly demand and call forth a tributary tear. So great was our regard for him; so great our dependance upon him, in this place, that we very sensibly and tenderly feel the impoverishing state—the awful frown of a Sovereign Holy God. The tears of Weathersfield are plentifully wept over the dust of the dead and honored deceased. He deceased in the 69th year of his age, and left a mournful widow and six children—four sons and two daughters." Madam Sarah Chester, d. 25 Jan., 1797, ae. 75.—*W. C. R.*

Children (Weth. Rec.):

1. John (Col.), b. 18, bp. 22 Jan., 1748-9. FAM. 7.
2. Leonard, b. 18 Sept., bp. Oct., 1750. FAM. 8.
3. Sarah, b. 12, bp. 16 Aug., 1752 ; m. 16 Oct., 1782, Thos. **Colt**, of Norwich, (*C. Geneal.* says Canterbury, Ct.). *Issue:*
    i. Frances (Colt), m. Rev. Parker **Adams**, of Johnstown, N. Y.
    ii. Sally (Colt), m. John **Knickerbocker**, of Waterford, N. Y.
    iii. Thomas C. (Colt), m. Mary Ann **Morgan**, of Htfd., Ct.
    iv. Stephen (Colt), m. Betsy **Throop**, of Norwich, Ct.
4. Abigail, b. 27 May, 1754, m. Joseph **Webb**, of Weth., 22 Nov., 1774 ; she d. 16 Mch., 1827.—*Weth. Ins. Issue:*
    i. Sally (Webb).
    ii. Harriet Blackly (Webb).

   iii. Joseph Harper (Webb).
   iv. Eliza Bancker (Webb).
   v. Frances Chester (Webb).
   vi. John Haynes (Webb), b. 1786 ; became a prominent mecht. at Albany, N. Y. ; d. at Htfd, Ct.
   vii. Thomas Chester (Webb), d. yg.
   viii. Amelia (Webb).
   ix. Thos. Chester (Webb).
   x. Henry (Webb).
   ix. Charles Barrel (Webb).
5. Stephen, b. 28 Oct., bp. 1 Nov., 1761. FAM. 9.
6. Thomas, b. 7, bp. 15 Jan., 1764. FAM. 10. Six infs. of this fam. d. betw. 1756 and 1760—three (b. at a birth) lived respectively 1 hour, 11 days, 17 weeks. *Hannah* and *Eunice* (twins) were bp. betw. 19 June and 16 Sept., 1759 ; and *Thomas* was bp. 2 Nov., 1760.—*W. C. R.*

FAM. 7. Col. JOHN,[5] (*Col. John,[4] Maj. John,[3] Capt. John,[2] Leonard,[1]*), b. 18 Jan.,

1748-9; grad. Y. C. 1766, and A. M. at H. C. 1775; sett. Weth.; m. 25 Nov., 1773, Elizabeth (dau. Hon. Jabez) **Huntington**, of Norwich, Ct., she was b. Nov., 1757. As early as 1771 he was a Lieut. in the militia, and in May, 1772, began his public career as a deputy in the General Assembly, a place he filled in 16 more sessions between 1774 and 1787, in the last four being Speaker of the House. On the news of Lexington and Concord he hastened to the front at the head of a picked body of about 100 men which ranked as the most select body in the provincial army of that period, and were distinguished at Bunker Hill. In Jan., 1776, he was promoted to Major, and in March was one of the first officers to enter Boston after the evacuation of the British. In June, app. Col. of one of the regiments raised to serve under Washington at N. Y., and was engaged in battle of L. I. Soon after was made Brigade commander, and was present at battles of White Plains and Trenton. At close of 1776 he was recommended for a Colonelcy in the new Continental Army, but on account of the condition of his personal affairs he declined the appointment and retired to private life, to the great regret, particularly, of Gen. Washington. In May, 1777, received the commission as Justice of the Peace, and was thenceforth much engaged in public business, and was often appointed on important committees by the General Assembly. From 1785 till death was a Judge of the Hartford Co. Court. In 1788 elected to the upper House of the Assembly, or Governor's Council, and held this till 1791, when Pres. Washington app. him Supervisor of U. S. Revenue for the District of Conn., from which he was removed by Jefferson in 1801; and in 1803 he resumed his seat in the Council till 1808, when a paralytic attack obliged him to retire from public business. The following advertisement in the *Conn. Courant* prob. marks the date of his retirement from public life. "The undersigned, being in ill-health, yet grateful for the partiality manifested by the freeman, requests them no longer to consider him a candidate for a seat at the Council Board.—*John Chester.* Wethersfield, March 25, 1809." A member of the State Convention for the ratification of the Constitution of the U. S. in 1788. He died after a little over a year of prostration, Nov. 4, 1809, in his 61st year. His widow survived till July 1, 1834, and died at Burlington, N. J., in her 78th year. Had 6 sons and 6 daughters.—See, also, our Chapt. XI, Vol. I.

Children (Weth. Rec.):

1. Elizabeth, b. 10, bp. 13 Nov., 1774; m. Eleazer Fitch **Backus,** of Albany, N. Y., 8 June, 1807.—*Conn. Courant & W. C. R. Issue:*
   i. Rev. John C. (Backus), D. D., of Baltimore, Md.
   ii. Rev. J. Trumbull (Backus), D. D., of Shenectady, N. Y.
   iii. Elizabeth (Backus), d. unm.
   iv. Mary (Backus), m. Jas. **Bayard,** Esq., of Philadelphia, Pa.
2. Mary, b. 20, bp. 25 Apl., 1779; m. Capt. Ebenezer **Welles,** of Brattleboro, Vt., 8 June, 1806.—*Conn Courant. Issue:*
   i. John (Welles).
   ii. Charles (Welles).
   iii. Henry (Welles).
3. Hannah, b. 27, bp. 28 Oct., 1781; m. Chas. **Chauncey,** Esq., L.L. D., of Phila., 26 Sept., 1808; he b. in New Haven, 1777; grad. Y. C. 1792; d. 30 Sept., 1849; she d. 6 Feb., 1821.—*W. C. R. Issue:*
   i. Charles (Chauncey), grad Y. C. 1828; d. 1831.
   ii. Elizabeth (Chauncey).
   iii. Susan Vaux (Chauncey), d. 1836.
   iv. Hannah (Chauncey).

v. vi. 2 sons, d. inf.
4. Sarah, b. 17, bp. 22 June, 1783; d. unm.
5. John (Rev.), b. 17, bp. 21 Aug., 1785. FAM. 11.
6. Charlotte, b. 20, bp. 25 Mch., 1787; d. 19 July, 1844, unm.
7. Henry, b. 3, bp. 17 Oct., 1790; d. 1 Mch., 1791.—*W. C. R.*
8. Julia, b. 15, bp. 25, 1792; m. 12 Apl., 1816, Matthew C. **Ralston,** of Philadelphia; d. 8. Apl., 1835. *Issue:*
   i. Sarah (Ralston).
   ii. Robert (Ralston).
   iii. Hannah Chester (Ralston).
9. Henry, b. 23, bp. 29 Dec., 1793; grad Union Coll. 1814; lawyer in Phila.; d. 1848, unm.
10. William, bp. 20 Dec., 1795.
11. William (Rev. et. D. D.), b. 20 Nov., 1798; grad U. C. 1815; D. D. Wash. Coll. Pa.; pastor of Pres. Ch. at Hudson, N. Y.; Sec'y Presb. Bd. Education, Phila; m. 1826, Frances M. **White,** of Hudson, N. Y.
12. George, b. 14 June, bp. 22 July, 1798; d. 22 Feb., 1801.
13. Charles, bp. 10 Feb.; d. 10 Sept., 1802.

FAM. 8. LEONARD,[5] (*Col. John,*[4] *Maj. John,*[3] *Capt. John,*[2] *Leonard,*[1]) b. 1750; grad. Y. C. 1769; sett. at Weth.; m. 12 (one acc. says 19) Sept., 1776, Sarah (dau. Col. William) **Williams,** of Pittsfield, Mass., by his 2d wife,——— Welles. By 1783 he had reached the rank of Major of the State Militia. In the strifes subsequent to the Revolution he was subject to criticism by the friends of law and order, and is pilloried in "The *Anarchaid,* a political poem, in 1786, under the name of "Lazarus." He d. of yellow fever in N. Y. City, 17 Aug., 1803, ae. 53; having but recently removed there from Weth.; she d. 3 May, 1835, ae. 76, bu. in N. Y. City.—*W. Ins.*

Children (*Weth. Rec. & W. C. R.*) Those starred[8] bp. 22 June, 1788:

1. Leonard Williams Pepperell, b. 20 Dec., 1777; m. Sabra **Roath**, of Norwich, Ct.; went to sea in H. B. M.'s brig *Quebec*, and was never heard of more; left one ch.
2. Hannah (*Chester Gen.* says, Sarah), b. 8 Aug., 1779; m. ————— **Leffingwell.**
3. Henrietta,* b. 8 Mch., 1781; m. Rev. Mr. **Briggs,** of Boxford, Mass.; 1 ch. d. at No. Rochester, 7 Aug., 1852.—*W. Ins.*
4. Sophia.* b. twin to Henrietta; d. 7 Nov., 1822 at Raleigh, N. C.—*W. Ins.*
5. John Noyes,* b. 20 Mch., 1783; shipmaster; went to sea bound to Java; never heard of again.
6. Sally Williams,* b. 2 Nov., 1784; d.

Liverpool, Eng., 10 June, 1844, ae. 60.—*W. Ins.*
7. William Williams,* b. 13 July, 1786; m. 13 Nov., 1818, Hannah **Sutherland,** of Blenheim, N. Y., who d. 8 Jan., 1863— s. p.; he founded the well-known firm of W. W. Chester & Co., N. Y. City, where he d. 4 Mch., 1869.—*W. T. R.*
8. Thomas Leonard, b. 20 Aug., bp. 12 Oct., 1788. FAM. 12.
9. James Davidson Colt, b. 13 Aug., 1792; dr. in Conn. River, 9 Sept., 1801.—*W. T. R.*
10. Abigail Webb, b. June, 1796; d. Feb., 1801.—*W. Ins.*

FAM. 9. STEPHEN,[5] (*Col. John,*[4] *Maj. John,*[3] *Capt. John,*[2] *Leonard,*[1]) b. 1761; grad. Y. C. 1780; Sheriff of Htfd. Co.; m. 5 Nov. 1788, Elizabeth (dau. of Chief Justice Stephen *Mix*) **Mitchell,** who was b. 11 Sept., 1770 and d. 22 Dec., 1852; he d. 6 Dec., 1835.—*W. Ins.*

Children (*Weth Rec.*,) those starred bp. 19 Apl., 1807.

1. Elizabeth, b. 15 Sept., 1789; d. 1 Oct., 1851 (*W. Ins.*), unm.
2. Maria, b. 17 May., 1791, bp. 5 Aug., 1810; m. Hon. Lewis **Strong,** of Northampton, Mass.; she d. 22 June, 1866; 10 ch. and 8 gd-ch.
3. Stephen Mitchell,* b. 18 Oct., 1793; grad. Y. C. 1813; mcht.; d. 14 Apl., 1862 (*W. Ins.*), unm.
4. Donald,* b. 25 July, 1795; grad Y. C. 1814; mcht.; d. 29 Sept., 1835, unm.—*W. Ins.*
5. Stephen, bu. 1 Oct., 1798, ae. 1.
6. Walter, b. 8 Oct., 1798; d. 28 Sept., 1799.—*W. Ins.*
7. Hannah Grant,* b. 27 May, 1800; d. 12

Mch., 1872, ae. 71 yr. 9 mo.
8. Walter,* b. 20 Nov., 1804; m. Henrietta **Lyman,** of Cazenovia, N. Y., 22 Apl., 1828; he d. 7 Apl., 1880 (*W. Ins.*); she d. 26 Sept., 1882 (*W. Ins.*); 6 ch. and 11 gd-ch.
9. Catharine,* b. 10 Nov., 1806; m. 7 May, 1829, Leonard W. **Belden,** M. D., of Springfield, Mass.; she d. 31 Jan., 1881 (*W. Ins.*), leaving 1 ch.; Dr. B. d. 26 Oct., 1839, ae. 38.—*W. Ins.*
10. Julia Buck, b. 23 Aug. 1809, bp. 8 Apl., 1810; d. 8 Apl., 1835, unm.—*W. Ins.*
11. Emily, bp. 5 Aug., 1810.—*W. C. R.* (?)
12. John, b. 23 Jan., bp. 6 June, 1813; m. Cath. M. **Morrell** of Detroit, Mich., 14 June, 1837; d. 18 Nov., 1852; 3 ch.

FAM. 10. THOMAS,[5] (*Col. John,*[4] *Maj. John,*[3] *Capt. John,*[2] *Leonard,*[1]) b. 1764; grad. Y. C. 1780; m. 26 Mch., 1795, Esther Margaret (dau. Joseph) **Bull,** of Htfd., b. 29 Sept., 1777, and d. 22 June, 1844, ae. 67—*W. Ins.;* he d. 2 Oct., 1831.

Children:

1. Aurella Louisa, b. 19 May, 1796; d. 19 May, 1876.—*W. Ins.*
2. Alfred (Rev.), b. 17 Mch., 1798; grad. Y. C. 1818; m. 24 Aug., 1826, Matilda **Chetwood,** of Elizabethtown, N. J.; he d. N. Y., 2 July, 1871; wife, b. Apl., 1802, d. 10 June, 1879.
3. Caroline, b. 26 Jan., 1801; m. 2 June, 1825, John **Knickerbocker,** of Waterford, N. Y.; she d. 20 Apl., 1869.—*W. Ins. Issue:*
   i. John (Knickerbocker), d. unm.
   ii. Thomas Adams (Knickerbocker), m. Helen **Jones,** of Penn Yan, N. Y.
   iii. Esther Margaret (Knickerbocker), m. Henry T **Walbridge,** of Saratoga Spgs., N. Y.; had (a) John Henry (Walbridge); m. H. O. V. **Agan,** of Saratoga, N. Y.—had *John K.; Benjamin K.,* and *Margaret Caroline;* (b) Thomas Chester (Walbridge), b. 1851; m. Annie E. **Carter,** of Phila; had *Leonard K.,* b. 1883; *Charles

Carter,* b. 1887; (c) Caroline (Walbridge), unm.; (d) William Gedney (Walbridge); m. (1) Esther Adin **Schaeffer,** of Phila; m. (2) Margaret **Ritchle;** has one ch. *William R.;* (e) Louise Chester (Wallridge), d. unm.; (f) Louie C. (Wallridge), m. Louise R. **Castle,** of Sandwich, Kan., has 4 dau.
   iv. Jane Chester (Knickerbocker, m. William Orr **Cunningham,** of Troy, N. Y.; res. Washington, D. C.; has one son *Seymour* (*Cunningham*), of Litchfield, Ct.
4. Mary Jane, b. 10 Nov., 1804; m. Prof. Sylvester **Hovey,** of Amherst Coll.; d. 11 Jan., 1840; had one son, Prof H., d. 6 May, 1840.—*W. Ins.*
5. Elizabeth Huntington, b. 31 Oct., 1807; m. James M. **Bunce,** of Htfd. Co.; d. 6 Mch., 1861; 6 ch.

FAM. 11. Rev. JOHN,[6] D. D., (*Col. John,*[5] *Col. John,*[4] *Maj. John,*[3] *Capt. John,*[2] *Leonard,*[1]) b. 1785; grad. Y. C. 1804; D. D. from U. C. 1821; sett. Nov., 1810, at Hudson, N. Y., where he remained until 1815, when he became the pastor of the Second Presb. Ch., in Albany, N. Y., and served that congrg. until 1827. As a preacher, he was able and useful, affectionately esteemed by his flock, and universally respected by the community at large; he m. Rebecca (dau. of Rob't) **Ralston,** of Philadelphia where he d. 12 Jan., 1829.

His published works were:

1. *A Sermon delivered before the Berkshire and Columbia Missionary Society*, at their annual meeting at Canaan, Sept. 21st, 1813. Hudson, N. Y., 1813, 8 vo. pp. 39.

2. *A Sermon in Commemoration of the Landing of the New England Pilgrims*, delivered in the Second Presb. Ch., Albany, N. Y., Dec. 22, 1820. Albany, N. Y., 1820., 8 vo. pp. 32.

3. *Knowledge and Holiness the Sources of Morality*. A sermon delivered by appointment, before the Albany Moral Society, Oct. 5, 1821, in Albany. Albany, N. Y., 1821, 8 vo. pp. 32.

Soon after his dth. in 1829, a small volume, entitled "Obituary Notices of Rev. John Chester, D. D.," was pub. at Albany. This includes a sermon by Rev. Mark Tucker, then of Troy, N. Y., on Dr. Chester.

Children:

1. Sarah Ralston, m. Rev. Samuel B. **Jones.**
2. Elizabeth Huntington.
3. Hannah Chauncey; m. Jonathan H. **Harbrusk.**
4. Marion Dorsey; d. unm.
5. Mary Welles, m. Martin B. **Inches.**
6. Rebecca Ralston, m. Abram Suydam **Mesier.**

FAM. 12.   THOMAS LEONARD,[7] (*Leonard,*[6] *Col. John,*[5] *Col. John,*[4] *Maj. John,*[3] *Capt. John,*[2] *Leonard,*[1]) b. 1788; m. 15 Oct., 1815, Eliza **Sidell,** who was b. 10 Sept., 1796. He d. N. Y. City, 17 May, 1870.—*W. Ins.*

Children:

1. William Henry, b. 17 Sept., 1816. FAM. 13.
2. Caroline Sarah, b. 5 June, 1818; d. 2 Dec., 1860.
3. John Noyes, b. 25 Sept., 1820. FAM. 14.
4. Eliza, b. 8 Oct., 1822; d. Aug., 1827.
5. Charles Thomas, b. 6 Jan., 1826. FAM. 15.
6. Edward, b. 12 July, 1828; m. Aug., 1848, Sophia **Hoffman.**
7. Stephen, b. 19 Sept., 1830; m. 25 Feb., 1868, Caroline Georgine **Harris,** of Htfd.
8. Henrietta, b. 18 Sept., 1832; d. 24 Apl., 1834.
9. Julia, b. 5 Dec., 1835; m. 31 Aug., 1866, Rev. O. W. **Whittaker,** of Mass.
10. Emeline, b. 20 Apl., 1840; d. 24 Dec., 1841.

FAM. 13.   WILLIAM HENRY,[8] (*Thomas Leonard,*[7] *Leonard,*[6] *Col. John,*[5] *Col. John,*[4] *Maj. John,*[3] *Capt. John,*[2] *Leonard,*[1]) b. 1816; m. 8 June, 1838, Eliza K. **Priest,** of N. Y., who d. 14 Mch., 1846; he m.(2) 9 Oct., 1850, Mary **Cooper,** of Eng. He was in the Union Army during the Civil War, and wounded at Gettysburg, and d. 10 July, 1862.

Children (by 1st Marr.):

1. Eleanor Kip, b. N. Y. City, 28 May, 1840.
2. Eliza Priest, b. Brooklyn, N. Y., 28 Feb., 1846.

(By second marriage):
3. William Fernando, b. San Juan, Cuba, 25 June, 1851.

4. Thomas L., b. N. Y. City, 22 Apl., 1854.
5. John, b. 31 Mch., 1856; d. Aug., 1863.
6. George Washington, b. 4 July, 1858; d. 14 Mch., 1859.
7. Stephen, b. 29 Nov., 1859.

FAM. 14.   JOHN NOYES,[8] (*Thos. L.,*[7] *Leonard,*[6] *Col. John,*[5] *Col. John,*[4] *Maj. John,*[3] *Capt. John,*[2] *Leonard,*[1]) b. 1830; m. 4 Feb., 1862, Fannie A. **Harris,** of Htfd., Ct.

Children:

1. Walter Harris, b. 27 Nov., 1863; d. 26 July, 1864.
2. William Williams, b. 30 Sept., 1866.

FAM. 15.   CHARLES THOMAS,[8] (*Thos. L.,*[7] *Leonard,*[6] *Col. John,*[5] *Col. John,*[4] *Maj. John,*[3] *Capt. John,*[2] *Leonard,*[1]), b. 1826, grad. Y. C. 1845; m. 17 June, 1856, Lucretia **Roberts.**

Children:

1. Charles Frederick, b. 10 May, 1857; d. 25 Aug., 1862.
2. Mary Roberts, b. 4 Mch., 1863.
3. William Sidell, b. 7 Dec., 1865.
4. Susan Guion, b. 8 Dec., 1867.

"The aged Mrs. Chester," d. 3 Oct., 1755.—*N. C. R.*

FREDERICK O. & Luretia, had

1. Oliver Benedict, b. 31 Aug., 1834.   3. Abigail, b. 5 Aug. 1838.—*R. H. C.*
2. Sarah Eunice, b. 26 Mch., 1836.

WILLIAM, m. Patty **Goodrich**, 16 Aug., 1795.—*S. C. R.*

CHURCH, JOHN, m. Anne **Curtis**, 11 Dec., 1735; she prob. the wid. Anne C. who d. 3 Nov., 1790, in 85 yr.—*S. C. R..;* he d. 5 Apl., 1775 in 75 yr.—*W. Ins.*

Children (Weth. Rec. dths. from S. C. R.) :

1. John, b. 27 Oct., 1736; d. 1 Apl., 1811, in 75th yr.
2. Hepzibah, b. 20 Feb., 1738; d. 5 Jan., 1782, in 44th yr.
3. Anne, b. 20 Feb., 1740; d. 26 Jan., 1832, in 92d yr.
4. Christian, b. 17 Feb., 1742; d. 2 [ ] July, 1821, in 79th yr.
5. Elisha, b. 15 Sept., 1747; d. 18 Feb., 1800, in 53d yr.—*S. C. R.; Conn. Courant; Weth. Ins.*

JAMES, d. 4 Nov., 1805, ae. 2-7-12—*W. Ins.*

JONATHAN, ae. 44, d. 11 Aug., 1804.—*W. C. R.; W. Ins.,* say 1801 ae. 41 yrs., his wife Dosha M., d. 10 Nov., 1848, ae. 80.—*W. Ins.*

A JONATHAN, of Weth., m. (pub. 2 May, 1812) Fanny **Kellogg,** of Sheffield, Mass.—*Sheff. T. Rec.*

MOSES, ae. 23, bu. 8 Sept., 1818, in W. I., at St. Petre, Guadaloupe.—*W. C. R.* & *W. Ins*

Wid. ——— Church, a son of d. 4 Nov., 1805.—*W. C. R.*

Note. Miss MARY C. BRISTOL, of 93 Madison Ave., N. Y. City, who is working (1901) on a hist. of the C. family which sett. in Great Barrington, Mass., betw. 1748 and '50, has been told that a *Moses and* poss. a *David,* of that family, came from Weth. and that they were desc'ts of Capt. Church of Indian War fame; also that, in a pub. geneal. of the C. famliy, by Arnold, of Providence, R. I., these two names do not appear.

MARY ANN (wife of Roderick Grimes) b. 21 Sept., 1793; d. 29 Feb., 1872.

MOSES, ae. 23, bu. 8 Sept., 1818, in W. I. at St. Petre, Guadaloupe,—*W. C. R.; W. Ins.,* wid. ——— Church, a son of d. 4 Nov., 1805.—*W. C. R.*

CHURCHILL,* *(Churchell)* JOSIAH, **CHURCHELL,** as he himself spelt the name, must have been in Weth. by 1638, the year he married Elizabeth (dau. of Nathaniel and Elizabeth *Deming*) **Foote.** He may have come to Weth. two or three years earlier, but nothing is definitely known about him until he appears as the fortunate husband of a daughter of Nathaniel Foote.

The first entry relating to his real estate in Weth. reads as follows:

---

* It is understood that a full genealogy of the Mass. and Conn. Churchills is being prepared, by the co-operation of Mr. N. W. Churchill, of BOSTON, and Rev. GEORGE N. BODGE, of Westwood, Mass. It is understood that a claim is made by some that the family derives from the De Corncey (Cornelio), of France, renowned long before the Conquest, and that it is related to the well-known English family of Churchills. This, however, is not yet proven, and the Weth. Churchills "take no stock" in such a claim.—H. R. S.

In the compilation of the Churchill records, we acknowledge our great indebtedness to the local acquaintance and genealogical accuracy of Hon. E. STANLEY WELLES, of Newington ; as well as to GEORGE DUDLEY SEYMOUR, ESQ., of New Haven, Ct., a descendant of the Newington Churchills, who has furnished the autographs and portraits which accompany this family sketch, as well as the interesting engravings, illustrative of the Capt. Charles Churchill Mansion, in our Chapter XVII.—H. R. S.

"The 2d month & 28th daie 1641 the lands of Josias Churchell lying in Weth. on Connecticutt river

One pece whereon his howse standeth con: six acr* more or lesse Theands [the ends] abutt against the hie waie west & great mea: east The sides against the waie into the great mea: South & the howse lott of John Jesiope (Jessup) North"*

This homestead was on the East side of High street, on the North corner of an ancient road leading to the "Great Meadow" and the river. It faced the Southern extremity of the Common, which stretched North from his house to the river. But he did not reside here all his life, for under the heading Dec., 1659, we have this entry: "The Hom lot of Josias Churchell which he bought of Mr. Tentor [Taintor] which was Gildeslieves formerly, living in Weth. on Connecticut River."†

This homestead of Richard Gildersleeve was on the West side of High street a few doors South of Josiah Churchell's earlier home.

It is diff. to glean much of interest from the recs. abt. the first sett. of Weth., but *Hinman's* estimate of Josiah Churchell in his *Genealogy of the Puritans* would seem to be true: "He was a gentleman of more than a medium estate for the time in which he lived, and of reputation in the colony."

Though he held no positions of the highest importance in Weth., he was quite actively eng. in pub. affairs. He was a juror at the Particular Court in June, 1643, June, 1649 and March, 1651; at the "Quarter" Court, December, 1664, and September, 1665, and at the County Court, October, 1666, March, 1670, and March, 1675. He was elected a constable in February, 1657, and February, 1670, and was chosen one of the two town surveyors in February, 1666 and 1673.

Josiah Churchell executed his will the 17th of November, 1683. The inventory of his estate was taken 5 January, 1686-7, by James Treat and John Buttolph, selectmen of Weth., and amounted to £618-12-6.

It shows that he owned at the time of his death two home-lots and one hundred and ten acres of land. He left his son Joseph "that house and hom lott he now lives on" together with several other pieces of land, and a fifty acre lot "at ye west end of Weath. bounds" in the newly settled tract to be known, a generation later, as the parish of Newington.

His son Benjamin received a number of pieces of land, and the old homestead at the decease of his mother. The daughters, as was customary in those days, had to be content with their proper shares of the "moveable estate."

The inventory itemizes "a graet chist" and "2 bibells and other books." This "graet chist" probably reappears in the inventory of his son Joseph which specifies a chest with the initials "J. C." as well as a piece of "turkie work."

The precise date of Josiah Churchell's death is unknown, but it prob. occurred in 1686. His wife, Elizabeth (Foote) died 8 Sept., 1700, aged about 84.

Children:

1. Mary b. 24 Mch. 1639; m. (prob.) Samuel (s. of Richard) **Church**, of Hadley, Mass.; he d. 13 Apl., 1684. His wife's dth. is not given.—See Judd's *Hadley*, pp. 461-2. *Issue:*
  i. Mary, b. 23 Jan., 1665; m. 1684, Samuel **Smith**, and d. 18 June, 1700.
  ii. Samuel, b. 19 Aug., 1667.
  iii. Richard, b. 9 Dec., 1669; m. 24 Jan., 1696, Sarah **Bartlett**, and was slain by the Indians 15 Oct., 1696.

  iv. Mehitable, b. 11 Jan., 1672; m. Nehemiah **Dickinson**.
  v. Josiah, b. 10 Apl., 1673.
  vi. Joseph, b. 26 May, 1678; d., unm., 1721.
  vii. Benjamin, b. 1 Sept., 1680.
  viii. John, b. 24 Dec., 1682.
2. Elizabeth, b. 15 May, 1642; m. 31 Oct., 1660, Henry **Buck**, of Weth.; he d. 17 July, 1712, ae. 86 yrs.; date of wife's dth. unknown. *Issue:*

* *Weth. Town Recs.* I, p. 204.
† *Ibid.*, p. 205.

i. Henry.
ii. Samuel, b. 2 Feb., 1664.
iii. Martha, b. 15 Oct., 1667.
iv. Elizabeth, b. 6 June, 1670.
v. Mary, b. 12 Mch., 1673.
vi. Sarah, b. 25 July, 1878.*
vii. Ruth, b. 4 Dec., 1681.
viii. Mehitable, b. 4 Jan., 1684.—See Timlow's *Southington*, p. 35.
3. Hannah, b. 1 Nov., 1644; m. (perhaps) 9 Jan., 1666-7, Samuel **Royce**, of New London and Wallingford. She prob. d. before Nov. 1683, as she is not ment. in her father's will of that date.—See Caulkin's *New London*, p. 294.

4. Ann, b. 1647; m. ———— **Rice**, as shown by her father's will.
5. Joseph (Sgt.), b. 7 Dec., 1649. FAM. 2.
6. Benjamin (Lieut.), b. 16 May, 1652. FAM. 3.
7. A son, d. at age of one year.
8. Sarah, b. 11 Nov., 1657; m. ———— **Wickham**, as indicated by her father's will. While it is stated that she married Cornet Thomas Wickham, of Wethersfield, the records plainly show that he married Mary ————, for his wife and that his children, six at least, were born of this Mary.—*E. S. W.*

FAM. 2. Sgt. JOSEPH,[2] (*Josiah*,[1]), b. 7 Dec., 1649; m. 13 May, 1674, Mary ————; he was one of the beneficaries named in the will of his maternal grandmother Elizabeth (Deming) (Foote) wid. of Gov. Thomas Welles. In an indenture dated Nov. 30, 1688, he is styled "husbandman."†

The property on which he lived was inher. from his father and appears to be the ho.-lot described as belonging to Josiah Churchell under date of Dec., 1659, in the following language:

"On pece a ho-lot whereon a house standeth contaings three ac (acres) more or less the ends abutt against the streat east and Mr. Wells weast the sids against the Hom lot of Sam Welles South and John Hubburd North."

In the inventory of the estate of Joseph Churchell his home lot is mentioned as consisting of three acres which would indicate that he passed his life on the homestead devised to him by his father. It is interesting to note the gradual promotion of Joseph Churchell to position of weight in his native place. At the age of 30 he was one of the town surveyors; three years later his name appears as one of the listers or assessors; the following year—1684—he was elected a collector of taxes. In 1689 he was chosen constable; he was again made lister in 1695, and at the annual town meeting held Dec. 27, 1697, "Sergt." Joseph Churchell was elected a selectman; at the next annual town meeting held Dec. 26, 1698, "Sergt." Churchell was re-elected selectman. and was serving in that capacity when he d. April 1, 1699,‡ at the age of 49. He left a comfortable estate of £461.

Mary, the wid. of Joseph Churchell lived to an advanced age. She is ment. as "Widow Mary, Senior" in the distribution of her son Nathaniel's est., April 2, 1728. It would appear that it was her est. which was invent. July 4, 1738, if so, she probably died that year.

His heirs according to a valuable memorandum at the end of the inventory were: *Children* (*Weth. Land Recs.*, I, 1640, p. 17.):

1. Mary (Edwards), 25 yrs., b. 6 Apl., 1675.
2. Nathaniel, eldest son, 22 yrs., b. 9 July, 1677. FAM. 4.
3. Eliza, 21 yrs., m. Richard **Butler.**
4. Dina, 18 yrs.
5. Samuel (Ens.), 11 yrs. FAM. 5.
6. Joseph, 9 yrs.
7. David,
8. Jonathan.§ FAM. 6. } 7 yrs., b. abt. 1693.
9. Hannah, 3 yrs.

FAM. 3. Lieut. BENJAMIN,[2] (*Josiah*,[1]), b. May 16, 1652, m. July 8, 1676, Mary ————.

At the age of 23 he was elected a surveyor, and thereafter during a public life of unusual activity his services in that capacity were in constant requisition. He

* This Sarah Churchill m. Sergt. John (*Dan'l*,[1] *Rose*,[2] *Robt.*[3]) **Rose.** Their dau. Anne (Rose), m. Elisha[4] **Coleman.** Their son Peleg[5] (Coleman), m. Rebecca **Dickinson.** His son Elisha[d] (Coleman), m. Hannah **Loveland.** Their dau. Abigail[7] (Coleman), m. Nathan W. **Pelton.** Their dau. Elizabeth Anne[8] (Pelton), m. Philo S. **Newton.** Their dau. Anna C.[9] (Newton), m. Geo. Fuller **Hawley.**
† *Wethersfield Town Records*, Vol. 3, p. 284.
‡ This date appears in the heading of the inventory of his estate on file at the Probate Office, Hartford, Conn.
§ A Jonathan had (*N. C. R.*) William, bp. 5. Nov., 1727; Benjamin and Hezekiah (twins), bp. 22 Sept., 1731, "abt. 14 days, possibly."

early held the offices of collector, lister and constable. At the age of 37 he was chosen a selectman and served a number of yrs. in that position. He was chosen on a comm. to build a school house in 1677. In 1698 he was one of a comm. of five to "new seat y⁰ meeting house." For his.ldd. ppy. see Chapt. VII, Vol. I. As surveyor he was not only selected by his townsman to lay out tracts of land in Weth., but he was also on several occasions appointed by the General Assembly on committees of survey for other towns.

He was app. May 8, 1701, Lieut. of the trainband at the north part of Weth. Strangely enough his death is not entered on the records. He was living in April, 1728,¹ but the tax list of Weth. for 1730 does not contain his name. His wife Mary, d. Oct. 30, 1712.

Children (Weth. Rec.):

1. Josiah, b. 8 Jan., 1676-7. FAM. 7.
2. Prudence, b. 2 July, 1678.
3. Abigail, b. 18 Feb., 1680-81.

FAM. 4. NATHANIEL,³ *(Joseph,² Josiah,¹)*, b. 1677; m. October 9, 1701,, Mary (dau. of John) **Hurlbut,** of Midd., by his wife Mary (dau. of John & Honor *Treat*) **Deming,** of Weth. He rem. from the old Wethersfield parish, across Cedar Mountain to the Westernmost Society of the town near Farmington bounds. He was active in furthering an exchange of lands in that region with Far., and his name appears in the request of a committee dated April 7, 1715, and in a petition to the General Assembly at its May session of the same year.

He must have d. soon after this, for the inventory of his estate was taken Feb. 28, 1715-16. Jabez Whittlesey and Benjamin Churchell distrib. the est. which was appraised at £371 5s. 6d. His wid. Mary was living as late as 2 April, 1728, when the distrib. was made.

Children (Weth. Rec.):

1. Nathaniel, b. 29 Oct., 1703 (bp. same month, *Mix*). FAM. 8.
2. John, b. 19 Jan., 1705-6 ; rem. to Chatham, Ct. ; m. 8 Jan., 1727, ——. *Issue:*
 1. Mary.
11. John.
3. Daniel, b. 3, bp. 5 Nov., 1710. FAM. 9.
4. Josiah, bp. 8 Aug., 1714.—*Mix.*
5. Stephen (?).
6. Solomon (?).

FAM. 5. Ensign SAMUEL,³ *(Joseph,² Josiah,¹)*, b. —— 1688, d. in Newington parish July 21, 1769. He m. June 26, 1717, Martha **Boardman,** b. Dec. 18, 1695; d. a wid. Dec. 14, 1780. She was the 6th child of Daniel and Hannah *(Wright)* Boardman of Wethersfield, and a gd-dau. of Samuel Boardman of Claydon, near Oxford, Eng., one of the first settlers of Weth. and for many years one of its most prominent citizens. Samuel Churchell res. in New. parish in a house on the hill-side just South of the present res. of Miss Mary Churchill.* He lies buried in the New. churchyard where there is a stone to his memory. Like his father and gr-father, he was active in affairs of church and town.

In one of the Weth. deeds he is termed a "smith." His name appears frequently on the records of the New. Soc. He was a member of the prudential committee and served several times on th school committee. He was on various commit-

---

* Samuel ·Churchill bo't ld. in New. as early as 1712, for on p. 14, Vol. 6, of the *Weth. Town Rec.,* is rec. a deed from Joseph Allen to Samuel Churchill, conveying a "certain fifty-two acre lott formerly Held and Claimed by Mr. Nicholas Moorcock of Boston in y⁰ County of Suffolk within her Majesties province of y⁰ Massachusets bay in New England, Brewer, S⁴ lot Scituate Adjoyning to y⁰ land of Cap⁴. Robert Wells on y⁰ South ; y⁰ lands of Jonathan Deming North ; upon y⁰ East & West Commons." Dated, January 18, 1711. Allen bought this "Lott of Wood-Land of Nicholas Moorcock and Amy his wife, Sept. 7, 1704.—*Weth. Town Recs.,* Vol. 3, pp. 374 & 5.

New. Ch. Rec., gives names of Sarah, Olive and Stephen, *gd-ch.,* of Ens. Samuel, bp. on his wife's account. 23 Nov., 1760.

tees of repairs for the meeting house school house, &c., and one vote of the
Society taken June 26, 1721, in anticipation of the settlement and ordination of
the Rev. Elisha Williams is of peculiar interest. It reads:—

Voted and agreed as followeth: Samuel Hunn, Jabezeth Whittlesey, Richard
Borman, *Samuel Churchel* should undertake to make twenty thousand bricks
for Mr. Elisha Williams, to take the care, and provide hands and all things for
said work.

At a meeting of the Society held Dec. 20, 1732, Samuel Churchill and 2 others
were appointed on a Committee "to seat our meeting house."

Appointed at its May session 1746 by the General Assembly to an Ensigncy, he
afterwards bore the title of Ensign. He d. 21 July 1767.—*W. Ins.*

Children (Boardman Genealogy):

1. Giles, b. 11 June, 1718; m. and sett. in
   Stamford, N. Y.
2. Samuel, b. 27 Apl., 1721.—See *Appendix* to
   this genealogy.
3. Charles (Capt.), b. 31 Dec., 1723. FAM. 10.
4. Jesse (Dea.), b. 31 Aug., 1726. FAM. 11.
5. Benjamin, b. 10 Apl., 1729; m. Abigail
   Barnes, of Bristol, where he sett. and d.

3 June, 1819.—*B. Ch. Rec.*
6. William, b. 6 Nov., 1732; m. (1) Ruth
   Tryon; m. (2) Abiah **Wildman.**
7. David (?).
   New. Ch. Rec. give names of Sarah, Olive
   and Stephen, *gd-ch.* of Ens. Samuel, bp.
   on his wife's account, 23 Nov., 1760.

FAM. 6. DAVID,[3] (*Joseph,[2] Josiah,[1]*), m. Dorothy —————.

Children (Weth. Rec.):

1. Dorothy , b. 3 Oct., 1726.
2. Elizabeth, b. 1 Feb., d. 19 June, 1729.
3. Betty, b. 9 June, 1731; d. 21 May, 1754.—
   W. Ins.

4. David, b. 16 Oct., 1733, bp. 10 Jan., 1735
   (*N. C. R.*); d. 9 Jan., 1775.—*W. Ins.*
5. Anne, b. 23 Oct., 1737.
6. Joseph, b. 31 May, 1743.

FAM. 7. JOSIAH,[2] (*Benjamin,[2] Josiah,[1]*), b. 1676-7; constable 1711; on school
comm. 1714; m. 1706, Elizabeth (dau. Mr. Thomas) **Toucey**, who d. 28 Oct.,
(Sept.—*W. Ins.*) 1751, in 50th yr.; he d. 22 Aug., (July—*W. Ins.*) 1751; is
called, in *Co. Ct. Rec.*, an attorney.

Children (Weth. Rec.):

1. Arminel, b. 20 (or 26) Feb., 1708-9 (*Mix
   MSS.* say bp. 7 Feb., perhaps 27, 1708-9).
2. Prudence, b. 20, bp. 24 Dec., 1710.—*Mix.*
3. Hezekiah, b. 20, bp. 24 Aug., 1712 (*Mix*);
   d. 24 June, 1714.
4. Mary, b. 6, bp. 17 (*Mix*) June, 1716.

5. Sarah, b. 11, bp. 17, *Mix*, June, 1716.
6. Josiah, b. 28 June, 1720; d. 28 Feb., 1791
   in 71st yr. (*W. Ins.*); poss. the Josiah who
   m. Eunice **Deming**, 2 May, 1751.—*Weth.
   Rec.*

FAM. 8. NATHANIEL,[4] (*Nath'l,[3] Joseph,[2] Josiah,[1]*), b. 1703, m. Rebecca **Griswold.**

Children (Weth. Rec.):

1. Abigail, b. 28 Sept., 1727.
2. Mary, b. 22 Aug., 1729.
3. Nathaniel, b. 25 June, 1731.
4. Rebecca, b. 10 Feb., 1734.

5. Lucy, b. 3 May, 1736.
6. Janna, b. 20 Feb., 1738.
7. Amos, b. 5 Mch., 1743; m. Lydia **Cole**, of
   Meriden, Ct., and sett. at Midd. (?).

FAM. 9. DANIEL,[4] (*Nath'l,[3] Joseph,[2] Josiah,[1]*), b. 1710; m. 16 June, 1736, Abigail
White.

Children (Hurlbut Genealogy):

1. Ruth.
2. Sarah.
3. Abigail, d. yg.
4. Elisha.
5. William.
6. Benjamin.
7. Daniel.
8. Abigail.

FAM. 10. Capt. CHARLES,[4] (*Samuel,[3] Joseph,[2] Josiah,[1]*), b. in New. parish Dec.
31, 1723, d. there Oct. 29, 1902. He m. Nov. 19, 1747, Lydia (dau. of Josiah
and Mabel *Wright*) **Belden**, and a descendant of Richard Belden of Weth., the
emigrant. Her paternal grandmother was Dorothy Willard, a descendant of
Major Simon Willard, one of the founders of the town of Concord, Mass., and
celebrated in the early annals of the Massachusetts Colony. They were m. by

the Rev. Joshua Belden of Newington whose kinswoman she was. She b. Sept., 1725, d. March 19, 1805.

To give a detailed sketch of Capt. Charles Churchill* would almost be giving the history of Newington parish for the last half of the 18th century. Perhaps no name appears so frequently as his during that period. In the highest sense of the term, he was a public spirited gentleman. For thirteen years in succession, he was a member of the Society's Committee; chosen Moderator of the Society's Meeting Dec. 7, 1778, he was called upon, after 1781, to preside at those meetings year after year until 1801, the year before his dth. He was placed on many committees of weight and confidence, and on Aug. 31st, 1786, as the Church Records state, "Charles Churchill, Esq. was chosen to the office of deacon." He was app. Captain of the 10th Company or trainband in the 6th militia reg. by the General Assembly at its May session 1762, and for twenty years on the Society Records his name is inscribed as *Capt. Charles Churchill.*

Throughout the Revolutionary War he gladly sacrificed his own interest for the sake of his country. With Capt. Martin Kellogg and other leading citizens of Weth., he was on the first committee app. by the town to take action on the impending war, at a town meeting held June 16, 1774, to consider the Resolution passed on the second Thursday of May preceeding by the Colonial House of Representatives.

At town meetings held April 7th, 1777, July 2nd, 1778 and June 19th, 1780, he was placed on other important committees appointed for raising men for the line, and providing food and clothing for the soldiers and their families. It is current in his family that he was untiring during the war in securing food and clothing for the troops in the field.

He entertained his company more than once at his fine house, and it is said at such times its five great baking ovens were kept going at the same time, and that he roasted a whole ox in the ample fire place in the cellar.

In the *Record of Connecticut Men in the War of the Revolution*, he is listed (p. 548) as Captain of one of the Militia Companies that turned out to repel Tyron's invasion of New Haven, July 5, 1779; he also appears (p. 626) as Captain in the 6th Militia Regiment, but unfortunately nothing further is recorded of his field services. It is told of him that at one time when he was off at the war with his three sons, Levi, Charles and Samuel, his wife sent him word of the difficulty she was having in running the farm without his or their aid. His reply shows the intrepid spirit of the man: "But I left you Benjamin and Joseph," meaning the younger sons Silas and Solomon.

During the last twenty years of his life, Capt. Charles Churchill appears on the Society Records as *Charles Churchill, Esq.* Such a change of titles indicates that when he laid aside the duties of a soldier, he assumed those of a Justice of the Peace.† To qualify himself better to discharge the duties of this office, he collected a library of law books, some of which are still in existence. It is interesting to note here that his Will, one of considerable length, is entirely in his own handwriting. His est. was appraised at $3834.80 by Abel Andrus and Lemuel Whittlesey. Besides managing a farm of one hundred and twenty acres, Capt. Churchill conducted a tannery and in the tax lists was liberally assessed for a "faculty" or trade. He was also licensed as a "taverner" or inn-keeper, by County Court, in June, 1747. It is related that he always prayed standing before the "bowfat" cupboard in the "North Room" as the Wainscoted parlor in his house was called.

---

* Unlike his father and his forbears, he spelt the name Churchill.
† App. Justice of the Peace, at May session of Gen. Assembly, 1778.

MARCIA (OR MARY) BOARDMAN,
WIFE OF SAMUEL CHURCHILL.

SAMUEL,
SON OF CAPTAIN CHARLES CHURCHILL.

By Courtesy of Geo. D. Seymour, Esq.

There are no portraits in existence of Captain Charles or his wife, but some leaves sewed into a little book found with other papers in Samuel Churchill's house, contain the following entry which, in a way, takes the place of other portraiture. The entry is incomplete and I do not identify the handwriting, but from the context I feel sure that these tributes were written by one of Samuel Churchill's children.

"March 25th 1805.

Feb. 10th, Sunday, Grandmother came over to our house, said she did not feel very well, & wanted that I should make her some tea, most of the family had gone to meeting. I was very glad to please her in any thing that she required, because that she was always so good to us all—she drank some tea, thanked me for my trouble and went home. I think that was the last time that ever she came into our house; she was taken sick pretty soon after; she died March 19th. She never spoke after Sunday afternoon till she died, Tuesday night (3 o'clock) but was in the utmost distress that could be.

Grandmother had six children and 39 grandchildren and great grandchildren when she died. Oh may all follow her pious example, and walk in the paths of virtue as she walked, whose loss we mourn. O what a kind, kind mother we have lost, I think she was as tender of her grand-children as own mothers are. Oh how often have I experienced her goodness, but not only me, but all of her dear offsprings. Oh how often has she spoke kindly unto me, and took my hand and told me, that I was born to hard fortune. (She said my hands indicated hard Labor.)

I think I shall never forget my dear Grandmother, nor my Grandfather neither, I think of him many times, and particularly I have heard him read, and in his prayers, he used to have that passage—Man Loveth Darkness rather than light because his deeds are evil,—and many more passages, when I hear mentioned, brings my Grandfather to mind. Oh that his children were as good, as kind, as Charitable to the poor as their parents were. It is striking that they had six Children living at their Death & only one that ever made any public profession of Religion, that one a minister, (the Rev. Silas) altho a minister he will not save his brethren, from" (here the writing breaks off.)

The old lady's interest in palmistry gives a natural touch to this simple record of her last days.

Captain Churchill and his wife Lydia lie buried in the churchyard at Newington Center.

Children (Weth. Rec.) bp. from N. C. R.:

1. Hannah b. 11, bp. 12 Jan., 1748-9; d. 13 Jan., 1749.
   "March 28th, 1751, we had a son born and lived about half an hour and then died."— *Old Record.*
2. Levi, b. 28 May, bp. 7 June, 1752; d. 12 Feb., 1836; m. 30 Oct., 1771, Elizabeth (dau. of Joseph) **Hurlbutt**, Jr. FAM. 12.
3. Mary, b. 22, bp. 23, d. 27 Sept., 1753.
4. Charles, Jr., b. 3, bp. 4 May, 1755. FAM. 13.
5. Samuel, b. 15, bp. 16 Apl., 1757. FAM. 14.
6. Hannah, b. 28. bp. 31 Dec., 1758; d. 25 Jan., 1838; m. (1) 27 Apl., 1786, Seth **Kilbourn**, who d. 27 Oct., 1802; m. (2) 8 June, 1806, Stephen **Webster**.
   "July 18th, 1761, we had a son born and lived an hour and died."—*Old Record.*
7. Solomon, b. 29 July, bp. 5 Aug., 1764. FAM. 15.
8. Silas (Rev.), b. 5 Apl., 1769. FAM. 16.

FAM. 11. Dea. JESSE,[4] (*Ens. Samuel,*[3] *Joseph,*[2] *Josiah,*[1]), b. 1726; m. (1) 3 Nov., 1750—*R. H. C.,* Jerusha **Gaylord**, of Far.; m. (2) 29 Nov., 1769 Sarah[4] (dau. Nath'l,[3] Nath'l,[2] Samuel,[1]) **Boardman**, and wid. of Nicholas **Cady**, of Stepney; m. (3) 15 June, 1778, wid. Elizabeth **Belden**, who d. 3 July, 1794 ae. 58—*W. C. R.* He, at first, res. in Bristol, Ct.,; but rem. to and res. at New. where he d. 7 May, 1806 in 80 yr.—*W. C. R.*

226 GENEALOGIES AND BIOGRAPHIES OF ANCIENT WETHERSFIELD.

Children (Boardman Geneal.; b. Weth.):

1. Jesse (Rev.), b. 18 Mch., 1757. FAM. 16a.
   (By second marriage):
2. Ithamar, b. 1 Nov., 1772; m. Elizabeth Blinn; d. 4 Sept., 1852.
3. Sally, b. 1774; m. Cyrus **Ranger.**
4. Nathaniel Cady, bp. 20 Oct., 1776.— *W. C. R.*
5. Martha, m. Benajah (s. Israel) **Boardman,**

of New.
(NOTE.—The *Boardman Geneal.* credits Rev. Jesse with two other ch., names not given. *Weth. Ins.* give a *Jerusha,* d. 1 July, 1849, ae. 63, who may be one of the two; *Mabel,* d. 31 July, 1879, ae. 89, who may have been the other.—H. R. S.

FAM. 12. Capt LEVI, (*Capt. Charles,*), b. 1752; m. 30 Oct., 1771, Elizabeth (dau. Joseph, Jr., & Hannah) **Hurlbut,** who was b. 28 Dec., 1748; res. in New.; he prob. m. (2) Hannah **Belden,** 12 Jan., 1785— *W. C. R.;* he d. 12 Feb., 1836, ae. 76.—*W. Ins.*

Children (bp. New. Ch. Rec.):

1. Elizabeth, bp. 27 Jan., 1773.
2. Noble, bp. 17 Jan., 1779; m. 12 Oct., 1802, Olive **Stoddard,** of Weth.
3. Charles Belden, bp. 5 Mch., 1786; m. Elizabeth **Hubbard,** both of Weth., 24 Feb., 1807.
4. Octavia, } bp. 11 Mch., 1787, twins.
5. Dau., }
6. Ch. ae. 3, bu. 16 Feb., 1791—*W. C. R.,*— prob. the ch. given in *W. Ins.,* as Samuel

(s. of Mr. Levi & Hannah); d 17 Feb., 1791, in 4th yr.
7. Silas,
8. Caroline,
9. Benjamin, } bp. 5 Jan., 1800.
10. Hannah, }
11. Sophia, }
12. Mary, }
13. Son, bp. 31 May., 1807.

FAM. 13. CHARLES,[5] Jr., (*Capt. Charles,*[4] *Samuel,*[3] *Joseph,*[2] *Josiah,*[1]), b. 1735; d. 16 Sept., 1818; rem. to Chapel Hill, nr. Newborn, N. C.; m. a Southern woman and had

Children:

1. Chappell McClure.
2. Claudius Belden.
3. Clinton Greene.
4. Constant Woods.
5. Crispen Osborne.
6. Cleopus Washington; this family rem. to New Orleans, Lou.

FAM. 14. SAMUEL,[5] (*Capt. Charles,*[4] *Ensign Samuel,*[3] *Joseph,*[2] *Josiah,*[1]), was b. in New. parish April 5, 1757, and d. there Dec. 10, 1834; he m. Mercy **Boardman,** July 16, 1778, in Rocky Hill, Aug. 2, 1757, (dau. of Jonathan & Martha) Boardman, a soldier of the old French War and a descendant of Samuel Boardman, of Cleydon, Oxfordshire, and afterwards of Weth. (See *Boardman Genealogy.*)

Samuel Churchill was a farmer and lived across the road from his father Capt. Charles Churchill, in a house built for him by his father. He was a man of great piety, and perhaps not without humor, for he is said more than anything else to have enjoyed reading that Psalm which constantly reiterates:—"His Mercy endureth forever."[*]

Children:

1. Chislieu, b. 4, bp. 17 Dec., 1779. FAM. 17.
2. Mary Ann. b. 25 Aug., 1782, bp. 19 Jan., 1783; d. unm. Feb., 18, 1848.
3. John, b. 11 Apl., 1785. FAM. 18.
4. Josiah Belden, b. 29 Aug., bp. 30 Dec., 1787; m. (1) Octavia **Churchill,** his cousin, (2) Phoebe Maria **Thompson.**
5. Charles, b. 12 Sept., 1790; m.. Matilda **Johnson.**
6. Mercy, b. 10 Nov., bp. 15, 1792; d. unm. 7 May, 1866.—*W. Ins.*
7. Samuel, b. (twin to Mercy); d. inf.
8. Charlotte, b. 3 Dec., 1795, bp. 10 July, 1796; d. unm. 7 Apl., 1864.—*W. Ins.*
9. Harriet, b. 12 Feb., bp. 3 June, 1798; d. unm. 12 July, 1825.—*W. Ins.*
10. Lucy, b. 6 Feb., bp. 26 July, 1801; d. unm. 30 Mch., 1883.—"Aunt Lucy".—*W. Ins.*

Mary Ann (called Polly), Mercy, Charlotte, Harriet and Lucy, daughters of above family, were a quintet of old maids who lived and died in the old homestead. Of them Charlotte was in every way the most accomplished. She was what they used to call in those days a "dressy" person, and seems to have been

───────

* A covert allusion to his wife's Christian name?

CHARLOTTE, DAUGHTER OF SAMUEL CHURCHILL.

By Courtesy of Geo. D. Seymour, Esq.

a woman of unusual charm and good breeding. Lucy lived on alone in the old homestead and died at 82 with no one, as she often said, "to lean on."

FAM. 15. SOLOMON,⁵ (*Capt. Charles,⁴ Ensign Samuel,³ Joseph,² Josiah,¹*), b. 1764, in New. parish where he passed his uneventful life as a farmer. He m. (1) Lucretia, (daughter of Job) **Marsh**, of New Hartford. He died June 16, 1842. She d. Nov. 2, 1811, ae. 48 years. He m. (2) Chloe **Deming**. Though he did not profess religion until late in life, he was a man of piety and a strict Sabbatarian. Indeed, the tradition survives that he took the Mosaic injunction so literally that he interdicted the cracking of nuts on the Lord's Day. A group of butternut trees near the house gives colour to the tradition, the very existence of which shows that the question was raised. We may be certain that his daughter Julia stood with him in opposition to such Sabbath breaking. With him, regularity of attendance on divine worship was one of the chief concerns of life. It is related that one wild Sabbath morning he started out on horse back in the teeth of a tremendous snow storm. As he was floundering through the drifts in front of the parsonage, Priest Belden came to the door and hailed him, "Where are you going, Mr. Churchill?" "To meeting," came the response. "Well," shouted back the dominie, "you had better come in here, as I am not going out in such a storm." His grandson, Leonard Churchill Hubbard, describes him (1903) as he appeared about 1820. "He was of medium height, a rather stocky-looking man, round face, kind spoken, and jovial for one of his years." There is no portrait of him, but a half humorous silhouette has been preserved showing him as he appeared when carding, with tufts of wool clinging to his clothes. Solomon's second consort, Chloe **Deming**, whom he m. 24 June, 1814, was, at that time an old maid of fifty, and they were not happy. She d. 3 Nov., 1838 ae. 73—*W. Ins.* He d. 16 June, 1842 ae. 78.

Children (by first marr.) :

1. Julia, b. 31 May, 1792, bp. 18 Aug., 1805 ; d. 16 Sept., 1822—*W. Ins.*—was long ago canonized, by the family, as its saint. As a Sunday School teacher she has been described as "fervently prayerful." Every family tradition testifies to her pure piety and to her fortitude in affliction for she was a life long sufferer. Her voluminous journal, still preserved, reveals her gentle and pious character on every page. She found little place in it for aught but notes on the sermons which she heard from Sunday to Sunday and for the record of her religious experiences. It contains, however, some valuable references to the beginnings of the Newington Sunday School. She also wrote verses addressed to different members of her family and elegies lamenting the departure of local worthies. The making of verses seems to have been the pastime with the Newington Churchills of that generation. Her cousins, the daughters of her uncle Samuel, expressed themselves in the same way. Verse making, indeed, seems to have been about the only form of diversion allowed by those Calvanistic households ; the product is invariably poor. I quote from a small pamphlet entitled "The Semi-Centennial of the Wethersfield and Berlin Sunday School Union, 1832-1882." p. 27 ;— "The Sunday School in Newington, in its beginning, was the voluntary enterprise of some young ladies of the church." Julia Churchill was one of the teachers. This pamphlet contains the following extracts from the journal above referred to : "June 20, 1819, Sabbath. Attended church in the day time and in the evening. This day hath been solemn. A Sabbath

school was established in this place. Four little children were committed to my care to instruct on the Sabbath. O Lord, help me to do my duty toward them, and wilt thou touch their young and tender minds by the influences of thy Spirit." "August 15th. My little class is increased from four to seven. My heart feels for their souls. O Lord, wilt thou be their heavenly teacher. O, impress their young and tender minds with a sense of religion. Although they are young, only about four and five years of age, yet Lord, thou are able to make them think of thee and of themselves. Thou art able to perfect praise out of the mouths of these babes. Do, Lord." "November 4th. The Sunday school is now out, and this day the scholars received their premiums. I commit my little class to thee, O Lord. Bless them, I pray thee. O, may they be trained up for God. May they become new creatures. O Lord, prepare them for heaven." These extracts are fair samples of the journal of this devoted woman, and truly illustrate the spirit which animated her, and probably the other founders of the school.

2. Nancy, b. 17 Mch., 1795, bp. 18 Aug., 1805 ; m. 3 Apl., 1826—*W. C. R.*—Leonard Chester (son of Timothy and Abigail), **Hubbard**, then of New., but afterwards of Berlin, Ct., as his second wife. For his first wife he married Elizabeth, the daughter of Deacon *Levi*, son of Captain *Charles Churchill*, and had one daughter. *Abigail Deming*, who died young. This Elizabeth Churchill (called *Betsy*) seems to have been a young woman of spirit, with a dash of romance

and a streak of fun, if her character can be gleaned from her love letters, some of which have been preserved.

NANCY CHURCHILL, her first cousin, and successor in the affections of Mr. Hubbard, must have been quite a different person. When her mother died, Nancy mothered the family and took care of her father's household until her marriage. Her elder sister, Julia, was a confirmed invalid, the other children were young, and the tradition is that Nancy found her burdens heavy. She had jet black eyes, black hair, and an unusually white skin. Her silhouette shows a firm chin and a *retrousse* nose. She was a woman of great decision of character, brought up her family in the fear of God, and lived to a great age. In her later years she was tenderly cared for by her family, but she never relinquished her authority, nor gave up the strict Sabbath Day observance which she had been bred to in her father's household. The writer once spent a Sunday with her son, Leonard, with whom she made her home, and well remembers the austere character of the day. In the morning she sat by the window reading her Bible, and secular conversation was avoided. In the afternoon a discussion of some old pieces of the family furniture was broached. The old lady moved uneasily and did not withhold a rebuke for such an invasion of the Sabbath. She had the air of a Prophetess. Rembrandt would have painted her *con amore*. *Issue, (b. Newington):*

i. Leonard Churchill (Hubbard), b. 15 Jan., 1828; m. at Berlin, Ct., 6 Oct., 1859, Mary Jane (dau. of Thos. Clark & Abigail Andrews *Flagg*) **Arnold**, of Berlin; he was edu. at the Wesleyan Acad. at Wilbaham, Mass; farmer; was a deacon of Berlin Cong'l Ch., a man of fine appearance and refinement; had (*a*) Leonard Clarence (Hubbard), b. 24 Jan., 1865; m. 19 Mch., 1898, Louisa **Junge**, of N. Y. City; (*b*) Eleanor Arnold (Hubbard), b. 1 Mch., 1870.

ii. Kasson (Hubbard), b. 6 Dec., 1831; d. 6 Apl., 1834.

iii. Elizabeth (Hubbard), b. 25 Jan., 1835; m. 6 Dec., 1855, Henry **Francis**, of Berlin; had b. at New Britan, (*a*), James H. (Francis), b. 1 Nov., 1860; (*b*) Grace E. (Francis), b. 9 Apl., 1862; m. John D. **Garvie**, of N. Brit.

iv. Abigail (Hubbard), b. 31 Oct., 1837; d. New Britain, 20 Apl., 1898.

3. Chester, b. 6 May, 1798, bp 18 Aug., 1806. FAM. 19.
4. Cynthia, b. 30 Oct., 1801, bp. 18 Aug., 1805; m. 21 Nov., 1822, Cyrus **Webster**, of New., later of Berlin, farmer; she d. 11 May, 1869, at B. A devout, even tempered woman, she was for many years in poor health and showed great patience under this affliction. Her husband was industrious and firm of purpose; interdicted the cracking of nuts and whistling, or any kind of play on the Lord's Day; resolute in rebuking the ungodly and profane; a leader of the choir and an adept in the use of the tuning fork. *Issue (b. New.)*:

i. Chester Churchill (Webster), b. 10 Nov., 1825; m. at N. 3 May, 1852, Marilla (dau. Oliver) **Richards**, of N., where he d. 30 Dec., 1861; *issue:* (*a*) David Clarke (Webster), who m. a **Jones,**; (*b*) Oliver (Webster); (*c*) Charles (Webster), m. a **Honiss**; (*d*) Nellie (Webster).

ii. Chauncey (Webster), b. 26 May, 1828; m. 1853, at Canton, Ill., where he res. (1903); m. Mary (dau. Rich. & Kate Fouts) **Johnson**; she d. 1872.

iii. Charles Selah (Webster), b. 22 Nov., 1834; m. 12 Oct., 1858, at B., Julia S. **Higgins**; had (*a*) Harriet Churchill Webster, b. 1870; m. (1) 1898, Hon. Frank L. **Wilcox**, of B.; (2) Cyrus, b. 3 Sept., 1874; d. 5 Sept., 1891.

5. Jemina, b. 19 Nov., 1805, bp. 18 May, 1806; d. unm. 9 June, 1899, at New Britain, Ct., while on a visit to her niece, Mrs. Francis, dau. of her sister Nancy. She was born in the fine house built by her grandfather, Captain Charles Churchill, and one of her earliest recollections was of standing in front of its carved doorway and watching a family of wrens go in and out of a fissure in the woodwork near the carved pilasters. She lived a useful life, spent principally in the families of her sisters, Nancy and Cynthia. As a young woman she learned not only to spin, but also to weave—a rarer accomplishment—and a fine blanket of her weaving is still preserved. As the writer remembers her, she was a very "smart" old lady, erect in carriage, prim without severity, scrupulous as to the details of her old fashioned dress, and pleasant spoken. It was a great pleasure to hear her talk. Like her father, Solomon Churchill, she set great store on divine worship and rarely failed to go to meeting, to the end of her days.

FAM. 16. Rev SILAS,[5] (*Capt. Charles,*[4] *Ensign Samuel,*[3] *Joseph,*[2] *Josiah,*[1]), was b. in New. parish April 5, 1769; d. at New Lebanon, N. Y., March 1, 1854. He m. Rhoda, (dau. of the Rev. Joshua and Anne) **Belden**, of New., Oct. 12, 1797. She b. May 29, 1766, and d. at N. L., N. Y., May 28, 1823. *R. H. C.* says Rev. Silas m. a second time. He was grad. from Yale College in 1787, studied theol. with his father-in-law and settled at New Lebanon, N. Y. Emulating the example of his father-in-law served in the ministry of the Presbyterian church of that place, his sole pastorate, for almost fifty years.

Children:

1. Belden, b. — 1798; a farmer who d. in Omaha, unm. at an advanced age.
2. Silas, Jr., b. June, 1800; a farmer in New Lebanon, N. Y.; a Deacon in his father's church for over fifty years. FAM. 19 *a.*
3. Deborah, b. ——; m. Rev. John **Beach**, and d. in Ohio.
4. Charles (Rev.), b. —— ——; d. in 1855

at New Lebanon, N. Y. He was grad. at Williams College and studied theology, but his health becoming undermined, he never settled in the ministery. He m. Mary Ann **Bowman**, and left two children, one of whom, Thomas, a farmer, is still living in New Lebanon.

SOLOMON, SON OF CAPT. CHARLES CHURCHILL.

By Courtesy of Geo. D. Seymour, Esq.

FAM. 16a. Rev. JESSE,[5] (*Dea. Jesse*,[4] *Ens. Samuel*,[3] *Joseph*,[2] *Josias*,[1]), b. 1757 ; m. in W., 22 Nov., 1786, Hannah[5] (*dau. Charles*,[4] *Timo.*,[3] *Daniel*,[2] *Samuel*,[1]), sett. in Hubbartam, Vt., as a Cong. minister; rem. abt. 1808 to Winfield, Herk. Co., N. Y., where he lived and d. In war of 1812, was an army chaplain. His wife d. H. 10 Dec., 1804, leaving a large fam. of young ch.; and he m. 2 Aug., 1807, Olive (dau. of John and aunt of Hon. Samuel J.) **Tilden**, b. 1771.

Children (Boardman Gen.) all b. in H. except the eld. who was b. in Glast.:

1. Betsy, b. 1 Dec., 1787.
2. George, b. 11 Oct., 1789, rem. Ill.; many yrs. memb. Ill. Leg.
3. Giles, b. 26 Dec., 1791.
4. William Boardman, b. 1 Mch., 1794; m. Alinson **Humes.**
5. Polly, b. 12 Apl., 1796.
6. Norman Smith, b. 5 Nov., 1799 ; m. Anna **Eggleston;** sett. Galesburg, Ill. ; d. 20 Sept.,

1886 ; an elder in the Ch., and active Christian.
(*By second marriage*) :
7. Lucena Ann, b. 31 Jan., 1809 ; who m. 10 Sept., 1834, Chas. W. **Hull,** of New Lebanon, N. Y. ; their son, James W. Hull, is Pres. of Berkshire Ins. Co., Pittsfield, Mass.

FAM. 17. CHISLIEU,[6] (*Samuel*,[5] *Capt. Charles*[4] *Ens. Samuel*,[3] *Joseph*,[2] *Josiah*,[1]), b. 1779; m. 31 Mch., 1806, Celinda **Hurlbut,** who was b. 12 Jan., 1786 and d. 27 Nov., 1863, ae. 77. He d. 9 July, 1857.

Children:

1. Chauncey, b. 8 Feb., 1808 ; m. Abigail **Webster,** and d. 23 June, 1868, on his return from the South ; was farmer in New. ; had :
   i. Edward Chester (Churchill), b. 7 Dec., 1839 ; d. 18 Jan., 1840.
   ii. Henry Andrews (Churchill), ; d. 25 Feb., 1842, ae. 3 yrs.
   iii. Sarah Virginia Thomas (churchill) ; d. 13 Mch., 1868.
2. Calvin, b. 16 Mch., 1810 ; went South and was a Meth. minister in Georgia.
3. Sarah, b. 6 Sept., 1812 ; m. John **Sheppard,**

of Portland, Ct.
4. Mary Ann, b. 26 Apl., 1814 ; m. 20 or 26, *W. T. R.*, Nov. 1834, Flaad **Weir,** who was b. 21 Sept., 1802, and d. 27 Nov., 1812 ; she d. 11 Dec., 1893.*
5. Clarissa, b. 20 Jan., 1818 ; m. 31 Oct., 1838, Truman **Weir,** who was b. 2 Sept., 1816, and d. 14 Aug., 1873.
6. Samuel Seymour, b. 28 Feb., 1825 ; m. 11 Nov., 1846, Louisa **Hunt,** of Vernon, Ct. ; he d. 2 Apl., 1900; she d. 19 Sept., 1894. FAM. 21.

FAM. 18. JOHN,[6] (*Samuel*,[5] *Capt. Charles*,[4] *Ensign Samuel*,[3] *Joseph*,[2] *Josiah*,[1]), b. at New., April 11, 1785, d. there 17th Sept., 1823, of a fever, on his way home to New Hartford from the South. He is buried back of the New. church. "In memory of Mr. John Churchill who died Sept. 17, 1825, A. E. 38."

He m. in New. 9th Sept., 1811, at "Ten Rod" the home of the bride's father by the Rev. Joab Brace, to Laura (dau. of Capt. Absalom and Lorraine *Patterson*) **Wells**, of Newington. She was b. at New. 23rd July, 1789, and d. 3rd July, 1877, at Bristol, where she is buried. She was a descendant in the 7th generation from Gov. Thomas Welles. After their marr. they rem. to New Hartford, Conn., where her brother, Absalom Wells, Jr., had bought a farm. John Churchill bought a farm in New Hartford and his widow lived there for several years after his death until she removed to Bristol, where her daughter Laura (Mrs. Lora **Waters**) had married and settled. John Churchill was a man of gentle nature rather than a man of force. He was a man of medium stature, rather slender in build, with regular features, blue eyes and brown hair. His portrait painted in 1812, portrays a man of attractive personality. Her portrait painted at twenty-three, shows a face not beautiful, but very pleasing and full of strength and animation. She was tall, in complexion fair, with blue eyes and brown hair. An accomplished horsewoman, she made before her marriage two trips on horseback to Lebanon, N. Y., where she visited her Uncle Stephen Patterson, who had removed there from New. Her father,. Capt. Absalom Wells was so proud of her accomplishments as a horsewoman that he

---

* *Weth. Recs.* say that Mary Ann Churchill m. 20 Nov., 1834, *Francis Wyer* ; and *W. Ins.* say, that Mary Ann, wife of Flavel Weir ; d. 10 Mch., 1861, ae. 25.—H. R. S.

gave her a saddle upholstered in embossed red velvet, very handsome for the time. What opportunity she could have had for dancing in the quiet village of Newington the writer does not know, but remembers very well of her telling him of having danced through two pairs of satin slippers in an evening. Her father's family living at "Ten Rod" seemed to carry the burden of Calvanism lightly and lived freely and easily, dispensing always a generous hospitality. Her husband's family, on the other hand, took their religious beliefs very hard. Left when very young with a family of five children to bring up, and with nothing but a farm in New Hartford, she displayed unusual courage and resource. In her later years, and as the writer remembers her, her deportment was simple and dignified. She was calm in her judgments, discreet and charitable of others. She often referred to her girlhood days at "Ten Rod," and was very proud of her Wells and Patterson blood. She is portrayed with her dau. Laura (afterwards Mrs. **Waters**) then at the age of 6 mos.

Children:

1. Laura, b. 23 July, 1812; m. Lora **Waters**, of Bristol, 21 Oct., 1833; she d. 11 Oct., 1892, s. p. at B.; a woman of large frame, favored her mother's folks in build and coloring; as a young woman taught school. Having no children, she adopted as a small baby her own first cousin, Sophia Wells, the daughter of her mother's brother Ralph, and brought her up as her own and left her property to her and her children. She was a capable business woman, fond of dress and had great pride in the appointments of her house. The writer recalls the impression of splendor made upon him as a little boy, by her parlor which was hung with paper representing scenes in Paris—a continuous picture extending clear around the room with the blue Seine winding in and out between bridges and palaces, and here and there a triumphal arch and a memorial column. It was a beautiful paper in its tones of blue, delicate French gray and white, and decorative, if not accurate. All this glory was set off by a deep toned velvet carpet, a big table with an oval top of finely veined verde antique, and portraits of Mr. and Mrs. Waters at about the time of their marriage, over the chimneypiece, in which it was painted. He d. 1880.
2. John, b. 16 Sept., 1814. FAM. 20.
3. Electa, b. 5 Apl., 1818; m. at Bristol, Ct., 28 July, 1844, Henry Albert **Seymour**, who was b. at New Htfd. 22 Jan., 1818; res. in N. H. until 1846, when they *rem. to Bristol, Ct., where she d. 10 Dec., 1873, and where he d. 6 Apl., 1897. His family has been established in New Hartford since the first settlement of the town, early in the 18th Century. Previous to that they had lived in Hartford and West Hartford, the progenitor of the family, Richard Seymour, having settled in Hartford about 1639. On first coming to Bristol, Mr. Seymour was prominently identified with town affairs. When, in 1870, the Bristol Savings Bank was incorporated, he became the President of the Bank, and held that office up to the time of his death. Electa Churchill Seymour had a brilliant complexion, dark blue eyes, very dark brown hair, and remarkably beautiful hands. She was a vivacious and witty talker, and greatly beloved by her own family circle and neighbors,—a loyal, hospitable and gracious woman. *Issue:*
    i. Laura Electa (Seymour), b. New Htfd., Ct., 5 Apl., 1846.
    ii. Henry Albert (Seymour), b. Bristol, Ct., 2 Apl., 1847; is a pat. law., of Wash-

ington, D. C.; m. at W. 30 Oct., 1872, Mary Marilla (dau. of Gen. Mortimer Dormer & Marilla *Wells*) Leggett, b. at Warren, O., 2 Aug., 1853; he grad. from Columbian Law School of Washington, D. C. Rem. to Washington 1870. Clerk in U. S. Census office, subsequently Examiner in U. S. Patent Office, Law Clerk to Commissioner of Patents and a principal Examiner in Patent Office. Has been extensively engaged in electric litigation, yachtsman, member of New York Yacht Club, of Metropolitan and Cosmos Clubs of Washington, D. C.; have b. at Washington, D. C., (a) Laura Leggett (Seymour), b. 11 Nov., 1873; (b) Rae Mortimer (Seymour), b. 24 Aug., 1877; (c) Helen Wells (Seymour), b. 16 Dec., 1878.
    iii. Mary Harriet (Seymour), b. Bristol, Ct., 22 July, 1849; m. at Bristol, 18 Oct., 1871, to Miles Lewis **Peck**, b. at Bristol, 24th July, 1849, (son of Josiah Tracy and Ellen *Barnard*) Peck of Bristol. They had: (a) Josiah Henry (Peck), b. 5th Mar., 1873, at Bristol, Ct., B. A. Yale Col. 1895, LL.B. Harvard Law School; (b) Howard Seymour (Peck), b. 17th May, 1874, at Bristol, Ct., B. A. Yale Col. 1896, (c) Hilda Margaret (Peck), b. 19th April, 1881, at Bristol, Ct., Vassar Col. 1903; (d) Rachael Keziah (Peck), b. 6th Jan., 1883, at Bristol, Ct.; (e) Mary Miles Lewis, (Peck), b. 22nd Jan., 1895, at Bristol, Ct.
    iv. Lilla Wells (Seymour), b. at B., 10 May, 1852; d. B. 7 Nov., 1854.
    v. John Churchill (Seymour), b. at Bristol, Ct., 5 June, 1853; d. 5 June, 1853.
    vi. Grace Ella (Seymour), b. at Bristol, Ct., 13 July, 1856; m. at Bristol, 11 Oct., 1881, William Shurtleff **Ingraham;** b. 25 April, 1857, at Bristol, (s. of Edward & Jane Eliza *Beach*). *Issue:*
        i. Faith Allen (Ingraham), b. 30 Apl., 1886, at Bristol, Ct.
        ii. Edward (Ingraham), b. 20 Dec., 1887, at Bristol, Ct.
        iii. Dudley Seymour (Ingraham), b. 14 Aug., 1890, at Bristol, Ct.
        Faith Ingraham assumed the name of "Allen" on learning that she had an ancestress named "Faith Allen" who was hung for witchcraft on Gallows Hill, Salem, in 16—, along with the Rev. John Burroughs.

Mr. John Churchill, of Newington and New Hartford, and his wife, Laura Churchill Welles, with their daughter, afterwards Mrs. Waters. From portraits painted by Sam'l Broadbent, about 1811–12.

By Courtesy of Geo. Dudley Seymour, Esq.

vii. George Dudley (Seymour), b. at Bristol, Ct., 6 Oct., 1859; patent lawyer of New Haven, Conn.; grad. from the Hartford Public High School, 1878, and from the Law School of Columbia University, Washington, D. C., 1880; degree of LL. M., 1881, in the office of his brother, Henry A. Seymour, of Washington, from 1878 to 1883; opened office in New Haven, October, 1883; has confined himself to patents and patent law exclusively; interested in literature and the fine arts, a student of family history, Secretary (1903) of the Society of Colonial Wars in the State of Connecticut; member of the Century Club of New York, Cosmos Club of Washington, D. C.; Graduates Club of New Haven, etc.; unm.

viii. Helen Wells (Seymour), b. at Bristol, Ct., 29 Jan., 1864; d. at Bristol, 12 July, 1866.

4. Absalom Welles, b. 29 Mch., 1820. FAM. 21.

5. Charles, b. 25 May, 1822. FAM. 22.

FAM. 19. CHESTER,[6] (*Solomon,*[5] *Capt. Charles,*[4] *Ensign Samuel,*[3] *Joseph,*[2] *Josiah,*[1]), was b. in New. parish May 6, 1798; m. (1) Celinda (dau. Seymour & Deborah) **Hurlbut,** b. Chatham, Ct., and bp. 10 Aug., 1788; he m. (2) Aug. 24, 1826, Lucretia, (dau. of Francis and Nancy *Judd*) **Olmsted,** of West Hartford, Conn. His nephew Leonard Churchill Hubbard says of him, "He was of medium build, well proportioned, pleasing in his address, an active and attractive man." His wife was a very unusual woman. She was better educated than most of the women of her day, having studied Latin, surveying, navigation, &c., under Dr. Strong of Hartford. She taught a school of as many as seventy pupils in the north part of that city, and gave instruction in Latin. After her husband's death she taught school for a while in Newington. She was a woman of great energy of mind and had a wonderful memory.

Chester Churchill started out for himself at the age of 18. He taught school when 19 in Booneville, N. Y. A little later he began to carry goods South and became prosperous. He had a warehouse in Hartford early in the thirties and shipped goods from that point to places in the South. His health soon failed however, and he was obliged to spend his winters in a warmer climate. While on his way to Augusta, Georgia, he grew rapidly worse and died Nov. 7, 1837, at Rappahannock, Va., where his remains are buried. His wife, Lucretia (Olmsted) Churchill d. in New., Conn., March 8, 1875, ae. 75 years.

Children (*Weth. Rec. & Ins.*):

1. Francis, b. 23 July, 1828; d. 24 Jan., 1834.
2. Julia, b. 3 Nov., 1831. She was a woman of fine culture and very handsome. She went South after her father's death to look after his landed interests there and married James **Watkins,** Esq. She d., without issue, in Tenn., 17 Feb., 1870.
3. Mary, b. 28 Oct., 1836, bp. 8 Oct., 1837. She lives (1903), unm., in the house built by Capt. Charles Churchill for his son Samuel.

FAM. 19a. SILAS,[6] Jr., (*Silas,*[5] *Capt. Charles,*[4] *Ensign Samuel,*[3] *Joseph,*[2] *Josiah,*[1]), b. in New Lebanon, N. Y., 1800; m. (1) Clarissa **Avery,** of New Lebanon; m. (2) Cornelia **Lynd,** of Hartford, Conn., who d. 17 Aug., 1896.

Children:

1. Francis E., b. 12 Sept., 1826; d. in Burlington, Iowa, 26 Apl., 1896; m. Catharine **Whitmore,** of Brooklyn, N. Y., 16 Aug., 1852, and left 4 children. He was at the head of a large wholesale drug store.
2. Mary, m. Rev. Henry E. **Decker.** They both died at Turin, N. Y.
3. William T., b. 21 Dec., 1830; came to Hartford, Conn., at the age of 16, where he still lives (1903); m. 25 Apl., 1883, Alice S. **Woodbridge,** of Portland, Me.; born in Manchester, Conn., in 1843; no children.
4. Silas Payson, b. 1832; d. 29 July, 1894, at Cleveland, Ohio, where he was a druggist; he was a deacon in the Plymouth Congregational church of that city.
5. Ellen, b. 1834; m. a brother of the Rev. H. E. **Decker,** her sister's husband, and died shortly after her marriage at the age of 22.
   (*By second marriage*):
6. Martha, m. John **McWilliams,** and is living in New Lebanon.
7. Joseph, is living in Oregon.
8. Alfred, d. in the Civil War.
9. Anna, m. Charles **Cooper,** of Watertown, N. Y., and died.
10. Alice, d. young.

FAM. 20.. JOHN,[7] of Bristol, Ct., (*John,*[6] *Samuel,*[5] *Capt. Charles,*[4] *Ensign Samuel,*[3] *Joseph,*[2] *Josiah,*[1]), b. 16 Sept., 1814; m. at Bristol, 4th Nov., 1841, Ann Eliza **Hendrick.** He d. at B. 28th June, 1887; was bu. with Masonic Honors. She d. at B. 20th Dec., 1892, ae. 70 years. John Churchill was a man of large frame, slow in movement and deliberate in thought and of speech, a student of nature, a great lover of plants and flowers, formed an extensive collection of such Indian implements as are to be found in Connecticut, fond of the game of chess, lived retired and took no part in public affairs; a man of sterling nature and sober judgment. His wife was a tall, angular woman, old fashioned and a home lover, of more than common intellectual force. In her later years she became interested in women's suffrage and a good reader of literature on that subject; a strong minded woman.

Children:

1. Electa, b. at Bristol ; d. at B., 4 Jan., 1880, ae. 36 yrs. ; she m. at B. 13 Sept., 1865, Austin D. **Thompson,** b. at Barnard, Vt., son of Nathan Parkhurst and Elvira (*Ellis*) Thompson of Bristol. He (Austin) saw three years of service in the Civil War. *Issue:*
   i. Eva (Thompson), b. Bristol.

ii. Austin (Thompson), b. Bristol.
2. Lucy Augusta, b. 8 Jan., 1850, at B., unm.
3. John B., b. at B. 27 Feb., 1859 ; m. at B. 16 Nov., 1898, Ella (dau. Jefferson W. & Mary) **Steele,** of New Britain, Ct.
4. Ann Eliza, b. at B. ; d there 12 Oct., 1856, ae. 9 yrs.

FAM. 21.   SAMUEL SEYMOUR,[7] (*Chislieu,*[6] *Samuel,*[5] *Capt. Charles,*[4] *Ensign Samuel,*[3] *Joseph,*[2] *Josiah,*[1]), farmer of New., b. Feb. 23, 1825, and d. there April 2, 1900. He m. Nov. 11, 1846, Louise (dau. of Erastus & Tryphena *Clark*) **Hunt,** of Vernon, Conn.—*N. C. R.;* she b. Jan. 23, 1825, and d. Sept. 19, 1894.

Children:

1. Dwight, b. 5 May, 1849.
2. George F., b. 11 Dec., 1858; is one of Newington's representative citizens. He has held various town offices and has for a long time been one of the Registrars of Electors. He was a member of the General Assembly in 1899, and a Delegate to the Constitutional Convention of 1902. He married 23 Aug., 1888, Anna (dau. of William P.) **Wickham,** of East Hartford. *Issue:*
   i. Almeron, b. 27 July, 1889.
   ii. Louisa, b. 12 Sept., 1898.

FAM. 22.   ABSALOM,[7] (*John,*[6] *Samuel,*[5] *Captain Charles,*[4] *Ensign Samuel,*[3] *Joseph,*[2] *Josiah,*[1]), b. 1820; d. Apr. 10, 1875, at Shirley, Mass., m. at Littleton, Mass., April 2, 1844, Harriet Mason, (dau. of John Mason and Harriet *Whitcomb*) **Porter,** of Littleton, Mass. Absalom Wells Churchill was above average height, had dark hair, blue eyes, clear, finely cut features and was pale of complexion. His height, type of face and dignity of bearing gave him marked distinction; to this he added a fine old fashioned courtesy. His sweet and genial nature and enjoyment of company won him many friends. He lived for a time in Nashua, N. H., where he had a farm and represented that town in the Legislature in 1855. In September, 1862, he joined the 53rd Massachusetts Regiment of Volunteers. Hardly robust enough for active service as a soldier, he was detailed as soon as he enlisted to the Quartermaster's Department and remained there during his year of service. He was a member of the Unitarian church from 1843 to the time of his death. Though a member of the Unitarian Communion, he adhered to the old Calvanistic view of Sabbath observance and governed his family accordingly. He was a Mason and an Odd Fellow.

Children:

1. Harriet Wells, b. 6 Apl., 1845, at Harvard, Mass. ; m. at Shirley, Mass., 30 Nov., 1869, Charles Langdon **Bailey,** of Manchester, N. H. *Issue:*
   i. Annie Mason (Bailey), b. 20 Mch., 1872, at Shirley, Mass.

ii. Joseph Wells (Bailey), b. 4 Apl., 1874, at S.
2. Augusta Porter, b. 10 July, 1847, at Groton, Mass.
3. Mary Kendall, b. 12 Oct., 1851, at Nashua, N. H.; m. 30 Oct., 1879, Henry **Richardson,**

of Waltham, Mass. *Issue:*
  i. Wells Churchill (Richardson), b. 26 Aug., 1880, at W.
  ii. Amy Porter (Richardson), b. 8 July, 1886, at W.
4. Clarence Mason, b. 6 Oct., 1853, at Nashua, N. H.; d. 12 July, 1855, at Bristol, Conn.
5. John Mason, b. 8 Apl., 1862, at Groton Junction (now Ayer), Mass.; m. at Waltham, Mass, 22 Nov., 1883, Laura A. **Linscott**, of Maplewood, Me. *Issue:*
  i. Laura Waters (Churchill), b. 23 July, 1884, at W.
  ii. Harriet Mason (Churchill), b. 9 June, 1887, at W.

FAM. 22. CHARLES,[7] of Bristol, (*John*,[6] *Samuel*,[5] *Captain Charles*,[4] *Ensign Samuel*,[3] *Joseph*,[2] *Josiah*,[1]), b. at New Hartford, 25 May, 1822; m. at Middletown, Conn., 3 May, 1843, Alice (dau. of Otis and Celestia *Taylor*) **Phillips**, b. at Canton Conn., 3 Jan., 1826. He d. at Bristol, 16 Nov., 1891. She d. at Bristol, 20th Oct., 1899. He was a lumber merchant. He was above medium height, spare in figure though well built, and had regular features, brown hair, lively blue eyes and a fresh complexion. In his later years he bore a remarkable likeness to Joseph Jefferson, the actor. He was a man of active physical habit, a fluent talker and a wag, the liveliest of all his brothers and sisters unless it was his sister Electa. He was devoted to Alice Phillips, his wife, and never stopped courting her. As a girl she was considered unusually handsome and made a fine looking woman. She was a home-loving woman and found her entire pleasure in her husband and family. She was a famous cook. Better "Election cake" than her's was never baked. They never recovered from the loss of their son, Charles, who went to the war and died in a rebel prison.

Children:

1. Charles, b. at Bristol, 27 Aug., 1844. At the age of 18 he enlisted in the 16th Reg. Co. K., Conn. Vols., and went to the front; was taken a prisoner at the battle of Antietam, and after nearly two years of privation and suffering as a prisoner of war, died in the prison at Florence, S. C., 3 Nov., 1864. He was a manly, fine fellow, and to good looks added unusual personal charm; a great favorite with his schoolmates. After his death it was recalled that as a school boy he was fond of reciting "A Soldier of the Legion Lay Dying in Algiers."
2. Laura Waters, b. at Bristol, 10 June, 1846; m. at B., 6 Nov., 1866, Charles Levi (son of Frederick & Freelove *Frisbie*) **Frisbie**, of Plainville. He (Frederick) was b. in Litchfield and his mother was a Moulthrop; she (Freelove) was born in Milton Society, Litchfield; had *Nellie Alice* (Frisbie) and *Charles Churchill* (Frisbie), both born in Plainville, Ct. *Issue:*
  i. Nellie Alice (Frisbie); m. (1) Elmore C. **Whitman**, of Bristol, by whom she had Harry Churchill, and from whom she was divorced; she m. (2) A. L. **Bradley**, of New Marlborough, by whom she had one son, Churchill Frisbie.
  ii. Charles Churchill (Frisbie) ; m.

Annie C. **Wentz**, of Naugatuck, and had (*a*) Churchill Roswell, b. in Naugatuck; d. at New Britain, 1892, ae. 6 yrs.; (*b*) Charles Churchill, b. in N.; d. in New Brit., 1902, ae. 4 yrs.; (*c*) Howard, b. in New Brit., 1900.
3. Alice Electa, b. at Bristol, 8 July, 1848; m. at Bristol, 17 Apl., 1872, William W. (son of William & Isabella *Scott*) **Russell**, of Preston, Lancashire, Eng.; b. 17 Oct., 1845. *Issue:*
  i. William Walter, b. 29 May, ——, d. young.
  ii. Ernest Churchill, b. 17 Nov., 1882; m. 6 May, 1903, at Los Angeles, Cal., Anne (dau. Jacob) **Mayer**, of Alta Vista, Kansas; living in California.
4. John Welles, b. June, 1851 at Bristol; d. 1856.
5. Mary Charlotte, b. 18 Dec., 1856; m. 14 Dec., 1882 at Bristol, Erwin H. (son of Elias & Nancy *Botsford*) **Perkins**; b. 15 Feb., 1841.
6. Arthur Clarence, b. 5 June, 1858; d. 13 June, 1861.
7. Annie Charlien, b. 12 June, 1861; m. 18 May, 1887, at Bristol, Roswell O. (son of Isaac W. & Ellen S. *Olmsted*) **Beach**, who died 13 Dec., 1895 of consumption; he was b. 28 Sept., 1861.

APPENDIX.

In Mr. Samuel Joseph Churchill's excellent *Genealogy* AND BIOGRAPHIES *of the Connecticut Branch of the* CHURCHILL FAMILY *in America*, pub. 1901, is given the following line from this SAMUEL,[4] (son of Ensign Samuel,[3] s. of Joseph,[2] s. of Josiah,[1]), b. 27 Apl., 1721. He m. Thankful **Hewitt**, and sett. at Sheffield, Mass. fm. which town he was one of the first volunteers in the alarm party, which, in 1757, went to the relief of Fort Edward, N. Y. His ch. were all b. in S., but, in 1774 or '75 he traded his farm there (valued at $3,000) for

3,000 acres of ld. in Hubbartown, Vt., where he rem., cleared a place, and erected a house. His family suffered much, in July, 1776, fm. an attack by a party of tories and Indians, under a Capt. Sherwood—the result of Gen. St. Clair's retreat fm. Ticonderoga—and started to return to their old Sheffield home—a trip, by the roundabout course they took, of some 350 miles—reaching S. in abt. 3 weeks. Samuel, the father, who had been taken prisoner at Ticonderoga, escaped and rejoined his distressed family; but two of his sons, who had also been capt. remained prisoners until Oct. when they were re-capt. by American soldiers. In the autumn Churchill rem. to Castleton, 10 miles fm. home, but not until the winter of 1778, did he feel it safe to return to his home at H., where he spent the remainder of his days, dying in Jan., 1801, ae. 80. His wife d. Sept., 1801, ae. 80. They had 10 ch. the second of whom was

JOSEPH,[5] b. 28 Feb., 1749; m. 7 Dec., 1773, Ann (or Amy) **Stiles**; was much employed by the early Vermont settlers in their ld. operations, as agent, surveyor, etc.; was J. of P. and Selectman for many yrs.; possessed great bodily strength. He d. 21 Mch., 1820, ae. 72; the eldest of his 12 ch. (all of whom lived to maturity) was

AMOS, b. 1 Oct., 1774; m. 20 Jan., 1799, Nabbe **Haven**, who d. 2 Sept., 1842; and had 5 ch.; a remarkable man. At age of 81, he wrote a *History* of Hubbardtown, Vt., (pub. 1855); he m. (2) Chloe **Smith**, of Brandon, Vt., 1846; he d. 2 Mch., 1865, ae. 91. His eld. son was

SAMUEL SUMMER, b. 1800; m. at Hubbardtown, Vt., 22 Mch., 1820, Polly **Richardson**, who d. 8 Jan., 1862, ae. 59. He d. 23 Jan., 1845. Of their 9 ch. the youngest

SAMUEL JOSEPH, b. H., 1 Nov., 1842; enl. at first call for vols. in Civil War, in Batt. G. 2d Ill. Light Art., served under Grant in the West, was present at siege and surrender of Vicksburg, Miss.; re-enl. in 1864; m. (while furlough, May, '64) Adelia Augusta **Holmes**; was promoted Corp'l; was in battle of Tupelo, Miss., and for an act of special bravery in action at battle of Nashville, Tenn., was awarded, by the U. S. War Dep't, a medal of honor; was hon. disch. Sept. 1865; rem. to Missouri, 1866; wife d. 1877, leaving 5 ch.; he m. (2) 4 Aug., 1870, Louana (dau. Rev. Jacob) **Grant;** res. Lawrence, Kan., 1st Ass't Insp. Gen. Dep't Kansas Grand Army of the Republic; City Councilman, etc. He is the author of a *Geneal. and Biog. of the Conn. Branch of the Churchill Family in America*, pub. 1901, and confined to the rec. of his own line of descent fm. Samuel of the 4th generation.

(Communicated by Mr. A. E. MERRITT, Washington, D. C.)

CLAPP, NORMAN,[6] first resident of the name in Weth., was directly descended from Capt. Roger Clap, b. at Salome Regis. Co., Devon, Eng., 1609, who came to New Eng., 1630, in the *Mary and John*, with others who sett. at Dorchester, Mass., and who in 1635 rem. to Windsor, Ct.

NORMAN CLAPP,[5] traced his descent from this well known figure in early N. Eng history, through *Elijah*,[4] of Htfd., Ct., *Thomas*,[3] of Northampton and Htfd.. Elder *Preserved*,[2] of Northampton, Capt. *Roger*,[1] of Dorchester, Mass. He was the 2d s. of Elijah[4] & Mary Benton, and was b. in Htfd.; sett. in Weth. and m. 2 Aug., 1782, Huldah **Wright**, of Weth., who d. ae. 29, Sept. 15, 1800, *W. C. R.*, and perhaps he m. (2) Mary Frances **Wright**. Norman Clapp d. 6 May, 1830, ae. 69.—*W. C. R.* See Benton Gen.

Children (Weth. Rec.):

1. Roswell, b. 16 Dec., 1783; m. and had, at least, 3 sons (besides several daus.—names unknown), viz.: *Alexander, William* and *Charles*. He was, for many yrs. the principal storekeeper in Weth.; his old store still standing on Main Street. He d. 5 Nov., 1852.
2. John (Capt.), b. 10 July (*Fam. Rec.*, 10 Feb.), 1786. FAM. 2.
3. Norman, b. 3 May, 1793; m. had 3 ch.; his dau. Rhoda, m. Chas. **Blake**, wid'r, of Springfield, Mass., whose first wife was a Pease.
4. Charles, b. 5 Nov., 1796; m. Sarah **Buck**, 17 Dec., 1818—*W. C. R.;* and d. 27 May, 1869. He d. 27 Jan., 1882.—*W. Ins.* She b. Avon, Ct., 9 Dec., 1795; d. 28 Jan., 1874, ae. 78 yrs., 6 mos. *Issue:*
   i. Elizabeth Ann (Clapp), b. 26 Feb., 1821; m. Sylvester **May** (as 2d wife).

ii. Sophia D., b. ————; m. Samuel A. **Castle**, who d. 3 June, 1882, ae. 52. Mrs. May and Mrs. Castle are still living (1902) in Weth.
5. Huldah.
   (In Beckley Cemetery (Berlin) is bu. a Miriam Clapp, wife of Norman Beckley, who d. 24 Sept., 1879, ae. 85, who may have been a dau. of Norman & Huldah (Wright) Clapp, and sister of Roswell,[6] John,[6] Norman[6] and Charles[6] Clapp.
   There was another Charles Clapp (called 2d, on rec.) in Weth., who m. Hetty **Buck**, 13 Dec., 1821—*W. C. R.,* and d. 28 Jan., 1882, ae. 87. They had dau. Catharine, bp. 3 Sept., 1828, and bu. 11 Feb., 1830.—*W. C. R.* His wife was a sister of Sally Buck, who m. Charles (s. of Norman) **Clapp,** 17 Dec., 1818; their relation to one another is not clear.)

FAM. 2. Capt. JOHN,[6] (*Norman,*[5] *Elijah,*[4] *Thomas,*[3] *Eld. Preserved,*[2] *Capt. Roger,*[1]) b. 1786; m. 2 Nov., 1806, Mary (dau. John & Mary) **Kilby.** Capt. John was dr. in North River, 28 Mch., 1822, ae. 36. His wife, b. 14 Aug., 1787, d. 16 Sept., 1876, ae. 89 yr. Her nobility of character and Christian virtues were known to all who had the privilege of her acquaintance.

Children:

1. Elias, b. Aug., 1807; d. Weth., 11 Dec., 1879—*W. In.* (called on *tombstone*, Elias W.), ae. 72 yrs., 4 mos.; a man of fine intellect; had a sweet and melodious voice, highly cultivated and he was well versed in the science of music. In his early yrs. he led a Bohemian sort of life, traveling extensively over the U. S.; was supp. to have been marr., but no rec. can be found.
2. Huldah Wright, b. 17 Sept., 1808; m. 17 June, 1827, John B. **Alden**—*W. C. R.;* a lineal desc't of John A., of the Mayflower; he b. 26 May, 1806; d. 1 Feb., 1868. She d. 2 Jan., 1899, ae. 90 yrs. *Issue:*
   i. Jane Olivet (Alden), b. 12 Mch., 1828; d. 3 Dec., 1883; m. Pliny **Robinson**, of Holyoke, Mass., who d. 7 Aug., 1886; had dau. Ada Louise (Robinson), who m. Frank J. **Sheldon**, of Springfield, and d. 19 Mch., 1884.
   ii. Eunice Brown (Alden), b. 19 June, 1829; m. Chester B. **Canterbury**, of Belchertown, Mass., who d. 1 Apl., 1898; s. p.
   iii. John Brown (Alden), b. 1 June, 1831; d. 28 Dec., 1896; m. Jane **Beemis**, b. 6 May, 1835; had Frederick (Alden), who is m. and has family.
   iv. Clarissa Anna (Alden), b. 25 Aug., 1833; d. 29 Sept., 1833.
   v. Arthur Rowley (Alden), b. 5 Aug., 1834; d. 30 Dec., 1834.
   vi. Sarah Elizabeth (Alden), 26 Oct., 1835; m. (1) Rich. **Frost,** 27 Nov., 1861; he d. 1875; m. (2) John A. **Turner,** 8 Sept., 1884; s. p.
   vii. James Henry (Alden), b. 5 Nov., d. 30 Dec., 1837.
   viii. Birdsey Brainard (Alden), b. 12 Feb., 1839; rem. to Strathalbyn, So. Australia, and m. and had a family.
   ix. Preston Dwight (Alden, b. 25 Feb., 1841; d. 22 July, 1869; served in Civil War, in 22 Reg., Mass. Vols., Co. I; m. but s. p.
   x. James Henry (Alden), b. 12, d. 21 Feb., 1845.

xi. Alfred Leslie (Alden), b. 16 May, 1846; d. 25 Aug., 1849.
xii. Elwin Herbert (Alden), b. 27 June, 1848; twice m.
xiii. Francis Marion (Alden), b. 4 Dec., 1850; d. 22 May, 1852.
3. Mary, b. twin to Huldah; m. 12 Feb., 1832, in Newington, Ct., Luther **Dart;** rem. to Chautauqua, N. Y.; she d. had family.
4. Elizabeth, b. 1810 or '11; d. 18 Jan., 1879, ae. 68; m. Alfred **Simpscn**, of Wallingto'd, Ct., 24 Aug., 1827—*W. T. R.;* had 3 sons:
   i. Walter (Simpson), m. and rem. to Muscatine, Iowa, where he and his wife d.
   ii. Henry (Simpson), prob. m. and d.
   iii. Samuel (or Geo.), living in Wallingford, Ct.
5. Clarissa Blinn, b. 6 Dec., 1812; m. Edwin **Merritt**, of Htfd. He b. 14 Dec., 1808; d. 29 Oct., 1891, ae. 83; she d. 30 June 1853, ae. 40 yrs., 7 mos. *Issue:*
   i. Augustus Edwin (Merritt), b. 19 Apl., 1833; m. (1) 5 Oct., 1859, Annie M. **Schall,** of York, Pa., who was b. 23 Jan., 1840, and d. 27 Jan., 1861; he m. (2) 1 May, 1862, Josie **Brashears,** of Washington, D. C., b. 17 Aug., 1837; he had (*by first marr.*): (*a*) William E. H. (Merritt), b. 27 Nov., 1860; (*by second marr.*): (*a*) Mary Elizabeth, b. 8 Sept., 1863;* (*b*) Stella Louise, b. 7 May, 1866; (*c*) Joseph (Merritt), b. 30 May, 1867; d. 1 June, 1867; (*d*) Harry Brashears (Merritt), b. 1 Jan., 1869; (*e*) Lillian Angela (Merritt), b. 5 May, 1871; (*f*) Florence Adele (Merritt), b. 27 May, 1874. Mr. Merritt m. (2) 30 Apl., 1854, Marie **Stearns,** of Ware, Mass., b. 14 May, 1826, by whom he has dau. Emma St. Clair, b. 8 Aug., 1855, who m. 29 Oct., 1879, Harry Loomis **Cattrell,** of Williamsport, Pa.; has dau. Hattie M., b. 16 Aug., 1881.
   ii. Marie Louise (Merritt), b. 19 Aug., 1835; m. 22 June, 1859, Samuel Junius **Bestor,** b. 5 June, 1832; d. 10 Feb.,

* Mary Elizabeth Merritt, m. 12 Oct., 1887, Eugene D. **Carusi,** of Wash., D. C. *Children:* Frances de Sales (Carusi), b. 14 Nov., 1888; d. Mch., 18 1889; Stella Mary (Carusi), b. 7 May, 1891; Edwin Stanford (Carusi), b. 11 July, 1892; d. 1 Mch., 1893; Alene Beatrice (Carusi), b. 16 Dec., 1894.

1875. *Issue:* (a) Lena Louise (Bestor), b. 5 Nov., 1864; m. Colin H. **Barbour**, of Htfd., 25 Jan., 1893; have (a) Francis (Barbour), b. 3 Dec., 1894; (b) Howard Gladding (Bestor), b. 7 Mch., 1866; m. N. Y. City, 11 July, 1888, Ida Burnside (dau. Capt. Pillsbury) **Andrews**; s. p.; (c) Robert Loomis (Bestor), b. 19 Feb., 1893.

iii. Orrin Clapp (Merritt), b. 28 May, 1837; m. Mary Louise **Potter**, 4 Mch., 1857; he d. 13 Mch., 1887, ae. 50; she d. 13 May, 1893; had (a) Mary Louise (Merritt), b. 23 Sept., 1858; m. James H. **Linton**, 25 Nov., 1875; (b) Edwin Porter (Merritt), b. 29 Feb., d. 3 Nov., 1862; (c) Cora Lee (Merritt), b. 6 Aug., 1864; d. 20 Sept., 1871; (d) Charles Bestor (Merritt), b. 3 Sept., 1866; m. Margaret **Donshoe**, 13 Oct., 1888; had Cora Louise (Merritt), b. 13 July, 1889; Estelle (Merritt), b. 17 Jan., 1897; (e) Orrin Emmett (Merritt), b. 9 Oct., 1870; d. 3 June, 1899.

iv. Mary Jane (Merritt), b. 2 June, 1840; d. 30 July, 1841.

v. Jane Elizabeth (Merritt), b. 30 Aug., 1842; m. Daniel **Shepard**, 29 Sept., 1859. *Issue:* (a) Chas. E. (Shepard), b. 6 May, 1861; m. 23 May, 1889, Grace Gorton **Geer**, b. 16 Feb., 1867; had Helen Geer (Shepard), b. 26 June, 1890, Charles Gilbert (Shepard), b. 5 Apl., 1892, Elizabeth (Shepard), b. 2 Oct., 1897; Harriet (Shepard), b. 1 Aug., 1898. Mr. Chas. E. Shepard, res. Htfd., is Gen'l Agt. for Aetna Life Ins. Co. for State of Conn.

vi. George Sunmer (Merritt), b. 16 Aug., 1844, served as private in 16th Conn. Reg. Vols., 1862-1865; participated in Battles of Antietam, Fredericksburg and Fall of Richmond, and after his disch. was engaged in settling the war accts. of the State of Conn.; m. 1 Aug., 1867, Louise **Illingworth**, b. Eng., 26 July, 1849. *Issue:* (a) Geo. Prescott (Merritt), b. 27 July, 1869; m. 14 Apl., 1897, at Htfd., Florence **Kibbe**, b. 13 July, 1872; had Ethel Louise (Merritt), b. 22 Aug., 1899; Alfred Illingworth, b. 17 Feb., 1901; (b) Harry Clayton (Merritt), b. 20 Mch., 1871; (c) Frederick Marshall (Merritt), b. 27 Jan., 1874; (d) Stella Louise, b. 17 July, 1887.

vii. Edwin, Jr. (Merritt), b. 3 Oct., 1847; d. 28 Jan., 1853.

viii. Mary Anna (Merritt), b. 3 Mch., 1850; m. (1) John B. **Bartholomew**, of Htfd., 6 Dec., 1867; from whom she obt'd divorce; she m. (2) Geo. B. **Jewett**, of Htfd., 6 Mch., 1874, and her s. by Bartholomew took Jewett's name. She was divorced from Mr. Jewett and m. (3) 27 Jan., 1890, Wm. F. **Manning**, at Williamsport, Pa.; had *issue* (by *first marr.*): (a) Edwin Augustus, b. 31 Mch., 1869; m. 18 Apl., 1888, Sarah Josephine **Mahon**, of Htfd.; had Marjorie St. Clair (Bartholomew), b. 14 Feb., 1889; William Ellsworth, b. 23 Jan., 1891; Oliver Augustus, b. 8 Mch., 1895; James Gilbouns, b. 8 July, 1897.

6. John, b. abt. 1814; d. 25 Dec., 1839, in Htfd.; m. Jane Ann **Beers**, of New Lond., b. 1812. He was educ. at Bap. Theol. Inst., Suffield, Ct., and ord. to the ministry. He d. 25 Dec., 1869, at Htfd.; wid. m. (2) 1845, Ezra L. **Backus**, Hebron, Ct., and d. 27 Dec., 1889; by first marr. had one ch. who d. inf.; by second marr. a dau. Mrs. Lucy Backus Jacobs.

7. Harriet Maria, b. 7 July, 1817; m. 2 Aug., 1840, Ariel Collins **Pease**, who d. 12 Oct., 1843; she m. (2) ——— **Griswold**, and d. 22 Aug., 1847; no issue by second marr. *By first marr.* had:

i. Ellen Harriet (Pease), b. 4 Apl., 1841; m. 18 May, 1856, Clarence **Killy**. by whom she had 2 ch.

ii. Jonathan Ariel (Pease), b. 5 Dec., 1842; m. 4 Jan., 1868, Elizabeth **Rogers**, of Springfield; had (a) Hattie B. (Pease), b. 24 May, 1869; d. 6 Aug., 1870; (b) Charles B. (Pease), b. 23 June, 1872; d. 24 July, 1894; (c) George R (Pease), b. 16 June, 1874; m. Mary Gertrude **Davis**, 12 Dec., 1900; res. Bethel, Vt.; (d) Lizzie L. (Pease), b. 20 June, 1878; m. res. Keene, N. H.; (e) Ellen S. (Pease), b. 15 Apl., 1880; m. John C. **Gilman**, 27 Feb., 1901; res. Bethel, Vt.; (f) Ariel C. (Pease), b. 29 Aug., 1885; res. Springfield, Mass.

8. Daniel, b. 25 Aug., 1818; m. Elizabeth P. **Beedle**, of Weth., Ct., 13 Jan., 1841, (*W. C. R.* says 27 Jan., 1842), who was b. 5 May, 1824. He d. 5 Oct., 1853, ae. 35.— *W. Ins. Issue:*

i. John B., b. 4 July, 1842; m. Leila F. (dau. Roswell) **Blodgett**, of Htfd., 17 Sept., 1867; had (a) John Roswell (Clapp), b. Htfd., 10 June, 1871; m. and res. H.; (b) Bently J. (Clapp), b. 6 Nov., 1844; d. 12 July, 1845; (c) Sherman R. (Clapp), b. 13 Mch., 1846; m. 5 Sept., 1866, Mary F. **Winship**; had several ch.; (d) Henry (Clapp), b. 4 Sept., 1847; d. 11 Aug., 1848; (e) Edward (Clapp), b. 2 Apl., 1852; d. 1 May, 1852; (f) Daniel F., b. 10 Jan., 1854; d. Dec., 1873.

John B. Clapp rec'd an academic educat. and was for a time clerk in a store in Weth., kept by Roswell Clapp. He enl. 21 July, 1862, in 16 Conn. Reg., and at Antietam displayed marked bravery, which advanced him to the 1st lieutenancy of Co. D, of that reg't, com. dated from the day of the battle. In Jan., 1863, he was made Adjt. and at siege of Plymouth, N. C., in 1864, rec'd brevet rank of Capt. for gallantry. The capture of the 16th Reg. at P. made him a prisoner for nearly a yr. On his ret. home he was app. Capt. of Co. F, of Weth. 1st Reg., which position he held until Asst. Adjt. Gen., on staff of Gen. C. H. Prentice of 1st Brig.; in 1817, he was prom. to Lieut.-Col. of the Reg., and became its Col. in 1874. In 1878, he was app. Brig.-Insp. on staff of Gen. Steph. R Smith, which position he retained until his prom. to staff of Gov. P. C. Lounsbury as Commissary Gen.

He held many civic offices and was engaged in the iron trade at Htfd. from 1868 till his dth., 14 July, 1899. His wife d. at Madison, Ct., 22 May, 1893; and his only son Roswell survived him and succeeded to his business in Htfd.

CLARK, (*Clarcke*). The first of this name in Weth. appears to have been

JOHN, who came, prob. 1635, from Watertown, Mass.,—*see Chapt. VII, Vol. I.; acc.* to *Savage* (I. 396) he was at Saybrook, 1640; later at Milford. (Seems by one acc. to have been at New Haven, prior to going to S.); at Saybrook was an influential citizen; rep. that town in Gen. Ct., 1651-64, and was named in the Col. Charter of 1662, as one of its 19 grantees. *Savage* credits him with several ch.

THOMAS, of Weth., (whether related to the foregoing, is not known); m. 9 Dec., 1710, (dau. by a second wife of Stephen) **Hurlbut;** had a ho-std. in Weth. 1726; he d. 3 Apl., 1767.

Children (Weth. Rec.):

1. Phebe, b. 25, bp. 26 (*Mix Rec.*) Aug., 1711 ; d. 21 Dec., 1712.
2. William, b. 19 June, 1713 ; *Mix Rec.* says bp. 21 *Jan.*
3. Martin, b. 9, bp. 15 (*Mix Rec.*), 1715.
4. Elisha, bp. 2 Mch., 1716-17.—*Mix Rec.*

5. Elisha, b. 23 Mch., 1717-18.
6. Phebe, b. 27 Jan., 1719-20.
7. Hannah, b. 23 June, 1721-22.
8. Mary, b. 9 June, 1724.
9. Thomas, b. 25 Apl., 1728. FAM. 2.

FAM. 2. THOMAS,[2] (*Thomas,*[1]) b. 1725; m. 17 June, 1756; he d. ae. 63, bu. 16 Jan., 1793; she d. May, 1806.—*W. C. R.*

Children (Weth. Town and Ch. Rec.):

1. Martin, b. 20 July, bp. 21 Aug., 1757 ; d. 16 Dec., 1762.
2. Roger, b. 1 Dec., 1759. FAM. 3.
3. William, b. 30 May, 1762.
4. Rufus, b. 2, bp. 16 Sept., 1764. FAM. 4.
5. George, b. 1 Dec., 1766 ; d. 29 Sept., 1775. —*W. C. R.*
6. Moses, b. 4 Jan., 1769 ; bp. Jan. or Feb.

FAM. 5.
7. Mary, b. 15 Feb., 1771.
8. Olive (son), b. 23 Oct., bp. 18 Dec., 1774.—*W. C. R.*
9. George, b. 7 Jan., bp. 22 Feb., 1778. FAM. 6.
10. Sally, bp. 22 Oct., 1780.

FAM. 3. ROGER,[3] (*Thomas,*[2] *Thomas,*[1]) b. 1759; m. 8 Feb., 1781, Eunice **Latimer,** who d. ae. 53, bu. 10 July, 1815,—*W. C. R.*, a wid. as rec. shows the bp. of Martin, her "s. by a former marr.," 1 Aug., 1824.

Children (Weth. Ch. Rec.);

1. Ch., b. 4 Sept., 1783.—*W. C. R.*
2. Elizabeth, bp. 12 Dec., 1784.
3. Lucintha, bp. 7 Jan., 1787.
4. William, bp. 30 May, 1790 ; d. Mch., 1792, ae. 2 yr.—*W. C. R.*
5. Inf. bu. Aug., 1794.—*W. C. R.*
6. Clarissa, bp. 22 Nov., 1795—*W. C. R.; bu.* 26 June, 1814.

7. Chauncey, bp. 21 Dec., 1800.
8. **Welthea,** bp. 24 Oct., 1802 ; bu. 19 Apl., 1822.

William Nathaniel, "s. of Roger," bp. 6 Aug., 1820.
Lydia, bp. 3 June, 1821.—*W. C. R.*

FAM. 4. RUFUS,[3] (*Thomas,*[2] *Thomas,*[1]) b. 1764; m. 4 Aug., 1785, Tryphena (dau. Ebenezer) **Jackways,** (Jaques?) who d. 2 Nov., 1798.

Children (Canaan, Ct., Rec.):

1. James Harvey, b. 19 Nov., 1786.
2. John Harmon, b. 27 July, 1788.
3. Elizabeth Lois, b. 11 Apl., 1790.

4. Tryphena Salina, b. 10 Apl., 1792.
5. Thomas [Alvan], b. 25 Feb., 1795. FAM. 7.

FAM. 5. MOSES,[3] (*Thomas,*[2] *Thomas,*[1]) b. 1769; m. 28 Aug., 1786, Mary **Hurlbut,** who d. ae. 33, 4 Oct., 1800; he m. (2) prob. July or Aug., 1801, being then described as "Moses of Old Soc'y," Martha ———; he d. 14 May, 1848, ae. 80; his wife Martha d. 1 Sept., 1841, ae. 75.—*W. Ins.*

Children, (W. C. Rec.) by 1st Marr.:

1. Daniel, b. 16 Jan., 1793.
2. Henry, b. 1 Dec., 1795.
3. Thomas, b. 5 Mch., 1797.
(*By second marriage*):
4. Inf. bu. 30 Mch., 1804, ae. 6 wks.
5. Lois, bp. Oct., 1804.

6. Martha, bp. 6 Oct., 1805 ; prob. the M. who m. 27 Dec., 1829, David **Goodhue,** of Far.
7. Mary, bu. 12 June. 1806, ae. 17.
8. Sylvester, bp. 14 Oct., 1810.

FAM. 6. GEORGE,[3] (*Thos.,*[2] *Thos.,*[1]) b. 1778; m. at Norfolk, Ct., Lydia **Jackways,** (Jacques,) 23 Apl., 1794, (*Norfolk Cong. Ch. Rec.*) ; abt. 1803, rem. from Weth. with his young family to Willsborough, N. Y. Abt. 1807, he started on horseback, on a journey to Conn., taking quite a sum of money with him for the purpose of transacting some business, and was never again heard from. —*Letter of Dr. James M. Cooley, of Glen Cove, L. I.*

Children:

1. Orrin, b. Weth., Ct., 2 Jan., 1798; d. at Willsborough, N. Y., Sept., 1885, ae. 87 yrs., 8 mos., 20 d.
2. George, sett. in Mich.; d. —————.
3. Calvin, sett. in Ohio; d. —————.
4-8. Five daus.

FAM. 7. THOMAS ALVAN,[4] (*Rufus,*[3] *Thos.,*[2] *Thos.*,[1]), m. (1?) Alma **Wells,** 5 Apl., 1809; m. (2) Almira L. **Lawrence,** 1 Feb., 1827.*

Children (family Bible Rec.):

1. James H., b. 1 Jan., 1828.
2. John H., b. 19 Jan., 1832.
3. Ellen L., b. 18 Aug., 1833.
4. Caroline L., b. 8 Oct., 1836.
5. Juniette A., b. 15 May, 1838.
6. Rufus, b. 3 July, 1840.

7. Theresa A., b. 29 Dec., 1842.
8. Amanda M., b. 3 Jan., 1845; to whose dau. Mrs. Cornelia E. **Newton,** of Grand Rapids, Mich., we are indebted for the rec. of the line from Rufus.[2]

Miscellanea, (from Weth. T. Rec.):

WILLIAM, m. (1) Susannah —————; m. (2) Margaret —————. He d. Dec., 1711.

Children:

1. Mary, b. 18 June, 1669.
2. Susannah, b. 25 Dec., 1671.
3. William, b. 29 Jan., 1673; drowned, 8 Apl., 1708; "in Glast., riding over a hollow when the flood set in on the low land—ae. abt. 33."
4. Matthias, b. 9 Feb., 1677.

5. Elizabeth, b. 28 Aug., 1679; m. ————— Morie [Morey?], see father's will.
(*By second marriage*):
7. Abigail, b. 4 Feb., 1706-7—dau. of Margaret wid. bp. 14 Nov., 1708.—*Mix MSS.*
8. Thomas,—see father's will.

S. W. A. thinks this William may have been the Wm. of Dorchester, Mass., whom *Savage* finds no trace of after 1664. He rec'd at Weth., from the Town, 1677, a piece of ld. on wh. to build a house.—See Chapt. VII, Vol. I, and appears on Weth. Ld. Recs. as late as 1696. His s. *William*, is ment. in a deed of 6 June, 1694, as son-in-law of wid. Mary Smith. William Clark's Senior's Invent. £35-05-00, was taken 11 Feb., 1711-12; his will dated 15 Jan., 1711-12; gives to his wife Susannah, s. Thomas, dau. Elizabeth (Morie), bal. to his other ch. Son Thos. whom he names as his exec[r] refused to act and adm. was gr. to the wid.—*Htfd. Co. Prob.* [Acc. to the will—where is the 2d wife, *Margaret*, who should have been ment. as wid. instead of *Susanna*, the first wife? A discrepancy somewhere.]

SAMUEL. Acc. to Rev. E. W. CLARK'S *Hist. and Geneal. of Samuel Clark, Sr.*, pub. 1892, orig. from Devonshire, Eng., came to Weth., 1636, and was one of the 20 men from W. who estab. Stamford, Ct. There was a Samuel who had a house-lot in Weth. before 1640, see Chapt. VII, Vol. I), at which date he rem. to S.; whether he was a s. or other relative of John, ment. at the head of this family, on our pages, we know not, but name of his fam. (as given in *Clark Gen.*, above referred to) remained in Weth.

CLEVELAND, (*from Step. & W. Ch. Rec.*):

EDWARD, ae. 19, bu. 29 Aug., 1834.

FREEMAN, m. 11 June, 1812 (or '11?) Harriet **Kelly,**(?) who d. 15 Sept., 1842, in 49 yr.; FREEMAN, s. of Joseph, bp. 14 Apl., 1793; FREEMAN, an inf., d. ae. 8 mos., bu. 11 Sept., 1824.

---

* This may have been a marr. of the T. who d. 25 Dec., 1814, ae. 38.—*N. C. R.*

JOSEPH, of [Martain?] Mass., m. Rebecca **Collins**, betw. 25 Jan., 1787 and 5 Mch., 1789; had SARAH, bp. 8 Nov., 1789, and m. Asa **Dow**, of Western N. Y., June, 1811; NANCY, bp. 31 Oct., 1790, m. John **Dowell**, Apl., 9, 1809,—*S. C. R..;* DAVID, bp. 19 Aug., 1798; an *inf.* d. 17 July, 1804; an *inf.* d. 7 Feb., 1806; JOSEPH prob. one of this family, d. 7 Feb., 1813 in 14 yr.—*S. C. R.*

HENRY I., Irene, wife of, d. 5 Nov., 1868 ae. 43.—*W. Ins.*

MOSES, m. Mary ————, had MOSES, b. 23 May, 1745.—*W. Rec.*

CLOUD, PETER, of N. Y., m. Lucy **Burnham,** 4 June, 1834; she d. 10 Apl., 1858, ae. 61.—*Weth. Ins. & Step. Ch. Rec.*

CLOUGH, JOSEPH, of Springfield, m. Fanny **Goodrich,** 10 Sept., 1798.

COE, (*Coo, Coe,*) This family came to America fm. Co. Suffolk, Eng., where acc. to Fox's *Book of Martyrs* III, 349, folio ed., one "Roger Coo, of Milford, was burned by Queen Mary, Sept., 1555, at Yexford, in that shire.

ROBERT, b. 1596, at Long Milford, Co. Suffolk, Eng., who seems to have been the first of the name in this country, and with his wife Anna, b. 1591, and 3 sons, sailed fm. Ipswich, Suffolk, in the ship *Francis*, the last day of Apl., 1634, reaching Boston, Mass., in June following, and sett. at Watertown, where he was made a freeman, 3d. Sept., same yr. His homestead in Weth. was located on N. W. cor. of present Main and Broad Sts., and is now occupied by the Adams family.—See Chapter VII, Vol. I. He was one of the 7 Watertown men to whom the W. ch. gave a letter of dismission in order to found a ch. "on the Connecticut," 1636; and when the troubles arose in the Weth. ch. which led to the emigration of a portion of its memb. elsewhere in 1640, he with Andrew Ward, in behalf of some 20 others, purchased for £33, the land at Rippowams, in the New Haven Colony, and there founded the Town of Stamford. At the Gen. Ct. in New Haven, 5 Apl., 1643, a court was estab. at S. and Mr. Coe was app. one of the assist. judges. He was prob. also, one of the Stamford Comm. sent in 1643 to L. I., to examine the country there, and in the following yr. 1644, he with the Rev. Rich'd Denton and other S. residents formed the first Eng. settlement at Hempstead, L. I., which was then within the Dutch government. In 1652, he rem. to Mespath, L. I., and aided in estab. the settlement of Middleburg (now Newtown, L. I.), where he was a magistrate and prominent citizen. In 1653, he was one of a deputation sent to Boston to invoke the aid and protection of the New Eng. Colonies agst. the Dutch and Inds., who were conspiring agst. the Eng. sett. on L. I.; and in Nov., same yr., he was deputed, with delegates fm. the other Eng. towns on L. I. to confer with the burgomasters of New Amsterdam, on plans for the common safety. Early in 1656, he was a first sett. in Jamacia, L. I.; both he and his s. Benjamin rec'g gt. of ld. and a signer of the certificate of purchase of the town's ld. fm. the Inds., 21 Mch., 1656. He was app. a maj. 1659, and rep. the town in Gen. Convention at Htfd. May, 1664, being there app. Commissioner for Jamaica. Full of active duties and public honor he d. abt. 1672, ae. 76 yrs. *Hinman* speaks of him as "a worthy man and much respected in Weth." and records of all the towns in which he res. testify to his high character and the pub. esteem in which he, as well as his son John, were held. He had 6 pieces of ld. rec. to him in Weth., and 14 acres at Stamford, which attest the consideration in wh. he was held.

Children (*b. Eng.*):

1. John, b. abt. 1626. | 2. Robert, abt. 1627. | 3. Benjamin, abt. 1629.

These sons all accompanied their father in his various removals; so that their subsequent personal history and the genealogies of their families does not properly pertain to Weth. history.

JOHN, the eldest son, was a man of distinction in Newton, L. I., mag., dep and over-seer; and prominent in all town affairs. His 5 sons seem to have remained in Long Island.

ROBERT, the 2d s., rem. fm. Stamford to Stratford, C.; his descendants form the Stratford line.

BENJAMIN, the youngest, spent his life in Jamaica, L. I., but a gd-son, Benjamin, b. 1702, rem. to Newark, N. J., and d. 1787; his descts. are numerous in N. J.

See *Record of the Coe Family*, 1596-1856, by David B. Coe, New York, 1856, 8vo., 14 pp.; and The *Coe-Ward Memorial and Immigrant Ancestors*, Meriden, Ct., 1897, 8vo., 136. There was also org. in July, 1898, a "*Coe* Association" for the purpose of collecting, compiling and publishing a genealogy of the family in America—of which Rev. Edw. B. Coe, D. D., of N. Y. City is President, and Mr. David Coe, of Stratford, Ct., Sec'y, to whom all enquiries or genealogical contributions must be addressed.

TIMOTHY COE, of Durham, Ct., m. Polly **Callendar**, of Weth., 10 Jan., 1803.— *S. C. R.*

JOHN, invent. (personal) £121-05-05, taken by Samuel Curtis, Samuel Butler and Joseph Flowers—*Ct. Rec.*, 3 Oct., 1738. Invent. exhib. by Jonathan Carter, admr.—*Htfd. Co. Prob.*

COLE, SAMUEL, (s. of Henry & Mary* Rusco Cole—See Chapt VII, Vol. I), m. Iydia ——————, 25 Sept., 1679—(*Weth. Rec.*) ; he must have d. before 1 Apl., 1718, on which date an agreement as to the sett. of his estate was made and signed by the wid. and her 2 ch. before Hez. Wyllys, Clerk of Prob. Ct.: wid. living 1723.—See Chapt. VII, Vol. I.

Children (*Weth. Rec.*) :

1. Joseph, b. 12 Sept., 1781. FAM. 2. | 2. Lydia, b. 8 Jan., 1684.

[Note, there was a SAMUEL res'd Ry-H. who was hayward 1701; fence viewer, 1702; whom S. W. A. seems to think was a s. of Samuel and Lydia above; but it is quite as poss. that these items refer to Samuel, Sen[r] rather than to the supposed s. Samuel, of whose birth we have no rec. at Weth.]

FAM. 2. JOSEPH,[2] (*Samuel,*[1]), b. 1681, m. Abigail (dau. Sgt. John) **Riley,** 13 Jan., 1708-9; he was fence-viewer in Ry-H. 1716, appraiser of cattle, 1728. He was dr. 20 Nov., 1733, ae. 51 yrs.—*Weth. Ins.*

Child (*Weth. Rec.*) :

1. John, b. (and bp. bp Mrs. Mix) 13 June, 1710.

---

* *Htfd. Mass., Hist.* (I, 257) gives marr. of Henry Cole to *Sarah* (dau. William) Rusco, 10 Dec., 1646. He rem. to Midd.

JOSEPH—*Ct. Rec.*, 4 Feb., 1734-5, account exhib. by White Cole, wid. adms. his dau. White Cole chose Daniel Goodrich to be her guardian—*Ct. Rec.*, 1 June 1737. David Goodrich, Jr., of Weth. to be guardian to Lydia Cole, dau. of sd. dec'd, late of Stepney parish—ae. abt. 2 yrs.—*Htfd. Co. Prob.* (See *Cowles.*)

LYDIA, wid., invent. £321-16-04, taken 31 Dec., 1734, by Gideon Goodrich and Benj. Wright. Invent. £32-09-08 in Midd., taken 30 Dec., 1734, by Nath'l White and Eleazur Gaylord—*Ct. Rec.;* 18 Mch., 1734-5, adm. gr. to John Cole, a son of sd. dec'd. Rec. £100 with Jacob Riley.—*Htfd. Co. Prob.*

COLEMAN, (Assistance acknowledged fm. the *Coleman Family*, by Rev. Lyman Coleman, 1867; Mr. *Fred M. Steele*, of Chicago, and Mrs. ANNA C. N. HAWLEY, of Hartford, Ct.), THOMAS, the ancestor of all who bear the name in Conn. and West., Mass., is said to have been b. abt. 1600 in Evesham, near the head-waters of Shakespeare's "sweet stream of Avon," Co. Worcester, Eng.; emig. to N. Eng. abt. 1634-5; appears at Weth. among its first sett., 1636, and had lds. assigned to him 1639—See Chapt. VII, Vol. I; became a prominent man in Weth.; in 1639 was app. by Ct. to appraise damages; a juror in 1639, '41, '45, '47 and '48; rep. to Gen. Ct. 1650, '51, '52, '53, '56, and repeatedly after; in 1654 app. by Gen. Ct. to "join with the Dep. Gov. (and 2 others) to see to the pressing of men and procuring necessaries in Weth., to attend the exped. to Narragansett in the Ninigret War;" often chosen admr. of estates and ap-praiser of personal and ldd. est. He seems to have been of a somewhat litigous spirit; and is found among those memb. of the Weth. Ch. who became involved in the celebrated "Htfd. Controversy," and with a majority of that ch. entered (Apl. 18, 1659) into that compact which resulted in an emigration from the three River towns which settled Hadley, Mass., under the leadership of Rev. John Russell, of Weth. Acc. to *Conn. Col. Rec.*

date of Mch., 1658, the Gen. Ct. freed him "fm. watching, warding and training, if he proved he was over 60 yrs. of age;" if so he was prob. b. in 1598 and was 37 yrs. old when he sett. in Conn. He was made a freeman in 1661, Hadley, Mass., whither he went with the emig. above referred to.

The name of his first wife (whom he undoubtedly m. in Eng.) is unknown; she is supp. to have d. in Weth. abt. 1640-1. He m. (2) Mrs. Frances (wid. of Hugh, Sr.) **Wells,** of Weth. He d. Hadley, 1 Oct., 1674, ae. abt. 76; his wid. d. at H., 16 Mch., 1678. His will. *Northampton, (Mass.,) Prob. Ct. Vol. I. 175.,* mentions ch. and gd.-ch.: Lands in Weth. to his two sons John and Noah equal; House, farms and lds. in Hadley to son Noah "except lott in little Ponsett, etc.," to Thomas Coleman my son John's eldest son; to dau. Deborah am't which 2 deacons of ye church shall judge suitable prov. it exceeds not £100. "To Dau. y⁰ wife of Philip Davies £ 20—her ch £5 ea—" "To Dau. Trott's ch. £4 apiece" "To son John's ch. £4 apiece" "To yᵉ schools in Hadley £5." 2 sons John & Noah joynt. executors of this my last will &c. "To my son-in-law Thomas Wells I give all my part of yᵗ which is in England due for yᵉ rent of y⁰ House at Evesham, & to his son John Wells, now dwelling with me £10 with provisos &c—dated 29 Sept., 1674—& signed by his signature & seal, Dec. 30, 1674. The 2 deacons Richᵈ Goodman & Peter (Felton or Tilton) raised Deborah's legacy from sixty pounds to £100. John & Rebecca Russell testified to his signing of will, of his sound mind at the time &c. &c.—Inventory taken Oct. 7, 1674, by Richᵈ Goodman Peter ——ton John Smith—Total Sum—£907-15-01. *Hinman,* p. 658, says, Coleman was app. by Part., Ct., 1639, with Francis Norton, to appraise damage done in a field of corn; in 1645, he and Nath'l Dickinson were app. by the Prob. Ct. to take invent. of Mr. Parkman's est.; he was dft. in Ct. 19 May, 1647; in 1654, app. by Gen. Ct., with Edw'd Stebbing, to draw rules for sealing leather; app. dep. the same session; took chge. of Ab'm Easton's est. until adm. was sett. by Ct. in 1647. Evidently was a man much respected and esteemed; his ch. and gd-ch. married into the very best families of Weth. He was a lge. ld. holder also.—See Chapt. VII, Vol. 1; *Land Rec.* 153; a part of the ppy. ment. in his will was in Evesham, Co. Worcester, Eng. The will of Wid. Frances Coleman is also at Northampton Prob. office—Vol. I, p. 199. She mentions, Dau. Mary Wells, Son John Wells, Dau. Gilburt; gr.-ch. Jonathan & John Wells, John Wells (his son), gd.-ch Thomas Wells, (Daus. of my son Jno. Wells, Sarah & Mary), Dau. Mary Wells, son John Wells (his wife) Dau. Deboro.

Children (by first marriage):

1. John Dea., b. abt. 1635, in Eng., as supp. FAM. 2.
2. Esther b. abt. 1637; m. Philip Davies, of Htfd. *Issue:* Three ch. daus.
3. Sarah, b. abt. 1639; m. Rich'd Treat, Jr., of Weth. (bro. to Gov. Rob't Treat); he d. 1669; she d. 23 Aug., 1734, ae. 92. *Issue:*
    i. Richard (Treat), b. 14 Feb., 1662.
    ii. Sarah (Treat), b. 8 June, 1664; m. Ephraim Goodrich.
    iii. Mary (Treat), b. 8 Oct., 1666; m. Thos. Chester.
    iv. Thomas (Treat), b. 14 Dec., 1668; m. Dorothy (dau. Dr. Rev. Gershom) Bulkely.
4. Noah, b. abt. 1640; drew lds. in Ind. Purchase, 1673; on common, to run So. line of Farm., 1661; freeman in Mass., 1671; d. Hadley. 20 July, 1676; m. 27 Dec., 1666, Mary (dau. John & Elizabeth) Crow, of Hadley, Mass.; she b. 1643, m. (2) 16 Sept., 1680, Peter Montague. For

ch. see Judd's *Hadley Hist.*, p. 464.
(*By second marriage*):
5. Deborah, b. abt. 1645; m. Daniel Gunn, of Milford, Ct., abt. 1672. He s. of Dr. Jasper Gunn, of Htfd. *No issue.*
Note.—One of Thomas, daus. seems to have m. a Thos. Wells (see will of Thos. Coleman, Sr., before given), as, in *Weth. Ld. Rec.*, I, 168, is notice of lds. of Thos. Wells, of Weth., etc., which "he bo't of Mr. Parke and of Thos. Coleman, his father-in-law." If this be so—it must have been a *second* marr. of whichever dau. of T. C. it was; most likely of Esther. The Thos. Welles in question is elsewhere spoken of as Thos. Wells, 2d. It is difficult to determine *which* Thos. W. he was, but *poss.* it may have been Thos. (s. Samuel) of Glast., b. 1693, who m. a first wife, whose name is unknown and whose progeny by 2d wife (a Pitkin) in 1715, may be found in *Goodwin's Notes*, p. 269.

FAM. 2. Dea. JOHN,[2] (*Thomas*,[1]), b. Eng. abt. 1635; made a freeman in Ct. 1658, and in Mass., 1672; had home-lots in Weth. 1659—See Chapt. VII, Vol. I; rem. to Hadley, with Rev. John Russell, and may have been a signer of the agreement to sett. at H., at the time of the Htfd. Controversy. He m. (1) Hannah (dau. John) **Porter,** of Windsor, 29 May, 1663; she was b. 4 Sept., 1642, and was slain by Inds., with her inf. dau., 19 Sept., 1677; he m. (2) Mehitable (wid. Hez.) **Root,** of Northampton, 11 Mch., 1679; he m. (3) Mary (wid. Thos.) **Stebbins,** of Spyfld., and dau. Robert Day, 16 Dec., 1696; she had previously been the wid. of Sam'l **Ely,** of Springfield and d. 7 Oct., 1725, ae. 84. Dea. John d. 2 Jan., 1711, ae. 76. Will of John[2] Coleman on file at Prob. office Northampton, Mass., Vol. 3, P. 261—dated 19 Jan., 1711. Very lengthy, ment. wife Mary, son Nath[1] son John Land in Weth. acc. to Deed of gift, to Noah's chil. son Ebenezer Lands in Weth. £10. Dau. Hannah Nash & Sarah Field £5. ea. Wives of Thomas Nash & John Field sons Ebenezer & Nath[1], executors & "my loving friend & kinsman Sam[1] Partridge Sen[r], helpful as an overseer &c. Signed with his signature & seal. Wit. by Eleaser Frary, Jonath[n] Frary & Nath[1] Smith, who app. before Sam[1] Partridge Esq[r] judge of Probate for Hampshire Co., 20 Feb., 1711-12. Sam[1] Partridge & Noah Coleman were sons-in-law of John Crow.

Children (by 1st marriage—Coleman Gen.):

1. Thomas, b. 3 Mch., 1664; d. at Hatfield, 1674.
2. Hannah, b. 14 Feb., 1667; m. Aug., 1685, Thos. (only surviving s. of Timo. & Rebecca) Nash, of Htfd.; d. July, 1722, ae. 55; had 5 ch.; he d. 19 Jan., 1728.
3. John, Jr. (Lieut), b. 11 Apl., 1669. FAM. 3.
4. Noah, b. at Hatfield 20 Dec., 1671; m. Hannah ———, by whom he had 3 sons and a dau.; rem. from Hat. to Colchester, Ct., abt. 1705, as one of its first sett.; d. there 1711, ae. 40 yrs.; wid. d. 1765 at great age.

Invent. taken 20 Dec., 1711 by Michel Tantior, Thomas Day and Samuel Loomis. *Ct. Ord.* 15 July, 1714—Hannah the wid. to be guardian to *Noah*, ae. abt. 11 yr; to *Joseph*, 8 yrs.; *Hannah*, 13, d.; she gave bond with John Coleman of Weth.; distrib. 1715 to above.

5. Sarah, b. Hatfield, 15 Feb., 1673; m. John (s. John & Mary) **Field**, of Hat., who was b. 11 May, 1672; *no issue found.*
6. Bethia, b. Hat., 14 Oct., 1676; she and her mother killed by Inds. 21 Sept., 1677, she being then 11 mos. old.—*A. C. H.*

Savage gives him (I, 431) two more ch., viz:
7. Ebenezer, Hatfield, Mass., b. 29 Aug., 1680; m. 11 Mch., 1705, Ruth **Nichols**, and sett. at Colchester, where he d. 1740, ae. 60; 7 ch. He was Deputy to General Court from Colchester, 1715-1717 (twice), May and Oct., and 1720.—*Col. Rec.*, Vol. V, VI, VIII, "est. of Eben'r Coleman late of *Hebron*, dec.
8. Nathaniel (Dea.), b. 18 Oct., 1684; m. Mary Ely; res. and d. at Hatfield 1755.

FAM. 3. Lieut. JOHN,[3] (*Dea. John,[2] Thos.,[1]*), b. 1669; sett. at Weth., where he was a large ld.-holder, both by inheritance and purchase.—See Chapt. VII, Vol. I, and a prominent man of affairs; collector, 1700; fence-viewer, 1713; drew ld. in allotment of 1694; will dated 7 May, 1746; he m. 24 Apl., 1695, Hannah (dau. James & Dorcas *Weede*) **Wright**, b. 1670, and she b. 1676, d. 1 Aug., 1741, ae. 71.—*Weth. Ins.* (Tombstone inscrip. which would make her b. 1670.) He is designated as "Lieut." on all *Town Recs.* His invent. of est. taken 1735, amt[d]. to £1,912-15-03. He died about 1708.

Children (Weth. Rec.):

1. Mary,[1] b. 13 Dec., 1695-6.
2. John, b. 12 May, 1698. FAM. 4.
3. Thomas (Capt.), b. 6 (bp. 8 *Mix MS.*) June, 1701; he d. in 1735, and we find, in *Htfd. Prob. Recs.* of Distributions, the following receipts of his bros. and sisters, co-heirs to his est. "We, the subscribers, Co-heirs to the est. of Capt. Thomas Coleman, dec'd, having 26 & 27 June, 1735, distributed to ourselves, by full consent and agreement of s[d] co-heirs, acknowledge the receipt of the several sums annexed to our respective names, as follows: *John Coleman, Jr.*, £268-05-00; *Elisha Coleman*, £268-05-00; *Nathaniel Coleman*, £268-05-00; Ebenezer and *Hannah Sage*, £268-05-00; Johnathan, Jr. and *Tabitha*

Bigelow, £268-05-00; *Mary* Owen, as Atty. of Aaron Owen, £268-05-00. All signed—sealed 27 June 1735. Nath'l Burnham in behalf of John Coleman, Jr., and Nath'l Coleman, at a Court of Probate held at Htfd., 4 Feb., 1737-8, exhibit the foregoing agreement. *Test.* Jos. Talcott, Jr., Clerk.*
4. Hannah, b. 25 Sept., 1704, Deed of gift to Hannah & Tabitha, Vol. 8, p. 245.
5. Elisha, b. 8 Oct., 1707. FAM. 5.
6. Tabitha (*Weth. Ld. Rec.*, VIII, 62 and 245); m. Jonathan **Bigelow**, Jr., of Htfd.†
7. Nathaniel, *Land Records*, deed of gift, Vol. 8, p. 62.
8. Ebenezer (*A. C. H.*).

FAM. 4. JOHN,[4] (*John,[3] John,[2] Thos.,[1]*), m. abt. 1726, Comfort (dau. of Samuel) **Robbins**, of Weth.; she d. ae. 71, bu. 22 Oct., 1786.

Children (Weth. Rec.):

1. Comfort, b. 29 Aug., 1727.
2. John, b. 27 July, (bp. 10 Aug. *Mix MS.*) 1729.
3. Elizabeth, b. 24 (bp. 31 *Mix MS.*) Oct., 1731.
4. Hannah, b. 19 (bp. 23 *Mix MS.*) Sept., 1734.
5. Thomas, b. 28 May, 1737.
6. Mary, d. 1 Sept., 1741, ae. 18 mos.—*Weth. Ins.*

FAM. 5. ELISHA,[4] (*Lieut. John,[3] Dea. John,[2] Thos.,[1]*), b. abt. 1707; m. abt. 1737, Anne **Rose**, b. 20 Apl., 1701, prob. the "wid. Ann' bu. 1 Apl., 1777—*W. Ch. Rec.;* like his predecessors he was a man of means and large est.; will (Htfd. Co. Prob. Off., Bk. XIX, 76) Invt. date on outside of original but inside June y[r] 6, 1763, gives invent. of est. as £804-13-3, date of Prob. Ct., Nov. 4, 1766; wife and Peleg Coleman, exec.; will dated, 29 Sept., 1762; will of Elisha[4] Coleman, Book 19, p. 76, Htfd. Probate. To son Peleg. To son Zadock. To Daughter Anne To Daughter Hope To Mary, gr.-dau., dau. of dau. Anne "Two sons & two daughters". Inventory date June 6, 1763. Making him abt. 56 yrs. at death. "Wid. Anne" Coleman d. 1 Apl., 1777.—*W. C. R.* Mrs. Ann Coleman, res. do. "Peleg, eldest son double portion To the Heirs of Mary Francis

* *W. Ld. Deeds*, viii, 62, 245, and *H. Co. Prob. Rec.*, XIII, 59; and in add. to the above heirs is ment. Mary (wife), a son *Owen;* and John Coleman.
† Among their descendants was the late Henry Barnard, LL. D., of Htfd., who d. July, 1900, a most distinguished scholar and educator.

To the Heirs of Mable Weaver, & To the Heirs of Ladoe Coleman. The sd. Mary, Mabel & Zadock being children of sd. Deceased." Elisha's wife was 7 yrs. older than he & therefore abt. 62 yrs. when he died.

Children (*Weth. Rec.*):

1. Peleg, b. 19 Aug., 1738. FAM. 7.
2. Anne, b. 22 Dec., 1739.
   i. Mary (ment. in gd-fthr's will).
3. Zadock, b. 27 Aug., 1746. FAM. 8.
4. Hope (ment in will).
5. Mabel, ment. only in the Invent. of Zadock's wid.—as Mabel (Weaver).

FAM. 6. NATHANIEL,[4] (*Lieut. John,*[3] *Dea. John,*[2] *Thos.,*[1]), b. ——, ——; m. Ruth **Beadle,** 19 Jan., 1743-4, who d. 20 Feb., 1750-1; he m. (2) 23 Nov., 1752, Comfort (wid. Mr. John) **Loveman,** of Glast., who d. 21 Oct., 1786.—*Weth. Ins.* He d. 16 Apl., 1767, in 55th yr.—*Weth Ins.*

Children (*Weth. Rec.*):

1. Mary, b. 3, bp. 7 Mch., 1744-5.
2. Benjamin, b. 21, bp. 26 Apl., 1747.
3. Sarah, b. 30 July, 1749; d. 6 Aug., 1749.
4. Apphia, b. 4 Feb., 1750-51.
   (*By second marriage*):
5. Nathaniel, b. 30 Dec., 1755.

FAM. 7. PELEG,[5] (*Elisha,*[4] *Lieut. John,*[3] *Dea. John,*[2] *Thos.,*[1]), b. 1738; m. 6 Dec., 1760-1, Rebecca (dau. Thos. & Hannah *Hurlbut*) **Dickinson,** b. 24 Feb., 1741-2; he was a man of much activitys eng. in sett. est. and a large ld.-holder. Invent. realized $3,734.17, mostly ld.; s. Elisha and Elias Francis execs.; the son d. two mos. after his father. He, Peleg, d. 18 Apl., 1823, ae. 85—*W. C. R., Weth. Ins.;* wife Rebecca bu. 14 Sept., 1775, ae. 35.—*Weth. Ins.* His home-lot was on Hartford or Sandy Lane, reaching nearly thro' to Prison St. and down to High St., upon which he built a substantial brick ho., with barn and necessary farm bldgs. His adm. on his father's, his mother's and his aunt Anne Coleman's estates.—*Htfd. Prob. Rec.,* XX, 69; XXII, 162. His will, dated 17 Jan., 1823, devises ppy. in Weth. and Glast.; by its terms his ch. and gd.-ch. enjoyed the use of the homestead up to the time of its sale by heirs of his gd-son Chauncey Coleman, to Wm. Mygatt for a seed warehouse, a few yrs. ago. The large elm tree now standing, it is said, was planted by Peleg himself. Among items of real estate ment. in will were: "Black Bird Pond" lot in meadow; the "May Pasture"; The Plain; a right in the Fishing Place, Wright's Island; and "Minchaug" Wickham lot in Glast.; m. and had William, Alfred and Curtis, ment. in their gd.-father Peleg's will. Also Boardman Lot & Mountain Lot and Deming Lot (to gr-sons William, Alfred & Curtis, 3 sons of my late son Thomas, Land called "Coal Plain") To gr.-son William, the fishing place at Wright's Island. Mrs. Abigail Coleman Pelton was the last heir living. When this est. was sold to Mr. Meggat, & by her sale it passed out of the Coleman family where it had been for 3 generations, the original house being in good condition when removed.

Children (*Weth. Rec.*):

1. Thomas, b. 10 Feb., 1761, bp. 18 Apl., 1762; d. 1 June, 1818. FAM. 8½.
2. Sarah, b. 2 Jan., 1763; d. 20 Mch., 1848; m. Wm. **Rhodes.**
3. Elisha, b. 2 Jan., 1764-5; bp 8, d. 23 June, 1823. FAM. 9.
4. Anne, b. 4 Feb., 1767; d. 9 Oct., 1850.
5. George, b. 4, bp. 14 Feb., 1768-9.—*A. C. H.*
1767.)
6. Anne, b. 23 Feb., 1769.—*A. C. H.*
7. George, b. 10 Jan., 1771.
8. John, b. 10 July, 1773, bp. 5 Feb., 1775.—*W. C. R.*
9. Son, bu. 19 Sept., 1775, ae. 13 mos.—*W. C. R.*

FAM. 8. ZADOCK,[5] (*Elisha,*[4] *Lieut. John,*[3] *Dea. John,*[2] *Thos.,*[1]), b. Aug. 27, 1746; m. 28 Sept., 1774, Hannah **Goodrich,** of Weth,; he d. 15 Mch., 1776, ae. 32; he bp. 11 Mch., 1778.—*W. C. R.*

Children (Weth. Rec.) :

1. Ch. bu. 18 Aug., 1775.—*W. C. R.*

2. Zadock, b. 16 Dec., 1776, bp. 10 May, 1778 (rec. as of Hannah, wid of Zadock).

FAM. 8½. THOMAS,[6] (*Peleg,*[5] *Elisha,*[4] *Lt. John,*[3] *Dea. John,*[2] *Thos,*[1]), b. 1761 ; m. Salome **Kilby**, 6 Nov., 1782 ; he d. 1 June, 1813—*Weth. Ins. & W. C. R.;* wid d. ae. 67, bu. 9 Dec., 1831.—*W. C. R.*

Children:

1. George, bp. 9 Feb., 1794.—*W. C. R.*
2. Rebecca, }
3. Hannah, } bp. 16 Feb., 1794.
4. Thomas, }
5. Polly, }
6. Mary, d. 9 June, 1793, ae. 5 yr. 9 mos.—

Weth. Ins.
7. Anne, bp. 19 Nov., 1797.—*W. C. R.*
8. Samuel, bp. 22 Aug., 1813.—*W. C. R.*
9. William, }
10. Curtis, } bp. 22 Aug., 1813.—*W. C. R.*
11. Alfred, }

FAM. 9. ELISHA,[6] (*Peleg,*[5] *Elisha,*[4] *John,*[3] *John,*[2] *Thos.,*[1]), b. 1765 ; m. 1788, Hannah **Loveland**, b. 1765, who d. 5 May, 1819, ae. 53—*W. C. R. & Weth. Gen.;* he d. 23 June, 1823, ae. 59.—*Weth. Ins.*

Children:

1. John, b. 22 Jan., 1788 ; bp. 4 Dec., 1796 ; d. 13 Aug., 1819.
2. Horace, b. 25 Oct., 1790 ; bp. 4 Dec., 1796 ; d. 15 Oct., 1805, at Isld. of Gaudalaupe, W. I. ; bu. Oct., 1808.—*W. C. R.*
3. Hannah, b. 17 Jan., 1792 ; bp. 4 Dec., 1796 ; d. 8 Mch., 1870 ; m. Samuel **Woodhouse**, Jr., 22 Dec., 1814. He d. at sea, 11 Jan., 1817. *Issue:*
   i. Samuel Woodhouse, Jr., b. 13 Aug., 1815, who m. Mary Ann (dau. Capt. James) **Blinn**, 18 May, 1842, who d. 7 Apl., 1885 ; had (a) Hannah (Woodhouse), b. 14 Feb., 1843 ; m. Sea-Capt. Lewis **Williams**, of Oakland, Cal. ; (b) Harriet Merriman (Woodhouse), who m. (1) ———— **Capron**, by whom she had dau. Grace (Capron) ; m. (2) Stephen M. **Wells**, of Weth ; (c) Catharine Landers, m. David L. **Robbins**, of New. ; had dau. Bertha (Robbins) ; (d) Samuel Newton (Woodhouse), b. 29 June, 1849 ; m. 1877, Elvira **Dudley**, of Guilford, Ct. ; 4 sons.
4. Ch., ae. 2, d. 6 Aug., 1796.—*W. C. R.*
5. Elisha, bp. 5 Sept., 1796. *Weth. Ins.* says d. 4 Sept.
6. Elisha, b. 10 Sept., 1797 ; bp. 16 and d. 20 Oct., 1798.—*W. C. R.*
7. Abigail, b. 29 Nov., 1799 ; m. 2 Dec., 1818, Nathan William **Pelton**, of Chatham, Ct., b. 18 Sept., 1799, who d. 4 Feb., 1884, ae. 84. She d. 6 Nov., 1877, ae. 78. *Issue:*
   i. Hannah (Pelton), b. 1 Apl., 1820 ; m. (1) Frank R. **Smith**; m. (2) Daniel P. **Bunce**, of Waterbury, Ct., 29 Sept., 1847, who d. 4 July, 1880. She d. 16 Jan., 1883 ; had (a) James Arton (Bunce), d. ae. 4 yrs. ; (b) Chauncey Coleman (Bunce), d. inf.
   ii. Elizabeth Anne (Pelton), b. 13 Aug., 1822 ; bp. 1 Sept., 1824 ; m. 1 Dec., 1841, Philo Sloeum **Newton**, b. 29 Mch., 1811, who d. Htfd., 2 May, 1891. She living (1904). *Issue:*
     i. Anna Coleman (Newton), who m. m. 8 July, 1808, George Fuller **Hawley**, M. D., of Htfd., Ct. *Issue (only child)* :
       i. George Burton (Hawley), b. 14 May, 1869, (grandson of Dr. G. B. Hawley. The founder of the Htfd. Hospital, and gt-gd-s. of Dr. Silas Fuller of the Htfd. Retreat for the Insane) ; after grad. at Htfd. High School and the Mass. Ins. of Technology, Boston, is now General "Inspector" of the

Central Union Telep. Co.
   ii. Philo Woodhouse (Newton), b. 10 Dec., 1849 ; m. 17 Apr., 1890, Mrs. Angelica Augusta Holden **Thompson**, of Worcester, Mass., a druggist, in 1868, Hospital Steward of 1st Reg. C, N. G. ; in Nov., 1871, rem. to Geo. In 1872, ret. to Htfd. and re-enl. as Hospital Steward in his old regt., where he served until 1885. Also memb. of Vet. City Guard of Htfd. Since 1888, has been active in Masonic circles ; in 1898, was elected Eminent Commander of Washington Commandery, K. T., and is also a 32d degree Mason.
8. Eliza, b. 17, Nov., 1801 ; d. 22 Mch., 1870 ; m. Henry **Buck**, of New Haven ; he d. 19 Apl., 1873. *Issue:*
   i. Frances Johnson (Buck), b. 9 Jan., 1831 ; d. 1 Apr., 1892 ; m. 17 Apl. 1854, Siloam Short **Marsh** of Toland Ct., and had :
     (a) Edwin Rice (Marsh), b. 27 Jan., 1857 ; m. 2 June, 1887, Anna (Gooch) **Clarke**, b. 6 Nov., 1863 ; 2 sons and 1 dau.
   ii. Sarah Brown (Buck), b. 9 Jan., 1831 ; res. old homestead.
   iii. George (Buck), b. 6 July, 1832 ; d. 6 July, 1879.
   iv. Caroline Elizabeth (Buck), b. 15 Oct., 1834.
   v. Sidney Wadsworth (Buck), b. 27 Oct., 1836 ; d. 13 May, 1894.
   vi. Jane Eliza (Buck), b. July, 1840 ; m. ———— **Bassett.**
   vii. Henry Chauncey (Buck), b. 6 Nov., 1843 ; m. ————
9. Sally, b. 17 Dec., 1803 ; d. 22 Nov., 1875 ; m. 4 Dec., 1828, Allen B. **Holmes**, b. 13 Nov., 1795.
10. William, b. 1 Dec., 1805 ; d. 1 Aug., 1839 ; (Weth. Ins.) ; m. 2 Apl., 1833, Mehitable **Griswold**,—*W. C. R.*
11. Chauncey Coleman, b. 25 Dec., 1810 ; d. 13 Oct., 1865 ; m. 30 Oct., 1844, Sarah Rose (dau. of Stephen & Martha) **Willard**; she d. 29 Dec., 1863. *Issue:*
   i. Mary Robbins (Coleman), b. 17 Sept., 1845.
   ii. Helen Maria (Coleman), b. 6 Oct., 1848 ; d. 1853.
   Mary R. C. and John H. **Phelps** were m. 28 Dec., 1867. They had 2 d. inf. ; Ruth (Phelps), b. 5 Mch., 1888.
12. Maria, b. 25 Dec., 1810 ; d. 22 Aug., 1871, unm.

COLFAX, (Colefax, Colefox) WILLIAM, recorded his purchase of a homestead in Weth., 1647 (See Chapt. VII, Vol. I); was a carpenter; res. in W. until dth. in 1661; he m. Alse ————.

Children (Weth. Rec. and notes furnished by FRED M. STEELE, *of Chicago, Ill.)* :

1. Elizabeth, b. Apl., 1653.
2. John, b. 1 Feb., 1654-5; d. 1681; his bro. Jona. had his est.
3. Mary, b. Feb., 1656-7; m. Henry **Arnold,** a sett. at Htfd. Acc. to *Hinnman* she was a sister of John C. (above), who d. 1681, and also of the wife of Jos. Bidwell; if so, Elizabeth above must have marr. Bidwell. Her *issue,* by Arnold, were:
  i. Sarah (Arnold), m. John (s. Rich. S.²) **Case;** he d. 24 Feb., 1725.

ii. Henry (Arnold), Jr.
iii. Elizabeth (Arnold), m. 27 Jan., 1714, Ebenezer **Fox** (s. of Rich'd & Bethia *Smith* Fox). Eben'z'r Fox d. 20 Feb., 1746; see *Glast. Centenn.,* p. 189.
4. Jonathan (Sgt.), b. Feb., 1658-9. FAM. 2.
  NOTE.—*Savage* (I, 432) ment. a William, whom he surmises may be "perhaps, a s. of Wm. of Weth."

FAM. 2.   Sgt. JONATHAN,² (*Wm.,*¹) , b. 1659; dr. ld. in 1694 allot.; was surveyor Dec., 1699; m. 28 May, 1696, Sarah ————. He served in several Ind. and Fr. campaigns; d. 17 Dec., 1711, ae. abt. 53. His invent., taken by Michael Griswold, Ab'm Kilborn and Josiah Belding, amt. £170-12-10—*Ct. Rec.;* 3 Mch., 1711-12, adm. gr. to wid. Sarah; distrib. 5 Apl., 1714 to ch.—

See, also, Chapt. VII, Vol. I. His wid. m. (2) Rob't **Webster,** who, as appears by *Ct. Recs.* of 17 Mch., 1717-18 and 5 Jan., 1719-20, was app. guardian of the Colefax ch.

Children (bp. Mix MS.) :

1. Sarah, b. 3 Mch., 1696-7.—*Weth. Rec.*
2. John, ae. 18, acc. to the Ct. Order of 5 Jan., 1719-20; bp. 15 Feb., 1701-2.
3. Hannah, ae. acc. to the Ct. Order of 5 Jan., 1719-20; bp. 16 Sept., 1711.
4. Jonathan, ae. 12, bp. 10 Aug., 1707.
5. Elizabeth, } bp. 13 Aug., 1699 ; ment in
6. Mary,   } distrib. of father's est. 5 Apl., 1714.

GEORGE, of N. Lond., m. Mary **Robbins,** of Weth., 2 Oct., 1777.—*N. Ch. Rec.*

COLLINS, (mostly a Stepney family) SAMUEL, m. Martha ————, 26 Oct., 1704.

Children (Weth. Rec., bp. Mix) :

1. Samuel, b. 21 Jan., 1704-5; bp. 29 Apl., 1705; d. 6 Nov., 1784 in 80 yr.
2. Jonathan, b. 8 Oct., 1706. FAM. 2.
3. Nathaniel, bp. 25 Apl., 1708—"prob. over 6 mos. old."
4. Martha, b. 9 July, bp 18 Sept., 1709.
5. David, b. 13 May., bp. 1 June, 1712. FAM. 3.
6. Daniel, b. 27 Aug., bp. 10 Oct., 1714.
7. Hannah, b. 7 June, bp. 1 Sept., 1717.
8. Mary, b. 11 Apl., 1720.
9. John, b. 8 Jan., 1722-23; d. 8 Oct., 1741 in 19 yr.—*Weth. Ins.*
10. Benjamin, b. 13 Nov., 1724. FAM. 4.
11. James, b. 30 Oct., 1727. FAM. 5.

FAM. 2.   JONATHAN,² (*Samuel,*¹), b. 1706; m. Rebina **Smith,** 2 June, 1731; wid. Rebina d. 28 Apl., 1776.—*S. C. R.*

Children (Weth. Rec. & S. C. R.) :

1. Isaac, b. 27 Feb., 1731-2; m. Esther **Belding,** 5 Sept., 1754; he d. 27 Apl., 1776.—*S. C. R.;* Wid. Esther d. 23 Nov., 1810 in 77 yr.—*S. C. R.;* Mercy, who was bp. 6 Oct., 1765, and the ch. of Isaac who d. 23 Feb., 1775, were prob. his ch.—*S. C. R.*
  Issue:
  i. Simeon (Collins), b. 19 Jan., 1755; prob. the S. who d. 1826 in 72d yr.
  ii. Mary (Collins), bp. 13 Oct., 1765.
  iii. Esther (Collins), bp. 29 Nov., 1765.
  iv. Ch., d. 23 Feb., 1775.
  v. The wid. of Isaac "lately dec'd," had dau. Prudence (Collins) bp. 23 June, 1776.

2. Robert, b. 5 June, 1734; d. 28 ———, 1802 in 69th yr.
3. Charles, b. 6 Oct., 1736.
4. Anna, b. 14 July, 1738.
5. Prudence, b. 20 Sept., 1740.
6. Olive, b. 13 Mch., 1742-3.
7. Charles, b. 11 Nov., 1746; d. 1826 in 80th yr.—*S. C. R.*
8. Rachel, b. 20 July, 1749 ; d. 26 May,1795, ae. 46.—*S. C. R.;* the recs. say: "the first that d. of 3 at a birth."
9. Rebina (triplet), b. 20 July, 1749; m. Samuel **Rockwell** (prob), 20 Oct., 1779— *W. C. R.*
10. Kezia (triplet), b. 20 July, 1749.

FAM. 3. DAVID,[2] (*Samuel,*[1]), b. 1712; m. Sarah **Cole**, 11 Nov., 1742; he d. 28 June, 1795, ae. 84.—*S. C. R.*

Children (Weth. Rec.) :

1. Abigail, b. 4 Dec., 1742.
2. Lucy, b. 5 Dec., 1745.
3. Josiah, b. 26 July, 1748; d. 22 Nov., 1749.
4. Josiah, b. 26 Sept., 1750; d. 25 Dec., 1825

in 76th yr.—*S. C. R.*
A Rhoda, dau. David, d. 16 May, 1772.—*S. C. R.*

FAM. 4. BENJAMIN,[2] (*Samuel,*[1]), b. 1724; m. Bathsheba **Dimock**, 30 Jan., 1755.

Children (Weth. Rec.) :

1. Moses, b. 6 Jan., 1756.

FAM. 5. JAMES,[2] (*Samuel,*[1]), b. 1727; m. 5 Nov., 1747, Elizabeth **Riley**,; he d. 3 Apl., 1805, in 78th yr.; wife d. 14 Oct., 1803 in 75th yr.—*S. C. R.*

Children (Weth. Rec.) :

1. Elizabeth, b. 2 May, 1748; poss. the E. of Ry-H who m. Thos. **Parsons, Jr.**, of Far., 6 Nov., 1777.—*W. C.R.*
2. Patience, b. 9 Nov., 1749.
3. Lydia, b. 5 June, 1752.

4. Zebediah, b. 16 July, 1755; d. ae. 45, 25 Mch., 1806.—*S. C. R.*
5. Martha, bp. 21 Mch., 1766.—*S. C. R.*
6. Roger, bp. 6 May, 1770.—*S. C. R.*

COLTON, SAMUEL, m. Mabel **Bibbard**, betw. June 19 and 16 Sept., 1759 (*L.*); ALANSON, m. Lucy **Deming**, of Weth., 25 Oct., 1821—*N. C. R.;* ALANSON, a ch. of, ae. 4 mos., d. 8 June, 1828; ch., ae. 1 d. 23 Aug., 1825—*N. C. R.;* GEORGE, of Htfd., m. Mary **Welles**, 11 Dec., 1783.

COLVIN, GILES, d. 31 Mch., 1815, ae. 34.—*C. L. C.*

COMSTOCK, WILLIAM, had ld. at Weth., 1641, first mention of his being in Conn.—(See Chapt. VII, Vol. I). He and John Sadler, for slandering Rich. Wyles, of Windsor, were before the ct. at Hartford, 1644 and '49; after which he disappears fm. Weth. and Htfd. rec.; and reappears at New Lond. Nov., 1650, voting upon the subject of co-operating with Mr. Winthrop to estab. there a corn-mill; and, in 1660-1, with John Gallup and others he appl. for a ho-lot. In 1651, seems to have become a sett. citizen of N. L., and wrought at the mill-dam with others; prob. had passed midd. life when he came to Weth. and Htfd., the rec. of which town and also that of N. Lond, have no note of; his son *Daniel* had m. a dau. of John Elderkin and sett. at latter place as early as 1661-2, "being received, with others, by the men, among the fathers." "Old Goodman Comstock" was app. sexton, 25 Feb., 1661-2 "to order the youth in the meeting-ho., sweep the meeting-ho., and beat out dogs at 40s pr. yr.; dig all graves and have 4s for a grave for a man or a woman, and 2s for children, to be paid by the survivors." His s. *John* was app. 1665-6, on a comm. to divide the town of Saybrook fm. that of Lyme, where he sett. Miss Calkins thinks Wm. C. was of New Lond. as early as 1649, and lived to old age at his ho. on Post Hill, that his wife Elizabeth was ae. 55 in 1663 (b. 1608) and a foreigner, as no other ch. seem to be found on record, except Daniel and John, unless a dau. Elizabeth.—See Calkin's *Hist. N. Lond,* and Hinman's *Puritan Settlers,* 2d Edit. But there appears to have been a *Samuel* and *Christopher.*—(See *Savage.*) Concerning the former, and probable relation of William, Samuel, John and Christopher, Mr. Wm. G. Comstock, of Watertown, Mass., thus speaks, in a letter to S. W. A. (1894): "That Samuel Cumstock gave bonds in 1648, for satisfying what damage Mr. Robbins shall sustain for want of his servant," would seem to indicate that Samuel, if a servant, was a *young* man, in 1648. The name Samuel Comstock, appears in Providence, R. I., 1654-1660 where he died. Daniel's name appears, also, in Providence, for some yrs. prior to 1665 when the name appears in New Lond. The reappearance of Christian names in the several families is also significant. *Samuel*, of Prov., named one son Daniel; another (seemingly his) Samuel. *Daniel*, of New Lond. named sons, Daniel and Samuel. *John* named children William, John, Samuel, Elizabeth and Christian. *Christopher*, named ch. Daniel and Elizabeth—and the latter who m. Edward Shipton, named ch. William and Elizabeth. 29 ch. in these five families were b. betw. 1651 and 1677, indicating a similarity of age in the respective parents. The similarity of age, the reappearance of Christian names, the association of Daniel and Samuel in Prov.; of Daniel and Samuel in New Lond.; of Samuel and William in Weth.; and Miss Caulkins' opinion, or impression in regard to Christopher and Samuel, all seems to fortify the conclusion that William and Elizabeth Comstock had *five* ch. viz. Elizabeth, Samuel, Daniel, John and Christopher."

WILLIAM G., and wife Adeline ———— had

Children (b. in Weth.).

1. Franklin Greene, b. 27 May, 1838.	5. William Greene,	
2. Jabez Knikht, b. 7 Feb., 1841.	6. Frederic,	
3. Mary Emma, b. 13 Nov., 1842.	7. Ralph Tracy, b. 18 Mch., 1849.	
4. Amy, b. 27 May, 1845. b. 13 Feb., 1847.	8. Robbins Tracy, b. 24 Oct., 1855.	

CONE, ANDREW D., b. 16 Aug., 1824; d. 21 Apl., 1897; his wife Sarah J., b. 21 Dec., 1845; d. 19 June, 1886.—*Weth. Ins.*

EDWARD, of Midd., m. Eunice **Belden.**

DANIEL, of E. Hadd., m. Abigail **Griswold,** of Weth., betw. Apl., 20 and Sept., 28,   .—*W. Ch. Rec.*

JARED, of Bolton, m. Elizabeth **Williams,** 15 Jan., 1784.—*W. T. R.*

JOSHUA, m. Mehitable **Blinn,** 20 Feb., 1781.—*W. T. R.* Wid. ae. 69, bu. 22 Nov., 1776.—*W. Ch. Rec.*

MEHETABLE, d. 8 Apl., 1837, ae. 80.—*Weth. Ins.*

COLTMAN, *Savage* (I. 431) speaking of the name *Coultman* (or Coulman) and *Coleman*, remarks, "in old writing, *e* is freq. taken for *t*; and *u* for *a* is a common error." (*Coultman*) JOHN, who was (acc. to *Hall Ancestry*, p. 167, and *Lechford's Note Book*, p. 280) son of Thos., blacksmith, of Newton Harcoate, Weston, Leicestershire, Eng., first appears in the Conn. Colony abt. 1645; his homestead lot rec. in Weth., 26 Mch., 1647 (See Chapt. VII, Vol. I); appears to have been a servant, or in someway employed in the fam. of Mr. Leonard Chester; and when afterward (1653,) he rec'd a gt. of ld. from the Town, it was coupled with the condition that he should build a house thereon and live in it for seven yrs, "he being so changeable, ever since he was his own man." In 1648, he had become part owner of the Chester Mill (of wh. prob. he had previously been the manager); and in Nov., 1668, was given by the Town, a piece of ld. near to the Mill, he was the Town schoolmaster in 1666-7 and for some yrs. after. His services to the Chester fam. seem to have been pleasantly recognized in Mrs. Leonard Chester's (then wid. of Hon. Rich'd Russell, of Charlestown, Mass., will in 1688, by a gift to this servant of nearly 50 yrs. before—see *Chester*, Vol. I, p. 637. He is said (writer in *N. Y. Mail & Express*,) to have rem. to Branford, Ct. He m. 21

(one rec. says "abt. the 24th" Sept., 1667, Mary ——————, who after Mr. Coltman's dth. (which was abt. 1696—some say 1688 or '89) m. (2) —————— **Sherman.*** Mr. Coltman's est. val. at £142.

Children (Weth. Rec.) :

1. Mary, b. 29 Nov., 1672; m. 3 May, 1693, David (s. of David and Elizabeth *Kirby*) **Sage**, of Midd., Ct., who was b. 1 Feb., 1665 and d. at Weth. 3 Aug., 1744; had 2 ch. *Savage* m. her, in 1684 to John Nash. of Norwalk, he must be wrong, as she

then would have been only 12 yrs. old.
2. Elizabeth, b. 14 Jan., 1677.
3. Anna, b. 11 Mch., 1680-1; m. 13 Nov., 1701, William (s. of Peter & Johanna) **Blinn**, of Weth., who was b. 1 July, 1675 ; she d. Weth., 17 Oct., 1724 ; had 7 ch.

COOK, ANNIS (wid) d. 8 Sept., 1850, in 93d yr.—*S. C. R.*

ERASTUS F., of Oppenheim, N. Y., m. Mary Porter **Beldin**, 22 May, 1821.—*W. T. R.* had *issue* (1) Mary, bp. 8 July, 1820, ae. 3; (2) Mary Parsons, bp. 23 Mch., 1828—*W. C. R.;* a dau. of Erastus. d. 8 July, 1830, ae. 3—*W. C. R.;* FLORILLA, wife of Albro Griswold, 1805-1895, LITTLE CATHARINE, 1838-1841—*Weth. Ins.;* GEORGE, of St. Armand, Lower Canada, m. Sarah **Hooker**, of Far. 28 (?) Sept., 1810—*S. C. R.;* JUSTUS, m. Mary **Goodrich**, (*alias* Webster) 21 Dec., 1795— *N. C. R.;* MARIA (wid.), of Htfd., d. 8 Oct., 1832, in 33d yr.—*S. C. R.;* NATHAN, of Salisbury, m. Anna **Grimes**, 8 July, 1784.

COOLEY, CYNTHIA M., of Ry-H., m. Wm. **Porter,** Jr., of Lee, Mass., 5 Nov., 1837.—*W. T. R.*

LORIN, of Granville, Mass., m. Susan **Blinn**, of Berlin, 31 Dec., 1833.—*N. C. R.*

COOLIDGE, OBADIAH, m. Elizabeth ——————. (It looks very much as if this might be the same Obadiah, of Sherborn, Mass., who acc. to *Savage* (I,452) was a "s. of Simon, and m. 28 Feb., 1687, Elizabeth **Rouse**, of Htfd., had 7 ch., rem. 'to Watertown, and d. 16 May, 1707." If so, his fam. was *started* in Weth.)

Children (Weth. Rec.) :

1. Elizabeth, b. 26 Feb., 1688.
2. Obadiah (*Hinman* says, "b. or d., prob.

b.") Sept. 25, 1689.
3. Hannah, b. 26 Mch., 1690-1.

SAMSON, m. Clarissa **Ward**, of N. Y., 26 Nov., 1838.—*W. T. R.*

COOMBS, ANDREW, bu. 7 Oct., 1796; his wife Mary, ae. 80, bu. 27 Jan., 1791— *W. C. R., Weth. Ins.;* ELIZABETH, of W., m. Luke **Watson**, of E. W., 24 Oct., 1808—*W. C. R.;* HANNAH, m. Truman **Starr**, Esq., of Goshen, 21 Apl., 1829; JOSEPH, (prob. the J. bu. 23 May, 1798, ae. 52—*W. C. R.*, and perhaps the J. who m. Dorcas **Markam** (Markham) 31 Oct., 1770—*W. C. R.*, was himself, with his son Joseph, bp. 19 Feb., 1775, d. 4 June,, 1775; Joseph's wife d. 3 Mch., 1803, ae. 36—*W. C. R.;* (2) Andrew, bp. 29 Mch., 1778 (poss. the A. whose dth. is given at head of this paragraph) ; (3) Oliver, bp. 10 Sept., 1780; (4) Sarah bp. 5 Jan., 1783; (5) Solomon, bp. 4 June, 1785—*W. C. R.;* JOSEPH, Jr., (prob. the J. given above, b. 1775), m. Elizabeth **Rhodes**, 18 Oct., 1789, who d. ae. 26, bu. 3 Mch., 1803, he had ch. d. 20 Sept. 1784—*W. C. R.*, JOSIAH, m. Eliza **Woodhouse**, 5 Jan., 1826. *Children (W. C. R.)*: (1) Mary Elizabeth, b. 31 July, bp. 15 Dec., 1826; (2) David Woodhouse, b. 2 Mch., bp. 29 July, 1829; (3) Daniel A., ae. 2, bu. 13 Oct., 1830—*W. C. R.;* (4) Lucy Ann, bp. 18 Sept., 1831; JOSIAH, m. Hannah **Phelps**, both of Weth., 2 Apl., 1778—*W. C. R.;* he d. ae. 70, bu. 8 Feb., 1821—*W. C. R.;* his wid. bu. 30 Mch., 1832; had—*W. C. R.*, inf. bp. 9

---

* *Savage* says Mary Coultman married John **Nash**, but elsewhere marries him to Mary **Combs**, whose age was rather more suitable to his own. At the date of John Nash's marriage Mary Coultman was eleven and a half years old.

Sept., 1780—*W. C. R;* MARY, of W. m. Marcus **Ives**, of Goshen, 24 Oct., 1810—
W. C. R.; MERCY, d. 31 Dec., 1840, ae. 87—*W. Ins.;* SARAH, of W. m. Arden
Eaton, of Castleton, Vt., 21 Jan., 1801—*W. C. R.;* SOLOMON, m. Molly **Griswold**, 18 Oct., 1797; WILLIAM, m. Seely (Celia?) **Webster**, of Weth., 5 June,
1777; had inf. bu. 11 Aug., 1779.—*W. Ins.*

COOPER, WILLIAM, of Midd., m. Jeanette **Riley**, 28 Oct., 1802.—*W. C. R.*

COPLEY, NATHANIEL, m.. Mary **Treat**, 6 Apl., 1766—*N. C. R.*

NATHANIEL, d. 26 Mch., 1773.—*S. C. R.*

NOAH, d. 5 Aug., 1765.—*S. C. R.*

COREY, (Cory) AMASA, of Htfd., m. Harriet **Myers**, 26 April, 1809.

CALVIN, had an inf. d. 12 Jan., 1848.—*S. C. R.*

OLIVER, m. Hannah **Adams**, 27 Nov., 1788; he d. 26 Feb., 1847, in 88th yr.; his
wife d. 11 Jan., 1835, in 67th yr.—*S. C. R.*

Children (Weth. Rec. & S. C. R.):

1. William, bp. 1 Aug., 1790.
2. Elizabeth, bp., 27 Sept., 1795.
3. Emily, bp. 6 May, 1798.
4. Sally, bp. 9 Nov., 1799; prob. the ch. who d. 10 Nov., 1799.
5. Ch. bp. 3 Oct., 1801.
6. Oliver, bp. 23 Aug., 1801; d. 1 Oct., 1801.
7. Sally, bp. 12 Oct., 1806.
8. Calvin Francis, bp. 30 Oct., 1808— *S. C. R.;* m. Martha E. **Goodrich**, 9 Nov., 1836, who d. 30 Apl., 1851, ae. 42.— *W. Ins. & S. C. R.*
9. Eliza Ann, bp. 30 Aug., 1812.
10. James Henry, bp. 10 Jan., 1815.
11. A twin inf. d. 10 Jan., 1815.
12. A twin inf. d. 12 Jan., 1815.

MARTHA, bp. 2 Sept., 1792—*S. C. R.;* m. Nathan **Lee**, and d. 26 Mch., 1830, in
29th yr.—*W. Ins.*

WILLIAM, had Molly, bp. 14 Apl., 1765; Oliver, bp. 10 Aug., 1866; Ruth, bp. 6
Mch., 1768, d. 11 Apl., 1769; Ruth bp. 10 Dec., 1769.

Wid. PATIENCE, d. 18 Feb., 1800, in 68th yr.—*S. C. R.* (in 69th—*W. Ins.*)

CORNISH, JAMES, of Weth., on 17 Aug., 1710, "being bound in His Majesty's
service, for Port Royal," made a will (being then unmarried) in which he
gave to his sister Damaris his lds. in Weth., and also his chest and clothes
then in the custody of his uncle George Wolcott, for her use during her life,
and then to descend to her eldest son and his heirs forever; will proven 2
July, 1711. He may have been the James, who, with his bro. George, res. in
Windsor, contributed to the sum raised in Conn. for the poor of the other
colonies, 1676, each 6s. and 3d. He and his bro. Gabriel, of Westfield (who
m. Elizabeth, dau. of Geo. Wolcott, 15 Dec., 1686) seem to have res. at Windsor,
Westfield, Saybrook and elsewhere on the Conn. River, frequently in the capacity
of school-masters.—See, also, *Hinman*, 2d edit., pp. 723-4.

CORNWALL, HARVEY B., m. Janette L. **Goodrich**, 24 Feb., 1850(?).

CORWIN, ISRAEL, a ch. of, d. 31 Aug., 1775.—*S. C. R.*

COTTON, Rev. JOHN, (s. of Rev. John, of Boston, whom *Savage* styles "the most
distinguished divine of that age," in this country) was b. at B., or at Plymouth, 13 or 22 Mch., 1639-40; grad. H. C., 1657; served the Weth. ch. fm.
1660 to June, 1663 (but was not sett. there—See p. 322, Vol. I); was made
freeman, 14 Mch., 1660 and m. at Weth., 7 Nov., 1660, Joanna (dau. Dr.
Bryan) **Rossiter**, of Guilford; ret. to Boston 1663, where as *Savage* says (I,

462) he "had the unhappiness of being excom. by his father's Ch. for three aggravated [immoral] offences, May, 1664, I presume without pub. prosecution; and happily, long after dth. of his pious father, but after an open confess. was restored next month." He then went to Martha's Vineyard, where he acquired the Ind. language; rem. to and preached at Guilford, 1664; was ord. at Plymouth, 1667, where he was dismissed, 5 Oct., 1697, *Savage* says, "under very unpleasant circumstances;" was then called to Charleston, S. C., where he arrived 7 Dec., 1698, and there labored until his dth. of yellow fever, 17 or 18 Sept., 1699, ae. 59.[1] His vocabulary of Indian words (pub. in *Mass. Hist. Soc. Collect.* III Series, Vol. II, pp. 155-257) is of considerable value in the study of the Ind. languages of New Eng.

Hinman says (2d. Edit. 735-6) that the Rev. John Cotton, had ch. b. at Weth.— but they do not appear on the *Weth. Rec.*, tho' they can be found in *Savage*. Acc. to same authority, his wife *Hannah* (unless this is an error of the pen for *Joanna*, there must have been a *second* marr.) d. 12 Nov., 1702, ae. 60. *Hinman* credits him with the following.

Children (prob. b. at Weth.):

1. John, b. 1661.
2. Elizabeth, b. 1663; m. (1) Rev. James **Alling**, of Salisbury, Mass., and by him "became the mother of a noble family;" she m. (2) Rev. Caleb **Cushing**, her first husband's ministerial successor.—Authorities: *Savage's Dict.; Sibley's Harvard Graduates, I, 496-508; Chapin's Glast. Centennial; Hinman's Puritan Settlers.*

COUCH, THOMAS, (assistance rec'd fm. Wm. S. Granger, of Providence, R. I.), first appears in Weth. when he bo't a lot fm. John Stiles —(See Vol. I, p. 262); he m. (1) Rebecca ——————, 22 Nov., 1666, who d. 1 Mch., 1671-2; he must have m. (2) as appears fm. name of his wid. Hanna ——————, given in his will. He d. (prob. 24 Mch.) 1687; his invent. taken 30 Aug. of that yr. by James Treat, John Robbins and John Buttolph amt. £81-11-00; will ment. wid. Hanna, adm'x; and the 9 ch. ment. below; to eld. s. a double portion and to the other ch. an equal share as they shall come of age; also, ment. made of a legacy to the ch. fm. Uncle Simon Couch.—*Prob. Ct. Rec.* Couch drew 57 acs. in ld. div. of 1670.—See, also, Chapter VII, Vol. I.

Children (Weth. Rec.):

1. Susannah, b. 12 Oct., 1667 (ae. 20 at father's dth).
2. Simon, b. 11 Dec., 1669 (ae. 18 at father's dth.); in 1722 rec'd gt. of 6,000 acr. in Glast.; 68 ac., £34, and under this grant 34 acr., 123 rods, in 1725.—*Hinman*, p. 737.
3. Rebecca, b. 15 Feb., 1671-2 (ae. 15 at father's dth.).

(By second marriage):

4. Hannah, ae. 1
5. Thomas, ae. 12
6. Mary, ae. 11
7. Sarah, ae. 8 } at father's dth. FAM. 2.
8. Abigail, ae. 6
9. Martha, ae. 3

FAM. 2. THOMAS,[2] (*Thomas,*[1]), b. 1675, m. Sarah **Hurst,** of Deerfield, Mass., 16 Dec., 1713. He d. 1 Dec., 1751; wid. b. at D., 26 July, 1685, d. Weth., 16 Oct., 1757.

Children (Weth. Rec. & Mix Rec.):

1. Sarah, b. 27, bp. 14 Nov., 1714.
2. Hannah, b. 27, bp. 29 May, 1716.
3. Elizabeth, b. 23 Aug., 1718; she may have been the E. adm. to Sandisfield (Mass.) Ch. 31 Aug., 1766, from 1st Ch. Weth.—

R. H. C.

4. Thomas, b. 9 May, 1721.
5. Ebenezer, b. 28 Sept., 1723.
6. Benoni, b. 5 June, 1727. FAM. 3.

FAM. 3. BENONI,[3] (*Thos.,*[2] *Thos.,*[1]), b. 1727; m. 28 July, 1754, Phebe **Miller,** who was b. 15 Nov., 1732, at Midd., d. 13 July, 1821, at Sandisfield, Mass. He d. at S. 7 June, 1807—*S. Recs.;* tho' *fam. Rec.* give 1813, the former date prob. the correct one.

* See Chapt. I, p. 322, *Note.*

Children (*Weth. Rec.*) :

1. Samuel, b. 18, bp. 22 June, 1755.
2. Thomas, b. 26 Apl., bp. betw. Apl., and May, 1757.
3. William, bp. 13 May, 1759.
4. Mary (or Mercy), bp. 26 Sept., 1762.
5. Stephen.
6. Stephen.
7. John.
8. Lois.
9. Phebe, b. Sandisfield, Mass., 17 Sept., 1774; m. at S. 1791, Simeon **Granger, Jr.**, of W. Spgfld., Mass., who was b. 17 Mch., 1770 at W. S., and who d. Pittsford, Vt.,

9 Nov., 1834; wid. d. at P. 6 Feb., 1840. *Issue:*
  i. Lyman (Granger).
  ii. Chester (Granger), m. Mary Page (dau. of Esq. Cephas) **Smith,** of Sandisfield, Mass., and Suffield, Ct.
  iii. Rensselaer (Granger).
  iv. Edward (Granger).
  v. Dudley (Granger).
  vi. Livingston (Granger).
  vii. Mary Ann (Granger).
      See *Smith Family.*

COULSIN, (*Colson*) JOSEPH, res. in Htfd.; m. Margaret **Morgan,** at Weth., 2 July, 1701—*W. T. R.*

JOSEPH, m. Lois **Brooks;** had James, b. 30 Oct., 1780.—*W. C. R.*

COVEL, EPHRAIM, of Glast., m. Abigail **Riley,** 19 Oct., 1785. (A query of *G. A. T.* in *Boston Transcript*, of 13 May, 1901, ment. a Mathew C.—"believed to have been of Weth., where he joined the Revol. army, in Capt. Elijah Wright's Co.—and that he was previously of Killingly and had sons *Silas* and *Benjamin*.)

COWAN, (*Cowing*) ISRAEL, m. Lois **Standish,** 27 May, 1773; she 'wid. Lois," d. 2 Feb., 1815, in 71st yr.—*S. C. R.*; their ch. d. 31 Aug., 1775—*S. C. R.*

SHUBAEL, of Htfd., m. Anna **Smith,** 26 Oct., 1809.—*S. C. R.*

COWLES, JOSEPH. Invent. of est. taken 18 Dec., 1733, by Benj. Wright, Jacob Williams, and David Goodrich—amt. £518-03-10.—*Ct. Rec.* 1 Jan. 1733-34, adm. gr. to White Cowles, wid. Rec. £200 with Jacob Williams. (*Note.* Samuel Smith, of Midd., and White Smith his wife sett. ld. in Stepney parish that was distrib. to White Cole.—*Htfd. Co. Prob.*)

ERASTUS, m. (1) Elizabeth ————, who d. ae. 28, bu. 24 Apl., 1822—*W. C. R.*; m. (2) 16 Jan., 1823, Sally **Hudson**—*W. C. R.*; had (*W. C. R.*) (1) Hintland; (2) Elizabeth, bu. 1 Sept., 1822, ae. 4½; (3) Samuel Chauncey—all bp. 19 Apl., 1822. *Note.* Dates of marr. and bp. do not agree—but are given as found on *W. C. Recs*: HANNAH (wid.) ae. 77, bu. 20 Feb., 1829—*W. C. R.*

KIRTLAND Cowles (son of Erastus) m. Mary **Deming.** He d. 15 Dec., 1885; she d. 1 Nov., 1888.

Children (*from Family Bible*) :

1. Oliver, b. 20 June, 1837.
2. William, b. 12 Oct., 1839.
3. Ralph, b. 30 Dec., 1841; Corpl. Co. F, 14 Conn. Vols.; d. 28 Aug., 1891.
4. Elizabeth, b. 20 Jan., 1845.

5. Alice, b. 10 Jan., 1848.
6. Thomas S., b. 15 Mch., 1851; m. Mrs. Kate **Heslin,** who d. 15 May, 1903.
7. Frederick, b. 23 June, 1855; d. 10 Apl., 1857.

COWNEY, MICHAEL, of Waterbury, m. Mehitable **Williams,** 10 Apl., 1783.— *W. C. R.*

CRABBE, RICHARD, early at Weth., prob. came with Robert Coe*; had 7 lots of ld. allotted to him in W. (See Chapt. VII, Vol. I); apparently a man of good personal reputation; rep. W. in Gen. Ct., 11 Apl., 1639, Jan., 1639-40, two sess. in 1640 and in Apl., 1641, before he rem. with others, to Stamford, where he rec'd a home-lot in Nov., 1641; was one of the 7 men app. at S.'s first Town-meeting, to order the affairs of the new town. He may have been at S. earlier, as he, (or some one of the same name), was on the roll of freemen for election of mag., 16 June, 1639, and 9 Apl., 1640, was pres. as dep.; he must have been a citizen of some note, as he had 10 acs. of ld. assigned him, prob. N. of the present limits of the town, since he is spoken of later as res. in Greenwich; and became involved in the troubles which arose betw. that town and the New Haven Col., whose jurisdiction G. denied; complaint having been made to the N. H. gov't that the people of G. permitted drunkenness and harbored many servants, and joined persons in marr. without lawful authority. The *Gen. Ct.* ord. Crabb and others who had been most stubborn, to be arrested and punished. —*Hinman* (2d Edit.) 740. It is quite prob. that Crabb was somewhat broader minded than his neighbors, and being withal of a courage equal to his convictions, he proved a hard man to handle. In 1658, he seems to have been the cause of trouble in the ch.—because he harbored some Quakers and read Quaker books—even if he was not himself one of that belief. Also, he did not fully agree with the Puritan, as to the sanctity of the Sabbath, and was contemptuous of the ministry—for all of which the ch. dealt with him, and he was finally fined £30 and put under £100 bonds for good behavior; was also ord. to make pub. acknowledgment of his errors at St. to the satisfaction of Francis Bell and others; in 1660, being apparently still unregenerate, he was ord. to be arrested.

CRAFTS, (Craft, Croft). The Am. ancestor of this fam. was prob. *Griffin* Crafts, who came fm. Eng., 1630, with Gov. Winthrop's party, and sett. at Roxbury; m. Dorcas (dau. John) **Ruggles.**

Children:

1. John, b. 10 July, 1630; appears first at Branford, Ct., then at Weth.—*Hinman,* 2d edit. [There was also a John Crafts, ae. 20, pass. in the *America,* for Va., 23 June, 1635, who seems to have been of Branford, afterwards of Weth.]
2. Samuel, b. 12 Dec., 1637.
3. Moses, b. 28 Apl., 1641; was in Branford, Ct., 26 Oct., 1683, when he deeded ld. to Jona. Fisher, being in the deed described as "sometime of Branford, now of Weth., yeoman." He was chosen hayward at Weth. 1684; was surveyor, 1700. See Chapt. VII, Vol. I. He m. (prob. a. 2d marr.) 24 Jan., 1667, Rebecca (dau. of Peter) **Gardner;** and was among the early sett. of Deerfield, but after the destruction of that town by Ind., 1673, he rem. to Roxbury, Mass., for a short time, then to

Hatfield, then to Weth. (*Savage,* I, 471.) His s. *Thomas,* b. abt. 1662-3, rem. to Deerfield with parents, and with them, res. after King Philip's War at Hatfield, and then came to Weth., where he was living 1702. *Thomas* (s. of above Thomas) was at Hadley as early as 1676; he d. Feb., 1692; m. 6 Dec., 1683, Abigail (dau. John) **Dickinson.** Several families of this name are given in the *Hist. of Whately, Mass.* The induction of the name Crafts, as a Christian name, into Weth. families, was, we think prob., with the naming (1727) of Capt. Crafts Wright, s. of Timothy & Sarah (*Walker*) W., and gd-s. of Samuel & Rebecca (*Crafts*) Wright. This Samuel *may have* been the Samuel, given as the 2d s. of Moses above, b. 1637.

CRAIGE, ————, had s. Peregrine, bp. 14 June, 1789.—*S. C. R.*

CRAMPTON, STEPHEN P., of Htfd., m. Mary **Wright,** 28 May, 1829.—*S. C. R.*

* Robert Coe, of Jamaica, L. I., 9 May, 1661 (*Dutch MSS., N. Y., Sec. State's Office,* IX, p. 600) refers, in a petition, to Richard Crabbe as his bro-in-law.

CRANE. The *Crane Gen.*, by ELLERY B. CRANE, of Worcester, Mass., (2 vols. 8vo., 1895, 1900) to which we are largely indebted, among other sources, for information cont. in the following hist. of the Weth. Cranes, says that:

FAM. 1. BENJAMIN CRANE, b. abt. 1630, was in Weth. as early as 1655, poss. earlier, and prob. fm. Mass. (*Savage* says fm. Medfield) ; was made freeman in Weth., 12 May, 1658, had lds. rec. to him in W. Feb., 1656, and acquired much other ld. estate.—See Chapt. VII, Vol. I. He seems to have been a tanner, by trade. *Savage* says he m. Elinor **Breck,** of Dorchester, Mass., 12 Sept., 1656; but, however, that may have been. *Weth. Rec.* estab. the fact that he m. at W. 23 Apl., 1655, Mary (dau. of Wm. & Sarah *Charles*) **Backus,** and that, 24 Feb., 1656, the Town of Weth. gr. him a home-lot. His tan-yard, located abt. a mile S. of the Vil. of Weth. was for many yrs. known as the "Old Crane Tannery Place," and, on his dth. fell to his s. John; he served as juror, 1664; drew ld. in 1670 allotment; was rated among Weth. inhab., 15 Jan., 1673, to pay town 4s. 5½d; in 1682, with others petit. Gen. Ct. for liberty to erect a plantation in the Wabaynissit Country (Windham Co.). Mr. Benj. Crane d. 31 May, 1691; invent. of est. val. at £526-12-00, taken 13 Feb., 1692, by Henry Crane, Jona. Deming and Nathaniel Foote. His wid. d. 8 July, 1717.

Children (Weth. Rec.—those starred fm. Crane Geneal.):

1. Benjamin, b. 1 Men., 1655-6. FAM. 2.
2. Jonathan (Lieut.), b. 1 Dec., 1658. FAM. 3.
3. Joseph, b. 1 Apl., 1661. FAM. 4.
   FAM. 4.
4. John, b. 21 (30 *Crane Gen.*) Apl., 1663. FAM. 5.
5. Elijah,* b. 1665. FAM. 6.

6. Abraham,* b. 1668. FAM. 7.
7. Jacob,* b. 1670; res. and d. Ry-H. (Weth.) ; d. abt. 1718-19 ; Invent. est. £77-02-04.
8. Israel, b. 1 Nov., 1671. FAM. 8.
9. Mary,* b. 1673 ; m. 21 May,   , Wm. **Warner,** of Weth. ; 7 ch.

FAM. 2. BENJAMIN,[2] Jr., (*Benj.,*[1]), b. 1655-6; m. 12 May, 1686, Mary **Chapman,** (prob. dau. of Edward, of Windsor), who d. 5 Sept., 1687, ae. 22; he m. (2) Martha (dau. Samuel & Mary *Betts*) **Boardman;** he was drowned 20 June, 1693; his wid. m. (2) 5 June, 1697-8, Samuel **Terry,** of Enfield, Ct., and d. 1743, ae. 77, having had 5 sons and a dau. by her Terry husband. Benjamin's est. was invent., 1693, at £55-13-10; he was a tanner; his life, tho' brief, was samewhat eventful; he was one of the Weth. men most active in opposing the usurpation of Gov. Andross in 1687-90, and his outspokeness led to an attempt to arrest him under a special writ entrusted to a person (not a civil officer) with a file of soldiers, who broke into his house but failed to find him, tho' they greatly endangered the life of his wife, who was, at the time, *enciente*. A full account of this matter will be found in page 214 of our first volume. For ldd. ppy. see Chapt. VII, Vol. I.

Children (Weth. Rec.):

1. Benjamin, b. 7 Nov., 1690 ; d. May, 1693.
2. Isaac, b. 19 Aug., 1692 ; d. 16 Sept., 1712, and by will left ppy. to his four half bros.

(Terry), as "he counted they were his nearest relatives."

FAM. 3. Lieut. JONATHAN,[2] (*Benj.,*[1]) m. Deborah (dau. Francis) **Griswold,** 19 Dec., 1678, who was b. 1661 and d. abt. 1704. He was an early and prominent citizen of Windham, Ct., 1691, where he built a grist-mill, and was commis. Ens. Oct., 1695; in 1703, he was Lieut. and licensed by the Ct. to keep an inn; in 1704, at a reorganization of the Windham trainband, in view of the Indian outbreak, he was its Lieut., and in 1726, was one of the first set of jurymen empanelled in Co. of Windham, in Ct. of Common Pleas. He was a man high in public trust and full of good works as a citizen, and, as his tombstone says "lived a Pious and Godly life and left ye earth for heaven," Mch. 12, 1735, in 77th, yr.

Children (Crane Gen.) :

1. Sarah, b. 16 Nov., 1680.
2. Jonathan, b. 2 Feb., 1684.
3. John, b. 1 Oct., 1687.
4. Mary, b. 20 Oct., 1689 ; m. Jacob **Simons,** 1710.
5. Hannah, b. 7 Mch., 1692.

6. Isaac, b. 6 Apl., 1694.
7. Joseph, b. 17 May, 1696.
8. Elizabeth, ¡ twins, b. Feb., 1698 ; d.
9. Deborah, ⸳ 1698.
10. Abigail, b. 15 Feb., 1700 ; m. David **Knight,** 24 Dec., 1718 ; res. Norwich, Ct.

FAM. 4. JOSEPH,[2] (*Benj.*,[1]), b. 1661; m. Sarah (dau. John) **Kilborne,** 10 Dec., 1684 ; he d. 28 Nov., 1707, ae. 46 yrs., 7 mo., 27d.; Joseph lived in S. end of Ry-H. on the Midd. road; invent. taken 22 Dec., 1707-8—amt. £233-00-06 ; wid. m. (2) a Mr. **Leonard,** and subseq. rem. fm. Weth.

Children (Weth. Rec.) :

1. Sarah, b. 10 Dec., 1685 ; d. 24 June, 1686.
2. Sarah, b. 15 Mch., 1686-87 ; m. Moses **Goff, Jr.,** 5 July, 1711, who d. 1711, ae. 24 ; she m. (2) ———— **Toole** (or Tooley), as it seems to be in *Prob. Rec.*
3. Hannah, b. 4 Aug., 1689 ; m. ———— **Purple** before her father's dth. acc. to *Hinman.*
4. Mary, b. 31 Aug., 1692 ; d. 27 or 28 Sept., 1701.
5. Benjamin, b. 21 May, 1694.

6. Joseph, b. 25 Nov., 1696 ; d. 28 Sept., 1712.
7. Hester, b. 7, bp. 11 Sept., 1698 ; d. 6 Sept., 1701.
8. David, b. 27 Apl., bp. 4 May, (*Mix*) : d. 12 Sept., 1701, wanting 12 days of 15 mos. old.
9. Esther, b. 28 Aug. (bp. Aug. *Mix*) 1702 ; m. ———— **Pullus.**
10. Susan, b. 1704 or '5 ; m. ———— **Poole.**
11. Isaac, b. (and bp. *Mix*) 20 Oct., 1707.

FAM. 5. JOHN,[2] (*Benjamin*,[1]) b. 1663; m. Abigail (dau. of Nath'l) **Butler,** 27 Oct., 1692 ; rem. with his bro. Jonathan to Windham, where he built, in 1691-2 ; was a blacksmith, but ret. to Weth. and succeeded to his father's bus. as a tanner; he d. ae. 31, 21 Oct., 1694. Invent. of his est. amt. to £417-06-04 ; his wid. m. (2) 23 Feb., 1696-7, Samuel **Walker,** formerly of Weth., but afterwards of Stratford, Ct., who were app. adm'rs on his est. and 5 June, 1709-10, rendered an account to the Prob. Ct., showing that there then remained £23-09-09 of moveables, and £262-00-00, for the son and heir—a minor.

Child (Weth. Rec.) :

1. Josiah, b. 22 Mch., 1693-4.

FAM. 6. ELIJAH,[2] (*Benjamin*,[1]) b. 1665; m. (1) Mary (dau. Samuel, Jr.) **Sherman,** of a Weth. fam. which had rem. to Stratford, where she was b., 1666. They rem. aft. July, 1692, to Fairfield, Ct., where they became memb. in full communion of the ch. in Stratford parish, Oct., 1699; she d. before Mch., 1720; he m. (2) Abigail (dau. of Samuel) **Adams,** of F. He d. prior to Feb., 1727.

Children:

1. Abigail, bp. 29 May, 1698 ; prob. d. before 1716.
2. Deborah, bp. 2 Apl., 1699 ; prob d. before 1734.
3. Mary, bp. 15 Sept., 1700.
4. Israel, bp. 28 Mch., 1703 ; prob. d. before 1724.
5. Comfort, bp. 16 June, 1706 ; m. Joseph **Goodwin.**
6. Elijah, bp. 7 Nov., 1708 ; m. 3 Aug., 1732, Elizabeth (dau. Henry & Sarah *Frost*)

Wakeley, of Fairfield ; res. at Stratford ; d. 3 Oct., 1740 ; wid. m. (2) Benajah **Mallory,** 1743.
7. Jabez, bp. 9 May, 1714 ; res. Norwalk.
8. Abigail, bp. 29 June, 1716 ; prob. d. before 1734.
(*By second marriage*) :
9. Sarah.
10. Elizabeth.
11. Israel.
12. Benjamin.

FAM. 7. ABRAHAM,[2] (*Benjamin*,[1]), b. 1668 ; m. Hannah ————; he d. 5 July, 1713, ae. 45. Invent. of est. £345-03-07. He dr. lds. in 1694 allot.; was fence-viewer, 1699.

Children (Weth. Rec.) :

1. Mary, b. 7 Feb., 1697; bp. 3 Apl., 1708—
   Mix; m. (1) James **Treat**, Jr., 11 Aug.,
   1731, who d. 1762; m. (2) Nath'l **Copley**,
   of Weth.; 5 ch. by first marr.
2. John (Sgt.), b. 14, bp. 17 Mch., 1700.
   FAM. 9.
3. Abraham, bp. 29, 3d mo., 1702.—*Mix.*
4. Benoni, b. 20 Aug., bp. 3 Sept., 1704—
   —*Mix;* res. Weth.; living as late as
   1754; had lds. in New.

5. Hannah, b. 26 May, 1706.
6. Lucy, b. 25, bp. 30 July, 1710—*Mix;* m.
   Joseph **Forbes**, of Weth., 23 Dec., 1732.
7. Abraham, b. 5 Oct. (dec'd 11—*Mix*), 1713;
   one acc. says 1714; on the books is the
   following: "Mem[a]. Abraham Crane's
   birth afores[d], viz.: in 1714, is a manifest
   mistake, as appears by past evidence."
   FAM. 10.

FAM. 8. ISRAEL,[2] *(Benjamin,[1])*, b. 1671; m. 13 Sept., 1695, Lydia (dau. James)
Wright, who d. 28 Apl., 1707—acc. to *Prob. Rec.;* he was collector in 1700;
large ld.-owner; est. invent. at £444-19-6; he was prob. a tanner.

Children (Weth. Rec. & Prob. Rec.) :

1. Lydia, b. 4, bp. 10 *(Mix* Aug., 1701).
2. Hannah, b. 24, bp. 29 Nov., 1702; m. Timothy (s. of Daniel) **Bordman**, 21 Dec., 1721;
   "a Godly woman;" 10 ch.
3. Elizabeth, b. 23, bp. 24—*Mix*, Sept., 1704;

m. John **Russell**, Jr., 1 Dec., 1725; d.
10 Nov., 1745; 6 ch.
4. Martha, b. 10 Mch., 1705-6; prob. never
   marr.

FAM. 9. Sgt. JOHN,[3] *(Abm.,[2] Benj.,[1])*, b. 1700; m. Lydia **Curtis**, 30 Mch., 1737,
who d. 1 Aug., (*W. C. R.* says bu. 1 Aug.) 1790, ae. 78; res. Weth.; a large ld.-
holder; prob. the John licensed as tanner, Feb., 1727.—*Co. Ct. Rec.*

Children (Weth. Rec.) :

1. Ruth, b. 2 Feb., 1737-8.
2. John, b. 10 Sept., 1739. FAM. 11.
3. Lydia, b. 23 May, 1741; bp. 13 June, 1745;
   m. Simon **Giffin**, at (Ry-H.) Weth., 12
   Dec., 1771; 3 ch.
4. Hannah, b. 6, bp. 14 Oct., 1744; m. 23

Aug., 1764, at Weth., Thomas **Kilbey**;
sett. W.; 5 ch.
5. Curtis, b. 27 Mch., 1747. FAM. 12.
6. William, b. 7 Apl., 1749. FAM. 13.
7. Elizabeth, b. 30 June, 1750.

FAM. 10. ABRAHAM,[3] *(Abm.,[2] Benj.,[1])*, b. 1713-4; m. Rebecca (dau. Thos. &
Rebecca *Meekins*) **Hulburt**, 15 Mch., 1738-9, who united with Weth. ch. 1739 and
d. 13 Nov., 1794, ae. 82. He d. 5 (25—*Weth. Ins.*) Mch., 1756, in 43d yr.; adm.
on est. gr. June. 1756.

Children (Weth. Rec.) :

1. Abraham, b. 16 Dec., 1739. FAM. 14.
2. David, b. 29 Nov., 1741; served in Revol.
   War, 1776-1781; d. without issue, Sandisfield, Mass., abt. 1820; pensioner.
3. Elijah, b. 9, bp. 15 Jan., 1743-4. FAM. 15.
4. Benjamin, b. 18, bp. 20 July, 1746; said
   to have d. before Dec., 11, 1776.

5. Hezekiah, b. 28 Sept., 1748. FAM. 16.
6. Rebecca, b. 22 Nov., 1750; d. inf. 4 Oct.,
   1751.
7. Mary, b. 5, bp. 12—*W. C. R.*, Nov., 1752;
   m. John **Adams**, 6 Dec., 1771; 4 ch.
8. Joseph, b. 13 Aug., 1755. FAM. 17.

FAM. 11. JOHN,[4] *(John,[3] Ab'm,[2] Benj.,[1])*, b. 1739; m. Ruth ————; sett. Weth.;
served in Revol. War, in Capt. Oliver Hanchett's Co. (10th) of Suffield; 2d Reg.,
Col. Spencer, May 11—Dec. 17, '75 in and abt. Boston; said to have d. in camp
before Sept., 1777.

Children (W. C. R.) :

1. Rhoda, bp. 6 Aug., 1764.
2. Rebecca, bp 23 June, 1765; perhaps m.
   Sol. **Latimer** (?).
3. Ashbel, b. 30 June, 1766; bp. 14 Nov.,
   1770. FAM. 18.

4. Charles, prob. the "ch. of John," bp. 14
   Jan., 1770.
5. John, bp. 21 Sept., 1777.
6. Ruth, bp. 21 Sept., 1777.

FAM. 12. CURTIS,[4] *(John,[3] Ab'm,[2] Benj.,[1])* b. 1747; m. 6 Oct., 1774, Elizabeth
Palmer, who d. Milford, N. Y., 15 June, 1848. He d. Eaton, N. Y., 10 Oct.,
1828; prob. left Weth. shortly after close of Revol. War. He served in Col.
S. B. Webbs Add. Regt., 1778-1785; d. prior to the first pension act, but his
wid. rec. a pension from 1837 until her dth.

Children (*Weth. Rec.*) :

1. William, b. 27 June, 1775; bp. 7 Jan., 1776; d. at Charleston, S. C., yell. fever.
2. Curtis, b. 24 June, bp. 21 Sept., 1777. FAM. 19.
3. Elizabeth, b. 28 Mch., 1784; bp. 11 Sept., 1785.
4. Henry, b. 28 Nov., 1785; bp. 29 Oct., 1786 ; m. Elizabeth Cassety; sett. at Eaton, N. Y.; 5 ch.

5. Nancy, b. 4 Nov., 1788; bp. 17 Feb., 1793.
6. Charles, b. 4 Mch., 1791; bp. 17 Feb., 1793; d. Eaton, N. Y., 15 Feb., 1826.
7. Lydia Platt, b. 14 July, 1794; bp. 11 Oct., 1795; m. David Crowfut, and d. Preble, N. Y., Dec., 1821.
8. John William, b. 3 or 31 July, 1797, at New Htfd., Ct.; bp. 18 Feb., 1798; d. Southwick, Mass., 29 Aug., 1803.

FAM. 13. WILLIAM,[5] (*Sgt. John,*[4] *Ab'm,*[3] *Ab'm,*[2] *Benj.,*[1]) b. Weth., 1749; m. Rebecca ————, res. Gt. Barrington, Mass., after the Revol. War; who d. 19 Dec., 1829; was a farmer and tailor: see Chapt. XI, Vol. I, for account of his Revol. services; rem. after the war to Gt. Barrington, Mass., will dated in May, 1818; wid Rebecca d. 19 Dec., 1819.

Children (*Crane Gen.*) :

1. William, who m. Sally Pierson, had *Harriet* and *William Whiting;* is reported to have gone to Mich., and that he was a Methodist Minister.
2. Whiting, who m. Ann Pelton, had *Albert Louis, Aurelia Loiza,* and d. before his father.
3. Sally.

FAM. 14. Capt. ABRAHAM,[4] (*Ab'm,*[3] *Ab'm,*[2] *Benj.,*[1]) b. Weth. 1739; m. Mary (prob. dau. Joshua) Robbins, of W., who d. 20 May, 1813, ae. 67.—*Weth. Ins.* He d. 29 June, 1808, ae. 69,—*Weth. Ins.;* was a tanner; united with W. Ch., 1774; Invent. $4,809.57, including 33 sides of sole leather.

Children (*W. C. R.*) :

1. Mary, b. 1767; d. Dec., 1773.
2. Abraham (Capt.), b. 1770; bp. 5 Feb., 1775. FAM. 20.
3. Huldah, b. 1774; d. 25 May, 1813.
4. Benjamin, bp. 5 Feb., 1775. FAM. 21.
5. Mary, bp. 16 Apl., 1775; m. Simeon Hanmer, 17 May, 1798, at Weth.
6. Lucy, bp. 7 (or 21) Sept., 1777 ; m. Samuel Hanmer, Jr., 15 Mch., 1798, at Weth.
7. Eunice, bp. 23 Apl., 1780; m. Samuel Lockwood, 27 Sept., 1809, at Weth.

FAM. 15. ELIJAH,[4] (*Ab'm,*[3] *Ab'm,*[2] *Benjamin,*[1]), b. 1744, at Weth.; m. Martha Bush, of Colebrook, Ct.; was a tanner; res. Weth. until abt. 1769, when he rem. to Sandisfield, Mass., and farmed; he d. at S., 30 Aug., 1806; was a Revol. soldier. (See Chapt. VII, Vol. I).

Children:

1. Rebecca, b. 17 Feb., 1771; m. Rossiter Robbins; rem. to Cincinnati, Ohio; d. in So. Carolina, 1830.
2. Martha, b. 24 May, 1772 ; joined the Lebanon (N. Y.) Shakers.
3. Damaris, b. 1 Jan., 1774.
4. Elijah, b. 25 May, 1775. FAM. 22.
5. Elias, b. 17 May, 1780; m. at Bethlehem Ct., 17 Sept., 1810, Esther Raymond. He, a farmer at Sandisfield, Mass.; she d. 18 Apl., 1849, at S., and he d. at S., 22 Jan., 1853. Issue:
   i. Milo Raymond (Crane), b. 27 Apl., 1811; res. Berlin, Ct.
6. Barnabas, b. 17 Mch., 1781; m. Elizabeth
Cobb; d. 11 Aug., 1857; s. p.
7. Silas, b. 18 Apl., 1784; m. Clarissa ————: res. W. Stockbridge, Mass.; d. before July, 1825; 8 ch.
8. Prudence, b. 31 Oct., 1786.
9. Abraham, b. 21 June, 1789 ; m. Betsy (dau. William & Tabitha *Sparrows*) Twing (or Twining), of Tolland, Ct.; he d. at Canton, Ct., 12 Mch., 1864 ; 2 ch.
10. Lucy, b. 6 June, 1791.
11. Mary, b. 28 Sept., 1793; prob. the M. who m. 25 Feb., 1813, Benjamin Stillman Kelsey, of Saybrook.—*W. C. R.*
12. Hopeful, b. 16 Mch., 1796.

FAM. 16. HEZEKIAH,[4] (*Ab'm,*[3] *Ab'm,*[2] *Benjamin,*[1]) b. 1748; m. 29 Dec., 1771, Mary Dix, b. 1750, who d. 13 Jan., (19th *W. Rec.*), 1875, ae. 95. He d. 10 Mch., 1800; was a blacksmith; prob. served in Revol. as private in a militia Co., which joined Gen. Gates' Army of the North, 1777.

Children:

1. Sarah, b. 7 May, 1772; bp. 3 July, 1774 ; m. Thos. Harris, of Weth., 1797; she d. 7 Feb., 1829.
2. Mary, b. 17 Jan., bp. 3 July, 1774 ; m. Levi Hatch. *Issue:*
   i. Samuel (Hatch) ; b. 15 July, 1795 ; d. 18 July, 1798.
3. Leonard, b. 15 Aug., bp. 1 Dec., 1776 ; lost at sea, 1797, or '99.
4. Samuel, b. 25, bp. 27 June (or July), 1779. FAM. 23.

5. Hezekiah, b. 5, bp. 14 Jan., 1781; d. 19
   May, 1827; m. Dosha Morley (Mosley ?)
   (wid. of Jonathan) **Church,** who d. 10
   Nov., 1848, ae. 80; he d. 19 May, 1827.
   Issue:
   i. Jane Gray (Crane), b. 10 Apl., 1810;
   m. Martin **Porter,** Far., Aug., 1837;
   had (a) Edward Romanta (Porter);
   (b) Clarissa Jane (Porter; (c)
   Nellie Webster (Porter).
   ii. James (Crane), lost at sea in youth.

6. Thomas. b. 1 Mch., bp. 17 Aug., 1783;
   d. 27 May, 1787.
7. Lancelot, b. 12 Feb., 1785; bp. 15 Jan.,
   1786; d. 17 July, 1866, unm.
8. Rebecca, b. 14 Mch., bp. 13 Apl., 1788; m.
   William **Robbins;** she d. 29 Oct., 1866—
   W. Ins.; 9 ch.
9. Emily, b. 19 Dec., 1790; bp. 16 Jan., 1791;
   m. 24 Mch., 1815, Dr. Ashbel **Robertson,**
   of Weth.; she d. 13 May, 1860.

FAM. 17. JOSEPH,[4] ($Ab'm.^3$ $Ab'm,^2$ *Benjamin,*[1]), b. 1755, at Weth., m. 3 Dec.,
1778, Abigail (dau. Jacob) **Dix,**—*W. C. R.;* res. at Weth.; d. 21 June, 1811;
wid. d. 27 Mch., 1813, ae. 48.—*W. Ins.;* a Revol. soldier.—See Chapt. VII, Vol. I.

Children:

1. Joseph, b. 1779; d. 10 bp. 13 Mch., 1784;
   W. C. R. says bu. 16 Feb., ae. 5 (?).
2. Abigail, b. 1781; d. 2 Oct., 1783.
3. Joseph, 17 Aug., 1784; bp. 17 Apl., 1785;
   m. Mary **May,** at Weth., 20 Nov., 1803.
   FAM. 24.
4. Abigail, b. 29 Aug., 1786; d. 5 Oct., 1819.
   —*W. Ins.*
5. George, b. 12 Aug., 1788. FAM. 25.
6. Justus, b. 22 Nov., bp. 5 Dec., 1790; m.

   Anna **Fosdick,** of Weth., 5 Mch., 1812.—
   W. C. R. Issue:
   i. Abby (Crane), b. 10 Mch., 1817.
7. Sally, b. 29 Dec., 1792, bp. 13 Jan., 1793;
   m. John **Harris.**
8. John, b. 13 Nov., 1794; bp. 6, d. 7 Jan.,
   1795.
9. David, b. 28 May, 1797. FAM. 26.
10. William, b. 4; bp. 27 June or July, 1800;
    d. 9 Aug., 1820.—*W. Ins.*

FAM. 18. ASHBEL,[6] (*John,*[4] *John,*[3] $Abm.,^2$ $Benj.,^1$) b. 1770; m. ——, sett. in
Worcester, N. Y., abt. 1796, rem. to Cobleskill, N. Y.

Children:

1. John, b. 4 Mch., 1793.
2. Betsy, b. 29 Sept., 1795.
3. Charles, b. 14 Mch., 1797.
4. Lydia, b. 24 Mch., 1799.
5. Hannah, b. 17 June, 1801.

6. Ashbel, b. 10 Apl., 1803.
7. Rebecca, b. 3 Oct., 1805.
8. Abigail, b. 16 Apl., 1808.
9. Ruth, b. 27 Oct., 1811.

FAM. 19. CURTIS,[5] (*Curtis,*[4] *John,*[3] $Ab'm,^2$ $Benj.,^1$), b. Weth., 28 Aug., 1777; m.
(28 Aug., acc. to Fam. Rec., but 28 Oct. by *Weth. Ch Rec.,*) 1800, Lucy (dau.
John & Mary *Crane*) **Adams,** of Ry-H., b. 25 Nov., 1777. He d. at sea 16
Sept., 1810, in the schr. *Sally,* of which he was first mate and super-
cargo, and which was capsized at Barnegat Shoals, while bound for the
Bermudas. The wid. and dau. rem. with some of her husband's family to
Angelica, N. Y., where she d. 3 May, 1867, in 91st yr.—Letter of C. C. Gardiner.

Child:

1. Mary, b. 25 July, 1801, bp. 11 Oct., 1807
   —*W. C. R.;* m. 22 Jan., 1822, Lyman
   Gardiner, at Eaton, N. Y. She d. Angelica,
   N. Y., 29 Apl., 1844. Of their 13 ch. the
   eldest, Curtis *Crane* Gardiner, b. 1822;

   is a prominent lawyer in St. Louis, Mo.;
   served in the War of the Civil Rebell.,
   and is the author of the Genealogy of
   Lyon Gardiner and His Descendants, pub.
   1900.

FAM. 20. Capt. ABRAHAM,[5] Jr.,($Ab'm,^4$ $Ab'm,^3$ $Ab'm,^2$ $Benj.,^1$), b. 1770, Weth.;
m. 9 Feb., 1797, Huldah **Hanmer,** of W. where they sett. She d. 15 May,
1813, ae. 67.—*W. C. R.* He m. (2) 9 Mch., 1834, Prudence Wright **Treat,** who
d. 17 Jan., 1861, ae. 74. He d. 20 Dec., 1842, ae. 72.—*W. Ins.;* was a tanner.

Children (*Weth. Rec.*), all bp. 27 Oct., 1811:

1. Mary, b. 27 Jan., 1798.
2. William Hanmer, b. 25 Oct., 1799.
3. Abraham, b. 13 Nov., 1801; m. 24 July,
   1833, Elizabeth T. (**Palmer**—*W. C. R.*).
   He d. at Hillsboro, Geo., 20 May, 1845—
   W. Ins.; she d. at Evans Mills, N. Y.,
   18 Oct., 1865, ae. 59.
   (From *Crane Geneal.*)
4. Martia, b. 1803; poss. the *Marcia* who m.

   1 Jan., 1840, James G. **Peck,** of Bristol,
   Ct.
5. Ralph, b. 8 June, 1805.
6. Edmund, b. 8 Mch., 1807; m. Amelia
   Johnson, 1849; is a farmer; their s.
   Edmund, Jr., b. 30 Apl., 1851, is a State
   Prison official at Htfd.
7. Eliza, b. 1811; m. J. R. **Crocker;** d. 6
   June, 1839, ae. 28.—*W. Ins.*

FAM. 21. BENJAMIN,[5] (*Abm.*,[4] *Abm.*,[3] *Abm.*,[2] *Benj.*,[1]) b. Weth., 1775; m. Sally **Lockwood**, 7 Sept., 1794, at W., and with his bro., Ab'm, succeeded to their father's tannery bus. He d. before 11 Apl., 1816, ae. 44.—*W. C. R., Weth. Ins.*

Children (Weth. Ch. Rec., W. C. R.):

1. Benjamin, ae. 2 ; bu. 19 Aug., 1798.
2. John, bp. 18 Aug., 1798.
3. Benjamin Robbins, bp. 18 Nov., 1798.
4. Sarah, bp. 18 Nov., 1798.
5. Samuel Lockwood, bp. 7 Sept., 1800 ; res.
   Pittsfield, Mass.
6. James.
7. Ira R., bp. 17 Jan., 1805 ; m. 1859, Lucy R. **Rawdon**; res. W. Farmington, Ohio.
8. Henry, bp. abt. 1807.

FAM. 22. ELIJAH,[5] (*Elijah,*[4] *Abm.*,[3] *Abm.*,[2] *Benj.*,[1]) b. 1775; m. Honor **Adams**, at Weth., 20 May, 1798; he then of Sandisfield, Mass., where his father had gone. They both d. Sheffield, Mass., he on 13 Mch., 1863, she 22 Apl., 1836. She was adm. to Sheffield Ch. from Weth. Ch., Nov. 3, 1833.— *R. H. C.*

Children (bp. Weth.):

1. Sarah, b. 1 May, 1800.
2. Harriet, b. 6 Aug., 1802 ; m. Josiah **Robbins**, 1826 ; res. Weth. ; 4 ch.
3. Calvin Camp, b. 28 Oct., 1805, at Sandisfield, Mass. ; m. Lucretia **Wolf**, 1828 ; res. Gt. Barrington, Mass. ; d. 1881.
4. Sarah Adams, b. June, 1807 (or 26 Feb., 1810 ?) ; bp. 3 Apl., 1808.—*W. C. R.*
5. George, b. 26 Feb., bp. 6 May, 1810 ; d. 18 Apl., 1850.
6. Royal, b. 23 May, bp. 4 Oct., 1812.— *W. C. R.*
7. Elizabeth C., bp. 19 May, 1816.
8. Martha Bush, b. 22 Nov., 1820 ; bp. 1 July, 1821—*W. C. R.;* d. 15 Aug., 1850 at Sheffield.

FAM. 23. SAMUEL,[6] (*Hez.*,[5] *Abm.*,[4] *Abm.*,[3] *Abm.*,[2] *Benj.*,[1]) b. 1779; m. at Weth., 9 Mch., 1799, Dorothy **Benton**, who d. 29 Apl., 1842; he lost at sea 24 Apl., 1852.

Children:

1. Nancy, b. 15 Jan., 1800 ; d. 19 Aug., 1831 ; m. Royal **Treat**, of E. Htfd., 6 Mch., 1828—*W. C. R.;* had 1 dau.
2. Ch., ae. 3, bu. 25 June, 1804.—*W. C. R.*
3. Leonard, b. 19 Sept., 1801 ; d. 29 June, 1802.
4. Harriet, b. 15 June, 1803 ; m. (1) ———— **Vall**; m. (2) **Hathaway.**
5. Emily, b. 17 Nov., 1805 ; m. Sylvester **Woodhouse**, as 2d wife ; 2 ch.
6. Mary, b. 19 Oct., 1807 ; d. 15 July, 1811.— *W. C. R.*
7. Leonard, b. 5 July, 1809 ; lost at sea, 1828.
8. Samuel, b. 23 July, 1813 ; d. 24 Apl., 1852.
9. Ch., ————, ae. 1½, bu. 28 Jan., 1816.
10. Mary, b. 3 Oct., 1815 ; d. 25 May, 1819.
11. Son, ————, ae. 4, bu. 10 Dec., 1820.— *W. C. R.*
12. Horace, b. 23 July, 1817 ; d. yg.
13. Jane, b. 19 Oct., 1819 ; m. Dr. Chas. **Austin**, 4 May, 1840 ; rem. to Albany, N. Y. ; he d. 1881 ; 7 ch.

FAM. 24. JOSEPH,[5] (*Joseph,*[4] *Ab'm,*[3] *Ab'm,*[2] *Benj.*,[1]), b. 1779; m. and res. Weth.; he d. 17 Oct., 1805.

Children:

1. Joseph Chauncey, b. 7 Mch., 1804 ; bp. 4 May, 1806 ; m. Sarah **Bushnell**, of Saybrook ; sett. at Norway, N. Y. ; he d. 21
   Feb., 1859 ; 3 ch.
2. Mary Ann, bp. 4 May, 1806 ; m. James **Wright**; rem. to Indiana, abt. 1850 ; 4 ch.

FAM. 25. GEORGE,[5] (*Joseph,*[4] *Ab'm,*[3] *Ab'm,*[2] *Benjamin,*[1]) b. 1788; m. Sarah **Kelsey**, 19 Apl., 1818; was a sea-capt., d. 28 Nov., 1824, at Bridgeport, Ct.; she d. 13 Dec., 1856, at Fairfield, N. Y.

Children:

1. Sarah Susan, b. 20 May, 1819 ; d. 4 Dec., 1820.
2. Emeline, b. 1 Jan., 1821 ; m. Jas. L. **Morehouse**; res. Fairfield, N. Y. ; d. 18
   Aug., 1888 ; 4 ch.
3. Louisa Maria, b. 4 Nov., 1822 ; d. 15 May, 1825.
4. George, b. 1 Oct., 1824 ; d. 28 Mch., 1825.

FAM. 26. DAVID,[5] (*Joseph,*[4] *Ab'm,*[3] *Ab'm,*[2] *Benj.*,[1]) b. 1797; m. 25 Sept., 1822, Pamelia (dau. Levi & Sarah **Grant**) **Deming**, who was b. 8 Nov., 1800 and d. 28 Dec., 1872. He d. 23 Apl., 1848, ae. 50½.—*W. T. C.*

Children:

1. Maria F., b. 24 Sept., 1823 ; d. 20 July, 1887.—*W. Ins.*
2. David, b. 13 Mch., 1826. Fam. 27.
3. Sarah, b. 29 Oct., 1829.
4. Juliette, b. July, 1833.

5. Levi D., b. 26 June, 1835 ; d. 2 Dec., 1847. —*W. Ins.*
6. Abigail. b. 21 July, 1838 ; m. Rev. S. D. **Jones.**

Fam. 27. DAVID,⁶ (*David,⁵ Joseph,⁴ Ab'm,³ Ab'm,² Benj.,¹*) b. 1826; m. Katharine **Callahan**, 13 Feb., 1861; he d. 29 Jan., 1882; res. Weth.

Children:

1. George, b. 8 Sept., 1863.
2. Edith A. b. 14 Apl., 1866.

3. Harry W., b. 11 Dec., 1868 ; is P. M. (1903) at Weth.

CRAUFUT, JOSEPH, of Berlin, m. Olive M————? 29 Mch., 1816.—*S. C. R.*

CRITTENDEN, ELIZABETH C., m. Cheney **Wright**, of Htfd., 21 Oct., 1826.— *W. C. R.; Ichabod's* son Lucius d. at St. Iago, Dec., 1822,—*W. C. R.;* William had Elizabeth, bp. 31 July, 1833.—*W. C. R.*

ICHABOD & Betsey had (*W. T. R.*) Joseph Lyman, b. 22 July, 1821; Lewis Thomas, b. 2 Nov., 1828; and Lucius, d. St. Iago., W. I., bu. Dec., 1822.

CROFT, Mr. MOSES, d. 30 Dec., 1718, in 80 yr.—*W. Ins.*

CROSBY, JOSEPH, of Htfd., m. Maria **May**, 27 Nov., 1834.

CROW, EUNICE, ae. 60, bu. 27 Feb., 1803.—*W. C. R.*

CROWELL, BENJAMIN, from Weth., sett. at Midd.; m. Sarah **Johnson**, of M., 30 Sept., 1708.—*Ch. Rec.*, see *Hinman*, 2d edit. 768. He d. 24 Jan., 1752; wid. d. 5 Dec., 1767.

CROWFOOT, (*Crowfoort, Crofoot, Crofut*), JOSEPH, ment. by Savage (*Gen. Dict. N. Eng., 1, 480,*) as at Springfield, Mass., in 1658; freeman, 1672; m. 14 Apl., 1658 ;, Mary (dau. John) **Hillier**, of Windsor, Ct., in 1663 had assigned to him, with three others, the 10th of the 10 principal seats in the S. meeting-house, which speaks fairly well for his social position; in 1665 he was fined, with 15 others for absenting himself from town-meetings; and in King Philip's War, 1676, he was one of the 150 men under Capt. Wm. Turner, who fought the Inds. at the memorable fight at Turner's Falls, his name being on the List of Soldiers approved by a committee of the Gen. Ct., as entitled to a land bounty for their services in this affair (see Bodge's *Soldiers of King Philip's War*, pp. 201-08). He d. it is said at Northampton, Mass. 1678.

Children (b. Springfield) :

1. Joseph, b. 29 Apl., 1660. Fam. 2.
2. Mary, b. 4 Oct., 1661.
3. John, b. Aug., 1663.
4. Samuel, b. 13 Oct., 1665.

5. James, b. 23 Jan., 1667.
6. Daniel, b. 23 Jan., 1669.
7. Matthew, b. 5 Apl., 1672.
8. David, b. 11 Oct., 1674.

Fam. 2. JOSEPH,² (*Joseph,¹*) b. 1660; m. 30 Dec., 1686, Margaret ————, who d. 1733; he was gr. lds. (20 acr.) in Weth., 1697 (See Chapt. VII, Vol. I), also in 1736 inherited his father's right to lds. in Mass., gr. by Gen. Ct. to the soldiers (or their descendants) who served in the Turner's Falls fight.—see

Bodge's *Soldiers of King Philip's War.* Crowfoot, Joseph, pltif. in suit, died before June, 1727, and his wife Margaret, of Bramford, was administratrix, Feb., 1727-8;—*Co. Ctt. Rec.;* poss. he had d. as early as 1722, as would appear from the following: Joseph Crowfoot Invt. 37-14--06 taken 1st October, 1722 by Ephriam Goodrich Jonathan Curtis Court Record 2nd. October, 1722 Adms. to Margaret Crowfoot widow of the Deed.

Children (Weth. Rec.) :

1. Mary, b. 25 Dec., 1687 ; d. abt. 1 Aug., 1689.
2. Margaret, b. 8 Mch., 1689.
3. Joseph, b. 12 June, 1692.
4. Elizabeth, b. 14 Aug., 1693.
5. Mary, b. 14 Jan., 1695.
6. Mehitable, b. 1 July, 1697 ; bp. 24 Mch., 1699-1700.—*Mix.*

7. Sarah, b. 19 Mch., 1700 ; bp. 30 Nov., 1701— *Mix;* d. inf.
8. Ephraim, b. 27 July, 1705. FAM. 3.

The name (acc. to *Savage* and *Hinman*) early passed out of Weth. to Midd., where it is still found : probably through the line of Ephraim (FAM. 3, below).

FAM. 3. EPHRAIM,[3] (*Joseph,*[2] *Joseph,*[1]) b. 1705 ; m. 26 July, 1753, (he then being 48 yr. old) Mary **Williams**, of Cromwell (Midd. Upper Houses) ; it is poss. that he might have had a previous wife; as acc. to the Geneal. in *The Owl,*[*] the Cromwell recs. show a marr. of a Margaret Crofoot to Mark **Hodgkins**, 25 Dec., 1739; also, of Abigail Crofoot to John **Cole**, 18 Aug., 1743. These may have been Ephraim's ch. by a first wife, or, again they might be his bro. Joseph's ch. It is prob. that Ephm. lived to a good old age, and that he d. in Berlin, about 1795; also, that he d. intestate; for there is on the B. recs. a deed, dated 20 Apl., 1795, exec. by Elisha and Joseph C. of B., for ld. descended to them by their father Ephm., dec'd, and which, from the description was prob. the fam. homestead.

Berlin Ld. Recs. also show several conveyances between that date and 1830, in which appears the names of Francis, Ira, Sylvester, and Ephm., Jr., Crofoot, all prob. ch. of Ephm. or his bro. Joseph.

Ephraim & Mary Crowfoot had the following *children*, as far as known:

1. Elisha, b. 1754 ; in 1797, when abt. 43 yrs. old he rem. to West Turin, Lewis Co., N. Y. (See Hough's *Hist. Lewis Co., N. Y.*, 230-1), where he d. 29 Mch., 1813, in 60th yr. ; wife d. 16th same month. *Issue :*
   i. Mary,) who, acc. to above history,
   ii. John, } did not rem. to N. Y.
) with him.
   iii. Isaac, b. 1784 ; at one time Judge of Co. Ct. ; and later a res. of Fond du Lac, Wis.
   iv. Rachel, who d. 11 Mch., 1813.
   v. James, res. at Turin, N. Y. ; his gd-dau. Mrs. Addie Comfort Dewey, of Constableville, N. Y., has fam. rec. wrote.
   vi. Anson, d. 23 July, 1825.

   vii. David, d. 2 Sept., 1814.
2. Joseph, res. in Berlin and held much landed ppy. ; name appears often in real estate affairs betw. 1795 and 1821 ; wife's name Hannah ; poss. he was the Joseph who served in Capt. Seth Seymour's Co. Col. Mead's Reg., Conn. troops, for one month and was disch. 24 Nov., 1776.
3. Ephraim, b. 1757 ; res. Berlin ; was a soldier in Revol. and when he mad- appl. for pension, 28 May, 1818, was 61 yrs. old, had served 3 yrs. in Cont. service, a part of the time in Capt. Darius Wilcox's Co., Col. Baldwin ; his wid. Lois (as per her appl. for her husband's pension, 13 June, 1837, was a res. of Midd. and ae. 79.

Miscellanea :

IRA, of Midd., m. Amelia **Belden**, 31 May, 1821.—*S. C. R.;* d. 2 Nov., 1846 in 67.— *S. C. R.*

CROCKER, HANNAH, d. 6 Dec., 1829, ae. 78.—*W. T. R.*

MARY, wife of Oliver, d. 4 Feb., 1814.—*N. C. R.*

SUSAN, m. Hiram Goodrich, 13 Apl., 1820.—*W. T. R.*

JOHN, of Derey, N. Y., m. Mary N. **Pilsbury**, 20 Aug., 1828.—*W. C. R.*

Rev. Z., d. Upper Midd., ae. 46.—*S. C. R.*

---

[*] *The Owl,* a very neat little magazine (now in its 2d volume), pub. at Kewaunee, Wis., by Geo. Dikeman Wing, is devoted almost entirely to genealogical and historical articles ; and among others, to the genealogy of the Crowfoot family.

CULVER, (*Step. Ch. Recs.*) ABIGAIL, of William, d. 6 Apl., 1782; CLARINDA, of Edward 1st, bp. 26 Oct., 1788, d. 7 Feb., 1789; CLARINDA, of Edward, 2d, d. 13 Sept., 1787; EDWARD, m. Hetty **Williams,** 29 (?) Jan., 1796; EDWARD, d. 28 Feb., 1823, in 73d yr.; had John bp. 2 Sept., 1781, Mehitable bp. 25 Aug., 1782, Jemina, bp. 9 May, 1784, Clarinda bp. 16 Apl., 1786, Clarinda, d. 7 Feb., 1789, in 1st yr., Clarinda bp. 6 Oct., 1778.—*W. C. R.* EDWARD'S wife d. ae. 35, Jan. 13, 1789.—*W. C. R.* ELETHA, (or Estelle) dau. Christopher C. & Frances) d. 3 May, 1853, ae. 3 yr. 6 mo. 22 d.—*Weth. Ins.;* ABNER, d. 28 Apl., 1869, ae. 72; BETHIAH, d. 13 Jan., 1789, ae. 35; EDWARD, d. 28 —, 1823, ae. 12; GEORGE W. d. 12 Apl., 1855, ae. 28; JEMINA, wife of Jeremiah, d. 10 Feb., 1792, "on Long Island" in 76 yr.— *S. C. R.;* FREDERICK D., d. 6 Oct., 1862, ae. 27; LORENZO D., d. 1 Apl., 1866; OTIS A., d. 9 May, 1866, ae. 26. The three foregoing, all members of Co. K. Eleventh Reg., Conn. Vols., (are sons of David A. & Sarah Culver, RUHAMAH (dau. Gershom & Phebe) d. 27 Sept., 1780, ae. 21 yr. 31 d.

CURTIS, (*Curtiss, Courtis, Curtice*). Assistance acknowledged from Mr. JAMES SHEPARD, of New Britain, Ct., and Mr. CHARLES B. CURTIS, of New York City. There are three distinct families of this name in Conn., and two individuals, JOHN and THOMAS CURTIS, brothers, were among the very early settlers of Weth. What little is known of JOHN, as concerning Weth. history, is to be found in our Chapt. VII, Vol. I.

1. THOMAS, b. 1598, an early sett. here, where his eld. ch. was b. 1639; had a cattle ear-mark recorded (*W. T. V.*), in 1653; was relieved by an order of the Gen. Ct., 21 May, 1657, from training, watching and warding; he d. 13 Nov., 1681, ae. 83,[1] in Htfd., a man of good reputation and large estate (See Chapt. VII, Vol. I.) am'g acc., to invent. taken 9 Dec., 1681, by Nath'l Boreman, Samuel Butler and Wm. Warner, to £717-13-09; adm'n gr. to his sons, John, Joseph and James, and Mr. Kimberly; his s. Samuel having rec'd his portion by deed, before his father's dth. His ch. agreed to a division of the est. which was made by Lieut. James Treat, Stephen Chester and Mr. Samuel Wolcott, under a decree of the *Prob. Ct.,* dated 2 Mch., 1681-2. His wife's name was Elizabeth ————. There is a fam. trad.—unsupported by any rec —that he was a physician.

Children (*b. in Weth.*) :

1. John,* (Sgt.), b. 1 Jan., 1639. FAM. 2.
2. James,[2] b. 15 Sept., 1641; m. Abigail ————, 8 July, 1686 ; the Town gave him in 1685, a ¾ rod add. to the width of his ho-lot ; he was constable in 1686.
3. Joseph,[2] b. "the last day of March," 1644. FAM. 3.
4. Samuel,* b. 1 Apl., 1645. FAM. 4.
5. Isaac,* b. [   ], 1647 ; was taxed, 1673,

to pay for the purchase of the "Five Mill" tract ; rem. to Woodbury, Ct., where *Cathren* says he was a late settler; and had a ho-lot there in 1682.
6. Elizabeth, b. ————— ; m. 26 May, 1674, John **Stoddard,** Jr.
7. Ruth, ————— ; m. Eleazur **Kimberly,** sometime Sec'y of the Colony of Conn.

FAM. 2. Sgt. JOHN, (*Thomas,*[1]) b. 1639; m. 20 Nov., 1666, Lydia —————, was made freeman, 1658; res. Weth., see Chapt. VII, Vol. I. Invent. of est. taken 18 Mch., 1714-15, am't to £1127-18-07; his will ment. all the ch. except the John and Lydia ment. below, and then dec'd.

---

[1] *Savage* is in error in saying that he was at Wallingford, Ct., in 1670 ; evidence to that effect is lacking. The Wallingford Curtis is that of Richard, previously of Dorchester, Mass.—*C. B. S.*

[2] *James* and *Joseph* are prcb. the parties who, in ——, were (with Thos. Hurlbut, Jr., and Thos. Wickham) sentenced by the *Gen. Ct.* to imprisonment during the Court's pleasure, for agreeing to rob Richard Smith's water-melon-patch, and *not only stealing* five melons, *but afterwards boasting of it.*

The stealing of watermelons, indeed, does not seem to have been viewed with that laxity of opinion in those early times, with which it is in the present day. In Rev. Mr.

Children (Weth. Rec.) :

1. John, b. 10 Dec., 1667. FAM. 5.
2. Thomas (Capt.), b. 15 Sept., 1670. FAM. 6.
3. Lydia, b. 1 Mch., 1673.
4. Dorothy, b. 15 May, 1674; m. Isaac **Bridgman.**
5. William, b. 12 Mch. (Oct. in *Hinman*), 1677. FAM. 7.

6. Elizabeth, b. 13 Nov., 1679; m. Joseph **Woodruff.**
7. Jonathan (Dea.), b. 13 Aug., 1682. FAM. 8.
8. Abigail, ————; m. —— **Lewis.** (Marriages of above from the father's will.)

FAM. 3. JOSEPH,[2] (*Thomas,*[1]) b. 1644; was surveyor, 1681; haywarden, 1697; for ld-ppy. see Chapt. VII, Vol. I; m. 8 Feb., 1674, Mercy ————; he d. 31 Dec., 1683; Invent. est. amt'd to £271-09-00.

Children (Weth. Rec.) :

1. Meribah, b. 10 Mch., 1673-4; d. 15 Jan., 1683-4.
2. Joseph, b. 10 Mch. (*Hinman* says *Jan.*), 1674-5. FAM. 8a.
3. Mary, b. 2 Sept., 1677.

4. Sarah, b. 23 Sept., 1679.
5. Thomas (Capt.), b. 24 Nov. or Dec., 1680. FAM. 9.
6. David, b. 29 Nov., 1682. FAM. 10.

FAM. 4. SAMUEL,[2] (*Thomas,*[1]) b. 1645; m. 20 Feb., 1683, Sarah ————; res. Weth.; ld-ppy. see Chapt. VII, Vol. I; d. 26 Nov., 1688, ae. abt. 42 yrs.; est. distrib. 1706-7, by Philip Alcock and Nath'l Boreman, according to a "deliberate consideration" and "loving agreement to prevent further trouble," by his heirs—amount'd to £130-01-03. He was a weaver.

Children (Weth. Rec.) :

1. Samuel, b. 23 Nov., 1684. FAM. 11.
2. Elizabeth, twin to Ruth, b. 17 May, 1687 :

d. 10 July, 1687.
3. Ruth, twin Elizabeth, m. Ebenezer **Hale.**

FAM. 5. JOHN,[3] (*John,*[2] *Thomas,*[1]) b. 10 Dec., 1677; dr. lds. in 1694, allot.; collector, 1692; Town school committee 1702; m. 3 Apl., 1690, Elizabeth (dau. Joseph & Mary) **Wright;** he d. 8 (7 acc. to *Prob. Rec.* and *W. Ins.*), Nov., 1712; his will devised to his wife, the use of all his lds. and his negro servant, Jacob, also to his ch. Invent. £1004-15-09.—*Htfd. Co. Prob.*

Children (Weth.) :

1. Martha, b. 17 Jan., 1690-1; m. Richard **Robbins.**
2. Lydia, b. "abt. the middle" of Nov., 1693; d. "abt. the middle" of Apl., 1696.
3. Mary, b. 5 July, 1696; m. John **Welles.**
4. Rachel, b. 25 (bp. 31—*Mix*) Oct., 1698.
5. John, b. 8 (bp. 9—*Mix*) Feb., 1700-1; "only surviving son" at time of his father's dth.; m. Elizabeth (dau. Richard,

Jr.) **Lord;** in 1721, the *Prob. Ct.,* directed him to take his father's ho-std. and pay their shares of the est. to his sisters Elizabeth and Hannah ; rem. to New Lond. and d. at Canterbury. Ct., 31 Oct., 1727.
6. Josiah, b. 17 Nov., 1703.
7. Elizabeth, b. 18 Mch., 1707.
8. Hannah, b. 12 Dec., 1711; in 1721 Mrs. C. was app'd guardian of these daus..

FAM. 6. Capt. THOMAS,[3] (*John,*[2] *Thos.,*[1]) b. 1670; m. 17 Mch., 1714-15, Rachel (dau. John) **Morgan,** of Groton, Ct., who d. 5 Feb., 1730. Her mother Elizabeth, was a dau. of Dep-Gov. William **Jones,** of New Haven, by his wife Elizabeth, dau. of Gov. Theophilus Eaton, of New Haven—and she m. (1) a **Williams,** and (2(John **Morgan.** Capt. Thomas Curtis was a sea-captain; his will dated 3 Aug., 1734, and he d. 1741; Inventory taken 23 Mch., 1744, by John Stillman and Josiah Wolcott (*Htfd. Prob.*) am't to £123-07-06.

Mix MSS. Rec., we find that it was considered a matter for Church discipline. "Dec. 26, 1703. I publickly reprove Benj. Churchill, Jun[r]. It was testified against him that he moved Wm. Goodrich, Jun[r]., to go get Watermelons, and went with Benj., Leete & Wm. Goodrich, Jun[r]., to Mrs. Dennison's, where they (that is, Leete and Goodrich) got Watermelons—tho' he [Benj. Churchill] would not. Ben[jn] Churchill owned he went wth them, and counseled them; tho' he said he also [dis]suaded them. But, refusing to express some[thing publickly ?] I openly reproved him." Ben.'s father, Benj[n] Churchill, Sen[r]., was also brought into this matter before the Church, as being under suspicion of encouraging his boy to withold public confession of his fault.

* A record filed with the Inventory of John Crouse in *Prob. Ct. Office,* at Htfd., gives the ages of these children at date of same, thus, *Joseph,* ae. 9 yrs.; *Henry,* ae. 7 yrs.; *Sarah,* abt. 5 yrs.; *Thomas,* ae. 3 yrs.; *David,* 1 yr. old—*C. W. M.*

Children (Weth. Rec.) :

1. Ambrose, b. 23, bp. 25 Mch., 1716; d. unm.,
   ae 77, 23 July, 1792.—*W. C. R.*
2. James, b. 11 Sept., 1718. FAM. 12.
3. Experience, b. 12 Nov., 1720; m. ———

Hinsdale.
4. Waitstill, b. 22 July, 1723; d. unm.
5. Rachel, b. 5 Feb., 1727; d. unm.
6. Thomas (Dea.). FAM. 13.

FAM. 7.   WILLIAM,[3] (*John,*[2] *Thos.,*[1]) b. 1677; lister, 1702; fence-viewer 1709;
m. 8 Jan., 1702, Ruth (dau. Nath'l) **Butler.**

Children (Weth. Rec.) :

1. Gideon, b. 10, bp. 11 (*Mix*) July, 1703;
   d. Nov., 1704.
2. William, b. 23 Aug., 1705; d. unm. abt.

1742.
3. Charles, b. 13, bp. 19 (*Mix*) Mch., 1709-10.
4. Lydia, bp. 19 Apl., 1713.—*Mix.*

FAM. 8.   Dea. JONATHAN,[3] (*John,*[2] *Thomas,*[1]), b. 1682, in Weth.; m. 5 June,
1705, Hepzibah, (dau. Thos. & Anna *Hawkes*) **Hastings,** of Htfd., (prob.
though written Hatfield in *Rec.,* and one acc. says Hadley), who was b. 16
Apl., 1682. Prob. res. in Ry-H. section of Weth., for which, in 1713, he was
chosen surveyor. Invt. of est. taken 1 or 7 Aug., 1733, exhib. by wid. as adm'x.

Children (Weth. Rec.) :

1. Anna, b. 31 Mch., 1706.
2. Christian, bp. (*Mix*) — Aug., 1707.
3. Abigail, b. 11 Oct., 1708.
4. Thomas, b. 8 Oct., bp. 17 Dec., 1710.—
   Mix.
5. Eleazur, b. 16 Sept., bp. 26 Oct., 1714-15.

—*Mix.*
6. Jonathan, b. 26 Dec., 1714; bp. 6 Feb.,
   1714-15.—*Mix.* FAM. 14.
7. John, b. 5 Jan., 1721; d. 6 Sept., 1785. in
   65th yr.—*S. C. R.*

FAM. 8.ª   JOSEPH,[3] (*Joseph,*[2] *Thos.,*[1]), b. 1675-6; m. 7 Dec., 1708, Dorothy (dau.
Joseph) **Edwards,** who d. 18 Apl., 1760 in 79 yr.—*W. Ins.* He d. 31 Dec.,
1765 ae. 92.

Children (Weth. Rec.) :

1. Dorothy, b. 30 June, bp. 21 Aug., 1709.
2. Katharine, b. 25, bp. 31 Dec., 1710.
3. Joseph, b. 22, bp. 25 Jan., 1712-13. FAM. 15.
4. Daniel, b. 29 Apl., 1715; prob. the D.
   who was licensed by the *Co. Ct.,* Apl.,
   1735, "to prosecute the art and mystery

of tanning leather;" res. in Lorrington,
and had 2 ch., 1737-54.
5. Sarah, b. 23, bp. 26 May. 1717.
6. Zachariah, b. 13 Sept., 1719. FAM. 16.
7. Josiah, b. 12 Dec., 1721. FAM. 17.

FAM. 9.   Capt. THOMAS,[3] (*Joseph,*[2] *Thos.,*[1]), b. 1680; was m. 30 Dec., 1703, by
Rev Steph. Mix, to Mary (dau. John & Rebecca) **Goodrich,** of Weth., who
was b. 4 Sept., 1680. Her sister Abigail, m. Daniel, (bro. of Thomas) **Curtis,**
and both families rem. to Torrington, Ct. Capt. Thomas bo't ld. in Farmington,
23 Feb., 1703-4, from Benj. Judd, but later rem. to Torrington, sometime
after he sold his Far. ppy., as per a deed of date of 20 Jan., 1746, in which he,
(described as "late of Far", now of Torrington), conveyed to Rob't Booth, his
"ho-lot and dwelling-lot * * *bd. E. upon the line betw. F. and Weth". This
deed is witnessed by his s-in-law Daniel Dewey. He was selectman, dep. to
Gen. Ct. and a Capt. in Maj, Roger Wolcott's Reg't. He d. 20 Jan., 1752.

Children (Weth. Rec. & Mix. Rec.) :

1. Rebecca, b. 28, bp. 29 Apl., 1705; m. 27
   Jan., 1731, Daniel **Dewey** (or Deming?),
   of New Britain.
2. Mary, b. 23 Mch., 1706-7, bp. 27 Mch., 1709.
   Mix.
3. Sybil, b. 23 Oct., 1708 (bp. 27 Mch., 1709
   Mix) ; m. 10 Dec., 1730, Ebenezer **North,**
   after his removal to Torrington.
4. Zebulon, b. 16 Jan., 1710-11, bp. 6 May,
   1711. FAM. 18.
5. Elnathan, b. 22 Mch., 1713.

6. Thomas, b. 6 June, 1715; named in
   Torr. Rec. as 6th ch. of Capt. Thomas.
7. Mary, b. 9 July, 1716.
8. Prudence, b. 13 Oct., 1718; m. Joseph
   Lee.
9. Lydia, b. 9 July, 1721; m. 14 Feb., 1743,
   James **Woodruff.**
10. Lois, b. 3 Mch., 1725-6; m. Timothy **Judd.**
11. Mercy, b. 20 Jan., 1726-7; supp. to have
    m. Capt. John **Warner.**
12. Sybil, b. 23 Oct., 1728.

FAM. 10.   DAVID,[3] (*Joseph,*[2] *Thos.,*[1]) b. 1682, at Weth.; Abigail (dau. John)
Goodrich, 25 Apl., 1706.

Children (Weth. Rec.):

1. Joseph, bp. 2 Mch., 1706-7.—*Mix*.
2. Allyn, b. 18 (bp. 23—*Mix*) May, 1708. FAM. 19.
3. Anna, b. 18 (bp. 23—*Mix*) July, 1710.

4. David. FAM. 20.
5. Abigail, bp. 18 Apl., 1714; father spoken of as res. in Farmington.

FAM. 11. SAMUEL,³ (*Samuel*,² *Thos.*,¹) b. 1684; m. Susannah **Allen**, 2 Feb., 1709-10; invent. est. £1554-07-02.

Children (Weth. Rec. & Mix Rec.):

1. Elizabeth, b. 7, bp. 11 Mch., 1710-11.

2. Samuel, b. 28, bp. 31 Aug., 1712. FAM. 21.

FAM. 12. JAMES,⁴ (*Thos.*,³ *John*,² *Thos.*,¹), b. 1718; m. 18 May, 1749,—W. C. R. Elizabeth **Kilborn**; he d. ae. 73, bu 16 May, 1790; she perhaps the "wid. of J." who d. 19 Mch., 1803—W. C. R.

Children (Weth. Rec.):

1. Elizabeth, b. 3, bp. 22 Apl., 1750; m. 15 Jan., 1778, John **Bigelow**, of Htfd.— *C. B. C.*
2. Hannah, b. 12 Jan., 1752.
3. Martha, b. 8 Dec., 1753, bp. 13 Jan., 1753-4; m. John **Boardman**.—*C. B. C.*

4. Mary, b. 11, bp. 25 Apl., 1756; m. Simeon **Deming**.—*C. B. C.*
5. James, bp. betw. 4 June and 4 Sept., 1758. FAM. 22.
6. Thomas, bp. 1763.
7. Rachel, m. Aaron **Warner**.—*C. B. C.*

FAM. 13. Dea. THOMAS,⁴ (*Thos.*,³ *Jonathan*,² *John*,¹); m. 8 Jan., 1741, Dorothea (dau. Edward & Dorothy *Prescott*) **Bulkeley**, of Weth., b. 11 Sept., 1716. and d. (wid) 7 Dec., 1801, in 86 yr.—*S. C. R.* Dea. T. d. 6 Nov., 1789 ae. 80.—*S. C. R.*

Children (Weth. Rec.):

1. Dorothy, b. 5 Dec., 1741; d. before 1806; s. p.
2. Josiah (Capt.), b. 11 May, 1744; d. 12 May, 1832, in 88th yr.—*S. C. R.*
3. Charles, b. 7 Mch., 1746.
4. Rachel, b. 9 Apl., 1748; perhaps the R. of Ry-H. who m. 11 Jan., 1787, Joseph **Goodrich**, of Weth., but *C. B. C.* thinks she m. Daniel **Riley**.
5. Wait, b. 1 Jan., 1751; d. 11 Mch., 1808, ae. 58 (*S. C. R.*); m. Millicent **Goodrich**, 23

Feb., 1786 (*S. C. R.*); the Wid. Millicent d. 1826, in 71st yr.—*S. C. R.*
6. Eleazer, b. 14 Mch., 1753.
7. Mary, b. 6 Oct., 1755; d. 20 Jan., 1807.— *S. C. R.*
8. Thomas, d. 28 Nov., 1763, in 5th yr.— *W. Ins.*
9. Hepzibah, b. 1757; d. 4 Jan., 1807; m. 7 July, 1784, Capt. Jason **Boardman**; Capt. J. B. m. (2) Lydia **Deming**.—See *Boardman Geneal.*

FAM. 14. JONATHAN,⁴ (*Dea. Jona.*,³ *John*,² *Thos.*,¹), b. 1714; m. 27 Mch., 1755, Hannah—prob. "the Wid." **Whaples**,—N. C. R. He d. 20 June, 1783 in 69 yr.—*S. C. R.**

Children (Weth. Rec. & N. C. R.):

1. Joseph, b. 12, bp. 25 Apl., 1756.
2. Hannah, b. 24, bp. 26 Mch., 1758.
3. Miles, bp. 19 Apl., 1761.

4. Jonathan, bp. 8 [June?] 1766 (*S. C. R.*); perhaps the J. who m. Hannah **Wright**, 5 Aug., 1789.

FAM. 15. JOSEPH,⁴ (*Joseph*,³ *Joseph*,² *Thos.*,¹), b. 1713; m. 31 Oct., 1732, Silence **Williams**; rem. to Goshen, Ct., abt. 1740; in 1750 rem. to Dutchess Co., N. Y.— *Hinman* 784.

Children:

1. Mary, b. 22 May, 1733.

2. Honor ("of Joseph, Jr."), bp. 5 Oct., 1740; 7 children b. in Goshen.

FAM. 16. ZACHARIAH,⁴ (*Joseph*,³ *Joseph*,² *Thos.*,¹), b. 1719; rem. to and sett. at Goshen, Ct., abt. 1748—(his bro. Joseph had sett. there in 1740); bo't land there 1749 and res. there until abt. 1750, when he rem. to Dutchess Co., N. Y.— *Hinman* 784.

*Mr. CHAS. B. CURTIS considers this Jonathan to be the son of *Ebenezer*⁴ (*Dea. Jonathan*,³ *John*,² *Thos.*,¹). In favor of this suggestion is the fact that this Jonathan is called on *W. Rec.*, "Jonathan, 2d."

Children:

1. Mary, b. Dec., 173—.
2. Hezekiah, b. May, 1735.
3. Hannah, b. Dec., 1736, d. —.
4. John, b. 17 May, 1738.
5. Honor, b. 12 Sept., 1740.

6. James, b. 10 Feb., 1743.
7. Dorothy, b. 12 Jan., 1745.
8. Joseph, b. 24 Jan., 1747.
   (See *Hinman*, pp. 780-781; tho' he is obscure.)

FAM. 17. JOSIAH,[4] (*Joseph,*[3] *Joseph,*[2] *Thos.,*[1]), b. 1721; m. 3 Dec., .1747, Mary **Kilborn,**—*N. C. R.*, who d. 7 Oct., 1799.—*Weth. Rec.* He d. ae. 79, bu. 4 Oct., 1800—*W. C. R.;* poss. the Josiah who served in the Revol. 1777, in Capt. Henry Champion's Colchester Co.

Children:

1. Levi, b. 26 June, bp. 2 July, 1749. FAM. 23.
2. Ruth, b. 6 Dec., 1751.
3. Josiah, b. 26, bp. 28 Aug., 1757; m. either, 2 Jan., 1777, Mabel **Bulkeley,** of Step. (*W. C. R.*); or 28 Dec., 1780, Eunice **Hunn** (*W. T. R.*); perhaps both.
4. Ebenezer, b. 31 Jan., bp. 3 Feb., 1760; m. 4 Apl., 1781, Rebecca **Latimer,** who was

b. 12 Dec., 1754.—*S. C. R. Issue:*
   i. Josiah (Latimer), (bp. 14 Nov.,
   ii. Rebecca (Latimer) (1784.
   iii. William Kilborn (Latimer), bp. 25 June, 1786.—*W. C. R.*
   iv. Timothy Hale (Latimer), bp. 9 Mch., 1788.

FAM. 18. ZEBULON,[4] (*Thos.,*[3] *Joseph,*[2] *Thos.,*[1]), b. 1710-11, res. in Far.; m. 3 July, 1735, Lydia (dau. Nath'l & Elizabeth *Woodford*) **Cole,** who was b. 1 Aug., 1719; he d. 1798.

Children:

1. Elizabeth, b. 4 June, 1737.
2. b. in Torrington.—*C. B. C.*

3. b. in Torrington.—*C. B. C.*
4. b. in Torrington.—*C. B. C.*

FAM. 19. ALLEN,[4] (*David,*[3] *Joseph,*[2] *Thos.,*[1]), b. 1708; m. Ruth ——————.

*Children (*b. in Torrington, Ct.,—C. B. C.*):*

1. Martin,* b. 14 Mch., 1725.
2. Solomon,* b. 1729.
3. Elihu,* b. 12 Nov., 1732.
4. Hannah,* b. 12 Nov., 1735.
   (*Born in Weth.*):

5. Chloe, b. 31 July, 1738.
6. Medad, b. 18 May, 1740.
7. Ebenezer, b. 6 Nov., 1741; d. Mch., 1742.
8. John, b. 30 Nov., 1742.
9. Anna, b. 24 Mch., 1748.

FAM. 20. DAVID, (*David* ——————————,), b. 1709; m. *Abigail;* he d. ——, 1776.

Children (Weth. Rec.):

1. Huldah, b. 25 Nov., 1738; m. Anesimus **Titus.**
2. Elizur, b. 11 Sept., 1740.
3. Achrah, b. 25 Aug., 1742.
4. Abigail, b. 10 June, 1744; m. Jonathan **Botsford.**
5. David, b. 14 Mch., 1746.

6. Ashbel, b. 25 Aug., 1748.
7. Joshua, b. 2 Jan., 1751.
8. Sarah, b. 2 Jan., 1751; m. Michael **Hinnman.**
9. Joanna, b. ——.
10. Caleb, b. 9 Feb., 1755.
11. Hull, b. 2 Feb., 1759; m. Lois **Hurd.**

FAM. 21. SAMUEL,[4] (*Sam'l,*[3] *Sam'l,*[2] *Thos.,*[1]), b. —— ——————; m. 28 Oct., 1736, Lois **Belding.** The "wid. Lois" d. Apl., 1785.

Children (Weth. Rec.):

1. Samuel, d. 1 Aug., 1737, ae. 14 d.—*Weth. Ins.*
2. Lois, b. 24 Feb., 1739-40.
3. Hannah, b. 6 Feb., 1741-42.
4. Samuel, b. 30 Mch., bp. before 1 June, 1744; m. 17 Oct., 1764, Mehitable **Goodrich.**
5. Susanna, b. 23 June, 1746.

6. Daniel, b. 25 Nov., 1748.
7. Margaret, b. 5 Mch., 1752; prob. the M. who m. 16 Apl., 1777, Elisha **Brewster,** Jr., of Midd.—*W. C. R.*
8. Eunice, b. 7, bp. 8 Dec., 1754.
9. Joseph, b. 15, bp. 16 June, 1765.
10. Lois (of Samuel, Jr.), bp. 12 Mch., 1769.

FAM. 22. JAMES,[5] (*James,*[4] *Thos.,*[3] *John,*[2] *Thos.,*[1]), b. 1768; m. 6 Apl., 1788. Sarah (dau. Ezekiel) **Fosdick,** who bp. 6 May, 1792—*W. C. R.*, d. (wid.) 13 May, 1852, at Auburn, N. Y. He d. 19 June, 1811.

Children (Weth. Rec. & W. C. R.) :

1. Sarah, b. 4, d. 18 Apl., 1789.
2. James, b. 4 May, 1791, bp. 3 Mch., 1792.
3. Sally, b. 28 Nov., 1792, bp. 25 Apl., 1793.
4. Mary, b. 8 Nov., 1794, bp. 1 Feb., 1795.
5. Roswell, b. 20 Aug., bp. 6 Nov., 1796.
6. Samuel Fordick, b. 8 Sept., 1799, bp. 15

June, 1800. FAM. 24.
7. Charles Chauncey, b. 20 Dec., 1803, bp. 17 June, 1804.
8. James, b. 29 Mch., bp. 6 July, 1806.
9. Anna Bacon, b. 20 Apl., bp. 21 Aug., 1808.

FAM. 23. LEVI, (*Josiah, Joseph. Joseph, Thomas, ————,*), b. 1749; m. 4 Jan., 1779, Rhoda (dau. Thos. & Mary *Camp*) **Stoddard**, of Weth. (*N. C. R.*) b. 30 Oct., 1754; rem. to Lenox, Mass., where he d. 29 June, 1833, ae. 84.

Children (W. C. R.) :

1. Josiah, b. 31 Oct., 1779, bp. 2 Apl., 1780. FAM. 25.
2. Thomas Stoddard, b. 14 Jan., bp. 22 Apl., 1781.
3. Lucy, b. 7 Aug., bp. 3 Nov., 1782.
4. Chloe, b. 13 Mch., bp. 26 June, 1785.
5. Lydia, b. 2 Mch., bp. 6 May, 1787.
6. Joseph Edwards, b. 9, bp. 25 Oct., 1789.
7. Rhoda, b. 30 July, bp. 23 Oct., 1796.

FAM. 24. SAMUEL FOSDICK,[6] (*James,*[5] *James,*[4] *Thos.,*[3] *John,*[2] *Thos.,*[1]), b. 1799; m. (1) 7 Dec., 1826, at Penn Yan, N. Y., Amelia (dau. Robert) **Boyd;** m. (2) 1 Dec., 1831, Mary (dau. Perley & Alice *Howe*) **Phillips.** He d. 24 Feb., 1871.

Children (C. B. C.) :

1. Charles Boyd, b. 24 Sept., 1827; m. (1) Harriet Augusta **Adams;** m. (2) Isabel (dau. Andrew E. & Sarah *Cornell*) **Douglass,** b. 4 May, 1848; res. N. Y. City. *Issue:*
   i. Elicott Douglass, b. 7 Sept., 1877, at Rye, N. Y.
   ii. Charles Boyd, b. Dec., 1878, in N. Y. City.
   iii. Isabel Woodbridge, b. 9 Aug., 1880 at Newport, R. I.
   iv. Ronald E., b. 12 Mch., 1883, in N. Y. City.

FAM. 25. JOSIAH,[6] (*Levi,*[5] *Josiah,*[4] *Joseph,*[3] *Joseph,*[2] *Thos.,*[1]), b. 1779; was of Lenox, Mass.; m. 29 Apl., (or 2 Aug.) 1802, Anna (dau. James) **Butler—** *W. C. R.;* who d. 29 Mch., 1803, ae. 24; he m. (2) 17 Feb., 1805, Betsy **Butler,** who d. 1 Apl., 1863; he d. 26 Apl., 1863, ae. 83.—*W. Ins.*

Children (Weth. Rec. & W. C. R.) :

1. Hezekiah Butler, b. 11 Mch., 1806.
2. Betsy Ann, b. 28 Feb., 1808; m. George Perry, of Oxford, Ct., 23 Dec., 1830.— W. C. R.
3. Maria, b. 6 June, 1810, bp. 2 June, 1811; prob. the M. who m. Henry B. **Oatman,** 21 Jan., 1816.—W. T. R.; his 1st wife was her sister Lavinia.
4. Emily, b. 31 Mch., bp. 15 Aug., 1813; d. 14 Sept., 1840, ae. 27.
5. Josiah (M. D.), b. 3 Apl., prob. bp. 1 Sept., 1816.—W. C. R.; res. Boston, Mass.; d. London, Eng., 1 Aug., 1883.
6. Lavinia, b. 7 July, bp. 26 Nov., 1820; m. 6 Dec., 1840, Henry B. **Oatman,** of Oxford, Ct., who d. 18 Aug., 1895, ae. 82; she d. 13 Feb., 1842, ae. 22. *Issue:*
   i. Henry L (Oatman), b. 31 Dec., 1841; d. 17 July, 1848, ae. 6 yrs., 6 mos.— W Ins.
7. Levi (M. D.), b. 5 May, bp. 7 Sept., 1823; res. Philadelphia, Pa.

DALIBE, (*Doliber, Dellabor, Dalliber,* and more recently *Doliver*) JONATHAN (*W. C. R.*) had *Abigail* bp. 24 June, 1787; d. 22 Oct., 1788; *Abigail* bp. 8 Aug., 1790.

JONATHAN, (prob. same as the foregoing), d. ae. 29, New Lond., Mch., 1792.

DANA, Rev. Dr. JAMES, of New Haven, m. Mrs. Abigail **Belding,** 10 Oct., 1796; she d. 17 Mch., 1798; he d. 18 Aug., 1812.

FRANCES MARIA, wife of D. G. **McLean,** b. 6 Mch., 1826; d. 27 Oct., 1872.— *Weth. Ins.*

DANFORTH, (communicated by Miss SARAH G. WILLIAMS, of Hartford, Ct.), fm. Framlingham, Co. Suffolk, Eng., abt. 90 miles N. E. of London, and 12 fm. the North Sea—a place once of some importance, but now chiefly noticeable for a great church and the ruins of a once magnificent castle, was the birthplace of NICHOLAS, the progenitor of the Danforth family of America. He was the son of Thomas and Jane (Sudbury) Danforth, and, in 1634, came, with his six children, on the ship *Griffin* to Newtown, now Cambridge, Mass. On board the same vessel, which brought 200 passengers to these shores, was also his brother-in-law, Rev. Zachariah **Symmes**, afterwards minister of Cambridge. And by the same vessel, came the order of the Privy Council, calling for the surrender of the Charter of the Mass. Colony. Danforth became quickly and prominently identified with the community at Newtown, but lived only 3½ yrs. after. By his wife Elizabeth **Symmes**, he had the following:

Children:

1. Elizabeth, bp. 3 Aug., 1619; m. Oct., 1639, And. **Belcher**, of Sudbury, later of Cambridge, who d. 1673; 6 ch.
2. Maria, bp. 21 May, 1621; d. in Eng.
3. Anna, bp. 3 Nov., 1622; m. 1646, Matthew **Bridge**; had 7 ch., of whom the ygst.

Elizabeth (Belcher), m. Capt. Benj. **Garfield**, and thus became the ancestors of Pres. James A. Garfield; she d. 2 Dec., 1704.
4. Thomas, bp. 20 Nov., 1823. **FAM. 2.**

FAM. 2. THOMAS,[2] (*Nicholas,*[1]), b. 1623; m. Mary **Withington**, 23 Feb., 1644. He was made freeman 1643; in 1650, was treasurer of H. C., wh. office he held for 19 yrs.; for 1657 and '58 a rep. to the Gen. Ct., of Mass.; 1659, chosen an Assistant, and annually re-elected for 20 yrs.; in 1679 and until the dissolution of the Col. Gov't in 1686, he was deputy-governor, associated with the venerable Gov. Bradstreet and virtually exerting all the influence pertaining to the higher position; and for 7 yrs. he was the President of Maine, at that time a subordinate province of Mass. For over 30 yrs. he was Recorder of Middlesex Co., Mass., and a part of that time its Treasurer; fm. 1662 to 1679, he was a commissioner from Mass., to the New Eng. Confederacy, which negotiated treaties with the Indians; and, fm. 1690 to 1692, was Lieut.-Gov. of New Hampshire. In 1692, he was an Associate Judge of the Superior Ct., of Mass.—and up to the time of his death.

Children:

1. Samuel, grad. H. C. 1671; d. 1676 in Eng.
2. Dau., m. Rev. Joseph **Whiting**, of Lynn, Mass., afterwards of Southampton. L. I.
3. Mary, m. (1) Sol. **Whipps, Jr.**, of Charlestown; m. (2) Thomas **Brown**, of Sudbury, Mass.
4. Elizabeth, m. Francis **Foxcroft**, Esq., of Cambridge (s. of a former mayor of Leeds, Eng.), and their dau. Phebe, m. Lt-Gov. Samuel **Phillips**, founder of Phillips' Academies at Exeter and Andover. Madam P. was distinguished for personal beauty and culture, and her portrait graces the Library of Andover Theol. Sem'y: through her dau. Mary Ann, who m. Wm. Guy **Brooks**, she was the grandmother of the late Bishop Philips **Brooks**, b. 1835: also of John, Arthur and William, all clergymen.
5. Samuel (Rev.), on the dth. of his father,

being then in his 12th yr. was placed in tht care of Rev. Mr. Shepard, under whom he was fitted for coll. and grad. H. C., 1643, in the second class which issued from that institution; served as tutor for some 5 yrs. thereafter, pursuing his theol. studies, and, in 1650 was ord. colleague to the Rev. John Eliot, pastor at Roxbury, Mass., and known as the "Apostle to the Indians." At R. he served in the ministry for 25 yrs. until his dth. in 1674.
6. Jonathan, was at age of 25, a first settler at Billerica, Mass., where for 40 yrs. he was a ld-surveyor of note; and for 22 yrs. Town Clk.; also, Selectman, rep. to Gen. Ct., and Capt. in the militia; and his house, one of the "fortified" or garrisoned houses of the town in 1675, was only destroyed in 1880.

The *Wethersfield Danforths* are descended from Thomas Danforth,[5] of Midd., Ct., (*s. Thomas,*[4] *Rev. Samuel,*[3] *Rev. Samuel,*[2] *Nicholas,*[1]), who was b. 2 June, 1731, at Taunton, Mass., d. at Midd., Ct., 8 Aug., 1782; he m. 20 Feb., 1755, Martha **Jacobs,** b. 1732, at Mansfield, Ct., and d. 12 May, 1792.

Children:

1. Thomas, b. 2 June, 1756. **FAM. 2.**
2. Joseph, b. 17 Aug., 1758; m. Sarah **King.**
3. Sarah, b. 27 Feb., 1761; m. Oliver **Boardman.**
4. Samuel, b. 17 May, 1763; d. 30 July, 1764.
5. Edward, b. 20 Mch., 1765; m. Jerusha **Moreley.**

6. Jonathan, b. 14 Dec., 1766; m. Lucy **Ward.**
7. William, b. 7 Feb., 1769; m. Huldah **Scovel.**
8. Daniel, b. 25 Jan., 1771; m. Lucinda **Montague.**
9. Samuel, b. 10 Apl., 1774; m. Melinda **Seymour.**

FAM. 2. THOMAS,⁶ (*Thos.,*⁵ *Thos.,*⁴ *Rev. Samuel,*³ *Rev. Samuel,*² *Nicholas,*¹), b. 1756; m. 11 Jan., 1775, at Midd., Elizabeth **Tallman,** b. 19 Sept., 1754, at New London, Ct.; he d. 15 Jan., 1840, at Rocky Hill; she d. 30 Dec., 1826, ae. 72, at Ry-H. Mr. Tallman rem. to Ry-Hill, with his family, May 19, 1778, having started there, in 1777, a large trade as a pewterer, which he continued until 1818. His account books show that he dealt in almost everything to be found in a country store, including almost every possible sort of hardware goods of the period, especially in the pewtering line. He mfd. all kinds of tin and brittania ware, japanned and pewter gds., and worked in and sold articles of brass and lead—having a factory supplied with horse-power. He, also, did a large business in sending out tin peddlers and had an extensive retail business at the store, with people fm. Weth., Newington, Berlin, New Britain, Farmington, Glastonbury, Marlbugh, Colchester and other Conn. towns. He also maintained a similar factory in Philadelphia—and, with his family, spent some winters there in charge of it; and the stamp of T. D. on his gds. was a well recognized guarantee of reliability not only near home, but at more distant points. For several yrs. fm. 1794, his son-in-law, Richard Williams, was associated with him in business.—(See also Dr. Griswold's Chapter on Rocky Hill, Vol. I, p. 907.) In 1783, Mr. Danforth built a fine house at the Centre; he had a brother res. at Midd., and bros. and sisters at Hartford, to whom his home was a delightful "half-way house" of family reunions.

Children:

1. Hannah, b. 16 Oct., 1775, at Midd.; m. 25 Sept., 1794, Richard **Williams** (?); she d. 3 Jan., 1815 at Ry-H. *Issue* (b. *Ry-H.*):
   i. Richard (Williams), b. 10 Nov., 1796; d. 31 Jan., 1797.
   ii. Richard (Williams), b. 12 Dec., 1797; d. 4 Jan., 1798.
   iii. Otis (Williams), b. 13 Mch., 1799, at Htfd.; d. Buffalo, N. Y., 12 May, 1831, unm.
   iv. Caroline Danforth (Williams), b. 20 July, 1801, at Htfd.
   v. Almira (Williams), b. 31 July, 1803, at Htfd.; m. 1823, Archibald **Robbins.** See *Robbins.*
   vi. Elizabeth Tallman (Williams), b. 3 Dec., 1808, at Htfd.; d. 3 Aug., 1883, at Clinton, Iowa.
2. Martha, b. 4 Aug., 1777; m. 7 July, 1796, Simeon (s. Simeon & Sarah *Rose*) **Robbins,** who was b. 2 Apl., 1774, and d. 1 Sept., 1833, at Frazersburg, Ohio. *Issue:*
   i. Eliza (Robbins), bp. 29 July, 1798; d. 12 Dec., 1802.
   ii. Martha (Robbins), b. 10 Apl., 1801; m. Horace (s. Nathan & Melinda) **Marsh,** of Kirkland, N. Y., in 1821; she d. at Esmond, Ill., 8 June, 1867; he d. 1854; they had (a) Myra Frances (Marsh), b. 12 Mch., 1827; (b) Henry Danforth (Marsh), b. 2 Mch., 1834; m. 1855, Sarah **Camp.**
   iii. Eliza (Robbins), b. 29 June, 1803; m. 12 Oct., 1832, Horatio Nelson (s. Jonah) **Byington** of New Htfd.
   iv. Elnora L. (Robbins), bp. 20 Apl., 1806. d. 24 Jan., 1809.
   v. Almira A. (Robbins), b. 14 June, 1808; m. 1830, Gates Warren (s. Warren & Hannah *Gates*) **Chapman.** *Issue:* Edward Talman (Chapman), b. 1834; Frederick Robbins (Chapman), b. 1836; William Henry (Chapman), b. 1842.
   vi. Elnora L. (Robbins), bp. 5 May, 1811; m. Sam. H. L. **Hall,** 20 May, 1857, at New Htfd., N. Y., a gd-son of S.

   Holden Parsons, Maj. Gen. in the Conn. Contin. Line; mcht. in Binghamton, N. Y.; memb. N. Y. State Senate, etc.
3. Sarah, b. 17 Sept., 1779; m. 16 Nov., 1797, Luther (s. Peter & Bathsheba *Miller*) **Goodrich,** who was b. 16 July, 1776, at Westfield, Ct., and d. at RY-H. 12 Nov., 1832. Mr. Goodrich was a sea-captain, long captain of the slp. *Almira,* in trade with N. Y., Boston and Southern ports. *Issue:*
   i. Sarah (Goodrich), b. E. Hadd. 1 July, 1800; d. 10 July, 1825, Ry-H.
   ii. Miranda (Goodrich), b. 8 Aug., 1803 at E. H.; d. 25 Feb., 1828 at Ry-H.
   iii. George (Goodrich), b. 8 Sept., 1805 at E. H.; m. 21 May, 1828, at Bristol, Ct., Charlotte Lucinda (dau. Ira & Cynthia *Shaylor* **Ives,** b. 1809; had (a) Almira Miranda, b. 1829; (b) Augustus Ives, b. 1833; (c) Geo. Luther, b. 1836; (d) Samuel Root, b. 1839; Geo., the father, m. (2) Mrs. Charlotte (Upson) **Birge,** 1880.
   iv. Hepsey Penfield (Goodrich), b. 24 Jan., 1809; m. 1846, at Ry-H., Wm. P. **Dorrance;** rep. the town of Andover, Ct., in Senate of Conn.; P. M., etc.; had (a) Wm. Gershom, b. 1847; d. 1877; (b) Geo. Henry, b. 1849.
4. Elizabeth, b. 23, bp. 30 Aug., 1789; m. 25 Mch., 1819, Merriam **Williams,** of Ry-H., b. 3 July, 1785; he d. 10 May, 1857; she d. 29 Mch., 1752 at Ry-H. *Issue:*
   i. Thomas Danforth (Williams), b. 4 Dec., 1819; d. 4 Dec., 1881.
   ii. Martha Tallman (Williams), b. 21 Dec., 1821; d. 27 Aug., 1871.
   iii. Mary Elizabeth (Williams), b. 2 Feb., 1826; d. 12 Dec., 1829.
   iv. Elizabeth Morton (Williams), b. 31 Dec., 1830; d. 2 Mch., 1901.
   v. Sarah Goodrich (Williams), b. 16 Aug., 1834.
5. Thomas, b. 6, bp. 8 July, 1792. **FAM. 4.**
6. Almira, b. 7, bp. 9 Nov., 1794; d. at Ry-H. 12 Dec., 1801.

FAM. 3. THOMAS,[7] (*Thos.*,[6] *Thos.*,[5] *Thos.*,[4] *Rev. Samuel*,[3] *Rev. Samuel*,[2] *Nich.*,[1]), b. 1792; m. 13 Sept., 1827, Mary Williams (dau. Capt. Joseph & Mary *Bulkeley*) **Butler**, (*Weth. Rec.* call her Mary *Ann*) who was b. 8 Jan., 1805, and d. 28 May, 1858, at Ry-H. He was early associated with his father, at Ry-H. and Philadelphia, in hdwe. mfr., and later spent several winters in Augusta, Geo., engaged in the same business, tinning, pewtering, etc. He d. 23 Mch., 1836. —(*S. C. Rec.*)   This and Fam. No. 4 and 5, fm. Mrs. MARY B. DANFORTH.

Children (*b. Ry-H.*) :

1. Henry Tallman, b. 1 June, 1828 ; bp. 31 Dec., 1830. FAM. 4.
2. Mary Bulkley, b. 13 May, bp. 31 Dec., 1830.
3. Ellen Cornelia, b. 5 Apl, bp. 5 July, 1833 ; d. 3 Apl., 1834.
4. Walter Williams, b. 4 Apl., bp. 4 Sept., 1835. FAM. 5.

FAM. 4.   HENRY TALLMAN,[8] (*Thos.*,[7] *Thos.*,[6] *Thos.*,[5] *Thos.*,[4] *Rev. Samuel*,[3] *Rev. Samuel*,[2] *Nich.*,[1]), b. 1828; m. N. Y. City, 1 June, 1857, Evelyn Augusta **Snyder**, who was b. 18 Nov., 1829, and d. 20 Nov., 1884.

Children:

1. Mary Williams, b. 8 Mch., 1858 ; m. 29 Jan., 1880, at Bklyn., N. Y., Herbert C. **Smith**. *Issue:*
   i. Evelyn C. (Smith).
   ii. Delia Crosby (Smith).
   iii. Mary Williams (Smith).
2. Henrietta, b. 14 June, 1860 ; m. 16 June,
1880, Chas. **Frasier**. *Issue:*
   i. Evelyn (Frasier).
   ii. Mary (Frasier).
   iii. Henry Danforth (Frasier).
3. Sarah Snyder, d. 2 Apl., 1869.—*Weth. Ins.*
4. Thomas Snyder, b. 22 June, 1874.
(And several ch. d. inf.)

FAM. 5. WALTER WILLIAMS,[8] (*Thos.*,[7] *Thos.*,[6] *Thos.*,[5] *Thos.*,[4] *Rev. Sam'l*,[3] *Rev. Sam'l*,[2] *Nich.*,[1]), b. 1835; m. 19 June, 1856, at Branford, Ct., Frances Eliza (dau. Samuel & Betsy *Blackstone*) **Averill**, who was b. 7 Nov., 1838. He d. Branford, Ct., 21 July, 1886.

Children (*b. Ry-H.*) :

1. Mary Jane, b. 4 May, 1857 ; m. 24 Dec., 1874, Albert W. (s. Wm. & Amelia A. *Shelley*) **Baldwin**, of Madison, Ct. ; b. 10 Mch., 1849. *Issue* (*Branford, Ct.*) :
   i. Rufus Isbell (Baldwin), b. 15 June, 1875.
   ii. Arthur Snow (Baldwin), b. 3 Mch. 1877.
2. Elizabeth Averill, b. 8 May, 1860.
3. Florence Bulkley, b. 9 May, 1863 ; d. 23 Nov., 1899.
4. Samuel Blackstone, b. 1 May, 1862 ; d. 9
Aug., 1862.
5. Susan Robbins, b. 1 Aug., 1865 ; m. 2 June, 1897, James Clayton **Clark**, of Forest Grove, Oregon, where they res.
6. Thomas Lawrence, b. 18 May, 1867.
7. Henry Tallman, b. 21 July, 1869, at Branford, Ct.
8. Josephine Barnes, b. 3 Oct., 1871 ; m. I. Gilbert **Hedges**, 20 Dec., 1893.
9. Walter Williams, b. 16 Nov., 1873.
10. Frances Virginia, b. 29 Apl., 1875.
11. Reginald Standish, b. 26 Aug., 1878.

DANIELS, JOHN, of E. Htfd., m. Julia **Burnham**, 18 Mch., 1827.—*W. C. R.*

SUSAN, m. Lorenzo **Marks**, of Simsbury, 11 June, 1834.—*W. T. R.*

CHARLES S. His wife Jane H. **Savage**, wid. of Sam'l W. **Morris**, b. 31 May, 1825, d. 30 Apl., 1894.—*Weth. Ins.*

LAURA WILDER—1826-1896.

DANIELSON, FRED, of Lake Sago, m. Abigail **Gaylord**, of Danville, Vt., 3 May, 1797.—*W. C. R.*

DARLING, HENRY, of Midd., m. Esther **Wright**, 19 Oct., 1805.—*W. C. R.*

DART, LUTHER, m. Mary **Clapp**, of Weth., 12 Feb., 1832.—*N. C. R.*

DAVIS, EBENEZER, m. Rachel **Andrus**, of Weth., 30 May, 1777.

JERUSHA, "grand-dau. to Naomi **Goffyt**" is gone away to Providence—this maid lived at Warwick [R. I.], bp. and owned the Covenant, 26 Feb., 1709-10.— *Mix MSS.*

WILLIS PHILANDER, m. Mary **Tucker**, both of New., 6 Oct., 1840; had (*N. C. R.*) *Mary Ellen* bp. 19 Nov., 1848; *Henry Willis* bp. 28 Aug., 1842; *Eugene M.* bp. 30 Aug., 1846.

HUGH, had Thomas Wilson, bp. 13 Jan., 1850.

DEANE. This family, consisting of *Silas, Barnabas, Simeon, Barzillai, Jesse, David*(?) and *Hannah*, were the children of Silas Deane, a blacksmith of Groton, Ct., and most of them seem to have been more or less identified with Weth., after the coming here of Silas, about 1761.

1. SILAS, (Hon.) the most prominent and probably the eldest of the number, was a man of good education, active, intellect and superior ability. He was of medium stature, and fine personality—a true gentleman of his day. His career has been fully noticed in Vol. I, pp. 491-7. His res. in Weth., now occupied by E. Hart Fern, Esq., is still standing and in a good state of preservation. While yet abroad in France, Mr. Deane had a house erected for him in Hartford, under the superintendence of his bro. Barnabas. This house, of which pictures and description are given in the *Hartford Daily Currant*, of Aug. 14, 1901, was then the finest in Hartford. Its design was French, from plans and specifications forwarded by Mr. D., from Paris, and in some of its architectual features unique. When erected, its E. (or true) front faced on Front St., but the mutations of time, have left it some distance from that street, and facing on Grove St.; and despite the changes made by successive owners, it still retains an air of aristocratic lineage which marked the period of great luxury preceding the French Revolution. The Hon. Silas probably never occupied it—though his bro. Barnabas did, and it passed into the hands of Daniel Buck, a well-known Commerce St. merchant; then to those of Nelson Hollister, and is now owned by Timothy I. Long. Mr. Deane m. (1) the wid. Mehitable (Nott) **Webb**, who d. in 1767, ae. 34; he m. (2) Elizabeth **Saltoustall**. Mr. Deane had but one son, *Jesse*, b. 24 June, 1764, who married and had a dau., Philura, who m. Horatio **Alden**, of Hartford, and had children. *Hinman* (1st edit.) to whom we are indebted for some of this fam. hist., says that Mrs. Alden rec'd fm. her father, a large estate. Jesse Deane d. at Hartford, in 1828.

2. BARNABAS, was a merchant, whose valuable Revolutionary services have been noted in Chapt. XI of our Vol. 1. He was a bachelor; res. in Hartford in the Esq. Daniel Buck ho.; owned several wharves and stores in that city; was partner with John Caldwell, Esq., in a large distillery, and also with Jeremiah Wadsworth. Esq., and Gen. Greene of R. I.; his will, dated Oct., 1794; his est. amt'g to £10,208-11s; after bequests and payment of debts, was divided equally betw. his sister Hannah (wife of Josiah) Buck, and his bro. John.

3. BARZILLAI, died at Weth. 1788; unm'd; his bro. Barnabas his adm'r.

4. SIMEON, of Weth. in Apl., 1777, being about to make a journey to a distant part of the country, made a will, and having no family, gave his nephew (Jesse, s. of Silas) all his books and wearing apparel, to his nephew, s. of his sister Hannah (Deane) Buck, a debt due to him fm. his bro.-in-law, Josiah Buck, and the avails of certain tickets in the U. S. Lottery; and the remainder of his ppy. to his bro. Barnabas, his sister Hannah (Buck) and his nephew, Jesse, s. of his bro. Silas.

5. JOHN, d. at sea, 1788; without issue.

6. JESSE, d. at sea without issue.

7. DAVID, d. young.

8. HANNAH, m. Capt. Josiah Buck, of Weth., where their descendants now live.

DEMING, (*Demon, Dement*).   Among the settlers of Weth. prob. as early as 1635 or '36, were two persons of this name, and prob. brothers—JOHN and THOMAS.

THOMAS, was a ship-builder, or carpenter.   On Sept. 22, 1648, the town "voted—that Thomas Demon, ship-carpenter, should have a lot upon the Common, by the Landing Place [the present "Cove"], to build a house on and for a Worke-yard; and Lieut. Bosie [James Boosey] and Nathaniel Dickinson was appointed to set out this lot."—*Ld. Recs. Weth. Savage* says, (11, 35) that he m. 24 July, 1645, Mary **Sheaffe**, of Far. and rem. to Southampton, and thence to Easthampton, L. I., where his posterity is still living.

(Much kindly help on this family has been given us by Mr. JUDSON K. DEMING, of Dubuque, Iowa, who has a history of the D's now in print.   But, even with his aid, we fear we may not have avoided certain dislocations in the proper alignment of families; but which we have had neither time or eyesight to investigate more fully.—H. R. S.)

JOHN DEMING, to whom lds. were gr. by the Town in 1636 and '45—see Chapt. VII, Vol. I; was adm. freeman, 1645; was selectman in 1647-8 and later; rep. the Town in the Gen. Ct., 1649-'61; and was one of the patentees named in the Charter of 1662. He m. abt. 1637, Honor (dau. Richard) **Treat;** and his will (dated 26 June, 1690) was proven 21 Nov., 1705, in which yr. as supp. he died. He was evidently a prominent and influential citizen; his desc't's were numerous and many have been distinguished. One of his legatees is mentioned in his will, as his cousin Sarah Wyer (Wyard?).

Children (named in his will):

1. John (Sgt.), b. 9 Sept., 1638. FAM. 2.
2. Jonathan (Sgt.)., b. 1639. FAM. 3.
3. Samuel, b. 1646. FAM. 4.
4. David. FAM. 5.
5. Ebenezer. FAM. 6.
6. Rachel, m. (1) Capt. John (s. of James) **Morgan,** 16 Nov., 1665; after her dth. he m. (2) Elizabeth **Williams.** *Issue (by first marr.)*:
   i. John (Morgan), b. 10 June, 1667; m. Ruth **Shapley.**
   ii. Samuel (Morgan), b. 9 Sept., 1669; m. Hannah **Avery.**
   iii. Isaac (Morgan), b. 24 Oct., 1670; m. twice—second marr. to Abigail **Skiffe,** 1715.
   iv. Hannah (Morgan), b. 8 Jan., 1674; m. Rev. Eph'm **Woodbridge,** 1704.
   v. Mary (Morgan), b. May, 1675; m. ———— **Williams;** d. 1754, ae. 89.
   vi. Sarah (Morgan), b. 13 Apl., 1678; m. John **Ames,** 1694.

vii. James (Morgan), b. abt. 1680; m. Bridget ————.
7. Frances, m. Richard **Beckley.**
8. Mary, m. John (*Savage* says Thomas) **Hurlbut,** of Midd., Ct. *Issue*:
   i. John (Hurlbut), b. 8 Dec., 1671.
   ii. Thomas (Hurlbut), b. 20 Oct., 1674.
   iii. Sarah (Hurlbut), b. 5 Nov., 1676.
   iv. Mary (Hurlbut), b. 17 Nov., 1678; d. inf.
   v. Mary (Hurlbut), b. 17 Feb., 1780.
   vi. Ebenezer (Hurlbut), b. 17 Jan., 1683.
   vii. Margaret (Hurlbut), b. 1685.
   viii. David (Hurlbut), b. 11 Aug., 1688.
   ix. Mehitable (Hurlbut), b. 23 Nov., 1690.
9. Hannah, m. Thomas **Wright.***
10. Sarah, m. Samuel **Moody,** of Hadley, Mass.; (supp. to be only s. of Dea. John of H., and gd-s. of George of Moulton Co. Suffolk, Eng.); she d. 29 Sept., 1717. *Issue*:
   i. Sarah (Moody), m. John **Kellogg,**

---

* See Note to JOHN² (FAM. 2) Beckley.

23 Dec., 1680 ; d. 19 Sept., 1689.
ii. John (Moody), b. 24 July, 1661 ; sett. at Htfd, Ct. ; d. 5 Nov., 1732, ae. 71.
iii. Hannah (Moody), b. 5 Mch., 1663 ; d. unm., 6 Jan., 1713.

iv. Mary (Moody), m. (1) Alex. **Panton,** 30 June, 1689 ; m. (2) James **Mason,** 29 June, 1698.
v. Samuel (Moody), b. 28 Nov., 1670.
vi. Ebenezer (Moody), b. 23 Oct., 1675.

FAM. 2. Sgt. JOHN,[2] (*John,*[1]), b. 1638; m. at Northampton, 20 Sept. (or, by another res. 12 Dec.) 1657, Mary (or Mercy, dau. Joseph) **Mygatt,** of Htfd.; he was a selectman, 1662; rep. to Gen. Ct., 1669 and '72; on a commis. to run the N. line of Town, 1651; in 1692 he was called a "knacker," *i. e.* "a maker of small work, or rope maker," as were his father and bro. David, also.— *J K. D.;* for ld. holdings see Chapt. VII, Vol. I; he d. 23 Jan., 1712; wid. d. 4 Sept., 1714.

Children (*Weth. Rec.*) :

1. John ("the Drummer"), b. 9 Sept., 1658. FAM. 7.
2. Joseph, b. 1 (or 2) June, 1661 ; rem. to Woodstock, Ct.
3. Jonathan, b. 12 Feb., 1662. FAM. 8.
4. Mary, b. 1 July, 1666.
5. Samuel, b. 25 Aug., 1668.
6. Jacob, b. 26 Aug., 1670. FAM. 9.
7. Sarah, b. 17 Jan., 1672.
8. Hezekiah (acc. to *Chapin* and *Talcott*). FAM. 10.

FAM. 3. Sgt. JONATHAN,[2] (*John,*[1]), b. 1639; m. (1) Sarah (prob. dau. of John) **Graves,** 21 Nov., 1660, who d. 5 June, 1668; he m. (2) Elizabeth (dau. Josiah) **Gilbert,** of Nayaug, 25 Dec., 1673, who d. Weth., 3 Sept., 1714, leaving (by a nuncupative will) her ppy. (all personal) to her 2 daus., Mary and Ann—adm'n gr. Oct. same yr. to Jonathan Deming, Jr., and John Edwards of Weth. Sgt Jonathan d. 8 Jan., 1699-1700, "ae. as he supp. abt. 61"—*Weth. Rec.* Invent. of his est. val. at £550-14-04; will dated 27 Mch., 1696.—*Htfd. Co. Prob.* See, also Chapt. VII, Vol. I.

Children (*Weth. Rec.*) :

1. Jonathan, b. 27 Nov., 1661. FAM. 11.
2. Sarah, b. 12 Aug., 1663 ; m. 31 July, 1681, Jonathan **Riley**; 9 ch.— See *Riley.*
3. Mary, b. 11 July, 1665 ; m. 26 Nov., 1685, Joseph **Smith.**—See *Smiths*—unattached.
4. Comfort, b. 5 June, 1668 ; m. (1) 18 May, 1693, Nathaniel **Beckley,** who d. 29 Oct., 1697; m. (2) (acc. to *Talcott*) 2 Feb., 1710, Thomas **Morton**; 3 ch.—See *Beckley.*
   (*By second marriage*) :
5. Elosie (in *Prob. Rec.* this name looks like *Elusia;* is prob. meant for Eluse, Luce?), b. 16 Feb., 1674 or '76 ; m. 15 May, 1707, John **Edwards.**—*Talcott.*
6. Elizabeth, b. 12 June, 1677 ; m. 23 Nov., 1699, Richard **Beckley**; 3 ch.—See *Beckley.*
7. Thomas, b. 27 Nov., 1679. FAM. 12.
8. Charles, b. 10 Jan., 1681 ; m. Anna (dau. Thomas) **Wickham,** 5 Sept.. 1706 ; m. (2) at Boston, Sarah **Meers.** *Issue :*
   i. ——— (Wickham), bp. 18 May, 1707.
   ii. Anna (Wickham), b. 28 May, 1711.
9. Benjamin, b. 20 (Jan. or July), 1684. FAM. 13.
10. Jacob, b. 20 Dec., 1689. FAM. 14.
11. Mary, b. 24 Oct., 1692 ; m. Gershom **Butler,** 1719 ; d. 22 Apl., 1771.
12. Anna, b. 1 Oct., 1695 ; m. 20 Mch., 1712, Nath'l **Wright.** *Issue :*
    i. Elias (Wright), b. 12 Mch., 1713.
    ii. Lucy (Wright), b. 17 Jan., 1716.
    iii. Elizur (Wright), b. 30 Jan., 1719.
    iv. Nathaniel (Wright), b. 21 June, 1722. (Sgt. Jonathan Deming's will also ment. "my son-in-law," *John Williams.*)

FAM. 4. SAMUEL,[3] (*John,*[2] *John,*[1]), b. 1648; m. (acc. to *Savage,* II, 35) 29 Mch., 1694, Sarah *Bucke* (gd.-dau. of John) **Kirby.** He d. 6 Apl., 1709 "in his 63d yr., near out." A prob. order for distrib. of his est., 6 Mch., 1715-16, shows his wid. m. (2) Jonathan **Church.**

Children :

1. John, b. 7 (or 27) Dec., 1694. FAM. 15.
2. David (Lieut.), b. 29 Dec., 1696. FAM. 16.
3. Samuel, b. 12, bp. 18 June, 1699. FAM. 17.
4. Honor, b. 16, bp. 28 Dec., 1701 ; m. (1) 16 Oct., 1729, Hez. **Goodrich;** m. (2) 5 July, 1733, Dr. Thomas **Perrin.**
5. William, b. 10 May, 1705 ; m. 22 Jan., 1730,

Prudence (dau. Josiah) **Churchill.** "*William,* of William," bp. 13 Aug., 1732, and who m. 14 July, 1774, Elizabeth **Griswold** (*W. C. R.*), and poss. James, bp. 11 Oct., 1730, were prob. ch. of this William & Prudence.

FAM. 5. DAVID,[2] (*John,*[1]), b. abt. 1652, m. 16 July, (or Aug.) 1678, Mary ———. *Savage* says he res. some yrs. at Cambridge, and afterward at Boston, Mass., where he d. 1725.

Children (Weth. Rec.) :

1. David (Rev.), b. 20 July, 1681 ; grad. H. C., 1700 ; minister at Medway, Mass.
2. Samuel, b. 9 Aug., 1683.
3. Honor, b. 9 May, 1685 ; d. 13 May, 1713.
4. Mehitable, m. Henry **Howell.**

FAM. 6.   EBENEZER,[2] (*John*,[1]), m. Sarah ————, 16 July, 1677 ; he was constable 1692 ; for ld-holdings see Chapt. VII, Vol. I ; he d. 2 May, 1705 ; an agreement of the heirs to divide the est. signed 1 May, 1710, ment. all the ch. given below.

Children (Weth. Rec.) :

1. Ebenezer, b. 5 May, 1678. FAM. 18.
2. John (Dea.), b. 26 July, 1679. FAM. 19.
3. Sarah, b. 6 (or 9) Jan., 1681 ; m. Dea. Joseph **Talcott,** 5 Apl., 1701 ; who d. 3 Nov., 1732 ; she d. 19 Mch., 1755. *Issue:* i. Josiah (Talcott), b. 27 Jan., 1702.
ii. Hezekiah (Talcott), b. 19 Mch., 1704 ; d. 31 Aug., 1734.
4. Ephraim (Lieut.). FAM. 20.
5. Josiah (Mr.). FAM. 21.
6. Prudence, m. Dea. Thomas **Wright,** 4 Oct., 1705 ; d. 24 Oct., 1706.

FAM. 7.   JOHN,[3] "the Drummer," (*Sgt. John*,[2] *John*,[1]), b. 1658, dr. lds. in the 1694 allot. ; m. 5 June, 1684, Mary (dau. wid.) **Graves.**—See Chapt. VII, Vol. I.

Children:

1. Abigail, b. 7 Oct., 1693.
2. Nathaniel, b. 2 Sept., 1696. FAM. 22.
3. Mary, b. 27 (bp. 29—*Mix*) Sept., 1700.

FAM. 8.   JONATHAN,[3] (*Sgt. John*,[2] *John*,[1]), b. 1663 ; m. 27 Oct., 1687, Martha (dau. Henry) **Buck.**—See Chapt. VII, Vol. I.   He d. prob. abt. close of 1719.

Children (Weth. Rec. & Mix Rec.) :

1. Isaac, b. 26 July, 1688-9
2. Anna, b. 20 Sept., 1690,
3. Noadiah, b. 20 Feb., 1693 ; m. Ruth ————. *Issue (Mix Rec.)* : i. Hezekiah, b. 6, bp. 9 Feb., 1728-29. ii. Dudley, bp. 4 July, 1731. (Noadiah's invent. of est. was taken 23 Aug., 1739 ; am't £681-12-00 ; adm. gr.
to wid., who may be the "Wid. Ruth," who d. 3 Oct., 1754 (*N. C. R.*) ; this fam. rem. 1749 to Pittsfield. Mass.
4. Abigail, b. 14 Mch., 1695 (or '98 ?).
5. Gideon, b. 29 Feb., bp. 5 May, 1700. FAM. 23.
6. Martha, b. 30 Aug., bp. 23 Sept., 1704.
7. Grace (acc. to *Talcott*).

FAM. 9.   JACOB,[3] (*Sgt. John*,[2] *John*,[1]), b. 1670 ; m. (acc. to *Talcott Geneal.*) Elizabeth (dau. Rich. & Elizabeth *Tuthill*) **Edwards,** of Htfd., 14 Mch., 1695 ; she m. (2) ———— **Hinckley,** of Kingston, R. I.

Children (Talcott Geneal.) :

1. Jacob, b. 1696.
2. Timothy, bp. 26 Mch., 1698.
3. Abigail, b. 21 Jan., 1700.
4. Lemuel, b. 1702.

FAM. 10.   HEZEKIAH,[3] (*John*,[2] *John*,[1]) ; m. Lois (dau. John) **Wyard,** 22 Nov., 1700 ; was hayward 1702 ; sheep-master 1703 ; rem. to and d. in Far., 1747.

Children (Weth. Rec.) :

1. Hezekiah, b. 10, bp. 20 July, 1703 ; m. Hannah (dau. Abia) **Warren,** 17 Aug., 1734 ; had large family.
2. Benjamin, b. 20 July, 1705.
3. Eunice, b. 29, bp. 30 May, 1708.
4. Lois, b. 24, bp. 28 Jan., 1710-11.
5. Elisha, bp. 8 Mch., 1712-13.
6. Zebulon, bp. 3 July, 1715.
   And others.

FAM. 11.   JONATHAN,[3] (*Jonathan*,[2] *John*,[1]), b. 1661 ; m. Abigail (dau. Zerubabel & Experience *Strong*) **Filer,** of Windsor Ct., 5 Jan., 1708-9. He was then 47 yrs. old, and this was prob. his 2d marr. ; his first wife having been Sarah **Barr,** of Midd. He may have been the Jona., who was a blacksmith, and whose ho. was one of the six "fortified" houses, in Feb., 1703-4. He was res. in Weth. in 1685, and prob. the same Jona. who was lister, in 1700 ; for his ld-holdings, see Chapt. VII, Vol. I. He was named, with his mother Elizabeth, as one of the executors of the will of his father, Jonathan, Sr.. which will he presented to the

Ct. of Prob. 27 Mch., 1700. As the Town had given to Jonathan D., Senior, 15 acres of ld., after the making of this will, and as there was no mention made in the will as to its disposition, the Court gave the said 15 acres to his son (this) Jonathan, Jr. "for his kindness to his father"—a tribute to his personal characacter of which his descendants may well be proud. His wid. m. (2) Abraham **Waterhouse**, of Saybrook, and d. 24 Dec., 1754.

Children (Weth. Rec.) :

1. Daniel, b. 5 Nov., 1709; bp. 15 Jan., 1709-10; being "abt. 2 yrs. old." FAM. 24.

2. Charles, b. 26 June, 1714. FAM. 25.

FAM. 12. THOMAS,[3] (*Jona.,[2] John,[1]*), b. 1679; m. Mary (dau. Thomas dec'd) **Williams**, 2 June, 1698; he d. 31 Jan., 1746-7; she d. 24 Aug., 1751.—*Weth. Rec.* They res. in 'Step. parish.

Children (Weth. Rec. & bp. Mix MSS) :

1. Lucy (*Eunice* in *Bp. Rec.*), b. 9, bp. 19 Mch., 1698-9; m. Elihu **Dickinson**.
2. Mary, b. 17 Mch., bp. May, 1700-1; m. Gideon **Hurlbut**, 30 Dec., 1725.
3. Elizabeth, b. 27 Sept., bp. Oct., 1703; m. Joseph **Belden**.
4. Daniel, b. 18 May, 1705. FAM. 26.

5. Abigail, b. 6 Nov., 1706; d. 16 Mch., 1708-9; *Talcott* says 1707.
6. Hannah, b. 22, bp. 25 Sept., 1708-9; m. Samuel **Williams**.
7. Thomas, b. 16 (bp. 24—*Mix*) Feb., 1711-12. FAM. 27.

FAM. 13. BENJAMIN,[3] (*Jonathan,[2] John,[1]*), b. 1684; m. Mary (dau. Thomas) **Wickham**, 4 Feb., 1706-7;* abt. 1732, rem. from Weth. to Goshen, Ct.,—tho' poss. not directly, as he is spoken of in 1736, as of Midd. He was apparently well along in yrs. at time of this removal, and during his last days he was probably in feeble health, as he turned over his ppy. to his ch., and was cared for by one of his sons. He d. 1772. He may have been the B. licensed by Co. Ct. June, 1731, as a "taverner." See, also, Chapt. VII, Vol. I.

Children (Bp. Mix. MSS.) :

1. Jonathan, b. 29 July, bp. 3 Aug., 1707; d. yg.
2. Benjamin, b. 19, bp. 24 July, 1709.
3. Sarah, bp. 26 Aug., 1711; m. Jno. **Riley**.
4. Prudence, bp. 2 Aug., 1713; m. James **Wright**.
5. Jonathan, bp. 20 May, 1716. FAM. 28.
6. Mary, b. 27 Jan., 1718-19; m. Capt. and Dea. Edmund[4] (*Capt. John,[3] Dea. John,[2] Thos.,[1]*) **Beach**.

7. Wait, b. 27 Sept., 1724; a blacksmith by trade; "armorer" in Fr. War, in 3d (Col. Fitch's) Reg.; d. at Ft. George, N. Y., in 1758; res. in Goshen, Ct.; was twice marr.; left 2 ch.
8. Dau., b. and d. 2 June, 1732 (1731—*Weth. Ins.*); was the first one bu. in Ry-H. Cemetery.—*Weth. Ins.*
9. Elias, b. 7 Nov., 1721.

* An exhaustive exam. of *Weth. T.* and *Ld. Recs.*, and of *Htfd. Co. Prob. Recs.*, made in 1899, by Mr. Edwin Stanley Welles, for Mr. Fred. M. Steele, of Chicago, Ill., establishes by apparently uncontrovertible proofs, the fact that this Benjamin was not (as tradition had it) from a branch of the Mass. fam., and a distinct importation into Weth., but that he was the son of *Jonathan,[2] John,[1]* the Weth. settler. The evidence (all circumstantial) is thus briefly stated by Mr. Welles, as condensed from documents accompanying his report to Mr. Steele: "The facts are these: (Ann Wickham) Deming, who m. Charles Deming, a bro. of Benj. Deming, sells out her interest in her gd-father's (Thomas **Wickham's**) estate at the same time that Benj. Deming and Mary his wife, and Jonathan **Carter**, and Elizabeth (**Latimer**) his wife sell out their interest in the same ppy. to Gideon Wickbam, of Southold, L. I.; prob. s. of Thomas Wickham, Jr. Now, Benjamin Wickham was not descended from the Demings, and had not himself any interest in the est. of Thomas Wickham, Sr. On the other hand, Ann Wickham, who m. his bro. Charles, is called, in the deed, gd-dau. of Thomas W., or Thos. W. is called her gd-fthr. (Prob. at this time her husband was dead.) Benjamin Deming's interest, therefore, came from his wife Mary, who, I believe was the sister of Ann (Wickham) Deming, and the gd-dau., also, of Thos. Wickham, Sr. Moreover, the *Prob. Recs.* strengthen this belief, as Benjamin Deming was app. adm[r] on the est. of Thomas Wickham, Jr., in place of Gideon Wickham, who declined, no doubt, because of his distance from Weth. As his est. was small, there was, unfortunately, no distrib. recorded to show who were his heirs. You will see that there is no doubt that Benjamin Deming was the s. of Jonathan D., and that he remained in Weth. until (at least) 1732. In 1736, he is called "of Midd." The *Ch. Bap. Rec.*, also, show that he was in Weth. from 1710-16, and, if they were not so faulty, would prob. reveal more.—*Authorities consulted, Weth. Ld. Rec.*, I, 1, 17, 77, 220; IV, 18, 19, 20, 29, 91, 252; V, 101. *Htfd. Co. Prob. Rec.,* XI, 23, 59. *Mix Rec.*

FAM. 14. JACOB,[3] (*Jonathan*,[2] *John*,[1]), b. 1689; m. (1) 3 Nov., 1709, Dinah (dau. Josiah) **Churchill**; she d. 3 Oct., 1751, ae. 69.—*C. L. C.;* m. (2) Abigail (wid. of Timothy) **Jerome.**

Children (Weth. & Mix Recs.) :

1. Dinah, b. 18 and bp. Oct., 1710; d. 13 Nov., 1710.
2. Joseph, b. 12 Nov., 1711, bp. 6 July, 1712. FAM. 29.

FAM. 15. JOHN,[4] (*Samuel*,[3] *John*,[2] *John*,[1]), b. 1694; m. Elizabeth (dau. Capt.) **Perkins**, of Norwich, Ct., 25 Nov., 1727.

Children (Weth. Rec.) :

1. John, b. 19 Oct., 1728.
2. Daniel, b. 1, bp. 6 Dec., 1730.
3. Honor, b. 11, bp. 18 Mch., 1732-3. We are inclined to think that we must add to this family a Capt. *Jabez,* of Norwich, Ct., who appears somewhat prominently in the affairs of that town, from 1760 to 1799. In Nor., 1760, he was one of 4 allowed to be "seated before y[e] pulpit," while his father (John) and his bro. (John) were seated in "the sixth seat, in y[e] meeting-ho." In 1775 and 1777 he was the Society Collector ; in 1790 and 1791 was on a School-Committee, and the *Chelsea Courier,* date of 23 Oct., 1799, gives

dth. at sea, of "Mr. Jabez Deming, 2d mate, son of the late Capt. Jabez Deming," —while the *Norwich Courier,* of 16 May, 1799, gives the death, at Preston, of a Mr. Jabez D., ae. 57 ; prob. the "late" Mr. J. D., referred to above. This would make Capt. Jabez, Sen., to have been b. abt. 1743, in Mch. of which yr. his father, John, "of Weth.," bo't an estate in East Norwich. Capt. Jabez's wife was Lucy **Stoddard**, of Groton ; m. prob. abt. 1771 ; she d. a wid. 6 May, 1830, leaving a dau. Lucy, b. 1783, who m. James **Gidbings**—and was the maternal gd-mother of Mrs. Joseph H. Johnson, of Minneapolis, Minn.

FAM. 16. Lieut. DAVID,[3] (*Samuel*,[2] *John*,[1]), b. 1696; m. Martha (dau. Sgt. John) **Russel**, 28 Jan., 1724-5; he d. 17 Feb., 1771 in 75th yr.; she d. 1 Sept., 1763, in 62 yr.—*Weth. Ins.*

Children (Weth. Rec. except * who were appar'tly b. at Sandisfield)* :

1. Martha, b. 15 Apl., 1726 ; m. Nathn'l **Goodwin**; 8 ch.
2. Mehitable, b. 27 May, 1727 ; m. Nathan'l **Stillman**; 10 ch.
3. David,* b. 16 (bp. 17, *Mix*) Aug., 1729. FAM. 30.
4. Mary, bp. 14 Mch., 1730-1.—*Mix.*
5. Mary, b. 8 Mch., 1732.
6. Abigail, b. 29 Apl., 1733, bp. 7 Apl., 1734 ; d. same yr.
7. Elizabeth (twin), b. and d. 5 Apl. 1734.
8. Abigail (twin), b. 5 Apl., 1734 ; m. Capt.

Elizur **Goodrich**, 24 Sept., 1760 (*Bible Rec.*) ; 6 ch.
9. Solomon,* b. 1 Dec., 1736.
10. Elizabeth, b. 8 Mch., 1738-9, m. Jonathan **Welles**. *Issue:*
    i. Jennette (Welles).
11. John,* b. 14 Mch., 1743. FAM. 31.
12. Simeon, b. 5 Mch., 1748.
13. Anna, b. ——— m. Asa **Talcott**. *Issue:*
    i. Asa (Talcott).
    ii. Mitty (Talcott).
    iii. Hannah (Talcott).

FAM. 17. SAMUEL,[3] (*Sam'l*,[2] *John*,[1]), b. 1699; m. Katharine (dau. Richard) **Treat**, 16 June, 1726; prob. the wid. Cath. who, ae. 72, was bu. 14 Sept., 1778.— *W. C. R.*

Children (Weth. Rec.) :

1. Treat, b. 28 Sept., (bp. Oct., 1, *Mix*), 1727.
2. Sarah, b. 10 (bp. 15, *Mix MS.*) Mch., 1729-30.
3. Katharine, b. 18 (bp. 21 *Mix*) Jan., 1732-33.
4. Samuel, b. 10 Dec., 1735.
5. Rebecca, b. 10 Oct., 1738 ; d. 6 July, 1758.
6. Mabel, b. 24 Aug., bp. 4 or 9 Sept., 1743.
7. Deliverance, b. 3 Dec., bp. —, 1746 ; d. 30 Aug., 1782, ae. 35.—*W. C. R. & Weth. Ins.*; prob. the D. who m. 5 May, 1773 (*N. C. R.*) Sarah [**Smith**, of Weth. *N.*

C. R.] who (wid.) was bu. 23 Oct., 1795 ; had Sarah bp. 8 Nov., 1778 ; bu., ae. 17, 18 Oct., 1795 (*Stephney*) ; ch. ae. 2 Sept., 1783. Billy and David bp. 6 July, 1777.
8. Richard, b. 11, bp. 15 Apl., 1750.
9. Richard, b. 12 Apl., bp ———, 1755 (*W. C. R.*) ; d. ae. 55, 4 Mch., 1805 ; *Weth. Ins.*, had a s. Richard, b. 12 Oct., 1784, who m. Abigail (dau. Sam'l & Anne) **Boardman**, 13 Dec., 1808, and had 11 ch.—For fam. rec. see *Boardman Gen.*, pp. 170, 328, 329.

FAM. 18. EBENEZER,[3] (*Ebenezer*,[2] *John*,[1]), b. 1678; m. Rebecca, (dau. Lieut. James) **Treat**, 27 Dec., 1704; she d. 26 Dec., 1753, in 68 yr.—*W. Ins.;* he was a hatter, and ld-holder in Weth. and New.; he d. 16 Apl., 1763.

Children (Weth. & Mix Recs.) :

1. Elizabeth, b. 6 Mch., 1705-6.
2. Joseph, b. 24, bp. 25 Jan., 1707-8. FAM. 32.
3. Oliver, b. 31 Dec., 1709, bp. 1 Jan., 1710. FAM. 33.
4. Ebenezer, b. 17, bp. 22 Dec., 1712. FAM. 34.
5. Timothy, b. 7, bp. 13 May, 1716. FAM. 35.
6. Moses, b. 1 Mch., 1719-20. FAM. 36.

FAM. 19. Dea. JOHN—,[3] on Recs. as "y[e] 3rd," (*Ebenezer,[2] John,[1]*), b. 1679; see Chapt. VII, Vol. I; m. (1) 5 June, 1712, Mary (dau. Joseph) **Curtis,** who d. 21 Dec., 1723; m. (2) Wid. Madam Katharine **Dewey,** (dau. John *Beckley*), 12 Aug., 1731; he was, with Ephraim, a signer of the petition for a separate parish at West Farms (Newington), and, while res. there, was called "Deacon". He d. 1 May, 1761, ae. 82; wid. d. 24 Dec., 1768.—*N. C. R.*

Children (Weth. & Mix Recs.):

1. Jedidiah, b. 15 Apl., bp. 31 May, 1712; d. unm. 1787.
2. Nichols, b. 25 Oct., bp. 7 Nov., 1714; d. 8 May, 1764.—*Annals of Newington* gives

this date as 1754.
3. Elizur, b. 5 Oct. (or 6 Nov.,), 1716; d. 11 Aug., 1736, unm.—*W. Ins.*

FAM. 20. Lieut. EPHRAIM,[3] (*Ebenezer,[2] John,[1]*), one of signers of 1812, for parish at West Farmes; m. Hannah (dau. John) **Belden,** 19 Jan., 1716, Lt. Ephraim d. 14 Nov., 1742.—*W. Ins.;* was a prominent man in New. Ch. and parish.

Children (Weth. & Mix Recs.):

1. Dorothy, b. and bp. 21 Oct., 1716.
2. Janna, b. 2 Nov., 1718. FAM. 37.
3. Honor, b. 18 May, 1721.
4. Stephen, b. 25 Aug., 1723. FAM. 38.

5. Waitstill, b. 18 May, 1726. FAM. 39.
6. Hannah, b. 4 Aug., 1728; m. Capt. Peter **Burnham.**
7. Lydia, b. 26 Mch., 1732; m. Elisha **Welles.**

FAM. 21. Mr. JOSIAH,[3] (*Ebenezer,[2] John,[1]*) b. abt. 1688; m. (1) Prudence (dau. Capt. James) **Steele,** 8 Dec., 1714; who d. 10 July, 1752.—*N. C. R.,* ae. 73; prob. m. twice, as we find the following (otherwise unappropriated) in *N. C. R.*— "Mr. Josiah Deming and Experience **Smith,** m. 11 Aug., 1756." He grad. Y. C. 1709; studied theol., but was never ord.; a prominent man in New parish.

Children (Weth. Rec.):

1. Elisha, b. 13 Dec., 1715, bp. 1 Jan., 1715-16.—*Mix.* FAM. 40.
2. Penelope, b. 17 Oct., 1717.

3. Zebulon, b. 25 Oct., 1719.
4. Solomon, b. 8 July, 1722. FAM. 41. And others.

FAM. 22. NATHANIEL,[4] (*John,[3] Sgt. John,[2] John,[1]*), b. 1696; m. Mary **Webb,** 25 Jan., 1721-22.

Children (Weth. Rec.):

1. Lois, b. 1 June, 1722, bp. 3 Dec., 1727 (*Mix MSS.*): m. Josiah **Churchill.**
2. Eunice, b. 11 Feb., 1724, bp. 3 Dec., 1727—*Mix MSS.*
3. Charles, b. 4 Sept., 1725.

4. Elisha, b. 8 Apl., 1728 (bp. 13 Apl., 1729, *Mix*); d. 15 Nov., 1731.
5. Hannah, b. 15 May, bp. 4 June, 1732.
6. Sarah, b. 6 Feb., 1738.

FAM. 23. GIDEON,[4] (*Jona.,[3] Sgt. John,[2] John,[1]*), b. 1700; m. Elizabeth **Case,** of Htfd., 5 Nov., 1729; he d. 1779.

Children (Weth. Rec.):

1. Gideon, b. 11, bp. 13 Sept., 1730.
2. Peter, b. 22 Dec., 1733. FAM. 42.
3. Temperance, b. 15 Nov., 1735.
4. Mary, b. 23 Aug., 1738.
5. Jonathan, b. 23, bp. 27 July, 1740. FAM. 43.

6. Sarah, b. 7 Sept., 1742.
7. Mabel, b. 25 Jan., bp. 3 Feb., 1744-45.
8. Abigail, bp. 27 Sept., 1747.—*W. C. R.*
9. Martha, b. 2 Sept., 1748.
10. Charles, bp. betw. 10 Apl. and May, 1751 or 7 (?).

FAM. 24. DANIEL,[4] (*Jona.,[3] John,[2] John,[1]*), b. 1770; m. 19 Nov., 1729, Mehitable (dau. Rev. Noadiah & Mary *Hamlin*) **Russell,** of Midd.; he d. at sea, 23 Apl., 1748. In the Rev. Mr. Russell's diary, his bereaved dau. Mrs. Daniel Deming thus records her loss, "my husband departed from his own house, 25 Mch., 1748. April the 9th, he sailed out of New London, and d. Apl., the 23d day. July 24th, news came of his dth." Mrs. Mehitable (Russell) Deming b. 27 May, 1704, d. 6 Jan., 1784, at Ry-H., in 80th yr.

Children (Weth Rec. & Family papers furnished by Mr. Wickmore):

1. Jonathan, b. 14 Sept., 1730; prob. the Jona. who d. 31 Mch., 1799, in 69th yr.
2. Abigail, b. 29 Sept., 1732; m. John **Goodrich,** 8 Oct., 1761; d. 12 June, 1799.

3. Mary, b. and d. 24 (25 *W. Ins.*) 1734.
4. Lydia, b. 24 Dec., 1738; m. Ebenezer **Goodrich.**

Fam. 25. CHARLES,⁴ (*Jona.,³ Jona.,² John,¹*), b. 1714, m. Dorothy **Belden,** 20 Dec., 1750; he d. 6 Feb., 1752.

Child (Weth. Rec.):

1. Mary, b. 23 Jan., 1752.

Fam. 26. DANIEL,⁴ (*Thomas,³ Jona.,² John,¹*), b. 1705; m. Eunice (dau. Abraham) **Williams,** 10 Mch., 1735; he d. 20 Oct., 1745; the "wid. Eunice" d. 6 Oct., 1768.—*S. C. R.*

Children:

1. Giles, b. 18 Feb., 1735-6. Fam. 44.
2. Abraham, b. 29 May, 1738; prob. the A. who m. Olive **Smith**; had Luther, bp. 8 Mch., 1767; Elijah, bp. 10 Sept., 1769; Eunice, bp. 5 Apl., 1722; Frederick, bp. 31

July 1774; prob the ch. who d. 24 Feb., 1775, and 3 other sons who left desc'ts.
3. Hannah, b. 12 Mch., 1742-3; d. 29 Sept., 1746.

Fam. 27. THOMAS,⁴ (*Thomas,³ Jona.,² John,¹*), b. 1712; m. 19 Dec., 1734, Elizabeth (dau. of Ens. Samuel) **Smith.** He d. 29 Sept., 1755.

Children (Weth. Rec.):

1. Elijah, b. 9 May, 1735. Fam. 45.
2. Abigail, b. 1 Mch., 1737.
3. Ozias, b. 11 May, 1739; d. 19 July, 1745.
4. Elizur, b. 9 May, 1741; prob. the E. who was bu. 20 June, 1813, ae. 75.—*W. C. R.*

5. John, b. 9 (or 19) Apl., 1743.
6. Elizabeth, b. 22 Nov., 1747.
7. Ann, b. 8 Mch., 1749.
8. Sarah, b. 30 Apl., 1752.

Fam. 28. JONATHAN,³ (*Benjamin,⁴ Jonathan,³ John,² John,¹*), b. 1716; m. Sarah (dau. Silas) **Richmond.** This may be the Jona. who d. 22 June, 1727; invent. of whose est. am't to £1246-14-04, real estate. He may have been the Jona. licensed as a "taverner" by the Co. Ct., in Dec., 1722 and Feb., 1727.

Children (bp. Mix MSS.):

1. Sarah, bp. 26 Aug., 1711; m. Jno. **Riley.**
2. Prudence, bp. 2 Aug., 1713; m. James **Wright,** and d. at Winsted, Ct., 1 Feb., 1717.

3. Dorcas, m. Lieut. Jno. **Wright.**—See *Boyd's Hist. Winchester,* Ct., pp. 115, 263.
4. Lucy, m. Charles **Wright.**
5. Jonathan, bp. 20 May, 1716.

Fam. 29. Lieut. JOSEPH,⁴ (*Jacob,³ Jona.,² John,¹*), b. 1711; m. (1) Martha **Hart,** 16 Dec., 1736, both of Far., who d. 26 Nov., 1748, in 33d yr.;—(*C. L. C.*); m. (2) Elizabeth **Wright,** 2 Aug., 1750; he d. 28 Feb., 1774, in 63 yr.— *Weth. Ins.*

Children (Weth. Rec.):

1. Joseph, b. 22 Aug., 1739.
2. David, b. 12 Jan., 1742.
3. Gideon, b. 21 Apl., 1744; d. 10 Nov., 1748.— *C. L. C.*
4. Asahel, b. 27 May, 1748.
(*By second marr.*):

5. Elizabeth, b. 20 Dec., 1752.
6. Abigail, b. 9, d. 20 Oct., 1755.
7. Mary, b. 24 Feb., 1758.
8. Huldah, b. 19 Mch., 1760.
9. Gideon, b. 27 Sept., 1762; perhaps the G. who d. 31 Mch., 1779, in 69th yr.

Fam. 30. DAVID,⁵ (*Lt. David,⁴ Samuel,³ Sgt. John,² John,¹*), b. 1729; m. Elizabeth [**Robbins,** *W. Ch. Rec.*] 12 Mch., 1754; rem. to Sandisfield, Mass.—*S. T. R.*

Children:

1. Elizabeth, b. 2 Sept., bp. 27 Oct., 1754; d. 31 Dec., 1839, ae. 84.—*Weth. Ins.*

2. Sarah, b. 1, bp. 7 Nov., 1756.
3. Simeon, bp. 16 Oct., 1763.—*W. C. Rec.*

Fam. 31. JOHN,⁶ (*Lt. David,⁴ Samuel,³ Sgt. John,² John,¹*), b. 1743; m. 18 Dec. 1777, Elizabeth **Welles.**—*W. C. R.*

Children (Weth. Rec.):

1. Elizabeth, b. 9 Feb., 1780; prob. the E. who d. 13 Nov., 1814, ae. 33.
2. John, b. 16 Nov., 1782.
3. Abigail, b. 2 Dec., 1787.

4. Achsah, b. 11 May, 1790.
5. Amos, b. 16 Oct., 1792.
6. Laura, b. 7 Oct., 1794.
7. Julia, b. 15 July, 1796.

FAM. 32. JOSEPH,[4] (*Ebenezer,[4] Ebenezer,[2] John,[1]*), b. 1708;* m. Elizabeth **Francis,** 8 Jan., 1735-6; res. Newington.

Children (Weth. Rec.):

1. Sarah, b. 24 May, 1737.
2. Francis, b. 12 Jan., 1739; d. 20 Dec., 1819, in 81st yr.—*W. Ins.* FAM. 46.
3. Aaron, b. 16 Oct., 1740; d. 12 Jan., 1740-1.
4. Aaron, b. 29 Mch., 1744; prob. the A.

who m. Lydia **Stoddard,** 14 Nov., 1771.— *N. C. R.*
5. Elizabeth, b. 1, bp. 8 July, 1750.
6. Titus, bp. 6 Mch., 1760.

FAM. 33. OLIVER,[4] (*Ebenezer,[3] Ebenezer,[2] John,[1]*), b. 1709; m. Lucy **Hale,** 3 Apl., 1735; he d. ae. 79, bu. 30 Sept., 1789.

Children (Weth. Rec.):

1. Lemuel, b. 16 Oct., 1735. FAM. 47.
2. Abigail, b. 20 May, 1738.

3. Oliver, b. 21 Mch., 1741-2.
4. Lucy, bp. 26 Apl., 1752.

FAM. 34. EBENEZER,[4] (*Ebenezer,[3] Ebenezer,[2] John,[1]*), b. 1712; m. Amy **Bunce,** prob. the E. Jr., who was found guilty by a jury of the *Co. Ct.,* Apl., 1745, for disturbing public worship, during the religious excitement attending the preaching. of the Bap. minister, Ebenezer Frothingham.—See p. 599, Vol. I.

Children (Weth. Rec.):

1. Ebenezer, b. 2 June, 1742. FAM. 48.
2. Amy, b., bp. 3 Sept., 1743.
3. Rebecca, b. 10 June, 1745.
4. Jerusha, b. 17 Feb., 1747.
5. Elizabeth, b. 8 July, 1748; d. Oct., '49.
6. John, b. 6 Dec., 1749.
7. Simeon, b. 16 Sept., 1751; m. Mary **Curtis,** 1 Apl., 1778 (*W. C. R.*), and may have been the same who m. 21 May, 1797,

Elizabeth **Deming.**
8. Elizabeth, b. 16 Oct., 1752 or '53.
9. Hester, b. 25 Dec., 1757; m. 23 Dec., 1777, Nathan'l **Baldwin,** of Stonington.—*W. C. R.*
10. Jesse, b. 17 June, 1760; d. 10 June, 1843, ae. 83 (*W. Ins.*); he m. Sarah ————, who d. 10 Mch., 1837, ae. 71.—*W. Ins.*

FAM. 35. TIMOTHY, (*Ebenezer, John, John,*), b. 1716; m. Susannah **French,** (prob. *Francis*) "as he saith, of Shatford," 5 Dec., 1740; he d. ae. 74, bu. 25 June, 1789.—*W. C. R.;* wid. d., ae. 85, bu. 19 Oct., 1801.—*W. C. R.*

Children (Weth. Rec.):

1. Eliakim, b. 1 Aug., 1741.
2. Charity, b. 29 Nov., 1742.
3. Sabra, b. 14, bp. 24 Feb., 1745; d. 9, bu. 10 Apl., 1776, ae. 31.—*W. C. R.* & *Weth. Ins.*
4. Abel, b. 11 Mch., bp. 3 May, 1747; m. Mary **Benton;** he d. 6 May, 1820, ae. 73.— *Weth. Ins.* FAM. 49.

5. Eli, b. 18 Aug., bp. before 19 Nov., 1749; m. Wid. Sarah **Ames.** FAM. 50.
6. David, b. 22 or 23 Oct., 1755, bp. betw. 25 Jan. and 25 Apl.
7. Mary, b. 18 Jan., bp. 18, 1758 (rec. ment. Mary and also a Sarah, twins).
8. Daniel, b. 10 Apl., bp. 2 May, 1762.

FAM. 36. MOSES,[4] (*Ebenezer,[3] John,[2] John,[1]*), b. 1720; m. 10 Nov., 1748, Martha **Welles**—*W. C. R.;* wid. d. ae. 83, bu. 31 Dec., 1811. He d. July, 1811, ae. "since Mch.," 92.

Children (Weth. Rec. & N. C. R.):

1. Martha, b. 16, bp. 19 Nov., 1749.
2. Judith, b. 18, bp. 24 Mch., 1754.
3. Elizabeth, b. 28 Nov., 1756.
4. Moses, b. 9, bp. 14 Jan., and d. 23 Jan., 1759.
5. Moses, b. 19 July, bp. before Sept., 1760;

m. and had *Laura,* bp. 22 Nov., 1799, and *Sally* (or Harriet acc. to one acc.), who d. ae. 5, bu. 17 Oct., 1803.—*W. C. R.*
A *Moses* d. 16 Jan., 1795, ae. 74 yr. 4 mos. *C. L. C.,* who may have been this one.

FAM. 37. JANNA,[4] (*Lieut. Ephraim,[8] Ebenezer,[2] John,[1]*), b. 1718; m. 14 June, 1750, Anne **Kilbourne;** he d. 24 July, 1796, ae. 78.—*W. Ins.;* res. New.; wid. d. 12 Apl., 1813, in 86 yr.—*W. Ins.*

Children (bp. from N. C. R.):

1. Elizur, b. 3 Feb., bp. 24 Mch., 1751; m. Lavinia (?) **Francis.** FAM. 51.
2. Elias, b. 11, bp. 12 Apl., 1752; m. Martha **Welles.** FAM. 52.
3. Daniel, b. 31 Dec., 1753, bp. 6 Jan., 1754.

4. Thomas, b. 27 Oct., bp. 2 Nov., 1755; d. 29 Sept., 1827.—*N. C. R.*
5. Anne, b. and bp. 6 Mch., 1758.
6. Eunice, b. 4, bp. 13 Apl., 1760.
7. John, b. 4, bp. 16 May, 1762.

*We confess to some uncertainty as whether this Joseph was the son of *Ebenezer,* FAM. 18, or of *Jacob,* FAM. 14. The difference between the ages of the two Josephs was but 2 yrs.

8. Chloe, b 25, bp. 28, 1765.
9. Honor, b. 6, bp. 18 May, 1767.
10. Gad, b. 19 June, bp. 6 Aug., 1770.
11. Levi (Dea.), b. 27 Aug., bp. 4 Oct., 1772; he d. 1 Jan., 1847, ae. 74; his wife, Sally,

d. 10 Mch., 1855, ae. 72; and a Sally S. "wife of Levi" (prob. a first marr.), d. 24 May, 1827, ae. 47.—*W. Ins.; dau.* Caroline, d. 23 Mch., 1842, ae. 32.

FAM. 38. STEPHEN,[4] (*Ephraim,*[3] *Ebenezer,*[2] *John,*[1]), b. 1723; m. Hannah **Goodrich,** 29 Jan., 1747; res. New.; he d. 24 Apl., 1790; wid. d. 16 Dec., 1799, ae. 75.—*W. Ins.*

Children (Weth. Rec. & N. C. R.):

1. Abigail, b. 2, bp. 6 Dec., 1747.
2. Rosanna, b. 3, bp. 9 Dec., 1750; d. 7 Jan., 1821, ae. 73.—*W. Ins.*
3. Sylvia, b. 22, bp. 27 Jan., 1754; d. 6 June, 1758.
4. Leonard, b. 18, bp. 19 Sept., 1756; d. 14

Aug., 1758.—*N. C. R.*
5. Sylvia, b. 5, bp. 8 July, 1759; "his second of the same name," d. 18 Apl., 1809, ae. 51.—*W. Ins.*
6. Leonard, b. 7, bp. 11 Sept., 1763; d. 1 Apl., 1787.

FAM. 39. WAITSTILL,[4] (*Benjamin,*[3] *Jonathan,*[2] *John,*[1]), b. 1724; m. Hannah **Lusk,** 31 Oct., or 1 Sept., 1758; he d. 10 Mch., 1776.

Children (Weth. Rec. & N. C. R.):

1. Elizabeth, b. 17, bp. 20 May, 1759.
2. Ephraim, b. 26 Feb., bp. 1 Mch., 1761; prob. the E. who was bu. 2 Mch., 1807, ae. 59, which would make him b. 1759.—*S. C. R.*
3. Ezekiel, b. 4, bp. 6 Apl., 1763.
4. Frederick, b. 17, bp. 19 May., 1765.

5. Lucretia, b. 19, bp. 22 Mch., 1767.
6. Selah, b. 7 Mch., bp. 7 May, 1769; prob. the S. who m. Sarah **Jerome,** 24 Feb., 1793.—*N. C. R.*
7. Roger, b. 19 July, bp. 22 Sept., 1771. FAM. 53.
8. Lyman, b. 2, bp. 13 June, 1773.

FAM. 40. ELISHA,[4] (*Mr. Josiah,*[3] *Ebenezer,*[2] *John,*[1]), b. 1715; m. Elizabeth **Williams,** 13 Mch., 1744-45,—*W. C. R.; she d. 1 Oct., 1779; he bu. 5 Sept., 1781.—W. C. R.*

Children (Weth. Rec. & W. C. R.):

1. Ephraim, b. 25, bp. 26 Jan., 1745-6; m. Martha **Deming.** FAM. 54.
2. Josiah, b. 1, bp. 2 Aug., 1747.

3. Anne Williams, b. 28 Mch., 1750.
4. Prudence, b. 30 Jan., bp. 4 Feb., 1753.

FAM. 41. SOLOMON,[4] (*Mr. Josiah,*[3] *Ebenezer,*[2] *John,*[1]), b. 1722; m. 27 Oct., 1748, Sarah **Kirkham,—***W. C. R.; res. New.; rem. to Pittsfield, Mass; they were the first marr. couple to reside in Pittsfield, Mass., arriving there in 1752, horseback (he on the saddle, she on a pillion behind); he built a log cabin, and, some yrs. later, a frame ho., the first framed building in P. Mrs. Deming was a woman of great courage and energy, and much of her household furniture is still preserved in the Athenæum at P., the citizens of which town erected to her memory a neat obelisk monument. She was b. in Weth., 1726, and d. at P. Feb., 1818, ae. 92.—Geo. A. Shepard.*

Children (Weth. Rec. & N. C. R.):

1. Rhoda, bp. 31 Jan., 1747-8.
2. Asa., bp. 4 Dec., 1748.

3. Noadiah, b. 14, bp. 16 July, 1749.
4. Abigail, bp. 29 Sept., 1754.

FAM. 42. PETER,[5] (*Gideon,*[4] *John,*[3] *Sgt. John,*[2] *John,*[1]), b. 1733; m. 6 Feb., 1763, Jerusha **Welles,—***W. C. R.; who d. 13 Jan., 1789, in 51 yr.; he prob. m. a second time, as W. C. R. gives marr. of Peter, to Mehitable **Stillman,** both of Weth., 10 Nov., 1793; and dth. of "wid. of Peter", 10 Aug., 1830, ae. 80. He d. 27 Sept., 1813, ae. 80.*

Children (Weth. Rec.):

1. Abigail, b. 10, bp. 19 Nov., 1765.
2. Elizabeth, b. 9 Nov., 1767.
3. Jerusha, b. 22 July, 1772.

4. Martha, b. 14 July, bp. 25 Aug., 1776.
5. Jonathan, b. 2 Oct., bp. 6 Dec., 1778; d. 13 Aug., 1783.—*W. Ins.*

FAM. 43. Lieut. JONATHAN,[5] (*Gideon,*[4] *John,*[3] *Sgt. John,*[2] *John,*[1]), b. 1740; m. 27 Jan., 1763, Jerusha (dau. Capt. Jacob & Eunice *Standish*) **Williams,** b. 1736. He was made Ens. of 9th Co. 6th Reg. Mil., in May, 1773; and in

May, 1774, Lieut. of 8th Co., in same reg't,—*Conn. Col. Rec.* XIII, 557 and XIV, 275. Lieut. Jonathan d. at Ry-H. 31 Mch., 1799; his wid. d. 21 Jan., 1815, in 79 yr.—*S. C. R.*

Children (Weth. Rec.) :

1. Mehitable, b. 15 Jan., 1764.
2. Daniel, b. 20 Feb., bp. 3 Mch., 1765.
3. Abigail, b. 19, bp. 23 Nov., 1766 ; m. 22 Mch., 1792, Asabel (s. of Lieut. Elisha & Thankful *Johnson*) **Savage** (*S. C. R.*), who went to Berlin, Ct., Mch., 1769, and d. at Sheffield, 22 Feb., 1850. *Issue:*
   i. Norman (Savage), b. 21 Dec., 1792 ; m. Elizabeth **Brown.**
   ii. Hamlin (Savage), b. 6 Feb., 1795 ; m. Sophia **Loring.**
   iii. Lyman (Savage), b. 16 Apl., 1797 ; m. Harriet **Holmes.**
   iv. Marietta (*Savage*), b. 22 Feb., 1799, v. Sarah Jerusha (Savage), b. 8 May, 1801 ; m. Ignatius **Loring.**
   vi. Abigail (Savage), b. 29 Apl., 1803 ; m. 2 Sept., 1824, Andrew (s. of Wyllis & Martha *Morse*) **Bartholo-**

mew, of Sheffield, Mass., b. 1802 ; d. 1879—they had (a) Asahel L. (Bartholomew), b. 24 June, 1826 ; (b) Martha E (Bartholomew), b. 30 Dec., 1827 ; (c) Henry A (Bartholomew), b. 28 Jan., 1830 ; (d) Emily M. (Bartholomew), b. 21 Nov., 1832 ; (e) Pauline Abigail (Bartholomew), b. 20 Nov., 1835 ;* (f) Jemima M. (Bartholomew), b. 12 Feb., 1838 ; (g) Norman Andrew (Bartholomew), b. 31 Mch., 1840 ; d. Feb., 1843.
4. Hamlin, b. 26 June., bp 8 July, 1770 ; d. 11 Oct., 1776.—*W. Ins.*
5. Harriet, b. 19, bp. 22 May, 1774 ; poss. the H. who m. 8 June, 1807, Rev. Wm. Lightbourn **Strong,** of Somers, Ct.—*Conn. Courant.*
6. Lydia, b. 9 May, 1777.

FAM. 44. GILES,[5] (*Daniel,[4] Thomas,[3] John,[2] John,[1]*), b. 1736; m. Hannah **Wright,** who d. 9 Feb., 1799, in 72d yr.; he d. 19 Oct., 1824, ae. 89.—*S. C. R.*

Children (S. C. R.) :

1. Asahel, bp. 7 July, 1765.
2. Hannah, bp 15 Nov., 1767.
3. Lydia, bp. 27 Nov., 1768.
4. Silence, bp. 7 June, 1772 ; prob. the S. who

d. 4 Oct., 1839, ae. 68.
5. Mercy, bp. 26 June, 1774.
6. Luman, bp. 31 Aug., 1776.

FAM. 45. Capt. ELIJAH, (*Thos., Thos., Jona.,*), b. 1735; m. 29 Jan., 1756, (*W. C. R.*,) Lucy **Sage,** prob. of Midd., whither he rem. and in Cromwell ("Upper Houses" of Midd.,) his wife is named *Rebecca*; in 1765 she was adm. to S. church 21 Sept., 1766, and d. 20 Feb., 1800, ae. 74; then he rem. to Sandisfield, Mass., where the dth. of his wife *Lucy* is rec. in 1810, and again the dth. of his wife *Naomi*, in 1822; so that he seems to have marr. 4 times. Elijah did good service in Revol. War, his name appearing as *Capt.* in list of officers, chosen by 11th company, Sandisfield, Berkshire Co. Reg., and accepted by Mass., Council, 6 May, 1776; as Capt., in Muster and Pay rolls of Col. Ashley's Berkshire Co. Reg., ordered to Saratoga by Gen. Gates,—enl. 26 Apl., disch, 20 May, 1776; as Capt. on Muster and Pay rolls of same Reg. ordered to Fort Edward, by Gen. Schuyler, enl. July 8, 1777, served 20 days; as Captain in same Reg., ordered to Bennington by Brig. John Fellows, enl. 16 Aug., 1777, served 6 days; and as *Capt.* in same Reg., ordered to Saratoga by Gen. Gates, enl. 19 Sept., 1777, served 30 days,—(For war acc. of Capt. Deming's military services and fam. hist., we are largely indebted to Mrs. Calvin C. Spencer, of Suffield, Ct.)†

Children (Weth. Rec., the two eldest given by *Hinman)* :

1. Mary, b. 4 Nov., 1756.
2. Thomas, b. 21 Jan., 1759.
3. Ozias, b. 1762 ; d. 7 Aug., 1847. FAM. 55.
4. Mehitable, bp. 14 Oct., 1764.

5. Hepsah.

Others, as supp.—one or two of whom joined the Shaker Community.

---

* Pauline Abigail Bartholomew, m. 10 Sept., 1856, Manly Horatio **Wickmore.** *Issue:*
1. Lillian E. (Wickmore), b. 25 Aug., 1858.
2. Frances E. (Wickmore), b. 13 Dec., 1859.
3. Cornelia Pauline (Wickmore), b. 17 Apl., 1865.
4. Arthur Manley (Wickmore), b. 19 Mch., 1867; grad. Wms. Coll., 1890; Univ. of Minn. Law School, 1893 ; here finished this line of descent from Jonathan Deming[5]
5. Townsend Bartholomew (Wickmore), b. 31 Mch., 1869.
† There was an Elijah, son of Gamaliel & Rebecca (Kellogg), who was m. 1751. *Children:* Elizabeth, first-born, date unknown ; Mary, second, ·b. Oct. 5, 1752. It may be that the two Elijahs, being synchronous, have been confused.—(*Times,* April 8, 1901.)

FAM. 46. FRANCIS,[5] (Joseph,[4] Ebenezer,[3] Ebenezer,[2] John,[1]), b. 1739; m. (1) 13 July, 1762, Mary **Camp**, who d. 19 Aug., 1782; he m. (2) Elizabeth **Churchhill**, 21 Aug., 1783,—N. C. R.; she d. 31 Dec., 1839.—N. C. R.

Children (Weth. Rec.):

1. Nancy, b. 11, bp. 12 Dec., 1762.
2. Robert (Ens.), b. 9, bp. 25 Dec., 1763; prob. the R. who m. Lucy **Blinn**, 17 Jan., 1786 (N. Ch. R.); he 1. 19 Dec., 1814, ae. 51.
3. Barzillai, b. 21, bp. 30 Mch., 1766; m. 22 Apl., 1790, Sophia **Smith**.
4. Joseph, b. 23 July, bp. 10 Sept., 1769.
5. Mary, b. 15 Oct., 1770.

FAM. 47. Capt. LEMUEL,[5] (Oliver,[4] Ebenezer,[3] Ebenezer,[2] John,[1]), b. 1735; m. Hannah **Standish**, he d., ae. 54, bu. 25 Apl., 1790.—Weth. Ins.; she d. 3 Dec., 1826, ae. 88.—Weth. Ins.

Children (Weth. Rec.):

1. Josiah, b. 7 June, bp. 8 Oct., 1758.
2. Hannah, b. 31 May., bp. before 18 Sept., 1760; d. 27 Apl., 1773.
3. Allyn, b. 19, bp. 26 Sept., 1762; he d. 15 Apl., 1847 (Weth. Ins.); m. Prudence **Woodhouse**, 28 May, 1791; *Patience*, "wife of Allyn," ae. 69, d. 9 Sept., 1834; Roswell, bu. 15 Nov., 1800; Allyn S., dr. bu. 14 June, 1821, ae. 27 (W. T. & Ch. Rec.); Patience, bp. 1 Aug. 1819.
4. Levi, b. 25 Nov., bp. 2 Dec., 1764; m. Sarah (dau. Aaron & Mabel *Easter*) Grant, of E. Windsor, Ct., 18 Dec., 1792; d. 27 Sept., 1848, ae. 83.—Weth. Ins. Had

Issue:
i. Sarah.
ii. Orrin.
iii. Pamela, m. David **Crane**.
5. Rhoda, b. 3, bp. 5 Apl., 1767.
6. Huldah, b. 8 Oct., 1769; m. Lemuel **May**.
7. Lucy, b. 31 Mch., 1772.
8. Oliver, b. 1, bp. 6 Nov., 1774.
9. Hannah, b. 16, bp. 24 Nov., 1776; m. Matthew **Francis**, and d. 12 Feb., 1842.
10. Asenath, bp. 18 Apl., 1779; m. John **Stillman**; she d. 10 Oct., 1841, ae. 62.—Weth. Ins.
11. Lemuel, bp. 14 July, 1782.

FAM. 48. EBENEZER,[5] (Ebenezer,[4] Ebenezer,[3] Ebenezer,[2] John,[1]), b. 1742; m. 4 Jan., 1769, Mabel **Deming**, who prob. was the "wife of Ebenz." who d. 9 June, 1813. He d. 24 Feb., 1824, in 83d.—Step. C. R.

Children (Weth. Rec.):

1. Mabel, b. 23 June, 1769.
2. Joseph, b. 6 Nov., 1772.
3. Gideon, b. 12 Apl., 1775; bu. 15 Nov., 1800, ae. 25 (W. C. R.), and perhaps, also, the G.
who m. Milly **Flint**, 6 May, 1800.—W. C. R.
4. Rebecca, b. 14 Nov., 1778.
5. Ebenezer, b. 7 May, 1782.
6. Sarah, b. 15 Aug., 1785.

FAM. 49. ABEL,[5] (Timothy,[4] Ebenezer,[3] John,[2] John,[1]), 1747; m. (1) 27 Sept., 1770, Mary **Benton**, who d. 12 Feb., 1811, ae. 60; m. (2) ———, who, (wid.) d. ae. 65, bu. 12 Feb., 1829.

Children (Weth. Rec.):

1. Rhoda, b. 19 Nov., 1771, bp. 28 Aug., 1774.
2. Lydia, b. 28 Nov., 1773, bp. 28 Aug., 1774.
3. Mary, b. 18 Jan., bp. 3 Mch., 1776.
4. Sabra, b. May, bp. 2 Aug., 1778.
5. Prue, b. 31 Oct., 1780; bp. 8 July, 1781.
6. Isaac, b. 7 Nov., 1782.
7. Jared, b. 5, bp. 12 Dec., 1784; prob. the
J. who m. Charlotte **Porter**, 25 Jan., 1807.
8. Titus, b. 3 Sept., 1786; bp. 30 June, 1799.
9. Emily, b. 14 July, 1791; bp. 30 June, 1799.
10. Harriet, b. 29 Oct., 1793; bp. 30 June, 1799.

FAM. 50. ELI,[5] (Timothy,[4] Ebenezer,[3] John,[2] John,[1]), b. 1755; m. 8 Feb., 1778, Sarah (wid. of Robert) **Ames**. (sic.)

Children (Weth. Rec. & W. C. R.):

1. Benjamin, b. 30 Mch., 1777; (sic.).
2. Hannah, b. 10 Dec., 1778; bp. 24 Jan., 1779.

FAM. 51. ELIZUR,[5] 2d., (Janna,[4] Lieut Ephraim,[3] Ebenezer,[2] John,[1]), b. 1751; m. 5 or 6 of May, 1773, Lucina **Francis**; he d. 5 Dec., 1827, ae. 77. (N. C. R., ae. 78); she d. 9 Dec., 1818, ae. 66.—Weth. Ins.; res. New.

Children (Weth. Rec.):

1. Elizur, b. 20, bp. 26, d. 28 July, 1774; so says orig. Weth. Rec., or we might suppose him to have been the E. who d. 20 Aug., 1779, ae. 5.—W. C. R.
2. James, b. 29 July, 1776; bp. 27 Apl., 1777.
3. Anne, b. 19 Oct., 1780; bp. 6 May, 1781.
4. Elizur, b. 18 May, bp. 20 Oct., 1782; d. 11 Dec., 1847, ae. 66.—W. T. R.
5. Nancy, b. 9 Apl., bp. 27 Aug., 1786.

FAM. 52. ELIAS,[5] (*Janna*,[4] *Lieut. Ephr'm*,,[3] *Ebenezer*,[2] *John*,[1]), b. 1752; m. Martha **Welles**, 26 Nov., 1778, who d. 5 Aug., 1813, ae. 63,—*N. C. R.; he d. 13 May, 1814, ae. 62.—W. Ins.; res. New.

Children (Weth. Rec.) :

1. Enos, b. 20 Aug., bp. 31 Oct., 1779 ; m. 2 Jan., 1803, Prue **Lusk**—*N. C. R.;* had *Lucy*, b. 8 Jan., 1805 ; *Martha*, d. 19 Apl., 1834, in 13 yr. ; *Levi*, d. 17 Sept., 1808, ae. 8 mos. ; *Prudence*, d. 27 Feb., 1823, ae. 4; *Marietta*, d. 22 Nov., 1827, ae. 4 yr.—*W. Ins.*
2. William, b. 25 Feb., bp. 13 May, d. 19 Aug., 1781.
3. William, b. 13 Oct., 1782.
4. Martha, b. 2 Dec., 1785 ; bp. 29 Jan., 1786 ; poss. the M. who m. 13 May, 1804,

Bartholomew **Lathrop**, of Harwinton.
5. Lucy, b. 13 May, bp. 10 Aug., 1788 ; d. 4 Dec., 1800.—*W. Ins.*
6. Jedidiah (Dea.), b. 7 Sept., bp. 21 Nov., 1790 ; prob. the Jed. who m. (1) Mary ———— [Lusk ?], who d. 18 May, 1827, ae. 37 ; m. (2) Ann **Wells**, 21 May, 1834. —*W. T. R.* She b. 1 Aug., 1804 ; d. 25 May, 1879 ; he d. 4 May, 1868 ; he had dau. Mary Lusk, who d. 29 July, 1841, ae. 23.
6. Lydia, b. 1 July ; bp. 31 Aug., 1794.
7. Lucy, b. 4 Dec., 1800.

FAM. 53. ROGER,[6] (*Waitstill*,[5] *Benjamin*,[4] *Jona.*,[3] *John*,[2] *John*,[1]), b. 1771; m. Mabel, who d. 26 Jan., 1811, ae. 44.—*Weth. Ins.*

Children (W. C. R.) :

1. Roger, bp. 9 Sept., 1798; the "son" who d. Oct., 1803, ae. 4.
2. Gideon, bp. 24 Aug., 1800.
3. Ch. ae. 13 mos. bu. 8 Aug., 1803.
4. William, bp. 11 Apl., 1803.
5. William, bp. 23 June, 1805.
6. Ebenezer, bp. 19 Oct., 1806.

FAM. 54. EPHRAIM,[5] (*Elisha*,[4] *Mr. Josiah*,[3] *Ebenezer*,[2] *John*[1]), b. 1746, m. Martha **Deming**, 27 June, 1771; res. New., d. 16 July, 1783; he is spoken of as "the late E." in bp. rec. of his youngest dau.

Children (Weth. Rec.) :

1. Martha, b. 1 May, 1772 ; bp. or b. (?) 15 May, 1774 (?).
2. Infant, bu. 2 June, 1776.
3. Betsy, b. 23 Feb., bp. 3 May, 1778.
4. Nancy, b. 11 Jan., bp. 11 Feb., 1781.
5. Mehetable, bp. 17 Aug., 1783 ; d. Mch., 1830, ae. 47.

FAM. 55. OZIAS,[6] (*Elijah*,[5] *Thomas*,[4] *Thomas*,[3] *Jonathan*,[2] *John*,[1]), b. 1762; m. 2 Jan., 1788, Louisa **Ely**, of Holyoke, Mass.

Children:

1. Elizur, b. 13 June, 1790 ; d. 27 Apl., 1849.
2. Hannah, b. 2 May, 1793.
3. Louisa, b. 16 Jan., 1796 ; d. 19 Nov., 1832.
4. Russell, b. 6 May, 1798.
5. Harriet, b. 4 Aug., 1803 ; d. 22 Nov., 1827.

DENNISON, MARY, Invent. £376-05-0¾, taken 23 June, 1721, by Edwd. Bulkley, Jonathan Deming, Ebenezer Belding,—*Ct. Rec.;* 4 July, 1721, adm. to Joshua Robbins, her son[-in-law?]. Order to Dist. to Joshua Robbins, eld. son, to Richard Robbins,[3] Samuel, Robbins,[2] sons of the dec'd, the heirs by agreement divide part of the lds.—*Htfd. Co. Prob. Rec.*

DENNY, Mr. THOMAS, m. Martha ————, who d. 5 Feb., 1790, ae. 31; they had *John Allen*, who d. 11 Sept., 1789, ae. 19 mos.—*Weth. Ins.*

DENTON, Rev. RICHARD.—See pp. 144-145, Vol. I.

DEORRANCE, WILLIAM, of Andover, Ct., m. Hezp. B. **Goodrich,** 6 May, 1846.

DERRICK, (*Derrick? Deorick?*) of St. Croix, Isld.; m. Lucy **Goodrich,** 15 Sept., 1839.

DEVOTION, Mr. JOHN.—See Chapt. VII, Vol. I.

DEWEY, DAVID, m. Esther, **D**————, 12 Feb., 1755.—*N. C. R.*

LUCY, (dau. of David), d. 22 Oct., 1748, ae. 5 yr. 11 mos.—*C. L. C.*

RHODA, (dau. of David), d. 15 Oct., 1748, ae. 11 yrs. 10 mos.—*C. L. C.*

DEWING, HIRAM'S, inf. d. d. 20 July, 1851.

DEWITT, MARTHA, d. 5 Apl., 1841, ae. 68.—*Weth. Ins.*

ABRAHAM VAN HORN, m. Martha **Belding**, 22 Aug., 1792.—*W. C. R.*

HENRY ALBERT, d. Petersburg, Va., 12 Sept., 1820.

DEWOLF, (*Dewoolf*,), Mrs. PRUDENCE, d. 16 June, 1737, in 61 yr.—*Weth. Ins*

BALTHAZER, ancestor of prominent families in Rhode Island, and Nova Scotia, of Senator Dolph and many other persons of distinction; lived in Weth. before his removal to Lyme, Conn. See Salisbury's *Family Histories & Genealogies.* See, also, Chapt. VII, Vol. I.

CHARLES, of Ashfield, Mass., m. Abigail **Blinn**, 20 Nov., 1828.

DEUSLAR, ELIHU, of Windsor, Ct., m. Mary **Rhodes**, 21 Nov., 1832.

DIBBLE, ABIGAIL an orphan, who lived with Rich Butlor, bp. 17 July, 1715.— *Mix. MSS.*

DICKINSON, (*Dykinson, Dykenson, Dykensonne, Dickemsonne*). Much kindly help on this family rec'd from Mrs. C. S. PRINCE, and Mrs. A. C. HAWLEY, of Hartford. Contrary to a fam. trad. which claims a Scotch origin, the author of the *Morton Memoranda*, p. 131, traces its descent from Walter de Caen, a kinsman and companion of William the Conqueror, and through him to Rollo, first Duke of Normandy; also that Walter wedded the dau. of the last Saxon lord of Kenson, and was afterward known as Walter de Kenson. In this he is supported by the author of the most recent genealogy of the D. fam.,[1] who traces the Weth. Settler, Nathaniel Dickenson, back thro' 14 gen. to the said Walter de Kenson.

Just when the fam. took the Anglicized form of the surname is unknown, but prob. in the early part of the XIV Century. Its two most ancient forms were *Dickenson,* then *Dicconson.* The former appeared in the reign of Henry VIII; but it is not until a century later that the second syllable is spelled with an *i,* which is clearly a corruption of the original orthography.

The *arms* of the family, as given by the *Morton Mem.,* are "Vert. a cross betw. 4 hinds' heads, coupled, or, — Motto, *Esse quam videri—i. e. "to be,* rather than seem to be." These arms are said to date from Henry VIII's reign, and were used by John de Caen, of Kenson, in the time of Edward I; their heraldic meaning (being, that the green field of the shield and the 4 hinds' heads,) signify that the orig. bearers were rangers of the Royal forests—most likely Epping, in Co. York; the cross, added in the time of the last crusade signifying that the D's participated in that holy war. These, however, do not accord with the arms assigned to them by the author of the D. genealogy—viz.— those of Yorkshire and Bradly—"*Az fesse ermine,* betw. 2 lions passant, or. *Crest, a demi lion rampant per pale erminoise et azure.*" The arms first described were those of one Hugh Dickinson, who lived abt. 1422, the supp. ancestor of the Americans, and who d. 1523.

Deacon NATHANIEL DICKINSON, an early Settler in Weth. was the s. of William & Sarah *Stacey* Dickinson, of Ely, Cambridge, Eng., where he was b. 1600, and with his wife Anna (Gull) and 3 ch., came to Watertown, Mass., in 1634; to Weth., 1636, perhaps 1637, where he seems speedily to have become a prominent citizen; was on the Jury, Oct., 14, 1642 (*Col. Rec.* I. p. 76); was

OLD DICKINSON LETTER.

Facsimile of a letter of Nathaniel Dickinson, an original settler of Wethersfield and later of Hadley, Mass., to Samuel Foreman of Wethersfield, October 10, 1666.

Original in possession of William F. J. Boardman.

app. Town Clerk, or "recorder," 1 Dec., 1645 (perhaps earlier—*Col. Rec.*, I. 76) the earliest town vote rec. on the oldest extant *Weth. Recs.*, being in his handwriting; was dep. to Gen. Ct. 1646-56; townsman, 1647-8; his homestead rec. to him 1649—(See Chapt. VII, Vol. I) ; and Oct., 1654, one of a comm. of 3 app. by the Ct. to advise with the constables of the 3 River Towns, abt "pressing men for the exp. into the Ninigret country," in the Narr. War. When the movement on the part of many dissatisfied members of the Weth. Htfd. and Windsor chhs., took place, Apl., 1659, for the emigration to Hadley, Mass., he and his sons, Nath'l and John, were present and active among the 59 persons concerned, and the father was one of the delegates chosen to lay out the new plantation East of Northampton. The three were also of the 29 present at a town meeting, Oct., 1660, at which rules and regulations for the new enterprise were adopted and signed. At Hadley, as at Weth., he became the first Town Clerk; was Town assessor; a magistrate; a member, at its formation, 1663, of the Hampshire Troop under Capt. Pyncheon; and connected with the founding of Hopkin's Acad., of which he was one of the first trustees; when Maj. Pyncheon purchased the Hadley tract, he accepted Mr. D. and Nath'l Ward as reps. of the planters, and they signed the final sett., 29 Oct., 1663. In both communities, Weth. and Hadley, he was justly esteemed as an upright, intelligent, active and capable citizen, bearing well his share in the labors, privations and dangers incident to a frontier life. Worn out at last by these, especially those incurred in the defense of Hadley, and the Ind. war of 1675-6, and depressed by the tragic loss of his 3 sons in that strife, he d. 16 June, 1676, a noble example of Puritan godliness, and manly loyalty to duty. His will, dated 29 May, 1676, describes him as "late of Hatfield, now of Hadley."

Dea. Nathaniel Dickinson, m. Jan., 1630, at East Bergholst, Co. Suffolk, Eng., Anna (wid. of William) **Gull.**

Children (Dickinson Genealogy & Weth. Rec.) : 5 births only rec. at Weth.

1. John, b. 1630, in Eng. FAM. 2.
2. Joseph, b. 1632, in Eng.; res. Nh., was a freeman of Conn., 1657; res. Nh., 1664-74; then rem. to Northfield, Mass.; was killed in battle, 4 Sept., 1675; m. at Hadley, 1665, Phebe (dau. John & Phebe *Berbridge*) **Bracey**, who was gd-dau. of Wm. Bisby, gent. of London, Eng. He was a deacon in Had. Ch.; seems to have gone to Weth. abt. 1661; prob. did not stay long; had 5 ch.—See Chapt. VII, Vol. I.
3. Thomas, b. 1633, in Eng. FAM. 3.
4. Anna, (or Hannah), b. 1636; m. (1) Jan., or June 16, 1670, John **Clary, Jr.**; m. (2) Enos **Kingsley**, of Nhm.
5. Samuel, b. "abt. the middle of July, 1638;" m. 4 Jan., 1668, Martha **Bridgman**; res. at Hadley; for his posterity, see Judd's *Hist. Hadley.*
6. Obadiah,* b. "abt. the middle of April," 1641. FAM. 4.
7. Nathaniel, b. 1644, acc. to D. *Geneal.*, p. 33; *Weth. Rec.*, or acc to some auth. (p. 33); not ment. in his father's will, but distinctly identified as his son, by Nath'l, Sen., in a deed in *Weth. Ld. Rec.*, Vol. II. p. 13½, dated 1 Apl., 1661; but Judd prob. gives date of birth,

Aug., 1643, more correctly; he **res.** in Hatfield; was 3 times m.; his posterity is given in Sheldon's *Deerfield*, II, p. 144.
8. Nehemiah, b. "abt. the middle of Aug., 1643, (Judd says "abt. 1644") ; m. and res. Had.; for post. see Judd's *Hadley*; had 14 ch. For *Weth. Ld. Rec.*, see Chapt. VII, Vol. I.
9. Hezekiah, b. "the last of Feb." 1645; mcht. at Had., Hat. and Spgfld.; m. 4 Dec., 1679-80, Abigail (dau. Samuel) **Blakeman**, of Stratford; was the father of Rev. Jonathan D., b. 22 Apl., 1688; grad. Y. C., 1706; pastor of 1st Pres. Ch., of Newark, N. J., and first Pres. of Coll. of N. J. (Princeton); was a phys. as well as a minister, was a D. D., and as a writer on divinity, was classed with Jonathan Edwards. Orcutt's *Hist. Stratford* says Hez., s. Nath'l, came to St., abt. 1679, from Weth.; m. there; rem. to Conn. River & thence to Spgfld.
10. Azariah, b. 4 (or 10) Oct., 1648; res. Hadley; slain in the Swamp Fight at Whately, Mass., 25 Aug., 1675; m. Dorcas ———, who m. (2) Jonathan **Marsh**, and d. 15 Aug., 1675, ae. 69.
11. Frances, acc. to D. *Gen.;* ment. in will of Nath'l.

FAM. 2. Sgt. JOHN,[2] (*Nathaniel*,[1]), b. 1630; m. at age of 17, Frances ———, —*Weth. Rec.;* the *Foote Gen.* supplies her family name, *Foote* (dau. of Nathaniel) and that they m. at Weth. 1648. He was a surveyor of highways, 1651; one of a comm. to run the S. line of Weth., 1659; for ld.-rec. see Chapt.

* The D. *Geneal.* gives 1639, as date of Obediah's birth, which (in the face of *Weth. Rec.*) could not be, unless, poss., a previous Obed. was b. and d. after Samuel.

VII, Vol. I; rem. to Hadley with his father, 1659; he was killed in the Falls (Turners) Fight, in King Philip's War, 19 May, 1676; his wid. m. (2) Francis **Barnard**, of Hadley.

Children (born in Weth.) :

1. Hannah, b. 6 Dec., 1648; m. (1) Samuel **Gillet**, of Hat., who was killed in same battle as her father; she m. (2) 5 May, 1677, Stephen **Jennings**; 4 mths. after was herself capt. by Inds. and carried into Canada, whence she escaped the next yr.; in 1708, her son Joseph Gillet was wounded and her dau.'s husband killed, and in 1710, her husband (Jennings) was killed by Ind. (*Given by Judd, and also D. Gen.*) ;
2. Mary, b. 1650 ; m. Samuel **Northam**, of Hat., Deerfield and Colchester, Ct.
3. Jonathan, b. 1654; d. before Mch., 1678.
4. Sarah, b. 1656; m. (1) 11 Dec., 1677,

Samuel **Lane**; m. (2) 27 Feb., 1691, Martin **Kellogg**.
5. Rebecca, b. abt. 1658; m. 11 Feb., 1691, Joseph **Smith**,, and d. 16 Feb., 1731, ae. 73.
6. Elizabeth,[3] b. abt. 1660; d. before Mch., 1678.
7. Abigail, b. 1662; m. (1) 6 Dec., 1683, Thos. **Croft**; m. (2) 30 Nov., 1704, Samuel **Crowfoot**.
8. Mercy, b. 1664 (*Judd* says 1668) ; m. 8 June, 1688, Joseph **Chamberlain**, of Hat. and Colchester, Ct., and d. 30 June, 1735, ae. 67.
9. Mehitable, b. 1666 ; m. 26 June, 1689, John **Ingram**, Jr.

FAM. 3. THOMAS,[2] (*Nathaniel,*[1]), b. 1634, *D. Gen.;* m. (acc. to *D. Gen.* 7 Mch., 1668, at Had., Hannah (ygst. dau. John & Elizabeth *Goodwin*) **Crow**, b. at Htfd., 13 July, 1649; he was freeman in Ct., 1657; and of Mass., 1661; was an early sett. of Had., but ret. to Weth. abt. 1678; and d. there, 1716; will dated, 7 June, 1710, at W.,—*Htfd. Co. Prob. Rec.,* IX, 146; his lds. rec.—*Ld. Rec.,* I, 106; he was fence-viewer on E. side Conn. River, 1691; in 1703, the town gave him "the piece of ld. which his ho. stands on" in Weth.; his wife was memb. of So. Ch., Htfd., 23 Jan., 1680.—*So. Ch. Rec.*

Children (acc. to Judd's Hadley) :

1. Elizabeth, b. 6 Dec., 1668; m. Benjamin **Adams**, of Weth.
2. Hannah, b. 20 May, 1670 ; m. Samuel **Leffingwell**; res. Norwich; d. before her father.
3. Thomas, b. Had., 15 Feb., 1672 ; m. 1694, Mehitable **Meekins**, at Hat., where he d. 1723.
4. Esther, b. 22 Jan., 1674 ; m. (1) Nath'l

Smith, of Htfd.; m. (2) Hez. **Porter**, of Htfd.
5. Mehitable, b. 20 Oct., 1675 ; d. inf.
6. Nathaniel, b. 15 Nov., 1677 ; bu. 26 Jan., 1678.
7. Elihu,[3] b. 1678.
8. Ebenezer, b. 1679 ; bp. in So. Ch., Htfd., 7 Nov., 1679. FAM. 5.

FAM. 4. Sgt. OBEDIAH,[2] (*Nathaniel,*[1]), b. 1641; accompanied his father to Hadley, 1659, took part in King Philip's War; in 1677 his ho. was burned by Inds., and he, wounded and with ch., capt. by Inds., but he escaped fm. captivity in Canada; he returned to Weth. in 1679; he and (2d wife) memb. of Weth. ch., 1694—*Mix MSS.*) ; he was constable, 1687-8; dr. ld. in allot. of same yr; comm. to lay out ld. in 1694. He m. (1) 8 Jan., 1668-9, Sarah (dau. Wm.) **Beardsley**, of Stratford; m. (2) 1690, Mehitable **Hinsdale**, of Hadley, or Hatfield, Mass., she was not living in 1702—(*Htfd. Co. Prob. Rec.,* VII) ; he d. 10 June, 1698, in 58th yr.; his seal on will (dated 7 June, 1698) tho' defaced, still bears traces of the "lion passant" described on the D. arms. Invent. £678-08-08 taken 7 July 1698, by William Warner, Joseph Churchill, William Goodrich. Will dated 7 June, 1698: I give to my three sons, Daniel, Eliphalet and Noadiah Dickinson, to my dau. Sarah Smith, to Mehetabell Dickinson, to each £40, not counting the wearing apparel or the child's clothes that were her mother's, my former wife. I give to my wife Mehetabell Dickinson—the use of my housing & home-lot, etc., for her comfort and the bringing up of the two children I had by her—while she remains my widow I give her the use of my son Noadiah's estate until he come to the age of 21 years—and that of my dau. Mehetabell until 18 years of age or shall be married. If my son Obadiah be living he to have an equal share with my sons. Obadiah Dickinson & Witnesses. John Chester, Samuel Northam—I give my servant Sarah Couch a cow, my son Eliphalet to be executor.—Court Records, 1st Sept., 1698, Will & invent. Proven.

Children (Judd's Hadley and D. Geneal.):

1. Sarah, b. 20 Aug., 1670; m. ————
   Smith (acc. to father's will).
2. Obadiah, b. 29 Jan., 1672—see Chapt.
   VII, Vol. I; prob. a sailor and apparently
   d. intestate, before 8 Mch., 1700, as an
   invent. of his est. adm. upon by his
   bros. Daniel and Eliphalet, and exhib.
   8 Apl., 1701 (*Htfd. Co. Prob. Rec.*), amt.
   to £55, 02s., and included 92 pieces of gold
   that came from Madagascar; and his
   father's will also refers to him as to
   one, "whom he knows not whether alive
   or dead."
3. Daniel, b. 26 Apl., 1674; prob. the D.

who had dau. Elizabeth, bp. 9 Feb., 1706-7.
   —*Mix Rec.*
4. Eliphalet, b. ————, 1676. FAM. 6.
   (*By second marriage*):
5. Noadiah, b. 2 Aug., 1694; prob. m. and
   d. 3 June, 1745, in 50 yr. (*W. I.*), as
   Abigail, "wid. and relict" of N. D., late
   of Weth. dec'd, was app. adm'x, 4 Mch.,
   1746—*Prob. Rec.*; also Eliphalet, ment.
   as an heir, 1748 (?).
6. Mehitable, b. 11 June, 1696; m. ————
   Frary, of Deerfield, acc. to conveyance
   deed of her bro. Eliphalet, 1749.

FAM. 4½. ELIHU,[3] (*prob. s. Thos.,[2] Nath'l,[1]*), b. 1678; m. Mary (dau. Jonathan)
Smith, 13 Nov., 1718, who d. in 27th yr., Nov. 13, 1720—*Weth. Ins.;* he m. (2)
Lucy **Deming**, 2 Apl., 1724.

Children (Weth. Rec.):

1. Mary, b. 26 Jan., 1725.
2. Hannah, b. 28 Feb., 1727.
3. Samuel, b. 28 Oct., 1729.
4. Esther, b. 30 Jan., 1732.
5. Ebenezer, b. 21 Feb., 1734; m. (1) Mabel
   ————; m. (2) 12 July, 1762, Lucy
   ————, and had (*W. R. and N. C. R.*),
   Hannah, bp. 11 Oct., 1761 (*by sec. marr.*);
   Orrin, bp. 28 Sept., 1766; *Ebenezer*, b. 9
   June, bp. 4 Aug., 1771; *Sarah*, bp. 6 Aug.,

1777; *Orrin*, b. 10 June, bp. 19 Sept., 1779;
   inf. bu. 3 Apl., 1779; *Ebenezer*, d. ae.
   2, bu. 8 Aug., 1777; *Huldah* and *Ashbel*,
   "of Ebenezer, dec'd," bp. 6 Aug., 1780—
   W. C. R.; *Ebenezer*, d. 15 Nov., 1813, ae.
   48—*W. C. R.; Lucy*, wid. of Ebenezer,
   ae. 59; bu. 29 July, 1799.—*Wetht. Ins.*
6. Experience, b. 17 Apl., 1736.
7. Moses, b. 15 Apl., 1738.
8. Elizabeth, b. 4 Mch., 1739-40.

FAM. 5. EBENEZER,[3] (*Thomas,[2] Nathaniel,[1]*), b. 1679; m. 3 Apl., 1707, at Weth.,
Susannah (dau. John & Hannah *Bidwell*) **Waddams.** He d. 19 July, 1752, in
72d yr. (Mrs. A. C. Hawley): Ebenezer was especially remembered in a deed
of gift from his father Thomas,—(*Weth. Town Rec.*, IV, 33) "for the natural
love and affection which I have unto my loving son, Ebenezer, in considering he
hath been so serviceable to me, and spent his time hitherto in being helpful to
carry on and advance concerns for my subsistance."

Children (Weth. Rec.):

1. Thomas, b. 29 Dec., 1707; bp. 4 Jan.,
   1707-8.—*Mix MS.* FAM. 7.
2. Anne, b. 6, bp. 10 Sept., 1710—*Mix MS.;*

d. in 14 days, 20 Sept.
3. Susanna, d. 8 Sept., 1736, in 65th yr.—
   Weth. Ins.

FAM. 6. ELIPHALET,[3] (*Obadiah,[2] Nathaniel,[1]*), b. 1676; m. Rebecca (dau. Jacob)
Brunson, of Far., Ct., 24 Nov., 1697. He d. 9 Sept., 1733, ae. 54 "and a half";
wid. d. 2 May, 1755, ae. 76.—*Gravestones in Rocky Hill.* His will dated 6
Feb., 1728-9; proven, 4 Sept., 1733; invent. taken 30 Oct., 1733, amt. £633·01·01.
—*Htfd., Prob. Off.* See, also, Chapt. VII, Vol. I.

Children (Weth. Rec.):

1. Sarah, b. 8 Nov., 1698.
2. Obadiah, b. 14, bp. 17 (*Mix MSS.*) Aug.,
   1701. FAM. 8.
3. Eliphalet, b. 1, bp. 8 (*Mix MSS.*) Aug.,
   1703;* ment. by his bro. Eleazer as
   living 1761.

4. Rebecca, b. 28 Dec., 1705.
5. Eunice, b.* 22, bp. 25 (*Mix MSS.*) July,
   1708; m. John **Francis.**
6. Lois, b. 18 Aug., 1710; d. 8 Nov., 1712.
7. Eleazer. b. 23, bp. 24 (*Mix MSS.*) Aug.,
   1712. FAM. 9.

FAM. 7. THOMAS,[4] (*Ebenezer,[3] Thomas,[2] Nathaniel,[1]*), b. 1707; m. 3 Mch., 1734-5;
Hannah (dau. Thos. & Rebecca *Meekins*) **Hurlburt;** res. Weth.; will dated 12
May, 1782; he d. ae. 75, bu. 30 May, 1782—*W. C. R.;* wid. bu. 11 or 14 Oct.,
1786, ae. 86.—*W. C. R.*

---

* It is noticeable that the *Mix MSS.* also records under date of Sept. 19th, this same yr.
(1703), the bp. of a child of Eliphalet Dickinson—could these have been twins—one of
which, from frailness of health, could not be bp until later than the other?—*H. R. S.*

Children (Weth. Rec.) :

1. Hannah, b. 28 Mch., 1736.
2. Ebenezer, b. 4 Dec., 1736; perhaps the E. W. C. R., and prob. the same who had *Ebenezer*, b. 9 June, 1771; *Orran*, 10 June, 1779.
3. Susanna, b. 23 Feb., 1738-9; m.———— **Fox**.
4. Rebecca, twin Sarah, b. 24 Feb., 1741-2; m. Peleg **Coleman**; their s. Elisha Cole-

man, m. Hannah **Loveland**; their dau. Abigail Coleman, m. Nathan W. **Pelton**; their dau. Elizabeth Anne Pelton, m. **Philo** Slocum **Newton**; their dau. Anna C. Newton, m. Dr. Geo. Fuller **Hawley**.
5. Sarah, b. twin to Rebecca, who d. ae. 35, bu. 25 Sept., 1775.—*W. C. R.*
6. Thomas, b. 20 Aug., 1744; bp. 24 Mch., 1745.

FAM. 8. OBADIAH,[4] (*Eliph.*,[3] *Obad.*, *Nath'l*,[1]), b. 1701; m. 22 Nov., 1733 (*Midd. Town Rec.*), Hannah (dau. Capt. Joseph & Elizabeth *Foster*) **Rockwell**, of Midd., where they res. until after the birth of four ch., then rem. to Weth. and res. and d. in Stepney parish, Rocky Hill; he 23 April, 1782, in 81st yr., she 23 May, 1781, in 77th yr. Will dated 15 June, 1776; off. for prob., 11 May, 1782; ment. wid. and all ch. given below; also, the dec'd dau., Lois. *Htfd. Prob. Rec. XXV.*

Children (rec. in Midd.) :

1. Lois, b. 28 Oct., 1734; m. and d. before her parents, in 1776.
2. Elizabeth, b. 19 Nov., 1736; m. ———— **Galpin**.
3. Obadiah, b. 2 May, 1739. FAM. 10.
4. Elias, b. 20 Feb., 1742; m. Ruth **Savage.** FAM. 11. (*Born in Weth.*):
5. Hannah, b. 24 Feb., 1745; d. unm. 26 Sept., 1810.—*Weth. (Step.) Ins.*

FAM. 9. ELEAZUR,[4] (*Eliph.*,[3] *Obad.*,[2] *Nathaniel*,[1]), b. 1712; m. Jermima **Nott**, 20 Apl., 1737; he d. 24 July, 1768—*S. C. R.;* wid. Jermima d. 6 June, 1776—*S. C. R.;* res. Stepney.

Children (Weth. Rec.) :

1. William, b. 6 Oct., 1737.
2. Daniel, b. 29 Oct., 1738; d. 31 Jan., 1754, in 16th yr.—*Weth. Ins.*
3. Mary, b. 17 Sept., 1740.
4. Jacob, b. 16 Dec., 1741.
5. George, b. 1 Mch., 1743-4 (*sic.*).
6. Noadiah, b. 20 Nov., 1745.

FAM. 10. OBADIAH,[5] (*Obad.*,[4] *Eliph.*,[3] *Obad.*,[2] *Nath'l*,[1]), b. 1739; m. E. Windsor, Ct., Elizabeth (only dau. of John) **Smith**,—See *E. W. Prob. Rec.*, XXIII, p. 77. John Smith & wife d., he 1733, she in 1775, both bu. in E. W. old cemetery. (Mrs. C. S. **Prince**, to whom we are indebted for aid in disentangling a very "kinked" line of descent.—*H. R. S.*

Children (b. at E. Windsor, names and births from Stiles' Windsor, Ct., Marr. from M. C. B. in N. Y. Mail & Express. Ans. 3673.)

1. Obadiah, b. 25 Mch., 1770 : *E. W. Ch. R.* gives bp. as 18 ; m. (1) 26 July, 1796, Mary (dau. Thos.) **Morse**, of W. Boylston, Mass. ; m. (2) ———— **Johnston**; d. at Union Village, Broome Co., N. Y., 1848.
2. Seth, b. 9, bp. 12 Jan., 1772.
3. Elizabeth, b. 20 Feb., 1774.
4. Hannah, bp. 24 Mch., 1776.
5. Horace, b. 6 Feb., 1778.
6. Mary, b. 28 Jan., 1780.
7. Anson, b. 28 Mch., bp. 7 Apl., 1782.
8. Ethan, b. 28 Sept., 1784.
9. Lois, b. 14 June, 1787 ; m. Erastus **Cole**; died 1861.

FAM. 11. ELIAS,[5] (*Obad.*,[4] *Eliph.*,[3] *Obad.*,[2] *Nath'l*,[1]), b. 1742; m. 25 Dec., 1766, Ruth **Savage,** of Cromwell; res. Stepney parish, Weth. He d. 29 Nov., 1822, in 81st yr.—*Weth. Ins.*; wid., late Elias D., d. 7 Dec., 1834.—*Step. C. Rec.*

Children (Weth. Rec., bp. Step. Ch. Rec.) :

1. Lois, b. 2, bp. 7 Aug., 1768 ; d. 29 Jan., 1802.—*S. C. R.*
2. Harvey, b. 29 Mch., bp. 7 Apl., 1770. FAM. 12.
3. Rockwell, b. 18, bp. 24 Nov., 1771; d. Stepney, 9 June, 1794, in 23d yr.
4. Sarah, (Sally on *T. Rec.*), b. 19 Sept., 1776 ; m. John (brother to Sabrina) **Cas**-

well; res. in So. Glast.
5. Seth, b. 8, bp. 19 June, 1774. FAM. 13.
6. Burrage, b. 4 July, bp. 10 Oct., 1779 ; d. 22 Aug., 1786.—*Step. Rec.*
7. Elias, b. 18 July, bp. 25 Aug., 1782 ; d. 26 Aug., 1786.
8. Lucy, b. and bp. 24 Apl., 1785 ; d. 1860.
9. Dau. in 7th yr.; d. 4 Oct., 1804.—*S. C. R.*

FAM. 12. HARVEY,[6] (*Elias,[5] Obad.,[4] Eliph.,[3] Obad.,[2] Nath'l,[1]*), b. 1770; m. 7 Oct., 1792, Hannah **Grimes**, who d. at Stepney, 1 Sept., 1831, ae. 62; he d. Raleigh, N. C., 1822, ae. 52.—*Weth. Ins.*

Children (Weth. Inscrips.):

1. Rockwell, d. at sea. Sept., 1824, ae. 22.
2. Susan, d. 8 Oct., 1826, ae. 12.
3. William,* d. Sept., 1823, ae. 19; lost at sea.
4. Elias, d. in Mississippi, 1837, ae. 30.
5. Mary, d. 24 May, 1830, in 22 yr.
6. Harvey.

FAM. 13. SETH,[6] (*Elias,[5] Obad.,[4] Eliph.,[3] Obad.,[2] Nath'l,[1]*), b. 1774; m. (1) 20 May, 1798, Jerusha (dau. Gurdon & Mercy) **Goodrich**, who d. 5 Mch., 1799, in 23d yr.—*S. C. R.*; he m. (2) Sabrina **Caswell**, who d. 29 May, 1810, in 31st yr.— *S. C. R.*; Step. Rec. say 29th yr.; he d. 26 Oct., 1836, in 63d yr. in P. H.

Children (Weth. Rec. by first marriage):

1. Jerusha, bp. 16 June, and d. 11 Nov., 1799, ae. 9 mos., 20 d.—*S. C. R.*
2. Seth, (called, by a gt-gd-dau., who identifies him, as "2d son of Elias & Jerusha.") He prob. the one who m. 24 Jan., 1813—

S. C. R., Mary (dau. Alex.) **Grimes**, who d. 10 Mch., 1860, ae. 88.—*Weth. Ins.* A Seth had Lester bp. 2 Sept., 1810.— Burrage bp. 5 July, 1807.—*S. C. R.*

We come now to an OBADIAH, whom we cannot locate. He is denominated "Jr." on the *Town Rec.*, poss. to distinguish him from some other O. of the same generation, perhaps fm. O., son of Eliphalet, of Fam. 6; who was for a long time a serious "bother" to us, as well as to other genealogists, but whom (thanks to Mrs. CHAS. SEELEY PRINCE, of Hartford, Ct., we have at last successfully married and credited with a family.—See FAM. 10. "Obadiah, the son of Eunice [Williams], and as she saith, of Obadiah Dickinson, "was born June 15, 1730." This item fm. the WILLIAMS' entries in the *Weth. Recs.*, seems to throw some light on "Obadiah, Jr.'s" parentage; a question which has seriously vexed other genealogical enquiriers, besides myself; and though it satisfactorily accounts for his being called "Jr.," in a family which is unusually prolific of the name Obadiah, it still fails to reveal *which* Obadiah (*Obadiah's* Obadiah, or *Seth's* Obadiah, or some other O.) was his father. But it makes no difference now— his life is lived and his descendants are as respectable, so far as we know, as any of the name who were born *in vinculae matrimonii*.

This Obadiah, *Jr. is stated by Weth. Rec*, (bk. 2, p. 77) to have m. 28 Mch., 1750, Mary (dau. Samuel & Mary) **Collins**, b. 11 Apl., 1720, who d. 25 Sept., 1794— *Ry-H. Ch. Rec.*; was deeded a saw-mill, 1765.—*Weth. Ld. Rec.*, XII.

Children (Weth. & Step. Rec.):

1. Wait, b. 10 Nov., 1751. FAM. 2.
2. Eunice, b. 15 Dec., 1752; m. 7 Apl., 1774, Thomas **Bunce**.—*Step. Rec.*
3. Ozias, b. 17 May, 1754. FAM. 3.
4. Christian [Christy Ann], b. 29 Nov., 1755 or '57; m. 16 Apl., 1772, Seth **Belding**.

FAM. 2. WAIT, (*Obad, Jr.*, ——————————,), b. 1751; m. at Stepney, 19 Mch., 1772—*S. C. R.*, Abigail **Russell**, of S., who d. 24 May, 1827, ae. 78.— *W. (R.) Ins.* He d. 7 (1, Step.) Apl., 1835, ae. 83.—*W. (R.) Ins.*

Children (Stepney Ch. Rec.):

1. Elizur, bp. 4 Apl. or Aug., 1773. FAM. 4.
2. Charles, b. 25 Sept., (?), bp. 26 Oct., 1774; d. ae. 56, bu. 23 Dec., 1830.—*W. C. R.* —poss. the C. who m. Eleanor **Libby**, 13 Jan., 1805.—*S. C. R.*
3. Olly (dau.), bp. 14 Apl., 1776.—*S. C. R.*
4. Elva (dau.), bp. 6 Nov., 1785.
5. Nabble, bp. 25 Aug. or Oct. (?), 1789.
6. Russell, bp. 2 Nov., 1794; m. Hepzibah ——————————, who d. 4 July, 1826, ae. 31; m. (2) Sarah ——————————, who d. 26 July, 1861, ae. 67; he d. 26 May, 1881, ae. 86.— *W. (R.) Ins.*

FAM. 3. OZIAS,[2] (*prob. s. Obad. Jr.,[1]*), b. 1754; m. (1) 27 Oct., 1772, —————— **Goodrich**; m. (2) 7 July, 1805—*S. C. R.*, Chloe **Belding**; res. Ry-H.

* There is, in Stepney Burial Ground, a tombstone rec. death of William, s. of Harvey and Rachel Dickinson, who d. Plymouth, Ct., 15 Oct., 1870, ae. 37 yrs., 9 days; prob. son of Harvey & Hannah. B. A.

Children (bp. Stepney):

1. Moses, bp. 2 May, 1773.
2. Dorcas, bp. 14 Nov., 1773, (*sic.*) prob. '75.
3. Eunice, bp. 3 Mch., 1776.
4. Ozias, bp. 6 Mch., 1785.
5. Mabel, bp. 13 Apl., 1788.
6. A son.

O. had Polly bp. 8 Apl., 1781.
O. had s. Bethume bp. 16 June, 1782.— *S. C. R.*
O. had Harley bp. 4 Oct., 1795.
O. had Truman bp. 21 Aug., 1791.

FAM. 4. ELIZUR,[3] (*Wait,*[2] *Obad. Jr.,*[1]), b. 1773, m. 11 Mch., 1798, Polly **Bunce,** b. 16 Apl., 1777; res. and d. in Stepney, where he d. 8 May, 1848, in 77th yr.; she bp. 15 Feb., 1801, d. 3 Jan., 1843, ae. 66.—*W. (S.) Ins. & Step. Rec.*

Children (Family Bible & W. C. R.):

1. Celestia, b. 8 May, 1798; bp 15 Feb., 1801; d. 24 Sept., 1804.—*W. (S.) Ins.,* d. 17 Oct., 1829.—*W. C. R.* (?)
2. Jalon, b. 5 July, 1800; bp. 15 Feb., 1801. FAM. 5.
3. Norris, b. 28 Feb., bp. 11 July, 1802; d. 9 Oct., 1804.—*Step. Graveyard.*
4. Ransom, b. 21 May, bp. 5 Aug., 1804. FAM. 6.
5. Norris, b. 6 Aug., bp. 25 Oct., 1807; m.

Priscilla **Church,** of Ludlow, Vt., who d. at Evanston, Ill. (her dau. Mrs. Julius Watson, res. 310 Ridge Ave., Evanston, Ill.)
6. Mary Bunce, b. 3 May, bp. 30 Aug., 1812; m. Chester **Belden,** of Stepney, where she d. 1 Oct., 1878; he m. again. *Issue:*
   i. Elizur Dickinson (Belden), b. 1842; d. in Rebel prison in War of Civil Rebell., 2 Nov., 1864.

FAM. 5. JALON,[4] (*Elizur,*[3] *Wait,*[2] *Obad. Jr.,*[1]), b. 1800; m. Miranda (dau. Ebenezer) **Roberts,** of Westfield Soc., Midd., who was bu. 17 Oct., 1829; he m. (2) 19 Oct., 1831, Laura (dau. Simeon) **Stillman,** of Weth., b. 29 Apl., 1805; he d. 5 May, 1896—*W. Ins.*; wid. d. 12 June, 1890.—*W. Ins.* He was by occupation a tinner. This calling he exalted by bringing to it, not only the best skill within his power, but beauty of character, and on the whole few Wethersfield men have better deserved the epitah, "Well done, thou good and faithful servant."

Child (by first marriage):

1. Henry H., b. 27 May, 1827; d. unm., Brooklyn, N. Y., 2 Feb., 1897. Biog. by B. A. He was familiarly known as "Doctor" his long career as a pharmacist began when, in early youth he was appr. to Dr. Cooke, then the prop. of the only drug store in Weth. Later he went to Brooklyn, N. Y., where after serving as a clerk for several years he entered in business for himself; at first on Atlantic Ave., but eventually on Montague St., on the cor. of Hicks St., and there he remained until his retirement from business in 1886. He retained his res. in Brooklyn until May, 1890, when he returned to the old homestead at Weth. "Doctor" Dickinson was, in his day, one of the best known residents of the Heights section of Brooklyn, where he was much liked for his peculiarly genial qualities and a conspicuous element of gentleness.

FAM. 6. RANSOM,[4] (*Elizur,*[3] *Wait,*[2] *Obad. Jr.,*[1]), b. 1804, m. (1) 28 Mch., 1827, Eliza **Bingham,** who d. bu. 12 Dec., 1828—*W. C. R.*; m. (2) Lucy N. **Smith.** He d. 1 Feb., 1835, ae. 31 (*W. (S.) Ins.*); she d. 2 Feb., 1835, ae. 27.—*W. (S.) Ins.*

Children (by first marriage):

1. William H., b. 10 Dec., 1828; d. 1853.
2. Eliza, b. 22 Aug., 1830.
(*By second marriage*):
3. Ransom M., b. 25 Nov., 1832; res. Mc-

Minnville, Ore.
4. Lucy, S., b. 24 Jan., 1835; m. Thos. Griswold **Adams;** res. Weth.

And, while we are among the *Obadiahs* of this family, we had better "call in" another Obadiah, tho' he is not exactly within our bounds, yet so near a neighbor that it will be safer to have our thumb on him, if ever he should be wanted by a wandering genealogist. This is he: Lieut. OBADIAH DICKINSON,[5] (*Lieut. Obadiah,*[4] *Azariah,*[3] *Joseph,*[2] *Nathaniel,*[1] *the Settler*), b. at East Haddam. Ct., Jan., 1754, m. at H., 27 Oct., 1774, Susannah (dau. Rich.) **Knowles,** b. 4 Feb., 1755.

Children (Hadd. Rec.):

1. Jonah, b. 12 May, 1775.
2. Obadiah, b. 20 Nov., 1776. FAM. 2.
3. Aaron, b. 1 Jan., 1779.
4. Susanna, b. Feb., 1781.
5. Sarah, b. 18 Jan., 1783.
6. Darius, b. Mch., 1785.

7. Bathsheba, b. 8 May, 1787.
8. Esther, b. 26 June, 1789.
9. Mary, b. 4 July, 1791.
10. Elizabeth, b. 20 Dec., 1793.
11. Amanda, b. 9 Nov., 1795.

JALON DICKINSON.

HENRY H. DICKINSON.

FAM. 2. OBADIAH,⁶ (*Lieut. Obad.,⁵ Obad.,⁴ Azariah,³ Joseph,² Nath'l,¹*), b. 1776; m. 12 May. 1805, Cynthia (dau. Reuben) **Shailor**, by whom he had 6 ch.; m. (2) 13 Dec., 1817, Martha **Smith**, by whom he had 4 ch.; his s. was

FAM. 3. OBADIAH,⁷ (*Obad.,⁶ Lieut. Obad.,⁵ Obad.,⁴ Azariah,³ Joseph,² Nahtaniel,¹*), b. at Hadd., Mch., 1812; m. Henrietta **Shipman.** He was a portrait painter and has sons res. at Deep River, Ct.

DILLINGS, (Dillins) ABRAH, m. 3 Apl., 1833. Sarah **Griswold**—*N. C. R;* Sarah W. his wife, d. 25 Oct., 1865, ae. 57—*W. Ins.*; ALBERT (s. Abrah & Sarah W.) d. 9 Sept., 1864, ae. 29—*W. Ins.*; ALFRED, d. 10 Feb., 1859, ae. 34. Frances, his wife, d. 19 July, 1877, ae. 38—*W. Ins.*; ABIGAIL, bp. 22 Aug., 1784; poss. the "dau. of Wid. D.," ae. 2, bu. 19 July, 1786; or poss. dau. of William, below; CHARLES H., and Eliza K., had Charlie, d. 25 Apl., 1878, ae. 8m. 9d.; DESIAH (Desire?), had Sarah, bp. betw. 14 Mch. and 1st Sept., —— (*W. C. R.*); ELIAS, (who d. 26 Jan., 1852, ae. 72) and Polly (who d. 15 Jan., 1859, in 78th yr.) had (*W. Ins.*) Lawry, d. 25 Oct., 1817, ae. 16; also Walter, d. 15 May, 1857, ae. 37; ELIZABETH (*alias* Grimes) had Sarah, b. 14 Feb., 1763—*Weth. Rec.;* ELIZABETH, bp. 28 Apl., 1776—*W. C. R.;* LAURA A., (dau. of Eleazer) of Ry-H., m. Nelson **Batsford**, of Meriden, Ct., 4 Mch., 1847—*W. T. H.;* LAURA, ae. 16, d. 16 Oct., 1817; NELSON, m. 20 Oct., 1841 (he being rec. as "of Weth., Vt.") Harriet **Rockwell**—*N. C. R.;* he d. 27 Nov., 1850, ae. 38; his wid. d. 29 May, 1856, ae. 37; had Mary E., d. 6 Feb., 1861. ae. 18—*W. Ins.;* Ella, b. 22 Jan., 1848—*W. T. R.;* WILLIAM, m. Hannah ————, he d. ae. 43, bu. 16 Apl., 1786, had, (*W. C. R.*) (1) Abigail, bp. 30 Jan., 1774; (2) Elizabeth, bp. 28 Apl., 1776; (3) inf. son bp.? 26 Feb., 1778; (4) Rebecca, bp. 25 Feb., 1778; (5) Elias, (see above) bp. 15 Aug., 1779, d. 23 Jan., 1832, ae. 56—*S. C. R.;* (6) Jesse, b. 5 Oct., bp. 30 Dec., 1781; WILLIAM, a res. of Weth., Apl., 1743.— *Co. Ct. Rec.*

DILLINGWOOD, CHARLES, m. Polly **Richards,** of Weth., 20 Aug., 1801.

DILLOWS, (poss. a misspelling of Dillings) WILLIAM, had William bp. 30 Apl., 1769, "in the mother's right."

DIMOCK, (*Dimmock, Dymoke, Dymoocke, Dimok, Dimak, Demoke, Demock*) This record mainly furnished by Mrs. KATHARINE SEARLES MCCARTNEY, of Wilkes-barre, Pa. This fam. ranks among the oldest in Gt. Britain. Burke's *Landed Gentry* gives the origin of the name thus: "Owen Ap. Bleden Ap. Tudor, 7th" in desc. fm. Tudor Trevor, Lord of Hereford and Whittington, in Salop, founder of the "Tribe of the Marches" had two sons, viz.:

1. Thomas Ap. Owen.
2. Owen Vychan, whose gt-gd-son, Madoc Ap. Ririd, m. Margaret (dau. of Ithel Anwyl, a chieftain of Tegenel (as most of Flintshire was then called by the Welch) and had a son David Ap. Madoc (called, according to the Welsh custom) "Dai Madoc"—"Dai" being the diminutive of David Ap. Madoc. He m. Margaret (dau. and heiress of Tudor Ap. Ririd, of Penley, by whom he acquired the estate of Penley, and, in turn, had a son and heir, David Ap. Dai Madoc, whose name, by mutation, became David Dai Madoc—(that is, David the son of Dai Madoc—and gradually became David Damoc, or Dymock as it

is interchangeably written in ancient MSS.—hence *Damoc*, or *Dymock* became the surname of the family.

Arms. It would appear, fm. an examination of the five or six arms of this family in Burke's *General Armory*, that those of the Scrivelsby Manor Dymocks (The Champions) are identical with those of the Penly Hall (Co. Flint) and the Ellemere (Co. Salop) branches. The family motto is *Pro Rege et lege Dimico.*

To the family of Dymoke of Scrivelsby Manor, belongs the hereditary right of furnishing the "Champion of England," a conspicuous personage at the Coronation Banquets of the English Kings—and whose special function on these occasions, consisted in riding into the Banquet Hall, upon horseback and fully accoutred in armor, and there proclaiming in a loud voice the rightful succession of the newly-crowned king to the throne, at the same time throwing down his mailed glove, in wager of defence against any one who should offer to dispute the claim. The exercise of this hereditary function, or right, was generally rewarded by the present of a golden cup from the Royal hand, and certain fees, privileges and prerequisites, and was, we believe, maintained down to the coronation of George IV. The office has been held in tne family of the Scrivelsby branch of the Dymocks, since the coronation of Richard II, when it was by the Court of Claims, adjudged to Sir John Dymoke, who claimed it by reason of his marr. to the Lady Margaret de Ludlow, dau. and heir. of Sir. Thomas Ludlow, Knt. Champion of Eng. (son of Sir Thomas) Ludlow, by Johanna his wife, who was dau. and heir. of Philip Marmion, Lord of Scrivelsby, to whose gt-gd-father, the manor of Scrivelsby was gr. to Henry II.

In *Scrivelsby The House of the Champions*, by Rev. Samuel Lodge, M. A. Canon of Lincoln and Rector of Scrivelsby, it is stated that the name Scrivelsby is supposed to be derived from that of the manor in Gloucestershire, the orig. seat of the family of Dymock; and that it was so called in accordance with the ancient belief in Totems, as deriving "its distinctive appellation from the oak tree from which it may be supposed the Dymokes believed. themselves to have *originally sprung.*"

THOMAS, first of the name in New Eng., was one of those created freeman, between 18 May, 1631, and 23 Aug., 1636, at Dorchester, Mass. (*D. Ch. Rec.*) ; he was a memb. of the D. ch. which was org. in Eng. at the time of its setting sail with Winthrop's fleet; and at D. he remained until 1636, when he rem. to Scituate, whence, after a short res. he rem. to Hingham; and, in 1639 he, then "Elder" Thomas Dimmock, together with the Rev. Joseph Hull, was interested in a grant of lands in Barnstable, Mass., with which town his whole subsequent life was clearly identified. He and Mr. Hull seem to have divided all the town offices and committees between them—and evidently were *the* trusted ones of the community in all public matters requiring the exercise of sound judgment, executive abilities and responsibility. He was adm. a freeman of the Plymouth Col. 3 Dec., 1639; a deputy 1640, '41, '42, '48, '49 and '50, and in June, 1640, he, with Mr. Freeman of Sandwich, were constituted a court (the first estab. in Barnstable Co.) to "hear and determine all causes and controversies within the three townships, not exceeding 20s." In June, 1644, he was re-app. a mag. or assis't to Mr. Freeman, the Chief Justice of the inferior court and assistant associate of the higher court. Sept. 2, 1642, Mr. D. was app. by the Col. Ct. as one of the Council of War; on 10 Oct., 1642, was elected lieut.

(the highest rank in the local militia) in B. County; and the Ct. approved of the choice. In 1650, he was one of the Plym. Col. Commis'rs app. to confer with Commiss'rs of the Mass. Col., concerning the Shawamet and Pawtoxet lds. Aug. 7, 1650, he was ord. an Elder of the B. ch. of which he had been an orig. memb.; in 1654, he leased his farm, and res. in B. until his dth. in 1658 or '59.

The place of Elder and Lieut. Dimmock's birth and resid. in Eng. has never been exactly determined, but a tradition held by every branch of the family, that he belonged to the line of the Champions, has been somewhat corroborated by an aged member of the family residing at Horncastle, Eng., early in the last century, who stated to Rev. Samuel Lodge, M. A. the author of the *Hist. of the Champions*, before mentioned, that "to the great sorrow of the family at the time, one of its members joined the Puritan movement and went to New Eng. early in the 17th Century." It is, also, a well known fact that Edward Fiennes, Lord Clinton and Earl of Lincoln, favored the Puritan movement; and as Sir Robert Dymock of Scrivelsby,—marr. into Earl's family it has been believed by the early descendents of Thomas Dimock that, at the Earl's house, he became imbued with the Puritan faith and policy. His gt-gt-gd-s., Lieut. David Dimock, born 1745, at Wethersfield, delighted in his declining years to narrate to his grand-dau. the mother of the writer, stories of how his ancestors lived in Eng., and of their functions (as Champions) at the Royal Court.

Elder and Lieut. Thomas Dimmock is said to have m. at Barnstable, Ann **Hammond**, of Watertown, Mass., before his rem. to B.

Children:

1. Timothy, bp. (by Rev. Mr. Lothrop) 12 Jan., 1639-40; was the first of the Eng. who d. in B., bu. 17 June, 1640, "in the lower side of the Calves' pasture."
2. Mehitable, bp. 18 Apl., 1642; m. Richard **Child**, of Watertown, Mass., 1662; d. 18 Aug., 1676, ae. 34. *Issue:*
   i. Richard (Child), b. 30 Mch., 1863.
   ii. Ephraim (Child), b. 9 Oct., 1664.
   iii. Shubael (Child), b. 19 Dec., 1665; m.; he was insane; d. in

iv. Mehitable (Child).
v. Experience (Child), b. 26 Feb., 1679-70.
vi. Abigail (Child), b. 16 June, 1672; m. Joseph **Lathrop**, of B.
vii. Ebenezer, twin Hannah, b. 10 Nov., 1674; d.
viii. Hannah, twin Ebenezer; m. Joseph **Blish**, of B.; d. 11 Nov., 1732.
3. Shubael, bp. 15 Dec., 1644. FAM. 2.

FAM. 2. Ens. and Deacon SHUBAEL,[2] (*Elder and Lieut. Thos.,*[1]), b. 1644; m. Apl., 1663, Joanna (dau. John) Bursley, who was bp. in Mch., 1645-6, and d. Mansfield, Ct., 8 May, 1727, ae. 83. He was the only s. of Eld. Thos., who lived to mature age; inher. his father's est. and in 1688 res. in his father's "fortified" ho. in B. The house wh. he built for himself in Mansfield, 217 yrs. ago, is still in good repair, and of the class known as "high single houses"— containing the same no. of rooms, fronted either due N. or due S., so that on clear days, the shadow of the ho. acted as a sun-dial to the inmates—the only time-piece they could consult, (*Otis' Barnstable Families*); he was later for a short time, a resid. of Yarmouth, Mass.; was a selectman in B. and deputy to Col. Ct., 1685-6 and 1689, after the expulsion of Sir Edward Andros; was an Ens. in militia; in 1693 rem. to Mansfield, Ct., where he was known as "Deacon." The orig. Ch. Cov't. signed by him is framed and hangs upon the walls of the present Cong. Ch. in Mansfield. He d. Sunday, 29 Oct., 1732, in 91st yr.; his wife d. 8 May, 1727, ae. 83; both bu. in M. Cemetery.

Children:

1. Thomas (Capt.), b. Apl., 1664. FAM. 3.
2. John, b. June, 1666. FAM. 4.
3. Timothy, b. Mch., 1668. FAM. 5.
4. Shubael, b. Feb., 1673. FAM. 6.
5. Joseph, b. Sept., 1675. FAM. 7.
6. Mehitable, b. 1677.
7. Benjamin, b. 1680. FAM. 8.
8. Joanna, b. 1682; m. 6 Oct., 1709, Josiah **Conant**. *Issue:*
   i. Shubael (Conant), b. 15 July, 1711,

Judge of Ct., and memb. Gov's Council of Safety at commencement of Revol. War.
   ii. Josiah, b. 1722.
   iii. Isaac, d. yg.
   iv. Isaac, b. 1727; d. yg.
9. Thankful, b. Nov., 1684; m. 28 June, 1706, Dea. Edmond **Waldo**, of Windham, Ct.; she d. 13 Dec., 1757.

FAM. 3. Capt. THOMAS,[3] (*Dea. Shubael,*[2] *Eld. & Lieu. Thos.,*[1]), b.   · ;
m. Desire **Sturgis**, a lineal desc't of John Howland, of "Mayflower" fame.
Capt. Thos. was in the military service against the Fr. and Inds. in the Eastern
country and was killed at battle Canso Sept. 9, 1697, bravely but perhaps
rashly refusing to take shelter as others did.

Children:

1. Mehitable, b. Oct., 1686; m. Capt. John **Davis**, 13 Aug., 1705; d. May, 1775, æ. 89 ; having been blind for some yrs. previously. *Issue* (*b. Barnstable*) :
   i. Thomas (Davis), b. 1 Oct., 1706 ; m. 17 Nov., 1726, Susan **Sturgis**.
   ii. John (Davis), b. 8 Sept., 1708; m. twice.
   iii. Solomon (Davis), b. 5 Apl., 1711 ; d. 1712.
   iv. William (Davis), b. 10 Apl., 1713; d. 1713.
   v. Solomon (Davis), b. 24 June, 1715; m. twice.
   vi. Mehitable (Davis), b. 10 Aug., 1717; m. 4 times : (1) Dr. James **Hersey**; (2) John **Russell**; (3) as 2d wife of John **Sturgis**; (4) her cousin Hon. Daniel **Davis**, by whom she had (*a*) Daniel (Davis), (*b*) Louisa (Davis), m. William **Minot**, of Boston ; and (*c*) Charles Henry (Davis), Rear Admiral U. S. N., b. Boston, Mass, 16 Jan, 1807.[*]

   vii. William (Davis), b. 24 Aug., 1719 ; m. Martha **Crocker**, Feb. 2, 1745.
2. Temperance, b. June, 1689 ; m. 2 June, 1709, Benj. **Freeman**, Harwich.
3. Edward (Capt.) b. 5 July, 1692. FAM. 9.
4. Thomas (Ens.), b. 25 Dec., 1694. FAM. 10.
5. Desire, b. Feb., 1696 ; m. Dec., 4, 1719, Job **Gornam**; she d. 28 Jan., 1732-3; he m. (2) 1736, Wid. Bethiah **Freeman**, of Fairfield, Ct., who d. 1762. *Issue* (*by first marriage; b. Barnstable*) :
   i. Temperance (Gorham), b. 23 July, 1721; m. 29 Oct., 1741, her cousin John **Fuller**.
   ii. Thomas (Gorham), b. 13 Aug., 1723 ; m. (1) Hannah **Gorham**; m. (2) Wid. Rebecca **Jones**.
   iii. Edward (Gorham), b. 12 Sept., 1725 ; d. yg.
   iv. Desire (Gorham), b. 17 Mch., 1727.
   v. Job (Gorham), b. 6 Nov., 1730 ; d. yg.
   vi. Sarah (Gorham), b. 15 Aug., 1736 ; d. yg.

FAM. 4. JOHN,[3] (*Dea. Shubael,*[2] *Eld. & Lieut. Thos.,*[1]), b. 1666; farmer; rem. 1709
to Falmouth, Mass.; his home in Barnstable now owned by Mrs. Wm. W.
Sturgis; he m. Nov., 1689, Elizabeth Lombard or **Lambert**.

Children (*b. Barnstable*) :

1. Sarah, b. Dec., 1690.
2. Anna (or Hannah), b. 1692.
3. Mary, (b. 1695).
4. Theophilus, b. 1696 ; m. Sarah (dau. Benjamin) **Hinckley**, 1 Oct., 1722.
5. Timothy, b. July, 1698. FAM. 11.

6. Ebenezer, b. Feb., 1700.
7. Thankful, b. Apl., 1702.
8. Elizabeth, b. 20 Apl., 1704 ; m. 1750, John **Lovell**.
9. David, bp. 19 May, 1706.

* Rear Admiral Davis, m. 22 Dec., 1843, Harriet (dau. Elijah & Harriet *Blake*) **Mills**, of Northampton, Mass., and U. S. Senator. *Children:*

1. Freeman (Davis), Lieut. U. S. N.; d. 1867.
2. Charles Henry (Davis), now Capt. U. S. N. FAM. 2.
3. Frank Du Pont, d. 1879.
4. Anna Cabot Mills, m. Henry Cabot **Lodge**, of Boston. *Issue:*
   i. Constance (Lodge), m. Augutus Peabody **Gardner**, of Boston ; has a dau. Constance.
   ii. George Cabot (Lodge), m. Elizabeth M. F. (dau. of Judge John) **Davis**, of

U. S. Ct. of Claims. They have (*a*) Henry Cabot (Lodge), b. 5 July, 1902 ; (*b*) John Davis (Lodge), b. 23 Oct., 1903.
5. Evelyn, m. Brooks **Adams**, of late Charles Frances Adams, of Boston ; *no issue.*
6. Louisa Minot, m. Henley (s. of Rear Admiral S. B.) **Luce**; has (*a*) Stephen Bleecher (Luce).

FAM. 2. Capt. Chases Henry Davis, m. 1857, Louise **Quackenbush**, of Albany, N. Y. *Children:*

1. Elizabeth. | 2. Charles Henry. | 3. Daniel.

FAM. 5. TIMOTHY,³ (*Dea. Shubael,² Eld. & Lieut. Thos.,¹*), b. 1668; m. Abigail **Doane,** of Eastham, who d. 1718. He rem. to Mansfield, Ct., and thence to Ashford, Ct., where he d. 1733.

Children (b. Mansfield, Ct.) :

1. Timothy, b. 2 June, 1703.
2. John, b. 3 Jan., 1704-5.
3. Shubael, "ye second of mansfield," b. 27 May, 1707. FAM. 12.

4. Daniel, b. 28 Jan., 1709-10.
5. Israel, b. 22 Dec., 1712.
6. Ebenezer, b. 22 Nov., 1715.

FAM. 6. SHUBAEL,³ (*Dea. Shubael,² Eld. and Lieut. Thos.,¹*), b. 1673; res. Barnstable, Mass.; m. (1) Bethiah (dau. of John & Hope *Howland*) **Chipman,** he m. (2) Tabitha (dau. Meletiah) **Lothrop,** a descendant of Rev. John Lothrop, May 4, 1699; she d. 24 July, 1727; he d. 16 Dec., 1728, both bu. in "Old Meeting House Hill." His father, on his removal to Mansfield, Ct., gave him a share of his estate. His son:

1. Samuel,⁴ b. 7 May, 1702. FAM. 13.

FAM. 7. JOSEPH,³ (*Shubael,² Eld. & Lieut. Thos.,¹*) b. 1675; m. 12 May, 1699, Lydia (dau. Dr. John) **Fuller,** who was b. 1673 and d. in E. Hadd., Conn., 6 Nov., 1755, ae. 80(?). On his rem. from Barnstable his house came into possess. of the Sturgis family, and taken down abt. 1830.

Children (Otis' Barnstable) :

1. Thomas, b. 26 Jan., 1699-1700.
2. Bethiah, b. Feb., 1702; m. 1726, Samuel **Annable;** 22 Oct., 1751, was dismiss. to Ch. in Scotland, Ct.
3. Mehitable, b. 22 Nov., 1707; m. Thos. **Crocker,** 1727; d. 1729.
4. Ensign, b. 8 Nov., 1709; m. Abigail ————, of Sandwich, Mass., 19 Oct., 1731. *Issue:*
   i. Thomas (————), b. 1732.

   ii. Mehitable (————), b. 1735.
   iii. Joseph (————), b. 1740.
5. Ichabod, b. 8 Mch., 1711.
6. Abigail, b. 31 June, 1714; m. Thos. **Annable,** 1 Apl., 1758, as his 3d wife. *Issue:*
   i. Abigail (Annable), b. ————.
   ii. Joseph (Annable), b. ————.
7. Pharoah, b. 2 Sept., 1717.
8. David, b. 22 Dec., 1721.

FAM. 8. BENJAMIN,³ (*Dea. Shubael,² Elder & Lieut. Thos.,¹*), b.   ; m. Mary ————; rem. with his father, to Mansfield, Ct.

Children (b. Mansfield, Ct.) :

1. Perez, b. 18 June, 1704; d. Aug., 1714.
2. Mehitable, b. 8 June, 1706; d. 6 Dec., 1713.
3. Peter (Perez in *Cor. Recs.*), b. 5 June, 1708; m. Mary **Baylo.**
4. Mary, b. 14 Sept., 1710.
5. Shubael, b. 22 June, 1715.

6. Joanna, b. 26 Mch., 1713; d. 1716.
7. Mehitable, b. 6 Aug., 1719.
8. Josiah (?), b. 17 Feb., 1722.
9. Isaac, }   d. 1724.
   }twins.
10. Jesse, }   d. 1727.

FAM. 9. Lieut. EDWARD,⁴ (*Capt. Thos.,³ Dea. Shubael,² Eld. & Lieut. Thos.,¹*), b. 1692; m. 1720, Hannah ————; he was a Lieut. in Mil., his commiss. dated 15 Feb., 1744, O. S.; he was Capt. of 1st Co. 7th Mass. Reg., in exped. against Louisburg.

Children:

1. Anna, b. 23 Nov., 1721; m. Thos. ———— 7 Mch., 1749.
2. Thomas, bp. 23 July, 1725; d. yg.

3. Edward, b. 17 Mch., 1726; d. yg.
4. Thomas, b. 16 Mch., 1727; m. Elizabeth **Bacon,** 7 Oct., 1755.

FAM. 10. Ens. THOMAS,⁴ (*Capt. Thomas,³ Dea. Shubael,² Eld. & Lieut. Thos.,¹*), 1694; rem. to Mansfield, Conn., d. in Cuba, in the King's service, 1741; m. 9 Nov., 1720, Anna (dau. Hezekiah) **Mason,** a gd-s. of Maj. John Mason, of Norwich, Ct.

Children (*b. in Mansfield*):

1. Silas, d. 31 Dec., 1721.
2. Son, d. 1722.
3. Thomas, b. 25 Oct., 1723; d. Nov., 1726.
4. Jesse, b. 6 Feb., 1725-6; m. 8 Feb., 1750, Rachel **Kidder**, of Dudley; had family.
5. Anna, b. 27 Feb., 1727-8.
6. Desire, b. 23 Jan., 1732-8; m. Timothy **Dimock**, of Coventry; John, s. of "Deziah,,

Dimock, bp. 20 Mch., 1757.—*W. C. R.* (?)
7. Lot, b. 14 Feb., 1733-4; m. 8 May, 1760, Hannah **Gurley**; had Roger, b. 27 Dec., 1761.
8. Seth, b. 5 June, 1736; d. 4 July, 1748.
9. Hezekiah, b. 3 Dec., 1739; m. Alice **Ripley**, 12 Jan., 1750.

FAM. 11. TIMOTHY,[4] (*John*,[3] *Dea. Shubael*,[2] *Eld. & Lieut. Thos.*,[1]), b. 1698; rem. to Mansfield, Ct.; m. Ann (dau. Joseph,[3] *Maj. Wm.*,[2] *Gov. Wm.*,[1]) **Bradford**, 15 Aug., 1723.

Children (*b. Mansfield, Ct.*):

1. Ann, b. 23 May, 1724; m. 2 Sept., 1740, Ebenezer **Clark**.
2. Timothy, (Capt.), b. 8 Apl., 1726. FAM. 14.
3. John, b. 24 Mch., 1727-8.
4. Joanna, b. 28 Aug., 1730; m. John **Babcock**.
5. Josiah, b. 2 Mch., 1732.

6. Simeon, b. 19 Sept., 1735; d. 1737-8.
7. Slyvanus, b. 18 June, 1738.
8. Oliver, b. 31 Dec., 1740; m. Sarah (dau. Samuel **Gurley**, of M.; she d. 1790; he d. 10 Feb., 1823.
9. Dan., b. 13 May, 1743. FAM. 15.

FAM. 12. SHUBAEL,[4] (*Timothy*,[3] *Ens. and Dea. Shubael*,[2] *Eld. and Lieut. Thomas*,[1]) b. 1707; m. 25 Jan., 1739, Esther (dau. of Samuel) **Pierce**, who d. 10 Mch., 1805, in 90 yr. He d. 26 June, 1788, in 82d yr.

Children:

1. Jeduthan, b. 13 Dec., 1739.
2. Esther, b. 4 Jan., 1743.
3. Ephraim, b. 2 Mch., 1744.
4. Ichabod, b. 13 Mch., 1746.
5. Edward, b. 5 June, 1748. FAM. 16.

6. Samuel, b. 29 Nov., 1750.
7. Eliphalet, b. 12 Mch., 1753; d. same yr.
8. Abigail, b. 12 Mch., (one acc. says 14 June), 1755.
9. Shubael.

FAM. 13. SAMUEL,[4] (*Shubael*,[3] *Dea. Shubael*,[2] *Elder and Lieut. Thomas*,[1]), b. 1702; m. Hannah (dau. Joseph & Hannah *Cobb*) **Davis**, 1 June, 1740; res. for several yrs. at Saybrook, Ct., where he was Justice of the Peace in 1746, '47, '48, '49, '49 and '50, and again 1755; app. 1755 1st Lieut. in Conn. Mil. in Capt. Josiah Griswold's Co., and afterwards Capt. of said Co., which office he resig. 1755,—*Conn. Col. Rec.*, VIII, 196, 269, 352, 416, 503, VIII. 394; Mrs. D. was· dismiss. to the 1st Ch. in Tolland, 1740; and subsequently they seem to have res. in the Rocky Hill Dist. of Weth. Otis in his *Barnstable Families* says that both d. at B. But we must take into consideration the facts that their son, Lieut. David, in relating the circumstances of his enlisting in the Revolutionary war, says that his father's parting words were "God bless you, my Son. Go and defend the liberties of your country, and never surrender them;" and that both of his parents died the same year, while he was in the ser- vice—without his seeing them again. Now, David enlisted either at Wethersfield or Middletown, and it is not probable that, in the then disturbed state of the country, and difficulties of travel, etc., that the aged couple ret. to B. but rather Saybrook, where they prob. d.[*]

Children (*all b. Barnstable, except the last*):

1. Mehitable, b. 25 Apl., 1722 (?).
2. Samuel, b. 17 Oct., 1726; d. Albany, 1755.
3. Hannah, b. 26 Nov., 1728.
4. Shubael, b. 31 Jan., 1731; rem. to Nova Scotia; had *issue:* Daniel, who had sons, Joseph, George, David, and (Rev.) An- thony V.

5. Joseph, b. 19 Feb., 1733; d. 1826, at Weth.; had s. Joseph.
6. Mehitable, b. 29 Sept., 1735.
7. Daniel, b. 28 May, 1738; res. in Eastern part of Conn.; was a mariner.
8. David (Lieut.), b. Ry-H. (Weth.). FAM. 17.

[*] There has been some doubt as to the identity of this Samuel, but Mrs. McCartney's researches show that there was no other Samuel Dimock who res. at Saybrook, where, as is supposed, both he and his wife died.

Fam. 14. Capt. TIMOTHY,[5] (*Timo.,*[4] *Shubael,*[3] *John,*[2] *Eld. & Lieut. Thos.,*[1]), b. 1726; m. 11 Mch., 1749-50, his cousin Desire (dau. *Ens. Thos.*[4] *Capt. Thos.,*[3] *Ens. Shubael,*[2] *Eld. Thos.,*[1]) **Dimock,** res. Coventry, Ct.

Children (Coventry Recs.) :

1. Desire, b. 22 Jan., 1757; m. Joseph **Boss,** 9 Aug., 1769.
2. Eunice, b. 9 Feb., 1753; m. 18 Dec., 1771, Israel **Gurley,** Mansfield, Ct.
3. Anne b. 15 Sept., 1754.
4. Lois, b. 12 May, 1756; m. 25 Feb., 1779, Stephen **Turner,** of Mansfield, Ct.
5. Sybil, b. 18 Mch., 1758; m. 8 Sept., 1776, Jeremiah **Fitch,** of M.

6. Lucy, b. 22 May, 1760; d. July, 1779.
7. Timothy, b. 22 Aug., 1762.
8. Daniel, b. 20 Feb., 1765; m. Anne **Wright,** 16 Nov., 1786. Fam. 18.
9. Mason, b. 22 June, 1767; m. 16 Jan., 1787, Anne **Robertson,** of Covington, Ct.
10. Rhoda, b. 10 Aug., 1770.
11. Roger, b. 5 Aug., 1772.

Fam. 15. DANIEL,[5] (*Timothy,*[4] *John,*[3] *Dea. Shubael,*[2] *Eld. and Lieut. Thomas,*[1]), b. 1743; m. 3 May, 1764, Phebe (dau. Stephen) **Turner.**

Children (Coventry Recs.) :

1. Molly, b. 28 Mch., 1765.
2. Eunice, b. 10 Nov., 1766.

3. Levinia (?), b. 1 June, 1769.
4. Diantha, b. 7 May, 1772.

Fam. 16. EDWARD,[5] (*Shubael,*[4] *Timothy,*[3] *Ens. & Dea. Shubael,*[2] *Eld. & Lieut. Thomas,*[1]) b. 1749; m. (1) Penniah **Hinckley,** by whom he had 6 ch., all of whom d. inf.; he m. (2) Esther, (dau. Joshua) **Tilden.** She d. 4 July, 1850; he d. 19 Sept., 1836.

Children:

1. Martial, b. 27 May, 1791; d. 25 Mch., 1879.
2. Ebor, b. 31 Dec., 1792; d. 11 Apl., 1841. Fam. 19.
3. Penniah, b. 4 Jan., 1795; d. 4 Jan., 1800.
4. Joshua Tilden, b. 26 Mch., d. 4 Jan., 1853.
5. Eunice, b. twin to Joshua T.; d. Oct., 1882.

6. Walter, b. 3 Aug., 1799; d. 3 Aug., 1802.
7. Amanda, b. 1 June, 1801; d. 3 July, 1802.
8. Edward, b. 12 July, 1803; d. within 10 yrs.
9. Esther, b. 12 July, 1803; d. 25 Mch., 1848.
10. Abigail T., b. 13 May, 1808; d. 26 July, 1850.
11. Shubael P., b. 13 July, 1811; d. 31 Aug., 1865.

Fam. 17. Capt. DAVID,[5] (*Samuel,*[4] *Shubael,*[3] *Dea. Shubeal,*[2] *Eld. & Lieut. Thos.,*[1]) b. 1745; m. 1767, Sarah (dau. Warren & Mary *Paine*) **Greene,** of Eastham, Mass., who rem. to Midd., Ct., before 1756. He res. in Stepney parish and was a soldier in the Lexington Alarm, Apl., 1775; later served under Col. Comfort Sage; was in battle of Harlem Heights and Long Island. He rem. his family, during the war to Vt. for safety, and he was commiss. Lieut. by Gov. of that State, and was in battle of Bennington, Vt.; rem. abt. 1790 to Wyoming Valley, Pa., where he res. until dth. of his wife in 1813, after which he removed to Montrose, Pa., where he d. 14 Aug., 1832, at the home of his son Rev. Davis Dimock. On the day of his burial all the places of business in the town were closed as a testimony of respect to a Revol. patriot. His title of Capt. was probably derived from the fact that he at one time was engaged in traffic on the Hudson River, betwn. Albany and N. Y. City, until his sloops were destroyed in a gale, after which he relinquished the business.

Children:

1. Davis, (Rev.), b. 27 May, 1776 in Ry-Hill, Weth. Fam. 20.
2. A son (Asa?), b. in Conn.
3. Mehitable, m. Jared **Clark,** of Middletown

and East Haddam.
4. Ch. d. 13 Oct., 1775.—*S. C. R.*
5. Ch. d. Nov., 1775.—*S. C. R.*

Fam. 18. Capt. DANIEL,[6] (*Lieut. Timothy*[5] *Timothy,*[4] *John,*[3] *Shubael,*[2] *Thos.,*[1]) b. 1765; m. 16 Nov., 1786, Anne, b. 20 Feb., 1765, (dau. of Eleazer & Anne *Marsh*) **Wright,** of Windham, Ct.; res. in Coventry, where he became a large land holder. He d. 1 Aug., 1833; she d. 26 Jan., 1832, ae. 65 or 66.

Children (*b. Coventry, Ct.*) :

1. Anne, b. 18 Aug., 1787 ; m. 26 Nov., 1807, Milton **Clark**, of Coventry.
2. Parthene, b. 9 Apl., 1789.
3. Lucinda, b. 18 Mch., 1791 ; m. 24 June, 1811, George **Perkins**, of Hebron, Ct.
4. Sally, b. 23 June, 1793 ; m. 5 Nov., 1818, Step. B. **Pomeroy**, of Norwich, N. Y.
5. Harty, b. 24 Dec., 1794 ; m. 28 Mch., 1822, Chauncey **Griggs**, of Tolland, Ct., and their son, Chauncey Griggs, Jr., one of the most successful lumbermen and bankers

in the West ; res. at Tacoma, Wash.
6. Clara Maria, b. 14 Sept., 1796 ; d. 21 Aug., 1849.
7. Eliza, b. 24 May, 1798 ; m. Bishop **Davenport**, 11 Aug., 1825.
8. Timothy, (Dr.), b. 17 Apl., 1799 ; d. 28 Apl., 1874. **FAM.** 21.
9. Desiah, b. 31 Mch., 1802 ; m. Balzaman **Belknap**, of Ellington, Ct., 14 Oct., 1824.

FAM. 19. EBOR,[6] (*Edward,*[5] *Shubael,*[4] *Timo.,*[3] *Ens. & Dea. Shubael,*[2] *Eld. & Lieut. Thos.,*[1]) b. 1792 ; m. 25 Nov., 1817, Roxy **Mumford**, who d. 21 Feb., 1875. He d. 11 Apl., 1841.

Children:

1. Roxana Maria, b. 9 Dec., 1817.
2. Miner Mumford, b. 28 Feb., 1819 ; d.
3. Walter Tilden, b. 7 Feb., 1821 ; d.
4. Abigail, Adeline, b. 18 Feb., 1824 ; d.
5. Edward Valentine, b. 14 Feb., 1826 ; still living.*
6. Sarah Mervins, b. 8 Aug., 1828 ; d. 1901.
7. Orville, b. 16 Mch., 1831 ; d.
8. Ebor, b. 25 May, 1834 ; d. 5 Aug., 1898 ; m. Eleanor Mary (dau. Geo.) **Beck**, 10 Oct., 1861 ; he d. 5 ——., 1898. *Issue:*
   i. George Beck (Dimmick),* b. 16 Aug., 1862, unm.
   ii. Eugene Ebor (Dimmick), b. 3 Sept.,

1864 ; d. 28 Oct., 1870.
   iii. James Orville (Dimmick), b. 19 Dec., 1866 ; m. 23 Feb., 1898.
   iv. Sarah Amelia (Dimmick), b. 30 May, 1869, single.
   v. Jesse (Dimmick), b. 15 Oct., 1871, single.
   vi. Edgar Allen (Dimmick), b. 6 Nov., 1873 ; d. 7 Aug., 1874.
   vii. Henry Laurens (Dimmick), b. 1 Aug., 1876 ; m. 3 Dec., 1901.
   viii. Eleanor Lorencie (Dimmick), b. 2 Jan., 1880, single.

FAM. 20. Rev. DAVIS,[6] (*Lieut. Daniel,*[5] *Samuel,*[4] *Shubael,*[3] *Shubael,*[2] *Eld. & Lieut. Thos.,*[1]) b. Ry-H. (Weth.), 27 May, 1776, d. in Montrose, Pa., 1858; he m. 1796, Elizabeth (gr-dau. Judge John & Lydia *Gardner*) **Jenkins;** rem. with his father to Pa., and early ent. the Baptist ministry—and was the pioneer minister of that denomination in Luzerne and Susquehanna Cos., Penn. In 1800 he sett. at Montrose, Pa., where he rec'd the app't of Associate Judge, which position he held for 27 yrs, as long as it was an appointive office. He was a man of inexhaustible energy and personal magnetism—preached over 8000 sermons and bp. 2000 persons. His journal is a complete history of the times, and his biog. was written (tho' not pub.), by Mrs. Lydia Dimock Searles. He was for many yrs. editor of a Christian Magazine; and also studied and practiced medicine, to meet the needs of the community in the new country to which he had removed. He is also noticed in Benedict's *Hist. of the Baptists,* (p. 612) as one of the organizers of the Bridgewater, (Pa.), Baptist *Association.*

Children:

1. Sarah, m. Nehemiah **Scott.**
2. Benjamin, m. —— **Chamberlin.**
3. Asa, editor and memb. of Ohio State Senate ; m. —— **Burnett.**
4. Betsy, m. Hubbard **Avery.**
5. Davis, b. 1803. Hon. Davis Dimock, Jr., d. at Montrose, Pa., in 39 yr. of age ; reared upon a farm, until at age of 22, he became the editor of the *Montrose Gazette,* the title of which he changed to that of *Susquehanna Register,* which he continued to edit and publish for seven yrs. In 1832, he was adm. to the bar and speedily attained an extensive practice and a leading position in his profession. In 1840, he became, by a large majority vote, a (Democratic) member of

the U. S. Congress, where he attended most faithfully to his duties until compelled to leave them, by the inroads of disease, from which he died Jan. 13, 1842. Honest, frank and manly in all his dealings with his fellowmen ; mild and unassuming in manner, yet loyal to every duty of his family, social or political relations, and above all, a sincere and humble Christian, he left a name to be loved and remembered, by all with whom, in life, he had been associated.
6. Lydia, b. 11 July, 1811 ; m. 29 Oct., 1832, Leonard **Searle**. She was a woman of fair literary attainments ; a grad. of Hamilton Acad. (now Colgate Univ.), and a writer and authoress of great force. She

---

* The record of this line from *Edward* of 5th gen. furnished by this gentleman, res. Scranton, Pa.
Authorities consulted by Mrs. Henry F. Dimock and by Mrs. K. S. McCartney: *Otis' Barnstable Families;* Manfield (Conn.) *Town and Church Recs.;* also *T. and Ch. Rec. of Coventry.* Conn. ; *Diary of Rev. John Lathrop of Barnstable.*

d. 24 July, 1881. *Issue:*
  i. Davis Dimock (Searle), b. 25 Mch.,
    1836; unm.
  ii. Katherine Elizabeth (Searle), b.
    17 May, 1838; m. Wm. H. **McCartney**,
    of Boston, a Capt. of Artillery, in
    the Civil War; has ch. (a) Eleanor,
    b. 21 Sept., 1873; (b) William H., Jr.,

b. 25 Dec., 1875.
  iii. Josephine (Searle), m. B. Stuart
    Bentley; has (a) Louise, who m.
    Harry **Gibson**, of Williamsport, Pa.
  iv. Hetty (Searle), m. Wm. M. **Miller**;
    dec'd; *no issue.*
  v. Leonard (Searle), Jr., d. s. p.

FAM. 21. Dr. TIMOTHY,[7] (*Capt. Daniel,[6] Capt. Timothy,[5] Timothy,[4] John,[3] Shubael,[2] Lieut. & Elder Thomas,[1]*), b. 1799-1800; m. (1) Mary Ann **Moody**, of Granby, Mass.; m. (2) Laura (dau. Rev. Chauncey) **Booth**, who d. 15 Jan., 1872, a lady of excellent abilities and good sense. He was educated at the common schools, supplemented by instructions from Rev. Chauncey Booth, pastor at Coventry, and at the Beacon Acad. at Colchester, Ct. His med. studies were in the offices of Dr. Chauncey Burgess, of Coventry, and Prof. Jonathan Knight, of New Haven, and he grad. M. D. at Y. C. 1823. After a few yrs. practice at Granby, Mass., he sett. 1837 in his native town, where he was a very successful practitioner for nearly 45 yrs. His superior mental endowments, good judgement, his faithful and self-reliant character, uprightness and gentlemanly bearing rendered him a favorite with his patients and with his brother practitioners as a consultant. He was a memb. of the Conn. State Med. Soc., and in 1858, of its standing committee on exam. for degrees; and for many yrs. a regimental surgeon in the Conn. Militia; also, a member of the Conn. Legisl. (lower house) in 1838, and Senator for the 21st Dist. in 1846. He was a Freemason of high degree, and for 46 yrs. a memb. of the Cong'l Ch. In person, tall, symmetrical and prepossessing, "Dr. Dimock," in the words of one who knew him "was a man who carried a great deal of light with him." He died 29 April, 1874. He left a large landed est. which is kept, by his son, under a high state of cultivation.

Children (b. Coventry):

1 Mary Elizabeth, b. 1840; d. 1842.
2. Henry Farnum, b. 28 Mch., 1842. FAM. 22.
3. Maria Farnum, b. 2 Oct., 1843; d. 13 Aug., 1861.

(*By second marriage*):
4. Daniel (M. D.), a practicing physician; served in the army of the War of Civil Rebellion.

FAM. 22. HENRY FARNUM,[7] (*Dr. Timo.,[6] Capt. Daniel,[5] Lieut. Timo.,[4] John,[3] Shubael,[2] Thos.,[1]*) b. 1842; m. 5 Sept., 1867, Susan Collins (dau. Gen. James *Scolly*) **Whitney**, of Brookline, Mass., he grad. Y. C. 1863; attended Harvard Law School and was adm. to bar of N. Y. 1865; was a memb. of the law firm of Dimock & Whitney, till 1870; in 1875, was app. by Gov. Tilden Commiss'r of Docks, N. Y. City; was a memb. of Committee to devise a plan for the government of cities of New York State; was a Director and Treas. of the Metropolitan Steamship Co.; Director of Boston & Maine R. R. Co.; Knickerbocker Trust Co., of N. Y.; Bank of No. America; N. Y. Loan & Improv't Co., and Dominion Coal Co., of Nova Scotia. See also, Stiles *Hist. Anc. Windsor*, II, 113.

Child:

1. Susan Maria, b. 18 Nov., 1869; m. 1900, | Cary **Hutchinson.**

Capt. SAMUEL. We have not been able to prove satisfactorily his place in the family line—but, Mrs. McCartney thinks he was a son of *Joseph*, (the No. 5 of FAM. 15) b. 1733, s. of *Samuel,[4] Shubael,[3] Dea. Shubael,[2] Thomas,[1]* and it seems most prob. that he came into Wethersfield from the Mansfield, (Ct.), branch of the Dimock family.

Be that as it may, he was one of the most active and best known ship-builders of Stepney during the first quarter of the XIX Century; later he kept tavern in the old Wait Robbins' inn, known to a still later generation as the Shipman place. He m. (1) 4 July, 1782 (*S. C. R.*) Rebecca (dau. Gershom & Thankful) **Bulkeley,** who d. 14 Oct., 1798, ae. 38,—*W.* (*S.*) *Ins.;* he m. (2) 25 Mch., 1799, Mary (dau. Elisha & Lydia) **Goodrich,** who d. 3 Nov., 1803, ae. 38,—*W. Ins.;* he m. (3) 8 Oct., 1804, Eunice ——————, who d. 25 Jan., 1827, ae. 58; he d. 27 Dec., 1820, in 61 yr.—*W. Ins.*

Children (*S. C. R.*) :

1. Andrew, bp. 3 June, 1787; d. 5 June, 1796, in 9th yr.
2. Andrew, bp. Jan., 1800; d. 17 Jan., ae. 11 d.
3. Andrew, bp. 28 June, 1801.
4. Jared Goodrich (Dea.), bp. 5 June., 1803.

FAM. 2.
5. Frederick Warner, bp. 5 Oct., 1806.
6. Lucy Robbins, bp. 27 May, 1811.
(A Samuel whom we cannot connect with *this* Samuel, had a son *Moses* bp. (*S. C. R.* 31 July, 1774.)

FAM. 2.   Dea. JARED GOODRICH,[2] (*Captain Samuel,*[1]) united with the Stepney Ch. during the pastorate of the Rev. Calvin Chapin; was chosen one of its deacons on 14 Oct., 1838, an office which he held with fidelity until his dth., 22 Dec., 1888, at the age of 88 yrs. and 8 mos.—during all of which period he had never absented himself from the communion service but once, and then owing to illness.   His mother having died during his infancy, he was adopted into the family of his uncle Jared Goodrich, who for a continuous period of 25 yrs. played the bass-viol in the Stepney meeting-house, and Dea. Dimock succeeded him in the same service without interruption for 28 yrs., and up to the time when a melodeon was introduced into the services of the church.   He became a member of the choir at age of 11 yrs. under the tuition of Dr. Daniel Fuller, and from 1834 to 1880, led the singing at the weekly prayer meetings and similar occasions.   His life was faithful, honest, helpful, without hatred, bigotries or any uncharitableness, full of good works and such, in every respect, as becometh a Christian.

Dea. Dimock, at the age of 20, loved and courted the dau. of Josiah Butler—but church bigotry interposed an unforseen obstacle.   This was five years after the adoption of the new constitution in Connecticut, under which those who so chose could withdraw from the support of the established order of the old Ecclesiastical societies; and there was much consternation and more bitterness among those who had been opposed to the new departure.   The question had entered into politics, the federalists denounced and the democrats advocated the change.   Neighborhood feeling from political and denominational differences was much more pungent and uncharitable than it is at the present day. Josiah Butler had "signed off" from the support of the old and sacred church of the Pilgrim Fathers; and the good uncle and aunt of the future deacon were of those who felt that this step should rule him out of their friendship; and the daughter came into a share of the hard feeling.   So there was opposition to the courtship of young Jared; under the stress of which he determined to leave home and go to sea.   He applied for the place of cabin boy on board of a vessel about to leave East Haddam under command of Captain Ashbel Boardman, an acquaintance, formerly of Rocky Hill; but the messenger returned him word that the berth was filled.   The mortuary record of Stepney parish has the entry, in the writing of Dr. Chapin, 4 November, 1823, Ashbel Boardman. aged 34, William Sage Butler, 36, Gideon Goff, Jr., 26, Oliver Corey, "sailed from Martinico, and have not been heard from."   So young Dimock, perforce, remained at home with his good uncle Jared and Aunt Deborah Goodrich, to finally marry the Butler girl and reach an honorable old age.

He m. (1) 7 Dec., 1823, (*S. C. R.*), Sophia (dau. Josiah) **Butler,** who was (as an adult) bp. 6 July, 1834, and d. 30 Apl., 1854, ae. 50 yrs.; he m. (2) 20 Mch.,

1855, Sarah M. (dau. Fred'k, Sen.,) **Robbins,** who d. 5 July, 1801, ae. 80.—
W. Ins.

Children:

1. Samuel, bp. 6 July, 1834 ; m. Mary Sophia **Smith;** res. Ry-H.
2. Andrew, bp. 6 July, 1834 ; m. Susan **Merrick,** of N. H. ; res. in Boston.
3. Mary Olivia, bp. 29 Apl., 1836 ; d. 27 Feb.,
1840, ae. 4.
4. Selina Harper, bp. 31 Aug., 1838 ; m. Wm. J. **Willis,** of N. Y., and d. 15 Feb., 1862, ae. 24.

JOSEPH,[6] Sen., (b. at Ry-H., and, perhaps, also, a brother of *Samuel,*[5] preceding, and s. of *Samuel,*[4] *Shubael,*[3] *Dea. Shubael,*[2] *Thos.,*[1]), d. at Granville, N. Y., ae. 89; his wife Elizabeth (Williams) d. 11 May, 1807, ae. 71.—(Information given by Joseph W. Dimock, 1887).

Children (bp. S. C. R.) :

1. Mary, b. 1764; bp. 3 Jan., 1765 ; m. prob. in 1787, Elias **Williams, Jr.;** she d. 3 Dec., 1788, in 24th yr.—*W. Ins.*
2. Elizabeth, d. 17 Mch., 1773.
3. Ch., d. 3 May, 1768 ; possib. this was the "Hannah, dau. of Joseph," bp. 6 Dec., 1767.—*S. C. Rec.*
4. Davis, bp. 28 June, 1772 ; d. at Haddam,
Ct., of yellow fever, 30 Aug., 1798, ae. 26 yrs., 2 mos., 6 d.—*S. C. R.;* had m. 8 July, same yr., Eleanor **Williams;** he was prob. a mariner.
5. Joseph (Capt.), b. 11, bp. 14 May, 1769. FAM. 2.
6. Ch., d. 26 Sept., 1776.

FAM. 2. Capt. JOSEPH, Jr., *Joseph, etc.,*) b. 1769; was dr. at Bermuda, W. I., Mch., 1, 1819, ae. 49; m. 12 Aug., 1789, Sarah **Warner,** who d. 6 Mch., 1819, ae. 46.

Children:

1. Moses, b. 3 Jan., 1790 ; lost at sea, Mch., 1812, unm.
2. Moses, lost at sea, Sept., 1823. (One of the above Moses was bp. 18 Mch., 1792.—*S. C. R.*)
3. William Davis, b. 7, bp. 30 Dec., 1792 ; lost at sea, Mch., 1812, unm.
4. Rachel, b. 1, bp. 28 Dec., 1794 ; d. 21 July, 1844, ae. 47.
5. Sally, b. 19 Jan., bp. 7 May, 1797 ; d. at Terre Haute, Ind., ae. 87.
6. Marrianne, b. Feb., bp. 26 May, 1799 ; d. 9 May, 1882, ae. 83.—*W. Ins.*
7. Joseph W., b. 15 Mch., bp. 23 Aug., 1801.
FAM. 3.
8. Abigail Maria, b. 28 May, bp. 21 Aug., 1803 ; d. 27 May, 1863 ; m. Phineas B. **Whitman,** of New Haven, 23 Jan., 1828.— *W. T. R.*
9. Walt Warner, b. 28 July, bp. 22 Dec., 1805 ; d. 5 July, 1808.
10. Walt Warner, b. 4 Oct., 1808 ; bp. 4 June, 1809 ; d. 10 Mch., 1810.
11. Mary Jane, b. 21 May, bp. 18 Aug., 1811 ; d. at New Haven, 1 Aug., 1845.
12. Elizabeth, b. 26 May, 1815 ; bp. 5 May, 1816.
13. An inf. dau. d. Jan., 1814.

FAM. 3. JOSEPH W.,[3] (*Capt. Joseph, Jr.,*[2] *Joseph,*[1]) , b. 1801; was a successful mcht. at Htfd.

Children:

1. Joseph Judson, b. Jan., 1827 ; d. Baltimore, Md., 1862.
2. Jane Maria, d.
3. Jannette H., d.
4. Sarah W., d.
5. William D., b. 1837 ; d. N. Y., 1873.
6. Jane Amelia, d.
7. James D., d.

Some Conn. families— of the Mass. stock.

PEREZ,[4] (*Benj.,*[3] *Dea. Shubael,*[2] *Thos.,*[1]), b. 1708; m. 5 Nov., 1725, Mary **Baylo.**— *Mansfield (Ct.) Ch. Rec.,* contain some error of transcription which "mixes things," somewhat, but this is the way we "piece it out."

Children:

1. Samuel, b. 27 Nov., 1726.
2. Benjamin, b. 9 Nov., 1728.
3. Gideon, b. 23 May, 1732.
4. Shubael, b. 1 Dec., 1736.
5. Mary, b. 9 Oct., 1739.

OLIVER,[5] (*Timo.,*[4] *John,,*[3] *Dea. Shubael,*[2] *Thos.,*[1]), b. 1740; m. Apl., 1764, Sarah (dau. Sam'l) **Gurley,** of Mansfield, Ct.

Children:

1. Oliver, b. 13 June, 1766.
2. Lucinda, b. 25 June, 1768.
3. Sarah, b. 6 June, 1770.
4. Samuel, b. 2 Mch., 1773.

5. Dan., b. 1 Mch., 1775.
6. Eunice, b. 26 Nov., 1778.
7. Oliver Ward, b. 20 June, 1780.
8. Sophia, b. 30 Apl., 1782.

DIMOND, (*Dimon, Diamond*), (*from W. C. R.*), ABIGAIL, had a son (*sic.*) of William Merrett, b. 11 July, 1785.

ABIGAIL (wid.) d., ae. 78, bu. 27 Mch., 1829.

ABIGAIL had *William*, bp. 19 Sept., 1790.

ABIGAIL, (wid.), had *Sarah* and *Elizabeth* bp. 26 Jan., 1784.

WILLIAM, m. Hannah, and had *Jesse* b. 5 Oct., 1781.—*W. T. R.*

DISBROW, (*Disbro', Disborough*), NICHOLAS, of Weth., d. 1683; est. val. abt. £300.—*Children.*

1. Dau., m. Obadiah **Spencer.**
2. Dau., m. Samuel **Eggleston.**

3. Dau., m. John **Kelsey.**
4. Dau., m. Robert **Flood.**—*Hinman.*

DIX, (*Dyx, Dickes, Deckes, Decks, Dixe*), LEONARD, one of the earliest sett. of Weth., was the son of Edward & Deborah Dix, who came from Eng., to Watertown, Mass., in the fleet with Gov. Winthrop, 1630. The father appears to have d. in W. prior to the removal of the family to Conn., leaving a wid., *Deborah*, and three ch. The wid. Deborah m. (2), 16 Oct., 1667, Richard **Barnes,** of Marlboro, Mass., by whom she had 5 ch. betw. 1669 and 1683.—See Bonds *Watertown*, pp. 198, 753.*

Children:

1. Leonard. Fam. 2.
2. John, who was in Htfd., 1676; ment. in Ld. Rec. Htfd., 1678; taxed there in 1683; sold his ho. and ld. 1686; owned ld. in Hoccanum, nr. mouth of Hocc. River, 1679; he and wife (Mary Bidwell) joined Second Ch., Htfd., 10 Sept., 1686, at which time they had the following ch. bp.,

viz.: Sarah, who m. 18 Aug., 1696, Samuel (s. of Uath'l) Hunn; she d. 6 Mch., 1753; John, b. 1684; d. 6 Mch., 1770, ae. 86; and 10 Apl., 1687, John & Mary (Bidwell) Dix had these other ch. bp., viz.: Margaret, Daniel, Elizabeth; and July 3, 1687, Susanna; and May 12, 1687, Joseph.
3. William, who d. Htfd., 1676.

FAM. 2. LEONARD,[2] (*Edward,*[1]), b. prob., abt. 1644-5, was (acc. to Savage), in Weth., 1645, (perhaps first to Htfd., for a little while), married Sarah ————, abt. 1645; then was in Branford, 1648, where he rec'd a gt. of ld.; was soon afterwards again at Weth., where he also had gts. of ld., and a lot in the vill. on which he res. from abt. 1650 until his dth. See Chapt. VII, Vol. I. Is ment. on the Town's books, as buying lds. (See, also, Chapt. VII, Vol. I), and, in 1657, as having taken up a stray heifer; was constable, 1672; surveyor of highways, 1684. Acc. to Prob. Ct. Rec., he d. 7 Dec., 1696. His will dated 24 Mch., 1696-7, provides for his wife Sarah, (who d. 1709) and bequeaths to two sons, John and Samuel, and to 3 daus., Mercy, Hannah and Elizabeth, and to his son-in-law, John **Francis.** He also had a s. William, who had d. some time before the date of the will—prob. unm. It appears by this will that he had previously given lds. to his two sons, and the balance of his real estate he gave to his s. Samuel, the use of certain portions being reserved for the support of the wid.; and in this devise he ment. the "last division of ld. gtd. him by the Town," and the lds. on the E. side the Great River, "being the Indian Purchase." His personal est. consisted of a horse, 2 cows, a heifer,

---

* Pope's *Pioneers of Mass.*, p. 140, gives acc. of another EDWARD DIX, first of Charlestown, then of Watertown, Mass.; whether a relative of the Edward who was father of the Weth. Leonard, is not known.

swine, a large number of agricultural implements and mechanical tools, a "great musket," a "long fowling piece," swords, belts, household goods, etc., all appraised at £53-10-00; his indebtedness £3-08-00.—*Htfd. Prob. Rec.* His wid. d. 27 Mch., 1709, her will proven 4 Apl., 1709; Invent. of her est. £10-15-03.

Children (all prob. b. Weth.) :

1. Sarah, b. 1658 ; m. 10 Feb., 1680, John **Francis** ; she d. 3 Apl., 1682.
2. John, b. 1661. FAM. 3.
3. Mercy, m. Moses **Goff**, 1687; she d. 20 Dec., 1711. *Issue:*
  i. Moses (Goff), b. 6 Feb., 1687 ; d. 2 Sept., 1712.
  ii. Jacob (Goff), b. 19 Feb., 1690.
  iii. Jerusha (Goff), b. 23 Sept., 1693 ; d. 8 Oct., 1712.
  iv. Benjamin (Goff), b. 30 Apl., 1696.
  v. Ephraim (Goff), b. 4 Mch., 1698.
  vi. David (Goff), b. 29 Apl., 1702.
5. Hannah, m. John **Rennals** (Reynolds), Nov., 1693 ; he d. 10 Dec., 1750; she. d. 7 Apl., 1733. *Issue:*
  i. Hannah (Reynolds), b. 18 Aug., 1695.
  ii. John (Reynolds), b. 8 Feb., 1699.
  iii. James (Reynolds), b. 18 Oct., 1703.
  iv. Jonathan (Reynolds), b. 27 Mch., 1707.
6. Samuel. FAM. 4.
7. Elizabeth, m. ——— **Vincent.**
4. William (?).

FAM. 3. JOHN,[3] (*Leonard,*[2] *Edward,*[1]) b. 1661 Weth.; hayward, 1686; surveyor of highways, 1704; in which yr. also the selectmen apprenticed to him Thos. Powell, a ch., then 2 yrs. old; m. Rebecca ———————, who d. 17 (or 24) Nov., 1711, ae. 60 yr. 1 mo.; he d. 2 Nov., 1711, ae. 50, and that his wid. d. next mo. Invent. of est. taken 27 Jan., 1711-12, amt. £83-12-05; sons John and Leonard, admr's.—*Htfd. Co. Prob. Rec.* John, Sr., occup. his father's ho-stéad, now that of Russell Adams.

Children (Weth, Rec.) :[*]

1. John, b. 17 or 20 Feb., 1684-5. FAM. 5.
2. Rebecca, b. 17 Mch., 1686-7.
3. Leonard, b. 27 Jan., 1688-9. FAM. 6.
4. Elizabeth, b. 3 Apl., 1691.
(*Weth. Recs.* show the marr. of a Sarah (dau. of John) Dickes to Samuel **Hunn**, 18 Aug., 1696, which would make *her* b. prob. abt. 1678, ae. 18. Does she belong to this family?)

FAM. 4. SAMUEL,[3] (*Leonard,*[2] *Edward,*[1]), m. 19 June, 1684 (or 22 Apl., 1686?), Mary Collins (dau. of Rich'd) **Moore,** 22 Apl., 1686 [but one Weth. Rec. says, with prob. more correctness, 19 June, 1684]; see Chapt. VII, Vol. I. Samuel Dix (yoeman) invent. £516-13-11 taken 9 May, 1735, by Jonathan Belding, David Goodrich and Ebenezer Belding, Jr. Will dated 21 February, 1733-4. I give to my wife, Mary Dyx, all my estate real and moveable both house and negro man named Reuben, during their natural lives and after the decease of my wife I give all my house, lands and moveable estate to my grand-son, Charles Nott, with the negro man, except £5 to be given to my dau. Sarah Nott. I appoint my wife, Mary Dyx, to be executrix and after her decease, Johnathan Nott, to be executor to pay and deliver to my dau. Sarah Nott the sd. £5, and the lands, moveable estate with the negro man to Charles Nott. Samuel Dyx. Witness, Aaron Goff, Step. Hellyer and Hez. Grimes. Court Record, 22 Apl., 1735. Proven.—*Htfd. Co. Prob. Rec.*

Child (Weth. Rec.) :

1. Sarah, b. 6 June, 1685 ; m. 3 Apl., 1707, | Jonathan **Nott;** she d. 30 June, 1757.

FAM. 5. JOHN,[4] (*John,*[3] *Leonard,*[2] *Edward,*[1]), b. 1685; m. Sarah (dau. John) **Waddams,** 9 June. 1709.

---

* EDWARD, of Watertown, Mass., was b. 1616, and Leonard, 1624 ; bringing them presumably into the same generation. Moreover, Edward's wife was *Jane* (not Deborah) *Wilkinson. Pope* gives an Edward of Charlestown : Ch. memb. 1630 ; and says he rem. to Watertown ; but *Savage* thinks he must be distinguished from the "youth of 19," who embarked Jan. 16, 1635, and m. Jane Wilkinson, upon landing, and that the Charlestown man was an older man of the same name. If so, may not Deborah and our line poss. be connected with the Charlestown Edward?—*Mrs. N. D. Hanmer Kendall.*

Children (Weth. Rec. & Mix) :

1. Samuel, b. 28 Feb., bp 4 Mch., 1710-11.
   FAM. 7.
2. John, b. 6 (bp. 9—*Mix MSS.*) Aug., 1713.
3. Sarah, b. 30 Mch., 1721; m. Joseph **Smith**,
   2 Dec., 1741. *Issue:*

    i. Roger (Smith), b. 7 July, 1742.
    ii. Sarah (Smith), b. 26 Feb., 1746-7.
4. Moses, b. 15 Mch., 1723-4. FAM. 8.
5. Benjamin, b. 27 May (bp. 8 June—*Mix MSS.*), 1729 ; d. 4 Sept., 1755.

FAM. 6. LEONARD,[4] (*John*,[3] *Leonard*,[2] *Edward*,[1]), b. 1689; m. Abigail (dau. Jacob) **Gibbs**, of Windsor, 15 Apl., 1714; he d. 11 July (22 Oct.) 1730. Invent. est. £887-17-10; wid. m. (2) prob. Wm. **Nott**, as these ch. in 1734 chose the "father-in-law" (*i. e.* step-father) William Nott and wife, as their guardians.— *Htfd. Co. Prob.* See, also, Chapt. VII, Vol. I.

Children (Weth. Rec & Mix) :

1. Abigail, b. 25, bn. 30 Jan., 1714-15 ; m.
   Elisha **Griswold**, 29 May, 1735. *Issue:*
       i. Abigail (Griswold), b. 26 Mch., 1736.
       ii. Lois (Griswold), b. 12 June, 1739 ; d.
           21 Sept., 1741.
       iii. Simeon (Griswold), b. 9 Aug., 1742.
       iv. Rhoda (Griswold), b. 4 Oct., 1748.
2. Leonard, b. 25 (bp. 26—*Mix MSS.*) May,
   1717 ; d. 25 Sept., 1741.
3. Hannah, b. 14 (or 19) Nov., 1719 ; m.
   Elisha **Boardman**.
4. Rebecca, b. 10 Apl., 1722 ; m. Ezra **Belden**,
   of Far.

5. Jerusha, b. 3 May, 1724 ; m. Ebenezer
   Kilby, 5 Nov., 1761. *Issue:*
       i. Abigail (Kilby), b. 5 July, 1762.
       ii. Jerusha (Kilby), b. 9 Mch., 1764.
       iii. Ebenezer (Kilby), b. 20 Nov., 1766 ; d.
           1767.
       iv. Huldah (Kilby), b. 4 Nov., 1770.
       v. Allen (Kilby), b. 15 Aug., 1772.
       vi. Ebenezer (Kilby), b. 21 May, 1775.
6. Jacob, b. 14 Apl., 1727. FAM. 9.
7. Charles, b. 11 (bp. 19—*Mix MSS.*) July,
   1730. FAM. 10.

FAM. 7. SAMUEL,[5] (*John*,[4] *John*,[3] *Leonard*,[2] *Edward*,[1]), b. 1711; m. Mary (dau. Sam'l & Mary *Stebbins*) **Williams**, 7 Feb., 1739-40; he d. 8 Jan., 1779—*W. C. R.; she* d. Feb., 1779.

Children (Weth. Rec.) :

1. Elizabeth, b. 16 May, 1741 ; d. unm. 22
   Nov., 1822.
2. Sarah, b. 2 Aug., 1742 ; m. Capt. Thos.
   Newson, who d. 1811, ae. 46 ; wife Sarah
   d. 1 Apl., 1794. *Issue:*
       i. John (Newson), b. 1760 ; d. 1806.
       ii. Sarah (Newson), b. 1765 ; m. Capt.
           Elisha **Williams**, Jr. ; d. 1811.
       iii. Elizabeth (Newson), b. 1768 ; d. 1808.

    iv. Mary (Newson), b. 1774 ; d. 1793.
    v. Lydia (Newson), b. 1779 ; d. 1819.
    vi. Nancy (Newson), b. 1786 ; d. 1812.
3. Leonard, b. 3 Mch., 1743-4 ; bp. before 1
   June, 1744.
4. John, b. 9 Aug., bp. before Sept., 1 1745.
5. Samuel, bp. 2 Aug., 1747. FAM. 11.
6. Mary, b. and bp. 1 Apl., 1750 ; m. Hez.
   Crane.—See *Crane*.

FAM. 8. MOSES,[5] (*John*,[4] *John*,[3] *Leonard*,[2] *Edward*,[1]), b. 1724; m. Hannah **Dickinson**, Sept. 1, 1744 ; he d. 25 Sept., 1798, ae. 75—*W. C. R.;* letters of admn. on his est. given to his s. Moses, of Far.

Children (Weth. T. and C. Recs.) :

1. Jerusha, b. 11, bp. 18 Nov., 1744.
2. Rhoda, b. 13 Aug., 1746 ; m. 19 Dec., 1764,
   Rhodes.
3. John, b. 26 Sept., 1748.
4. Ozias, b. 6 Dec., 1750. FAM. 12.
5. Hannah, b. 26 May, 1753 ; d. 30 Sept.,
   1753.

6. Hannah, b. 3 Dec., 1754.
7. Rebecca, bp. 23 Sept., 1759.
8. Mary, bp. 24 May, 1762.
9. Son, ae. 12, bu. 23 Oct., 1776.—*W. C. R.*
10. Dau. (prob. Mary), ae. 13 ; bu. 3 Dec.,
    1776.—*W. C. R.*
11. Moses, m. Ruth **Crane**, 7 Nov., 1792.

FAM. 9. JACOB,[5] (*Leonard*,[4] *John*,[3] *Leonard*,[2] *Edward*,[1]), b. 1727; m. Mary ————, he d. 27 May, 1790; she d. 24 Oct., 1784, ae. 57.—*Weth. Ins.*

Children:

1. Leonard, bp. 24 Dec., 1748. FAM. 13.
2. Mary, bp. 10 Nov., 1768 or 9 (*Ch. Rec.*) ;
   m. Ebenezer **Wright**.
3. Abigail, bp. 1764 ; m. Joseph **Crane**, 3
   Dec., 1778 ; she d. 27 Mch., 1813.—See
   Crane.
4. Jesse, bp. 19 Dec., 1765 (or *Ch. Rec.*,
   1766) ; m. (1) as we supp. ————,
   as we find, *W. C. R.*, of "wife of Jesse

Dix," bu. 10 June, 1809 ; he m. (2) Experience (*Pelton*, wid. of Leonard) **Boardman**, of Weth., 4 Feb., 1810, and who d. 1807, leaving all his ppy. to his wid. He seems to have had no issue by either marriage. See *Boardman Geneal.*, 336. Mr. Jesse Dix d. 19 Jan., 1826.—*W. C. R.*
5. Jacob, bp. 25 May, 1766. FAM. 14.

FAM. 10. Lieut. CHARLES,[5] (*Leonard,[4] John,[3] Leonard,[2] Edward,[1]*), b. 1730; m. (1) Martha (Mary, in *W. Ins.*) **Baxter,** 24 Jan., 1753; who d. 25 Aug., 1762, in 32d yr.; he m, (2) Lydia —————, who d. 17 Apl., 1765, ae. 39; m. (3) Sarah (wid. Seth) **Hooker,** of Berlin, Ct., who d. 8 Feb., 1803, ae. 68—*W. C. R.* Lieut. Charles Dix d. ae. 81, bu. 13 June, 1812.—*W. C. R.* He was a lieut. in Col. Canfield's Reg. in the Revol. War. His last will and test. was made 16 May, 1809. He d. 1812. His will ment. his dau. Martha Griswold, to whom he gave the homestead in wh. he res., and "one-half of the Collyn lot," so called, as well as the remainder of his personal ppy. To his s. Charles he gave "all the ld. in the Great Meadow" and the "lot called the Pumman"; also, lds. to his gd-sons, George, Elisha, Harvey and Charles, sons of his son Elisha.

Children (Weth. Ch. Rec.):

1. Elisha, bp. 1 June, 1755. FAM. 15.
2. Moses, bp. 16 Mch., 1760.
3. Charles, b. 9 Dec., 1764. FAM. 16.
4. Martha; m. Moses **Griswold,** 3 Apl., 1782.

FAM. 11. SAMUEL,[6] (*Samuel,[5] John,[4] John,[3] Leonard,[2] Edw'd,[1]*), b. 1747; m. Sarah **Palmer,** 15 May, 1775, both of Weth.—*W. C. R.;* he d. 17 Sept., 1778, ae. 30. A wid. Sarah Dix m. 26 July, 1798, Benj. **Roberts,** of E. Htfd.

Children (Weth. Ch. Rec.):

1. Abigail, bp. 18 Feb., 1776; m. Charles **Crane.**
2. John, bp. 16 Mch., 1777; rem. to Champlain, N. Y., before 1805.
3. Mary, bp. 2 May, 1779; m. Samuel **Rhodes,** 27 June, 1797; she d. 14 Nov., 1860. *Issue:*
   i. Emily (Rhodes), b. 8 Feb., 1799; d. 7 Dec., 1824.
   ii. Samuel (Rhodes), b. 2 May, 1803; d. 13 June, 1804.
   iii. Mary (Rhodes), b. 7 Sept., 1805; d. 25 Sept., 1805.
   iv. Mary (Rhodes), b. 15 Dec., 1806; m. Henry **Hale;** d. 1873.
   v. Samuel (Rhodes), b. 18 Sept., 1808; d. in Buffalo, N. Y., 17 Sept., 1861.
   vi. Sarah (Rhodes), b. 18 June, 1810; d. 23 June, 1842.
   vii. John (Rhodes), b. 28 Mch., 1812; m. Jenette **Jerome.**
   viii. Marsha (Rhodes), b. 14 Feb., 1814; d. 12 Mch., 1819.
   ix. Louisa A. (Rhodes), b. 2 Apl., 1818; m. Joseph **Treat,** 1842; d. 8 Feb., 1881.
   x. Jonathan W. (Rhodes), b. 31 Mch., 1823; d. Louisville, Ky., 13 Feb., 1850.

FAM. 12. OZIAS,[6] (*Moses,[5] John,[4] John,[3] Leonard,[2] Edw'd,[1]*), b. 1748; m. —————; was a Revol. soldier. Query? Did he rem. to Vt. as we find in *W. Ch. Rec.* of bp. of Jerusha, dau. of Ozias Dix of Brattleboro, Vt., bp. in Weth. 13 Feb., 1785.

Children (Weth. Ch. Rec.):

1. Leonard, bp. 1 May, 1774.
2. Ozias, bp. 1 May (?), 1774; son d. 8 Sept., 1775.
3. Lydia, bp. 21 July, 1776.
4. John, bp. 19 July, 1778.
5. Samuel, bp. 11 Mch., 1781.

FAM. 13. LEONARD,[6] (*Jacob,[5] Leonard,[4] John,[3] Leonard,[2] Edw'd,[1]*), b. 1748; m. (1) 19 Oct., 1780, Mary **Goodrich,** who (with inf. son d.) 2 Dec., 1786, ae. 30— *W. C. R.;* m. (2) Susanna **Hollister,** of E. Hadd., 14 June, 1787, who d. 26 Apl., 1788, ae. 22—*W. C. R.;* m. (3) wid. Mary **Forbes,** 4 Sept., 1788; he d. 13 Feb., 1798; wid. m. Joseph **Adams.** May be the L. who d. 15 Feb., 1794, ae. 44, at W. I.—*W. C. R.*

Children (Weth. Ch. Rec. & W. C. R.):

1. Ch. bp. 7 Sept., 1782.
2. Rhoda, ,b. 2 Dec., 1782; bp. 7 Sept. 1782; d. 1782.
3. Rhoda, bp. 30 Nov., 1783; d. 25 Aug., 1784.
4. Leonard, b. 6 June, bp. 21 July, 1785.
(*By second marriage*):
5. Timothy Hollister, b. 11 Apl., bp. 1 June, 1788.
(*By third marriage*):
6. John, b. 15, bp. 21 June, 1789; d. before 1820.
7. Samuel, b. 24 Oct., 1781; bp. 20 Apl., 1792.
8. Mary (Mariah), b. 22 May, 1794; prob. the Mariah Goodrich, dau. of Leonard, bp. 14 Sept., same yr.

FAM. 14. JACOB,[6] (*Jacob,[5] Leonard,[4] John,[3] Leonard,[2] Edward,[1]*), bp. 1766; m. 21 Jan., 1790, Sarah **Hanmer,** who d. 8 May., 1849, ae. 80.—*W. Ins.* He d. 28 Jan., 1843, ae. 77.—*W. Ins.*

Children (W. C. R.):

1. Jacob, b. 1791; d. unm., 23 July, 1823.
2. William, b. ——, 1802; bp. 25 Sept., 1808. Fam. 17.
3. Sarah, b. 1804; bp. 25 Sept., 1808; m. 23

May, 1844, Joseph **Welles**; she d. s. p., 18 Oct., 1875.
4. Roswell, b. 9 May, 1807; bp. 25 Sept., 1808. Fam. 18.

Fam. 15. ELISHA,[8] (*s. of Lieut. Chas.,*[5] *Leonard,*[4] *John,*[3] *Leonard,*[2] *Edw'd,*[1]), b. 1755; m. (1) ——————; m. (2) Rose **Andrus,** who after his dth.; m. (2) Appleton **Holmes,** and res. many yrs. in Glast. He d. ae. 52; bu. 22 Nov., 1806.— W. C. R.

Children (W. C. R.):

1. Alvin, bp. 10 Dec., 1775.
2. Sarah, bp. 22 Jan., 1777; m. John S. **Riley;** had dau. Henrietta.
3. Orrin, bp. 1 Apl., 1781; m. Nancy **Blinn;** rem. to Torrington, Ct.; from 1820-29, res. at Parma, N. Y.
4. George, bp. 20 Oct., 1783; was his father's execr.; rem. to Parma, N. Y.; poss. this G. was the one who m. 19 Sept., 1805, Olive **Hubbard,** both of Weth., 1st Soc. —*S. C. R.*
5. Elisha Harvey, bp. 19 June, 1785. Fam. 19.
6. Charles (known as Charles 2d), b. 12 Apl., 1788; bp. 14 Mch., 1790—*W. T. R.;* m. at age of 16, Polly **Blinn,** of and in the Old Soc'y, 22 Nov., 1804.—*S. C. R.;* rem. to Vernon, N. Y., abt. 1805, and was

res. there in Sept., 1825; had *issue:*
   i. Horace, b. 4 Nov., 1805; d. 12 Dec., 1806.
   ii. Horace, b. 14 Nov., 1807.
   iii. Mary.
   iv. Edwin.
   v. Caroline.
   vi. Sarah Jane.
   vii. Hiram.
   viii. Ch. d. in 3d. yr., 29 Apl., 1816.— *S. C. R.*
   ix. Son, b. 18 Sept., 1825.
(The above names taken from a letter written by him on the above date, and addr. to his stepmother, Mrs. Appleton **Holmes,** of Glast.—*Hon. E. E. Farman.*)

Fam. 16. CHARLES,[6] (*Lieut. Chas.,*[5] *Leonard,*[4] *John,*[3] *Leonard,*[2] *Edw'd,*[1]), b. 1764; m. 5 Mch., 1786, Prudence (dau. John & Hannah *Curtis*) **Welles,** of Newington, who was b. W. 12 Nov., 1766, and d. Vernon, N. Y., 15 Dec., 1845; they rem. to Torrington, Ct., and as stated in hist. of that town, erected there the first tannery. His first 4 ch. were b. in T., and abt. 1795, he ret. to Weth.; from there, in 1802, he rem. to Vernon, Oneida Co., N. Y., where he bo't a tract of ld. in So. part of the town, adjoining the Oneida Ind. Reservation, on which he res. till his dth. 1850. He bro't with him to his new home sufficient means to enable him to maintain, fm. the first, an independent financial position, and which he maintained during his life. His lds. were well and picturesquely situated; and he built here a tannery, shoe shop, flax-mill and rope-walk, and his farm was ever a busy place. He treated his Ind. neighbors with great kindness and tact, and secured their lasting friendship. A grand-son relates that he often saw the Inds. seated near the house, on logs that had been drawn for cutting up into firewood, and being served with food under the direction of Mrs. Welles. These industrial bldgs. have all been swept away in the course of time, and are supplanted by the modest farm house in which resides one of Mrs. Dix's grand-daughters.

Children:

1. Lydia, b. 6 Apl., 1787, in Torrington, Ct.; d. 27 Aug., 1870, in Vernon, N. Y.; m. 10 Apl., 1807, in Vernon, N. Y., David Phelps **Flint,** b. 1781, in Bolton, Ct., and d. 10 Nov., 1850, in Vernon, N. Y. *Issue* (b. *Vernon*):
   i. John S. (Flint), b. 21 Sept., 1811.
   ii. Samuel (Flint), b. ——————.
   iii. Amelia (Flint), b. 27 Jan., 1814; d. 10 Aug., 1889, in V.
   iv. Lucy (Flint), b. 28 May, 1816.
   v. Hiram (Flint), b. 28 Sept., 1818.
   vi. Milan (Flint), b. 15 Jan., 1826.
   vii. Ira Thomas (Flint), b. 3 Dec., 1828.
2. William, b. 7 June, 1789, in Torr. Fam. 20.
3. Erastus, b. 15 Apl., 1791. in Torr.; d. 1844, at Ausable Forks, N. Y. Fam. 21.
4. Ara, b. 14 July, 1793, in Torr.; d. 4 Sept., 1826, in Vernon, N. Y. Fam. 22.

5. Martha, b. 12 Dec., 1796, in Weth., Ct.; she m. at Vernon, N. Y., 8 Mch., 1814, Zadock (s. of Rosswell & Abiah *Hutchins*) **Farman;** they rem. to New Haven, N. Y., where she res. until her dth., 23 Dec., 1863. Zadock Farman was b. Bath, N. H., 24 Apl., 1791; came with his father to Oneida Co., N. Y., in 1803; thence, 1806, to New Haven, N. Y., where his mother (a dau. of Capt. Jeremiah Hutchins, of Bath, N. H.) d. 18 Sept., 1809; and his father d. 27 Oct., 1839. He d. N. H., 9 Apl., 1854. His wid. m. (2) 6 May, 1855, Ora **Lawton,** b. 10 Feb., 1797, in Schoharie Co., N. Y., and d. 12 Mch., 1884, at No. Scriba, N. Y. *Issue* of Zadock & Martha Farman:
   i. Samantha (Farman), b. 2 Apl., 1816; d. 28 Feb., 1835, in N. Haven, N. Y.;

E. E. Farman.

m. 21 Mch., 1834, Levi Warren **Whit-ney**, who d. North Scriba, N. Y., 1 Oct., 1890. *No issue.*

ii. Charles Dix (Farman), b. 11 Nov., 1820; d. 17 Jan., 1889, in Gainesville, N. Y.

iii. Henry (Farman), b. 14 Mch., 1823; d. 12 Mch., 1899, in Knoxboro, N. Y.

iv. Prudence Hannah (Farman), b. 19 Feb., 1827; d. 21 July, 1828, in N. H.

v. (Hon.) Elbert Eli (Farman), jurist and diplomat, New Haven, Oswego Co., N. Y., Apl. 23, 1831. On the paternal side he is descended from an old Maryland family of planters, that settled near Annapolis, in 1674. He prepared for college at the Genesee Wesleyan Sem'y; grad., A. B., at Amherst, 1855, and three years later as A. M. Immediately on leaving college he took an active part in public political discussions in support of John C. Fremont in the presidential campaign of 1856. He studied law at Warsaw, N. Y., and was admitted to practice in 1858. From 1865 to 1867, he travelled and studied in Europe. In January, 1868, he was app., by Governor Fenton, Dist. Att. for Wyoming Co., and was elected for the two following terms to the same position, serving until 1875. In March, 1876, he was app. by President Grant Diplomatic Agent and Consul-General at Cairo, Egypt. He held this position until July 1st, 1881, when President Garfield on the last day of his public service, on the personal recommendation of Secretary Blaine, designated him as one of the Judges of the mixed tribunals of Egypt. This was a life position with a liberal salary, but he resigned in the fall of 1884, and returned to the U. S., taking an active part in the Republican campaign of that year.

In 1880, while Agent and Consul-General, he, with Geo. S. Batcheller were app. by Pres. Hayes, delegates on the part of the United States, to act on an International Commission instituted to revise the judicial codes of Egypt for the use of the mixed tribunals. He was engaged in this work one year. In January, 1883, he was designated by Pres. Arthur as a member of the International Commission, organized to determine the amounts to be paid to the people of Alexandria for damages arising from the riots, bombardment, burning and pillage of that city in June and July, 1882. This commission examined, in eleven months, over ten thousand claims, and awarded upon them over $20,000,000. During this work he continued to hold his position in the courts, generally sitting one day in the week. Mr. Farman was the U. S. representative in Egypt during the most interesting period of its modern history: was in Cairo during the dethronement of the Khedive Ismail Pasha, and the installation, in his place, of his son Tewfik, and afterward witnessed the riots at Alexandria, and the bombardment and burning of that city.

When Gen. Grant visited Egypt Mr. Farman presented him to the Khedive, and acted as interpreter at all their interviews. He also accompanied him on his famous voyage up the Nile. While Consul-General he sent to the department at Washington voluminous reports upon the agriculture, people, commerce, politics, and finance of Egypt, many of which

have been officially published. By direction of the Dep't of State at Washington, made at his suggestion, he negotiated with Egypt a treaty relating to the extinction of the slave traffic in that country and its provinces. Although this treaty was completed and verbally assented to by the Egyptian government, it failed of execution on account of a sudden change of the ministry.

He took, in other ways, a deep interest in the condition of the slaves in that country, and on his application and through his personal efforts in their behalf at different times, fifteen slaves were liberated by the government on the ground of their ill treatment by their owners. He successfully conducted the negotiations for the increase of the number of American judges in the mixed tribunals, and Philip H. Morgan, afterwards U. S. Minister Plenipotentiary and Envoy Extraordinary to Mexico, was appointed to the position thus created. He also conducted the negotiations for the obelisk, and to his friendly personal relations with the Khedive, Ismail Pasha, and the members of his cabinet, as well as to his diplomatic skill, New York City is indebted for the gift of that ancient monument.

Mr. Farman made, while in Egypt, extensive collections of ancient coins, scarabs, bronzes, objects in porcelain, and other antiquities which he has since classified, and some of which collections are loaned to, and now on exhibition in the Metropolitan Museum of Art in New York City. In 1882, Amherst college conferred upon him the degree of LL.D On his leaving Egypt he received from the Khedive the decoration of "Grand Officer of the Imperial Order of the Medjidieh," a distinction rarely conferred. Mr. Farman is a member of the Union League Club, and of the Society of the Sons of the Revolution of New York City, and of the New York Bar Association. He has been twice married, (1) 24 Dec., 1855, at Madison, O., Lois **Parker**, a niece of Rev. Joel Parker, D. D., of N. Y. City. She was b. at Gainesville, N. Y., 13 June, 1832; d. at Warsaw, N. Y., 21 June, 1881; m. (2) 1883. Sarah Adelaide, (dau. of Hon. David H.) **Frisbie**, of Galesburgh, Ill., and b. 9 Mch., 1855.

Since his return from Egypt, he delivered an occasional lecture and made political speeches, but has been principally engaged in the management of his private affairs. *Children* (b. Warsaw, N. Y., all by second marr.) :

i. Lois Elbertine, b. 21 Dec., 1884.

ii. Elbert Eli, b. 27 Dec., 1886.

iii. Maria Louise, b. 7 July, 1889.

vi. Samuel (Farman), b. 6 Dec., 1835; res. Fillmore, N. Y.

6. Hannah, b. 8 Dec., 1799, in Weth., Ct.; m. (1) 1823, John (s. David & Sukey) **Powers**; b. Saratoga, N. Y., who d. Staiford, N. Y., 10 Aug., 1832; m. (2) 2 July, 1838, in Stafford, N. Y., Clark **Daniels**; b. Danville, Ct., 18 Sept., 1794, and who d. Stafford, N. Y., 6 Nov., 1893, in his 100th yr. Mrs. Daniels d. Stafford, N. Y. 27 Feb., 1878. *Issue:*

i. Cornelia (Powers), b. 10 Nov., 1824, in Vernon, N. Y.; m. (1) 31 Dec., 1840, Stephen **Daniels**, s. of Clark Daniels, her mother's second husband, and b. in Stafford, N. Y., 25 Dec., 1818;

d. 13 Aug., 1877, in Almena, Mich.;
she m. 2nd in Almena, John Johial
Hughson; b. 23 Apl., 1856 in Hammond, N. Y.; no issue by either
marr.; res. Almena, Mich.
ii. Catherine (Powers), b. 20 Oct., 1828
in Stafford, N. Y.; d. 21 Aug., 1887
in Pioneer, Mich.; m. 28 June, 1845,

Wm. Sumner **Parker**; 5 ch.
7. Inf. ae. 15 mos. bu. 12 Dec., 1800.
8. Charles, b. 1 May, 1802, in Weth. Fam. 23.
9. Samuel, b. 14 July, 1805, in Vernon,
N. Y.; d. V. 27 Mch., 1807.
10. Eli Richards, b. 6 Oct., 1807, and d. 18
May, 1852, at V. Fam. 24.

Fam. 17. WILLIAM,[7] (*Jacob,*[6] *Jacob,*[5] *Leonard,*[4] *John,*[3] *Leonard,*[2] *Edw'd,*[1]), m. 9 or
10 Oct., 1825, Lucy **Barrett,** who d. 22 Dec., 1871, ae. 68; he d. 16 July, 1844.—
W. *Ins.*

Children:

1. Dau., bu. 10 Oct., 1831, ae. 4 yrs.
2. Chauncey B.
3. Franklin.
4. Ralph, m. and had three ch.: Edward,
Bella and Lucy.
5. Stephen.
6. Cornelia F., d. 12 Oct., 1832, in 4 yr.—

W. *Ins.*
7. Cornelia, b. 13 Dec., 1838; m. John
Warner, of Weth.; she d. 16 Feb., 1869.
8. Martha B., b. ————; m. Luther W.
Adams, of Weth.; she d. 1879.
9. William H., d. 6 Oct., 1840, in 4 yr.

Fam. 18. ROSWELL,[7] (*Jacob,*[6] *Jacob,*[5] *Leonard,*[4] *John,*[3] *Leonard,*[2] *Edw'd,*[1]), b. 1807;
m. Nancy **Robbins,** 1 Mch., 1830; he d. 29 Oct., 1858; she bp. 7 Aug., 1831, and
d. 26 Apl., 1878.

Children (A. R. & W. C. R.):

1. Jacob, b. 18 Dec., 1830; bp. 25 Sept., 1831.
Fam. 25.
2. Charles Robbins, b. 26 Mch., bp. 31 July,
1833; d. 5 May, 1878.
3. Roswell Newton, b. 19 Mch., 1835; d. 10
Feb., 1899. Fam. 26.
4. Ellen Nancy, b. 1 or 21 July, 1838; m.
Caleb J. **Hanmer,** 3 May, 1859, who was b.
24 Nov., 1833 and d. 15 May, 1887. *Issue:*
i. Elizabeth (Hanmer), b. 16 Aug., 1860;
d. 26 Mch., 1863.

ii. Nellie D. (Hanmer), b. 2 Sept., 1862.
iii. Frederick C. (Hanmer), b. 24 Oct.,
1864; d. 21 Apl., 1896.
iv. M. Gertrude (Hanmer), b. 13 Jan.,
1871.
5. Sarah Hanmer, b. 23 Nov., 1840; m. John
H. **Boardman;** she d. 1 Mch., 1898. *Issue:*
i. Carrie E. (Boardman), b. 1 Sept., 1870.
6. James, b. 6 Feb., 1843; d. 9 May, 1854.
7. Dwight, b. 28 July, 1846; d. 7 Aug., 1864.

Fam. 19. ELISHA HARVEY,[7] (*Elisha,*[6] Lt. *Charles,*[5] *Lenoard,*[4] *John,*[3] *Leonard,*[2]
Edw'd,[1]), b. 1785, m. (1) Sarah **Look;** m. (2) Betsy **Hopkins;** res. in Springfield, Mass., in employ of U. S.; in 1820, was res. at Rowe, Mass.

Children:

1. Alvira, b. 8 Feb., 1812.
2. Austin, b. ————, 1814.
3. Samira, b. 8 Feb., 1815; m. John S.
Riley, July, 1832.
4. Thomas F., b. 1 Aug., 1820. Fam. 27.

5. E. Sherman, b. 10 Apl., 1822; m. Mary
Stanford, 1844. Fam. 28.
6. Rosette, b. 26 July, 1826; m. Chas. **Peck,**
19 May, 1847; 3 ch.

Fam. 20. WILLIAM,[7] (*Charles,*[6] Lieut. *Chas.,*[5] *Leonard,*[4] *John*[3], *Leonard,*[2] *Edw'd,*[1]),
b. 1789, in Torr.; m. in Vernon, N. Y., 11 July, 1811, Hannah **Deming;** res.
at V. until 1831, when he rem. to Pittsfield, Mich., and in 1868, to Dover,
Mich., where he d. 19 Mch., 1876; wife d. at D., 20 Aug., 1880.

Children:

1. Clarissa, b. 14 June, 1812, in Vernon,
N. Y.; m. at Pittsfield. Mich., 4 Oct., 1842,
Newton A. **Prudden.** *No issue.*
2. Julia, b. 23 Mch., 1815, in Augusta, N. Y.;
m. 15 Jan., 1838, in Pittsfield, Mich., Conrad
Holmes, b. 25 Mch., 1814, in Clarkson,

N. Y. *Issue:*
i. William Francis (Holmes), b. 22 Dec.,
1838; d. unm. 4 Mch., 1863.
ii. Charles Isaacs (Holmes), b. 12 June,
1850, in Dover, Mich.; m. 10 Apl., 1874;
res. Clayton, Mich.

Fam. 21. ERASTUS,[7] (*Chas.,*[6] Lieut. *Chas.,*[5] *Leonard,*[4] *John,*[3] *Leonard,*[2] *Edw'd,*[1]), b.
1791; m. (1) Sally (dau. David & Sukey) **Powers,** of Augusta, N. Y.; m. (2)
Catherine **Reiner.** He d. 21 June, 1844, at Ausable Forks, N. Y.

Children:

1. Lovina, b. 12 Jan., 1815; in Vernon, N. Y.; d. unm. 18 May, 1835, in Augusta, N. Y.
2. David, b. 9 Feb., 1817, in V.; d. 6 Aug., 1847, in Randolph, N. Y. FAM. 29.
3. John, b. 1823; d. unm. in Danville, Ky., in the Union Army, War of Civil Rebellion.

4. Caroline Maria, b. 20 June, 1820, in V.; d. 26 Feb., 1821.
5. Lorinda, b. 8 July, 1832, in V.; d. 15 Nov., 1887, m. 26 Oct., 1853, Frank Tilden, in V.
6. Leander, b. 1835, in V.; d. 7 Sept., 1842; accidental dth.

FAM. 22. AKA,[7] (*Chas.,[6] Lt. Chas.,[5] Leonard,[4] John,[3] Leonard,[2] Edw.,[1]*), b. ————; m. Lydia **Richards**, 31 Dec., 1816, in Vernon, N. Y. He d. 4 Sept., 1826, at Vernon, N. Y.

Child:

1. Oliver, who res. at Nettle Creek, Ill., in 1891; 6 ch.

FAM. 23. CHARLES,[7] (*Chas.,[6] Lt. Chas.,[5] Leonard,[4] John,[3] Leonard,[2] Edw',[1]*), b. Weth., 1802; m. (1) 12 Mch., 1836, Mary **Alden;** m. (2) 20 Apl., 1859, at LeRoy, N. Y., Florilla **Olmstead**, b. 8 Dec., 1819. He d. LeRoy, N. Y., 8 Mch., 1862.

Children (E. E. F., all by first marriage):

1. Helen Miriam, b. 27 May, 1839, in Stockbridge, N. Y.; d. 1 July, 1896, at Gd. Rapids, Mich.; m. 15 Apl., 1862, at LeRoy, N. Y., Dr. John Byron **Parker**, who b. 1839, d. at Asheville, N. C., 1895. *Issue (b. Grand Rapids, Mich.):*
   i. Joe Dix (Parker), b. 13 Oct., 1872; d. unm., res. Grand Rapids, Mich.

ii. Helen Amelia (Parker), b. 25 June, 1874; m. 10 Nov., 1896, Marshall Otis (son of Oscar & Mary Elizabeth *Peck*) **Straight;** res. Detroit, Mich.
2. William Henry Harrison, b. 22 Dec., 1846; d. 10 Aug., 1857, in Augusta, N. Y.
3. Leander Vaughn, b. 23 July, 1843, in Augusta, N. Y. FAM. 30.

FAM. 24. Eld. RICHARDS,[8] (*Chas.,[7] Lt. Chas.,[6] Chas.,[5] Leonard,[4] John,[3] Leonard,[2] Edw'd,[1]*) b. —; m. 25 Dec., 1839, Cath. **Foot**, b. 16 July, 1814, of Augusta, N. Y. He d. Vernon, N. Y., 18 Aug., 1852; wid. m. (2) 7 Oct., 1858, Solomon W. **Wells**, (son of Daniel Wells and bro. of Prudence Dix), and d. 6 Feb., 1886, at Augusta, N. Y.

Child (by first marriage):

1. Ella Orianna, b. 4 Jan., 1847, in Vernon, N. Y., the orig. homestead of her gd-fth. Charles **Dix**, where she (1901) res.; she

m. 10 Feb., 1874, Gay Henry **Rodemore**, in V., who was b. V., 14 Oct., 1850; addr. Knoxboro, N. Y. *No issue.*

FAM. 25. JACOB,[8] (*Roswell,[7] Jacob,[6] Jacob,[5] Leonard,[4] John,[3] Leonard,[2] Edw'd,[1]*), b. 1830; m. (1) Jane **Brewer**, 10 Apl., 1856; m. (2) Louise **Brewer.**

Children (A. R.):

1. Edward B., b. 18 Oct., 1857. FAM. 31.
2. Charles, b. 30 Apl., 1860.
3. Dwight R., b. 5 Feb., 1865.
4. Jennie L., b. 4 May, 1870.

5. Milton, b. 13 Aug., 1872; d. same yr.
6. Alice, b. 9 Feb., 1877.
   (*Bu second wife*):
7. Lewis A., b. ————.

FAM. 26. ROSWELL NEWTON,[8] (*Roswell,[7] Jacob,[6] Jacob,[5] Leonard,[4] John,[3] Leonard,[2] Edw'd,[1]*), b. 1835; m. Helen Maria **Bulkley**, 13 Apl., 1864; he d. 10 Feb., 1899.

Children (A. R.):

1. Eva Sarah, b. 27 Jan., 1866.
2. Mary Bulkeley, b. 26 Sept., 1867; d. 23 Apl., 1893.
3. Frank Robbins, b. 12 July, 1870.

4. Herbert Newton, b. 9 Sept., 1872.
5. Carrie Elizabeth, b. 23 Nov. 1874.
6. Leonard Roswell, b. 7 Sept., 1880.

FAM. 27. THOMAS F.,[8] (*Elisha Harvey,[7] Elisha,[6] Lt. Chas.,[5] Leonard,[4] John,[3] Leonard,[2] Edw'd,[1]*), b. 1820; m. (1) Zilpha **Stone**, 8 Aug., 1841; m. (2) Sylvia **Streeter**, 8 Oct., 1854.

Children (A. R.):

1. John F., b. 26 May, 1843.
2. Lydia E., b. Dec., 1846.
3. Elisha Harvey, b. 1849.

4. W. Rosette, b. 1852.
   (*By second marriage*) :
5. Gilbert A., b. 1862.

FAM. 28. E. SHERMAN,[8] (*Elisha H.,[7] Elisha,[6] Lt. Chas.,[5] Leonard,[4] John,[3] Leonard,[2] Edw'd,[1]*), b. 1822; m. Mary **Stanford**, 1844.

Children (A. R.):

1. Mary, b. ————; m. T. **Marcy.**
2. Lucien, b. 1 Apl., 1855.

3. Flora, b. 1850.

FAM. 29. DAVID,[8] (*Erastus,[7] Chas.,[6] Lt. Chas.,[5] Leonard,[4] John,[3] Leonard,[2] Edw'd,[1]*), b. 1791; m. 19 Aug., 1846, Rebecca Scott **Marble**, in Clinton, N. Y., b. 9 Sept., 1819, and who d. 4 Apl., 1892, in Randolph, N. Y.

Children (E. E. F.):

1. Harriet Josephine, b. 4 Aug., 1847, at Assyria, Mich; m. 2 Oct., 1867, Milton **Randall**, at Toll, N. Y.; res. Ensley, Mich.; 4 children.
2. Leander Marble, b. 19 June, 1849, in Vernon, N. Y.; m. Emma **Stone**; 4 ch.; res. Randolph, N. Y.
3. Theodore Velascl, b. 13 Sept., 1852, in Stockbridge, N. Y.; m. Mary **Slat**; res.

Ensley, Mich.
4. David Jay, b. 31 Jan., 1855, d. 21 May, 1859.
5. Charles Emery, b. 23 Dec., 1857, in Stockbridge, N. Y.; m. 22 Aug., 1881, Lillie **Hull.**
6. Ida May, b. 17 Feb., 1883.
7. Florence Irene, b. 5 May, 1889.
8. Ray Elton, b. 20 Oct., 1890.
   (6, 7, 8, all b. in Conewango, N. Y.)

FAM. 30. LEANDER VAUGHN,[8] (*Chas.,[7] Chas.,[6] Lt. Chas.,[5] Leonard,[4] John,[3] Leonard,[2] Edw'd,[1]*), b. ——, ——;m. 29 Sept., 1868, at Jeff. City, Mo., Mary (dau. Geo. & Cath. *Argus*) **Conn**, b. 1843, at W. Bedford, O.; he was a memb. of Co. I, 6th U. S. Cavalry, in 1864; res. Jefferson City, Mo.

Children (b. Jeff. City, Mo.):

1. Helen Miriam, b. 7 Jan., 1870.
2. Jessie Minnie, b. 20 Sept., 1871.
3. Dora, b. 13 Feb., 1873; d. 19 Mch., 1887.
4. Charles Angus, b. 4 Jan., 1875; m. 8

Dec., 1898, ———— (dau. James H. & Julia *Price*) **Davis**; res. Jeff. City, Mo. *No issue.*
5. Mary Blanche, b. 28 July, 1877.

FAM. 31. EDWARD B.,[8] (*Jacob.,[7] Roswell,[6] Jacob,[5] Leonard,[4] John,[3] Leonard,[2] Edw'd,[1]*), b. 1851; m. Lenora **Lamb**, 20 Oct., 1881.

Children (A. R.):

1. E. Leon, b. 22 Oct., 1883.

2. Grace V., b. 1 July, 1885.

DODGE, CALVIN, m. 26 Feb., 1799 Huldah **Robbins;** had (*W. C. R.*) Dan'l Robbins, Fidelia, Henry Sherman, and Calvin, bp. 28 Sept., 1808.

CHAMPION'S dau. Mary, d. Sept., 1828, ae. 13-4; his inf. son d. 8 Apl., 1825.—*W. C. R.*

JAMES COOK, of New Boston, N. H., m. Mary **Baxter**, 23 Dec., 1813.—*W. C. R.*

JOSEPH, m. Elizabeth **Flowers**, 22 Jan., 1777.—*W. C. R.*

DOGAN, (*Dugan*) DENNIS, m. Mary **Welles**, both of Weth., 3 July, 1774—*W. C. R.; he* d. ae. abt. 85, 13 Dec., 1813.—*S. C. R.*

DOTY, DANIEL.—See Chapt. Vol. I.

MILO, of Htfd., m. Catharine **Wells**, 21 Feb., 1838.—*N. C. R.*

DOUGLAS, JONATHAN, of Shelter Island, m. wid. Emily **Wells**, 19 Feb., 1824.—*W. C. R.*

DOW, EDMUND, m. Sarah **Stillman,** 9 Dec., 1750; d. 3 Mch., 1786, ae. 58.

Children (Weth. Rec.) :

1. Charles, b. 25, bp. 29 Apl., 1751.
2. Helen, b. 1 Dec., 1752.
3. Sarah, b. 9 Apl., 1754.

4. Edmonde, b. 1 Jan., 1756 (prob. the father of Huldah and Charlie, bp. 29 Apl., 1781.— *W. C. R.*

POLLY, of Weth., m. Stephen **Skinner,** of Htfd., 22 Apl., 1779.—*W. C. R.*

SAMUEL, prob. the S. who m. Abigail **Bulkeley,** 12 Dec., 1793; and was himself bp. 15 Mch., 1795; and had Samuel bp. 17 Jan., 1795; and Samuel Stillman, bp. 28 Feb., 1796; Huldah, bp. 21 Dec., 1797, and William bp. 16 Mch., 1800.

SALLY (adult) bp. 30 May, 1781—*W. C. R.;* SARAH, m. Sol. **Wadsworth,** of E. Htfd., 11 Jan., 1836.—*W. T. R.;* SARAH, wife of Samuel, bp. 6 May, 1821. SARAH, (wid.) d. 21 Feb., 1800, ae. 71. JOHN, m. 17 June, 1806, Lucy **Andrus.**—*N. C. R.* JOHN, had s. John Churchill, bp. 13 Aug., 1830.—*N. C. R.* JOHN CHERRY, m. (1) 23 Aug., 1825, Laura **Churchill,** of Weth., who d. 27 May, 1830—*W. Ins.;* he m. (2) 10 Oct., 1832, Martha **McCarter,** (*N. C. R.*) who d. 24 Nov., 1854, ae. 41.—*Weth. Ins.*

Children (N. C. R., by first marriage) :

1. Samuel, bp. 11 Feb., 1827; d. 9 Nov., 1827, ae. 10 mo. 4 d.—*Weth. Ins.*
2. Inf. d. Sept., 1830, prob the John bp. 13 Aug., that year.—*Weth. Ins.*
   (By second marr.—*Weth. Ins.*)
3. Laura C., bp. 3 Aug., 1834 ; d. 20 Mch., 1853.

4. Mary Abilene, bp. 30 Sept., 1838 ; d. 8 Nov., 1855.
5. Martha Urania, bp. 31 July, 1836 ; d. 27 Nov., 1859.
6. John Newell, bp. 15 Nov., 1845.

LUELLA, d. 9 Aug., 1867, ae. 14.—*W. Ins.*

MEHITABLE, (adult) bp. 22 Oct., 1789.—*W C. R.*

DOWD, GAYLORD, m. Olive M. **Welles** (?), 16 Dec., 1840?

DOWELL, (or *Dorrell?*) JOHN, had Joseph Cleveland and Thomas Gibbs, bp. 12 July, 1818.—*W. C. R.*

NANCY, (wid.) d. 28 Dec., 1833, ae. 42, or 43.—*W. C. R.*

DRAPER, PRINCE, m. Sybil **Goodrich,** 23 Feb., 1792.—*New.*

AARON, of Roxbury, m. Ruth **Beadle,** 19 Aug., 1779—*W. C. R.;* had ch bu. 19 June, 1789.—*W. C. R.*

DRINKWATER, (*N. Rec.*) THOMAS, m. Nancy **Kilborn,** 17 Oct., 1810.—*W. T. R.*

Children:

1. Nancy Maria,
2. Harriet Amanda,   bp. 19 Aug., 1821.

3. Horace Kilborn, bp. 19 Aug., 1821.
4. An inft. of, d. 12 Apl., 1811.—*N. C. R.*

DRISCOLL, FLORENCE, owned ppy. at Weth. and Springfield; d. insolvent, 1678.— *Hinman.*

DUCASSE, JOHN, mentioned in Goodwin's *Geneal. Notes,* as "Capt. John Ducasse, a French officer in our Revolution," m. 13 Oct., 1778 (*N. C. R.*) Mary (dau. of Charles) **Whiting,** by his wife Honor, dau. of Esq. Hezekiah Goodrich, of Weth. Capt. Ducasse d. in 1780, and his wid. m. (2) Capt.

Samuel **Wyllis**, or Willis, of No. Carolina, 2 June, 1788—*N. C. R.;* she d. 27 Oct., 1799.—(*Goodwin.*)   Capt. and Mrs. Ducasse had a dau. Harriet Lavergne, b. 21 July, 1779.   The following is a copy of an old document, relating to Capt. Ducasse, found in the first volume of *Town Votes of Weth.,* p. 83:

"Pour Valeur receive (?) Je payerai a M. Jean Andre Violene, on ordre, le somme de deux Mille trea (?) cents soixante dix—news (?) Dollars argent, dis continent, on la valeur equivalente en espece mouneyee (?) a sa demande.

Jⁿ. Ducasse.

Wethersfield, 12 October, 1779.
 Pʳ. 2379 Dʳ.

For value received I will pay to Mr. Jean Andre Violene, or to his order, the sum of two thousand three hundred and seventy-nine Dollars, in Continental money, or the equal value thereof in coined specie, whenever he shall demand it.

Jⁿ. Ducasse.

Wethersfield, 12 October, 1779.
 P. 2379 Dʳ.

I certify the above to be a true and literal translation of the original Note, as laid before me by Mr. Violene.

Wethersfield, 15th of May, 1780.

B. Romans.

The above Translation is a true one.

Elizur Goodrich.

DUDLEY, ASHBEL, of Midd., m. Hannah **Woodhouse,** 5 Mch., 1781.—*W. C. R.*

ELIZUR, m. Anne **Hurlbut,** 8 June, 1801.—*N. C. R.*

ISAAC, of Midd., m. Anne **Woodhouse,** 19 Jan., 1785.—*W. C. R.*

DUGAN, (See *Dogan.*)

DUMORRIS, JOHN, a "denizen" of Weth. in 1721—*Co. Ct. Rec.* DENIZENS, on HIGHWAYS.   In March, 1701-2, the "inhabitants" of the town, in town meeting, directed Capt. John Chester, Lieut. James Treat, Lieut. Wm. Warner and the Rev. Stephen Mix, to examine into the "plaints" which had been made "of sum ronge done unto" the inhabitants, by "denesens on hie ways"

"Inhabitants" were persons who had been "admitted" as such, by vote of the town, and their male resident descendants of full age; and they had rights, as owners of the highways and commons, which mere "denizens" did not possess. It is presumable that the latter had, in some cases, "squatted," to use a modern phrase of contempt—on the highways and public lands of the town; and hence, the vote above mentioned.—*S. W. A.*

DUNHAM, SOLOMON, m. Elizabeth **Ives,** 2 Mch., 1758.

Children (*Weth. Rec.*) :

1. Elizabeth, b. 3 Dec., 1758.
2. Warner, b. 4 Dec., 1760, "of Boston ;" m. Mary **Andrus,** of Weth., 9 Mch., 1812.—*N. C. R.*
3. Solomon, b. 18 Jan., 1762.
4. Elishama, b. 17 Feb., 1764.
5. Lucy, b. 5 Mch., 1766.
6. Mary, b. 25 Oct., 1768.
7. Reuben, b. 13 Feb., 1773.

SOLOMON, d. July or Aug., 1786.—*W. I.*

WILLIAM, m. Nancy **Peck,** of Kens., 27 Feb., 1812.—*N. C. R.*

DAVID, of Sheffield, m. Lucretia **Adams,** 5 Aug., 1779.—*W. C. R.*

JOHN, Jr., b. Feb. 6, 1784; d. May 2, 1826; m. at Berlin, May 11, 1807, wid. Lois **Smith,** b. in Beckley Quarter, Wffd., Nov. 16, 1778, dau. Elias & Lois (*Lee*) **Beckley,** and wid. of Elnathan Smith, who d. at Berlin, Feb. 22, 1801. Mrs. Lois Dunham d. at New Haven, July 22, 1833.—*Htfd. Times,* Aug. 18, 1902.

DUNN, Capt. RICHARD, d. 17 May, 1791, ae. 69 or 70—his wife Mary d. 16 Aug., 1788, ae. 62—formerly of Newport, R. I.—*W. Ins; S. C. R.* says d. 15 Aug.. 1789 in 65 yr. Their dau. Mary (wife of Alex. Grimes) d. 26 Feb., 1823, ae. 75.—*W. Ins.*

SAMUEL, m. Susannah **Curtis,** 25 Oct., 1767—*W. C. R.;* he and his dau. *Mabel,* bp. 29 May, 1768—S. C. R.; had *Eunice,* bp. 24 Feb., 1771.

D[unn?] JAMES had Elizabeth, Anna and Mary bp. 22 July, 1781.

DUPLESSE, —————, a res. of Weth. abt. 1730.—*Co. Ct. Rec.*

DUPRE, (*Dupee, Dufee?*) Lucretia Griswold, wife of Simeon *alias* Senio,) whom she m. 26 Apl., 1771 (or '77) ae. 32, bu. 28 Aug., 1779—*W. C. R.;* SIMEON, bu. 28 Dec., 1811—*W. C. R.;* WID. (prob. of above) d. ae. 82, bu. 9 Dec., 1828; she was bp. 26 Aug., 1779—*W. C. R.;* SIMEON, (prob. s. Simeon & Lucretia) m. Jermina **Goodrich,** both of Weth., 21 Dec., 1783—*W. C. R.;* WILLIAM, of N. Y., m. Maria **Hills,** of New., 30 Apl., 1839.—*W. T. R.*

DURANT, JOHN, (See Chapt. VII, Vol. I) m. Margaret —————, 14 Jan., 1678-9.

Children (Weth. Rec.) :

1. Ebenezer, b. 22 July, 1681.
2. Eunice, b. 12 Nov., 1682.
3. John, b. 30 Nov., 1685.

4. Miles, b. 24 Jan., 1686-7.
5. Daniel, b. 16 Sept., 1688.

DURKEE, (*Dirkee*) FELIX, s. of Azor & Clarissa, b. 11 Sept., 1828.—*W. T. R.*

DURRAN, (wid.) fm. Southampton, L. I., d. at P. H. 2 Jan., 1828, ae. 59 yrs.— *W. C. R.*

DWIGHT, Dr. NATHANIEL, m. Rebecca (dau. Appleton) **Robbins,** 24 June, 1798; she d. 28 Apl., 1848, ae. 77.—*W. Ins.*

Dr. Dwight was a very skillful physician, educated under Dr. Cogswell of Htfd.; practiced in several places; finally located in Weth. In 1812, he relinquished practice and sett. in the ministry at Westchester; in 1820, resumed med practice at Providence, R. I., and later at Norwich, Conn. He died of Lake fever while on a visit to Oswego, N. Y., in 1821, ae. 61. Mrs. Dwight was, in her youth, a beautiful woman and a meek and devoted Christian. *Issue:*

Children (Weth. Rec.) :

1. John Allen, b. 10 Sept., 1800 ; bp. 19 Apl., 1801.—*W. C. R.*
2. George Robbins, b. 3 Nov., 1802 ; bp. 23 Oct., 1803—*W. C. R.;* m. at Weth., Sarah **Smith,** 22 Feb., 1832—*W. C. R.;* followed the sea for many years ; then sett. as a farmer in Dunkirk, N. Y., where he d. s. p., 24 Aug., 1868.
3. Theodore Mason (Rev.), b. 17 Dec., 1804 ; m. Angela **Hunt,** of New Brunswick, N. J., 16 Sept., 1833, who d. 12 Oct., 1836, at Richwood, Ga. ; he m. (2) 23 Nov., 1842, at Collinsville, Ct., Almira (dau. Alex.) **Collins,** of Midd., who d. 4 Sept., 1846,

at Gallatin, Tex. Children (*by first marr.*) : Gilbert Snowden (Dwight), b. Columbia, S. C., 2 Apl., 1835. (*By sec. marr.*) : Mason Collins (Dwight), b. Weth., 3 Oct., 1843.
4. Henry Cecil, b. 22 Oct., 1806 ; d. 27 Sept., 1807.
5. Harry Cecil, b. 6 Nov., 1807 ; a Harry Cecil d. 29 Sept., 1875, ae. 65—*W. Ins.,* hence b. 1810.
6. Nathaniel Appleton, b. 6 June, 1809 ; d. 25 July, 1809.
7. Nathaniel Appleton, b. 23 May, d. 30 Aug., 1810.

GEORGE S. Sgt. Co. K, 41st Ohio Inf., d. 14 July, 1864.—*W. Ins.*

EASTMAN, JOHN R., of Pawling, N. Y., m. Adeline **Gibbs,** 24 Nov., 1833.—
W. T. R.

EATON, ARDEN, of Castleton, Vt., m. Sarah **Combs,** 21 Jan., 1801.

EDWARDS, JOHN, early at Weth., his first rec. of ld. being ent. "the 2nd. mo.
and the 26th day, of 1641, (*Weth. Ld. Rec.* I, 220),—see also Chap. VII, Vol. I.,
Savage says "he had prob. lived at Watertown," Mass., but *Mem. Hist. Htfd.
Co.* claims him, with his s. Thomas, as of those coming together from places
other than Watertown. He had the care of the Weth. Meeting ho. 1659;
was also Town Drummer; in Feb., 1661-2 was consignee, on acc. of Mr.
Abraham Finch, of 2 hogsheads and one tierce of sugar from Barbadoes, to be
delivered a't New Lond., by Mr. John Crow of Htfd., an owner of the ship
Tryall,—a vessel built and owned in Weth.: in 1657, he bo't the homestead of
Ab'm Finch, whose wid. he marr., his first wife having d. before he came to
Weth. Mr. John Edwards d. 27 Dec., 1664. Invent. taken, 2 Mch., 1664-5,
included 9 horses and colts and 15 hogs.—*Htfd. Co. Prob. Rec.* III, 28. His
wid. Dorothy (Finch) Edwards m. (2) Thomas (or Rich.) **Towsley,** (Towsy,
or Toucey?) of Saybrook, 1676 and d. 13 Nov., 1712.

Children (Weth. Ld. Rec. II, 8; Talcott's N. Y. & N. Eng. Fam.):

1. Thomas, b. 1621; d. 27 July, 1683, ae. abt. 62.—*Weth. Rec.* FAM. 2.
2. Abraham, b. 12 Aug., 1637, acc. to *Savage;* but *Talcott* thinks by sec. wife.
(*By second marriage*):
3. John (Corp'l), b. 16 Dec., 1638; killed in King Philip's War, 1675, as appears from the following doc. in *Htfd. Co. Prob. Office,* III, 156: "The deposition of Benjamin Adams and Samuel Williams testify that, being in the late service agt. the enemy, in the Company of John Edwards of Weth., the sayd Edwards, being mortally wounded, did order that his estate should remayne to his mother, her lifetime, and after her decease, willed that his bro.

Joseph Edwards should inherit all the estate," 20 Jan., 1675; in Ct., 12 Apl., 1676. —For landed ppy, see Chapter VII, Vol. I.
4. Esther, b. June, 1641, "ae. 23 in June, last" 1664.
5. Ruth, b. Dec., 1643, "ae. 21 in Dec., last" 1664.
6. Hannah, b. Jan., 1645, "ae. 19 in Jan., last" 1664.
7. Lydia (?), b. July, 1646, "ae. — last July", 1664.
8. Joseph, b. May, 1648, "ae. 16 in 1664." FAM. 3.
(The ages given of the five children above from Invent. of father's est., 2 Mch., 1864-5. —*Htfd. Co. Prob. Rec.,* III.

FAM. 2. THOMAS,[2] (*John,*[1]) b. 1621, as may be inferred from the rec. of his dth.,
27 July, 1683. Invent. est. £61-12-00, he is called (*Weth. Rec.,*) abt. 62 yrs.
old; but is ment. by others, as arriving in New Eng. in 1635, ae. 20, which
would make him b. 1615 (see *N. Eng. Reg.,* III 184—"passengers for Virginia,
20 June, 1635,—in the *Philip,* the men have been exam. by the Minister of the
Town of Gravesend,, etc.," *Thos. Edwards,* ae. 20); lds. rec. to him *Weth. Ld.
Rec.* I, p. 49; III, 160. See also, Chapt. VII, Vol. I; seems also to have had an
interest in lds. at Totoket, (Branford), in 1647; he was made a freeman
28 Feb., 1642-3; but there is no rec. of marr. or family—only 2 daus., viz.,

1. ELIZABETH, who (acc. to *Goodwin's Notes,* pp. 54, 55), became in 1645, the first
wife of John **Goodrich,** of Weth., and who d. in childbed, 5 July, 1670,
and a dau.

2. RUTH, who (see *Weth. Ld. Rec.* II. 11, 161, 189, 252), m. Samuel **Heall,** (or
Hale), Jr., 20 June, 1670.

Thomas Edwards Invt. (in part) £118-00-00, taken 12 November, 1712 by John
Hubbard Sen., & Francis Smith. Court Record, 4 March, 1711-12, Samuel and
Mary Hale of Glastonbury gr-children. Cited to appear and take Adms.
Adms. was gr. to his son-in-law Samuel Hale "now Dec'd." Adms. unfinished
the Court now grant Adms. to Thomas Kimberly in right of his wife Ruth,
Kimberly a gr-d. to sd. Thomas Edwards. Court Record, 7 April, 1713, upon

motion of Thomas Kimberly this Court orders the Lands of Thomas Edwards late of Wethersfield Dec'd. Distributed & Divided, to Samuel Hale of Glastonbury a gr-child of the Sd. Deed. and to Mary Hale & to Ruth Kimberly the two gr-daughters of the sd. deceased.

Elizabeth (Edwards) Goodrich's 6th ch. *Hannah*, b. 1659, became the first wife of Zachariah (s. John) **Maynard**, of Sudbury, Mass., and their s. Moses Maynard, b. abt. 1702, of S., m. Lois **Stone**, of Farmingham, Mass., 1723-4; their 2d ch. and eld. s. Samuel, b. 1726, m. Sarah **Noyes;** their s. Daniel Maynard m. Hannah **Harrington**, 1776; their dau. Lucy Maynard, m. Daniel **Newton**, 1803; their s. Philo Slocum Newton, m. Elizabeth Anne **Pelton**, 1841; their dau. Anna C. Newton (to whom we are indebted for help in the Edwards gen.), m. Geo. F. **Hawley**, M. D., of Hartford, Ct., 1868.)

JOSEPH,[3] (*John*,[2] *Thos.*,[1]), m. Sarah ——————, 12 Nov., 1670; he d. 12 (10 *Prob. Rec.*), Dec., 1681; Invent. est. £162-19-04.—*Htfd. Co. Prob.;* was one of earliest sett. in Stepney parish, (Rocky Hill), see Chapt. VII, Vol. I.

Children (Weth. Rec.) :

1. Sarah, b. 20 Oct., 1671; m. —————— **Webster.**
2. Mary, b. 25 May, 1674; m. —————— **Conklin.**
3. Hannah, b. 21 Nov., 1676; m. James **But-** ler, b. May, 1703; d. 11 June, 1742.
4. John, b. 30 May, 1679. FAM. 2.
5. Dorothy, b. Sept., 1681; m. Joseph **Curtis,** 7 Dec., 1708; d. 18 Apl., 1760.

FAM. 2. JOHN,[3] (*Joseph*,[2] *Thos.*,[1]), b. 1679; m. Luce **Deming**, 15 May, 1707; he d. 25 Mch., 1716, ae. abt. 37; Invent. est. £598-04-09.—*Htfd. Co. Prob.;* fence-viewer, 1704; tithing-man Dec., 1713. See Chapt. VII, Vol. I.

Children (Weth. Rec.) :

1. Sarah, b. 16 (bp. 17—*Mix*) Dec., 1710; m. David **Goodrich**, of Glast., 1729, who d. 11 May, 1790, ae. 80, at G.; their s. John (Goodrich), m. Abigail **Deming**, as his sec. wife. His first was prob. a **Church.**
2. Ann, b. 2 Jan., 1712-13; d. 3 July, 1713.
3. John, b. 1 Aug., 1715. FAM. 3.

FAM. 3. JOHN,[4] (*John*,[3] *Joseph*,[2] *Thos.*,[1]), b. 1715; m. Rebecca **Blinn,** 23 Feb., 1743; he d. 25 Apl., 1796, in 81 yr. "John Edward's wid." d. 16 June, 1813, ae. 68.—*S. C R.*

Children (Weth. Rec.) :

1. Joseph, b. 4 Apl., 1743; prob. the J., of Midd., who m. Eleanor **Bulkely;** d. 6 Jan., 1812, in 69th yr.—*S. C. R.*
2. John, b. 5 May, 1745; d. 17 Mch., 1801, in 56th yr.—*S. C. R.*
3. Lucy, b. 26 Feb., 1747.
4. Sarah, b. 3 Mch., 1749; d. 4 Mch., 1836, in 87th yr.—*S. C. R.*
5. George, b. 13 Apl., 1751.
6. Rebecca, b. 13 Feb., 1753; d. 31 Dec., 1842, in 90 yr.—*S. C. R.*
7. Martha, b. 6 Mch., 1756.

JOSEPH EDWARDS Court Record 1st March 1725-6 Invt. 14 March 1725-6 We Subscribers being present at the dwelling house of Jonathan Pratt, in Wethersfield when Joseph Edwards lay sick and in our presence declared his will. That his lame brother Nathaniel Edwards, whom he supposed was not able to maintain himself, he gave one half of his estate and that the other half he gave to be equally divided amongst all his brothers and sisters and at the time was in his right mind etc. 5 February 1724-5; and he dyed on the 7th February; or about two days after he made his will as aforesaid Signed Jonathan Pratt. Samuel Churchill Churchill Edwards—under *Oath* Adms to Samuel Churchill & Churchill Edwards.

The following genealogy is due to the painstaking labors, (both by personal visitation and correspondence) of Mrs. GEORGE H. BUTLER, of Cromwell, Ct.

DAVID, (s. of Josiah and Mary *Churchill*) **Fdwards,** b. in E. Hampton, L. I., 6 Apl., 1707; in Mch., 1723-4, chose James Francis as his guardian.—*Htfd. Co. Prob.* He and a bro. Churchill Edwards, both served as troopers in the Canada expedition, and the two are said to have sett. N. of the Little River, which separates Cromwell (formerly "the Upper Houses" of Midd.) fm. the city of Midd.; m. Mary (dau. Joseph, s. of Dea. Richard) **Butler,** (see *Butler,* in this Vol.) b. 1703; he d. 7 Jan., 1795; she d. 10 July, 1786.

Children:

1. Anna, b. 1735 ; m. Jehiel **Williams; she** d. 30 Nov., 1810.
2. Mary, b. 1737-8 ; m. Ebenezer **Backus,** 25 Nov., 1760.
3. Sarah, b. 18 May, 1740 ; m. Rev. Edward **Eells,** Jr., 27 Jan., 1763 ; she d. 4 July, 1769.
4. Joseph, bp. 7 Mch., 1742 ; m. Eleanor **Bulkeley;** he d. 29 Feb., 1776.
5. Martha, bp. 18 Mch., 1744 ; m. Zebulon **Stocking,** 16 Apl., 1765 ; she d. 14 Nov., 1790.
6. Hepzibah, bp. 9 Feb., 1746 ; d. 23 Nov., 1796 ; m. Jeremiah **Goodrich.**
7. David, bp. 24 Dec., 1749. FAM. 3.

FAM. 2.   DAVID,[3] (*David,[2] Josiah,[1]*), bp. 1749; m. (1) Rosanna (dau. of Samuel) **Hubbard,** of Htfd., who d. 1 Oct., 1795; m. (2) 8 Sept., 1796, Mary **Wells,** of Haddam, who d. 4 Jan., 1860; he d. 23 Oct., 1825.

Children:

1. Mary, b. 6 Oct., 1797 ; d. 6 Feb., 1883 ; m. abt. 1820, Joseph C. **Johnson.**
2. Sarah, b. 17 Mch., 1799 ; m. 20 Nov., 1831, Edward P. (s. of Phineas E. & Phoebe *Dibble*) **Jones,** of Westbrook, Ct. ; she d. 30 Jan., 1886. *Issue:*
   i. Edward W. (Jones), b. 6 Sept., 1833 ; d. 1 Jan., 1834.
   ii. Edward R. (Jones), b. 22 May, 1835 ; d. 4 Feb., 1901 ; m. Martha **Parker.***
   iii. Adelaide E. (Jones), b. 29 Mch., 1838 ; m. Ralph **Stocking.**†
   iv. Wells P. (Jones), b. 14 May, 1842 ; m. Martha Laura **Parker.**‡
3. Daniel, b. 14 Feb., 1802. FAM. 3.

FAM. 3.   DAVID,[4] (*David,[3] David,[2] Josiah,[1]*), b. 1802; m. 9 July, 1841, Louisa (dau. Allen & Sally *Stocking*) **Sage,** gd-dau. of Samuel & wid. Eleanor Bulkely Edwards Sage. He d. June, 1895. She, b. 25 Dec., 1812, d. 28 Nov., 1883, ae. 72.

---

* EDWARD R. JONES m. Martha L. (dau. of Rich. & Laura Clark) **Parker,** of Cromwell. Ct., b. 19 July, 1841. *Children:*
1. Frederick Parker (Jones), b. 21 May, 1864 ; m. 28 Dec., 1886, Louise **Deming;** he d. 28 Sept., 1888. *Issue:* (a) Eunice, b. 3 Feb., 1888, in Midd. ; (b) Bessie, b. 25 July, 1889 ; d. 30 July, 1893.
2. Corrine Louise (Jones), b. 23 Apl., 1867 ; m. 18 Dec., 1889, Adolp **Miellez.** *Issue:* (a) Walter, b. 8 Oct., 1890.
3. Howard (Jones), b. 19 Sept., 1870 ; d. July, 1871.
4. Charles W. (Jones), b. 20 Sept., 1873 ; m. Eugenia (dau. Chas. & Helen *Edwards*) **Penfield,** 8 July, 1896. *Issue:* (a) Clarence Raymond, b. 25 June, 1898 ; (b) Howard Penfield, b. 10 Sept., 1899.
5. Walter Edward (Jones), b. 9 Apl., 1876 ; d. 5 Jan., 1890.
†ADELAIDE E. JONES, m. 12 June, 1836, Ralph (s. Geo. & Sarah *Pelton*) **Stocking,** b. Cromwell, 16 Apl., 1830. *Issue:*
1. Fred'k Ralph (Stocking), b. 13 Nov., 1856 ; d. 6 Feb., 1863.
2. Nellie Elizabeth (Stocking), b. 7 Aug., 1858 ; m. John **McFadyen,** of Htfd., (s. of James & Janet), 26 Jan., 1886.
3. Adelaide Edward (Stocking), b. 8 Aug., 1860 ; m. Edgar Miles (s. Geo. & Mary M. *Lewis*) **Beckley,** M. D., b. 4 July, 1856. *Issue:*
   i. Florence Daisy (Beckley), b. 2 June, 1880.
   ii. Adelaide Mary (Beckley), b. 31 Dec., 1881.
   iii. Kate Louise (Beckley), b. 15 July, 1884.
   iv. Helen Hughes (Beckley), b. 1 Aug., 18—.
   v. Eddie Stocking (Beckley), b. 19 Jan., 1900.
4. Edward Wells (Stocking), b. 4 Nov., 1862 ; m. Ida H. **Byles,** 8 Jan., 1890.
5. Herbert Latimer (Stocking), b. 21 May, 1871.
‡ WELLES P. JONES, m. Laura (dau. Rich. & Laura Clark) **Parker,** 1869. *Children:*
1. Clifton Meacham, b. 22 Feb., 1871.
2. Adelaide Martha, b. 15 May, 1872 ; m. 27 June, 1894, Andrew J. **Sommers,** of Brooklyn, N. Y. *Issue:*
   i. Clinton (Sommers), b. 3 Apl., 1895.
   ii. Andrew (Sommers), b. 20 June, 1900 ; d. 6 June, 1901.
3. Howard Wells, b. Oct., 1879 ; d. July, 1880.

Children:

1. David Arthur, b. 6 May, 1842 ; m. June 1868, Hannah **Bidwell**, Glast. ; *no issue.*
2. Ellen Louisa, b. 9 Feb., 1844 ; m. 1 Jan., 1866 (?), Charles T. **Penfield**; had dau. Eugenia, b. 12 Oct., 1868 ; m. Chas. (s. Ed. Wells) **Jones.**
3. Harriet Sage, b. 7 Mch., 1845 ; m. Jan.,

1867, Myron **Austin**, of Woodstock, Windham Co., Ct., b. 29 Jan., 1840 ; (s. of Dwight & Mary A. *Butler*) **Austin**, of Greenich, R. I. ; 9 ch.
4. Inf. d. 17 Aug., 1847.
5. Albert Allen, b. 25 Nov., 1848.
6. Ch. d. 6 Dec., 1853, ae. 11 mos.

EELLS, Rev. JOHN, of Glast., m. Sarah **Welles**, 24 Dec., 1776.—*W. T. R.*

HANNAH, m. Wakefield **Utlay**, of Pomfret, Ct., 13 July, 1799. (?)

ELLIS. (See, also, *Allis*). ABEL, d. 3 July,, 1816, ae. 60.—*C. L. C.*; THANKFUL, wid. of Abel, d. 27 Jan., 1829, in 76th yr.—*C. L. C.*; WILLIAM, had *Mary* bp. 25 Nov., 1711, *Lydia*, bp. 11 Oct., 1713—*Mix Rec..; m* Lydia **Webster**, of Weth., 16 Sept., 1816.—*W. T. R.*

ELDRIDGE, BENJAMIN, of Chatham, Mass, d. at Weth., 13 Nov., 1796. ae. 21.

CATHARINE, m. Herman **Laflin**, of Southwick, Mass., 9 July, 1806.—*W. C. R.*

ELSEN, (*Elesen, Elson, Elsing, poss. Olsen.*) ABRAHAM rec. a homestead lot in Weth. wh. he had prob. owned some time before.—See Chapt. Vol. I. ; but *Savage* thinks may have res. there some 10 yrs. before. He d. 1648; estate valued at £221; ord. lds. to be rented for 4 yrs. for support of his ch. ; gave the "lot at the Meadow gate" to the ch. of his friend B—— Gardiner; remainder to his wife Rebecca, except the ho. and home lot wh. he gave to her two sons, *Benjamin* and *Job*, after her dth.; the inference being (as he is not cred. on *Weth. Rec.* with any sons) that they were her sons by a previous marriage—tho' perhaps, going by the name of Elsen. His wid. (acc. to *Savage*) m. (2) next year. Jarvis **Mudge.**

Children (Weth. Rec.) :

1. Sarah, b. 17 Mch., 1643-44.
2. Hannah, b. 15 Aug., 1645 ; d. inf.
3. Hannah, b. 14 Aug., 1646 (incorrectly copied by *Hinman*, as "Mariah").

JOHN, (prob. bro. of Abraham), homestead rec. in 164 [7?]; m. wid. of Benjamin **Hilliard**; no issue; see *Savage*, as to his dth., prob. 1648, and that his wid. m. Thomas **Wright.** See Chapt. VII. Vol.I.

ELY, JUSTIN, Jr., of W. Spgfld., m. Abigail **Belden**, 1 Mch., 1809.

MARGARET, dau. of *Dolphin*, d. 27 July, 1768.—*S. C. R.*

EMERY, Rev. R., d. 7 Jan., 1821, ae. 26.—*N. C. R.*

EMERSON, Rev. JOSEPH, (s. Daniel & Anna *Fletcher*) **Emerson**, b. at Hollis, N. H., 13 Oct., 1777; grad. H. C., 1798; was tutor there, 1801-1803, meanwhile studying theology; was ord. pastor at Beverly, Mass., 21 Sept., 1803-1816; estab. an academy for young ladies at Byfield, Mass., taught a ladies school and served in the ministry, at Saugus, Mass., 1821-23; sett. in Weth., 1825, where he conducted a seminary for young ladies, with great success until his death, May 14, 1833, ae. 46 yrs.

Mr. Emerson m. Oct., 1803, Nancy (dau. of Ebenezer and Rebecca) **Eaton**, who was b. at Framingham, Mass., 28 May, 1779, and d. at Beverly, Mass., 15 June, 1804; he m. (2) Eleanor (dau. Thos. & Martha) **Reed**, b. Northbridge,

Mass., 19 Dec., 1777, and d. at Leicester, Mass., 7 Nov., 1808; he m. (3) 1810, Rebecca (dau. John & Rebecca *Barton*) **Hazeltine,** b. Bradford, Mass., 17 Sept., 1782; sister of Mrs. Judson, the missionary. They res. at Beverly, Byfield and Weth.

Mr. Emerson was, in his day and generation, an eminent and very successful educator, and writer of books upon educational subjects. He gave frequent and admirable lectures upon history, astromony, the Millennium, and other topics; was greatly interested in the subject of Education generally, and especially that of women—his schools being the first advanced schools for girls in this country; and Mary Lyon who founded South Hadley Seminary, and Miss Grant, the founder of Ipswich Acad., were among his pupils.

His mental activity may be inferred from the following list of his published works:

1. *Plan. and Specimens of a Reference Catechism.* 1807.
2. *A Sermon preached before the Mass. Missionary Society,* on *"Christian Economy."* Boston, 1813.
3. *Writings of Miss Fanny Woodbury,* who died at Beverly, Nov., 15, 1814, aged 23 years, selected and edited by Joseph Emerson, 1815.
4. *The Evangelical Primer,* containing a minor Doctrinal Catechism, and a minor Historical Catechism, to which is added the Westminister Assembly's Shorter Catechism. 3rd Edition, with 73 cuts. Boston 1811, 12 mo. pp. 72.
5. The same, 9th Edition, Boston, 1817, 12 mo., pp. 72.
6. The same, with new engravings, Boston, 1825, 12 mo., pp. 72. (Note. 1st edit. pub. 1809?) Of this Primer, 201,000 copies are said to have been sold.
7. *Lectures on the Millennium,* Boston, 1818, 12 mo., pp. 288.
8. *Outline of a Course of Astronomical Lectures,* with an Appendix, containing an explanation of the most important terms relating to Astronomy, Boston, 1819, 12 mo., pp. 67.
9. *A Union Catechism* founded upon Scripture History, Boston, 1821, 12 mo., pp. 120.
10. *Questions adapted to Whelpley's Compend of History,* Boston, 1816, 12 mo., pp. 60.
11. The same, Third Edition, Boston, 1821, 12 mo., pp. 60.
12. The same, Tenth Edition, Boston, 1829, 12 mo., pp. 69.
13. *Female Education.* A Discourse delivered at the Dedication of the Seminary Hall in Saugus,, Jan. 15, 1822. To which is added The Little Reckoner, consisting principally of Arithmetical Questions for Infant Minds, Boston, 1822, 12 mo., pp. 40.
14. *A Compend of History from the earliest times * * * * By Samuel Whelpley, A. M., Eighth Edition with corrections and important additions and improvements. By Rev. Joseph Emerson, Two Volumes in One, Boston (?) 1825, 8 vo.,
15. The same, New York, 8 vo., pp. 218 & 283. The above text book had many editions.
16. *Prospectus of the Female Seminary at Weth., Ct.,* comprising General Prospectus, Course of Instruction, Maxims of Education, and Regulations of the Seminary * * * * Weth., A. Francis, printer, 1826, 12 mo., pp. 60.
17. *Recitation Lectures upon the Acquisition and Communication of Thought,* proposed for the Ensuing Season, Weth., 1826, 8 vo.
18. *Letter to a Class of Young Ladies,* upon the Study of the History of the United States, Boston, 1828, 12 mo., pp., 36. (This little work, written at a period when American literature possessed but few works relating to Am. history, shows an extensive acquaintance with, and keen discrimination of such works

of the kind as had then been published; and forms, even at the present late day, an admirable introduction to a course of reading in American history. It clearly reveals in its author, the possession of a fine historic instinct and criticism.— *H. R. S.*)

19. *Letter to the Members of the Genesee Consociation, N. Y.*, together with an Explanatory Communication addressed to a Friend in Reading, Mass., Boston, 1829, 12 mo., pp. 23.

20. The same, Fourth Edition, Boston, 1829, 8 vo., pp. 15.

21. The same, Rochester, 1828.

22. The same, Brooklyn, Ct., 1829, 8 vo.

23. *Questions and Supplement to Goodrich's History of the United States*, Boston, 1831, 12 mo., pp., 204.

24. *Questions and Supplement to Watts on the Improvement of the Mind*, Boston, 1831, 12 mo., pp. 68.

25. *The Improvement of the Mind*, by Isaac Watts, D. D., with Corrections, Questions and Supplement. By Joseph Emerson, revised Stereotyped Edition, Boston, 1832, 12 mo., pp. 234.

26. *The Poetic Reader*, containing Selections from the most approved authors, designed for Exercises in Reading, Singing, Parsing, Hermeneutics, Rhetoric and Punctuation. To which are prefixed Directions for Reading, Weth., 1832, 8 vo., pp. 19 & 25.

27. The same, 1828 (?)

28. A pamphlet defending *Free Masonry*.

Publications relating to Mr. Emerson, are:

Sermon preached at the Ordination of Rev. Joseph Emerson, Beverly, Sept., 21, 1803, by Rev. Nathaniel Emmons, Salem, [1803], 8 vo., pp. 31.

The Conversion of Mrs. Eleanor Emerson, from an Account written by Herself. Am. Tract Society publication, No. 133, pp. 20.

The Christian Mourning with Hope, a Sermon delivered at Beverly, Nov. 14, 1808, on occasion of the Death of Mrs. Eleanor Emerson, late Consort of the Rev. Joseph Emerson. By Samuel Worcester, A. M. * * * * To which are annexed Writings of Mrs. Emerson, with a brief Sketch of her Life, Boston, 1809, 12 mo., pp. 120.

A reply of the Genesee Consociation to the Letter of the Rev. Joseph Emerson of Weth., Connecticut * * * Hartford, 1829, 8 vo., pp. 34.

The same, Rochester, 1829, 8 vo., pp. 43.

Life of Rev. Joseph Emerson, [with an Appendix] by Rev. Ralph Emerson, Boston, 1834, 12 mo., pp. 454.

For the above list of Mr. Emerson's works, we are indebted (as, also, in many similar cases) to Mr. Benj. Adams' careful MSS. *Bibliography of Books relating to Weth.* or written by Weth. men.

Children (From The Ipswich Emersons):

1. Nancy, b. 14 July, 1806; d. 16 Dec., 1864.
2. Luther, b. 29 Nov., 1810; m. Catharine **Minor**; d. 9 Feb., 1867.
3. Alfred, b. 5 Apl., 1812; m. 18 Oct., 1847, Martha C. **Vose**; he grad. Y. C. 1834.
4. Edwin, b. 1814; d. 1816.
5. ———, b. 1816; d. 1816.
6. Eleanor, b. 1817; d. 1819.
7. Ellen, b. Dec. 1819; d. 23 Jan., 1848.
8. Edwin, b. 1821; d. 1840.
9. John, b. 2 Apl., 1823; d. 19 Nov., 1851.
10. Ch. ae. 9 wks. bu. 4 Sept., 1828.
11. Ann Rebecca, b. 5 July, 1829; d. 24 Sept.

EUSTIS, ROSWELL, of Auburn, N. Y., m. Betsy **Wells,** 3 Oct., 1820.

EVANS, (*Evance*) JOHN, "Gentleman," rec. homestead in Weth., 1640, but he had rem. some two yrs. before to Quinnipiack (New Haven), of which town and colony he became a very prominent citizen.—See Chapt. VII, Vol. I.

EWER, Rev. SETH & Elizabeth had Harriet Newell, b. 22 Jan., 1824.—*W. T. R.*

FAIRFIELD, GEORGE H., of Htfd., m. Eunice R. **Butler,** 2 June, 1847; their inf. d. 23 Jan., 1848, in E. Htfd.— *S. C. R.*

JONATHAN T., of Pittsfield, m. Julia Ann **Butler,** 12 Nov., 1840; they had Joseph Butler, bp. 30 Apl., 1847.—*S. C. R.*

FARLEY, HENRY, was chosen chimney-viewer, 7 Dec., 1713.

FARNSWORTH, Dr. JOSEPH, (*s.* of *Joseph, s* (by his 2d wife) of the *Samuel* "of Dorchester in the Bay" who was m. 1677 to Mary (dau. of Thomas and Mary) **Stoughton,** of Windsor—(See Stiles *Anc. Windsor* II, 249) ; grad. Y. C. 1736.

FAXON, CHESTER, of W. Htfd., m. Sarah **Deming,** of W., 12 June, 1833.— *N. C. R.* Dr. JOSEPH, m. (1) Oct., 1741, Mary **Blinn**; he m. (2) Honor **Williams**; she "the wife of Dr. Joseph" d. 15 Feb., 1784.

Children (*Weth. Rec., by first marriage*) :

1. Mary, b. 1 Aug., 1742.
2. Joseph, b. 12 Aug., 1744.
3. Martha, bp. 11 May, 1746.
4. William, b. 11, bp. 12 May, 1747.

5. Philip, b. 11 Nov., 1747 (*sic*).
6. James, b. — Aug., 1749, bp. 5 Aug., 1750.
7. Abigail, b. 10 Aug., 1753 ; *W. C. R.* says bp. 22 *July* 1753.

FENNER, THOMAS, d. 1647.

FERGUSON, JAMES, d. Oct., 1834, ae. 48; his wid. d. 1 Dec., 1834, ae. 44.— *W. C. R.*

FERRE, HENRY, m. Lauretta (dau. of Jesse) **Goodrich,** 26 Sept., 1833, who d. 22 Feb., 1848, at Savannah, Geo., ae. 43; he m. (2) Mrs. Harriet J. **Smith** (dau. of the late Francis Stillman,) 1 June, 1849?—*W. T. R.*

Children :

1. James Clifford, b. 10 Mch., 1836 ; d. 23 Nov., 1870, ae. 34.
2. Helena Estelle, b. 18 Dec., 1839.

(No member of the family at present time in the town.)

FERRIS, JEFFRY, orig. at Boston; freeman at Watertown, Mass., May, 1635; next found at Weth., where he had home-lot rec. 1641—(See Chapt. VII, Vol. I) ; rem. to Stamford, with first Weth. emigration, and 1636, was among the Greenwich petit. for admission to New Haven jurisdiction. He d. 1666; for further notes see Huntington's *Hist. Stamford.*

The name Ferris derives fm. the Leicestershire house of *Friers* fm. Henry, s. of Gualchelme de Ferriers, to whom William the Conquerer gave large grants of land in Co's Stafford, Derby and Leicester. The name of *Ferre* (represented modernly in Weth.) is prob. also of the same derivation.

FIELDS, NATHAN, of E. Guilford, m. Sarah **Callender,** 29 Nov., 1801—*S. C. R.;* she was bp. 20 June, 1802.—*S. C. R.*

FRED (Fiels) of Berlin, m. wid. Oner (Honor?) **Edwards,** 28 ——, 1800.

FILLEY, JEMIMA, ae. 88, d. 23 Aug., 1844.—*W. T. R.*

FINCH, ABRAHAM, prob. fm. Watertown, where, acc. to *Winthrop,* he lost his wigwam and all his gds. by fire in Sept., 1630; was freeman, 3 Sept., at W., 1634; was at his coming to Weth., abt. 1634-5, an aged man, and called "Old Finch," in distinction fm. his s. Ab'm, who was also the head of a family. For ld-rec. see Chapt. VII, Vol. I. He had sons *Abraham, Daniel* and prob. *John.*

1. ABRAHAM, Jr., was the one who was killed in the massacre of Apl., 1636, leaving an only s., Abraham 3d, then a minor, and who was adopted by his gd-fthr., "Old Finch." His wid. Dorothy, (said by Nath'l Foote, in *Foote Geneal.* to have been a dau. of Matthew Mitchell), m. (2) John **Edwards;** and m. (3) Rich. **Tously,,** of Saybrook, but by 1676 was the 3d time a wid. The ch. by her first marr. (Abraham 3d) rem. to Saybrook with his mother, where he was a freeman in 1658; d. unm'd and gave his ppy. to his (Edwards) sisters and bros., the ch. of his mother by her 2d husband.—See, also, Chapt. VII, Vol. I.

2. DANIEL, res. Weth. 1641, and was in 1636, constable; the first officer of the kind app. in the Colony; for ld-rec. in Weth., see page 200, Vol. I; became one of the orig. pprs. of Stamford; and, 1653, rem. to Fairfield, where he m. 1657, Elizabeth (wid. John) **Thompson,** of F. and d. Mch., 1667; his will ment. s. Nath'l with gd-ch. Abraham, and 3 daus.

3. JOHN—concerning whom see Judge *S. W. A.'s* remarks on page 269, Vol. I. He d. 1657; invent. est. taken 9, 12 mo., 1658.—*Htfd. Prob. Rec.*

A. SAMUEL, is also credited by *Savage* (See Vol. II, p. 160) as res. "sometime at Weth."

FISH, ELIAKIM, m. Sarah **Launcelot,** 18 Oct., 1769.—*W. C. R.*

HORACE, of Glast., m. Abigail **Blinn,** 10 May, 1812.

ROBERT, of Weth., emigr. to Stamford, Ct., early as 1640.

FISK, BENJAMIN, of Midd., m. Sarah **Deming,** of Weth., 8 Dec., 1757.— *W. C. R.*

BENJAMIN, of Midd., m. Mary **Deming,** 30 Jan., 1766.—*W. C. R.*

ALFRED M., of Htfd., m. Sarah **Callender,** 1 May, 1843.—*S. C. R.*

FITCH, Mr. THOMAS, (s. of *Mr. Samuel* teacher in Htfd., and later of Milford, who was a rep. to Gen. Ct., 1654-55, and who m. Mrs. Mary, wid. of Worshipful Mr. Wm. Whiting, of Htfd.) was b. 1652; m. (1) Abigail (dau. William —the Settler) **Goodrich,** he m. (2) Sarah (dau. Samuel & Mary *Robbins*) **Boardman,** of Weth.; he d. intestate, 17 Oct., 1704, ae. 52—*W. R.;* invent. £111-3-0; constable, in Dec., 1679; drew ld. in 1694 allotment; was rate-maker; 1685; was Town schoolmaster in 1699, and leather-sealer, 1702; res. E. side Broad St., between ch. and Fletcher's Lane. See, also, *Boardman Geneal.,* pp.

196, 197. His 1st wife d. 8 Nov., 1684. Thomas Fitch died 18 October, 1704; Invent. £111-03-00, taken 13 Nov., 1704, by John Curtis, Sen., John Goodrich, Daniel Boardman (the children with invt.) Samuel Fitch, Abigail, the wife of Abraham Kimberly, Sibbel, the wife of Joseph Hurlbut and Martha Fitch. Court Record 26 April, 1705—Adms. to Sarah Fitch, widow relect of Thomas Fitch, dec'd.

Children (Boardman Gen.) :

1. Thomas, b. 20 July, 1681 ; d. yg.
2. Sybil, b. 2 Nov., 1684 ; d. 18 Dec., '84, "as" *Savage* says "did the mother in 5 days." *(By second marriage)* :
3. Abigail, m. Ab'm **Kimberly**, of Newton, Ct., 11 Feb., 1696 ; he was s. of Maj. Ab'm K., who was of the "Albemarle Colony," and killed in the Indian fight there, and gd-s. of Thomas K., formerly of New

Haven.—*Htfd. Times*, 16 June, 1902.
4. Sybil, m. Joseph **Hurlbut**, 27 Apl., 1704 ; for ch.—see *H. Geneal.*
5. Martha, d. unm. 2 Feb., 1713—*W. R.;* her invent. of estate, taken 3 Sept., 1713— val. £8-12-08 ; adm. gr. to her mother.
6. Samuel, b. before 1697—in 1713, being then a minor, chose William Whiting to be his guardian.

FLAGG, SAMUEL, adm. to full comm. in New South ch. of Boston, 5 Apl., 1727; adm. to full comm. in 1st ch. of Htfd., 1 Mch., 1740-1, by letter fm. Rev. Mr. Checkly; and he and wife bu. in gds. of said ch. in Htfd. He d. 30 Apl., 1757; wid. d. 22 Mch., 1769. He left est. val. £130-09-00; will gave wife ½ of real est. for life and 1/3 chattels forever; also names daus. *Sarah* and *Elizabeth,* whose names do not appear on *Ch. Recs.* He m. 24 Dec., 1730, Sarah (dau. Jonathan & Sarah *Sanford*) **Bunce**, of Htfd.

Children (Weth. Rec.) :

1. Sarah, b. 14 Dec., 1731 ; prob. the ch. rec. in *Mix MS.* under date of 12th Feb., as "Flagg's first ch."—*Weth. Ch. Rec.*
2. Mary, bp. 19 Aug., 1733.
3. Samuel, bp. 21 Mch., 1735-6. FAM.
4. Abigail, bp. 26 Mch., 1738.
5. Joseph, bp. 9 Mch., 1739-40.
6. Hannah, bp. 3 Jan., 1740-1.
7. Susanna, bp. 23 Sept., 1743.
8. Jonathan, bp. 1 Sept., 1745.
9. Benjamin, bp. 18 Mch., 1753.

FAM. 2. Dr. SAMUEL,[2] (*Samuel,*[1]), m. 22 May, 1760, Martha **Bigelow**, of Htfd.; res. in E. Htfd., practiced medicine; was one of the first members of the Conn. Med. Soc. He d. 20 Nov., 1814.

Children:

1. Martha.
2. James.
3. Samuel (Dr.), b. 2 Apl., 1766 ; m. Mary **Wyles**; d. in Bernardston, Mass., 30 July, 1804.
4. William.
5. Hezekiah.
6. Elizabeth.
7. Soffa (Sophia?).

(*Assistance acknowledged from Stanley G.* Flagg, Esq., of Philadelphia, Pa.)

ABIJAH, m. Thankful **Seymour**, 7 Feb., 1782; she bp. 15 Dec., 1793.—*N. C. R.*

ABIJAH, of Htfd., m. Thankful **Woodhouse**, 20 Nov., 1791.

BENJAMIN B., m. Hannah **Meeks**, 24 Sept., 1823.

FLETCHER, JOHN, from Watertown, abt. 1635, homestead rec. 16 Mch., 1640 (See Chapt. VII, Vol. I) ; m. dau. of wid. Joyce **Ward**, before 1640.—*See Savage.*

FLINT, ALLAMEN, of E. Htfd., m. Sally **Deming**, 4 June, 1807 ; AMANDA A., m. James **Benton**, 9 May, 1833; HIRAM, d. 14 Apl., 1840, in 24th yr.—*S. C. R.;* JANE A., of Ry-H., m. Wm. F. **Whitney**, of Harvard, Mass., 1 Jan., 1840; JARED W., of Ry-H., m. Sally **Frances**, 20 Nov., 1828; JARED W., d. 31 Dec., 1841, in 37th yr.—*S. C. R.;* JOHN'S dau. ae. 4, bu. 2 Dec., 1813; JOHN, d. 31 Aug., 1854, ae. 76—*S. C. R.;* JOHN, m. Mary **Ackley**, 18 Nov., 1804—*W. C. R.;*

JOHN'S wife d. 30 Aug., 1847, in 65th yr.—*S. C. R.; JOHN* F., ch. of, d. Palmer, Mass., 16 Oct., 1846—*S. C. R.*, in 3d yr.; MARY, (prob. wife of Joshua) bu. 18 Jan., 1830, ae. 53—*S. C R.; MARY* C., of Ry-H., m. Asaph U. (or N.) **Thomas,** of New Britain, Ct., 29 Nov., 1835.

RAY, m. Mary **Kilby,** 3 Feb., 1774; he d. ae. 78; bu. 6 Feb., 1826; had (*W. Ch. Recs.*) :

1. Mary, bp. 18 Dec., 1774.
2. Melly, bp. 21 July, 1776.
3. Joshua, bp. 30 Aug., 1778; prob. the J. who d. 14 Jan., 1830, ae. 51.—*W. C. R.*
4. Polly, bp. 1 Apl., 1781; may be the P. who m. Robert **Starkweather,** of E. Windsor, 21 Sept., 1806.
5. James, bp. 27 Apl., 1783; poss. the J. of

Ray. bu. 4 Sept., 1783.
6. Rhoda, bp. 15 or 18 Aug., 1784.
7. Rebecca, bp. 18 Mch., 1787; prob. the R. who m. Martyn **Cables,** of Htfd., 23 Feb., 1806.
8. James, bp. 20 Nov., 1791.
9. William, bp. 20 Nov., 1791.

WILLIAM, m. Harriet **Abby,** 9 June, 1814.

FLOOD, (*Floyd*) ROBERT, sett. 1677, on lds. in Rocky Hill, gr. by Town—(See Chapt. VII, Vol. I) See *Savage.* He m. Abigail ————, he d. 16 Dec., 1689, ae. abt. 43; invent. of his est. (val. £117-14-00) taken 6 Feb., 1689-90; his wid. m. (2) before 1695 Matthew **Barnes.**

Children (*Weth. Rec.*) :

1. George, b. 7 Aug., 1670 ; d. 20 July, 1683.
2. Robert, b. 18 Mch., 1674 ; drowned 20 June, 1684.
3. Abigail, b. 26 Mch., 1676.

4. John, b. 27 Apl., 1678.
5. Thomas, b. 15 Aug., 1680.
6. Mary, b. 6 Jan., 1682.
7. George, b. 28 Jan., 1685.

MARY had *Lucy Welles,* b. 22 Nov., 1756

FLOWER, (*Flowers*). Assistance on this family acknowledged fm. Mrs. M. E. FLOWER SMITH, of Chicago, Ill. A *Flower Geneal.* was pub. some yrs. ago, by Albert Welles in the *Am. Fam. Antiquarian.* It is understood that a geneal. of the Virginia and Maryland families of this name, is in preparation by Col. C. Dudley Teetor, of New York City.

LAMROCK, first of the name in Conn. appears at Htfd., 1684 or '85; b. at Whitwell, Co. Rutland, Eng., 1660; m. 1686, Lydia (dau. of Joseph) **Smith;** by his wife Lydia, who was a gd-dau. of Rev. Ephraim Huit of Windsor, see Stiles' Hist. *Ancient Windsor,* Ct., Vol II, p. 415, had 8 ch. of whom

FAM. 2. JOSEPH,[2] b. 24 July, 1706, m. 25 Oct., 1727, Sarah (dau. Sgt. Samuel) **Wright,** of Htfd., b. 25 Apl., 1706. He d. 20 Feb., 1869.

Children (*Weth. Rec.*) :

1. Sarah, b. 26 Nov., (bp. 8 Dec., *Mix MSS.*) 1728; m. Nath'l **Leonard,** of Sheffield, Mass. *Issue:*
  i. Huldah (Leonard).
  ii. Sarah (Leonard).
  iii. Nathaniel (Leonard).
  iv. Mary (Leonard), ⎫ twins.
  v. Lucy (Leonard), ⎭
  vi. Abigail (Leonard).
  vii. Nathaniel (Leonard), m. ———— **Tibbitts.**
2. Joseph, b. 15 (bp. 22 *Mix MSS.*) Mch., 1729-30. FAM. 3.
3. Ozias, b. 22 Dec., 1731. FAM. 4.
4. Rebecca, b. 13 (bp. 18, *Mix MSS.*) Nov., 1733 ; m. Capt. Nath'l **Saltonstall,** of New London. *Issue:*
  i. Gurdon F. (Saltonstall), b. 18 May, 1750 ; d. at Cincinnati, O., 1836, ae. 78.

ii. Rebecca (Saltonstall), b. 1756; m. 1778, Wm. **Evans,** of Newark ; family rem. to Marietta, O., and, after her dth. to Cleveland, O.
  iii. Sarah (Saltonstall), b. 1758.
  iv. Joseph L. (Saltonstall), b. 8 June, 1763.
5. Lydia, b. 9 Sept., 1735; m. (1) Daniel **Granger;** m. (2) Sam. **Polmeo.**
6. Abigail, b. 17 July, 1737 ; m. Jesse **McIntire.**
7. Luce, b. 12 Apl., 1739 ; m. (1) ———— **King;** m. (2) Dr. Timo. **Horton.**
8. Samuel, b. 17 Jan., 1741-2. FAM. 5.
9. Timothy, b. 12 (bp. 16) Oct., 1743. FAM. 6.
10. Elisha, b. 10 (bp. 22) June, 1746 ; rem. to Natchez, Miss., and d. there.
11. Josiah, b. 17 Apl., 1748; rem. to and d. at Natchez, Miss.

FAM. 3. JOSEPH, (Joseph,[2] Lamrock,[1]), b. 1730; m. 20 Jan., 1749, Hannah **Pierce,**
of Weth. He d. 29 Sept., 1793—Weth. Ins.; she, b. 9 Oct., 1733, d. 26 Dec.,
1794, in 61st yr.—Weth. Ins.

Children (Weth. Rec.) :

1. William, b. 5 Oct., 1751; m. Hannah
   Flower, a cousin, of Ashfield, Mass.; their
   s. Phincas,[5] b. 1779, m. Rebecca Jones;
   their s. Calvin,[6] b. 1814; m. Hannah
   Phillips; their s. James M.,[7] b. 1835, m.
   Lucy L. Cones; their s. Elliott,[8] poet and
   writer.
2. Hannah, b. 10 (bp. 13) Jan., 1754; m. 1796,
   John Burgee.
3. Rhoda, b. 1 (bp. 6) June, 1756; m. 1773,
   Elias Griswold.
4. Elizabeth, b. 7 (bp. 14 ?) Sept., 1758; m.
   23 Jan., 1777, Joseph Dodge; both of Weth.
   —N. C. R.
5. Simeon, b. 14 Jan., 1760-1. FAM. 7.
6. Joseph, b. 14 June, 1763; m. 19 Nov., 1783,
   Mehitable Curtis.
7. Sarah, b. 14 Dec., 1765; m. (1) Jesse
   Deming; m. (2) a Belden; her dau.,
   Sarah Deming (by 1st husband), b. 7 May,
   1808; m. Francis Griswold; res. at Midd.,
   Ct. Issue:
      i. Louise (Griswold), m. Apollos Mark-
         ham.
     ii. Florence (Griswold), m. ——— Pat-

terson; res. Bridgeport, Ct.
  iii. Robert, res. Weth.
   iv. Albert, m. Mary Ann Griswold; res.
       (1889) at Rocky Hill, Ct.
    v. Harriet, m. ——— Williams, New
       Britain, Ct.
   vi. Florence, m. ——— Viberts, of
       Manchester, Ct.
  vii. Elizabeth, ⎫ school teachers.
 viii. Sarah,   ⎭
   ix. Jenie.
    x. Everett.
       (By second marriage) :
   xi. Lois (Belden), b. 3rd Mch., 1781; d.
       1826; m Joseph Warren Flower.
8. James, b. 23 (bp. 27) Mch., 1768.
9. Rebecca, b. 8 (bp. 14) Oct., 1770.
10. George Gardiner, b. 30 May, 1773 (1776,
    Weth. Rec.), bp. 15 Aug., 1779; m. Re-
    becca Deming, 21 Apl., 1795.
11. Artemus, b. 10 Oct., 1778, bp. 15 Aug.,
    1779; m. Mary ——— (Weth. C. Rec.),
    which also gives bp. of their dau. Caro-
    line, 24 Mch., 1809, and of a ch. who d.,
    ae. 3 mos., bu. 18 Oct., 1805.

FAM. 4. OZIAS,[3] (Joseph,[2] Lamrock,[1]), b. 1731; m. (1) ———; m. (2) 6 Mch.,
1775, Abigail **Miller.** He d. at Feeding Hills, Mass.

Children :

1. Belinda, b. 9 May, 1781; m. 1787, Ranford
   Rogers.
2. Rebecca, b. 26 May, 1767.

3. Josiah, b. 26 Sept., 1771.
4. Horace. b. 11 Sept., 1773. FAM. 8.
5. Frederick.

FAM. 5. Col. SAMUEL,[3] (Joseph,[2] Lamrock,[1]), b. 1742; m. 21 June, 1770, Sarah
McIntire, who d. 2 June, 1808, ae. 61; he d. at Feeding Hills, Mass., 28 Oct.,
1815. For Col. F's Revol. services, see Mass. Soldiers and Sailors of War of
Revol., V. 809, also, Flower Geneal.

Children :

1. Sarah, b. 31 Jan., 1772; m. 1790, Ebenezer
   Ripley, of Feeding Hills, Mass. Issue:
      i. Lester (Ripley), b. 11 Dec., 1792; d.
         Richmond, Pa.
     ii. Alfred (Ripley), b. 9 Nov., 1794; d.
         at Sullivan, Pa.
    iii. William Cooper (Ripley), b. 13 Oct.,
         1797.
     iv. Francis (Ripley), b. 20 Jan., 1802; d.
         1806.
      v. Nancy (Ripley), b. 2 Jan., 1804.
     vi. Lucy (Ripley), b. 14 Apl., 1806.
    vii. Samuel (Ripley), b. 25 Nov., 1808.

 viii. Dwight (Ripley), b. 12 July, 1812.
2. Francis, b. 29 July, 1773.
3. Samuel, b. 9 May, 1775.
4. Henry, b. 23 Apl., 1777; poss. the Henry
   who m. Lydia Horton (?), both of Springfield, 29 Jan., 1806.
5. Alfred, b. 6 June, 1780; m. Harriet
   Leonard.
6. Lucy, b. 5 Aug., 1783; m. 1808, John G.
   Norton.
7. Elisha, b. 8 Apl., 1786.
8. Nancy, b. 15 Oct., 1790.

FAM. 6. TIMOTHY,[3] (Joseph,[2] Lamrock,[1]), b. 1743; m. (1) 1766, Anna **Smith,**
of Lyons, Ct.; m. (2) 24 May, 1784, Hannah **Spencer,** of Somers, Ct.; m. (3)
14 Dec., 1809, Martha **Jones,** of Groton, Ct. He d. 18 Oct., 1834.

Children :

1. Roswell, b. 27 May, 1767. FAM. 9.
2. Anna, b. 29 Apl., 1769; m. Joseph Phelan,
   Esq.
3. Timothy, b. 26 Oct., 1771. FAM. 10.
4. Betsy, b. 25 Nov., 1773.
5. Lydia, b. 6 Jan., 1776.

6. Joseph Warren, b. 10 May, 1778. FAM. 11.
7. Bernice, b. 9 Aug., 1780.
   (By second marriage) :
8. Spencer, b. 3 Jan., 1785. FAM. 12.
9. Ebenezer, b. 3 Sept., 1787. FAM. 13.
10. Daniel, b. 19 Oct., 1790.

FAM. 7. SIMEON,[4] (*Joseph*,[3] *Joseph*,[2] *Lamrock*,[1]), b. 1761; m. 3 Jan., 1778, Honor **Montague,** of Weth.; she d. ae. 70; bu. 23 Feb., 1831.—*W. C. R.*

Children:

1. Joseph.
2. James.
3. Harriet, b. 1796, d. 1865; m. Thomas Lock-row. *Issue* (b. Berlin, Ct.):
   i. Mary Ann (Lockrow), m. Joseph **Plodwell.**
   ii. Sophia (Lockrow), m. Edwin C. **Pinks.**
   iii. Caroline (Lockrow), b. 1824, d. 1883;

m. Hilliard Earl **Sawyer;** had:
i. Delancy P. (Sawyer), So. Meriden, Ct.
ii. Sarah A. (Sawyer).
iii. Chas. Hilliard (Sawyer), res. Vinita, Ind. Ter.
iv. Chas. H. (Sawyer), Lancaster, O.
4. David B., b. 11 Sept., 1802; m. 1825, Frances **Whipple.**

FAM. 8. HORACE,[4] (*Ozias*,[3] *Joseph*,[2] *Lamrock*,[1]), b. 1773; m. Artemesia (dau. Maj.) **McIntire,** and b. Feeding Hills, Mass. Her father was a Revol. soldier. Mr. Horace Flower was a noted Latin scholar in his day.

Children:

1. Honor, b. 6 Aug., 1795.
2. Frederick, b. 11 July, 1797; m. 1820, Kezia **Hallock;** he d. 1879.
3. Frances, b. 9 Aug., 1799.
4. Horace, b. 9 Oct., 1801.
5. Josiah, b. 19 June, 1803; m. 1833, Mary **McCreary.**
6. Daniel Ostrander, b. 14 May, 1809; m. Harriet **Cable.**
7. Marvin, b. 12 Apl., 1812; m. 1839, Almira **Hitchcock;** 7 ch.
8. Marcus T. C., b. 8 Oct., 1814. FAM. 14.
9. Ann, b. 1818; d. Oct., 1885.

FAM. 9. ROSWELL,[4] (*Timo.*,[3] *Joseph*,[2] *Lamrock*,[1]), b. 1767; m. 5 Dec., 1794, Huldah **Austin,** of Rupert, Vt.

Children:

1. Joseph, b. 27 Jan., 1795; m. Maria Flower **Leonard.** FAM. 15.
2. Betsy, b. 10 Feb., 1797; m. 11 Dec., 1834, James **Weed.**
3. Abigail, b. 5 Mch., 1799; m. James **Shelton.**
4. Roswell A., b. 18 Dec., 1803; d. 1807.
5. Emily, b. 13 Jan., 1806; m. Grandison **Sherman;** she d. 1879.
6. Julia, b. 19 Jan., 1807; m. 1827, Morehouse **Sherman.**
7. Roswell, b. Dec., 1808; m. 1838, Phebe **Peek;** rem. to Iowa, 1866; his s. Dr. Dwight Flower, is a prominent phys. at Monticello, Wis.
8. Huldah, b. 25 Apl., 1811; m. Fred. **Cramer.**
9. Anna, b. 22 Oct., 1814; m. Fred. **Brewer.**

FAM. 10. TIMOTHY,[4] (*Timo.*,[3] *Joseph*,[2] *Lamrock*,[1]), b. 1771; m. Feb. 17, 1800, Clarissa **Phillips,** who was b. 16 Feb., 1785, and d. 11 Apl., 1863? He d. 17 Jan., 1869, ae. 90; res. W. Rupert, Vt.

Children:

1. Elizabeth, b. 2 July, 1802; m. Warner **Hopkins.**
2. Clarissa, b. 22 June, 1804; m. Gus. **Wyman.**
3. Bernice, b. 29 Aug., 1806; m. ———— **Comstock.**
4. Thankful, b. 29 Apl., 1809; m. Silas **Spencer.**
5. Timothy, b. 11 Nov., 1811; d. unm. 1890.
5. Elihu, b. 27 Aug., 1813; d. 1897; m. Theodora **Hastings.**
7. Horace, b. 13 Feb., 1816; m. Delia **Rogers.**
8. LeGrand, b. 9 June, 1819; d. 12 May, 1870.
9. Cynthia, b. 11 Mch., 1821; d. unm.
10. Lydia H., b. 14 July, 1823; m. Sol. **Moore.**
11. Lucinda, b. 19 Oct., 1827; m. St. John **Sanborn.**

FAM. 11. JOSEPH WARREN,[4] (*Timo.*,[3] *Joseph*,[2] *Lamrock*,[1]), b. 1778; m. (1) (and is then named as of W. Springfield, Mass.) 6 Feb., 1797, Lois (dau. V. & Sarah *Flower*) **Belden,** who was b. 3 Mch., 1781, at Weth., and d. 28 Nov., 1826; Joseph Warren Flower m. (2) Ann **Stephens;** he d. 1834, at Clayton, Jeff. Co., N. Y.

Children (b. Weth.):

1. Henrietta, d. inf.; prob. the ch., ae. 13 mos., bu. 16 Aug., 1798.—*W. C. R.*
2. Lorenzo Warren, b. 25 July, 1800; d. 1822.
3. Mahala Deming, b. Mch., 1802; m. Moses **Harmon,** of Clayton, N. Y.
4. Henry, b. 30 June, 1805; d. inf.
5. Louisa Henrietta, b. twin to above; m.

Rev. Elisha Pratt **Cook,** of Lorraine, N. Y.; d. 25 Dec., 1876, at Oswego, N. Y. *Issue:*
i. Helen Maria (Cook), b. 12 Apl., 1824.
ii. Byron Flower (Cook), b. 8 June, 1826; d. 1858.
iii. Mahala Antoinette (Cook), b. 4 Nov.,

1828; d. Apl., 1891; m. J. **McLean**, of Oswego, N. Y.; had: (a) Mary Elizabeth (McLean), m. Mr. ————, of Chicago; (b) Louisa (McLean), m. ————; (c) Frank Flower (Mc-Lean), of N. Y. City.
6. Timothy Smith Madison, b. 22 May, 1808; d. 13 Oct., 1863.
7. Joseph Manly, b. 28 Feb., 1812; d. 10 Apl., 1853.
8. Sarah Ann (b. Lorraine, N. Y.); m.

Perly **Wickes.**
9. Elam LeGrand, b. Apl., 1819; d. at Weeping Waters, Neb., of which place he was a pioneer.
(By second marriage):
10. George Warren, b. Clayton, N. Y.
11. Stephen Warren, b. 21 Aug., 1832, at Clayton, N. Y.; res. (1901) Toledo, O.; wealthy and memb. Bd. of trade; m. Nellie ————; s. p.

FAM. 12. SPENCER,[4] (*Timo.,[3] Joseph,[2] Lamrock,[1]*), b. 1785; res. Feeding Hills, Mass.

Children:

1. Lester, b. 10 Aug., 1807; d. 24 Mch., 1895, at Htfd., Ct.
2. Hannah, b. 19 Mch., 1809; m. ———— **Holliday**; d. 9 May, 1899.
3. Julia, b. 2 Mch., 1811; m. ———— **Ely.**
4. Nancy, b. 5 Apl., 1813; m. ———— **Worthington**; d. 9 May, 1882.
5. Spencer L., b. 8 Aug., 1815; res. Htfd.,

Ct., (1900).
6. Cornelius, b. 1 Apl., 1818; d. 18 July, 1888.
7. Homer, b. 26 Apl., 1820; d. 23 Apl., 1868.
Issue:
　i. Homer, of Feeding Hills, Mass.
　ii. Mrs. Lois M. **Smith**, of W. Htfd., Ct.
8. Henry E., b. 15 Nov., 1822.

FAM. 13. EBENEZER,[4] (*Timo.,[3] Joseph,[2] Lamrock,[1]*), b. 1787; m. Ann **Granger,** of Feeding Hills, Mass., b. 1781, was a prominent and wealthly business man of Htfd., of which city he was at one time (1853) Mayor; an active memb. of Episc. ch. and owner of lines of steamboats plying betw. Htfd. and New York and Boston.

Children:

1. Margaret, b. Sept., 1819; d. 24 Feb., 1834.
2. Henrietta, b. ————; d. 19 Apl., 1834.

The death of these ladies was signalized by a poem written by Mrs. Sigourney.

FAM. 14. MARCUS T. C.,[5] (*Horace,[4] Ozias,[3] Joseph,[2] Lamrock,[1]*), b. 1814; m. 20 Nov., 1836, at Comorant, O., Sybil **Brooks;** res. (1900) at St. Paul, Minn.

Children:

1. Cordelia, b. Dec., 1838.
2. Mark D. (Gen.), b. 31 Mch., 1842; enl. as private in Co. C, 7th Reg., Ill. Vol., Apl., 1861, until Aug., same yr., when term expired and he re-enlisted July, 1862, in Co. A, 36th, Reg., Ill. Inf. Vols. for 3 yrs., or during the war. June, 1863; was prom. Capt., and served as Asst. Adjt-Gen. until

June, 1865, when he was hon. mustered out, and rem. to Minn., where (Mch., 1867) he was app. Adjt-Gen. of the State of Minn., which he resigned after 6 yrs. incumbency. Res. in St. Paul, Minn.; has dau. *Grace.*
3. Lydia, b. 25 Oct., 1853.
4. May, b. 18 Apl., 1860.

FAM. 15. JOSEPH,[5] (*Roswell,[4] Timo.,[3] Joseph,[2] Lamrock,[1]*), b. 1795; m. 1820. Maria Flower **Leonard.**

Children:

1. Mary, m. Wm. **Stearns.**
2. Dwight, d. yg.
3. Byron, b. 1838; d. (as a Surgeon) in War of Civil Rebell., 1863.

4. Julia, m. Henry **Smith**; their only s. Kirby Flower (Smith) is (1900) Prof. in John Hopkins Univ., Baltimore, Md.

JOSEPH, m. Mary **Francis**, 29 Nov., 1821.—*W. T. R.*

MARY W., m. Edward D. **Wills**, of Htfd., 25 Oct., 1846.

WILLIAM, of Willimantic, Ct., m. E. Maria **Pilsbury**, of Weth., 18 Dec., 1849.— *W. T. R.*

FOOTE. This most reputable Conn. family, commenced its American history in Weth., yet, owing to an apparently inconquerable migratory tendency in its earlier representatives, the *name* had entirely disappeared from the town by the end of the third generation. Through its various early intermarriages with other Weth. families, however, the history of these early generations possess

Colchester, Conn., and Hadley, Hatfield, Deerfield and other old towns in Western Mass. The family has also been fortunate in having had its history written by a competent hand, half a century ago.*

NATHANIEL FOOTE, the emigrant ancestor, b. Eng. 1593, came to New England with his wife Elizabeth (sister of Mr. John **Deming**, also one of Weth's first settlers, for many years a Magistrate of the Conn. Colony and one of the patentees named in its Charter) whom he had married about 1615, in England. They had seven children, all, with, perhaps, the exception of the youngest, born in England.

It is by no means certain that Mr. Foote, as some have asserted, was the *first* settler at Weth., but it is probably true that he was one of the first ten men, known as "adventurers," who absolutely first settled here; and that he was the largest holder of so-called "Adventurer's lands." In the original lay-out of the town, 1640, he received a home-lot of ten acres, at South End of Broad St., East side, and gradually became the owner of other pieces of ld., partly in the Great Meadow, east of his home-lot, and amounting in all to over 400 acres. See Chapt. VII, Vol. I. In 1641-2-4, he represented the town in the General Court,* an, evidence of the respect and confidence in which he seems to have been held by his fellow-townsmen. In May 1637, when the little army under Capt. John Mason was being provisioned for the memorable Pequot campaign, it was "ordered yᵗ that there shalbe 1 hogg pʳvided att Wythersfeild for the design in hand, wch. [*i. e.* the *hogg*, not the expedition] is conceived to be Nathaniell Footes"—a compliment, certainly from the Col. authorities, to Mr. Foote's ability in raising good pork!

His wife was Elizabeth Deming, whom he m. in Eng., abt. 1615. He d. in 1644, ae. abt. 51 yrs.; his wid. m. (2) abt. 1646, Mr. Thomas **Welles**, Magistrate, afterwards Governor of the Colony, whom also she survived, dying 28 July, 1683, ae. abt. 88 yrs. That she was a woman of character and a good wife, is evidenced by the fact that her first husband (Foote) dying intestate, she was by the Particular Court to whom the inventory of his estate was presented, "admitted to administer the estate;" and by the will of her second husband (Welles) "she was to enjoy and improve" his whole estate, so long as she remained a widow, · · · · "that she may keep the better hospitality."

A conspicuous feature in the history of the first generations of the Foote family, is the deaths, sufferings and captivities of its members, and of those connected with them by marriage, at the hands of the Indians.

Child (*Weth. Rec.*) :

1. Nathaniel, b. Eng., abt. 1620. FAM. 2.
2. Robert (Lieut.), b. Eng., abt. 1627; m. (says *Savage*) Sarah ——, 1659 ;* rem. to Wallingford, Ct.; d. ae. 52; his wid. m. 1686, Aaron **Blachley**, of Branford, and later rem. to Guilford, Ct.; Foote's ch. were 8, b. betw. 1660 and 1672.—See Goodwin's *Geneal. Foote Fam.*
3. Elizabeth, b. Eng., abt. 1616 ; m. Josiah **Churchill**, of Weth., 1638, who d. abt. 1 Jan., 1686; she d. 8 Sept., 1700; 7 ch.; see *Churchill.*
4. Mary, b. Eng., abt. 1623 ; m. (1) 1642, John **Stoddard**, of Weth., who d. 1664 ; m. (2) 1674, John **Goodrich**, Sen., of Weth., who d. 1680 ; m. (3) Lieut. Thos. **Tracy**, of Norwich, Ct., who d. 1685 ; Mrs. Mary (Stoddard-Goodrich) Tracy d. ———— ; had 7 ch., all by first husband.—See *Stoddard.*
5. Frances, b. Eng., abt. 1629 ; m. (1) 1648, John **Dickenson**, of Weth., but later of

* THE FOOTE FAMILY, or the descendants of Nathaniel Foote, one of the first settlers of Weth., Conn. * * * * By Nathaniel Goodwin, Hartford, Press, of Case, Tiffany and Co., 1849, 8 vo., xlvi, 360 pp.
* *Conn. Col. Rec.*, I, 6, 7, 69, 70-113.
* We owe it to Mr. JAMES SHEPARD, of New Britain, Conn., that we now have this Sarah's full name. She was the dau. of Wm. Potter and after Foote's death, she m. Aaron **Blatchley**, or Blakesley, as rec. in the following item from the *New Haven Ld. Rec.*, Vol. V, p. 130 : "Sarah **Blachley**, *alias* **Foote**, *alias* **Potter**, acknowledges that she has received her full share in the estate of her father, William Potter, of New Haven, deceased—23 Aug., 1796.

Hadley, Mass., who d. 1676; m. (2) 1677, Francis **Barnard**, of Htfd., later of Hadley, as his second wife; had 10 ch., all by first husband.*
6. **Sarah**, b. abt. 1632; m. 1652, Jeremiah **Judson**, of Stratford; she d. 1673, ae. abt. 41; he m. (2) wid. Cath. **Fairchild**; she had 7 ch.—See Goodwin's *Geneal. Notes.*
7. **Rebecca**, b. abt. 1634; m. (1) abt. 1657, to Lieut. Philip **Smith**, orig. of Weth., later (after 1659) of Hadley, Mass., who d. 19 Jan., 1685; "murdered with an hideous

witchcraft," of which Rev. Cotton Mather's account will be found in Chapter XIII, Vol. I, of this History. Mrs. Philip Smith m. (2) Maj. Aaron **Cooke**, of Windsor, Ct., and later a first settler of Northampton, Mass., 2 Oct., 1688, she being then 54 and he 78 yrs. of age; he d. 1690, ae. 80, and Mrs. Cooke d. 6 Apl., 1701, ae. 67. By Lieut. Smith, she had 8 ch., concerning whom see Goodwin's *Geneal. Notes;* also our *Smith* and *Stillman Genealogies.*

FAM. 2. NATHANIEL,[2] (*Nath'l,*[1]), b. abt. 1620; m. 1646, ld-owner in Weth., see Chapt. VII, Vol. I, Elizabeth (dau. Lieut. Samuel) **Smith,** of Weth., later of Hadley, Mass.; he d. 1655, ae. 34; wid. m. (2) Wm. **Gull,** of Weth., later of Hadley, by whom she had 4 ch. She survived her second husband. Will and invent. dated 23 Sept., 1656.—See State Off., Vol. 2.

Children:

1. Nathaniel, b. 10 Jan., 1647. FAM. 3.
2. Samuel, b. 1 May, 1649; was of Hatfield; m. Mary **Merrick,** of Springfield, Mass., 1671; d. 7 Sept., 1689; his second s. Samuel was slain by Ind., at Deerfield, 1704; for descts. see Judd's *Hadley,* p. 495.
3. Daniel, b. 1652, was of Stratford, Ct.; m. (1) Sarah ————; m. (2) May.
————.
4. Elizabeth, b. 1654; m. 10 Nov., 1670, Daniel (s. of Wm.) **Belden,** of Hatfield, but later

of Deerfield, Mass.; but b. Weth., 30 Nov., 1648, and d. at D., 14 Aug., 1732; his wife was killed by Ind., 16 Sept., 1696.—*Hatf. T. Rec.* At the attack in Deerfield, Sept. 26, 1696, at which time, also, the following of their 14 ch. were capt., wdd. or killed by Ind., viz.: *Elizabeth,* b. 1673, capt.; *Esther,* b. 1683, capt.; *Samuel,* b. 1687, severely wdd.; *Abigail,* b. 1690, wdd.; and *John,* b. 1693, and *Thankful,* b. 1695, killed.

FAM. 3 . Quarter-Master NATHANIEL,[3] (*Nath'l,*[2] *Nath'l,*[1]), b. 1647; m. Margaret (dau. Nath'l & Margaret) **Bliss,** of Springfield, Mass., 2 May, 1672; sett. Hatfield, Mass., where he res. two yrs.; then res. successively at Stratford, Bramford and finally at Weth., (See Chapt. VII, Vol. I), where he d. 12 Jan., 1703. ae. 55 yrs. 2 days; wid. d. Colchester, Ct., 3 Apl., 1745, ae. 95. His death prevented another removal which he had planned, to a new settlement prospected by him at "Jeremy Farms" since called Colchester, Ct., which was on ld. gr. to Mr. F. by the Ind., "as a consideration of love and affection" to be utilized as he saw fit, except 50 acres which they desired him to reserve for himself and heirs forever. The settlement was commenced in 1710—but failing health prevented his being one of the company, and his wife and ch. after his dth. became the first settlers of Colchester. Mr. Foote was a house-carpenter and also practiced as an attorney in the Colonial Courts.

Children (Weth. Rec., except the two eldest daus.) who were b. Hatfield:

1. Sarah, b. 1672; m. Thos. **Olcott,** of Htfd.
2. Margaret, b. 1 Dec., 1674.
3. Elizabeth, b. 23 June, 1677-9; m. Robt. **Turner,** of Weth.; later of Coventry, Ct.
4. Mary, b. 24 Nov., 1679; m. Daniel **Rose,** of Weth.; later of Coventry, Ct.
5. Nathaniel,* b. 9 Sept., 1682. FAM. 4.
6. Ephraim, b. 11 Feb., 1685.
7. Josiah, b. 27 Sept., 1688.
8. Joseph, b. 28 Dec., 1690; of Htfd. and Colchester; m. 12 Dec., 1719, Ann **Clothier,** prob. of N. Lond. (*Htfd. Times*), 25 Mch., 1901.
9. Eunice, b. 10 May, 1694.
All rem. to Colchester with their mother, abt. 1703-4.—See Judd's *Hadley,* p. 494.

FAM. 4. Capt. NATHANIEL,[3] (*Nathaniel*[2] *Nath'l,*[1]), b. Weth., 8 Sept., 1682; d. Colchester, 20 Aug., 1774. He was app. Ens. by the Gen. Ct., 1721; *Lieut.,* May,

---

* Of these *Hannah Dickinson,* the eldest, m. Samuel **Gillett,** of Hatfield, who was killed in the Ind. fight at Turner's Falls, in 1676. She m. (2) Stephen **Jennings,** of Hatfield, and in 1677, was captured by Indians, six months after her marriage, and carried to Canada, but was soon released; a daughter b. soon after her return was appropriately named "Captivity." But the family's ill luck did not stop here. In 1690, they rem. to Brookfield, where, in one of the Ind. surprises so common to that locality, Mr. Jennings, with five others, engaged in making hay, July, 1710, were ambushed and killed. The daughter Captivity, before referred to, m. Abigah **Bartlett,** and he too was killed by Ind., Oct., 1708.
The third dau. *Sarah Dickinson,* m. (1) Samuel **Lane,** of Hadley, later of Suffield, Mass., by whom she had 5 ch., b. in S.; she m. (2) 1691, Martin **Kellogg,** of Hatfield, and Deerfield, Mass., later of Suffield, by whom (as his 2d wife, she had 4 ch., 3 of whom were capt. at the Deerfield massacre), and had Ind. experiences in Canada, as will be more fully seen in our *Kellogg Genealogy.*
* From this Nathaniel, 4th, descends (Capt. *Aaron, Amasa,* of Colchester, who m. 5 Mch., 1820, Lydia Worthington **Tracy**) JOSIAH ISHAM, ESQ., of Middletown and Brooklyn, N. Y., b. 20 Oct., 1825; m. Frances Maria **Spirman,** of Attlebury, N. Y.

'32, *Capt.* '36; dep. to Gen. Ct. for C., 1724, 1725, '26, '27, '28, '29, '30, '31, '32, '38, '39, '42, '43, '44, '45, '46,—23 sessions in all; he was app. Justice for Htfd. Co. by the Gen. Ct. for yrs. 1731-1763 incl.—a period of 31 yrs. continuous service. He m. (1) Ann **Clark,** of Lebanon, Ct., who d. 1736; m. (2) Hannah **Coleman.** He had 9 ch.

From Daniel his 4th ch. and 3d son, we trace the following lines. *Daniel,*[4] b. 6 Feb., 1717, in Colchester, d. there 27 Dec., 1801; was a dep. to Gen. Ct. for 21 sess. and Justice of Htfd. Co. for 12 yrs.; he m. (1) 1743, Marg't **Parsons,** of Springfield, Mass., m. (2) Wid. Mary **Skinner.** He was gt-gd-fthr. of Rev. Henry Ward Beecher; had 12 ch. Of these, *Isaac,*[5] his 2d ch. and s. b. 1746 rem. to Stafford, Ct., in 1773; and in 1794 rem. to Smyrna, then in Herk. now in Chenango Co., N. Y., where he d. 27 Feb., 1842, in his 97th yr. He was rep. to Gen. Ct. of Conn. from Stafford, 8 sess. betw. 1779 and '90; served in Revol. War in 2d Reg. (Col. Lamb's) Artillery, May 1, '72—11 Apl., '83; was one of the delegates to Convention at Htfd. which ratified the Constitution of the U. S.; was elected from Herk. Co., N. Y., to the State Assemb., 1798, 1802-3, and in 1804-5 was a memb. of the Senate of N. Y. State. In 1810 was app. first Judge of Chenango Co., N. Y.; had 8 ch. of whom the 7th, *John,*[6] b. Stafford, Ct., 1786; was a lawyer, Counsellor in Chancery, and U. S. Dist. Atty.; res. Hamilton, N. Y., where he d. 23 July, 1884, in 99th yr. His 1st wife was Mary B. **Johnson;** his 2d Harriet (dau. of Judge Ebenezer *Foote,*) of Delhi, N. Y., and wid. of Dr. Bryan. Of his 11 ch. his 3 ch. and 2d s. *John Johnson*[7] b. 11 Feb., 1816; m. Mary **Crocker,** b. 12 May, 1819, dau. of Hon. Amos. Crocker, of Hamilton, N. Y., by his wife Mary **Owen.** He was a prominent man in Central N. Y. and during the Civil War was very active in the raising and organization of regiments in that portion of the State. He was the first Central New Yorker to subscribe for Government bonds, and in every way an ardent patriot; State Senator 1858-59; Auditor of the N. Y. City P. O. under Post Master Thos. L. James, and his system of rules and regulations for the reorganization and reformation of that office have since been adopted by the U. S. P. O. Dep't, in the larger post-offices of the U. S. In 1900 he was res. in Belvidere, Ill.

Children:

1. Mary Annette, b. Hamilton, N. Y., 9 Sept., 1840; m. 2 Sept., 1862, Hon. Enos **Clarke,** a prominent lawyer of St. Louis, Mo.

2. John Crocker,[8] b. H., 20 Sept., 1841. FAM. 2.
3. Harriet Foote, b. H., 22 May, 1848; res. (1900).

FAM. 2.   JOHN CROCKER,[7] (s. *John J.,*[6] *John,*[5] *Daniel,*[4] *Nath'l.*[3] *Nath'l,*[2] *Nath'l,*[1]), b. 1841; grad. from Madison (now Colgate) Univ. 1864; rem. from Hamilton to Belvidere, Ill., Sept., 1869; mcht.; memb. Ill. Soc. Sons of Revol.; Missouri Soc. of Colonial Wars; N. Y. Soc. of Founders and Patriots; and Conn. Soc. of Mayflower Descendants.

He m. in N. Y. City, Apl. 24, 1867, Helen (dau. Judge Samuel *Bostwick*) **Garvin,** and who is also a lineal descendant of Mr. Mathew Mitchell, one of the first sett. of. Weth.

Children:

1. Mary Helen, b. 11 Apl., 1868; m. 21 July, 1897, Rev. Harry Edward **Purniton,** of Chicago, Ill., who is a grad. of Colgate Univ. (1894); of Theol. Dept. Chicago Univ. (1897); pastor of Broadway Bap. Ch., Denver, Col., for a yr.; and of Bap. Ch., Marquette, Mich. *Issue:*
   i. Raymond Chivers (Purniton), b. Denver, 17 Nov., 1898.

2. Maria Garvin, b. 21 Sept., 1870.
3. Florence Annette, b. 24 Oct., 1875.
4. John Garvin, b. 7 Feb., 1877.
   (This branch of the Foote family possesses a coat of arms gr. upon their ancestor (James Foote) by Charles II, of Eng.; described as a shield, divided by a chevron, with quarterings of clover leaves. *Crest,* an oak tree. *Motto,* "Loyalty and Truth.")

DANIEL, of Wintonbury, m. Martha **Stillman,** 14 Jan., 1747-8.—*W. C. R.*

FORBES, (Communicated mostly by JOHN S. GOODWIN, Esq., of Chicago, Ill.),
JAMES, b. prob. in Scotland, m. Catteran (Catharine) ————; sett.
prob. at Burnside, in E. Htfd., Ct., abt. 1645? where he d. intestate, 27 Nov.,
1692; adm. gr. on his est. at Htfd., 11 Jan., 1602-3; he is said to have settled
first at Windsor, Ct., *Hinman* credits him with 15 ch. in all; but those ment.
below are all which appear on *Prob. Ct. Recs.* There are indications that James
Forbes of East Htfd., was the Capt. James Forbes, of Culloden, Scotland, who
m. Agnes Munro, in 1643, and by her had ch. who "came to be men and women,"
and that "Catteran" was his second wife.

Children:

1. John, m. Mary **Griffin.** FAM. 2.
2. David,* m. 1671, Sarah **Treat.**
3. Dorothy, m. William **Roberts.**
4. Mary, m. Daniel **Gains.**

5. Sarah, m. Joseph **Collier.**
6. James,* m. (1) Sarah **Williams**; m. (2)
   . Mrs. Elizabeth **Buckland.**

FAM. 2.   JOHN,[2] (*James,*[1]), b. E. Htfd.; m. Mary (dau. John) **Griffin;** res. in
Htfd., where he d. intestate, 4 May, 1713.

Children:

1. John,† bp. 8 Dec., 1695; m. (1) Abigail
   ————; m. (2) Anne ————.
2. Mary, bp. 12 Mch., 1697-8; m. John **Russell,** Jr.

3. Lydia, bp. 1700; m. Joel **Clark.**
4. Joseph, bp. 170—. FAM. 3.
5. Samuel,‡ bp. Sept., 1703; m. Mary **Thompson.**

FAM. 3.   JOSEPH,[3] (*John,*[2] *James,*[1]), b. 170-, in E. Htfd.; m. 23 Dec., 1732, Lucy
(dau. Abraham & Hannah) **Crane,** who was b. 25 July, 1710, in Weth.; he was
a tanner; res. in Weth. and, perhaps, in East Haven, as Mrs. Lucy Crane
Forbes d. there 10 Aug., 1797; she was not quite as old (90) as stated on her
tombstone; Joseph F. was "licensed to be a tanner," *Htfd. Co. Ct. Rec.*, Feb.,
1731; and on Thos. Hurlbut's account book was charged for "shoes for Mary,"
1761, "shoes for Sarah," 1766; and "for Aaron," 1769. He d. Weth. abt.
1770.—(*W. C. R.*) Fam. trad. gives him 7 sons and a dau., but record proof
only gives him 6 sons and 2 daus.§ Joseph, Joseph Jr., John, Daniel, and
Elijah subscribed, 1761, to the bldg. of the Weth. Church.

Children:

1. Joseph, Jr., b. 1731. FAM. 4.
2. John. FAM. 5.
3. Aaron. m. untraced.
4. Daniel. FAM. 6.
5. Sarah, b. 27 Sept., 1745; m. 20 Oct., 1779,

   James **Hale;** she d. 19 Mch., 1824.
6. Elias. FAM. 7.
7. Elijah (Capt.), b. 5 Sept., 1739. FAM. 8.
8. Mary, m. at Weth., Simeon **Hurlburt,** 3
   Oct., 1768.

FAM. 4.   JOSEPH,[4] (*Joseph,*[3] *John,*[2] *James,*[1]), b. 1731, Weth.; m. (1) Sarah
Treat; m. (2) Abigail ————; res. in Weth., where his first wife d.
before 1766; as in 1766-8-9-11-12, Joseph 3d and Sarah, minor ch. of Joseph,
Jr., appeared by their father and guard. in the est. of James Treat. Joseph
F., Jr., was at sea in 1774. The est. of Mrs. Sarah (Treat) Forbes was not
prob., however, until May 23, 1780, her s-in-law, Theodore Hale, being app.
adm'r—this was the same yr. her husband's est. was prob.;' they res. Weth.
where he was bu. 4 Jan., 1776, ae. 45,—*W. C. R.*; adm. gr. on his estate
to his wid. Abigail, 20 Dec., 1780; she m. (2) John **White,** Jr., who was
app. guard. of Nathaniel Forbes, of Weth., a minor.

---

* These two sons are the ancestors of the Hartford Forbes family.
† John, ancestor of the Canaan, Ct., Forbes.
‡ Samuel, ancestor of the New Haven, Ct., Forbes.
§ In fact, Mr. Benj. Adams states, "We *know* Mary and Sarah were ch. of Joseph Forbes."

Children (by 1st marr.) :

1. Sarah, bp. 15 Nov., 1774; m. Theodore **Hale.** *Issue:*
   i. Abigail (Hale), m. (1) a **Smith**; m. (2) a **Kellogg.**
   ii. Sarah, b. 8 Aug., 1780; m. Zaccheus (s. of Zacch.) **Brown,** of Southington, Ct., 16 Oct., 1808; he d. Dec., 1861; she d. 3 Nov., 1872, both bu. at New.; they had (a) William (Brown); (b) Horace Hale (Brown), b. 22 Dec., 1810; (c) Martin (Brown); (d) Abigail (Brown); (e) Walter Francis (Brown); (f) Sarah Ann (Brown; (g) Henry Gillett (Brown).
   Horace Hale (Brown), b. 1810; m. 14 May, 1845, Harriet S. **Smith.** He d.

27 Jan., 1879, at New Britain, Ct.; had a dau. Kath. Maria (Brown), b. Sept., 1857, who m. 23 Oct., 1895, Wm. F. **Brooks**; res. New Britain, and has Katharine (Brooks), b. 14 July, 1899.

2. Joseph, 3d.
   (*By sec. marr.; all of whom were bp. by Rev. Abraham Jarvis, of Midd.*) :
3. Lucy, bp. 6 Nov., 1774; m. Asa **Lord,** of Htfd.
4. Ashbel, bp. 6 Nov., 1774.
5. Nathaniel, bp. m. (1) Ruth ————; m. (2) a **Lyman.**
6. A son, bu. 17 Jan., 1776; this may pos. be the Ashbel above.

FAM. 5. JOHN,[4] (*Joseph,[3] John,[2] James,[1]*), b. Weth., res. in Weth., where "John, reputed son of John Forbes" was bp. John Forbes, according to the statement given by Mrs. Thomas Chester Forbes, (b. 1803), of Danville, Ill., (d. 1895), left Weth. and settled at Cork Ireland, where he m. an Irish woman; gave a ship to his nephew Aaron (s. of Elias); adopted a son whose parents' name was Burke and d. in Ireland, abt. 1820. Mr. Thos. C. Forbes rec'd a part of his est. and stated that John's adopted son Burke, m. his adopted father's wid. when she was upwards of 90, in order to prevent her est. from coming to the Forbes fam. in America. From some of the old estate receipts, it is learned that the name of John's wife, was Thomasine. This leads to the enquiry as to who were Capt. aand Thomasine Forbes, of Guilford, Ct., whose dau. Lucy was bp. 19 June, 1768.

Children:

1. John, "reputed son of John Forbes." FAM. 9. | 2. ———— (Burke), adopted son.

FAM. 6. DANIEL,[4] (*Joseph,[3] John,[2] James,[1]*), b. Weth.; m. (*W. C. R.*) 14 Dec., 1775, Lydia (dau. Thos. & Abigail) **Hurlbut,** who was b. 21 Dec., 1748; they res. Weth.; he d. at Norfolk, Ct., 1779; fam. trad. says he was a sea-captain; his wid. Lydia and Ozias Hurlbut, of Weth., sett. the est.; she "wid. Lydia Forbes" joined the Weth. Church in 1782; she m. (2) 16 July, 1788, Isaac **Buck,** of Far. On 25 Feb., 1780, Elida (Lydia?) Forbes settled an acc't at Weth. of Daniel Forbes, of Winchester, Ct., dec'd.

Children (W. C. R.) :

1. Alma, bp. 7 July, 1782.
2. Daniel J., bp. 7 July, 1782; was in early yrs. a mariner; and (acc. to *Norfolk Prob. Recs.*) bo't ld. in Torrington; he d. 1779 (1799 ?); wid. m. (2) Ozias Hurl-

burt, of Weth., who, with wife took adm. on Forbes' est.—*Conn. Quarterly,* III, 239. See, also, *American Ancestry,* under S. Waldo Forbes. FAM. **6a.**

These three following families (6a, 6b, 6c) furnished by letter of S. WALDO FORBES, Forestville, Ct.

FAM. 6a. DANIEL J.,[5] (*Daniel,[4] Joseph,[3] John,[2] James,[1]*), b. 1782; m. 1802, Belinda (dau. Regin & Sarah) **Gridley,** of Far.

Child:

1. Samuel Gridley, b. 18 Aug., 1803. FAM. **6b.**

FAM. 6b. SAMUEL GRIDLEY,[6] (*Daniel,[5] Daniel,[4] Joseph,[3] John,[2] James,[1]*), b. 1803; m. 8 Apl., 1828, Ellen E. (dau. John & Eunice *Eddy*) **Hamlin,** of Far. He d. 10 Jan., 1868; she d. 5 Oct., 1899 ae. 93.

Children:

1. Samuel Waldo, b. 4 May, 1830. Fam. 6c.
2. Emily M., b. 19 Feb., 1836; m. 8 Jan., 1861, Sam'l N. **Chapin,** b. 8 July, 1836.
   Issue:
   i. Jennie Estelle (Chapin), b. 4 May,

1868.
ii. Wilfred Herbert (Chapin), b. 19 Aug., 1872.
iii. Gertrude Lillian (Chapin), b. 16 Nov., 1878; m. Russel **Clark.**

Fam. 6c. SAMUEL WALDO,[7] (*Samuel G.,[6] Daniel, Jr.,[5] Daniel,[4] Joseph,[3] John,[2] James,[1]*), b. 1830; m. 6 Sept., 1852, Huldah (dau. Geo. H. & Huldah *Woodruff*) **Clarke.**

Child:

1. Lena, b. 20 May, 1863; m. 1 Oct., 1885, Carlyle F. (s. of Wallace & Eliza *Fuller*) **Barnes.** *Issue:*
   i. Fuller Forbes (Barnes), b. Mch.,

1887.
ii. Harry Clarke (Barnes), b. 20 Nov., 1889.

Fam. 7. ELIAS,[4] (*Joseph,[3] John,[2] James,[1]*) b. Weth; m. 26 Nov., 1755, Abigail (dau. Thomas & Sarah *Hitchcock*) **Shepard,** who was b. 15 June, 1736; he d. 1760; wid. m. (2) ———— **Stowe;** m. (3) Jonathan **Goodrich,** and d. 17 Apl., 1821, in Branford, Ct.

Children:

1. Abigail, m. Maj. Thomas **Potter.**
2. Elias, m. Hannah **Gorham.**
3. Aaron, b. 1760; m. (1) Abigail E. **Green;**

m. (2) his cousin Sarah **Forbes;** he was the Aaron to whom his uncle John (Fam. 5) gave a ship.

Fam. 8. Capt. ELIJAH,[4] (*Joseph,[3] John,[2] James,[1]*), b. 1739 at E Htfd., m. (1) Mary **Hale,** or Hall; m. (2) Eunice **Chester,** 4 Sept., 1785; was a sea-capt.; res. in New Haven, Ct., where his first wife d. 20 Sept., 1784; his 2d wife, Eunice, by whom he had no issue, d. 27 May, 1812. Capt. Elijah d. 12 Jan., 1814, in N. H.

Children (by 1st marr.):

1. A son, b. 15 Oct., 1768; d. same day.
2. Mary (Polly), b. 9 Apl., 1771; m. Elihu **Lyman.**
3. William, b. 17 Mch., 1775; m. (1) Mary **Hinman;** m. (2) Clarissa **Hinman.***
4. Benjamin (Capt.), b. 20 Nov., 1777. Fam. 10.

5. Sarah, b. 16 Mch., 1779; d. 24 Aug., 1779.
6. Sarah, b. 29 July, 1780; m. her cousin Aaron. See Fam. 7.
7. Elizabeth, b. 29 Oct., 1783; m. (1) Capt. Barnabas **Mulford;** m. (2) Luke **Moody.**

Fam. 9. JOHN,[5] (*reputed son of John,[4] Joseph,[3] John,[2] James,[1]*), m. 19 Apl., 1784, Mary (dau. Zephaniah) **Hatch;** res. in Weth., where he appears to have d. shortly after his marr. as the "Wid. Mary Forbes" joined Weth. Church, 30 Apl., 1786; she m. (2) 4 Sept., 1788, Leonard **Dix;** m. (3) Joseph **Adams,** by whom she had one ch.

Child (by 1st marr.):

1. Mary, b. 15 Aug., 1784; bp. 30 Apl., 1786 | —W. C. R.; m. Samuel **Blinn.**

Fam. 10. Capt. BENJAMIN,[5] (*Elijah,[4] Joseph,[3] John,[2] James,[1]*), b. 1777, in New Haven, Ct.; m. 4 Aug., 1801, at N. H., Sarah (dau. John & Lucretia *Warner*) **Scott;** he was a ship-capt.; res. N. H., where he d. 24 Jan., 1824. Mrs. Forbes d. 8 Feb., 1841; she was a dau. of Stephen,[5] (*Robert,[4] Seth,[3] Robert,[2] Andrew,[1]*), **Warner,** and Mary,[6] (*Samuel,[5] Joseph,[4] Comfort,[3] Thomas,[2] Dr. Thomas[1]*) **Starr.**

Child:

1. Thomas Chester, b. 12 Nov., 1803. Fam. 11.

---

* Ancestor of the Derby, Vt., Forbes.

FAM. 11. THOMAS CHESTER,[6] (*Capt. Benj.*,[5] *Elijah*,[4] *Joseph*,[3] *John*,[2] *James*,[1]), b. 1803, at New Haven, Ct., m. (1) 31 May, 1826, at Midd., Ct., Mary Elizabeth (dau. Thomas & Clarissa *Treadway*) **Sill**,[6] (*Micah*,[5] *Thos.*,[4] *Joseph*,[3] *Capt. Joseph*,[2] *John*,[1]); he was a mcht. and capitalist; Episcopalian; res. fro. 1831 in Danville, Ill., where Mrs. Forbes d. 27 Aug., 1872. Her mother Clarissa[6] Treadway, was dau. of Amos,[5] Josiah,[4] James,[3] Josiah,[2] Nathaniel **Treadway**[1] and Eunice[5] his wife, dau. of Josiah,[4] Nathaniel,[3] Nathaniel,[2] Nathaniel[1] **Foote.** Mr. Thomas Chester Forbes, m. (2) at Danville, Ill., 29 Jan., 1874, Mary Elizabeth (dau. William & Cath. Ann *Cannady*) **Hessey**, b. at D. He d. 5 Jan., 1895.

Children (by first marriage):

1. Harriet Brown, b. 7 Nov., 1827; d. 13 June, 1833.
2. Henry Sill, b. 21 Oct., 1829; m. (1) Lucy H. **Wright**; m. (2) Georgia **Dunn**; m. (3) Mrs. Kate (Johnson) **Harris.**
3. Sarah Scott, b. 22 Aug., 1831; m. (1) Alex. Y. **Harrison**; m. (2) Robert **Davison.**
4. Thomas Richard, b. 22 Dec., 1833. FAM. 12.
5. Frederick A., b. 30 June, 1837; d. 29 Sept., 1837.
6. William, b. 7 Jan., 1839; d. 4 Dec., 1858.
(By second marriage):
7. Cordelia Catharine, b. 8 Jan., 1876.
8. Caroline Chester, b. 4 Feb., 1879.

FAM. 12. THOMAS RICHARD,[7] (*Thos.*, *Chester*,[6] *Capt. Benj.*,[5] *Capt. Elijah*,[4] *Joseph*,[3] *John*,[2] *James*,[1]), b. 1833, in Danville, Ill.; m. 1 Sept., 1857, at D., Anna Eliza (dau. William & Margaret *Daris*) **Robinson**, b. Attica, Ind.; Mr. F. d. at Danville, Ill., 21 Nov., 1860. He was a Deputy Co. Clerk.

Children:

1. Mary Elizabeth, b. 9 June, 1859; m. 7 Oct., 1880, John Samuel **Goodwin**, of Chicago, Ill., who was b. 16 Mch., 1859, in Edinburg, Ind., a s. of Rev. William Rees & Susan Ann *Keeley* Goodwin; lawyer; they res. in Beloit, Wis., until Sept., 1888, since then in Chicago. Mrs. G. was educ. at Rye Sem., N. Y.; has traveled extensively; is a memb. of the Arctic Club, of Chicago. *Issue:*
    1. Suzanne (Anna), b. 15 Dec., 1886.
2. Anna, b. 4 July, 1861; d ———.

Miscellenea: JOTHAM, of Waterbury, Vt., m. Nancy **Olmstead**, 8 Jan., 1805; they had (*S. C. R.*) Mary Ann, bp. 20 Sept., 1807, and Caroline, bp. 7 (or 21) May, 1809.

MARY, (wid.) had Mary, bp. 30 Apl., 1786.—*W. C. R.*

ABIGAIL, (wid.) son of, d. 17 Feb., 1776.—*W. C. R.*

FORDHAM, GIDEON, "of L. I." had (*S. C. R.*):

1. Silas, bp. 16 Apl., 1781.
2. Apollos, bp. 8 Mch.
3. John, bp. 8 Mch., and d. 12 May, 1782.
4. John, bp. 30 Mch., 1783.
5. Polly, bp. 4 June, 1786.

FORTUNE, LUKE, d. 4 May, 1817, ae. 76—*Weth. Ins.;* m. 18 Jan., 1776, Prudence **Buck;** she d. 17 Jan., 1825, ae. 87.—*W. C. R.*

Child (Weth. Rec.):

1. James, b. 8 Oct., 1777; bp. 26 July, 1778. | FAM. 2.

FAM. 2. JAMES,[2] (*Luke*,[1]), b. 1777; m. 5 Nov., 1797, Betsy (dau. of the late Capt. Ashbel) **Riley.**

Children (Weth. Rec. & W. C. R.):

1. Mary Bennett, b. 17 Mch., bp. 6 Oct., 1799; m. James **Treat**, and d. 4 Oct., 1840, ae. 41. *Issue (Weth. Ins.):*
    i. Mary Elizabeth (Treat), d. 2 Aug., 1841, ae. 19 yr.
    ii. James Porter (Treat), d. 18 July, 1851, ae. 18.
2. Luke, b. 19 Mch., bp. 19 Apl., 1801; d. in Texas, ae. 30, bu. 30 July, 1831.—*W. C. R.*
3. James, b. 19 Aug., bp. 27 Nov., 1803.
4. Elizabeth Buck, b. 29 July, bp. 25 Aug., 1806; m. George **Story**, 10 Oct., 1836.
5. Roswell Riley, b. 8 Oct., bp. 1 Nov., 1807; d. 20 Dec., 1826, ae. 19, in Jamaica, W: I.
6. Prudence Buck, b. 3 Dec., 1809; bp. 8 Apl., 1810.
7. Ashbel Riley, } twins, b. 17 Nov., bp. 15
8. Justus Riley, } Dec., 1811.
9. Jennette Riley, b. 4 Sept., 1813; bp. 9 Apl., 1815; bu. 3 Aug., 1832.
10. Lavinia Morgan, bp. 16 Mch., 1817; d. 26 Sept., 1817.
11. Ezekiel Riley, b. 1 Jan., 1822.

FOSDICK, (*Fosdyke*). This name probably originally a "name of place" with which the family were connected—viz., (*fosse* and *dyke*—a channel cut, by order of Henry VIII fm. the Great Marsh (or Fen) near Lincoln, Eng., to the river Trent.—See Arthur's *Family Surnames*, 132. Mr. EZEKIEL, m. (1) Abigail (dau. Capt. Samuel Jr., & Abigail) **Wright**, b. 11 Mch., 1723-4; they were res. of Weth. in Apl., 1744—*Co. Ct. Rec.;* she d. 7 Nov., 1755, ae. 31 (*Weth. Ins.*); he m. (2) 22 Sept., 1756, wid. "Anna" **Wells,** who d. 27 Dec., 1808, ae. 76.—*Weth. Ins.* He d. 2 Jan., 1786, ae. 66.—*Weth. Ins.*

Children (*Weth. Rec.*) :

1. Abigail, b. 10 Dec., 1745.
2. Clorinda, b. 9 Mch., 1748; bp. (adult) 28 Jan., 1776.—*W. C. R.*
3. Alvin, b. 9 Mch., 1750.
4. Rhoda, b. 17 Nov., 1751.
(*By second marriage*) :
5. Ezekiel, b. 19 Sept., 1757.
6. William, b. 9 Aug., 1759.
7. Anna, b. 20 July, 1761.

8. Susannah, b. 10 June, 1763.
9. Sarah, b. 16 May, 1766.
10. Ruth, b. 1 Oct., 1768.
11. Elizabeth, b. 15 June, 1772; bp. 4 Jan., 1784.
12. Mary, b. 27 July, 1774; bp. 4 Jan., 1784.
13. Samuel, b. 3 June, 1778; bp. 4 Jan., 1784; prob. the S. who d. at Gaudaloupe, W. I., recorded 25 Dec., 1799.

WILLIAM,[2] (*Ezekiel,*[1]), b. 1759; m. Anna **Robbins,** 8 Mch., 1781; she prob. the "Anna" N. (adult) bp. 4 Jan., 1784—*W. C. R.;* d. ae. 52, bu. 21 May, 1811; he d. before Nov., 1796.

Children (*W. C. Rec.*) :

1. Ch. bu. 24 Apl., 1782.
2. Annar.
3. George.
4. Ezekiel

5. Anna.
6. Horace Boardman, d. 8 Aug., 1812.—*W. C. R.*
7. Anne.   (All bp. 6 Nov., 1796.)

JAMES, (*W. C. R.*) had:

Children:

1. Polly, bp. 19 Dec., 1790; prob the inf. bu. 19 Dec., 1790.
2. Inf. bu. 1 Aug., 1792.

3. Inf. bu. 14 Mch., 1795.
4. Thomas, bp. 14 Mch., 1795. } Poss. the same.

ASENATH, ae. 76, bu. 27 Dec., 1808.

PRUDENCE, wid. of *Ezekiel*, d. ae. 61, bu. 4 Feb., 1822.—*W. C. R.*

FOSTER, SAMUEL, of Southampton, L. I., b. 12 June, 1739, m. 4 Sept., 1769—*S. C. R.*, an Elizabeth **Webb**, said to have been a niece of Gen. Samuel B. Webb, of Weth. Her mother is said to have been a Bulkeley. She used to relate that she had dined and danced with Gen. Washington at her uncle's (Gen. S. B. W.'s) home, in Weth., which event was the crowning glory of her life. Her portrait and that of her dau. Katharine, and of the latter's husband, Sam'l Bryan, painted in 1824, are now in possess. of Mrs. SAMUEL F. LYONS, of Brooklyn, N. Y.[†] (*Weth. Recs.* give this marr.—without date—and the following children: those marked * are supplied by Mrs. Lyons) Mr. Samuel Foster d. 13 Nov., 1797, in 59th yr.—*S. C. R.*

Children:

1. Elizabeth, b. 25 Aug., 1770; bp. 9 June, 1771—*S. S. R.;* d. 6 Oct., 1775, in 6th yr. —*Weth. Ins.*
2. Mary, b. 27 Nov., 1771; bp. 16 Feb., 1772; d. 15 Jan., 1854.
3. Samuel, b. 25 Aug., 1774; *Weth. Recs.* say 5 Sept., 1773, and that he was lost at sea Jan., 1793.
4. Elizabeth, b. 22 Apl., 1777 (*Weth. Rec.,* 1776) ; m. Titus **Chapman,** Mch., 1796; d. 8 May, 1807.

5. Martha,* b. Feb., —— (?).
6. Cleopatra,* b. 12 Sept., 1780; m. (1) John W. **Lyons,** of N. Y. City, July, 1806; m. (2) John W. **Wetherslim;** d. 10 Apl., 1859. FAM. 2.
7. Katherine,* b. 18 May, 1783; m. Samuel **Bryan,** of Hudson, N. Y., Dec., 1799; d. 29 Oct., 1860. *S. C. R.* gives bp. of Cath. Webb, (dau. Samuel) Foster, 29 June, 1783; prob. same as this Katherine.

† To Mrs. Clara M. H. Lyons, of Brooklyn, N. Y., we are indebted for this family record, taken from a Family Bible in possession of her late husband Samuel Lyons, and collated by ourselves with data from the *Foster* items in the *Weth. Recs.* But we have not been able to identify the parentage of Elizabeth Webb, *alias* Foster.

Roswell Fox, M. D.

Fam. 2. CLEOPATRA, (dau. Samuel & Elizabeth *Webb*), m. 1806, John W. **Lyons,**
of N. Y. City; *issue:*

1. George L. (Lyons), b. 26 Nov., 1808; d.
17 Sept., 1837; lost at sea *en route* to
Europe.
2. Samuel B. (Lyons), b. 10 Jan., 1811; m.
America **Hyatt,** of Ky.; had daus. *Cleopatra* and *Susan*, and a son *Geo. B.*, who
m. Carrie **McCarthy,** niece of Justin McCarthy, M. P.

3. Robert Campbell (Lyons), b. 29 Nov., 1812;
d. 18 Jan., 1853; m. Hannah Hudson **Cook,**
of L. I., 5 Jan., 1835. Fam. 3.
4. Catharine B. (Lyons), b. 8 Jan., 1815;
m. Dr. Wm. **Hansel,** of Philadelphia, 3
Oct., 1839; d. 1 Aug., 1886; left no surviving children.

Fam. 3. ROBERT CAMPBELL LYONS, (John W. & Cleopatra Foster) by his wife
Hannah H. **Cook,** had

Children:

1. Samuel Francis, b. Aug., 1840; m. Clara
Mitchell **Howell,*** and had a son, *Robert*

Kerr Lyons.
2. Mary, b. 12 Sept., 1849.

BARTHOLMEW, m. Mary ————.

Children (Weth. Rec.):

1. Ann, b. 9 July, 1694.
2. Timothy, b. Apl., bp 14 May—*Mix Rec.*,

1699.
3. Mabel, b. Apl., bp. 11 May, 1701.

MEHITABLE, (adult) bp. 9 July, 1786.—*S. C. R.*

FOWLER, HARVEY, s. of ————, d. ae. 7, 3 Apl., 1822.—*W. C. R.*

FOX. (Foxe) CHRISTOPHER, BENONI,* who sett. in Glast., was son of
Eliphalet, s. of *Thomas,* of Concord, Mass., and m. (1) at C. Mary **Ball,** 23 May,
1711; m. (2) 12 Sept., 1712, Experience **Page;** after the birth of their 3d ch.
they rem. to Hartford, Ct., 1817, finally sett. in Glast.; d. 15 Dec., 1650. Invent.
£16-17-00, taken by Nathaniel Dickinson and John Nott. Boatswayne of the
ship *Tyral*, of Weth. Account rendered by John Saddler, of Weth., for charges
for 9 weeks and 2 days care and expense in the sickness of Christopher Foxe,
The Court gave Saddler power to admr. the estate, 21 Feb., 1650-1.—*Htfd. Co.
Rec.*

Children:

1. Joseph, b. 1713.
2. Benjamin, b. 1714.
3. Eliphalet, b. 1715-16.
   (*By second marriage.; b. at Glast.*):
4. David, b. 1717.

5. Ephraim, b. 1719.
6. Experience, b. 1721.
7. Mary, b. 1725.
8. Sarah, b. 1727.

RICHARD, of Weth. m. Beriah (dau of the first Richard) **Smith,** of Weth., resided
in present Glast.—*Savage*, II, 196. See, also, Chapt. VII, Vol. I. *Ld. Recs.*
show that they had 11 ch.: their s. *Abraham*, who rem. to Glast. had sons
Abraham, William and *Jonah*, and dau. *Ruth* who was b. abt. 1725; poss. other
ch. also.

THOMAS, m. Mary (dau. Thos. & Mary) **Boardman,** 6 Nov., 1729.

Children (Weth. Rec.):

1. Thomas, b. 17, bp. 21—*Mix MSS.* Feb.,
1730-1.
2. John, b. 24 Dec., 1732.
3. Elisha, b. 25 Mch., 1735.

4. Amos, b. 16 Dec., 1736. Fam. 2.
5. Prudence, b. 10 Feb., 1738-9.
6. Martha, b. 21 Aug., 1742.

Fam. 2. AMOS,* (*Thos.,*)), b. 1736; m. 12 Mch., 1761 (1) Susannah **Dickinson,—**
W. C. R., who d. 7 Jan., 1778; m. (2) 14 Mch., 1779, wid. Jerusha **Kilby.**

Children (*Weth. Rec.*) :

1. Hannah, b. 20 Dec., 1761.
2. Amos, b. 23 June, 1763.
3. Martha, b. 26 Jan., 1765.
4. Mary, b. 24 Dec., 1766.
5. Thomas, b. 13, bp. 18 Dec., 1768.

6. George, b. 15 ; bp 28 Oct., 1770.
7. Abigail, b. 27 May, 1773 ; *poss.* the Abig. who m. John Charles **Dennis**, both of Weth., 15 Nov., 1787.
8. Inf., bu. 18 July, 1775.

THE FOX ARMS.

ROSWELL* (M. D.) b. 14 Nov., 1825,† in Lebanon, Ct., prepared for Y. C. at the academies at Wilbraham, Mass., and Colchester, Ct., studied medicine with Dr. Elisha Pinney, of Yantic, then took one course at Med. Dep't Y. C., completing his course, and finally grad. fm. Med. Dep't of University of City of New York, in 1847; and then located in Weth., where he continued in active practice and the honorable esteem of his fellow citizens until his death. In May, 1848, he married Anna Maria (dau. of Hon. Samuel A.) **Gager,** of Bozrah, Ct., and they had the pleasure of celebrating their Golden Wedding in 1897. Dr. Fox d. at Weth. 25 Oct., 1898 aged 72 yrs., being then one of the oldest medical practitioners in the state. He was long an honored member of the Htfd. Co. Med. Association, which he represented at the meetings of the Conn. State Med. Society. It was well said of him by one of the most eminent of his fellow practitioners,‡ that "No physician could have more fully the confidence of the community than he did, as was fully and amply proved by his long and unusually successful career, no man could be more devoted to his profession. With rare singleness of purpose, foregoing the allurements of ease and pleasure he surrendered himself to the welfare of his patients, faithfully and anxiously watching over them, joined with that benevolence so expressive in his countenance. He was without guile and abhorred ostentation. Honesty of purpose and entire freedom from selfish ends inspired confidence in all who sought his counsel and that confidence then grew into close personal friendship. Whatever is exemplary in dealing justly with his fellow-men, in speaking evil of no man, in bountifully befriending the poor, in sacrificing self for the good of others, in leading a blameless life, these virtues were features in his upright and Christian life. He was also deeply interested in the welfare and prosperity of the Town and State in which he lived. He had been a member of the Wethersfield Congregational Church nearly half a century."

* According to orig. MSS. in possess. of this Fox family, corroborated by Eng., historical data arranged by the late Roswell Fox, M. D., and completed by his son Charles James Fox, M. D., the Eng. lineage of this Fox family is as follows :
Sir Stephen Fox, was b. shortly after Charles I ascended the throne, and d. shortly after the accession of George I. His son Henry (the first Lord Holland) married the eld. dau. of the second Duke of Richmond (her gt-gd-mother being Dutchess of Portsmouth, tracing her ancestral lineage to Charles II, of Eng., and Henry IV, of France. To this Henry (Lord Holland) were born three sons, viz.: Charles James, Stephen and Thomas—the latter came to America and sett. in Concord, Mass., in the latter part of the 16th Century.
The Fox *arms* as here given are copied from a picture "worked in worsted," which was in the possess. of "Capt." Roswell Fox, the gt-gd-fther. of Dr. Chas. James Fox, of Willimantic, Ct. The motto is *Et vitam imponders Vero*—"Sacrifice even Life for Truth."
† Son of *David Austin Fox,*[7] by his wife Wealthy (dau. Nath'l Saxton, of Lebanon, Ct. ; s. of Capt. *Roswell Fox,*[6] by his wife Phebe (dau. Jabez) **Hough,** of Bozrah, Ct.; s. of *Joseph Fox,*[5] b. New London, Ct., by his wife Hannah **Crocker;** s. of *Benjamin Fox,*[4] who d. New London, 1746 ; s. of *Samuel Fox,*[3] of Montville (Fox's Mills), Ct.; s. *Samuel Fox,*[2] b. 1650 ; s. of *Thomas Fox,*[1] of Concord, the American emigrant ancestor.
‡ *From an Obit. by Melancthon Storrs, M. D., of Htfd., read at the Annual Meeting of the Htfd. Co. Med. Soc.,* 1899.

Edward G. Fox, M. D.

CHARLES JAMES FOX, M. D.

Children:

1. John Gager, b. 7 Apl., 1852; d. 17 Mch., 1853.
2. Charles James (M. D.), b. 21 Dec., 1854; receiving his preliminary education in the district and private schools of Weth., he fitted for Yale College at the Htfd. High School; fitted for clasical course and passed exams. at Y. C., but finally began the study of medicine with his father—taking also regular and special courses of lectures and clinical instruction at the Med. Dep't of Univ. of City of New York, and at Bellevue and the Charity Hospitals of that city. Grad. Feb., 1876, he immediately commenced his professional life as Physician-in-Chief at the Hartford City Hospital, where he served until Apl., 1877, since which time he has practiced in Willimantic, Ct., where (as elsewhere) he ranks as one of the most active and intelligent members of the profession in the state. He is a member and former Pres. of the Windham Co. Med. Soc., which he rep. as Fellow to the Conn. Med. Soc'y's sessions of 1879, '81, '84, '92. '94, '95 and '98; also, memb. of Conn. State Med. Association, and Chairman (1895) of its Committee on Matters of Profess. interest; was Windham Co.'s Member of the Centennial Committee in 1891, to make arrangements for the Conn. State Society's Centennial of 1892, and has frequently rep. the State Soc'y in other State organizations; he is also a permanent memb. of the Am. Med. Asso., of the International Med. Congress, and of the U. S. Board of Examining Surgeons (at Willimantic) of the Willimantic Bd. of Trade, a 32d degree Mason, an Odd Fellow, a Knight of Pythias, and a founder in W. of the Royal Arcanum, of which he has been a Med. Examiner since its organization. He is, also, a non-resident memb. of the staff of Backus Hospital at Norwich, Ct.; chairman of delegates of Conn. State Med. Assoc. to Nat. Med. Assoc., at Atlantic City, N. J., in 1900; Surgeon-Gen. (1886-88) of the Nat. Guard of Conn., and memb. of the Conn. Assoc.

of Military Surgeons; and app. on a committee of 15 to draft a new charter for the City of Willimantic; he, also, holds membership in the Am. Assoc. for the Advancement of Science; in the Conn. Hist. Soc., and the Conn. Sons of the Am. Revolution, and Associate member of Francis S. Long Post, Grand Army of the Republic; Republican in politics, public-spirited and progressive in public affairs and loyal to the highest interests of whatever concerns the welfare of his native State, or the community in which he dwells; his life is one of professional and personal beneficence and usefulness. He m. 15 May, 1886, Lillian (dau. Rev. Horace) **Winslow;** she d. 17 Sept., 1887.
3. Edward Gager (M. D.), b. 8 Aug., 1859. Grad. from the High School and fitted for college under private tutors; began to read medicine with his father, Roswell Fox, M. D., in 1878; attended three full courses of lectures at the Univ. of the City of New York, Med. Depart., and grad. in Feb., 1883; also received private instruction while attending lectures. Dr. Fox has practiced medicine in his native town since 1883. He is a member of the Conn. State Med. Soc.; of the Am. Med. Assoc., and of the Htfd. Co. Med. Soc. He is now a physician and surgeon in charge of the Conn. State Prison, app. 1891; health officer from 1888 to the present time and is now (since 1900) medical examiner of the town; also medical examiner for a large number of life insurance companies; delegate from the Conn. State Med. Soc., in 1889 and 1900, to the Am. Med. Asso.; to the N. Y. State Med. Soc., in 1888, and Fellow from Htfd. Co. Med. Soc., to the Conn., State Soc., in 1889. He is, also, member of the Conn. State Assoc. of Military Surgeons, as well as of the National body. Dr. Fox is a Mason and Knight Templar; married 26 Oct., 1892, Miss Frances Stoddard **Wells,** of Weth., Conn. They have one son *Kenneth Lewis.*

FRANCIS, (In the compilation of this family record, we are much indebted to a MSS. genealogy belonging to Mr. WM. F. J. BOARDMAN, of Htfd.; and, in one line, to Miss Chatfield's pamphlet, referred to in another place.—*H. R. S.**) ROBERT. His name first occurs in *Weth. Rec.* in connection with the birth of his dau. Susannah, 1652; his ld. rec. commences March, 1652—(See Chapt. VII, Vol. I.) From whence, or exactly when he came to Weth. it is impossible now to ascertain.† Evidently he was then a young man, as he subsequently had a no. of ch.; he was made freeman 1669; and his dth. occurred in 1712: he was fence-viewer, 1671-2; surveyor of highways, 1675, and a memb. of Rev. Mr. Mix's congregation. His wife's name was Joane ————, who d. 19 or 29 Jan., 1704-5, ae. 76. He d. 2 Jan., 1711-12, ae. 83.—*Weth. Ins.*

Children (Weth. Rec.):

1. Susanna, b. 1 Nov., 1651; m. 15 Apl., 1671, John **North.**
2. Robert, b. 6 Nov., 1653; d. before 1705.
3. Mary, b. 11 (or 12) Oct., 1656; m. Jacob (s. Michael) **Griswold,** of Weth., 10 Dec., 1685; *N. Y. Mail & Exp.,* 3 May, 1897.
4. John (Sgt.), b. 4 Sept., 1658; d. 28 Dec., 1711.—*Gr. Stone.* FAM. 2.
5. Abigail, b. 14 Feb., 1660.
6. James, b. 1 Mch., 1662; d. 14 Feb., 1664-5.
7. Sarah, b. 15 Aug., 1664; m. 26 Feb., 1691, Wm. **Powell.**

* Dr. Charles E. Francis, of Stamford, Ct., has nearly ready for press, the *Francis Family Genealogy, Htfd. Times,* 27 Apl., 1903.
† Individuals of the name ment. in Francis' *Register of First Settlers of Mass.,* earlier than 1651, are *John,* of Braintree, whose wife Rose, d. 1659; *Richard,* of Cambridge, made

FAM. 2. Sgt. JOHN,[2] (*Robert,*[1]), b. 1658; was fence-viewer, surveyor of highways, constable, and (1702) school-rate collector—*T. V.*, 184, 220, 227; m. (1) 16 Jan., 1680, Sarah ————, who d. 3 Apl., 1682, ae. 24; he m. (2) Mercy [Chittenden] 16 Jan., 1683, who d. 13 Oct., 1745, ae. 83—*Weth. Ins.;* he d. 28 Dec., 1711, ae. 53, five days before his father. Invent. val. £713·07·00; est. div. by agreement 13 Apl., 1716.—*Htfd. Co. Prob. Rec.*

Children (by 2d wife—Weth. Rec.):

1. John, b. 12 Oct., 1684. FAM. 3.
2. James, b. 13 Oct.,1685-6. FAM. 4.
3. Siberance, b. 23 Aug., 1687; m. David Griswold.
4. Mary, b. 26 May, 1689; m. Samuel Griswold (as ment. in father's will).
5. Thomas, b. 4 Feb., 1690. FAM. 5.
6. Robert, b. 13 Feb., 1692; d. 25 Mch., 1695.
7. Abigail, b. 8 Mch., 1694-5; m. Nath'l Hale.
8. Robert, b. 25 Jan., 1696-7. FAM. 6.
9. Joseph, b. 9 Nov., bp. — (*Mix MSS.*), 1698; Sett. at Wallingford, Ct.; had 10 ch., 4 of whom were *Samuel,* b. 1729; *Amos,* b. 1736; *Asa,* b. 1739; *Josiah,* b. 1745.—*A. L. F.,* Glenbrook, Ct.
10. Daniel, b. 18 Sept., bp. 22 (*Mix MSS.*) Sept., 1700.
11. Hannah, b. 5 Feb. (bp. 28—*Mix MSS.*), 1702-3; m. Thos. Cadwell, of Htfd.
12. Sarah, b. 6 (bp. 11—*Mix MSS.*) Mch., 1704-5.
13. Prudence, b. 24 (acc. to *Mix MSS.* bp. 11) Jan., 1707-8; m. Charles Hollister, of Glast., 5 Apl., 1729.—*Hall Gen.,* p. 65.
14. Mercy, b. 27 Jan., 1709-10.

Note.—The six sons of this fam. sett. in different towns of Conn. *Daniel,* in a deed of 1725, is ment. as of Durham; afterwards, 1746, in a deed given by him and Joseph, he is located in Killingworth, and *Joseph* in Wallingford. *Thomas* Sett. in Newington, and *James* in Berlin. *John* and *Robert* remained in Weth.

FAM. 3. JOHN,[3] (*John,*[2] *John,*[1]), b. 1684; m. (1) 30 Dec., 1708, Mary **Hatch**, in Weth., who d. W., 15 July, 1718, in 50th yr. (gr-stone.) Her gr-stone, in Weth. cemetery, next that of her husband, gives her age as 50, making her his senior by 16 yrs.—perhaps an error of the stone-cutter; m. (2) 12 Feb., 1719, Abigail (dau. of Nath'l & Eunice) **Stoddard**, of Weth., who d. 22 Aug., 1723, ae. 26; he m. (3) Eunice **Dickinson**, 16 Oct., 1735; he res. on cor. nr., where No. brick school-house is, and where the later John and his s. Elias once res.; was hayward, 1704, licensed inn-keeper, Mch., 1707; trad. says he was a very powerful athletic man. He kept a tavern (licensed Feb., 1727—*Co. Ct. Rec.*) many were the feats he is said to have performed; such as taking in his arms a professional bully who had come to fight and tossing him into the briar bushes near which he (Francis) was at work; outrunning another when challenged to a race, as he was on his way to his daily labor, though at the same time carrying an ox-yoke and chain; tossing into the street, fm. the door of his house, two riotous men, together, one fm. each hand, etc. etc. Others of this family were also noted for physical strength. He d. 14 (or 19) Sept., 1749, in 65th yr.—*Weth. Ins.;* the wid. Eunice d. 21 May., 1770.

Children (Weth. Rec.):

1. John, 1st., b. 28 Sept., bp. 1 Oct. (*Mix MSS.*), 1710; d. 15 May, 1738. FAM. 7.
2. Elisha.
3. Mary, m. a **Bassett** (prob. Jonathan), who, by wife Mary, had 7 ch. (1739-1753), res. in Weth.
(*By third marriage*):
4. Lydia, b. 4 June, 1738.
5. Eunice, b. 15 Aug., 1741; m. 3 Nov., 1762, Abigah **Tryon**, a soldier of the Revol.
6. John, 2d, (Capt.), b. 28 June, 1744; m. Rhoda **Wright**. FAM. 8.
7. Mercy, b. 6 Feb., 1746-7; d. 6 July, 1747, ae. 5 mos.—*Weth. Ins.*

FAM. 4. JAMES,[3] (*John,*[2] *Robert,*[1]), b. 1685, m. (1) 3 Nov., 1713, Elizabeth (dau. John) **Howard**; m. (2) Abigail (dau. Abr'm) **Warren**, 30 Sept., 1731; surveyor of highways in Weth., 1715; sett. in Berlin, Ct.; she d. 13 Apl., 1728, in 39th yr.—*Weth. Ins.*

freeman in 1646, d. Mch., 1687, leaving sons *Stephen,* b. 1644, and *John,* b. 4 Jan., 1650, John and Richard first, first ment. above, may (either) have been the father of Robert of Weth.

Robert, by deed, 1705, gives to his "well beloved and only s. John," for the prevention of all trouble and discord among his ch., certain lds.; and this fact seems to prove that, of his sons, John alone had lived to yrs. of maturity, and also that the daus. were then living.

Children (by first marriage—Weth. Rec.):

1. Anne, b. 23 Aug., (bp. 5 Sept.—*Mix MSS.*), 1714.
2. Elizabeth, b. 18 June, 1716-7.

3. Mary, b. 5 Feb., 1721-2. (*By second marriage*):
4. Elijah, b. 25 Feb., 1732-3. FAM. 9.

FAM. 5. Sgt. THOMAS,[3] (*John*,[2] *Robert*,[1]), b. 1690; appraiser of cattle, 1719; m. (1) 19 Mch., 1717-18, Abigail (dau. Jacob) **Griswold**; he res. and d. in New.; was several times app. on church and school committees; adm. to communion in ch., 4 July, 1762; m. (2) Anne ————, who d. 8 Feb., 1752; m. (3) Sarah **Smith**—*New. Ch. Rec.*; who d. 8 Feb., 1752. He d. 26 Apl., 1774, in 85th yr.—*Weth. Ins.*; wife Abigail and daus. *Abigail* and *Anna*, bu. beside him.

Children (Weth. Rec.):

1. Abigail, b. 7 Dec., 1718.
2. Josiah, b. 18 Sept., 1722. FAM. 10.
3. Samuel, b. 22 Jan., 1724-5.
4. Lydia, b. 12 June, 1729; m. Robert **Sanford.**
5. Ann, b. 19 Oct., 1732; m. Samuel **Steele.**

6. (John of Thos. Fr[ancis ?], bp. 31 Dec., 1732.—*Mix MSS.*)
7. Hezekiah, b. 11 Mch., 1737-8; m. Deborah ————. FAM. 11.
8. Mabel, b. [27 Dec.], 1740; m. 1767, Uriah **Goodwin.**

FAM. 6. ROBERT,[3] (*John*,[2] *Robert*,[1]), b. 1697; m. Elizabeth **Butler;** sett. Weth. on father's homestead; he d. 21 Feb., 1777, ae. 80 (*Weth. Rec.*); she d. 20 May, 1767 or '9, ae 69.—*Weth. Ins.*

Children (Weth. Rec.):

1. Samuel, b. 8 Feb., 1723; m. ———— **Brigden.** FAM. 12.
2. Elizabeth, b. 17 Apl., 1726; d. unm., ae. 63, bu. 4 or 14 Feb., 1789.—*W. C. R.*
3. Honor, b. 13, bp. 14 (*Mix MSS.*) Apl., 1728; m. John **Bulkley.** *Issue:*
   i. John (Bulkley).
   ii. Francis (Bulkley).
   iii. Benjamin (Bulkley).

   iv. William (Bulkley).
   v. Edward (Bulkley).
   vi. Honor (Bulkley).
   vii. Elizabeth (Bulkley).
   viii. Sarah (Bulkley).
4. William, b. 11, bp. 15 (*Mix MSS.*) Feb., 1729-30. FAM. 13.
5. Timothy, b. 8, bp. 11 (*Mix MSS.*) Mch., 1732-3. FAM. 14.

FAM. 7. JOHN the 1st,[4] (*John*,[3] *John*,[2] *Robert*,[1]), b. 1710; m. Mary (dau. Edward) **Dodd**, of Htfd.; invent. £781-11-02, taken Dec., 1738; adm. gr. to wid.; he d. 15 May, 1738; his wid. m. Peter **Ayrault**, of Weth., in 1744, as J. F.'s ch. abt. that time, chose their father-in-law, P. A., as their guardian—*R. H. C.;* prob. the J. F. who rec'd license as a taverner, Dec., 1722, fm. Co. Ct.

Children:

1. John, bp. 2 July, 1744; d. in Colonial army.
2. Josiah, b. 1735; m. ————. FAM. 15.

3. Eunice, bp. 13 Aug., 1745.
4. Charles. FAM. 16.
5. Mary, d. unm.

FAM. 8. Capt. JOHN,[4] or John the 2d, (*John*,[3] *John*,[2] *Robert*,[1]), b. 1744; m. 20 Sept., 1764, Rhoda (dau. Elias, Nath'l, Joseph, Thos.) **Wright;** she d. 27 Mch., 1816, ae. 73 (gr.-st.) ; he was a soldier of the Revol. (See Vol. I, Chapt. XI) ; he d. ae. 80, 31 May, 1824—see *Midd'x Gazette* of June 2d (Tuesday) 1824, which says he d. "Sunday last." *Weth. Ch. Rec.* gives his bu. as 30 May.

Children (Weth. Rec.):

1. Jennet, b. 13 Jan., 1765; d. Weth., unm.
2. John, b. 22 Feb., 1767. FAM. 17.
3. Olla, b. 9, bp. 20 Aug., 1769; d. 31 Jan., 1770.
4. Daniel (Capt.), b. Dec., 1770. FAM. 18.
5. Matthew (s. John), ae. 3 or 4, bu. 4 Feb., 1776.—*W. C. R.*
6. Matthew, bp. 4 Feb., 1774; ment. on bp. rec. as being bp. when 3 or 4 yrs. of age.

—*W. C. R.* FAM. 19.
7. Olla, b. 1775; m. 23 June, 1803, Simeon **Welles**, who d. 12 Nov., 1837.
8. Elias, b. 1783. FAM. 20.
9. Rhoda, b. 31 Oct., 1778; m. Dea. Ebenezer **Stillman**, 16 May, 1797; she d. 27 Apl., 1833, ae. 54. Dea. S. d. 11 Dec., 1854, ae. 78; res. Weth.; had 12 ch.

FAM. 9. ELIJAH,[4] (*John*,[3] *John*,[2] *Robert*,[1]), b. 1733; m. Hannah **Buck**; res. in Berlin, Ct.; rep. B. in Gen. Assembly, May, 1808; prob. notice for sett. of his est. appeared in *Conn. Currant*, for 29 Sept., 1812; his sons James and Elijah, Exec'rs.

Children:

1. James. FAM. 21.
2. Elijah, prob. the one who rep. Town of Berlin in Gen. Assemb., 1822—*Conn. Courant;* m. Jane **Clark**. *No issue.*
3. Selah, prob. the S. who m. Roxa **Bulkley,**

of Step., 25 Feb., 1793—*Step. Rec.;* had Mary Lyman, bp. 7 Sept., 1794, and Roxa Bulkley, bp. 9 Oct., 1796.—*S. C. R.*
4. Justus. FAM. 22.

FAM. 10. JOSIAH,[4] (*Thomas*,[3] *John*,[2] *Robert*,[1]), b. 1722; m. Milicent (dau. Nath'l & Sarah *Buck*) **Stoddard**, 26 Feb., 1746-7; she d. 5 July, 1800, ae. 71 (*Conn. Currant*); he d. 10 Nov., 1798, in 76th yr., at New.—*Weth. Ins.*

Children (Weth. Rec., bp. fm. N. C. R.):

1. Elias, b. 30 Apl., bp. 1 May, 1747; is prob. the E. to whom *N. C. R.* gives 25.
   Rachel and *Elias* (twins), bp. June, 1772, of whom *Elias*, bp. privately 24, d.
2. Justus, b. 8, bp. 11 Nov., 1750. FAM. 23.
3. Lucina, b. 7, bp. 8 Apl., 1753; m. Elizur **Deming**.
4. James, b. 4, bp. 7 Dec., 1755; an officer in Revol. War; mcht. in Weth., after the war; prob. the James, father of the following ch. whose *bps.* are rec. in *W. Ch. Rec.:* George, bp. 30 June, 1782; Miles Coe, bp. 6 Apl., 1783; Justus Chauncey, bp. 27 Feb., 1785; James, bp. 28

Jan., 1787; Sarah, bp. 12 Dec., 1790; Thomas, bp. 9 Sept., 1792; d. 21 Apl., 1794.
5. Asa, b. 8, bp. 13 Nov., 1757. FAM. 24.
6. "John of Josiah," bp. 4 Feb., 1759; prob. belongs to this family.
7. Allen, b. 23, bp. 26 Oct., 1760; an Allen (perhaps this one) m. Esther **Hotchkiss**, 13 May, 1797.—*N. C. R.*
8. Roger, b. 29 Apl., bp. 1 May, 1763; former res. at W. Htfd., Ct. FAM. 25.
9. Achsah, dau. of Josiah, bp. 5 Feb., 1764; prob. belongs in this family.
10. Sarah, b. 6, bp. 16 Apl., 1769; m. Aaron **Hunt.**

FAM. 11. HEZEKIAH,[4] (*Sgt. Thomas*,[3] *John*,[2] *Robert*,[1]), b. 1738; m. Deborah **Blinn,** 7 Oct., 1762; res. New.

Children (New. Ch. Rec.):

1. Roswell (?), b. 27 Dec., 1762—*Weth. Rec.;* bp. 6 Apl., 1763.
2. Hosea, b. 13 (*Weth. Rec.*), bp. 21 Oct., 1763 or 1764.
3. Thomas,   } twins, bp. 17 Aug.,1766.
4. Sarah (or Selah ?), }
5. Amanda, bp. 1 Oct., 1768.
6. Harriet, bp. 12 June, 1770 (or 4).
7. Adonijah, bp. 9 Aug., 1772; d. 2 Aug., 1778.
8. Hezekiah, bp. 16 Feb., 1777.
9. Truman (?), d. 5 May, 1782.

FAM. 12. SAMUEL,[4] (*Robert*,[3] *John*,[2] *Robert*,[1]), b. 1723; m. 27 Nov., 1751, Joanne **Bridgon**; sett. at Southwick, Mass., tho' prob. not in early life, as his ch. are reg. rec. on *Weth. Rec.* His sons all enl. in Revol. army fm. Mass.; after the War they rem. to Essex Co., N. Y., and the sons all sett. in Girard township, Erie Co., Pa.

Children (Weth. Rec.):

1. Samuel, b. 21, bp. 29 Oct., 1752.
2. William, b. 21, bp. 27 Jan., 1754; m. 1783, Agnes (dau. Jedidiah & Sybil *Case*) **Loomis**, of Windsor; *Htfd. Times*, 14-28 July, 1902.
3. Sarah, b. 17, bp. 23 Nov., 1755.
4. Levi, b. 9 June, 1757.
5. Simeon, bp. 19 Jan., 1757. (Poss. 4 and 5 were twins.)
6. Thomas, b. 11 Apl., 1759.

FAM. 13. WILLIAM,[4] (*Robert*,[3] *John*,[2] *Robert*,[1]), b. 1730, m. 1 Oct., 1753, Phebe **Woodhouse**, of Weth.; was an early sett. at Pittsfield, Mass., where he d. 13 Mch., 1818; his name is in P. recs. in 1772 as having a fam. of 9 persons—had 2 ch. rec. in P.

Children:

1. Robert.
2. William.
3, 4, 5. Daughters (prob. 3), of which *Ruth*

and *Elizabeth*, "dau. of Wm.," bp. 9 Dec., 1759 (*W. C. R.*) may be two.

Capt.

Daniel Francis

FAM. 14. TIMOTHY,[4] (*Robert*,[3] *John*,[2] *Robert*,[1]), b. 1732-3; m. Elizabeth **Hanmer,** 10 Mch., 1762; res. on old fam. homestead; d. 3 Aug., 1807, ae. 75—*Weth. Ins.;* poss. the Mrs. Elizabeth F., who d. at Weth., 9 Aug., 1814 (*Conn. Currant*) was his wid. more likely (as per *Weth. Ins.*) ; she d. 30 July.

Children (*Weth. Rec.*) :

1. Robert, b. 26 Apl., 1763. **FAM.** 26.
2. Lucy, b. 23 Mch., 1765-6; m. Caleb **Griswold,** of Weth.
3. James, b. 25 May, 1767. **FAM.** 27.
4. Honor, bp. 20 Aug., 1769.
5. David, b. 18 June, 1772 ; m. and sett. Charleston, S. C., d. 1801, leaving one

ch. which also d. soon.
6. Honor, b. 19, bp. 25 Sept., 1774 ; m. Daniel **Welles,** a bro. of her bro. James Francis' wife; had several daus. d. at Trenton, N. Y. Mr. W. m. (2) and had 2 ch.

FAM. 15. JOSIAH,[5] (*John*,[4] *John*,[3] *John*,[2] *Robert*,[1]), b. 1735; m. at Htfd., Abigail **Spencer**, 12 Aug., 1759; she b. 8 May, 1737, d. P., 13 May, 1814, dau. of Obadiah Spencer; he d. 2 Mch., 1814, acc. to *Mail & Exp.*, 15 May, '97; rem. abt. 1792, to Pittsfield, Mass., where he and his s. Josiah, Jr., were memb. of the the Baptist Ch.

Children (*facts fm. ROLLIN COOK of Pittsfield, Mass.*) :

1. John (Rev.), b. 1759; rem. to Pittsfield, Mass., 1780; prob. had 4 ch.; he m. (1) Anne **Hubbard,** who d. 19 Sept., 1801, ae. 41; both he and wife were orig. memb. of Bap. Ch. in P., in 1800; and he was ord. in 1806; he m. (2) Lucy H. ————, who d. Suffield, 27 Jan., 1845, ae. 77; he was a Revol. soldier.—*Pittsfield Recs.*
2. Luke, b. 23 Feb., 1772 ; m. 18 Oct., 1798, in Pittsfield, Mass., Mehitable **Sackett** (dau. of Capt. Daniel & Mehitable *Cadwell*), b. 4 Dec., 1779; he d. 20 Aug., 1849; res. P.; had 10 ch.—*Pitts. Rec.*
3. Abigail, b. Htfd., 27 Jan., 1758; not named in father's will.
4. Anna.
5. Josiah, b. 3 Dec., 1765; m. at Weth., 6 Feb., 1797, Sarah **Boardman**; in 1800, was an orig. member of the Bap. Ch. at P., where he res., and where the births of 9 ch., are recorded.
6. Eldad, b. 10 Jan., 1768 ; m. Anna **Stephens.**
7. Lydia, b. 1760 ; m. 3 times; not ment. in father's will.
8. Hannah.
9. Aohsah.

FAM. 16. CHARLES,[5] (*John*,[4] *John*,[3] *John*,[2] *Robert*,[1]), m. ———— poss. "Anne, wife of Chas." who was bp. 1 Jan., 1775; a Charles was bu. 22 Oct., 1776.— *W. C. R.*

Children:

1. Huldah, bp. "privately, being sick"—*W. C. R.*, 4 Sept., 1758.
2. Charles, bp. 6 Nov., 1774. **FAM.** 28.
3. Huldah, bp. 6 Nov., 1774.
4. Simeon, bp. 6 Nov., 1774. **FAM.** 29.
5. Melicent, bp. 6 Nov., 1774.
6. George, bp. 10 Dec., 1775. **FAM.** 30.

FAM. 17. Capt. JOHN,[5] (*Capt. John*,[4] *John*,[3] *John*,[2] *Robert*,[1]), b. 1767; m. Huldah **Bulkeley,** (7 or) 8 Nov., 1792. He was a seafaring man and d. 22 Jan., 1835, ae. 68—gr.-st.; she d. 14 Apl., 1833, ae. 68—*Weth. Ins.* acc. to *Weth. Rec.;* but a notice in *Conn. Currant* gives date of 8 May.

Children (*deaths fm. Weth. Ins.*) :

1. Caroline, b. 21 Apl., 1794 ; d. 9 Apl., 1871, ae. 77.
2. Huldah, b. 16 Jan., 1796; d. 1 May, 1878, ae. 82.
3. John, b. 30 July, 1797; d. New Orleans, 15 Oct., 1840, ae. 43.
4. James Bulkeley, b. 9 June, 1799; d. 16

Dec., 1850, ae. 51.
5. William, b. 12 Mch., 1801; d. 21 Nov., 1872, ae. 72.
6. Stephen, b. 14 Dec., 1802. **FAM.** 31.
7 Albert b. 5 Dec., 1808; prob. the A. who m. Sarah Ann **Robbins,** 15 Nov., 1837; he d. 15 June, 1844, ae. 35.

FAM. 18. DANIEL,[5] (*Capt. John*,[4] *John*,[3] *John*,[2] *Robert*,[1]), b. 1770; m. Mehitable (dau. Elizur) **Goorich,** 5 June, 1799, who was b. 13 June, 1777. He was a mariner (See Chapt. on Maritime Hist., Vol. I) ; res. in Weth. in the brick ho. since occup. by Wm. P. Fay, W. side of High St.; he d. 9 (*Weth. Ins.* says 14) Jan., 1837; she d. 16 Dec., 1845.—*gr. st.*

Children (*W. T. & W. C. R.*) :

1. Abigail Deming, b. 18 Dec., 1801, bp. 25 Apl., 1802 ; m. Calvin Francis; she d. 25 Oct., 1865, in Chatham, Ill.—See Fam. 45.
2. Mary, b. 6 Nov., 1803, bp. 29 Apl., 1804 ; m. William Boardman, 5 Jan. (3 July?) 1828.—See B. Fam.
3. Jannet, b. 1 Jan., bp. 8 June, 1806 ; d. unm. 30 May, 1823, ae. 17 y. 5 mos.— Weth. Ins.
4. Daniel, b. 7 Dec., 1808. Fam. 32.
5. Elizur Goodrich, b. 18 Feb., 1811 ; d. unm. 31 July, 1874 ; rem. in early life to Albany, thence to Buffalo, N. Y.; later to St. Louis, Mo. ; again to Alexandria, Va., where he res. and d. much respected.
6. Anson Wright, b. 7 Mch., 1813 ; d. New Haven, 20 Feb., 1896 ; m. 13 Apl., 1837, Ann Hart, of New Britain ; she d. 28 Feb.,

1839 ; he m. (2) 22 Feb., 1844, Harriet (Russell), wid. of Stephen Warner, of Plymouth, Ct., who d. New Haven, Ct., 17 June, 1889. By 1st wife, Mr. A. W. F. had dau. Laura Ann, b. 9 Feb., 1839 ; by 2d wife, sons Willard, Samuel, and Walter.
7. Honor Goodrich, b. 22 July, 1815 ; m. 14 Mch., 1837, Wm. Hanmer; she d. Weth., 20 Feb., 1897.
8. John Newton, b. 9 Sept., 1817 ; m. 24 July, 1844, Eveline (dau. Hosea) Harris, of Weth. (W. T. R.) ; he d. 6 June, 1867. Fam. 33.
9. Julius Edward, b. 11 Jan., 1822 ; d. 1 Aug., 1881, unm., at Buffalo, N. Y.; was in the drug trade ; successful, and in his will, besides private legacies, made valuable bequests to his adopted city.

Fam. 19. MATTHEW,[5] (*Capt. John,*[4] *John,*[3] *John,*[2] *Robert,*[1]), b. 1774 ; m. Hannah Deming, 7 July, 1799 ; he d. in Feb., 1840, ae. 66 (*gr. st.*) ; she d. 12 Feb., 1842, ae. 65.—*Weth. Ins.*

Children (*Weth. Rec. except those* *) :

1. Alfred, b. 6 Oct., 1799 ; printer ; m. Emeline Buck, 2 Mch., 1827 ; he d. 24 Jan., 1875 ; she d. 10 Jan., 1890, ae. 90 ; no issue.
2. Hannah,* b. 13 Oct., 1801 ; d. 24 June, 1802. —W. C. R.
3. Matthew,* ae. 8 mos., bu. 24 June, 1802.
4. Jannet,* b. 4 Oct., 1803 ; d. 7 Nov., 1804.
5. Levi, b. 4 Feb., 1806 ; d. 31 Mch., 1867 (Weth. Ins.), unm.; carriage maker at

Htfd. ; rem. to New Haven, Ct., where he d.
6. Hannah Standish, b. 26 May, 1808 ; d. 25 June, 1848 (Weth. Ins.) ; m. 26 May, 1844, John N. Littlefield, of Lyme, Ct. ; no issue.
7. Matthew, b. 10 Jan., 1813. Fam. 34.
8. Hiram, b. 13 Sept., 1816. Fam. 35.

Fam. 20. ELIAS,[5] (*Capt. John,*[4] *John,*[3] *John,*[2] *Robert,*[1]), b. 1783 ; m. Mary Wells, 4 Oct., 1803, who d. 28 and her infant 29 Jan., 1823, ae. 37 or 38; he m. (2) 7 Apl., 1824, Sarah Griswold; he d. 22 Sept., 1836, ae. 53.—*Weth. Ins.*

Children (*by first marriage*) :

1. Polly, b. 7 Feb., 1804.
2. Lucy, b. 6 May, 1808 ; m. 8 Mch., 1832, Benj. Twissell, of Meriden, Ct.—Midd'x Gaz., 14 Mch., 1832.
3. Chloe Ann, b. 17 Feb., 1812.
4. Elias, b. 7 Mch., 1816.
5. Thomas, b. 27 Nov., 1817.
6. Julia Wells, b. 7 July, 1820; who m.

Joseph B. Twiss, of Montreal, Canada, 9 Aug., 1837.
(By second marr.) :
7. Elizabeth, b. 3 Mch., 1825.
8. Henry, b. 15 Nov., 1827.
9. George W., b. 22 Feb., 1829.
10. Sarah, b. 28 Nov., 1831.
11. Caleb, b. 6 June, 1833.

Fam. 21. JAMES,[5] (*Elijah,*[4] *James,*[3] *John,*[2] *Robt.,*[1]), b. ———— ; m. Lydia Stanley.

Children:

1. Ursula.
2. Laura.
3. James (Sylvia, ae. 68, wife of James Fr., d. at Berlin, Ct., 21 Mch., 1822.— Conn. Courant.)

4. Romeo, of Berlin, m. Cath. Andrews, 7 Dec., 1812.—Conn. Courant. From same paper we get the dth. of Romeo B., (s. Romeo) at Berlin, 22 May, 1822.

Fam. 22. Major JUSTUS,[5] (*Elijah,*[4] *James,*[3] *John,*[2] *Robert,*[1]), b. May, 1822 ; m. Abigail Stanley; Capt. Justus d. Berlin, 14 Feb., 1819—prob. this Conn Currant Justus.

Children:

1. John. Fam. 36.
2. Jessie.
3. Abi.
4. George.

5. Horace.
6. Laura, (dau. Major) Justus Fr. ; m. Nov., 1816, Mr. Grandison Barber.—Conn. Courant of 26 Nov.

Fam. 23. JUSTUS,[5] (*Josiah,*[4] *Thos.,*[3] *John,*[2] *Robert,*[1]), b. 1750. (This Justus is the starting-point of Miss Chatfield's interesting pamphlet, entitled *Family Records of some of the Descendants of Robert Francis, of Weth.* pub. in Apl., 1900, and fm. which we take some of the facts given in this line of descent fm. the Settler.) Justus Francis was a Soldier of the Revol.—see our Chapt. on the Revol. War in our 1st vol.; he res. in Newington, and was a prominent man in town and church, in bldg. ch. edifices, selecting pastors, etc. He m. (1) 6 May, 1773, Keturah **Andrus,** who d. 14 Aug., 1780—*Weth. Ins.;* he m. (2) Mary (dau. of Rev. Joshua) **Belden,** of New., 3 July, 1783, who d. 5 Mch., 1785, in 30th yr.; he m. (3) 9 Nov., 1786, Lois (dau. Hezekiah) **Andrus,** b. 1763, and who d. 20 July, 1813, ae. 49—*Weth. Ins.;* he m. (4) Ruth **Barber,** of Bloomfield, Ct.; he d. New., ae. 76, 8 Jan., 1827.—*Weth. Ins.*

Children (New. T. and C. Recs.; by first marr.) :

1. Appleton, b. 9 Aug., bp. 24 Dec., 1780 ; m. Charlotte **Webster,** 18 Nov., 1805 (*W. T. R.*) ; d. at Berlin, ae. 53, 14 Feb., 1832.—*Conn. Courant.* Bernard J. (s. of Appleton), d. New Orleans, 10 Sept., 1820, ae. 22.—*Conn. Courant.*
(*By second marr.*) :
2. Keturah Andrus, b. 19, bp. 28 Mch.; d. 19 Apl., 1784.
(*By third marr.*) :
3. Harvey, b. 27 Jan., bp. 3 May, 1789 ; d. 27 Jan., 1869 ; m. 27 Nov., 1828, Abigail **Kilborn,** who d. 18 Sept., 1860.

4. Anson, b. 4 Nov., 1790, bp. 16 Jan., 1791 ; d. 14 Nov., 1868. FAM. 37.
5. Newman, b. 25 June, bp. 11 Aug., 1793. FAM. 38.
6. Cyrus, bp. 4 Mch., 1795 ; d. yg.
7. Alfred, bp. 11 Jan., 1796. FAM. 39.
8. Cyrus, b. 16 Dec., 1797. FAM. 40.
9. Laura, bp. 15 Mch., 1800.
10. Erastus, b. 16 Nov., 1802 ; bp. 27 Feb., 1803. FAM. 41.
11. Mary, b. 28 June, bp. 28 Aug., 1808 ; m. ——— **Butler;** descts. res. W. Htfd.

FAM. 24. ASA,[5] (*Josiah,[4] Thos.,[3] John,[2] Robert,[1]*), b. 1757; m. 8 Mch., 1781— *W. C. R.,* Prudence **Warner,** of Weth.; he rec. at time of marr. as of Htfd.; he served in Revol. War (See Chapt. VII, Vol. I) ; had a carriage mfy. in Htfd. The wid. Prudence d. at H., 14 Oct., 1841, ae. 84, *Conn. Currant* of 15th.

Children (b. Htfd.) :

1. William, b. 4 Aug., 1784 ; d. at Boston, 26 June, 1804.
2. John, b. 1 Dec., 1785 ; m. (1) Lucy **Dyer,** of Windham, Ct., 12 Oct., 1815 ; she d. at Royalton, Vt., 27 Feb., 1822, ae. 26 ; he m. (2) Rebecca **Wheeler,** of Ashford, N. H., 20 Apl., 1823, who was living 1876 ; he d. Royalton, Vt., 1843, ae. 58.
3. Ann Lockwood, b. 12 Nov., 1787 ; m. 1809, Ira **Webster,** of W. Htfd., Ct. ; d. at Wallingford, Ct.
4. George, b. Htfd., 25 June, 1790 ; m. Martha (dau. Reuben & Eliz'th **Stevens**) **Wads-**

worth, 30 Nov., 1818 ; acc. to *Conn. Courant* m. 14 Dec., 1819 ; he d. 7 Mch., 1873 ; he had 5 ch., of whom Dr. Chas. Edwd., of N. Y. City, b. 1828, is said to be preparing a gen. of the *Francis Family.*
5. Asa, b. 8 Nov., 1791 ; m. Nancy **Parkhurst,** of Lebanon, N. H., Oct., 1824 ; she d. 24 Mch., 1830 ; he m. (2) Jane **Wallace,** of Milford, N. H., in 1833 ; he d. at Middlebury, Vt., 1 (or 16) Dec., 1862.
6. Henry, b. 30 Nov., 1793 ; d. 30 Nov., 1794.
7. Henry, b. 31 Mch., 1796 ; m. (2) May, 1825, Emily **Cheeney.** FAM. 42.

FAM. 25. ROGER,[5] (*Josiah,[4] Thomas,[3] John,[2] Robert,[1]*), b. 1763 ; m. Dec., 1790, Eliza beth **Andrews,** who d. 1 Sept., 1845 ; he d. 16 Sept., 1839.

Children (Miss C. E. C.'s book) :

1. Charles, b. 12 Aug., bp. 30 Sept., 1792 ; d. unm. 17 Oct., 1835.
2. Amzi (Rev.), b. 31 July, bp. 21 Sept., 1794. FAM. 42a.

3. Betsy, bp. 4 Nov., 1797 ; d. a few days after.—*New. Rec.*
4. Julia Ann, b. 1 June, 1800 ; d. 17 Apl., 1810.
5. Chester, b. 21 Feb., 1812. FAM. 43.

FAM. 26. ROBERT,[5] (*Timothy,[4] Thos.,[3] John,[2] Robt.,[1]*), b. 1763 ; m. 8 May, 1788 Anne (dau. Josiah) **Francis;** sett. at New.; she d. 23 Aug., 1845, ae. 83 ; m. (2) Lydia **Deming,** 14 Jan., 1846 ; she d. 7 Mch., 1872, ae. 77. He d. 13 Feb., 1855, ae. 92.—*Weth. Ins.*

Children (Weth. Rec.) :

1. Abigail, b. 20 Oct., 1789 ; m. ——— **Hubbard,** of Bloomfield,. Ct.
2. Robert, b. 24 Oct., 1791 ; poss. the R. N. Fr. (s. Capt. Robt.), who d. in Geo., Apl., 1826.
3. Anna, b. 11 Sept., 1793 ; d. 18 Mch., 1795.
4. John, b. 31 Jan., 1795 ; m. 18 Apl., 1830, Maria (dau. James) **Francis;** he d. 24 Aug., 1859.

5. Anna, b. 3 Dec., 1796 ; m. 3 May, 1820 (*Conn. Courant*), Benj. **Belden,** of W. Htfd.
6. Joseph, b. 10 Mch., 1800 ; d. 18 Apl., 1826, of fever in Geo.
7. Timothy, b. 3 (or 5) Oct., 1801 ; d. 13 May, 1838, from exposure at a fire in Vicksburg, Miss.; prob. the Timo. who m. 27 Dec., 1828, in Weth., Esther N.

Miner; she d. 25 May, 1880, ae. 73 yrs.
9 mos. *Issue:*
  i. Timothy, d. 5 Apl., 1836, ae. 11 mos.
  ii. Ellen E., d. 7 Apl., 1854, ae. 21 yrs.
  iii. John M., (Capt. Co. I, 25th Reg.
    Conn. Vols.) d. at Baton Rouge, 9
    July, 1863, ae. 32.—*Weth. Ins.*

8. Heman, b. 23 Mch., 1804; d. 8 May, 1825,
   at home, of fever contracted at the South.
9. Lidia, b. 16 Nov., 1805; m. 1833, Joseph
   Camp (*Conn. Courant* of 29 Jan.); d.
   25 Apl., 1837.
10. Asaph, b. 20 July, 1808; sett. at Mendon,
   Ill.

FAM. 27. JAMES,[5] (*Timo.,[4] Robert,[3] John,[2] Robert,[1]*), b. 1767; m. 31 Jan., 1793, Pamelia (dau. Joshua) **Welles.** He d. 23 Sept., 1852, ae. 85; she d. 4 Dec., 1848, ae. 80.—*Weth. Ins.*

Children:

1. Pamela. b. 14 Sept., 1793; d. 11 Aug., 1827;
  m. 13 Apl., 1820 (*W. C. R.*) Ransom **Tom-**
  linson, of Derby, Ct.; sett. at Glast., Ct.,
  11 Aug., 1827. *Issue:*
    i. Jane (Tomlinson).
    ii. James (Tomlinson).
    iii. Welles (Tomlinson).
2. James Hanmer (Rev.), b. 28 May, 1796,
  bp. 1 Dec., 1816 (*W. C. R.*); grad. Y. C.
  1826; sett. as Cong'l minister at Dudley,
  Mass., 1831; in 1840, was sett. in Westfield,
  So. Midd., Ct., where he d. 11 July, 1863.—

Weth. Ins.
3. Clarissa, b. 29 June, 1798; d. 5 Dec., 1834;
  m. Joshua **Goodrich.** *Issue:*
    i. Francis (Goodrich).
    ii. Elizabeth (Goodrich).
    iii. James (Goodrich).
    iv. Mary (Goodrich).
4. Walter, b. 10 Mch., 1800; d. Geo., 17 Jan.,
  1834 (*Weth. Ins.*); a trader at the South.
5. Maria, b. 24 Dec., 1801; m. John[6] (s.
  Robt.[5]) **Francis,** who d. 24 Aug., 1850, ae.
  55; she d. 26 June, 1868.—*Weth. Ins.*

FAM. 28. CHARLES,[6] (*Chas.,[5] John,[4] John,[3] John,[2] Robert,[1]*), bp. 1775?; m. Sarah **Adams,** 16 June, 1799.

Children:

1. Sally, b. July, 1802, (*W. C. R.* say Sarah,
  bp. 29 Nov., 1801—may have been an

earlier Sarah who d.); m. Hosea **Harris.**
2. Charles, b. 3 Jan., 1803. FAM. 44.

FAM. 29. Dea. SIMEON,[6] (*Chas.,[5] John,[4] John,[3] John,[2] Robert,[1]*), b. ————; m. 26 May, 1793, Mary Ann **Adams;** she d. 18 Sept., 1822, ae. 49—*Weth. Ins.;* he d. ae. 54, 7 Sept., 1823.—(*Middx. Gaz.,* 2 Oct., 1823.)

Children (*Weth. Rec.*):

1. Charles, b. 19 Mch., 1794; prob. the Charles
  2d, who m. Elizabeth **Haskell,** 4 Dec., 1820.
2. Simeon, b. 8 May, 1796; prob. the Simeon
  who m. Eliza **Rumsey** at N. Lond., 26
  Dec., 1820.—*Conn. Courant.*
3. Mary Ann, b. 9 Aug., 1798.
4. Calvin, b. 12 June, 1802. FAM. 45.
5. Josiah, b. 14 Jan., 1805.
6. Edwin, b. 9 Oct., 1808.
7. Huldah, b. 10 May, 1810.
8. Allen (Hon.), b. 1814; rem. to Illinois,
  where, with his bro. Maj. Francis, he estab.
  the *Ill. State Journal*, which was conducted
  with ability and success for 27 yrs. In
  1861, he was app. by Pres. Lincoln, as

U. S. Consul at Victoria, B. A., and took
up his permanent res. at that port; res.
after 10 yrs. service and engaged in the
fur industry; was again app. Consul at
Victoria, from which position he was
transferred by Pres. Arthur, in 1881, to a
similar duty at St. Thomas, where he d.
4 Aug., 1887, from injuries rec'd in a
railroad collision, ae. 70 (?). He was the
author of a little work entitled *My Home
of Fifty Years Ago,* pp. 15, pub. N. Y.,
1874, which refer to the old Simeon Francis
place on West Hill, in Weth., now owned
by John Hanmer, Esq.
9. Newton.

FAM. 30. GEORGE,[5] (*Charles,[4] John,[3] John,[2] Robert,[1]*), b. 1775; m. Sarah **Butler,** 5 Oct., 1801, who was b. 26 Apl., 1778 and d. 20 Sept., 1825 (*W. Rec.*) ae. 47; he m. (2) Mary (wid. of Eli) **Stoddard,** 3 May, 1835,—*W. C. R.* He d. 21 Nov., 1858, ae. 84, she d. 4 Feb., 1866, ae. 78.—*Weth. Rec.*

Children (*Weth. Town & Church Rec.*):

1. Eliza Scott, b. 4 Apl., 1828.
2. Stephen Bulkely, b. 9 Feb., 1830.
3. James Bulkely, b. 26 Feb., d. 17 Dec., 1834,
  ae. 10 mos.—*Weth. Ins.*

4. Edwin Elisha, b. 29 Mch., 1837.
5. Lewis Henry, b. 27 July, 1839.
6. Elisha Stevens, bu. 18 Aug., 1855, ae. 12.—
  W. C. R.

FAM. 31. STEPHEN,[6] (*John,*[5] *Capt. John,*[4] *John,*[3] *John,*[2] *Robert,*[1]), b. 1802; m. Elizabeth Secor **Stevens**, 3 Oct., 1827; she d. 11 Apl., 1847, ae. 42.—*Weth. Ins.;* he d. 4 Oct., 1864, ae. 62.—*Weth. Ins.*

Children (*Weth. Rec.*) :

1. Sally, b. 29 Mch., 1802, bp. 22 Aug., 1803; d. 12 Sept., 1803.—*Weth. Ins.*
2. John Butler, b. 29 June, (*July,* Weth. Ins.) bp. 28 Oct., 1804 ; d. Sept. 1806.
3. Sarah, bp. 12 July, 1806.
4. Sally, b. 5 June, bp. 12 July, 1807 (one rec. says 1810; prob. incorrect) ; m. (1) Jared W. **Flint**, of Ry-H., 20 Nov., 1828 ; m. (2) ——— **Robbins**.
5. Lucy, b. 10 Oct., 1810, bp. 2 June, 1811 ; m. 9 Oct., 1831, Seneca C. **Hemmingway**, of

Lane, Mass.—*W. C. R.*
6. John Butler, b. 29 Jan., bp. 15 Aug., 1813 ; m. Hannah J. **Hart** in Waterloo, N. Y., 22 Apl., 1838 ; d. at Waterloo, N. Y., 13 Apl., 1902 ; *no issue*.
7. George, b. 25 Feb., bp. 6 Aug., 1815, then of Waterloo, N. Y.; m. Huldah (dau. John) **Stillman**, 25 May, 1840 ; *no issue*.
8. Martha, b. 18 June, bp. 3 Oct., 1819 ; m. Eli **Stoddard**.

FAM. 32. DANIEL,[5] (*Capt. Daniel,*[4] *John,*[3] *John,*[2] *Robert,*[1]) b. 1808; m. 16 Mch., 1835, Elida (dau. Moses & Grace *Carson*) **Long**, of Albany, N. Y.; rem. to Buffalo, N. Y., where he was a mfr. of Britannia ware, and celebrated his Golden Wedding, 16 Mch., 1685. During the Patriot War of 1837, Mr. F. was requested by Gov. Scott to pull the stroke oar in the truce boat sent by the Gen. to the two armed schooners lying in Niagara River, with despatches requesting their Commander not to fire upon the Barcelona, then acting as a supply ship to the troops stationed on Navy Island. The Caroline had formerly been employed in this work, but had been fired upon and sent adrift down the River. The Br. troops at Chippewa were then firing upon Navy Island with hot shot.—*Newspaper.* Mrs. F. d. Buffalo, N. Y., 10 July, 1897.

Children :

1. Grace Long, b. 11 Jan., 1836 ; m. 15 Sept., 1859, Frederic Lyman **Danforth**, of Midd., Ct. ; res. Buffalo, N. Y. *Issue :*
   i. Frederic Wm. (Danforth), b. 15 July, 1860 ; m. Grace Myrtle **Wilcox**.
   ii. Francis Lobdell (Danforth), b. 18 Aug., 1862 ; m. Suzette **Barnes**.
   iii. William Edgar (Danforth), b. 28 Sept., 1864.
   iv. Grace Elida (Danforth), b. 4 Jan., 1876.
2. Jennie Gardner, b. 22 Dec., 1837 ; res. Buffalo, N. Y., unm.
3. Edward Gardner, b. 7 Dec., 1839 ; d. 24 Feb., 1842.
4. George Webster, b. 13 May, 1845 ; d. 15

Sept., 1894 ; m. 16 July, 1874, Frances E. (dau. Noah H. & Fanny *Foster*) **Gardner**; res. Buffalo, N. Y. *Issue :*
   i. Alice Gardner (Francis), b. 10 July, 1879.
   ii. Edith (Francis), b. 21 Sept., 1885.
5. William Carson, b. 6 Feb., 1847 ; d. 27 Apl., 1889 ; m. 15 June, 1876, Gertrude C. (dau. G. R. & Jane *Townsend*) **Wilson**. *Issue :*
   i. Guilford Wilson (Francis), b. 30 Apl., 1877.
   ii. William Carson (Francis), b. 21 May, 1879.
   iii. Florence Gertrude (Francis), b. 9 Aug., 1885.

FAM. 33. JOHN NEWTON,[6] (*Daniel,*[5] *John,*[4] *John,*[3] *John,*[2] *Robert,*[1]), b. 1817; m. 24 July, 1844, Evelina (dau. Hosea) **Harris**, of Weth., and d. 6 June, 1867, of yell. fever, at sea, near Carthagena, S. A., and was bu. on a small island near the coast; was Capt. of ship *Sicanee;* "beloved as a father and husband, esteemed and respected as a gentleman and citizen, and worthy the name of an efficient Christian."

Children (*b. Weth. & New Haven*) :

1. Albert Newton, b. 10 June, 1845. FAM. 46.
2. Henry Harris, b. 24 Oct., 1847. FAM. 47.
3. John, b. N. H., 10 Apl., 1850 ; d. 30 May, 1850.
4. Harriet Evelina, b. N. H., 25 Sept., 1851 ; m. 30 Aug., 1878, Marcus E. **Robertson**; d. Galesburg, Ill., 17 Sept., 1890. *Issue* (*b. Htfd., Ct.*) :
   i. William H. (Robertson), b. 16 Aug., 1870 ; d. 1885.
   ii. Maud F. (Robertson), b. 17 Sept., 1880 ; d. 1885.

iii. Grace E. (Robertson), b. 8 Jan., 1884.
   iv. Lena F. (Robertson), b. 1886.
4. Mary Elida, b. N. H., 21 July, 1854 ; res. Htfd., unm.
5. Daniel, b. 31 May, 1857, in Chatham, Ill.; d. Weth., 31 Mch., 1865.
6. John Newton, b. Weth., 2 Apl., 1860 ; d. there, 2 Oct., 1861.
7. William Hanmer, b. Weth., 12 June, 1862 ; m. 11 Apl., 1887, Kate G. **Karey**; res. Htfd.

FAM. 34. MATHEW,[6] (*Matt.*,[5] *John*,[4] *John*,[3] *John*,[2] *Rob't*,[1]) b. 1813; m. Lucy **Seymour**, (dau. James), of Htfd., Ct., 22 Nov., 1838; she was b. 27 June, 1816; they sett. on a farm at Weth., where he d. 10 Jan., 1886; she d. 27 Jan., 1892.

Children:

1. Edward M., b. 1 Dec., 1841. FAM. 48.
2. Fannie, b. 2 Nov., 1846.

3. Alfred L., b. 14 Aug., 1851.

FAM. 35. HIRAM,[6] (*Matt.*,[5] *John*,[4] *John*,[3] *John*,[2] *Robert*,[1]), b. 1816; m. Elizabeth **Bowe**, 16 Sept., 1849; res. some yrs. at the South; rem. to Berlin, Ct., then to Meriden, where he was res. 1876.

Children:

1. Alice E., b. 1 July, 1850.
2. Elbert, b. 11 May, 1852.
3. Adella, b. 4 June, 1853; d. 21 Dec., 1853.
4. Levi, b. 6 Sept., 1854.

5. Ralph, b. 14 Jan., 1856.
6. Willis, b. 28 Apl., 1857.
7. Emma B., b. 14 Mch., 1864.

FAM. 36. JOHN,[6] (*Justus*,[5] *Elijah*,[4] *James*,[3] *John*,[2] *Robert*,[1]), b. m. Sophronia **Lusk**, of New Britain, Ct.

Children:

1. Lydia.
2. John. FAM. 48a.

3. Horace.
4. Oliver.

5. Abi.
6. Justus.

FAM. 37. ANSON,[6] (*Justus*,[5] *Josiah*,[4] *Thos.*,[3] *John*,[2] *Robert*,[1]), b. 1790-1, at Medford, Minn., 14 Nov., 1868; when a ygman, he rem. with a bro. to Wethersfield Springs, N. Y., where they cleared a home lot and res. the greater part of his life. He m. (1) 18 Sept., 1814, Almira **Owen**, of Ashford,—*W. T. R.;* m. (2) Betsy **Hatfield**, who d. 1829; he d. 14 Nov., 1868.

Children:

1. Anson, who res. at Sandusky, O., dep., Collector of the port and expr. agent; d. in State of Washington; m. Cordelia **Easton**.
2. Edwin, m. Chloe Anna **Tilton**; res. Sandusky, O.; d. 5 Aug., 1849. *Issue (b. at S.)* :
    i. John Wesley (Francis), b. 21 Oct., 1845; m. 24 Dec., 1874, Dora A. **Reeve**; served in the Civil War; had *issue:* Vinne R., Floyd E. and Eva R.
    ii. Elmira Elizabeth (Francis), b. 24 Jan., 1847.
    iii. Lucy (Francis), b. 31 May, 1849.
3. Owen (Lieut.), killed in Mex. War, 19 Oct., 1846; unm., bu. in Mexico.

4. Cyrus, b. 18 Apl., 1823.
5. Isaac, b. 8 July, 1827.
6. Betsy O., b. 18 Oct., 1831; m. Chas. **Jones**, 23 Apl., 1848. *Issue:*
    i. Clarissa O. (Jones), b. 16 Apl., 1849.
    ii. Helen (Jones), b. 11 Apl., 1851; d. 11 Sept., 1887.
    iii. Emma (Jones), b. 23 Dec., 1853; d. 6 Feb., 1854.
7. Mary Elizabeth, b. 13 Dec., 1832; m. Geo. H. **Partridge**.
8. Cynthia, b. 19 Aug., 1835; m. 1861, James **Hayes**.—See *C. E. C.'s Pamphlet.*
9. Martha A., b. 16 Aug., 1837; m. 9 Oct., 1855, Herman B. **Johnson**; 7 ch. and 18 gd-ch.

FAM. 38. NEWMAN,[6] (*Justus*,[5] *Josiah*,[4] *Thomas*,[3] *John*,[2] *Robert*,[1]), b. 1793; m. at Glast., 15 Feb., 1834, Octavia (dau. Jonathan) **Strickland**, this marr. was announced in *Conn. Currant*, issue of 2 Mch., 1835, who d. 13 Jan., 1843, ae. 34.— *Weth. Ins.* He d. W. Swanzey, N. H., 13 Aug., 1865, ae. 72.—*Weth. Ins.*

Children:

1. Roselle Bunce, b. 9 Oct., 1836; m. 5 Nov., 1856, Geo. A. **Capron**; res. (1900) at W. Swanzey, N. H.; 4 ch.

2. Martha Octavia, b. 4 July, 1842; m. 9 July, 1867, Henry H. **Onthrop**; res. (1900) Midd., Ct.; 2 ch.

FAM. 39. ALFRED,[6] (*Justus*,[5] *Josiah*,[4] *Thomas*,[3] *John*,[2] *Robert*,[1]), b. 1796, rem. with his bro. Anson, to Weth. Springs, N. Y., farmer and blacksmith; d. at Magnolia, Wis., Nov., 1851; m. 25 Aug., 1818, Nancy **Deming**, of Weth.— (*N. C. R.*) ; b. 1798, who d. 18—.

Children (*b. Weth. Springs, N. Y.*) :

1. Lucy Deming, b. 28 Dec., 1819 ; d. 12 Feb., 1839.
2. Louisa Ruth, b. 22 Aug., 1822 ; m. 20 May, 1857, James H. **DeRomer,** of Rock Co., Wis.
3. Franklin Justus, b. 6 Nov., 1825 ; d. 27 May, 1840.
4. William Pratt, b. 18 May, 1827 ; m. 2 July, 1863, Celia **Fredenberg,** b. Schoharie Co., N. Y., 1842. *Issue:*
   i. Anna Flora (Francis), b. 13 Feb., 1866 ; d. 1 July, 1891.

ii. Mary Alberta (Francis), b. 3 Nov., 1869 ; d. 2 Jan., 1873.
5. Nancy Jane, b. 3 Apl., 1829 ; d. 21 July, 1839.
6. Alfred Orostes, b. 6 Oct., 1831 ; d. June, 1889 ; printer ; m. Mary **Follet;** res. St. Paul, Minn.
7. Albert Butler, b. 25 Nov., 1837 ; unm.
8. Helen May, b. 28 Mch., 1840 ; m. 1861, Geo. C. **Moon;** res. Missoula (?), Mont. ; 4 ch.

FAM. 40. CYRUS,[6] (*Justus,[5] Josiah,[4] Thomas,[3] John,[2] Robert,[1]*), b. 1797 ; m. (1) 22 June, 1823, Sabra **Blinn,**—(*S. C. R.*) ; who d. 5 July, 1824, ae. 22; m. (2) Nancy Dorrance **Platt,** who d. 23 July, 1850, ae. 47. He d. crushed by ox-cart in New. 22 Oct., 1845.—*Weth. Ins.*

Children (*by first marr.*) :

1. Blinn, b. 10 Mch., 1824 ; d. 15 Nov., 1895 ; m. 1848, Lucy **Hart.** *Issue:*
   i. Julia Sabra (Francis), b. 1849 ; m. Harry C. **Butler.**
   ii. Laura Hart (Francis), b. abt. 1850 ; d. abt. 1885 ; unm.
   iii. Jane (Francis), b. abt. 1850 ; d. 1888 ; m. 1874, Niles C. **Beckwith.**
   iv. Henry Newton (Francis), b. 6 Nov., 1853 ; m. 10 Sept., 1878, Emily I. **Pettis,** of Putnam Co. ; res. Narragansett, R. I.
   v. John Woodruff (Francis), b. 1855 ; res. Southington, Ct. ; 7 ch.
   vi. Geo. Blinn (Francis), b. W. Htfd., 31 Jan., 1857 ; m. Apl., 1880, Florence Louise **Green.** Is Chief Eng., R. I. Suburban Railway, and for 20 yrs. a well known railroad engineer ; res. Providence, R. I.
   vii. Hattie L. (Francis), b. 1865 ; res. W. Htfd.
   viii. Lucy Alberta (Francis), b. 1868 ; m.

Henry **Atwood;** res. Southington, Ct.
(*By second marriage*) :
2. Pratt, b. 22 Sept., 1831 ; m. Adaline **Hurd;** res. Brooklyn, N. Y. *Issue:*
   i. Arlan Pratt (Hurd), b. 30 May, 1858 ; m. 17 June, 1886, Kate M. **Atwood;** 1 ch.
   ii. Fred Wilson (Hurd), b. 16 Sept., 1863 ; res. Brooklyn, N. Y.
3. Cyrus (Rev.,), b. 17 June, 1838 ; m. 24 Sept., 1867, Harriet **Miner,** who d. 1873 ; m. (2) Ida **Terry,** 1894 ; he grad. Y. C., 1863 ; at New Haven Theol. Sem., 1867 ; miss'y in Atlanta, Ga., for 27 yrs. and 20 yrs. teacher in Atlanta Univ. ; rem., 1894, to Brookfield, Ct., as pastor of Cong'l Ch. *Issue:*
   i. Dwight Terry (Francis), b. 18 Nov., 1894.
   ii. Alfred West, b. 11 Mch., 1896.
4. Nancy Dorrance, b. 29 Dec., 1841 ; m. 1866, Lucian H. **Adams;** miss. to Turkey, where she d. abt. 1890 ; had 4 ch.

FAM. 41. ERASTUS,[6] (*Justus,[5] Josiah,[4] Thos.,[3] John,[2] Robert,[1]*), b. 1802 ; m. (1) 17 July, 1825, Bertha B. **Stoddard,** she d. 9 Mch., 1852,—*Weth. Ins.*; he m. (2) 30 Dec., 1852, Cornelia **Stoddard,** b. 27 Aug., 1813, and who d. Dec., 15, 1877; he d. at New. 28 Aug., 1858, ae. 56.—*Weth. Ins.*

Children (*b. New.*) :

1. Charles James, b. 16 Dec., 1825 ; d. 20 Nov., 1877 ; m. 18 June, 1863, Ellen **Boynton.** *Issue:*
   i. Hubert C. (Francis), b. 7 July, 1865.
   ii. Thomas A. (Francis), b. 6 June, 1868.
   iii. Charles S. (Francis), b. 13 Jan., 1877.
2. Theodore J., d. 16 Mch., 1860.

3. Laura L., d. 3 Apl., 1829 ; ae. 5 yrs.
4. James H., d. ae. 3 yrs., 3 May, 1839.
5. Flora, J., b. 6 Oct., 1842 ; m. 15 Sept., 1874, Henry **Luce;** res. New. ; 1 ch.
6. Ellen M., b. 9 May, 1845 ; m. 5 Jan., 1870, Leonard N. **Beecher;** res. Southington, Ct.
7. May C., b. 9 June, 1851 ; m. 17 Apl., 1879, Frank N. **Pierce;** res. West Carmel, Ct.

FAM. 42a. Rev. AMZI,[6] (*Roger,[5] Josiah,[4] Thomas,[3] John,[2] Robert,[1]*), b. 1794 ; m. (1) 10 May, 1824, Eliza **Talcott,** who d. 17 Aug., 1829; m. (2) 15 Feb., 1832, Mary S. **Hedges,** who d. abt., 1896; he d. 18 Oct., 1845.

Children (*by first marr.*) :

1. Roger Andrews, b. 21 May, 1826 ; d. 11 July, 1885 ; m. Isabel **Hedges.** *No issue.*
2. Samuel Talcott, b. 21 July, 1829 ; d. 29 Jan., 1831.

(*By second marriage*) :
3. Mary Amelia, b. and d. 1836.
4. Samuel Talcott, b. 1839 ; d. 1841.
5. Henrietta Elizabeth, b. 23 July, ——; m. James **Talcott;** 5 ch.

FAM. 42. HENRY,[6] (*Asa*,[5] *Josiah*,[4] *Thos.*,[3] *John*,[2] *Rob't.*,[1]), b. 1790; m. 2 May, 1825, Emily **Cheeney**, of Manchester, Ct., who d. 22 Apl., 1871; he living in 1876.

Children:

1. Emily C.
2. Elizabeth S., d. ————.
3. Roselle M., d. ————.
4. Adelaide G., d. ————.

5. Henry, m.; d.; *no issue.*
6. Mary G.
7. Rebekah W.
8. Rose S.

FAM. 43. CHESTER,[6] (*Roger*,[5] *Josiah*,[4] *Thomas*,[3] *John*,[2] *Robert*,[1]), b. 1812, m. 4 Sept., 1832, Lucy **Halsey**, who d. 20 Feb., 1895; he d. 10 Aug., 1893.

Children:

1. Sarah Jane, b. 3 Sept., 1836; d. 26 Aug., 1896.
2. Samuel Halsey, b. 8 Dec., 1837; m. 24 Apl., 1861, Martha L. **Barber**; 3 ch.
3. Roger Newton, b. 14 Nov., 1839; m. 15

June, 1869, Emeline A. **Chadwick**; res. Elmwood, Ct. *No issue.*
4. Charlotte Augusta, b. 30 Oct., 1841; m. 1866, Hugh G. **Montgomery**; 6 ch.

FAM. 44. CHARLES,[6] (*Chas.*,[5] *Chas.*,[4] *John*,[3] *John*,[2] *Robert*,[1]), b. 1803; m. at Weth., 5 Oct., 1823, or '25, Emily **Blinn**,—*S. C. R.* Is this the Chas. who m. Elizabeth Haskell, 4 (or 17) Dec., 1820(?) He d. 9 Apl., 1885, ae. 82; she d. 20 Dec., 1883, ae. 81.—*Weth. Ins.*

Children (W. C. R.):

1. Martha, bp. 29 Oct., 1828.
2. Sarah A., d. 12 Sept., 1828, ae. 8 mos.—*Weth. Ins.*
3. Charles, bp. 31 Jan., 1831; d. 6 May, 1862.
4. Lucy Blinn, bp. 3, d. 11 Aug., 1833, ae. 13 mos.—*Weth. Ins.*
5. Lucy Blinn, bp. 3 Aug., 1833; d. 27 July,

1880.—*Weth. Ins.*
6. Daniel, prob. the D. W. Francis, whose wife Marietta d. 9 Apl., 1891, and whose ch. *Allen B.*, d. 22 July, 1888, and *Alice R.*, d. 6 June, 1894.—*Weth. Ins.*
7. Emily, d. ————.
8. Emily.
9. Jennie.

FAM. 45. CALVIN,[6] (*Dea. Simeon*,[5] *Chas.*,[4] *John*,[3] *John*,[2] *Robert*,[1]), b. 1802; m. 21 Oct., 1823, Abigail Deming (dau. Capt. Daniel) **Francis**, of Weth.; he d. Athens, Ill., 27 June, 1886, ae. 84 yrs. 15 d.; she d. at Chatham, Ill., 23 Oct., 1865.

Children:

1. Janette, b. 18 Aug., 1824; m. 4 Jan., 1844, Abner Banks **Hall**, of Athens, Ill. *Issue:*
   i. Ida Francis (Hall), b. 26 July, 1856; m. 30 Sept., 1875, Thos. **Croft**; had (*a*) Sally May (Croft), b. 12 Oct., 1876; (*b*) Michael Abner (Croft), b. 10 July, 1878; (*c*) Ida Janette (Croft), b. 31 May, 1880; (*d*) Margaret Araina (Croft), b. 19 Feb., 1882; (*e*) Samuel Lewis (Croft), b. 24 Feb., 1884; (*f*) Nora Belle (Croft), b. 13 Feb., 1886; (*g*) Flora Dell (Croft), b. 7 Dec., 1887; (*h*) Bessie (Croft), b. 14 Feb., 1791; (*i*) Kittie (Croft), b. 28 May, 1893.
   ii. Abigail Jane (Hall), b. 23 May, 1859; m. James H. **Parrish**; had (*a*) James Francis (Parrish), b. 8 Jan., 1888; (*b*) Matilda Janette (Parrish), b. 19 Apl., 1890.
   iii. Calvin Francis (Hall), b. 18 Oct.,

1861; m. 13 June, 1888, Carrie **Whitehurst**; had (*a*) Earl Abner (Hall), b. 16 Mch., 1890; (*b*) Everett Raymond (Hall), b. 16 Dec., 1892.
2. Mary, b. 21 Jan., 1828; m. 21 Dec., 1848, Barney Cook **Whitney**, of Athens, Ill., who d. 2 Sept., 1892, ae. 68 yrs., 3 mos.; a soldier of the Union Army. *Issue:*
   i. Chas. Francis (Whitney), M. D., b. 29 Apl., 1857; m. 1880, Anna Eliza **Hall**; had (*a*) Ella Mabel (Whitney), b. 7 Mch., 1883; (*b*) Charles Earl (Whitney), b. 31 Aug., 1890.
   iii. Calvin John (Whitney), b. 8 May, 1860; m. 27 Nov., 1887, Rose **Christen**; had (*a*) Geo. Clinton (Whitney), b. 22 Feb., 1888; (*b*) Frank (Whitney), b. 30 June, 1890; (*c*) Henry Allen (Whitney), b. 12 July, 1892; (*d*) Grace Mary (Whitney), b. ————.

FAM. 46. ALBERT NEWTON,[7] (*John N.*,[6] *Daniel*,[5] *John*,[4] *John*,[3] *John*,[2] *Robert*,[1]), b. 1845; m. 16 Jan., 1878, Emma A. **Shepard**; res. Htfd.

Children:

1. Albert Newton, b. 2 Dec., 1878.
2. Edmund Henry, b. 26 Jan., 1880.
3. Genevieve, b. 14 Oct., 1882.

4. Emma Elizabeth, b. 8 Feb., 1884.
5. Raymond Shepard, b. 17 Aug., 1888.

FAM. 47. HENRY HARRIS,[6] (*John N.,[5] Daniel,[4] John,[3] John,[2] Robert,[1]*), b. Weth., 24 Oct., 1847; m. 24 Oct., 1876, Sarah Alice (dau. Samuel W.) **Bidwell,** of Htfd., where they res.

Child:

1. Leila May, b. Union City, Ct., 17 May, | 1878.

FAM. 48. EDWARD M.,[7] (*Matthew,[6] Matthew,[5] John,[4] John,[3] John,[2] Robert,[1]*), b. 1841; m. Elizabeth M. (dau. Walter & Jane *Bulkeley*) **Edwards,** 24 Mch., 1870.

Children:

1. Everett M., b. 26 Sept., 1872; m. 1 Dec., 1898, Mary I. **Dickinson;** s. p.
2. Bernice E., b. 14 Jan., 1874; m. 26 May, 1897, Everett Clayton **Willson.** *Issue:*

1. Francis Clayton (Willson), b. 10 May, 1900.
3. Inf. dau., b. and d. 23 July, 1875.

FAM. 48a. JOHN,[7] (*John,[6] Justus,[5] Elijah,[4] James,[3] John,[2] Robert,[1]*), m. Mary **Camp,** 16 Sept., 1832.

Children:

1. John Allen, b. 2 Apl., 1833; unm.
2. Jane E., b. 6 Apl., 1835.
3. Albert, b. 31 Dec., 1836. FAM. 49.

4. Edward, b. 16 Jan., 1839. FAM. 50.
5. Christiana, b. 20 Feb., 1841.
6. Charles, b. 8 July, 1845. FAM. 51.

FAM. 49. ALBERT,[8] (*John,[7] John,[6] Justus,[5] Elijah,[4] James,[3] John,[2] Robt.,[1]*), m. Elizabeth **Kearney;** res. Columbus, Geo.

Children:

1. Jane. 2. John.

FAM. 50. EDWARD,[8] (*John,[7] John,[6] Justus,[5] Elijah,[4] James,[3] John,[2] Robert,[1]*), b. 1839; m. Sarah **Hill,**

Children:

1. Christiana, b. 30 Sept., 1858. | 2. Mary, b. 3 Mch., 1861.

FAM. 51. CHARLES,[9] (*John,[8] John,[7] John,[6] Justus,[5] Elijah,[4] James[3] John,[2] Robt.,[1]*), b. 1845; m. Hannah **Sykes,** 1868.

Children:

1. William, b. 11 Jan., 1869.
2. Edward, b. 21 Feb., 1871.

3. Albert, b. 7 Jan., 1873.
4. Arthur, b. 27 Nov., 1875.

FRANKLIN, ROSWELL G., d. 5 Feb., 1848, in 34th yr.—*S. C. R.*

MOSES E., m. Lucinda **Goodrich,** 7 Apl., 1808.—*S. C. R.;* had Elizabeth Maria, and Rockwell Goodrich, bp. 13 Nov., 1816.—*S. C. R.*

FRARY, (or Franey) MARY, of John, bp. 10 Dec., 1782.—*N.;* JOHN m. Abigail **Stoddard,** 26 Nov., 1750.—*N.*

FRASER, ALEXANDER, m. Lucretia **Wright,** 8 Dec., 1766.

Children (Weth T. & Ch. Rec.):

1. Bille, b. 4 July, 1767.
2. Charles, b. 19 Oct., 1768; d. 15 or 16 Sept., 1775.
3. Elias, b. 4 Oct., 1770; d. 1 Oct., 1775.
4. Alexander, b. 28 Sept., 1772.

5. James, b. 12 Sept., 1774; bp. 19 Jan., 1777.
6. Elizabeth, b. 25 Oct., 1776; bp. 19 Jan., 1777.
7. Lucy, bp. 10 Jan., 1780.

MRS. had dau. *Olive* bp. betw. 10 Apl. and May, 1757.

SIMEON, of New City, N. Y., m. Anne **Loveland,** 11 Jan., 1784.—*W. C. R.*

DAMARIS m. 20 Sept., 1759, Simeon **Judd,** of Far.—*W. C. R.*

FROTHINGHAM, EBENEZER, of Weth., found guilty by jury, for false and railing speeches agt. Rev. James Lockwood, Apl., 1745. Vol. R. Case 154, 756, *Co. Ct. Rec.* See, also, Chapt. XIII, Vol. I.

FROW, (*Fro*), Thomas, "a mariner, d. suddenly and untimely," coroners inquest, Oct., 1709. *Rec. Ct. of Assistants.* He may have been a s. of David Frow, au Irish servant at Northampton in 1668, as mentioned by *Savage,* II. 213.

FULLER, EPHRAIM, of Weth., bo't ld. in Tyringham, (Mass.) Equivalent, 1770. *Conn. Quart.* II. 397.

DANIEL, (Rev.) pastor at Willington, Ct., m. Lucy (dau. Jona.) **Goodrich,** 7 Aug., 1723.

Children (Weth. Rec.) :

1. Hester, b. 24 Oct., 1824.
2. Lucy, b. 3 Dec., 1726.
3. Abigail, b. 23 Feb., 1729-30; "a dau. of

Mr. Daniel, pastor at Willington," bp. 1 Mch., 1729.—*Mix MSS.*

FREDERICK, m. Anne **Barrett,** 17 Sept., 1782; he d. ae. 50, bu. 8 Mch., 1814.

Children (Weth. Rec.) :

1. Mary, b. 14 Dec., 1782; prob. the inf. d. 4 Sept., 1783.
2. Horace, b. 20 Mch., 1785.
3. Martha, b. 8 Feb., 1787.
4. Wilson, b. 16 Feb., 1789.

5. Benjamin Chapman, b. 8 Mch., 1791.
6. Anne, b. 5 Apl., bp. 21, and d. 22 Oct., 1795.
7. Anne, b. 23 July, 1796.
8. Cornelia Green, b. 31 Oct., 1801.

Miscellanea: ABEL m. Hannah **Rhodes**—*N. C. R.*; AMBROSE m. Rhoda **Williams,** of Weth., (?) 14 Apl., 1771—*N. C. R.* DANIEL, M. D., d. 16 Dec., 1843 in 69th yr.; his wife d. 21 Oct., 1835 in 54 yr.—they had (1) *Amanda,* (2) *Walter,* (3) *Josiah Butler,* and (4) *Edward,* all bp. 26 July,, 1818—*S. C. R.*; DANIEL, (prob. the foregoing) had a (twin) *inf.* wh. d. 9 Nov., 1807.—See, also, as to Dr. DANIEL, on Chapt. XIX, Vol. I; HENRY, of Colchester, m. Chloe **Webster,** of Weth., 23 Mch., 1815—*W. T. R.*; JOSIAH BUTLER, (s. of Dr. Daniel) d. at New Orleans, ae. 22, in Sept., 1833; LEVI m. Eunice **Wells,** 2 May, 1776—*N. C. R.*; MARTHA m. Justus B. **Stevens,** of Granby. Ct., 24 Oct., 1822—*W. C. R.*; NOAH, m. Ellis **Brown,** 3 Jan., 1757—*N. C. R.*; ORRA, d. 1 Nov., 1827 ae. 20—*N. C. R.*; WALTER, an inf. of, d. 2 Oct., 1842; a *ch.* of d. 5 Nov., 1844 , at Rahway, N. J.; a *ch.* of, d. 11 Apl., 1841 at N. Y—*S. C. R.*

FULLERTON, NATHANIEL, ae. 21, bu. 31 Jan., 1796.

GAINS, (*Gaines*), JAMES, of Glast., m. Lydia **Loveland,** 7 Jan., 1790.

JAMES, bu. 12 July, 1799—*W. C. R.*; had a ch., ae. 2, bu. 5 Oct., 1794.—*W. C. R.;* had *Sylvester*, bp. 5 Oct., 1794.

GALPIN, (communicated by Mr. E. S. TILLOTSON.) SAMUEL, b. 3 Apl., 1785, at Midd., p(rob. a desc't of Philip, of New Haven and Fairfield); the first of the name in the township, came here from Berlin, Ct., abt. 1807 or 8; m. 10 Apl., 1810, Caroline (dau. John & Sarah *Buck*) **Woodhouse;** soon after marr. purchased of Capt. Gurdon Montague the house on the W. side of Broad St., until recently occupied by his gd-son, Albert H. Galpin. That he was highly esteemed by his fellow townsmen is amply evidenced by the following list of offices held by him during 50 yrs. previous to 1862, taken from a memorandum in his own handwriting, viz: Lister and assessor, 18 yrs.; Board of Relief, 1 yr.; Selectman, 15 yrs.; Constable, 9 yrs.; Collector of Town & State taxes, 5 yrs; Justice of the Peace, abt. 20 yrs.; Director of State's Prison, 1 yr.; County Commis'r 3 yrs.; Town Clerk, 1 yr.; Clerk of the First Eccl. Soc., 37 yrs.; Committee to hold Loan and collect Parsonage money, 28 yrs.; Collector of First Eccl. Soc., 4 yrs.; Collector of Broadstreet School Dist., 15 yrs.; Notary Pub., 6 yrs.; Repres. to Gen. Assembly, 1839; Executor, or Adm'r of 34 estates— Total 166 yrs. of pub. service—an honorable record, truly!
Mr. Galpin d. 17 Mch., 1864, ae. 79; his wid. d. 30 Jan., 1875, ae. 89.

Children (*bp. W. C. W.*) :

1. Albert, b. 5 Sept., 1811; bp. 27 July, 1817. FAM. 2.
2. Samuel H., b. 18 Oct., 1812; bp. 27 July, 1817; grad. Y. C., 1835; taught schl. at Glast., Ct., and Natchez, Miss., 1842-44; stud. theol. at and grad. from Theol. Instit. of Conn (East Windsor Hill), 1844; but ill health and weakness of voice turned him again to teaching, at Lexington, Ky., until in broken health, 1853, he became station agent of the P. H. & F. R. R., at Bristol, Ct. In 1864, he rec'd an app't in Treasury Dep't at Washington, D. C. He m. Mary Anne **Perrin,** of E. W. Hill, who was bp. 1 Dec., 1816. —*W. C. R. Issue:*
   1. Samuel Arthur, b. 5 Jan., 1846; ent.

Y. C., 1866, but prevented from grad. by ill-health. He grad. Law Dep't Col. Univ., Washington, D. C., 1872; was in employ of Customs and Indian Dep'ts; m. 1880, Clara R. **Larned,** of Htfd.; rec'd a hon. degree of A. M., from Y. C., 1880; res. in New Haven, where he is Pres. of the New Haven Clock Co.; in 1901, presented Y. C. with $1,000, as the basis of a fund for a Latin prize, in memory of his father.
3. John, b. 12 Aug., 1816; bp. 29 July, 1817. FAM. 3.
4. Caroline, b. 27 June, 1821; bp. 21 July, 1822; m. 10 May, 1842, Albert S. **Welles,** of Weth.; she d. 27 Aug., 1850.

FAM. 2. ALBERT,[2] (*Samuel,*[1]), b. 1811; m. 4 July, 1843, Esther Maria, (dau. of Chas.) **Washburn,** of Far. Mr. W. was, at one time Warden of Newgate Prison, Granby. She d. 17 Dec., 1871, ae. 59; he m. (2) 25 Sept., 1873. Jerusha B. **Perrin,** of Rockville, Ct., who d. 23 Aug., 1892, ae. 75. He d. 5 Oct., 1892. Following in his father's footsteps, he held the office of Town Clerk for 45 yrs.; Town Treas. from 5 Oct., 1874 until death; Selectman, Assessor, Clerk of the Eccl. Soc. for many yrs., and sett. over 30 estates.

Children:

1. Albert Hillyer, b. 16 Jan., 1847; unm.; succeeded his father as Town Treas. until 18 Apl., 1898; also, as Town Clerk to date (1901), and has benn Clerk of Eccl.

Soc., since Dec., 1884; Repr. to the Gen. Assembly, 1886.
2. Hubert Drayton, b. 17 July, 1849. FAM. 4.

FAM. 3. JOHN,[2] (*Samuel,*[1]), b. 1816; m. 19 Sept., 1842, Cornelia (dau. Capt. Gurdon) **Montague;** rem. to New Haven, where he res. until his dth., 19 Oct., 1857. For yrs. he was in the stationary and book binding business, under firm name of Galpin & Osborne, in that city.

Children (b. New Haven) :

1. Emma Cornelia, b. 16 Sept., 1844; m. Pierce N. (of Hannanes) **Welch**; Mr. W. was many yrs. Treas. of City of N. H.;

had several ch.
2. Caroline Maria, b. 6 Nov., 1846; unm.; res. N. H.

FAM. 4. HUBERT DRAYTON,[3] (*Albert*,[2] *Samuel*,[1]), b. 1849; m. 24 Sept., 1878, Kate Helena **Sexton**, of Aurora, Ill., where he still resides—since abt. 1860.

Children (b. Aurora, Ill.) :

1. Katharine Esther, b. 23 Sept., 1879.
2. Hubert Sexton, b. 22 Jan., 1882.

3. Albert Lee, b. 29 June, 1884.
4. Arthur J., b. 17 Nov., 1887.

GARDNER, BENJAMIN, adm. inhab. 27 Dec., 1686; ld. rec., see Chapt. VII, Vol. I.; m. Margaret ————, 21 June, 1688; he was prob. a mariner and d. at sea, as the invent. of his est. was made by James Patterson and Benj. Churchill, 27 Feb., 1713-14— amt. £175-04-02; the *Ct. Rec.* of 5 Jan., that yr., says, "whereas Benj. Gardner, late belonging to Weth. has been long absent abroad, at sea, and is supp. to be dead,"—adm. was gr. to his wid. Margaret; and 2 Aug., 1715, his son Peter Gardner, ae. 12 yr., chose John Skinner to be his guardian: same date his dau. Margaret was named as being 13 yrs. of age; aand son Moses, 19 yrs. old, as "being now absent at sea," and before 6 Sept., 1715 his dau. Sarah had been m. to ———— **Howard.** *Htfd. Co. Prob. Ct.*

Children (Weth Rec., bp. Mix Rec.) :

1. Samuel, b. 14 July, d. 13 Aug., 1689.
2. Benjamin, b. 5 Sept., 1690; d. 26 Mch., 1707.
3. Sarah, b. 1 Aug., 1692; m. ———— **Howard.**
4. Martha, b. 27 Dec., 1694; m. Samuel **Gardner**, of Muddy River, 1 Jan., 1712-13.

5. Moses, b. 23 May, 1697.
6. Rebecca, b. 1, bp. 5 Mch., 1698-9; d. 18 Oct., 1702.
7. Margaret, bp. 30 Nov., 1701.
8. Margaret, b. 20, bp. 30 Nov., 1702.
9. Peter, b. 26, bp. 27 Feb., 1703-4.
10. John, b. 23 July, 1706.

SAMUEL, in Weth., 1641; for ld-holdings see Chapt. VII, Vol. I.

GEORGE, (*s. Thos. Jr.*,[2] *Thos.*,[1] b. 1572); an eminent mcht. at Salem, Mass., b. 1679 in Eng.; m. Elizabeth (wid. of John) **Orne,** of Salem, and his dau. Hannah, m. Lieut. John **Buttolph,** of Weth. Geo. Gardner's will (*Salem Rec.*) ment. this wife Eliz'th, sons Samuel and Ebenezer and Hannah (Buttolph), and her son; he left a large est. and app. his "loving friend, Capt. John Allen," also, his friend Caleb Stanley, to oversee the carrying out of his will.

GAREY, NATHANIEL & Sarah had (*Weth. Rec.*) Timothy, b. 6 Apl., 1726.

GARNSEY, SETH, of Westfield, m. Mehitable **Jenning,** 1 Apl., 1787.—*W. C. R.*

GARRETT, JOSEPH, a Sgt. in the Fr. War; bo't ppy. in Weth., 1705.—See p. 391, Vol. I.; m. Sarah (dau. Jacob) **Johnson,** 2 June, 1702; had *Ch.* (*Weth. Rec.*) Prudence b. 27 Sept., 1711—she was bp. by Rev. Mr. Mix.

GATES, GIDEON, of Derby, Ct., m. Lucy **Blinn,** 27 Oct., 1812.—*N. C. R?*

GAYLORD. EDWIN GAYLORD of W. Htfd., m. Lucy **Camp,** of Weth., 16 Mch., 1813.—*W. T. R.;* their s. Joseph Camp, bp. 2 Oct., 1825.—*N. C. R.;* LUCY Ann d. 19 May, 1848, ae. 31 ;SALOME, of Lucy, bp. 11 Apl., 1800.—*N. C. R.;* EDWIN, d. 23 Jan., 1862, ae. 75; Lucy C., his wife, d. 18 Mch., 1837, ae. 67.

STEPHEN, of Bristol, m. Anne **Rhodes,** 19 July, 1796.—*W. C. R.*

SAMUEL, of Ens. Joseph, d. 6 Mch., 1755, in 10 mo.

GEARS, (*Geers*) GEORGE, cowkeeper to the Town, 1655—*W. T. V.* I, p. 45; prob. the Geo. mentioned by *Savage*, as of New Lond., 1659—for whose desc'ts see *Savage* II, 239.

GIBBS,—GREGORY and JOHN—(See Chapt. VII, Vol. I.) Those of this name in Weth. were undoubtedly of the Windsor stock. They were:

JACOB,[4] (*prob. Jacob*,[3] *b.* 1700, *s. of Jacob*,[2] *s. of Giles*[1]) (See Stiles' *Ancient Windsor*, II, 288); who m. Mary —————.

Children (*Weth. Rec.*):

1. Mary, b. 1 Oct., 1737.
2. Jerusha, b. 23 Sept., 1742.
3. Jacob, b. 25 Feb., bp. betw. 14 Mch., and Sept., 1745.
4. John, b. 30 June, 1747; prob. the son bp. "on wife's acc't" 16 Aug., same yr.—*W. Ch. R.* He is prob. the J. who d. 9 Dec., 1835, ae. 89—*S. C. R.*, and who m.

13 May, 1773, Elizabeth **Weed** (or Mead); they had John bp. 28 July, 1776; d. 3 Sept., 1795, in 22 yr.; Jerusha, bp. 14 Oct., 1781; Betsy, bp. 22 May, 1785; Abigail, bp. 13 Apl., 1788; Millie, bp. 15 Nov., and d. 23 Dec., 1795; the mother d. 20 Mch., 1820, in 67th yr.—*S. C. R.*

EBENEZER, (prob. the E. b. 1703 and bro. of foregoing Jacob), m. Ruth —————.

Ch. (*Weth. Rec.*):

1. Ozias, b. 20 Aug., 1731; his bp. rec., 12 Dec., 1731, by Rev. S. Mix, who says of

the father "*who came firstly from Windsor.*"

JOHN and GREGORY were at Weth. betw. 1636 and 1640, and JOHN rem. to Quinnipiac (New Haven) 1639.—*Mail & Express*, 6 July, 1901.

JOHN, of Weth., a rep. to Gen. Ct., Mch., 1638.—*Savage*, II. 246.

JOHN, d. 9 Dec., 1835, in 89th yr.—*W. C. R.; Weth. Ins.* has it 8 Dec., 1836, ae. 87.

JACOB, d. 1 Apl., 1848, in 73d yr.—*S. C. R.*; his wife d. 22 Mch., 1830, in 52d yr.—*Weth. Ins.*

MARY, wife of *Jacob*, d. 27 Feb., 1787, in 82nd yr.—*Weth. Ins.*

HARRIET, wife of Jacob, d. 22 Mch., 1830, ae 51.—*Weth. Ins.*

LEMUEL, m. at Weth. 21 Jan., 1790, Martha (dau. of Elias & Patience) **Hurlbut,** b. 11 Feb., 1770, in W.

MEDAD, m. Eleanor (dau. Elias & Patience) **Hurlbut,** 30 Dec., 1792; b. 25 July, 1760, at W.—*N. Ch. Rec. & Hurlbut Genealogy.*

MARY, of Ry-H. m. Farrand **Hartwell,** of Charlotteville, N. Y., 27 Nov., 1834.— *W. T. R.*

GIFFEN, SIMON, d. ae. 80, Nov., 1820; his wife d. ae. 73, Dec., 20, 1813.— *W. C. R.*

GILBERT, JOSIAH, first heard of, as *Savage* says, in 1651, and a bro. of John of Htfd., and poss. s. of William of Windsor; he m. Elizabeth —————, who d. 17 Oct., 1682, ae. 50; he m. (2) wid. Mary **Ward.** (*Savage*); was a lister in Weth., 1665, or earlier; also, constable; surveyor of highways, 1667; drew lds. in allotments of 1670 and 1694; bo't ld. of Mr. Willard, Dec., 1668, and of Gershom Bulkeley, 1671.—See Chapt. VII, Vol. I. Josias Gilbert, witness in controversy Hollister *vs.* Bulkely, testified, Oct. 14, 1684, that he was 56 yrs. old and that in 1651 he entered upon Lt. Hollister's farm at Nayaug, as his tenant and held it 12 yrs.; had frequent disturbance fm. Mr. John Latimer, who complained of trespass. Josias' bros. Jonathan and John were on the place.—*Private Controversies*, III.

This wid. Mary Ward, it is thought, was prob. the wid. of John **Ward**, of Midd., who d. abt. 1683-4, and, if so, she was dau. of Wm. **Harris**, of Midd., tho' the name is not ment. in the sett't of the Ward est. John Ward had a son, then 18 yrs. of age; and his wife was *enciente* at the time of her husband's dth. Josiah Gilbert m. wid. Ward in Jan., 1687-8—and, under date of Aug., 1695, we have the following doc. (*Prob. Office*) giv'g "An account of what estate Mary Ward carried to Josiah Gilbert's house when married to him," viz:

February 1687-8	3 cows	£12-00-00
	1 horse	5-00-00
	8 swine	14-00-00
	10 bushels Ind. corne	1-05-00
	Paid Ens. Ward for Jos. Gilbert to Hay sold Ensign Ward	1-15-00
	To cash	08-00

To summer work of 2 boys one 14
   yrs. old; the other capable of
   earning his victuals, and returned home before Winter.
The summers' work of Mary, abt.
   16 yrs. of age.
The use of the cows, the summer.
The charge of bringing up Jno.
   Gilbert, son of Josiah, fm.
   March last week 1689 to this
   present April, 1696—7 years.

An acct. of what was returned to ye said Mary Ward after her husband's decease:
   2 cows   £ 8-00-00

She was to receive 40s annually, now 7 yrs., she
   has received 46 shillings of Benjamin Gilbert—still due £11-14-00
Also, Benjamin withholds 2 acres of ye best of ye land,
   whereby she loses 20 shillings per year   6-00-00

Still due the widow on future account   £17-14-00

August, 1695.
The Contract for marriage is as follows:

In the year of our lord 1681
The condishens hearof that whear the within bounders JOSIAH GILBERT shall by the grace of god marry and take to wife one MARY WARD widow, if the said Josiah after the said maridge had and solomised hepen to dey [die] before the said Mary that then the said Jos. shall leave the said Mary tow romes in the west end of the dwelling house now in being with one third part of his barn and out houseing told yards and with all freedom and convenience therein as also one third part of his orchard on the South side and foure akers of land tow akers of it abounding one the great river east and a deviding fence north and the orchard west and the other tow akers one the South side of Divident brook whare the said Mary shall make Choyce with convenient ways for transportation and forty shillings yearly in Corent pay of this contory to be paid att the said house by the asins of the said Josiah G: to the said M: or his asins after the

deth of Jo: to be employed and Disposed to the proper use of the said Mary W: During her life and if after hir widowhod to Return the housing unto the cares [heirs] or asins of the said Jo: it is further granted that the said Mary W: shall after mared Solomised bring the improvement of his premises according to Law now unto the free use of the said Josiah G. with thirty tow pounds of her joynter portion and the other thirty tow is for hir att time before hir deth to Declare and make hir will devise and give att hir plesur to what parson or parsons and unto whet use or parpos as shee will att hir plasure and allso do permet hir executors to prove, declare and proforme hir will without interruption in Conformation hear of we set to our hands, October ye 18

Witness Daniel Harris.
　Isaac Johnson.

Jo. Gilbertt.
Mary Ward.

Mch. 2, 1695-6.—Jacob Williams, who had m. Josiah Gilbert's dau. *Sarah* and Simon Willard, the husband of his dau. *Mary*, make complaint (doc. in *Prob. Ct.* office) that the est. of Josiah Gilbert "hath now of long time been undivided, as to an absolute settlement, and is suffering thereby," and call upon "our respected Uncle Francis Whitmore," of Midd., to petition the County Court, at its next session, to order an equal distribution of the same.

Josiah Gilbert d. in 1684, and in Mch., 1696-7, acc. to *Court Rec.*, John Chester having orig. been app. distributor to the est. with others, but having declined to act, the duty was given to Capt. Joseph Wadsworth and Mr. Joseph Mygatt.—(*Htfd. Prob. Rec.*, Vols. IV and VI.)

Children (*Weth. Rec.*):

1. Benjamin, b. 22 Sept., 1652. FAM. 2.
2. Elizabeth, b. 28 Mch., 1654; m. Jona. **Deming**, Sr., as his second wife, 5 Dec., 1673, and d. 3 Oct., 1714.
3. Lydia, b. 88 Dec., 1656; m. John **Riley.**
4. Josiah, b. 12 Sept., 1659; d. 2 Feb., 1704-5; will dated 24 June, 1704; Invent. est. taken 15 Feb., 1704-5, £85-16-02; he devises to bros. and sisters; and gives his "cooper's tools" to his cousin Josiah, son of his sister Mary (**Willard**), and his "new Bible" to her daughter Mary.
5. Sarah, b. 1 Dec., 1661; m. Jacob Wil-

liams.
6. Eleazer (Ebenezer ?), b. 20 Sept., 1663.
7. Moses, b. 12 Apl., 1666.
8. Caleb, b. 10 June, 1668.
9. Mary, b. 18 Nov., 1670; m. Simon **Willard.**
10. Amy, b. 12 Apl., 1672; adm'n on whose est. was gr. to Jacob Williams, of Weth., 1 Jan., 1739-40.—*Htfd. Prob.*
11. John, named only in div. of est. at Prob., as youngest of the ch.—*Savage,* II. 250.

FAM. 2. Sgt. BENJAMIN,[2] (*Josiah,*[1]) b. 1652; m. Mary (dau. John) **Riley,** 25 Nov., 1680; collector, 1686; lister, 1690; drew lds. in allotment of 1694; repaired the bridge (Goffe's) 1698. He d. 9 Dec., 1711, ae. abt. 59. His wife d. 17 Oct., 1682, ae. abt. 50.—*Weth. Rec.*

Children (*Weth. Rec.*):

1. Mary, b. 22 Nov., 1681.
2. Hannah, b. 13 Mch., 1688-9.

3. Keziah, b. 7 Oct., 1691.

The *Christian Lane Cemetery,* (within the present bounds of Weth.) retains the several *Gilbert* memorials. See pages 610-613, Vol I.

GILDERSLEVE, (*Col. Rec. Gyldersly,* also, *Guildersleve*), RICHARD. From whence he came into the Conn. Col. is not known; but he had a lot rec. to him in Weth., Mch., 1640, which he sold in 1643; while at Weth. was convicted by Gen. Ct. of uttering "pernitious speeches," tending to the detriment and dishonor of the commonwealth, fined £20 and bound over, under bond of £20. In 1636 was app. by Gen. Ct., to take invent. of gds. of John Oldham (who had been murdered by Inds.) and report to next Court; rem. to Stamford, with first emig. fm. Weth., where (acc. to *Savage*) he had res. for 5 yrs. previous to 1641; and rep. St. in

Gen. Ct., held at New Haven; in 1663 was of Hempstead, L. I.—See Chapt. VII,
Vol. I; also Huntington's *Hist. Stamford.* (Rev. John E. Peters, of Camden,
N. J., is preparing a life of Richard Gildersleeve, 'Sen., and a Genealogy of the
Gildersleeve family.)

GILES, SAMUEL, m. Prudence **Smith,** 4 Apl., 1790.—*W. C. R.*

GILLITT, (*Gillet, Jillet*) JOHN, adm. inhab. Mch., 1697, m. Sarah (dau. Wm.)
Tryon, 7 Apl., 1697; he owned Cov't and was bp. 20 July, 1712.

Children (*Weth. Rec., bp. Mix MSS.*) :

1. Abel, b. 10, bp. 13 Mch., 1697-8.
2. William, b. 15, bp. 17 Mch., 1699-1700.
3. John, b. 16, bp. 21 June, 1702. FAM. 2.
4. Hannah, b. 26, bp. 28 Jan., 1704-5.

5. Sarah, b. 23, bp. 29 Feb., 1707-8.
6. Samuel, b. 15, bp. 16 July, 1710.
7. Mary, bp. 5 Sept., 1714.

FAM. 2. JOHN,[2] (*John[1]*,), b. 1702; m. Mary (dau. Jacob) **Williams,** 29 Aug., 1727.
Mary, wife of John, owned Cov't 18 Feb., 1727-[28].

Children (*Weth. Rec., bp. Mix MSS.*) :

1. Mary, b. 14 Feb., 1728.
2. John, b. 18, bp. 21 Sept., 1729.
3. Sarah, b. 2, bp. 9 May, 1731.

4. Ann, bp. 18 Feb., 1732-3.
5. Abigail, bp. 20 Oct., 1734.

JONATHAN, m. Elizabeth **Steel,** Dec. 28, ————? —*N.*

CHARLES C., described in rec. of marr. as "of Newington," published 11 Aug.,
(Weth.) m. 18 Oct., 1815, Louisa (dau. of Uriah & Lois *Hinckley*) **Lathrop,**
of Pittsfield, Mass.—*Pitts. Rec.*

EBENEZER, of Lebanon, m. Roesy **Rhodes,** of Weth., 12 Jan., 1812.—*N. C. R.*

GLADDING, (*Gladden*)—*S. C. R.*

JOHN, d. 6 Aug., 1814, in 42d yr.; *inf.* of, d. 23 July, 1814.—*S. C. R.*

RHODA, (wid.) d. in P. H., 6 Feb., 1823, in 48th yr.

RHODA, m. Edward **Borson,** of New Bedford, Ct.—*W. C. R.*

JOSIAH, bu. 5 Sept., 1804.—*W. C. R.*

JAMES, d. 21 Mch., 1836, ae. 56.—*Weth. Ins.*

HULDAH, m. John **Russell,** of Stilton(?) or Shelton, 31 July, (or 6 Aug.—*N. C.
R.*) 1820.—*W. T. R.*

GLEASON, SAMUEL S., of Tolland, Mass., m. Eliza W. **Guild,** 2 Mch., 1817.

GLYN, PEGGY, ae. 34, killed by lightning, 23 Aug., 1786.—*W. C. R.*

GOFF, (*Goffe, Goofe, Goft.*) Furnished by Mr. HOMER W. BRAINARD, of Hartford, Conn., who says that, in his researches among families of this name, he
has frequently met with the tradition that they were descended from, or connected with William Goffe, Cromwell's General, and one of the Judges of
Charles I, who was obliged to flee England at the Restoration, 1660-62, and took
refuge at New Haven and elsewhere; finally dying (as the consensus of the
best historical evidence seems to prove) in Hadley, Mass., where he with his
associate Judge Whalley, was secretly harbored for many years by Rev. Mr.
Russell, minister of Hadley, and who had formerly been minister at Weth. Mr.

Brainard, however, finds no evidence supporting this claim of kinship between the regicide Judge and the Weth. Goffs. Dwight, in his *Strong Genealogy* makes an equally impossible claim that the line of descendents of Hezekiah Goff, of Killingly, Woodstock and Middletown was so connected; but Mr. Brainard shows that this line derives, probably, fm. Anthony of Woburn and Billerica, Mass. Nor has it yet been ascertained whether Gen. Wm. Goffe left any male issue. He had daus. and at least one son, Frederick, but whether any more, is not evident. If he did, they were doubtless still in Eng., in 1662. Gen. Goffe was the son of Rev. Stephen Goffe, a rector in Surrey, Eng., who is said to have had a large family. Perhaps some of them came to America. Gen. Goffe was a staunch Puritan.

The name appears in Southeastern England, (Hertfordshire has a place called Goff's Oak) and is prob. of Flemish origin.

PHILIP GOFFE was the first of the name in Weth., where he sett. before 1649; was not among the settlers of 1635-6, and prob. did not come fm. Watertown, Mass. He was Town Crier, 1651. He built the first house within the present bounds of Rocky Hill (nearer Weth. Centre than to the present village of Rocky Hill) in 1655.—See Chapt. VII, Vol. I. A brook, flowing into the Connecticut River just north of Ry-H. still retains his name, though none of the name have lived near it for a century and a half. Cattle ear-mark rec. *W. T. V.*, 1, p. 5; app. Town Crier, 1651 (p. 38). He was adm. freeman in Weth., Oct., 1669, and d. ———— 1674, leaving wife Rebecca and five children. No Goff tombstones, except a few of the present century, remain in any Weth. cemetery.

Children (* *Weth. Rec.*):

1. Jacob, * b. 15 Aug., 1649. FAM. 2.
2. Rebecca, * b. 7 Oct., 1651.
3. Philip, * b. 2 Mch., 1653. FAM. 3.
4. Moses, * b. 30 May, 1656. FAM. 4.
5. Aaron, b. 1658. FAM. 5.

FAM. 2. JACOB,[2] (*Philip,*[1]), b. 1649; fence-viewer, 1675; m. 5 Dec., 1679, Margery (dau. John & Dorothy *Lord*) **Ingersoll**, of Htfd., Northampton and Westfield, Mass., b. at N., Jan., 1656; he d. at Weth., 21 Oct., 1697; his wid. had her taxes abated the next yr.; inventory of est. taken 12 Nov., 1697-8, exhib. in Ct. by wid., 6 Apl. 1699—amt. £136-03-06; he owned upwards of 100 acres of ld. (See Chapt. VII, Vol. I) house, 5 cows, a horse, mare and colt, steers, calves, sheep, bees and books; was evidently a well to do farmer; his wid. m. (2) Jonathan **Buck**, of Weth., and at May sess. of 1700, of Gen. Assembly, was empowered to sell her late husbands lds. to pay his debts. Thos. Morton of Weth. was discharged fm. his guardianship of Mary (dau. of Jacob) Goff, to which he was chosen 1708, 7 July, 1712.

Children (*Weth. Rec.*):

1. Jacob, b. 5, d. 14 Nov., 1680.
2. Moses, b. 10 Mch., 1681; d. before 1708.
3. Mabel, b. 3 Oct., 1690; m. 30 Oct., 1707. Daniel **Andrews**; had 7 ch.—*Andrews*

Memorial.
4. Mary, b. 15 Nov., 1693; m. John **Andrews**, of Weth.; 2 ch.—*Andrews Memorial.*
5. Eunice, b. 27 Mch., 1696.

FAM. 3. PHILIP,[2] (*Philip,*[1]), b. 1653; dr. lds. in 1694 allot.; surveyor of highways, 1716; m. Mrs. Naomi (wid. of John) **Reynolds,** and dau. John and Ann Latimer, b. Weth., 4 Apl., 1648; in 1704 Philip and wife were fined 20s by the Ct. at Hartford, for not attending service at the Meeting-house on the Lord's Day. They plead that they could not in conscience attend, and would not go to the meeting on the Sabbath in the public meeting-house. Mrs. G. was again fined, 1710, with Moses Goff Sr. and Hannah, wife of Aaron Goff, for not attending divine service.—*Co. Ct. Rec.* He d. 7 Mch., 1724-5.—*Midd. Rec.*

Children (Weth. Rec.):

1. Philip, b. 24 June, 1685. FAM. 6.
2. Nathaniel, b. 13 Sept., 1687.
3. Naomi, b. 1 Oct., 1692.
4. (Prob. others.)

FAM. 4.   MOSES,[2] (*Philip*,[1]), b. 1656; m. 1687, Mercy ——————, who d. 20 Dec., 1711, in an epidemic that prevailed in Weth.; he was a farmer—See Chapt. VII, Vol. 1; d. 12 Oct., 1712; will, dated 30 Sept., 1712—(*Htfd. Prob. Rec.*, VIII, 148); invent. £335-12-06, a fair estate; all ch. except Moses, named in will; s. Jacob* and cousin Philip Goffe, executors; witnesses, Gideon Belden, Eben'r Prout; appraisers, Sam'l Williams, Sam'l Smith, Joseph Grimes. Est. divided equally among ch. except extra to Jacob his s.

Children (Weth. Rec.):

1. Moses, b. 6 Feb., 1688; Hayward, 1708; m. Sarah (dau. Joseph, dec'd, & Sarah) **Crane,** 5 July, 1711; he d. Weth., 15 Dec., 1711, "ae. abt. 24;" their ch. Moses, d. 17 Jan., 1712; wid. m. (2) John **Tooley,** or Tobey, of Midd. (?); she m. (3) Thes. **Marks** (?).
2. Jacob, b. 19 Feb., 1690; d. Weth., 23 Mch., 1723; prob. not m.; his invent. taken by Joseph Grimes and Philip Goffe, covers 3 pp. in *Htfd. Co. Prob. Rec.*, and shows him to have been in comfortable circum-stances—a carpenter by trade; adm. on his est. granted to his bro. Ephraim, 6 Aug., 1723.
3. Jerusha, b. 23 Sept., 1693; d. 8 Oct., 1712.
4. Benjamin, b. 30 Apl., 1696; John Reynolds, of Weth., chosen his guardian, 1713.
5. Ephraim, b. 4 Mch., 1699; chose his cousin Philip Goffe, Jr., of Weth., to be his guardian, 6 Sept., 1714. FAM. 7.
6. David, b. 29 April, 1702; John Dix, of Weth., opp. his guardian, 17 Apl., 1717. FAM. 8.

FAM. 5.   AARON,[2] (*Philip*,[1]), b. 1658; m. 19 Jan., 1681, Hannah (dau. Henry) **Cole** [I supposed him to be the H. C., who m. in Htfd., in 1648; rem. to Midd. abt. 1654, and finally, after 1670, to Wallingford, but the Midd. recs. do not give him a dau. Hannah; she might have been dau. Henry Cole, Jr., b. 1647.] Aaron G., d. Feb., 1711-12; adm. to est. granted to wid., 3 Mch., 1711-12.—*Htfd. Prob. Rec.*, VIII, 126. Invent. of est. £101-08-06. He was a farmer; occup. ho. and shop in Weth., 10 acres ld. therewith and abt. 100 ac. at Pilgrim's Harbour (now in Meriden) Meriden, Ct.

Children (Weth. Rec.):

1. Solomon, b. 7 Feb., 1685. FAM. 9.
2. Aaron, b. 10 Mch., 1689; prob. the A. who dr. ld. in 1694 allot. FAM. 10.
3. Gershom, b. 12 Mch., 1691. FAM. 11.
4. Samuel, b. 30 Apl., 1698. FAM. 12.

FAM. 6.   PHILIP,[3] (*Philip*,[2] *Philip*,[1]), b. 1685; m. 15 Dec., 1703, Mary (dau. Thomas & Hannah) **Couch,** b. abt. 1676; he d. 7 Mch., 1724-5, at Midd.; adm. on est. granted to s. Philip, 4 July, 1727, delay prob. that this s. might reach legal age. Philip[3] rem. with sons Philip[4] and Nath'l[4] to a place S. of Knowles' Landing in Midd. (now in Middle Haddam) abt. 1720—the family being the first white settlers in that region. *Midd. Deeds* show ld. bo't by Philip, Nathaniel and Aaron Goffe, fm. 1724 onward. He was in Weth. late as 1714-15.

Children (Weth. Rec.):

1. Philip, b. 15 Oct., 1704. FAM. 13.
2. Mary, b. 9 Dec., 1705.
3. Nathaniel, b. 4 Sept., 1707. FAM. 14.
4. Naomi, b. 4 Mch., 1709; bp. 26 Apl., 1740,
   at Midd.,Haddam.
6. Jerusha, b. 13 Oct., 1715; bp. 26 Apl.,
5. Abigail, b. 24 May, 1713.
   1740, at Midd. Haddam.

FAM. 7.   EPHRAIM,[3] (*Moses*,[2] *Philip*,[1]), b. 1699; m. Oct., 1732, Mary **Viets;** he d. 1744; adm. on est. gr. to wid. and to Aaron Goffe, 1744-45—*Htfd. Co. Prob. Rec.*, XIV, p. 54; inventory £861-18-11 (Vol. XIV, 165) Jan. 24, 1745.

Children (Weth. Rec.):

1. Ephraim, b. 11 Jan., 1734.
2. Mercy, b. 22 June, 1735.
3. Mary, b. 24 Jan., 1737.
4. David, b. 9 May, 1738.
5. Jacob, b. 11 Mch., 1740.
6. Benjamin, b. 20 Sept., 1745; d. 11 Sept., 1746.

FAM. 8. DAVID,[3] (Moses,[2] Philip,[1]), b. 1702; m. Lydia ————, [perhaps **Boardman**—see Boardman Gen.]; he d. 1734, betw. 5 Mch. and 2 Aug.; will (Htfd. Co. Prob. Rec., XII, 260-1); wife and Daniel Andrew, exec's; est. £300; res. in Stepney, now Rocky Hill.

David Goff (Stepney) Invt. £333-04-03, taken 2 August, 1734, by John Dyx Ephriam Williams, Jonathan Belding.

Will dated, 5 March, 1734, I give to my wife Lydya, to my son Moses, to Elijah, to my dau. Jerusha.   DAVID GOFF. O

Witness Benjamin Wright, Jonathan Renals, Ephraim Goff.

Court Record, 28 Sept, 1734.   Proven.

Children (Weth. Rec.):

1. Moses, b. 1724 or '25; was of Weth., on Mch. 1, 1749-50.
2. Elijah, b. 1729 or '30; chose his step-father, John Tailor, of Weth., as his guardian, 18 Mch., 1746-7; being then 17 yrs. old.
3. Jerusha, b.· ————.

FAM. 9. SOLOMON,[3] (Aaron,[2] Philip,[1]), b. 1685; m. (1) abt. 1710, Elizabeth ————, who d. 5 Jan., 1712-13; he m. (2) 6 Jan., 1714-15—(Midd. Rec.) Mary (dau. Abraham) **Doolittle**, of Midd., and Wallingford, Ct.; they res. in that part of Wall. which is now in Meriden.—See Davis' Wallingford Hist., 124.

Children (Weth. Rec.):

1. Elizabeth, b. 9 Mch., 1711; d. yg. | (Other ch. b. Wallingford.)

FAM. 10. AARON,[3] (Aaron,[2] Philip,[1]), b. 1689; m. Margaret ————; he d. abt. 1751; res. Stepney parish, Weth.; will, dated 1 Apl., 1751—Htfd. Prob. Rec., XVI, 141; witnesses, Josiah Grimes, Jonathan Latimer, Jonathan Boardman, Jr.

Children (Weth. Rec.):

1. Bathsheba, m. Jonas **Wright**, 7 Feb., 1739-40. Issue (Midd. Rec.):
   i. Lois, b. 3 Mch., 1740-41.
   ii. John, b. 3 Aug., 1743.
   iii. Jonas, b. 28 Jan., 1749.
2. Elisha, inher. father's ho. in Stepney;
2 ch. of an Elisha G., whose deaths are rec. in Ch. Rec., of Portland, Ct., 14 June, 1758, and Jan., 1765, may be ch. of this Elisha.
[No other ch. ment. in will.]

FAM. 11. GERSHOM,[3] (Aaron,[2] Philip,[1]), b. 1691; m. 3 Dec., 1724, Elizabeth **Holcomb** (Simsbury Rec.); she may have been his 2d wife; sett. Simsbury, Ct.

Children (b. Simsbury, Ct.):

1. Ashbel, b. 6 Sept., 1725; m. Hannah ————. Issue:
   i. Elizabeth, b. 12 Dec., 1753.
   ii. Oliver, b. 4 Feb., 1756.
2. Isaac, d. in Simsbury, 14 Sept., 1760; m. Rebecca **Dickinson**, of Haddam, as shown by a Hadd. deed of 1752.

FAM. 12. SAMUEL,[3] (Aaron,[2] Philip,[1]) b. 1698; m. Elizabeth **Hollister** (b. abt. 1699-1700), (dau. of Jonathan & Elizabeth Williams), of Stepney parish Weth. and gr-dau. of Amos Williams, he poss. this Sam., d. 12 Sept., 1781, in 86th yr.—S . C. R.

Children (Weth. Rec.):

1. Martha, b. 27 Sept., 1724.
2. Elizabeth, b. 12 Aug., 1728; d. ————.
3. Ambrose, b. 12 Apl., 1731.
4. Josiah, b. 6 Feb., 1734.
5. Patience, b. 14 May, 1738.
6. Hannah, b. 26 May, 1741.
7. Stephen. b. 5 Sept., 1743.
8. Elizabeth, b. 15 June, 1746.

FAM. 13. PHILIP,[4] (Philip,[3] Philip,[2] Philip,[1]), b. 1704; m. abt. 1725, Sarah ————; He was bp. at Midd. Haddam, 13 Sept., 1741, and his wife Sarah was bp. 19 Sept., 1742, on uniting with the ch.; their older ch. were bp. 14 Mch., and 19 Sept., 1742. Later they were reckoned as belonging to East Hampton parish (orig. 1743-8), but they may have lived all the time on the same farm.

Children (*b. Midd., given in order of baptism*):

1. Philip, b. abt. 1725. FAM. 15.
2. Samuel, b. abt. 1727. FAM. 16.
3. Jacob, b. abt. 1729.
4. Joseph, b. abt. 1733.
5. Sarah, b. abt. 1735; m. 23 Oct., 1730, Benj. **Carrier,** of Midd. (?)
6. Benjamin, b. abt. 1738. FAM. 17.
7. Gideon, b. abt. 1740; bp. 15 Aug., 1743.

FAM. 18.
8. Thankful, b. abt. 1744; bp. 28 Sept., 1746; m. 2 Oct., 1766, Thomas **Hill;** she was adm. to full communion in E. Hampt., Ct., 31 July, 1771; had a family; res. in E. part of parish, from whence they rem. in 1800.

FAM. 14.   NATHANIEL,[4] (*Philip,[3] Philip,[2] Philip,[1]*), b. 1707; m. Jershua ————; abt. 1733; he d. after 1777 in Midd. (Midd. Haddam parish); farmer; petit'd for the formation of Midd. Hadd. parish, Oct., 1738; his 4 oldest ch. bp. at Midd. Hadd., 26 July, 1741; the others at intervals later.

Children (*b. Midd.*):

1. Anne, b. abt. 1734.
2. John, b. abt. 1736. FAM. 19.
3. Abigail, b. abt. 1738; m. 7 July, 1768, Edward **Corvell** or Covell.
4. Mary, b. abt. 1740; bp. 6 Dec., 1741.
5. Ruth, b. abt. 1744; bp. 8 Apl., 1744.
6. Keziah, b. abt. 1746; bp. Dec., 1746.

7. Ezekiel, b. abt. 1749; bp. 30 July, 1749. FAM. 20.
8. Nathaniel, b. abt. 1752; bp. 15 Oct., 1752. FAM. 21.
9. Stephen, b. abt. 1755; bp. 12 Oct., 1755; d. in Chatham, 15 Feb., 1777; prob. unm.

FAM. 15.   PHILIP,[5] (*Philip,[4] Philip,[3] Philip,[2] Philip,[1]*), b. Midd., abt. 1727; m. 1755, Desire **Green,** who d. 22 Apl., 1767, at E. Hampton; he farmer, d. at Chatham, Ct., (E. Hampt. parish) 27 Oct., 1779.

Children (*b. Midd. & Chatham*):

1. Mercy, b. 1756, bp. 12 Jan., 1757; m. Zacheus **Cook,** Jr., 18 Jan., 1776.
2. Benjamin, [Green], bp. 9 Oct., 1757; was a Revol. soldier; killed 24 June, 1781.
3. Timothy, bp. 27 July, 1760; a Revolu-

tionary soldier.
4. Philip, bp. 17 Aug., 1766; m. 19 Oct., 1787, Chloe **Cole;** prob. rem.
5. James, bp. 2 June, 1776 (67?).

FAM. 16.   SAMUEL,[5] (*Philip,[4] Philip,[3] Philip,[2] Philip,[1]*), b. Midd., abt. 1727; m. 12 Apl., 1753, Hannah **Tom[son,** kins, or as?] (rec. prob. worn or defective), who d. and he m. (2) 26 Sept., 1771, Mary (prob. dau. of Thos.) **Cuningham,** she d. 13 Dec., 1823, ae. 84. He d. E. Hampton, 3 Jan., 1823, ae. 98; res. in E. pt. S. E. Hampt., Soc. nr. the Colchester Marlborough line, N. E. of farm of late Henry S. Gates.

Children (*b. Midd.*):

1. Dorothy, b. 1754; d. 21 Nov., 1815, ae. 61, unm.
2. Joseph, b. 1757; d. yg., unm.
3. Joshua, b. 1759, bp. 26 Aug., 1759. FAM. 22.
4. Samuel, b. 1761, bp. 20 June, 1762.
5. Thomas, b. 1766 (?), bp. 5 Apl., 1767.

(*By second marr.*):
6. Hannah, b. 1772 (?), bp. 5 Mch., 1775.
7. Joseph, b. Sept., 1781, bp. 16 Oct., 1781. FAM. 23.
8. Thankful, b. Sept., 1784, bp. 4 Apl., 1785; d. 9 May, 1798.
9. Patience, b. 1784, bp. 4 Apl., 1785.

FAM. 17.   BENJAMIN,[5] (*Philip,[4] Philip,[3] Philip,[2] Philip,[1]*), b. abt. 1738; m. abt. 1760, Prudence **Johnson,**? [her maiden name preserved in an extant deed]; he d. 31 May, 1787, in Chatham, (E. Hampt.); she m. (2) 2 Mch, 1794, Daniel **Smith,** of Midd. Hadd., and d. 1817.

Children (*b. Midd-Chatham*):

1. Josiah, b. abt. 1760; prob. the eldest son, as he was adm'r on his father's est. 1777. FAM. 24.
2. Benjamin. FAM. 25.
3. James. FAM. 26.
4. Jacob. FAM. 27.
5. Asahel.

One of these Nos. 2, 3, 4, 5, b. 16 Jan., 1767, at Easthampton, but which, it is impossible to tell.
(Doubtless there were daus. in this family, but it is impossible to tell, owing to loss of records kept by the first E. pastor, Rev. John Norton.)

FAM. 18.   GIDEON,[5] (*Philip,[4] Philip,[3] Philip,[2] Philip,[1]*), b. abt. 1740; m. 18 Feb., 1762, wid. Huldah (*Hubbard*), wid. of Joseph **Arnold,** is called Gideon, Jr., in *Ch. Rec. of Midd. Hadd.*; res. in Haddam, (middle parish E. of River).

Children (b. Haddam):

1. Lament (dau.), b. 6 May, 1762; m. Amos **Shepard**, 11 Nov., 1784.
2. Abner, bp. 4 Dec., 1763.
3. Huldah, b. 18 Feb., 1766; m. Sylvanus **Freeman**, Jr., 1 Jan., 1787; sett. Butternuts, N. Y.
4. Elizabeth, b. 11 Aug., 1768.
5. Asa, b. 10 Sept., 1771. FAM. 28.
6. Lucy, b. 11 Sept., 1772.
7. Anna, b. 26 Mch., 1775.
8. Joseph Arnold, b. 2 July, 1780. FAM. 29.

FAM. 19. JOHN,[5] (*Nath'l,[4] Philip,[3] Philip,[2] Philip,[1]*), b. abt. 1737-8; m. 24 Oct., 1765, Mary (dau. John & Lydia) **Rich**, who came from Eastham, Mass., and who was b. 29 Apl., 1743. "Mrs. Polly Goff, who d. of an epidemic fever 1815, ae. 61," could not have been wid. of John,[5] if the age is rightly given; he was a farmer, res. in Midd. Hadd. parish—below the landing and Chestnut Hill; he d. Feb., 1813, ae. 75; est. invent. in *Midd. Prob. Ct.* X 451; estate small, but he had owned much ld. earlier; amt. of Invent. £483-61; Ichabod Pierce, adm'r.

Children (b. Chatham):

1. John, b. abt. 1766-7. FAM. 30.
2. Lydia, b. abt. 1769-70; m. (as 2d wife) Ichabod **Lucas**, 17 Mch., 1796.
3. Mary, b. abt. 1772-3; m. 26 May, 1796, Ichabod **Pierce**.
4. Anne, b. abt. 1775; m. John **Ely**, 29 Mch., 1819, and had a son Elisha Goff *Ely*.
5. Elisha, b. abt., 1777.
6. Elijah, b. abt. 1779. FAM. 31.
7. ———, b. Jan., 1781; d. 12 Feb., 1781.

FAM. 20. EZEKIEL,[5] (*Nath'l,[4] Philip,[3] Philip,[2] Philip,[1]*), b. abt. 1749; m. 18 Jan., 1776, Hannah (Higgins), wid. Abner **Hubbard;** prob. rem.; a Revolut. soldier.

Children:

1. Stephen, b. 4 May, 1777.
2. Elizabeth, b. 5 July, 1782; d. 30 June, 1798.
3. William, b. (?)

FAM. 21. NATHANIEL,[5] (*Nath'l,[4] Philip,[3] Philip,[2] Philip,[1]*), b. abt. 1752, m. 1773, Mary ———; he d. in Chatham, 5 June, 1777; wid. m. 10 Jan., 1782, Samuel Rich.

Child:

1. ———, d. 27 Nov., 1775, ae. 13 mos.

FAM. 22. JOSHUA,[6] (*Sam'l,[5] Philip,[4] Philip,[3] Philip,[2] Philip,[1]*), b. abt. 1759; m. 26 Aug., 1787, Hannah **Barnstable,** at E. Hampton; he was a Revol. soldier in Capt. Darrow's Co., of Chatham; rem. prob. to Ohio.

FAM. 23. JOSEPH,[6] (*Sam'l,[5] Philip,[4] Philip,[3] Philip,[2] Philip,[1]*), b. 1781; m. 23 Nov., Clarissa **Welch**, who d. 27 June, 1824, ae. 41; he m. (2) 21 Nov., 1824, Lucy, sister of his 1st wife; res. E. Hampt. till abt. 1831.

Children:

1. Mary, m. Silas **Hills;** she d. 16 Apl., 1884.
2. Clarissa.
3. Amelia, d. yg.
4. Gurdon Saltonstall. FAM. 34.
5. Joseph Nelson, b. 1808. FAM. 35.

FAM. 24. JOSIAH,[6] (*Benj.,[5] Philip,[4] Philip,[3] Philip,[2] Philip,[1]*), b. abt. 1760; m. 7 Feb., 1782, Anna (dau. Duel ?) **Rowley;** they joined East Hampton Ch., 23 May, 1784; he was a Revol. soldier; this family rem. prob. to Turin, N. Y.

Children:

1. Duel, b. 1 Jan., 1786, bp. 26 Feb., 1786 (*E. Hampt.*); m. Vianna **Pelton**, of Chatham, now Portland, 7 Feb., 1782. *Issue:*
   1. Duel, b. 27 Feb., 1809, in E. Hampt.
2. Lucy, b. 1782, bp. 30 May, 1784, in E. Hampt.; d. 27 Aug., 1784, ae. 2 yrs.
3. Florilla, b. 11 Jan., 1804.
   (Prob. others.—See *Josiah* in *Miscellanea* of this family.)

FAM. 25. BENJAMIN,⁶ (Benj.,⁵ Philip,⁴ Philip,³ Philip,² Philip,¹), b. abt. 1764; m. 5 Feb., 1786, Abigail (dau. Othniel) **Brainard,** of Chatham, Ct.; she b. 1767 and 'd. 23 July, 1823, ae. 56.

Children (b. Chatham):

1. Benjamin, b. Oct., 1787; d. 16 Dec., 1788.
2. Nell, b. 1792; d. 19 Mch., 1827, at Midd. Hadd., ae. 35; Capt. in Militia in War of 1812.
3. Phila, m. John **Cole;** *issue* by Cole:
   i. Prudence (Cole), m. a **Kelsey,** of Hadd.

   ii. Eliza (Cole), m. Asaph **Young.**
   iii. Lucy (Cole).
      Mrs. Phila Cole, m. (2) Justin **Smith,** and had *issue:*
   iv. Catharine (Smith), m. Lyman **Howse** (or Howe ?).
4. Julia, bp. 25 Aug., 1799; d. unm.

FAM. 26. JAMES,⁶ (Benj.,⁵ Philip,⁴ Philip,³ Philip,² Philip,¹), m. 30 Mch., 1786, Mary **Carrier;** res. E. Hampt., where they were ch. members; she dismissed to Ch. in Burton, O., April, 1840.

Children (b. Chatham):

1. Alfred, b. 1786, bp. 23 Sept., 1787. FAM. 32.
2. Benjamin, bp. 25 Oct., 1789.
3. Prudence, b. 1794, bp. 24 Aug., 1794; d. 10 June, 1803.
4. Orren, bp. 15 June, 1806; d. 1 June, 1809,

ae. 3½.
5. Cyrus, b. and bp. 27 Dec., 1807. FAM. 33.
6. Titus Carrier, b. abt. 1834; rem. to Trumbull Co., O.

FAM. 27. JACOB,⁶ (Benj.,⁵ Philip,⁴ Philip,³ Philip,² Philip,¹), m. (1) Anne ————; who d. 12 Nov., 1788, ae. 20; m (2) 24 Jan., 1792, Sarah **Taylor.**

Children (b. Chatham):

1. Anna, b. 1803; m. Luther **Rich,** who d. 30 June, 1869, ae. 65; she d. 28 July, 1887, ae.

84.—*E. Hampton Cemetery Inscrp.*

FAM. 28. ASA,⁶ (Gideon,⁵ Philip,⁴ Philip,³ Philip,² Philip,¹), b. 1771; m. wid. Jemima **Bailey.**

Children:

1. Asa, bp. 7 Dec., 1794.
2. Elizabeth, bp. 20 June, 1796.
3. Miranda, m. 2 Feb., 1820, Ephraim **Hall.**
4. Abner.

5. Allen, m. ———— **Hubbard,** of M————
6. Jemima, m. Jabez B. **Young** (s. Asaph & Abigail **Brooks**), 31 Dec., 18—.

FAM. 29. JOSEPH ARNOLD,⁶ (Gideon,⁵ Philip,⁴ Philip,³ Philip,² Philip,¹), b. 1780; m. Temperance (dau. Daniel & Hurlbut) **Brooks,** 28 July, 1807; res, at Haddam Neck; he d. 14 Dec., 1837; she d. 1 Apl., 1858, ae. 73.

*Children (those * named in a deed, Vol. XXIX, 536, 1835, as heirs of J. A. G.):*

1. Francis J., b. 1808; d. 16 Sept., 1893, ae. 84 yrs., 8 mos.; family.
2. Joseph F.,* m. Chloe **Case.**
3. Hubbard Hurlburt,* b. 12 Jan., 1818; d. 12 Mch., 1890, ae. 72 yrs., 2 mos.; m. Louisa Elizabeth (*Russell*) **Brooks,** 26 Jan., 1845; res. Hadd. Neck. *Issue:*
   i. Calvin R.,⁸ b. 6 Nov., 1847; d. 28 Aug., 1860.
   ii. H. Goff, b. 1840; d. June, 1874, ae. 34.
4. Hatzell J.,* b. 1816; d. June, 1874, ae. 58; estate distributed 1 July, 1875, to Rebecca H.⁸ Goff, Harriet L.,⁸ Julia

R., the last one not then of legal age; her sister Harriet app. her guardian.
5. Arba Bradley,* b. 2 Apl., 1822; m. 14 Sept., 1845, Harriet K. (dau. Deming & Elizabeth *Wheat Dexter*) **Brooks,** of Hadd. Neck; farmer; rem. to New Hamburg, N. Y.; Episcopalian. *Issue:*
   i. Leander Dexter, b. 26 Aug., 1847; d. 17 Dec., 1847.
6. Susan S., b. ————; m. 11 Nov., 1849, Luke **Burr;*** res. Chatham.
7. Ansel, m. 12 June, 1825, Mary Ann **Smith.**
8. Asa, m. 3 May, 1841, Lucinda **Church.**

FAM. 30. JOHN,⁶ (John,⁵ Nath'l,⁴ Philip,³ Philip,² Philip,¹), b. abt. 1766-7; m. (1) abt. 1790, Vesta **Freman**— no doubt dau. of Barnabas and Ann. F., of East Hampton—prob. (orig. bp. rec. lost), b. 1771 and who d. 1816 ae. abt. 45 yrs.; he was m. (2) 8 Sept., 1816, Hannah **Cobb,** b. in New Lond., Feb., 1780, d. 14 Aug., 1836, at Midd. Haddam, ae. 76 yr. 7 mos. John Goff d. abt. 1831? ae. 77.

Children (by 1st marr.) :

1. Simeon, b. 16 Jan., 1792. FAM. 36.
2. Cyrus, b. 1794 ; d. in West or South, single.
3. William, b. 1796 ; lost at sea ; single.

4. Jesse, b. 1803 (?). FAM. 37.
5. Sylvester, b. 16 July, 1804. FAM. 38.
6. Alfred, b. 1807. FAM. 39.
7. Henry, b. 1815-16. FAM. 40.

FAM. 31. ELIJAH,[6] (*John*,[5] *Nath'l*,[4] *Philip*,[3] *Philip*,[2] *Philip*,[1]) ; m. (1) Elizabeth ————, who d. 3 June, 1813, ae. 35; m. (2) Anne **Cobb,** b. New Lond. (sister of bro. John's wife), res. Midd. Hadd.

Children (by 1st marr.) :

1. Giles, b. 13 Feb., 1796.
2. Elijah. FAM. 41.
(*By second marriage*) :
3. George, m. 9 Aug., 1862, Fannie (dau. Orren & Lucy *Goff*) **Grover.**
4. Elizabeth Ann, m. Harvey **Lucas,** as his sec. wife ; bu. at E. H. ; m. (2) William

Clark, of Midd. Hadd. *Issue :*
　i. Ralph D.
　ii. Ebenezer.
　iii. Sarah Frances, m. Lewis **Hailng.**
　iv. Harriet.
　v. Wm. Clark, Jr.

FAM. 32. ALFRED,[7] (*Jas.*,[6] *Benj.*,[5] *Philip*,[4] *Philip*,[3] *Philip*,[2] *Philip*,[1]), b. abt. 1787 ; m. (1) Sally **Frasier,** who d. 19 July, 1847, ae. 59; he m. (2) Charlotte (dau. Jacob), **Goff,** Mch., 23, 1822, who d. 12 May, 1880, ae. 84.

Children (by 1st marr.) :

1. Sally Prudence,[8] b. 1 Mch., 1809 ; m. Mr. **Crompton;** d. 9 Jan., 1841, ae. 32.
2. James, b. 27 Nov., 1810 ; d. 17 Feb., 1828.
3. Two sons, b. 2 Feb., 1815.
4. Daughter, b. 14 Mch., 1816.
5. Daughter, b. 12 July, 1817.
6. Timothy Dwight, b. 26 Mch., 1818 ; m. Evelina (dau. Evelina) Cook, of Windsor ; d. 12 June, 1886 ; she d. June 12. *Issue :*
　i. Sarah E.
　ii. Lucy A.
(*By second marriage*) :
7. Mary, b. 25 Mch., 1822 ; m. ———— **Maynard;** d. 18 Nov., 1863, ae. 41.
8. Horace, b. 24 Mch., 1823 ; d. 8 Mch., 1865, in Ohio.
9. Lucy Ann, b. 22 Nov., 1824 ; m. Orren **Grover.**

10. Warren, b. 8 May, 1826, m. Cornelia **Strong.**
11. Dau. b. 18 d. 20 Feb., 1828.
12. James, b. 11 Mch., 1829 ; m. Callsta **Rich;** he d. 4 Dec., 1862, in army ; she m. (2) Jas. **Dingwell.**
13. Florilla, b. 5 Mch., 1831 ; m. Sylvester **Cook;** d. 6 Mch., 1868.
14. Charlotte, b. 25 June, 1832 ; m. ————.
15. Elizabeth, b. 21 Oct., 1834 ; m. ———— **Root;** res. Coventry, Ct. ; had a son John now res. N. Lond.
16. Orren L., b. 3 Mch., 1837 ; m. ———— **Butler:** soldier of Civil War (Union) ; d. 30 May, 1895.
17. Cerena, b. 16 Sept., 1842 ; m. (as second wife) Julius T. **Smith.**
18. Irena (?).

FAM. 33. CYRUS,[7] (*James*,[6] *Benj.*,[5] *Philip*,[4] *Philip*,[3] *Philip*,[2] · *Philip*,[1]), bp. 1807 ; m. 3 Jan., 1832, Laura **Crowley,** and was killed 15 Apl., 1839 by bursting of a grindstone in a scythe mfy. in E. Hampton; wid. m. (2) William Riley **Carpenter,** and d. N. Lond., Ct.

Children :

1. Laura Prudence, b. 5 Apl., 1833 ; m. And. J. **Hobson;** res. N. Lond.
2. Frances M., b. 16 July, 1836 ; m. (1)

———— **Case;** m. (2) Lyman D. **Calkins;** res. N. Lond.

FAM. 34. GURDON SALTONSTALL,[7] (*Joseph*,[6] *Sam'l*,[5] *Philip*,[4] *Philip*,[3] *Philip*,[2] *Philip*,[1]). m. Chloe Maria **Tilden,** of Lebanon (?) d. abt. 1889; she d. E. Hampton, 12 Mch., 1900, ae. 80.

Children :

1. Lucius, m. Mary (dau. Silas D.) **Buckley;** res. E. Hampt. ; bell mfr. *Issue :*
　i. Eugene, m.
　ii. Lucius, m.

　iii. Matilda, m.
　iv. Otis, } twins ; m.
　v. Olla, }
　vi. ————.

FAM. 35. JOSEPH NELSON,[7] (*Joseph*,[6] *Sam'l*,[5] *Philip*,[4] *Philip*,[3] *Philip*,[2] *Philip*,[1]), b. 1808; m. 5 Nov., 1831, Florilla **Veazey**, who d. 8 Nov., 1878, ae. 70; he d. 22 Oct., 1889, ae. 81; res. E. Hampton.

Children (b. E. Hampton):

1. George.   2. Charles. | (Prob. others.)

FAM. 36. SIMEON,[7] (*John*,[6] *John*,[5] *Nath'l*,[4] *Philip*,[3] *Philip*,[2] *Philip*,[1]), b. 1792; m. 15 July, 1816, Lavinia (dau. Geo. ?) **Rich**, b. 24 Mch., 1793, in Midd. Hadd. she d. 21 Oct., 1885. He was in War of 1812, for many yrs. a ship carpenter at M. H., res. on Hog Hill. He d. 8 Mch., 1884, in 93 yr.

Children (b. Midd. Haddam):

1. Norman, b. 15 Dec., 1817. FAM. 43.
2. Seth, b. 1 June, 1819; d. 5 Dec., 1849; single.
3. Jeremiah, b. 5 July, 1821; m. Harriet **Button**. FAM. 44.
4. Lovinia, b. 8 June, 1823; m. Alonzo

Butler.
5. William Henry, b. 21 Aug., 1825; m. (1) Caroline **Cone**, of Ware, Mass., who d. abt. 1864; m. (2) in the West, ————; res. Delta, Col.

FAM. 37. JESSE,[7] (*John*,[6] *John*,[5] *Nath'l*,[4] *Philip*,[3] *Philip*,[2] *Philip*,[1]), b. 1802; res. many yrs. in Peconic dist. of Portland, Ct., where he was pound keeper in 1841; m. 26 Jan., 1831, Mary **Tryon**, of Midd. He d. 29 May, 1886, at Cromwell.

Children (b. Chatham-Portland):

1. Elizabeth, b. 1831; m. ———— **Spencer**, of Midd.; bu. 31 Aug., 1851, at P.
2. Jane, d. Midd.
3. Belle, b. ————; m. Leroy **Nobles**; res. Htfd.; but now in Midd.
4. Edward, res. Midd.; served in Civil War.
5. Sarah Ellen, m. Samuel **Tryon**; res. Bloomfield, Ct.
6. Catham, m. William **Moore**; res. College Ave., Annapolis, Md.
7. Isabel, d. Portland.
8. Mary Charlotte, b. 1845; d. Htfd., 21 Nov., 1896; m. 1 Aug., 1864, Asahel **Ingraham**, then of Colchester, who served in 13 Conn. Vols. and is now in Soldiers' Home at Noroton; had son Frederick.

FAM. 38. SYLVESTER,[7] (*John*,[6] *John*,[5] *Nath'l*,[4] *Philip*,[3] *Philip*,[2] *Philip*,[1]), b. 1804; m. 11 July, 1830, Sarah Tracy (dau. Joshua & Lydia *Isham*) **Worthington**, of E. Hadd., b. 18 Feb., 1809, in Colchester, Ct., and d. 20 May, 1851, ae. 42, by stroke of lightning. He was a shoemaker and dealer; res. in N. part of E. Hadd., near Chatham line; after dth. of wife, res. in E. Hadd.; memb. of Meth. Ch., and an upright man. He d. 5 Nov., 1885.

Children:

1. Sarah Almira, b. 25 Feb., 1832, in E. Hadd.; m. Nov., 1863, Oliver F. **Emmons**, of E. H., where they res. *No issue:*
2. Henry Augustus, b. 20 Aug., 1834, in Chatham. FAM. 45.
3. Mary Eliza, b. 31 Oct., 1836; m. 13 May, 1856, Wm. R. **Brainard**, b. 16 July, 1832, (s. of Enos Lewis & Emily *Scovil* Brainard), res. Htfd., Ct. *Issue:*
  i. Homer Worthington (Brainard), b. 30 May, 1864; res. Htfd.
  ii. Margaret Fuller (Brainard), b. 21 Mch., 1871; res. Htfd.
4. William Ellsworth, b. 21 Jan., 1839. FAM. 46.
5. Cynthia Levantia, b. 10 Jan., 1841; m. Henry S. **Gates**, of Chatham, who d. 10 Mch., 1899; farmer; wid. res. East Hampt. *Issue:*
  i. Ruth (Gates), b. 3 Dec., 1870; m. 6 Nov., 1890, Eugene B. (s. of Lucius) **Goff**, of E. H.; *no ch.*
  ii. Harry Augustus (Gates), b. 14 Oct., 1872; d. 8 Nov., 1891.
  iii. Mary Naomi (Gates), b. 30 Oct., 1881.

FAM. 39. ALFRED,[7] (*John*,[6] *John*,[5] *Nath'l*,[4] *Philip*,[3] *Philip*,[2] *Philip*,[1]), b. 1807; m. Adaline **Giddings**, who d. 9 July, 1885; he d. 27 Feb., 1885; shoemaker at Moodus, E. Hadd.

Children:

1. Jane, m. Elijah **Wetherell**, of Moodus, Ct. (as sec. wife); m. (2) 28 Nov., 1849, Geo. W. **Lester**, of E. Hadd.
2. Franklin, m. ———— **Davis**, of Darien.
3. Charles, m. Emma **Crowinnshield**; res. New York.
4. Orlando, res. Yankton, Dak.

FAM. 40. HENRY,[7] (*John*,[6] *John*,[5] etc.), b. 1816; d. 21
Dec., 1880, ae. 64; m. 7 Aug., 1842, Emeline **Hall.**

Children:

1. Frederick, soldier in Civil War, res. E. Htfd.
2. Sarah.
3. Mary Louisa, m. 23 Feb., 1865, Benajah **Lester.**

FAM. 41. ELIJAH,[7] (*Elijah*,[6] *John*,[5] *Philip*,[4]), m. Lucy
——————, who was bu. 14 Sept., 1847, Portland, Ct.; he prob. m. again.

Children:

1. Miles (or Giles), drowned at Midd. Hadd., 13 Aug., 1841, ae. 12 yrs.

(*By second marriage*):
2. Martin. FAM. 42.
3. Stephen, d. at sea.

FAM. 42. MARTIN,[7] (*Elijah*,[6] *John*,[5] *Philip*,[4]) b. 1796
m. 1 Mch., 1825, Marietta Hall (dau. Abijah & Chloe *Freeman*), **Markham,**
b. 11 Sept., 1809, d. 14 Feb., 1839. Ship carpenter at Midd. Hadd.; he m. (2)
3 Oct., 1842, Rachel **Brainard.** He d. 3 Feb., 1846.

Children:

1. Giles, res. Cobalt; Chatham, Ct.
2. William Henry, b. abt. 1820; m. 31 Oct., 1847, Nancy Diana **Strong,** b. 31 May, 1831.

Issue:
i. Fred. Wm. Augustus, brass moulder, New Haven, Ct.

FAM. 43. NORMAN,[8] (*Simeon*,[7] *John*,[6] *John*,[5] *Nath'l*,[4] ,), b. 1817; m.
m. 17 Sept., 1846, Emeline **Flood,** who d. 6 Apl., 1855, ae. 26; he m. (2) her
sister Phebe **Flood;** he d. at Norwich, Ct., 20 Mch., 1900, in 83d yr.; was nearly
all his life a ship builder at Midd. Hadd. and Gildersleve (Portland), Ct.

Children:

1. Robert, res. Gildersleeve, Ct.
2. John, res. New Haven, Ct.
3. Mrs. James **Lord,** Warehouse Pt., Ct.
4. Mrs. C. W. **Tubbs,** Norwich, Ct.

FAM. 44. JEREMIAH,[8] (*Simeon*,[7] *John*,[6] *John*,[5] *Nath'l*,[4] ,), b.
1821; m. 8 Jan., 1846 in Portland, Ct., Harriet **Button;** he d. Higganum, Ct.,
abt., 1886.

Children

1. Dau!
2. Dau.
3. Son, who res. at So. Frances, Midd.

FAM. 45. HENRY AUGUSTUS,[8] (*Sylvester*,[7] *John*,[6] *John*,[5]), b.
1834; m. 27 Dec., 1855, in Binghamton, N. Y., Ellen Carter (dau. Col. Jacob
Carter & Louise *Dunham*) **Robie,** of B.; has been a dealer and mfr. of shoes
for 45 yrs.; a substantial and respected citizen; memb. and trustee of the
Cong. Ch.

Children (b. Binghamton, N. Y.):

1. Lillie Belle, b. 3 Feb., 1857; m. Aug., 1878, Chas C. **Pratt,** of New Milford, Pa.; 4 ch.
2. Sarah Louise, b. 20 June, 1859; d. May,
1883; single.
3. Nellie Robie, b. Dec., 1860; d. yg.
4. Charles Henry, b. 8 May, 1875; res. B., in bus. with father; single.

FAM. 46. WILLIAM ELLSWORTH,[8] (——————————————), b.
1839; m. 1858, Julia (dau. Henry & Julia Ann *Watson*) **Holdridge,** b. Colchester, Ct., who d. 19 Jan., 1893, at Htfd. He d. 11 Mch., 1892, in Htfd.;
res. in E. Hadd., So. Windsor, Manchester and Htfd., Ct.

Children (b. E. Hadd.) :

1. Carrie Adaline, b. 22 Apl., 1859 ; m. (1) Alexander **Hamilton;** m. (2) 10 Apl., 1884, Horace Porter **Fox,** res. Htfd., Ct. *No issue.*
2. Hatsued Sylvester, b. 20 Oct., 1861 ; d. 29 Apl., 1899, Htfd. ; m. 14 Mch., 1881, Angeline (dau. John) **Tryon,** then of Manchester, Ct. ; she now res. Schenectady,

N. Y. *Issue:*
  i. Harry H., b. 2 Oct., 1882, in Htfd.
  ii. Robert b. 17 Dec., 1884.
3. William Ellsworth, b. 18 Mch., 1863 ; d. 12 Nov., 1898, in Midd., res. Htfd. ; single.
4 Estella, b. 27 Jan., 1867 ; m. 4 Nov., 1886, Charles **Glazier,** b. 23 Nov., 1852 ; res. Htfd. *No issue.*

The following are probably descendants of Philip of Wethersfield, perhaps of the Simsbury or Wallingford branches.

DAVID GOFF was a Revolutionary soldier. He was in 1767, one of the petitioners for the incorporation of the town of Winchester. He removed to Sharon later. The story of his remarkable escape after being taken prisoner by the British, is told in Sedgwick's *History of Sharon, Ct.* His wife's name was Mary ————, and he had:

Children:

1. Irena, b. 9 Jan., 1770.
2. Sarah, bp. 10 Feb., 1771.
3. Esther, b. 10 Nov., 1772.

Perhaps the Sharon records may disclose others.

In Tillotson's *Wethersfield Cemetery Inscriptions* I find:

THANKFUL GOFF d. Apr. 10, 1849, aged 78 yrs. And in the same book, (Rocky Hill Cem.), I find:

GIDEON GOFF d. Aug. 18, 1849, aged 88 yrs.—*S. C. R.* Anna, [Nath'l m. 21 Aug., 1786.—*S. C. R.*] his wife, d. Feb. 6, 1809, aged 54.—*S. C. R.* Mehitabel, his [second] wife, d. Aug. 29, 1838—*S. C. R.*, aged 64. Hezekiah, their son, [bp. 4 Oct., 1789—*S. C. R.*], d. Apr. 27, 1790, aged 8 mos.—*S. C. R.* Lydia, their dau., [bp. 24 Aug., 1794—*S. C. R.*], d. Jan. 12, 1795, aged 7 mos. Gideon Jr., [bp. 14 Oct., 1798—*S. C. R.*], d. at sea, Dec., 1, 1823, aged 26. *S. C. R.* give them Anna Deming, bp. 20 May, 1792; and Abigail, bp. 11 Nov., 1787.

In my records I find the following: *East Middletown,* (since Chatham, and Portland, *Congregational Church Records.* June 20, 1811, GIDEON Goff of Northfield and Mehitabel **Barlow,** of Newport. This is probably the second marriage of the above Gideon. Where the places mentioned are, I am not sure. Northfield may be the town in Massachusetts and Newport may be the town in New Hampshire, but I don't feel certain of this identification. I have found a few traces of Goffs in Saybrook, Ct., but have not been able to trace out their connections. There are also some in Glastonbury, doubtless of the Philip line. Other Goffs in Connecticut, *not descendants* of Philip[1] of Wethersfield.

ANTHONY[1] GOFF was an early settler at Woburn and Billerica, Mass. By wife, Sarah, he had recorded at Woburn, Joseph, b. Nov. 1, 1687, and James, b. June 3, 1689; both died soon. March 5, 1718 among the proprietors of Ashford, Conn., was Anthony Goff, and families of this name have been found in Killingly, (Thomsan parish) Plainfield, and Pomfret (Abington parish) and Woodstock, Ct.—See Miss Larned's *History of Windham County.* The meeting house in Thomson parish was begun in 1720, and finished in 1733, Hezekiah[2] Goff being the contractor, and doing the fine inside work. I suppose that this Hezekiah[2] was a son or relative of Anthony.[1] He lived in Killingly. *Woodstock* records have the following:

HEZEKIAH³ GOFF (probably a son of the Hezekiah² of Killingly); m. Oct., 31, 1743 at Woodstock (?) [acc. to the church records] Bethia **Morris,** dau. of   Morris, b.   . Their daughter Betty,⁴ bapt. Apl. 3, 1748. Sometime later he removed to Middletown, Conn., for on the Middletown records we find: Children of Hezekiah Goff and Bethiah his wife.

Children:

1. Asa, **b.** 7 Jan., 1749-50.
2. Betty, b. 26 June, 1750; O. S.
3. Bethiab, b. 2 Feb., 1752.
4. Hezekiah, b. 26 June, 1754.
5. Jonathan, b. 4 Mar., 1757.

6. William, b. 14 May, 1759.
7. David, b. 16 Oct., 1761.
8. Hannah, b. 26 Feb., 1764.
9. Sarah, b. 3 July, 1766.
10. Elizabeth, b. 26 Apl., 1769.

Hezekiah³ Goff died in Middletown; in the probate records there is found an application for administration on the estate [insolvent] of Hezekiah Goffe, deceased.

HEZEKIAH⁴ and probably all his brothers removed to Vermont [See Hemenway's *Historical Gazeteer of Vermont*], probably to Richford or that vicinity. Perhaps the Hezekiah Goff who was in Deerfield, Mass., from 1784 to 1796, is the same. Hezekiah was a soldier (private) in the 8th Reg. 9th Co., Capt. Filer, in the Revolutionary war; the company was raised mainly in Haddam and Chatham.

JONATHAN was in Warner's Company, 3rd. Regiment Connecticut line; probably also William and David.

Jonathan Goff and Hydia **Harding,** were married Apr. 3, 1796, in Chatham or Middletown. This may perhaps be Jonathan son of Hezekiah.³

HANNAH GOFF,⁴ dau. Hezekiah,³ m. Michael **Braddock,** b. July 20, 1765, in Birmingham, England. In 1779-80 it is said that he came to America in the British Army, but purchased his discharge and settled in Connecticut. He died March, 13, 1828, aged 63, in Middletown or Middle Haddam. His wife Hannah died Aug., 18, 1804, aged 39. Some of their descendants can be found in the *Strong Genealogy,* but much of what is said there about her being a descendant of Gen. William Goff, the regicide Judge of Charles I, is in mention, or twisted tradition.

Another Goff family in Connecticut.

ROBERT¹ GOFF, of Rehoboth, Mass., m. May 8, 1733, Hannah **Horton,** of Rehoboth, b. May 28, 1704. Their oldest son

COMFORT² GOFF was born in Rehoboth, Sept. 25, 1734, and m. there Jan. 20, 1757, Susannah **Guernsey,** b. June 24, 1737, probably dau. Seth Guernsey of Rehoboth.

Soon after his marriage he removed to Connecticut and settled in that part of Colchester which is now Marlboro. About 1783 he removed with his sons to Winchester, Ct., (See Boyd's *Annals of Winchester*), or perhaps only Comfort, Jr., Enoch and Guernsey, his sons, did so. See Boyd's Winchester, pp. 286, 320. He died in Rush, N. Y., in 1819, aged 85. About 1804 Brainards, Rowleys, Goffs, Tuppers, and Wm. Allen and wife, also Prestons, Carletons and Wilcoxes, mostly from Chatham and Winchester, Ct., settled in Rush, Monroe Co., N. Y. From there many of them went, about 1832, to Genesee and Macombe Cos., Michigan. Their descendants live at Grand Blanc, Mich., now.

Children:

1. Charles,[3] b. 1758 or '59; d. 13 Oct., 1832, in Rush, N. Y., aged 73, acc. to U. S. pension record. He was a Revolutionary soldier. He m. Deborah **Hill**, of Colchester, dau. of Thomas and Deborah (or perhaps of Daniel Hill), b. 1756; d. in Rush, N. Y., 7 Jan., 1818, ae. 62. The gravestone of Charles Goff, in Rush, is said to give his age as 79. If so, he was b. in 1753 or 4, and could not be a son of Comfort, but I prefer to follow the pension record and the family tradition, which says that he was a son of Comfort. He m. (2) Anna (wid. of Eli) **Brainard**. Her maiden name was **Strong**, and she was born in Chatham, Ct. *Issue (by first marriage):*
   i. Elizabeth, b. 1778 or 79; m. 22 Feb., 1798, at Midd. Hadd., Ct., John **Tapper**, of that parish. Their children were: Reuben, Newell, Alden, Harrison, Benajah, Alexander, Charles.
   ii. Esther, b. 21 Aug., 1780; m. 13 (or 3) Aug., 1800, at Midd. Hadd., William **Allen**, b. 11 Feb., 1777, in Stonington, Ct., s. of David and Elizabeth (Goff) Allen; went to Rush, N. Y., and Michigan (?). *Children:* Hannah, b. 22 June, 1801, in Chatham, Ct.; David, Ellsworth, Jason, Isaac, Hopkins, Enoch Goff, Asenath, Hopkins again, Deborah and Alvin.
   iii. Hannah, b. ————; m. 16 Sept., 1801, at Midd. Hadd., Ct., Daniel **Remington**; settled in Macomb Co., Mich.
   iv. Asenath, b. ————; m. Alfred (s. of Eli & Anna *Strong*) **Brainard**. *Children:* Alva, Gurdon, Eli, Ira, Alice.
   v. Deborah, b. ————; m. Ira **Preston**; sett. Macomb Co.
   vi. Charles W.,[4] b. ————; m. Asenath **Brainard**. *Children:* Juliet, who m. John (nephew of Daniel) **Remington**, before mentioned; he was, 1810, in Htfd., Ct.; Asahel, Madison, Asenath, who m. ———— **Van Tiffiin**.
2. Elizabeth, b. ———— (?); possibly she may have been the oldest; m. ————,

David **Allen**, of Stonington, Ct. In 24 Oct., 1779, David Allen and wife joined the church at East Hampton (Chatham). He was a Revolutionary soldier, and is said to have lived to be upwards of a hundred years old. *Children:* William,[4] b. 11 Feb., 1777, already mentioned; David, d. in inf.; Mary, who m. ————. **Foote**; Rachel, who m. ———— **Drake**. David Allen may, possibly, have been from Rehoboth, where that name is numerous. Possibly Elizabeth was *sister* of Comfort Goff, or some other relation.
3. Guernsey, b. ————; m. 31 Dec., 1789, Asenath (dau. Dudley & Windwell *Ackley*) **Brainard**, of Midd. Hadd. He was in Winchester, in 1794, but sold out that year. He was made blind by accident, but became a basket-maker, and was active and intelligent. Had a family.
4. Squire, b. ————; m. Experience **Brainard**, dau. Dudley Brainard above. Had a family.
5. Enoch, b. ————; m. ————, and had a family; lived in Colchester and Winchester.
6. Comfort, b. ————; m. 10 Mch., 1781, in Chatham, Amelia **Pelton**, of that town (now Portland); went to Winchester, and Rush, N. Y.; was a Revolutionary soldier.
7. William, b. ————; it is said that he remained in Connecticut.
8. Hannah.
9. Rachel.
10. Beloved.
11. Harvey.

(Further information about Comfort Goff's descendants may be obtained from Miss Lucy A. Brainard, 4 Atwood St., Htfd., Ct., or Miss Rose Van Tiffiin, 1400 S. Saginaw St., Flint, Mich.)
(Goff families were numerous at Salem, Boston, Dorchester, Cambridge, Mass., and Londonderry, N. H., but I do not find that any of them came to Connecticut. Those in Providence, R. I., are, I believe, descts. of Richard and Robert of Rehoboth.)

GOLDRICK, JOHN, b. 1803; d. in Weth., where he had res. many yrs., 8 Sept., 1887, ae. 84; he contributed many poems to the Hartford papers; his wife Jane **Berry**, d. 8 May, 1867, ae 56.—*Weth. Ins.*

GOODALE, (*Goodell*), ALMIRA, m. Charles **Seldon**, of Chatham, 5 May, 1833.—*W. T. R.*

BENJAMIN, a ch. of, in 2d yr., d. 17 Dec., 1846.

EBENEZER, m. Leora **Rich**, 28 Apl., 1833.—*W. T. R.*

EBENEZER, d. 18 Feb., 1847, ae. 66; his wife Sally d. 29 Dec., 1832, in 48 yr.; their dau. Fanny, d. 24 Feb., 1823, ae 10 yrs; their dau. Lucy Ann, d. 9 Apl., 1826, ae. 3 yr., 8 mo.—*Weth (S) Ins.*

FANNY, d. 24 Feb., 1823, in 11 yr.—*S. C. R.*

EMELINE, (wife of Horace **Adams**), d. 14 Dec., 1883, ae. 75.—*Ibid.*

FRANCIS (dau. Ebenezer), m. Seldon **Deming**, 1 Mch., 1846.—*W. T. R.*

NELSON, wife of, d. 14 Jan., 1840, ae. 35—*S. C. R.*; their inf. d. 12 Jan., 1840.—*S. C. R.*

PHILO CHAPELLE, m. Elizabeth Prudence **Belden**, 1 Dec., 1833.—*S. C. R.*

WALTER, of Htfd., m. Julia Ann **Stoddard**, 7 Mch., 1838.—*W. R.*

GOODFELLOW, THOMAS, was, in 1673, apprentice to Henry Buck (black-smith), had been previously serving under John Cherry. He was a s. of Thomas, of Htfd., where, *Porter* says he was res. before 1639, and had a lot but did not settle, either sold or forfeited it. Came to Weth., abt. 1674. For ld-holding at Weth., see Chapt. VII, Vol. I. He m. abt. 1681, Mary (eld. dau. Peter) **Grant;** he d. 25 Nov., 1685; invent. of his est. taken by Sam'l Talcott and Nath'l Bowman, of Weth., amt'd to £49-04-06; the *Prob. Ct. Rec.* (1685-6), provides that the wid. (who was made adm'r), should "bring up the children—if she could give them anything it is desirable she should."

Children (*Weth. Rec.*) :

1. Mary, b. 10 Apl., 1683.
2. Thomas, b. 26 Mch., 1684.
3. Samuel, b. 31 Oct., 1685.
4. Timothy, b. 3 Jan., 1687 (1686-7 ?).

GOODHUE, DAVID, of Far. m. Martha **Clark,** 27 Dec., 1820.

GOODRICH, (*Guttridge, Goodridge*). Two of this name, JOHN and WILLIAM, brothers, were among the first settlers of Weth. Genealogies of their respective families (brief, as to *John*), are given in Goodwin's *Genealogical Notes*. Other contributions to the history of the family are (1) The *Goodrich Family Memorial*, Parts 1 and 2, compiled by Edwin Hubbard, Chicago, Ill., 1883-4, 8 vo. Mr. Hubbard d. 1890 and two parts only were pub.—containing 109 pp.; and (2) *The Goodrich Family in America*, a Genealogy of the descendants of John and William Goodrich, of Weth., Ct., Richard Goodrich, of Guilford, Ct., and William Goodridge of Watertown, Mass., etc. By Lafayette Wallace Case, M. D., Chicago, Ill., 1889, 8 vo. 417 pp. This last named work we have not seen.

Goodwin, in his *Notes*, p. 70, presents strong presumptive evidence of the relationship of JOHN and WILLIAM, of Weth., to the Rev. William G., of the estab. Church of England, who died in Hedgasett, Co., Suffolk, Eng..* which fact, together with more recent investigations, since Goodwin wrote, identifies them as natives of that part of Eng. At their first coming to New Eng. they

---

* In 1678, there d. in Hegessett, Suffolk Co., Eng., childless, the Rev. Wm. Goodrich * * * * leaving a will in wh. he bequeathed certain specified real and personal estate to his wife Rebecca during her natural life, with remainder to one of the sons of his brother Jno. Goodrich and to one of the sons of his brother Wm. Goodrich, naming them.
Rebecca, the widow of the Rev. Wm. G., d. in Nov., 1698, after which (8) Jonathan Goodrich, the s. of (1) John G., Sr., and (15) John Goodrich, s. of (2) Wm. G., were entitled to receive about £200 sterling from the estate.
The Rev. Wm. G., of Hegessett, Eng., was probably brother-in-law of (1) John and (2) Wm. G., of Weth., Ct. May 18, 1703, (8) Jonathan G. appointed Nicholas Hallman, mariner, of New Lond., to take possession of his estate in Hagessett, Eng. For the will of Rev. Wm. G., of Hegessett. Eng., and letters rel. thereto, see *"Private Controversies,"* v. 5 pp. 239, *Secy. of State's Office,* Hartford, Ct.

(From Vol. V, p. 240-243, *State Archives*.)
"No. 240. A letter from Henry Bull, 23 Nov., 1692, to 'Cozen' Goodrich, mentions "your Aunt, my one s. John, a Minister, and my son-in-law, Thomas Winlock, who m. my dau."

No. 241. Addressed "Dear Brother." Bury [St. Edmonds, Eng.], 24 Nov., 1698. "My kind love to you and yrs. This is to desire you to send to my Cousins the Goodriches to let them know that their Aunt is dead, and was bu. the 18 day of this inst. Nov. * * * * yr loving brother Henry Bull."

Page 242.   From Bury [St. Edmonds], Ye 16 of July, 1678.
"Cozen Goodrich :
This is to inform you that your brother [Rev.] William is lately dead, he dyed in Hegessett, near Bury in the County Suffolk, and left no children ; the sum of his Last Will and Testament, this he has given to his wife all during her natural life, after her death he has bequeathed to your Relations, as followeth, viz. to Joseph, the eldest son of his brother John, he has given his house and ground at Hegessett above said, and £100 in money if the [said] Joseph shall then be living, else to second son, or failing there, to the eldest dau. of his brother John. He has also given one Copyhold ground, in value near £100 and £100 in money to John, the eldest son of his brother William, after the

located at Watertown, Mass., where William rec'd and rec. several pieces of ld.; and they came prob. with the first general emigr. from Wat. to Weth, 1636, where, also, they rec'd ld. grants—as see Chapt. VII, Vol. I.*
The Goodriches of England were of an ancient lineage, antedating the Norman Conquest, at which time many of the name were in possession of lands, lordships and titles, which after the manner of those times, suffered confiscation at the hands of the Conqueror. "Doomsday Rolls" are especially full of the name, which originally was Goderic—that is "Eric," prefixed by the name of the Deity. From the number enrolled as clergy, of various ranks, it is probable that many of the name sought, in the service of the Church, that refuge from absolute poverty and dependence to which they had been reduced by the confiscation of their estates. Goodrich Castle, a noble fortalice, and erected soon after the Conquest on the banws of the river Wye, as a protection for the West of England against the incursions of the Welsh, but, still remains (though in ruins since the War between Parliament and Charles the First,) indissolubly connected with the history of the family.

THE *JOHN* GOODRICH FAMILY OF WETHERSFIELD.

JOHN GOODRICH, the eld. of the two bros. who came to Weth., was b. prob. at or near Bury St. Edmunds, Eng., and prob. was at Weth., as early as 1644—in which yr. he had lds. rec. to him, and later in 1666. See Chapt. VII, Vol. I. In 1645, he m. (1) Elizabeth (dau. Thomas) **Edwards,** of Weth., who d. in childbed, 5 July, 1670; he m. (2) Apl., 1674, Mary (dau. of the first Nath'l) Foote, and wid. of John **Stoddard**, late of Weth. In the *Weth. Ld. Recs.* III, 53, as also in *Private Controversies*, III, 49, 50, *MSS. Archives, Sec'y State's Office*, is to be found rec. of an ante-nuptial contract betw. Mr. G. and the wid. Stoddard, dated 4 Apl., 1674, explaining why and how she was to be provided for, and why she is not ment. in his will. Mr. Goodrich d. Apl., 1680, and his will exhib. to the Prob. Ct., 2 Sept., same yr.; the will was not allowed; admin. was gr. to Lt. Samuel Steele, Daniel Rose and Josiah Goodrich, with an order for distrib.; (the eld. s. John had d.); to Joseph, the eld, surviving son, was given £190; to Jonathan, £190; each of the 3 daus. rec'd £90; and the wid. £4 pr. an. "with her ante-nuptial agreement."* Invent. of est. taken 6 Apl., 1680, by Samuel Steele, John Wolcott and Nathaniel Boreman, am't £651-10-00. The wid. m. (3) Lieut. Thomas **Tracy**, of Norwich, (formerly Weth.),—See *Foote, Stoddard* and *Tracy*. Mr. G. was juryman, 4 Dec., 1645; 4 Mch., 1646; 7 Sept., 1748.--*Col. Rees.*, and, with Michael Griswold, was app. Constable for Weth, 1663 or '64.—*Co. Ct. Rec.* III. 12.

---

decease of his wife. if then living, or next then failing, to William the son of his brother William and his heirs forever, all to be enjoyed after the death of his wife whom he hath app'd sole executrix, myself and one Mr. John Goodrich of Hawleigh to be Supervisors.
My wife is yet living, who was your Cozen Jane Coates, and desires to be kindly remembered to you. I am also your loving Kinsman   HENRY BULL."
* There is a trad. (not, however, satisfactorily supported) in the family, that John and William were orphans and came to New Eng., from South Wales, abt. 1664, with their mother's bro., a William Stillman, and that they first sett. in the New Haven Colony.
* This agreement, executed "in consideration of £180 in lds. and other ppy. which were to be handed to him, on marriage" provided that in case of Mr. G.'s dth. before her, "she should receive back all the said lds. and ppy., and also £4 per yr., out of his own proper estate, and that if any of said est. and ppy. should have been disposed of, the value of same should be made good to her," out of certain designated meadow lds:, duly described. This contract was witnessed, Apl. 4, 1674. before Josiah Churchill, Joseph Wright and Hugh Wells.

Children (Weth. Rec.,* all by 1st marr.) :

1. Elizabeth, b. 2 Nov., 1645; m. Daniel **Rose**, of Weth., 1664.
2. John, b. 5 (*Goodwin* has it 8) Sept., 1647; sett. in W.; d. May, 1676; leaving a wid. Mary, and a dau. Mary, b. 23 Apl., 1676.
3. Mary, b. 15 Dec., 1650; m. abt. 1677, Thomas **Read**, Jr., of Sudbury, Mass.
4. Joseph, b. 10 June, 1653; rem. to Sudbury, where he d. Oct., 1680; s. p.; his will (*Middlesex Co., Mass., Prob.*) devises ppy.

to his bros. and sisters.
5. Jonathan. FAM. 2.
6. Hannah, m. (1) abt. 1679, Zachariah (s. John & Hannah *Axtell*) **Maynard, of** Sudbury, Mass., who had at one time, res. in Weth., or Glast, (his name being found on rec. of both towns), b. 7 June, 1647, and d. 1724; she d. 1719.—See *Hist. Farmingham, Mass.*, 322, for issue.

FAM. 2.   JONATHAN,[2] (*John,*[1]), sett. in Weth.; m. Abigail (dau. Moses) **Crafts,** 3 Dec., 1691. This Jonathan is identified as the son of John Goodrich, the Settler; and also, as of Hedgesett (or English) line, by the following docs. preserved in the *Conn. State Archives*, Sec'y State's Office, V. 243.

"Be it known unto all men, by these Presents, that I, Jonathan Goodrich, of Wethersfield, * * * Tailor, one of the sons of John Goodrich, late of Weth., aforesaid, husbandman, deceased, for divers good causes * * * have * * * constituted and appointed my friend Nicholas Hallam, of New London, in the county of New London, * * mariner, my true and lawful attorney, to act for me in the realm of England to enter into and upon certain Messuage, or Tenement * * * lying and being in Hegesett, in the County Suffolk, in the Kingdom of England, formerly belonging to and being in the possession of William Goodrich, of Hogesett aforesaid, Clerke, and now of Right belonging to me * * * to do, execute and accomplish all and whatsoever I myself might or could do personally * * * * * * Jonathan Goodrich.

Witness, Hezekiah Willis ⎱
Caleb Stanley, Jr.   ⎰   18 May, 1703.

Test, Eleazer Kimberly, Sec'y.

By the Gov. Council,
J. Winthrop.

John Winthrop, Esq., Governor of Her Majesty's Colony of Conn. * * greeting * * this 20th May, 1703, appeared before me, sd. John Winthrop in Hartford, William Warner, age about 57 years, and Thomas Welles, aged about 41 years, both of Wethersfield. * testify from personal knowledge and acquaintance with John Goodrich, late of Weth., husbandman, deceased, living & conversing with him many years, and that said John Goodrich had a reputed son named Joseph Goodrich, who hath been dead for about 22 yr., and died without issue.

And the said William Warner and Thomas Welles further declare that the sd. John Goodrich left another son at his decease, named Jonathan Goodrich, who now (since the sd. Joseph, his death) is reputed only son surviving lawfully begotten and that Jonathan Goodrich aforesaid, taylor, a person who was present at the time of taking the oath upon whose request this Certificate is granted & claims estate lying in Hegesett, County Suffolk, Eng., devised to him by the last will and testament of William Goodrich, sometime of sd. Hegesett, Clerke. Said Jonathan Goodrich, about 38 yrs. of age married and his several children living.

J. Winthrop.

Eleazor Kimberly, Sec'y.   (Colon. Seal)

Children (b. Weth.) :

1. Jonathan, b. 1 Feb., 1692-3.
2. Abigail, b. 28 Nov., 1694; m. Samuel (s. of Samuel) **Wright,** of Weth., 2 Jan., 1717-18.
3. Moses, b. 19 July, 1697.

4. Lucy, b. 9 (bp. 17—*Mix MSS.*) Sept., 1699; m. Daniel **Fuller**, of Weth., 7 Aug., 1723.
5. Rebecca, b. 24 (bp. 28—*Mix MSS.*) Dec., 1701-2.

THE *WILLIAM* GOODRICH FAMILY, OF WETHERSFIELD.

Ensign WILLIAM GOODRICH,* b. near Bury St. Edward, Co. Suffolk, Eng., m. at Htfd., 4 Oct., 1648, Sarah (dau. Matthew & Elizabeth) **Marvin**, of H.; he was app., with Mr. Robbins, constable for Weth., at the Ct. of 7 Mch., 1649,— *Htfd. Prob. Rec.* II. 2; was adm. freeman of Conn., 15 May, 1656; dep. from Weth. to Gen. Ct., during 5 sess. (May, 1662—Oct.,1666); was a grand juror, May, 1662; comm'd Ens. of Weth. Train-band, by Gen. Ct., 11 May, 1665, (*Col. Rec.* II. 17), and is so styled on all pub. recs. until his dth. in 1676. His wid. m. (2) as his second wife, Capt. William (s. John) *Curtis,* of Stratford, Ct., who d. 21 Dec., 1702. She d. at S., near close of same yr.; her will, dated 21 Oct., 1697, adm. to prob. 7 Jan., 1702-3; by her second marr. she had no issue.

The inventory of Ens. Wm. Goodrich's estate, amt'g to £915-03-06, taken 14 Nov., 1676, by John Belding, Samuel Wright, and John Robbins, Townsmen— shows an account of what he gave his daus. *Abigail* and *Elizabeth,* as their marr. "settting out"—viz:

"An acc't of what his son Thomas Fitch (who m. the dau. *Abigail*) rec'd of his father (in-law) Goodrich, as follows:

To silver	£20-00-00	To one chest & box	£0-09-00
" a horse	4-00-00	To putor [pewter]	2-11-00
" a cow	4-00-00	" brass cittel [kettle]	1-02-00
" a bed & furniture	8-00-00	" a Iron pote	0-08-00
" Linen	9-03-00	" a brass cittell ⎱	
" cushions	0-16-00	" 2 skilletes ⎰	0-18-00
" serge for cushion	0-16-00	" a box & heaters†	0-05-00
" a cubbard cloth		" woodden ware	0-12-00

| | | *as footed on old paper* | £52-00-00 |

An account of [what] his son Robbard Welles [who m. the dau. *Elizabeth*] received of his Father Goodrich—To 2 cows, £8; to 2 steers, £8; to putor, £2-05; to feather-bed, one bolster, and blanket, £4; to Linen, £9-13; to curtains £0-13; to porke, £1-08; to 7 bushels Ind. corne, £0-17-06; to one cittel, £1-05 to one scillet, £0-06; to a bason, sarge [serge] & worsted, £0-16; to a trunk, £0-16; to wooden ware, £0-09; to what he received in silver, £4-12-00—footed £43-00-06.

On the back of the inventory is the following memorandum of the ages of Ens. William's sons, at date of the making of this document, viz: John Goodrich is 24 yrs. old y⁰ 20th day of May next. William Goodrich is 17 yr. old y⁰ 8th Feb'y next. Ephraim Goodrich is 14 yrs. old y⁰ 2d June next. David Goodrich is 10 yrs. old y⁰ 4th March next."—*Htfd. Co. Prob. Rec.* III. 175.

---

* There appears to have been another William Goodrich (ment. by *Savage* under the head of Goodrich), who res. in Watertown, Mass., and d. 1647, and whose wid. Margaret, as the wife of John Hale, d. 3 Feb., 1683.
† Probably a warming-pan and heating irons.

Children (Weth. Rec.) :

1. William, twin Sarah, b. 8 Aug., 1649 ;
   d. yg.
2. Sarah, twin William ; m. 20 Nov., 1667,
   John, Jr., (s. John & Joanna *Treat*)
   Hollister, of Glast., b. 1642 ; she d. 1700.
3. Mary, b. 13 Nov., 1651 ; m. 1667, Joseph
   (s. Dea. Rich. & Elizabeth) **Butler,** of
   Htfd., who d. 1732, ae. 85 ; she d. 1 June,
   1735.
4. John, b. 20 May [* * 1652—*Weth.
   Rec.*] 1653. FAM. 2.
5. Elizabeth, b. 1658 ; d. 17 Feb., 1698 ; m.
   9 June, 1675, Capt. Robert (s. John &

Elizabeth) **Welles,** of Stratford. Capt.
Welles m. (2) Mary ————, by whom
he left *no issue.*
6. William(Lieut.), b. 8 Feb., 1661. FAM. 3.
7. Abigail, b. 5 June, 1662 ; m. 15 Sept., 1680,
   Thomas (s. of Samuel & Susanna *Whiting*) **Fitch,** of Weth., who d. 7 Nov., 1884 ;
   he m. (2) Sarah (dau. Samuel) **Boardman,**
   of Weth., by whom he had 4 ch. For his
   ch. by Abigail Goodrich, see *Fitch.*
8. Ephraim (Capt.), b. 2 June, 1663. FAM. 4.
9. David (Col.), b. 4 May, 1667. FAM. 5.

FAM. 2. JOHN,[2] (*Ens. William,*[1]), b. 1653; sett. Weth.; m. 28 Mch., 1678, at
Charlestown, Mass., Rebecca (dau. Capt. John "mariner") **Allen,** of C. He d.
abt. 1737, ae. 84.

Children (Weth. Rec.)

1. Sarah, b. 10 Apl., 1679 ; m. 26 Oct., 1699,
   Ab'm **Kilborne,** of Weth., who d. 9 Mch.,
   1713, ae. 38.—See *Kilborne.*
2. Rebecca, b. 11 Nov., 1680 ; m. 28 Dec.,
   1699, David **Wright,** of Weth. ; she d.
   10 Apl., 1703 ; he m. (2) Mary (dau.
   Lieut. Jona.) **Belden,** of W., 1710.—See
   Wright.
3. Mary, b. 4 Sept., 1682 ; m. 30 Dec., 1703,
   Thomas **Curtis,** of Weth. ; she d. 5 Feb.,
   1730 ; he m. (2) Rachel (dau. John)

Morgan, of Groton. *Issue (by first marriage) :* Rebecca, b. 28 Apl., 1705.—*Weth.
Rec.*
4. Samuel, b. 24 May, 1684 ; d. 7 May, 1706,
   ae. nr. 22.
5. Abigail, b. 27 Apl., 1686 ; m. 25 Apl., 1706,
   David **Curtiss,** of Weth.—See *Curtiss.*
6. John, b. 9 June, 1688. FAM. 6.
7. Allen, b. 13 Nov., 1690. FAM. 7.
8. Ann, b. 1 Sept., 1692.
9. Jacob, b. ————. FAM. 8.

FAM. 2. Lieut. WILLIAM,[2] (*Ens. Wm.,*[2]), b. 1661; m. (1) Grace (dau. John &
Grace) **Riley,** of Weth., 22 Nov., 1680; she d. 23 (*Weth. Ins.* 17) Oct., 1712,
ae. 51; he m. (2) 5 June, 1714, Mrs. Mary Ann (wid. of Dr. Nich.) **Ayrault,**
who d. 27 Aug., 1741, in 60th yr. Lieut. William d. 27 Dec., 1737, ae. 76.
Inventory of est. taken 27 Dec., 1737 by Ephriam Goodrich, Isaac Riley
and David Wright, amts. to £3,079-05-03. Will (dated same day as invent.)
beq. estate to wid. and sons Benjamin and Joseph, the latter being app. exec'r.
He gives to his wife ½ of his negro man George "*forever,*" and the pasturage
of two milch cows; to his s. Benjamin one acre of ld. in Weth. Plain and 5
roods in West Swamp; and to his s. Joseph, 10 acres in the West Swamp,"provided he maintain the fence and suffers my beloved wife to pasture two cows
there during the time she remains my widow;" he also gives Joseph one acre in
Weth. Plain and ½ of the negro George. Will was presented for probate 28th
Dec. (the day after testators dth.) ; but acc. to the *Ct. Rec.* the whole family
(wid. and ch.) promptly appeared before the Court, in person or by their legal
representatives, in opposition to the confirmation of Joseph as executor. The
case was postponed and the exhibition of the inventory Aug. 1, 1738, evoked a
request from the wid. that her dower should be set out to her—which the Ct. app.
Capt. Thos. Welles, Lt. Eleazur Goodrich, and Dea. Thomas Wright to do; but on
Aug. 5, 1739, the set out of dower was refused, and Dea. Thomas Wright, Jonathan Burnham and Benjamin Stillman were then app. to settle the matter, and
William Goodrich was app. admr.

Children (Weth. Rec. & Mix Rec.) :

1. William, b. 3 Aug., d. 16 Nov., 1681.
2. William, b. 2 July, 1686 ; m. FAM. 9.
3. Benjamin, b. 29 Sept., 1688. FAM. 10.
4. Joseph (Lieut.), b. 29 Feb.,1691-2. FAM. 11.
5. Isaac, b. 18 Aug., 1693. FAM. 12
6. Ann, b. 25 Mch., 1697 ; m. Robert **Powell,**
   of Weth., 3 Feb., 1717; she d. 28 Dec.,
   1783.
7. Ephraim, b. 12, bp. 17 Sept., 1699 ; sett.
   at Weth.; m. 5 Oct., 1726, Susan (dau.

Dr. Daniel) **Hooker**—*Weth. Rec.;* he d.
1728.
8. Ethan, b. 1702 ; supp. to have d. in early
   life, as he is not ment. in father's will.
   (*By second marriage*) :
9. Elizabeth, bp. 8 Jan., 1715-16.
10. Lucenia, m. 8 Aug., 1723, Rev. Daniel
    Fuller, of Willington, Ct.—See *Bond's
    Watertown,* 666, foot note.
11. Eunice.

FAM. 4.   Capt. EPHRAIM,[2] (*Ens. William,[1]*), b. 1663; m. (1) 20 May, 1684, Sarah (dau. Maj. Richard & Sarah *Coleman*) **Treat**, of Weth., 20 May, 1684, who d. 26 Jan., 1712, in 48th yr.—*Weth. Ins.* He m. (2) being then styled "Lieut.," Jerusha (wid. Capt. Thomas **Welles**, of Weth., and dau. of Capt. James **Treat**, of W.) 25 Dec., 1712. Capt. Ephraim d. 27 Feb., 1739, ae. 76; wid. d. 15 Jan., 1754, in 76th yr.—*Weth. Ins.*; res. in Stepney.

Children (all of whom, by 1st marr. sett. in Glast. except Gideon and Sarah); dates * thus—*Htfd. Times*—12 May, 1902.

1. Richard, b. 27 Feb., 1685. FAM. 13.
2. Ephraim, b. 21 Dec.,* 1693. FAM. 14.
3. Sarah, b. 1698 ; m. Rich. **Butler**, of Stepney, Weth., 18 Dec., 1725, who d. 27 Oct., 1757 ; she d. 6 May, 1795, in 98th yr.
4. William, b. 21 Feb., 1699.* FAM. 15.
5. David (Dea.), b. 3 Oct., 1699.* FAM. 16.

6. Thomas, b. 27 Sept., 1701. FAM. 17.
7. Gideon, b. 7 Feb., 1705.* FAM. 18.
   (*By second marriage*) :
8. Oliver, b. 14 Sept., bp. 3 Oct., 1714.—*Mix MSS.* FAM. 19.
9. Gurdon, b. 29 Dec., 1717. FAM. 20.

FAM. 5.   Col. DAVID,[2] (*Ens. William,[1]*), b. 1667; m. (1) 7 Mch., 1688-89 Hannah (dau. Thomas Jr. & Elizabeth *Chittenden*) **Wright**, of Weth., who d. 27 Apl., 1688 (*Weth. Rec.*) ae. nr. 28; he m. (2) 1 Dec., 1698, Prudence (dau. Benj. & Mary) **Churchill**, of Weth.; she b. 2 July, 1678, d. 9 May, 1752. "Sgt." David was app. May, 1704, as Lieut. of the Htfd. Co. militia ordered to march to the relief of Hampshire Co., Mass., then threatened by Inds.; and in Dec. of same yr. had another campaign. In that of 1709, he served as Capt., Adjt., and Regimental Qr. Master; in Feb., 1712, was on duty, as Capt. in Hampshire Co., and again in Aug., 1723, and in Oct., of the latter yr. was a memb. of the Col. Committee of War, and re-app. (with rank of Col.) in 1725. With but few intervals, he rep. Weth., as dep. to the Gen. Ct. fm. 1716 to 1740; serving also in various committees. In Nov., 1724, he became a memb. of the Gov'r's Council, continuing to serve as such afterwards, and during most of his life was Justice of the Peace, and many yrs. a Justice of the Quorum. He res. Weth. where he d. 23 (28?) Jan., 1755, in his 88th yr.

Children (Weth. Rec. & Mix MSS.) :

1. Josiah, b. 15 June, 1690. FAM. 21.
2. Elizabeth, b. 19 Nov., 1691 ; m. Allen (s. John) **Goodrich**, 29 Dec., 1709.—See FAM. 7, of this Gen.
3. Elizur (Col.), b. 30 Mch., 1693 ; m. 22 Apl., 1714, Anna (dau. of Cornet Samuel & Mary *Ellery*) **Talcott**, of Glast. Col. Elizur d. 4 Apl., 1774, ae. 81 ; his wid. d. 3 Jan., 1776, ae. 83. The following mention of him appeared in the *Conn. Courant*, of Apl. 26th : "On the 4th inst., Apl., d. at his ho. in Weth. Col ELIZUR GOODRICH had just completed his 81st yr. He bore a fair and honorable character through life, and particularly in the various and important offices he sustained in the service of the public. He was many yrs. a Justice of the Peace ; and in the yr. 1745, served as Lieut.-Col. in the Expedition against Louisburg, where, by his genial conduct, his great humanity and benevolence, he obtained the estimation and love of the officers and soldiers. In the yr. 1755, he was app. as Col. of a regiment raised in this Colony for the expedition against Canada, and during the campaign was taken sick and continued a long time in a low state of health. He has been many times a memb. of our Gen. Assemb. but for some time before his dth. declined all pub. business. He was, a very long time, a memb. of the Ch. of Christ in this place, a constant and devout attendant upon the worship of God, and so continued to the last. His fear and love of God, his universal kindness and tenderness to his neighbors, render his memory truly precious." His epitaph reads : "Sacred to the Memory of | Col[nl] ELIZUR GOODRICH, | who in the Cours of a long Life | sustained & adorned | the Characters of the Citizen the | the Soldier, the Patriot & the Christian | by a faithful discharge of his | duty in there respective stations. | Go, traveler & Imitate his Vertues | his piety in this Life & trust in | divine mercy for happiness in the Next | died April 4th, 1774 | Aged 81. Also, Mrs. Ann Goodrich. | Wdo. Col[nl] Elizur Goodrich, | who d. Jan[y] 27 3[d] 1776, Aged 83." They had *no issue.*
4. David (Dea.), b. 8 Dec., 1694. FAM. 22.
5. Abigail, b. 2 Apl., 1697 ; d. 3 (or 28 ?) Sept., 1712.
   (*By second marriage*) :
6. Hezekiah, b. 28 June, 1709—*Weth. Rec.*, but acc. to *Mix MSS.*, bp. 4 Feb., 1699 ; prob. these dates should be reversed. FAM. 23.
7. Prudence, b. 18, bp. 22 June, 1701 ; m. Esq. David (s. of John) **Hubbard**, of Eastbury, Soc. Glast., who d. 13 Oct., 1760, in 63d yr. ; she m. (2) Judah **Holcomb**, Esq. ; she d. 29 Nov., 1783, ae. 83 yr. *Issue (by first marr.)*, several ch., of whom was Capt. Elizur Hubbard, b. 1736, who m. Lois (dau. of James) **Wright**, of Weth., who d. 15 Sept., 1794, ae. 49. Capt. H. m. (2) Huldah ——. *G. Mem.* says Judith **Holcomb**, who d. 26 Apl., 1807, ae. 55. He d. 14 Sept., 1801; his s. (by first marr.) David E.

Hubbard, bp. 15 Mch., 1778, m. Pamella (dau. Elisha & Penelope) **Hollister**, of Glast., b. 6 Oct., 1779; she bp. 26 Apl., 1781.
8. **Sarah**, b. 12, bp. 14 Mch., 1702-3; m. (1) ———— **Lord**; m. (2) ———— **Ward**; m. (3) ———— **Starr** (*G. Mem.*); she d. 1784.
9. Mary, b. 15 Dec., 1704; m. a s. of Peter **Bontecau**; she d. 1760.—*G. Mem.*
10. Hannah, b. 2, bp. 3 Aug., 1706; d. 1773; m. Isaac (s. of Isaac & Hannah *Dickinson*) **Hubbard.**—*G. Mem.*
11. Jeremiah, b. 9, bp. 11 Sept., 1709. FAM. 24.
12. Anna, b. 14, bp. 17 Feb., 1711-12; m. (1)

———— **Reynolds**; m. (2) ————
Jones; d. 1784.—*G. Mem.*
13. Zebulon, b. 22, bp. 29 Nov., 1713. FAM. 25.
14. Benjamin, b. and bp. 13 Nov., 1715; m. 5 Oct., 1737, Hannah (dau. Daniel & Hannah *Ketchum*) **Olmstead**, b. prob. at Ridgefield, Ct.; they sett. in Hancock, Mass., where he d. 14 Mch., 1797; had 14 ch., of whom 7 became Shakers.— *R. H. C.*
15. Abigail. b. 18 Jan., bp. 2 Feb., 1717-18; m. ———— **Russell**; d. 1761.—*G. Mem.*
16. Charles, b. 7 Aug., 1720. FAM. 26.
17. Millicent, b. 23 Jan., 1722-3; m. Dea. Nathan **Olmstead**, of Ridgefield, Ct.

FAM. 6. JOHN,³ (*John,² Ens. Wm.,¹*), b. 1688; m. 5 June, 1712, Mary (dau. prob. of John) **Tillotson**, "formerly of Saybrook," Ct., who d. 31 May, 1740.—*Weth. Rec.*

Children (*Weth. Rec.*):

1. Samuel, b. (*and bp.—Mix*) 26 July, 1813; d. July, 1714.
2. Abraham, b. 3, bp. 4 Sept., 1715; m. Hannah **Collins**, 16 Sept., 1742—*Weth. Rec.*,

Wid. Hannah d. 19 May, 1773.
3. Sarah, bp. 11 Sept., 1715.—*Mix MSS.*
4. Mary, b. 20 May, 1718.

FAM. 7. ALLEN,³ (*John,² Ens. Wm.,¹*), b. 1690; m. 29 Dec., 1709, Elizabeth (dau. Capt. David & Hannah *Wright*) **Goodrich**, of Weth., where they sett., but later rem. to Far., where she d. 25 Aug., 1726; he m. (2) 10 Dec., 1729, Harriet **Seymour**, of Kingston. He d. Far.

Children (*Weth. Rec. & Mix MSS.*):

1. Elizabeth, b. and bp. 19 Oct., 1710.
2. Elisha, b. 22, bp. 23 Sept., 1712. FAM. 27.
(*By second marriage*):
3. Abigail, b. 13, bp. 19 Dec., 1714; m. 26 Dec., 1734, Dea. Elijah (s. of Dea. Thomas & Mary *Thompson*) **Hart**, who d. 21 Jan., 1809.—*G. Mem.*
4. Jedidiah, b. 24 July, 1717. FAM. 28.
5. Samuel, b 23 Apl., 1720. FAM. 29.

6. Allen, b. Far., 18 Aug., 1726.
(*And acc. to G. Mem. by sec. mar.*)
7. John, b. 26 Mch., 1734; m. 1757, Hannah (dau. Daniel & Rebecca *Curtis*) **Dewey**; he d. 27 Apl., 1817.—*G. Mem.*
8. Asahel, b. ————; m. (1) Abigail (dau. Jona.) **Gilbert**; m. (2) May, 1775, Sarah **Woodruff**.—*G. Mem.*

FAM. 8. JACOB,³ (*John,² Ens. Wm.,¹*), b. ————; m. 12 Sept., 1717, Benedicta (dau. Nath'l) **Goodwin**, of Htfd., who d. 1746, at Windsor, Ct., and was bu. at Weth. (*Wintonbury Ch. Rec.*): this fam. rem. to Wintonbury, Mch., 1745.

Children (*Weth. Rec.*):

1. Hannah, b. 31 Aug., 1719. The *G. Mem.* says she m. 27 Apl., 1749, Job, 2d (son Jeremiah & Hannah *Burnham*) **Drake**.
2. Rebecca, b. 14 Apl., 1721; m. Reuben **Loomis**, 1745.—*G. Mem.*
3. Elijah, b. 3 July, 1724; sett. Windsor, Ct., and m. Margaret **Gillett**, of Windsor.—See Stiles' *Ancient Windsor*, II, 300, for further mention.
4. Ruth, b. 22 May, 1727.

5. Stephen, b. 21 (bp. 24—*Mix*) Jan., 1731; m. Rachel **Gillett**, of Wintonbury (Windsor), where he sett.—See Stiles' *Ancient Windsor*, II, 301.
6. Sarah, b. 21 Oct. (bp. 4 Nov.,—*Mix MSS.*), 1733; m. a **Gillett**.—*G. Mem.*
7. Jacob, m. a **Goodrich**, of Wintonbury; had two sons, Jacob, who rem. to Hancock, Del. Co., N. Y.; and Stephen.—*G. Mem.*

FAM. 9. WILLIAM,³ (*Lieut. Wm.,² Ens. Wm.,¹*), b. 1686; m. May, 1706, Margaret (dau. of "Goodman") **Orvis**, of Far.; sett. and for 10 yrs. res. at Litchfield; thence rem. to Sheffield, Mass., thence to Sharon, Ct., acc. to Woodruff's *Litchfield Register.*

Children (*Weth. Rec. & Mix MSS.*):

1. Deborah, b. 8 Jan., 1707.
2. Samuel, b. 29 June, bp. 4 July, 1708.
3. Margaret, b. 1 June, 1710; d. ae. 8 days.
4. William, b. 5, bp. 6 May, 1711; m. Miriam ————; d. 1 Sept., 1777.
5. Ethan, b. 9 July, 1713; bp. 26 Dec., 1714 —*Mix MSS.*; d. 2 days old.
6. Jared, b. 11, bp. 12 July, 1714; m. Esther ————.
7. Margaret, b. 28 May, and "on night following 4th day [June 5] bp. at his ho."—*Mix MSS.*

8. Elnathan, b. 6, bp. 8 Dec., 1718; m. 1740, Elizabeth **Showers**.—*G. Mem.* (To this fam. Woodruff's Geneal. Reg'r of *Inhabs. of Litchfield, Ct.*, 1720-1806, adds from *L. Recs.*):
9. David, [m. Martha (dau. Ebenezer & Abigail) **Mudge**.—*G. Mem.*]
10. Anne, b. 20 Mch., 1722.
11. Elisha, b. 5 Jan., 1724-5.
12. Solomon, b. 7 Mch., 1726-7.
13. Lucy, b. 18 July, 1729.

FAM. 10. BENJAMIN,³ (*Lieut. Wm.,² Ens. Wm.,¹*),, b. 1688; m. 7 Mch., 1715-16, Grace (dau. Ebnz'r.) **Kilbourn**, of Glast.; he d. 11 May, 1742, ae. 54, bu. in New. Est. distrib. by fam. agreement, 1751; fam. all sett. in Far.

Children (Weth. Rec) :

1. Benjamin, b. 21 July, 1717. FAM. 30,
2. Ebenezer, b. 22 Sept., 1721; m. Abigail **Collier**, 25 Aug., 1766.
3. Timothy, b. 17 Feb., 1724; m. an **Ashley**; sett. Far. The *G. Mem.* gives him the following ch.: *William* and *Timothy*, both rem. to Vergennes, Vt.; *Ashley, Chauncey, Benjamin, Ebenezer*, b. 1771; d. 1839; m. Submit **Norton**, who d. 1836.

4. Daniel, b. 19 Feb., 1726; res. Woodbury, Ct., 1760.
5. Waitstill, b. 9 Jan., 1829; res. 1760, in Woodbury, Ct.; m. 5 June, 1755, Mercy (dau. Hezekiah,⁴ *John*,³ *Rev. Sam'l*,² *Rev. Thos.*¹) **Hooker**, of Woodbury; she b. 8 Jan., 1727.—*Boardman Gen.*
7. Sarah, b. 19 Apl., 1731; d. 20 June, 1751 or '58, unm.

FAM. 11. Lieut. JOSEPH,³ (*Lieut. Wm.,² Ens. Wm.,¹*), b. 1691; m. Mehitable (dau. Nath'l) **Goodwin**, of Htfd., 23 Dec., 1714; she d. 31 Jan., 1768, in 77th yr.—*Weth. Rec.*

Children (Weth. Rec.) :

1. Mehitable, b. 20 (bp. 25—*Mix*) Mch., 1716.
2. Nathaniel, b. 15 July, 1717. FAM. 31. (*G. Mem. gives, also*) :
3. Daniel, b. 26 June, 1723.

4. Thomas, b. 7 Apl., 1726.
5. Samuel, b. 15 June, 1729.—*Fam. Bible.* FAM. 32.

FAM. 12. ISAAC,³ (*Lieut. Wm.,² Ens. Wm.,¹*), b. 1693; sett. Weth. m. Mary (dau. Samuel) **Butler**, of Southold, L. I., formerly of Weth., 19 Nov., 1718; he d. Dec., 1727.

Children (Weth. Rec.) :

1. Mary, b. 26 Sept., 1719; m 23 June, 1743, Jonathan (s. Dea. Samuel & Hannah

White) **Gipson**.

FAM. 13. RICHARD,³ (*Capt. Eph'm,² Ens. Wm.,¹*), b. 1685; sett. in Glast., but, by deed fm. him to Thos. Welles, of G., 1725, it appears that he was then in Midd. (prob. at "Upper Houses,"); he m. (1) at Glast., 18 May, 1709, Hannah (dau. Dr. Charles) **Bulkeley**, of New Lond.; she d. 23 Sept. (or 21, *Weth. Ins.*) 1720, ae. 30. He m. (2) 23 Apl., 1721, Mehitable (dau. Sam'l) **Boardman**, b. 1703 or '05. He d. 7. Apl., 1759.

Children (Glast. Rec.) :

1. Ann, b. 6 Mch., 1710; m. Stephen **Miller**, 2 July, 1730.—*G. Mem.*
2. Richard, b. 13 July, 1712; d. 1 Sept., 1714.
3. Sarah, b. 6 July, 1715; m. 12 Sept., 1734, William **Tryon**.
4. Gershom, b. 5 May, 1717. FAM. 33.
5. Richard (Lieut.), b. 23 July, 1719; m. Martha ———; he d. 11 Mch., 1767. (*By sec. marr. acc. to G. Mem.*) :
6. Charles, b. 1721; d. 15 July, 1807; m. Susanna ———.
7. Joshua, b. 3 Mch., 1723; m. 12 Feb.,

1746, Hannah **Bliss**.
8. Solomon, b. 18 June, 1725.
9. Zaccheus, b. 28 Feb., 1731; m. (1) 5 Apl., 1750, Rachel **Cornwell**, b. 1731, who d. 20 May, 1759; he m. (2) Abiah (dau. Samuel & Abiah *Boardman*) **Stocking**, of Chatham, Ct.; he m. (3) a **Butler**; he m. (4) ——— **Buck**; rem. to Avon, Genesee Co., N. Y.; acc. to *G. Mem.*; had 6 ch.
10. Eunice, b. 7 Sept., 1734.
11. Peter, b. 2 Oct., 1737; m. Silence ———, b. 1739; d. 11 Aug., 1763.

FAM. 14. EPHRAIM,² (*Capt. Eph'm,² Ens. Wm.,¹*), b. 1693; sett. at Glast.; m. 10 July, 1715, Hannah (dau. James & Ann *Welles*) **Steele**, of Weth., b. 18 Mch., 1697; he prob. d. 1728; invent. of his est., taken 3 Apl., that yr., val. £488-02.

Children (Weth. Rec.) :

1. Abigail, b. 10 July, 1716.
2. James, b. 21 Jan., 1718; rem. to Vt.
3. Charles (Capt.), b. 9 Nov., 1720. FAM. 34.
4. Ephraim, b. 9 Dec., 1722. FAM. 35.
5. Hannah, b. 16 May, 1725. (*G. Mem.* adds to this family the

following) :
6. John.
7. Ashbel.
8. Abner, b 1729.
9. Mary.

FAM. 15. WILLIAM,³ (*Eph'm,² Ens. Wm.,¹*), b. 1701; sett. Glast.; m. 4 Apl., 1728 Rachel (dau. Capt. Thomas) **Savage**, who d. 20 Sept., 1787, ae. 84; he d. 16 Dec., 1787, ae. 86.

Children (Glast. Rec.) :

1. William, b. 20 Jan., 1729; res. Glast. [m. (1) Mehitable ———, by whom he had (*a*) Mehitable and (*b*) Thirza; m. (2) Mary **Hollister.**—*G. Mem.*]
2. Stephen, b. 2 May, 1732; res. Glast. [d. 23 Sept., 1816; m. Dorothy ———, by whom he had 9 ch.—*G. Mem.*]
3. Elisha, b. 27 May, ——; res. Glast.; had

(*G. Mem.*) 10 ch.
4. Jehiel (twin), b. 16 Sept., 1741 [m. Prudence **Miller**; res. Glast.; 10 ch.—*G. Mem.*]
5. Jemima (twin), b. 16 Sept., 1741 [m. 19 Feb., 1767, Thos. **Hollister.**—*G. Mem.*]
6. Mary, b. 18 Nov., 1745 [m. 14 Jan., 1767, Thomas **Matson.**—*G. Mem.*]

FAM. 16. Dea. DAVID,[3] (*Capt. Eph'm,[2] Ens. Wm.,[1]*), b. 1699; res. Glast., m. 13 Feb., 1729, Sarah (dau. John) **Edwards;** he d. 7 June, 1779; his gravestone reads, "whom, at his evening prayer, fell down in an instant and never saw to make any motion after, being in the 74th yr. of his age. His wid. d. 11 May, 1790, in 80th yr.

Children (Glast. Rec.) :

1. John (Capt.), b. 16 June, 1730. FAM. 36.
2. David, b. 22 May, 1732. FAM. 37.
3. Walt, b. 8 Feb., 1736. FAM. 38.
4. Lucy, b. 24 Feb., 1738; m. 14 Mch., 1754, Benjamin (s. Eleazur) **Kilborn**, of Morristown, N. J. (one acc. says Elisha Goodrich, and d. 1807).
5. Rhoda, b. 17 Dec., 1739 [m. 27 Nov., 1760, Gideon, Jr. (s. Gideon & Batsheba *White*) **Sage.**—*G. Mem.*]
6. Isaac, b. 2 May, 1743; m. Hannah **Strickland,** and had:
   i. Catharine, b. 1757 (?).
   ii. Julia, b. 1758 (?).
7. Elizur, b. 8 Aug., 1745; m. Sarah **Kimberly,** who d. 1810; he d. 1798; fam. rem.

from Glast. to Granville, N. Y., 1796, and (in 1798) to Auburn, N. Y.
8. Sarah, b. 20 June, 1747 [m. 20 Nov., 1765, Isaac **Talcott**, bro. of her bro. (Capt. John's) wife Prudence; she b. 29 Aug., 1710; d. 6 Aug., 1815.—*G. Mem.*]
9. Honor, b. 8 Apl., 1749; m. 26 Jan., 1786, Daniel **Miles.**
10. George, b. 13 Aug., 1751; m. Sarah **Welles;** rem. to Gill, N. Y.; had:
    i. Alfred.
    ii. George, who m. 1816, Honor **Welles,** of Glast.
11. Prudence, b. 14 Apl., 1754 [m. 23 Nov., 1786, Noah (s. of Eph'm) **Goodrich;** b. 4 Sept., 1763.—*G. Mem.*]

FAM. 17. THOMAS,[3] (*Eph'm,[2] Ens. Wm.,[1]*), b. 1701; m. 26 Nov., 1719, Hannah (dau. John) **Reynolds,** of Weth.

Children (Weth. Rec.) :

1. [Peter, m. Bathsheba **Miller**, of Berlin; had 12 ch.—*G. Mem.*]
2. James, b. 2 Mch., [*May, G. Mem.*] 1721;

m. and had 5 ch.; res. Glast.
4. Daniel, b. 26 June, 1723.
5. Thomas, b. 7 Apl., 1726.

FAM. 18. Capt. GIDEON,[2] (*Capt. Eph'm,[2] Ens. Wm.,[1]*), b. 1695; sett. at Stepney, Weth.; rem. to Midd. (Upper Houses); m. 1718, Sarah, [**Goodrich**—*G. Mem.*]; d. 9 Aug., 1769, in 74th yr.—*Weth. Ins.*

Children (S. C. R.) :

1. Sarah, bp. 29 June, 1718.
2. Jerusha, bp. 16 Dec., 1720.
3. Elijah, b. 5 June, 1725, bp. 1726. FAM. 39.
4. Gideon (Lieut.), b. 15 Dec., 1727; m. 13 Oct., 1756, Anna ———; res. Weth.; the Pittsfield (Mass.) *List* of 1772, names Gideon Goodrich and a gravestone in P. commemorates Mrs. Eunice (wife of John) **Baker,** and dau of Lieut. Gideon Goddrich; d. 1 Oct., 1783, in 26th yr. Lieut. G. was a Revol. soldier.—*R. H. C.;* he had also a dau. Jerusha, b. 1 Mch., 1760, who m. Geo. **Stevens** (*G. Mem.* says), of Oxford.
5. Lois, b. 12, bp. 13 Apl., 1729 [m. John, (s. Joshua & Sarah) **Robbins;** b. 31 Mch., 1713; d. 1768.—*G. Mem.*]

6. Caleb, b. 1 Sept., 1731; m. Huldah **Butler;** rem. early to Pittsfield, Mass.; tailor by trade; quarter-master in Revol. Army at time of Burgoyne's surrender; had 14 ch.; was living in 1858.—*R. H. C.;* his dau. Rhoda was the gd-mother of M. R. Huck, of Ticonderoga, N. Y.
7. Ebenezer, b. 18 Mch., 1733. FAM. 40.
8. Eunice, b. Apl., 1735.
9. Joshua, b. 18 May, 1738; may have been the J. who had (*S. C. R.*):
    i. Ezra, bp. 9 July, 1766.
    ii. Mercy, bp. 7 Aug., 1768.
    iii. Jason, bp 21 Oct., 1770.
10. Walt, b. 10 Jan., 1740.—See *Miscellanea.*
11. Levi, b. 10 June, 1750.

FAM. 19. OLIVER,[3] (*Capt. Eph'm,[2] Ens. Wm.,[1]*), b. 1714; sett. in Stepney, Weth.; m. 26 June, 1740, Temperance **Wright,** of Step.; he d. 23 Sept., 1780, in 66th yr.; she d. 4 Oct., 1803, in 80th yr. He is prob. the Capt. O., who (acc. to *N. Lond, Gazette,* issue of 13 Nov., 1778) "in a privateer schr. of 4 carriage guns," sailed fm. that port, "last Friday, and the same day was taken by a [Br.] privateer schr. of 8 guns, fm. Newport."

Children (Weth. Rec. & S. C. R.) :

1. Roger, b. 4, bp. 18 Oct., 1741. FAM. 41.
2. Sarah, b. 28, bp. 31 July, 1743.
3. Prudence, b. 10, bp. 11 Aug., 1745.
4. Temperance, b. 10, bp. 11 Oct., 1747.
5. Oliver, b. 19 Sept., bp. 8 Oct., 1749 [m. 3 Feb., 1771—*S. C. R.*, Sarah (dau. Oliver) **Butler**—*G. Mem.* (perhaps her sur-name was *Warner*—*H. R. S.*], and it is prob. the O. who d. at Ry-H, 6 Apl., 1830; she prob. the "wife of O." who d. 17 July, 1810, ae. 58—*S. C. R.*, and of whose dth. the *Conn. Courant* gives the date as 30 Aug., 1810. An Oliver, prob. this one, had (*S. C. R.*) 2 twins daus., d. 25 Feb., 1781; *Oliver*, bp. 1 Aug., 1784; *Ralph Warner*, bp. 28 Aug., 1785; *Pamela*, bp. 25 Aug., 1787; *Archibald*, bp. 25 Oct., 1789; *Lucretia*, bp. 14 Aug., 1791; an inf. d. 29 June, 1793. Three ch. cr. on *S. C. R.* to Oliver Good-

rich, viz : *James Wright*, bp. 21 June, 1812; *Sarah*, bp. 29 May, 1814; *Chauncy Wells*, bp. 18 Aug., 1816; were prob. ch. of Oliver, Jr., b. 1784.
6. Melicent, b. 28 Oct., bp. 3 Nov., 1751; d. 12 July, 1752.
7. Melicent, b. 25, bp. 29 Sept., 1754 [m. John **Gilbert**, of Hebron, Ct.—*G. Mem.*]
8. Pollicene, b. 15 May, 1757.
9. Ezekiel, b. 22 Apl., 1759; d. 19 Sept., 1783. —*S. C. R.*
10. Lucretia, b. 8 May, 1761. (As these are not rec. on *Weth. Rec.*, the dates given are prob. those of bp.)
11. Chloe, bp. 8 Sept., 1765.
12. Wealthy, bp. 13 Oct., 1771.
13. Oxinia, bp. 6 Feb., 1774. (These may belong to this fam. unless they may belong to Oliver, Jr., No. 5.)

FAM. 20. Capt. GURDON,[3] (*Eph'm*,[2] Ens. *Wm.*,[1]), b. 1717; res. Step. Weth.; m. 7 June, 1739, Abigail (dau. Gideon & Elizabeth *Seymour*) **Belden,** who was b. 1721 and d. 22 Feb., 1787, in 66th year.—*W. Ins.* He was a mariner, and d. 24 Jan., 1794, in 77 yr.—*S. C. R.*

Children (S. C. R.) :

1. Gurdon, bp. 31 Aug., 1740; d. 2 Oct., 1741.
2. Jerusha, bp. 26 July, 1741 [m. 6 Feb., 1783, Geo. **Stevens**—*G. Mem.*] ; prob. an error—see Lieut. *Gideon*, FAM. 18.—*H. R. S.*
3. Experience, bp. 25 Sept., 1743 ; d. 24 July, 1746.
4. Gurdon, bp. 12 Jan., 1745, and d. 2 Dec., 1815, in 70th yr.—*S. C. R.* [m. ———, and had dau. Eunice, b. 24 May, 1761— *G. Mem.* ; which would make her father marr. at age of 16?] ; it is more prob. that her birth-date should be 1771; and her father may have been the G. who m. Mercy ———, and whose s. *Barnabas*, d. 10 Apl., 1800, in 22d yr. (*S. C. R.*) ; and another s. *Silas*, d. at Newport, R. I., Sept., 1800, in 24th yr.—*Weth.* (*S.*) *Ins.* Gurdon & Mercy had dau. *Jerusha* bp. 1 Oct., 1775.—*S. C. R.*, who m. Seth **Dickenson,** and d. 5 Mch., 1799, in 23d yr., and their dau. *Jerusha* (*Dickinson*), d. 11 Nov., 1799, ae. 9 mos. 20 d.—*Weth. Ins.* A Gurdon, poss. the same, had *Rebecca*, bp. 10 May, 1767, and *Issac*, bp. 11 Nov., 1764.—*S. C. R.*
5. Elizabeth, bp. 12 Nov., 1747

6. Abigail, bp 12 Nov., 1749.
7. Ephraim, bp. 7 Apl., 1752 [m. Deborah **Thomas**—*G. Mem.*]
8. Jemima, bp. 7 Apl., 1754.
9. Elizur, bp. 10 Sept., 1756 ; d. 22 (*W. Ins.* 20) Aug., 1798, in 42d yr.—*S. C. R.* ; m. 13 Aug., 1778, Abigail **Grimes**; she d. 11 Oct., 1795, in 38th yr. ; poss. he was the E. who m. 6 Mch., 1796, Martha **Bulkeley.**
10. Ichabod, bp. 10 Sept., 1758 ; m. 1788, Binah [Rebina?] **Goodrich,** who d. 10 June, 1813, ae. 43 ; m. (2) 11 Oct., 1815, Wid. Mary **Butler**; prob. the "wife of I." who d. 17 Apl., 1826, ae. 77. He d. 3 Sept., 1844, ae. 88 (should be 86—*S. C. R.*) ; they had (*W. Ins. & S. C. R.*) *Lucinda*, bp. 13 Sept., 1789 ; *Jasper*, bp. 13 Apl., 1791 ; *Nathan*, d. May, 1793, ae. 1 mo. ; *Rockwall*, bp. 13 July, 1794, who d. 21 June, 1815, ae. 20—*W. Ins.*; Admiral (name afterwards changed by parents to *Ichabod*, bp. 23 Apl., 1797 ; *Ira*, bp. 26 May, 1798 ; *Jonathan Welles*, bp. 31 May, 1801 ; *Luther*, bp. 31 July, 1803 ; *James*, bp. 5 Oct., 1806 ; *William Henry*, bp. (first bapt'm in new Step. meeting-ho.) 23 Oct., 1808 ; *Maria*, d. 21 Feb., 1811, ae. 1 mo.

FAM. 21. Esq. JOSIAH,[3] (*Col. David*,[2] Ens. *Williams*,[1]) b. 1690; sett. in Weth., in Weth., but rem. to Tolland, Ct.; m. (1) 5 Dec., 1711, Sarah (dau. Esq. Sam'l) **Porter,** of Hadley, Mass., who d. 3 July, 1726, ae. 34; he m. (2) Sarah (eld. dau. Rev. Stephen) **Mix,** of Weth., abt., 1727. He d. S., 1731, ae. 41; wid. d. Weth., 1748.

Children (Tolland & Weth. Recs. & Mix. Rec.) :

1. Joanna, bp. 17 Aug., 1712.—*Mix MSS.*
2. Joanna [b. and d. Sept. 1713—*G. Mem.*]
3. Josiah, b. 22 Aug., bp. 1 Sept., 1717 ; m. (1) Grace **Grant**, of Tolland ; m. (2) Mary **Porter**; res. Tolland—for ch. see *G. Mem.*
4. Sarah, b. 8 Sept., 1715 ; d. 15 June, 1724.
5. Aaron, b. 25 Sept., 1719 [m. 1745, Dorcas **Cook,** of Hadley, where they res. ; 6 ch.— *G. Mem.*]
6. Samuel, b. 1 Nov., 1721 ; [m. 1741, Elizabeth (dau. Capt. Charles) **Whiting,** of

Tolland, Ct., where they res. ; 8 ch.— *G. Mem.*]
7. Son, ⎰
8. Son, ⎱ twins, b. and d. 23 Nov., 1723.
9. Sarah, b. 5, d. 10 Mch., 1725.
10. Joanna, b. and d. 17 June, 1726. (*By second marr.*) :
11. John, b. 16 May, 1728 ; d. 19 Mch., 1755.
12. David, b. 10 Feb., 1730 ; m. 1755, Hannah (dau. Cornet Joseph) **Boardman,** of Weth. ; rem. to Stockbridge, Mass. ; 11 ch.—See *G. Mem.* and *Boardman Gen.*

FAM. 22. Dea. DAVID,[3] (*Col. David,[2] Ens. William,[1]*), b. 1694; m. 21 Dec., 1721 Hepzibah (dau. Ens. Jonathan, dec'd,& Mercy *Hubbard*) **Boardman**, of Hatfield, Mass., b. 16 Feb., 1702-3 and who d. 9 Dec., 1782, ae. 82.—*W. Ins. & S. C. R.* Dea. David d. 14 July, 1785, in 91 yr.—"46 yrs. a Deacon"—*gravestone*, Ry-H. bu-gd.

Children (*Weth. Rec.*) :

1. Abigail, b. 11 Oct., 1722 ; d. 10 Nov., 1723.
2. David, b. 2 Sept., 1724.
3. Alpheus, b. 4 Mch., 1727. FAM. 42.
4. Josiah, b. 5 May, 1731. FAM. 43.
5. Hezekiah, b. 9 Apl., 1733. FAM. 44.
6. Elizur (Rev.), b. 18 Oct., 1734. FAM. 45.
7. Hepzibah, b. 19 Jan., 1737 ; [m. David **Belden**, 3 Aug., 1769.—*G. Mem.*
8. Abigail, b. 8 Mch., 1739.
9. Mercy, b. 17 June, 1741 ; m. 10 July, 1788, Asahel **Waterman**, of Chatham, Ct.
10. Hannah, b. 29 Aug., 1743.

FAM. 23. HEZEKIAH,[3] (*Col. David,[2] Ens. William,[1]*), b. 1700; m. 16 Oct., 1729, Honor (dau. Sam'l, dec'd) **Deming**, of Weth.; he d. 9 Oct., 1732; his wid. m. (2) 5 July, 1733, Dr. Thos. Perrine, of W., she d. 3 Sept., 1778, ae. 77.

Children (*Weth. Rec.*) :

1. Elizur (Capt.), b. 8 Oct., 1730. FAM. 46.
2. Honor, b. 22 Feb., 1732 ; m. (1) 18 May, 1749, Charles (s. Charles & Elizabeth *Bradford*) **Whiting**, of Norwich, Ct., by whom she 6 ch ; she m. (2) 14 Nov., 1774, Rev. Joshua (s. Silas & Abigail *Robbins*)

Belding, of New. parish ; was his 2d wife, and by him had only a son, Hezekiah (Belden), b. 17 Feb., 1778, who d. 22 Mch., 1849, being at that time Town Clerk of Weth. Mi.3. Honor Belding d. 21 Aug., 1801, in 70th yr.

FAM. 24. JEREMIAH,[3] (*Col. David,[2] Ens. William,[1]*) ; m. 6 July, 1732, Ruth, (dau. Thomas) **Kimberly**, of Glast.; sett. in Weth.

Children :

1. Ruth, b. 22 Nov., 1732 ; m. 5 Oct., 1753, Enoch **Smith**.
2. Prudence, b. 25 Oct., 1736.
3. Sarah, b. 14 June, 1738.
4. Mary, b. 13 Nov., 1740.

FAM. 25. ZEBULON,[3] (*Col. David,*   ), b. 1713; m. 8 Jan., 1735-6 (acc. to *Talcott*, 23 Oct., 1737) Ann, (dau. James & Elizabeth *Howard*) **Francis**, joined ch. in New Britain, Ct., 21 May, 1758, by letter from ch. at New.

Children (*Weth. Rec. & G. Mem.*) :

1. Mary, b. 23 Aug., 1737 ; m. 6 Dec., 1759, Samuel, (s. Wm. & Rebecca *Hun*) **Smith**; b. 1732, who d. 16 May, 1802 ; she d. 13 Feb., 1819.
2. Elizabeth, b. 4 June, 1739 ; m. 23 Nov., 1758, Thomas (s. Thos.) **Lusk**.
3. Phebe, b. 9 July, 1741.
4. Zebulon, b. 11 June, 1744 ; m. 5 Oct., 1759, Oner [Honor?] **Whaples**; rem. to Lebanon,
N. Y.—*G. Mem.* ; was a Quaker [Shaker?].
5. Ann. b. 23 Nov., 1746 (prob. the A. "dau. of Zeb." b. 24 Nov., 1751.—*N. C. R.*) ; m. 1764. Herman **Judd**, of Far., b. Feb., 1744.
6. Melicent, b. 24 Jan., 1752 ; m. Sol. **Hollister**.
7. Elijah. b. 3 June, bp. 13 July (*N. C. R.*), 1755.
8. David, b. 14 Dec., 1757 ; m. 25 Sept., 1783, Huldah **Booth**.

FAM. 26. Capt. CHARLES,[3] (*Col. David,[2] Ens. William,[1]*), b. 1720; m. (1) 25 Dec., 1747, Lucy (dau. Samuel) **Ward**, of Midd.; m. (2) Hannah, sister of his first wife, who, b. 1741, d. 10 Apl., 1826; he d. 15 Nov., 1815, at Pittsfield, Mass., ae. 90. He rem. to P. 1752, driving the first horse and wagon that ever entered that town; he built the first ho. there; was Captain in the Continental Army; present at the battle of Bemington; served through the war; was first town Treasurer of P. and a dep. to Mass. Gen. Ct., 1764, '69 and '70.—*R. H. C.;* may have been the Charles G. who (2 Sept., 1776) was published as an enemy to his country, by a committee of citizens of P.—but on 23d of same mo. he replied by publishing his justification (on appeal) by the Mass. assembly.—*Conn. Courant.* (There was another *Charles* Goodrich (s. of Eph'm, s. of Ens. Wm.,), b. in same yr. as this Charles, viz. 1720, whose rec. has been somewhat confused by all the genealogists who have tried to state it. Perhaps, we also, haven't been altogether successful in stating it correctly. —*H. R. S.*)

Children (Weth. Rec.) :

1. David, b. 3 Mch., 1746.
2. Abigail, b. 1 Mch., 1748.
3. Dorcas, b. 14 Mch., 1750.

4. Mary, b. 17 May, 1752.
   (*R. H. C.* says he had 5 ch. by 1st and 5 by 2d wife.)

FAM. 27. ELISHA,[4] (*Allen,[3] John,[2] Ens. William,[1]*), b. 1712; m. Rebecca (dau. Samuel & Hannah *North*) **Seymore**, 21 Nov., 1734; res: Berlin, Ct.; she prob. the "wife of Elisha" who d. 2 May, 1792, ae. 81.—*W. C. R.*

Children:

1. Elisha, b. 12 Mch., 1736.

2. Josiah, b.

FAM. 28. JEDIDIAH,[4] (*Allen,[3] John,[2] Ens. Wm.,[1]*), b. 1717; m. Mary (dau. Samuel & Mercy *Leet*) **Hooker.** He d. 13 Oct., 1803; she d. 13 June, 1800; res. Remington, Soc. Berlin.*

Children (G. Mem.) :

1. Mercy, b. 1 Jan., 1751; d. 22 Apl., 1804; m. 19 Nov., 1790, Joshua **Welles.**
2. Abigail, b. 30 Oct., 1754; d. 9 Apl., 1811;

m. 25 May, 1773, Isaac (s. Isaac & Tabitha *Norton*) **Lee**, who d. 11 Apl., 1828.
3. Thomas, b. 20 June, 1762; d. 1 July, 1764.

FAM. 29. SAMUEL,[4] (*Allen,[3] John,[2] Ens. Wm.,[1]*), b. 1720; m. 10 June 1747, Elizabeth **Whiting.**—*W. C. R.*†

Children (Weth. Rec.) :

1. Samuel, b. 7, bp. 17 July, 1748.
2. Wealthiam, b. 24 Sept., bp. before Oct., 1750.
3. Melicent, b. 29 Nov., bp. 3 Dec., 1752.
4. Elizabeth, b. 28 Feb., bp. 2 Mch., 1755.
5. Porter, b. 11 May, bp. during the mo.,

1757.
6. Solomon Porter, b. 28 Feb., bp. 2 Mch., 1760.
7. Anne, b. 15, bp. 25 Apl., 1762.
8. Eliphalet, b. 30 Sept., bp. 7 Oct., 1764.

FAM. 29. Lieut. BENJAMIN,[4] (*Benj.,[3] Lieut. Wm.[2] Ens. Wm.,[1]*), b. 1717; m. wid. Sarah **Dewey**, 8 Mch., res. New.; he d. 15 Apl., 1787, ae. 70; she d. 19 Nov., 1782, ae. 71.—*W. Ins.*

Children (Weth. Rec.) :

1. Lois, b. 7 Dec., 1744; d. 8 Oct., 1749.— *W. Ins.*; m. Capt. Levi (s. Edw'd) **Spalding.** 1778, as his 2d wife; a Revol. pensioner.
2. Bela, b. 20, bp. 27 Dec., 1747; d. 17 Sept., 1751.—*W. Ins.*

3. Rhoda, b. 23, bp. 25 Mch., 1750.
4. John, b. 21, bp. 25 Aug., 1754. FAM. 46a.
5. David, b. 16, bp. 20 Mch., 1757; prob. the D. who d. 22 Aug., 1822, ae. 66—*N. C. R.;* and whom *G. Mem.* make him to have m. Belinda **Steele.**

FAM. 31. NATHANIEL,[4] (*Lieut. Joseph,[3] Lieut. Wm.,[2] Ens. Wm.,[1]*), b. 1719; m. Martha **Deming.** 25 Aug., 1744, who d. 1 Apl., 1801, ae. 76.—*W. C. R.;* he res. Weth., d. 7 May, 1797, ae. 78.—*W. C. R.*

Children (Weth. Rec.) :

1. Nathaniel, b. 20, bp. 23 Dec., 1744. FAM. 47.
2. Mehitable, b. 29 Mch., bp. 5 Apl., 1747.
3. Joseph, b. 6 Oct., bp. betw. Oct., and Nov. 19, 1749; prob. the J. who m. 5 Dec., 1785, Rhoda **Wolcott**—*Weth. Rec.;* she was prob. the "wife of Joseph" who d. ae. 43, bu. 20 Oct., 1796; and he *may* be (by error of fam. rec's) the J. who d. ae. 79, bu. 12 Feb., 1829, which would

make him b. 1750.
4. Isaac, b. 23 Mch., 1752. FAM. 48.
5. Martha, b. 4, bp. 10 Nov., 1754.
6. Mary, b. 9, bp. 16 Jan., 1757.
7. Rebecca, bp. 16 Sept., 1759.
8. Abigail, (b. twin to Rebecca).
9. Simeon, b. 7 Dec., 1762. FAM. 49.
10. Sarah, b. 1 Nov., 1765.

FAM. 32. SAMUEL,[4] (*Lieut. Joseph,[3] Lieut. Wm.,[2] Ens. Wm.,[1]*), b. 1729; m. 27 May, 1751, Dorothy (dau. Charles) **Treat**, who was b. 15 Apl., 1731 and d. (*Fam. Bible*), 19 July, 1786; he d. 25 Oct., 1777, (*Fam. Bible* says 27 July, 1826.

---

* A "Jeh'a Goodrich" enlisted June 22, marched July 10, 1776, "In Capt. Welles's Company, Col. Chester's Regiment." Was this the Jedidiah Goodrich who d. in New Britain, in 1803.—*Htfd. Times*, May 19, 1902.
† The *G. Mem.* gives (p. 72) the marr. of this Samuel, 24 Sept., 1747, to Martha (dau. John & Sarah *Lee*) **Langdon**, and an entirely different family of children.—On what authority, I know not.—*H. R. S.*

Children (G. Mem. and copies from Fam. Bible furnished by Mrs. E. P. Bronson, of Nashville, Tenn.):

1. Daniel, b. 8 Feb., 1751-2 ; d. 19 Nov., 1773.
2. Dorothy, b. 9 June, 1755 ; m. 9 Jan., 1777, William (s. of Enoch & Mary *Bidwell*) Kelsey, of Berlin, Ct.
3. Bathsheba, b. 21 July, 1757 (*Fam. Bible*, 1756) ; d. 22 Dec., 1776.
4. Samuel, b. 23 Feb. ; d. 27 Mch., 1760.

5. Elizabeth, b. 30 Sept., 1761 (1762—*Fam. Bible*).
6. Rachel, b. 12 Aug., 1764 ; d. 29 May, 1793, in Wethersfield, Vt.
7. Abigail, b. 23 Oct., 1768 (1767—*Fam. Bible.*)

FAM. 33. GERSHOM,[4] (*Rich.,*[3] *Lieut. Eph'm,*[2] *Ens. Wm.,*[1]), b. 1717; m. Elizabeth **Savage,** who b. 1707, d. 24 Apl., 1761; he d. 18 June, 1789; res. Chatham, Ct.

Children (G. Mem.):

1. Nathaniel, b. 1 July, ——; m. 19 Dec., 1773, Prudence **Stocking.**
2. Hezekiah, m. (1) 22 Oct., 1770, Submit (dau. Elisha) **Stocking;** m. (2) Anne **Southmayd.**

3. Giles, b. 12 Jan., 1755 ; m. 27 Oct., 1774, Hannah **Stancliff.**
4. Jeremiah, m. 3 June, 1770, Hepzibah **Edwards.**
5. David, m. 9 Nov., 1772, Penelope **Holcomb.**

FAM. 34. CHARLES,[4] [see Note to FAM.], (*Eph'm,*[3] *Eph'm,*[2] *Ens. Wm.,*[1]), b. ; m. 20 Nov., 1745, Mary (supp. dau. of Samuel) **Belden.**

Children (Talcott Gen.):

1. Lucy, bp. 6 Nov., 1748—*W. C. R.;* m. Isaac **Jones.**
2. Charles, bp. 26 Aug., 1750—*W. C. R.;* d. inf.
3. James, d. inf. 12 July, 1752—*W. C. R.* (*By second marr.*) :

4. Lucy, b. 24 Apl., 1776 ; m. Erastus **Pratt;** d. 1866, in 90th yr.
5. Charles (Rev.), b. 22 Apl., 1778 ; m. Amelia **Jones,** 17 Sept., 1797; had 10 ch.; res. at Penn Yan, N. Y., and Pittsfield, Mass.

FAM. 35. EPHRAIM,[4] (*Eph'm,*[3] *Eph'm,*[2] *Ens. Wm.,*[1]), b. 1722; we believe this to be the Eph'm, who m. (*Weth. Rec.*), 17 Nov., 1748, Rebecca **Goodrich,** who d. (*Weth. Ins.*), 23 Apl., 1805, in 77 yr.; and that he also m. (2) Penelope **Hale,** (or Tryon, or was she a wid. Hale, or a wid. Tyron, when marr.? and who d. at Tioga, N. Y., 15 Nov., 1826. He d. 25 Apl., 1826, in 75 yr.—*W. Ins.*

Children (Weth. Rec.):

1. Ephraim, b. 22 Jan., 1750.
2. Susannah, b. 12 May, bp. 7 June, 1752.— *W. C. R.*
3. Rebecca, b. 10 Mch., 1754-5, bp. 23 Mch., 1755.—*W. C. R.*
4. Nicholas, bp. 25 Dec., 1757.—*W. C. R.*
5. Penelope, b. 7 Feb., 1762.—*G. Mem.*
6. Noah, b. 31 Aug., 1764 ; m. (1) Prudence (dau. David & Sarah *Edwards*) **Goodrich,** who was b. 14 Apl., 1754 ; m. (2) Ruth **Stratton;** he d. 19 July, 1834. *Talcott,*

who also hints at "other names" of ch. of this fam. of Ephraim's (*G. Mem.*), gives Noah's birth as 4 Sept., 1763.
7. Jemima, b. 3 Nov., 1765.—*G. Mem.*
8. Sarah, bp. 9 June, 1765.—*W. C. R.*
9. Ruth, b. 13 Dec., 1767.—*G. Mem.*
10. Penelope, b. 22 Oct., 1769.—*G. Mem.*

(It will be seen that we have four different authorities contributing to the make-up of this fam.—as a result of which there too may be found two or three misplacements.)

FAM. 36. Capt. JOHN,[4] (*Dea. David,*[3] *Eph'm,*[2] *Ens. Wm.,*[1]), b. 1730; m. (1) Prudence, (dau. Col. Elizar ? Ruth *Wright*) **Talcott,** 17 June, 1752, who d. 18 Oct., same yr.; he m. (2) 8 Oct., 1761, Abigail (dau. Daniel, Jr.) **Deming;** res. in Glast. where he d. 12 Oct., 1774; wid. d. 12 Jan., 1799, ae. 68.

Children (Talcott Gen.):

1. John, b. 3 July, 1752.
2. Mary, b. 17 Apl., 1763 ; m. Wm. **Stillman;** res. Sheffield, Mass.
3. Russell, b. 6 Feb., 1765 ; d. unm. 1837, at Columbus, Tenn.
4. Abigail, b. 1 Aug., 1767 ; m. Geo. **Talcott,** 9 Feb., 1786 ; d. 27 June, 1854.
5. Jared, b. 15 Mch., 1769 ; m. June, 1798,

Louisa **Loveland;** d. 19 Sept., 1804. (A Jared also m. Deborah **Griswold,** of Step., 15 Sept., 1793.—*W. C. R.*)*
6. Amelia, b. 5 Jan., 1771 ; m. (1) Sam'l R. **Smith,** Sept., 1797 ; m. (2) —— **Pilkin;** m. (3) Elisha **Chapman,** and d. 1828.
7. Hope, b. 28 Mch., 1773 ; d. 4 July, 1774.— *G. Mem.*

* A Mrs. Lois, wife of Capt. Jared Goodrich, d. 2 Apl., 1803, ae. 27, at Glast.—*Conn. Courant.*

FAM. 37. DAVID,[4] (*Dea. David,[3] Eph'm,[2] Ens. Wm.,[1]*), b. 1732; m. 7 Nov., 1754, Prudence (dau. Josiah) **Benton,** who d. 27 June, 1799; he d. 15 Oct., 1808; res. Glast.

Children (G. Mem.):

1. Katurah, b. 3 Apl., 1755; m. 20 Jan., 1780, Elijah **House.**
2. Israel, b. 7 Nov., 1756; d. 1779, in Revol-War.
3. Roswell, b. 20 Jan., 1760.
4. Hannah, b. 14 Feb., 1762; m. 17 Oct., 1779, John **Hale.**
5. Anne, b. 1 Oct., 1763.
6. Prudence, b. 20 July, 1766.

7. David, b. 2 Apl., 1769.
8. Asa, b. 10 Sept., 1772.
9. Jesse, b. 14 Nov., 1773; prob. m. Abigail **Hanmer,** 23 Dec., 1802; had (*W. T. R.*) (1) *Lucetta*, b. 26 May, 1804; (2) *Jane*, b. 30 Nov., 1808; (3) *Sally*, b. 27 Aug., 1815; (4) *Mary Ann*, b. 1 Apl., 1818.
10. Israel, b. 15 Oct., 1779.
11. ————.

FAM. 38. Capt. WAIT,[4] (*Dea. David,[3] Eph'm,[2] Ens. Wm.,[1]*), b. 1736, a mariner; m. Hannah **Boardman;** he d. 21 Sept., 1809, ae. 74.—*W. C. R.*

Children (G. Mem.):

1. Lucretia, b. 1757; d. 1 Aug., 1759.
2. Jeduthan, b. 8 July, 1759; dr. at sea, 5 Feb., 1787.
3. Grove, b. 14 June, 1761.
4. Rhoda, b. 20 Mch., 1763; m. 28 Feb., 1781, James **Strain.**
5. Wait, b. 11 Aug., 1765.

6. Lucretia, b. 21 June, 1767.
7. Anson, b. 18 June, ———; m. Eunice **Andrews.**
8. Nancy, } twins, b. 14 June, 1772.
9. Kitty, }
10. Hannah, b. 19 Nov., 1775; d. 12 Oct., 1777.
11. Samuel—twin to Hannah.

FAM. 39. ELIJAH,[4] (*Capt. Gideon,[3] Capt. Eph'm,[2] Ens. Wm.,[1]*), b. 1725; m. Lydia (or Mary?) **Wright,** of Ry-H., 25 Jan., 1749; he d. 8 Mch., 1803, ae. 77,—*S. C. R.*; she d. 10 Feb., 1804, ae. 74.—*W. Ins.*

Children (Weth. Rec.):

1. Ozias, b. 2, d. 11 Nov., 1750.
2. Lydia, b. 3 Nov., 1751; [m. 3 Dec., 1768, Samuel **Warner.**—*G. Mem.*]
3. Israel, b. 1 Aug., 1754.
4. Mary, prob. the M., "dau. of Elijah," bp. 7 July, 1765—*S. C. R.*; m. as his 2d wife, Sam'l **Dimock,** and d. 3 Nov., 1803, ae. 38.

5. Elijah, bp. 27 Apl., 1770, and d. 5 Nov., 1772.—*S. C. R.*
6. Catharine, d. 5 Sept., 1799, ae. 46.—*W. Ins*
7. Jerusha, m. William **Ames,** and d. 15 Dec., 1793, in 26th yr.

FAM. 40. EBENEZER,[4] (*Gideon,[3] Eph'm,[2] Ens. Wm.,[1]*), b. 1733; m. 10 Jan., 1760, Lydia **Deming;** he d. 19 Sept., 1813, in 81st yr.—*S. C. R.*

Children (Weth. Rec.):

1. Phila [Philo ?], b. 27 Jan., 1760-1; d. 17 May, 1821. This is the man. prob. who is called in *S. C. Recs.*, Filer, Phila, *Filor*, etc.; *S. C. R.* say he m. 9 Oct., 1783, Lucretia **Williams,** and had (1) Laura, bp. 20 June, 1784; (2) Lucy, bp. 19 Mch., 1786; (3) Erastus, bp. 16 Mch., 1788; (4) Sylvester, bp. 4 Oct., 1789; (5) Austin, bp. 6 Nov., 1791; (6) Henry, bp. 24 July, 1796; (7) Evelina, bp. 20 May, 1798; and (8) Caroline, bp. 14 June, 1801.
2. Mehetable, b. 15 Apl., 1762; m. Ashbel

Riley, and d. 14 Jan., 1790.
3. Gideon, b. 19 June, 1764; m. Eunice **Warner;** rem. to Saratoga Co., N. Y.
4. Lois, b. 27 Dec., 1765; bp. 5 Jan., 1766; m. ——— **Butler;** she d. 23 Apl., 1784.
5. Honor, b. 6, bp. 11 Dec., 1768—*S. C. R.*; m. Isaac **Goodrich.**
6. Esther, b. 12, bp. 19 Aug., 1770—*S. C. R.*; m. James (s. John) **Riley;** rem. to Erie Co., N. Y.
7. Ruth, bp. 14 Feb., 1773.—*S. C. R.*

FAM. 41. ROGER,[4] (*Oliver,[3] Eph'm,[2] Ens. Wm.,[1]*), b. 1741; m. Prudence ———, of Chatham, Ct. He d. 1 Nov., 1828, in 88 yr., leaving 5 ch., 75 gd-ch., and 79 gt-gd-ch.; his wife d. 25 ———, 1819, in 78 yr.—*S. C. R.*

Children (S. C. R.):

1. Lemuel, bp. 24 Feb., 1771; m. (1) Elizabeth **Taylor.**
2. Chester.
3. Asahel, bp. Jan., 1768.
4. Allen, b. twin to Asahel. (*W. C. R.* say Asahel d. at Wilmington, N. C., Aug., 1802; his bro. *Allen*, and "another bro. *Chester*, sailed a yr. ago for Lisbon and have not been heard of

since.")
5. Josiah.
6. Nancy, bp. 18 May, 1766.
7. Roger.
8. Rhoda, m. a **Wolcott.**
9. Gershom, m. a **Goffe.**
10. ———, m. a **Morgan.**
11. Rosanna, bp. 5 Feb., 1769.—*S. C. R.*
12. Prudence, bp. 6 Dec., 1772.—*S. C. R.*

13. Barzillai, bp. 7 June, 1776—*S. C. R.;* we judge him to have been the B. who (*S. C. R.*) had (1) *Roxy,* bp. 29 July, 1798; (2) an inf. bp. and d. 2 Jan., 1800; (3) *Maria,* bp. 22 Nov., 1801; (4) a child, d. 3 Nov., 1802, in 2d yr.; (5) *Clarissa Maria,* bp. 12 June, 1803; (6) *Aaron Horsford,* bp. 2 June, 1805; (7) *Adeline,* bp. 7 June, 1807; (8) *Julia Etty* (Juliette ?), bp. 7 May, 1809, and poss. (9) *Ralph Warner,* bp. 18 June, 1815; (10) a child, bp. 30 Mch., 1818, prob. the inf. who d. 1 Apl., that yr.; (11) *Caro-* *line Sophia,* bp. 1 July, 1821.—See *Miscellanea B.*

14. Clarissa, bp. 10 Oct., 1779.

15. Oliver, bp. 1 Aug., 1784; prob. the O. who m. Esther ————, 7 Mch., 1811. —*W. C. R.* (*S. C. R.,* also, give bp. of "Asahel, s. of Roger," 31 May, 1776, and dth. of "Asahel, s. of Roger," as 11 June, 1776; and the bp. of "Asahel and Allen, twin sons of Roger," 28 Jan., 1781; this Roger must have been the No. 7 of preceding fam.)

FAM. 42.   ALPHEUS,[4] (*David,*[5] *David,*[2] *Ens. Wm.,*[1]), b. 1727; m. Hepzibah (dau. Jonathan) **Hubbard,** 27 Dec., 1753; res. Ry-H.; he d. 24 June, 1803, ae. 80.—*S. C. R.*; she d. 17 Aug., 1793, ae. 59.—*Weth. Ins. & S. C. R.*

Children (Boardman Gen.):

1. David, b. 12 Dec., 1754; m. Huldah (dau. Ebenezer & Mary *Butterick*) **Gilbert,** 25 Sept., 1783.
2. Anne, b. 18 Nov., 1756; m. 25 May, 1783, Dea. Seth (s. of Nath'l & Martha *Norton*) **Hart;** she d. 27 June, 1799.
3. Jeremy, bp. 9 Oct., 1763 (1761 ?).—*S. C. R.*
4. Alpheus, b. 1766; m. Roxana ————, who d. 22 Apl., 1813, ae. 49—*S. C. R.;* he d. 2 May, 1852, ae. 86.—*S. C. R. Issue* (*Weth.* (*S.*) *Ins.*): (1) *Catharine,* d. 1804, ae. 4 yrs.; (2) *Solomon,* d. Feb., 1815, ae. 3 yrs.; (3) *Sally,* d. 1828, ae. 20

yrs.; (4) a child, d. 15 Mch., 1816— *S. C. R.,* which, also gives dth. of "wife of Alpheus," ae. 35. (An Alpheus had *Tryphina,* bp. 20 Jan., 1771; *Caty,* who d. 26 Sept., 1806, who may have been of this family.

The *Goodrich Family,* 1889, p. 74, says that "*Mary,* dau. of Alpheus Goodrich, of Ry-H., b. 1765; m. 11 Nov., 1794, Thos. [Holmes ?] **Greenwood.**" If so, she belongs betw. Jeremy and Alpheus, Jr., in this family—tho' her bp. res. does not appear in *S. C. R.*)

FAM. 43.   JOSIAH,[4] (*David,*[3] *David,*[2] *Ens. Wm.,*[1]), b. 1731. Here we are again in doubt as to wives. Acc. to *Weth. Rec.,* Josiah m. Mary **Hubbard,** 22 Feb., 1766, [incorrectly given in *N. Eng. Gen. Rec.,* XVIII. 54, as 1758]. But another rec. (*W. C. R.*), gives him two wives, viz., (1) Ruth **Gilbert,** whom he m. 10 Sept., 1767, and who d. 14 Aug., 1777, ae. 35; and (2) Abigail **Wright,** whom he m. 25 Feb., 1779; both of Weth.*

Children (Weth. Rec. & W. C. R.):

1. Lydia, b. 25 Sept., bp. 6 Nov., 1768. (*By second marriage*):
2. Ruth, b. 6, bp. 12 Dec., 1779.—*W. C. R.,* prob. the "dau. 10 mos. old," bu. 4 Sept., 1780.

3. Elizur, b. 18, bp. 22 July, 1781.
4. Josiah, b. 9, bp. 11 May, 1783.
5. Levi, b. 9, bp. 11 Dec., 1785.
6. Sophia, b. 23 Feb., bp. 1 Mch., 1789.
7. Harriet, b. 22 May, bp. 2 June, 1793.

FAM. 44.   HEZEKIAH, (*David,*   ), b. 1733; m. Jerusha **Butler;** res. in Weth.; she d. 4 Apl., 1794, in 53 yr.—*W. Ins.;* he d. 21 Nov., 1788, in 56 yr.

Children (Weth. Rec.):

1. Eleazer, b. 2 Nov., 1760; d. 22 Feb., 1777.
2. Eli (Esq.), b. 20 Nov., 1762; m. (1) Rhoda (dau. Capt. Moses & Martha) **Williams** (?); she d. 1 Apl., 1815, in 51st yr.—*Weth. Ins.;* he m. (2) 10 June, 1817, Sally (dau. Simeon & Sarah) **Robbins,** who d. 12 Feb., 1840, ae. 60.—*W. Ins.* Esq. Eli d. 26 Jan., 1821, in 59th yr.—*S. C. R.*
3. Hannah, b. 30 Nov., 1765.
4. Hezekiah (Rev.), b. 28 Feb., bp. 2 Apl., 1769; who, as we learn from an obit. in *Conn. Courant,* of 26 Feb., 1802: "d. [7 Feb.] at Rutland, Vt., in 19th yr. of his ministry; a native of Weth.; while he was of tender yrs. his father d., and he rec'd his education under the patronage of his uncle, the Rev. Mr. G., late

of Durham; he was grad. Y. C., 1785, and 1 July, 1793, was inducted into the pastorate at R." The *G. Mem.* says he m. in Aug., 1793, Mary (dau. of Belcher & Abigail) **Richards,** of Princeton.
5. Joseph Butler, b. 12 Nov., bp. 30 Dec., 1772; d. 22 June, 1774.
6. Joseph, b. 12 Jan., 1774; d. same mo.
7. Joshua, b. 21 July, bp 10 Sept., 1775— *S. C. R.* says he m. 25 Oct., 1800—*S. C. R.,* Nancy (dau. Charles & Mary Griswold) **Bulkeley,** who d. 11 Apl., 1839, in her 64th yr.—*S. C. R.;* and had (*S. C. R.*): (1) *Walter Butler,* bp. 22 May, 1803; (2) *Oliver Butler,* bp. 27 May, 1804; (3) *George William,* bp. 27 Apl., 1806; (4) *Martha Eliza,* bp. 16 Apl., 1809; (5) *Eli,* bp. 22 Sept., 1811.

* *G. Mem.,* also, gives Mary Hubbard as Josiah's wife, as does my correspondent *R. H. C.,* and the latter informs me that some of their ch. rem. to Benson, Vt.

FAM. 45. Rev. ELIZUR, (*Dea. David, Col. David,*), b. 1734, in Step. Weth.; grad. Y. C., 1752 and was tutor there 1753. "So deeply interested was he in mathematics and astronomy, that in the busiest scenes of his subsequent ministry, he rarely failed to calculate the eclipses of each successive yr., and when the Aurora Borealis of 1780 made its appearance, he drew up one of the fullest and most accurate accounts of it ever pub., with exact drawings of the auroral arch. In Nov., 1756, he was ord. pastor of the Cong. Ch., at Durham, Ct., in which office he continued until his dth. He gave 14 hrs. daily to severe intellect. labor; was an accomplished teacher, having prepared some 300 yg. men for college and public life; and was also an active friend of the Am. Rev., preaching on the right of resistance and urging his people to lay down their ppy. and lives in the conflict. He pub'd several sermons, and left behind him some hundreds of elaborate essays on difficult passages of Scripture."—*G. Mem.* He d. 22 Nov., 1796, while on a visit to Norfolk, Ct. We find two dates given for his dth., viz., 22 Nov., 1796, and 21 Nov., 1799, while his funeral sermon was preached by Rev. Dr. Dwight, on 25 Nov., 1797. *Goodwin* gives it as 21 Nov., 1797,—prob. the correct date.

His published works were:

1. *The Duty of Gospel Ministers to take Heed to themselves and their Flock.* A Sermon preached at the Ordination of the Rev. Mr. Roger Newton, at Greenfield, Nov., 18, 1761. Boston, 1762. 8 vo. pp. 30.

2. *A Sermon preached at the Installation of the Rev. Mr. Benjamin Boardman,* in the Pastoral Office over the Second Church of Christ in Hartford, May 5, 1784. Hartford, 1784. 8 vo. pp. 29.

3. *A Sermon preached July 6, 1786, at the Ordination of the Rev. Samuel Goodrich,* to the Pastoral Office of the First Church of Christ in Ridgefield. Fairfield, 1787, 8 vo. pp. 29.

4. *The Principles of Civil Union and Happiness Considered and recommended.* A Sermon Preached before His. Excellency, Samuel Huntington, Esq., LL. D. Governor and Commander in Chief, and the Honorable the General Assembly of the State of Connecticut. . . . On the Day of the Anniversary Election, May 10, 1787. Hartford, 1787, 8 vo. pp. 58.

5. *A Sermon delivered at the Ordination of Rev. Matthew Noyes, A. M.,* to the Pastoral Charge of the Church of Christ in Northford, Aug., 18, 1790, New Haven, 1790. 8 vo. pp. 31.

The Sermon preached at Rev. Mr. Goodrich's funeral was the following: *A Discourse preached at the Funeral of the Rev. Elizur Goodrich,* Pastor of the Church in Durham, Nov. 25, 1797. By Rev. Timothy Dwight, New Haven [1797], 8 vo. pp. 39.

Rev. Mr. Goodrich m. 1 Feb., 1759, Katharine (dau. Hon. Elihu & Mary *Griswold*) **Chauncey,** of Durham; who d. 8 Apl., 1830.

Children (Goodwin & Talcott Gen's.):

1. Chauncey (Hon.), b. 1759; grad. Y. C., 1779, tutor there for next 2 yrs.; then commenced study of law in Htfd., became eminent in his profess.; was chosen memb. State Leg., 1793; in 1794, elected a Rep. to U. S. Congress, of which he was a memb. 6 yrs.; a Counsellor of the Conn. State Gov't, 1802-1807, when he was app. U. S. Senator, which office he held until 1813, when he became Lieut.-Gov., of the State of Conn.; in 1812, was Mayor of City of Htfd. He m. (1) 1 Oct., 1789, Mary Ann (dau. Gov. Oliver & Laura *Collins*) **Wolcott,** who d. 20 Mch., 1805— *Conn. Courant;* he m. (2) Abigail (dau. Dr. ————) **Smith,** of Htfd. Hon. Chauncey G. d. Htfd., 18 Aug., 1815.

2. Elizur (Hon.), b. 24 Mch., 1761. FAM. 50.

3. Samuel (Rev.), b. 12 Jan., 1763. FAM. 51.

4. Elihu Chauncey, b. 16 Sept., 1764; d. 1802, unm.

5. Charles Augustus, b. 2 Mch., 1768; grad. Y. C., Sept., 1786; d. 1804, unm.

6. Nathan, b. 5 Aug., 1770; d. yg.

7. Catharine, b. 2 Dec., 1775; m. Oct., 1799, Rev. David **Smith,** D. D., of Durham; she d. 1845.

Capt. *Elizur Goodrich*

MRS. ABIGAIL (DEMING) GOODRICH.

By Courtesy of Wm. F. J. Boardman, Esq.

FAM. 46. Capt. ELIZUR, (*Hez., Col. David,*   ),
b. 1730; m. 25 Sept.,1760.—*W. C. R.*, Abigail (dau. David & Martha *Russell*)
Deming, who d. 21 Nov., 1813, at Weth., in 80 yr.—*W. C. R.* Capt. G. was
a mariner and d.—(*Conn. Currant*), 19 Apl., 1785, of small-pox on the island
of Maria-galante,, one of the French W. I. possessions, and was there bu. under
a large tree, his name being cut in its bark to mark his grave. In the Rev.
War he was an ardent patriot—(see Vol. I. p. 317), and served in the ranks.
He was prob. the Capt. E. who rep. Weth. in the Assembly, Oct., 1776,—*Conn.
Current.*

Children (Weth. Rec.) :

1. Abigail, b. 24 Apl., 1762; bp. 2 and d. 5 May, 1829, ae. 67—*W. C. R.*; kept a private school in Weth.; will dated 16 Apl., prob'd 1 July, 1829.
2. Hezekiah, b. 9 May, 1764; bp. 11 and d. 13 June, 1765.—*W. Ins.*
3. Hezekiah, b. 11 May, bp. 1 June, 1766; grad. Y. C., 1785; rem. to Greenville Dist., S. C., and there marr.; rem. to Circleville, O., where for many yrs., he was a Circuit Judge. He had two or more ch., a dau. *Abigail*, who m. Nath'l **Kyle,** and res. at Salem, Ill., and d. 22 Dec., 1854, leaving *issue: Hezekiah Goodrich* (Kyle), and *Mary* (Kyle), who d. before her mother, and *Newton, Margaret, Oscar* and *Theresa,* who m. a **Paynter.**
4. Honor, b. 17, bp. 27 Nov., 1768; m. 24

Dec., 1795, Phinehas **Hurlbut,** of W. Htfd.; she d. 20 Nov., 1809. *Issue:*
   i. Phineas (Hurlbut), b. 1797; **Mr. H.** m. (2) Hannah **Andrus,** of Weth., by whom he had
   ii. Hosea Goodrich (Hurlbut), bp. 13 Oct., 1815; m. a **Fields.**
5. Elizur, b. 18 Aug., 1771; a sea capt., d. at sea, 16 Aug., 1794, ae. 23.—*W. C. R.*
6. Mary, b. 1 May, 1773; m. Jan., 1809, James **Wright,** of Weth., who d. 7 Nov., 1821, ae. 58. *Issue:*
   i. John Goodrich (Wright), b. 13 Nov., 1809; d. 29 May, 1888.
   ii. Charles (Wright), b. 29 Oct., 1811; d. 11 Aug., 1885.
7. Mehitable, b. 9 June, bp. 27 July, 1777.— *W. C. R.*

FAM. 46.ᵃ JOHN, 3d., (   ); m. Abigail
Price, 1 Oct., 1776.

Children (Weth. Rec.) :

1. Bela, b. 4 Feb., 1777.
2. Joseph, b. 19 Feb., 1778.
3. Lucy, b. 12 Oct., 1779.
4. Levi, b. 3 Nov., 1782.
5. Abigail, b. 24 Jan., 1785.

6. Dorothy, b. 28 July, 1786.
7. Austin, b. 12 Nov., 1787.
8. John, b. 30 July, 1793.
9. Rhoda, b. 8 Aug., 1796.

FAM. 47. Capt. NATHANIEL, Jr.,⁵ (*Nath'l,⁴ Lt. Joseph,³ Lt. William,² Ens.
William,¹*), b. 1744; m. 17 (21 *W. C. R.*), Apl., 1765, Lucy **Hanmer,** of
Weth.; res. Weth. She bu. at New Haven.

Children (Weth. Rec. & W. C. R.) :

1. Martha, b. 29 May, bp. 31 July, 1765.
2. James, b. 27, bp. 29 Oct., 1769. **FAM. 52.**
3. George, b. 18 Feb., 1772; lost at sea, Sept., 1794—*W. C. R.*; bu. at L'Ause-a-Veau, on S. coast of Martruico Isld.
4. Lucy, b. 15 Apl., bp. 8 May, 1774; m. 8 June, 1812, Samuel **Buck.**

5. Levi, b. 30 July, bp. 11 Aug., 1776.—*W. C. R.*
6. Ashbel, b. 7 Oct., 1781; bp. 28 Apl., 1782— *W. C. R.;* d. 10 Aug., 1808.—*W. C. R.*
7. Allyn, b. 22 May, 1785; bp. 29 Jan., 1786— *W. C. R.;* d. Martinico, W. I., 1812; a sailor before the mast.

FAM. 48. ISAAC,⁵ (*Nath'l,⁴ Lt. Joseph,³ Lt. Wm.,² Ens. Wm.,¹*), b. 1752; m. 15
Feb., 1784, Elizabeth **Raymond,** of New Lond.; he d. at Waterford, N. Lond.,
ae. 62, 27 Sept., 1813.—*W. R. C.;* wid. d. ae. 72, bu. 3 June, 1833.—*W. C. R.*

Children (Weth. Rec. & W. C. R.) :

1. Elizabeth, b. 6 Feb., 1785; bp. 19 Mch., 178b.
2. Joshua (Dea.), b. 5 Dec., 1789; bp. 21 Feb., 1790; m. Clarissa **Francis,** 14 Feb., 1822; had *issue* (*W. C. R.*):
   i. Joseph, bp. 31 Aug., 1823, prob. the J. who d. 8 Nov., 1825.
   ii. Caleb Raymond, bp. 28 Aug., 1825; d. Dec., 1825, ae. 9 mos.
   iii. Joseph, Francis, bp. 1 July, 1827.
   iv. Pamelia, bp. 17 May, 1829.
   v. James, bp. 20 June, 1831.
   (*W. C. R.,* also, says "Wife of Dea. Joshua" d. ae. 36; bu. 4 Dec., 1834.)

3. Mary, b. 25 Dec., 1791; prob. the ch. bp. 19 Feb., 1792.
4. Charlotte, bp. 19 Feb., 1792.—*W. C. R.*
5. Joseph, b. 31 July, 1795; perhaps the J. who took his A. B. degree at Y. C., 18 Sept., 1821, and Nov. 7, 1822, m. at Southington, Ct., Martha (dau. Selah) **Barns.** They were going as missionaries to the Sandwich Islands, and were m. in public, and a sermon preached by Rev. Mr. Ogden (from Psl. II, 6), after which a collection was taken up for the A. B. F. M., to be applied to the S. I mission.

FAM. 49. SIMEON,[5] (*Nath'l*,[4] *Lt. Joseph*,[3] *Lt. Wm.*,[2] *Ens. Wm.*,[1]), b. 1762; m. 10 Jan., 1788, Hannah **Welles,**—(*W. C. R.*) He d. 16 Aug., 1847, in 84 yr.; she d. 4 May, 1844, ae 84.—*W. Ins.*

Children (Weth. Rec. & W. C. R.):

1. Simeon, b. 19 Feb., bp. 8 Mch., 1789.
2. Hannah, b. 5, bp. 19 Dec., 1790.
3. Rhoda, b. 21 Jan., prob. the R. bp. 24 Mch., 1793.
4. Daniel, b. 4 Sept., bp. 5 Nov., 1795; bu. 9 Feb., 1801.
5. Elizur, b. 20 Feb., bp. 13 May, 1798; d. 10 Feb., 1854, ae. 56; he m. (1) 16 July,

1832—*W. C. R.*, Jerusha W. **Stillman**, who d. 2 Jan., 1835, ae. 31; he m. (2) 4 Apl., 1845, Prudence B. **Fortune**, who d. 25 Mch., 1864, ae. 56. *Weth. Ins.* give rec. of dths. of following ch.: (1) *Henry E.*, d. 16 Dec., 1865, ae. 9; (2) *Riley Fortune*, d. 1 Sept., 1848.—*W. C. R.*

FAM. 50. Hon. ELIZUR,[5] (*Rev. Elizur*,[4] *Dea. David*,[3] *Col. David*,[2] *Ens. Wm.*,[1]), b. 1761, at Durham, Ct.; m. 1 Sept., 1785, Anne Williard (dau. Daniel & Esther) **Allen.** He d. New Haven, Ct., 1 Nov., 1849; grad. Y. C., 1779, where he was tutor for next two yrs.; commenced practice of law in N. H., 1783; elected member. U. S. Congress, 1801; Collector of Port of N. H.; memb. many yrs. of Conn. Leg.; Judge of Co. Ct., 13 yrs.; Judge of Prob. Ct., 17 yrs.; Mayor of N. H., 1803-22; 9 yrs. Prof. of Law in Y. C., resigning in 1810. His wife d. 17 Nov., 1818.

Children (Talcott Gen.):

1. Elizur, b. 3 Oct., 1787; m. Eliza (dau. Gen. Henry) **Champion**, of Htfd., 25 Oct., 1818.
2. Chauncey Welles, b. 29 Oct., 1790; m. Oct., 1816, at Amherst, Mass., Frances

Juliana (dau. Noah, LL. D., the Lexicographer) **Webster.**
3. Nancy, b. 1 Jan., 1793; m. Hon. Henry L. **Ellsworth**, of Windsor, Ct., who d. 15 Jan., 1847.

FAM. 51. Rev. SAMUEL,[5] (*Rev. Elizur*,[4] *Dea. David*,[3] *Col., David*,[2] *Ens. Wm.*,[1]), b. 1763; m. 29 July, 1784, Elizabeth (dau. Col. John & Sarah *Worthington*) **Ely.** He was installed, June 1811. pastor of the 3d. Cong. Ch., at Berlin, Ct., where he d. 19 Apl., 1835; wid. d. 3 Mch., 1837.

Children (Talcott Gen.):

1. Sarah Worthington, b. 7 Aug., 1785; m. (1) Amos **Cooke**, of Danbury, June, 1815; m. (2) Hon. Fred'k **Wolcott**, of Litchfield, Ct.
2. Elizabeth, b. 26 Apl., 1787; m. Rev. Noah **Coe.**
4. Abigail, b. 29 Nov., 1785; m. Samuel **Whittlesey.**
5. Charles Augustus (Rev.), b. 19 Aug., 1790; m. June, 1818, being then "of Winchester, Mass.," Sarah (dau. Rev. Dr. Benoni) **Upsen**, of Berlin. He grad. Y. C., 1812; was pastor of Cong. Chh. at Worcester, Mass., and Berlin, Ct.; author of *Lives of the Signers;* A *History of the U. S.;* and the *Universal Traveler;* he d. at Htfd., 4 Jan., 1860.
6. Catharine, b. 4 Dec., 1791; m. Sept., 1817, at Berlin, Ct., Daniel **Dunbar**, Esq., of Berlin.
6. Samuel Griswold, b. 19 Aug., 1793, in Ridgefield, Ct. He is better known as "Peter Parley;" from 1828-1842, he edited *The Token* at Boston; from 1841-54, edited *Merry's Museum* and *Parley's Maga-*

zine. His "Peter Parley" books won him a great popularity, evidenced by the fact that the *nom de plume* was attached to over 70 spacious volumes. Among the 200 books pub. by him were *The Poetical Works of John Trumbull* (1820); *Tales of Peter Parley abt. America* (1827), and similar works on Europe, Asia, Africa and other countries. He was at one time U. S. Consul to France; he m. (1) Adaline (dau. Gen. Stephen R.) **Bradley**, of Westminister, N. Y., who d. 24 June, 1822—*Conn. Courant;* he m. (2) at Boston, Jan., 1826, Mary **Boot.** He d. at New York, 9 May, 1860.
7. Elihu Chauncey, b. 18 Nov., 1795; d. 9 June, 1797.
8. Mary Ann, b. 29 May, 1799; m. Mch., 1819, Hon. Nath'l B. **Smith**, of Woodbury, Ct.
9. Emily Chauncey, b. 25 Nov., 1801; d. 22 Oct., 1803.
10. Emily Chauncey, b. 13 Nov., 1805; m. Rev. David **Mead.**

FAM. 52. JAMES,[6] (*Capt. Nath'l*,[6] *Nath'l*,[5] *Lt. Joseph*,[3] *Lt. Williams*[2] *Ens. William*,[1]), b. 1769; m. 17 July, 1790, Elizabeth (dau. of John & Sarah *Wright*) **Bulkley;** he was a sailor; when young rem. to New Haven, Ct., commanded several vessels with distinction, was in the China trade; was taken in the ship *Confederacy* to Nantes, by a French privateer, and also, (acc. to fam. trad.), commanded a privateer in the War of 1812; he was associated with the late Henry Farnham in the Construction of, and was President of the "Canal

Railroad;" and d. at N. H., greatly respected by his fellow citizens, 17 Oct., 1858. His wid. b. 1779, d. at N. H., 12 Oct., 1864.

Children (*b. New Haven, Ct.*):

1. John Bulkeley, b. 23 July, 1801; d. 18 July, 1828, being then capt. of a ship at Callao, Chili; unm.
2. James Wright, b. 23 July, 1803; d. unm., about 1869.
3. Elizabeth, b. 19 June, 1807; m. 14 Sept., 1825, Thos. H. **Bond**; d. abt. 16 Mch., 1864. *Issue:*
   i. John Goodrich (Bond), b. N. Haven, 17 Oct., 1829; d. unm., 4 Feb., 1891, in Binghamton, N. Y.
   ii. Josephine Maria (Bond), b. Orange, N. Y., 9 Oct., 1843; m. 10 June, 1863, Edward Mitchell **Le Moyne**, had: (*a*) Elizabeth Goodrich (Le Moyne), b. 22 Apl., 1864, in N. Y. City; m. Wm. Theo. **Jones**, 22 Apl., 1890; (*b*) Josephine Clara (Le Moyne), b. N. Y., 19 Nov., 1868; unm.; (*c*) Henrietta (Le Moyne), b. 27 Dec., 1872; res. N. Y., unm.; (*d*) Mary Mitchell (Le Moyne), b. N. Y., 30 Jan., 1874, unm.
4. William, b. 2 Mch., 1809. FAM. 53.
5. Mary B., b. 6 Dec., 1811; d. 6 Sept., 1815.
6. Charles, b. 2 Apl., 1814; d. 20 Sept., 1815.
7. Sarah Maria, b. 6 Feb., 1817, at Htfd.; m. 3 June, 1835, Caspar Fred. **Uhlhorn;** he b. St. Thomas, 7 Apl., 1811; d. 1862. *Issue:*
   i. John Fred'k (Uhlhorn), b. 25 Mch., 1836; d. 5 Dec., 1862.
   ii. Harriet Elizabeth (Uhlhorn), b. 24 June, 1838; m. 27 May, 1863, James Brewster **Cone.**
   iii. Maria Goodrich (Uhlhorn), b. 30 Sept., 1840; d. 24 Jan., 1851.
   iv. Frances Augusta (Uhlhorn), b. 22 Aug., 1842; d. 1 Aug., 1896; m. 3 June, 1861, Jacob **Lorillard.** *Issue:* (*a*) Jacob; (*b*) Augusta, m. Wm. **Sands,** has ch.; (*c*) Ernest, m. Elizabeth **Scriven.**
   v. Amelia B. (Uhlhorn), b. 30 July, 1844; m. 26 Apl., 1866, Ezekiel Noyes **Trowbridge;** d. 31 Jan., 1867.
   vi. Catharine Mason (Uhlhorn), b. 13 Mch., 1847; d. 30 Jan., 1852.

FAM. 53. WILLIAM,[7] (*Capt. James,[6] Capt. Nath'l,[5] Nath'l,[4] Lt. Joseph,[3] Lt. William,[2] Ens. William,[1]*), b. 29 Mch., 1809; m. 22 Dec., 1840, Sarah Ann **Bearden,** of Knoxville, Tenn.; made several sea voyages, as supercargo; then sett. at Philadelphia as a broker and when himself broken, in 1857, retired to New Haven, Ct. Successful in early life in business, he was less so in later yrs. A disciple of Isaac Walton, he could make. and cast the alluring fly; a modern Nimrod, when he pulled the trigger, the bird dropped; fond of his dog and his horse; genial, jovial, kindly, his memory abides with his children a soft haze of loving kindness. He d. 4 July, 1883, at N. H.

Children:

1. James, b. 15 Oct., 1841; m. 15 Dec., 1869, Sarah (dau. of David) **Lockett**, of Macon, Miss., and d. 13 Mch., 1882; s. p.
2. William, b. 12 Jan., 1845; m. 29 Sept., 1875, Helen (dau. of Anthony, Jr.) **Groves**, of Chesnut Hill, Pa. No issue. Served in the Civil War, as follows: 1st Lieut., Co. G, 15th Conn. Vols., 25 Aug., 1862; Asst. Provost Marshall, Dist. No. 6a, 27 Aug., 1864; Aid-de-Camp to Brig.-Gen. J. N. Palmer, Dist. No. 6a, Mch. 21, 1865; mustered out, 27 June, 1865.
3. Caspar Frederick, b. 7 Jan., 1847. FAM. 54.
4. Henry Whitney, b. 11 Nov., 1848; d. 22 Jan., 1849.
5. Joseph King, b. 13 Jan., 1850; m. (1) 17 Apl., 1882, at Boston, Mass., Mrs. Harriet **Lovejoy,** *nee* **Wingate;** m. (2) 12 May, 1896, Mary (dau. of J. B.) **Kramer,** of Carlisle, Pa.; m. (3) Jenny **Sponsler,** of Carlisle; has two young sons, res. in Japan.
6. Sarah Ann, b. 8 June, 1852; m. 26 Sept., 1871, William **Earp,** of Phila., since dec'd. She has one dau.:
   i. Ellen Fobes (Earp), b. 26 Feb., 1873.
7. Harriet Whitney, b. 27 Feb., 1859; m. 13 Feb., 1888, Wm. T. **Kirk,** Jr., of Phila. *Issue:*
   i. Alan Goodrich (Kirk), b. 30 Oct., 1888.
   ii. Dorothy (Kirk), b. 10 Feb., 1891.
   iii. William T. (Kirk), b. 5 May, 1895.

FAM. 54. Capt. CASPAR FREDERICK, U. S. N.,[8] (*William,[7] Capt. James,[6] Capt. Nath'l,[5] Nath'l,[4] Lt. Joseph,[3] Lt. William,[2] Ens. Wm.,[1]*), b. 1847; m. 4 Sept. 1873, Eleanor (eld. dau. of Charles E. **Milnor,** Esq., of New York and his wife Susan E. **Stephens,** of Newark, N. J.) Mrs. Eleanor Goodrich was b. N. Y. City, 1850, and is a gd.-dau. of the late Rev. Geo. Milnor of St. George's P. E. ch., New York City, and a descendant of several of the old Dutch families of New Amsterdam; also fm. the Ely family of Conn., and the Perkins family of Mass.

Captain Goodrich was app. acting midshipman from Connecticut (the New Haven district) at the Naval Academy, Dec. 10, 1861, went through the four years' course in three years; grad. Nov. 22, 1864, at the head of his class; served on the European station until 1868, in the frigate *Colorado* and the tender *Frolic;* on the *Brazil* instructor in Physics and Chemistry till 1874; on the China Station on board the *Tennessee* and *Kearsarge* till 1877; at the Torpedo Station till 1880, as Executive Officer of the *Lancaster* in Europe till 1884, when he brought home the *Thetis* and *Alert* for the Greely Relief Expedition. During this cruise, he commanded the sailors and marines landed at Alexandria after the bombardment; served as military and naval attache on the staff of Sir Garnet Wolseley and made an exhaustive report which is still considered the standard history of the Bombardment of Alexandria and the Telel-Kebir Campaign of 1882. After this cruise, was member of the statutory board to examine torpedoes for adoption in the naval service; of the board which planned the Naval War College; Inspector of Ordnance at the Washington Navy Yard, where he organized the Gun Factory on lines which still prevail and built some of the earlier of the new rifled guns for the Navy; member, in 1885, of the Endicot Board on Fortifications and other Defenses; Inspector of Ordnance in charge of the Torpedo Station 1886-1889; commanded the *Jamestown* 1891, the *Constellation* 1892, the *Concord* 1893-1894 (on the China Station with a tour of four months in Bering Sea protecting the seal herd); then lecturer at, and afterward President of, the Naval War College. Promoted to Captain in 1897. Just before the breaking out of the Spanish War established the Coast Signal Service and immediately took command of the auxiliary cruiser, the American Liner *St. Louis* in which he scouted, cut cables, captured blocade runners, carried dispatches, had the first fight with the batteries at Santiago (for which he got a special medal), landed Shafter's Army, brought Cervera and 700 of his men north, carried troops to Porto Rico and seized Arroyo. Transferred to the *Newark*, he had the last battle of the war at Manzanillo and only lost the fruit of his victory [wh. cost the Spaniards 300 in killed and wounded] by the premature signing of the protocol of peace (for this action he got another special medal). His last cruise was in command of the *Iowa* on the Pacific Station. Is now (1903) in command of the *Minneapolis* pending his promotion to rear admiral.

Children:

1. Eleanor, b. 19 Oct., 1876; m. 1 June, 1901, Douglas **Campbell**, son of Col. John Campbell, U. S. A.
2. Milnor, b. 20 Dec., 1878; d. 20 Oct., 1880.
3. Caspar, b. 4 May, 1881; midshipman, U. S. N.
4. Garnet Wolsely, b. 22 Oct., 1882; d. 5 July, 1883.
5. Gladys, b. 14 June, 1886.

JOHN (poss. the J. s. of Ephraim, FAM. 14) m. 11 Aug., 1743, Anne **Riley.**

Children (Weth. Rec.):

1. John, b. 12 Mch., 1745.
2. Seth, b. 23 Mch., 1747; prob. the S. who d. 20 Oct., 1834, in 88th yr., and had (S. C. R.): Gideon, bp. 27 June, 1773; Rachel, bp. 1 Apl., 1781; d. 4 Oct., 1783; Joel, bp. 13 July, 1783; Samuel, bp. 18 May, 1794, and had a ch. d. 12 June, 1776.
3. Abigail, b. 11 May, 1749.

JONATHAN, m. Sarah **Steele,** 27 Nov., 1740, who d. 18 Sept., 1775; he d. 7 July, 1772.

Children (Weth. Rec.):

1. Jonathan, b. 28 Aug., bp. 1 Sept., 1741.
2. Luce, b. 17 Oct., bp. 10 or 12 Nov., 1743.
3. John, b. 11, bp. 20 Apl., 1746.

JOHN 2d, m. Jerusha **Deming,** 5 May, 1773—*N. C. R.;* she prob. the J., wife of Dea. John, who d. 2 Sept., ——, ae. 76.—*Weth. Ins.*

Children (Weth. Rec.):

1. John, b. 29 Sept., 1774; d. 24 Sept., 1775.
2. Jesse, b. 26 Aug., 1780.
3. John, b. 21 Dec., 1782; d. 20 Mch., 1783.
4. Sally, b. 1 Mch., 1784.

JOHN, m. Mary **Hale**, 5 Apl., 1770; she prob. the "wife of John" who d. ae. 52, bu. 13 Dec., 1798—*W. Ins.;* he prob. the J. who d. ae. 86, bu. 23 Dec., 1830.— *W. C. R.*

Children (Weth. Rec., bp. W. C. R.) :

1. Amos, b. 31 Mch., 1771 ; d. 17 Oct., 1775.
2. Abigail, b. 7 June, 1773.
3. John, b. 13 Dec., 1774 ; bp. 1 Jan., 1775.
4. William, b. 17, bp. 20 July, 1777.
5. Benezer, b. 14 Dec., 1779 ; bp. 6 Feb.,

1780.
6. Anne, b. 11 Oct., 1781 ; bp. 6 Jan., 1782.
7. Mary, b. 28 Sept., 1783 ; bp. 4 Jan., 1784.
8. George, b. 11 Oct., bp. 13 Dec., 1788.

MICHAEL, m. Elizabeth **Hill;** poss. the M. who advertised a farm of 30 acres for sale at Sandisfield, Mass., in *Conn. Courant,* 28 Sept., 1801.

Children (Weth. Rec.) :

1. Elizabeth, b. 9 June, 1774.
2. Alvin, b. 22 Apl., 1776.

3. Bayley, b. 30 May, 1778.
4. Walter, b. 11 Sept., 1780.

WAIT. There were three Goodrich men of this name res. (contemporaneously) in Weth., viz. 1. A son of Dea. David, (FAM. 16,) and b. 1736; 2. A son of Capt. Gideon (FAM. 18), and b. 1740; 3. A son of Capt. Wait (FAM. 28) and b. 1765. As each of these were mariners, and each carried the prefix of "Captain," it has been impossible for me to satisfactorily disentangle their respective family lines.

The *American Mercury,* pub. at New London, Ct., states, under date of Aug. 4, 1804, that a Capt. Wait Goodrich, Jr., d. at sea, 27th ulto, ae. 38, (*W. C. R.* mention his death, as of a fever, at sea, in Aug., under date of Dec., 1803,) "leaving an aged father, a wid. and 3ch." This date of death, with age given identifies him with the Wait, b. in 1765, s. of Wait, b. 1736 and gd-son of Dea. David. The same paper, under date of 28 Sept., 1809, records the death (on 21st) of a Capt. Wait in his 74th yr. which would make him to have been b. in 1735 or '36, and s. of Dea. David, and evidently the "aged father" of the Capt. Wait before mentioned as b. 1765.

The *third* Wait, (b. 1740. and s. of Capt. Gideon,) is prob. the W. ment. on the recs. as Wait, Jr.. of Glast. He m. 17 Dec., 1789, Lucy **Balch,** of Weth., who was b. 21 Dec., 1763 and d. 17 July, 1854. They had (*W. C. R.*) a dau. d. 29 Jan., 1797, ae. 4; Lois, bp. 28 June, 1795, d. 27 May, 1822, ae. 27; Anson, bp. 30 July, 1797; Grove, bp. 4 Aug., 1799, prob. the s. wh. d. ae. 15 mos., 16 Dec., 1802; Charles Anson, bp. 29 Nov., 1801; also, a Lucy, who d. 8 Feb., 1873, having, 7 May, 1811, m. a Raphael **Fontaine,** by whom she had 3 ch. To return to the other Capts. Wait, the one b. 1736 and his s. Capt. Wait, b. 1765—the elder one of these, we think, must have been the one referred to in the following extracts from the *Conn. Courant,* of 25 Dec., 1772. "Sailed from New London, the ship *Mississippi,* Capt. Goodrich, bound for Pensacola and Mississippi, having on board a company of Military Adventurers to reconnoitre the lds. lately gr. by the Crown to Maj. Gen. Lyman and the Company of Adventurers"; and, again, under date of Dec. 14, 1773, "Sailed for Midd. the sloop *Adventurer,* Capt. Wait Goodrich, master, with abt. 30 passengers, to settle on the borders of the Mississippi." A similar notice appeared in the *Courant* of same month. This Wait, we think, was the one who m. Olive **Williams,** 26 Jan., 1789—*S. C. R.* She, in Oct., 1819, being then a res. of Weth., petit. the Co. Ct. for a divorce from him, on the ground of desertion. He had rem. to Franklin, Del. Co., N. Y., and the *Conn. Courant* of 17 Dec., 1823, contains an advertisement from him inviting his wife O. to return. According to *S. C. R.* and *Weth. Inscript.,* this couple had *Cynthia*, bp. 9 and d. 27 Jan., 1801; *Otis*, who was bp. 2 May, 1802 and d. 22 Aug., 1808, ae. 6 yrs. 7 mo.; *Russell*, bp. 3 July, d. 3 Feb., 1809, ae. 1 yr. 10 d., and perhaps, also, *Louis*, bp. 9 Nov., 1806, and *Orinda*, bp. 5 July, 1810.

WAIT, (evidently another family,) had *Susannah*, bp. 5 Jan., 1761 *Sybil*, bp. 1 May, 1768; *Marius*, bp. 9 Dec., 1770; *Lois*, bp. 28 June, 1795; *Edwin*, bp. 21 Oct., 1799; a *dau.* bu. 29 Jan., 1797 ae. 4, and a *dau.* bu. 13 Aug., 1798, ae. 1 yr.

Wid. GOODRICH, d. 11 Sept., 1775, ae. 69.—*W. C. R.*

GOODWILL, MARY ANN, m. John **Hurlburt,** 2d, 1 Jan., 1832.

GOODWIN, (*Goodin*) CALEB, of Htfd., m. Harriet **Williams,** 3 Sept., 1811.

EZEKIEL, m. Eunice **Goodrich,** 4 Oct., 1780.

HORACE, m. Lydia **Andrews,** 29 Mch., 1808.—*W. T. R.*

JANE, m. James A. **Clifford,** of Savanah, Ga., 7 Oct., 1833.—*W. T. R.*

JOHN 1st, had a ch. ae. 13 mos. bu. 30 Oct., 1784.—*W. C. R.*

JOHN, (s. of Mr. Thomas) bp. 4 ———, 1740.

LUCY, m. John **Robbins,** of Rochtester, N. Y., 7 May, 1828.—*W. T. R.*

OLIS W., ae. 22, bu. 5 Apl., 1830.—*W. C. R.*

SARAH ("I think") dau. of Isaac, bp. 16 Mch., 1728-9.—*Mix MSS.*

SARAH ELIZABETH, (dau. Stephen B.) bp. 26 June, 1825—*W. C. R.;* m. Erastus A. **Kingsbury,** of Manchester, Ct., 26 Dec., 1849.—*W. T. R.*

STEPHEN B. d. 14 Sept., 1849, ae. 66, had (1) Mary Ann, bp. 6 Apl 1823—*W. C. R.;* bu. 30 Dec., 1823 *W. C. R.;* (2) Sarah Elizabeth, bp. 26 June, 1825; (3) Stephen Buckland, bp. 30 June, 1830.—*W. C. R.*

THOMAS, "late of Boston, now of Weth." ment. in *Co. Ct. Rec.,* June, 1734; prob. the T. given by *Weth. Rec.* as father of the following ch. by his wife Abigail ————, viz.: Jacob, b. 12 Aug., 1735, and Gale (Gail?) b. 6 Jan., 1737-8.

GORHAM, HENRY, d. 9 Feb., 1824, in 8th yr.—*S. C. R.*

GRAHAM, (see also *Grimes*) JOHN, m. Hannah **Hun,** 21 Apl, 1768.—*Weth. and N. C. Rec.*

Children:

1. Samuel, b. 20 June, 1771—*Weth. Rec.;* bn. 16 Aug., 1772.—*New. Ch. Rec.*
2. Clara, b. 10 June (*Weth. Rec.*), bp. 13 (*New. Ch. Rec.*), 1773.
3. Mary, bp. 25 June, 1775.—*New. Ch. Rec.*
4. Hannah, bp. 3 Aug., 1777.—*New Ch. Rec.*
5. Sarah, bp. 23 May, 1779.—*New. Ch. Rec.*
6. Wealthy, bp. 17 June, 1784.—*New. Ch. Rec.*

JASPER, m. 28 Dec., 1823, Lois **Williams;** he d. 10 Mch., 1841, in 69th yr.— *S. C. R.*

MARTHA, ae. 70, d. 19 May, 1825.—*N. C. R.*

DANIEL, of Suffield, m. Lydia **Goodrich,** of W., 10 May, 1790 or 6?

GRANNIS, ANSON, (*S. C. R.*) wife of, d. 5 Sept., 1830, in 31st yr.; dau. of. d. in Htfd., 9 Oct., 1841; a son d. 23 Apl., 1836.—*S. C. R.*

GRANT, AZARIAH and Abigail, had Abigail, b. 8 Nov., 1774.—*Weth. Rec.*

ROSWELL, m. Fluvia **Wolcott,** both of E. Windsor, 20 Aug., 1783.—*W. C. R.*

GRAVES, NATHANIEL, b. Eng., 1629, s. of Thomas & Sarah, of Htfd. and Hatfield; m. 16 Jan., 1655, Martha (dau. of John & Mary) **Betts,** who was b. Eng., 1625, and d. 13 Apl., 1701, ae. 75 yrs., "as some think"—*Weth. Rec.* They res. in Weth., on E. side of Broad St., at its So. end. He was a juror in Ct. of May, 1659 and '60; surveyor, 1661; constable, 1674; fence-viewer, 1668; drew ld. in 1670 allot.; for his real est. see Chapt. VII, Vol I; was early on the tax-list.—See *W. T. V.,* 9-12. He d. 28 Sept., 1682, ae. abt. 50. Invent. of est. 30 Oct., 1682, val. £439-02-08. Mrs. G.'s invent. amt'd (1702) to £22-16-01.

Children (Weth. Rec.) :

1. Sarah, b. 4 Oct., 1656; m. Samuel (prob. s. of Lesly) **Bradfield,** who rem. to Branford, 1646.
2. Mary, b. 11 Nov., 1658; m. 5 June, 1684, John[3] (s. *Sgt. John,[2] John,[1]*) **Deming,** who d. 25 Sept., 1729.
3. Rebecca, b. Feb., 1660-61—*Prob. Rec.;* living, unm., 7 Mch., 1683-4.
4. Nathaniel, b. 1662—*Prob. Rec.;* d. 5 Jan., 1681.
5. Martha, b. July, 1667; m. 9 Apl., 1691, Sgt. John **Russell;** she d. 15 July, 1740; he m. (2) Susannah **Nichols.**
6. Abigail, b. 15 Oct., 1668; m. Sgt. Ebenezer (s. John & Lydia) **Belden.**

BENJAMIN, b. 1676; rem. to Colchester abt. 1709, where he d. 1752, and in *Colch. Rec.* is spoken of as prob. coming from Hatfield, Mass. But this is more than doubtful, as the date of his birth does not correspond, and his childrens' names are entirely different fm. those of the Hatfield Benjamin's, who was s. of *John,[3] Isaac[2]* and *Thomas,[1]* who rem. fm. Htfd. to Ht. abt. 1660. Benjamin of Colchester, had *Benjamin,* Jr., who sett. in E. Hadd., *Jedidiah, Jonathan, Ruth, James, Harris* and 5 daus.—(*Letter of John C. Graves, to S. W. A.,* 1889.)

JOHN, of Weth., bro. of Nath. above and b. in Eng., freeman, Conn., 1654, had 5 ch. b. there before his rem., 1659-60, to Hadley, and 5 after b. at H.; the last, "perhaps," as Savage thinks, by 2d wife, who was wid. of John **Wyatt,** of Hadd. Of those 10 ch. nine were living in 1692. John, the father was killed by Inds., 19 Sept., 1677; his wid. m. (2) Wm. **Allis,** and (3) Samuel **Gaylord.** For ld. holdings in Weth., see Chapt. VII, Vol. I.

ISAAC, of Htfd., a bro. of foregoing Nath'l and John, was, in 1648, engaged in building Goffe's bridge in Weth. He "keyed" it down.—*W. T. V.,* I, p. 32. See Judd's *Hist. Hadley,* and for family, *Savage* II, 294.

GRAY, JOHN W.'s ch. d. Glast., 3 July, 1853.—*S. C. R.*

GREEN, BERIAH, of Pawlet, Vt., m. Maria **Deming,** of Middlebury, Vt., 21 Jan., 1821.—*N. C. R.*

JOHN, d. 14 Feb., 1840, ae. 62—*N. C. R.;* his wife Phillis d. 23 May, 1850, ae. 72; their dau. Martha, d. 28 Jan., 1843, ae. 24.—*W. Ins.*

JOEL, T. m. Cath. B. **Webb,** in Brooklyn, N. Y., 2 Aug., 1848.—*S. C. R.*

JAMES, inf. d. 18 July, 1856.

JOSEPH.—See Chapt. Vol. I.

SAMUEL.—See Chapt. Vol. I.

WILLIAM, m. Rhoda **Smith,** 3 July, 1817.

GREENWOOD, Holmes, m. **Mary Goodrich,** 11 Nov., 1794—*S. C. R.;* had (*S. C. R.*) Rodney, bp. 16 Sept., 1798.

PARSONS, m. (1) 27 Feb., 1777 (*W. C. R.*) Sarah **Latimore,** who d. 1 Sept., 1788—*W. C. R.,* (prob. d. 31 Aug., and bu. 1 Sept.) ; he m. (2) Mary **Wilson,** 14 June, 1789.

Children (Weth. Rec. & W. C. R.):

1. William, b. 22 Jan., 1778 ; bp. 11 ——, 1779.
2. Elizageth, b. 4 Apl., bp. 14 May, 1780.
3. Parsons, } twins, b. 6 Mch., bp. 28 Apl.,
4. Sarah,   }   1782.
5. Samuel, b. 22 Oct., 1783 ; bp. 9 Jan., 1785.
6. George Frasier, b. 6 Aug., bp. 24 Sept., 1786.
7. John, bp. 30 Aug., bu. 22 Dec., 1788.

THOMAS, (? See Holmes Greenwood above) m. Mary (dau. Alpheus **Goodrich,** of Ry-H. had:

Children (Weth. Rec.):

1. Thomas Jefferson, b. 1803, was early thrown upon his own resources, and in his early years was a peddler. He accompanied his Uncle Jeremy Goodrich to Chenango Co., N. Y. [Letter of G. E. Congdon, of Waterman, Ills., 1901.]
2. Rodney, who was lame.

GREER, HENRY S., of Cromwell, m. Martha A. **Chambers,** 29 Oct., 1854.— *S. C. R.*

GRIDLEY, Dr. HORATIO, of Woodbury, m. Mary **Welles,** 9 Dec., 1823.

GRIFFIN, SIMON, m. 12 Dec., 1771, Lydia **Crane.** He d. Nov., 1820, ae. 80; she, ae. 73, d. 20 Dec., 1813.

Children (Weth. Rec.):

1. George, b. 19 May, 1772. | 2. Anna, b. 19 Nov., 1774. | 3. John, b. 6 Feb., 1777.

GRIMES, (prob. orig. *Grihme,* or *Grihmes,* sometimes *Graham*) is the name of an old Step. family—concerning which the *Town's Recs.* give us much less than one should like to know—the mortuary records of *Weth. Ins.* giving us the most of what we do know.

JOSEPH, of Htfd., the earliest whose name we find on *Weth Rec.,* dr. ld. in 1694 allot.; fence-viewer at Ry-H., 1705, Vol. I, 24 Nov., 1686, Deborah (dau. John) **Stebbins,** who d. 21 Jan., 1711-12; he res. in Step.; his will, dated 19 Apl., 1733; invent. taken 21 Nov., 1734; amt. £943-00-06, devises to all the 7 ch. (given below) then living.

Children (Weth. Rec.):

1. Mary, b. 3 Apl., 1688.
2. Henry, b. 9 Jan., 1690-1. FAM. 2.
3. Joseph, b. 12 Oct., 1693 ; d. 22 Jan., 1712.
4. Josiah, b. 17 Dec., 1696 ; prob. the Josiah, "bachelor," who (*S. C. R.*) d. 28 Jan.,
    1781, ae. 84—or 86, acc. to *Weth. Ins.*
5. Hezekiah, b. 26 Sept., (bp. 6 Oct.—*Mix*), 1700. FAM. 3.
6. Christopher, b. 6 (bp. 16—*Mix*), 1703. FAM. 4.
7. Deborah, b. 24 May, 1706.

FAM. 2. HENRY,[2] (*Joseph,*[1]), b. 1690-1; hayward, 1710; m. Mary (dau. Zachariah) **Seimer** [Seymour] 2 Aug., 1711.

Children (Weth. Rec.):

1. Zebulon, b. 5. d. 12 Feb., 1711-12.
2. Mary, b. 30 Oct., 1713.
3. Deborah, b. 13 Feb., 1715-16.

Fam. 3. HEZEKIAH,[2] (*Joseph*,[1]), b. 1699; m. Abigail ————, who "wid. Abigail" d. 25 Mch., 1792, in 90th yr.—*S. C. R.* He d. 24 Sept., 1775.—*S. C. R. Weth. Ins.*

Child:

1. Martha, d. 19 Oct., 1754, in 3d yr., conse- | quently b. 1731.—*Weth. Ins.*

Fam. 4. CHRISTOPHER,[2] (*Joseph*,[1]), b. 1703; m. 13 Oct., 1726, Abigail **Williams.**

Children (Weth. Ins.):

1. Honor, b. 26 July, 1727.
2. Christian, b. 26 July, 1729.
3. Abraham, b. 20 Apl., 1732.

4. Abigail, b. 7 July, 1734.
5. Lucretia, b. 31 July, 1737.

Fam. 1. ALEXANDER, (*prob. s. of Alexander*, who d. 21 Apl., 1771,) and b. (acc. to date and age at dth.) 1744; m. 17 Aug., 1769—*S. C. R.*, Mary (dau. Capt. Richard) **Dunn**, of Newport, R. I.; he d. 25 Mch., 1840, ae 96.—*Weth. Ins. & S. C. R.*

Children (Weth. Rec.):

1. Ch., d. 21 Apl., 1771.—*S. C. R.*
2. Mary, b. abt. 1772; m. Seth **Dickinson**, and d. 10 Mch., 1860, ae. 88.
3. Nathan, b. abt, 1774; d. at Launce Vaux, W. I., 2 Aug. (S. C. R.—Sept.), 1796, ae. 19 (22).—*Weth. Ins.*
4. Hezekiah, b. abt. 1775; d. 19 Dec., 1833, ae. 58—*S. C. R.; his wife Sally, d. 12 Dec., 1822, ae. 46.—Weth. Ins.*
5. Samuel, b. abt. 1777, d. at Point Petre, W. I., 12 Sept., 1794, ae. 17.—*S. C. R.*
6. Sophrania, b. abt. 1780; d. 29 Aug., 1861, ae. 81.—*Weth. Ins.*
7. Henry, b. abt. 1784; d. Antiqua, 17 June,

1803, ae. 19.—*Weth. Ins.*
8. Richard (Capt.), d. in Texas, ae. 68; his s. *William Bradford*, went with him; in the bus. of cattle-raising; later rem. to Kansas City, where he was, for a time, a large drygoods dealer and pres. of First Nat. Bk. of that city.—*R. W. G.* (Perhaps, betw. Sophriana and Henry above, we ought to put Capt. *William*, who was lost at sea, Sept., 1819, ae. 37 (consequently b. 1782); and whose wife Mary [Jagger], they were m. 23 Apl., 1809, d. 18 Apl., 1845, ae. 58—*Weth. Rec.;* and, also, *Roderick*, b. 3 Oct., 1786.—See Fam. 2.

Fam 2. RODERICK,[3] (*Alexander*,[2] prob. *Alex.*,[1]), b. 1786; m. 22 Oct., 1816 (*W. C. R.*) Mary Ann **Church**, who was b. 21 Sept., 1793, and d. 29 Feb., 1872.—*Weth. Ins.* He was a large mcht. at the Rocky Hill landing, for many yrs. A Roderick (whether this one or not, we know not) m. 27 June, 1824, Charlotte **Bradford.**—*S. C. R.*

Children (Weth. Ins.):

1. Marshall, b. 16 Jan., 1818; d. Sherman, Tex., 2 June, 1868. *S. C. R.* credit him with being bp. 6 May, 1838, and with s. William Johnson, bp. 4 Sept., 1846, and with dau. Lucy Auraild [Ayrault ?]; bp. 17 Mch., 1750.
2. Lucy, b. 25 Jan., 1820; m. John H. **Brainard**; she d. 4 Dec., 1873; he (*J. H. B.*) b. 15 Apl., 1827; d. 2 Dec., 1891.
3. Mary Ann, b. 28 Feb., 1822; m. 6 Aug.,

1851 (*S. C. R.*) (as his sec. wife), Frank W. **Shipman**; she d. 11 Jan., 1894.
4. Agnes, b. 27 July, 1824; m. Frank W. **Shipman**; she d. 7 Feb., 1847; he b. 1821, d. 6 Nov., 1863. Frank D. Shipman (s. by first wife), b. 20 Sept., 1862; d. 16 Jan., 1882.
5. Donald, b. 9 June, 1826; d. 13 May, 1865.
6. Gertrude, b. 26 Aug., 1831; d. 12 Jan., 1860.

RODERICK, son of "Uncle Aleck," at the Landing, mcht., was in Leg. of 1831; a man of more than ordinary intelligence and information. His store, during the latter part of his life was the resort of the chief men of the Democratic party in Rocky Hill. It was "Uncle Roderick" who bestowed the name of the "Barbary States" upon the Windham county towns. After an election and when the first returns answered favorably for his party, he was wont to say to his associates, "Let's wait a little, we havn't heard fm. the Barbary States yet."

JOSIAH, Jr., b. abt. 1743; d. 13 Jan. 1797 in 54 yr.—*Weth. Ins.;* m. (1) Abigail ————, who d. 12 Nov., 1771, in 23d yr.—*S. C. R.;* m. (2) 14 June, 1773, Mehitable **Warner**, who d. 27 Sept., 1802, in 53d. yr.; their dau. Betsy, d. 27 Sept.

GRINOLAW, JOHN, d. ae. 23, 10 July, 1838.—*N. C. R.*

GRISWOLD.[*] "The English Griswolds were an ancient county family, established at Solihull, Warwickshire, Eng., prior to 1400; the name being generally written as Greswold; but, without doubt, the "e" in the first syllable had the Latin sound as "i," short, for it was often written Griswold, or Gryswold, and sometimes with a terminal "e." The family had a pedigree, and were entitled to a coat-of-arms, viz., *Arg. a fesse qu. betw. two greyhounds current, Sa.* "They were descended from a certain John Griswold, who about the middle of the 14th century, came from Kenilworth, married and settled in Solihull, and by *Burke,* the family is called Griswold of Kenilworth and Solihull." (Information derived from the late Hon. Seneca O. Griswold's personal researches, as given in Stiles' *Hist. Genealogies of Ancient Windsor, Conn.,* Vol. II, p. 347-351, to which the reader is referred for much more information of an interesting character, concerning the English history of the family.) The same authority says, "The family was one of local distinction, they held county offices, were summoned by the Sheriff with the other gentlemen of the county, to be present at the proclamation of Acts of Parliament, and sworn to defend them. They sought and obtained wives from the local families, and an alliance with their daus. was considered honorable. As primogeniture prevailed, it follows that, in a family extending through so long a period, there would be poor as well as rich, and they spread into a number of adjoining parishes. They were not of the nobility, but belonged to the middle class landed gentry—that devout, patient and, above all, valiant race which has contributed so much to make England, for centuries, the foremost of nations."

The *Connecticut* Griswolds, are descendants of the brothers EDWARD and MATTHEW, who came to Windsor in 1639, (See Stiles' *Hist. & Geneal. of Ancient Windsor,* Vol. II, p. 347); and of MICHAEL who, some years later, came to Weth. No positive proof has as yet been obtained that this Michael was a brother, or in any way related to Edward and Matthew of Windsor; yet there is a possibility of such a relationship; and the Rev. F. W. Chapman, who compiled an extensive Griswold Genealogy (never published), wrote to a correspondent of ours in 1874, saying, "I have documentary evidence that he was a bro. of Edward and Matthew; also of Francis, who sett. in Cambridge, Mass., and d. without male heirs."—Concerning Francis, *Charleston Rec.* give sufficient evidence as coming from Eng., 1636, freeman at Cambridge, 1645, etc. Concerning this same point, Mrs. E. E. Salisbury of New Haven, Ct., thus writes to Judge Adams, in 1889, "In regard to *Michael* Griswold, Mr. Salisbury and I have, for yrs. been searching for the ancestry of Edward and Matthew, sons of George, of Kenilworth, [Co. Warwick, Eng.] The early recs. there are destroyed and the Eng. fam. is extinct. Matthew owned a house and ld. there which he left in the occup. of his bro. Thomas. The education of the bros., and their high pub. and private *status* in this country give evidence that they belonged to the gentry of Eng., but we can trace their pedigree no further." While the knowledge of the relationship between the Killingworth and Lyme branches of Griswolds has been always retained, we can find no tradition of relationship to Michael Griswold of Weth. If it existed, all trace of it seems to have been lost." (Of the two opinions thus given, our judgment rests with that of Mrs. Salisbury.—*H. R. S.*)

[*] In making up this genealogy of the Griswolds of Weth., I have been considerably aided by an incomplete genealogy, and notes, found among the MSS. of the late SHERMAN W. ADAMS, who was not unjustly proud of his connection with the family.—*H. R. S.*

MICHAEL GRISWOLD, b. in Eng., a mason by trade, yeoman in civil rank, owned lds. in Weth. as early as 1640 (?) and was the only "freeman" of the name, in the town, in 1659. He had cattle ear-mark rec.,—*W. S. V.*, I. p. 2; pd. fence tax 1647, (p. 29). He held the offices of constable, assessor and appraiser of lds. Resided on the place now (1880) occupied by Harvey Hurlburt's heirs, in Black Lane, so called (Cornelia Hurlbut and her sister, Mrs. Burdett, being his descendants, through his youngest son Michael), and the old brown house which they occupy in Back Lane, stands upon the site of their emigrant ancestor's house.—See picture, p. 726. Michael's will was probated 18 Nov., 1684, evidently only a few days after his death, as he executed a codicil thereto Sept. 22d, 1684. His estate inventoried at £628 ; he gave to his wife, Ann, the home lot for life, then to go to his son Michael; to his oldest son Thomas he gives the house where Thomas then lived with barn and 1½ ae. of ld ; also, other pieces of ld.; to his son Isaac, one half of the homestead bo't of Luke Hitchcock and other lds.; to Jacob, his 3rd son, among other lds. 16 acres at "Two-Stone Brook," (now Griswoldville), being ld. given him in 1674, by the Town—which ld. with other pieces purchased by Jacob, has remained in the G. family to this day. This will prob. drawn by Gershom Bulkely—is rec'd in Vol. V. p. 205, *Htfd. Prob. Ct. Rec.*

Michael Griswold, died 26 September 1684 Invt. £628-01-00 taken by Samuel Talcott, Samuel Butler, Timothy Hide.

Will dated 10 December 1678—I give to my wife Anne Griswold to my son Thomas Griswold to Jacob to Michael to my d. Hester Bradley and to her d Ann Abigail Mary & Hester. to my my d. Abigail Lattin and to her d Ann Lattin to my d Sarah Hills to my son in law Obadiah Wilcox I appt. my wife Ann Griswold Executrix if she survive me if not my eldest surviving son to be executor

Michael Griswold   O

A Codicil date 22 September 1684
Witness John Buttolph Eleazer Kimberly   Proven 18 December 1684

Children (Weth. Rec.) :

1. Thomas, b. 22 Oct., 1646. FAM. 2.
2. Hester, b. 8 May, 1648, m. ————
   Bradley. *Issue :*
   i. Ann (Bradley).
   ii. Abigail (Bradley).
   iii. Mary (Bradley).
   iv. Hester (Bradley).
3. Mary, b. 28 Jan., 1650 ; m. Obadiah **Wilcox.**
4. Michael, b. 14 Feb., 1652 ; d. in childhood.

5. Abigail, b. 8 June, 1655 ; m. ————
   Lattin. *Issue :*
   i. Ann (Lattin).
6. Isaac, b. "abt. the last of" [30 Sept.] 1658.
7. Jacob, b. 15 Apl., 1660. FAM. 3.
8. Sarah, b. "last of Sept.," [30 Sept.], 1662 ; m. ————— **Hill** (or Hills).
9. Michael (Ens.), b. 7 Mch., 1666-7. FAM. 4.

FAM. 2. THOMAS,[2] (*Michael,*[1]) b. 1646; surveyor of highways, 1675; constable, 1690; see Chapt. VII, Vol. I; m. Mary (dau. Henry) **Howard,** 28 Nov., 1672; Mary "wife of Thomas Grisold," d. 29 Oct., 1718, ae. 71 yr.—*Weth. Ins.*

Children (Weth. Rec.) :

1. Thomas, b. 11 Jan., 1673-4.
2. Jacob, b. 5 Feb., 1675. FAM. 5.
3. Isaac, b. 20 Oct., 1678. (Was *noncompos*.)

On auth. of H. Woodruff, N. Y. City.
4. Michael, b. 28 Jan., 1680. FAM. 6.

FAM. 3. JACOB,[2] (*Michael,*[1]), b. 1660; m. Mary (dau. Dea. Joseph & Mary *Stoddard*) **Wright,** 10 Dec., 1685; he d. 22 July, 1737, will dated 1735; she d. 25 Apl., 1735, in 71 yr.—(*Weth. Ins.*) He was prob. the first settler at "Two-Stone" now Griswoldville, where he inher. ld. from his father, and where he also bo't ld. and blt. the older G. house in which Thomas, Sr., s. of Ezra, afterwards lived. In his will (dated 10 Feb., 1735-6) he gave his home lot to son and Ephraim, and makes it appear that he had already given sons Jacob, Michael and Ebenezer, their portions in advance; will proven, 2 Aug., 1737.

Jacob Griswold Sen. Invt. £268-17-09—(He Died 22 July 1737) Taken 18 August, 1737, by John Stilman Jonathan Williams Jonathan Belding. Will dated, 10 February, 1735-6. I give to my son Josiah Griswold Land in Newington. I give to the heirs of my eldest son John Griswold Decd. to Jeremiah the eldest son of the Decd. to John, to Hannah, to Thankful, to Mabel, children of my son John Griswold, Decd. I give to my son Jacob, to Ebenezer, to Ephraim, I give to my eldest d. Mary Ellis £110. to Sarah £110. to Esther £110. Lydia £110. I appoint my son Josiah to be sole executor.

Jacob Griswold   O

Witness Thomas Wright, Elisha Meeks, Joseph Pyncheon. Proven 2 August, 1737.

Children (*Weth. Rec. & Mix MSS.*) :

1. John, b. 25 Sept., 1686. FAM. 7.
2. Mary, b. 19 June, 1688; m. 1709, Wm. Ellis (see *Allis*), of Kensington.
3. Jacob (Capt.), b. 26 Mch., 1690; rem. to Litchfield, Ct., of which he is called the first settler. Woodruff's *Geneal. Reg. of Inhabitants of Litchfield*, 1720-1780, gives the family of a Jacob from Weth., also, the families and descendants of *Elijah, Jacob, Jeremiah* and other Griswolds of the New Milford stock. There is still (and, perhaps, will ever be) some incertitude as to which *Jacob*, this "first sett. of Litchfield" was—whether it was Jacob (s. of *Thos.*[2] s. of *Michael*,[1]) b. 1675, and given FAM. 5 in this geneal. or Jacob[2] (s. *Jacob's Micheal*[1]) b. 1660, FAM. 3, in our list. Our own opinion is that it was the former. Orcutt (*Hist. New Milford, Ct.*, p. 64) in giving a list of "new sett. of L. betw. 1713 and 1720," says, "JACOB Griswold fram Weth., came to N. M., 1713," being made freeman in latter town that yr.; bo't a right of Hugh Gray, 11 Jan., 1713-14, but his home lot was laid out to him 17 Nov., 1713, next N. of the "ministry lot" gr. to Rev. Mr. Boardman, which was the 6th on the W. side the street in the Town Plot. This lot he sold in 1716; was res. 1720, in L. where he was one of the first sett." The *Annals of Litchfield* say that in May, 1722, while at work alone in the field abt. a mile E. of present L. Court House (Ind. name Bantam) was surprised by two Inds., who bound him and took him northward with them, until by nighttime they had reached a place now called Canaan (18 miles from L.), near Hanatowne Falls. That night the Capt. managed, while his captors slept, to loose his pinions and escaped to his home, carrying with him their guns. Orcutt, also, connects with Capt. Jacob, in this emigr. to and sett. of Litchfield, two other bros. JOHN and DAVID. We cannot figure it out that way. It is more prob. they were *cousins*, and all grandsons of Michael, the Settler, of Weth.— See our FAMS. 3, 4, and 5.

4. Anna, b. 14 Aug., 1693; d. 4 Aug., 1723.
5. Sarah, b. 18 Mch., 1695-6; m. as his 3d wife, 16 Dec., 1718, John Belden, 3d.— See *Belden*.
6. Hester, b. 13 Mch., 1696-7.
7. Joseph, of Jacob G., Sr., bp. 21 Aug., 1698.—*Mix* (?).
8. Josiah, of Jacob, bp. 20 Aug., 1699; bp. 5 Jan., 1700—*Mix*; prob. d. yg.
9. Josiah (Maj.), b. 4, bp. 5 (*Mix*) Jan., 1700-1. FAM. 8.
10. Ebenezer (Lieut.), b. 25 Oct., bp. 1 Nov., 1702. FAM. 9.
11. Ephraim, b. 23, bp. 24 Sept., 1704.
12. Lydia, b. 4 (bp.7—*Mix*) Sept., 1707.

FAM. 4. Ens. MICHAEL,[2] (*Michael*,[1]), b. 1666; m. Elizabeth (dau. Wm.) **Burnham,** 12 May, 1692; she d. 9 Sept., 1741; he was collector, 1692; chimney viewer, 1794—See Chapt. VII, Vol. I; commis. 1710 by Gov. Saltonstall, as Ens. of So. trainband in Weth.;* he d. 24 July, 1742, in 76th yr.—*Weth. Ins.;* will dated, 1741.

Children (*Weth. Rec. & Mix MSS.*) :

1. David, b. 25 Mch., 1693; d. ———.
2. Jonathan, b. 6 Oct., 1695.
3. Joseph, b. 28 Dec., 1697.
4. Stephen, b. 14, bp. 19 Aug., 1700.
5. ——— Elizabeth, b. 21, bp. 25 Apl., 1703; m. ——— **Bunce.**
6. Caleb (Capt.), b. 8 May, 1706. FAM. 10.
7. Elisha, b. 6, bp. 7 (bp. prob. 25) Feb., 1708-9. FAM. 11.
8. Nathaniel, b. 23, bp. 24 ———, 1711-12. FAM. 12.
9. Anna, bp. 2 or 9 Jan., 1714-15.

---

* Commission in poss. "of Miss Kate Knowles," of Htfd.

FAM. 5. JACOB,² (*Thos.*,² *Michael*,¹), b. 1675; m. Abigail (dau. Stephen) **Hand,** of Guilford, 30 Nov., 1696; she d. 18 Apl., 1747, in 67th yr.—*Weth. Ins.*

Children (Weth. Rec. & Mix MSS.):

1. Joseph, bp. 21 Aug., 1698.
2. Lydia, bp. 11 Feb., 1699-1700.
3. Hezekiah, b. 16 Oct., 1697; d. ————.
4. Abigail, b. 1, bp. 7 Dec., 1701.
5. Rachel, b. 8 Apl., 1705.
6. Rebecca, b. 25, bp. 28 Sept., 1708.

7. Experience, b. 11, bp. 12 Mch., 1709-10.
8. Irene, b. 5, bp. 9 Aug., 1713.
9. Lydia, bp. 25 Mch., 1715-16.—*Mix.*
10. Lydia, b. 17 Mch., 1716-17.
11. James (or Janna), b. 16 Sept., 1719.
12. Mindwell, b. 19 Feb., 1723-4.

FAM. 6. MICHAEL, Jr.,² (*Thos.*,² *Michael*,¹), b. 1680; m. Mary (dau. Sgt. Benjamin) **Gilbert,** 27 Jan., 1703-4.

Michael Griswold 2nd died 20 April, 1731—Invt. £919-06-04, taken 11 May, 1731, by Michael Griswold, Nathaniel Burnham and Jacob Griswold. Will dated 2 Apl., 1731. I give to my son Benjamin Griswold my Homested with buildings, reserving the use of one-half to my wife during her natural life and the Black-smith Shop and tools thereof with the ground sd. shop covers reserved for my son Michael Griswold so long as he shall uphold and work in sd. shop and no longer. My brother Samuel Griswold and Father Thomas Griswold, my dau. Prudence Griswold I give to my son William ½ my lot at Newington, and the other half to my son Michael Griswold. I give to my son Phineas Griswold 1½ acres of land I bought of my brother Samuel which was part of my father's home-lot, who is to have ⅓ of the use during life with house & barn, at the de-cease of my father to be divided between my son Phineas & son Ensign Michael Griswold. I give to my d. Prudence to my d. Keziah—wife & son Benjamin to be executors.

MICHAEL GRISWOLD O

Witness Nathaniel Burnham, Michael Griswold, Nathaniel Griswold. Proven 4 May, 1731.

Children (Weth. Rec. & Mix MSS.):

1. Benjamin, b. 10 Apl., 1705; d. ————.
2. Prudence, b. 22 Jan., 1706-7.
3. William, b. 22, bp. 26 Sept., 1708. **FAM. 13.**
4. Michael, b. 18 Feb., 1710-11; m. Sarah **Howard,** 23 May, 1746
5. Phinehas, b. 26 Dec., 1714. The *Hurlbut Geneal.* gives the fam. of a *Phinehas,* for which we can find no place unless here; yet dates of his birth and marr. would make him 50 yrs. old at time of latter event, not imposs., but improb. He m. 23 Aug., 1764, Lois (dau. Amos & Hannah) **Hurlbut,** b. Weth., 21 May, 1744; after the birth of a number of ch.,

they rem. to Winchester, Ct., and are there bu. *Children:*
  i. Phineas, bp. 28 July, 1765.
  ii. Lois, bp. Jan. or Feb., 1769.—*W. C. R.*
  iii. Benjamin.
  iv. Matthew.
  v. Amos.
  vi. Martha, bp. 19 June, 1774.—*W. C. R.*
  (*Born in Winchester*):
  vii. Polly, b. 1 Feb., 1778.
  viii. Bena, b. 26 Dec., 1779.
  ix. Sabia, b. 26 Aug., 1781.
6. Kezia, b. 10, bp. 20 Dec., 1717.

FAM. 7. JOHN,³ (*Jacob*,² *Michael*,¹), b. 1686; m. 18 Jan., 1710-11 (*Weth. Rec.*) Mabel (dau. Daniel and sister of Rev. Daniel) **Boardman,** and rem. to New Milford, Ct., abt. 1717 (Orcutt's Hist. *New Milford,* 708). He d. at N. M. (be-fore his father) 24 Dec., 1719; he owned the first mill erected in N. M. Orcutt's Hist. gives the rec. of an agreement with the Town Committee of N. M. in ref-erence to this mill. *Orcutt* also says (p. 42) that John G. came fm. Weth. in 1716, a relative of Jacob and Daniel G. who preceded him thither. He built his mill in what is now Lanesville, accord'g to agreement, prob. 1717; but had not rec'd payment, when by some sudden illness he d. leaving a fam. of yg. ch., one being bu. after his decease. See pp. 66-67 Orcutt's *New Milford.*

*Children (those thus starred * are fm. Weth. Rec.):*

1. Jeremiah,* b. 16 Nov., 1713. **FAM. 14.**
2. John, b. 1 Mch., 1720. **FAM. 15.**
3. Hannah,* b. 33 (*Sic.*) Nov., 1711; bp. 25 Nov., 1711.—*Mix.*
4. Thankful, b. 1715; m. Thos. **Starr;** rem.

to Salisbury, Ct.
5. Mabel, b. and bp. 1718.
6. John, b. 1 Mch., 1720; m. Phebe **Collins;** had 6 sons.

FAM. 8. Maj. JOSIAH,[3] (Jacob,[2] Michael,[1]), b. 1700-1, major of cavalry in several French and Ind. War Campaigns; res. in and prob. blt. the house in Griswoldville known as "Broadbent House;" m. Mabel (dau. Josiah and Mabel Wright) Belden, 17 Aug., 1727; she b. 9 Feb., 1707-8, d. 13 Dec., 1789, ae. 83 (Weth. Ins.) Maj. J. d. 24 May, 1769, in 69th yr.—Weth. Ins.

Children (Weth. Rec. & Fam. Rec. found by S. W. A. in possess. of J. Wells Griswold of Weth. Those starred thus * not on Town Rec.):

1. Josiah, b. 30 (bp. 10—Mix MS.) June, 1728. FAM. 16.
2. Mabel, b. 6 (bp. 10—Mix) May, 1730; d. 18 (Fam. Rec., but 13, Weth. Ins.) Dec., 1736.
3. John, b. (and bp.—Mix) 30 Apl., 1732; m. Abigail Stanley, 15 Mch., 1756; she d. 6 June, 1795, in 66 yr.; he d. 19 Nov., 1763. Issue:
   i. Abigail, b. 21 June, 1761.
4. Jacob, b. 20 (bp. 23—Mix MS.) June, 1734; m. 17 Nov., 1755, Susannah Bowen; he d. 2 Sept., 1768.—Fam. Rec. and W. C. R. FAM. 17.
5. Ozias, b. 16 Jan., 1735-6. FAM. 18.
6. Justus, b. 26 Dec., 1737; d. 18 Aug., 1760.

—Fam. Rec. and Weth. Ins.
7. Mabel, b. 13 (bp. 15—L. Rec.) June, 1740.
8. Mary, b. 5 Nov., 1741; m. John Robbins, a man of wealth; she d. 24 Jan., 1772.— Fam. Rec.
9. Rebecca,* b. 19 Feb., 1742-3; d. same day.
10. Rebecca,* b. 7 Sept., 1744; m. 2 Jan., 1765, Col. Noadiah Hooker, of Farmington.†
11. Daniel, b. 28 Dec., 1746. FAM. 19.
12. Sarah,* b. 26 May (bp. betw. 29 and17 July—L. Rec.), 1748; she d. 27 Mch., 1754, in 6th yr.—Weth. Ins.
13. Chloe, bp. 10 June, 1750.
14. Lydia,* b. 13 (bp. 20) May, 1753.

FAM. 9. Lieut. EBENEZER,[3] (Jacob,[2] Michael,[1]), b. 171—; m. 13 Dec., 1734, Deborah (dau. Henry) Grimes; who d. 7 June, 1765, in 50th yr.—Weth. Ins. He d. 7 Dec., 1772, in 71st yr.—Weth. Ins.

Children (Weth. Rec.):

1. Elias, b. 22 Feb., 1734-5; d. 18 May, 1741. —Weth. Ins.
2. Zebiel, b. 22 June, 1738; m. (1) Lucy ———, who "d. in travail," 16 Oct., 1770, ae. 28, and he prob. m. again—as W. C. R. give bp. of two of his daus.. Lucy, bp. 2 Oct., 1774; Esther, bp. 9 Feb., 1777; and L. C. R. gives Ebenezer (Grimes), bp. 22 July, 1781.
3. Elizur, b. 10 Aug., 1742; d. 9 Nov., 1744.— Weth. Ins. & Rec.
4. Timothy, b. 24, bp. 28 Oct., 1744. FAM. 20.

5. Anne, b. 10 Oct., 1746.
6. Elias, b. 6, bp. 7 Oct., 1750; m. Rhoda (dau. Joseph) Flower, 8 Dec., 1773. Issue:
   i. Elias, b. 4 June, 1775.
7. Elizur, b. 30 Oct., bp. 4 Nov., 1753; m. Tryphena Burge, who was b. 18 July, 1757; his s. Chester, m. his cousin Rhoda, dau. of his father's bro. Elias.—(Letter of B. H. G., Baltimore, Md., a gd-s. of Chester, 1890.)
8. Sarah, b. and bp. 7 May, 1758.

FAM. 10. Capt. CALEB,[3] (Michael,[2] Michael,[1]), b. 1706; m. Abigail Bunce, 30 July, 1730; he d. 20 Dec., 1754, in 49th yr.—Weth. Ins.

Children (Weth. Ins.):

1. Caleb, b. 25 and bp. 31 Oct., 1731 (Mix MS.); d. 23 Sept., 1762.—Weth. Ins.
2. Jonathan, b. 30 Aug., bp. 2 Sept., 1733 (Mix MS.); d. 28 Nov., 1756 in 24th yr.— Weth. Ins.
3. William, b. 14 Jan., 1735-6. FAM. 21.
4. Timothy, b. 19 Mch., 1737-8; d. 27 June,

1791, ae. 53.—W. C. R.
5. Abigail, b. 8 Nov., 1740.
6. Michael, b. 28 Oct., 1742; d. 27 Apl., 1745 in 4th yr.—Weth. Ins.
7. Prudence, b. 22, bp. 29 July, 1744.
8. Elizabeth, b. 12, bp. 22 June, 1746.
9. Sarah, b. 11, bp. 21 May, 1749.

FAM. 11. Capt. ELISHA,[3] (Michael,[2] Michael,[1]), b. ————; m. Abigail (dau. Leonard dec'd) Dix, 29 May, 1735; was commis. 1756, Lieut. in Troop of horse, 6th Reg.; prom. Capt. 1761, Gen. Court; he d. 15 Apl., 1780—W. C. R.; wid. d. ae. 95, bu. 13 Feb., 1809.

† In order to prevent the cost of Administration upon Maj. Josiah's estates, the following persons, who style themselves the "natural heirs of Mrs. Mabel Griswold, late of Weth., dec'd, sign an agreement to leave the final adjustment of the est. to Messrs. Chester Welles and Appleton Robbins. This doc. dated 16 Mch., 1790, is signed by

John Robbins.
Noadiah Hooker & Wife.
Charles Z. Bulkeley.
Edward Bulkeley (son of Chas.).
Ozias Griswold.
Josiah & Catharine Griswold.
Jerusha [Janette (?)] Griswold.
Hosea Bulkely.

Jerusha Griswold.
Martha Griswold.
Charles Bulkley, Jr.
Joseph Riley.
Abigail Griswold.
Cunlot Griswold.
Amasa Adams, Jr.

Children (Weth. Rec.) :

1. Abigail, b. 26 Mch., 1736.
2. Lois, b. 2 June, 1739; d. 21 Sept., 1741, ae. 2 yrs. 3 mos.—*Weth. Ins.*
3. Lois, b. 8 June, bp. before 1 Sept., 1745.
4. Simeon, b. 9 Aug., 1742. FAM. 22.

5. Rhoda, b. 4 June, 1748; d. 22 Sept., 1752.
6. Elisha, b. 11, bp. 17 June, 1753; d. ae. 70; bu. 8 Feb., 1821.—*W. C. R.*
7. Rhoda, b. 4 June, 1757; m. Capt. Francis **Bulkeley**; d. 6 Mch., 1795 in 38th **yr.**

FAM. 12. NATHANIEL,[3] (*Michael*,[2] *Michael*,[1]), b. ————; m. Mabel **Griswold,** 27 Jan., 1737-8.

Children (Weth. Rec.) :

1. Frederic, b. 3 July, 1739; m. 11 Sept., 1775, Mary **Dickinson**, both of W.—*W. C. R.* Issue:

i. Molly, b. 21 Dec., 1776, bp. 29 June, 1777.—*W. C. R.*
2. Felix, b. 10, bp. 17 Aug., 1746.

FAM. 13. Capt. WILLIAM,[4] (*Michael*,[3] *Thos.*,[2] *Michael*,[1]), b. 1708; m. to Martha **Tapley**, in the ch. of St. Mary Magdalen, London, Eng., 17 Nov., 1761, by Termery Mathews—*Weth. Rec.;* he d. 7 Sept., 1806, in 72d yr.—*Weth. Ins.;* she d. 8 Sept., 1789, ae. 47. *Weth. Ins.*

Children (Weth. Rec.) :

1. Edward, b. 15 June, 1762.
2. Benjamin James, b. 6 May, 1769; d. 19 Aug., 1793, on way home from W. I., ae. 24.—*Weth. Ins.*

3. Martha, b. 3 June, 1771.
4. Charlotte, b. 20. bp. 29 (*S. C. R.*) Aug., 1774; m. Capt. William **Webb.**
5. Sarah, bp. 10 Oct., 1779.—*S. C. R.*

FAM. 14. JEREMIAH,[4] (*John*,[3] *Jacob*,[2] *Michael*,[1]), b. 1713; m. Hannah ————; res. New Milford, Ct.

Children (Orcutt's Hist. New Milford, Ct.) :

1. Seth, b. 30 May, 1740.
2. Asahel, b. 23 Jan., 1743-4.

3. Mabel, b. 5 Mch., 1746.

FAM. 15. JOHN,[4] (*John*,[3] *Jacob*,[2] *Michael*,[1]), b. 1720; m. 29 Nov., 1750 Phebe **Collins;** res. New Milford, Ct.

Children (Orcutt's Hist. New Milford, Ct.) :

1. John, b. 15 Sept., 1751.
2. Nathan, b. 5 Mch., 1756.
3. Adonijah, b. 11 June, 1759.

4. David, b. 29 July, 1761.
5. Asaph, b. 17 Oct., 1766.
6. Doctor, b. 30 Nov., 1770.

FAM. 16. Lieut. JOSIAH,[4] (*Maj. Josiah*,[3] *Jacob*,[2] *Michael*,[1]), b. 1728; m. (1) 21 May, 1750 (*W. C. R.*) Deborah **Williams**, who d. 14 Aug., 1763, in 29th yr.; he m. (2) Mercy **Miller,** 7 Oct., 1764, who d. 3 Nov., 1819, in 82d yr.—*Weth. Ins.* This is prob. the J. G. mentioned in *W. Ch. Rec.*—thus: ¡22 June, 1766, "Josiah Griswold made confession for *breaking the Sixth Commandment in a certain degree*, by shaking Elnathan Boardman," etc. It must have been somewhat by a stretch of the imagination that the case, for disciplinary consideration by the ch. could have been brought within the limits of the commandment forbids us to kill. Still, it is to the credit of Josiah's conscience that he made confession. He was a clothier and d. 20 Oct., 1802.

Children (Weth. Rec. & Fam. Rec.) :

1. Chloe, b. 30 Jan., 1750 (*sic*) ; prob. 1750-1.
2. Solomon, b. 27 Aug., 1751. FAM. 23.
3. Constant, b. 29 Mch., 1753 ; m. 27 Dec., 1780, Rebecca **Boardman.** FAM. 24.

(*By second marr.*) :
4. Nancy, b. 10, bp. 17 Nov., 1765 ; d. 1 Oct., 1781 in 16th yr.—*S. C. R.*
5. Deborah, b. 18 Mch., bp. 10 Apl., 1768.— *S. C. R.*

FAM. 17. JACOB,[4] (*Maj. Josiah*,[3] *Josiah*,[2] *Michael*,[1]), b. 1734; m. (1) 17 Nov., 1755, Susannah **Bowen;** m. (2) 25 Dec., 1785, Rachel **Warner** (*S. C. R.*), who d. 22 Nov., 1789.

Children (Weth. Rec. by second marriage):

1. Jacob, bp. 12 Nov., 1786 (*S. C. R.*); d. 2 Feb., 1848; prob. the J. who m. 12 Nov., 1807, Lydia **Wright** (*S. C. R.*); had (*a*) a ch. who d. 27 Sept., 1811; (*b*) Alonzo, bp. 5 June, 1814; (*c*) **Alfred**, bp. 8 Sept., 1816; (*d*) Sally, bp. 27 Oct., 1818; (*e*) Wyllys Williams, bp. 14 Nov., 1821; (*f*) Lydia
Wright, bp. 15 July, 1823; (*g*) **Cornelia**, bp. 2 July, 1826; (*h*) Sarah Wilkinson, bp. 3 July, 1829; (*i*) Eliza Ann, bp. 4 Oct., 1831; (*j*) Jennie, bp. 4 July, 1834; (*k*) Martha, bp. 2 Sept., 1836.
2. Wait, b. 9 Feb., bp. 6 Apl., 1788.
3. Rachel Warner, bp. 20 Oct., 1811.

FAM. 18. OZIAS,[4] (*Maj. Josiah,[3] Jacob,[2] Michael,[1]*), b. 1735; m. 11 Dec., 1766, "Anner" (*sic.* both on Records and gravestone) dau. of Thomas & Mary *Francis* **Stanley**, of Stanley Quarter, New Britain; she d. 26 July, 1825, ae. 83.—*W. Ins.* He d. 4 Dec., 1815, ae. 86 yrs., 3 mos.—*W. Ins. & W. C. R.*

Children (Weth. Rec. & W. C. R.):

1. Anner, b. and bp. 12 Sept., 1762; m. Samuel **Welles**; she d. 15 Sept., 1828, ae. 65.
2. Mary, b. 18 Mch., bp. 5 or 1 Apl., 1764; m. Elisha **Welles**; she d. 1834, ae. 70.
3. Lucy, b. 20, bp. 21 Apl., 1765; d. 17 Aug. or Oct., 1774.
4. John, b. 29 Nov., 1766; d. 16 (or 19) Sept., 1775.
5. Justus, b. 26 Apl., 1768. FAM. 25.
6. Samuel, b. 26 Jan., bp. in Feb., 1770; m. Eunice **Collins**; he d. Nov., 1833, ae. 63 yrs. 10 mos.
7. Lydia, b. 8 (6 *Fam. Bible*) Oct., 1771; m. John **Woodbridge**; she d. 1826.
8. Ozias, b. 7, bp. 8 Aug., 1773.
9. Thomas, b. 11, bp. 16 July, 1775. FAM. 25.
10. Lucy, b. 17 or 27 (11 *Fam. Bible*) Apl., 1777; m. Ephraim **Willard**.
11. John, b. 9, bp. 25 Apl., 1779; m. (1) 26 Jan., 1803 (*W. C. R.*) Esther **Welles**, who d. 11 July, 1813 in 33d yr.—*W. Ins.*; m. (2) Harriet **Welles**; he d. 26 Feb., 1826, ae. 55.—*S. W. A.*
12. Sarah, b. 20, bp. 25 (*sic*) Mch., 1781; d. 9 July, 1800.
13. James, b. 21, bp. 24 Aug., 1784. FAM. 26.
14. Mabel, b. 26 Feb., bp. 15 Mch., 1786; d. 31 May, 1804, ae. 19.—*W. C. R.*
15. Nancy Clark, b. 10, bp. 14 Sept., 1788; m. George **Morgan**.

FAM. 19. DANIEL,[4] (*Maj. Josiah,[3] Jacob,[2] Michael,[1]*), b. 1746; m. 23 Nov., 1769, Jerusha **Gibbs**—*S. C. R.*; he d. 26 Jan., 1786, in 40th yr.—*W. C. R.*; wid. bu. 25 Feb., 1804, ae. 63.

Children (Weth. Rec.):

1. Josiah, b. 6 Sept., 1771; d. 16 Sept., 1802, in 32d yr.
2. Daniel, bp. 15 Aug., 1773.—*S. C. R.*
3. Daniel, b. 29 Oct., bp. 5 Nov., 1775 (*W. C. R.*); d. 31 Aug., 1783.
4. Jacob, b. 4, bp. 11 Jan., 1778 (*W. C. R.*); d. 31 Aug., 1783.
5. George, b. 25, bp. 29 Apl., 1781; prob. the Geo. who m. Eunice **Williams**, 18 Apl., 1802.—*W. C. R.*; whose ch., ae. 2, d. July, 1827; and dau. Hannah, bp. 1 Jan., 1828; and dau. Clarissa d. June, 1822, ae. 20.—*W. C. R.*

FAM. 20. TIMOTHY,[5] (*Ebenezer,[4] Elias,[3] Jacob,[2] Michael,[1]*), b. 1744, m. 17 Jan., 1765, Hannah **Tryon** (*W. C. R.*), who d. 4 Apl., 1815, ae. 74.—*W. Ins.* He d. 27 June, 1791, ae. 53.—*W. C. R.*

Children (Weth. & W. C. Rec.):

1. Jonathan, b. 19, bp. 25 May, 1766. FAM. 27.
2. Hannah, b. 21, bp. 26 June, 1768; d. 24 Oct., 1772.
3. Timothy, b. 11 June, bp. 1 July, 1770; d. inf.—tho' he may have been the T. who d. N. Y. 22 July, 1795.—*W. C. R.*
4. Hannah, b. 24 Oct., 1772.
5. Moses, b. 2 Aug., bp. 1 Oct., 1775.—*W. C. R.* FAM. 28.
6. George, b. 12 Apl., bp. 29 June, 1777; d. 18 Dec., 1801, ae. 25.—*Weth. Ins.*
7. Abigail, b. 24 Jan., bp. 27 June, 1779; d. 24 Nov., 1805, ae. 27.—*Weth. Ins.*
8. Hannah, b. 24 Nov., 1782, bp. 4 May, 1783.

FAM. 21. Capt. WILLIAM,[4] (*Capt. Caleb,[3] Michael,[2] Michael,[1]*), b. 1736; m. 18 Oct., 1759, Elizabeth **McCloud**. He was prob. the Wm. who. d. ae. 41, 14 Nov., 1776.—*W. C. R.* He d. ae. 41, bu. 14 Nov., 1776; she d. 28 Oct., 1771, in 34th yr.—*Weth. Ins.*

Children (Weth. Rec.):

1. Elizabeth, b. 7 Feb., bp. 20 Apl., 1760.
2. Caleb, b. 25, bp. 28 Nov., 1762. FAM. 29.
3. William, b. 1, bp. 11 May, 1766; prob. the Wm. who m. Lucy **Deming**, 10 Apl., 1788;
and prob. the Wm. who d. ae. 14, at Charleston, S. C., Oct., 1802, was their son.
4. James, b. 9, bp. 13 Nov., 1768.

FAM. 22. SIMEON,[4] (*Elisha,*[3] *Michael,*[2] *Michael,*[1]), b. 1742; m. 4 May, 1769 (*W. C. R.*) Mary Ann **Ayrault,** who d. 14 Sept., 1824, ae. 79. He d. 21 Nov., 1785, ae. 44.—*W. C. R.*

Children (*Weth. Rec. & W. C. R.*) :

1. Lois, b. 27 Apl., 1771, bp. 13 Nov., 1774 ; d. 14 Sept., 1840.
2. Simeon, b. 13 (*Fam. Rec.*) Mch., 1773, bp. 13 Nov., 1774. FAM. 30.
2. George, b. 1 (*Fam. Rec.* 5) Apl., 1775, bp. 28 Apl., 1776 ; d. unm. 22 Jan., 1851 (more prob. 18 Dec., 1801, ae. 25.— *W. C. R.*
3. Nabbe (Abigail), b. 5 May, bp. 5 (*W.*

C. R. 6) July, 1777 ; d. 26 Jan., 1802.— *W. C. R.*
4. Wealthy, b. 14 Aug., bp. 31 Oct., 1779 ; m. James **Hurlbut,** 1804. *Issue:*
　i. Henry (Hurlbut), b. 1804.
　ii. Jane Ann (Hurlbut), b. 1806.
　iii. Abigail (Hurlbut), b. 1808.
5. Polly, b. 9 Aug., 1783 ; d. 26 May, 1794.— *Fam. Rec.*

FAM. 23. SOLOMON,[5] (*Josiah,*[4] *Maj. Josiah,*[3] *Jacob,*[2] *Michael,*[1]), b. 1751; m. 2 Feb., 1775, Sarah **Deming**—*S. C. R.;* he d. 17 Aug., 1777.—*Weth. Ins.*

Children (*Weth. Rec.*) :

1. Josiah, b. 21 Nov., 1775, bp. 7 Jan., 1776.— *S. C. R.* FAM. 31.
2. Solomon (acc. to *S. W. A.*) ; prob. the

Sol. who d .2 Jan., 1830, in 49th yr.
3. Sarah, b. 4 Nov., 1777.

FAM. 24. CONSTANT,[5] (*Josiah,*[4] *Maj. Josiah,*[3] *Jacob,*[2] *Michael,*[1]), b. 1753, at Ry-H.; m. at Cromwell, Ct., 27 Dec., 1780, Rebecca (dau. John) **Boardman,** of Ry-H., who d. 20 Mch., 1825, ae. 65.—*Weth. Ins.* He d. 11 Apl., 1839, ae. 87.—*S. C. R.*

Children (*Boardman Genealogy & S. C. R.*) :

1. Solomon, b. 24 Oct., 1781 (*Weth. Rec.*), bp. 26 May, 1782.—*S. C. R.*
2. Josiah, bp. 24 Oct., 1790.
3. Sylvester, bp. 11 Dec., 1791.
4. Deborah, bp. 6 July, 1794 ; m. Wm. **Olds;** res. in Ind. and Ky.
5. Frederic, bp. 14 May, 1797.
6. Nancy, bp. 24 June, 1787 ; m. Mr. ——

Hugh, of Berlin, Ct.
7. Nabby, m. Mason **Smith;** res. in **Phila.,** Pa.
8. Amanda, m. Joseph **Hubbard;** res. Cromwell, Ct.
9. Ashbel. (*S. C. R.* gives an Ashbel Boardman bp. 10 Oct., 1784, "s. of Constant.")

FAM. 25. JUSTUS,[5] (*Ozias,*[4] *Maj. Josiah,*[3] *Jacob,*[2] *Michael,*[1]), b. 1768; m. 29 Dec., 1791, Prudence **Wells;** he d. 1 Aug., (one rec. says 31 July) 1803, ae. 35—*W. C. R.;* she d. 22 Nov., 1739, ae. 73.—*Weth. Ins.*

Children (*Weth. Rec. & W. C. R.*) ;

1. Inf. bu. 17 Oct., 1792.
2. Inf., d. 6 Jan., 1793.—*W. C. R.*
3. Justus, b. 5 Nov., 1793, bp. 23 Nov., 1794.

4. Mary, b. 15 Nov., 1795.
5. Abigail, b. 23 Aug., 1798, bp. 13 Jan., 1799.

FAM. 26. THOMAS,[5] (*Ozias,*[4] *Maj. Josiah,*[3] *Jacob,*[2] *Michael,*[1]), m. (1) 22 July, 1799, Mary (dau. Elisha Jr., & Mary *Welles*) **Wolcott;** m. (2) Rhoda **Wright,** he d. 24 Feb., 1850; she d. 4 June, 1847.

Children (*W. C. R.*) :

1. Thomas, b. 7 Dec., 1899 ; m. Jerusha **Wells,** 4 May, 1830 ; he bu. 13 Oct., 1878, ae. 79. FAM. 2.
2. Franklin Wolcott, b. 27 Dec., 1801 ; d. 27 Jan., 1814, ae. 13.
3. Stanley, bp. 22 Jan., 1804.
4. Mary Welles, b. 11 Aug., 1806 ; m. Welles

Adams.
5. Mabel Belden, b. 20 Nov., 1810, bp. 23 June, d. 19 Sept., 1811.
6. Mabel Belden, bp. 1 Nov., 1812 ; m. Geo. **Stillman.**
7. Franklin Wolcott, b. 28 Mch., 1815, bp. 28 Mch., 1816 ; d. 21 Sept., 1886.

FAM. 27. JONATHAN,[6] (*Timothy,*[5] *Ebenezer,*[4] *Elias,*[3] *Jacob,*[2] *Michael,*[1]), b. 1766; m. (1) Huldah **Francis,** 7 Oct., 1790, who, with inf. d. 25 Sept., 1797, in 29th yr. —*W. C. R.;* m. (2) 31 Mch., 1799, Melicent **Davis** (*Weth. Rec.* say Melicent *Francis*), who d. 20 Mch., 1816, ae. 43.—*Weth. Ins.*

Children (Weth. Rec.):

1. Nancy, b. 16 July, 1791.
2. Mary, b. 22 Dec., 1793.
3. Timothy, b. 1 June, 1795 ; m. 19 Apl., 1821, Laura **Standish**, who d. 29 June, 1838, ae. 42 ; he d. 27 Mch., 1837, ae. 42.—*Weth. Ins. Weth. C. Rec.* say he also m. Emeline **Hill**, 13 Nov., 1821. *Issue:*
   i. Jane Eliza, b. 30 May, 1822.
   ii. Timothy, bp. 22 June, 1823.—*W. C. R.*

iii. John Miles Standish, b. 31 Aug., 1826.
iv. Huldah Isabella, b. 14 Apl., 1828.
(By second marriage):
4. Charles, b. 24 May, 1800.
5. Huldah, b. 27 Aug., 1802.
6. Melicent, b. 4 Mch., 1805 ; d. 8 Mch., 1806.
7. Melicent, b. 27 Sept., 1807.
8. Harvey, b. 18 Apl., 1810.

FAM. 28. MOSES,[6] (*Timothy,[5] Ebenezer,[4] Elias,[3] Jacob,[2] Michael,[1]*), b. 1755; m. Martha **Dix**. He d. apparently, in 1795, as the ch. whose bp. is given below, are ment. as ch. of "wid. of Moses."

Children (W. C. R.):

1. Sylvester, ⎱ bp. 27 Dec., 1795.
2. Martha, ⎰

(Poss. a s. Moses—of whose birth and bp. we have no record.)

FAM. 29. Capt. CALEB,[5] (*Capt. William,[4] Capt. Caleb,[3] Michael,[2] Michael,[1]*), b. 1762; m. 18 Oct., 1787, Lucy **Francis**, who d. Aug., 1849, ae. 84—*Weth. Ins.;* he d. June, 1837, ae. 74.—*Weth. Ins.*

Children (Weth. Rec.):

1. Elizabeth, b. 8 Mch., 1788 ; d. 21 Apl., 1813, ae. 25.—*Weth. Ins.*
2. Sally, b. 27 June, 1790.
3. Lucy, b. 3 Sept., 1792 ; d. 22 June, 1856, ae. 62.—*Weth. Ins.*
4. Francis (Capt.), b. 1 Apl., 1795. FAM. 32.
5. Prudence, b. 25 Aug., 1797.

6. Caleb, b. 7 Nov., 1799. FAM. 33.
7. Sylvester, b. 22 Apl., 1802.
8. William, b. 6 Sept., 1804 ; poss. the Wm. who m. 16 Mch., 1834, Julia Ann **Gibbs.**—*S. C. R.*
9. Walter, b. 6 Feb., 1807 ; d. 18 Jan., 1817, ae. 10.—*Weth. Ins.*

FAM. 30. SIMEON,[5] (*Simeon,[4] Elisha,[3] Michael,[2] Michael,[1]*), b. 1772; m. (1) 27 Oct., 1799, Joanna **Riley**, who was bp. 29 Mch., 1807 (*W. C. R.*) and d. 1 July, 1808, ae. 34; m. (2) 26 Mch., 1812, Sarah **Kentfield** (or Kenfield), of E. Htfd. (*W. C. R.*), who d. 8 May, 1845, ae. 64. He d. 9 Jan., 1858, ae. 86.

Children (Fam. Rec.):

1. Sylvester R., b. 22 June, 1800 ; prob. the S. Riley bp. 4 and d. 9 Dec., 1806.—*W. C. R.*
2. Mehitable, b. 9 Aug., 1805 ; m. Wm. **Coleman**. *Issue:*
   i. Martha (Coleman), m. Wm. **DeBlois**, of N. Y. ; has (a) Edward (DeBlois) ; (b) Ar'hur (DeBlois) ; (c) Hetty (DeBlois) who m. Louis N. **Crane**, of Fishkill-on-the-Hudson, N. Y.
   ii. Horace (Coleman), d. unm., ae. 24.
   iii. Frances (Coleman), m. Arthur **Baker**, of Htfd.
3. Mary Ann, b. 10 Feb., 1803 ; m. Capt. Elisha **Latimer**, of Htfd. *Issue:*
   i. Laura (Latimer), m. Geo. **Knowles**, of Htfd.
   ii. Sarah (Latimer), m. (1) Kingsbury

Bidwell; m. (2) S. B. **Grosvenor**, of Htfd. ; has *Grace*, who m. a **Woodis**, of Worcester, Mass., and *Mary*.
   iii. Charles (Latimer), m. (1) Lucy **Chapman**, and had dau. *Lucy*; he m. (2) a **Dustin**, of Mich.
   iv. George (Latimer), m. a **Neff**, of Ry-H. ; he d. ae. 28, s. p.
4. Diantha, b. 16 Oct., 1807 ; m. Osmond **Harrison**, of Weth., and d. 1897; he d. 1895, ae. 96, s. p.
(By second marriage):
5. Julia, b. 4 Sept., 1817 ; d. unm. 4 Mch., 1845.
6. Charles Frederick, b. 13 Oct., 1821 ; d. unm.
7. Henry, b. 25 Jan., 1825 ; d. unm. 29 Sept., 1854, ae. 28.—*W. Ins.*

FAM. 31. JOSIAH,[6] (*Solomon,[5] Josiah,[4] Maj. Josiah,[3] Jacob,[2] Michael,[1]*), b. 1775; res. at Stepney; m. 14 Jan., 1798, Charlotte **Adams**; he d. at Step. 19 Dec., 1832; she d. 3 Sept., 1847.

Children:

1. Charlotte (Griswold), b. 9 July, 1799 ; m. 2 June, Horace **Blinn**.
2. Sarah Deming (Griswold), b. 11 Feb., 1801 ; m. 3 Sept., 1823, Chester **Wilcox**; she d. 15 Jan., 1852.
3. Josiah (Griswold), b. 3 Dec., 1802 ; m. Eliza **Cumings**; d. 3 Dec., 1841.
4. Solomon (Griswold), b. 2 Jan., 1805 ; m. 11 Nov., 1827, Elizabeth W. **Arnold**; he d. 23 Aug., 1853.
5. Melissa (Griswold), b. 9 Jan., 1807 ; m. 10 Mch., 1831, Walter **Warner**; d. 1898.

6. Mercy Miller (Griswold), b. 2 Mch., 1809 ; m. 26 Nov., 1829, Russel **Adams**; she d. 30 Aug., 1865.
7. William (Griswold), b. 12 Apl., 1811 ; m. Julia A. **Gibbs**; d. 14 Aug., 1880.
8. Martha (Griswold), b. 2 Apl., 1813 ; d. 25 Jan., 1833.
9. Lester (Griswold), b. 15 July, 1815 ; d. 3 Feb., 1816.
10. Mary (Griswold), b. 16 Mch., 1817 ; m. James **Reilly**, 24 Oct., 1847.

FAM. 32. Capt. FRANCIS,⁶ (*Capt. Caleb,⁵ Capt. William,⁴ Capt. Caleb,³ Michael,²
Michael,¹*), b. 1795; m. 26 May, 1825, Sarah P. **Deming**, (*S. W. A.*); he d.
12 May, 1851, ae. 56.—*Weth. Ins.*

Children (Weth. Rec.):

1. Walter Augustus, b. 4 Aug., 1826; d. 1
   Aug., 1831.—*W. C. R.* and *Weth. Ins.*
2. Francis Marion, b. 23 Nov., 1828; d. 25
   Aug., 1864, ae. 35.—*Weth. Ins.*
3. Sarah Augusta, b. 27 July, 1831; d. 25
   July, 1852, ae. 21.—*Weth. Ins.*
4. Albert Deming, b. 29 July, 1834; m. Mary
   A. ————; he d. 26 Apl., 1889, ae. 54
   yrs., 9 mos. *Issue:*
   i. Emma L., d. 27 Feb., 1869, ae. 7 yrs.,
      7 mos.
   ii. Albert A., d. 9 Mch., 1876, ae. 3 yrs.,
      8 mos.

5. Louisa Catherine, b. 5 July, 1836.
6. Robert Bruce, b. 20 Mch., 1839; d. 11
   Apl., 1842, ae. 3 yrs.—*Weth. Ins.*
7. Robert Palmer, b. 5 July, 1842.
8. Ella Hand, b. 28 Sept., 1844; d. 20 Dec.,
   1851.—*Weth. Ins.*
9. Martha, d. 2 Apl., 1855, ae. 8 yrs.—*Weth.
   Ins.*
   (There was a W. A., poss. a second W. A.,
   who m. Louisa A. ————, (who d. 17
   Jan., 1871, ae. 51), who had *Alfred W.*, who
   d. 28 Sept., 1876, ae. 2 yrs., 4 mos.—*Weth.
   Ins.*)

FAM. 33. CALEB,⁶ Jr., (*Capt. Caleb,⁵ Capt. Williams,⁴ Capt. Caleb,³ Michael,²
Michael,¹*), b. 1799; m. Mary Robbins (dau. Stephen) **Willard**, 21 Dec., 1830.

Children (Weth. Rec.):

1. Stephen Willard, b. 25 Oct., 1831; d. 28
   Oct., 1838.—*Weth. Ins.*
2. Ellen Maria, b. 8 Oct., 1833; d. 16 May,
   1839.—*Weth. Ins.*
3. Cornelius, b. 17 May, 1835; d. 14 Apl.,

1838.—*Weth. Ins.*
4. Cornelius, b. 11 Apl., 1840.
5. Clarissa Ashley, b. 19 ————, 1841.
6. Eugene Willard, b. 24 Feb., 1844.

FAMILIES UNATTACHED.

In the first volume of *Town Votes of Wethersfield* appears the following entry:
"THOMAS GRISWOLD, junior; his ear marke is a crop on the neare ear, and a
halfpenny on the under side of the fare, the [   ] slit toward the lowar
side." This is dated March 14, 1673. It appears from this that there was a
Thomas Griswold not the son of Michael, nor of Michael's son Thomas, and
whether he was of the same stock is not known. Probably he was related to
George.—*S. W. A.* Possibly he is the Thomas (s. of George) of Windsor, b.
1658, and head of the FAM. 7 of the Windsor Griswolds.—See Stiles' *Hist. &
Geneal. Anc. Windsor, Ct.*, Vol. II, p. 352.

GEORGE, "the sonne of George and of Marget his wife, was born the seventeenth
day of Mch., 1653"—*Weth. Ld. Rec.*, Vol. I. Could this, by mistake of a 5 for
a 3, be the Geo., 2d s. of Mr. Edward Griswold,² (see Stiles' *Anc. Windsor, Ct.*,
II, p. 351), and if so, if b. 1633, he was 71 yrs. old at time of his dth., 1704.

MOSES, who d. 1 Dec., 1829, ae. 53—*W. C. R.*; and who m. Nancy **Robbins**,—both
of 1st Soc'y.; she d. 30 Sept., 1820, ae. 42.—*Weth. Ins.* See also MOSES,
FAM. 28.

Children:

1. Moses, who d. ae. 8 mos; bu. 26 Mch.,
   1806.—*W. C. R.*
2. Chauncey, who d. ae. 19 mos.; bu. 16
   (June ?), 1814.
3. Moses Henry,
4. George Robbins,
   bp. 6 Oct., 1816.—*W. C. R.*

Then there was a MOSES who m. Elizabeth **Basconn**, 5 Nov., 1828; and whom we
cannot properly locate (except his marr.
be a 2d marr. of Moses above, the husband
of Nancy), but who was prob. the father
of *Elizabeth*, bp. 7 Feb., 1830.—*W. C. R.*

SAMUEL, m. Mary (dau. of Sgt. John) **Francis**, 11 Mch., 1707-8.

Children (Weth. Rec., bp. Mix MSS.):

1. Mercy, b. 4 July, bp. 22 Aug., 1708; d.
   17 Feb., 1711-12; marked ill in bp. rec.
2. Samuel, b. 5 bp. 12 Feb., 1709-10.
3. Lucy, bp. 11 Nov., 1711.
4. Jared b. 8, bp. 11 Jan., 1712-13.
5. Lucy, b. 8, bp. 12 Dec., 1714.

6. Jeremiah, b. 12 Aug., 1716.
7. Jeremiah, b. 8, bp. 9 Feb., 1717-18.
8. Moses, b. 2 Nov., 1719.
9. John, b. 23 June, 1721.
10. Mary, b. 23 June, 1723.

Fam. 2. JAMES STANLEY,[6] (*James*,[5] *Ozias*,[4] *Maj. Josiah*,[3] *Jacob*,[2] *Michael*,[1]), b. 1815; m. (1) 1 Sept., 1841, Prudence **Churchill;** m. (2) Lucy S. **Swift,** 16 June, 1858; m. (3) Eunice **Clark,** 26 Apl., 1876.

Children (Fam. Bible):

1. Martha Amelia, b. 9 Jan., 1844; m. 16 Oct., 1872, Frank H. **Belden.** *Issue:*
   i. Prudence G. (Belden), b. 15 May, 1819.
   ii. James A. (Belden), b. 14 Jan., 1883.
2. James Dixon, b. June, 1848. Fam. 5.

Fam. 3. WAIT ROBBINS,[6] (*James*,[5] *Ozias*,[4] *Maj. Josiah*,[3] *Jacob*,[2] *Michael*,[1]), b. 1820; m. (1) Piera L. **Roberts,** 1 Sept., 1846, and who d. 4 Aug., 1848— *S. C. R.;* m. (2) 13 Apl., 1852, Lewey A. **Bierce,** who d. 29 Jan., 1901. He d. 15 July, 1887.

Children (Fam. Bible):

1. Piera Roberts, b. 23 June, 1847.
2. Lucy Robbins, b. 4 Aug., 1848; d. 12 May, 1873.

(By second marriage):
3. Wait R., b. 10 May, 1853; d. 7 Feb., 1878.
4. Peter Pierce, b. 3 Feb., 1855.

Fam. 4. ALBERT CLINTON,[6] (*James*,[5] *Ozias*,[4] *Maj. Josiah*,[3] *Jacob*,[2] *Michael*,[1]), b. 1827; m. 13 Jan., 1853, Caroline Louise **Goodrich.**—*S. C. R.*

Children (Fam. Bible):

1. William Goodrich, b. 4 May, 1854.
2. Clara.
3. May.
4. Samuel.
5. Nellie.

Fam. 5. JAMES DIXON,[7] (*James Stanley*,[6] *James*,[5] *Ozias*,[4] *Maj. Josiah*,[3] *Jacob*,[7] *Michael*,[1]), b. 1840; m. H. Addie **Johnson,** 20 Sept., 1870.

Children:

1. Lillian P., b. 14 May, 1872.
2. Grace M., b. 10 Feb., 1874.
3. James S., b. 13 Mch., 1876.

THOMAS,[5] (*Thomas*,[4] *Ozias*,[3] *Maj. Josiah*,[2] *Michael*,[1]), b. 1784; 4 May, 1830, m. Jerusha (dau. Joseph) **Welles,** who was b. 28 Feb., 1811 and d. 27 Dec., 1898.

Children (Family Recs.):

1. Joseph Welles, b. 29 Aug., 1831; m. Sept., 1857, Mary **Chapman;** he d. Nov., 1894.
2. Thomas Newton, b. 30 Jan., 1834; m. 10 Mch., 1858, Jennette **Butler.**
3. Charles Fayette, b. 22 Mch., 1836; m. 13 Dec., 1865, Caroline **Hale.**
4. Edward Payson, b. 6 Aug., 1838; d. 19 Jan., 1879; m. 13 June, 1865, Mary **Browning.**
5. Mary Ann, b. 3 Mch., 1841; d. 3 Dec., 1875.
6. Robert Southgate, b. 9 Feb., 1849; m. 17 Dec., 1873, Ida **Griswold.**
7. Jerusha Frances, b. 30 May, 1851; d. 16 Aug., 1854.

JAMES,[5] (*Ozias*,[4] *Maj. Josiah*,[3] *Jacob*,[2] *Michael*,[1]), b. 1784, m. 22 Jan., 1812—*S. C. R.*, Lucy **Robbins,** who d. 19 June, 1855, ae. 72.

*Children (Fam. Bible, those mkd. * bp. 17 June, 1821.—W. C. R.):*

1. Lucy Robbins,* b. 9 Nov., 1812; m. Nov., 1835, George **Smith.** *Issue:*
   i. Edgar Robbins (Smith), b. 20 June, 1840.
   ii. Albert Griswold (Smith), b. 22 June, 1844.
   iii. Maria Delphine (Smith), b. 6 June, 1846.
   iv. Harriet Marian (Smith), b. Sept., 1850.
2. James Stanley,* b. 1 May, 1815. Fam. 2.
3. Martha Amelia,* b. 21 Oct., 1817; d. 17 Nov., 1834.—*W. C. R.*
4. Wait Robins,* b. 15 June, 1820. Fam. 3.
5. Henry Morgan,* b. 13 Jan., 1823; d. ae. 24 yrs. and 12 d.
6. Nancy Morgan, b. 2 Dec., 1825; d. 23 Jan., 1857.
7. Albert Clinton, b. 4 Sept., 1827. Fam. 4.

GROSSMAN, NELSON, m. Mary M. **Weldon,** of Glast., Apl., 1833.

GUILD, JEREMIAH'S wife d. ae. 20, 27 Sept., 1801; their inf. d. 1 Sept., 1800, and a s. d. 27 Mch., 1804, ae. 15 mos., prob. the same Jeremiah who m. Martha **May,** 15 Apl., 1802.—W. C. R..

ELIZA W., of Weth. m. Sam'l S. **Gleason,** of Tolland, Mass., Mch., 1817.—W. C. R.

GULL, WILLIAM, appears in Weth. in 1648, when he was chosen cattle-herder for the Town (W. T. V., I, p. 31), also, 1655 (Ibid., p. 45); he m. after 1654, Elizabeth, dau. Lieut. Samuel **Smith,** and wid. of the 2d. Nathaniel **Foote;** rem. to Hadley, 1663, where he was freeman, 1673; d. 1701.—See Chapt. VII, Vol. I.

Children (*b. Weth.*):

1. Mary, m. 21 Nov., 1676, Rob't **Bardwell.**
2. Ann, m. 1680, Jonathan **Root,** and is ment. in her father's will, 1701, as then living. (*b. at Hadley, Mass.*):

3. Esther, b. 21 Nov., 1665; m. Joseph **Gillet;** dec'd before her father, whose will ment. a ch. of hers.
4. Mercy, b. 27 June, 1668; m. Jeremiah **Alvord.**

GUSTIAN, (*Gustin, Justin?*) LYDIA, d. 18 Feb., 1782, in 64th yr.—S. C. R.

HALE, (*Haill, Heall, Hall*). A Glast. fam., mostly desc. fm. SAMUEL **Jr.** and THOMAS, sons of Samuel, Sen. Chapin (*Hist. Glast.,* 167) says, "The Hales are supp. to have come fm. Wales, and are said to have been men of large size and uncommon strength;" in evidence of which he relates a story (similar to what has been related of certain other men in other towns) of *a* Mr. Hale of Glast., who was challenged by the "bully" of another town, to a trial of strength. Mr. Hale, whom he met on the road with a load of cider in barrels, accepted the challenge and then knocking the bung out of a barrel, raised it to his lips, by the chine, and, after taking a drink, offered it to his astonished would-be opponent to do likewise—who thereupon backed out of the appointed test of strength.

SAMUEL HALE, Sen.[*], b. 1615, came early to New Eng.; was a soldier in the Pequot War, received for his services a lot in "the Soldier's Field"; ; owned lot in Htfd. in 1639, on E. side the River; in 1643 res. in Weth., where he was selectman, 1647 (W. T. V.); rem. to Norwalk, where he res. in 1655 and rep. that town in Gen. Ct., 1655-7, and in '60; ret. again to Weth. in 1660, altho' he did not dispose of all his N. pp. until 1669, in which yr. (14 Apl.) he exch. ld. with the Town of Weth. (W. T. V., I, p. 17). He hired the Gov. Welles estate, which appears to have been on the E. side of the Great River; and it is an evidence of the then existing lack of conveniences of domestic life, that the ho. had no staircase, and the 2d floor was reached only by a ladder, See, also, Chapt. VII, Vol I. He m. Mary ——————. He d. Nov., 1693; the Invent. of his estate, taken 13 Nov., 1693, by Eleazur Kimberly and Joseph Hills, gives a val. of abt. £100 personal estate. His will, dated 6 Dec., 1692, mentions that he had already given his sons Samuel, John, Thomas and Ebenezer "considerable portions in lds.;" then proceeds to devise to his s. Samuel "my musket and my two horse brands;" to John, "the best pair of my wearing shoes that I shall leave at

[*] THOMAS (brother of Samuel, the Settler) a soldier in Peq. campaign of 1637; prob. was never res. in Weth., but was in Htfd. first, and later in Norwalk; had sons *Thomas* and *Ebenezer* to whom, in 1672, he gave 56 ac. of ld. in Naubuc; Thomas, Jr., was, in 1688, fence-viewer for East side of River; in 1690, surveyor of highways, and, Feb., 1691, one of the promoters of the new church at Naubuc.

my decease;" to Ebenezer. "all my right and title to 3 score acres of ld. gr. to me by the Gen. Court for my services in the Pequot War, also, my great Bible and all the rest of my books, except one I gave my dau.-in-law Naomi [Kilbourn, wife of his son Thomas]; to his son Thomas he gives a "great iron pot, grindstone, Peas Hook and all my casks and barrels that have been used to hold corn;" to his daus. Marre, Rebecca and Dorothie, each, one of his "great pewter platters and to Rebecca, his "three-pint pewter pot;" to his gd.-sons, John and Thomas, sons of his s. John, "my interest in the tract of ld. lying on the E. side of the Town of Glastonbury, and being six mile in length and five in breadth, to them and their heirs forever;" he also remembers his gd.-child, Abigail Benjamin, dau. of his dau. Dorothie, and appts. sons Samuel and Thomas his executors. Signed, Samuel X Halle.—*Htfd. Co. Prob. Rec.* The wid. Hale d. 19 Jan., 1711-12.—*W. Rec.*

Children (Weth. Rec.) :

1. Martha, b. 2 Oct., 1643.
2. **Samuel**, b. 12 Feb., 1644-5. **FAM. 2.**
3. John, b. 21 Feb., 1646-7. **FAM. 3.**
4. Mary, b. 29 Apl., 1649.
5. Rebecca, b. 29 Oct., 1651.
6. Thomas, b. 1653 (not on *Weth. Rec.*). **FAM. 4.**
7. Bennezer (*sic*), b. 29 July, 1661. See

Chapt. VII, Vol. I, also under *Ebenezer*.
8. Dorothy (acc. to Chapin's *Glast. Centennial*, p. 166), was prob. the "one of the daus. of Samuel Hale, who m. Caleb **Benjamin**, and had dau. Abigail, ment. in her gd.-father's will, and who m. Dr. Ebenezer **Hills**."

FAM. 2.   Lieut. SAMUEL,[2] (*Samuel,*[1]), of Glast., b. 1644-5; m. 20 June, 1670, Ruth (dau. Thomas) **Edwards**, who d. 26 Dec., 1682, ae. abt. 30; he m. (2) 1695, Mary (dau. Samuel & Elizabeth *Hollister*) **Welles**, b. 23 Nov., 1666. He, with his bro. John, were petitioners to Gen. Ct. 1690, for a town incorporation.— See, also, Chapt. VII, Vol. I. He d. 1711: "Here lieth inhumed the body of Mr. Samuel Hale, Esq., of late one of Her Majestie's Justices of the Peace, who d. on the 18th day of Nov[r] Anno Dom., 1711, and in the 67th yr. of his age."— *Weth. Ins.* Wid. Mary Hale d. 18 Feb., 1715.

Samuel Hale, Glastonbury, Invt. £1400-05-05, taken 30 May, 1712 by Samuel Smith, Samuel Welles, Thomas Treat, Richard Smith. Will dated 20 February, 1708-9, I give to Samuel Hale my eldest son, to Jonathan, to David, to Benjamin. I give to Jonathan, Land which I had, have and ought to have for my wive's portion of the estate of her late father Capt. Samuel Welles, reserving the use thereof for my wife during her life. I give to my dau. Mary Hale, to my dau. Ruth Kimberly, to my grand sons Eleazer, Thomas and Samuel Kimberly. I give to my wife Mary Hale and make her residuary legatee.

SAMUEL HALE, Sen. (Seal.)

Witness Caleb Stanley, Thomas Bunce, Jr. Another Proviso is added 18 March, 1709-10. Witnessed, Thomas Hooker, Caleb Stanley, Jr. Signed, sealed, proven, 19 December, 1711.

Children (Weth. Rec. & Chapin's Glast. Cent.) :

1. Ruth, b. 14 Jan., 1670; d. 7 May, 1671.
2. Samuel, b. 14, d. 15 June, 1673-4.
3. Samuel, b. 13 June, 1675; m. John **Day**, of Colchester.—See Chapin's elaborate note on this marr., *Glast. Centen.*, 166-7, *note*.
4. Samuel (*Weth. Town Rec.*), b. 17 July, 1677.
5. Ruth, b. 1 Dec., 1681; m. Thomas (s. of Hon. Eleazer) **Kimberly**. He d. 29 Jan., 1730, ae. 48; she d. 14 May, 1737, ae. 55. (*By second marriage*) :
6. Jonathan (Capt.), b. 21 Aug., 1696; he m. (1) 28 Nov., 1717, Sarah (dau. Dea. Benj.) **Talcott**, who d. 15 Jan., 1743, in 44th yr.; he m. (2) Hannah ————, who d. 26 May, 1749, in 54th yr.; he prob. m. (3) Mrs. Mary ————, "former wife of Mr. Josiah **Hollister**, Jr., late

wife of Jonathan **Hale**, Esq.," who d. 18 Jan., 1780, in 82d yr.—*Weth. (Gl.) Ins.* Esq. Jonathan d. 1772. "Here lies Interred the Remains of Jonathan Hale, Esq., who having served his Generation in Several Offices of Trust with Faithfulness, fell asleep, July 2d, A. D. 1772, in the 76th year of his Age."—*Weth. (Gl.) Ins.* His s. *Elizur*, b. Glast., 15 Jan., 1724-5, grad. Y. C., 1742; studied med. and surgery and sett. (1746) in practice in Glast. He was an excellent phys. of dignified, though rough exterior, witty and sarcastic, but benevolent and very useful; he abounded in kind deeds, was generous in the use of his ppy. and advice to the needy. He d. at G., 27 May, 1790, in his 66 yr.; he m. 23 Mch., 1749, Abigail (dau. Joseph

& Martha *White*) **Hollister**, of G., who. d. 9 Oct., 1807, ae. 79. The Rev. Albert Hale (Y. C., 1827) was his gd-son.— *Yale Biog.*, 708. 7. David, b. 7 Jan., 1700; d. 31 Mch., 1718.	8. Joseph, b. 10 July, d. 4 Aug., 1702. 9. Benjamin, b. 22 July, 1707; m. 30 Jan., 1729, Hannah (dau. Benj. & Sarah *Hollister*) **Talcott**, b. 1706.

FAM. 3. JOHN,[2] (*Samuel*,[1]), b. 1647; dr. ld. in 1673 allot.; bo't Sam'l Smith's 15 acs. in the West Fields, 1675; signed agreement, Feb., 1691, for new church on E. side River; m. Hannah ————, 8 May, 1668. He helped repair meeting-house.—*W. T. V.*, 1, p. 19. He d. 19 July, 1709, "abt. 60 yrs. old."— *Glast. Town Rec.*

Children (Weth. Rec.):

1. John, b. 7 Feb., 1668.* 2. Samuel, b. 3 Apl., 1671. 3. Hannah, b. 1 June, 1673. 4. Thomas, b. Sept., 1675; he, then of Glast., m. Mercy (dau. John & Mary) **Hurlbut**; rem. to Chatham; for fam. see *Hurlbut Geneal.*, p. 406. 5. Rebecca, b. 1, d. 15 Nov., 1681. 6. Ebenezer, b. 24 Dec., 1682; Rev. Mr.	Mix's *Bp. Rec.* give bp. of following ch. of Ebenezer, supp. to be this one; *Hannah*, bp. 23 Mch., 1706; *Dorothy*, bp. 21 Mch., 1707-8; *Joseph*, bp. 12 Mch., 1709-10; *Gideon*, bp. 6 July, 1712. This family rem. to Midd. where *Ch.* and *Town Recs.* preserve many dates—an interminable and confusing line of Ebenezers, etc.—*A. C. N. H.*

FAM. 4. THOMAS,[2] (*Samuel*,[1]), b. 1653; m. 30 Oct., 1679, Naomi (dau. John & Naomi) **Kilbourn,** b. 1656; he d. 23 Dec., 1723; she d. 17 May, 1735, in 79th yr.—*Weth. Ins.* See Chapt. VII, Vol. I.

Children (Weth. Recs.) marr. fm. Glast. Centenn., p. 167:

1. Naomi,* b. 30 Sept., 1680. 2. Mary,* b. 20 Nov., 1682; m. Edward **Benton**, 16 Oct., 1702 (*Glast. Town Rec.*); 3 children. 3. Thomas,* b. 17 Sept., 1684; m. Susannah (dau. Nathaniel) **Smith**, 11 Jan., 1722. Could this have been a 2d marr. of Thomas, Jr.? For the Glast. grave-yd. holds the remains of one "Marcy Hale, Wife of Thomas Hale, Junr" who d. 21 Aug.,	1719, ae. 38; "Here lies on whos life thrads cut asunder she was strekd dead by a clap of thunder."—*Weth. (Gl.)* Ins. Mr. Thomas Hale d. 4 July, 1750, in 66th yr.—*Weth. (Gl.) Ins.* 4. Timothy, b. 1692. FAM. 5. 5 Nathaniel, b. 1694. FAM. 6. 6. Ruth, m. Benj. **Hollister.** 7. Eunice, m. Ebenezer **Kilborn.**

FAM. 5. TIMOTHY,[3] (*Thos.*,[2] *Samuel*,[1]), b. 1692; m. (1) Sarah (dau. Lt. Samuel & Sarah *Boardman*) **Frary**, who was b. 1700, and d. 20 Sept., 1770, in 70th yr. (*Weth. (Gl.) Ins.*). He d. 9 Aug., 1784, in 92d yr.

1. Timothy, Jr. (Capt.), b. 3 Aug., 1727.	FAM. 8.

FAM. 6. NATHANIEL,[3] (*Thos.*,[2] *Samuel*,[1]), b. 1694; hayward, 1714; m. Abigail (dau. John) **Francis**, 17 May, 1717; he d. 10 Jan., 1738-9; Invent. est. taken 5 Feb., 1738-9, amt. £567·07·06; adm. gr. to wid. and Oliver Deming of Weth.— *Htfd. Prob. Ct. Children (Weth. Rec.)*:

1. Lucy, b. 6 Sept., 1718. 2. Bennezer, b. 26 Jan., 1719-20. FAM. 9. 3. Justus, b. 29 June, 1725; m. 28 Feb., 1749-50, Martha **Wright**—*Weth. C. R.*; had	*Adine*, bp. 6 May, 1753. 4. Hezekiah, b. 29 (bp. 31—*Mix*) Aug., 1729. FAM. 10.

FAM. 8. TIMOTHY, Jr., Capt.,[4] (*Timothy*,[3] *Thos.*,[2] *Sam'l*,[1]), m. Hannah (daus. Benj. & Hannah *Talcott*) **Hale.**

Child (fm. Chart. by J. Buckingham, of Zanesville, O.):

1. Philo, b. 16 Mch., 1785; d. 29 Oct., 1847; m. Caroline M. **Butler.** 2. Hannah, b. 14 Nov., 1786; m. Rev. Prince **Hawes**; d. 5 Mch., 1827. 3. Timothy, b. 14 Oct., 1788; m. Ann **Hale**; d. 19 July, 1819. 4. Benjamin, b. 16 Sept., 1790; m. Lavinia **Talcott**; d. Sept., 1859.	5. Eunice, b. 22 Oct., 1792; m. Ebenezer **Buckingham**; d. 28 Feb., 1843. 6. Anna, b. 9 Mch., 1795; m. Alvah **Buckingham**; d. 23 Sept., 1867. 7. Jerusha Merrick, b. 19 Sept., 1797; m. Eben P. **Sturges**; d. 25 Apl., 1847. 8. Lucy, b. 22 Mch., 1800; m. Sol. **Sturges**; d. 25 July, 1859.

---

* *Glastonbury Town Rec., Book A*, p. 31: "*John Hale Junior*" (*marr. not given acc.*): Mary Hale, dau. of John Hale, Junr., & Mary his wife, was born, Nov. 10, 1697; John Hale, son of, b. March 10, 1699-1700; Samuel Hale, son of, b. Feb. 27, 1701; Ann Hale, dau. of, b. May 30, 1705; Benoni Hale, son of, b. Jan. 23, 1706; Abigail Hale, dau. of, b. Dec. 20, 1708; Thankful Hale, dau. of, b. Feb. 26, 1710; Hannah Hale, dau. of, b. Oct. 27, 1712; Sarah Hale, dau. of, b. Aug. 15, 1714.

FAM. 9. BENNEZER,[4] (*Nath'l*,[3] *Thos.*,[2] *Samuel*,[1]), b. 1720; m. 2 Jan., 1744-5, Anne **Woodhouse**, who was bu. 17 June, 1807, ae. 88; (*W. C. R.* show another Anne, wid. of Bennezer **Hale**, who d. ae. 86, 16 Sept., 1805—which ?). Bennezer bu. 19 Dec., 1798, ae. 36. He prob. the B. who d. 3 July, 1784. *Children (Weth. Rec.)* :

1. James, b. 27 Sept., bp. 6 Oct. (*L. MSS.*), 1745.
2. Mary, b. 28 Sept., 1747.
3. William, b. 10 Mch., 1749-50; prob. the Wm. who d. W. I., Oct., 1811, and m. Martha **Griswold**, 29 Nov., 1809, and whose wife *Martha* had s. *William*, bp. 29 Nov., 1809 ; and ch. bp. 7 July, 1816. —*W. C. R.*
4. Anne, b. 5 Apl., 1752; may have been the

A. who m. 22 Jan., 1777, Amasa **Wade**, of Winchester, Ct.
5. Theodore, b. 1, bp. 8 Dec., 1754. FAM. 11.
6. Abigail, b. 1, bp. 7 May, 1758.
7. Nathaniel, b. 13 July, 1763 ; bu. ae. 39, 16 Jan., 1802.—*W. C. R.*
8. Horace, } ch. of the "late Benne-
9. Huldah, } zer," bp. 22 Sept.,
10. Benezer, } 1799.
11. Mary Goodrich, }

FAM. 10. HEZEKIAH,[4] (*Nath'l*,[3] *Thos.*,[2] *Sam'l*,[1]), b. 1729; m. 15 Jan., 1756, Abigail **Hanmer**.—*W. C. R.*   *Child (Weth. Rec.)* :

1. Francis, b. 14 Mch., 1757.

FAM. 11. THEODORE,[5] (*Bennezer*,[4] *Nath'l*,[3] *Thomas*,[2] *Samuel*,[1]), b. 1754; m. 20 Oct., 1779—*W. C. R.*, Sarah **Forbes**, of Weth.   *Children (Weth. Rec.)* :

1. Rhoda, b. 21 June, bp. 23 Dec., 1781.
2. Prudence, b. 4 Jan., bp. 30 Mch., 1783.
3. Betsy, b. 14 Feb., bp. 18 June, 1786.

4. Sarah, b. 20 May, 1789 ; bp. 31 Jan., 1790 ; bu. 4 June, 1827.

EBENEZER, (prob Hale), m. Theda ————, who d. a wid., 19 June, 1842, ae. 89.—*Weth. Ins.*   *Children :*

1. Simeon, b. 1790. FAM. 2.

2. Theda, b. abt. 1779 ; d. 29 Aug., 1853.

FAM. 2. SIMEON,[2] (*Ebenezer*,[1]), b. 1790; m. Lucy **Covel**, 17 Nov., 1817, who d. 30 Oct., 1831, ae. 41; he m. (2) Nancy **Johnson**, 19 Aug., 1833; she d. 13 July, 1885. He d. 5 Apl., 1869, ae. 79.

Children (Weth. Ins. & Rec.) :

1. Mary, b. 14 Sept., 1818; bp. 13 June, 1819 ; d. 31 July, 1843, ae. 25.
2. Simeon, b. 13 Nov., 1820. FAM. 3.
3. John, b. 1 Dec., 1822.
4. Walter, b. 22 Mch., 1825 ; d. Calif., 19 June, 1869, ae. 44.
5. Matthew, b. 21 Aug., 1827.
6. Eliza, b. 15 Jan., 1830.
    (*By sec. marr., Weth. Ins.*) :

7. Ellen, b. 16 May, 1837 ; d. 21 Oct., 1838.
8. Nancy, b. 15 Mch., 1839 ; d. 8 Dec., 1839.
9. Lucy, b. 27 May, 1834 ; d. 1 Feb., 1845.
10. Lewis, b. 18 Aug., 1836.
11. Nathan, b. 7 Feb., 1841 ; d. 12 Oct., 1862 ; memb. Co. A, 16 Reg., Conn. Vols.
12. Cephas, b. 2 Jan., 1848.—*W. T. R.*
13. Hannah, b. 28 Dec., 1842.
14. Celia, b. 29 Aug., 1844.

FAM. 3. SIMEON, Jr.,[4] (*Simeon*,[3] *Ebenezer*,[2] *Simeon*,[1]), m. Mary Sophia ————.

Child (Weth. Rec.) :

1. Harriet, b. 10 Oct., 1847.

HALL. (Confusion frequently arises in the mind of the readers of old records, betw. the names of Hall and Hale, especially when both names exist in the same town. The antique chirography and sometimes careless writing of old town-clerks may be accountable for some of this; but the fact remains that it is very easy to mistake one name for the other.)

JOHN, fellow discoverer, with Oldham, of Weth., 1634; a soldier in Pequot war fm. Htfd., 1637; of New Haven, 1639-40; a founder of Wallingford 1670.—See James Shepard's Monograph on *John Hall, of Wallingford*, p. 24.

JOHN, m. Rebina ————, who was left a wid. by his dth. in 1692.—See Chapt. VII, Vol. I.

John Hall. Invt. £247-04-07 taken 23 November 1692 by Nathaniel Boreman & Obadiah Dickinson—the Widow Rebinah and Elizabeth dau. 9 months old— Court Record, 7 December 1692 Adms to the widow Rebinah Hall. one third of the personal estate to the widow forever the use of ⅓ one third of the Real Estate during life—and the use of all until the child comes of age then to inherit 2/3 of the estate. (Overseer not mentioned.) (*Htfd. Co. Prob. Rec.*)

Child (*Weth. Rec.*) :

1. Elizabeth, b. 25 Feb., 1691.

EDWARD, in Weth. abt. 1670; had his tax list rec. *W. T. V.*, I, p. 12; he d. 26 Aug., 1682. Invent. of est. taken 20 Sept., 1682, by John Kilbourn and Thomas Wright, amt. £7-08-00; ment. *Anna*, his wid. and their ch. *Mary*, ae. 2 yrs.— *Htfd. Co. Prob.*

MARY, d. 12 Feb., 1711-12.—*W. R.*

ARCHIBALD, m. Harriet **Deming**, (*N. C. R.*), 17 Aug., 1806.

Children (*N. C. R.*) :

1. Cornelia Hale, bp. 5 May, 1822.
2. Royal Sereno, b. and bp. 20 Dec., 1816.
3. Samuel Talmage, b. and bp. 19 Aug., 1807 ; of Weth. ; m. Harriet **Hart**, of Berlin, 1 Feb., 1829.—*N. C. R.*
4. Lucinda Deming, b. and bp. 5 May, 1809 : m. Sidney **Curtis**, of Auburn, N. Y., 2 Sept., 1834.
5. Roby William, b. and bp. 22 Jan., 1811.
6. Jonathan Barton, b. and bp. 1811.

GEORGE, of E. Haddam, m. Mary **Deming**, 6 Nov., 1804; had *Eliza Ann*, bp. 10 Nov., 1805.—*W. C. R.*

RICHARD—See Chapt. VII, Vol. I.

ISAAC, of Leydon, N. Y., m. wid. Lois **Bulkeley**, 20 Dec., 1800.

SAMUEL T., of Westfield, Mass., m. Harriet **Hart**, of Berlin.

SARAH, of Weth., m. Zaccheus **Bronson**, of Killingly, 5 Oct., 1808.

HAMLIN, BENJAMIN L., of Htfd., m. Abigail **Goff**, 12 May, 1817.

HAMMOND, THOMAS m. Jane ————.

Children (*Weth. Rec.*) :

1. Thomas, b. 14 Aug., 1737. | 2. Samuel, b. 2 Apl., 1743.

HANCOCK, Mrs. CATHARINE, ae. 42, bu. 13 Nov., 1810.—*W. C. R.*

Wid. MARGARET, d. 18 Sept., 1789.—*W. C. R.* Her tombstone (*Weth. Ins.*) says, "In Memory of Mrs. MARGARET HANCOCK, who was eminent for Piety, Exemplary in virtue, an accomplished instructress of children in that useful Employment, with Honor to herself & profit to her Friends. She spent many years with an unshaken Faith in her Redeemer, and joyful hopes of an eternal Bliss; she serenely departed this Life, Sept. 18th, 1789, in the 60th year of her Age, Lamented by all."

THOMAS, jailor, 1691; res. Beckley Quarter.

HAND, DANIEL, d. 31 Aug., 1795, in 2d yr.—*S. C. R.*

JONATHAN, the wife of, d. 23 Oct., 1789, ae. 33—*S. C. R.;* she had Sylvanus, Harriet and Hannah, bp. 29 Nov., 1795. Daniel, bp. 26 Aug., 1795.

JONATHAN, m. Hannah **Beachgood**, 7 Feb., 1790.—*S. C. R.*

HANDY, THOMAS, of Chatham, m. Lydia C. **Arnold**, of E. Hadd., 26 Aug., 1825.

(Acknowledgements for help on this family are due to H. W. CRANE and ALFRED
HANMER.)

HANMER, (*Hanmore*). It is prob. that the Weth. families of this name descend
fm. the Hanmers of Boston, Scituate, Duxbury and Marshfield, referred to in
Pope's *Pioneers of Mass.*, 210, *Deane's Hist. of Scituate*, 278, etc., in all of
which John is given as first of the name, and as prob. located at S. 1638, with
sons *John, Joseph* and *Isaac*, and daus. *Rebecca, Hannah* and *Bethiah;* his
wife's name Hannah. Thomas Stiles, of Windsor (Stiles' *Ancient Windsor*, II,
704) also m. a BETHIAH **Hanmer**, fm. Scituate, and a John Brooks, of
Windsor (*Idem.* 117) m. Susannah **Hanmore**, 1652, so that these items seem
to indicate the starting point of the H. family in Weth.

FRANCIS, m. Hannah **King**, 15 July, 1704 (*Boston Rec.*) and they shortly after
rem. to Weth. where she d. 18 Dec., 1745. In Sept., 1717, she obtained a
divorce fm. her husband.—(*Rec. Sup. Ct.*)

Children (*Weth. Rec.*):

1. Mary, b. in Boston, July, 1706.

2. Francis, b. "abt. the middle" of June,
1709. FAM. 2.

FAM. 2.   FRANCIS, Jr.,[2] (*Francis,[1]*), b. 1709; m. 4 May, 1731, Elizabeth **Curtis,**
(*Boardman Gen.* says **Mills,**) he d. ae. 82 (d. 19—*Weth. Ins.*), bu 28 Dec.,
1790 (*W. C. R.*); wife of Fr., d. 10 Feb., 1787, in 67th yr.—*Ibid.*

Children (*Weth. Rec.*):

1. John (Capt.), b. 2 Aug., 1731; d. ae. 68,
25 Dec., 1799—*W. C. R.*; an inf. of wife
of John, bu. 5 Apl., 1793.—*W. C. R.* A
Rev. soldier.
2. Elizabeth, b. 16 Aug., 1733.
3. Abigail, b. 13 July, 1735.
4. Anne, b. 8 Dec., 1737; d. same night.

5. Francis, b. 23 Mch., 1739. FAM. 3.
6. Samuel, b. 16 Apl., 1741. FAM. 4.
7. Anne, b. 9 Aug., 1743.
8. Lucy, b. 4 Nov., 1745.
9. James, b. 10 Dec., 1747. FAM. 5.
10. Hannah, b. 21 Apl., 1750.
11. Martha, b. 6 Jan., 1753.

FAM. 3.   FRANCIS,[3] (*Francis,[2] Francis,[1]*), b. 1739; m. 13 Sept., 1762, Rhoda (dau.
Joseph, Sam'l, Sam'l), **Boardman**—*W. C. R.* He d. 4 May, 1816, ae. 77.—
W. C. R.; she d. 29 Nov., 1801, ae. 60.—*Conn. Courant.* He was a Revol. soldier.

Children (*Boardman Geneal.*):

1. Rhoda, m. 20 Oct., 1784, Elizur **Wright,**
of Canaan; rem. to Portage, O.
2. Mary, m. 27 Nov., 1788, Capt. Geo. **Boardman,** of Weth., and Schenectady, N. Y.
3. Hannah, m. Dr. Silas **Castle,** of Roxbury, Ct.

4. Lucy, m. 12 Feb., 1789, Isaac **Johnson,**
of Auburn, N. Y.
5. Simeon (Capt.), m. Mary **Crane.** FAM. 6.
6. Francis. FAM. 7.
7. Irvin (twin to Francis), d. yg.

FAM. 4. SAMUEL,[3] (*Francis,[2] Francis,[1]*), b. 1741; m. 10 Dec., 1767, Sarah **Willis**
(dau. of Jona. W. ,of Windsor?),—*W. C. R.*; he d. ae. 72, 3 Oct., 1813; a
Sarah, "wid. of Samuel," d. 13 Apl., 1818, ae. 76,—*W. C. R. & Weth. Ins.* He
was a Revol. soldier.

Children (*W. C. R.*):

1. Sarah, b. 1769, bp. 8 May, 1774; d. 1876;
m. Jacob **Dix.**
2. Abigail, b. 15 Aug., 1770, bp. 8 May, 1774;
m. Nath'l **Robbins.**
3. Huldah b. 30 July, 1773, bp. 8 May, 1774;
m. Abraham **Crane.**
4. Samuel, b. 20 Oct., 1776.
5. Samuel, b. 4 Dec., 1778. FAM. 7.

6. Elizabeth, bp. 10 Sept., 1780; m. Joseph
Harris, of Htfd., 19 June, 1800.—*W. C. R.*
7. Pruey (Prudence), b. 26 Sept., bp. 1 Dec.,
1782; d. 29 Nov., 1866, ae. 84.—*Weth. Ins.*
8. Nancy, b. 12 Feb., bp. 19 June, 1785;
m. 11 Feb., 1808, Caleb **Pond,** of Htfd.
9. Joseph, b. 23 Nov., 1787, bp. 27 Apl., 1788.

FAM. 5.   JAMES,[3] (*Francis,[2] Francis,[1]*), b. 1747; m. 5 May, 1767, Elizabeth
Ayrault, who d. 18 Oct., 1837, ae. 88,—*W. C. R.*; he d. 9 or 10 Dec., 1789, ae.
42.—*Weth. Ins.* A soldier of the Revol., prob. a mariner.—See Chapt VII, Vol. I.

Children (*Weth. Rec.*) :

1. James, b. 18 Aug., 1767; m. Abigail **Wells**, 19 Feb., 1795.
2. Elizabeth, b. 4 Jan., 1769.
3. Polly, b. 5 Oct., 1770.
4. Lydia, b. 10 July, 1772.
5. A son, bu. 21 Sept.,1775, ae. 14 mos.
6. John, b. 30 July, 1774; d. 10 Oct., 1775.

7. Patty, b. 25 Feb., 1776.
8. John, b. 25 Feb., 1778.
9. Clara, b. 5 Feb., 1780.
10. Abigail, b. 27 Dec., 1781.
11. Lydia, b. 3 Jan., 1784.
12. Morgan, b. 18 Feb., 1786.
13. Lucy, b. 25 July, 1788.

FAM. 6. SIMEON,[4] (*Francis,[3] Francis,[2] Francis,[1]*), b. abt. 1771; m. 17 May, 1798, Mary **Crane;** he d. ae. 40, bu. 7 Nov., 1813; Mary, his wid., d. ae. 38, bu. 14 Nov., 1813.

Children (*W. C. R.*) :

1. Mary, d. ae. 14; bu. 28 Aug., 1813.

2. Harriet ("of the late Simeon"), bu. 10 Nov., 1822, ae. 11.

FAM. 7. SAMUEL, Jr.,[3] (*Samuel,[2] Francis,[1]*), b. 1778; m. Lucy **Crane,** 15 Mch., 1798; she d. 17 Sept., 1827, ae. 50; he d. 16 Nov., 1852, ae. 72. He a Revol. soldier.

Children:

1. Sarah, b. 1798; d. 1876.
2. John, b. 1801.
3. Samuel, b. 1804. FAM. 8.
4. Lucy Ann, b. 1806; d. 1884, unm.
5. Nancy, b. 1809; d. 1886, unm.

6. Henry (Rev.), b. 1815; m. Emily A. **Latimer;** d. in Wisconsin.
7. Charles, b. 1818; d. 1896, unm.
8. Eliza, b. 1812; d. 1900, unm.

FAM. 8. JOHN,[5] (*Samuel,[4] Samuel,[3] Francis,[2] Francis,[1]*), b. 1801; m. 14 Jan., 1833, Hannah Belden **Churchill;** he d. 1881; she b. 1805, d. 1886.

Children:

1. Caleb J., b. 27 Nov., 1833. FAM. 9a.
2. Elizabeth, b. 8 Oct., 1835; unm.
3. Mary Ann, b. 8 Aug., 1837; m. Elizur Stillman **Goodrich,** 19 Oct., 1859; 2 ch
4. Charles Henry, b. 18 Oct., 1839; m. Clara

Elizabeth **Way.**
5. Felicia Havens, b. 6 Sept., 1842; m. Dudley **Wells,** 15 Oct., 1862.
6. John, b. 16 May, 1849; m. Fannie Rebecca **Bulkeley,** 28 Jan., 1874; 4 ch.

FAM. 9. FRANCIS,[4] (*Francis,[3] Francis,[2] Francis,[1]*), b. abt. 1770; m. (1) 11 Jan., 1798, Huldah **Dickinson,** who d. 4 May, 1862—*Weth. Ins.;* m. (2) ————— **Forbes,** He d. ae. 42, bu. 28 Oct., 1814.—*Weth. Ins.*

Children (*W. C. R.*) :

1. Francis, d. 7 May, 1811, ae. 2 yrs., 2 mos. *Weth. Ins.*
2. Lucy.
3. Chauncey ("s. of the late Fr., Jr."), ae. 11, bu. 17 Feb., 1816.
4. William, b. 16 Nov., 1863. •FAM. 10.
5. Thomas.

6. Walter.
7. Huldah Maria ("dau. of Wid. Huldah") bp. 3 Nov., 1824; poss. the Maria who d. ae. 36, bu. 12 July, 1848.—*Weth. Ins.*
8. Hannah (of Wid. Huldah), bp. same time with Huldah Maria, above; m. ————— **Pratt.**

FAM. 9a. CALEB J.,[6] (*John,[5] Samuel,[4] Samuel,[3] Francis,[2] Francis,[1]*), b. 1833; m. 3 May, 1859, Ellen Nancy (dau. Roswell & Nancy *Robbins*) **Dix.** He d. 15 May, 1887; a prominent bus. man in Weth. (firm of Adams & Hanmer) wholesale tobacco dealers; first selectman of town for many yrs.; rep. Weth. in Leg. 1872 and '73; vestryman of Trinity Ch.; memb. St. John's Lodge F. and A. M. and of Washington Commandery K. T. of Htfd.; a man of excellent judgment and public spirit.

Children:

1. Elizabeth.
2. Nellie, m. Eugene S. **Kendall.**
3. Frederick Caleb, m. Nellie T. **Ridgeway.**

4. Gertrude, m. John **Latimer;** d. 4 Mch., 1904; 2 ch.

FAM. 10. WILLIAM,[5] (Francis,[4] Francis,[3] Francis,[2] Francis,[1]), b. 1803; d. Jan. 29, 1862; m. 14 Mch., 1837, Honor Goodrich (dau. Capt. Daniel and Mehetabel Goodrich) Francis; b. 22 July, 1815, d. ————. He was a builder and a successful farmer. Their children, excepting four who died in infancy, viz.: Maria A., Hattie E., Frederic, Jeannette, are as follows:

Children:

1. William Francis, b. 18 Feb., 1840; unm.; res. Wethersfield.
2. Thomas Newton, b. 27 Feb., 1841; unm.; res. Wethersfield.
3. Julius Edward, b. 25 June, 1842; m. Maria **Belden**, of Weth.; res. Providence, R. I.
4. Walter, b. 18 Nov., 1843; m. Elizabeth S.

Johnson; res. Hartford, Conn.
5. Mary Francis, b. 16 Oct., 1847; m. Albert E. **Warner**; res. Weth.
6. Katharine Badger, b. 25 Sept., 1854; m. Augustus **Sargeant**, who d. 26 Jan., 1885. He was warden of Conn. State Prison. Katharine d. 20 Mch., 1893.

HANSET, (Hanchet, Hanshet), THOMAS, ld. owner in Weth., 1642,—See Chapt. VII, Vol. I; m. Deliverance (dau. George) **Langton**, acc. to *Savage*, who thinks him to have been, perhaps, a bro. of John, of Boston, Braintree and Roxbury. Thomas rem. to New Lond., 1651, where he res. 3 yrs.; was at Northampton abt. 1660; was deac. 1668; rem, to Westfield; thence to Suffield, where he d. 11 June, 1686. His wid. m. (2) 14 Dec., 1686-7, Jonathan **Burt**.

Child (Weth. Rec.):

1. John, b. 1 Sept., 1649.

HARLOW, ADELIA, d. 12 Sept., 1854.

HARRINGTON, JOHN, signed the covenant for the estab. of new church at Naubuc, 13 Feb., 169-, see *Savage*.

HARRIS, (Harriss, Herress). [Assistance acknowledged from Miss MARY J. HARRIS, Weth., Conn.,* and from a record prepared by the late Nath'l H. Morgan, of Htfd.] The original emigrant ancestor of this family seems to have been THOMAS, 1630, who kept the ferry between Winnisimmet and Charlestown, Mass., and who d. 11 Apl., 1661, ae. 90. His wid Elizabeth m. (2) a Dea. Wm. **Stilson**, (Savage says Stetson), who, in 1680, testified that Thos. Harris had kept the ferry 49 yrs. ago and that having m. the wid. Harris, he had continued the ferry. The sons are ment. by Savage as being of Boston, Chelsea, Ipswich, Rowley, Mass., and Midd., Ct. Elizabeth Harris (Stetson or Stilson) d. 16 Feb., 1670.

Children:

1. Anthony, m. Elizabeth ————, and d. Chelsea, 30 Dec., 1651.
2. John, m. Amy ————. See *Savage*.
3. Thomas, m. 15 Nov., 1647, Martha (dau. Margaret) **Lake**; his will prob. 14 Sept., 1687.
4. William, m. Edith ————; rem. to

Rowley, thence to Charlestown, Mass., and later to Midd., Ct.; wife d. 5 Aug., 1685; he d. 1717.
5. Daniel, m. Mary (dau. Joseph) **Weld**, of Roxbury; d. Nov., 1701.—*Wyman's Gen. & Estates of Charlestown.* FAM. 2.
6. Ann, m. Elias **Maverick**.

FAM. 2. Capt. DANIEL,[2] (Thomas,[1]); m. Mary (dau. Joseph) **Weld**, of Roxbury; res. at Rowley, sold his pp. in R. in Aug., 1652, and rem. to Midd., Ct., there in 1660 was app. to keep an inn; was a Lieut. in 1661, and Capt. later had ho. and lot in R. and was a carpenter and wheelwright; he d. last of Nov.,

---

* Miss Harris states that all the Harris families in Weth. are descendants of this Thomas and Anne (Miller) Nott Harris. A family tradition says that the first of the name here were two brothers, John and Thomas by name, who came up from New London in a boat, as far as Middletown and traded their boat for land in Wethersfield. The Thomas Harris of our Record has no brother John, but still there may be a kernel of truth in the story.

1701; wid. d. 1711. His will ment. all of his ch. as living, except dau. Sarah (**Bidwell,**) and prob. Joseph. Invent. £509-9, pres. to Ct. by s. John, 19 Dec., 1701.

Children (Midd. Rec.)

1. Mary, b. 2 Apl., 1651, at Rowley; m. 26 Oct., 1669, Isaac **Johnson,** of Roxbury.
2. Daniel, b. 15 July, 1653. **FAM. 3.**
3. Joseph, b. 12 Feb., 1655.
4. Thomas, b. 20 May, 1657.
5. Elizabeth, b. 22 Mch., 1660; m. John **Hunnewell.**
6. Sarah, b. 17 Feb., 1661; d. soon.
7. Sarah, b. 3 Sept., 1663; m. Samuel **Bidwell.**
8. William, b. 17 July, 1665; prob. the Corp'l Wm. H., in Orcutt's *New Settlers of New Milford,* p. 66; m. Elizabeth **Johnson;** prob. the couple cr. on *Weth. Rec.* with dau. Eunice, b. 1 Mch., 1712; and she prob. the E., "wife of Wm.," on list of ch. memb. in New Milford, Ct., 1718, "recommended from Weth."—Orcutt's *N. Milford.*
9. John, b. 4 Jan., 1668.
10. Hannah, b. 11 Feb., 1670; m. (1) ———— **Cook;** m. (2) ———— **Sprague.**

FAM. 3. Capt. DANIEL,[3] (*Daniel,[2] Thos.,[1]*), b. Midd., 1653; m. 14 Dec., 1680, Abigail **Barnes,** who d. 22 May, 1723, her tombstone says, "Here lies one dead which in life was my loving, pious wife." He m. (2) Elizabeth (wid. of Samuel) **Cook,** of Wallingford, 5 Jan., 1727. He d. 18 Oct., 1735 in 82d yr. Wm. Harris distrib. his est.

Children:

1. Abigail, b. 7 Feb., 1683.
2. Mary, b. 11 Jan., 1686.
3. Daniel, b. 2 Oct., 1688; had (*Conn. Quart.,* II, 399) *Merriman,* b. July, 1713; *Daniel,* b. 10 Apl., 1715; *Moses,* b. 20 May, 1717; *John,* b. 26 Feb., 1719; *Thomas,* b. 9 May, 1722.
4. Joseph, b. 1 Mch., 1691.
5. Patience, b. 15 May, 1693; d. 15 Aug., 1777.
6. Thomas (prob.) b. 1695. **FAM. 4.**

FAM. 4. THOMAS,[4] (*Daniel,[3] Daniel,[2] Thos.,[1]*), b. 1695, fm. New London as family trad. hath it, sett. Weth., where he m. 18 Dec., 1729, Anne (dau. John & Patience *Miller*) **Nott,** who was b. 29 July, 1699, and d. 9 Oct., 1769—*Weth. Ins.;* he d. Spring of 1774. Will pres. to Ct. by s. Hosea. Invent. £885-3-6. He was a tanner, Nov. 1733, *Co. Ct. Rec.* From this Thomas & Anne Harris descended all the Harris families in Weth. The house built by Thomas Harris of the fourth generation, in 1755 still stands on South Hill in a good state of preservation. The frame of the house just North of it was raised by his son Hosea on the day of the battle of Lexington, April, 1775, and was burned in 1902.

Children (Weth. Rec. bp. Mix.):

1. Anna, b. 26 (29—*Weth. Ins.*) Nov., 1730; d. 29 Jan., 1731.—*Weth. Ins.*
2. Anne, b. 29, bp. 26 Mch., 1732; d. 28 May, 1736.
3. Sarah, b. 18 Feb., bp. 3 Mch., 1733-4; m. 8 Sept., 1755, Elisha **Robbins.**
4. Hosea, b. 11 Feb., 1736. **FAM. 5.**
5. Mehitable, b. 28 Apl., 1738; m. ———— **Robbins.**
6. Anna, b. 8 Apl., 1740; m. 24 Mch., 1768, Stephen **Willard.**
7. Thomas, b. 7 May, 1743. **FAM. 6.**

FAM. 5. HOSEA,[5] (*Thos.,[4] Daniel,[3] Daniel,[2] Thos.,[1]*), b. 1736; m. 11 Dec., 1760, Eunice Boardman **King,** wid. of David King. He d. ae. 56, 11 Apl., 1792—*W. C. R.;* his wid. d. 2 Apl., 1813, ae. 80.—*Weth. Ins.*

Children (Weth. Rec. and Boardman Geneal.):

1. Mehitable, b. 14 June, bp. 4 Oct., 1761; m. Thos. **Belden,** of Htfd.
2. Eunice, b. 29 June, bp. 3 July, 1763; m. Moses **Montague;** she d. 5 Apl., 1841.
3. Mary, b. 10 Sept., 1765; m. Thos. **Welles,** 2d.
4. Hosea, b. 18 Nov., bp. 6 Mch., (*sic.*) 1768; d. ae. 23, in W. I., Feb., 1794.
5. John, b. 13 July, 1770. **FAM. 7.**
6. Joseph, m. Elizabeth **Hanmer.** **FAM. 7a.**
7. Anna, bp. 4 Sept., 1774; prob. m. Cary **Leeds,** of Stamford.
8. Lucy.

FAM. 6. THOMAS,[5] (*Thos.,[4] Daniel,[3] Daniel,[2] Thomas,[1]*), b. 1743; m. Abigail (dau. Joshua, Jr. & Mary *Welles*) **Robbins,** 26 July, 1770,—*W. C. R.,* who was b. 29 Apl., 1749. He d. 27 Dec., 1774, (*Weth. Ins.* say Dec., 1775), from effects of injury rec'd at a barn-raising; wid. m. (2), as his 2d wife, Dr. Josiah **Hart,** and d. 8 Aug., 1796.

Children (Weth. Rec.):

1. Thomas, b. 8 Feb., 1771; bp. 4 Sept., 1774. FAM. 8.
2. Abigail, b. 6 June, 1773; bp. 11 Sept., 1775; m. (1) Josiah Griswold; (2) Sam'l

Broadbent; he d. 27 Jan., 1874.
3. Sarah, b. 26 Apl., bp. 11 June, 1775; m. 5 Jan., 1800, Chester Wolcott, of So. Windsor, Ct.

FAM. 7. JOHN,[6] (*Hosea,*[5] *Thos.,*[4] *Daniel,*[3] *Daniel,*[2] *Thos.,*[1]), b. 1770; m. Martha (dau. Maj. William) Russell, 21 Nov., 1790; he d. 4 Apl., 1858; she b. 14 Aug., 1760, d. 31 Mch., 1853.—*W. Ins.*

Children (Weth. Rec.):

1. John, b. 30 Apl., 1791. FAM. 9.
2. Clarissa, b. 14 Mch., 1794; m. Capt. Humphrey Woodhouse; she d. 5 Apl., 1871.
3. Mary, b. 20 Aug., 1796; m., as his 2d wife, Chauncey Wolcott; she d. 25 May, 1888.
4. Hosea, b. 22 July, 1799. FAM. 10.
5. Timothy Russell, b. 15 Mch., 1802; m. Julia (dau. Rob't) Robbins, 25 Nov., 1824.—*W. C. R.;* he d. 20 Feb., 1853; had

Julia Robbins, bp. 24 June, 1827.
6. Walter, b. 24 Aug., 1805. FAM. 10a.
7. William, twin to Walter.
8. Henry, b. 8 May, 1808. FAM. 11.
9. Martha, b. 19 Apl., 1811; m. John Blinn, and d. 1 Feb., 1876.
10. Cordelia, b. 9 Oct., 1814 or '15; m. John Blinn; she d. 11 May, 1893. Wells. FAM. 12.

FAM. 7a. JOSEPH HARRIS,[6] (*Hosea,*[5] *Thos.,*[4] *Daniel,*[3] *David,*[2] *Thos.,*[1]), b. Feb. 15, 1774, d. Sept. 16, 1832; m. Elizabeth Hanmer. She was b. 13 July, 1780, d. 9 Sept., 1860.

Children:

1. Joseph, b. 29 July, 1802; d. Nov., 1844.
2. Edward, b. 8 Nov., 1806; d. 17 Nov., 1868.
3. Henry, b. 8 Jan., 1809; d. 6 Jan., 1873.
4. George, b. July, 1810; d. 16 Sept., 1858; m. Evelina Maden, of Cuba; had 3 ch., *Joseph, Ellen* and *George.*

5. Elizabeth, b. 5 Nov., 1812; d. 8 Apl., 1899.
6. Samuel, b. 8 June, 1814; d. 6 July, 1897; m. Jane C. Wood, of N. Y., b. 24 Aug., 1824; d. 3 Feb., 1873; had one child, *Elizabeth,* who m. W. R. Pierce.

FAM. 8. THOMAS,[6] (*Thos.,*[5] *Thos.,*[4] *Daniel,*[3] *Daniel,*[2] *Thomas,*[1]), b. 1771; m. 8 Feb., 1797, Sarah (dau. Hez'h & Mary *Dix*) Crane. He d. 2 Feb., 1829, ae. 58; she d. 5 days later, both of typhoid.

Children (Weth. Rec. & W. C. R.):

1. Sally, b. 25 Dec., 1797, bp. 13 Jan., 1799; m. Sylvester Woodhouse; d. Nov., 1828.
2. Thomas, b. 20 Aug., bp. 1 Dec., 1799; d. 4 Sept., 1857, unm.
3. Mary, b. 21 Feb., bp. 19 July, 1801; m. 10 Feb., 1833, Washington Hatch; she d. 1 Apl., 1872.
4. Abigail, b. 28 Nov., 1802, bp. 20 June, 1803; d. 8 Mch., 1876, unm.
5. Hezekiah Crane, b. 18 June, 1804, bp. 26

Oct., 1806; d. 12 June, 1812.
6. Eliza Hart, b. 10 Apl., bp. 26 Oct., 1806; m. Wm. Talcott; d. 31 Mch., 1883.
7. Emily, b. 29 Mch., 1808; d. 15 Jan., 1829, unm.
8. Jane, b. 3 Oct., 1810; d. 24 July, 1896, unm.
9. Hezekiah, b. 7 July, 1814; d. 9 Aug., 1894, unm.
10. Chauncey, b. 28 Sept., 1816; m. Emeline Wells.

FAM. 9. JOHN,[7] (*John,*[6] *Hosea,*[5] *Thos.,*[4] *Daniel,*[3] *Daniel,*[2] *Thos.,*[1]), b. 1791; m. Sarah (dau. Joseph & Abigail *Dix*) Crane. He d. 3 Feb., 1869; she d. 1 Oct., 1859.

Children (Weth. Rec.):

1. Abigail, d. 2 Apl., 1890, ae. 69 (*W. Ins.*); m. Justus G. Churchill.
2. Clarissa, d. 3 Nov., 1831, ae. 10.—*Weth. Ins.*

3. Sarah, m. Henry King.
4. John, b. 29 June, 1826. FAM. 14a.
5. Lucy, d. 30 July, 1903; m. Frank C. Wilcox.

FAM. 10. HOSEA,[7] (*John,*[6] *Hosea,*[5] *Thos.,*[4] *Daniel,*[3] *Daniel,*[2] *Thos.,*[1]), b. 1799, d. 16 Oct., 1874. He m. Sarah Frances (dau. Chas. & Sarah *Adams*) Francis, 7 Aug., 1821. She was b. 30 July, 1801, d. 27 Dec., 1854.

Children:

1. Charles, b. 22 Feb., 1822; d. 1828.
2. Evelina H., b. 3 Oct., 1824; m. Capt. John Francis.
3. Francis H., b. 24 Jan., 1829; m. Emeline Bradley. FAM. 15.

4. Henry H., b. 9 Sept., 1834; unm.
5. Sarah A., b. 29 Oct., 1837; m. Dr. H. H. Sprague, of Deerfield, Mo.
6. Mary L., b. 19 Mch., 1844; m. Frederick Morton, of Rocky Hill, Ct.

Chauncey Harris.

FAM. 10a. WALTER, b. in Weth., 1804, d. Apl., 8, 1881; he m. 15 Aug., 1836, Caroline M. **Orcutt,** Schoharie, N. Y., b. 25 Aug., 1818, who d. 22 Mch., 1898.

Children:

1. Georgine C., b. 17 June, 1837; d. 19 July, 1898.
2. Francis A., b. 13 Feb., 1839; d. 13 Feb., 1877.
3. Walter Clifford, b. 14 Apl., 1841; d. in Mexico, 1883.
4. Albert W., b. 11 Feb., 1843.
5. H. Tudor B., b. 10 Mch., 1845; res. and is in bus. in N. Y. City.

FAM. 11. HENRY HARRIS,[7] (*John*,[6] *Hosea*,[5] *Thos.*,[4] *Daniel*,[3] *Daniel*,[2] *Thos.*,[1]), b. 8 May, 1808; m. Frances (dau. Wm. & Rebecca *Crane)* **Robbins.**

Children:

1. Marshall H., b. 29 July, 1835; d. 27 Sept., 1901; m. Honor **Woodhouse.** FAM. 16.
2. Fannie, m. Edwin R. **Curtiss,** of Glast.
3. Luther, unm.; d. 1888.
4. Martha R., d. 1885; m. Frank **Young.**

FAM. 12. CHAUNCEY,[7] (*Thos.*,[6] *Thos.*,[5] *Thos.*,[4] *Daniel*,[3] *Daniel*,[2] *Thos.*,[1]), b. 1816. He was the youngest of a family of 10 ch., both father and mother died within a week of each other, leaving him an orphan at twelve. The loss of most of the fingers of his right hand when a mere child, shut him out from many occupations, and when a young man he turned to teaching for a livelihood, beginning work in a district school near his own home, and teaching afterwards in Bristol and Meridan, Ct., Hempstead, L. I., and at Rock Island, Ill. In 1844 he became principal of the So. Dist. School in Htfd., which position he held to the end of his life. His death, 12th Feb., 1875, was felt as a public loss by the whole community. In his character were blended indefatigable industry, peculiar quietness of manner and self- control, a genius for management and superintendence, and a combination of gentleness with firmness, of justice with kindness, of positiveness with patience—all dominated by an unfaltering sense of fidelity and a considerate courage.

For a number of years he was also in charge of the Hartford Orphan Asylum— but as the labors of the two positions began to tell upon his not too rugged health, he relinquished the latter and built for himself a residence on South Hill, in Weth., on a farm which he owned, and in which his family now reside. He had the faculty of securing the respect and unbounded confidence of every one with whom he came in contact; and his substantial, wholesome piety no one could doubt. It was well said of him that, "If the *flame* of his piety was less visible than in some others, the *heat* of it was more penetrating and pervading." Mr. Harris m. 6 May, 1840, Emeline (dau. Geo. L. and Prudence *Deming*) **Welles.**

Children:

1. George W., b. 25 Mch., 1847. FAM. 13.
2. F. Estelle, b. 1 Oct., 1849; m. 17 Oct., 1877, E. Newton **Loveland.**
3. Mary J., b. 25 Oct., 1854.
4. Emma L., b. 31 July, 1857.
5. Charles Edward, b. 23 Oct., 1859; d. 29 Mch., 1861.
6. Charles Chauncey, b. 14 Jan., 1863. FAM. 14.

FAM. 13. GEORGE WELLS,[8] (*Chauncey*,[7] *Thos.*,[6] *Thos.*,[5] *Thos.*,[4] *Daniel*,[3] *Daniel*,[2] *Thos.*,[1]), b. 1847; m. (1) Alice Josephine (dau. Henry) **Rowe,** of Baltimore, Md., 12 Jan., 1871; m. (2) Lillie S. (dau. Chas.) **Mills,** of W. Htfd., 28 Sept., 1876.

Children:

1. Alice J. Rowe, b. 17 Mch., and d. 4 July, 1872.
(*By second marriage*):
2. Chauncey Karl, b. 1 Feb., 1879.
3. George Mills, b. 3 Feb., 1883.
4. Marjorie Sillman, }
5. Rodney Wells, } b. 6 June, 1890.

416   GENEALOGIES AND BIOGRAPHIES OF ANCIENT WETHERSFIELD.

FAM. 14. CHARLES CHAUNCEY,⁵ (Chauncey,⁷ Thos.,⁶ Thos.,⁵ Thos.,⁴ Daniel,³ Daniel,² Thos.,¹), b. 1863; m. 11 Dec., 1889, Carrie R. (dau. Josiah G. & Ellen Warner) **Adams.**

Child:

1. Burton A., b. 2 July, 1891.

FAM. 14a. JOHN⁸ (John,⁷ John,⁶ Hosea,⁵ Thos.,⁴ Daniel,³ Daniel,² Thos.,¹), b. 1826, m. Roxanna **Losey,** 6 June, 1853. He d. 15 Feb., 1870.

Children:

1. William E., b. 4 Feb., 1855; m. Helena **Weingarten,** 6 Sept., 1882. *Issue:* i. Wm. Henry, b. 20 June, 1883.
ii. Sidney James, b. 6 Dec., 1884.
2. Frank, b. 20 Mch., 1857; d. 24 Sept., 1859.
3. James H., b. 22 Feb., 1863.

FAM. 15. FRANCIS H.,⁸ (Hosea,⁷ John,⁶ Hosea,⁵ Thos.,⁴ Daniel,³ Daniel,² Thos.,¹), b. 24 Jan., 1829; m. 22 Oct., 1856, Emeline W. **Bradley.**

Children:

1. Emma F., b. 16 Oct., 1857; m. 2 Sept., 1885, Benj. H. **Cobb.**
2. Richmond Russell, b. 27 Dec., 1859; m. 23 Nov., 1886, Jane R. **Perkins;** has (a) Dorothy P., b. 29 May, 1888; d. 5 Mch., 1891; (b) Marguerite F., b. 30 Apl., 1892.
3. Charles Hosea, b. 11 Mch., 1863; m. 18 Oct., 1894, Minnie C. **Earle;** has dau. Mildred E., b. 24 May, 1902.
4. Francis Bradley, b. 18 Nov., 1870; m. 30 June, 1898, Susie H. **Wrisley;** has ch. Ruth H., b. 8 May, 1899.

FAM. 16. MARSHALL,⁸ (Henry,⁷ John,⁶ Hosea,⁵ Thos.,⁴ Daniel,³ Daniel,² Thos.,¹), b. 1835; m. Honor (dau. Manna and Honor Goodrich) **Woodhouse;** d. 27 Sept., 1890. She b. 14 May, 1834.

Children:

1. Carrie T., b. 31 Jan., 1864; m. George **Royce.**
2. Henry A., b. 28 Oct., 1868; m. Annie **Griswold;** has Dorothy, b. 30 Jan., 1901.
3. Annie L., b. 11 Dec., 1872; m. F. W. **Weildon.**
4. Luther, b. 14 Feb., 1874.

HARRISON, (Harison), JOHN, early at Wetn., from Watertown,—See Chapt. VII, Vol. I.; m. Katharine ————, 4 May, 1653; d. 1664 or '66; cattle earmark rec.—W. T. V., 1. 5; Town Crier, 1653—(Idem. 43); Savage (II,366) says he was a mcht.; freeman in Conn., 1657; d. 3 Aug., 1665, leaving large estate—invent. at £929. His wid. Catharine, was indicted as a witch—see Chapt. XVII, Vol. I.

Children (Weth. Rec.):

1. Rebecca, b. 10 Feb., 1654.
2. Mary, b. 8 June, 1655.
3. Sarah, b. 9 Mch., 1657.

JARED, bp. 7 Nov., 1879, m. Caroline **Loveland,** 30 Apl., 1829; she (wid.) d. 16 Mch., 1862, ae. 63; their dau. Mary Gilbert, bp. 16 Oct., 1831, d. 17 June, 1861, ae. 30; Caroline Elizabeth, bp. 30 June, 1830, d. 14 Feb., 1856, ae. 26; Theodore Talcot, bp. 4 Aug., 1833, d. 2 Sept., 1843, ae. 10 yr. Mr. Jared Harrison d. 11 Feb., 1846.

MARTHA, m. Noah **Butler,** 13 Jan., 1806.

OSMUND, b. 9 Oct., 1798, he d. 30 Mch., 1895 ae. 96 yrs. 5 mos. 21 d.—being then the oldest memb. of the Cong'l Ch. in Weth., as well as of the Conn. Soc'y of the Sons of the Revolution. He m. Diantha **Griswold,** who was b. 16 Oct., 1807, and d. 24 Feb., 1837; he m. (2) Prudence **Griswold,** who survived him.

REUBEN, an inf. of, bu. 16 Aug., 1794.—W. C. R.

SAMUEL, of Far., m. Hannah **Butler**, of Weth., 10 Mch., 1785.

SAMUEL, d. 2 Sept., 1830, ae. 45.

SAMUEL, m. 7 Aug., 1808, Sally **Lattimer**, she bp. 3 Mch., 1814,—*W. C. R.*; she d. 3 Mch., 1814, ae. 27—*W. C. R.; Issue: Sarah,* bu. 3 Mch., 1814; *William, Samuel Crane,* and *Sarah Lattimer,* bp. 11 Oct., 1818,—*W. C. R.;* the latter m. Wm. A. **Reeves,** 18 Feb., 1838.

THEODORE, d. 20 May, 1836, ae. 80.—*Weth. Ins.;* his wife d. ae. 76, bu. 20 July, 1829.—*W. C. R.*

TIMOTHY, of Branford, m. Clarinda **Fosdick,** of Weth., 14 Mch., 1776.—*W. C. R.*

THOMAS, of Saybrook, m. Chole **Wright,** 17 Apl., 1780.—*W. C. R.*

HART, Dr. JOSIAH, *(son of Dea. Elijah,)*, b. in that part of Farmington, (Kensington parish, now New Britain), 28 Apl., 1742; grad. Y. C. 1762; studied med. under Dr. Jared Potter, of East Haven; in 1765, m. Abigail **Sluman,** of Stonington, and soon afterwards sett. in Weth., where his wife d. 4 June, 1777, of small-pox. He m. (2) 25 or 27 Mch., 1778,—(*W. C. R.*), Abigail (wid. of Thomas) **Harris,** and dau. of Joshua **Robbins,** of Weth. He seems, from the evidence of entries in his account book, now in the possession of Mr. WM. F. J. BOARDMAN, of Htfd., to have commenced practice in February, 1762, the first of the legible entries being on the 22nd of that month and year. These entries, which are continued regularly down to 1700, disclose the materia medica and the methods of practice that prevailed during the closing quarter of the last century. The cost of visits receives an interesting illumination from the old record. A few of these old records, the sums appearing in pounds, shillings and pence, will be of interest to the modern practitioner. There is a singular variation for the same service, but that may be due to the sympathy and good-heartedness of the old-time doctor. Taking the twenty years from 1766 until 1786 general data appears to be, the year being given: 1766, bleeding 6d., visit 9d., emetic 6d., visit night 2s., 1766, emetic 6d., night visit 2s., 1777, two vomits 2s. (1768) a vomit 9d., 1779, visits for twenty-four days, one each day, £1, 14s., 1768, accidental visit and bleeding 2s., 3d., 1768, visit 1s., cathartic 9d., emetic 9d., bleeding 6d., 1774, night visit and bleeding, 2s. 6d., 1785, delivering wife 12s., 1786, delivering wife 8s.

The doctor's pay came in every conceivable commodity that could be produced in a country neighborhood. It comprised wheat, pork, butter, veal, pasturing cows, onions, wool, making hay, hay, shoes, wood, boards, work, flax, spinning, corn, beef, shad, potatoes, schooling, pewter, "cyder," horse keeping, swamp wood, rum, pork barrel, cheese, brooms, tallow, boots, vinegar, oats, Indian corn in the ear, hoeing corn, mowing, threshing, winter apples, "soaling" shoes, curry combs, chestnut rails, brandy, pigs, cloth, honey and tobacco.

In 1767 Dr. Hart received two barrels of "cyder" from William Loveland, in connection with his account, the cost being 10 shillings. In March, 1769, he received six gallons of molasses from Joseph Butler at 15 shillings; two loads of wood from William Hurlbut, in March, 1768, were credited at 13 shillings.

Sugar to the amount of 15 shillings and 6 pence was furnished by Prescott Bulkley to the doctor, in 1768, in connection with his account. Now and then there is an an "accidental visit." Exactly what that signified does not appear from the accounts. But it is presumed that the accidental visit was when the doctor happened to be going by and was called in. This was different from a regular call, when he was sent for by the patient.

A night visit, "all night" visit, as the record shows, cost the Dickinson family in Newington 9 shillings. Thirty bunches of onions were received or credited at 6 shilling and 3 pence. An accidental visit and bleeding, March 27, 1768, cost Jacob Dix 1 shilling and 6 pence. From Mr. Dix the doctor received wheat and flax and 1,000 shingles at an expense of one pound. John Benton, in 1769, paid the doctor in onions, Indian corn and seed wheat. A gallon of rum about the same time cost 4 shillings and 6 pence. In 1770 Josiah Hurlbut paid in onions 37 "ropes," the credit being 6 shillings and 2 pence. In November, 1769, Hezekiah Hurlbut paid his account in full in cash, 1 pound, 8 shillings and 9 pence. The account embraces not less than 225 manuscript pages, and this is believed to be the only instance where there is a payment of an account in full in cash.

One of the most remarkable entries in the book, as showing an open winter and pasturage into the month of January, is shown on page 72. It gives credit to John Belding as follows: By pasturing cows from 27th of June, 1769, till 8th of January, 1770. There was also credit for wheat at 4 shillings a bushel.

Not frequently *medicine was returned to Dr. Hart by his patients and was credited in the accounts.* Dr. Hart was one of the delegates from the Htfd. Co. Med. Soc. to the first meeting of the Conn. Med. Soc'y, at Middletown, in Oct., 1792; and a member of the Gen. Assembly from Weth. in 1789. In 1793 he became a deacon in the Weth. Ch. The death of his second wife, (Abigail Robbins, wid. Thomas Harris), 8 Aug., 1796, at the age of 49 led him to give up practice and rem. to Marietta, O., where his two surviving sons had settled. There he m. (3), Anna (dau. of William) **Moulton.** He d. at Lowell, O., of spotted fever, Aug., 1812; his wife survived him only a few hours. The Dr. was an honored and useful member of the Army Medical service during the War of the Revolution.—See Chapt. XI, Vol. I.

Children (Weth. Rec.) :

1. Abigail, b. 3 Feb., bp. 20 Apl., 1766.
2. Josiah, b. 10 Dec., 1768, bp. 10 Jan., 1768-9 ; d. 15 Jan., 1769.
3. Hannah, b. 24 ——, 1769.
4. Emily, b. 3 Feb., 1771.
5. Josiah Sluman, b. and bp. 10 Jan., 1773 ; d. 1 Jan., 1792.—*W. C. R.*
6. William, b. 4, bp. 12 Mch., 1775 ; prob.

the Wm. who m. Sarah **Waterhouse,** 5 Sept., 1797.—*W. C. R.*
7. Thomas, b. 14 Dec., 1776, bp. 16 Mch., 1777. (*By second marr.*) :
8. Betsy, b. 22 Dec., 1778, bp. 3 Jan., 1779.
9. Clarissa, bp. 21 Sept., 1783.—*W. C. R.*
10. Cynthia, bp. 12 Oct., 1788.—*W. C. R.*

SETH, who d. 12 Dec., 1813, in 54 yr., m. (1) Anna ——, who d. 26 June, 1799, in 36 yr.; m. (2) 10 Nov., 1799, Wid. Lydia **Bull,** who d. 5 Mch., 1812, in 50 yr.—*S. C. R.*; m. (3) Lucy **Boardman,** 9 Aug., 1812.—*S. C. R.*

Children (W. Ins., & S. C. R.) :

1. Nabby, bp. 29 Oct., 1786.
2. Roxy, bp. 6 Nov., 1791 ; poss. the inf. who d. 26 June, 1794.
3. Norman, bp. 14, d. 28 Aug., ——, ae. 3 mos. 10 d.
4. Selah (twin), b. 1 and bp. 2 Oct., 1796 ; d. 7 Oct., 1796.—*W. Ins.*
5. Seth (twin), b. 1 and bp. 2 Oct., 1796 ; d. Oct., 1796.—*W. Ins.*
(*By second marr.*) :
6. Caroline, bp. 11 Oct., 1801 ; d. 26 Feb., 1812, in 11th yr.—*W. Ins. & S. C. R.*
7. Lucius, bp. 31 July, 1803 (*S. C. R.*) began in the pewtering bus. abt. 1845-6 ; formed

a bus. connection with Thos. Danforth Boardman, of Htfd., and rem. to N. Y. City as business mng'r of firm of Boardman & Hart, mfrs. of block tin and brittania ware. Plated and silverware ultimately came into their line of mfre. and Mr. Hart (Lewis Hart & Co., Burling Slip) acquired a fortune. He was a man of cheerful, merry countenance, an active church, Sunday school and temperance worker, and was highly respected in both business and religious circles.
8. Norman, bp. 22 Dec., 1805.

HARTSHORN, JERUSHA, ae. 78, d. 31 Mch., 1825.—*N. C. R.*

HARTWELL, FARRAND, of Charlottesville [ ], m. Mary **Gibbs,** 27 Nov., 1834.

HASKELL, (*Hascall*), SQUIRE, m. Esther **Humphrey;** he d. 2 Apl., 1801, ae. 53.—*W. C. R.*

Children (*Weth. Rec.*) :

1. Mary, b. 29 Oct., 1789.

2. Joseph, b. 1 Feb., 1792.

ELIZABETH, bp. 6 Sept., 1818.

A. E., of Htfd., m. Martha A. **Gardner,** 25 May, 1854.

WILLIAM R., m. Jennie G. **Blinn,** who was b. 1860 and d. 1893; had—(*W. Ins.*), *Alice Elizabeth,* d. 6 Mch., 1885, ae. 2 wks. 3d.

HASTINGS, CHARLES H., m. Nancy **Whitmore,** both of Ry-H., 30 Sept., 1834; she d. 28 Feb., 1855, ae. 39; had:

1. Thomas, d. 18 Nov., 1847, ae. 2 yrs. 10 mos.

2. Thomas F., d. 10 Sept., 1851. Wid. d. 10 Aug., 1848, in 46th yr.

HATCH, ZEPHANIAH, m. 5 Dec., 1751, Esther **Dickinson,** who d. 9 Jan., 1822, in 91st yr.—*S. C. R.* He d. ae. 76, bu. 7 Mch., 1807; his wid. d. 10 Jan., 1822, ae. 91.—*W. C. R.*

Children (*Weth. Rec. & W. C. R.*) :

1. Luce, b. 6 May, 1752.
2. Jerusha, b. 11 June, 1755.
3 James, b. 26 Oct., 1757. FAM. 2.
4. Moses, b. 15 Mch., 1760. FAM. 3.
5. Mary, b. 13, bp. 18 Apl., 1762.
6. John, b. 22 Aug., 1764.
7. Simeon, b. 26 Nov., 1766. FAM. 4.

8. Samuel, b. 19 Feb., bp. 31 July, 1768.
9. Levi, b. 13 Oct., 1770. FAM. 5.
10. Esther, b. 10 Sept., 1772.
11. Elias, b. 19 Mch., 1774 [1775 *Fam. Rec.*], bp. 19 Mch., 1775.
12. Daniel, b. 26, bp. 30 Aug., 1778. FAM. 6.

FAM. 2. JAMES,[2] (*Zeph.,*[1]), b. 1757; m. (*W. C. R.*), 16 Mch., 1780, Mehitable **Adams,**—*W. C. R.*; he d. at sea, ae. 34, 23 Oct., 1791; she d. 19 Dec., 1831, ae. 72.—*W. C. R.*

Children (*Weth. Rec.*) :

1. Jerusha, b. 23, bp. 26 May, 1781.
2. Mehitable, b. 3, bp. 10 Aug., 1783; m. Daniel **Harris,** of Midd., 8 Mch., 1804.— *W. C. R.*

3. George, b. 15, bp. 24 July, 1785.
4. Sarah Kilborn, b. 21 June, bp. 27 July, 1788.
5. John, b. 21 Sept., bp. Oct., 1791.

FAM. 3. MOSES,[2] (*Zeph.,*[1]) b. 1760; m. Abigail **Loveland,** 21 July, 1785.

Children (*W. C. R.*) :

1. Levi Loveland, bp. 30 Apl., 1786.
2. Abigail, bp. 28 Oct., 1787.
3. Polly, bp. 9 May, 1790; d. ae. 11 mos., bu.

14 Feb., 1791.
4. Polly, bp. 3 Mch., 1793.
5. Esther, bp. 31 Jan., 1796.

FAM. 4. SIMEON,[2] (*Zeph.,*[1]), b. 1766; m. Rebecca **Kilborn,** 4 Apl., 1790.

Children (*W. C. R.*) :

1. George, bp. 21 Aug., 1791.
2. Lucy, bp. 31 Jan., 1796.

3. Mary, bp. 12 Nov., 1797.

FAM. 5. LEVI,[2] (*Zeph.,*[1]), b. 1770; m. 7 (*Fam. Rec.* 23), Dec., 1794, Mary (dau. Hez.) **Crane;** he d. 15 May, 1849, ae. 78; she d. 5 Feb., 1850.—(*Fam. Rec.*)

Children (*Weth. Rec.*) :

1. Samuel, b. 15 (*Fam. Rec.* 12) July, 1795, bp. 24 Sept., 1797; d. 18 (*Fam. Rec.* 12)

July, 1798.

FAM. 6. Capt. DANIEL,[2] (*Zeph.,*[1]), b. 1778; m. Salome **Beadle,** 1 Feb., 1801, who d. ae. 29, bu. 15 June, 1808; prob m. (2) Anna **Belden,** 23 Nov., 1808.

Children (*W. C. R.*) :

1. Daniel, b. 13 Mch., 1803.
2. Inf., ae. 2 mos. d. 2 Apl., 1805.
3. Henry, d. 15 Apl., 1807, ae. 4 wks.—

Weth. Ins.				
4. Henry, d.	8 Aug.,	1809,	ae. 4	mos.—
Weth. Ins.				

HAVENS, THOMAS. (Furnished by FRANK W. HAVENS, Esq., of Hartford, Ct.) There is an (unsubstantiated) trad. that he was a native of Weth., his mother having been an Elizabeth **Robbins,** of that town, who m. a sea-captain commanding a vessel trading between the Conn. ports and the West Indies, and who was lost at sea shortly after his marriage and prior to the birth of his son. It is believed by some however that Thomas, Jr., was of the Suffolk County, (N. Y.) family and came to Weth. when a young boy to learn the trade of ship carpenter. While no recs. have as yet been found to confirm this supposition the fact that his own and his children's names are constant family names among the Suffolk county family lends color to the claim. The fact is pretty well estab. that, long before he was of age, he was a workman in the ship yard of Benjamin Adams, then located at the Cove, and it is said that, up to the time of his death, his sons worked there with him; 30th Jan., 1783 he m. Lucinda Sept., 1828. His death occurred 14th Sept., 1825. The date of his birth was June, 1761. They both joined the Weth. Ch. in Jan., 1821.

Children (*bp. W. Ch. Rec.*) :

1. Sarah, b. 9 Aug., 1784, bp. 29 Oct., 1786 ; d. 16 Mch., 1805.
2. Sylvester, b. 19 Sept., 1785, bp. 29 Oct., 1786. FAM. 2.
3. Thomas, b. 19 Sept., 1787, bp. 14 Oct., 1787. FAM. 3.
4. Uzziel, b. 24 Nov., 1789 ; bp. 20 Dec., 1789. FAM. 4.
5. Nancy, b. 6 Mch., bp. 29 July, d. 16 Aug.,

   1792.
6. William Adams, b. 27 Oct., 1794, bp. 9 Feb., 1795. FAM. 5.
7. Henry, b. 14 May, 1796, bp. 26 Nov., 1797. FAM. 5.
8. Nancy, b. 6 July, 1798 ; d. 4 Aug., 1887.
9. Hiram, b. 17 May, 1803. FAM. 7.
10. Sarah.

FAM. 2. SYLVESTER,[2] (*Thomas,*[1]), b. 1785; m. Caroline Matilda **Hills,** of East Htfd., b. 1788 and d. 21 Apl., 1847; he d. 9 Oct., 1852; after his father's dth. rem. to Htfd. and was know as Capt. Sylvester; he built some of the most prominent bldgs. of that city, and was the "building mover" of the city. It is said he moved the first brick bldg. ever undertaken there.

Children:

1. George Hills, b. 16 Dec., 1813 ; res. and d. unm. 5 Oct., 1866, in Htfd.
2. Sylvester A., b. 28 Feb., 1815. FAM. 8.
3. Samuel Hayford, b. 16 Sept., 1819. FAM. 9.
4. Walter H., b. 29 Aug., 1821. FAM. 10.
5. Caroline Matilda, b. 29 Dec., 1817 ; m. 10 Apl., 1839, William C. **Learned,** who was b. 24 May, 1810, and d. 7 May, 1899. She d. 20 June 1868. *Issue:*
   i. Ellen G. (Learned), b. 10 Jan.; d. 29 Mch., 1892.
   ii. Everett C. (Learned), b. 7 June, 1843 ; m. 27 Dec., 1866, Fannie A. **Moore,** b. 15 July, 1844, and d. 26 May, 1903.
   iii. Charles F. (Learned), b. 12 July, 1844.
6. William H., b. 29 Apl., 1824 ; m. 24 Feb., 1850, Susan B. **Gates,** b. 29 Mch., 1826 ; he d. 11 Dec., 1872 ; was a bridge builder in Htfd.
7. Ann A., b. 9 July, 1828 ; m. 16 Oct., 1848, Geo. B. **Carey,** who was b. 20 July, 1823, and d. 8 May, 1902 : She d. 10 Apl., 1898. *Issue:*
   i. George Havens (Carey), b. 3 Jan., 1852 ; m. 11 Oct., 1876, Grace G. **Whitney;** had (a) Ralph Whitney (Carey),

   b. 25 Apl., 1881.
   ii. Frank Sumner (Carey), b. 3 Apl., 1854 ; m. 3 Feb., 1880, Ella Louise **Bissell,** b. 1 June, 1855. They have (a) Ruth Bissell (Carey), b. 29 Apl., 1884 ; d. 4 June, 1884 : (b) Hiram Bissell (Carey), b. 12 Apl., 1886 : (c) Harold Dearborn (Carey), b. 11 June, 1895.
8. Jane A., b. 9 July, 1828 ; m. 18 Feb., 1850, William H. **Miller,** who was b. 29 Apl., 1822, and d. 16 Oct., 1894. *Issue:*
   i. Ida Louise (Miller), b. 27 Sept., 1851.
   ii. Arthur Howard (Miller), b. 13 July, 1854 ; m. 4 May, 1880, Susan Nellie **Hale,** b. 27 July, 1859. They had (a) Elsie Louise (Miller), b. 11 Aug., 1881 ; (b) Bessie Hale (Miller), b. 14 Mch., 1886 ; (c) Ruth Havens (Miller), b. 3 Jan., 1890.
9. Ellen Sophia, b. 28 Feb., 1833 ; m. 22 Nov., 1852, Elisha Sumner **Risley,** who was b. 9 May, 1827 ; d. 21 Mch, 1897. She d. 4 Mch., 1895 ; was a singer of more than local reputation.

SUNRISE ACROSS THE COVE, LOOKING EAST—EARLY SPRING, WATER HIGH AND FROZEN.

Photo. by Albert W. Morgan.

FAM. 3. THOMAS,[2] (*Thomas*,[1]), b. 1787; m. 8 Nov., 1812, Patty **Blinn**, who was b. 14 June, 1788, d. 21 May, 1864. He d. 10 May, 1857; with his bros. Henry and Hiram was connected in the bldg. of a fleet of steamboats which ran in connection, by relays, between Htfd. and Bellows Falls, Vt. Later worked as a carpenter in Weth.; ever a useful and respected man.

Children:

1. Nancy Blinn, b. 24 Aug., d. 12 Sept., 1814.
2. Nancy Blinn, b. 13 July, 1817; d. 31 Mch., 1819.
3. Nancy Blinn, b. 7 Sept., 1819; d. 23 Sept., 1822.
4. Thomas, b. 16 May, 1821; d. 2 Nov., 1835.
5. Emily Blinn, b. 31 Jan., 1824; d. 6 Apl., 1892, unm.
6. Elizabeth Robbins, b. 1825; m. (as his 2d wife) Welles **Adams**; d. 1895.—See *Adams*.
7. Martha Celestia, b. 14 Mch., 1830; d. 9 Aug., 1830.
8. Horace Cary, b. 21 Nov., 1827; d. 17 Mch., 1899. FAM. 11.

FAM. 4. UZZIEL,[2] (*Thomas*,[1]), b. 1789; m. 1 Sept., 1813, Rachel **Jagger**, who was b. 17 May, 1792 and d. 14 May, 1870. He d. 14 Feb., 1825 at Matanzas, Cuba, whither he had gone to buy ship timber.

Children:

1. Mary, b. 2 May, 1814; d. 27 July, 1815.
2. Mary Melissa, b. 20 Feb., 1816; m. 17 July, 1846, Julius **Hollister**, who was b. 9 Jan. 1818—who is still living. She d. 25 Mch., 1895. *Issue:*
   i. Charles J. (Hollister), b. 21 June, 1851.
   ii. Arthur E. (Hollister), b. 23 Mch., 1853; d. 2 Jan., 1871.
3. William Grimes, b. 20 Feb., 1820; went to sea. as ship's carpenter—then was a cooper; m. a (half-caste) native woman of the Sandwich Islands. *Issue:*
   i. Acsah Emma (Havens), b. 21 Mch., 1864; d. 18 Jan., 1878.
   ii. Eva (Havens), b. 8 Apl., 1866; d. 3 Nov., 1897; both these daus. were adopted by Rev. Geo. Whipple (bro. of the late Bishop Whipple), who brought them to the U. S. and educated them.
4. Charles Hiram, b. 2 Apl., 1818; d. 24 Jan., 1847.
5. Hannah M., b. 19 Feb., 1822, d. 19 Apl., 1844.
6. Uzziel Adams, b. 13 July, 1824; d. 21 Jan., 1842.

FAM. 5. WILLIAM ADAMS,[2] (*Thomas*,[1]), b. 1793; m. 9 Jan., 1817, Mary **Waterbury**, who b. 1792, d. 6 Sept., 1865. Was the miller at the Adams' Mill, also, a farmer. He d. 29 Aug., 1865.

Children:

1. William Waterbury, b. 13 Nov., 1817. FAM. 12.
2. John, b. 19 Oct., 1819. FAM. 13.
3. Simeon, b. 22 Oct., 1821. FAM. 14.
4. Mary Waterbury, b. 4 Dec., 1823; m. 10 Apl., 1849, Seldon S. **Williams**. *Issue:*
   i. Mary F. (Williams), b. 6 Apl., ; d. 12 Sept., 1851.
   ii. Everett Seldon (Williams), b. 3 Dec., 1861; m. 28 May, 1902, Clementine **Seymour**; have (a) Clifton Seymour (Williams), b. 1 Apl., 1903.
5. Irene, b. 31 June, 1826; m. 3 June, 1851, Henry J. **Cleveland**, of Boston, Mass.
   She d. 9 Nov., 1869. *Issue:*
   i. Emma Irene (Cleveland), b. 2 Apl., 1852; m. Wells H. **Baker**, 1874.
   ii. Minnie F. (Cleveland), b. 24 Oct., 1856.
6. Huldah Waterbury, b. 1827; m. 25 Apl., 1872, Ebenezer **Wiswall**; she d. 9 Oct., 1888.
7. Ebenezer G., b. 23 Feb., 1829. FAM. 15.
8. Hiram, b. 3; d. 11 Feb., 1832.
9. Albert, b. Oct., 1833; d. 14 Apl., 1834.
10. Thomas, b. 16 June, 1835; m. 5 Dec., 1865, Mary A. **Denton**, who was b. 19 Aug., 1847; he was an engraver in Boston; rem. to and d. at Chelsea, Mass.

FAM. 6 HENRY, (—————————————), b. 14 May, 1796; m. 25 Dec., 1825, Chloe Wing **Keene**, of New York, b. 2 Aug., 1804, who d. 6 July, 1873. He d. 12 June, 1868; he was, with his bro. Hiram, a builder of boats on the Conn. River, and of locks on the Wilhampton and New Haven Canal; sett. at and d. Fair Haven, Ct.

Children:

1. Joseph T., b. 5 Feb., 1827. FAM. 16.
2. Russell H., b. 13 Dec., 1829. FAM. 17.
3. Frederick Adams, b. 13 Sept., 1830. FAM. 18.
4. Lucinda Adams, b. 17 Oct., 1831; m. 27 Mch., 1849, Henry L. **Thomas**, who d. 28 Jan., 1855; she d. 28 Aug., 1854. *Issue:*
   i. John Henry (Thomas), b. 25 Apl., 1851.
5. Edwin Martin, b. 5 Sept., 1837. FAM. 19.
6. George Leander, b. 8 Oct., 1838; m. 27 Dec., 1864, Ellen F. **Nye**; b. 9 Mch., 1840. He d. 14 Feb., 1895.

FAM. 7. HIRAM,[2] (*Thomas,*[1]), b. 17 May, 1803; m. 13 Feb., 1833, Mary Welles **Adams**, b. 25 Oct., 1811, d. 19 Nov., 1876. He d. 30 Oct., 1886..

Children:

1. Catharine Adelia, b. 27 Sept. ,1834 ; m. 19 Jan., 1870, Hon. Thomas **McManus**; b. 20 Jan., 1834.
2. Emma Eliza, b. 7 Oct., 1836.
3. Edward Newton, b. 10 Oct., 1838. FAM. 20.
4. Francis, b. 2 Dec., 1845. FAM. 21.
5. Charles Hiram, b. 15 July, 1849 ; d. 17 Sept., 1850.

FAM. 8. SYLVESTER A.,[3] (*Sylvester,*[2] *Thomas,*[1]), b. 1815; m. Olive H. **Goodwin**, 9 Dec., 1842. He was a pattern-maker; lived, marr. and d. in Htfd. 6 June, 1886.

Children:

1. Ralph G., b. 7 Dec.. 1842 ; d. ————.
2. Roselle, b. 11 May, 1845 ; d. 19 Mch., 1853.

FAM. 9. SAMUEL HAYFORD,[3] (*Sylvester,*[2] *Thomas,*[1]), b. 16 Sept., 1819; m. Eliza **Welles**, 20 July, 1842; she b. 19 Nov., 1817, d. 2 Apl., 1886. He d. 23 Sept., 1883; was for many yrs. a bridge-builder; res. in Htfd. and until nearly the end of his life an inspector and purchasing agent of the Htfd., Bos. & Fishkill R. R.; also for some yrs. Chief of the Htfd. Fire Dep't.

Children:

1. Alice Maria, b. 3 Oct., 1843 ; m. 3 Oct., 1864, Thomas Roland **Berry**; b. 3 Aug., 1841. *Issue:*
   i. Frederick Daniel (Berry), b. 1 May, 1866 ; m. 3 Oct., 1894, Ella Marshall **Harrison**; she d. 8 Apl., 1902.
   ii. Samuel Havens (Berry), b. 9 Dec., 1869 ; m. 18 Nov., 1896, Mary Jane **Courtice**; had:
   (a) Courtice Havens (Berry), b. 22 June, 1901.
2. Dudley Watson, b. 19 Sept., 1845 ; m. 20 May, 1867, Eva Jane **Cotney**. FAM. 22.
3. Hattie Adelaide, b. 27 June, 1848 ; m. 23 Dec., 1868, James **Morgan**. *Issue:*
   i. James Havens (Morgan), b. 7 Feb., 1875 ; m. 7 Dec., 1898, Adeline Sedgwick **Belden**; has a son James Belden (Morgan), b. 1 Oct., 1899.
   ii. Florence Estelle (Morgan), b. 11 Sept., 1882 ; unm.
4. Estelle Fidelia, b. 28 Oct., 1850 ; m. 17 Sept., 1872, Robert Chauncey **Northam**, 2d, who was b. 12 July, 1844 ; d. 7 May, 1881. *Issue:*
   i. Robert Chauncey (Northam), Jr., b. 15 Dec., 1873 ; m. 7 Oct., 1896, Elsie Estella **Dibble**; had (a) Robert Chauncey (Northam), b. 13 Nov., 1897 ; (b) Ruth Theresa, b. 27 Jan., 1904.

FAM. 10. WALTER H.,[3] (*Sylvester,*[2] *Thomas,*[1]), b. 1821; m. 7 Dec., 1843. Frances **Butler**, who was b. 3 July, 1820; res. in Htfd., where for many yrs. he held a position in the Htfd P. O.; was later a Street Comm'r; and at time of his dth. president of the Htfd. Co. Fire Ins. Co. He d. 16 June, 1876.

Children:

1. Frances B., b. 21 June, 1848 ; m. 11 Oct., 1876, Roderick Walton **Farmer**; b. 27 Apl., 1847. *Issue:*
   i. Walter Havens (Farmer), b. 25 Jan., 1879.
   ii. Alice Havens (Farmer), b. 6 May, 1887.
2. Mary Letty W., b. 9 Apl., 1851.
3. Ellen S., b. 30 Aug., 1854.
4. Sumner Risley, b. 8 Dec., 1858 ; d. 29 Mch., 1861.
5. Walter K., b. 24 Jan., 1862 ; d. 14 Dec., 1884.
6. George Hatch, b. 20 Aug., 1866 ; m. 6 Apl., 1893, Edith **Annis**, b. 27 Oct., 1869, s. p.

FAM. 11. HORACE CARY,[3] (*Thomas, Jr.,*[2] *Thomas,*[1]), b. 1827; m. (1) 12 May, 1852, Rhoda Fidelia **Welles**, who was b. 14 Nov., 1829; d. 5 Aug., 1870; He m. (2) 21 May, 1872, Sarah Elizabeth **Clark**, b. 2 Mch., 1829, who d. 13 Aug., 1886. He d. 17 Mch., 1899; was for many yrs. press sup't of the *Htfd. Courant;* later rem. to Providence, R. I., and again to Chicago, where his son Frank W. res. and there d.; bu. in Weth.

Children (by first marr.):

1. Frank Welles, b. 21 Feb., 1853.
2. Thomas Clifford, b. 16 Sept., 1860. FAM. 23.
3. Virginia Augusta, b. 29 Aug., 1855; d. 9 Mch., 1856.
4. Lizzie Adelaide, b. 22 Sept., 1865 ; d. 7 July, 1866.
5. Howard Burton, b. 31 Jan., 1867 ; d. 6 Mch., 1867.

FAM. 12. WILLIAM WATERBURY,[3] (*Wm. Adams*,[2] *Thomas*,[1]), b. 13 Nov., 1817; d. 13 Jan., 1901; m. (1) in 1846, Eliza **Burns**, who was b. 1818 and d. 31 Aug., 1865; m. (2) 16 Oct., 1867, Amanda **Seymour**, who was b. 17 Dec., 1824 and d. 19 Dec., 1890. He was a carpenter and ho-bldr. under whose supervision many fine houses were builded in Htfd., where he res. until abt. two yr. before his dth. when he rem. to Ry-H. where he d.

Children (all by first marr.) :

1. Gertrude M., b. 24 Oct., 1848 ; d. 17 Aug., 1899 ; m. 14 May, 1872, Geo. S. **Cleveland**, of Boston, Mass. ; had (only ch.) :
   i. Elsie H. (Cleveland), b. 30 Nov., 1881.

2. Florence B., d. 21 Apl., 1852, ae. 5 mos.
3. Florence A., d. 26 Aug., 1854, ae. 3 mos.
4. Lewis C., d. 19 Aug., 1857, ae. 3 mos.

FAM. 13. JOHN,[3] (*William A.*,[2] *Thomas*,[1]), b. 1819; m. (1) 13 Jan., 1848, Martha **Welles**, who was b. 9 Sept., 1820, and d. 18 Jan., 1887; he m. (2) 15 Mch., 1888, A. Maria **Adams**, b. 21 Jan., 1842; farmer; rem. to Missouri, where he farmed on a large scale; ret. to Weth. where he d. 9 May, 1898.

Children:

1. Irene A., b. 10 Dec., 1850 ; m. 7 Sept...1875, Stephen F. **Willard**, who was b. 7 Feb., 1851. *Issue:*
   i. Arthur C. (Willard), b. 29 July, 1876.
   ii. Thomas H. (Willard), b. 11 Feb., 1878.
   iii. Edward W. (Willard), b. 1 Apl., 1883.
   iv. Stephen F. (Willard), b. 1 Nov., 1885.
   v. John C. (Willard), b. 29 Mch., 1892.
2. Fannie A., b. 20 Jan., 1854 ; m. 22 Feb., 1875, Benj. F. **Pierce**. *Issue:*
   i. John H. (Pierce), b. 4 Aug., 1876.

ii. Irene A. (Pierce), b. 8 Mch., 1878 ; m. 15 Oct., 1900, Jas. H. **Stragner**.
iii. Benjamin F. (Pierce), b. 21 Nov., 1880.
3. Ashbel W., b. 17 Nov., 1855.
4. William A., twin to Ashbel W. FAM. 24.
5. John A., b. 17 Nov., 1855.
6. Martha Elizabeth, b. 21 Aug., 1862 ; d. 8 Aug., 1865.
7. Robert Martin, b. 18 Dec., 1867 ; d. 30 Aug., 1868.

FAM. 14. SIMEON,[3] (*William A.*,[2] *Thomas*,[1]), b. 1821; m. 3 June, 1851, Jeanette S. **Griswold**, who was b. 1821, and d. 23 Oct., 1863. He was an engraver and silversmith for many yrs. in Boston, but ret. to Weth. where he d.

Children:

1. Jeanette K., b. 1852 ; d. 19 Aug., 1886.
2. Charles H., b. 1854 ; d. 1893. FAM. 25.

3. Frankie W., b. 1858 ; d. 3 June, 1860.
4. Florence, b. 15 June, d. 15 Sept., 1861.

FAM. 15. EBENEZER G.,[3] (*William A.*,[2] *Thomas*,[1]), b. 1829; m. (1) 29 Nov., 1855, Melvina M. **Ruick**, who was b. 19 Mch., 1830, and d. 14 Apl., 1862; he m. (2) 9 Apl., 1866, Jennie A. **Martin**, who was b. 26 Nov., 1848, and d. 12 Nov., 1901; he was a farmer, and res. in So. Weth.

Children (by first marr.) :

1. Owen Ruick, b. 23 Aug., 1856 ; m. 27 May, 1887, Lillian S. **White;** b. 20 Apl., 1852 ; he res. in Ry-H.; Selectman and has rep. the town in the Legislature.
2. Nellie M., b. 27 Dec., 1858.
(*By second marriage*) :
3. Leila G., b. 7 July, 1868 ; m. 26 May, 1885, Frank G. **Sherwood**. *Issue:*
   i. Everett W. (Sherwood), b. 25 Apl.,

1888.
ii. Harold H. (Sherwood), b. 7 May, 1889 ; d. 2 Dec., 1892.
iii. Charles H. (Sherwood), b. 12 May, 1892.
iv. Philip R. (Sherwood), b. 21 Apl., 1895.
v. Lee S. (Sherwood), b 9 Jan., 1903.
vi. William C. (Sherwood).

FAM. 16. JOSEPH T.,[3] (*Henry*,[2] *Thomas*,[1]), b. 1827; m. 3 July, 1853, Mary Ann **Foote**, who was b. 24 Jan., 1826, and d. 8 June, 1896; he d. 2 Jan., 1897.

Children:

1. Eugene W., b. 15 Sept., 1854 ; d. 18 Dec., 1868.
2. Herbert A., b. 6 July, 1861 ; d. 21 Sept., 1862.

3. Grace J., b. 18 Sept., 1864 ; d. 26 July, 1865.
4. Frederick W., b. 3 Aug., 1866 ; d. 17 Apl., 1876.

FAM. 17. RUSSELL H.,³ (*Henry,² Thomas,¹*), b. 1828; d. 20 Apl., 1864; m. 21 Mch., 1861, Ann W. **Perkins,** who was b. 12 Sept., 1831, d. 23 Mch., 1900.

Children:

1. Edith Russell, b. 28 Aug., 1864; m. 7 Oct., 1896, John Francis **Donovan**; b. 28 May, 1871. *Issue:*
    i. Colton Francis (Donovan), b. 31 Dec.,

1899.
    ii. Nellie Doris (Donovan), b. 13 Apl., 1902.

FAM. 18. FREDERICK A.,³ (*Henry,² Thomas,¹*), b. 1830; m. (1) 27 May, 1851, Jemima **Dunham,** who was b. 17 Sept., 1831 and d. 9 Feb., 1887; he m. (2) Lydia V. M. **Hollister,** b. 10 Nov., 1840.

Children (by first marr.):

1. Ella, b. 1 May, 1853; d. 18 Jan., 1865.
2. Jennie W., b. 3 Feb., 1855; m. 5 June, 1895, Leslie E. **Adams**; b. 25 Feb., 1847.
3. Minnie Amanda, b. 2 May, 1863; m. 26 June, 1895, Homer Tomlinson **Partree,** M. D., b. 1 Dec., 1865. *Issue:*
    i. Eulalie (Partree), b. 19 June, 1896.
    ii. Pauline May (Partree), b. 17 July,

1897.
    iii. Gladys (Partree), b. 11 June, 1900.
4. May, b. 24 May, 1867; d. 11 Jan., 1892; m. 30 Jan., 1889, Geo. W. **Nichols**; b. 23 Oct., 1865. *Issue:*
    i. Ward C. (Nichols), b. 25 Aug., 1891; d. 11 Jan., 1892.

FAM. 19. EDWIN MARTIN,³ (*Henry,² Thomas,¹*), b. 1837; m. (1) 28 Aug., 1858, Julia Ann **Welles,** who was b. 9 Mch., 1835, and d. 7 Sept., 1883; m. (2) Caledonia **Adams.**

Children (by first marr.):

1. Irving Welles, b. 1 July, 1860; m. 17 Oct., 1883, Cora **Wolcott,** b. 11 Dec., 1862.
2. Lena Ruth, b. 7 Apl., 1866; m. 10 June,

1902, Augustus **Whiting,** who was b. 10 Aug., 1857.

FAM. 20. EDWARD NEWTON,³ (*Hiram,² Thomas,¹*), b. 1838; m. 5 July, 1861, Harriet E. **Callendar,** b. 15 Oct., 1842.

Children:

1. Charles Edward, b. 1862; d. 5 Sept., 1866.
2. Martha Adams, b. 10 Jan., 1863; m. 21

Jan., 1891, Burmaton **Gorden,** who was b. 14 May, 1855; she d. 29 Oct., 1903.

FAM. 21. FRANCIS W.,³ (*Hiram,² Thomas,¹*), b. 1845; m. May, 1870, Eliza Wright **Brainard,** who was b. 24 Sept., 1843. Studied law; but is now supervisor in the Htfd. Life Ins. Co., where he edits the Co.'s paper and other literature. Is a prominent Free Mason, and in 1898, Grand Master of the order in Conn. He has been most helpful in this Haven's Genealogy.

Children:

1. Frank Stuart, b. 17 Dec., 1871; grad. Y. C., 1896, with two yrs.' honors in Science; after 3 yrs. serivice in Kent Laboratory as teacher, and having a post-grad. course he obtained the degree of Ph. D.; is memb. of the Am. Chemical Socy., the

Am. Branch of the Eng. Chem. Socy.; Hon. memb. of the German Chem. Socy. of Berlin, and is connected in bus. with a large Chem. Mfg. Co., of N. Y., as expert chem. adviser.
2. Mary Catharine C., b. 21 Aug., 1876.

FAM. 22. DUDLEY WATSON,⁴ (*Sam'l H.,³ Slyvester,² Thomas,¹*), b. 1845; m. 20 May, 1867, Eva Jane **Cotney.** Res. Htfd. where is an inspector on the Water Bd.

Children:

1. Hattie Louise, b. 3 Feb., 1868; ; m. 20 May, 1889, Edwin Towne **Staples.** *Issue:*
    i. Eva Havens (Staples), b. 31 May,

1890.
2. Samuel Howard, b. 17 Jan., 1875.

FAM. 23. THOMAS CLIFFORD,⁴ (*Horace C.,³ Thomas Jr.,² Thomas,¹*), b. 1860; m. 14 Apl., 1885, Katherine Marie Louise **Cubbage,** who was b. Oct., 1861.

Children:

1. Elizabeth Katherine, b. 5 Feb. 1886.
2. Horace Edward, b. 31 Jan., 1888.

3. Florence Louise, b. 8 July, 1890.
4. Grace Adelaide, b. 17 Nov., 1891.

FAM. 24. WILLIAM A.,[4] (*John*,[3] *William A.*,[2] *Thomas*,[1]), b. 17 Nov., 1855; m. 9 Feb., 1880, Phebe S. **Brownell.**

Children:

1. Albert W., b. 26 Nóv., 1882.
2. Charles B., b. 9 July, 1884.

3. John T., b. 15 Oct., 1886.
4. Martha E., b. 5 Apl., 1889.

FAM. 25. CHARLES H.,[4] (*Simeon*,[3] *Wm. A.*,[2] *Thomas*,[1]), b. 1854; d. 1893; m. 21 June, 1883, Carrie E. (dau. of John) **Amidon;** he was a very skilful engraver and illustrator in Boston; but rem. to and d. in Weth. The leading systems of penmanship in use in U. S. are monuments of his genius and skill; and he could etch upon copper, without the use of wax, the finest script lines.

Child:

1. Lillian A., b. 26 June, 1887.

HAYFORD, SAMUEL, of Far., m. Thankful **Adams,** 22 Mch., 1791,—*issue, Samuel,* bp. after his father's dth., 12 Nov., 1792; d. 10 Jan., 1816, ae. 25.— *W. C. R.*; his wife Hannah, d. 15 Aug., 1878, ae. 91 yr. 8 mo.; their dau. *Julia Ann*, d. 9 Oct., 1830 ae. 16 yr.—*W. Ins.*

MARTHA, m. John A. **Tieburt,** of N. Y., 31 Oct., 1830.—*W. T. R.*

THANKFUL, m. Silas **Goff,** of Far., 12 May, 1814.—*W. C. R.*

HAYWARD, (See *Howard*).

HEMPSTED, JOSHUA, m. Anne **Buck,** 12 Dec., 1758.—*W. C. R.*

HENDERSON, JOHN S. R., of Queensbury, N. Y., m. Emily **Corey,** 14 Sept., 1817.

HENDY, JONATHAN. His nuncupative will rec. in *Htfd. Co. Prob.,* date 18 May, 1688. "He gave to his mother £10; to his sister Hannah **Belden,** £5; and all the rest of his estate to his brother Richard **Hendy,** and app. Benjamin Church-ill, Exer." Signed by Benjamin. Churchill and John Wiard. See, also, *Hand* and *Handy*, p. 409.

HENRY, LEMUEL, of Htfd., m. Martha Churchill **Steele,** 25 Aug., 1811.

HENSHAW, BENJAMIN, of Midd., m. Huldah **Sumner,** of Weth., 2 July, 1761.— *W. C. R.*

HENCY, (or *Hancy*) JOSEPH, was father of Lucy Blinn's ch. both of Weth., Feb. 1733.—*Co. Ct. Rec.*

HENDRICK, Benj., d. ae. 25, Nov., 25, 1822.—*N. C. R.*

HEIFFORD, wid. HANNAH had ch. bp. 24 Aug., 1823—viz.: Martha, Jane and Julia Ann—the latter d. 10 Oct., 1830.

HEMMENWAY, (*Hemmingway*) SENECA, m. Lucy **Francis,** 9 Oct., 1831.

EDWARD (*Hemmingway*), m. Sarah Ann **Francis,** 29 May, 1845.

HIGGINS, Dr. JOSEPH, d. 18 July, 1797, ae. 38; he m. 18 Dec., 1785, Nancy **Williams.** *Children (W. C. R. and W. Ins.):* Nancy, William Henry, Joseph Edwin, and Silas, bp. 6 June, 1796. William, bp. 19 July, 1796, who d. 12 Sept, 1797, in 9th yr. Mary, bp. 6 Aug., 1797.

DEUEL, of So. Glast, m. Fanny **Blinn,** 24 Mch., 1819.

HILL, *(Hills)* DAVID, of E. Htfd., m. Amelia H. **Talcott,** 14 Feb., 1822; he prob. the D. who d. 18 Oct., 1856 ae. 56.—*W. Ins.*

Children (W. C. R.):

1. David Henry, d. 25 Aug., 1824, ae. 1 yr. 2 mos.—*W. Ins.*
2. Amelia Talcott, bp. 2 Nov., 1825.
3. Huldah Elizabeth, bp. 10 Nov., 1829.
4. Inf., ae. 2 yrs., bu. 10 Nov., 1829.
5. David Henry, d. 1 May, 1833, ae. 2 yrs. 7 mos.
6. Harriet A., d. 20 July, 1838, ae. 6 wks.

BENJAMIN, m. Mary (dau. John) **Bronson,** 11 Jan., 1688.—*(Weth. Rec.)* Query: Can this be the B. who, acc. to *Savage,* was of New Haven, 1646, but rem. soon after taking the oath of fidelity?

WILLIAM, res. E. side the River, 1653; m. Phillis (dau. Richard) **Lyman,** of Htfd. (rem. to Fairfield?).—See *Hills.*

HILLHOUSE, NATHANIEL, d. 20 Apl., 1845, ae. 53.—*N. C. R.*

Dea. SAMUEL, of Montville, d. 22 Dec., 1834, ae. 74.

HILLIARD, BENJAMIN, whom *Savage* calls s. of Hugh, freeman of Salem, Mass., was cattle herder for Weth., 1648 (*Weth. T. V.,* I, 31); was, acc. to a bond executed by him and duly rec. on *Weth. T. V.,* I, p. 1, Mch., 15, 1649, the son-in-law of Thos. Wright. He had been fined by the Gen. Ct. £10 and ordered to procure a bond of that amt. to secure his good behavior for the next 12 mos. He secured his father-in-law, Wright, for this bond by transfer to him of "my house, and barne and home-lot, that was given me by my father-in-law, John **Elson,** in his last will and test. in reversion, after the dth. of my mother"— from which it seems that he had been twice marr. (1) to dau. of Elson; (2) to a dau of **Wright.** *Savage,* II, p. 421, seems to have been in error, in attributing these two marr. to Benjamin's mother, Margaret, wid. of his father Hugh, who d. 1670, and had, he says, no issue by either Elson or Wright.— See Chapt. VII, Vol. I.

JOB, (s. Hugh, of Salem, and bro. of Benj. above).—See Chapt. VII, Vol. I.

HILTON, JOHN, d. 1686, had (*Hinman*) John, ae. 11; Richard, ae. 7; Mary, ae. 14; Ebenezer, ae. 8 mos.

HINE, DANIEL S., the wife of, d. 24 Oct., 1832, in 25th yr.

HINSDEL, *(Hinsdale)* JOSEPH, m. Elizabeth ————; had (*Weth. Rec.*): 1. Abel, b. 20 June, 1750. 2. William, b. (and bp.—*N. C. R.*), 16 Feb., 1752.

HITCHCOCK, LUKE, *Savage* (II, 428) from whom we eke out some details to complete the meagre *Weth. Rec.,* says he came to Weth. fm. New Haven.—See Chapt. VII, Vol. I. *Weth. Rec.* say he m. Elizabeth ————, and that he d. 1 Nov., 1659. His cattle earmark rec. (*W. T. V.,* I, p. 2) and he was at one time a selectman at Weth. His will was dated 17 Oct., 1659. Invent. £452-00-00, taken 28 Nov., 1659, by John Russell, John Hubbard and Thomas Welles. He gave his wife full power to dispose of the est. but if she marr. again she was to have only her thirds, and give to his sons John, Luke and dau. Hannah £40, with her uncle's gift when they came of age. He desired Rev. Mr. Russell, with the church, to appoint overseers. This will, witnessed by John Russell, Thomas Coleman and Thomas Welles, was exhib. in Ct. I Dec., 1659.—*Htfd. Prob. Ct. Rec.* Among articles inventoried were 8 hives of *bees*, and 50 lbs. of *hops*. His wid. (says *Savage*) m. (2) 2 Oct., 1661, William **Warriner,** of Springfield, Mass., and (3) Joseph **Baldwin,** of Hadley.

Children:

1. Hannah, m. 2 Oct., 1661, Chiliab **Smith,** of Hadley.
2. John, (afterwards of Springfield)—see *Savage* for family.—See Chapt. VII, Vol. I.
3. Luke, b. (*Weth. Rec.*) 5 June, 1665; also of Springfield—and Sheriff of Hamnden Co., Mass.

JEREMIAH (Hickock), who d. H., 1827, in 49th yr.—*W. C. R.,* had Mary Caroline, who m Andrew **Williams,** 24 Feb., 1835; George Myron; Laura Olive; and Sydney Norton, bp. 26 July, 1818. Horace, bp. 22 Oct., 1820, and d. 14 July, 1822, in 3d yr. Horace Francis, bp. 3 Nov., 1822.

JAMES HENRY, of Waterbury, Ct., m. Sophia **Kilby,** 15 Apl., 1811.—*W. C. R.*

(*Hicox*) BENNETT (or Benoni), of Watertown, Ct., m. Harriet **Gibbs,** 30 Apl., 1802.

HOBBY, JONATHAN, of Boston, m. Sarah **Walker,** of Weth., 24 Apl., 1781.— *W. C. R.*

HODGE, (*Hodges*), d. 18 Jan., 1712-13 "in ye afternoon."—*Weth. Rec.* Invent. £36-15-03, taken 30 Jan., 1712-13, by John Goodrich and James Patterson; *Ct. Rec.,* 12 Feb., 1712-13, adm. gr. to Thomas Kircum of Weth.; final order to distr. est. to bros. and sisters equally, to *Thomas,* to *John,* to *Abigail,* all of Weth.—*Htfd. Co. Prob.*

JAMES, s-in-law to Thos. Kirkham, and s. to Dorcas, wife of Thos. Kirkham, which said James is now bound and apprenticed to Samuel Wright; b. 12 July, 1687.

HOGENS, JAMES, m. Mary ————.

Child (*Weth. Rec.*) :

1. James, b. 14 Mch., 1734-5.

JAMES, m. F———— **Minor,** 31 July, 1782.—*N. C. R.*

HOISINGTON, JOHN, who was a soldier in Capt. Samuel Wadsworth's Mass. Co. in King Philip's War, 1675-6, and on Feb. 8, 1678-9, took the freeman's oath at Hatfield; abt. 1689, was a signer, *at Weth.,* to a petition for the erection of a plantation at Wabaquesset, or Mattabeset Country, etc.—*A. Kidder.*

HOLBROOK, CHESTER, of Lebanon, m. Harriet **Deming,** 15 Feb., 1815.

HOLCOMB, ERASTUS, of Granby, m. Laura **Robbins,** 11 Feb., 1837.

EDMUND, of Granby, m. Mabel **Wells,** 13 June, 1833.

HOLDIN, (*W. C. R.*) CHANY, of Colebrook, m. Mary Stocking **Abbe**, 6 Jan., 1833.

EBEN, a ch. of, d. 3 Oct., 1825, in 2d yr.

EBEN MITCHELL, of Granby, Ct., m. Hepzibah **Goodrich**, 3 Nov., 1785.

ISAAC, m. Sarah **Potter**, 28 Feb., 1822; had inf., d. 2 Mch., 1823.

MARILLA, d. 29 Jan., 1838, in 18th yr.

WILLIAM, of Granville, Mass., m. Prudence **Belden**, 21 Feb., 1795.

WILLIAM, ch. of, d. 17 Mch., 1807, in 2d. yr.; had Edmund, bp. 8 Mch., 1807; Austin, bp. 3 Dec., 1797; Sylvester, bp. 11 Oct., 1801; Isaac, bp. 13 Oct., 1799.

HOLLEN, HORATIO P., m. Julia N. **Lewis**, 14 Nov., 1830; their inf. d. 4 Dec., 1832.

JOHN, m. Emeline **Goodrich**, 22 Apl., 1832.

HOLLISTER, [Authorities for this sketch; Goodwin's *Geneal. Notes; Talcott's N. Y. & N. Eng. Families;* Trumbull's *Hist. Conn.;* Hollister's *Hist. Conn., The Hollister Family,* by Dr. L. W. Case, Mss. of *Mrs. Anna C. N. Hawley,* of Htfd.]

John Hollister

Mr. (or later Lieut.) John Hollister is said to have been born in Glastonbury, Eng. but Mr. Alpheus Hollister of Hollisterville, Pa., says, "The H.—s were from Bristol, Eng., a good old family as early as Henry VIII. There was a Jno. Hollister, Lord of the Manor of Stinchcombe in 1608. Dennis H. was a member of Cromwell's Privy Council after the Protectorate was established. The name is derived from "Holly" and "Ter" or "Terre," which means Holly land or the place of Holly trees. There is still a hamlet in Eng. bearing the name of "Hollester" or Hollesterre." From this it appears that the name is Eng. and of Somerset County, Eng.

John Hollister seems to have located first at Weymouth, Mass.; was made freeman in Mass. 10 May, 1643; rep. to Mass. Gen. Ct., Mch., 1644; was a man of good family and education, and when he rem. in Nov. of that yr. to Weth., ("where," as *Savage* says, "he had been in 1642, where his son John was b. to him, as is said, strange as his res. seems at that day"), he quickly took a prominent position in the community. In June, 1646, was a juror of the Particular Ct. at Htfd., with Thos. Coleman and Nath'l Dickinson; dep. to Conn. Gen. Ct. Apl., 1645, at Sept. sess. of 1644, and subsequently re-elected to same 14 times. In Oct., 1654, was app. by Gen. Ct. one of a comm. of 3 "to press men and necessaries in each town" for an exped. then being sent out agt. the Inds.; and, again, in Feb., 1656, was, with others, app. by the Ct. to "give the best and safest advice to the Inds., if they agreed to meet and should crave their advice." These and many other legisl. appointments testify to the respect in which he was held both by the people and the authorities of the Colony. He was app. by the Ct., 7 Mch., 1649-50, as Lieut. of the Weth. trainband. Mr. H. was a large land-owner in the present Glast. portion of old town of Weth., then called Naubuck Farms, where he hld. lot No. 34 fm. the Htfd. S. line, orig. Mitchell's, who had early rem. to Stamford, containing 900 acs. and to wh. he added 10 acs. 1655. On this farm a dw-ho. and other necessary bldgs.

had been erect. before 1651, at which time Joseph Gilbert became his tenant and so remained until 1663. A considerable portion of this farm remained in possess. of the H. fam. till 1884, when, on the dth. of its owner, Mr. Chas. H., it passed into other hands. The "Old Red House," in which he lived is said to have been built in 1675. It is pleasantly located on the W. bank of Roaring Brook, facing S., on the road leading to the Ry-H. ferry.—(See, also, Chapt. VII, Vol. I). Mr. Hollister was collector for Weth., Mch., 1660.

He was a man of strong character and became very prominently involved in the controversy which arose in the Weth. ch. which ultimately resulted in the large emigr. to Hadley, 1659, under the Rev. Mr. Russell.—See Chapt. VIII, Vol. I, also Hollister's *Hist. Conn.*

He m. Joanna (dau. of the 1st. Hon. Richard) **Treat,** by his first wife Joanna, and he d. at Weth., leaving by his will dated 3 Apl., 1665, a large estate to wid. and 5 s. and 3 daus. Invent. 20 Apl., 1665; will gave to his eld. s. John, "his feather bed at Nayog," and his farm there, when he shall be 22 yrs. old, he also to pay to his widow 20 bu. of apples and 2 bbls. of cider yearly. Mr. H.'s inventory, ment. *wampum* £10—amt. of whole est. £1,642-1-6; ment. also "29 small swine." Wid. d. Oct., 1694. *Children:*

1. John, b. abt. 1642. FAM. 2.
2. Elizabeth, m. Samuel (s. of Gov.) **Welles,** 1659 ; not ment. in father's will—but her 3 daus. rec'd legacies.
3. Sarah, m. (1) 1674, Rev. Hope **Atherton** first min. of Hatfield ; m. (2) abt. 1679, Lt. Timo. **Baker,** of Northampton ; she d. 8 Dec., 1691.
4. Mary, m. John **Welles** (s. John, s. Gov. Thos.) of Stratford, abt. 1669.—See *Welles.*
5. Thomas. FAM. 3.
6. Joseph, d. 29 Aug., 1674, unm.
7. Lazarus, b. abt. 1656 ; d. Sept., 1709, single. See Chapt. VII, Vol. I. *Htfd. Co. Prob. Rec.* preserve the following, as to his est. and relatives : *Lazarus Hollister—* Invt. £260-16-09 taken 28 November 1709 by Thomas Steele & Thomas Chester— Court Record 6 February 1709-10 adm[s] to John or Johnathan Hollister—2 June 1712 report ad.[s] act. this Court Order Dist. to brothers & sisters—July 1712 Order to Distribute to Mary Welles sister ; to Heirs of John Hollister Dec ; to Heirs of Thomas Hollister Dec ; to Heirs of Stephen Hollister ; to Heirs of Elizabeth Hollister *alias* Welles ; to Heirs of Sarah Hollister *alias* Baker, late of Northampton, Dec. Distributions Lazarus Hollister Late of

Wethersfield Decd. 1713—Persons related to him : Mrs. Mary Welles of Hartford (Stratford) Mr. John Hollister[s] Children Glastonbury John, Joseph, Thomas, David, Ephraim & Elizabeth. Mr. Thomas Hollister[s] Children : Thomas, Johnathan, Mary, Harris, Abigail ; Mr. Stephen Hollister[s] Children : Gershom, Samuel, Gideon, Nathaniel, Hepzibah, Abigail, Ann, Eunice ; the Children of Elizabeth Hollister : Capt. Samuel Welles, Capt. Thomas Welles ; Children, the Heirs of Sarah Blackleach (?), Mary Hale, Ann Welles, Elizabeth Shelton, the Heirs of Sarah Baker Northampton, Decd. The persons that are concerned desire that Mr. Thomas Chester, Mr. Edward Bulkeley, a Mr. James Patterson may be appointed Distributors.
By Court Order July 12 to Mrs. Mary Welles sister of the Deceased ; to Heirs of John Hollister of Glastonbury Decd ; to Heirs of Thomas Hollester Decd ; to the Heirs of Stephen Hollister Decd ; to Heirs of Elizabeth Hollister *alias* Welles ; to the Heirs of Sarah Hollister *alias* Baker late of Northampton Decd.
8. Stephen, b. 1658. FAM. 4.

FAM. 2.   Sgt. JOHN,[2] (*Lieut. John,*[1]), b. 1642; m. 20 Nov., 1667, Sarah (eld. dau. Ens. Wm. & Sarah *Marvin*) **Goodrich,** who d. Glast., 1700. He was one of the principal men of Glast.; possessed much of his father's belligerent spirit and was a principal for many yrs. in the great law-suit *Hollister vs Bulkeley*, over certain boundary lines, which finally led to a re-survey, by order of the Ct., of all the lots fm. E. Htfd. line to Nayaug—See *State Archives,* also Chapt. VII. Vol. I, this work; also, Chapin's *Glast. Centenn.,* 180-3; was a selectman, 1650-1, 1653—*W. T. V.,* I, 26,37. He d. 24 Nov., 1711.

John Hollister Sen., Glastonbury, Invent. £79-06-09, taken 1st April, 1712, by Thomas Hall, Nathaniel Talcott, Samuel Hale.

Will dated 22 November, 1711—My will is that what I have already settled upon my sons John, Thomas, David, Ephraim, and daughter Sarah, shall be the whole of their portions of my estate. My son Joseph what I have settled upon him with 7 acres of land which I now give him shall be his portion of my estate. I give to my dau Elizabeth, single woman, all my moveable estate with a certain piece of land and all the estate of my brother Lazarus Hollister, that may fall to me and also what belongs to me of my late brother Joseph Hollister's estate, all to be to her and to her heirs forever.

JOHN HOLLISTER Sen. O

Witness Daniel Andrews, Tho. Kimberly—19 December, 1711. Joseph Hollister exhibits will and desires to have it proven, John objects. Will proven 1st September, 1712, Adms. to Elizabeth Hollister the daughter Joyntly with her brother Joseph Hollister with will annexed.

Children (Weth. Rec.):

1. John, b. 9 Aug., 1669, m. (1) 7 June, 1693, Abiah (dau. Lt. Thos.) **Hollister,** his cousin, who d. 28 Aug., 1719, ae. 47.—*W. Ins.*; he m. (2) Susannah ———; he d. 13 Dec., 1741, ae. 73.
2. Thomas, b. 14 Jan., 1671-2. FAM. 5.
3. Joseph, b. 8 July, 1674; m. (1) 27 Nov., 1694, Ann ———, who d. 5 Oct., 1712, in 34th yr.—*W. Ins.*; m. (2) Sarah ———, who d. 3 July, 1746, ae. 72.—*W. Ins.*; he d. 9 July, 1746; res. Glast.; est. invent. £997·02-10.—*Htfd. Co. Prob.* xv, 26-37.
4. Sarah, b. 25 Oct., 1676; m. Benj. **Talcott,** 5 Jan., 1698-9; he (s. Samuel & Hannah *Holyoke* Talcott) sett. at Glast; d. 15 Oct., 1715.
5. Elizabeth, b. 30 Mch., 1678; d. inf.
6. David, b. 20 Nov., 1681; he d. 27 Dec., 1753, in 76th yr.—*W. Ins.*; he m. Charity ———, who d. 12 Jan., 1786, in 89th yr.; est. val. at £9,923-20-03.—*Htfd. Co. Prob.,* xvi, 326.
7. Ephraim, b. 15 Mch., 1683-4; m. Elizabeth (dau. Tobias) **Green,** 1 Apl., 1707; admx. in Glast., 4 ch.; wid. d. 1733.
8. Charles, b. 29 July, 1686; d. before 11 Nov., 1711; prob. unm.
9. Elizabeth (acc. to *Savage*) "without date;" m. Dr. Joseph (s. Capt James & Ann *Wells*) **Steele,** of Kensington, 16 Feb., 1715.

FAM. 3. Lieut. THOMAS,[2] (*Lieut. John,*[1]), m. (1) Elizabeth (dau. John) **Latimer;** m. (2) abt. 1690, Elizabeth (wid. of Amos?) **Williams.**—See Chapt. VII, Vol: I. Lieut Thomas Hollister, Wethersfield. Died 8 November, 1701. Invt. £369-12-06, taken 19 December, 1701, by Benjamin Churchill, Isaac Boreman, Samuel Wright, Court Record, 9 March, 1701-2. Adms. to Elizabeth the Releet and Thomas eldest sons. The Admx. Elizabeth presented the estate that her dec'd. Husband died seized of in his own right also as adms. estate of Amos Williams dec'd 'Son. John Hollister chose John Hollister son of John Hollister of Glastonbury to be his guardian and son Joseph chose Walter Harris to be his guardian.

Children (Savage II, 450):

1. Thomas, b. 1672; prob. the T. who d. 12 Oct., 1741 in 70th yr.—*Weth. Ins.*
2. Jonathan.—See Chapt. —, Vol. I.
3. Joseph, b. 1675.
4. John, prob. d. or killed in service in Fr. and Ind. Wars. *John Hollister, Jr.*—Invt. £30-15-00 taken 2 July 1711 by Thomas Treat, Thomas Kimberly. Will date 13 September 1710—I John Hollister If I should not live to return home again I give to my Brother Thomas Hollister all that is mine and if I live to return home again he shall return it all to me again.— John Hollister. (*Court Record* 2 July, 1711, adms. to Thomas Hollister with will annexed.)
5. Sarah, m. John **Williams,** 24 Jan., 1695.
6. Mary, m. Walter **Harris,** of Weth.
7. Stephen, b. 20 Sept., 1681 (one *Weth. Rec.* says Stephen, s. of Lt. Thos. & Abigail, b. 15 Mch.; d. 26 Oct., 1681).
8. Abiah, or Abigail, d. 28 Aug., 1719; m. her cousin, ——— **Hollister,** 1693.

FAM. 4. Capt. STEPHEN,[2] (*Lieut. John,*[1])—See Chapt. Vol. I, m. (1) 1683, Abigail (dau. Matthias) **Treat;** m. (2) Elizabeth (wid. Jonathan) **Reynolds,** dau. of John Coleman, who was living 1727. He d. 2 Oct., 1709, in the camp at Greenbush, N. Y., of camp-fever. Capt. Stephen Hollister, Invent. £133-17-05, taken 30 March, 1790-1 by Thomas Welles sen. and James Steele. Court Record, 2 January, 1709-10 Adms. Joyntly to Elizabeth Hollister the Relect and Ebenezer Seamour Farmington, son-in-law of the dec'd Gershom Hollister, 17 years of age a son chose Capt. Thomas Welles to be his guardian also guardian to Nathaniel, age 8 years.

Children (Weth. Rec.):

1. Jerusha, b. 7 Jan., 1684; d. unm. 30 Sept., 1710.
2. Stephen, b. 12 July, 1686; d. unm. 29 Apl., 1707.
3. Abigail, b. 16 Aug., 1688; m. Ebenezer **Seymour,** of Far. 29 Dec., 1709.
4. Ann, b. 16 Mch., 1689-90; m. Robert **Boothe,** of Stratford, 27 Nov., 1712.
5. Gershom, b. 2 Apl., 1692; m. and had ch. (*Savage* also cr. him with the following):
6. Samuel, b. 1694; m. and res. Far. and Sharon.

7. Eunice. b. 1696; m. Ebenezer **Deming**;
app. her guardian, 5 May, 1712; she m.
Jona. **Seymour**, 23 Dec., 1714.
8. Gideon, bp. 24 July, 1698 (*Mix*); m. Rebecca **Sherman**, 28 Mch., 1722; d. 10 May,
1725; had *Sarah*, b. Nov., 1723; *Gideon*,
b. 21 Sept., 1725.—*Orcutt's Stratford*.
9. Daniel, b. 30 Apl., (*Mix*) 1700 (?) See

orig.
10. Nathaniel, b. 1702; Thos. Welles app.
guardian; bp. 7 Dec., 1701—*Mix*.
(*By second marr.*):
11. Stephen, b. 12 (bp. 18, *Mix*) Sept., 1709,
in Oct., 1724, being then 16 yrs. of age,
chose Sam'l Goff as his guardian.

FAM. 5. Lieut. THOMAS,[3] (*John,*[2] *John,*[1]), b. 1672; m. Dorothy (dau. Joseph)
Hills, who d. 5 Oct., 1741, in 64th yr.—*Weth. Ins.* He was a weaver, deacon, and lieut.; res. Glast. [Joseph Hill, prob. s. of Mr. William H., who came,
1632, to N. Eng. in the *Leon*, and whose will (*Htfd. Co. Prob.*, II, 29), dated 9
Sept., 1649, ment. a s. Jos. b. 15 May, 1650; he was a freeman at Roxbury,
Mass., 1632; m. (1) Phillis (of Rich.) Lyman and rem. to Htfd.; m. (2)
wid. Mary (dau. Andrew) **Warner**, and d. Htfd., July, 1683. Joseph H. prob.
sett. Glast. and in will (1713) *Htfd. Co. Prob.* ment. his dau. Dorothy Hollister.]

Children:

1. Josiah (Lieut.), b. 7 June, 1696; m.
Martha (dau. Wm.) **Miller**, of Glast.,
18 Jan., 1718, who d. 12 July, 1777, at
Glast., ae. 79; 5 ch.; he d. 3 Jan., 1749,
in 53d yr.—*Weth. Ins.*
2. Dorothy, b. 17 Oct., 1697; m. Abraham
(s. Richard & Beriah) **Fox**, 3 Jan., 1717.
3. Gideon, b. 23 Sept., 1699; m. Rachel
(dau. Nathaniel) **Talcott**, of Glast.,
where she was b. 6 Oct., 1706; she d.
G. 13 June, 1790, ae. 85; he sett. in Eastbury Soc. Glast.; Lieut., 1736; Deacon of
E. ch.; d. 15 Feb., 1785; bu. in E.; 9 ch.
4. Charles, b. 26 July, 1701; m. 5 Apl., 1729,
Prudence (dau. John) **Francis**, of W.
sett. Eastbury; d. 2 Feb., 1753.
5. Elizabeth, b. 17 Dec., 1703; m. as his
sec. wife, Wm. **Miller**, Jr., of Glast.,
14 Oct., 1731; 7 ch.
6. Hannah, b. 26 Dec., 1705; d. 12 Oct., 1712.
7. Thomas, b. 13 Jan., 1707; m. abt. 1 Jan.,
1734, Abigail **Talcott**, of G.; d. 31 Mch.,
1812; he d. 17 Sept., 1724.
8. Ruth, b. 13 Oct., 1710; m. Nehemiah

Smith, of Htfd.
9. Rachel, b. 27 July, 1712; m. Joshua
Talcott, of Bolton, 9 Jan., 1735; she d.
10 Mch., 1807.
10. Hannah, b. 16 Feb., 1714; m. Wm.
House, of Glast.
11. Eunice, m. 27 Nov., 1733, Thos. (s. of
John & Keziah *Williams*) **Loveland**, of
Glast.; their 3d ch., *Wm. Loveland*,[5]
m. 1758, Abigail **Adams**; their dau. Hannah,[6] m. Elisha[6] **Coleman**; their dau.
Abigail,[7] m. Nathan Wm. **Pelton**; their
dau. Elizabeth Ann Pelton,[8] m. Philo
Slocum **Newton**, 1841; their dau. Anna
Coleman Newton,[9] m. 1868, Geo. Fuller
Hawley, M. D., of Htfd., and their child
is Geo. Burton Hawley,[10] b. 14 May, 1869.
12. Susanna, m. 4 May, 1741, Benoni **House**,
of Glast.; (?) Susanna (dau. John,[8]),
m. Benoni **House**, 4 May, 1742.
13. Elisha (Dea.), b. 1732. FAM. 6.
(Births of these last three not rec., but
for proof of parentage see *Glast. Ld. Rec.*,
IV, 373.)

FAM. 6. Dea. ELISHA,[4] (*Thomas,*[3] *John,*[2] *John,*[1]), b. 1722; m. (1) Experience (dau.
Richard) **Robbins**, of Weth.; m. (2) Penelope (dau. Jonathan) **Graves**, Jr.,
& Margaret *Strong*, of Belchertown or Northampton, wid. of Elisha Dwight.
Dea. Elisha was a farmer, inn-keeper, an off. in Rev. War, and a man of
prominence. His wid. Penelope was esteemed a wonderful woman, of excellent
executive ability.

Children:

1. Roger, b. 16 Sept., 1749; d. 31 Aug., 1750.
2. Roger, b. 15 Sept., 1751; d. 3 Nov., 1751.
3. Martha, twin Lucy, b. 2 Sept., 1751; d.
10 Aug., 1753.
4. Lucy, twin Martha, d. 13 Sept., 1756.
5. Eunice, b. 27 Nov., 1754; m. Dr. Asa
Coleman, of Glast.; d. 30 June, 1840;
7 ch. See *Coleman*.
6. Experience, b. 30 July, 1757; m. Samuel
Risley, of Greenfield, Mass.; 4 ch.
7. Mehitable, b. 3 Aug., 1759; m. Rev.
——— **Chapin**; had dau. Mehitable,
m. Perez (s. of Capt. David E. &
Pamela *Hollister*) **Hubbard**. *Hollister
Geneal.* says their Mehitable d. 3 June,
1787; unm.
8. Martha, b. 7 June, 1762; m. Rev. Mr.
Chapin.

9. Lucy, b. 5 Apl., 1764; m. Allen **Goodrich**,
2 Dec., 1784.
(*By second marriage*):
10. Elisha (Dr.), b. 3 Sept., 1767; m. (1)
Aurelia (dau. Ebenezer & Eunice *Wright*)
Field; m. (2) Martha (dau. Dea. Elisha)
Munn; d. 8 Dec., 1833; 9 ch.
11. Penelope, b. 9 Mch., 1769; d. 11 July,
1773.
12. Roger, b. 23 May, 1771; d. 7 Jan., 1851.
13. Perez Graves, sea capt., d. at sea.
14. Hannah Dwight, b. 24 Aug., 1775; m. (1)
Rodolphus Wright **Field**, 14 Sept., 1797;
m. (2) Hon. Josiah **Pomeroy**; d. 16 June,
1867.
15. Pamela, b. 23 Mch., 1778; m. David E.
Hubbard.

Lieut. THOMAS, bro. of Lieut. JOHN, the foregoing Nayaug settler;
has, apparently no fam. cr. to him on *Weth. Rec.*; yet *Savage* (II, 449) gives

him the following ch. by his wife Elizabeth (dau. of John) **Latimer.** He is ment. on tax-list—*W. T. V.*, I. p. 12; selectman, 1649 (*Ibid.*, 35); lot gr. him by ch. and town in Weth., Dec., 1649 (*Ibid.*, 35).

Children:

1. Thomas, b. 1672.
2. Jonathan. FAM. 2.
3. Joseph, b. 1675.
4. John.

5. Sarah.
6. Mary.
7. Stephen, b. 20 Sept., 1681.
8. Abiah, or Abigail, d. 8 Nov., 1701.

FAM. 2. JONATHAN, (prob. b. abt. 1674, s. of Lieut. Thos & Elizabeth), m. Elizabeth **Williams,** 22 Sept., 1698. Prob. d. in 1714, as we find invent. of est. of Jona. Hollister, amt. £250-16-05, taken 24 June of that yr., by Philip Goff, Jr., and Joseph Grimes. *Ct. Rec.* 15 July, 1715. Adm. gr. to Elizabeth the wid. She to be guardian to her ch. "now under 14 yrs." of age; and invent. of lds. £253-00-00, taken by Samuel Williams and Joseph Graham. *Ct. Rec.* 3 Mch., 1723-4. Jacob Hollister, a minor, 19 yrs. of age, William Nott (Knott) to be his guard.; the Ct. app'd Joseph Graham, Samuel Williams and Joshua Robbins to make a new appraisement of the lds. of sd. dec'd; on same date, Eliz., the wid., exhibits accounts and received order to distr. to *Jonathan, Jacob, Stephen, Elizabeth* and *Mary* the children.—*Htfd. Co. Prob.*

Children (*Weth. Rec.*):

1. Jonathan, b. 28 Feb., 1698-9.
2. Ch., bp. 23 Apl., 1699 (*Mix Rec.*); perhaps the above Jona.
3. Elizabeth, b. 26 (bp. 29—*Mix*) Jan., 1701-2.
4. Jacob, b. 2 Oct., (bp. Dec.—*Mix*), 1704.

5. Stephen, b. 30 Mch. (bp. 2 May—*Mix*), 1708.
6. Mary, b. 3 (bp. 6—*Mix*) July, 1712; she is prob. the "Wid. Susannah," who d. 6 Mch., 1765.

JONATHAN, (*prob. the foregoing Jona., s. of Lt. Thos.*), m. Susannah **Lindsey,** 17 Mch., 1743; he d. 29 Oct., 1754.

Child (*Weth. Rec.*):

1. Jacob, b. 1 May, 1743.

ELIZAR, m. Mary (dau. Capt. & Esq. Jonathan & Mary) **Belding,** 13 Oct., 1757—*N. C. R.*; she d. 29 May, 1759, in 36th yr.—*Weth. Ins.*

EBENEZER, s. of Jerusha Hollister, dec'd, bp. 24 June, 1711, by Rev. Mix, who, in his record enters this sympathetic note: "This poor, illegitimate orphan, I spake with the Selectmen, some of them, that they would engage in behalf of the Town, for its Christian education, which was not, I suppose, dissented fm. by some of them. This ch. died, I think, before the next Lord's day after its baptism."

JESSE & *Lucy M.*, had Sarah Jane, d. ae. 1, 24 Aug., 1838; inf. d. 18 Aug., 1839.

LAZARUS, d. at beginning of Sept., 1709.—*Weth. Rec.*

ROBERT, had s. Roswell, who d. 24 Jan., 1853, ae. 4.

JOSEPH, of Glast., d. 8 Oct., 1746, in 50th yr; his wife Martha, d. 12 July, 1777, in 79th yr.—*W. Ins.;* prob. the Joseph who had two daus., who m. sons of Daniel Shelton—viz.: Mary, b. 1704, and d. 26 May, 1782; m. 11 May 1726, Joseph **Shelton;** and Esther, who m. Thaddeus **Shelton,** 17 Oct., 1733; she b. 1709, d. 6 May, 1778, at Huntington, L. I.

Daniel Shelton, the father of these husbands of the Hollister girls, came fm. Yorkshire, Eng., to Stratford, Ct., prob. in Spring of 1686, as a mcht.; he m. Elizabeth (dau. of Sam'l) **Welles,** of Weth., 4 Apl., 1692; res. at S. till 1717 or '18, then rem. to Long Hill, Huntington, Ct., where he d. 1728; wid. Elizabeth d. 1 Apl., 1747, ae. 77; had 10 ch.—See Orcutt's *Hist. Stratford*, II, 1279.

HOLMES. This old Weth. fam. is mostly connected with Stepney parish.

JONAS, m. Sarah ——————, 11 May, 1692; from *Co. Ct. Rec.* (Nov. 27, 1727) we learn that he was a ship-wright—See Chapt. VII, Vol. I; d. 1732. Invent. of ets. (amt. £583-07-05), taken 30 May, 1732, by Jonathan Curtis, Jacob Williams and Daniel Goodrich. *Ct. Rec.*, 5 Sept., '32, adm. gr. to Sarah the wid. and Benj. Wright, of Weth.; the son Wm. a minor (17 yrs.) chose his mother to be his guard.; the wid. dec'd before 4 June, 1734, when (as per *Ct. Rec.* of that date) adm. was gr. to Richard, eld. s. of Jonas, with Benj. Wright, but Sept. 28th, Rich., at his own req. was disch. fm. his adm. and the other adm'r (Wright) was gr. a longer time to sell the ld.; and in Mch., 1735-6, was directed by the Ct. to "sell the dwelling-ho. of the dec'd at Weth., Rocky Hill and 2 acs. ld. adjoining"— *Htfd. Co. Prob. Rec.*, which was accomplished by sale to Thos. Butler—deed 6 Apl., 1736—for £145.

Children (Weth. Rec., bp. Mix Rec.) :

1. Mabel, b. 20 May, 1693.
2. Hannah, b. 25 Dec., 1694.
3. Ann, b. 4 Dec., 1696.
4. Richard, b. 12 Feb., bp. 26 Mch., 1698-9.
5. Sarah, b. 16 Oct., bp. Nov., 1701.
6. Abigail, b. 28 Feb., 1703-4; bp. 25 Apl., 1704.
7. Martha, b. 6 Sept., 1708; bp. 6 Feb., 1708-9.
8. Jonas, b. 7 Mch., 1709.
9. Thomas, b. 7, bp. 11 Mch., 1710-11.
10. Phinehas, b. 24 Apl., 1713. FAM. 2.
11. William, b. 22 May, bp. 3 July, 1715. FAM. 3.

FAM. 2. PHINEAS,[2] (*Jonas,[1]*), b. 1713; m. Elizabeth **Grimes,** 5 Feb., 1736; she d. 7 Oct., 1783, in 67th yr.; he d. 5 July, 1785, in 72d yr.—*S. C. R.*

Children (Weth. Rec.) :

1. Jonas, b. 1 Sept., 1736; d. 22 May, 1815, in 79th yr.—*S. C. R.*
2. John, b. 22 Oct., 1738; prob. the J. who d. 16 Dec., 1821, in 84th yr.; his wife Mary, d. 19 Apl., 1807.—*S. C. R.*
3. Jehiel, b. 20 Sept., 1745.
4. Mary, b. 6 Oct., 1747.
5. Levi, b. 13 Feb., 1751; d. 1819, ae. 68— *S. C. R.; m.* 1788, Molly **Corey,** who d.

1 Apl., 1806; had Ralph, bp. 17 Oct., 1790, who d. 11 Sept., 1820, returning from St. Eustatia, W. I.—*S. C. R.;* Phineas, bp. 8 July, 1792; inf. d. 14 Sept., 1793; Levi, bp. 26 July, 1795; Phineas, bp. 25 June, 1797; Alma, bp. 14 Oct., 1798; Mary, bp. 31 Mch., d. 1 Apl., 1800.—*S. C. R.*
6. Sarah, b. 1 Nov., 1753.
7. Simeon, b. 24 Aug., 1755.

FAM. 3. WILLIAM,[2] (*Jonas,[1]*), b. 1715; m. Hannah **Hale,** 24 July, 1738; she d. 5 Aug., 1795, in 80th yr.—*Weth. (S.) Ins.*

Children (Weth. Rec.) :

1. Mabel, b. 16 Sept., 1738.
2. Ruth, b. 7 May, 1741.
3. Richard, b. 28 May, 1743.
4. Charles, b. 4 Sept., 1748. FAM. 4.
5. Appleton, b. 9 Nov., 1750; m. 14 Nov., 1771,

Lydia Goodrich; had Florinda, bp. 12 July, 1772; Richard, bp. 22 Aug., 1773; a son bp. 15 Jan., 1775.
6. Hannah, b. 26 July, 1754.

FAM. 4. CHARLES,[3] (*William,[2] Jonas,[1]*), b. 1748; m. Martha ——————.

Children (Weth. Rec.) :

1. Ruth, b. 15, bp. 17 July, 1774.
2. William, b. 7 Oct., 1776.
3. Polly, b. 22 May, 1778.
4. Howell, b. 16 Aug., 1779; prob. the son of Charles, bp. 10 Oct., 1779.
5. Patty, b. 28 Nov., 1781; bp. 20 Jan., 1782.
6. Josiah, b. 10 Aug., 1783.
7. Aaron Hale, (twins, b. 20 Aug., bp. 2
8. Annis, (Oct., 1785.
9. Polly, b. 17 Aug., 1792.

HOLTON, or (*Holtum; orig. Holtham*). This fam. tho' res. in Weth. does not appear at all on Weth. Rec., and we are indebted for what we know of it, to the *Boardman Geneal.*, whose author (the late Charlotte Goldthwait) gives the following carefully collected facts.

The name is found in early Eng. recs. in Warwickshire, Kent, and the City of London. The Amer. fam. is desc'd fm. JOHN Holtum, who rec'd a gt. of ld. in Springfield, Mass., 1671; rem. after 1682, to Lyme, Ct., where he had also a

gt. of ld. 1689 and he d. before 1699; his wid. rem. to Htfd. and m. (2) —————
Spencer, 4 ch. of whom the youngest was Joseph, b. 1693, and known as
DEA JOSEPH. Left an orphan at an early
age, he was br't up by Bevil Waters, of
Htfd.; m. 20 Mch., 1717-18, Abigail (prob.
dau. Benjamin & Elizabeth) **Hastings**, of Hatfield. His res. during the first
yrs. of his marr. life, was on the W. side of the present road to New., on the
Cedar Mountain, thus bringing him within the bds. of Weth.; the N. boundary
of his farm being the div. line betw. Weth. and Htfd. Thus, tho' living com-
paratively near to New. (which at the time of his marr. was just beginning
its distinct parochial existence)—and the first road above referred to not then
being opened—all his neighbors and ch. associations were in the parish of the
So. ch. of Htfd., 4 or 5 miles distant; which he attended and where all his ch.
were bap. His daus. m. into fams. of the Htfd. Rocky Hill neighborhood,
which then and long after formed an important part of the So. ch. parish and
he and his wife were bu. in the old bu-gd. of the Center Ch. Owing to the loss
of the So. ch. Rec. during a part of Joseph Holtum's connection with it, there is
no way of learning when he was chosen deacon, or how long he held the office.
He was a selectman of Htfd. in 1743, and his signature is freq. found on prob.
docs. as appraiser, distributor, or witness of wills, etc. He was a ppr. in
Harwinton, 1740, but exch. his ld. there for a homestead in Htfd. Dea. Holton
d. 3 Jan., 1770, in 77th yr.; his wife d. 28 Oct., 1753.—(*Sexton's Rec.* of
burials in Center Ch. yd.)

Children (Boardman Gen.) :

1. Abigail, bp. 18 Jan., 1718-19; d. 8 Sept., 1776, ae. 57; unm.
2. Samuel, bp. 18 Oct., 1721; bu. 25 Sept., 1758.
3. Elizabeth, bp. 7 June, 1724; m. 10 Nov., 1748, Medad **Webster**; had *Samuel* and *Joseph*.
4. Mary, bp. 15 Sept., 1728; m. Ebenezer **Catlin**; d. 14 May, 1803, ae. 75. *Children,* see *Boardman Geneal.*, p. 344.

HOOKER, Dr. DANIEL,[3] (*Rev. Samuel,*[2] *Rev. Thos.*,[1]), ygst. son of Rev Samuel
& Mary Willet, of Far. was b. 25 Mch., 1679, and was the first Far. born man
to receive a coll. education; grad. H. C., 1700, and after his father's dth. was
invited to succeed him in the ministry at Far., but declined. He became the
first tutor at Yale Coll., but soon resigned in favor of Rev. John Hart (who
subsequently m. his niece) who grad. Y. C., 1703, nominally the second, but
actually the first student to grad.; he also became the first A. B. of Yale.
Young Hooker studied medicine and was duly licensed to practice; and sett. in
Weth., (was living in Weth., Nov., 1711—*Co. Ct. Rec.*) where he continued in his
profession until his dth. He also studied law and was adm. to the Bar (Mch.,
1714-15—*Superior Ct. Rec.*) ; but, as there is no evidence of his ever having practiced law, it is probable that he studied it only with a view of being useful to
his patients, in the giving of advice, making of wills, etc., etc. He was surgeon to
the expedition against Canada, in 1711. He m. 24 June, 1707, Sarah (dau.
Dea. John & Esther *Newell*) **Standley**, of Waterbury, Ct., who was bp. at Wat.,
4 July, 1686; she d. 15 June, 1726, ae. 36.—*Weth. Ins.* He d. 1742, ae. abt. 63.

Children (b. Weth.) :

1. Susannah, b. 14 Apl., 1708; m. (1) 25 Oct., 1726, Ephraim (s. of Wm. & Grace *Riley*) **Goodrich**, who d. 1728, ae. 29; m. (2) Edward **Bailey**, 7 Jan., 1727 or 8, she [wid.] was bp. and owned cov't and her son Ephraim Goodrich, was bp. (*Mix MSS.*)
2. Daniel (Dr.), b. 22 Feb., 1710; m. 2 Apl., 1729, Sarah **Webster** (poss. a wid.); he d. 14 Sept., 1761, ae. 52, at Htfd.; had 3 ch.; their s. Daniel, prob. the son b.
15 Oct., 1730—*Co. Ct. Rec.*, and his son Daniel were also physicians in W. Htfd.; four Daniels, all doctors.
3. Sarah, b. 10 Sept., 1713; m. Benj. **Chamberlain**, of Midd.; d. 30 Oct., 1781, ae. 68, at Midd.
4. Hannah, m. 7 Sept., 1738, Reuben (s. Thos. & Rachel *Starr*) **Norton**, of Guilford, Ct.; she d. at G., 9 May, 1797, ae. 85.
5. Mary, m. Elijah **Peck**.
6. Margaret.

Capt. NOADIAH (s. of Capt. Joseph & Sarah *Lewis*) **Hooker** was b. 29 Aug., 1737, and m. 2 Jan., 1765, Rebecca (9th ch. of Major Josiah & Mabel *Belden*) **Griswold**, of Weth. He was an earnest and conspicuous patriot in the days preceding the Revol. War, memb. of the Far. committee of correspondence, Capt. of a band of Sons of Liberty, and on receipt of the Lexington Alarm of Apl., 1775, he raised the first troops enl. at Far. and marched in command of 100 vols. for Boston, where he arrived some three weeks in advance of other enl. men fm. Conn.; was commmis. Capt. by the Col. Assembly, and in July, '76, was made a Col., and in that capacity served until close of war. He rep. town of Far. for many sessions in the Conn. Gen. Assembly—only one man— John Treadwell having served more sessions than he, and only one other man, John Mix, having ever served as many; he was for 40 yrs. a J. P., and very prominent in Town and State affairs; many yrs. Treas. of Ch. Socy. and active in the erection of the Far. meeting-house; with Mr. Woodruff, the architect and builder, he personally inspected every piece of timber used in its construction; also went to Maine on horseback and purchased the shingles for the roof of the edifice, and the carefulness of his work is attested by the fact that those shingles were not repaired or replaced for more that 50 yrs. Rebecca, his wife, was a worthy mate of so good a man, and herself the dau. of a gallant major of the French wars, she exhibited her Griswold blood, during the Revol. War, by taking charge of a gang of British prisoners, when Far. was made a place of detention for them, and with them, working her husband's farm, while he was away fm. home, and raising produce for the use of the army—as, also, did many other Far. people.

Col. Hooker res. in Farmington, at the old, "Red College" as it was called, fm. the fact that his grand-son Edward Hooker (Y. C., 1805) afterwards conducted there, a high grade preparatory school for young men. Col. Hooker d. 3 June, 1823, ae. 86; his wife d. 9 Nov., 1816, ae. 72.

Children (b. *Far.*) :

1. Sarah, b. 10 Oct., 1765 ; d. 15 Oct., 1766.
2. John (twin), b. 24 Oct., 1766 ; d. 26 Oct., 1766.
3. Joseph (twin), b. 24 Oct., 1766 ; d. 25 Oct., 1766.
4. Sally, b. 16 Nov., 1767 ; m. George **Cooke**, of St. Armand, Can., whose 1st wife had been Hannah **Metcalf**, a cousin of Melinda Metcalf, wife of Dr. William Griswold Hooker. She d. 6 July, 1823, ae. 56, at St. Armand ; *no issue*.
5. Lucy, b. 16 Jan., 1771 : was at school, New Haven, and d. exactly at the moment when she became 17 yrs. of age, 16 Jan., 1788.
6. John, b. 21 June, 1774. Fam. 2.
7. James, b. 11 Sept., 1777. Fam. 3.
8. Abigail, b. 23 May, 1780 ; m. 6 Sept., 1804, Asahel (s. Asahel & Eleanor *Strong*) **Clarke**, farmer and lawyer, of Columbia, Ct. He grad. Y. Law Schl. ; he d. 14 Oct., 1865 at Peoria, Ill., in 90th yr. ; she d. at C. 9 Sept., 1839. *Issue* (*all* b. *at Columbia, Ct.*) :
   i. Nancy Hooker (Clarke), b. 31 July, 1805 ; d. unm., at Htfd., 3 Mch., 1873.
   ii. Ellen Strong (Clarke), b. 6 May, 1807 ; d. unm., 5 May, 1900.
   iii. Jane Rebecca, b. 4 May, 1810 ; d. unm., 16 Aug., 1892, at Htfd.

   iv. Samuel Strong (Clarke), b. 12 Mch., 1812 ; d. 5 Apl., 1813.
   v. Samuel Strong (Clarke), b. 7 Apl., 1814 ; m. 17 June, 1847, Cath. Elizabeth **Burns**; d. Peoria, Ill., 19 Nov., 1892.
   vi. Mary Ann (Clarke), b. 6 Nov., 1815 ; m. Henry H. **Smith**; d. 27 Nov., 1887, at Union Spgs., Ala.
   vii. Sarah Louisa (Clarke), b. 26 Sept., 1817 ; m. 2 Oct., 1842, Joseph D. **Hopper**; d. 23 Apl., 1854, at Montgomery, Ala.
   viii. Lucy Abigail (Clarke), b. 28 Apl., 1819 ; m. 23 Nov., 1855, Joseph D. **Hopper**; d. July, 1888, at Union Spgs., Ala.
9. Nancy, b. 1 Sept., 1782 ; m. 16 May, 1806, Martin (s. Elijah & Eunice *Gould*) **Cowles**, of Far. ; country mcht. and farmer ; she d. F. 29 Apl., 1808 ; he m. (2) ————. *Issue:*
   i. Lucy Hooker (Cowles), b. Feb., 1803 ; d. unm. 12 May, 1869, at Far.
   ii. Julius (Cowles), b. 1805 ; d. 19 Mch., 1805.
   iii. John Edward (Cowles), b. 1806 ; d. 4 Oct., 1818, at Far.
10. William Griswold (Dr.), b. twin to Nancy. Fam. 4.
11. Edward, Esq., b. 27 Apl., 1785. Fam. 5.

FAM. JOHN,[2] (*Col. Noadiah,*[1]), b. 1774, Far.; grad. Y. C., 1796; stud. law and settled at Columbia, S. C.; m. 6 Oct., 1808, Mary Ann (dau. Gershom & Mary) **Chapman,** of Columbia, S. C., who was b. 23 Oct., 1789. He was held in high esteem as a lawyer, and would soon have made a judge of one of the higher courts, had not his sudden death intervened, 28 July, 1815; no issue; his wid. m. (2) 1818, Dr. Geo. W. **Glenn,** Newberry Dist., S. C., and d. 15 Dec., 1872.

FAM. 3. JAMES,[2] (*Col. Noadiah,*[1]), b. 1777, was bred to the sea; became in later yrs. partially insane, and 14 June, 1840, when 63 yrs. old, m. wid. Janette **Sweet,** ae. 28; he d. at Far. 1 May, 1846; wid. m. (2) —————, and d. 16 Jan., 1890.

Children:

1. Noadiah Charles (who now calls himself Charles N.), b. 1841.
2. Jeanette, b. 1 Nov., 1844; m. 29 Sept., 1864, Eli **Moore,** as 2d wife.
3. Franklin (twin), b. 5 Dec., 1845.
4. James Frederick (twin), b. 5 Dec., 1845;

d. 1 Dec., 1864, ae. 19, in U. S. Army hospital; he was a gallant yg. soldier of the 2d Conn. Reg. Heavy Art., Army of the Potomac; now bu. in Gov't Cemetery at Arlington; his name is on the Far. Soldiers' Monument.

FAM. 4. WILLIAM GRISWOLD HOOKER,[2] (*Col. Noadiah,*[1]), b. Far., 1782; m. 20 Oct., 1807, Melinda (dau. David & Annie *Champion*) **Metcalf,** of Lebanon, Ct., b. 30 Oct., 1785; he was a physician at Middlebury, Vt.; later rem. to New Haven, Ct., where he became the first treas. of the N. H. Savings Bank, which office he held for many yrs. He d. N. H., 19 Sept., 1850; wife d. 28 Aug., 1865.

Children:

1. John Metcalf, b. 25 Oct., 1809; grad. Middlebury Coll.; studied med., and was abt. to est. himself in practice when he d. very suddenly.
2. Nancy Champion, b. 18 Oct., 1813; m. 26 Apl., 1837, Edward Lucas **Hart;** she d. at

Far., 21 July, 1880.
3. Samuel, b. 11 June, 1817; m. 28 May, 1844, Wid. Lydia Elizabeth (Strong) **Baldwin;** he d. at White Pigeon, Mich., 12 July, 1852.

FAM. 5. EDWARD,[2] (*Col. Noadiah,*[1]), b. Far., 1785; m. 24 May, 1812, Elizabeth (dau. Esq. Henry & Elizabeth *Prescott*) **Daggett,** of New Haven, Ct., b. 5 July, 1786; she was a niece of Roger Sherman. Mr.' H. grad. Y. C., 1805; stud. law, but never practiced; was, for a time, connected with the Faculty of So. Carolina College, Columbia, S. C.; then tutor at Y. C.; later at the head of a high grade collegiate school at Farmington, Ct., finally sett. down to literary pursuits and scientific farming, and the duties of a town official. He d. Far., 5 May, 1846; wid. d. Htfd., 2 Aug., 1869.

Children (all b. Far.):

1. Elizabeth Daggett, b. 1 May, 1813; m. 10 Sept., 1834, Hon. Francis **Gillette.**
2. John, b. 19 Apl., 1816; m. 5 Aug., 1841, Isabella **Beecher.**
3. Edward, b. 31 Dec., 1819; d. 20 May, 1821.
4. Edward (U. S. N.), b. 25 Dec., 1822. FAM. 6.
5. Mary, b. 3 May, 1825; d. 1 Oct., 1826.

FAM. 6. EDWARD,[3] (*Edward,*[2] *Col. Noadiah,*[1]), b. 1822; Commander, U. S. N. (retired). From Hammersley's *Officers of the Army and Navy (Regular) who served in the Civil War* we quote the following brief geneal. of this gentleman, to whose antiquarian and genealogical zeal we have been much indebted for facts in connection with our Weth. genealogies.

Commander Edward Hooker was bred to the sea in the Merchant Marine, commanding a ship when twenty-three years old. One of the earliest volunteers for the Naval Service in the Civil War, he was appointed Acting Master in July, 1861. His first service was in the gunboat *Louisiana,* and, while attached to that vessel, was severely wounded during a boat expedition, October 5th, 1861. He was the first officer of his grade wounded during the war, and as years roll around, these wounds caused him serious inconvenience. He took an active part in the Burnside Expedition while in the *Louisiana.* At Newberne that vessel fired the first and the last shot of the action. Soon after the capture of Newberne, he became the executive officer of the *Louisiana.* At the time of the Confederate attack upon Washington, N. C., in September, 1862, the ship was fought by Commander Hooker in the absence of the commanding officer, in a manner which caused high commendation from commanding officers of our own forces, and forced from the Confederates the admission that "Were it not for the gunboat, the Union garrison would have been captured; for the town was surprised at daybreak, the fortifications captured, and the guns turned on the garrison. The rapidity and accuracy of fire of the Louisana drove the Confederates off after they were in full possession."

For gallantry on this occasion, Commander Hooker was made Acting Volunteer Lieutenant to date from the day of the action. He was then ordered to a command in the blockade off Wilmington, and, soon after, to the command of a division of the Potomac Flotilla, in which command he continued until the end of the war. In 1864 he was ordered, with his division, to co-operate with General Grant's Army, and to clear the Rappahannock River, so that transports could reach Fredericksburg. This duty he performed, and remained at Fredericksburg until it was evacuated by our forces. His ship being then in urgent need of repairs, Commander Hooker was sent by Commander Foxhall Parker, commanding the flotilla, to the Washington Navy Yard, being then promoted to Acting Volunteer Lieutenant Commander.

After the war closed he took the store ship *Idaho* to the Asiatic Squadron; and while there was transferred from the volunteer to the regular navy list, commissioned Lieutenant, March, 1868, and Lieutenant Commander, December, 1868. He was, after this, Captain of the yard at League Island, Assistant light-house Inspector, and other duties, until in February, 1884, while on duty at the Naval Home, at Philadelphia, he was promoted to Commander. In December of that year he was placed upon the retired list by operation of law, and passed the remainder of his life in N. Y., where he d. in May, 1903.

He is a companion of the Loyal Legion, member of Rankin Post No. 10, Grand Army, Connecticut Society of Sons of the Revolution, the Brooklyn New England Society, Brooklyn Library Association, Long Island Historical Society, and Rhode Island Marine Society, and honorary member of other societies. A member of Aurora Grata Club, Brooklyn, and an active member of the Brooklyn Association of Masonic Veterans. Member of New York City, Rhode Island and Connecticut Associations Masonic Veterans. Hon. Life member Boston Commandery, U. S. Naval Association, member Hundred Year Club, and Naval Academy Athletic Association. He m. (1) 28 Mch., 1847, Elizabeth Moore **Wardwell;** m. (2) 11 May, 1851, Esther Ann **Battey.**

BRAINARD,[6] (*Hez.,*[5] *Hez.,*[4] *John,*[3] *Rev. Sam'l,*[2] *Rev. Thos.,*), b. 4 Mch., 1747, at Woodbury, Ct.; m. Mary (dau. Chas. & Dorothy *Belding*) **Deming,** of Weth., who was b. 23 Jan., 1752; res at Weth., until sometime betw. 1782 and '87, when they rem. to Middlebury, Vt. He was a Revol. soldier. He d. at Middlebury, Vt., 1812; ae. 60; wid. d. 1844, ae. 91.

Children (b. Weth.) :

1. John, b. 7 Jan., 1774; m. Sally **Briggs,** of Middlebury, Vt.; rem. to Cato, N. Y.
2. Charles, b. 26 Dec., 1776; m. Nancy **Pettibone,** poss. of Middlebury, where they res.
3. Calvin, b. 12 Oct., 1779; rem. to Cato, N. Y.
4. Electa, b. 26 Nov., 1782; m. Rosewell **Stevens,** of Middlebury, Vt.
5. Harris, b. 13 May, 1787, at Middlebury,

Vt., a prisoner of war, at Quebec, 1815; m. Betsy **Johnson,** prob. of M.; 2 ch.
6. Louisa, b. 14 Sept., 1790, at Middlebury, Vt.; m. at M., 12 Sept., 1812, Burnham **Phelps.**
7. Polly, b. 18 Mch., 1792; at Middlebury; d. 11 Dec., 1838, ae. 45; at Louisville, Ky.; m. 7 Jan., 1814, Burnham **Phelps,** whose first wife was her sister Louisa.

BYRON E., of Bristol, m. Maria R. **Williams,** 27 Mch., 1833.

ROGER, of Far. m. Anne **Kellogg,** of New., 30 July, 1747.—*W. C. R.*

URANIA, wife of A. B. **Doolittle,** d. 14 May, 1614, d. 8 Nov., 1895.—*Weth. Ins.*

POLLY W., d. 23 Mch., 1886, ae. 77.—*Weth. Ins.*

SARAH, (Mrs.), formerly wife of Seth **Hooker,** of Berlin and late wife of Charles **Dix,** d. Feb., 10, 1803, ae. 69.—*Weth. Ins.*

JAMES, d. ae. 38, 1 Jan., 1835.—*N. C. R.*

HOOPER, MARTIN, s. of Philip, d. 16 Oct., 1824, ae. 22.—*N. C. R.*

NANCY'S ch. d. May, 1815, ae. 1 mo. ? —*N. C. R.*

HOPKINS, (N. C. R.).   HORACE, m. Fanny ————; had *Henry Benjamin; George Botsford; Horace Root;* bp. 5 May, 1822; *Rollin Peck,* bp. 4 Sept., 1825.

Capt. BENJAMIN, who d. 6 May, 1834, ae. 41; m. 17 Mch., 1816, Harriet **Lusk,** of Weth.,—(*N. C. R.*), who d. 9 Apl., 1852, ae. 57,—*Weth. Ins.; had* —(*N. C. R.*) *Wyllis* bp. 23, Oct., 1825; d. 27 Aug., 1873, ae. 48—*Weth. Ins.; Delia W.,* bp. 19 Aug., 1821.

CALEB, had *Joseph* and *Ira,* bp. 29 May, 1796.

BENJAMIN, d. ae. 58, 19 Jan., 1810.

DELIA, of New., m. Dumont **Carey,** of Berlin, 10 May, 1842.—*N. C. R.*

DISETHEUS & *Eunice,* had *William,* bp. 27 Sept., 1821.—*N. C. R.*

ELIZABETH, had *Joseph,* bp. 10 July, 1774.

EDWARD, m. Elizabeth **Beadle,** 17 Aug., 1768.—*W. C. R.*

EBENEZER, m. Mary (dau. Samuel) **Butler,** 21 Jan., 1691.

HORNER, THOMAS, m. Phebe **Clark,** 4 Jan., 1739; she d. ae. 89, bu. 7 Jan., 1806. He d. 11 Nov., 1757, ae. 42.—*Weth. Ins.*

Children (Weth. Ins.) :

1. Thomas, b. 29 Sept., 1743; bp. 30 Dec., 1744 (*L.*); on the mother's right, he d. 6 Feb., 1816, in 73d yr.—*W. C. R.*
2. William, b. 23 Sept., 1745.
3. Mary, b. 24 Sept., 1747.

4. George, b. 12 Oct., 1749; d. 14 Oct., 1753, ae. 4 yrs., 14 d.—*Weth. Ins.*
5. Phebe, b. 10 June, 1751.
6. Margaret, b. 16 Dec., 1754.
7. Judith, b. 28 Apl., 1757.

THOMAS', dau. ae. 3, bu. 2 Mch., 1776.

LUCY, dau of Thomas, bp. 4 Dec., 1774.

PEGGY, of Weth., m. Epaphras **Thompson**, of Saybrook, 11 Jan., 1779.

HORSFORD, (*Hosford*), Dr. AARON, m. Esther ————. He "having for 30 yrs. practiced physic in this Society [Step.], d. 7 Apl., 1804, in 57 yr."—*W. Ins.;* she d. 18 July, 1828, ae. 77.—*W. Ins.*

Children (Weth. Ins.) :

1. Aaron, b. 27 Feb., 1772; m. 8 Nov., 1795, Roxy (dau. Capt. Oliver & Sarah) **Goodrich**, who d. 10 Dec., 1796, in 23d yr. ; their dau. Roxy G., bp. 7 Feb., d. 25 Mch., 1796. Mr. Aaron, d. 6 Feb., 1805, in 33d yr.—*W. Ins.*
2. Joel, d. 29 Oct., 1776, ae. 2 mos.—*W. Ins.*
3. Clarissa, b. 19 July, 1777.
4. Esther, b. 6 Apl., 1779; prob. the Etty who d. 8 May, 1840, ae. 61.—*S. C. R. et W. Ins.*
5. Othniel, b. 25 June, bp. 29 July, 1787.
6. Harley, b. 2 Jan., 1791; m. and had Aaron Adams, bp. 8 Nov., 1818.
7. Joel Hall, who d. 3 or 5 Sept., 1786, in 5 yr.—*W. Ins.*

An OTHNIEL m. Sarah **Willard**, both of Weth., 15 Jan., 1778—*W. C. R.*, and had (*S. C. R.*) Sally and Lydia, bp. 28 Oct., 1781; Charlotte and Lauretta, bp. 7 July, 1782.

ELISHA, of Far. m. Martha **Cole,** of New., 8 Apl., 1778.—*W. C. R.*

HORTON, TIMOTHY, Jr., of W. Springfield, m. Betsy **Hanmer,** 2 Feb., 1794.— *W. C. R.*

HAMILTON R., of Glast, m. Lucy **Bulkeley,** 1 Aug., 1844.

ROSWELL'S wife, d. 3 Dec., 1803, in 27 yr.

HOSKINS, RUSSELL, of Winchester, Ct., m. Hannah **Wells,** 1 Dec., 1791.—*W. C. R.*

EZRA, a patrol in State Prison, Weth., killed by convicts 30 Apl., 1833; monument erected by the State.—*W. Ins.*

HOUGH, JOHN, of Meridan, had John, bp. 27 Sept., 1767.

HOUSE, WILLIAM, a signer of the covenant for the Ch. at Naubuc, Feb., 1691.

JEREMIAH, of Glast., m. Fanny **Blinn,** of Weth., 11 Feb., 1821.—*N. C. R.*

CHAUNCEY, of Coventry, m. Polly (dau. Jonathan) **Wells,** 1 May, 1825? She d. ae. 26, 10 Sept., 182-?

HOVEY, EDMUND, of Mansfield, m. Sophia **Bulkeley,** 13 Apl., 1806.

HOWARD, (*Hayward*), HENRY, ho-lot ment. in *W. T. V.* I. p. 29, see also, Chapt. VII. Vol. I. *Savage* ment. him (II. 471) as of Htfd., but as having been at Weth., where he m. Sarah (perhaps sister of Rev. Samuel) **Stone,** 28 Sept., 1648, and had the following ch. all b. at Weth., besides two ment. in his will (the two last on list) etc.

Children:

1. Mary, b. 1651.
2. Sarah, b. 1653 ; m. John **Atchet,** or Adjet, and had *John* and *Samuel,* who d. before their father's dth.
2. Elizabeth, b. 1656 ; died before her father.
3. John, twin Lydia, b. 1661 ; see Chapt.

——, Vol. I.
4. Lydia, twin John, m. Joseph **Barnard.**
5. Mary, ment. in father's will ; m. Thos. **Griswold.**
6. Samuel, ment. in father's will; was a trader at Htfd.

JOHN, (prob. the J., s. of Henry, preceding), m. Mary ————, 1 June 1687, who
d. 27 Apl., 1698; he m. (2) Margaret (dau. John) **Stebbins,** 12 Nov., 1702.
He d. 15 Feb., 1720-21.   Est. invent, at £630-09-06.

Children (Weth Rec.) :

1. William, b. 29 Aug., 1687.   FAM. 2.
2. Elizabeth, b. 8 Sept., 1689; m. ————
   Francis, acc. to father's will.
3. Mary, b. 1 Nov., 1693 ; d. 25 Sept., 1695.
4. John, b. 2 May, 1696.

(By second marriage; bp Mix Rec.) :
5. Mary, b. 11 Oct., bp. 7 Nov., 1703.
6. Sarah, b. 20 Nov., 1705.
7. Lidia, b. 28, bp. 26 (*sic.*) Nov., 1708-9.
8. Jonathan, b. 1, bp. 3 Jan., 1713-14.

FAM. 2.   WILLIAM,[2] (*John,*[1]), m. Sarah (dau. Benj.,) **Gardner,** 16 Sept., 1714.
See Chapt. VII, Vol. 1.

Children (Weth. Rec.) :

1. Benjamin, b. 6 May, 1715.
2. Elizabeth, b. 17 Apl., 1717.

3. Sarah, b. 15 Dec., 1718.

HOWE, ————, of E. Haven, m. Phebe **Weaver,** 12 Jan., 1778,—*W. C. R.*

PERLEY, had *Horace* and *Henry,* (twins) bp. 17 and d. 22 Feb., 1793; s. *George,*
bp. Oct., 1791.—*W. C. R.*

HOYT, (*Height, on Weth. Rec.*), WALTER, has fence tax rec. 1647, *W. T. V.*
I. p. 29.   He is poss. the W. H. of Windsor, having had poss. some landed
interest at Weth.   See Chapt. VII, Vol. I.

JAMES JAUNCEY, (2d s. James J. & Mary) of Colbrook; dr. at Weth., 3 July,
1819, ae. 16 y. & 6 mo.   His father's dth. at C., is also rec. in Weth., 30 Sept.,
1812, in 43d yr.

HUBBARD, (*Hubert*), GEORGE, prob. from Watertown, Mass.   It is not at
all improbable that he may have been a bro. of the Samuel Hubbard (ment. in
Stiles' *Windsor* II, 414), who came from Mendeleham, Co. Suffolk, Eng.,
1633, sett. at Watertown, thence rem. 1635, to Windsor, Ct., where he was m.
1636-7 to Tare **Cooper,** ae. 28, and *began his m. life at Weth.,* whence he soon
rem. to Springfield, then Fairfield and finally to Newport, R. I.   He was an
important man in the Col., on a Comm. app. by the Gen. Ct. 1637, '39; and one
of those app. by the Ct., 1656, to survey Weth.; dep. to Gen. Ct. Aug. and
Sept. sess. of 1639; rem. abt. 1643-4 to Milford, Ct.; then, 1650, to Guilford,
thence to Midd., where he d. 1684, ae. abt. 80.   On *Weth. T. Rec.* I. p. 6,
his cattle ear-mark is rec. and (*Hubert, on rec.*), surveyor, 1653, (*Ibid.* I.
p. 43); constable, 1654, (*Ibid.* I. 44); see Chapt. VII, Vol. I; rep. to Gen. Ct.
after the Union of the Conn. and N. H. Colonies, 1655-6.   Tho' no *ch.* are rec.
to him on *Weth. Rec.,* his will, dated 23 May, 1682, with a cod. of Dec, 30.
names 3 sons and 5 daus. as follows, and Savage (II. 483) remarks that some
of his *ch.,* no doubt, d. before he came to Weth., prob. in Eng.   His wife d.
Sept., 1676.   His res. in Weth. on W. side High St., a few rods N. of Fort
St., on which the Prison now stands.

Children :

1. John. FAM. 2.
2. Daniel, bp. 26 May, 1644, at Milford.
3. William.
4. Mary, m. John **Fowler.**
5. Sarah, m. ———— **Harrison,** or Morrison.
6. Abigail, bp. 26 May, 1644, at Milford;
   m. Humphrey **Spinning;** their s. John

ment. in his gd-father's will, but with
no ref. to their parents, who prob. had d.
before date of his will.
7. Hannah, bp. 26 May, 1644, at Milford;
   m. (prob.) Jacob **Melyne,** or Melyen.
8. Elizabeth, unm. at date of father's will;
   but she m. later, John **Norton,** of Guilford, as his 2d wife.

FAM. 2. JOHN,[2] (George,[1]); m. Marie ————; see Chapt. VII, Vol. I; rem. to Hadley and there had 5 ch. born; rem. thence to Hatfield, where he d. before Mch., 1706, Judd's *Hadley Hist.*, says abt. 1705; and his will ,of 1702) prob. all his 7 ch. were then living. *Judd* says his wife Mary (**Merriam**?) of Concord survived him.

Children (*Weth. Rec.*) :

1. Marie, b. 27 Jan., 1650-1; acc. to *Savage*, d. yg.	3. Hannah, b. 5 Dec., 1656; acc. to *Savage*, d. yg.
2. John, b. 12 Apl., 1655.—See Chapt. VII, Vol. I.	4. Jonathan, b. 3 Jan., 1659.

DAVID, a grad. of Y. C., class of 1721, was 2d s. of John, Jr., of Glast., & Rebecca, and gt-gd-son of George the Settler. He spent his life on a farm in Eeastbury Soc'y,(now Buckingham, Ct.) ; rep. Glast. in Gen. Assemb. during 19 sessions, between 1724 and '35; was Capt. of 2d Co. of Glast. Trainband; d. Glast. 15 Oct., 1776, ae. 66; bu. in old burying gd. in B.; his wife was Prudence (eld. dau. David) **Goodrich**, of Weth., by his 2d wife Prudence **Churchill**; she m. (2) Judah **Holcomb**, and d. 29 Nov., 1783, in 83d yr., leaving several ch.

CHARLES M., s. of Gideon M and Emily, b. 19 Aug., 1847.—*W. T. R.*

CHARLES M., d. 7 Sept., 1849, ae. 2 yr.

DANIEL, of Berlin, m. Sarah **Belden**, 15 Dec., 1799.

HARVEY, wife of, d. ae. 25, bu. 26 May, 1822.

JAMES H., of Midd., m. Mary **Goodrich**, 23 Oct., 1825.

JAMES, d. 15 Jan., 1848, ae. 6 mos.

MOSES, ae. 60, bu. 6 Oct., 1819.

EMILY, of New., m. Joseph L. **Shepard**, of Westfield, Mass., 27 Apl., 1841.—*W. T. R.*

GEORGE, of Berlin, m. Lydia **Wright**, 18 Jan., 1786.

MARIA, of New., m. Stephen **Lamberton**, 30 Sept., 1834.—*W. T. R.*

SARAH, ae. 57 bu. 12 Sept., 1821.

WILLIAM, m. Martha **Hurlbut**, of Boston, 2 Apl., 1834, who d. 2 Jan., 1842, ae. 26,—*Weth. Ins.* He d. 15 July, 1888, ae. 76,—*Weth. Ins.; issue, William Henry,* d. 26 Feb., 1839, ae. 2 yr. 4 mos.; *Charles E.* d. 6 Jan., 1861, ae. 20.—Weth. Ins.

DOSITHEUS, (who d. 3 Feb., 1853, ae. 66, *Weth.* (*N.*) *Ins.*) ; m. Eunice ————, who d. 8 Jan., 1879, ae. 92.—*Weth.* (*N.*) *Ins. & (N. C. R.).*
Issue :

1. Marilla, bp. 7 May, 1826.	3. Emily, bp. 2 Sept., 1821 ; d. 15 Aug., 1873.—*Ibid.*
2. Orrin, bp. 2 Sept., 1821 ; d. 29 Nov., 1827, ae. 9 yrs.—*Weth.* (*N.*) *Ins.*	4. Eunice Maria, bp. 2 Sept., 1821.

HUBBELL, IRA, res. many yrs. in Ry-H.; m. (1) Irene **Strong**; m. (2) Uno [Eunice?] **Hart**, with whom he res. in Midd.; m. (3) Urania **Patton**; after her dth. 18 Nov., 1874, ae. 80—*Weth. Ins.*, he being then 80 yrs. old sold out his ppy., part of which had come to him by her., and rem. to Winchester, Ct., to the ho. of his bro-in-law, McPherson Hubbell, where he d., ae. over 90. His father was SILLIMAN [*Stillman?*] Hubbell, who enl. in the Revol. war from near Bethel, or Danbury, and at one time served under Gen. Putnam, at Greenwich, Ct.; was a Revol. pensioner.—Letter of AND. L. HUBBELL, 1900.

NATHAN, d. ae. 24, bu. 4 Nov., 1785.—*W. C. R.*

LUCIUS, of Huntington, m. Emily C. **Deming**, of Weth., 29 Mch., 1829.—*W. C. R.*

442   GENEALOGIES AND BIOGRAPHIES OF ANCIENT WETHERSFIELD.

HUDSON, JOHN, m. Elizabeth **Latimer,** 9 Oct., 1783.—*W. C. R.*; she d. ae. 65, bu. 13 Aug., 1822.—*W. C. R.*

JOHN, d. ae. 45, bu. 22 Dec., 1827.

JOHN, d. ae. 48, bu. 9 May, 1801.

JOSEPH, d. ae. 39, bu. 3 Apl., 1822.

SARAH, m. Erastus **Cowles,** 16 Jan., 1823.—*W. Rec.*

LENAH, bp. 3 Apl., 1814.

HULBURT,[*] (*Hurlburt, Hurlibut, Holebert,*)[†] THOMAS, acc. to tradition, a Scotchman, and b. 1610, is also supposed to have been one of the 11 male passengers, who embarked at London, 11 Aug., 1635, with wife and female servant and, in the *Bachelor,* in company with Capt. Lyon Gardnier,[‡] the Eng. engineer employed by the Conn. Patentees under patent issued by King Charles II, Lords Say and Seal, Brooke and others, to erect a fort at Saybrook, at the mouth of the Conn. River. Hurlbut may have been an employee of Capt. Gardiner, or a soldier under his command; at all events he was a blacksmith by trade, and was located at Saybrook with Gardiner, where he was conspicious for coolness and bravery in the fight with the Indians when they attacked the fort there in 1637. Fortunately for Mr. Hurlbut's record, his part in that encounter, was fully stated by Capt. Gardiner in his *Relation of the Pequot Wars,* (Mass., Hist. Soc. Coll. III, third series) written at the request of Maj. Mason, Thos. Hurlbut, Robert Chapman and others from memory, aided by some old papers, in June, 1660, some 23 years, after the skirmish, as follows: "In the 22d of February, I went out with ten men and three dogs, half a mile from the house [fort] to burn the weeds, reeds and leaves upon the neck of land, because we felled twenty timber-trees which we were to roll to the water-side to bring home, every man carrying a length of match with brimstone matches with him to kindle the fire in that. But when we came to the small of the Neck, the weeds burning, I having before this set two sentinels on the small of the Neck, I called to the men that were burning the weeds to come away, but they would not until they had burnt up the rest of their matches. Presently there starts up four Indians out of the fiery reeds, but ran away, I calling to the rest of the men to come away out of the marsh. Then Robert Chapman and *Thomas Hurlbut,* being sentinels, called to me saying there come a number of Indians out of the other side of the marsh. Then I went to stop them that they should not get the woodland; but *Thomas Hurlbut* cried out to me that some of the men did not follow me, for Thomas Rumble and Arthur Branch threw down their guns and ran away; then the Indians shot two of them that were in the reeds, and sought to get between us and home, but durst not come before us, but kept us in a half-moon, we retreating and exchanging many a shot, so that *Thomas Hurlbut* was shot almost through the thigh, John Spencer in the back into his kidneys, and myself into the thigh; two more were shot dead. But, in our retreat, I kept Hurlbut and Spencer still before us,

---

[*] THE HURLBUT GENEALOGY, or Record of the Descendants of Thomas Hurlbut, of Saybrook and Weth., Conn., etc., etc. By Henry H. Hurlbut, Albany, N. Y., 1888, 8 vo., pp. 545.
[†] This spelling, common on Weth. Rec., suggests the possible correctness of an idea already advanced that the name is an abbreviation of what was formerly *Haliburton.* A correspondent claims to have counted some twenty different spellings, from *Holabird* to *Hurlbut,* and *Our English Surnames,* pub. London, 1873, by Bardsley, says it belongs to the class of *nicknames,* like Shakespeare; being derived from an old weapon, called *Whirlbat,* which was held, or whirled by the hand.
[‡] Winthrop, however, says that Gardiner sailed in a Norsey (Norway) bark, 10 July, 1635.

we defending ourselves with our naked swords, or else they had taken us all alive, So that the two sore wounded men, [*Hurlbut* and Spencer] by our slow retreat, got home with their guns, when our two sound men [Rumble and Branch] ran away and left their guns behind them. But when I saw the cowards that left us I resolved to let them draw lots which of them should be hanged, for the articles [of war—or "general orders"] did hang up in the hall for them to read, and they knew they had been published long before. But, at the intercession of old Mr. Mitchell [Mr. Matthew Mitchell, like Hurlbut, afterwards of Weth.] Mr. Higgison and Mr. Pell, I did forbear. Within a few days after I went out with eight men to get some food for our relief, and found the guns that were thrown away, and the body of one man shot through, the arrow going in at the right side, the head sticking fast, half through the rib on the left side, which I took out and cleaned it, and preserved to send to the Bay [*i. e.* to friends at Boston] because they had said that the arrows of the Indians were of no force."

After the Pequot War, Hurlbut rem. fm. Saybrook to Weth., of which he became the first established blacksmith. In the *Col. Rec.*, we find that Mch. 2, 1642, he was fined 40*s* for "encouraging others in taking excessive rates for work and ware;" and, probably, if he practiced as he preached, he charged good prices for his own work. The fine, however, was remitted Feb. 5th, 1643. He seems to have held a good standing in Weth.; appraiser of the Elsen est., 1648; was Clerk of the Train Band in 1640; deputy to the General Court, Grand Juror, and Constable in 1644; collector of taxes, 1647—*W. T. V.*, I, p. 27; his earmark for cattle is also rec. p. 1 same vol. In 1671, Oct. 12, he rec'd a grant of 120 acres of land fm. the Gen. Court, for his services in the Indian wars— which, however, was not set off to him during his lifetime, being finally set off in 1694, on the petition of his grandson, John, Jr., of Midd. His landed possessions are given in Vol. I. p.—*Weth. Ld. Rec.*, 111 145. His res. in Weth. is supp. to have been on the site of the house occupied, in 1888, by Miss Harriet Mitchell, of the 6th generation. Trad. also says that that orig. house had a peculiar fascination for the Indians, so long as they remained in the vicinity; for, whenever they were in the village they were frequently to be seen peering in curiously at the windows. Acc. to *Hurlbut Geneal.* he d. abt. 1671, but acc. to his deed to his s. Stephen (*W. L. Rec.*, III, 145) he was alive May 18, 1682. His wife's name was Sarah ——————, but the defective early records of Weth. have preserved for us the record of birth of one only of his six sons, and no names, etc., of the daus., if there were any. Dr. C. G. Hubbard of Hornellsville, says she was Abigail (dau. Silas) **Belden**, of Weth. Mr. Hurlbut prob. d. soon after the grant of ld. fm. the Colony, viz.: Oct., 1671.

Children (*prob. b. in Weth.*) :

1. Thomas. FAM. 2.
2. John, b. 8 Mch., 1642. FAM. 3.
3. Samuel. FAM. 4.
4. Joseph. FAM. 5.
5. Stephen. FAM. 6.
6. Cornelius. FAM. 7.

FAM. 2. THOMAS,[2] (*Thos.*,[1]), b. abt. 1660; m. (1) Lydia [**Ketchum**,]—*S. D. A.*, who d. before 1675; m. (2) Elizabeth ——————; was a blacksmith and succeeded his father in bus. at Weth., the Town, Mch. 11, 1662, granting him a piece of ld. whereon to set a shop.—See Chapt. VII, Vol. I. He d. Sept., 1689-0; est. (invent. 6 Mch., 1690) including blacksmith tools, furniture etc., amtd. to £57, 19*s*. The Invt. gives name (Christian) of his wife and 4 ch. The author of *Hurlbut Gen.* thinks that his 1st wife, Lydia, was the mother of the eldest s. Thomas 3d, and that the second wife was mother of the other three.

Children:

1. Thomas, b. prob. in Weth., abt. 1660; supp. to have left Weth., abt. the time of his father's second marr.; was at Woodbury, before 1682, and was living there in 1698; m. and had (*bp. Woodbury, Ct.*):
   i. Jemima (Hurlbut), bp. Aug., 1680; supp. m. at Stratford, Ct., John **Blakeman**.
   ii. Jerusha (Hurlbut), bp. Apl., 1681-2,
   iii. Thomas, 4th, (Hurlbut), bp. Dec., 1684; prob. res. Wilton, Ct.
   iv. Gideon (Hurlbut), bp. Aug., 1688; rem. to Westport, Ct. (Green's Farms), where he d. 9 Mch., 1757, in 70 yr.; wife Margaret ———, d. 28 Feb., 1754, (*Will, Fairfield Co., prob.*

Office); had several children, of whom *Mary*, m. Nathan **Gray**, 24 July, 1735; and *Elizabeth*, b. 1710-18, m. Joseph **Ketchum**, at G. Farms, 8 Mch., 1749-50, and d. in The Oblong, after Mch., 1792-3; her son, Amos Ketchum, m. Arabella **Landon**, and their dau. (Mary K. Landon), m. Samuel Ackerly, M. D., father of the Rev. S. M. Ackerly, who m. Louise **DuBois**, and were the parents of the accomplished genealogist *Lucy D. Ackerly*, of Newburgh, N. Y.
2. Timothy, b. 29 Sept., 1681.—*Weth. Rec.*
3. Nathaniel, 7 yrs. old at father's dth.
4. Ebenezer, 4 yrs. old at father's dth.

FAM. 3. Sgt. JOHN,[2] (*Thos.,*[1]), was also a blacksmith, and after coming of age, worked at his trade at Weth. and Killingsworth.—See Chapt. VII, Vol. I, for ld-holdings. At age of 27, entered into contract, 25 Oct., 1669, with the first sett. of Midd. to locate there and "do the Town's work of smithing for seven yrs." He became a large landholder and prominent man in Midd.; was made freeman, 1671, and was Sergeant in th Train-band. He m. 15 Dec., 1670, Mary (dau. of John & Honor *Treat*) **Deming**, of Weth., who was b. 1655 and adm. to Midd. Ch. 5 Sept., 1675. Sgt. H. d. Aug. 30, 1690 (acc. to *Prob. Rec.*), ae. 48; est. £373, 15s, 6d; shop, house and home ld., £100; other lots, £160; cattle, etc., £46; smith's tools, etc., £10.

Children (b. in Midd.):

1. John, b. 8 Dec., 1671; farmer; Midd.; family.
2. Mary, b. 7 Apl., 1673; d. inf.
3. Thomas, b. 20 Oct., 1674; blacksmith; Midd.; family.
4. Sarah, b. 5 Nov., 1676; m. 1703, Joseph **Warner**, of Midd.
5. Mary, b. 17 Nov., 1678; m. 1701, Nath'l **Churchill**, of Weth.—See *Churchill*.
6. Mercy, b. 17 Feb., 1680-1; m. Thos. **Hale**,

of Glast.
7. Ebenezer, b. 17 Jan., 1782-3; farmer; Midd.; family.
8. Margaret, b. Feb., 1684-5; m. 1706, Timo. **Sage**, of No. Midd.—*Cromwell*.
9. David, b. 11 Aug., 1688; blacksmith; first at Upper Houses; (Cromwell) fam.
10. Mehitable, b. 23 Nov., 1690; m. 1714, Capt. Daniel **White**, of Midd. (Cromwell.)

FAM. 4. SAMUEL,[2] (*Thos.,*[1]), farmer, Weth., where he bo't, Dec., 1668, a ho. and home-lot; named in 1692, as res. in Weth.—Chapt. VII, Vol. I; the S. who d. 1712, in W. may have been him, tho' he may have rem. to Far. where some of his fam. were res.; no Prob. Rec. threw light on time of dth., etc.; tax-list.—*W. T. V.*, I, 12. He m. Mary ———; he d. 6 Dec., 1712.

Children (Weth. Rec.):

1. Stephen, b. 27 Dec., 1668. FAM. 8.
2. Nathan, b. 4 Oct., 1670. FAM. 9.
3. Mary, b. 16 Oct., 1672; m. Henry **Webb**, 10 Oct., 1695; 2 ch.
4. Sarah, b. 25 Dec., 1674.
5. Jonathan, b. 2 Mch., 1677. FAM. 10.
6. David, b. 7 July, 1679. FAM. 11.

7. Titus, b. 18 Dec., 1681.
8. Nathan, b. Apl., 1683; m. 27 Mch., 1703, Joshua **Bates**; 9 ch.
9. Samuel, b. 17 Jan., 1686-7. FAM. 12.
10. Elizabeth, b. 4 Jan., 1690-1.
11. Lemmon, b. 1 Aug., 1695.

FAM. 5. JOSEPH,[2] (*Thos.,*[1]), rem. to Woodbury, Ct., res. there as early as 1682; m. Rebecca ———, who d. 2 Feb., 1712; he prob. the "Joseph the aged" who d. at Woodbury, Ct., 13 July, 1732.

Children:

1. Joseph.
2. John.
3. Sarah.

4. Cornelius.
5. Jonathan.
6. Rebecca.

7. Mary, m. Josiah **Minor**.
8. Phebe, m. Josiah **Walker**, later of Litchfield.

FAM. 6. STEPHEN,[2] (*Thos.,*[1]), fm. a rec. on Weth Town Books, 23 Feb., 1694, of a gr. of ld. 8 by 70 ft. adjoining his home-lot, "to set a shop upon," it is inferred that he was a mechanic—poss. a blacksmith. He m. (1) Phebe ———,

12 Dec., 1678 (*Weth. Rec.*) ; the *Hurlbut Gen.* gives Mr. Edwin Stearns, genealogist, as auth. for statement that he m. on that date, *Dorothy* ————— ; it is
quite poss. he might have m. a second time, a supposition rendered more ten-
able by the names of his two daughters.

Children (*Weth. Rec.*) :

1. Stephen, b. 17 Sept., 1679.
2. Thomas, b. 28 Jan., 1680-1. FAM. 13.
3. Joseph, b. 10 July, 1683. FAM. 14.
4. Benjamin, b. 29 Oct., 1685 ; sett. Weth. ;
   prob. fthr. of Honor Hurlbut, bp. 12 Mch.,
   1731-2.
5. Phebe, b. 2 Aug., 1688 ; m. 3 Mch., 1709,
   John **Wiard**, of Weth.—See *Wiard*.
6. Dorothy, b. 5 Mch., 1690-1 ; m. 9 Dec.,
   1710, Thomas **Clark**, of Weth.—See *Clark*.

FAM. 7. CORNELIUS,[2] (*Thos.*,[1]), b. abt. 1654 ; m. Rebecca —————.

Children (*Weth. Rec.*) :

1. John, b. 27 Jan., 1686 ; lost at sea, 22
   Nov., 1701, with all the crew ; aged abt.
15.—*Hinman, N. E. Gen. Reg.*, XVIII, 58.
2. William, b. 28 Mch., 1689. FAM. 15.

FAM. 8. STEPHEN,[3] (*Sam'l,*[2] *Thos.*,[1]), b. 1668 ; sett. in New Lond., where, abt. 1696,
he m. Hannah **Douglas**; he d. 7 Oct., 1712.

Children (*b. New Lond.*) :

1. Stephen.
2. Freelove.
3. Mary.
4. John.
5. Sarah.
6. Titus.
7. Joseph.

FAM. 9. NATHAN,[3] (*Sam'l,*[2] *Thos.*,[1]), b. 1670, sett. in Weth.; m. 9 July (or 30
Dec.) 1699, Mary (dau. Peter) **Blinn**.

Children (*Weth. Rec. & Mix Rec.*) :

1. Gideon (Lieut.), b. 9, bp. 18 Feb., 1699-00.
   FAM. 16.
2. Anna, b. 2, bp. 10 Aug., 1701 ; m. 18 Apl.,
   1718, Noah (s. of John, Jr.) **Wadhams**,
   of Weth.
3. Peter, b. 12, bp. 19 (26?) Sept., 1703.
   FAM. 17.
4. Hezekiah, b. 28 Aug., 1705.
5. John, b. 30, bp. 31 Aug., 1707. FAM. 18.
6. Samuel, b. 12, bp. 14 Aug., 1709.
7. Mary, b. 25, bp. 28 Oct., 1711.
8. Elizabeth, b. 13, bp. 28 Oct., 1713.
9. Thankful, b. 16 Dec., 1717, bp. 3 Jan.,
   1717-8 ; "dangerously ill" says the *Mix
   Rec.*
10. Nathaniel, b. 15 June, 1720. FAM. 19.

FAM. 10. JONATHAN,[3] (*Sam'l,*[2] *Thos.*,[1]), b. 1677, sett. Kensington parish, Farmington, (now Berlin) ; m. (1) 27 July, 1699, Sarah **Webb** (*Weth. Rec.*) ; m. (2)
Abiah ————— (named in will) ; will (probated, 28 Mch., 1730) mentions
5 sons, 4 daus. The *Hurlbut Gen.* credits nativity of *all* his ch. to Kensington;
but the birth of the 5 eldest are rec. in Weth. He d. 1 Apl., 1730—seems to
have been of some prominence in town. Est., £716.

Children (* *Weth. Rec.*) :

1. Stephen,* b. 16 Mch., 1700 ; res. Kensington, Ct.
2. Jonathan,* b. 7 Apl., bp. 3 May, 1702 ;
   res. Southington, Ct.
3. Josiah,* b. 10 Oct., 1704 ; ment. in *Rec.*
   as s. of the 2d wife.
4. Abiah,* b. 18 June (bp. 20 July, *Mix*),
   1707.
5. Sarah,* b. 28 May (bp. 2 July, *Mix*), 1710 ;
   m. cousin, Samuel **Hurlbut**, 3d.
6. Mary, bp. in Weth. (bp. 5 Apl., 1713, *Mix*) ;
   joined K. ch. 1761.
7. Isaac, b. 1715.
8. James (Dr.), b. 1717 ; a physician of wide
   fame in Ct.; see Thacher's *Med. Biogra-
   phy ;* res. in Far., but d. in Weth. 11 Apl.,
   1794, ae. 77.
9. Martha, b. —————.

FAM. 11. DAVID,[3] (*Sam'l,*[2] *Thos.*,[1]), b. 1679 ; res. Weth.; m. —————.

Child :

1. Noah, bp. Weth., 8 Mch., 1712-3.—*Mix
   Rec.*

FAM. 12. SAMUEL,[3] (*Sam'l,*[2] *Thos.*,[1]), b. 1687 ; sett. in Weth. near the Far. (now
the Berlin) line ; bo't ld. in Berlin in 1736.

Child :

1. Samuel.
   The *Hurlbut Gen.* also thinks that he had
   son *John*, who went to Canaan, and that he
was the gd-father of Wm. S. Holabird, at
one time Lieu.- Gov. of Conn.

Fam. 13. THOMAS,[3] (*Stephen*,[2] *Thos.*,[1]), b. 1680-1; farmer, Weth.; m. 11 Jan., 1704-5, Rebecca (dau. John) **Meekins**, of E. Htfd., and gd.-dau. of the emigrant John Bidwell, of Htfd. He d. 10 Apl., 1761, ae. 81—*W. Ins.;* will dated, 19 Nov., 1755; proven, 25 Apl., 1761. Invent. of est., 1762, £781-03-04—*Htfd. Prob.* XXIII, 228; she d. 22 Mch., 1760—*W. Ins.,* acc. to *Co. Ct. Rec.,* Apl., 1737, he was a tanner.

Children (Weth. Rec.):

1. Stephen, b. 3 Feb., 1705-6; may have been the S. who with wife Mary, owned bp-cov't in New., Ct., 1765; had lds. in Weth. and Glast.; d. 19 July, 1767.—*Weth. Ins.* Est. val. £197; *no issue.*
2. Hannah, b. 8, bp. 14 Mch. 1707-8; m. 3 Mch., 1735-6, Thos. **Dickinson**, of Weth.; 6 ch.
3. John, b. and bp. 1 Oct., 1710. **Fam.** 20.
4. Rebecca, b. 12, bp. 18 Jan., 1712-13; m. 15 Mch., 1739, Ab'm **Crane**, of Weth.; 8 ch. Her dau. Rebecca, m. Peleg **Coleman,**

whose s. Elisha (Coleman), m. Hannah **Loveland**, whose dau. Abigail (Coleman), m. Nathan W. **Pelton**, and his dau. Elizabeth Anne (Pelton), m. Philo Slocum **Newton**, whose dau. Anna C. (Newton), m. Dr. Geo. Fuller **Hawley**, of Hartford.
5. Thomas, b. 19, bp. 20 Feb., 1714-15. **Fam.** 21.
6. Amos, b. 14 Apl., 1717. **Fam.** 22.
7. Elijah, b. 9 Dec., 1719. **Fam.** 23.
8. Elizabeth, b. 1721; supposed to have d. before her father.
9. Timothy, b. 16 June, 1722-23. **Fam.** 24.

Fam. 14. JOSEPH,[3] (*Stephen*,[2] *Thos.*,[1]), b. 1683; farmer in New., Ct., m. 27 Apl., 1704, Sybil (dau. of Thomas & Abigail) **Fitch**, of Weth.; members of New. Ct.; he d. 24 June, 1752.—*N. C. R.*

Children (Weth. Rec.):

1. Sybil, b. 4 Nov., 1705.
2. Charles, b. 4, bp. 9 Nov., 1707. **Fam.** 25.
3. Joseph, b. 10, bp. 11 (*Mix Rec.* says bp. 14) May, 1710. **Fam.** 26.
4. Josiah, b. 4 Mch., bp. 19 Apl., 1713-14
5. Sarah, b. 18 May, 1716; m. Sam'l (s. Thos. & Martha) **Hurlbut.**
6. Phebe, b. 3 July, 1718; m. 21 Feb., 1745, Elijah **Andrus;** 4 ch.
7. Abigail, b. 24 Apl., 1721; d. 28 June, 1740.
8. Martha, b. 27 Oct., 1723; memb. New. Ch.

1747; m. 10 Mch., 1748, Phineas **Cole.**
9. Fitch, b. 27 Feb., 1726; m. (1) ————, who d. 22 Feb., 1772 (*N. C. R.*); m. (2) 14 Apl., 1773, Wid. Jemima **Hunn**, of New.; prob. had *no issue.*
10. Elisha, b. 3 July, 1729; prob. sett. Canaan, Ct., and became the ancestor of the C. branch of the H. fam. Is said to have rem. to Vt., where his line is now numerous.

Fam. 15. WILLIAM,[3] (*Cornelius*,[2] *Thos.*,[1]), b. 1689, farmer, Weth.; m. 17 Apl., 1717, Susannah (dau. Josiah) **Brown**, of W.; he d. 24 Mch., 1760; Mrs. H. d. 22 Sept., 1756 (one acc. says '58).

Children (Weth. Rec. & Mix Rec.):

1. Ch. bp. 30 Mch., 1716-17.—*Mix.*
2. Martha, b. 30 Mch., 1718; m. Jonah **Griswold.**
3. Rebecca, b. 26 Mch., 1720; m. 1738, Benj. **Tryon**, of Weth.; 3 ch.—See *Tryon.*
4. Abigail, b. 23 Aug., 1722; m. Timo. **Belden,**

of Sheffield, Mass.; she d. 1 Jan., 1786.
5. Elizabeth, b. 21 July, 1725; m. Richard **Belden;** she d. 28 Feb., 1818.
6. William, b. 21, bp. 26 May, 1728. **Fam.** 27.
7. Josiah, b. 28 Jan., 1734-35. **Fam.** 28.

Fam. 16. Lieut. GIDEON,[4] (*Nathan*,[3] *Sam'l*,[2] *Thos.*,[1]), b. 1700; res. for sometime in New. parish, Weth.; but became one of the first sett. of Goshen, Ct., 1738; early memb. G. ch.; freq. held town offices; was living as late as 1791; wife d. 17 June, 1798; she was Mary (dau. Thos.) **Deming**, of Weth.; m. 30 Dec., 1725.

*Children (Weth. Rec. *)*:

1. Abigail,* b. 9 Dec., 1726; m. ———— **Baker;** sett. Lanesboro, Mass.; 2 ch.
2. Jeremiah,* b. 25 Nov., 1728. **Fam.** 29.
3. David,* b. 27 Dec., 1730; d. during Revol. War.
4. Samuel,* b. 8 Jan., 1733; d. unm. Glast. 7 July, 1817.

5. Elisha,* b. 14 Apl., 1736. **Fam.** 30.
6. James, b. (prob. in Goshen); "slender & feeble;" unm.
7. Molly, b. (prob. in Goshen); d. old and single.
8. John, b. (prob. in Goshen); d. unm.

Fam. 17. PETER,[4] (*Nathan*,[3] *Sam'l*,[2] *Thos.*,[1]), b. 1703; m. 12 Apl., 1727. Sarah (dau. Henry) **Webb**, of Weth., where they sett., but, before 1750, rem. to Htfd. E. side of River, nr. Glast., where he res. until 1766.

Children (Weth. Rec. & Mix Rec.) :

1. Elias, b. 16, bp. 28 July, 1728 ; sett. on farm in E. Htfd. next Glast. line, 1770.
2. Prudence, b. 13, bp. 17 May, 1730 ; m. 10 Apl., 1755, Samuel (s. of Nath'l & Rebecca) **Sage**, of Midd. ; rem. to Sandisfield, Mass. ; she d. S. Apl., 1811.
3. Sarah, b. 19 Aug., 1735 ; m. 10 Feb., 1757,

John **Buck**, of Weth. ; *no issue*.
4. Elizabeth, b. 23 Mch., 1737-38.
5. Mehitable, b. 8 May, 1740.
6. Jeremiah, b. 24 Mch., 1742-43 ; sett. on farm at E. Htfd. next Glast. line, 1770 ; had sons *Jesse* and *John*, who res. in Manchester, Ct.

FAM. 18. JOHN,[4] (*Nathan*,[3] *Samuel*,[2] *Thos.*,[1]), b. 1707 ; m. Jemima —————.

Children (b. Weth., H. Geneal.) :

1. Joanna, b. 26 Jan., 1734-5.
2. John, b. 26 Mch., 1737.

3. Jemima, b. 11 Jan., 1739-40.
4. Sarah, b. 1 Apl., 1746.

FAM. 19. NATHANIEL,[4] (*Nathan*,[3] *Samuel*,[2] *Thos.*,[1]), b. 1720, m. 17 Nov., 1742, Azubah **Fox**; supp. to have sett. on W. side of Weth., or in Far., nr. the W. line; he and wife adm. to Weth. Ch. 1743; he d. 26 Apl., 1791, ae. 71.— *W. C. R.*

Children (Weth. Rec.) :

1. Nathaniel, b. 19 Dec., 1744. FAM. 31.
2. Luce, b. 30 Apl., 1747.

3. Azubah, b. 2 Sept., 1750.
4. Mary, b. 8 Dec., 1752.

FAM. 20. Capt. JOHN,[4] (*Thos.*,[3] *Stephen*,[2] *Thos.*,[1]), b. 1710, sett. E. Htfd., farmer; m. (1) 2 Feb., 1738-9, Mary Anna (dau. Dea. William & Elibazeth) **Cowles** (or Cole) of E. H., who d. 31 Aug., 1739, ae. 21; he m. (2) 1 Oct., 1741, Mabel **Loomis**, of E. Windsor, Ct.; he d. 21 Apl., 1778; wid. d. 5 Aug., 1810, ae. 36.— *W. Ins.*

Children (b. E. Htfd.) :

1. Hannah, b. 25 Jan., 1739 ; m. Dea. Amasa **Loomis**, of E. Windsor, July, 1762 or '63 ; she d. 1 July, 1793 ; 10 ch. for whom see Stile's *Hist. Ancient Windsor*.
2. John, b. 11 July, 1742.
3. Joseph, b. 23 May, 1744.

4. Mabel, b. 23 Feb., 1746 ; m. Elisha **Benjamin**.
5. Samuel, b. 28 Aug., 1750. FAM.
6. Anna, b. 8 Apl., 1753 ; m. ———— **Roberts**, of Cazenovia, N. Y.

FAM. 21. THOMAS,[4] (*Thos.*,[3] *Steph.*,[2] *Thos.*,[1]), b. 1715 ; m. 12 Dec., 1744, Abigail, (dau. Silas & Abigail *Robbins*) **Belden**, of Rocky Hill; was a shoemaker in Weth.; member of Weth. ch., 1744, and still in 1774; his will, dated, 24 Sept., 1788; he d. ae. 76, 13 Nov., 1791; wid. d. ae. 87, 9 Feb., 1807.—*Weth. Ins.*

Children (Weth. Rec.) :

1. Jerusha, b. 2, bp. 13 Oct., 1745 (d. before 1788, *C. G. H.*).
2. Abigail, b. 2 Apl., 1747 ; d. unm. 5 June, 1834, ae. 87.—*Weth. Ins*.
3. Lydia, b. 21 Dec., 1748 ; d. before her father.
4. Anne, b. 14 Nov., 1750 ; d. before her father.
5. Hopeful, b. 24 Oct., 1752 ; d. before her father.

6. Silas, b. 13 Oct., 1754. FAM. 32.
7. Ozias, b. 13 Mch., 1757 ; m. 22 May, 1793, Eunice **Deming**, of N., where they res. ; she joined W. ch. 1803; he d. ae. 46, bu. 23 May, 1803 ; *W. C. R.* rec. bp. of twins of "late O. and wife Eunice," 2 Oct., 1803, *Mary* and *Thomas*.
8. Moses, b. 1 June, 1759.—Acc. to *Hurlbut Gen.*

FAM. 22. AMOS,[4] (*Thos.*,[3] *Steph.*,[2] *Thos.*,[1]), b. 1717 ; sett. Newington Soc.; m. (1) 10 June, 1742, Hannah **Wright**; they adm. to N. ch., 1747, m. Weth. ch.; she d. N., 25 July, 1756, in 39th yr.—*Weth. Ins.;* he m. (2) in N., 3 Mch., 1757, Sarah **Hills**, who owned Cov't, Dec., 1758, and d. 1764; he m. (3) in N., 10 Mch., 1766, Sarah **Latimer**; supp. to have d. 1777, adm. gr. on est., 28 Feb., 1777.

Children (Weth. Rec., others fm. bap. record of N.)* :

1. Lois,* b. 21 May, 1744 ; m. 23 Aug., 1764, Phineas **Griswold**.—See *Griswold*.
2. Samuel, b. abt. 1746. FAM. 33.
3. Solomon, bp. 2 Nov., 1748 ; d. 4 same mo.
4. Lemuel, b. 21, bp. 26 Aug., 1750. FAM. 34.
5. Hannah, bp. 10 May, 1752 ; m. 25 Oct., 1769, Levi **Bronson**.

6. Josiah, bp 2 Feb., 1755 ; d. May, 1756. (*By second marriage*) :
7. Amos, bp. 22 Oct., 1758 ; d. 13 Jan., 1759.
8. Anna, bp. 11 Nov., 1759 ; d. 24 Feb., 1760.
9. Stephen, bp. 28 Dec., 1760. FAM. 35.
10. Ruth, bp. 17 Jan., d. 24 July, 1762.
11. Martin, bp. 12 June, 1763 ; m. and rem. to Winchester, Ct. ; d. 1810.

FAM. 23. ELIJAH,[4] (*Thos.*,[3] *Steph.*,[2] *Thos.*,[1]), b. 1719; m. Elizabeth **Belden**; both adm. ch., 1744; res. Weth.; d. ae. 83, bu. 8 Feb., 1803; wid. bu. 1 Nov., 1810.— *W. C. R.*

Children (Hurlbut Geneal.) :

1. Elijah.
2. Simeon, prob. the Simeon whose wife Mary and daus. *Mary* and *Lois*, bp. 24 Apl., 1774; *Daniel*, bp. 12 Nov., 1775; and *Simeon*, bp. 6 Apl., 1777.
3. Levi, b. 28 Oct., 1748 (?).
4. Thomas.
5. Robert, we are inclined to think this is the Robert who m. Betsy **Curtiss**; his wid. Betsy, d. ae. 36, bu. 25 Feb., 1818,

and had *Robert*, ae. 5, bu. 15 May, 1811; A *Prudy* and *Robert* (of Wid. of Robt.) were bp. 16 Sept., 1787.—*W. C. R.*
6. Stephen, bp. betw. June 4, and Sept. 4, 1758.
7. Rebecca.
8. Hetty.
9. Elizabeth.
10. Mehitable, bp. 27 Mch., 1763 (?).
11. Eunice, bp. 4 Aug., 1765 (?).

FAM. 24. TIMOTHY,[4] (*Thos.*,[3] *Steph.*,[2] *Thos.*,[1]), b. 1723, farmer, Weth., and owned ld. in Glast.; memb. of ch., 1758, as also his wife; m. 5 Oct., 1757, Sarah **Clark**—*W. C. R.;* 16 Sept., 1772, he advertised his wife Sarah, but concludes by saying "if she will return to her duty to me and my family, I will receive her kindly and provide as well as I can for her;" he d. Aug., 1773; est. £398, 17s, distrib. by will, 1 May, 1780; wid. m. (2) ———— **Collins;** m. (3) **Chamberlain.**

Children (Weth. Rec.) :

1. Timothy, b. 12 Aug., 1758; bp. 8 Oct., 1758; learned carpenter's trade and was a farmer; rem. to Pittsfield, Mass., where he m. (1) in 1784, Mary (dau. Joshua) **Robbins,** of P., who d. 4 June, 1809, ae. 45; m. (2) Olive **Caldwell,** of P. who d. 16 Oct., 1855 or 6; he d. 12 July, 1838; had 14 ch., all b. Pittsfield.
2. Titus, b. 15 Apl., 1760.
3. Sarah, b. 17 Jan., 1762; m. (as supp.) Thos. (s. of Stephen) **Hollister,** of New Britain, Ct.; res. Western N. Y.
4. Philip, b. 30 Sept., 1764; d. 30 Nov., 1766.
5. Ruth, b. 22 Nov., 1766; m. Elisha **Chamberlain,** of Dalton, Mass., son of her mother's 3d husband.
6. Philip, b. 7 Jan., 1769; d. as supp. unm.

FAM. 25. Ens. CHARLES,[4] (*Joseph*,[3] *Steph.*,[2] *Thos.*,[1]), b. 1707, m. Martha ————, who joined Newington ch., 3 July, 1763; farmer; d. 14 June, 1787.

Children (Weth. Rec.) :

1. Prudence, b. 26 Nov., 1730; m. 1753, David **Lusk,** of Farm. (New Britain).
2. Anne, b. 4 Aug., 1732; m. at Canaan, Ct., 1764, Elijah **Kellogg;** she d. Starksboro, Vt., 17 Feb., 1815; 4 ch.
3. Mary, b. 10 Oct., 1734; m. Benajah **Taylor.**
4. Elias, b. 1 July 1739; d. 5 Sept., 1741.
5. Elias, b. 17 Feb., 1742. FAM. 36.
6. Jerusha, b. 18 Apl., 1744; m. 1780, Joseph **Wells,** of Weth.; she d. 18 June, 1805;
   one ch.
7. Martha, b. 11 Feb., 1747; m. Levi (s. Joseph, Jr.) **Hurlbut.**
8. John, b. and bp. (*N. C. R.*) 10 Apl., 1751. FAM. 37.
9. Charles, b. 1754, (added by *Hurlbut Gen.,* tho' with doubt); m. sett. W. Htfd.; 7 ch.; it was prob. his s. *Charles,* b. Weth.; who m. in New. Soc., Rhoda **Trumbull** (?), and had 4 ch.

FAM. 26. JOSEPH,[4] (*Joseph*,[3] *Steph.*,[2] *Thos.*,[1]), b. 1710; m. 8 Jan., 1735-36, Hannah **Wells,** of Weth.; res. in New. Soc., Weth.; memb. of N. ch., 1772; bo't farm in W. Htfd., on Far. and Weth. lines, where some of his sons settled; he d. 5 Dec., 1790.

Children (Weth. Rec., bp. N. C. R.) :

1. Hannah, b. 7 Nov., 1736; m. 16 Dec., 1756, Bela **Blinn.**
2. Christopher, b. 15 Dec., 1738. FAM. 38.
3. Abigail, b. 16 Jan., 1740-1; m. 24 Jan., 1760, Robert **Welles,** Jr., of New.
4. Levi, b. 20 Mch., 1743-4. FAM. 39.
5. Sybil, b. 10 Aug., 1746; m. 8 July, 1770, Eli **Tryon.**—*N. C. R.*
6. Elizabeth, b. 28 Dec., 1748; bp. 19 Feb., 1748-9; m. 30 Oct., 1771, Levi **Churchill.**
7. Joseph, b. 19, bp. 23 Aug., 1752; m. at Htfd., 12 July, 1776, Lindvilley (?) **Sedgewick;** res. W. Htfd.; 3 ch.; all d. yg.
8. Eli, b. 29 Mch., bp. 4 Apl., 1756; m. 26 Oct., 1785, Sarah (dau. Sam'l & Sarah) **Landers,** of New.; res. W. Htfd.; she d. 8 May, 1806, leaving a son Levi, Jr.
9. Unni, b. 17, bp. 18 June, 1758.
10. Esther, b. 30 June, bp. 6 July, 1760.

FAM. 27. WILLIAM,[4] (*Wm.*,[3] *Cornelius*,[2] *Thos.*,[1]), b. 1728; m. 21 Mch., 1759, Catharine **Deming,** of Weth., where he res., as his father had before him, on the W. side of Bell Lane (now W. Main St.); he d. 12 Dec., 1790—*W. C. R.*; his wid. adm. to Weth. ch., 1792; she m. (2) a **Belden** and d. 4 Jan., 1801 or '04.

Children (Weth. Rec.):

1. William, b. 6 Sept., 1762; m. 1787, Lydia (dau. of Dr. Hez.) **Porter**, of Northampton, Mass.; he d. 29 July, 1796; his wid. m. (2) Alex. Andrew **Johnson**, by whom she had a son Eleazer (Johnson), who studied med. with Dr. Porter and m. in Mexico, Marie Dolores **Calcaneo**, by whom he had 2 daus. *Julia* and *Lucretia*. Julia m. Dr. **DeVado**, of the City of Mexico, and Lucretia was unm., in 1884. Mrs. Lydia Hurlbut Johnson m. (3) Sulmon **Moulton**, by whom she had a son Julius (Moulton). By her first husband (Hurlbut), she had 2 sons, viz.: *William*, b. 1790; bp. 6 Feb., 1791; who d. 1871, and

James, b. 1792, and d. 1823. She d. 1852.
2. Sarah, b. 2 or 9 Dec., 1764; d. unm., 1820.
3. Catharine, b. 13 Oct., 1767; m. 3 Feb., 1799, Daniel **Hancock**, of Htfd., Ct.; she d. 13 Nov., 1810.
4. John (Capt.), b. 18 Aug., 1770. FAM. 40.
5. James, b. 27 Feb., 1773; bp. 16 Dec., 1792. FAM. 41.
6. Inf., bu. 8 Sept., 1788.
7. Nabby, twin Martha, b. 27 June, 1777; d. 8 July, 1777.
8. Martha, twin Nabby, d. 11 July, 1777.
(These two given by *Hurlbut Geneal.*)

FAM. 28. JOSIAH,[4] (*Wm.*,[3] *Cornelius*,[2] *Thos.*,[1]), b. 1735; sett. at Weth.; m. Mabel **Deming**, who d. 18 Jan., 1790, ae. 46.

Children (Weth. Rec.):

1. Rebecca, b. 21 Jan., 1768.
2. Mabel, b. 20 June, 1769.
3. Josiah, b. 24 Oct., 1770; m. Prudence **Curtis**, 23 Oct., 1796—*W. C. R.*; may have res. at Stave, Vt., or at Boonville, N. Y.
4. Sarah, b. 4 June, 1772.
5. Betsy, b. 4 May, 1774.
6. Treat, b. 3 Oct., 1776; said to have res. at Boonville, N. Y.

7. Abigail, b. 28 Apl., 1779.
8. Ashbel, b. 7 Feb., 1781; m. (1) 19 Mch., 1810, Lucy **Blinn**, of Ry-H., who d. 4 May, 1811; m. (2) Elizabeth (dau. Peter) **Stevens**, of Glast.; was an ingenious mechanic and d. Pawlet, Vt., 30 Apl., 1828; 6 ch.
9. Catharine, b. 16 Nov., 1784.

FAM. 29. JEREMIAH,[5] (*Gideon*,[4] *Nathan*,[3] *Samuel*,[2] *Thos.*,[1]), b. 1728; m. 23 Jan., 1751, Esther (dau. Sam'l) **Thompson**, of Goshen, Ct., where he res., and was in Capt. Ledgwick's Co. in the Quebec Exped. of 1775; is said to have d. during the Revol. War; she d. at Poultney, Vt.

Children (b. Goshen—Hurlbut Geneal.):

1. Lucia, b. 11 Mch., 1752.
2. Gideon, b. 11 Apl., 1754; m. and had family.
3. David, b. Mch., 1757; m. and had family.

FAM. 30. ELISHA,[5] (*Gideon*,[4] *Nathan*,[3] *Samuel*,[2] *Thos.*,[1]), b. 1736; m. Chloe (dau. Dea. Gideon & Lydia *Punderson*) **Thompson**, in New Haven; res. many yrs. and d. in Goshen, Ct., 17 Feb., 1808; she d. 24 Dec., 1814; he was a Revol. soldier.—See Cothren's *Woodbury*, p. 782.

Children (b. Goshen—Hurlbut Geneal.):

1. Huldah, b. 20 or 25 Mch., 1763 (68 ?); m. at G., 2 July, 1789, Nath'l **Merrills**, of Htfd.; sett. at Litchfield, Ct.; rem. to Dover, N. Y.; 8 ch.
2. Lorraine, b. 30 Mch., 1770; m. Andrew **Norton**; she d. 27 May, 1851.
3. Elisha, b. 7 Jan., 1773; m. Avis **Munson**, of Litchfield, Ct.
4. Chloe, b. 1777; m. Ebenezer **Dunbar**, of

Eaton, N. Y.
5. Truman, b. 1781; m. at Stratford, Ct., Mercy **Burton**; he d. 16 Dec., 1839; she d. 15 July, 1842.

(Elizabeth, dau. of Elisha H. [Hurlburt?], bp. 25 Jan., 1761, was, we think, of this family.)

FAM. 31. NATHANIEL,[5] (*Nath'l*,[4] *Nathan*,[3] *Sam'l*,[2] *Thos.*,[1]), b. 1742; m. (1) 27 Apl., 1772, Susannah (dau. Amasa) **Adams**, of Ry-H., who d. 4 Feb., 1800. ae. 63; he m. (2) Mrs. Sarah **Clark**, of E. Htfd., who d. 5 Jan., 1811; he d. 16 Aug., 1817.

Children (by 1st marr.):

1. David, bp. 15 Jan., 1775; prob. the D. (s. of N.), who d. at W. I., Sept., 1800.
2. Amasa, bp. 8 May, 1776; m. Rhoda **Kilby**.
3. Elizur, b. 29 July, bp. 24 Aug., 1777. FAM. 42.
4. Lucy Camp, bp. 18 June, 1786; m. James **Pearl**, of E. Windsor, 4 Jan., 1802.

(*By second marriage*):
5. Anderson.
6. Albert, m. Lucy **Forbes**, of Berlin, Ct.; s. p.
7. Sarah.
8. Nelson.

FAM. 32.   SILAS,⁵ (*Thos.,⁴ Thos.,³ Steph.,² Thos.,¹*), b. 1754; m. 16 Nov., 1792, Sarah **Kilby;** res. Newington Soc., Weth.; he d. 13 Oct., 1836, ae. 82.—*Weth. Ins.*

Children (Weth. Rec.) :

1. Alma, b. 27 Feb., 1793.
2. Hannah, b. 21 Dec., 1794 ; d. W., 30 Oct., unm., 1881.—*Weth. Ins.*
3. Abigail, b. 12 Nov., 1796; m. 9 May, 1822, Jeremiah **Ward**, and d. 1880 ; 4 ch.
4. Belden, b. 10 Feb., 1799 ; d. unm., 1862.
5. Laura, b. 10 Apl., 1801 ; m. Wm. **Mitchell**, a sailor ; she d. W., 1868, ae. 67. *Issue:*
   i. Henry (Mitchell), d. yg.
   ii. Harriet (Mitchell), who in 1888, res. on site of orig. dwelling of her emigrant ancestor Thos.
6. Jerusha, b. 11 Dec., 1803 ; m. Roswell **Cheppell**, of Glast. ; had dau. Jane.
7. John, b. 8 Feb., 1805 ; m. (1) **Mary Roberts**, of Newington, Ct. ; m. (2) 1 Jan., 1832, Mary (Ann ?) **Goodrich;** d., wid m. —— **Wing.** *Issue:*

i. Charles, m.
ii. William, d. inf.
iii. Sarah, m. res. N. Haven.
iv. Lewis, m.
v. Fanny.
8. James, b. 12 Mch., 1807 ; m. 23 Nov., 1831, Harriet **Deming**, of Newington, who d. 1877 ; he d. No. Guilford, Ct., 1882. *Issue:*
   i. Fanny, m.
   ii. Harriet, m. d. ; 3 ch.
   iii. Newton, m. ; no ch.
   iv. Henry, m. ; 2 ch.
   v. James, m. ; 7 ch.
   vi. Silas, m. res. Dunkirk, N. Y. ; no ch.
   vii. Barzillai, m. ; 2 ch.
   viii. Albert, d. ; 1 ch.
   ix. Emma, d. ; 1 ch.
   x. Alice, m. ; res. Midd., Ct. ; 1 ch.

FAM. 33.   SAMUEL,⁵ (*Amos,⁴ Thos.,³ Steph.,² Thos.,¹*), b. 1746; m. Torrington, Ct., 1 Dec., 1768, Rebecca (dau. Abel) **Beach;** rem. to Winchester, Ct., 1774, first of his family to go there, and blt. ho. there, now occup. by his gd.-son Samuel; was called *Capt.;* was among the first American importers of Merino sheep, and his sons Samuel and Lemuel were the first to bring into their part of Conn., imported Devon cattle; he rep. W. in 17 sess. of Gen. Assemb.; d. 23 Mch., 1831; she d. 27 Oct., 1829.

Children (Hurlbut Gen.) :

1. Silas, b. 6 July, 1769 ; d. 24 Dec., 1793.
2. Leonard, b. 18 May, 1771.
3. Margaret, b. 2 Mch., 1773.
4. Samuel, b. 13 Mch., 1775 ; d. 4 Oct., 1776.
5. Lucy, b. 6 Oct., 1777 ; m. —— **Hall.**

6. Rebecca, b. 30 Nov., 1779 ; m. —— **Church.**
7. Samuel, b. 2 Oct., 1783.
8. Lemuel, b. 30 Sept., 1785.

FAM. 34.   LEMUEL,⁵ (*Amos,⁴ Thos.,³ Steph.,² Thos.,¹*), b. 1750; farmer, Newington; m. 20 (or 22) Dec., 1773, Tabitha **Nott**, b. 21 Aug., 1752, of Rocky Hill; both adm. New., ch., 29 June, 1777; rem. to W. Htfd.; sold his farm, 82 acres, 1790, for £462; d. W. Htfd., 15 Aug., 1815; she d. 8 Feb., 1813.

Children (first five fm. Weth. Rec., remainder fm. W. Htfd. Rec., bp. fm. N. C. R.)

1. Hannah, b. 5 May, 1775; bp. "at point of dth." 28 Sept., 1776; d. same day.
2. Hannah, b. 10 Apl. (bp. 7 Sept.), 1777 ; m. Far., 5 Feb., 1797, John **Selden**.
3. Lemuel, b. 16 Nov., 1778 ; bp. 17 Jan., 1779 ; m. 8 Dec., 1802, Eunice **Whitman**, of E. Htfd., where he sett. ; adm. to ch., 6 Sept., 1799 ; d. 17 Jan., 1830 ; 2 ch., *Lucy Whitman*, bp. 29 Apl., 1804 ; *Fanny*, bp. 1806 ; d. 24 Apl., 1816.
4. William, b. 7 Apl., bp. 22 Oct., 1780.
5. Mercy, b. 17, bp. 28 Oct., 1781 ; m. 2 Sept., 1812, Barney **Collins**, of Htfd.
6. Prudence, b. 3 June, bp. 31 Aug., 1783 ; m. 6 Apl., 1807, Dea. & Col. Moses, Jr. (s. Moses⁴ & Anne *Seymour*) **Goodman**,

of E. Htfd. ; she d. 13 Sept., 1857.
7. Harlet, b. 11 Nov., 1784, bp. 27 Feb., 1785 ; d. 1847.
8. Samuel, b. 3 Mch., bp. 11 June, 1786.
9. Sarah, b. 13 Sept., bp. 9 Dec., 1787 ; m. 10 Sept., 1813, Chester (s. of Col. Timo. & Abigail *Skinner*) **Seymour**, of W. Htfd. ; she d. 18 Feb., 1866 ; 2 ch.
10. Martin, b. 18 June, bp. 16 Aug., 1789.
11. Thomas, b. 4 Aug., 1791, bp. 18 Mch., 1792 ; d. 23 Apl., 1795.
12. James Dimock, b. 12 Sept., 1792, bp. 3 Feb., 1793.
13. Elizabeth, b. 16 Jan., bp. 7 June, 1794 ; d. 22 Apl., 1795.

FAM. 35.   STEPHEN,⁵ (*Amos,⁴ Thomas,³ Steph.,² Thos.,¹*), b. 1760; m. Salisbury, Ct., Abigail **Meeker,** of Fairfield Co., Ct.; tho' very young, was a Revol. soldier, for which his wid. rec'd a pension; res. for a time in Vt., but later in Winsted, Ct., where he d. 1 May., 1807; wid. d. 14 May, 1854.

Children (Hurlbut Gen. & W. C. R.) :

1. "Clary" (Clara?) (twin?), bp. 9 Sept., 1787 ; m. 1825, Walter **Dickinson.**
2. Stephen (twin to Clara), bp. 9 Sept., 1787.
3. Inf., d. 21 Oct., 1788, ae. 6 wks.—*W. C. R.*
4. Eunice, b. 29 July, 1789 ; m. 1818, David H. **Hubbard.**
5. Clary (Clara?), bp. 4 Apl., 1790.
6. Amos, b. 13 (?) Feb., 1792.
7. Harriet, bp. 12 Feb., 1792.
8. Lucy, b. 21 Apl., 1794 ; m. Daniel **Phelps.**

9. Mary, b. 27 Aug., 1796 ; m. 1819, Charles **Clark.**
10. Samuel, b. 31 Oct., 1798.
11. Huldah, b. 15 Feb., 1801 ; d. 31 Oct., 1830, unm.
11. Silas, b. 27 Mch., 1803.
12. Clarissa, b. 18 Aug., 1806 ; m. Sherman **Goodwin.** (*W. C. R.* give inf., d. 21 Oct., 1788 ; and Roswell, bp. 29 June, 1794, bu. 29 Sept. same yr., ae. 13 mos., who poss. were of this family.)

FAM. 36. ELIAS,[5] (*Charles,*[4] *Joseph,*[3] *Stephen,*[2] *Thos.,*[1]), b. 1742; res. and m. in New., 4 Apl., 1764, Patience **Blinn;** both owned cov't N. ch., 1764; farmer.

Children (Weth. Rec. & N. C. R.) :

1. Mehitable, bp. 9 Sept., 1763.
2. Mehitable, b. 19 June, 1764 ; m. 23 Nov., 1803, John **Loveland,** Jr., as his 2d wife.
3. Elenor, b. 25 July, 1766 ; m. at Weth., 30 Dec., 1792, Medad **Gibbs.**
4. Martha, b. 1 Feb., bp. 15 Apl. (*N. C. R.*) ; m. at Weth., 21 Jan., 1790, Lemuel **Gibbs.**

5. Phebe, b. 25, bp. 31 Jan., 1773.
6. Absalom, b. 29 May., bp. 18 June, 1775.
7. Jemima, b. 2 June, bp. 12 Sept., 1779 ; m. Weth. 17 May., 1809, Joseph **Brace,** of Bloomfield, N. Y.
8. Inf., privately bp., being abt. to die, 10 Jan., 1784.

FAM. 37. JOHN,[5] (*Chas.,*[4] *Joseph,*[3] *Steph.,*[2] *Thos.,*[1]), b. 1751, m. 12 Jan., 1778, Judith **Homer,** of N. Soc., Weth., who was adm. N. ch., 1790, and joined Weth. ch., 1803 ; family rem. to Fabius, N. Y., where he d. 2 Mch., 1832 ; she d. 19 Nov., 1839.

Children (Weth. Rec., bp. N. C. R.) :

1. Lucy, b. 23 Jan., 1778, bp 9 May, 1790 ; m. Samuel **Fox;** 6 ch.
2. Mary, b. 28 Jan., 1782, bp. 9 May, 1790 ; m. ——— **Welch;** 4 ch.
3. William, b. 6 Jan., 1785, bp. 9 May, 1790.
4. John, b. 26 Feb., 1788, bp. 9 May, 1790.
5. Allen, bp. 7 Nov., 1790.—*N. C. R.*
6. Allen, b. 30 Sept., 1791, bp. New., 7 Nov., 1790 ; m. (1) ——— **Potter;** m. (2) ——— **Shoemaker;** d. Venango, Pa. *Issue:*
   FAM. 41.
   i. Mansel, b. 1815.
   ii. John, boatbuilder ; res. Pa.
   iii. Philomela.

iv. Calista.
(*By second marr.*) :
v. Harriet.
vi. Lydia.
vii. Hortense.
7. Chauncy, b. 22 July, bp. New. 6 Oct., 1793 ; res. Goshen, Ct. ; rem. to Mich. ; m. Polly **Fox.** *Issue:*
   i. Geo. Washington, b. Goshen, Ct., 6 Apl., 1823.
8. Hiram, b. 29 Jan., bp. at New. 7 May, 1797 ; became physician ; res. Fabius, N. Y., and Norwich, N. Y. ; m. 1820, Hannah **Eames;** 6 ch., b. Fabius, N. Y.

FAM. 38. CHRISTOPHER,[5] (*Joseph,*[4] *Joseph,*[3] *Steph.,*[2] *Thos.,*[1]), b. 1738; m. 19 Jan., 1764, Mary (dau. Gideon & Elizabeth *Case*) **Deming**— *W. C. R.;* both owned Cov't in N. ch, Mch. 31, 1765; he d. W. Htfd., 28 Mch., 1807; farmer; wid. d. 9 June, 1821.

Children (bp. fm. N. and W. Htfd. ch. Recs.) :

1. Phineas, bp. 14 Apl., 1765 ; m. (1) 24 Dec., 1795 (*W. C. R.* says 21 Jan., 1796) Hono: **Goodrich.** who was adm. ch. 3 Apl., 1802, and d. 20 Nov., 1809 ; he m. (2) 2 Jan., 1815, Hannah **Andrews,** of Weth. ; residing 1815 in Htfd. ; ch.—a son Phineas, and dau. Honor. FAM. 44.
2. Christopher, bp. 20 July, 1766 ; d. 1788.
3. Gideon, bp. 11 Sept., 1768 ; m. 5 Jan., 1793,

Anna **Gilbert,** of Htfd., who joined N. ch. 1802 ; she d. 10 July, 1808, ae. 38 ; 3 ch. bp. in N. ch.
4. William, bp. 19 May., 1771 ; d. Dec., 1835.
5. Samuel, bp. W. Htfd. 21 June, 1773.
6. Mary, bp. W. Htfd. 3 Mch., 1776.
7. Abigail, bp. W. Htfd. 3 July, 1778.
8. Arden, bp. W. Htfd. ——— ; m. ——— **Adams,** of Simsbury.

FAM. 39. LEVI,[5] (*Joseph,*[4] *Joseph,*[3] *Steph.,*[2] *Thos.,*[1]), b. 1744; m. (1) June, 1767, his cousin Martha (dau. Charles & Martha) **Hurlbut;** both owned Cov't N. ch., Dec., 1767, and adm. to same ch., 2 Apl., 1780; she d. 1787; he m. (2) 1788 or '89, Martha (dau. Sam'l) **Wells,** of New., who d. 18 May, 1808; he m. (3) at N., 30 July, 1809, Lois **Johnson,** of W. Htfd.; he d. 17 Mch., 1817.

Children (Weth. Rec. & N. C. R.) :

1. Roger, b. 1 Oct., bp. 27 Dec., 1767.
2. Levi, b. 17, bp. 22 Nov., 1772; d. 17 Apl., 1775.
3. Seth, b. 16, bp. 22 Jan., 1775; m. Elizabeth (dau. Thos.) **Steadman**; res. Far.; she d. 23 Apl., 1842; he d. Wintonbury—had s. *Levi.*
4. Levi, b. 13 July, bp. 2 Nov., 1777; m. and res. N. J.
5. Anna, b. 11 June, 1779; m. 8 Jan., 1801, Elizur **Dudley**, of Kensington Soc.
6. Barzillai, b. 13 June, bp. 5 Aug., 1781; m. 26 Aug., 1806, Lavinia **Wolcott**, of Weth.; rem. to Eagle, N. Y., 1815; d. Mch., 1858. *Issue;*
   i. Cornelia, b. 14 Apl., 1808 in Conn.; m. 26 Nov., 1827, Norman **Howes**; res. Eagle, N. Y.; 3 ch.
   ii. Barzillai, b. Conn., 9 Mch., 1810; m. and res. Eagle, N. Y.; 10 ch.
   iii. Gideon, b. Conn. 7 Feb., 1812.
   iv. Lois Naomi, b. Conn. 28 Jan., 1814;

   m. 11 May, 1835, Volney Richard **Beach**; rem. to Iowa; 6 ch. v-x. All b. Eagle, N. Y.
7. Sylvester, b. 5 Aug., bp. 17 Oct., 1784.
8. Charles, b. 29 June, bp. 23 Sept., 1787; d. 10 Mch., 1788.
  (By second marr.) :
9. Charles, b. Weth. 5 Sept., 1790, bp. New. 17 Jan., 1791; m. (1) 1811, Julia **Sage**, of Simsbury, who d. 7 Jan, 1842; m. (2) 21 Aug., 1842, Wid. Sally (*Corey*) **Boardman**, of Ry-H., later of Weth., who d. 6 June, 1859, ae. 53; 5 ch.—See *H. Geneal.*
  (By third marr.) :
10. Joseph, b. 1810, bp. New. 1 July, 1810 (*N. C. R.*); m. (1) a **Roberts**; m. (2) a **Trowbridge**; res. Waterbury, Ct.; one of the pprs. of the *W. American*; 3 ch.—See *H. Geneal.*
11. Martha, bp. (*N. C. R.*) 10 May, 1812; d. 13 Aug., 1813.

FAM. 40. Capt. JOHN,[5] (*Wm.,*[4] *Wm.,*[3] *Corn.,*[2] *Thos.,*[1]), b. 1770; built and occup. house in Weth., lately occup. by Levi Goodwin; was a famous navigator.—See our Chapter on *Maritime Hist. of Weth.* in Vol I. He d. in N. York, ae. 38, 6 July—*Weth Ins.*, 1808, of small pox; wid. d. same yr. He m. Anne ————, (prob. Anne Wright, 25 Aug., 1799); if so, she (wid. Anne) d. 5 Aug., 1810, ae. 36.

Child:

1. Anne (or Nancy), bp. 27 June, 1802; m. Dec., 1823, Henry Wadworth (s. of Gen. Nath'l & Cath. Wadsworth) **Terrey**, who was b. 3 Feb., 1799, and d. at Winsted, Ct. Mr. T. was a landscape gardener, and as such, at one time had charge of the laying out of Central Park, N. Y. City. *Issue (b. in Htfd., Ct.) :*
   i. Rose (Terrey), b. 7 Feb., 1827; m. May,

1873, Rollin H. **Cooke**, of Winsted, Ct., and Pittsfield, Mass; a well known authoress and poetess; pub. many short stories dealing with New Eng. life and a volume entitled *Steadfast;* she d. at P. 18 July, 1892; *no issue.*
   ii. Alice (Terrey), b. 3 Sept., ——, d. 1877; m. 23 Feb., 1856, Howard L. **Collins**, of Htfd., Ct.

FAM. 41. JAMES,[5] (*Wm.,*[4] *Wm.,*[3] *Corn.,*[2] *Thos.,*[1]), b. 1773; m. 1 Apl., 1804, Wealthy (b. 1779) dau. of Simeon Griswold and his wife Marian (gr.-dau. of Dr. Nicholas) **Ayrault;** he became a seaman at the age of 23—See our Chapter on *Maritime History of Weth.* in Vol I; he d. 20 Apl., 1852; he was, in 1827, a memb. of 3d Co., 2d Reg., Light Art., of Conn., Orrin Webster, Capt.; wid. d. 4 Sept., 1864.

Children (b. Weth.) :

1. James Hervey, b. 22 Dec., 1804. FAM. 43.
2. Jane Ann, b. 4 Oct., 1806; m. 1844, Dea. John **Pendleton**, of Williamansett, Ct.; she d. 1 Dec., 1880; *no issue.*
3. Abigail, b. 28 Oct., 1808; unm. 1891.

4. Catharine, b. 2 Dec., 1810; m. 1869, Dea. Merritt **Butler**, of Rocky Hill, Ct.; she d. 1892; he d. 1891, ae. 96; *no issue.*
5. Mary Ann, b. 14 Sept., 1814; m. 1842, Geo. L. **Tibbals**, of Milford, Ct.; she d. 1882.

FAM. 42. ELIZUR,[6] (*Nath'l,*[5] *Nath'l,*[4] *Nathan,*[3] *Samuel,*[2] *Thos.,*[1]), b. 29 July, 1771; m. 3 Jan., 1798 (*W. C. R.*), Mary (dau. Abel & Mary) **Benton;** served in War of 1812; d. 22 Apl., 1833; wid. d. 4 Aug., 1860, ae. 83.—*W. Ins.*

Children (Weth. Rec. & W. Ins.) :

1. Lavinia, b. 16 May, 1799; d. 16 Oct., 1861.
2. Susannah, b. 16 Feb., 1801; d. 17 July, 1822.
3. John, b. 15 Jan., 1803; d. 18 Jan., 1874.
4. Caroline, b. 14 May, 1805; d. 13 Dec., 1890, ae. 85.
5. Allen, b. 2 Jan., 1808; d. 10 Aug., 1832.

6. Mary, b. 31 July, 1810.
7. William (Capt.), b. 11 Nov., 1812. FAM. 44.
8. Elizur (Capt.), b. 7 May, 1815. FAM. 45.
9. Martha A., b. 8 Feb., 1819.
10. Eliza, b. 9 July, d. 17 Aug., 1821.

FAM. 43. JAMES HERVEY,[6] (*Jas.*,[5] *Wm.*,[4] *Wm.*,[3] *Corn.*,[2] *Thos.*,[1]), b. Weth., 1804; m. 9. Sept., 1832, Eliza (dau. Bridgman & Polly *Latham*) **Brown**, of Stonington, Ct.; he d. 1 Apl., 1876; she d. 4 Apl., 1856.

Children:

1. Maria, m. Geo. H. **Burditt**, of Boston, Mass.; *no issue;* res. Weth. and has been very helpful in regard to several Weth. genealogies.

2. Cornelia, res. Weth. (1888); unm., and with her sister Mrs. Burditt, res. in the home built in 1730, by Michael Griswold, 2d.

FAM. 44. Capt. WILLIAM,[7] (*Elizur*,[6] *Nath'l*,[5] *Nath'l*,[4] *Nathan*,[3] *Sam'l*,[2] *Thos.*,[1]), b. 1812; m. 20 Mch., 1846, Louisa H. (dau. Daniel & Louisa *Stockbridge*) **Bartlett;** he a sea-capt.; sett. at Weth.; d. 26 Sept., 1879; wid. d. 21 June, 1887.—*W. Ins.*

Children:

1. Adaline T., b. 22 Dec., 1848 (*W. C. R.* say 23 Dec., 1847); d. 30 May, 1872.—*W. Ins.*
2. Daniel B., b. 30 Oct., 1850.

3. Belle L., b. 29 Dec., 1852; m. 20 June, 1877, Henry **Davis.**
4. Lillie E., b. 21 Feb., 1857.

FAM. 45. Capt. ELIZUR,[7] (*Elizur*,[6] *Nath'l*,[5] *Nath'l*,[4] *Nathan*,[3] *Samuel*,[2] *Thos.*,[1]), b. 7 May, 1815; m. 1843, Clarissa (dau. Benj. & Abigail) **Weeks**, of Weth.; he, with his eld. bro. William were among the oldest and the last of the coasting-trade Captains betw. Weth. and New York in early part of 19th century; he rem. to the West and d. at Jamaica, Iowa, 21 Nov., ———, ae. 85.

Children:

1. John.
2. Henry.

3. Elizur, b. 31 May, 1849.—*W. C. R.*
4. Inf., bu. 17 Aug., 1850.—*W. C. R.*

HUNKEY, Mrs., d. 2 Oct., 1842, ae. 46.

HUNN, This Weth. family are descendants of GEORGE, who was of Boston, 1635; made freeman 17 May, 1637; was a tanner, and had est. at Braintree, and on Long Island, Boston Harbor. His will, dated 25 May, 1640, (*N. Eng. Gen. et. Hist. Reg.* VII. p. 31), ment. wife Ann, and sons, one of whom was *Nathaniel*, whom he bound out to James Johnson for 5 yrs. After his dth. his wid. m. —————**Philpot**, 16 Dec., 1651.

NATHANIEL,[2] *George*,[1]), b. 1626, was a shoemaker; memb. of the Anc. and Hon. Artill. Co., of Boston, 1662; acc. to *Savage* (II 499) is not heard of in B. after 1669, but was of Weth., 1673-1693; was twice marr., 1 to Sarah; 2d Rebecca —————d; he d. late in Sept. or early in Oct., 1704, ae. abt. 76 yrs.

Children (before rem. from Boston):

1. Sarah, b. 8 July, 1652.—*Savage.*
2. John, b. 16 Jan., 1656; d. 1657.—*Savage.*
3. Nathaniel, b. 1671. FAM. 2.
   (*By second marriage*):
4. George, b. Weth., 24 Dec., 1682; d. 19

Dec., 1712; inv. of his est. taken 1 Jan., 1712; valued at £19-18-06; prob. the G. ment. in Chapt. VII, Vol. I.
5. Samuel. FAM. 3.

FAM. 2. NATHANIEL,[3] (*Nath'l*,[2] *Geor.*,[1]), b. 1671; see Chapt VII, Vol. I., m. Martha (dau. Samuel) **Orvis**, 7 Dec., 1704; she m (2) John **Root**, Jr., of Far. Nath'l Sen., d. 7 Dec., 1712.

Children (Weth. Ins.):

1. Hannah, b. 4 Oct., 1705.
2. Nathaniel (Rev.), b. (bp.—*Mix*) 10 Sept.,

1708. FAM. 4.
3. Deborah, bp. 29 July, 1711.—*Mix MSS.*

Nathaniel Hunn Sen. Invt. £75-15-10 taken 7 December 1712 by Hezekiah Deming, John Stodder, John Root. Will dated 4 December 1712—I give to my wife I give all my Land to my son Nathaniel all my moveable estate to be equally divided amongst my children only my wife to have one third part of them I appoint my wife executrix—and desire Mr. Stephen Lee and Thomas Curtis to be Overseers.

NATHANIEL HUN   X   mark   O

Witness Stephen Lee, Thomas Curtis. Court Record, 12 February 1712-13 will now exhibit by Martha Hunn Executrix widow of the Deceased: *Htfd. Prob. Rec.*

FAM. 3.   SAMUEL,² (*Nath'l*,² *Geo.*,¹), b. 1671; m. Sarah (dau. John) **Dickes,** [*Dix*], 18 Aug., 1696; he d. 1 Nov., 1738, ae. 67,—*Weth. Ins.*; she bp. 10 Oct., 1686, d. 6 Mch., 1753; bo't ld. in Newington, Aug., 1696; was one of first sett. of that parish; with his bro. Nathan'l was in 1712, one of petitioners for separate ch. org.; and one of comm. of 3 to raise funds for building the first meeting house, etc.; in 1732 was agent of the New. parish, and prominent as its ch. rec. shows, in all its affairs. See, also Chapt. VII, Vol. Invent. taken 26 Apl., 1739, by Martin Kellogg and John Camp, val. at £925-09-06. Adm. gr. to Gideon Hunn and Jno. Whaples, of Weth. Margaret, wife of Geo. Hunn, owned cov't and bp. 20 July, 1712.—*Mix*. See, also, p. 759 Vol. I.

Children (Weth. Rec., bp. Mix):

1. Rebecca, b. 26 Aug., 1697.
2. Samuel, b. 26 Aug., bp. 5 Nov., 1699; d. 1 Nov., 1738.—*Mix. Rec.*
3. Sarah, b. 20 Oct., 1701; bp. 17 Aug., 1701; d. 6 Mch., 1753.
4. Jonathan, b. 12 Jan., 1704-5.
5. David, b. 2 Sept., bp. 3 Oct., 1708; d. 8 Sept., 1737.—*Weth. Ins.*

David Hunn Died 8 September 1737 Invt. 338-03-06 Taken 20 Dec. 1737, by Joseph Woodbridge, Peletiah Buck, Josiah Riley. Court Record 6 December 1737 Admˢ to William Smith of Farmington who married one of the Sisters of the Decᵈ Samuel Hun Jr Eldest brother of the Decᵈ refused Admˢ.—18 January 1737-8 upon complaint of the admˢ. Samuel & Gideon Hun. were brought before this Court to be examined upon Oath for concealing Divers goods Bills Notes etc. They plead that they are not now held to answer to any Interogatories but ought to be dismist in that they have not been bound over to this Court by an Assistant or Justice as per pleas on file will more fully appear this Court decide they are obliged here to answer—Samuel and Gideon Hun appealed to the Superior Court 5 December 1738 now examined before John Hooker J. P. and 6 February 1738-9 account of Admrs. Exhibit & allowed. (It appears here and elsewhere the Huns were right as to the law and their rights under it.—*C. W. M.*)

6. Gideon, b. 12 Mch., bp. 7 May, 1709-10. FAM. 5.
7. Ebenezer, b. 18 Jan., d. 4 Feb., 1711-12.
8. George, bp. 30 Sept., 1711.
9. Mary, b. 21, bp. 26 Apl., 1713; m. 1738, William⁴ (*Thos.*,³ *Sam'l*,² *Thos.*¹) **Welles;** she d. 19 Aug., 1756.
10. Thankful, b. 24 June, bp. 1 July, 1716.

FAM. 4.   Rev. NATHANIEL,⁴ (*Nath'l*,³ *Nath'l*,² *George*,¹), b. 1708; grad. Y. C. 1731, and studied for ministry; on recommendation of the Rev. Sam'l Whitman, of Far., he was adm. to memb. of the ch. at Stratfield [Bridgeport], 18 Mch., 1732-33. On the declination by his classmate, Stephen Mix, of a call to the ch. at Reading (now Redding), then known as the 4th Soc. in Franklin, Ct., young Hunn, was called, accepted and ord. there and served that parish until his dth. (prob. Aug. or Sept.), 1749, while on a visit to Boston. He m. 14 Sept., 1737, Ruth (dau. of the eminent lawyer John H. C. 1697) **Read,** of Boston and Redding, from whom the latter place was named. She d. at R., 8 Aug., 1766, ae. 66; no issue. Mr. Hunn published a work entitled, *The Wellfare of a Government Considered. A Sermon* [on 2 Chron. XII, 12], Preached before the General Assembly of Connecticut on the day of their Annual Election, May 14, 1747. N. London, 1747, 16 mo. pp. 35, "a sermon which had a timely reference to the recent provincial capture of Cape Briton, and an earnest lament over the disadvantages of a paper currency—owing to which cause the preacher's own salary of £100 had been gradually raised to £340, even that amt. being hardly a fair equivalent for the orig. sum.

He was, also, believed to be the author of an anonymous *Inquiry into the Consequences of Calvinistic Principles*, circulated in manuscript in 1749, and which elicited a reply from Rev. Moses Dickinson (Y. C. 1717),—*Yale Biog's*, 429.

FAM. 5. GIDEON,⁴ (*Samuel*,³ *Nath'l*,² *George*,¹), b. 1710; m. Rebecca ————————, she d. 23 Oct., 1793, in 86 yr.; he d. 29 Aug., 1785. in 76 yr.—*Weth. Ins.; res.* Newington, Ct.

Children (Weth. Rec.) :

1. Rebecca, b. 5 Mch., 1741; d. 21 Apl., 1778, in 39th yr.—*Weth. Ins.*
2. Jemima, b. 20 Aug., 1742.
3. Zadock, b. 17 Apl., 1743; he studied theology and was called to the pastoral office in Becket, Berkshire Co., Mass., Sept. 26, 1770, and ordained there June 5, 1771; dismissed Oct., 1778, and in 1795, removed to a farm in Canandaigua, N. Y., where he labored faithfully and usefully among the new settlers, and was long and affection-

ately remembered. Plain in his manners, sound in doctrine, fervent in spirit, instructive in conversation and preaching, and acceptable to his audience. He died in Canandaigua, May 12, 1801, having just completed his 58th year.—Dexter's *Yale Biogs.*
4. Enos, b. 1 Mch., 1745.
5. Thankful, b. 17, bp. 18 (*N.*) June, 1749.
6. Eunice, b. 1, bp. 3 (*N.*) May, 1752.

SAMUEL, m. Mary **Barnard**, 14 Mch., 1745; he d. 2 Aug., 1757.—*New. Ch. Rec.*

Children (Weth. Rec. & N. C. R.) :

1. Hannah, b. 21 Apl., 1747; bp. 1 May, 1748.
2. Sarah, b. 4, bp. 15 Jan., 1749.
3. Mary, bp. 15 Dec., 1751; d. 1 Jan., 1753.

DAVID, d. 24 Jan., 1856, ae. 77; wife Abigail d. 23 Feb., 1863, ae. 75.—*Weth. (N.) Ins.*

FAM. 2. ENOS, (*Gideon*,), b. 1745; m. Esther **Smith**, 28 Feb., 1774, she d. 6 June, 1817, ae. 63.—*Weth. Ins.* He d. 21 June, 1805, ae. 61.—*Weth. Ins. & N. C. R.*)

Children (N. C. R.) :

1. Elishaba (dau.), bp. 18 June, 1775; d. 13 (11—*N. C. R.*) Dec., 1839, ae. 65.—*Weth. (N.) Ins.*
2. David, bp. 2 May, 1779; m. Abigail; had *Albert Smith, Enos Higley,* both bp. 18 July, 1813.—*N. C. R.*
3. Rebecca, bp. 27 May, 1781; d. 25 July,

1860, ae. 78.—*Weth. Ins.*
4. Leister Chauncey, bp. 17 Oct., 1784; m. Caty **Goodrich,** 8 Nov., 1806; he d. 24 Mch., 1835, ae. 57; Wid. Katy, d. 7 May, 1836, ae. 51; had *Eliza,* d. 4 Aug., 1819, ae. 6; *inf.* 28 Mch., 1820; *Chauncey L.,* d. 15 Nov., 1817.—*W. C. R.*

HUNNESON, JACOB, had (*W. C. R.*) Henrietta, bp. 24 Mch., 1793.

HUNNEWELL, (*Huniwell, Honeywell*). Furnished by Mr. JAMES SHEPARD, of New Britain, Ct. JOHN, of Weth., said by Savage to have been a surveyor of roads, in 1682;* m. (1) Lydia, 1 Jan., 1679-80, who d. 10 Aug., 1683—(*Weth. Rec.*); he m. (2) Elizabeth (dau. Capt. Daniel & Mary Weld) **Harris,**† of Midd., Ct.; for lds. in Weth. Vol. 1 Chapt. VII; in *Weth. Ld. Rec.* III. p. 296, date of 28 Feb., 1682, he acknowledges himself indebted to Joseph Curtis, in "the sum of £8. 10 s., in consideration of 2 bbls. of cyder which I bought of him about last Oct., * * * to be paid in manner and form as follows, yᵗ is to say, one third part in wheat, one third part in grass, and one third part in Indian corne, all good and marketable." He rem. to Midd., where the birth of two of his ch. were rec., and d. there before 1706, as is shown by the following from *Htfd. Prob. Rec.* VII. 86,—"Bridget Honeywell, of Midd., a minor of abt. 14 yrs. of age, one of the daus. of John Honeywell,

---

* It is claimed that a *Roger H.,* arrived from Co. Essex, Eng., at Boston, 1645; *Arms* of the family are: Party per fesse sable and argent, 3 hawk's heads erased, countercharged. *Crest,* a bee-hive with bees volent—all ppr."
† As shown by numerous deeds relating to lds. that descended to her from her father, as rec. in *Midd. Ld. Rec.*

late of Midd., appeared in Ct. and made choice of her uncle Isaac Johnson, Sr., of Midd., to be her guardian,"—Aug., 5, 1706. The wid. Elizabeth H., d. before 4 Dec., 1710, when adm. on her est. was granted to John Honeywell, eld. son of her husband—(*Htfd. Prob. Rec.* VIII. 23), who rec'd a double portion, and his sisters each a single portion; ear-mark for cattle rec. *W. T. V. I. p.* 10.

Child (by 1st marr., Weth. Rec.) :

1. Mary, b. 10 Jan., 1682.
(*By second marriage*) :
2. Abiah, b. 1684 (her name variously spelled on the *Midd. Recs.*, Abiah, Abial, Biall, etc.), m. Abel **Tryon**, of Midd., and d. 30 Nov., 1756. (In *Midd. Ld. Recs.*, III, 199, is a deed, dated 4 Dec., 1718, wherein "Abil Tryon," with "Biall his wife," sell ld. that was set out from the est. of Thomas Harris to his sister, Elizabeth Hunnewell, dec'd, and Biall the wife of Abil Tryon, above named, being dau. to Elizabeth Hunnewell." Other rec. just as clearly prove Elizabeth and Bridget to be the daus. of John Hunnewell's second wife Elizabeth (**Harris**) thereby showing that she left three daus., altho' it might be otherwise inferred from the distrib. of her est. that she had only two. Mr. Tryon d. 29 Jan., 1761. *Issue;*
   i. Sarah (Tryon), b. 10 July, 1704; m. 10 May, 1727, Anthony **Siser**; "a seafaring man," who d. 21 Sept., 1753; 7 ch.
   ii. Eunice (Tryon), b. 10 Feb., 1705-6.
   iii. Thomas (Tryon), b. 7 May, 1708; m. 20 Dec., 1733, Mary **Andrus**; 10 ch.
   iv. Abel (Tryon), b. 3 Oct., 1710.
   v. William (Tryon), b. 2 Nov., 1712; m. 12 Sept., 1734, Sarah **Goodrich**; 4 ch.
   vi. Elizabeth (Tryon), b. 24 Oct., 1714.
   vii. Mary (Tryon), b. 24 Feb., 1716-17.
   viii. Charles (Tryon), b. 31 May, 1712; m. 8 Mch., 1738-9, Else **Griffin**; 6 ch.
3. Elizabeth, m. (as his second wife) Samuel **Williams**, of Stepney parish (Weth.), whose will dated 1 Feb., 1742-3, (see *Htfd. Prob. Rec.*, XIV, 190) names his first wife Abigail and 5 sons and 5 daus., and also heirs of dau. Elizabeth, and then refers to ld. in Midd., "that I bo't of my 2d wife's bros. and sisters." The only lds. deeded to him in *Midd. Recs.*, came from the Hunnnewells, thus showing that E. was his 2d wife; her identity is further proven by *Midd. Ld. Recs.*, III, 175, where Sam'l Williams of Weth., and Elizabeth, his wife, deed ld. that descends to her, "as a part of her portion set out to her by distrib. of her mother's

est. which ld. did descend to her by her father's last will, Capt. Daniel Harris, sometime of Midd.," dated 6 Aug., 1713; ch. (9 of whom are rec. at Weth.) *by first marriage to Mary Stebbins*, to whom he was m. 24 June, 1697:
   i. Amos (Williams), b. 27 Mch., 1695.
   ii. Samuel (Williams), b. 3 Feb., 1701.
   iii. Elizabeth (Williams), b. 28 Apl., 1700.
   iv. Deborah (Williams), b. 18 Apl., 1704.
   (*By second marriage*) :
   v. Susanne (Williams), b. 18 Oct., 1707.
   vi. Mary (Williams), b. 7 Mch., 1708-9.
   vii. Jonathan (Williams), b. 29 Mch., 1709-10; d. 7 Mch., 1710.
   viii. Jonathan (Willaims), b. 5 Dec., 1711; d. 20 Apl., 1713.
   ix. Joseph (Williams), b. 29 Jan., 1713.
   x. Sarah (Williams),   ⸲ Midd. Ld. Rec.,
   xi. Martha (Williams), ⸲   I, 376.
   xii. Benjamin (Williams).
   xiii. Elisha (Williams).
   xiv. Rachel (Williams).
   Last three named in father's will, but not otherwise identified.
4. John, b. 17 Apl., 1689; rem. from Conn. to New Jersey, before July 7, 1712, and deeds on *Midd. Ld. Rec.* show that he res. at Woodbridge, N. J., Nov., 1716, and at Hanover, N. J., Dec., 1733.
5. Bridget, b. 2 Oct., 1691; m. Jonathan **Roberts**, abt. 1716, (in Nov., 1714, she signed a deed with her maiden name, and signed one in 1718, as wife of Roberts), res. N. Haven 1729-1747; where had 2 ch. bp.; bo't ho. in East Haven, 1748. *Issue:*
   i. Molly (Roberts), b. 1717; d. 6 Mch., 1794; unm.
   ii. Rebecca (Roberts), b. 1721; d. 9 Sept., 1796; unm.
   iii. Thankful* (Roberts), b. at Meriden Ct., 24 Mch., 1729-30; m. abt. 1750 Joseph[4] (s. *Benj.*,[3] s. *Joseph*,[2] s Peter,[1]) **Mallory**, of New Haven; she d. E. Haven, Ct., 30 July, 1773, ae. 43; he m. 1774 (2) Eunice (dau. Benj. & Hannah *Abbot*) **Barnes**, 1774.
   iv. Jonathan (Roberts), b. at Meriden, Ct., 1 June, 1734; d. Southington, Ct., 16 Oct., 1788; m. Jemima **Abbot**.

Line of Descent of *JAMES SHEPARD*, of New Britain, Ct., from John Hunne well, of Weth., through his dau. Bridget (Hunnewell) Roberts.

FAM. 2. THANKFUL ROBERTS (3d ch. and dau.), of Jonathan and Bridget (Hunnewell) **Roberts**, b. 1729-30; m. abt. 1750, Joseph (s. of *Benj.*, *Joseph*, *Peter*,) **Mallory**, of N. Haven, she d. at E. Haven, 30 July, 1773, ae. 43; he m. (2) 1774, Eunice (dau. Benj. & Hannah *Abbot*) **Barnes**, they res. in E. H. until abt. 1780, when they rem. to Wolcott, Ct., & there united with ch. He d. Wolcott, 9 June, 1791; wid. d. 22 Nov., 1793. *Issue.*

1. Benjamin (Mallory), b. 1751; bp. 23 Mch., 1756; m. Eunice **Talmadge**, 19 Dec., 1774.
2. Elizabeth (Mallory), b. 1754.
3. Amos (Mallory), b. 1756.
4. Abigail (Mallory), b. 1760; m. Samuel **Cook**.—*Hist. Wallingford, Ct.*
5. Thankful (Mallory), b. 1762; m. Samuel **Shepard**, 1 Jan., 1787. FAM. 3.
6. Ezra (Mallory), b. 1767.
7. Joseph (Mallory), b. before 31 July, 1773; bp. 5 Mch., 1775.
   (*By second marriage*) :
8. Noah Woodruff (Mallory), bp. 5 Mch., 1775.
9. Eunice (Mallory), b. ————.
10. Elizabeth (Mallory).

FAM. 2. JONATHAN,[2] (*Jona.*,[1]), b. 1734; d. 16 Oct., 1788, in 55 yr., at Meriden, Conn.; rem. to Southington, abt., 1780. He m. Jemima **Abbott**.

Children:

1. William (Roberts), d. yg.
2. William (Roberts), res. Bristol, Ct.
3. Hannah (Roberts), b. East Haven, Ct., 1 Sept., 1760; m. 11 June, 1780, Nathaniel (s. Samuel & Hannah *Bronson*) **Shepard**, b. Htfd., 29 Aug., 1760; was a Revol. soldier; res. Southington and Kensington, Ct.; d. at K., 4 May, 1822; she d. K., 12 Sept., 1834.
4. Pamela (Roberts), b. E. Haven, 1761; m. Sol. **Alcox**, of Wolcott, 14 July, 1784, a sold. of Revol. War; she d. 20 Aug., 1810; he m. (2) Wid. Abigail **Goodyear**.
5. Betty (Roberts), m. Amasa **Bradley**, of Watertown, Ct.
6. Eli (Roberts), res. Southington, Ct., 1788.
7. Jemima (Roberts), res. Southington, Ct., 1788.

FAM. 3. THANKFUL MALLORY, (*Joseph & Thankful (Roberts) Mallory*), b. 1762; m. (as 2d wife) 1 Jan., 1787, Samuel **Shepard**, of Southington, b. Htfd., 4 May., 1754 (s of Samuel, John, John, Edward, of Cambridge, Mass.,), and bro. of Samuel Shepard, who m. Thankful (Mallory) Shepard's first cousin, Loraine Mallory, and of Nathaniel Shepard whose wife Hannah **Roberts**, was also first cousin of Thankful (Mallory) Shepard; he rem. with his father, from Htfd. to Southington, Ct., abt. 1761; served in Revol. War as private in Capt. Asa Bray's Co.; d. at S., Feb., 1803, as a result of exposure in the war 30 yrs. before; his 1st wife Rhoda **Hitchcock**, d. 8 Dec., 1785; his 2d, Thankful, m. (2) Clark **Royce**, 17 Jan., 1818; she d. 27 May, 1832, ae. 69.

Children:

1. Inf. (Shepard), d. 26 Nov., 1785.
2. Rhoda (Shepard), d. 8 Dec., 1785. (*By second marriage*):
3. Rhoda (Shepard), b. 27 Sept., 1787; d. Southington, 30 Dec., 1844; m. 12 Feb., 1807, Mark (s. Joel & Elizabeth *Atkins*) **Lane**.
4. Sophia (Shepard), b. 4 Jan., 1789; d. 31 Jan., 1845; m. Noah (s. Noah & Sarah *Curtis*) **Gridley**, whose first wife was Susannah **Andrus**.
5. Jerusha (Shepard), b. 15 Sept., 1790; m. 8 June, 1848, Ebenezer (s. Ebenezer) **Barnes**; he d. 9 June, 1825, ae. 37.
6. Amos (Shepard), b. 28 May, 1793; d. 2 Mch., 1829. FAM. 4.
7. Eunice (Shepard), b. 7 Aug., 1796; d. S., 17 Feb., 1872; m. 17 Oct., 1816, Solomon (s. Ebenezer & Ruth *Buckley*) **Stur**, of Ry-Hill (Weth.), 14 Sept., 1816; he d. at S., 31 Aug., 1868.
8. Oswell (Shepard), b. 27 July, 1799; d. Canaan, N. Y., 29 Nov., 1840; m. 20 Apl., 1825, Elizabeth Woodward (dau. Jared) **Heminway**, b. Southington, 23 Jan., 1804; she d. C., 22 Jan., 1847.
9. Joseph, b. 1801; d. 24 Jan., 1803.

FAM. 4. AMOS SHEPARD,[7] (*Samuel*,[6] *Samuel*,[5] *Samuel*,[4] *John*,[3] *John*,[2] *Edward*,[1]), b. 1793; m. 4 Oct., 1819, Statira (dau. Samuel & Lydia *Warner*) **Alcott**, who d. May, 1890. He was a soldier in War of 1812; after marr. rem. to Southington, where he res. until dth., 2 Mch., 1849. He spent most of his life in travel in Southern States, had considerable literary talent and many of his poems have been pub.

Children:

1. Samuel Royce (Shepard), b. S., 10 July, 1820; m. 1845, Lucy (dau. Hopkins) **Carter**; res. Rochester, N. Y.
2. Ann Sophia (Shepard), b. S., 19 Nov., 1822; m. 25 Nov., 1846, at Plainville, Ct., Lucius Edward (s. of Chester & Rachel *Bartlett*) **Strong**, of Northampton, Mass., who d. at Grand Forks, Dakota, 30 Sept., 1872.
3. Jane Emeline (Shepard), b. 6 Mch., 1827;
d. 21 May, 1832.
4. Henry (Shepard), of Crookston, Minn., b. S., 11 Aug., 1832.
5. Amos (Shepard), of Plantsville, Ct., b. there, 2 Nov., 1835; m. 19 Nov., 1864, Harriet **Harrison**.
6. James (Shepard), of New Britain, Ct., b. 16 May, 1838; m. 25 Sept., 1859, at Plymouth, Ct., Celia Adelaide (dau. Wm. G. & Lucy *Preston*) **Curtis**, of Bristol, Ct.

HUNT, ALEXANDER, (*Weth. Ins.*), late of N. Y., d. 21 Aug., 1790, ae. 60; his wife Abigail, d. 26 Aug., 1801, ae. 69; their dau. *Ann*, d. 4 Sept., 1783, ae. 21; their s. *John*, d. 9 July, 1780, ae. 20.

BLAYACH, a cousin of Mary **Collins** and Mary **Balyding**, and a nephew of Mr. Welles, d. unm'd, 1640.—*Hinman.*

JACOB STEELE, of N. Y., m. Cath. **Hunt,** 2 Jan., 1780.—*W. C. R.*

JOHN, ae. 20, bu. 10 July, 1780.—*W. C. R.*

ROBERT, of Glast., m. Keturah **Shipman,** 31 Mch., 1819.

HUNTER, BENJAMIN, of Glast., m. Anne **Palmer,** 8 July, 1789, she d. 15 June, 1806; had *inf.* ae. 6 wks. bu. 9 July, 1794; *ch.* bu. Oct., 1798; *inf.* bu. May, 1806. He d. ae. 48, bu. at New., Sept., 1813.

CATY, d. 10 Oct., 1825, at P. H., in 21st yr.

ROSWELL, had—(*N. C. R.*), *inf.* d. 18 Feb., 1806; *ch.* ae. 6 mos., bu. 22 Mch., 1817; *inf.* ae. 6 d., bu. 15 May, 1822; *inf.* ae. 6 mos., bu. 2 Oct., 1823; *inf.* d. 13 Jan., 1825, ae. 3 mos., and an *inf.* bu. Sept., 1826.

HUNTINGTON, JONATHAN, of Hadd., m. Mary **May,** 8 Mch., 1790.—*W. C. R.*

JOHN, had Abigail, bp. 5 Sept., 1784.

JOSIAH, had Wealthy, bp. 15 Sept., 1782; Nathaniel Gilbert, bp., 6 Nov., 1785; Josiah, bp. 24 June, 1787; Eleazur, bp., 10 May, 1789.

JOSIAH, m. Rachel **Hinsdale,** of W. Htfd., 30 Aug., 1808.—*W. T. R.*

Capt. SIMEON, of Norwich, m. Patience **Kenee,** 15 Jan., 1788.—*W. C. R.*

HUNTLEY, CHARLES, m. Frances **Judd,** both of Weth., 27 Aug., 1848.—*W T. R.*

HUTCHINS, Sgt. JOHN, d. 1681; left wid. and 2 ch. viz.; *Sarah,* ae. 4 and *Ann,* ae. 1½ yrs. Invent. of est. taken 30 Sept., 1681, by Nath'l Bowman, Samuel Butler and Wm. Warner; amt. £38; adm. gr. to wid. 1 Nov., 1681.—*Hinman.*

JOEL, m. Elizabeth **Goodrich,** 12 Apl., 1797.—*N. C. R.*

HYDE, THOMAS, of Lebanon, m. Achsah **Marsh.**

INGRAHAM. JAMES, m. Martha **Brewer,** 6 June, 1738.

Children (Weth. Rec.):

1. Martha, b. 24 Mch., 1740. | 2. James, b. 5 or 9 Feb., 1740-41.

IRELAND, SAMUEL, came to Weth., 1637, or earlier. For his ld. rec. see Vol. I, p. 280. He came to this country in the ship *Increase,* Apl. 15, 1635, with wife and child thus described in passenger list. *Samuel Ireland,* carpenter, [ae.] 32; *Marie Ireland,* uxor, [ae.] 30, *Martha Ireland,* [ae.] 1½. Chapin's *Glast Centenn.* mentions him as in Weth., 1634; Sept. 5, 1639, he was fined 10*s* "for contempt of ye Ct.", in not appearing vppon a warrant served vppon him." Upon his submission he pay'd 5*s* and was acquitted (*Conn. Col. Rec., I, 28*); d. at Weth., 1639, or certainly, prior to 1645, in Mch., of which year the invent. of his est. was exhib. to the Court by his late wid. (then m. to Robert **Burrows,**) and Jo. Edwards; the wid. "to have the thirds and the other two p'rts. to be for the children," Martha and Mary, whose portions (£30) was delivered to their stepfather (Burrows) by John Latimer, of Weth., in 1651.—*Conn. Col. Rec.,* I, 149. For Ireland's ld-holdings, see Chapt. VII, Vol. I.

IVES, MERRICK, of Goshen, Ct., m. Mary **Coombs**, 24 Oct., 1810.

PHILO, Sophia, wife of, d. 8 Apl., 1838.—*Weth. Ins.*

JAGGER. (*Gager*), JEREMIAH, from Watertown, Mass., 1636; soldier in Pequot campaign of 1637; rec'd a lot for services, 30 yrs. later; ho-lot rec. in Weth., 1640, see Chapt. VII, Vol. I.; rem. to Stamford, 1641; petit. the Ct., 1655, for remission of a fine, his petit. gt'd, "so long as he carry it well." *Savage* (II, 535), says that he was master of a trading vessel to the W. I., four yrs. before his dth., which was 14 Aug., 1658; left wid. Elizabeth, and sons *John, Jeremiah* and *Jonathan*, all sett. at S., and with families. Wid. m. (2) Robert **Usher.** Jagger's invent. appraised by Rich. Law and Francis Bell, 11 Dec., 1658, and given in on oath by Elizabeth (then) wife of Robert Usher, 19 May, 1659, amt'd to £472-17-00,—*Fairfield Co. Prob. Rec.* Robert Usher was exec'.

ABRAHAM, d. 17 Oct., 1833, ae. 80; wife d. ae. 69, 1827; had: *ch.*, d. 8 Jan., 1786, in 1st yr.; *Rhoda*, d. 24 or 27 June, 1797, in 3d yr.—*W. C. R.*

ABRAHAM, had *Mary, Rachel* and *Daniel*—poss., also *Nathan*— bp. 17 Sept., 1797; *Sylvanus* and *Lucy*, bp. 2 Oct., 1803.

DANIEL, d. 18 May, 1827, in 31 yr.—*W. C. R.*

LUCY LIZOR, (*Eliza?*) (adult), bp. 3 July, 1842.

MARGARET, wife of D. H. and dau of Wm. and Mary Grimes, d. 14 Apl., 1892, ae. 81.—*Weth. Ins.*

MARTHA ANN, m. Geo. Washington **Barber**, of Hebron, Ct., 30 Oct., 1831.

NATHAN'S wife Roxanna **Hart**, whom he m. 11 May, 1808, and who d. 21 Mch., 1841, in 51st yr.—*Weth. Ins.; dau.* d. 22 Mch., 1829, in 8th yr:; *Leander*, d. at E. Htfd., 11 Aug., 1851, ae. 19. Mr. N. J. d. 21 Mch., 1861, ae. 72.—*Weth. Ins.*

NATHAN, JR., had inf. bu. 14 May, 1817.—*W. C. R.*

JAMES, JOHN, ment. in Co. Ct. Rec. 1721, as "of Weth."

JOHN (Rev.) d. 9 Aug., 1729, ae. abt. 72 yrs.—*Weth. Ins.*

JANES, (*Jeanes, Jaynes*), Acknowledgment of aid is made to the *Janes Geneal.*, (pub. 1868), and to Mr. AUSTIN ROBERTSON, of Weth.

WILLIAM, was a prominent citizen and beloved school-teacher at New Haven for 17 yrs., where he rec'd £10 per. ann., for his services. Finally, the good people of Weth., invited him to come to them, "only by consent of the brethren," at N. H., as their schoolmaster, and prob. offered him better inducements in the way of salary. At a Gen. Court at New Haven, Oct. 3, 1650, it was propounded that a schoolmaster might be provided for the town. A committee was appointed, March 10, 1650.—It was propounded whether the town would allow any salary to Mr. Janes for teaching school.

May 19, 1651. For the incouragement of Mr. Janes in teaching school the court ordered he should have £10 for this year, &c.

Oct. 8, 1651. Mr. Janes informed the town that he is offered a considerable maintenance to go to Wethersfield to teach school.

Oct. 29, 1651. Mr. Janes desired to know of the town if they would not give
him liberty to go to Wethersfield to accept of the proffer made him to teach
school, for he hears there is another coming hither. He had liberty granted.
He was at Weth., however, only a few months, and ret. to N. H., and finally
(1656), rem. to Northampton, Mass. His wife, to whom he was m. in Eng.,
was Mary ————. Their *Children (Janes Geneal.)*, were:

1. Joseph, res. in Northampton, 1704.
2. Samuel, ditto ; had wife and 3 ch.
3. Benjamin, b. 30 Sept., 1672. FAM. 2.

4. Benoni, res. Northampton, 1704; wife and 4 ch.

FAM. 2.   BENJAMIN,[2] (*William,*[1]), b. 1672; m. Hannah (dau. of Samuel) **Hinsdale**, of Hadley. On May 13, 1704, a little vill. betw. Mt. Tom and Westfield,
Mass., was attacked by Indians. Of the five families there res., Benjamin's
bros., Samuel Janes, with his wife and 3 ch.; and Benoni Janes and 2 ch., were
killed, and Benjamin's wife Hannah, was knocked down and scalped, but survived
and was taken to Weth., so as to be under the care of Dr. Gershom Bulkeley,
and other surgeons. She ultimately recovered and lived to be over 80 yrs. of
age.   Benjamin and family rem. to Coventry, Ct., in 1712-13.

Children (b. in Mass.):

1. Hannah, b. 14 May, 1696; killed by Inds. 13 May, 1704.
2. Miriam, b. 7 Jan., 1700; killed by Inds. 13 May, 1704.
3. Nathan, b. 18 Jan., 1703; killed by Inds. 13 May, 1704.
4. Hepzibah, b. 14 Dec., 1706; d. inf.
5. Ebenezer, bp. (*Rev. Mr. Mix*) 5 Sept., 1708.
6. Silence, b. 1708 (perhaps twin to Ebenezer) ; m. Henry **Curtis.**

7. Hannah,* (twin), b. 16 June, 1710, bp. by *Rev. Mr. Mix*; m. John **Brown**, of Northfield, Mass.
8. Hepzibah,* (twin), b. 16 June, 1710, bp. by *Rev. Mr. Mix*; m. George **Hawkins**, of Coventry, Ct.
9. Seth, b. 1713; m. Sarah **Larrabee.**
10. Elisha, b. 1715. FAM. 3.
    (*Weth. Rec.*—These twins not ment. in *Janes Geneal.*)

FAM. 3.   ELISHA,[3] (*Benjamin,*[2] *William,*[1]), b. 1715; m. 23 Apl., 1740, Wid. Mary
Dimock; he d. in Coventry Ct., and after his dth., the family rem. to Canaan,
N. Y.

Children:

1. Elisha, b. 30 June, 1741; m. (1) Elizabeth **Davenport**; m. (2) Desire **Thompson.**
2. Bathsheba, b. 10 Feb, 1742; m. John **Tilden**, of Lebanon, Ct. *Issue:*
    i. Lois (Tilden).
    ii. Lucina (Tilden).
    iii. Ann (Tilden).
    iv. John (Tilden), d. 15 Aug., 1790.
    v. Oliver (Tilden).
    vi. Cynthia (Tilden).
    vii. Elmer (Tilden, m. Polly *Younglove* **Jones**; had (*a*) *John ;* (*b*) *Mary ;* (*c*) *Elizabeth ;* (*d*) *Moses Y. ;* (*e*) *Samuel J.*, the late distinguished lawyer and statesman, of N. Y. City ; (*f*)

and (*g*) *Henry* and *Henrietta* (twins).
3. Mary, b. 10 Feb., 1744.
4. Samuel, } twins, b. 6 Feb., 1747 ; d. inf.
5. Daniel, }
6. Benjamin, b. 3 Mch., 1748; m. Irene **Sawyer.**
7. Daniel, b. 1750; d. 4 Dec., 1770.
8. Jerusha, b. 27 July, 1752 ; m. 1 June, 1775, Moses **Badger.**
9. Tryphenia, b. 8 July, 1755; m. 18 Feb., 1773, Daniel **Robertson**, gd-father of Mr. Austin Robertson, of Weth.
10. Tabitha, b. 22 Feb., 1757.

LEONARD T., Sgt. Co. B, 10 Reg. C. Vols., d. 4 Sept., 1895.—*Weth. Ins.*

JENNINGS, JOSHUA, a joiner, *W. T. V..* I. 25, 20 Apl., 1647; his wife was Mary,
(perhaps dau. of Matthew **Williams**), m. 23 Dec., 1647; rem. to Fairfield,
Ct. See Chapt. VII; also, p. 220, Vol. I.

SIMEON, m. Elizabeth **Kilby**, 13 Dec., 1764.—*W. C. R. Children*,—(*Weth. Rec.*),
(1) *Mehitable*, b. 26 Apl., bp. 14 July, 1765; (2) *Simeon*, b. 17 Oct., 1766.

JOSEPH. See Chapt. VII, Vol. I.

www.ingramcontent.com/pod-product-compliance
Lightning Source LLC
Chambersburg PA
CBHW070629270326
41926CB00011B/1862